INTERNATIONAL COOKBOOK OF LIFE-CYCLE CELEBRATIONS

INTERNATIONAL COOKBOOK OF LIFE-CYCLE CELEBRATIONS

Updated and Revised

Lois Sinaiko Webb, Lindsay Grace Cardella, and Jeanne Jacob

GREENWOOD™

An Imprint of ABC-CLIO, LLC
Santa Barbara, California • Denver, Colorado

Library of Congress Cataloging-in-Publication Data

Names: Webb, Lois Sinaiko, author. | Cardella, Lindsay Grace, author. | Jacob, Jeanne, author.
Title: International cookbook of life-cycle celebrations / Lois Sinaiko Webb, Lindsay Grace Cardella, and Jeanne Jacob.
Other titles: Multicultural cookbook of life-cycle celebrations
Description: Second edition. | Santa Barbara, California : Greenwood, an imprint of ABC-CLIO, LLC, [2018] | Revised edition of: Multicultural cookbook of life-cycle celebrations / by Lois Sinaiko Webb. 2000. | Includes bibliographical references and index.
Identifiers: LCCN 2018008118 (print) | LCCN 2018010363 (ebook) | ISBN 9781610690164 (ebook) | ISBN 9781610690157 (hardcover : alk. paper) | ISBN 9781610693714 (paperback : alk. paper)
Subjects: LCSH: International cooking. | Holiday cooking. | LCGFT: Cookbooks.
Classification: LCC TX725.A1 (ebook) | LCC TX725.A1 W43 2018 (print) | DDC 641.59—dc23
LC record available at https://lccn.loc.gov/2018008118

ISBN: 978-1-61069-015-7 (hardcover)
        978-1-61069-371-4 (paperback)
        978-1-61069-016-4 (ebook)

22 21 20 19 18   1 2 3 4 5

This book is also available as an eBook.

Greenwood
An Imprint of ABC-CLIO, LLC

ABC-CLIO, LLC
130 Cremona Drive, P.O. Box 1911
Santa Barbara, California 93116-1911
www.abc-clio.com

This book is printed on acid-free paper ∞

Manufactured in the United States of America

This book is dedicated to Lois Webb with her passion of educating, experiencing, and sharing cultures. She was a storyteller, dear friend, and adopted grandmother to many. Every day, her warm smile, witty banter, and heartfelt kindness are missed. This final book was her "baby," and I am thankful for the support and dedication of Jeanne Jacob for her assistance in completing the revised text.

Contents

Contents

Contents

Contents

Contents

Contents

Contents

Contents

Contents

Contents

Contents

Contents

Contents

Contents

Preface

In all cultures, sharing food is a primary way of sustaining human relationships. In fact, the English word "companion" is derived from Latin and French words that mean "sharing bread together." Each society's culture is passed on to children through eating with the family, a setting in which individuals learn sharing, kinship and family values, and the traditions of the group.

Ever since finishing a cookbook about the countries and one about national holidays around the world, Lois Webb desired to write a cookbook about people and their family celebrations.

The first book, *Multicultural Cookbook for Students* (now in its second edition), gives an overview of a country: the geography, climate, terrain, and principal crops grown. The recipes included are the typical foods eaten by the majority of the people in that country.

The second book, *Holidays of the World Cookbook for Students* (also in its second edition) covers a country's most important celebration or its national holiday. The recipes included are for the dishes eaten in celebration of a special day or holiday.

This book, the *International Cookbook of Life-Cycle Celebrations*, now in its second edition, covers the life-cycle celebrations that take a person from birth to the grave and the food consumed on this journey. As one goes into the homes and lives of people around the world, doors of understanding open, barriers come down, and new light is shed on how other cultures share their most precious family moments.

Life-cycle events are often celebrated with food. A festive feast communicates many things: a family's wealth and success, status within the society, family ties, and religious devotion. A celebration feast usually means enjoying great quantities of more expensive foods. In most cultures, a meal becomes a feast only when special breads are baked, traditional dishes are prepared, and meat is on the table.

Preface

This book takes readers into the homes and kitchens of people in more than 140 countries. Each country listed has a short introduction describing the country's geographic location, relevant history, and ethnic and religious breakdowns. This information is followed by examples of local life-cycle celebrations, often unique to that country or a region of that country. (Rather than describing the same life-cycle events over and over for countries with similar ethnic and religious groups, we have included an overview at the beginning of the book outlining the important life-cycle events for the world's major religions. The reader is frequently referred to the appropriate section of this essay in these introductions.)

Following the introductions is an average of three or more recipes, made with readily available ingredients. The recipes are for dishes specifically prepared to commemorate a life-cycle celebration or for dishes that would be included in the celebration feast.

To expand the senses and make the taste buds more adventuresome, we included recipes for a few of the more unusual yet easily available foods, such as salt cod, herring, and caviar. To please the eye, there are recipes for decorative breads and Japanese sushi, as well as lovely birthday and wedding cakes and cookies. Recipes using edible gold and **silver leaf** (*vark*), used in India and other regions to decorate food for special occasions, have been added. For texture, recipes for unusual vegetables include yuca (cassava), chayote and prickly pear (cactus pear), and grain dishes. (All products are easily available at most supermarkets, health food stores, or designated ethnic markets.) A trip to an ethnic market can be delicious, informative, and fun. If an unusual food is in a recipe, detailed information about it appears in the Glossary of Food Terms starting on page xlv. These unusual foods and cooking terms are set in boldface type the first time they appear in a recipe, indicating their inclusion in the glossary.

All recipes in the book include the following:

- *Yield*, stating the number of people a recipe will serve or how many pieces it will make
- *Ingredients*, listing how much of each food item you need for the recipe
- *Equipment*, listing cooking equipment, such as pans, bowls, and spoons
- *Instructions*, telling you exactly how to make the recipe
- *Serving suggestions*, explaining how to plate and serve the finished product and. if necessary, how it is to be eaten

This second edition includes new and updated recipes, as well as a few countries not included in the original edition, such as Kosovo and Belize. While every single country and every possible celebration could not be covered in this single volume, great effort has been made to include representative countries and celebrations of every region of the world.

Acknowledgments

FROM THE FIRST EDITION

Special thanks to:

Mary Kegg

Kateri Angel (named after Tekakwitha, the first American Indian woman to become a Catholic saint)

Jean Ouimet, French Canadian

Ning Yu

Gretchen Facey

Ganesh N. Rajamani

Shirley Donahoo

Asghar Khan

Jan and John Blyth

Josie Wilson

Neala Gunderson

Olga Mire

Jean Seltzer

Harvey Belsky

Hedwig Somdah

FROM THE SECOND EDITION

Special thanks to my daughters, Cailyn Grace and Zoey Alessandra, and to my supportive husband Nick. As a family, our traditions are grounded in food and celebration. I am thankful for family and friends that continue to share their stories and traditions of celebration through so many milestones of life.

During the writing and research for her part of the book, Jeanne underwent medical treatment in Bonn, Germany, and wishes to thank Drs. Hanna and Hermann Liese for hosting her over two months and providing information on Rhineland funeral and other festive foods. Thanks also to Dr. Andreas Heinemann-Gruder and his wife Derya for their hospitality on several weekends in Bonn and for information on Turkish celebratory foods. In Leamington Spa, Warwickshire, UK, Jeanne wishes to thank former neighbors Avril Brooks and June Cranmer for their kind care and invaluable discussions on English and Welsh foods. And as well, deepest thanks go to Kaitlin Ciarmiello for her kind understanding and steadfast support throughout.

Getting Started

IMPORTANT: PLEASE READ THE FOLLOWING BEFORE YOU BEGIN TO USE THIS BOOK.

SAFETY TIPS

To make cooking an enjoyable experience, it's a good idea (1) to cook safely, (2) to think before you act, using common sense, and (3) to make sure that you, your cooking tools, and your kitchen are clean. All experienced cooks know the importance of these few simple rules.

Don't Cook Alone. Have Adult Help

Even apprentice chefs in restaurants never cook alone; an experienced cook is always present to teach food preparation and explain cooking equipment.

Keep Food at the Proper Temperature at All Times

Cold food must be kept cold, and hot food must be kept hot. Never cover food while it is cooling to room temperature because it takes longer to cool down, and there is a chance of bacteria forming. Cover to refrigerate or freeze. It is very important not to use spoiled food. If you think something may have spoiled, ask an adult if it should be discarded.

Prevent Fire Accidents

The kitchen's most dangerous equipment are stove top burners, where most home accidents occur. Always keep a fire extinguisher (designed for stove fires) within easy reach and in working condition. To prevent stove top accidents, follow a few simple rules:

Never turn your back on or walk away from a skillet or pan of hot cooking oil. Always have the necessary utensils and ingredients ready to go before heating the oil.

If the oil should begin to smoke or seems too hot, quickly turn off the heat.

Do not move the pan, and do not throw water in the pan as it could cause the oil to flame. It is best to turn off heat, allow it to cool down, and begin again. In case of fire, pour baking soda over it to smother it.

Never leave food that is cooking unattended, unless you are making a soup or stew with plenty of liquid and cooking on low heat. Even a soup or stew must be checked from time to time while it cooks to make sure it's not drying out, sticking, or burning. If the phone rings or there are other distractions while cooking, turn off the heat, and, using a pot holder, slide the pan to a cold burner. If the pot is too heavy, ask an adult to do it. Double-check the burner to make sure you turned it off. (A common mistake is to turn it up, thinking you have turned it to off.) When you return to the kitchen, if it hasn't been more than a few minutes, continue cooking where you left off.

When you finish cooking, before leaving the kitchen, make sure the oven and stove top burners are off.

Keep dry, heatproof oven mitts or pot holders handy. All metal spoons and handles get hot. Use wooden mixing spoons or plastic-handled metal spoons instead. Do not use all-plastic spoons or other cooking tools for mixing hot food because they will melt. Never transfer very hot food to plastic containers or plastic bags; some are not made to hold hot food and might melt.

When lifting the lid off a pan of hot food, always direct the open lid away from you so that the steam does not come toward your face.

Accidents do happen, however, and it is a good idea to have a first aid kit with burn and cut medication on hand.

Adjust the Cooking Time

Please note that the recommended cooking time given for each recipe is approximate. This time can vary, based on thickness of the pan, thickness of the ingredients, differing heat controls on stoves, and altitude.

Keep Knives Sharp

Dull knives can be dangerous, even more so than sharp knives. A dull knife can slip off food, causing accidents. Always cut food on a cutting board, and always have an adult standing by to help. Always carry a knife by the handle with the blade pointing toward the floor; never pass a knife to another person blade first, and do not put utility knives in a dishwasher or in a sink full of soapy water. It is not only dangerous, but it is also not good for the knives. Wash knives by hand, and keep them in a safe place away from small children.

Use Caution When Working with Hot Peppers

Cover hands with gloves or plastic baggies to prevent burning. Do not touch your eyes or face as you are working; if you do, splash them with cold running water.

Be Extremely Careful When Working around Hot Grease

Always have an adult help you when cooking with hot grease or oil. When you finish using the deep fryer or other pans with grease, immediately turn off the heat or unplug the pan. Double-check to make sure the burners are off, not turned to high, which is a very serious and common mistake many people make. Do not move the pan of hot grease until it is cool. Keep a kitchen fire extinguisher in working order and handy at all times. Accidents do happen, so be prepared.

CLEANLINESS IN THE KITCHEN

- Tie your hair back or wear something on your head, such as a bandana.
- Roll up your sleeves and wear an apron or some protection to keep your clothes clean.
- Do not touch any food or cooking equipment unless you have first washed and dried your hands. Wash your hands frequently while handling food to prevent cross-contamination. Raw chicken and raw eggs are two foods that can easily become infected by bacteria called *salmonella*. Raw chicken must be kept at a cold temperature (below 45°F) at all times. It is best to thaw frozen chicken in the refrigerator (this can take a day or so, depending on the size) or more quickly under cold, running water. When preparing the chicken, keep the work area and all utensils sanitized (to "sanitize" means to kill disease-causing bacteria by cleaning). Also, immediately after the chicken has been prepared and before any other food preparation, sanitize the work surface, utensils, and equipment again to prevent cross-contamination. Eggs keep well at 36°F. When buying eggs, look for the freshness date on the container, and check each egg to be sure there are no cracks.
- Wash all fresh fruits and vegetables before cutting.
- Have all the utensils and equipment clean, ready, and in good working order before beginning to cook.
- Wipe up spills and drips at once. Good cooks clean up after themselves and always leave the kitchen spotless.

Equipment and Methods You Need to Know About

Almost every recipe you will use from this book will require the following basic equipment:

- A set of measuring cups—probably nested cups in different sizes for measuring dry items, such as flour, and a liquid measuring cup with lines drawn on the sides to tell you how much liquid you have
- A set of measuring spoons for measuring small amounts of liquid and dry items
- A work surface, such as a countertop or tabletop, where you can put all of your equipment as you prepare your food
- A set of sharp knives for cutting and dicing ingredients

Each recipe will tell you what other equipment you will need—such as bowls, pans, or spoons—to make the food described.

Glossary of Food Terms

allspice. A spice made from the dried and ground berries of the Jamaica pepper tree. Allspice tastes like a combination of cloves, nutmeg, and cinnamon; hence its name.

almond paste. A pliable mixture of ground almonds, raw egg whites, sugar, and liquid. To avoid using raw egg whites, commercial almond paste is recommended for noncooking recipes, available at supermarkets in 6- to 8-ounce packages. Keep the paste well wrapped and refrigerated after opening. If almond paste becomes hard, it can be softened by heating for 2 to 3 seconds in a microwave oven or by placing it in warm oven.

appetizers (also French: *hors d'oeuvre*, literally "outside the works"). Small, light, decoratively presented finger food items eaten before the main meal, usually to appease hunger.

areca nuts. *See* **betel nuts**

arrowroot. A tasteless and colorless thickening agent.

atta (chapati flour). Very finely ground wheat flour, cream or pale yellow in color. Atta is ideal to use in unleavened flatbread recipes. Sifting out the coarse particles of bran in whole wheat flour, using a fine-mesh sifter, will produce flour with a texture similar to atta. Atta is available at all Indian and Middle East food stores and at some health food stores.

bamboo steamer basket. *See* **steamer pan**

basmati rice. Long grain, nonglutinous rice (each grain cooks separately from the other).

baste. To moisten with liquid at intervals while cooking.

beetroot. The English name for beets. *See also* **beets**

beets. A firm, round, dark red root vegetable with leafy green tops that are also edible and nutritious. Buy beets that are firm with smooth skin. Small to medium-size beets are the most tender. Beets will keep refrigerated for up to two weeks.

betel nuts. Hard round nuts, called *supari* by East Indians, that are really the astringent seeds of the betel palm (also arecca palm). Since ancient times, they have been chewed for their stimulating effect. After having been chewed awhile, the nuts soften and give off a peculiar taste. Chewing the betel nuts makes your lips, mouth, and teeth bright orange. Habitual chewing of the betel nut will stain the teeth black. The betel nut is used in many Hindu life-cycle rituals. *Paan*, the betel leaf, is spread with either white lime paste (*choona*) or red paste made from the bark of a tree (*katechu* or *kattha*). The paste is sprinkled with mixture of crushed betel nuts and spices and herbs, such as cardamom and aniseed. The leaf is folded into a small triangular wad and fastened with a whole clove. The *paan* is chewed as a digestive and mouth freshener. The betel leaf varies in taste from sweet to slightly bitter. In Papua New Guinea (PNG) chewing the betel nut (or in Pidgin, *buai*) is so common that people greet each other by asking, "Do you chew?" (meaning, "Do you chew betel nut?"). People chew it as a little pick-me-up, a bit like a midmorning cup of tea or coffee. The children of PNG, as young as 5 years old, take up chewing the betel with all the condiments, and they start by gnawing on the husks of the nut discarded by others. The nut is combined with mustard stick (*daka*) and crushed-coral lime (*cumbung*). The "chew" is foul tasting, and the lime used in the procedure is highly caustic and can cause terrible mouth sores

black-eyed peas. A white pea with a black eye, brought to the Southern United States from Africa in the 17th century with the slave trade.

blanch nuts. A process done to nuts to make it easier to peel off the skin. To blanch nuts, cover them with boiling water, and let them stand for 5 minutes. Drain, and, when cool enough to handle, the skins will easily peel off.

blanch vegetables. A process done to vegetables to make it easier to peel off the skin, to set color, to slightly soften the vegetables, and to remove the raw flavor. To blanch vegetables, fill a saucepan with 4 cups water for every cup of vegetables to be blanched. Bring water to a boil over high heat, and add vegetables. Bring water back to a boil for 1 to 3 minutes, depending upon size of vegetables. Remove at once from heat, drain vegetables in colander, and rinse them under cold running water to stop the cooking action.

blend. To mix two or more ingredients completely into one.

blender. An appliance with whirling blades that quickly crushes and blends food.

bok choy. Literally "white cabbage," a vegetable with thick white stems and long, narrow leaves.

boned (also bone). Term used to describe fowl, fish, or meat whose bones have been removed.

bread crumbs (also breadcrumbs). Dry bread crumbs and fresh (soft) bread crumbs used in various ways in different recipes. For best results, use what is called for in a recipe. Fresh white bread crumbs are made by trimming off the crust of white bread, cutting it into **cubes,** and processing it in food processor or blender, 1 to 2 slices at a time, to desired size of crumb. Dried crumbs can be made by trimming off crust and drying bread on baking sheet in an oven heated to 250°F until crisp and lightly toasted; either crush with rolling pin or in food processor. Dry plain or seasoned bread crumbs are available at all supermarkets.

bread doneness. A test to indicate whether a loaf of bread is done. To do this test, remove bread from the oven and from the pan, and tap the bottom of loaf with handle of dinner knife. If loaf sounds hollow, it is done. If it has a dull, thump sound, it is not done. Return to pan and oven, and continue baking for at least another 10 to 15 minutes.

breadfruit. A starchy fruit with a tough, bumpy or prickly skin. Fresh, the fruit is as big as a cannonball. It is eaten green or ripe and sometimes stands in for white potatoes. Breadfruit weigh from 2 to 5 pounds with cream-colored flesh, bland flavor, and texture that is often compared to grainy bread. It is cooked like squash or potatoes and can be used in both sweet and savory dishes. As it ripens, it becomes sweeter. It is available fresh, canned, or frozen at some supermarkets and at all Latin American food stores.

broccoli rabe (also *raab*, *rapini* [Italian], or rape). A vegetable related to both the cabbage and turnip family. It has a pungent, bitter flavor that has not been popular in the United States. It is very popular in Italy, where people fry or steam it and use it in soups and salads. It is available in some supermarkets and at all Asian and other ethnic food stores.

bulb baster. A kitchen tool that is used for moistening meat or fowl while it is baking. A bulb baster has a plastic or metal shaft with a heavy rubber bulb at one end. To operate, place the shaft opening in the pan drippings, and squeeze the rubber bulb. By releasing the bulb, the air comes back into the bulb, drawing the liquid from the pan up into the shaft. Squeeze the bulb again to **baste** the food.

bulgur (also bulghar or burghul). *See* **wheat berries**

bundt pan. A fluted pan with a center tube.

butterfly. To split a food (such as meat, fish, or shrimp) through the middle, leaving it intact at one end. The two halves are opened, like the pages of a book or butterfly wings. This procedure is generally done with a piece of meat or fish that is going to be stuffed. Shrimp are butterflied to make them look larger and more attractive.

cake boards. Square, rectangular, or round (**cake circles**) pieces of cardboard that are placed under baked cakes to keep them rigid. Before setting a cake on the cardboard, cover the side it will sit on with foil. To cover a circle board with foil, cut the foil about 2 inches larger than the circle. Wrap the excess foil over the edges, and press it down in pleats on the backside of the circle. Cake boards come in different sizes and are packed 6 or 12 of one size to a box. They are available at kitchenware and craft supply stores.

cake circles. *See* **cake boards**

candied fruit (also **glacé cherries**). A fruit, used in cakes, breads, and other sweets, that has been boiled or dipped in sugar syrup and sometimes dipped in granulated sugar. Chopped mixed candied fruit (fruitcake mix) and chopped pineapple, cherries, and citron come in 8-ounce (1-cup) and 16-ounce (2-cup) containers at most supermarkets. After opening, store candied fruit in an airtight container, and refrigerate.

candy thermometer. *See* **sugar syrup; thermometers**

carambola (also **star fruit**). Pale yellow green fruit, with five pointed ridges around the center core. When sliced crosswise, each slice is shaped like a star. Available at most supermarkets.

cassava (also **manioc** and **yucca**). A tropical root vegetable with hard white flesh covered by dark brown, hairy bark-like skin. It has to be peeled and cooked before eating. It is a staple food in African, Caribbean, and Latin American kitchens. Tapioca is made from cassava. Cassava is cooked whole, sliced, and pounded into pulp or ground into a coarse flour. Only sweet cassava is available in the United States; the bitter variety is poisonous until it is cooked. Cakes and breads are made from cassava meal, which is made from grated, sun-dried cassava. Cassava is available fresh and in meal and flour form in Asian and Latin American food stores and some supermarkets.

cauliflowerets. The white top part of cauliflower, broken or cut off from the stems.

chafing dish. A metal dish or pan heated from below with a flame, hot coals, or electricity, for warming or cooking food; the name comes from the French word *chauffer* (to heat).

chard (also **Swiss chard**). A green leafy vegetable with reddish stalks. Buy tender greens and crisp stalks. It will keep up to three days if refrigerated.

chayote (also **mirliton**). A tropical round or pear-shaped squash, 3 to 8 inches long, with a thin green skin. It has white, bland-tasting flesh around one soft seed. It is prepared like summer squash or can be stuffed and baked like acorn squash. They are available in the winter at most supermarkets. Buy chayote that are unblemished and firm.

chicken doneness. To check whether chicken is fully cooked, pierce thickest part of fowl with a knife. If juices that trickle out are clear, not pinkish, the chicken is done.

cilantro. *See* **coriander**

cinnamon sugar. To make cinnamon sugar, mix 3 tablespoons sugar with 1 teaspoon ground cinnamon.

citron. A fruit of the citrus family, resembling a large, lumpy lemon, cultivated for its thick rind, which is candied or pressed; its oil is used in making liqueurs, perfume, and medicine.

coarsely chopped. Cut into ¼- to ½-inch pieces. *See also* **finely chopped**

coconut, fresh grated. To prepare grated coconut, choose a coconut without any cracks and one that produces the sound of swishing liquid when shaken. Have an adult pierce the eyes of the coconut with an ice pick or skewer, drain the liquid, and save it for another use. After draining, break the coconut with a hammer, and remove the flesh from the shell, levering it out carefully with the point of a strong knife. Peel off the brown membrane, and cut the coconut meat into small pieces. In a food processor fitted with the shredding disk, shred the pieces a few at a time, or grate the coconut meat on the fine side of a grater. One large coconut yields about 4 cups of grated coconut.

cod, salt. *See* **salt cod**

collard greens (also collard). A type of cabbage with leaves that do not form a head. Buy fresh, crisp green leaves, avoiding leaves with a yellowish or wilted appearance. They are available at all supermarkets.

colander. A perforated, bowl-shaped container used to drain liquid from solids.

core. The center of fruit such as an apple, pear, or pineapple that has seeds or the tough fibrous part of vegetables such as on the bottom of cabbage or celery.

coriander. An herb related to the parsley family. When fresh, it is also called "Chinese parsley" or by its Spanish name, **cilantro**. Buy fresh coriander with bright green leaves. Keep refrigerated with stems in glass of water. Dried coriander seeds are available whole or ground, and the dried leaves are available crushed or ground. The seeds and leaves have different flavors, so, when adding to a recipe, be sure to use the proper kind.

cornstarch (or **corn flour**). Corn finely ground to the consistency of fine flour. Corn flour is the British term. It is often used for thickening liquids.

cornmeal. Coarsely ground corn often sprinkled on baking sheets to prevent breads from sticking. Also used to make corn bread.

couscous. A pasta that looks and acts like a grain. The tiny granules are made of semolina, the same hard durum wheat used for noodles. *Couscous* is the Arabic word for semolina. The term "couscous" refers to both the granules and the famous dish called "couscous." All North African countries have couscous recipes; the Moroccans sprinkle in saffron, Algerians add tomatoes, and Tunisians drizzle on *harissa*, a fiery red pepper sauce. Authentic North African couscous takes about an hour to prepare and requires three steamings. Precooked couscous, found in supermarkets, takes about 5 minutes to make. To cook, follow directions on package. The larger, pearl-size couscous from Israel is available at some supermarkets and Jewish and Middle East food stores.

crawfish. *See* **crayfish**

crayfish (also crawfish). Tiny lobster-like crustaceans that are usually found in freshwater. Live crayfish are seasonal and available only at certain times of the year. Packaged, frozen, cooked crayfish meat is available at most supermarkets all year long. It takes 5 pounds of live crayfish to pick out 1 pound of edible meat.

crème fraîche. A specialty of France, this thickened cream has a slightly tangy flavor and a smooth velvety texture. It is easy to make: Combine 1 cup heavy cream and

2 tablespoons buttermilk in a glass container. Cover, and let stand at room temperature (about 70°F) for 8 to 24 hours, or until very thick. Stir before covering, and refrigerate up to 10 days. *Crème fraîche* can be cooked in sauces and soups without curdling.

croquettes. A mixture of meat and/or vegetables formed into small cylinders, ovals, or rounds and fried until crisp and brown.

croûtes. French for a "crust," "shell," or "piece of bread" or dough used in various savory dishes. *En croûte* means "encased in pastry."

crudités. Raw vegetables, such as carrot, celery, and zucchini cut into finger-size pieces, and cauliflower and broccoli, broken into small **florets**, to accompany a dipping sauce as an **appetizer**.

cubed. To cut something into small (about ½-inch-size) pieces of uniform size. Compare to **diced**.

cuisine. A French term pertaining to a specific style of cooking or the food of a particular region or country.

dasheen. *See* **taro root**

deep fryer. A special container with a built-in thermostat used for quickly frying food. Fill deep fryer with oil according to manufacturer's directions. Heat to 375°F on deep fryer thermometer, or place the handle of a wooden spoon in the oil; if small bubbles appear around the surface, the oil is ready for frying. A wok, deep skillet, or saucepan with a cooking thermometer can be made into a deep fryer. A wok is ideal for deep frying. Its sloping sides enable one to decrease the amount of oil normally used for deep frying. To fry with a **wok:** Use only vegetable oil and fry in small batches. Some woks come with a semicircular wire rack that may be placed above the oil for draining food after it is fried. Drain again on paper towels. To remove food from the wok, use either a slotted metal spoon or spatula or metal tongs.

deveined. *See* **peeled and deveined**

diced. Food cut into very small (about ¼-inch) pieces of uniform size. Compare to **cubed**.

doneness. *See* **chicken doneness; bread doneness**

double boiler. Two pans that fit together with one resting partway inside the other; it usually comes with a cover that fits either pan. Food cooks in the top pan from the heat of the boiling water in the bottom pan. A double boiler can be made by placing a metal mixing bowl over a slightly smaller pan. The boiling water should not touch the bottom of the upper bowl.

drizzle. To lightly pour a liquid or sauce in fine lines over a surface. This is done when only a little liquid or sauce is needed, usually as a decorative touch. An easy way to drizzle is to put liquid or sauce into a squirt bottle with a small hole in the nozzle.

dry-roast. *See* **roasted nuts**

Dutch oven: A cast iron pot with a tight-fitting, domed lid that is used for slow cooking soups, stews, and cobblers.

egg wash. Combine 1 egg yolk with 2 tablespoons water or milk in cup, and, using a fork, gently beat to mix.

egg whites. *See* **eggs, separated**

egg yolks. *See* **eggs, separated**

eggs, separated. *How to crack and separate eggs:*

1. Wash your hands. Have three bowls ready: one for the yolks (the yellow part), one for the whites, and one to crack the eggs over.

2. Hold the egg in one hand; crack it with one light, sharp blow against the rim of the bowl, or crack lightly with the dull side of a table knife. Try to make an even, crosswise break in the shell.

3. Hold the cracked egg over an empty bowl; take it in both hands, with the cracks on the upper side, and pull the crack open with your thumbs, breaking it apart into halves. As you do this, some of the egg white will drip into the bowl underneath it. Hold the yolk-filled half shell upright so it cups the yolk. Empty any remaining egg white in the other half shell into the bowl.

4. Hold the yolk-filled half over the bowl, and carefully, so that the yolk doesn't break, pass it back and forth from one half shell to the other. As you do this, more egg white drips into bowl. When the yolk is free of egg white, put it into a separate bowl, and continue cracking remaining eggs the same way. If an egg is spoiled, it can be easily discarded when cracked into a separate bowl. Make sure no yolk gets in the white because the slightest fat from the yolk will keep the whites from whipping.

elastic. A term used for dough. When dough is elastic, it springs back when you pull on it.

fenugreek. A plant with pungent, bittersweet edible seeds. The seeds come whole or ground and are used in African and Middle Eastern cooking. Fenugreek is often combined with other spices to make Indian curries.

fillet. (also *filet*, the French spelling). A cut of meat or fish that has been trimmed of all bones and sometimes the skin. When ordering fillets from the fishmonger, always specify you want them skinless. Some fish fillets, such as tuna and catfish, are always boneless and skinless because the skin is tough and inedible.

filo. *See* **phyllo.**

finely chopped. To cut into very tiny pieces. It is the same as to **mince.** *See also* **coarsely chopped**

Finnan haddie. Smoked haddock, originally from the Scottish town of Findon; hence the name. Finnan haddie is available whole or in fillets at some supermarkets.

fish. When fish is opaque white and easily flakes, it is fully cooked. The flesh appears solid white (versus translucent light gray when raw). When poked with a fork, the fish easily separates into small chunks (flakes).

florets. Tender, edible tops of cauliflower and broccoli.

fold in. To combine a frothy light substance, such as beaten egg whites or cream, with a heavier one and not lose air or reduce volume or lightness. To fold in, stir in a continuous, gentle circular motion from the bottom of the container to the top. Continue to fold in until the ingredients are incorporated.

fresh white bread crumbs. *See* **bread crumbs**

froth. To make foamy by adding air to the mixture; this is done by vigorously beating or whipping.

fusion. Blending food and/or herbs and spices and/or cooking methods and techniques from a different culture, resulting in a new taste.

garnish. To put something on or around food, either to make it more colorful, such as adding a sprig of parsley; to make it more flavorful, such as adding syrup, icing; or to decorate it, such as with confectioners' sugar.

glacé cherries (also candied cherries). *See* **candied fruit**

glaze. To give a shiny appearance to both savory and sweet preparations. For savory foods, coat with a light sauce; for sweets, coat with sprinkled sugar or icing.

gold leaf. *See* **silver leaf**

grater. A metal kitchen utensil with different surfaces used for grating, shredding, and slicing. Graters are found in flat, cylindrical, or box shapes, and some have a handle across the top for a firm grip. The surface used for grating is perforated with rough-edged round holes that stick out, forming a rasp-like surface. Graters usually have two grating surfaces, one for finely grating things such as spices, and a larger rasp-like surface for coarse grating things such as cheese and bread crumbs. The shredder surface is perforated with ¼-inch round holes that have a raised cutting edge along the bottom side of each hole. The slicing surface has several parallel slits with a raised cutting edge along the bottom side of each slit.

grill. Cooking over heat on a perforated rack. The grill can be gas, electric, charcoal, wood, or combination. The food takes on a distinct grilled flavor, especially over a wood fire.

ground. The process of grinding different substances, ranging from coarse, used for ingredients such as meat, to fine powder, used for spices. Nuts can be ground in an electric blender, food processor, nut or coffee grinder, or **mortar and pestle.** Grind nuts, a few at a time, adding a little of the sugar called for in the recipe. Adding sugar to each batch prevents lumping up, which is caused by the oil in the nuts. The standard food processor can take 1 cup nuts and 2 teaspoons sugar. Use the on-off pulse method to grind; 6 to 8 pulses should be sufficient.

guava. The fruit of a tropical tree. It is available fresh, but it is best to buy it canned for a more consistent taste and texture.

half-sheet baking pan. A professional 18×13×1-inch baking pan. This is the maximum size pan that will fit in most home ovens.

heavy-bottomed. A saucepan with a thick bottom such as cast iron or enameled cast iron. Food cooks more evenly in this type of pan and is less likely to burn.

herring. A saltwater fish found in the cold waters of the North Atlantic and Pacific Oceans. Over a hundred varieties of herring have been found. It is eaten fresh, pickled, smoked, and salted and is very popular in Scandinavian and Eastern European countries.

hominy. Dried white or yellow corn kernels from which the hull and germ have been removed. Hominy is sold canned, ready to eat, or dried (which must be soaked in water before using). Hominy grits, or simply grits, come in three grinds—fine, medium, and coarse. They are generally available at supermarkets.

hors d'oeuvre. See **appetizers**

icing spatula. *See* **pastry spatula**

jalapeño. An easily available hot green pepper that can be bought fresh or pickled and canned at supermarkets. When working with peppers, it is best to wear plastic or rubber gloves to protect your hands. The heat of peppers is in the seeds, and so it is best to remove and discard the seeds and membrane before using.

julienne. Cutting food, especially vegetables, such as carrots, into matchstick-size shapes.

kiwi. A fruit known since ancient times in China (as *yang tao* [Chinese gooseberry]), it was introduced to New Zealand in 1906. When buying kiwi, select firm fruit. Kiwi that are soft can be mushy or mealy and lack flavor. To ripen kiwi, just leave in a bowl for a few days; do not refrigerate. To speed up ripening, place kiwi in a paper bag with a banana.

knead. To push down into the dough with the heels of hands. To knead, push down, turn the dough slightly, and repeat. Continue to turn and fold dough until it is smooth and elastic. As you knead, you will see the dough change from a flaky consistency to a more solid consistency that holds together. As you continue kneading, you will feel and see the dough become more and more elastic; it springs back each time you pick up the heel of your hand.

kosher salt. An additive-free, coarse-grained salt. It is used primarily in Jewish cooking.

lemon grass. A lemon-flavored, thick-stemmed grass that is widely used in South East Asia, especially in Thai cooking. It is often combined with flavors of coconut, chili, and ginger. Many varieties are available; some of them are called "sorrel," derived from the German word for "sour." Sorrel is also popular in French cooking. Lemon grass has long greenish-gray leaves with a white bulb-like base. (It looks something like a large green onion.) It has a sour-lemon flavor and fragrance. It is available fresh or dried in many supermarkets and in Asian food stores. Lemon grass is also called "citronella." Dried lemon grass needs to be soaked before using. Lemon grass is used only for flavoring; it is not to be eaten.

lentils. Probably the earliest cultivated legume, dating back as early as 8000 BCE. Lentils, which have a pleasant earthy flavor, come in many varieties. The most common are the brown or green lentils. Red lentils have a salmon color that turns yellow when cooked. Lentils don't require soaking, cook in about 20 minutes, and can easily turn mushy if left to cook too long.

liqueur. The name, derived from French, for sweet alcoholic beverages usually served at the end of a meal.

lukewarm. A cooking term used to refer to heating or cooling food to a specific temperature, usually between 110°F and 115°F on a food thermometer.

manioc. *See* **cassava**

marinade. A seasoned liquid used to coat foods in order to absorb flavor or to tenderize.

marinate. To soak food, especially meat, in a sauce (**marinade**) made up of seasonings and liquids.

marzipan. A sweet mixture of almond paste, sugar, and usually egg whites. It is pliable, like modeling clay, and is often tinted with food coloring and made into different shapes to decorate cakes and other sweets. It is available in cans or plastic-wrapped logs at most supermarkets.

meat mallet. A tool used to flatten meat to a uniform thinness and to break down the meat fibers, tenderizing the meat and permitting even cooking. Also known as "meat pounders," they come in different shapes and are made of wood or metal. Use a heavier blow on meat, a lighter pressure on breast of chicken. Place the meat between two sheets of plastic wrap to prevent it from sticking to the mallet or work surface. Pound outward as well as downward to spread the meat out evenly.

melon baller. A kitchen tool with small, bowl-shaped scoops of different sizes at either end of a handle. It is used for cutting out round balls from melons.

millet. A grain native to Africa and Asia; it is a high-protein staple usually made into porridge. In the United States, it is used mostly for animal fodder.

mince. To chop very fine.

mortar and pestle. A bowl (mortar) and a grinding tool (pestle), typically used to grind spices. Both are made of a hard substance. The mortar holds the ingredients, and the pestle is held in the hand and is used to mash or grind them. You can make a mortar and pestle by simply using a metal bowl or a hard surface for the mortar and a clean, smooth rock, small enough to hold in your hand, or the head of a hammer or wooden mallet for the pestle.

mung beans. A small, dried bean popular in Indian subcontinent and Asian countries. The bean has a green skin that must be removed before cooking. Cover the beans completely in water to soak for 4 hours. After soaking, rub the beans briskly between your palms, which will loosen the skins. Pour off soaking water and discard skins. The skinless yellow bean that remains is what is used for cooking. Dried skinless yellow beans are available in Asian food stores and need no presoaking. When cooked, they have a slightly sweet flavor and velvety texture. Cook according to directions on the package or the recipe. Bean sprouts grow from mung beans.

mustard greens. Dark green leaves of the mustard plant. They have a strong mustard flavor and are available fresh, canned, or frozen at supermarkets. Buy only fresh, crisp, young leaves. Do not buy yellowish, wilted looking greens; they are old and will have an unpleasant fibrous texture.

oven-ready. Meat, fowl, or fish that is ready to cook with no preparatory work. Have the butcher or fishmonger prepare the item you are buying so that it is ready for cooking according to your recipe, be it for the stovetop, oven, or grill. Fish must always be gilled, gutted, and scaled to be considered oven-ready.

paan. *See* **betel nuts**

papaya (also tree melon or *pawpaw*). A tropical fruit, usually weighing about 1 to 2 pounds. The skin of this creamy, orange-colored fruit is a vibrant green that ripens to yellow. When selecting papaya, gently press on the fruit; if it yields to the pressure, it is ripe for eating. Cut a papaya in half lengthwise and scoop out the small, shiny (and inedible) black seeds.

parboil. To partially cook food by boiling in water for a short time to remove the raw flavor. It also speeds up the preparation of dense foods when they are combined with other ingredients that require minimum cooking.

pastry bag. A cone-shaped paper, plastic, or cloth with an opening at both ends. A metal or plastic tip is fitted onto the tip end, and the bag is filled through the large top opening with a soft, smooth mixture, such as icing, whipped cream, or other foods. When the top opening is securely closed and the bag is squeezed, the mixture is forced through the tip. The tips come in different sizes and designs. Pastry bags and tips are available in hobby and craft stores, kitchenware sections of department stores, and supermarkets.

pastry blender. A kitchen tool made of several parallel rows of stiff metal wires, bent in a U shape. They are attached to either side of a 4- or 5-inch-wide handle. As you press the wires down into the flour mixture, in a chopping motion, the fat is cut into the flour, making tiny pea-size pieces.

pastry brush. Used for applying glazes to foods. It can be a 1-inch paint brush, but it should be soft and of good quality so that the bristles do not come out.

pastry spatula (also **icing spatula**). A straight, narrow blade used for applying smooth coatings of frosting to the tops and sides of cakes and for slicing and filling layer cakes. The best are made of flexible stainless steel. They come in different lengths, but the 9-inch-length blade is average.

peeled and deveined (shrimp). To peel shrimp, remove the hard shell that covers the edible flesh. This is done by holding the shrimp between the thumb and index finger of one hand and carefully pulling the tiny legs under the shrimp apart with the finger of the other hand. The shell should easily peel off. To devein shrimp, remove the visible black (sometimes white) vein running down the back of peeled shrimp.

Using a paring knife, cut the thin membrane while rinsing the shrimp under cold running water. Use the point of the knife to remove the vein.

phyllo (also **filo**). Pastry sheets used in Greek, Eastern European, and Middle Eastern cooking. Available in 1-pound boxes, each containing 22 paper-thin sheets, 14 by 18 inches in size (available in the freezer section of supermarkets [trade name Fillo]). The pastries are paper-thin and dry out quickly. Once the package is opened, keep the sheets you are not working with covered with a damp towel.

pigeon peas (also Congo peas, no-eyed peas). A tiny grayish-yellow legume native to Africa. They are popular in Southern states where they grow in long fuzzy pods. They are available dried, fresh, frozen, and canned in many supermarkets and in most Latin American and Indian food stores.

pine nuts. A seed from the cone of the stone pine tree (*Pinus pinea*). They are available at supermarkets but are less expensive in Asian or Italian food stores.

piri-piri. A spicy Portuguese sauce made of chopped chili peppers, olive oil, bay leaves, and lemon rind.

pith. The spongy tissue between the skin and flesh of citrus fruits such as oranges, lemons, and grapefruit.

pitted. Stony seeds or pits from fruit or vegetables, such as avocados, that have been removed.

plantains (also platanos). Cooking bananas that come in all sizes and are green, yellow, or black. They are good boiled, baked, fried, and broiled. Most supermarkets have them in the fresh produce section.

poach. To cook food gently in liquid held below the boiling point.

poi. See **taro root**

pomegranate. A golden red fruit, about the size of an apple. It grows on trees native to the Middle East. The fruit is full of tiny edible seeds imbedded in pith. The fruit dates back to ancient times and has been used in many religious rites.

proof. To dissolve and activate yeast in **lukewarm** liquid (sometimes with small amount of sugar); set yeast and water in warm place for 5 to 10 minutes until it is bubbly and expands.

puff pastry sheets (French: *pâte feuilletée*). Available frozen in most supermarkets; a 17¼-ounce box contains 2 sheets puff pastry, each 9½ inches square. Thaw, unwrap, and unfold pastry sheets according to directions on package. Puff pastry has to bake in a very hot, preheated oven to "puff up." Bake according to directions in each recipe. Puff pastry is made by folding and rolling dough and butter to produce many very thin butter-rich layers. During baking, the steam from the melted butter pushes the layers up to make the delicate flaky pastry.

punch down. To do this procedure, use a closed fist to punch down on the dough. This process releases the carbon dioxide air bubbles in the dough. After punching down the dough, remove it from the bowl, and turn it upside down on a lightly floured work surface.

purée. A French-derived word that means to mash, blend, process, or strain food until it reaches a smooth, lump-free consistency. Purée in a blender or food processor; adding a little liquid helps.

reduce. To boil rapidly until the amount of liquid is reduced due to evaporation. This is done to concentrate flavor in broth, to burn off alcohol in wine, and to thicken the sauce's consistency.

render. To melt fat over low heat to release the oil from animal tissue.

rosewater. A sweet, clear, liquid flavoring distilled from rose petals; the petals are often imported from Bulgaria. It is available in Middle Eastern food stores, specialty food stores, and pharmacies.

roasted nuts. To roast nuts, preheat oven to 400°F. Place nuts on a baking sheet and bake for 8 to 10 minutes, or until lightly browned. To dry-roast, put nuts or seeds in a dry pan with no liquid or oil. Shake the pan and stir with a wooden spoon until they lightly tan. Remove from heat at once so the nuts or seeds do not burn.

roux. *See* **white sauce**

salt cod. A Mediterranean staple, especially in Portugal, where it is said there are more than 365 different ways to cook it. In the United States, salt cod was of vital importance to the New England colonies, both for eating and exporting, but gradually fell into disfavor. This was partly due to the misconception that salt cod dishes are salty. In fact, the salt is used to preserve the fish, not flavor it. Salt cod is made by curing fresh cod in brine or rock salt and then drying it either in the sun or air (the traditional way) or in temperature-controlled drying rooms. When properly reconstituted, salt cod is no more salty than fresh fish. It is all in the soaking: Change the water every 4 hours during the soaking process, and refrigerate the soaking cod during the last half of the soaking; it becomes perishable after losing its salt. On average, salt cod fillets should be soaked for at least 12 hour and sometimes up to 36 hours. After soaking in the brine solution, salt cod must be soaked in cold water to soften it and remove its salt. The soaking time depends on how heavily the cod has been salted. Canadian salt cod, the type most commonly available in the United States, is often less heavily salted than other varieties and so needs less soaking. When the fish becomes soft and pliable, start tasting it. Salt cod with skin should be soaked for 48 hours; peel the skin off after soaking. Unlike some preserved foods, salt cod is very different from the fresh version. Salting and drying not only preserves the cod but also silkens the texture and enhances flavor, turning a bland fish into a distinctive product. Salt cod is sold by the pound in many ethnic markets. In food service terminology, "salt cod" refers to boneless fillet, while *bacala* means split, dried salt cod sold with the bone-in and skin-on. Other fish of the cod family are salted and dried and may also be called salt cod; the species name, such as pollock or haddock, should be on the package.

samovar. A large metal urn-like container used for heating water, usually for tea.

sausage casing. Casing used to hold a sausage mixture together in a tube shape. Natural casings are usually intestines of hogs and sheep, which are sold commercially cleaned. Soak in warm water for 2 to 3 hours, until casing is soft and pliable before using. Artificial casings need no preparation, but they are inedible and must be removed before eating the filling. Fill casing according to each recipe.

sauté. To fry in a small amount of oil. This term comes from a French word that means "to jump." The oil must be hot as you quickly cook the "jumping" ingredients; otherwise they absorb too much oil.

scald milk. To heat milk to just below the boiling point, when small bubbles form around the edge of the pan. Formerly, milk was always scalded to kill bacteria. Now, with pasteurized milk, air-dried milk solids, and canned milk, scalding is usually done to save time in dissolving the sugar and melting fat.

Scotch bonnet. A tiny pumpkin-looking capsicum, native to Jamaica, it is one of the hottest peppers known. Since they can be difficult to find, jalapeño peppers or ground red pepper can be used instead.

sear. To cook the surface of food, especially meat, quickly over high heat to brown the exterior. Searing does not "seal in" juices, as commonly thought, but it does improve the flavor and appearance.

section (citrus fruit). To peel the fruit and remove all the **pith**. To section, hold the fruit over a bowl to catch all the juices. Using a serrated paring knife or grapefruit knife, carefully cut down on both sides of the fruit's membrane to release each V-shaped section of edible fruit. Repeat until all edible fruit is removed from the membrane. Squeeze the membrane in your hand to release any remaining juice into the bowl. Discard membrane.

seed. To remove and discard seeds before cutting or chopping, usually for a fruit or vegetable. To seed tomatoes, cut in half and gently squeeze tomatoes over a small bowl. Discard juice, or cover and refrigerate it and the seeds for another use. This is the quickest and easiest way to remove seeds from a tomato.

self-rising flour. A type of flour containing leavening agents and salt for convenience.

segment. *See* **section (citrus fruit)**

semolina. Hard wheat flour (durum) that is excellent for making pasta and some breads.

separated. *See* **eggs, separated**

serrated knife. A knife that has saw-like notches along the cutting edge, such as on a bread knife.

sesame seeds. Used for flavoring in Middle Eastern and Asian cooking. Toast sesame seeds in skillet by cooking over medium heat, tossing frequently, until lightly browned, about 5 minutes. Spread out on a plate to cool. The best places to buy sesame seeds are health food and Middle Eastern food stores.

shallots. A variety of the onion family whose bulbs form small clusters. It has a mild flavor. Peel off the thin brown skin before cooking. Buy shallots that are firm, not wrinkling or sprouting, and store in a cool dry place.

short grain. The type of rice favored for most Japanese cooking. It is more absorbent than the more familiar long grain rice. If the rice you buy seems to have a gummy residue on the surface of the grains, put it in a strainer, wash under cold running water, and drain well. To continue, follow cooking directions on package or in recipe.

shuck. To remove shucks from corn or shellfish.

sift. To shake a dry, powdered substance (such as flour, baking powder, etc.) through a strainer/sifter to make it smooth and lump-free. *See also* **sifter**

sifter. A container, such as a flour sifter, with a strainer bottom used for sifting. *See also* **sift**

silver leaf (also *vark* or *varak*). Tissue-thin edible silver that is decoratively applied to sweet and savory dishes as a show of status and wealth by people in India and the subcontinent. To decorate, gently lay silver leaf on the food, and it self-adheres. Sometimes just a dab, no bigger than a pea, is added to small candies. Three pieces of 2- to 3-inch squares cost about $1.00 at Indian and Middle East food stores. Gold leaf is similar but more expensive than silver leaf.

simmer. To slowly cook food just below the boiling point.

simple syrup. Dissolve 1 cup sugar in ¾ cup water over medium heat. Bring to boil, and cook for 3 to 4 minutes, or until it reaches 220°F on a candy thermometer. Cool syrup, and refrigerate in jar with tight-fitting lid. Use as needed. *See also* **sugar syrup**

skimmer. A long-handled tool that has a round, slightly cupped, mesh screen or metal disk with small holes for removing food items from hot liquid.

slivered. Finely sliced

slurry. A paste made by stirring together water and flour or cornstarch. It is used to thicken hot soups, stews, gravy, or sauces. After adding slurry, continue to cook for several minutes for flour to lose its raw taste.

snow peas (also Chinese snow peas). A legume that is totally edible, including the thin crunchy pod. The French call it *mange-tout,* which means "eat it all." Buy snow peas with crisp, brightly colored pods. If they seem limp, they are probably old. Snow peas can be eaten raw or cooked. Trim off tips at both ends of the pod just before adding to salad or cooking. Rinse under cold running water and drain well. They are available fresh or frozen at most supermarkets and most Asian food stores.

sorghum. A grain similar to **millet**. It is eaten as porridge in Asian countries, and in Africa it is used for porridge and made into flour, beer, and molasses. In the United States, it is mostly used for forage.

star fruit. *See* **carambola**

steamer pan. A two-part pan with a tight-fitting cover. The upper pan is perforated and sits above boiling water in the lower pan. Food placed in the upper pan cooks by the steam from the boiling water. A steamer pan can be made by placing a metal **colander** into a larger saucepan with cover. The pan must be large enough so that the boiling water does not touch the upper container. The steamer basket (upper container) can be propped up with something heatproof, such as a wad of foil or small metal bowl placed in the water. A **bamboo steamer basket** placed in a **wok** makes an excellent steamer pan. Bamboo steamer baskets come in assorted sizes, are inexpensive, and are available in kitchenware stores and Asian food stores.

steamed pudding mold. Heatproof containers that are wider at the top with either plain or fluted sides and with attached cover. Some have a center tube enabling food to cook quicker. The molds come in different sizes. If you don't have a steamed pudding mold, you can make one using either a round-bottomed stainless mixing bowl or a 2- or 3-pound coffee can. Cans aren't tapered like the molds, but they work quite well. Cover the top with sheet of greased aluminum foil, placed greased side down, over the opening. Press the foil tightly against sides of the can and tie with string. It is important to prevent moisture from entering the container.

steep. To soak dry ingredients in liquid (usually hot) until the flavor is incorporated (infused) into the liquid.

sugar syrup (sweet syrup). To make it, heat 1 cup sugar and 1 cup water in small saucepan over high heat until sugar dissolves, about 1 minute. Add a small **pinch** of cream of tartar, stir, and boil rapidly until the syrup is pale golden caramel (310°F to 312°F on candy thermometer). Remove syrup from heat, and place it in a pan of hot water simmering on the stove. This will keep the syrup liquid. If the sugar syrup gets too firm, warm it to soften but do not reboil, or it will crystallize. Sugar syrup stages as it registers on candy thermometer: thread, 230°F to 234°F; soft ball, 234°F to 236°F; firm ball, 242°F to 248°F; hard ball, 250°F to 265°F; crack stage, 270°F to 290°F; hard crack stage, 300°F to 310°F. *See also* **simple syrup**

tamarind. Refers to the seed pod of the tamarind tree, about 5 inches long. When dried, its sweet-sour flavor is used to season food, much like adding lemon juice. Dried tamarind pods are available at all Asian food stores and some supermarkets. Tamarind paste, made from tamarind seeds, is more convenient and available in jars in all Asian food stores.

taro root. A plant of the arum family cultivated throughout Polynesia and the tropics for its edible, starchy roots. When the taro root is cooked and **puréed**, it looks very much like dehydrated mashed potatoes. In its natural state, its color varies from steel blue to pink to purple. Using taro, the Hawaiians make a pudding called *kulolo*. The leaves of the callaloo plant are eaten as a green vegetable. Like the taro root, the leaves must be cooked for at least an hour to remove a peculiarly irritating taste. A variety of taro grown in the Southern United States is **dasheen**.

temper. To raise the temperature of a cold liquid gradually by slowly stirring in a hot liquid.

thermometers. Refers to meat, cooking or candy, and deep fryer thermometers. Meat thermometers register the inside temperature of meat. Cooking or candy thermometer register heat to 400°F and are used for extremely hot ingredients. The best meat thermometer is called "instant," which gives a reading in just seconds. Deep fryer thermometers are built into the fryer equipment.

toasted nuts. *Toast in oven:* Spread nuts or seeds out on baking sheet, and put in preheated 325°F oven until lightly golden, 12 to 15 minutes. *Toast in skillet:* Heat medium skillet over high heat until a drop of water flicked across its surface evaporates instantly. Add the nuts or seeds, and, shaking the pan gently, cook for 2 to 3 minutes, until the seeds are lightly toasted. *See also* **sesame seeds**.

tomatoes, peeled. To peel tomatoes, drop each in boiling water for 1 to 2 minutes. Remove with a slotted spoon, and hold under cold water to stop the cooking action. If the skin has not already cracked open, poke the tomato with a small knife, and the skin easily peels off. *See also* **blanching**

trim or trimmed. To trim off the inedible parts on food products, such as the stems and root ends and blemish spots on fruits and vegetables, gristle and silver skin on meat, or rind on cheeses.

truss. To tightly bind together. When applied to poultry, it is done to keep stuffing inside the bird while it cooks. Trussing can be done by sewing up the opening or inserting several metal truss pins or skewers into skin on either side of the opening and lacing it closed with string (like lacing a boot).

turnips. A root vegetable with white flesh and skin. Buy small, firm, young turnips; as they age, they get a tough, almost woody texture. Wash and **trim** just before using. They can be cooked like potatoes. Turnip greens are best when young. They are available at all supermarkets.

vark **or** *varak. See* **silver leaf**

wasabi. A horseradish-like root grown in Japan and sold as a paste or powder at Asian markets. The powder is soaked in a little cold water for 10 minutes before using. It is served as a condiment for dipping.

water bath. A container with food placed in a larger shallow pan of water that is heated either on the stove or in the oven. The food cooks with less intense heat. Food is also kept warm. The French call it *bain marie*.

watercress. A member of the mustard family that grows in shallow streams. The crisp, deep green leaves are used as an herb, salad green, and garnish. Its flavor is peppery and slightly pungent.

wheat berries. Whole wheat grains that have not been cooked or processed in any way. If they are in good condition, they will sprout and can even be used as seed. Wheat berries can be cooked a long time to make porridge, and they can be cooked with less liquid for a shorter time to use much as you might use rice. With a blender, you can grind wheat berries into a coarse meal. Cracked wheat is wheat berry that has been coarsely chopped by steel blades. It cooks faster than whole berries but not as quickly as bulgur. Bulgur (also bulghar or burghul) refers to wheat berries that have been steamed, toasted, and cracked and then either finely or coarsely ground. Bulgur can be made by boiling the wheat berries about half an hour, until barely tender, draining them thoroughly, and toasting them in flat pan in a 250°F. (warm oven) for 1 to 1½ hours, or until completely dry. In the blender, pulverize the toasted berries to either coarse or fine grind. You can buy wheat berries, cracked wheat, and bulgur in bulk or boxed in health food stores and many supermarkets.

white sauce. A sauce made by stirring a liquid, such as milk or water, into a paste made of fat (usually butter) and flour; this paste is called **roux**. For thin sauce, use 1 tablespoon each of fat and flour for each cup of liquid; for a medium sauce, use 2 tablespoons each of fat and flour for each cup of liquid; for a thick sauce, use 3 tablespoons of each for each cup of liquid.

wok. A Chinese round-bottomed metal cooking pan with sloping sides and a large cooking surface suitable for stir-frying and steaming. A special ring trivet is used to adapt the wok to Western stoves.

yeast. A natural substance that helps breads and cakes rise. In home baking, two types yeast are used—compressed cake yeast or active dry granulated yeast. Both are living organisms and must be activated in warm liquid. One package of dry yeast may be used in place of 1 cake of yeast. To use, dissolve contents of package of dry yeast in ¼ cup **lukewarm** water. Sugar is added to yeast to quicken the action of the yeast. (Never add salt, it retards the yeast action.) When buying dry yeast, make sure it is active by checking the expiration date on package. One package of dry yeast (¼-ounce) contains 2 teaspoons yeast.

zest. The outer peel of citrus fruits, removed by grating or scraping off. It is important to remove only the colored outer peel, not the white pith beneath, which is bitter.

Introduction: What Is a Life-Cycle Event?

A life-cycle event, also known as a "rite of passage," is a person's progression from one stage of life to another. An individual's key life-cycle events—birth, puberty (coming of age), marriage, and death—are important occasions in most societies and cultures worldwide. Other personal milestones—celebrating birthdays and name days, graduating from school, getting the first job, paying off the mortgage, becoming a grandparent—are also times for marking a person's advancement in life. The events indentified as important vary from place to place, from time to time, and from one culture to another. Among most cultures, however, a new stage in life usually calls for a celebration, perhaps a ritual, and almost always food.

Sometimes life-cycle events are marked by an official rite of passage that formally removes individuals from an earlier status or role and places them officially in a new role that includes different rights and responsibilities. In other situations, life milestones are marked or celebrated without such an official rite, but with recognition and a celebration of other kinds. Some of these practices are defined by religious leaders or teachings. Some are the customs of the ethnic group or national community. Often, the life-cycle celebrations are surrounded with familiar customs and traditions, anticipated by all involved.

Many of these customs are rooted in religious traditions, but some of the beliefs can be traced back to more ancient customs. Today in most countries, these beliefs, often called "good luck" and "bad luck," are still very strong. For example, throwing rice at newlyweds to send them on their way at the end of a wedding is supposed to shower luck on their life together. Tying shoes on their getaway car is another act for good luck.

The groom seeing the bride before the wedding is sometimes considered bad luck. Consulting the stars for an auspicious date, rubbing oil on an infant during baptism to ward off the devil, and eating longevity noodles are all rituals that have been passed from generation to generation.

Life-cycle rituals vary from culture to culture and from nation to nation. Some customs are more understandable to outsiders than others. One of the goals of this book is to show the many ways that different cultures mark the milestones in individuals' lives.

In reading these descriptions, keep in mind that rituals vary, even within the same group and that this book limits its descriptions to the most obvious and easy to understand rituals. In addition, the rituals described in these pages tend to reflect an idealized version of the tradition, one that might not be followed in every household. For example, even though it is pretty safe to say that a cake is part of most weddings, not every wedding includes a special cake.

Throughout the world, life-cycle celebrations reveal the very heart of the family and the culture. Continuing the ancestral life-cycle customs and rituals gives continuity and a sense of belonging and substance to each new generation.

Religious Life-Cycle Rituals and Customs

To better understand life-cycle celebrations, it is important to know something about the role religion plays in these events. Throughout the world, religion and culture are entwined, and for many people, religion determines which life-cycle events are celebrated and when and how they are celebrated. Even people who do not consider themselves religious often turn to their religions when reaching these rites of passage. Keep in mind, though, that religious rituals are just one facet of the life-cycle celebrations; the other facets that determine how life-cycle events are celebrated include the family and social structure, the lifestyle, and the habitat of the celebrants.

Although there are countless variations among the world's religions, this introduction will describe the most important life-cycle rituals of eight of the major religions of the world: Indigenous religions, Judaism, Christianity, Islam, Hinduism, Buddhism, Shintoism, and Confucianism. This book cannot, of course, undertake the daunting task of explaining or comparing religions. Nor can it go beyond a simplified presentation of how life-cycle events are celebrated. Over time, with religions crossing borders, mountains, and oceans, life-cycle rituals and celebrations frequently have changed. Local people often have altered, added to, or fused religious and secular customs and rituals. Many of these local customs are described in the introductions to each country section of this book.

INDIGENOUS RELIGIONS

"Indigenous" or "traditional religion" is the umbrella term under which I have classified the religious traditions of tribes and other small groups of people. These traditions represent some of humans' most ancient interpretations of the world around them. Although these indigenous religions are grouped together in this book and also by anthropologists, the variations among religions in this category are immense. To give some idea of this diversity, consider that such groups include but are not limited to Africans, the Maoris of New Zealand, the Aborigines of Australia, and the Native Americans of the Western Hemisphere. Although indigenous religions are found throughout the world, most of the descriptions that follow apply to the indigenous life-cycle events of Africa because these religions have more followers in Africa than in other parts of the world.

Even though indigenous religions differ throughout the world and even in Africa, some general beliefs are fairly widespread. Some followers of indigenous religion believe that all things in nature have a soul and that spirits inhabit trees, water, animals, and all other things in nature, a belief system sometimes known as "animism." Other groups believe that the ancestral spirits (founders of the family, lineage, or clan) affect everyday life. Many followers of indigenous religions who have been exposed to other religions combine these beliefs with their traditional practices, incorporating rituals from both indigenous and introduced religions in life-cycle celebrations.

AFRICAN LIFE-CYCLE RITUALS

Life-cycle events in an African society following indigenous practices usually begin with an offering to the ancestral spirits. The offerings can be baskets of food left on the family shrine or a beverage, water or something stronger, taken out and poured over the ancestral burial ground. Popular ritual foods are honey, pumpkins, and yams.

Birth

Shortly after birth, it is important to name the newborn; usually an ancestral or "spirit" name is chosen. The name is chosen according to which dead ancestor has "returned" in the child. (See Death.) The name is more than a label; being given the name of an ancestor is to inherit something of his or her basic nature, qualities, and status.

Coming of Age (Initiation)

Among most ethnic groups, when the male reaches puberty, an initiation ceremony takes place, usually at the beginning of the dry season in May. The first stage of this ceremony is separation from all females, especially from mothers. Among most groups, circumcision is performed during this separation. The boys spend several months at camps, away from the village, where they undergo trials and are instructed in traditional beliefs and practices. Their return to the village as men is a joyful occasion, and great communal feasts are part of the celebration.

The initiation of girls is often performed on an individual basis, usually just before the first menstrual period. The initiation prepares young women for marriage, and usually no celebration is held, or at most a party is given for the immediate family.

Marriage

Throughout rural Africa, the betrothal and marriage rituals are tied to the age-old concern of collective survival. The rituals, steeped in tradition, might differ slightly from tribe to tribe, but, regardless of specific traditions, marriage is a union between families and communities rather than between two people. Marrying within the kin group is discouraged; however, the preferred marriage is with someone belonging to the same ethnic group. In traditional indigenous cultures, polygamy (one husband and many wives) has been the accepted family structure, in part because of the high death rate of women during childbirth.

Once a mate has been selected, the long, drawn-out courting process can take up to a year to complete in traditional cultures. The giving of premarital gifts and providing of services to each other's families help to cement the marriage agreement. Gifts from the groom's family to the family of the bride, given to validate the marriage contract, include such things as cattle, kente cloth, bags of money, beer, and food. In some communities, the men farm for their prospective in-laws as part of the nuptial contract.

In these traditional cultures, to have children is the most important responsibility of life. To be childless is to have failed the community, including the ancestors. A person without children cannot be an "ancestor" and does not participate in the continuity of communal life.

Until recent years, a girl had no say in her future. As Africa modernizes, women are speaking out, and in some communities they have the right to accept or reject the husband selected by their family. Some can actually choose their own husbands but not without first consulting the ancestral spirits for approval.

Death

In most traditional religions, ancestors are revered by the living. Not everyone who dies becomes an ancestor—only those who have children, who die without shame, and who are correctly buried.

Upon the death of a family member, a period of mourning forges links between the living and the dead. Those in mourning perform a number of rituals to ensure that the spirit of the dead person moves easily into the world of his or her ancestors. Families practice different rituals to retain the connection between this world and the next so that they do not lose contact with ancestors. For example, ancestral worshipers make offerings of food and drink at the grave, and some ethnic groups keep a private shrine or a "spirit house" within the family compound. When a favor is requested of the ancestor spirit, a sacrifice is made, usually a small animal such as a chicken or goat.

The most important link between ancestors and the living is the rebirth of the dead through the birth of a child. In this way, the relationship between ancestors and descendants is continuous and never ending.

In many of these societies, kings and chiefs are considered sacred, and they have elaborate funerals. To please their followers, it is important for ruling figures to be impressive in death, and so they are buried in full regalia. Not too many years ago, the wives and servants of the rulers were killed and buried along with the important men to help them in their afterlife.

JUDAISM AND JEWISH LIFE-CYCLE RITUALS

Judaism is the world's oldest monotheistic religion (belief in just one God), surviving for over 4,000 years. It has also given rise to the Christian and Islamic traditions. Although followers of Judaism can be found all over the world, its roots are in the Middle East, particularly the region around the country of Israel, which was founded in 1948 as a Jewish state.

Judaism has split into three branches—Orthodox, Conservative, and Reform—with numerous other small variations. Although all branches observe the same life-cycle events, each interprets the rituals differently. Orthodox Jews are the most pious and generally follow rituals and customs to their full extent. Most Conservatives accept some of the rituals and customs, while most Reform Jews follow them in moderation, if at all.

One important difference between the different Jewish groups is that Orthodox Jews follow strict kosher dietary laws. The word "kosher" means "fit" or "clean." The kosher rules apply to what can be eaten, how it is processed, and how it is prepared and served. Many Conservative Jews "keep kosher," while most Reform Jews don't observe the kosher laws.

In the state of Israel, the kosher dietary laws are the law of the land and are followed by most people. For Kosher Jews, eating shellfish, pork, and certain other animals is forbidden, and the animals they do eat must be slaughtered a certain way. Dairy products must not be eaten at the same meal with meat and poultry. Wine and the traditional bread, *challah* (recipe page 670), are ritual foods included in all life-cycle celebrations.

Birth

On the eighth day after a boy is born, friends and family gather for a ceremony, observed for millennia, a *brit milah*, the ceremony of circumcision (commonly referred to as a *bris*).

The *mohel*, a person trained to perform the circumcision, does so for male infants of all Orthodox and some Conservative and Reform parents. Followed by appropriate blessings and prayers, the *mohel* completes the procedure with the skill of a fine surgeon. The baby is then comforted in the arms of its mother while the family and a few close friends invited for the ceremony adjourn to another room for a light repast. Some Conservative and Reform Jews prefer to have a doctor perform the circumcision at the hospital before the newborn is taken home. The first Friday evening after the birth of a boy, the family holds a *shalem zachor*, a festive occasion to welcome him into the family. Sweet pastries and *nahit* (chickpeas or garbanzo beans) are traditionally served.

A ceremony fairly new to Judaism celebrates the birth of a girl. *Simhat habat* is Hebrew for "rejoicing over the daughter." When a girl is born, the family's rabbi (Jewish religious leader) announces her name to the congregation during Friday night synagogue services. To celebrate the occasion, some parents and grandparents provide sweets and beverages in the reception area for the congregation following the service.

Many Jewish children are given two names—a secular name and a Hebrew name. Some are named after people in the Bible. The Hebrew name is used throughout life: at the *bar* and *bat mitzvah*, at the wedding, and on the gravestone.

Orthodox Jews have many rituals and customs not practiced by the Conservative or Reform branches of Judaism. For instance, only Orthodox Jews delay a little boy's haircut until he is three years old, the age at which Orthodox boys traditionally begin to study the Torah (the first five books of the Bible).

Coming of Age

Jewish parents believe nothing is more important for their children than an education in both the secular and Hebrew schools. After a boy completes his Jewish learning, at age 13, a coming of age ceremony, a *bar mitzvah*, is held. For a girl, at age 12, a *bat mitzvah* is held. This ceremony is an important event in the lives of Jewish boys and girls because it means they are no longer looked upon as children and they are now received into the religious community. The bar and bat mitzvah ceremonies are a relatively recent development. Neither a ceremony nor a feast is called for in the Jewish religious law, but decades ago, Eastern European Jews began the practice of marking the day with a ceremony at the synagogue, followed by a simple party.

Although customs vary, the *bar* and *bat mitzvah* services take place during the weekly Sabbath service in the synagogue or temple. The young adults read in Hebrew from the Torah, and they are called upon to give a speech, usually thanking their parents and Hebrew teachers. At the close of the service, attended by family, relatives, friends, classmates, and regular members of the congregation, it is customary for the boy's or girl's parents to invite the attendees into the social hall of the temple or synagogue for a *kiddush*, the traditional Sabbath prayer over bread and wine. After the service, everyone is invited to the parent's home, a social hall, or restaurant for a celebration marked by plenty of food and the giving of gifts.

Another coming of age ceremony for Reform Jews is the confirmation ceremony that is celebrated after the completion of Hebrew high school. This practice arose out a belief by Reform Jews that 13 was too young an age for the coming of age ceremony. Today, most Reform Jews celebrate both the bar mitzvah and the confirmation.

Marriage

In Judaism, marriage is considered to be a holy covenant (agreement) between the bride and groom. Among the Orthodox and some Conservative and Reform Jews, a marriage document (*ketubah*) is signed by the bride and groom in which they promise to take care of each other and to make a Jewish home. This document describes the rights and obligations of the bride and groom.

A bride will often wear a face veil for the wedding, especially if she is Orthodox. If the veil is worn, a veiling ritual takes place just before the ceremony when the groom veils the bride after he verifies that she is actually the woman he plans on marrying. This symbolic ritual is a reminder of the lesson learned in the Old Testament by Jacob, who was tricked into marrying Leah instead of Rachel, his true love. Leah pretended to be Rachel and covered her face with her veil so that Jacob would not know the truth until the marriage was sanctioned.

A Jewish wedding can be held at any location, as long as an ordained rabbi officiates. By custom, all immediate relatives are part of the wedding party. The groom and then the bride are escorted down the aisle by their parents. Siblings can be attendants, and grandparents may have a place in the procession.

The wedding ceremony is performed under a *huppah* (wedding canopy), which represents the couple's future home. The *huppah* is often a large embroidered cloth, or it can be a blanket of fresh flowers and greenery; sometimes it is a prayer shawl (*tallit*) belonging to a relative. The *huppah* is held up by four poles, and it is considered an honor to be one of the four people selected to hold a pole upright during the ceremony. Symbolically, the pole bearers are showing loyalty to the marrying couple. Under the *huppah*, a table is set with two glasses and a bottle of ritual wine used for the *kiddush* prayer.

Depending on the couple's cultural background, personal preference, and local custom, the language of the service will vary, possibly combining Hebrew and English. After the introduction by the rabbi, wedding vows are exchanged; for Orthodox and some Conservative ceremonies, the groom then places a plain gold band (without engraving or breaks) on the bride's right index finger. If it is a Reform ceremony, it is usually placed on her left ring finger.

The rabbi then reads aloud the *ketubah* (the traditional marriage contract). At some point during the service, the bride and groom will each sip a glass of ritual wine while a traditional prayer, a *kiddush*, is recited. Near the end of the ceremony, the traditional seven blessings will be recited or sung. The Orthodox ritual is a little different. The bride may circle the groom seven times, representing the seven wedding blessings, before taking her place at his right side.

The *sheva brachot* (seven blessings) symbolize the seven days of creation and the completion of the marriage ceremony. The first blessing is upon the wine, the fruit of the vine. The second thanks God for his creation, and the third specifically praises God for his creation of human life. The fourth blessing acknowledges the separation of human life into man and woman. The fifth wishes for Jerusalem to be rebuilt and restored to its beautiful existence. The sixth declares hope that the new couple will be as happy as Adam and Eve were in the Garden of Eden. The seventh blessing thanks God for creating delight, mirth, gratification, pleasure, love, serenity, and brotherhood.

The ceremony ends with the tradition of crushing the wine glass used in the ceremony beneath the groom's heel. The glass is often wrapped in a napkin or handkerchief before the groom stamps on it. The breaking of the glass symbolizes the destruction of the Temple of Jerusalem and acts as a reminder that in life and in marriage, there are times of sorrow and joy. The shattered glass also reminds guests and participants of how fragile life is. After the groom breaks the glass, guest clap and cheer him and call out, *"Mazel tov!"* ("congratulations" or "good luck"). Immediately following the ceremony, some Jewish couples perform a traditional ritual known as *yichud* (union). The couple goes into a private room where they briefly eat some food together, usually chicken broth.

Housewarming

Chanukat habayit is the celebration for the family in their new home. It is a housewarming or a "dedication of the home." A *mezuzah*, a case containing small scrolls in Hebrew with two extracts from Deuteronomy (in the Old Testament), is fixed to the top right-hand side of the front door and each door inside the house. Prayers are said, and bread and salt are brought into the house before the festivities begin.

Death

After a death in a Jewish family, the funeral service is arranged as soon as possible, preferably within 24 hours of death. Funerals are kept very simple, even among wealthy families. No prayers for the dead are offered, but *kaddish*, a prayer of praise to God, is recited in their memory. When a parent dies, it is the responsibility of the children to say *kaddish* on their behalf. At Orthodox and some Conservative funerals, mourning family members make a small tear in their clothes (such as on a tie or scarf) as a mark of grief.

After the funeral, mourners are invited to the departed person's family home to partake in food and drink prepared by friends or family members other than mourners. This meal is known as *seudat havra-ah* (meal of consolation). Customs vary among the different communities and Jewish groups, but the food for *seudat havra-ah* always includes hard-cooked eggs as a symbol of life and another food whose roundness suggests the continuance and eternity of life, such as lentils or bagels. In Judaism, bread is the staff of life and is served at all meals. At a time of mourning, it is especially appropriate to eat bread as the symbol of life. The *seudat havra-ah* is a *mitzvah* (blessing), not a social event, and so mourners can drink a moderate amount of wine. Meat is symbolically the food of celebration and joy; therefore it is never served for *seudat havra-ah*.

Before entering the house, all the mourners must wash their hands. A pail of water and towels are placed just outside the front entrance of the house for this ritual. Following the funeral, a week of private mourning, called *shivah* (the seven days), is observed. During *shivah*, the grieving Orthodox Jews sit on low stools or on the floor. It is also the custom to cover mirrors and pictures hanging on the walls with cloth sheets.

On the anniversary of a parent's death, the children light a memorial candle (and recite the *kaddish*. Toward the end of every Friday night synagogue or temple service, the rabbi asks those mourning a loved one to join him in reciting the *kaddish*.

CHRISTIANITY AND CHRISTIAN LIFE-CYCLE RITUALS

Christianity is a universal religion with more followers than any of the other world religions. Christianity is a monotheistic religion (the belief in just one God) that grew out of Judaism. The Old Testament of the Christian Bible is the same as the Jewish Torah; however, Christians believe that Jesus Christ is the messiah prophesized in the Old Testament. The story of Jesus's life makes up the New Testament.

Over the centuries, cultural differences and variations in the way people worship have led to the formation of thousands of different branches, denominations, and sects within Christianity. The principal divisions in Christianity are the Protestant, the Catholic, and the Orthodox Churches. Despite these divisions, Christians share some common beliefs: Jesus Christ is the savior, Sunday is the official day of worship, and the Bible is the holy book of Christianity.

Almost all Christian churches celebrate life-cycle events with the designated rituals—baptisms, communion, confirmation, marriage, and death. The rituals and pageantry vary from simple in some Protestant churches to the symbolic pageantry in most Catholic churches and the grand opulence in the Orthodox churches. Besides these differences in religious sects, the geographic location, the traditions, and the customs of local people cause rituals to vary from one country to another. Although these differences exist, the foods associated with Christian rituals are fairly universal. Red wine or grape juice and breads and wheat grain products have a religious significance in most Christian church ceremonies.

PROTESTANT AND CATHOLIC LIFE-CYCLE RITUALS

Birth

Baptism is the most widely accepted way of becoming a member of the Christian faith. The word "baptism" is derived from Greek *baptizein*, meaning "to dip or immerse." Christian churches have infant baptisms and adult baptisms. When infants are baptized, they are either dipped into a baptism tub, called a font, or water is sprinkled on the infant's head by the minister (Protestant clergy) or priest (Catholic clergy). When an adult converts to Christianity, the baptism ceremony can be held in a church or in a river or lake. The various Christian groups observe the rituals in different ways. Among some groups, when a baby is born, parents select godparents to oversee the child's spiritual progress in case they are unable to do so. The godparents are expected to take part in the baptismal ceremony. For some groups, naming the child, the christening, is part of the ceremony.

Coming of Age

Christian churches that practice infant baptism almost always have coming of age ceremonies, known as "confirmation." Although confirmations can take place at anytime, they are usually held at the onset of puberty, at about age 14. At these ceremonies, a young person is "confirmed" to take a more active role in the church. To be confirmed, one has to attend classes to learn more about the Christian faith.

Catholic confirmation services are a little more extensive and include many symbolic rituals. In most denominations, the ceremony is performed by a high-ranking member of the church. An emotional ritual performed by the clergy is "laying hands" on the head of the person being confirmed. This ancient ritual symbolizes the passing on of the Christian faith from one generation to the next.

Betrothal and Marriage

Christian marriage traditions vary from church to church and even from family to family. Prior to marriage, the couple usually announces their intentions to marry, known as the "betrothal." The lengths of the betrothal period are different for each marriage, with no set time period. Some Christian groups have orientation classes at the church to prepare the couple for marriage.

A Christian wedding may be an elaborate, formal church ceremony with many attendants or a very simple affair with just the bride and groom before the minister. Most

Protestants hold their wedding ceremonies anywhere they like; they need not take place in the church. The wedding celebrations differ according to the customs of the country, ethnic group, city, village, and even the family.

Roman Catholic marriages must take place in the church to be officially recognized. The ceremony can be either without mass and only 20 minutes long or a more elaborate ceremony with a mass, lasting for an hour.

It is customary for the Roman Catholic priest to give instructions throughout the mass, which often vary from parish to parish. During the wedding ceremony, vows and rings are exchanged. Just before communion (see next paragraph) is served, the priest gives a sign of peace, and at that time the guests turn to their neighbors, shake their hands, and say, "Peace be with you" or some other friendly greeting. Close friends and relatives often hug.

In The Roman Catholic Church, communion is reserved for baptized Catholics. The Communion is the commemoration of Christ's Last Supper. It is the ceremony in which bread and wine are consecrated and taken to be the body and blood of Christ. (Episcopal and Orthodox churches also have communion ceremonies during weddings.) To take communion, members of the congregation walk down the center aisle to take the bread (usually a wafer) and wine and then return to their seats. After Communion, the signing of the register takes place, and the priest introduces the newly married couple to the guests. At this time, the guests will often applaud, depending on local custom.

Both Catholic and Protestant wedding ceremonies are usually followed by a wedding feast. It can be a simple meal for just the wedding party or an elaborate one for thousands of guests. The feast can be a wedding breakfast, luncheon, afternoon repast, supper, or extravagant wedding reception at any time of day or evening with feasting, drinking, dancing, singing, and merrymaking.

Death

Christian customs for mourning the dead vary from country to country and from parish to parish. When a Christian dies, the body is embalmed and then washed and dressed in clean clothing in preparation for burial and placed in a coffin. Another option is for the body to be cremated, or reduced to ashes. The family may choose to keep those ashes at a memorial site or cemetery, or they may be retained by family members to be kept on mantles or dispersed in a private setting. Depending upon local customs and the financial situation and wishes of the family, Christian funerals can take place either at home, a funeral home, a church, a public hall or a place dedicated by loved ones as special.

The evening before a Protestant funeral, it is customary for family and friends to view the body in either the home or funeral home. Catholics have a wake (prayer service), followed by the serving of food and drink. In fact, food and drink play an important role in the mourning process. As soon as friends and neighbors hear about a death, it is customary for them to bring platters, bowls, and baskets of prepared food and beverages to the home of the deceased to be shared by mourners.

On the day of the burial, Protestants generally have a service at the funeral home or church. Catholics may or may not bring the casket to the church for the mass. After the burial at the cemetery, the mourners go to the church hall or the home of the deceased to share in the food provided for the occasion.

It is customary for Catholics to have a memorial mass said in memory of a loved one 30 days after the death and again after one year.

EASTERN OR ORTHODOX CHURCH LIFE-CYCLE RITUALS

The Eastern or Orthodox churches are territorial or national. This arrangement is unlike the close-knit unity of the Roman Catholic Church, whose clergy are under the authority of the Pope, regardless of their location. The Orthodox churches of Greece, Russia, Armenia, Bulgaria, Serbia, and other countries are autonomous and have always been closely identified with their own country. The life-cycle rituals of Orthodox churches are more elaborate than those of other Christian churches.

Birth

Parents are allowed to bring their newborns to church for the first time 40 days after birth. At that time, the priest offers special prayers and blessings for the infant.

The baptism, usually held after the infant is three or four months old, is the first important event in a child's life. Baptism is the triple immersion of the baby by the priest in a baptismal tub filled with warm water. For the baptism, the baby's clothes are removed and discarded. After the triple dipping, the child is dried off by the godparents. The priest then performs the chrismation, anointing the child with oil (chrism). This symbolic act is performed to keep the devil from grasping the child. Another symbolic act is for the priest to snip off a lock of the child's hair, representing the child's first donation to the church.

After the immersion, the godparents dress the baby in their gift of new clothes, all white, a symbol of purity. They also give the infant a gold cross. The child is given a Christian name, usually chosen from one of the many saints and martyrs of the church.

Name Day: Catholic and Orthodox Christian

In some Catholic and Orthodox Christian communities, instead of celebrating a birthday, the children celebrate the "name day" of the saint or martyr they were named after. The name day is not the birth date of the child or the saint but rather the designated date on which the church elevated a holy or godly person or martyr to sainthood. Each country or region of the world, ethnic group, or church has its own collection of saints and martyrs.

Marriage

The traditional Orthodox wedding takes place in the church, and it is usually a very long ceremony with many symbolic rituals. Each country, ethnic group, or church adds its own unique traditions to some of the following basic rituals.

During the wedding, the bride and groom wear crowns or wreaths to signify their elevation to king and queen of the home they will share. The couple jointly sips red wine from a cup to signify their togetherness, and double rings are blessed and exchanged as a visual ritual of unity. The reception feast follows at the church hall, club or hotel ballroom, restaurant, or family home.

Death

Orthodox Christian funerals are marked by long, involved rituals and ceremonies that vary by the ethnic group, the church, the community, and, to some degree, the family's wishes.

The burial service is more intense and dramatic than that of the Roman Catholic Church service, taking it to a higher level of pageantry. Among some groups, it is customary for the family mourners to cut a lock of hair to be buried with the dead; this act symbolizes that not even death will sever the strong family ties.

ISLAM AND ISLAMIC LIFE-CYCLE RITUALS

Islam is the second largest universal religion, with followers in all parts of the world. Islam is a monotheistic religion with its roots in Judaism and Christianity. Muslims believe in the biblical prophets Adam, Noah, Abraham, Ishmael, Isaac, Jacob, Moses, and Jesus, but they believe that Muhammad is the last prophet sent by God and that his message is the final one. Although Muslims believe Jesus was a prophet, they don't believe he was the son of God or that he was crucified.

Islam cannot be separated from daily life and government and so provides a framework for both secular and spiritual life. Prayer, fasting, pilgrimage, and dietary requirements are some of the long held customs of the Muslim faith.

Muslims must pray five times a day, every day of their lives. At dawn each morning in Muslim communities, a *muezzin* (prayer announcer) enters the mosque (house of worship), climbs to the top of the minaret (tower), and, usually with the help of loudspeakers and a public address system, calls the faithful to the first of the day's prayers. They are called, if not actually to enter a mosque, at least to take the time to pray wherever they are. In most Islamic countries, it is a common sight to see Muslims praying by the side of the road or in the street.

On Fridays, the Muslims gather before noon at the mosque, and the prayer (*jum'ah*) is led by an *imam* (religious leader). In the mosque, the prayer area for the men is completely separate from the section designated for the women and children. The mosque also serves as a community center where children and adults are schooled in the Koran (the Islamic holy book).

Birth

In Muslim countries, the birth of a child is a joyous occasion. The birth of a boy is cause for a greater celebration than for the birth of a girl. When a boy grows up and marries, his wife and children become part of and strengthen his parents' extended family. Girls, however, leave their families and become part of their husband's clan when they marry.

To welcome a newborn baby into the world, an *imam* whispers the call to prayer into its ear. Another auspicious and joyous ceremony is when the baby is named. Guests are invited to a celebration feast. Roasted lamb is the traditional food served at this ceremony and at most other Muslim celebrations.

Coming of Age

The major event of a boy's life is his circumcision, which normally takes place sometime between the ages of seven and 12. It is a religious requirement for male Muslims. This ritual requires no celebration except perhaps a family dinner.

When a girl reaches puberty, she changes from the dress of a schoolgirl to the garments worn by women. From this time forward, she dons the veil (*hijab*, also *khimar*) in public. The veiling signifies that she is now a woman and is ready for marriage. Each Muslim country has its own identifiable veiling and rules of dress for women. It is often possible to tell not only a woman's country but also what region she is from and her status in life by the veil she wears. Varying in style, some veils cover just the hair and neck, and others leave only the eyes visible. Among the most devout Muslims, the veil not only completely covers a woman's head and face but it drapes down over her clothes to her ankles.

Marriage

Marriage rituals in most Muslim countries are basically similar, but some are very rigid, following Islamic law to the letter; others are a little more lenient. Most Muslim marriages are arranged by the parents, and because marriage is an agreement between families, a financial contract is drawn up to define the terms. The bride takes no part in the negotiations, nor does she see her husband until after they are married. The groom has to pay *mahr*, the bride-price, by giving the bride gold jewelry or other goods that are worth an agreed amount of money. In some countries, the bride's family, not the bride receives the money from the groom. If a groom is wealthy, he will give money to the family and jewelry to the bride.

The religious part of a marriage is very private and is performed separately from the more public celebration. According to strict Islamic law, at no time are men and women allowed to be together in the same room for any part of the wedding celebration or for any other occasion, for that matter. The religious part of the marriage ceremony is quite simple and is conducted by someone learned in *sharia* (Islamic law), usually the *imam*. In Islam, the *imam* is separated from the bride-to-be by a screen or closed door; he asks the bride if she will accept the prospective husband. If she agrees, the *imam* then goes to the groom and asks him, in the presence of four witnesses (they cannot be family members), if he will take the woman for his wife. His acceptance in front of witnesses makes the marriage valid, and then the *imam* officially records the contract.

According to Islamic law, polygamy (a husband with more than one wife) is allowed; a man can have no more than four wives at a time and, even then, only if he can afford to treat them all equally; otherwise, he must take fewer wives.

Hajj

The *hajj*, the pilgrimage to the Muslim holy city of Mecca, is the most important rite of passage in a Muslim man's life. Muslim men are obliged to make the pilgrimage at least once in a lifetime. The *hajj* must be performed during a specific month.

The Ka'aba is the sanctuary in Mecca to which all Muslims turn in prayer. The Black Stone is a sacred object set in the eastern wall of the Ka'aba. During the *hajj*, the faithful try to kiss or touch the stone. The Koran associates Abraham and Ishmael with the building of the Ka'aba.

Death

When a Muslim dies, the funeral is very simple, and the body must be buried within 24 hours. The placement of the grave is important because the body must face Mecca.

The body is washed and wrapped in a white cotton shroud. Muslims are not buried in coffins; a plank is placed at the bottom of the grave, and the body is laid on top of it. The face is covered with a cloth before the body is lowered into the ground. Men carry the body on a stretcher, or, in the case of a young child, the father carries the body in his arms. Male relatives sprinkle the grave with earth before it is completely covered. The final prayers are said for deceased at the cemetery. Muslim graves have no elaborate headstones. Only a small stone or marker is placed at the head and foot of the grave.

Muslim women do not accompany the body to the burial ground because it is not considered appropriate for them, as bearers of life, to visit a place of death.

It is the custom for friends and relatives to bring food for the immediate family for three days after the burial, and, in turn, the guests are offered coffee (but no food). Honey or dishes made with honey are often eaten after funerals. Muslims believe eating honey is soothing to the soul and eases the mental anguish associated with death. A widower has no required mourning period, but a widow must go into seclusion for several months after the death of her husband.

HINDUISM AND HINDU LIFE-CYCLE RITUALS

The origins of the Hindu religion are obscure, but elements of Hindu beliefs can be traced back at least several thousand years. It is a complicated religion with many different interpretations by the numerous sects. Each group has intricate and minutely detailed rituals, customs, and ceremonies that are deeply rooted in every stage of life.

Traditional Hindus attempt to achieve four objectives through life. The first objective is *dharma* (duty), followed by *artha* (material prosperity), *kama* (enjoyment), and finally *moksha* (salvation). To achieve these four objectives, Hindus divide life into four segments: *bramacharya* (celibacy—student life, learning); *grihastha* (family life—enjoying life years); *vanaprastha* (retirement—delegating responsibilities to younger generations); and finally *sanyas* (renunciation—giving up all responsibilities to prepare for death and the journey to the spirit world).

The most basic Hindu ceremonies, those pertaining to the life cycle, take place in the home. The four major life-cycle events are prenatal and birth, childhood, marriage, and death. Most Hindus keep a home shrine for daily prayer, which can be a shelf, a corner of a room, or in some homes a small room or closet. For the life-cycle ceremonies, family and friends gather around a family member who performs the ritual. When necessary, a priest is called in to take over the more complicated services.

The shrine contains pictures and/or statues of the gods and goddesses, saints, and ancestors. Other ritual necessities are a container of water for sprinkling and purifying the area, a bell, a lamp to wave in front of the gods, an incense burner, and a tray with flowers and food. The food offerings include fruit, freshly cooked rice, butter or *ghee*, and sugar. After a prayer is said over the food, family members eat it.

Food is an important element of Hinduism. The kitchen in a Hindu home is treated as part cooking room, part dining room, and part chapel. Since leather is considered unclean by Hindus, one may not cook or dine wearing shoes. Beef is banned because cattle are revered as sacred.

The Hindu food laws and restrictions do not simply prohibit certain foods in the same way Muslims and Jewish people are forbidden from eating pork. Hindu food restrictions and rituals are very complex; caste, ethics, aesthetics, and faith, as well as nutrition, hygiene, and diet, are all interwoven into the Hindu doctrines involving food. The specific rituals and customs extend not only to what food is eaten and why it is cooked a certain way but also to how and where it is served and eaten.

One unique feature interwoven in Indian society and Hinduism is the caste system that divides the Indian population into four main castes (*varnas*). The castes were established by Aryan priests after India was invaded by the Aryans around 1500 BCE. The caste divisions were originally based on racial or ethnic differences, with the Aryans occupying the higher castes. The highest caste are the *Brahmans* (priests and scholars); next are the *Kshatriyas* (nobles and warriors); below them are the *Vaishyas* (merchants and skilled artisans); and finally there are *Shudras* (common laborers). Beyond the actual castes are the *Harijans* (outcastes), who were given the dirty and degrading jobs. The outcastes were called "untouchables" because merely to touch an outcaste or even to be touched by an outcaste's shadow was considered a form of ritual pollution for members of the higher *varnas*. Although officially banned by the Indian constitution since 1949, some people are still considered *Harijan*.

Within the four Indian castes are thousands of subcastes (*jati*), usually confined to local areas or regions. A *jati* is usually connected to a particular occupation, such as trash collectors, rag pickers, snake charmers, farmers, and street sweepers.

Although the Indian caste system is stronger in rural areas, it still is a vital part of the Hindu religion and Indian culture. Indians' caste and subcaste positions affect the jobs available to them as well as their diet and religious practices, including how life-cycle events are celebrated.

Prenatal, Birth, and Early Childhood

Before birth, during the seventh month of pregnancy *simantonnayana* takes place, during which time prayers are recited, and then the mother's hair is parted by her husband with hopes of calming and relaxing her mind and body for birth. After birth, the placenta is honored through a burial as it nourished and provided nutrition for the baby. Another tradition is the naming ceremony that takes place on the 10th or 12th day after birth and is performed by a Hindu priest. The name is selected according to the baby's horoscope, and friends and relatives are invited to celebrate the event. Another ceremony, *annaprasana*, is held at six months when the infant is given its first solid food. The baby's first step and first birthday may also be observed with a religious ceremony and a party. Between the ages of one and five, girls experience a ceremonial ear piercing; this event too is reason to rejoice and have a party as it is supposed to ward off evil.

The *mundan*, first haircut, is a very auspicious event for baby boys between one and three years of age. The father is supposed to shave the head, but usually he just cuts a few hairs while reciting the appropriate Hindu verses; the task is finished by a barber.

The first hair is offered as a sacrifice to the gods. The hair cutting event always calls for a large celebration with plenty of food.

Coming of Age

The main adolescence ritual is *upanayana*, popularly known as the "thread ceremony." Only boys between the ages of eight and 12 in the upper three castes of the Hindu social system go through this ceremony. There are complex variations to this ritual for different Hindu sects. One of the basic principles behind this ceremony is to elevate the boy into manhood. Before the ritual, he eats his last meal with his mother, and after the completion of *upanayana*, he is expected to eat with the adult male family members. The "thread," or *upavita*, refers to a three-strand rope normally worn over the left shoulder and hanging under the right arm. It is a visible symbol confirming the boy's passing over into manhood.

Some of the ritual foods used in this ceremony are *ghee* (recipe page 142), coconut, corn, wheat, and rice.

Marriage

Most Hindus consider it a social obligation to be married within the religion, and marriages are arranged between members of the same caste (social group). The first thing parents have to do, with the consent of their offspring, is to find a suitable mate. Then an auspicious date and time for the marriage ceremony are chosen based on astrological charts. Nowadays, more and more parents, especially in urban areas, believe the dowry and good looks are more important than the agreement of stars. This has become possible because boys and girls are not married as children as they once were.

Hindu wedding ceremonies vary greatly, depending on geographical location, sect, family customs, and personal taste. Even within the same community, differences can be seen in the clothes, ornaments, rituals, food, and length of the wedding celebrations, which in some cases can last several days. Rice and *ghee* (recipe page 142) are important ritual foods.

The marriage (*vivaha*) is considered to be a gift-giving ritual by the father. He gives his daughter (*kanya*) as a gift (*dan*) to the boy's family. The biggest donation a father can make in his lifetime is *kanya dan* (the gift of his daughter).

A great many marriages take place in wedding halls, which are available on a rental basis. A priest officiates the wedding, which is held in front of a pit for the sacrificial marriage fire (*vivahahoma*). The fire is fueled by sprinkling it with *ghee*. Among most Hindus, it is the custom for the couple to circle the fire seven times, chanting vows and throwing in offerings such as rice.

During the ceremony the bride and groom each wears a garland of flowers around the neck, which they exchange with each other as a token of acceptance. The father of the bride offers her hand in marriage first of all to the gods, then to the groom. The groom then assures his father-in-law that he will take care of his bride.

At some point during the ceremony, the bride may stand on a stone, representing firmness and stability, to signify loyalty and faithfulness in the marriage. The rituals and customs extend to the wedding feast, making it an important part of the total marriage ceremony.

Retirement

The 60th birthday is a milestone in a person's life and is a very auspicious date. Making it to 80 years old is as good as reaching 100; it is called *sathabishekam*, which means 100. Both dates are reasons for a celebration feast with family and friends.

Death

Hindus view death as part of the never ending cycle of birth and rebirth. According to Hindu tradition, bodies are cremated after death. Very elaborate ceremonies may continue for several weeks after the cremation, which must take place as soon as possible after death. After someone dies, the body is immediately washed and dressed in fresh clothes. Men and widows generally are covered in white shrouds, although the customs and the color of the shroud cloth can vary greatly, even within the same Hindu group. Among some Hindus, a woman is decorated as for her wedding, and her shroud is orange.

Unlike other Hindu life-cycle celebrations, friends and family do not bring food to the families in mourning. Death memorial rituals can last for several days or up to a year after the death of a loved one, depending on the beliefs of the person performing them.

BUDDHISM AND BUDDHIST LIFE-CYCLE RITUALS

Buddhism originated in India in the sixth century BCE as an offshoot of Hinduism and soon spread to other countries. Buddha, the Enlightened One, was a Hindu prince whose philosophy grew into a separate religion. Buddha considered himself not a holy man but rather a teacher who simply wanted to inform and enlighten people about life and afterlife. Buddhism was accepted by people from all walks of life and all over the world. Many different interpretations of Buddhism have developed over the years in different countries.

Life-cycle events, such as births, coming of age, and marriages, are not considered to be spiritually significant by Buddhists, although monks may bless a new baby, a marriage, or a new house. In some countries, for example Thailand, temporary ordination and a short period in the monastery may serve as a boy's entry into adulthood.

Buddhists do consider burial ceremonies important occasions. Funerals reconfirm the Buddhist teachings that nothing is permanent and that rebirth follows death. The funeral takes place in a temple or funeral hall, where priests, accompanied by the sounds of bells, gongs, and hollow wooden blocks, recite prayers over the body placed on a bier or in a coffin. Mourners then burn incense before the corpse. Twenty-four hours or more later, the body is taken to be cremated or buried.

Most Buddhists build a family altar in their home and place an ancestral tablet and other sacred articles on it. The tablet is a small lacquered, gilded board containing a picture and the name of the deceased. Incense is burned on the altar, and family members pray before it.

Families traditionally mourn their dead for 49 days and then observe the first, third, seventh, and 13th anniversaries by asking a priest to give a prayer service for the dead.

Shintoism and Shinto Life-Cycle Rituals

Shintoism is a Japanese religion. Its origins are unclear, but some scholars believe it is the name given to combined religious practices, some dating back to prehistoric Japan. Others believe Shintoism is simply a way of life that grew out of a natural love for everything and everyone.

Japan has thousands of Shinto shrines, sacred places where spirits (*kami*) dwell. (In the Shinto religion, the source of all creation and the unexplainable essences of the universe are called *kami*.) Different shrines are visited for specific divine powers (*shintoku*). Students visit certain shrines to seek help with their studies, and sick people come to other shrines for their healing powers. Some shrines give protection from accidents, while other shrines are popular with couples seeking to bless their marriages.

Mostly life-cycle celebrations and community festivals take place at the shrines. The Japanese often combine religions, and it is not unusual for the same person to have had a Shinto wedding and a Buddhist funeral.

Birth and Early Years

It is common, though not universal, for a baby to be brought to the Shinto shrine by its mother or grandmother so that prayers may be said for its good health. *Hatsu miya-mairi* (first shrine visit) takes place on the 32nd day after birth for a boy and on the 33rd day for a girl. At this ceremony, the baby is introduced to the spirits (*kami*) and becomes a member of the shrine.

The *shichi-go-san* (seven-five-three) festival is held throughout Japan on the nearest Sunday to November 15. Parents with three- and seven–year-old boys and five–year-old girls dress them in traditional kimonos and bring them to the shrine for a ceremony. At the shrine, parents give thanks for their children's good health and growth so far and pray for their future.

Coming of Age (Seijin-no-hi)

Seijin-no-hi is on the second Sunday in January. The once-a-year coming of age ceremony is held for all who turn 20 throughout the year. On this day, Japanese youth are granted full rights as citizens. Families spend huge amounts of money on traditional clothing and photos for a ceremony that lasts less than an hour. Most women attend this ceremony in a colorful *furisode*, a long-sleeved kimono worn by single women.

Marriage

The *shinzen kekkon-sai* is a marriage ceremony before the *kami* (spirit). The majority of wedding ceremonies in Japan include Shinto rituals, while others are Western-style, Christian events, popular since World War II. Shinto weddings became popular in the early 1900s after the very first royal wedding was performed by Shinto priests. Some Shinto shrines have a special hall to accommodate wedding parties. If the ceremony is not held at the shrine, the priests often officiate at public wedding halls or hotel ballrooms.

Death

Buddhist monks are looked upon as ritual specialists, and they are often called upon to chant the *sutras* that will benefit the deceased and to conduct all funeral rites and memorial services; the funeral services for the two religions are very similar. To help the deceased on the journey to the beyond, mourners make offerings of paper "spirit money," along with wine, incense, and food, such as fish, fowl, and vegetables. Instead of burning incense as the Buddhists do, the Shinto mourners offer strips of white paper and twigs of the sacred *sakaki* tree.

Selecting a proper location for the grave is very important, and a *feng shui sien sheng* (a specialist in grave placement matters) is consulted for the best site. The heirs must maintain the grave, and they are expected to make occasional offerings.

Within 100 days of the burial, a memorial service is held in the home of the oldest male heir. The Shinto priest offers prayers and reads an account of the life of the deceased.

The Shinto ancestral tablet, containing a picture and the name of the deceased, is made of plain wood. It is dedicated by the priest and placed on the home altar along with joss sticks (special incense), which are lit and placed on the tablet. Newlyweds traditionally bow before the altar as a sign of respect.

According to Shinto beliefs, overseeing the proper funeral for a family member and making regular offerings to the ancestors are critical if the living descendants expect to have a successful, good life.

CONFUCIANISM AND CONFUCIAN RITES OF PASSAGE

Confucianism can be confusing to Western readers because it is more of a philosophy and way of life than a religion. Confucian teachings have influenced the beliefs and values of traditional societies in China, Korea, Japan, Vietnam, and Taiwan for centuries. Confucius (551–472 BCE) was a teacher who taught social and ethical reforms, not religion. Respectful relationships between all people—parents and children, one another, and elders—are fundamental to Confucians.

In the old Imperial China, Confucian officials regulated the traditional rites of passage and all aspects of public behavior. Under Communism, the great majority of Chinese people still hold fast to values that were first introduced by Confucius and his followers, even though religion is officially discouraged.

Throughout Asian countries, Confucian rituals are hard to identify because they are generally fused with other religions.

Death

Today, the most important rite of passage for Confucians is death. Confucians have great respect for their ancestors; when someone dies, the funeral is a memorable occasion. Colorful decorations and elaborate rituals are carefully attended to with the help of a religious leader. Family mourners chant prayers and offer sacrifices of food, especially rice. They symbolically burn paper money, and in some cases paper cars, planes, and images of servants, all necessary items that they believe will help the spirit of the dead make a more enjoyable journey into the world of its ancestors.

AFRICA

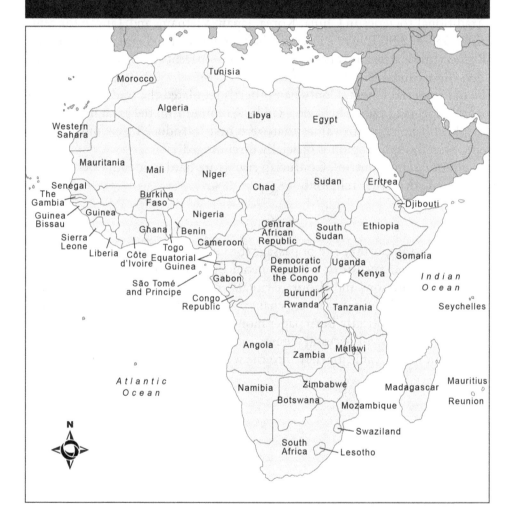

❧ 1 ❧

Africa

INTRODUCTION

Africa is the world's second largest continent, with perhaps the most diverse population in the world. There are well over a thousand ethnic groups and just about as many different languages. The majority of Africans are farmers and pastoralists in rural communities where the foods, religion, daily life, and celebrations of life passages have changed little for centuries.

Christianity and Islam are the most prevalent religions in Africa, while a small percentage of farmers and herders practice indigenous religious beliefs. African Christians follow the life-cycle rituals prescribed by the Church, and African Muslims follow those of the Koran. It is also very common for Africans to fuse traditional local religious practices with those of Christianity or Islam.

Five major African initiation rites or rituals are commonplace among most indigenous tribes: birth, adulthood, marriage, eldership, and ancestorship. Each rite is considered a new phase in one's life and identifies a role within the community. (See Indigenous Religions, page lxv and African Life-Cycle Rituals, page lxvi).

Today, African traditions and customs have been modified due to Western influences. Many of the events to celebrate individuals' life-milestones vary according to the family, its social status, and its wealth; the region where the people live; their communication skills; and their religious beliefs. However, throughout Africa, individuals' life-milestone celebrations are usually community affairs, and recognition of each person's progress through the key events of the life-cycle is important to everyone in the family, clan, and village.

Life is harsh in many parts of Africa, so an opportunity to celebrate the achievement of a life-milestone is a joyous occasion that usually includes feasting, dancing, singing, and the wearing of elaborate garments, ornate headdresses, and colorful jewelry.

In most African communities, the clothing a woman wears indicates whether she is single, married, or widowed. In southern Africa, among the *Ndebele* women, for instance, a bride's mother-in-law makes her a *jocolo*. This is a colorfully beaded five-paneled goat-skin apron that married women wear on ceremonial occasions. In parts of Western Africa, a married woman wears a large and elaborate head scarf that she folds and wraps in a manner that signals her social group and status.

African men and women often wear jewelry and other ornaments that communicate their stage in life. For instance, among the Maasai people in Kenya and Tanzania, women still stretch and adorn their ears with beads and hoops. However, today, fewer and fewer young boys stretch their ears. By the presence of certain colors of beads on her headband, a *Rendile* woman indicates that she is barren. A Samburu woman will wear a double strand of beads looped between her ears for each son who has passed into warriorhood. Male elders of the Turkana and Pokot tribes wear leaf-shaped aluminum pendants suspended from their nostrils to announce a daughter's engagement.

Some groups in Africa communicate their status by decorating their heads and bodies with paints and dyes. Henna dye is used in parts of northern and western Africa to paint intricate patterns on the hands, feet, and face. Although the dye is sometimes used by men and children, it is more commonly applied by women of marriageable age to show that they are looking for a husband or, in some societies, that they are about to be married. Body painting, piercing, tattooing, and scarification are other ways Africans traditionally indicate milestones they have reached in life.

In Africa, music is an important component of rituals, celebrations, and healing ceremonies. The rhythms have specific meanings, which are responded to by swaying, dancing, and sometimes singing. Different musical patterns signal distinct purposes, such as songs of warriors or hunting songs that can be performed only by men. Other music is limited to women and might be played only during childbirth or for girls' initiation rites.

Channeling between the spirit world and the world of humans is another important part of life-cycle events and celebrations in some western and central African communities. Channeling is done through masked dances (also known as masquerades). The identity of the person wearing the mask is hidden from the audience, and "the mask" (as the dancer is known) takes on the identity of the character represented. Combined with dance steps, gestures, songs, and sounds, the "mask" becomes a powerful and energetic force connecting the spirit world with the world of humans. Masquerades are usually performed by men—members of secret societies who begin their training as children. The services of the "masks" are especially effective for funerals.

North Africa

The majority of people living in the North African countries of Algeria, Libya, Morocco, Sudan, and Tunisia are Muslims, and consequently Islamic customs and laws dictate every facet of their lives and life-cycle events. (See Islam and Islamic Life-Cycle Rituals, page lxxvi.)

A *diffa* (feast) is part of most life-cycle celebrations, and it can be very elaborate or modest, depending on the importance of the event. No amount of money is spared for the *diffa* that celebrates a Muslim's return from his pilgrimage to Mecca. A nonstop feast can go on for two or three days in celebration of the most important rite of passage in a Muslim's life. Making the pilgrimage not only assures a Muslim a place in heaven, but he has the enviable title, *Hadji* (one who has made the pilgrimage to Mecca).

Strict Islamic modesty laws prevail throughout North Africa; however, exceptions are found in the chic Moroccan and Tunisian cities and resort areas. Exceptions are also found among the Berbers, the descendents of the pre-Arab inhabitants of North Africa, who make up a large part of the North African population. The Berbers eventually accepted Islam after the Arabs conquered North Africa in the seventh century CE. The free-spirited Berbers enjoy a much more liberated lifestyle than their Arab neighbors do. They are known to infuse ancient pagan beliefs into their Muslim rituals.

When an Arab Muslim boy is born, the first words uttered to the child are the call to prayer. A week later, this is followed by a ceremony in which the baby's head is shaved and an animal, such as a lamb or young calf, may be sacrificed. The sacrificial meat may be given to the poor.

Among the Berbers, the birth of a baby is a welcome addition to the family, whether it is a boy or girl, unlike the Arabs, who openly prefer boys. At birth, a Berber girl receives her first set of beads and a small amulet containing herbs and seeds believed to have magical powers to ward off evil spirits. At each stage of development, a Berber girl receives jewelry befitting her age and social standing.

The major event of a Muslim boy's childhood is circumcision, which normally takes place sometime between the ages of 7 and 12. A feast is often prepared for family and friends to celebrate the event.

Dating is taboo, and a public show of affection is frowned upon in most of North Africa. Arranged marriages are the norm among Arab Muslim families.

A few days after the marriage proposal has been accepted and the first agreement, "the giving away," has been completed, the women of the groom's family traditionally pay a visit to the bride's family. This phase of the negotiating ritual is called *kèmlet-àtiya*. The women come to welcome their new daughter- or sister-in-law into the family. The bride's mother traditionally serves everyone tea, a light repast, and honey, which is provided for good luck.

Wedding rituals can take more than a week to complete. During that time the groom traditionally sends new clothes to his bride, and she in return sends him trays piled with sugar, fresh butter, milk, a bunch of fresh mint leaves, dates (to signify wealth), and *kàb el ghzal*.

Although the women and men are usually kept in separate quarters during wedding ceremonies, they are almost always colorful and noisy affairs. One custom among urbanites is for all the men to get into their cars and drive around the streets in a convoy making as much noise as possible. The men celebrate until the early hours of the morning, often ending at sunrise, with the day's first call to prayer.

For all Muslims, the death ceremony is very simple, and there is no *diffa* (feast). The body is washed with clean, scented water and then wrapped in a *kafan* (white cloth).

The body is placed directly into the ground since coffins are not used and then turned onto his or her right side facing Mecca.

Algeria

Algeria is located in Northern Africa, bounding on the Mediterranean Sea, between Morocco to the west, Tunisia to the east, and Mauritania, Mali, and Niger to the south. Most Algerians are of mixed Arab and Berber descent. Nearly all are Muslims.

Algeria belonged to France for nearly 130 years, finally gaining its independence in 1962. The cooking of Algeria has strong French influences, although most people follow family traditions that have been passed from mother to daughter for generations. In Muslim North Africa where pork products are taboo, sheep are the main source of meat, and *méchoui*, a lamb roasted whole on a spit, is one of the cornerstones of the cuisine. It has been the main dish of weddings and other family celebrations for generations. Urbanites enjoy the lamb, but they generally have it cut up before roasting over a charcoal grill.

The men traditionally eat first and apart from the women. To eat, the men sit on carpeted floors around a low table (*tbla* or *mida*). Before touching the food, which is eaten with the fingers of the right hand, a servant or young family member takes a bowl of perfumed water around to each diner. According to Muslim tradition, the left hand must never touch food, as it is used only for personal grooming. A little water is poured over their hands, and then they are handed a towel (*ied ettas*) to dry them.

⚶ *Chorba 'dess* (Lentil Soup)

Yield: serves 6

2 tablespoons olive oil

¼ pound lean meat, (lamb, veal, or beef, or combination), **cubed**

1 large onion, **trimmed, finely chopped**

2 teaspoons **ground coriander**

8 cups water

1 cup **lentils**

2 large potatoes, quartered

2 large carrots, quartered

salt and pepper to taste

Equipment: Large saucepan with cover, wooden mixing spoon

1. Heat oil in large saucepan over medium-high heat. Add cubed meat, onions, and coriander. Stir until meat is lightly browned on all sides, 5 to 7 minutes.

2. Add water and lentils, and stir. Increase heat to high and bring to a boil. Reduce heat to simmer and add potatoes and carrots. Stir, cover, and cook until lentils are soft and potatoes are tender, 30 to 40 minutes. Add salt and pepper to taste before serving.

Serve with plenty of bread to mop up the broth. Soups are eaten along with the main dishes, not before the meal as in Western cultures.

ꙮ *Kaskasu bi'l-Lahm* (Lamb with Couscous)

This dish would be popular for a wedding feast in Algeria.

Yield: serves 5 to 6

¼ cup olive oil

2 medium onions, **trimmed, finely chopped**

3 pounds boneless lamb, trimmed and cut into serving-sized pieces

4 garlic cloves, trimmed, **minced**

16-ounce canned stewed tomatoes

8-ounce canned chickpeas, drained

1 turnip, trimmed, **coarsely chopped**

1 teaspoon cayenne pepper

1 teaspoon cumin

¼ teaspoon **allspice**

6 cups beef broth or water

2 large carrots, trimmed, sliced into 1-inch rounds

2 zucchini, trimmed, coarsely chopped

½ pound green beans, trimmed, cut into ½-inch-long pieces

salt and pepper to taste

For serving:

2 cups plain **couscous**, prepared according to directions on package, fluffed with fork

lemon wedges

Equipment: **Dutch oven** or large **heavy-bottomed** saucepan with cover, wooden mixing spoon

1. Heat olive oil over medium-high in Dutch oven or heavy-bottomed saucepan. Add onions and cook until soft, about 8 to 10 minutes, stirring frequently.

2. Add lamb, and brown on all sides, about 12 to 15 minutes over medium-high heat.

3. Add garlic, tomatoes, chickpeas, turnip, cayenne pepper, cumin, allspice, and broth or water, mix well. Bring to boil over high heat, cover, and reduce to simmer for 20 to 25 minutes.

4. Stir in carrots, zucchini, and green beans, mix well. Return to simmer and continue cooking for 1½ to 2 hours or until lamb is tender. Add more broth or water as needed if mixture becomes too thick. Add salt and pepper to taste.

Serve warm, ladled into individual bowls over a scoop of couscous. Add several ladles of broth and serve with a lemon wedge.

♪ *Chlada Felfel* (Tomato and Green Pepper Salad)

Salads and relishes are always served along with the meat dishes. This simple combination of vegetables is a typical Algerian salad.

Yield: serves 4 to 6

4 large yellow or red bell peppers, or combination	½ tablespoon wine vinegar
4 tablespoons olive oil	2 cloves garlic, **trimmed, minced**
	salt and pepper to taste

For **garnish:**

2 large tomatoes, thinly sliced	6 **pitted** black olives
	6 stuffed green olives

Equipment: Oven mitts, metal tongs, resealable plastic bag, medium serving platter, whisk, small bowl

1. Preheat oven broiler.

2. Set top oven rack about 4 inches under the broiler. Place whole peppers on broiler pan and place under broiler to blister all sides, 10 to 20 minutes. Wearing oven mitts and using metal tongs, turn peppers as they darken. When skin has patches of black, remove from oven with metal tongs and place in plastic bag and seal tightly. (This is done so that the peppers will sweat, and the skin will easily peel off when they cool enough to handle.) Peel off skin, remove seeds, and coarsely chop peppers. Pile chopped peppers in the center of a serving platter.

3. Prepare dressing: Whisk olive oil, vinegar, garlic, and salt and pepper to taste in small bowl.

4. Arrange tomato slices around peppers and drizzle with dressing. Garnish with black and green olives.

Serve with a chunk of ksra *(recipe page 14) to sop up the dressing.*

♪ *Makroud* (Semolina Pastry Stuffed with Dates)

A week prior to an Algerian wedding, *makrouds* and other desserts are prepared in the bride's home.

Yield: about 2 dozen

3 cups **semolina**

¼ cup sugar

½ teaspoon salt

½ teaspoon ground nutmeg

½ teaspoon ground cinnamon

½ teaspoon ground cloves

2 tablespoons roasted almonds, **finely chopped**

For filling:

12 ounces date paste or ground **pitted** dates (available at international markets or Middle Eastern markets)

½ cup vegetable oil, more as needed for frying

1 cup water

1 cup honey

2 tablespoons orange flower water (available at international markets or Middle Eastern markets)

1 cup confectioners' sugar, more as needed

1 cup almonds, finely chopped

½ teaspoon ground nutmeg

½ teaspoon ground cinnamon

½ teaspoon ground cloves

CAUTION: HOT OIL IS USED.

Equipment: Large mixing bowl, rubber spatula or mixing spoon, medium mixing bowl, **Dutch oven** or **heavy-bottomed** saucepan, deep fryer thermometer or wooden spoon, metal slotted spoon or **skimmer**, baking sheet with several layers of paper towels, small bowl

1. In a large mixing bowl, combine semolina, sugar, salt, nutmeg, cinnamon, cloves, almonds, oil, and water, mix well using rubber spatula. Roll into ball, cover, and refrigerate for 15 to 20 minutes.

2. Prepare filling: in medium mixing bowl combine dates, almonds, nutmeg, cinnamon, and cloves. Mix well and form into a ball.

3. Remove dough from refrigerator. Take a ping-pong-ball-size piece of dough and shape into ball. Using a finger, make an indention in center of ball. Fill with about 1 tablespoon filling mixture, seal, and reshape into ball. Place side by side on baking sheet until all mixture is used.

4. Prepare to fry. *Caution: Adult supervision required.* Add 2½ to 3 inches oil in Dutch oven or heavy-bottomed saucepan. Heat oil to 375°F on deep fryer thermometer, or place handle of wooden spoon in oil; if small bubbles appear around surface, oil is ready for frying.

5. Carefully fry 4 to 5 *makrouds* at a time for about 2 to 3 minutes or until golden brown. Remove using metal slotted spoon or skimmer, and set aside on paper towels to drain. Continue frying in batches.

6. In small bowl, combine honey and orange flower water, mix well. One at a time, dip *makrouds* into mixture, dust with confectioner's sugar and set aside. Continue until all cookies have been dipped and dusted.

Serve as a sweet treat for a wedding celebration or at the end of a meal.

⚘ *Khchaf* (Fruit Drink)

Yield: serves 6 to 8

2 quarts water	½ cup raisins
2 sticks cinnamon	sugar to taste

Equipment: Medium saucepan, mixing spoon, beverage glasses

1. Bring water with cinnamon sticks to boil in medium saucepan. Add raisins, reduce heat to simmer, and cook for 15 minutes. Stir in sugar. Remove from heat, and take out and discard the cinnamon sticks.

2. When liquid is completely cool, refrigerate for 30 to 40 minutes.

Serve in beverage glasses, adding a few raisins to each serving.

Libya

Libya, in northeastern Africa, borders the Mediterranean and Tunisia, Algeria, Egypt, Sudan, Chad, and Niger. Once called the Desert Kingdom of Africa, most of the nation's land is desert. The majority of Libyans are city dwellers, primarily in cosmopolitan cities along the coast. A small percentage of the population lives in villages or small settlements throughout the desert. Libyans are mainly Arabs and Berbers (see North Africa page 3), and almost all are Muslims. Islam, the state religion, provides the framework for both the secular and spiritual life of the nation. All life-cycle events are conducted and celebrated according to Islamic law and custom. (See Islam and Islamic Life-Cycle Rituals, page lxxvi.)

A week after baby is born, a shaving-the-head ceremony takes place, along with the sacrifice of a goat or lamb for the special occasion. A boy's childhood event of circumcision usually takes place between the ages of 7 and 12 and is always followed by a celebration.

For festive occasions, a goat or lamb is roasted, and as many as 40 other dishes are prepared for the feast. Diners sit on cushions on the floor and eat off a low table. They eat by dipping the fingers of the right hand into the food placed on the table. Traditionally, no plates or forks are used, but flat loaves of bread are broken into pieces and used to scoop up the food. Bowls of perfumed water are passed between courses so that diners may cleanse their fingers. There are often a dozen or so desserts and always a large fruit assortment, *fakha taza* (recipe page 11). Only water is served with food, and *coffee* is served after the meal.

⚘ *Beid Mahshi* (Stuffed Eggs)

A celebration feast always begins with the *mezze* (**appetizer**) table, with such dishes as *abrak* (stuffed grape leaves); pickled vegetables (available in jars at all supermarkets); black and green olives; cheeses; and plenty of bread. This recipe for *Beid Mahshi* is easy-to-prepare and has an unusual combination of flavors. Stuffed eggs are a symbol of fertility and life. They are prepared for most life-cycle celebrations.

Yield: serves 4

1 cup plain yogurt

2 teaspoons sugar

1½ teaspoons **ground** cinnamon, divided

4 hard-cooked eggs, shelled

1 tablespoon olive oil

½ onion, **trimmed, grated**

2 tablespoons fresh parsley, **finely chopped,** or 1 tablespoon dried parsley flakes

½ teaspoon paprika

salt and pepper to taste

Equipment: Small bowl, mixing spoon, plastic food wrap, medium shallow bowl, work surface, fork, serving plate

1. Prepare sauce: Pour yogurt into small bowl, add sugar and 1 teaspoon cinnamon. Stir well and cover with plastic wrap. Refrigerate until serving time.

2. Cut hard-cooked eggs in half lengthwise. Remove yolks and put into medium shallow bowl. Set whites cut-side up on work surface. Using fork, mash yolks in shallow bowl. Add olive oil, grated onion, parsley flakes, remaining ½ teaspoon ground cinnamon, paprika, and salt and pepper to taste. Stir to mix well.

3. Spoon egg yolk mixture equally into egg white halves and arrange them on a serving plate.

To serve, spoon yogurt sauce over tops of eggs, and eat as a midday snack or appetizer.

⚱ *Shorba* (Libyan Soup)

A great beginning to any celebration feast is a hearty bowl of *shorba*.

Yield: serves 4 to 6

2 tablespoons olive oil

1 onion, **trimmed, finely chopped**

4 cloves garlic, trimmed, **minced**

1 pound lamb, cut into 1-inch cubes

1 tablespoon turmeric

½ teaspoon cayenne pepper, or to taste

1 teaspoon curry powder

1 teaspoon cumin

14.5 ounces canned diced tomatoes

4 tablespoons tomato paste

14.5 ounces canned chickpeas, drained

6 cups water

¾ cup **orzo** (available at Middle Eastern or Italian markets)

salt and pepper to taste

½ cup fresh parsley, **coarsely chopped**

For serving:

lemon wedges

warm crusty bread

Equipment: **Dutch oven** or large **heavy-bottomed** soup kettle, mixing spoon, ladle

1. Heat olive oil in Dutch oven or heavy-bottomed soup kettle over medium-high heat. Add onions and garlic, **sauté** until soft, about 6 to 8 minutes, stirring frequently.

2. Add meat and sauté until brown, about 10 to 12 minutes.

3. Stir in turmeric, cayenne pepper, curry powder, cumin, diced tomatoes, tomato paste, chick-peas and water, mix well. Bring to boil over high heat, reduce to simmer for 25 to 30 minutes.

4. Stir in *orzo* and continue cooking for about 10 to 12 minutes or until orzo is **al dente**. Add salt and pepper to taste.

Serve warm, ladled into individual soup bowls; sprinkle with a pinch of parsley, and serve with a lemon wedge. Warm crusty bread is perfect for dipping.

✠ *Sayadia* (Fish with Lemon)

It is not unusual for celebration feasts to take four or five hours. The meal is eaten in a leisurely manner, and every bite of food is savored. This fish dish can be set on the mezze table, or, at a wedding banquet, it is often served to guests after the soup course and before eating the roasted lamb, *kabab barreh* (recipe page 629).

Yield: serves 6

¼ cup olive oil

1 clove garlic, **trimmed, minced**

8 tablespoons lemon juice

4 cups water

1 teaspoons crushed chili peppers, or **ground red pepper to taste**

salt and pepper to taste

½ teaspoon turmeric

3½ tablespoons fresh parsley, **finely chopped, divided**

2½ pounds skinless fish **fillets**, fresh or fresh frozen (thawed)

For **garnish:** 1 lemon, cut crosswise into thin slices

Equipment: Large skillet with cover, mixing spoon, fork, wide slotted spatula, serving platter

1. Heat oil in large skillet over medium-high heat. Add garlic, stir, and **sauté** until soft, about 1 minute. Add lemon juice, water, crushed chili peppers or ground red pepper to taste, salt and pepper to taste, turmeric, and 3 tablespoons chopped parsley. Stir well, bring to boil, and add fish fillets. Bring back to boil. Reduce heat to **simmer**, cover, and cook until fish is opaque white and flakes easily when poked with a fork, 12 to 15 minutes. Remove from heat, uncover, and allow fish to cool in liquid.

2. *Prepare to serve:* Using wide slotted spatula, transfer fish to serving platter. Either discard cooking liquid or cover and refrigerate for another use.

To serve, garnish fish with lemon slices, and sprinkle with remaining ½ tablespoon parsley. The fish is served at room temperature.

৬ *Hunkar Begendi* (Sultan's Pleasure)

Throughout the Middle East, this dish is traditionally served with lamb at life-cycle celebrations.

Yield: serves 6

2 eggplants (about 2 pounds total)

1 tablespoon lemon juice

¼ cup butter or margarine

1 cup half-and-half

½ cup **fresh white bread crumbs**

3 tablespoons grated Parmesan cheese

salt and pepper to taste

1 tablespoon **finely chopped** fresh parsley

1 green bell pepper, **trimmed, seeded,** cut crosswise into thin rings

Equipment: Fork, baking sheet, oven mitts, knife, spoon, food processor, rubber spatula, mixing spoon, medium saucepan, serving bowl

Note: *While processing, turn machine off once or twice and scrape down sides of container with rubber spatula.*

Preheat oven to 450° F.

1. Poke eggplant skin with fork in about 8 places and set on baking sheet. Bake in oven until soft and tender, 30 to 40 minutes. Using oven mitts, remove from oven and cool enough to handle. When cool enough to handle, cut in half, scoop out pulp, and put into food processor. Discard eggplant skin. Add lemon juice to pulp in food processor and process until smooth, about 1 minute.

2. Transfer eggplant mixture to medium saucepan. Add butter or margarine and half-and-half, and cook over medium heat, stirring frequently, until butter or margarine melts. Stir in bread crumbs, salt and pepper to taste, and Parmesan cheese. Stir and continue to cook over medium heat until thickened, 5 to 7 minutes.

To serve, transfer to serving bowl, sprinkle with chopped parsley and garnish with green pepper rings. Serve as a vegetable side dish with meat.

৬ *Fakha Taza* (Fresh Fruit)

A life-cycle feast usually includes dozens of different very sweet pastries and puddings, but nothing is more enjoyable to end a meal than platters of *fakha taza*. A combination of fruits is either set out on the buffet table for guests to peel and eat, or the fruits are made into a salad that is eaten at the end of the meal.

Yield: serves 6 to 8

1 **pomegranate**

1 cantaloupe, peeled, **seeded,** cut into ½-inch cubes

3 pears, **trimmed,** peeled, **seeded,** cut into ½-inch cubes

1 mango, peeled, cut into bite-size chunks

2 oranges, peeled, **pith** removed, cut into sections

2 cups strawberries, washed, drained, trimmed, cut in half

juice of 2 lemons

2 bananas, peeled, sliced crosswise ¼-inch thick

12 **pitted** dates, cut in half

Equipment: Paring knife, teaspoon, small bowl, large serving bowl, salad tools, plastic food wrap

1. Cut pomegranate in half and work on one half at a time. Remove tough outer skin and white **pith**. Carefully pull out edible seeds with your finger or a teaspoon and put in small bowl. Take care not to pierce the red seeds.

2. Put cubed cantaloupe, pears, mango chunks, orange sections, and strawberries into large serving bowl. Sprinkle with lemon juice. Using salad tools, gently toss to mix. Cover with plastic wrap and refrigerate until ready to serve.

To serve, add pomegranate seeds, sliced bananas, and dates, gently toss to mix, and serve at once.

Morocco

Morocco lies directly across the Strait of Gibraltar from Spain. On the east and southeast is Algeria; south of Morocco is the Western Sahara; and the Atlantic Ocean and Mediterranean Sea bound it on the west and north. The culture is a blend of Berber, Arab-Islamic, and African, with influences from France and Spain.

In the Berber culture, the women are allowed to select their own husband, which is unheard of among Arabs, whose marriages are strictly prearranged according to the laws of Islam. As a matter of fact, in Imilchil, Morocco, high in the Atlas Mountains, an annual three-day festival is held every September where Berbers come to sell and trade camels, sheep, and goats. Over the years, it has become known as the Bridal Fair, due to the influx of Berber women of the Ait Hadiddu tribe looking for husbands. The young women parade around wearing full-length, black-hooded cloaks. They all look alike except for the different colored, narrow stripes running down the back of each garment. They decorate their hoods with brightly colored ribbon and yarn from which they hang small pieces of jewelry in the shape of animal paws, such as a jackal or turtle foot. They believe the symbolic animal paws possess magical powers.

On the last day of the festival, couples make their choice, shake hands, and declare themselves engaged. The couple then formalizes their vows in front of a notary. Although a girl may meet her future husband at the fair, she returns home with her father when it is over. Once home, a meeting is arranged between the families. When both families can agree about dowry and the marriage contract, they give their consent. The marriage takes place about a year later.

Unlike the Muslim Arab women, who cannot remarry, divorced and widowed Berber women are free to remarry as often as they like, and the fair is a good place to select a new husband. They wear decorative pointed hoods, called *aquilous*, to distinguish them from single girls.

₡ Moroccan-Style Lemon Chicken with Olives

The following dish is a simple and elegant meal perfect for any festive celebration. In Morocco, a *tagine*, a casserole dish commonly used in North Africa, is often used to prepare this recipe. A *tagine* consists of two pieces—a plate-like bottom and a cone-shaped lid. The bottom doubles as a serving dish, which comes in handy for nomads. We suggest a heavy-bottomed skillet.

Yield: serves 4 to 6

1 teaspoon ground cumin

1 teaspoon ground paprika

½ teaspoon cinnamon

1 teaspoon turmeric

½ teaspoon pepper

1 tablespoon ginger root, **trimmed,** finely **grated**

2 tablespoons olive oil, more as needed

4 to 6 skinless, boneless chicken thighs or breasts

3 cloves garlic, trimmed, **minced**

1 onion, trimmed, **coarsely chopped**

1 preserved lemon (available at International or Middle Eastern Markets)

1 cup green olives, **pitted**

½ cup raisins

½ cup sliced almonds

½ cup water, more as needed

salt and pepper to taste

¼ cup fresh **cilantro, finely chopped**

Equipment: Small bowl, baking sheet, plastic wrap, sharp knife, large **heavy-bottomed** skillet with cover, tongs

1. Prepare marinade: In small bowl, combine cumin, paprika, cinnamon, turmeric, pepper, ginger, and 2 tablespoons olive oil, mix well. Add chicken pieces one at a time, evenly coat all sides, and transfer to baking sheet. Cover lightly with plastic wrap, and place in refrigerator to marinate for 45 minutes to 1 hour.

2. Place preserved lemon on clean work surface. Using sharp knife, remove peel and discard pulp. Using knife, carefully **julienne** lemon peel and set aside.

3. Remove chicken from refrigerator, set aside. Heat 2 tablespoons oil in heavy-bottomed skillet over medium-high heat. Add marinated chicken pieces one at a time and cook on each side about 6 to 8 minutes or until lightly browned. Stir in onions and garlic, reduce to medium-low heat, cover, and cook additional 8 to 12 minutes, adding more oil if necessary to prevent sticking.

4. Sprinkle lemon slices, olives, raisins, and almonds over top of chicken. Carefully pour ½ cup water into pan and bring to simmer over medium-high heat. Cover and cook additional 20 to 25 minutes, adding more water if necessary to prevent sticking. Check **chicken doneness.** Add salt and pepper to taste.

Serve warm over couscous. Sprinkle with cilantro before serving.

Ksra (Moroccan Anise Bread)

Bread is a staple, and no meal is complete unless great quantities of bread are on the table. Early each morning, most households prepare their own dough, which they take to the local baker who bakes it for them.

Yield: 2 small loaves

1 package dry active **yeast**

1½ cups **lukewarm** water, divided

1 teaspoon sugar

4 cups sifted all-purpose flour

½ cup whole wheat flour

2 teaspoons salt

½ cup lukewarm milk

1 tablespoon anise seed (available at supermarkets)

½ cup yellow **cornmeal**, more or less as needed

Equipment: Small bowl, mixing spoon, plastic wrap, large mixing bowl, wooden mixing spoon, lightly floured work surface, 2 greased dinner plates, greased baking sheet pan, kitchen towel, oven mitts

1. Place yeast in small bowl with about ¼-cup lukewarm water; stir to combine. Stir in sugar. Cover with plastic wrap and set aside in warm place for 10 minutes or until frothy.

2. In large mixing bowl, combine all-purpose flour, whole wheat flour, and salt. Using wooden mixing spoon, stir in yeast mixture and lukewarm milk. Gradually add just enough of remaining 1¼ cups lukewarm water to make stiff dough.

3. Transfer dough to lightly floured work surface, and **knead** for 15 to 20 minutes, or until dough is smooth and satiny. Knead in anise seed. (When necessary, lightly sprinkle flour on work surface to prevent sticking.)

4. Divide dough in half and shape each piece into ball. Place each ball on greased plate, cover with plastic wrap, and allow to rest for 10 minutes.

5. Using greased hands, shape balls into slightly flattened round loaves about 5 inches in diameter. Sprinkle cornmeal on greased baking sheet and set breads on top, allowing space between to rise. Cover with towel, and set in warm place to double in bulk, 1 to 2 hours.

Preheat oven to 400° F.

6. Gently prick the top of each loaf in three or four places with fork. Bake in oven for 10 minutes, reduce heat to 300°F for 35 to 40 minutes. (Test **bread doneness,** insert toothpick in center, and if it comes out clean, bread is done.)

7. Cool on wire cake rack for 10 minutes to firm up.

Serving bread with each meal is essential in Morocco. Bread is used to transport food from the platter to the mouth and to help mop up the sauces and cooking juices. Bread is broken, never cut, into pieces. (Cutting requires both hands to touch the food, which is taboo.) Ksra is delicious when eaten warm.

⚜ *Fresh Oranges (Moroccan Dessert)*

Meals usually end with fresh fruit, such as this simple recipe for sliced oranges. This is probably the most popular way of eating fresh fruit throughout the Middle East and North Africa.

Yield: serves 4

4 oranges, peeled

1 teaspoon **cinnamon sugar**

1 teaspoon **rosewater** (available at Middle Eastern food stores and pharmacies)

Equipment: Paring knife, small bowl, spoon, individual plates

Using a paring knife, remove the white stringy membranes from the oranges and divide into segments. Place the orange segments, slightly overlapping, on a plate and sprinkle with cinnamon sugar and rosewater.

Serve immediately.

Sudan

One of the largest nations on the African continent, Sudan has 500 miles of coastline along the Red Sea. It shares its other borders with Ethiopia and Eritrea to the east, South Sudan to the south, Chad and the Central African Republic to the west, and Egypt and Libya to the north.

Sudan has two distinct cultures (Arab and black African) and over 500 ethnic groups. There are great differences between the Dinka people who travel with their herds, subsistence farmers like the Zandes who work with ancient tools and farming methods, and the very Westernized Sudanese urbanites who enjoy high-tech living.

Most people living in the northern two-thirds of the country belong to the large Muslim community, which comprises about 70 percent of Sudan's total population. These Sudanese live in walled compounds, and most men wear *jellabiahs* (Arabic dress) and turbans. Women are covered with loose-fitting garments called *"tobes."* In the southern part of the country, however, most Sudanese are Christians or practice indigenous religions. These people live in clusters of beehive-shaped huts, and although many men wear *jellabiahs*, which are comfortable in the hot climate, they don't wear turbans. Women wear Western-style dresses.

The Muslims and Christians in Sudan have customized the standard rituals of their faith to include local traditions and beliefs. (See Islam and Islamic Life-Cycle Rituals, page lxxvi; Protestant and Catholic Life-Cycle Rituals, page lxxiii; and African Life-Cycle Rituals, page lxvi.)

The Dinka people have lived in the Sudan region since about the 10th century. Most are Muslims. They are seminomadic people who raise herds of cattle, which give their owners respect and status. With cattle, a man can purchase a bride, pay taxes, and buy staples. Cattle provide meat and milk for his family, and the smoke from burning cow dung keeps mosquitoes away.

The Dinkas are devoted to their cows, which they believe are a link with the spiritual world. When a Dinka boy reaches puberty, he is given a young calf. This becomes his "namesake ox," after which he himself is named. For the next few years, he identifies closely with the young bull, imitating and emulating it as the two mature together. Scarification signifies a boy's initiation into adulthood. This is done by making deep cuts across a boy's forehead to resemble horns. It is an ordeal that must be endured without any show of pain.

Among the Dinka, the family of a prospective husband is expected to pay the bride-price in the form of cattle. The number of cattle exchanged for the bride is negotiated between the future in-laws. A beautiful bride can cost a future husband many head of cattle, adding considerable wealth to her family. Thus, when Dinka girls reach marrying age, they are fattened up by their families to make them more desirable. To add to their allure, marriageable girls wear beaded bodices made of dozens of rows of tiny beads strung horizontally across the chest and back. The beads are applied in patterns that indicate the family's prosperity, and cowrie shells are attached to promote fertility.

⚶ *Bani-Bamia* (Lamb and Okra Stew)

All life-cycle celebrations in Sudan include a communal feast. This recipe for *bani-bamia* combines two African favorites, lamb and okra. Okra in Africa is known as "ladyfingers."

Yield: serves 4

2 tablespoons vegetable oil	3 cups water
2 onions, thinly sliced	salt and pepper to taste
2 cloves garlic, **trimmed, minced**	10-ounce package frozen whole okra, thawed
1½ pounds lean boneless lamb or other lean meat, cut into 2-inch chunks	For serving: 6 cups cooked rice, kept warm
1 cup canned tomato paste	

Equipment: Large saucepan with cover or **Dutch oven**, mixing spoon, small bowl, large serving platter

1. Heat oil in large saucepan or Dutch oven over medium-high heat. Add onions and garlic, stir, and **sauté** until soft, 3 to 5 minutes. Add lamb and brown on all sides, 7 to 12 minutes.

2. In small bowl, combine tomato paste with water. Add tomato mixture to lamb mixture in large saucepan. Add salt and pepper to taste and bring to boil. Reduce heat to **simmer**, cover, and cook until meat is tender, 45 to 50 minutes. Add okra and cook, covered, until okra is tender, 8 to 10 minutes.

To serve, spoon lamb mixture over cooked rice in large serving platter.

≀ Shorbat Robe (Yogurt and Cucumber Salad)

The foods of Sudan are a combination of Middle Eastern and African cooking. This easy salad recipe is served as a side dish with whole roast lamb (*méchoui*) (recipe page 27) for weddings and other special occasions.

Yield: serves 6

2 cucumbers, peeled, **finely chopped**

1 cup plain yogurt

salt and pepper to taste

2 cloves fresh garlic, **trimmed, minced**, or 1 teaspoon garlic granules

For **garnish:**

2 hard-cooked eggs, finely chopped

2 tomatoes, finely chopped

1 onion, trimmed, sliced

Equipment: Medium bowl with cover, mixing spoon, serving bowl

Put cucumber in medium bowl, **fold in** yogurt, salt and pepper to taste, and garlic, and **blend** well. Cover and refrigerate until ready to serve. At serving time, transfer to serving bowl, sprinkle with hard-cooked eggs, tomatoes, and onion slices.

To serve, place bowl of shorbat robe *on the table and have guests help themselves. To eat, tear off a piece of* khobaz arabee *(recipe page 682) and use to scoop up some onion, egg, and tomato with each bit of salad.*

≀ Roselle Tea (Hibiscus Tea)

Roselle tea is believed to have many healthy benefits, and dried hibiscus flowers are abundant throughout Sudanese markets. For any festive occasion, this beverage may be served hot or cold at the end of a meal.

Yield: serves 6 to 8

2½ cups dried hibiscus flowers (also *roselle*, available at international markets)

2 quarts cold water

1 cup sugar, more to taste

1 sprig mint (optional)

½ teaspoon ginger root, **trimmed, grated** (optional)

1 teaspoon orange flower water (available at international markets, optional)

Equipment: **Strainer**, large saucepan, 12-inch-square cheese cloth, large tea pitcher, wooden mixing spoon

1. Place hibiscus flowers in strainer, rinse with cold water, and drain well.

2. In saucepan, bring water to boil over medium-high heat. When water begins to boil, add rinsed hibiscus flowers, stir, remove immediately from heat, and let sit for 8 to 10 minutes.

3. Line strainer with cheese cloth.

4. Transfer hibiscus water from saucepan to pitcher using cheesecloth-lined strainer to remove flower pieces.

5. Stir in 1 cup sugar or more to taste. Add mint, ginger root, and orange flower water if desired, mix well.

Serve hot or cold after a festive meal.

Tunisia

Tunisia is the northernmost country in Africa. Its northern tip is only 85 miles from Sicily, in Italy. Tunisia is bounded on the north and east by the Mediterranean Sea. On the west, Tunisia is bordered by Algeria and on the south by Libya. Almost all Tunisians are Arabs and Muslims, and there is a heavy French influence, with many Tunisians speaking French as an additional language.

Today, many Tunisians still have arranged marriages; however, with urbanization, men and women have more opportunities to meet in social settings. The male may meet a young girl at school and request she be interviewed by his family to deem if she is an acceptable match. Traditionally, the bride's opinion was irrelevant, though today her wishes might be consulted.

It is the custom for the women to serve the men, and men and women do not eat together. The men sit around a low table on carpeted floors, backed with an assortment of decorative pillows. The table is usually an etched, brass tray set on carved legs. Eating is done with the thumb, forefinger, and middle finger of the right hand, using chunks of bread for scooping and dipping.

Harissa (also *Hrisa*) (Fiery Red Pepper Seasoning)

Tunisians prefer their food highly seasoned and use *harissa* in almost everything except desserts. *Harissa*, thinned with olive oil and tomato paste, is spread on bread and fed to babies to ward off sickness and evil spirits.

Yield: about ¾ cup

½ cup **ground** red pepper

¼ cup ground cumin

2 teaspoons salt

Equipment: Resealable plastic bag

Combine red pepper, cumin, and salt in resealable plastic bag. Seal top and shake bag to blend ingredients thoroughly. Refrigerate until ready to use.

Serve harissa *in a shaker or small dish, and sprinkle it carefully as a hot seasoning.*

✄ *Tajine Chakchouka* (Tunisian Baked Lamb Casserole)

A wedding banquet menu includes soup, bread, salads, **couscous,** and more than one *tajine,* or casserole. Everything is put on the table at the same time. Meat is a luxury in North Africa, so using it in *tajine* makes a little meat go a long way. Sometimes camel meat is added to *tajine,* but most are made with lamb, mutton, goat, or beef when rainfall is adequate and livestock plentiful. When the meat is left out, the *tajine* becomes a delicious vegetarian meal.

Tajine in Tunisia bears no relation to Moroccan *tajine.* The Tunisian version is like a quiche (a popular French savory pie made with eggs) and is normally served at room temperature.

Yield: serves 6 to 8

1 pound boneless lean lamb, cut into 1-inch cubes

1 teaspoon **ground** cinnamon

salt and pepper to taste

3 tablespoons olive oil

3 cups water

1½ cups onions, **trimmed, finely chopped**

3 large **tomatoes, peeled, coarsely chopped**

2 green bell peppers, stemmed, **seeded,** coarsely chopped

¼ teaspoon *harissa* (recipe page 18), more or less to taste

¼ teaspoon ground **coriander**

½ cup grated Parmesan cheese

½ cup finely crumbled white bread

6 eggs, lightly beaten

2 tablespoons melted butter or margarine

Equipment: Large mixing bowl, large skillet with cover, metal spatula, 3-quart ovenproof casserole, wooden mixing spoon, oven mitts

1. Put lamb cubes in large mixing bowl, sprinkle with cinnamon, salt, and pepper to taste. Toss to coat.

2. Heat oil in large skillet over medium-high heat. Add meat, turning meat with metal spatula to brown all sides, 5 to 7 minutes. Add water and bring to boil. Reduce heat to simmer, cover, and cook for 45 minutes. Using slotted spoon, transfer lamb to ovenproof casserole,

leaving juices in skillet. Add to juices in skillet onions, tomatoes, green peppers, ¼ teaspoon *harissa* (more or less to taste), coriander, and salt and pepper to taste. Stir well, and bring to boil over medium-high heat. Reduce heat to simmer, and cook for 15 minutes, until vegetables are tender.

Preheat oven to 350°F.

3. Transfer onion mixture to casserole dish of lamb and **fold in**. Gently fold in cheese, bread crumbs, and lightly beaten eggs.

4. Bake in oven for 45 minutes, or until top is golden brown. Just before serving, drizzle melted butter over top.

Serve directly from casserole. To eat as they do in Tunisia, use only the fingers of your right hand, scoop up a portion, and pop it in your mouth. According to Muslim tradition, the left hand must never touch food; it is used only for personal grooming.

Chunks of bread can be used instead of your fingers to scoop up the tajine.

੬ Yo-Yo (Tunisian-style Deep-fried Dough in Syrup)

Yo-yo is an inexpensive dessert that is easy to make and ideal to serve for large gatherings.

Yield: about 2 dozen

3 eggs	¼ cup sugar
¼ cup vegetable oil, more as needed for frying	2½ cups flour
¼ cup orange juice	1½ teaspoon baking soda
4 tablespoons **shredded** coconut, **finely chopped** (divided)	water, as needed

Syrup:	2 tablespoons lemon juice
1 cup sugar	1 cup honey
2 cups water	

CAUTION: HOT OIL IS USED.

Equipment: Medium mixing bowl, mixing spoon or rubber spatula, **sifter**, kitchen towel, small saucepan, sharp knife, **deep fryer** (use according to manufacturer's directions) or medium **heavy-bottomed** saucepan, deep fryer thermometer or wooden mixing spoon, slotted spoon or **skimmer**, baking sheet with several layers of paper towels, serving bowl, ladle

1. Prepare dough: Place eggs, ¼ cup oil, orange juice, 2 tablespoons coconut, and ¼ cup sugar in medium mixing bowl, and, using mixing spoon or rubber spatula, mix until smooth.

2. **Sift** in flour and baking soda. Using clean hands, **knead** until mixture forms soft dough. If dough is too firm, add water, a little at a time, if necessary. Cover with towel, and set aside for about 1 hour.

3. Prepare syrup: Place 1 cup sugar, 2 cups water, and lemon juice in small saucepan. Bring to boil over medium-high heat, stirring constantly until sugar dissolves. Reduce to simmer, stir in honey and remaining 2 tablespoons coconut. Simmer additional 10 minutes. Reduce heat to low, keep warm.

4. Using lightly floured hands, pinch off walnut-sized pieces of dough, one at a time. Using palms of your hands roll each into a ball, and slightly flatten it into disc. Place disc of dough on lightly floured work surface, and, using a sharp knife, carefully cut a ½-inch-wide X in center. Hold dough in one hand, and, with index finger of your other hand, gently poke a hole in center of the X cut. Set aside on clean work surface, and continue until all dough is used.

5. Prepare to deep fry: **Caution: *Adult supervision required.*** Have ready several layers of paper towels on baking sheet. Fill deep fryer with oil according to manufacturer's directions, or fill deep saucepan with about 3 inches of vegetable oil. Heat to 375°F on deep fryer thermometer, or place handle of wooden spoon in oil, if small bubbles appear around surface, oil is ready for frying.

6. Carefully slip 2 to 3 *yo-yos* at a time into oil, fry about 4 to 5 minutes or until golden on both sides. Using slotted spoon or skimmer, remove from oil and place on paper towels to drain. Continue until all *yo-yos* are fried.

7. Transfer to serving bowl. Carefully ladle warm syrup over *yo-yos*.

Serve warm as a sweet treat at the end of a meal for a wedding or other family celebration.

⚵ *Thé à la Menthe* (also *Etzai*) (Mint Tea)

In Muslim countries, alcoholic beverages are forbidden. Tea and coffee are served at all life-cycle celebrations. The ritual of preparing tea is as important as drinking the finished brew. Green leaf tea is combined with chunks of sugar chipped off a large cone. Many Moroccans use a **samovar**, or urn called a "*babour*," for making tea, while others prefer to brew their tea in small brass pots. The traditional way to drink tea in Morocco is from narrow, 3-inch-tall glasses.

Yield: serves 3 or 4

8 tablespoons green tea leaves	3 tablespoons sugar, more or less to taste
4 cups boiling water, divided	fresh mint sprigs to taste

Equipment: 2 6-cup teapots, 3 3-inch-tall heatproof glasses, 3 or 4 teaspoons

1. Put green tea leaves in a teapot, and pour in 1 cup boiling water; swirl liquid in pot for a minute, and then pour into second teapot. (This is called "washing the tea.")

2. Add 3 tablespoons sugar, more or less to taste, and mint leaves to taste. Pour in remaining 3 cups boiling water. Carefully pour tea mixture back and forth 3 or 4 times between two teapots. (This is done to oxygenate the prepared tea.)

3. North Africans have a saying that goes along with the tea drinking ritual. "The first tea is bitter, like life, the second is sweet like love, and the third is gentle, like death." To drink the

tea as they do in North Africa, repeat the entire process two more times: repeat the recipe with same amounts of water and sugar but no more tea or mint. At the end, everyone will have had 3 glasses of tea, each milder than the one before.

WEST AFRICA

The countries in the region of West Africa typically include Benin, Burkina Faso, Ivory Coast (Côte d'Ivoire), Gambia, Ghana, Guinea, Guinea-Bissau, Liberia, Mali, Mauritania, Niger, Nigeria, Senegal, Sierra Leone, and Togo.

⚘ *Salade Végétale Froide* (Cold Vegetable Salad)

Corn and sweet potatoes are popular crops grown throughout Western Africa. Vegetables are used in abundance for healthy nutritious meals. Meat is expensive; therefore the following dish is ideal to serve for a large family gathering or celebration.

Yield: serves 4 to 6

¼ cup peanut or vegetable oil

2 tablespoons lemon juice

½ teaspoon salt

½ teaspoon pepper

½ teaspoon cayenne pepper or to taste

1 green pepper, **trimmed, coarsely chopped**

1 onion, trimmed, **finely chopped**

1 celery stalk, trimmed, finely chopped

1 cup corn kernels, fresh, frozen (cooked according to directions on package) or canned, drained

4 cooked sweet potatoes; fresh, trimmed, peeled or canned, drained, cut into ½-inch cubes

For **garnish**: parsley

Equipment: Small bowl, **whisk**, large salad bowl, salad fork and spoon, plastic wrap

1. *Prepare dressing*: In small bowl **whisk** together oil, lemon juice, salt, pepper and cayenne, mix well. Set aside.

2. Place green pepper, onion, celery, corn, and sweet potatoes in salad bowl. Evenly pour dressing over top, and, using salad fork and spoon, toss to mix well.

3. Cover with plastic wrap and refrigerate for about 4 hours.

Serve chilled, garnished with a sprig of parsley.

⚘ *Akotonshi* (Stuffed Crabs)

Many coastal West African countries rely on treasures from the sea, and crabs are one of the most sought after due to their delicious flavor. *Akotonshi* is an ideal inexpensive dish served for any festive occasion. We suggest using fresh or frozen prepackaged lump crab meat, available at most supermarkets.

Yield: serves 4 to 6

2 tablespoon vegetable oil

1 onion **trimmed, minced**

2 bell peppers, trimmed, **finely chopped**

3 cloves garlic, trimmed, minced

¼ cup scallions, trimmed, finely chopped

1 tablespoon ginger root, trimmed, **grated** or 1 teaspoon ground ginger

1 tablespoon tomato paste

½ teaspoon paprika

½ teaspoon cayenne pepper or taste

2 pounds lump crab meat (available at most supermarkets)

½ cup plain **bread crumbs** (available at most supermarkets)

nonstick butter-flavored cooking spray

For serving: 4 to 6 lemon wedges

Equipment: Large skillet, wooden mixing spoon, 4 to 6 ovenproof ramekins about 4–5 inches in diameter and 1-inch deep, baking sheet, oven mitts

Preheat broiler.

1. Heat 2 tablespoons oil in skillet over medium-high heat. Add onion, bell peppers, garlic, scallions, ginger, tomato paste, paprika, and cayenne pepper, **sauté** 3 to 5 minutes.

2. Stir in crab meat, and sauté additional 3 to 5 minutes or until heated through.

3. Evenly transfer crab mixture to ramekins, and top with bread crumbs. Spray bread crumbs with nonstick cooking spray until moistened. Set ramekins on baking sheet, and broil for about 1½ to 2 minutes or until breads crumbs are golden brown. Carefully remove from oven using oven mitts.

Serve warm in individual ramekins garnished with a lemon wedge.

Burkina Faso

Burkina Faso is a landlocked country in West Africa, sharing borders with Côte d'Ivoire, Mali, Niger, Benin, Togo, and Ghana. The nation has more than 60 ethnic groups, the largest of which is the Mossi. For centuries, the Mossi resisted northern Muslim forces that tried to convert them to Islam. Today, most Muslims in Burkina Faso live in the north, and they account for a majority of the population. (See Islam and Islamic Life-Cycle Rituals, page lxxvi.) A small percentage of the population maintains indigenous religious beliefs. (See Indigenous Religions, page lxv.) The nation's small number of Christians are predominantly Roman Catholics, mostly urban dwellers. (See African Life-Cycle Rituals, page lxvi.)

In Burkina Faso, no traditional life-milestone event takes place without sorcery and contacting the spirits. Among Muslims, as soon as a baby is born, an amulet is placed in the swaddling to ward off the "evil eye." The baby and mother are kept in seclusion until the naming ceremony, which occurs when the child is about three months old. If the baby is a boy, there is always a great celebration. The next important event in a

Muslim boy's life is when he is circumcised at about seven years of age. Whole roasted lamb (*kabab barreh*) (recipe page 629) is traditionally prepared for the feast.

Muslim marriages are arranged by parents, usually between first cousins. The rituals begin when a spokesman for the groom, usually an uncle, comes to negotiate the bride-price with the bride's father or a family elder. The bride-price is paid, and the local religious leader sanctions the union. Islamic law allows a man to have four wives.

A unique indigenous wedding ceremony by Fulani Nomads takes place over four days. The family gathers from near and far for the celebration. The women use huge mortar and pestles to pound millet into flour while the men beat on drums. The bride then emerges from her home and ceremoniously says good-bye to her family. A feast takes place on the final day, celebrating the union of the couple. However, the husband does not emerge until the very end of the festivities to meet his bride. The couple returns to his home, and the bride wears a special veil for the next 40 days to signify her status as a newlywed.

Funerals among Burkina Faso's Bobo people can be dramatic events. When a person of wealth or importance dies, such as a village chief, a great funeral takes place about six months afterward. Dozens of masked dancers, each in the image of a different spirit, become increasingly energetic during the all-night ritual, performing spectacular acrobatics, taking giant leaps in the air, and looking for evil spirits that might prevent the deceased from going to paradise.

All life-cycle celebrations call for a feast, which must include meat, fish, or fowl. In rural areas, bush rodent is a tasty delicacy. In the cities, *broasheht* (recipe page 69) and grilled beef, chicken, rabbit, and goat are popular. Favorite beverages are nonalcoholic ginger beer and Senegalese *bissap*, a fruit juice drink.

⸎ *Yassa* (Chicken and Rice)

Yassa is the supreme West African party dish. It is a favorite for family gatherings, such as the party for a newborn or for the bride-price meeting. Spread a cloth on the floor, and put the large serving platter of *yassa* in the center. Guests must remove their shoes outside before squatting to eat. All guests, having washed their hands, eat only from the section of bowl in front of them. It is rude to reach across into someone else's section.

Yield: serves 8 to 12

4 to 5 pounds chicken, cut into serving-size pieces

8 cloves garlic, **trimmed, minced**

8 onions, trimmed, **finely chopped**

2 cups red wine vinegar

1 cup vegetable oil, more as needed

crushed dried chili pepper to taste

salt and pepper to taste

8 to 12 cups rice, cooked according to directions on package, keep warm

Equipment: Paper towels, large mixing bowl with cover or plastic food wrap, mixing spoon, large skillet, metal tongs, large roasting pan with cover, oven mitts, deep serving platter

1. Wash chicken pieces, place on several layers of paper towels, and pat dry.
2. Make **marinade:** Combine garlic, onions, vinegar, 1 cup oil, crushed chili peppers to taste, and salt and pepper to taste in large mixing bowl. Stir to mix well. Add chicken pieces and coat well with mixture. Seal bowl with cover or plastic wrap, and refrigerate to **marinate** for at least 4 hours. Remove from refrigerator once or twice, and toss to coat chicken pieces with marinade.

Preheat oven to 350° F.

3. Prepare to skillet-fry: *Caution: Adult supervision required.* Place large roasting pan near stove. Heat 2 tablespoons oil in large skillet over medium-high heat. Add chicken pieces, a few at a time, and fry until browned, 7 to 12 minutes on each side, reserving marinade. Using metal tongs, transfer to large roasting pan and continue frying in batches.
4. Pour marinade over browned chicken pieces, cover, and bake in oven for 45 minutes. Remove cover and bake for another 30 to 40 minutes until chicken is very well done. Test **chicken doneness.**

To serve yassa, cover bottom of deep serving platter with cooked rice and arrange chicken pieces over the top. Spoon tomato mixture from roasting pan over chicken and rice or serve in a separate bowl. To eat yassa as they do in Burkina Faso, gather a good amount of rice, chicken, and sauce in your right hand and form into a ball against the side of the platter. Squeeze it with your fingers until it's compact, then pop into your mouth. It is bad manners to start forming another ball while there is still food in your mouth. When you finish eating, clean off the part of the bowl in front of you with your hand and lick your fingers clean. If other people are still eating after you have finished, it is rude to watch them eat, although you can sit and converse with them, but keep your eyes focused on something else in the room.

⚘ Millet Bread

Millet is an important grain grown throughout Burkina Faso. During wedding ceremonies indigenous tribes pound millet into flour. The flour is then used to make breads and others dishes that will feed family and friends during the wedding celebration.

Yield: serves 6 to 8

2 teaspoons salt

1 cup **millet** flour (available at international markets)

2 cups **cornmeal**

2 cups oat flour

2½ cups water

2 tablespoons honey

2 eggs

2 tablespoons oil

2 packages of **yeast** (activate according to directions on package)

Equipment: Large mixing bowl, mixing spoon, medium mixing bowl, rubber spatula, medium-square, greased or nonstick baking pan, moist towel, toothpick, oven mitts, wire rack

1. In large mixing bowl, combine salt, millet flour, cornmeal, and oat flour. Mix well.

2. In medium mixing bowl, combine water, honey, eggs and oil, mix well. Carefully stir in activated yeast.

3. Using rubber spatula, fold egg and honey mixture into flour mixture, mix well.

4. Transfer to baking pan, cover with a moist towel, and set in warm place 30 to 40 minutes or until dough has doubled in size.

5. Preheat oven to 350°F.

6. Bake 25 to 30 minutes, or until bread is golden on top and a toothpick inserted in center comes out clean. Carefully remove from oven using oven mitts and set on wire rack to cool.

Serve in individual slices with a hearty meal for a wedding celebration or family gathering.

Gambia and Senegal

Gambia and Senegal are on the western "bulge" of Africa, along the Atlantic Ocean. Except for about 75 miles of coastline, English-speaking Gambia is entirely surrounded by French-speaking Senegal, which is bordered by Mauritania, Mali, Guinea, and Guinea-Bissau. Much of the population in both countries live in villages made up of compound-houses with extended families.

The majority of people in Gambia and Senegal are Muslims. Traditional local religions and customs are intermixed with Islam in both countries, especially in beliefs concerning death. Bad luck, childbirth deaths, and other sudden deaths are believed to be the work of witches, who steal people's souls immediately after birth or during circumcision, when a human is most vulnerable to attack. Also typical of the blending of Islamic and indigenous beliefs is the wearing of *jujus*. A juju is a leather amulet worn around the wrist, neck, waist, or ankle to bring good luck.

Much of African life centers on special events, such as weddings, baptisms, funerals, and village celebrations. Most celebrations in Gambia and Senegal include dancing, singing, and feasting.

Weddings are celebrated with great enthusiasm. On the day of the marriage, the legal and religious ceremonies are performed as early as possible so the day can be spent celebrating. The offering of kola nuts plays a special role in weddings, as well as on other special occasions. Biting into a kola nut is an age-old ceremony meant as a blessing. During a traditional wedding, the bride's grandmother and great-aunts take her to the marriage chamber, where they lecture her about the pleasures and perils of marriage. If the first night of marriage goes well, the next morning, guests shower the bride with gifts. Senegalese and Gambian Muslim men may have up to four wives, if they can afford to support them.

Circumcision is an important rite for Muslim boys that is performed shortly after they reach puberty. Among some Gambian ethnic groups, before the procedure, the boys are dressed like women and wear shells and jewels in their long hair. Afterward, still wearing their costumes, they stay away from people and live in special huts until healed. On returning to their village, they are honored with a feast.

When affluent Senegalese and Gambian family and friends gather for a circumcision or wedding celebration, *méchoui*—whole roasted lamb (recipe follows) or goat—is prepared for the event. The meat is brushed with a mixture of hot pepper sauce, water, and peanut oil. As it roasts, the surface of the meat becomes crusty and spicy, and the inside stays moist and soft. For urban dwellers, *méchoui* is baked in the oven.

Many other dishes are served along with the meat. For those who cannot afford *méchoui*, a little meat is added to rice and vegetables, such as *gombos* (okra). Most dishes are served with "broken rice," rice that has been broken into tiny granules. Originally, broken pieces of rice were used because they were all that the Senegalese could afford—whole grains were reserved for export. Eventually, broken grains became a staple of Senegalese cooking, and now rice is grown and broken, in order to supply the demand.

At feasts, family and guests assemble on the floor on a mat or cloth around platters of food. Eating is done only with the right hand, although some city dwellers use spoons.

⚱ *Méchoui* (Lamb Roast)

Yield: serves 15 to 18

8 to 10 pounds lean lamb roast or baron (saddle and two legs) of lamb

salt and pepper to taste

juice of 2 lemons

2 cloves garlic, **trimmed, minced**

2 tablespoons Dijon mustard

Equipment: Paper towels, large shallow roasting pan with rack, small bowl, mixing spoon, oven mitts, **bulb baster**, carving board, sharp knife, meat fork, large serving platter

Preheat oven to 450° F.

1. Wash lamb thoroughly and pat dry with paper towels. Place lamb on rack in large shallow roasting pan, and sprinkle with salt and pepper to taste.

2. Put lemon juice, garlic, and mustard in small bowl. Stir to mix well. Using your hand, rub mustard mixture over surface of lamb.

3. Place lamb in hot oven to **sear** for 35 to 45 minutes. Reduce heat to 325°F, and continue to bake for 3½ to 4½ hours, or until meat thermometer registers about 150°F for medium. Allow 20 minutes per pound for rare meat and 35 minutes per pound for well done meat. While baking, **baste** occasionally with pan drippings, using mixing spoon or bulb baster. Remove from oven, and let rest at least 20 minutes before carving.

4. Transfer meat to carving board, and, using sharp knife and holding meat in place with meat fork, cut across grain into thin slices and transfer to large serving platter. Set platter on the tablecloth set on floor.

Serve méchoui *with North African* chlada felfel *(recipe page 6) and* **couscous** *(cooked according to directions on package) seasoned with lamb drippings.*

♪ *Salade de Lentilles et de la Banana* (Lentil and Banana Salad)

Lentils are a staple of West Africa. This simple and easy to prepare dish is ideal to serve with any fish dish for a festive occasion or large family gathering.

Yield: serves 6 to 8

2 cups brown **lentils** (cooked according to directions on package), drained, cooled

3 tablespoons olive oil

1 onion, **trimmed, finely chopped**

1 red bell pepper, trimmed, **coarsely chopped**

2 cloves garlic, trimmed, **minced**

3 to 4 semiripe bananas, peeled and sliced into ½-inch rounds

4 tablespoons balsamic vinegar

3 tablespoons fresh **cilantro**, trimmed, coarsely chopped

2 tablespoons fresh parsley, trimmed, coarsely chopped

½ teaspoon cayenne pepper or to taste

salt and pepper to taste

½ cup peanuts, shelled, peeled, chopped

Equipment: Large serving bowl, medium skillet, mixing spoon, plastic wrap

1. Place cooked lentils in serving bowl and set aside.

2. Heat 2 tablespoons oil in skillet over medium-high heat. Add onion, bell pepper, and garlic, **sauté** 3 to 5 minutes, or until onions are soft and translucent. Transfer to serving bowl with lentils, gently mix well.

3. Carefully **fold in** bananas, vinegar, cilantro, parsley, cayenne pepper, and salt and pepper to taste, gently mix well. Cover with plastic wrap, and chill in refrigerator for 15 to 20 minutes, or until ready to serve.

Serve, sprinkled with chopped peanuts, as an accompaniment to roasted or grilled fish.

♪ *Dem Saint-Louis* (Stuffed Mullet, Saint-Louis Style)

Dem Saint-Louis is a specialty of Saint-Louis, a coastal town that was once the capital of Senegal. In Senegal, mullet is the fish used for this dish; however, any small, firm fish can be used. Rainbow trout is an excellent substitute.

Yield: serves 4

4 whole mullet or rainbow trout, 10 to 12 ounces each, cleaned, with head and tail intact

1 cup onion, **trimmed, finely chopped**, divided

½ cup green onions, finely chopped, divided

4 cloves garlic, trimmed, crushed, divided

14 ounces canned stewed tomatoes, **coarsely chopped**

salt and pepper to taste

4 ounces skinless fish **fillets, coarsely chopped** (such as cod, white fish, or tilapia)

2 eggs

½ cup tomato paste

¼ teaspoon **ground** red pepper, more or less to taste

1 cup fresh **bread crumbs**

1 tablespoon vegetable oil

Equipment: Paper towels, work surface, 12×9×1½-inch baking pan, mixing spoon, food processor, medium mixing bowl, rubber spatula, greased **pastry brush**, oven mitts

1. Layer several sheets of paper towels on work surface. Rinse each fish under cold running water, and drain on paper towels.

2. Put ½ cup onions, ¼ cup green onions, and 2 cloves garlic in baking pan. Add canned stewed tomatoes and salt and pepper to taste. Using mixing spoon, stir and spread mixture evenly over bottom of baking pan. Set aside.

Preheat oven to 350° F.

3. Prepare stuffing: Put fish fillets in food processor. Add eggs and tomato paste, and process until smooth and well mixed, about 1 minute.

Note: While processing, turn machine off once or twice, and scrape down sides of container with rubber spatula.

4. Transfer mixture to medium mixing bowl. Add salt and pepper to taste, remaining ½ cup onion, ¼ cup green onions, and 2 cloves garlic. Add ¼ teaspoon ground red pepper, more or less to taste, and bread crumbs, and stir until well mixed. Stuff each whole fish with processed fish mixture and place side by side on tomato mixture in baking pan. Any leftover stuffing can be shaped into egg-shaped balls. Slightly flatten leftover balls into patties and place in sauce around fish. Using pastry brush, brush top of each fish lightly with oil.

5. Bake in oven for 25 to 30 minutes, or until fish and stuffing are done.

To serve, cut each fish into 4 pieces, and serve directly from the pan.

⚒ *Boulettes de Poisson* (Fish Balls in Sauce)

In Gambia and Senegal, most people pick up the food and eat it with the fingers of their right hand. Rice, steamed millet, or **couscous** (cooked according to directions on package) is served with this dish.

CAUTION: HOT OIL IS USED.

Yield: serves 6 to 8

1 pound skinless fish **fillet** (such as cod, haddock, red snapper, or trout), cut in chunks	salt and pepper to taste
	4 tablespoons oil, divided
1 onion, **trimmed, finely chopped**	1 onion, trimmed, finely chopped
1 tablespoon parsley, finely chopped	1 cup tomato paste
½ cup **bread crumbs**	1 cup water
1 egg	**ground** red pepper to taste

Equipment: Food processor, rubber spatula, medium mixing bowl, mixing spoon, paper towels, 2 baking sheets, large skillet with cover, slotted metal spatula, serving platter

1. Put fish fillet chunks in food processor, add onion, parsley, bread crumbs, and egg. Process until smooth. Transfer mixture to medium mixing bowl. Add salt and pepper to taste.

Note: While processing, turn machine off once or twice, and scrape down sides of container with rubber spatula.

2. Prepare to skillet-fry: *Caution: Adult supervision required.* Place several layers of paper towels on baking sheet. Heat 2 tablespoons oil in large skillet over medium-high heat. Form fish mixture into egg-sized balls, flatten slightly, and place in skillet. Lower heat to medium, and fry on both sides, in batches, until lightly browned, 3 to 5 minutes on each side. Remove with slotted metal spatula, and place on paper towel–covered baking sheet to drain.

3. Heat remaining 2 tablespoons oil in same large skillet over medium-high heat. Add finely chopped onion and **sauté** until soft, 3 to 5 minutes. Stir in tomato paste, water, salt and pepper to taste, and ground red pepper to taste. Cook for 5 minutes, until slightly thickened. Reduce heat to **simmer**, and add fish balls. Cover and cook for 30 minutes.

To serve, transfer to a serving platter, and serve as finger food with other dishes.

⚜ *Noix de Coco Biscuits Lime* (Coco-nutty Lime Cookies)

This combination of flavors is a favorite among children and adults alike. It is ideal for a baptismal or wedding celebration.

Yield: about 1½ to 2 dozen

1 cup flour	1 cup sugar
1½ cups rolled oats	1 egg
1 cup shredded coconut	**zest** and juice of 2 limes
1 teaspoon baking powder	½ teaspoon vanilla extract
½ teaspoon salt	½ cup walnuts or peanuts, shelled, **finely chopped**
½ cup unsalted butter, room temperature	

Equipment: Medium mixing bowl, electric mixer or large mixing bowl with mixing spoon, greased or nonstick cookie sheet, oven mitts, spatula, wire rack

Preheat oven to 375°F.

1. In medium mixing bowl, combine flour, oats, coconut, baking powder, and salt, mix well and set aside.
2. In electric mixer or large mixing bowl, combine softened butter and brown sugar until light and fluffy. Add egg, lime zest, lime juice, and vanilla extract, mix well. Mixing constantly, add flour mixture, a little at a time, until well blended. **Fold in** nuts.
3. Drop tablespoons of batter onto cookie sheet. Bake in oven for about 7 to 10 minutes, or until golden on top. Carefully remove from oven using oven mitts. Let cool for 1 to 2 minutes on cookie sheet, then using spatula, transfer to wire rack to cool completely.

Serve as a sweet treat for children's celebration.

Ghana

Ghana (once known as Gold Coast) is situated just above the equator in West Africa, bordering the Atlantic Ocean, Togo, Burkina Faso, and Côte d'Ivoire (Ivory Coast). Ghana is home to more than 50 small ethnic groups. More than half of Ghana's people are Christians, and a small percentage are Muslims. The rest—mostly rural folk—practice indigenous religions. (See Protestant and Catholic Life-Cycle Rituals, page lxxiii; Islam and Islamic Life-Cycle Rituals, page lxxvi; and African Life-Cycle Rituals, page lxvi.)

The clothing Ghanaians wear tells a great deal. For important events—naming ceremonies, weddings, and funerals—men wear *kente* cloth, a beautifully patterned hand-woven textile. *Kente* cloth is made into a garment about the size of a bed sheet that is worn draped over the left shoulder, with the right shoulder left bare, toga-style. The designs and colors of the *kente* cloth differ for each specific occasion, and the intricate patterns are rich in symbolism. For example, *kente* cloth woven with threads of red, a Ghanaian color of mourning, is worn by men of the Akan people when they dance the funeral rituals.

In Ghana, the traditional belief is that when persons die, they are actually going on a journey, that life continues after death. Ghanaians often spend everything they have on funerals, and one of the hardest struggles in life is to make enough money for this occasion. Part of the cost is for highly individual coffins, which are created by woodcarvers to reflect objects of special importance to the customer. There is such a demand for these creative coffins that when a person dies before the coffin is ready, the body may have to be kept in a mortuary for several months. Families bury their dead with the comforts and adornments of life; for instance, handwoven cloth, jewelry, and money are placed in the coffin.

Ghanaians love festivals. Funerals draw large crowds: often hundreds of people come for a celebration that is more jubilant than sad. During a Christian funeral ceremony, there will be a blending of Christian and traditional practices, such as when the officiating cleric pours a libation over the coffin to ask blessings from the deceased.

⚔ *Aprapransa* (Palm Nut Stew)

Aprapransa is a delicacy of the Akwapim people; however, it is eaten by all Ghanaians. When it is prepared for special occasions, smoked **herring** is added to the dish. The recipe calls for palm butter, a pulp made from palm nuts. Canned palm butter is available in some Latin American and other specialty food stores; however, peanut butter is an acceptable substitute. Ghanaians always have cauldrons of cooked rice, *tuo zaafi* (recipe page 33), boiled yams, and stews such as this recipe to feed the throngs of people who come to a funeral and stay for the feast.

Yield: serves 4

1 tablespoon vegetable oil or red palm oil (available in Latin American food stores)

1 onion, **trimmed, finely chopped**

1 cup cooked **black-eyed peas**, dried (cooked according to directions on package) or canned

2 to 4 tablespoons palm butter or peanut butter

4 tomatoes, finely chopped, divided

water, as needed

3 tablespoons masa flour (available at all Latin American food stores and all supermarkets)

1 tablespoon lemon juice

salt and pepper to taste

Equipment: Large skillet, mixing spoon, serving bowl

1. Heat oil in large skillet over medium-high heat. Add onion, stir, and **sauté** until soft, 3 to 5 minutes. Add cooked black-eyed peas, palm butter or peanut butter, half the chopped tomatoes, and 2 cups water. Stir and bring to a boil. Reduce heat to **simmer**, and cook for 5 minutes, for flavor to develop.

2. Stir in masa flour, lemon juice, and salt and pepper to taste. Reduce heat to simmer. Cook, uncovered, for 10 to 15 minutes, or until thickened. Stir occasionally to prevent sticking.

To serve, transfer to serving bowl, and sprinkle the top with remaining chopped tomatoes.

⚔ *Fante Mbire Flowee Hkatenkwan* (Ginger Chicken and Okra)

This dish is prepared for a baptism celebration, first communion, or wedding feast. It is eaten with *tuo zaafi* (recipe follows).

Yield: serves 4 to 6

2½- to 3-pound chicken, cut into serving-size pieces

1 tablespoon ginger root, **trimmed, minced** fresh ginger, or 1 teaspoon **ground** ginger

1 onion, trimmed, **finely chopped**

8 cups water

2 tablespoons tomato paste

2 tomatoes, **cored,** finely chopped

1 cup chunky peanut butter

½ teaspoon ground red pepper, more or less to taste

1 cup eggplant, peeled, **cubed**

1 pound whole okra, fresh or frozen, **trimmed**

salt and pepper to taste

Equipment: Large saucepan with cover or **Dutch oven**, slotted spoon, trivet

1. Put chicken pieces, ginger, onion, and water in large saucepan or Dutch oven. Bring to a boil over high heat. Reduce heat to **simmer**, cover, and cook until chicken is tender, 1 hour. Using slotted spoon, remove chicken pieces and keep warm.

2. Add tomato paste, tomatoes, peanut butter, ground red pepper, more or less to taste, eggplant, okra, and salt and pepper to taste. Bring to boil over medium-high heat, stir, and cook 5 minutes. Reduce heat to simmer, cover, and cook 10 minutes. Return chicken pieces, and lay on top of vegetables. Cover and simmer for 15 minutes or until chicken is heated through.

To serve, set the saucepan or Dutch oven on trivet in the middle of the table and have guests help themselves.

⸎ *Tuo Zaafi* (Millet Porridge)

Muslims prepare roasted lamb, such as *méchoui* (recipe page 27), for their circumcision and wedding celebration feasts. Porridge made of different grains is an African staple eaten at every meal; it holds the same place in African cultures as bread in European countries and rice in Asian countries. *Tuo zaafi* is served with roasted meats, such as *méchoui* (recipe page 27).

Yield: serves 4

1 cup **millet** (available at all health food stores), soaked overnight

6 cups canned beef broth

2 tablespoons vegetable oil

1 onion, **trimmed, finely chopped**

1 potato, peeled, **coarsely chopped**

2 carrots, **trimmed**, sliced crosswise

1 cup finely chopped cabbage

½ cup milk

salt and pepper to taste

For **garnish:** 2 tomatoes, quartered

Equipment: Strainer, medium saucepan with cover, mixing spoon, medium skillet

1. Drain soaked millet in strainer placed over sink, and discard soaking water. Put millet in medium saucepan, add beef broth, and bring to boil over medium-high heat. Reduce heat to **simmer**, cover, and cook for 45 minutes, or until tender.

2. Heat oil in medium skillet over medium-high heat. Add onions, stir, and **sauté** until soft, 3 to 5 minutes. Add potatoes, carrots, and cabbage, and stir. Reduce heat to simmer, cover, and cook until vegetables are soft, 12 to 15 minutes.

3. Add potato mixture to cooked millet, and stir to mix well. Add milk, stir, and cook, uncovered, over medium-low heat to thicken to desired consistency, 7 to 12 minutes. (It can be either soupy or thick.) Add salt and pepper to taste.

To serve, garnish with tomato wedges. If mixture is soupy, you can drink it, or if thick, use the fingers of your right hand to scoop tuo zaafi *out of the container into your mouth. The left hand must never touch food; it is used only for personal grooming.*

✿ *Tatale* (Plantain Cakes)

Tatale, a traditional Ghanaian snack, is ideal to serve at the beginning of a baptism or a wedding feast.

Yield: serves 4 to 6

2 **plantains**, soft and black, peeled, **trimmed**, mashed (available at most supermarkets and international markets)

¼ cup **cornmeal**, more or less as needed

1 onion, trimmed, **finely chopped**

1 teaspoon vegetable oil, more as needed

salt and black pepper to taste

For serving: hot sauce (optional)

Equipment: Medium mixing bowl, mixing spoon, large **heavy-bottomed** skillet, spatula, serving plate covered with several layers of paper towels

1. Place mashed plantains in mixing bowl, add just enough cornmeal to bind plantains together, mix well. Stir in onion, 1 teaspoon oil, and salt and pepper to taste, mix well.

2. Heat 2 tablespoon oil in skillet over medium-high heat. Reduce to medium heat, drop 2 to 3 heaping tablespoons of mixture into skillet (mixture should spread out like a pancake). Cook about 2 to 3 minutes on each side or until golden brown. Fry in batches until all batter is used, adding more oil if necessary to prevent sticking. Set aside on paper towel–covered serving platter, cover, and keep warm.

Serve warm as a snack, adding a few drops of your favorite hot sauce (optional).

Guinea and Guinea-Bissau

The Republic of Guinea and its tiny neighbor Guinea-Bissau border the Atlantic Ocean on the west coast of Africa. Their closest neighbors are Senegal, Mali, Côte d'Ivoire, Liberia, and Sierra Leone.

In Guinea, more than 75 percent of the people are Muslims, and in Guinea-Bissau, about half are Muslims. Except for a few Christians in the urban areas, the rest of the people in both countries adhere to traditional local religions. (See Islam and Islamic Life-Cycle Rituals, page lxxvi, and African Life-Cycle Rituals, page lxvi.)

Muslims in Guinea and Guinea-Bissau combine local customs with general Islamic practices in all life-cycle celebrations. Traditionally, when a Muslim man in these countries is informed that his wife is pregnant, he must collect at least a three-month supply of firewood for the hot baths she will take after the delivery. Just after the birth, the mother drinks a spicy gruel made with potash. Four days after the birth, a soup made with the legs and jaw of a cow is prepared for the new mother.

Seven days after a birth, a naming ceremony is held for the baby. The father gives kola nuts to his parents, in-laws, friends, and neighbors. The ground in front of his house is thoroughly swept to set down carpets and mats for guests to sit on, and he must provide either a bull or ram to be sacrificed for this occasion. When the animal is being slaughtered, the *malaam* (Islamic religious leader) is told the name for the child. After the sacrifice, the *malaam* prays, blesses the child, and whispers the chosen name in its ear. A barber shaves the infant's head completely and—if it is the clan's tradition—he makes the desired tribal marks, called "scarification," on the child. After the rituals are complete, there is a dancing, singing, and feasting celebration.

Circumcision of boys at seven years of age is required by Islamic law, although some put it off until the child is about nine. A group of boys who undergo circumcision at the same time often feel a bond with one another that lasts a lifetime. A barber trained in circumcision performs the procedure. The boys live together until they are healed; they are kept away from other people and fed only millet or corn porridge. Once healed, the boys are washed, their heads are shaved, and they each receive a new *bante* (loincloth). They are then presented to the public at a celebration that includes a dance and a feast. A cow or lamb is slaughtered and roasted for the occasion.

When a Muslim dies in an urban area, he or she is buried in a communal cemetery. In rural areas, each family has its own burial area in their residential compound. The body is prepared according to specific religious rules. It is wrapped in a *kubba* (white cotton shroud) and carried to the burial site. The body is buried on its side with its face turned toward Mecca (the Islamic holy city).

After the burial, the bereaved family gives food to the poor, on behalf of the deceased: millet, corn, or bean cakes similar to *tamiya* (recipe page 47) and *tuo zaafi* (recipe page 33). A man has no designated mourning period after his wife dies, and he can remarry soon after her death. A woman is expected to mourn her dead husband for up to 4 months and 10 days. During the mourning period, widows do not comb their hair, nor do they wear jewelry or cosmetics.

⚓ *Poisson de Guinée* (Guinean Fish)

Saltwater and freshwater fishing is an important industry in both Guinea and Guinea-Bissau. When properly **garnished**, this fish dish would be perfect to serve along with other dishes at a life-cycle celebration.

Yield: serves 4 to 6

2 to 3 pounds skin-on fish **fillets** (such as trout, halibut, salmon, or red snapper)

8 tablespoons vegetable oil, divided

ground red pepper to taste

½ teaspoon ground cloves

salt and pepper to taste

1 onion, **trimmed, finely chopped**

2 tomatoes, finely chopped

For **garnish:**

2 hard-cooked eggs, peeled, sliced

2 tablespoons tomato paste

1 tablespoon **ground** dried shrimp (available at Asian food stores)

1 onion, sliced into ¼-inch-thick rings and separated, for **garnish**

1 plantain, sliced into ¼-inch-thick circles, for garnish

For serving: 4 cups cooked rice, kept warm

1 green bell pepper, **trimmed, seeded, julienned**

Equipment: Paper towels, medium shallow baking pan, plastic food wrap, large skillet, mixing spoon, medium bowl, oven mitts, fork, large serving platter

1. Rinse fish fillets under cold running water, drain, and pat dry with paper towels. Put fish into medium shallow baking pan. **Drizzle** both sides of fish with 4 tablespoons oil. Sprinkle with ground red pepper to taste, cloves, and salt and pepper to taste. Cover with plastic wrap and refrigerate for 1 to 2 hours while preparing sauce and garnish.

2. Prepare sauce: Heat 2 tablespoons oil in large skillet over medium-high heat. Add chopped onion, and **sauté** until soft, 3 to 5 minutes. Add chopped tomatoes, tomato paste, ground dried shrimp, and salt and pepper to taste. Stir to mix well. Reduce heat to **simmer**, and cook 3 to 5 minutes for flavor to develop. Transfer to medium bowl.

3. Prepare garnish: Heat remaining 2 tablespoons oil in large skillet over medium-high heat. Add onion rings, plantains, and salt and pepper to taste. Stir and sauté until lightly brown about 5 to 7 minutes.

Preheat oven to 350° F.

4. Remove plastic wrap from fish. Pour prepared sauce over fish. Bake in oven for 12 to 18 minutes until fish is opaque white and flakes easily when poked with fork.

Serve by making a mound of cooked rice on large serving platter with raised edge. Lay fish on top of rice, and spoon sauce over it. Garnish with sautéed onion rings and plantains. Arrange egg slices over the top, and sprinkle with julienned green pepper.

♪ Lime Cake

Lime cake is an example of the **fusion** of African and Western cultures using locally grown fruits.

Yield: serves 6 to 8

2½ tablespoons butter

2 eggs, well beaten

juice of 1 lime or 2 to 3 tablespoons bottled lime juice

zest of 1 lime

1½ cups flour

2¼ teaspoons baking powder

½ cup chopped peanuts, shelled, peeled

For serving: ice cream, whipped topping, or yogurt

Equipment: Electric mixer or medium mixing bowl with mixing spoon, medium, square, greased or non-stick baking pan, rubber spatula, oven mitts, toothpick

Preheat oven to 350°F.

1. In an electric mixer or in medium mixing bowl using a wooden spoon mix together sugar and butter until well blended. Stir in eggs, lime juice, flour, baking powder, and peanuts, mix well.

2. Transfer to baking pan, and bake for 20 to 25 minutes or until toothpick inserted in center comes out clean.

3. Carefully remove from oven using mitts and set aside to cool. Sprinkle lime zest over top of cake.

Serve with a dollop of ice cream, whipped topping, or yogurt as sweet treat for any family celebration.

Ivory Coast (Côte d'Ivoire)

Ivory Coast (formerly known as Côte d'Ivoire) is situated on the Atlantic coast, along the underside of the West African bulge. The neighboring countries are Liberia, Guinea, Mali, Burkina Faso, and Ghana. There are four major cultural groups in the Ivory Coast, within which are 60 different ethnic groups. Each ethnic group has its own lifestyles, rituals, and celebrations. Although the nation has two of the world's largest Roman Catholic cathedrals, only a small percentage of the people are Christians, most of them Protestants. Muslims, living mostly in the north, make up a small minority of the population as well. The majority of Ivorians follow indigenous religions. (See African Life-Cycle Rituals, page lxvi.)

The Baoulés are the largest ethnic group. Baoulés trace kinship through their mothers' families rather than their fathers', and although Baoulé women live with their husbands' families, women have superior authority in family matters. The land and power are passed down through a mother's family line to her sisters' sons rather than to her own.

Each Baoulé family line claims ownership of a ceremonial stool that represents the spirit of the founding ancestor of the mother's family. The male leader of the mother's family sits on this stool on important occasions, such as weddings.

Another large ethnic group in the Ivory Coast is the Sénoufo people, whose lifestyle, rituals, and customs are entirely different from those of the Baoulés. They believe a person's life is divided into seven-year phases, the most important being ages 14 through 21.

To prepare children for adulthood, the Sénoufo people have a secret society known as *lô*. Rigorous tests are part of the preparation for manhood, and each Sénoufo village has a "sacred forest" where these rituals take place in secret. The goal of *lô* is to preserve tribal traditions and folklore. The children are instructed over many years in the oral history and social mores of the Sénoufo people. Their education is divided into three seven-year periods ending with an initiation ceremony.

Sénoufo funerals are presided over by blacksmiths, even though they are of a low caste. Blacksmiths are believed to have a kinship with the earth that gives them special powers. During a funeral, the corpse is carried in a long procession through the village, while men in enormous grotesque masks follow along, chasing away the dead person's soul. Immune to evil spirits, the blacksmiths dig a hole and carefully position the body in the grave, after which they present the corpse its last meal. The funeral ends with a great communal feast and celebration.

₵ *Fruits de Mer et de la Salade de Fruits* (Seafood and Fruit Salad)

This colorful salad is a festive dish to serve for a funeral celebration.

Yield: serves 6 to 8

water, as needed

1 pound medium-sized shrimp, peeled, **deveined**

3 (3–5 ounces each) skinless fish **fillets** (such as snapper, bass, grouper, or tilapia)

3 **papayas, trimmed**, seeded, **coarsely chopped**

14.5 canned pineapple chucks, drained

juice of 1 lemon or 1 teaspoon lemon juice

2 avocados, peeled, seeded, coarsely chopped (sprinkle with lemon juice to prevent browning)

2 tablespoons mayonnaise

¾ cup fresh or canned grapefruit juice

hot sauce (optional)

salt and pepper to taste

For **garnish**: ½ cup peanuts, shelled, **finely chopped**

Equipment: Large kettle, slotted spoon or **skimmer, colander** or strainer, small mixing bowl, mixing spoon, cutting board, sharp knife, salad bowl, salad fork and spoon, plastic wrap

1. Fill kettle ½ full with water. Add shrimp and bring to boil over high heat, reduce to simmer, and cook for 3 to 5 minutes or until shrimp float to top and are opaque white. Using slotted spoon or skimmer, remove from water, and place in colander or strainer to drain, set aside to cool.

2. Carefully add fish fillets to simmering water. **Poach** for 5 to 7 minutes or until **fish** is **opaque white** and **flakes** easily when poked with fork. Using slotted spoon or skimmer, carefully remove fillets and place in colander or strainer to drain, set aside to cool.

3. When fish is cool enough to handle, place on clean work surface or cutting board and, using knife, carefully cut into 1-inch chucks.

4. In salad bowl, add shrimp, fish pieces, papaya, pineapple, and avocado, set aside.

5. In small mixing bowl, combine mayonnaise, grapefruit juice, and hot sauce, mix well.

6. Pour grapefruit dressing over seafood and fruit mixture; using salad fork and spoon, toss to mix well. Add salt and pepper to taste. Cover with plastic wrap and place in refrigerator to cool for 15 to 20 minutes or until ready to serve.

Serve salad chilled with peanuts sprinkled on top for garnish.

⚘ *Kedjenou à la N'Gatietro* (Chicken-in-a-Pot)

One of the country's most celebrated special occasion dishes is *kedjenou à la n'gatietro*. It is called "chicken-in-a-pot" because it is cooked in a *canari* (terracotta pot). In the Ivorian bush, the chicken is wrapped in banana leaves and cooked under the ashes of a fire instead of in a *canari*. Most dishes are served with rice and *attiéké*, one of the country's best liked specialties. *Kedjenou á la n'gatietro* can be prepared in a large electric slow cooker. Cook according to manufacturer's directions. Test for **doneness.**

Yield: serves 6 to 8

3 to 4 pounds chicken, cut into serving-size pieces	1 tablespoon ginger root, trimmed, grated, or 1 teaspoon **ground** ginger
salt and pepper to taste	1 bay leaf
4 onions, **trimmed, finely chopped**	1 cup water
1 (16-ounce) canned diced tomatoes	1 cup peanut butter
2 cloves garlic, **trimmed, minced**	ground red pepper to taste
	hot water, if necessary

Equipment: Large heatproof casserole with cover or **Dutch oven**, small bowl, mixing spoon, large serving platter

1. Sprinkle chicken pieces with salt and pepper to taste, and layer in large heatproof casserole or Dutch oven. Add onions, canned chopped tomatoes, garlic, ginger, bay leaf, and salt and pepper to taste.

2. Put water in small bowl, and add peanut butter and ground red pepper to taste. Stir to mix well. Pour over chicken mixture, and bring to boil over high heat. Reduce heat to **simmer**, cover, and cook for 1 to 1¼ hours, or until very tender. Add just enough hot water from time to time, if necessary, to prevent drying out. Test **chicken doneness**.

To serve, mound rice in center of large serving platter, arrange chicken pieces around the sides, and spoon sauce over top of rice.

Jamma Jamma (Spiced Greens)

Every feast includes assorted vegetables dishes, such as *jamma jamma*. Any combination of greens can be used to make this dish.

Yield: serves 4 to 6

3 tablespoons vegetable oil

1 onion, **trimmed**, thinly sliced

3 cloves garlic, trimmed, **minced**

½ teaspoon **ground** red pepper, or to taste

2 bunches **mustard greens, collard greens,** or spinach, or combination, trimmed, rinsed, **coarsely chopped**

¼ cup vegetable broth

salt and pepper to taste

Equipment: Large skillet with cover, mixing spoon

1. Heat oil in large skillet over medium-high heat. Add garlic and onion, and **sauté** until onion is soft, 3 to 5 minutes. Sprinkle in ¼ teaspoon ground red pepper, more or less to taste.

2. Stir constantly for about 30 seconds, and add greens. Reduce heat to medium, cover, and cook until wilted, 3 to 5 minutes.

3. Add broth and salt and pepper to taste, and stir. Cover and cook until tender, 5 to 7 minutes. Remove from heat and serve immediately.

Serve jamma jamma as a side dish with meat, chicken, or fish dishes.

Sauce Arachide (Peanut Sauce)

Sauces made with either palm nuts or peanuts are eaten to enhance the flavor of most dishes, much as Americans eat mustard or ketchup. This is a popular peanut sauce.

Yield: about 1½ cups

1 cup unsalted peanuts, shelled, **roasted**

2 cups water

salt to taste

1 teaspoon **ground** chili powder

2 tablespoons peanut oil

1 onion, **trimmed, finely chopped**

Equipment: Electric **blender**, rubber spatula, small saucepan, mixing spoon, small skillet, small serving bowl

1. Put peanuts in blender and add enough water (½ to 1 cup) to **blend** into smooth paste.

2. Bring remaining water to boil in small saucepan over high heat. Reduce heat to **simmer**, stir in peanut mixture, add salt to taste, and chili powder. Cook for 10 minutes.

3. Heat oil in small skillet over medium-high heat. Add onion and sauté until soft, about 3 minutes. Add onion to nut mixture, stir well, and continue to cook for 10 minutes more.

Serve sauce in small serving bowl, and everyone uses it as they like. It is often poured over jamma jamma.

Liberia

Liberia was founded in 1821 by African American settlers from the United States whose ancestors had been taken from Africa as slaves. Liberia lies along the Atlantic coast, on the western "bulge" of Africa. It shares borders with Sierra Leone, Guinea, and Côte d'Ivoire. It is one of the last West African countries with a significant rain forest (an estimated 44 percent of the nation's land). Most Liberians are subsistence farmers.

The population is made up of 16 ethnic groups. About 5 percent of the people are descendants of freed slaves from the Americas. A small percentage of the people are Muslims, and almost an equal number are Christians, the majority of whom are Protestants. Other Liberians practice local religions. Indigenous beliefs and customs are part of all life-cycle celebrations in Liberia. (See Islam and Islamic Life-Cycle Rituals, page lxxvi; Protestant and Catholic Life-Cycle Rituals, page lxxiii; and African Life-Cycle Rituals, page lxvi.)

The ethnic groups in Liberia have intermarried, and there is not the same strong sense of separation between groups as is found in most other parts of Africa. For example, there are secret societies in Liberia that are not restricted to a particular tribe—they are based on caste rather than on ethnicity. The men's society is called *poro*, and the women's is called *sande*. Liberian secret societies have rites and ceremonies that are similar to those of most African tribes, but they are also involved in areas beyond religion and the education of the young; for instance, they control the activities of indigenous medical practitioners, and they often judge disputes between members of high-ranking families.

Life-cycle celebrations in Liberia are communal, and they always involve music and dancing. Each community has its own drummers and musicians who play for weddings, school graduations, and other communal celebrations.

One of the most popular festive dishes is red nut stew, traditionally eaten with rice. Red nuts grow on oil palm trees, and, although they are plentiful in Liberia, they are not easily available in the United States.

A soup with many variations that has traveled up and down the West African coast is pepper soup. It is cooked outdoors in a cauldron. Red nut stew or pepper soup are often eaten to restore health at the end of the wedding celebration. Meat is added when the soup is prepared for celebration feasts.

⚘ *Pepper Soup*

Note: Use care when handling peppers. Wrap your hands in plastic wrap, or cover them with a plastic sandwich bag. If you accidentally touch your eyes, rinse them out at once under cold running water.

Yield: serves 4 to 6

1 pound lean stewing beef, cut into bite-size pieces

8 cups water

2 hot green chili peppers (**jalapeños**), **seeded, finely chopped**, or **ground** red pepper to taste

1 onion, **trimmed**, finely chopped

4 **new potatoes**, with skin on, washed, cut into bite-size pieces

2 tomatoes, trimmed, **peeled**, finely chopped

½ cup tomato paste

salt and pepper to taste

For serving: 2 cups cooked rice (cooked according to directions on package)

Equipment: Large saucepan with cover or **Dutch oven**, mixing spoon, ladle, individual soup bowls

1. Put meat, water, peppers or ground red pepper to taste, onion, potatoes, tomatoes, tomato paste, and salt and pepper to taste in large saucepan or Dutch oven. Bring to boil over high heat. Stir well and reduce heat to **simmer**.

2. Cover and cook until meat is very tender, 1 to 1½ hours.

To serve, divide cooked rice equally between 4 to 6 soup bowls, and ladle hot soup over the rice.

⚘ *Abala* (Savory Steamed Rice)

Several rice dishes are always on the menu for life-cycle celebrations. In Sierra Leone and Liberia, banana leaves are used instead of foil to encase the rice mixture.

Note: Use care when handling peppers. Wrap your hands in plastic wrap, or cover them with plastic sandwich bag. If you accidentally touch your eyes, rinse them out at once under cold running water.

Yield: serves 6

1 cup cream of rice cereal (available at all supermarkets)

¾ to 1 cup boiling water

1 hot green chili pepper (**jalapeño**), **seeded, finely chopped**

1 onion, **trimmed**, finely chopped

¼ cup vegetable oil

1 teaspoon salt

Equipment: Medium mixing bowl, mixing spoon, plastic food wrap, aluminum foil, work surface, **steamer pan**, metal tongs

1. Put cream of rice in medium mixing bowl. Stirring constantly, slowly add just enough boiling water (between ¾ to 1 cup) to make smooth, firm mixture. Add pepper, onion, oil, and salt, and stir well. Cool to room temperature, and cover with plastic wrap. Refrigerate for 1 hour to firm and chill.

2. Place 6 (8- or 9-inch-square) pieces of foil on work surface. Mound equal amounts of mixture in center of each square and enclose securely in foil.

3. Steam *abala*: Pour water into bottom of steamer, keeping it below, not touching, rack or container that holds the food. Stack foil-wrapped packages on rack or in container and bring to boil over high heat. Reduce heat to **simmer**, cover, and steam until rice mixture is fully cooked and holds together, about 2 hours. Open foil package to check doneness.

Note: *Check water level frequently during steaming to be sure there is at least 1 inch of water in bottom pan. Add more hot water, when necessary.*

To serve, each person is given an abala. Each guest opens his or her own and eats out of the wrapping, like eating a candy bar.

₡ *Kyekyire Paano* (Toasted Cornmeal Cookies)

Except in urban areas, most people in Africa don't have ovens; thus, few recipes call for baking. Cookies such as these can be made in homes with modern appliances, or they can be bought at a bakery. These cookies are served to guests who have come to a baby-naming party.

Yield: about 24 pieces

1 cup yellow or white **cornmeal**

1½ cups all-purpose flour

½ teaspoon salt

½ teaspoon nutmeg

½ cup butter or margarine, at room temperature

½ cup sugar

2 eggs, beaten

1 teaspoon lemon **zest**

Equipment: Baking sheet, oven mitts, metal spatula, flour **sifter**, small bowl, large mixing bowl, electric mixer or mixing spoon, plate

Preheat oven to 350°F.

1. Spread cornmeal in baking sheet, and place in oven or until lightly browned, about 20 minutes. Using oven mitts, stir with metal spatula so cornmeal toasts evenly. Remove from oven and cool to room temperature.

2. **Sift** flour, salt, and nutmeg into small bowl.

3. Put butter or margarine in large mixing bowl, add sugar, and beat with electric mixer or mixing spoon until fluffy and light, 1 to 2 minutes. Add flour, toasted cornmeal, salt, nutmeg, eggs, and lemon zest. Beat until well mixed. Leaving at least 1½ inches between, drop spoonfuls of dough onto baking sheet, making each cookie about the size of a ping-pong ball.

Increase oven to 375°F.

4. Bake in oven for 15 to 20 minutes, or until golden brown.

To serve, arrange cookies on plate, and set out as a snack with milk.

ℰ Chocolate-covered Almonds and Coffee Beans

Cocoa was introduced to West Africa from Latin America, and it is now a major export crop in such countries as Ghana, Côte d'Ivoire, Liberia, and Sierra Leone. Sweets at celebrations are eaten as a symbol of prosperity and good luck.

Yield: serves 6 to 8

2 cups dark chocolate chips   1 cup almonds, shelled

1 cup roasted espresso coffee beans

Equipment: **Double boiler,** rubber spatula, cookie sheet, wax paper, soup spoon

1. Melt chocolate in double boiler over medium heat, stirring frequently until chocolate is melted and smooth. Add coffee beans and almonds, mix well until all pieces are coated.

2. Cover cookie sheet with wax paper. Drop two heaping tablespoons of mixture onto wax paper to make each candy cluster, leaving space between. Continue until all mixture is used. Set in refrigerator or freezer to cool. When hardened, transfer to airtight container, separating layers with wax paper to prevent sticking. Store in cool place.

Serve with tea or a glass of milk.

Mali

Mali is a landlocked country in the Saharan region of West Africa. Its neighbors are Guinea, Senegal, Mauritania, Algeria, Niger, Burkina Faso, and Côte d'Ivoire. Almost all Malians are Muslims, and in every ethnic group in the nation, life-milestone events combine Islamic practices with indigenous customs and beliefs. (See Islam and Islamic Life-Cycle Rituals, page lxxvi, and African Life-Cycle Rituals, page lxvi.)

Traditionally, when a Malian man wants to marry, he has a friend or male relative visit the girl's father to make the request for him. The suitor brings kola nuts to his prospective in-laws—offering kola nuts as a gift signals respect. If the kola nuts are accepted, it indicates the father's consent to the marriage proposal.

Agreeing on a bride-price finalizes the marriage. Usually the bride-price is paid in installments over several years. The payment period is a time to strengthen the bond between families—or, if the bride doesn't fulfill her obligations to her husband, he can stop the payments, and she is returned to her father. It is not unusual for a father to offer another daughter or his unmarried sister or sister-in-law as a replacement for a returned bride, who is felt to have disgraced the family.

Among Mali's Malinke people, a naming ceremony takes place on the eighth day after a baby's birth. Early in the morning, the villagers arrive for the daylong celebration. After saying a blessing over the infant, the religious leader shaves the child's head; he then shares kola nuts and says a blessing over the ritual food of rice, honey, and sour milk. He prays that the child will bring pride and honor to the family and community. The baby's name is a secret to all except the parents and officials. After the father whispers the name three times in the baby's ear, he announces it to everyone present. Then the music, dancing, and feasting begin.

Konkonte D'Abam (Spiced Coconut Pudding Cake)

Konkonte d'abam is an ideal dessert to serve for the baby-naming feast.

Yield: serves 4 to 6

1 egg, beaten	1 teaspoon nutmeg
1 cup milk	½ teaspoon salt
2 cups all-purpose flour	1 cup grated coconut
1 cup sugar	2 tablespoons butter, melted
1½ tablespoons baking powder	½ cup raisins
2 teaspoons cinnamon	For serving: whipped topping or ice cream

Equipment: Small mixing bowl, whisk, medium mixing bowl, mixing spoon, nonstick or greased medium baking pan, oven mitts, toothpick, wire rack

Preheat oven to 375°F.

1. In small mixing bowl, whisk together beaten egg and milk, set aside.

2. In medium mixing bowl, combine flour, sugar, baking powder, cinnamon, nutmeg, salt and coconut, mix well. Gradually stir in milk and egg mixture, mix well. Stir in melted butter and raisins.

3. Transfer to baking pan, bake for 25 to 30 minutes or until toothpick inserted in center comes out clean. Carefully remove from oven using oven mitts, cool in pan for about 10 minutes. Turn onto wire rack to finish cooling.

Serve warm, cut into serving-size pieces with a dollop of whipped topping or ice cream.

Mauritania

Mauritania is in northwestern Africa, bordering the Atlantic Ocean, Morocco, Mali, Algeria, and Senegal. The Moors, who make up 75 percent of the population, live in the northern part of the country. They are nomadic pastoralists of mixed Arab and Berber descent who herd camels, sheep, and goats, depending on the region. The remaining 25 percent of the people are black Africans living in the southern region. One of the major southern groups is the Fulani, cattle herders who live mainly on milk, milk products, and millet, eating meat only for special celebrations

Each group has its own traditions and customs, with one common bond: Islam. (See Islam and Islamic Life-Cycle Rituals, page lxxvi.) In some places, traditional indigenous practices are combined with Islamic rites.

Fulani boys and girls are required to participate in a rite of passage ceremony before they are considered adults. The young boys must participate in a whipping match. The competition is held with a boy from a neighboring village. Each boy prepares for the ceremony by selecting a stick that is used to whip the other boy three times. The boy who hits the hardest and flinches the least while being hit is considered the winner of the match. People from both villages surround the boys during the ceremony and determine who the winner is.

Young girls must undergo hours of facial tattooing before they can be considered for marriage. During the tattooing ceremony, they must remain calm and not show signs of fear or weakness. After these rites of passage are conducted, the boys become men, and the girls are considered woman ready for marriage.

In Mauritania, the main dish served for the *kaliyoo*—the wedding or funeral feast—is whole roasted goat or lamb, or *meshwi* (recipe page 48). All meals begin and end with the ritual drinking of three small glasses of *at'tay* (tea). The tea-brewing and -drinking ritual is the same in Tunisia, and the tea is similar to *thé à la menthe* (recipe page 21).

✑ *Soupe de Potiron* (Pumpkin Soup)

For those girls and boys who have experienced the grueling coming of age rituals, a soothing and nourishing bowl of *soupe de potiron* is comforting.

Yield: serves 6 to 8

2 tablespoons vegetable oil

1 onion, **trimmed, minced**

2 (14.5-ounce) cans pumpkin puree or 2½ pounds fresh pumpkin, cooked, trimmed, mashed

3 cups chicken stock

¾ cup heavy cream

2 tablespoons tomato paste

2 tablespoons brown sugar

½ teaspoon ground ginger

½ teaspoon ground cinnamon

½ teaspoon cayenne pepper, or to taste

salt and pepper to taste

Equipment: Large saucepan, mixing spoon, **blender**

1. Heat oil in large saucepan over medium-high heat, add onions and **sauté** 3 to 5 minutes, or until soft.

2. Stir in pumpkin, broth, cream, tomato paste, brown sugar, ginger, cinnamon, and cayenne pepper, mix well. Stirring occasionally heat through. In batches, transfer to blender and purée until smooth. Return to saucepan and cook over medium-high heat until heated through. Add salt and pepper to taste.

Serve warm with crusty bread for dipping.

♂ *Tamiya* (Bean Balls)

Fritters, patties, and balls made with dried beans, peas, lentils, and rice are popular throughout Africa and the Middle East. This recipe is made with dried yellow or green split peas or white beans.

Note: This recipe takes 2 days.

CAUTION: HOT OIL IS USED.

Yield: serves 6 or 8

2 cups (about 1 pound) dried yellow or green split peas or white beans, soaked in water overnight, drained

1 egg

water, as needed

2 cloves garlic, **trimmed, minced**

1 onion, trimmed **finely chopped**

½ teaspoon **ground** turmeric

ground red pepper to taste

salt and pepper to taste

vegetable oil, for deep frying

Equipment: **Blender**, rubber spatula, medium mixing bowl, plastic food wrap, **deep fryer, deep fryer thermometer** or wooden spoon, paper towels, baking sheet, slotted spoon

1. Put drained split peas or white beans in blender, add egg, and **blend** until coarsely ground, not smooth, about 30 seconds. If necessary, add just enough water, about 1 or 2 tablespoons, to help mixture blend. (The mixture should be thick and coarse.) Transfer to medium mixing bowl.

2. Add finely chopped garlic, finely chopped onion, turmeric, ground red pepper to taste, and salt and pepper to taste. Cover with plastic wrap, and refrigerate for at least 2 hours to thicken.

3. Prepare to deep-fry: *Caution: Adult supervision required.* Place several layers of paper towels on baking sheet. Heat oil to 375°F on fryer thermometer, or oil is hot enough when small bubbles appear around a wooden spoon handle when it is dipped in the oil.

4. Form mixture into ping-pong-size balls, and fry a few at a time until golden brown, 1 to 2 minutes. Remove with slotted spoon, and drain on paper towels. Continue to fry in batches.

Serve warm as a starter or cold as a snack, or use to scoop up stew.

ⵣ *Meshwi* (Meat Kebabs)

Traditionally, *meshwi* is made with lamb, goat, or antelope, but it also can be made with beef. When made with lamb, the dish is called *lahm meshwi*. Rice would be served with *meshwi* since it is regarded as special occasion food, especially when served with *sauce arachide* (recipe page 40).

CAUTION: GRILL OR BROILER IS USED.

Yield: serves 4

2 pounds lean lamb, goat, or beef, cut into 1½-inch cubes

1 cup olive oil

salt and pepper to taste

½ teaspoon **ground** thyme

For **garnish**: 2 onions, **trimmed, finely chopped**, for **garnish**

Equipment: Medium bowl, mixing spoon, plastic food wrap, 8 wooden or metal 8- or 10-inch skewers (if using wooden skewers, first soak in water for at least 30 minutes so they don't burn when cooked), charcoal **grill** or broiler pan, oven mitts, metal tongs, large platter

1. In medium bowl, combine oil, salt and pepper to taste, and thyme. Add **cubed** meat, and toss to coat. Cover with plastic wrap, and refrigerate for about 4 hours to **marinate**, stirring frequently to coat.

2. Have an adult help prepare charcoal grill or preheat broiler.

3. Thread meat pieces tightly together on skewers. Place side by side on grill or broiler pan. Wearing oven mitts and using metal tongs, turn skewered meat to brown on all sides, and cook 15 to 20 minutes, or to desired doneness.

To serve, arrange skewers on large platter, and sprinkle with finely chopped onions, for garnish. Serve with cooked rice.

Niger

A landlocked country in Saharan Africa, Niger is surrounded by Mali, Algeria, Libya, Chad, Benin, Burkina Faso, and Nigeria. It shares not only its name, but a fair proportion of its people, with neighboring Nigeria. Niger's largest ethnic group, the Hausa people, have kinfolk living across the border in the northern two-thirds of Nigeria.

In both countries, the people are predominantly Muslims, although there also are small communities of Christians. All groups fuse local religious beliefs with Islam or Christianity, and rituals and customs vary greatly from group to group. (See Islam and

Islamic Life-Cycle Rituals, page lxxvi, and Protestant and Catholic Life-Cycle Rituals, page lxxiii.)

Although Niger is primarily a country of small villages, with the majority of people working as subsistence farmers, the nomadic Wodaabé people are herders who constantly travel with their cattle—a sign of wealth and prestige—over Niger's sub-Saharan steppe.

Most Wodaabé parents arrange the betrothal of their children, usually to a first cousin, when the child is born or is very young. Years later, after marrying, a Wodaabé man may have up to three more wives, but they must all be from outside his clan. If a marriage has not been arranged by the parents, a boy can abduct the girl he wants for his wife. By slaughtering a sheep, followed by a short celebration, the two are considered wed.

The Wodaabé are very concerned with physical appearance, and having beautiful children is of utmost importance to married couples. During courtship, to win the attention of the eligible girls, single men sometimes participate in a "beauty contest." The main event is a performance for which the men blacken their lips to make their teeth seem whiter. The men dance and perform for hours, displaying their looks and charisma to entice the young girls standing on the sidelines.

Some girls ultimately make a choice, and if a marriage proposal results, the man takes a calabash full of milk to her parents. If they accept, he then brings them the bride-price: three cattle that are slaughtered for the feast that follows.

Cattle are usually slaughtered and roasted for celebration feasts, which also include cauldrons of millet porridge, the same as *tuo zaafi* (recipe page 33).

¿ *Adalu* (Mashed Vegetable Medley)

The vegetables in this dish are staples throughout West Africa. *Adalu* is ideal to serve as an accompaniment with *bondo gombo* (recipe page 50).

Yield: serves 4 to 6

2 tablespoons vegetable oil

1 onion, **trimmed, finely chopped**

1 tomato, trimmed, finely chopped

14.5-ounce canned **black-eyed peas**, drained

1 cup frozen corn (cooked according to directions on package) or 14.5-ounce canned corn, drained

14.5 ounce canned yams, drained, **coarsely chopped**

½ teaspoon cayenne pepper, or to taste

salt and pepper to taste

Equipment: Large **heavy-bottomed** saucepan, mixing spoon, potato masher

1. Heat oil in saucepan over medium-high heat, add onions, and **sauté** 3 to 5 minutes, or until soft. Stir in tomato, black-eyed peas, corn, and yams, mix well. Sauté 5 to 7 minutes, or until vegetables are heated through. Remove from heat.

2. Using potato masher, mash vegetables until well blended.

3. Stir in cayenne pepper and salt and pepper to taste.

Serve warm as a side dish with bondo gombo *(recipe follows).*

Bondo Gombo (Lamb Gumbo with Whole Wheat Dumplings)

Lamb is a favorite meat of Muslims in Africa. In Africa, *gombo* means "okra," which is used in this lamb gumbo.

Yield: serves 6

4 tablespoons vegetable oil

2 pounds lean stewing lamb, cut into 1-inch cubes

1 onion, **trimmed, finely chopped**

3 tablespoons all-purpose flour

1 cup tomato paste

6 cups water

10-ounce package frozen sliced okra, thawed

salt and pepper to taste

For serving: whole wheat dumplings (recipe follows)

Equipment: Large saucepan with cover or **Dutch oven**, mixing spoon

1. Heat oil in large saucepan or Dutch oven over medium-high heat. Add meat and brown on all sides, 7 to 12 minutes. Stir in onions, reduce heat to medium and cook until soft, 3 to 5 minutes. Sprinkle in flour and stir until smooth. Add tomato paste and water and stir. Cover and **simmer** over medium heat until meat is tender, 1 to 1½ hours. Carefully **fold in** okra, and simmer until soft, 10 to 15 minutes. Add salt and pepper to taste.

2. Prepare whole wheat dumplings.

Serve the bondo gombo *from the cooking pot. Either arrange dumplings on top of gumbo or serve separately. Either way, the dumplings are used to sop up the meat sauce.*

Whole Wheat Dumplings

Yield: serves 6 to 8

1 cup whole wheat flour

1 cup water, more as needed

1 ½ teaspoons salt, divided

Equipment: **Double boiler** with cover, mixing spoon, medium saucepan, slotted spoon

1. Put flour in top pan of double boiler. Stir in 1 cup water and ½ teaspoon salt to make smooth paste. Fill bottom pan of double boiler halfway with water, and bring to boil over high heat. Reduce heat to **simmer**. Set flour mixture over simmering water, cover, and cook 30 minutes. Remove from heat.

2. Fill medium saucepan two-thirds full with water, and bring to boil over high heat. Add 1 teaspoon salt, and reduce heat to rolling boil. Drop dumplings, one tablespoonful at a time into water. Do not crowd pan. Cook 5 to 7 minutes. When dumplings float to the top, cook additional 5 minutes. Remove with slotted spoon and keep warm. Continue to cook in batches.

Use in the recipe for bondo gombo.

Nigeria

Nigeria is on the west coast of Africa, and shares its other borders with Benin, Niger, Cameroon, and Chad. It is divided into three very distinct regions—northern, southwestern, and southeastern—separated naturally by a Y-shaped division through the center of the country formed by the Niger River and its tributary, the Benue. The three regions differ in languages, religions, traditions, and alliances. The northern two-thirds of the country, known as the Holy North, is where the Muslim Hausa-Fulani people live. The southwest is home to the Yoruba people, about half of whom are Christian and half Muslim. The southeast is inhabited by the Ibos, who are mostly Roman Catholics.

Throughout Nigeria, puberty initiation rites and ceremonies are conducted for both boys and girls. Today, the initiation rites of most ethnic groups are painless, unlike *sharo,* a practice of the Fulani people of the north. *Sharo* has been illegal for many years, however, it is still practiced in remote regions of the country. It involves two boys, usually from neighboring villages. Each, in turn, must flog the other three times with a large stick. The boy being hit cannot show that he is feeling any pain, or he will be disgraced before the girls in the village and will not be able to marry.

There are several forms of marriage in Nigeria. In the south, Christian urbanites have monogamous marriages, while traditional Nigerian marriages are polygamous. In the Holy North, Muslim men marry up to four wives. In polygamous marriages, the first wife is usually the leader among the wives. Frequently, she is the only one for whom a full dowry has been paid.

During traditional courtship, the suitor's family visits the girl's family, bringing quantities of *mmanya*, a type of wine; this is called "the carrying of the wine." Libations are poured, and ancestors are called upon to bless the union.

In parts of Nigeria (as well as in neighboring Togo), a bride-to-be resides in a fattening room for 14 days prior to her wedding. Female family elders put her through an intensive feeding and beautifying regime, hoping she will be more pleasing to her husband.

In Nigeria, as well as in Togo and Benin, everyone in the clan or village takes part in the wedding feast. Meat is the main food, served with great quantities of pounded yams, fritters, grilled plantains, soups, porridges, and stews. After the wedding feast, a bride goes to her husband's home, thus confirming her marriage to the family. The Igbo community in eastern Nigeria then refer to her as *nwuye any,* which means "our wife."

In Eastern Nigeria, a man of importance is given two funerals. After his death, such a man is buried promptly and secretly. Although it is common knowledge that the man has died, people keep silent about it until the family is ready for the public announcement of a second funeral. Because of the expense of providing food and drink for everyone who attends, months—perhaps even years—may pass before the bereaved family can afford the festivities. The deceased man's estate is not distributed among his heirs until after the second funeral.

☙ *Ewa and Dodo* (Black-eyed Peas with Fried Bananas)

Black-eyed peas (*ewa*) and bananas (*dodo*) are a favorite dish in Nigeria. The following recipe is one of the many side dishes served at a wedding feast.

CAUTION: HOT OIL IS USED.

Yield: serves 6

1 cup plus 1 tablespoon vegetable oil, divided

1 onion, **trimmed, finely chopped**

6 cups cooked **black-eyed peas** with liquid, homemade or canned (cooked according to directions on package)

1 large tomato, trimmed, finely chopped

3 tablespoons canned tomato paste

7 ounces canned water packed tuna or salmon

ground red pepper to taste

3 bananas, peeled, cut crosswise into ¼-inch slices

salt and pepper to taste

Equipment: Medium saucepan with cover, mixing spoon, paper towels, baking sheet, large skillet, metal slotted spoon, serving bowl

1. Heat 1 tablespoon oil in medium saucepan over medium-high heat. Add onions, stir, and **sauté** until soft, 2 to 3 minutes. Add peas with liquid, chopped tomato, and tomato paste. Stir, reduce heat to **simmer**, and cook for 10 minutes. Using mixing spoon, **fold in** tuna or salmon, and salt and ground red pepper to taste. Simmer for 10 minutes without stirring. Cover and keep on medium-low heat.

2. Prepare to skillet-fry: *Caution: Adult supervision required.* Place several layers of paper towels on baking sheet. Heat remaining 1 cup oil in large skillet over medium-high heat. Add bananas and fry on both sides until golden brown, 3 to 5 minutes. Remove with metal slotted spoon and drain on paper towel–covered baking sheet. Sprinkle with salt and pepper to taste.

To serve, sprinkle dodo *(fried bananas) over* ewa *(black-eyed peas) in a serving bowl.*

♪ *Chinchin* (Fried Pastries)

Chinchin is simply fried dough sprinkled with sugar. It is popular under different names in almost every country in the world. Platters of *chinchin* are prepared for many life-cycle celebrations. They are a favorite sweet snack, especially among children.

CAUTION: HOT OIL IS USED.

Yield: about 2 dozen

2 cups all-purpose flour

1 teaspoon baking powder

1 teaspoon **ground** nutmeg

½ teaspoon salt

1 tablespoon vegetable shortening, at room temperature

¾ cup hot water, more or less as needed

vegetable oil, for deep frying

For **garnish**: confectioners' sugar

Equipment: Large mixing bowl, mixing spoon, kitchen towel, lightly floured work surface, lightly floured rolling pin, knife, **deep fryer**, deep frying thermometer or wooden spoon, paper towels, baking sheet, wooden spoon, slotted metal spoon or metal tongs, serving platter

1. In large mixing bowl, mix flour, baking powder, nutmeg, and salt. Using clean hands, **blend** in shortening until mixture resembles fine crumbs. Add just enough hot water, a little at a time, to make soft dough that holds together, leaving sides of bowl clean. Divide dough into 2 balls, and cover with towel to prevent drying out.

2. On lightly floured work surface, using lightly floured rolling pin, roll one ball into a rectangle, about ¼ inch thick. Sprinkle with flour if dough seems sticky. Using knife, cut dough into 1×6-inch strips. Cover with towel, and repeat with second ball.

3. Prepare deep fryer: *Caution: Adult supervision required.* Place several layers of paper towels on baking sheet. Heat oil to 375°F on fryer thermometer, or oil is hot enough when small bubbles appear around wooden spoon handle when it is dipped into the oil. Deep-fry in small batches, 3 or 4 at a time, until golden brown, 2 to 3 minutes. Remove with slotted metal spoon or metal tongs, and drain on paper towel–covered baking sheet.

To serve, stack pastries on serving platter, and sprinkle with confectioners' sugar, for garnish.

♪ *Grubombo* (Stewed Okra and Tomatoes)

Grubombo is a basic recipe throughout much of Africa. A hearty one-dish meal can be made by adding shrimp, cubed fish **fillets**, chunks of meat, chicken, sausage, or any combination of those ingredients to the okra mixture (*gombo* means "okra"). The Créoles of southern Louisiana learned how to make gumbo from the slaves who brought *grubombo* with them from Africa. Serve *grubombo* as a vegetarian dish over rice or as a side dish. It is best to use fresh okra (not canned) for the following recipe.

Yield: serves 6 to 8

2 tablespoons vegetable oil

2 onions, **trimmed, finely chopped**

1 pound fresh whole okra (small pods), trimmed

28 ounces canned whole tomatoes, **coarsely chopped**

1 **jalapeño (hot green chili pepper)**, trimmed, **seeded**, finely chopped

salt and pepper to taste

Equipment: Medium **heavy-bottom** saucepan with cover or **Dutch oven**, mixing spoon

1. Heat oil in medium heavy-bottomed saucepan or Dutch oven over medium-high heat. Add onions, stir, and **sauté** until soft, 3 to 5 minutes.

2. Add okra, tomatoes, and jalapeño, and bring to boil. Stir, reduce heat to **simmer**, cover, and cook until okra is tender, 10 to 15 minutes.

3. Stir in salt and pepper to taste. Simmer, uncovered, for 5 to 10 minutes to thicken.

Serve as a side dish or as a sauce over rice, meat, or chicken.

⚘ *Crab Imoyo* (Crab Salad with Shrimp)

Crab imoyo is a cold yet spicy dish. This elegant salad is ideal for a bride to make in order to impress the groom's family for their summer wedding feast.

Yield: serves 4 to 6

1 onion, **trimmed, finely chopped**

2 tomatoes, trimmed, finely chopped

1 tablespoon vinegar

juice of 1 lemon or 1 tablespoon lemon juice

2 tablespoons olive oil

1 tablespoon tomato paste

1 cup fish **stock**

1 pound lump crabmeat (available at most supermarkets)

½ pound medium-size cooked **shrimp**, peeled, **deveined**

½ teaspoon cayenne pepper, or to taste

salt and pepper to taste

For **garnish:**

1 bell pepper, trimmed, sliced into ¼-inch rings

lime or lemon wedges

Equipment: Small mixing bowl, mixing spoon, salad bowl, salad fork and spoon, plastic wrap

1. In small bowl, combine onion, tomatoes, vinegar, lemon juice, and oil, mix well. Set aside to marinate 15 to 20 minutes.

2. In salad bowl, combine tomato paste and fish stock, mix well. Stir in onion and tomato mixture, crabmeat, shrimp, cayenne pepper, and salt and pepper to taste, toss with salad fork and spoon to mix well.

3. Cover with plastic wrap and refrigerate 45 minutes to 1 hour, or until chilled through.

Serve chilled, garnished with bell pepper slices and lime or lemon wedges.

Sierra Leone

Sierra Leone is located on the Atlantic Coast of Africa, on the West African "bulge." It shares borders with Guinea and Liberia. It is one of the wettest countries in the region, with a rainy season that extends from May through November.

The two largest ethnic groups in Sierra Leone are the Temnes in the north and the Mendes in the south. The Temnes are Muslims and love pomp and pageantry. They incorporate their own elaborate ceremonies into the life-milestone religious rites prescribed by the Koran. The Mende people are known for their secret societies, which are responsible for training children in matters of tribal law and cultural traditions. Like most Sierra Leoneans, they follow indigenous religious practices. The Creoles are a small group of Christians who are descendants of slaves who returned to Africa from Great Britain and North America. (See Protestant and Catholic Life-Cycle Rituals, page lxxiii.)

In Sierra Leone, parents traditionally arrange marriages. In these arranged unions, the girls customarily have no say in whom they marry. Because brides have value and bring bride-price to the family, parents see to it that their daughters are attractive and well trained. In some ethnic groups, girls of marriageable age go through a fattening ceremony. They are kept in a special house for two to 12 months to be force-fed in order to achieve a well-rounded figure. Today, on the other hand, an educated woman may have a career and may be choosy about her husband. The bride-price in such a situation may be a sum of money to set the woman up in business.

Sierra Leoneans are always ready for a celebration. A wedding leads to days of visiting with friends, gift giving, and feasting. The wedding feast day usually begins early in the morning and continues far into the night.

Another occasion for the gathering of friends and relatives is the naming of a child, usually on the 28th day of its life. Again, the celebration begins early in the day with singing, dancing, and feasting. Parents give their children such names as the season of their birth, the day of the week on which they were born, or weather conditions on the day of birth.

✥ *Ogede Sise* (Boiled Bananas)

The Muslim wedding feast begins with *méchoui* (recipe page 27) or whole roasted lamb, such as *kabab barreh* (recipe page 629), vegetable dishes, and mountains of rice, or *abala* (recipe page 42).

The wedding and funeral feast for Christians and traditional practitioners would be *yassa* (recipe page 24), a specialty of most West African countries. It is made with lamb, fish, chicken, or even monkey. Serve with abala (recipe page 42), **couscous** (cooked according to directions on package), or *tuo zaafi* (recipe page 33). An added treat on the banquet table would be *ogede sise.*

Yield: serves 3 to 6

6 cups water	6 bananas, with skin on (Allow 1 or 2 bananas per person.)

Equipment: Medium saucepan with cover, slotted metal spoon or metal tongs, paring knife, serving platter

1. Pour water into medium saucepan, and bring to boil over high heat. Add bananas with skin on, and bring water back to boil. Reduce heat to **simmer**, cover, and cook 15 minutes.

2. Remove bananas with slotted metal spoon or tongs, and place on serving platter. Slit skins lengthwise with paring knife, and serve at once.

To serve, place platter of bananas on the table. Each person eats the banana out of the skin, either by breaking into bite-size pieces or by scooping it out using only the fingers of the right hand. The left hand must never touch food; it is used only for personal grooming. The bananas can also be eaten with a spoon or fork.

⸎ Grilled Squid

This recipe calls for squid, which is also known as *calamari. Calamari* must be rinsed thoroughly under cold running water inside and out. It is plentiful throughout the Atlantic Ocean, making it ideal for any celebration banquet such as a naming ceremony or a wedding celebration.

Yield: serves 6 to 8

4 tablespoons olive oil, more as needed	2 pounds squid tubes rinsed, cut into ¼ to ½-inch-wide rings
juice of 2 lemons or 4 tablespoons lemon juice	½ cup black olives
juice of 1 lime	½ cup peanuts, shelled, finely chopped
2 red chilies, **trimmed, finely chopped** or to taste	For serving: ¼ cup parsley for garnish, finely chopped
2 garlic cloves, trimmed, **minced**	

Equipment: Small mixing bowl, mixing spoon, large mixing bowl, plastic wrap, large skillet, spatula, serving bowl

1. In small bowl, combine 4 tablespoons olive oil, lemon juice, lime juice, red chilies, and garlic, mix well. Set aside.

2. Place squid rings in large mixing bowl and pour olive oil mixture over top. Using mixing spoon, carefully mix well to coat. Cover with plastic wrap, marinade in refrigerator for about 1 hour, stirring once or twice to evenly coat squid.

3. Heat 2 tablespoons olive oil in skillet over medium-high heat. Pour squid with marinade into skillet, reduce heat to medium, and **sauté** for 3 to 5 minutes, or until lightly golden. Transfer to serving dish.

4. **Fold** in olives and peanuts.

Serve garnished with parsley as a starter to the meal or as a side dish.

CENTRAL AFRICA

The countries typically included in Central Africa include Angola, Cameroon, Central African Republic, Chad, Democratic Republic of Congo, Equatorial Guinea, Gabon, and Republic of Congo.

Angola

Angola is on the southwest coast of Africa, bordered by the Democratic Republic of Congo and the Republic of Congo to the north, Zambia to the east, and Namibia to south. In the late 1400s, Portuguese colonists—slave traders and farmers—began settling in Angola. These Portuguese colonists imported chili peppers, maize, tobacco, tomatoes, pineapples, sweet potatoes, manioc, and bananas to Angola from Latin America. They also planted orange, lemon, and lime trees, and they introduced the domestic pig into Africa. Angola broke from Portugal and gained its independence in 1975.

The largest ethnic group in Angola is the Mbundu people, about half of whom are Christians, mostly Roman Catholics. Most Angolan Christians combine Church teachings with traditional religious practices when celebrating important life-cycle events. (See Protestant and Catholic Life-Cycle Rituals, page lxxiii, and African Life-Cycle Rituals, page lxvi.)

Baptism ceremonies take place within a few weeks after birth. The ceremony is followed by a celebration with singing, dancing, and a huge feast. Guests are expected to bring gifts for both the mother and the father, usually a small amount of money. Typically, a pig is slaughtered and roasted (recipe page 425) for the occasion.

As in many other parts of Africa, when boys reach puberty, they go through secret rituals to mark their transition to manhood. They are taken away to a camp for a month of seclusion where they are circumcised, educated in the social and moral values of the community, and put through rigorous tests of endurance. During this rite of passage, the leaders wear elaborate costumes representing the spirits of deceased chiefs and heroes. After the monthlong process, the boys return to the village as "new men."

Upon their return, there is a great celebration with a communal feast—ideally, meat roasted on a spit.

In Angola, a wedding ceremony can be very simple or quite lavish, depending on the family's wealth. If the family is poor, the ceremony is likely to be at home with just the couple, their families, and a religious leader. More expensive weddings might involve the entire community and take place in a rented celebration hall with music, dancing, and great quantities of food. Among Angola's Bantu people, cattle and sheep are currency, and meat is eaten only at weddings and funeral feasts.

⚭ *Bacalhau Gomes Sa* (Salt Cod with Boiled Potatoes)

The Angolans learned how to prepare and cook **salt cod** from the Portuguese. Today, Angolans love it as much as the Portuguese do. It is often on the menu at a celebration feast. Salt cod must be soaked overnight to soften it and to remove the salt before cooking.

Note: This recipe takes 2 days.

Yield: serves 4 to 6

1 to 2 pounds dried **salt cod** (available at Latin American food stores and some supermarkets), reconstituted according to directions on package

water, as needed

3 bay leaves

6 medium potatoes, washed

¼ cup olive oil

2 onions, **trimmed, finely chopped**

2 cloves garlic, trimmed, **minced**

1 green pepper, trimmed, **seeded**, finely chopped

¼ teaspoon oregano

½ cup fresh parsley, finely chopped

3 hard-cooked eggs, shelled, sliced

For **garnish:**

12 black olives

Equipment: Medium bowl, work surface, medium saucepan, slotted spoon, plate, **colander,** knife, vegetable peeler, large **heavy-bottomed** skillet, mixing spoon, serving platter

1. Put salt cod in medium bowl, and cover with plenty of cold water. Set on work surface to soak overnight.

2. The next day, transfer fish to medium saucepan, and discard soaking water. Cover fish generously with fresh cold water, add bay leaves, and bring to boil over medium-high heat. Reduce heat to **simmer,** and cook 20 minutes. Using slotted spoon, remove fish and transfer to plate. Discard cooking liquid, and clean medium saucepan.

3. Put potatoes in clean medium saucepan, and cover generously with fresh water. Bring to boil over high heat. Reduce heat to simmer, cover, and cook until tender, not mushy, 15 to 20

minutes. Drain potatoes in colander. When cool enough to handle, peel and chop into bite-size pieces.

4. Heat oil in large heavy-bottomed skillet. Add onions, garlic, and green pepper. Stir and **sauté** until onions and pepper are soft, 3 to 5 minutes. Reduce heat to medium, add potatoes, oregano, and parsley. Toss to mix well. Break fish into bite-size chunks, and carefully **fold in** to onion mixture. Heat through, 3 to 5 minutes.

To serve, transfer to serving platter, and garnish with olives and egg slices.

⚬ *Arroz de Coco e Papaia* (Rice with Coconut and Papaya)

Arroz de coco e papaia is a traditional Angolan recipe. It is an ideal dish to welcome home young boys after undergoing their puberty rite of passage.

Yield: serves 4 to 6

1 cup rice	½ teaspoon ground cinnamon
14.5 ounces-coconut milk, homemade (recipe page 225), or canned	1 **papaya, trimmed, seeded, coarsely chopped**
¼ cup water	½ cup shredded coconut

Equipment: Medium saucepan with cover, mixing spoon, fork, medium bowl, potato masher

1. Combine rice, coconut milk and water in saucepan, mix well. Bring to boil over medium-high heat, cover and reduce to simmer 15 to 20 minutes, or until liquid is absorbed and rice is cooked through. Remove from heat, fluff with fork, and stir in cinnamon.

2. In medium mixing bowl, using potato masher, mash half the chopped papaya. **Fold** in mashed papaya, remaining chopped papaya, and shredded coconut to rice mixture. Return to medium-low heat and heat through, stirring occasionally to prevent sticking.

Serve warm as a side with bacalhau gomes sa *(recipe page 58).*

⚬ *Broa* (Portuguese Corn Bread)

The Portuguese colonists brought their breads to Angola, where bread is now part of the national cuisine. *Broa* is one of Portugal's favorite breads.

Yield: 1 loaf

1½ cups **cornmeal**, divided	1 package active dry **yeast**
1½ teaspoons salt	1 teaspoon sugar
1 cup boiling water	¼ cup **lukewarm** water
1 tablespoon vegetable oil	2 cups sifted all-purpose flour, more or less as needed

Equipment: **Blender** or food processor, rubber spatula, large mixing bowl, mixing spoon, plastic food wrap, lightly floured work surface, kitchen towel, lightly greased baking sheet, oven mitts, wire cake rack

1. Pulverize cornmeal in blender or food processor, ½ cup at a time, until fine and powdery. The bread can be made without this step, but bread texture will not be as smooth.

2. Put 1 cup powdered cornmeal and salt into large mixing bowl. Stirring constantly, slowly pour in boiling water. Stir until smooth. Stir in oil, and let cool to lukewarm.

3. Stir to dissolve yeast and sugar into lukewarm water, leave for 5 to 10 minutes, until **froth** forms.

4. When cornmeal mixture is lukewarm, stir in yeast mixture. Beat in remaining cornmeal and 1 cup all-purpose flour to make soft dough. If mixture is sticky, add ¼ cup flour at a time, until smooth and no longer sticky. Cover with plastic wrap, and set in warm place to rise to double in bulk, 30 to 40 minutes.

5. Transfer dough to lightly floured work surface, **punch down** and **knead** in ¾ to 1 cup flour, enough to make firm dough. Knead for 3 to 5 minutes until dough is smooth and **elastic**. Shape dough into round ball, place on lightly greased baking sheet, and flatten to about 7 inches across. Cover with towel and let rise in warm place to double in bulk, 30 to 40 minutes.

Preheat oven to 350° F.

6. Bake in oven for 45 to 50 minutes, until golden brown and done. Test the **bread doneness**. Transfer to wire cake rack to cool.

Serve bread fresh from the oven for best flavor. Cut into slices, or break into chunks and use to sop up gravies and juices.

◎ *Cocada Amarela* (Yellow Coconut Pudding)

The Portuguese influence in Angola is evident in many dishes, including this dessert pudding. Desserts are something most Africans know nothing about. African languages have no word for dessert, so this dessert is called "pudding." This would be served as a refreshing ending at a first communion dinner or wedding feast.

Yield: serves 8

2 cups sugar

6 cups water

4 whole cloves

4 cups unsweetened finely grated coconut, homemade or canned (available at all Latin American food stores and most supermarkets)

12 eggs

For **garnish**: **ground** cinnamon

Equipment: Medium saucepan, mixing spoon, **candy thermometer** or cup cold water, slotted spoon, medium mixing bowl, whisk, individual dessert dishes

1. Put sugar, water, and cloves into medium saucepan. Stirring constantly, bring to boil over medium-high heat. Continue to boil briskly without stirring until syrup reaches 230°F on candy thermometer, or when a few drops spooned into a cup of cold water immediately forms coarse threads, 15 to 20 minutes. Reduce heat to low, and, with slotted spoon, remove and discard cloves. Add coconut, 1 cup at a time, stirring well after each addition. Continue to cook, stirring frequently, for 8 to 10 minutes, or until coconut becomes translucent. Remove pan from heat.

2. In medium mixing bowl, beat egg yolks with whisk until slightly thickened, about 1 minute.

3. **Temper** eggs: Stirring constantly, pour 1 cup hot coconut mixture into eggs and beat well. Slowly pour tempered egg mixture into coconut syrup, stirring constantly, until well mixed. Stirring frequently, cook over medium heat until mixture thickens enough to pull away from sides of pan, 7 to 12 minutes.

4. Spoon mixture into individual dessert dishes.

Serve at room temperature or refrigerate for about 2 hours. Before serving, sprinkle lightly with cinnamon.

Cameroon

Cameroon, located on the west coast of Africa, is bordered by Nigeria, Chad, the Central African Republic, the Republic of Congo, Equatorial Guinea, and Gabon. The area was free of colonial rule until the 1880s, when Germany gained control. After World War I, control was split between Britain and France. The legacy of this split is reflected in the fact that it is the only African nation where the French and English languages both have official status. Cameroon became an independent nation in 1960.

Indigenous religious beliefs (see African Life-Cycle Rituals, page lxvi) influence the Muslims (see Islam and Islamic Life-Cycle Rituals, page lxxvi) who live in the north and the Christians (see Protestant and Catholic Life-Cycle Rituals, page lxxiii)—mostly Roman Catholics—who live in the south. Many in Cameroon have never converted from local religions.

Among urban Christians, childbirth usually takes place in a hospital or clinic. A few weeks after the baby is born, friends and relatives are invited to a party called *born hause*. Guests bring gifts for the newborn, and the family provides food and drink during the daylong celebration.

Children are baptized when they are about 5 or 6 weeks old. Baby girls have godmothers and boys have godfathers, not godparents. Some parents have a second baptism for their child at the time of first communion, at about eight years of age. For first communion, girls wear white dresses with short veils, and boys wear white shirts and long black pants. Families share the work and expense for the communal feast and party, which generally takes place in a rented "celebration hall" after the church ceremony.

For traditional Africans, marriage is still a union of families; however, young Christian urbanites in Cameroon typically choose their own marriage partners. When a boy finds the girl he wants to marry, he must ask the oldest member of the girl's family for permission. The elder can be a grandparent, an aunt, or an uncle (female elders wield as much power as male elders). The elder accepts or rejects the suitor and asks a bride-price. The bride-price (also called the "dues") varies from group to group. A pig and goat, perhaps a cow, and a sum of money are typical components of the required dues. The boy's family then arranges to come with their son to meet with the elder of the girl's family; this is called "knock door." At this visit, the boy's family brings the requested bride-price items, and, if expectations are satisfied, the marriage is approved.

Christian men are allowed one wife, and Muslims can have up to four. Those adhering to local beliefs and practices may have as many wives as they can afford.

Weddings can take place at any hour of the day; however, the reception never begins before six in the evening. Wedding reception rituals are carefully orchestrated by a master of ceremonies (also called the "announcer"). He welcomes the guests and is in charge of all activities during the evening. During the reception, he sits with the bride and groom, the chairlady and chairman, and the best man at the "high table." The chairlady is a friend of the bride and makes a glowing speech about her. The chairman does the same for the groom. While the speech making takes place, platters of appetizers, popcorn, and boiled peanuts are brought to guests. The speech making usually takes three hours, after which a wedding cake is cut by the bride and groom, and wedding gifts are opened before everyone partakes in a buffet dinner. Toward the end of the evening, after much partying, a large pot of pepper soup (recipe page 42) is set out for guests, along with plenty of French bread (*gateau*) (recipe page 72); it settles their stomachs and sobers them up.

When a Christian dies in Cameroon, it is common for several hundred people—most of whom may be total strangers to the family—to come from miles around for the funeral. The body is placed in a coffin at the mortuary, and, after a requiem mass, at the church, it is interred in a cemetery. It is customary for family members and other mourners to throw a handful of dirt on top the casket after it is lowered into the ground. During the funeral, women friends prepare a funeral feast. Great quantities of food, including pigs, goats, and even a cow or two, are prepared for the crowd of mourners, who stay all week long.

Widows wear black for one year, and, at the end of the mourning period, there is another huge feast. Again, throngs of people show up to share in the memorial feast, which usually is announced over the radio. Again, livestock is slaughtered for the occasion. To prepare for the designated end of the mourning period, it is the custom for all family members to have garments sewn from the same fabric. This is done to show solidarity and to distinguish the family from other mourners.

🎼 *Egussi* (also *Eggusi*) (Steamed Fish Dumplings)

Egussi is a dish prepared for feasts held for special occasions. *Egussi* are seeds from a vegetable similar to squash or pumpkin. In Cameroon, the fish mixture is put in plantain leaves to cook. A good substitute for plantain leaves is quart-size heavy-duty plastic freezer bags wrapped in aluminum foil.

Yield: serves 10 to 15 people

water, as needed

2 pieces (about 1 pound) dried smoked fish (available at all African food stores and most multiethnic supermarkets)

1 to 1½ pounds fresh catfish **fillets**

3 cups *eggussi* seeds (available at all African food stores and most multiethnic supermarkets)

½ cup dried **crayfish** (available at all African food stores and most multiethnic supermarkets)

ground red pepper or **piri-piri** to taste (available at all African food stores and most multiethnic supermarkets)

salt to taste

½ cup vegetable oil

Equipment: Medium saucepan, slotted spoon, **colander**, knife, small bowl, work surface, electric **blender**, rubber spatula, large mixing bowl, 1 cup-size ladle or measuring cup, 6 or 7 quart-size plastic heavy-duty freezer bags, aluminum foil, **steamer pan**, metal tongs

1. Fill medium saucepan two-thirds full with water, and add dry smoked fish. Bring to boil over high heat and cook for 15 minutes. Add catfish fillets, and cook for 10 minutes more. Set colander in sink, drain both types of fish into colander, and cool enough to handle. Remove catfish from colander, and place on work surface.

2. Cut catfish fillets into ½-inch cubes and put in small bowl. After cooking, dried smoked fish becomes soft and pliable. Using your hands, carefully remove and discard skin and bones from smoked fish. Add edible smoked fish pieces to catfish cubes, making a total of 2 to 3 cups combined fish.

3. Pour *egussi* seeds out on work surface and carefully pick through them to remove and discard any broken shell or other debris.

4. Put 1½ cups egussi seeds in blender, add ½ cup water, and **blend** until smooth. Add just enough water, a little at a time, until mixture resembles smooth, thick milk shake, 3 to 5 minutes. Transfer to large mixing bowl.

5. Put remaining 1½ cups seeds in blender, and add dried crayfish and ½ cup water. Blend as before, adding just enough water, a little at a time, until mixture resembles a smooth, thick milk shake, 3 to 5 minutes. Add to first batch already in large mixing bowl, and stir with rubber spatula. Stir in dried, smoked fish and catfish, ground red pepper or *piri-piri* to taste (½ teaspoon for mild), salt to taste, and oil. Stir to mix well.

6. Fill each heavy-duty plastic bag with 1 cup of fish mixture. Press mixture to bottom of bag, press out air as you roll it up and seal top. (Each bag should be cylinder shaped, about 7 inches long.) Wrap each bag in foil to make watertight.

7. Fill steamer pan with at least 4 cups water, and bring to boil over high heat. Stack foil packages in steamer so that they are above boiling water. Cover tightly and cook for 1½ to 2 hours. Maintain water level, adding hot water to steamer pan as needed (about every 10 to 15 minutes). After 1½ hours, open package to check for doneness. When fish mixture is firm and holds together, it is done. If not done, continue steaming for about 30 minutes more.

To serve, remove foil and cut open plastic bag. For best flavor, serve at room temperature. Cut each fish dumpling crosswise into ½-inch thick slices.

♪ Moyin-Moyin (Black-eyed Pea Pudding)

Moyin-moyin is a savory side dish ideal to serve for a child's baptismal feast.

Yield: serves 4 to 6

2 (14.5-ounce) cans **black-eyed peas**, liquid reserved

14.5-ounce canned diced tomatoes

1 **jalapeño, trimmed, seeded, finely chopped**

2 onions, trimmed, finely chopped

½ teaspoon cayenne pepper, or to taste

1 tablespoon shrimp powder (available at International Markets)

salt and pepper to taste

water, as needed

Equipment: Food processor or **blender**, muffin pan, 1 package aluminum cupcake liners, large spoon, large cake pan, toothpick, oven mitts, wire rack

Preheat oven to 350°F.

1. Place black-eyed peas and reserved liquid in food processor or blender and **blend** on medium-low until smooth.

2. Add tomatoes, onions, jalapeño, cayenne pepper, shrimp powder, and salt and pepper to taste. Blend until smooth. If necessary, add water a little at a time, to form thick paste.

3. Line muffin pan with aluminum cupcake liners.

4. Spoon 3 to 4 heaping tablespoons of mixture into each cupcake liner or until about ⅔ full. Continue until all cupcake liners are filled.

5. Fill cake pan with ¼-inch hot water. Place muffin pan into cake pan.

6. Bake in oven about 30 to 40 minutes or until toothpick inserted in center of each bean pudding comes out clean. Carefully remove from oven, and set aside to cool. When cool enough to handle, remove bean puddings in cupcake liners and set on wire rack to finish cooling. Continue baking in batches until all mixture is used.

Serve warm as a side dish with dinner.

Central African Republic

The Central African Republic lies deep in the interior of Africa, just above the equator. The landlocked nation is surrounded by Cameroon, Chad, Sudan, South Sudan, the Democratic Republic of the Congo, and the Republic of Congo. The area was ravished by slave traders from the 16th to the 19th centuries. Ruled by France, the Central African Republic proclaimed its independence in 1960.

Country-wide, about one-quarter of the people are Roman Catholics, and there is also a small Muslim population in the north. The remainder of the population practices indigenous religions. (See Protestant and Catholic Life-Cycle Rituals, page lxxiii; Islam and Islamic Life-Cycle Rituals, page lxxvi; and African Life-Cycle Rituals, page lxvi.)

One of the 80 ethnic groups in the Central African Republic is the tropical forest foragers (Pygmies), who live in the rain forest in the southwestern section of the country. They are descendants of some of the earliest inhabitants of the region. The life-style of these hunter-gatherers is distinct from that of the village-based farmers who live throughout the rest of the country. As elsewhere in Africa, music accompanies the Pygmies' life-cycle celebrations; however, it is also a prominent part of all their daily tasks—cooking, hunting, gathering berries, and bartering. Among the tropical forest foragers, everyone is a musician—men and women, young and old alike. Everyone participates in singing, clapping, stamping, or playing musical instruments.

(See page lxvi for coming of age rituals.)

Marriage aims to strengthen existing families rather than establishing new ones. Parents arrange marriages for their children, and once the bride-price is paid, the marriage is confirmed.

Life-cycle celebrations in the Central African Republic give people a change from the routine of daily life. Along with music, life-cycle celebrations include feasts. If meat, fish, or chicken is available, it must be included. Beer made from millet is the beverage most men drink on a daily basis; however, palm wine is prepared for special celebrations and is used for the libations.

Egusi Potage (also *Eggussi Potage*) (Thick Meat Soup)

Ground *egusi* (also *eggussi*) seeds, a thickening agent used in this soup, are from the egusi melon, native to Africa. Egusi seeds are available in African food stores and multiethnic food markets. Pumpkin seeds can be substituted if *egusi* is unavailable. In West Africa, *egusi* potage is made with whatever meat is available, or it can be made with fish or fowl.

CAUTION: Use care handling peppers. Wrap your hands in plastic wrap or slip them in plastic sandwich bags. While handling peppers, if you accidentally touch your eyes, rinse them out at once under cold running water.

Yield: serves 4

1 cup *egusi* seeds or pumpkin seeds	½ cup dried **crayfish** or dried shrimp
water, as needed	1 pound lean boneless beef or lamb, **cubed**

2 tablespoons vegetable oil or palm oil
(available at ethnic food stores)

2 onions, **trimmed, finely chopped**

3 fresh chili peppers, **trimmed, seeded,** and
finely chopped, or 1 teaspoon **ground** red
pepper, more or less to taste

3 tomatoes, trimmed, finely chopped

1 bunch (about 10 ounces) fresh spinach,
washed and **coarsely chopped**

salt and pepper to taste

Equipment: **Blender,** rubber spatula, medium saucepan with cover, large skillet with cover,
mixing spoon

1. Put *egusi* or pumpkin seeds in blender, and pulse for 1 or 2 seconds to coarsely grind seeds.
   With blender running, add water, through feed tube a little at a time, to make a smooth mixture, the consistency of a milk shake. Turn off machine once or twice, and use rubber spatula
   to scrape down sides of container. Add dried crayfish or dried shrimp, and **blend** until smooth,
   about 10 seconds. Set aside.

2. Put beef or lamb cubes in medium saucepan, and add salt to taste. Add enough water to
   cover beef or lamb, and bring to boil over medium-high heat. Reduce heat to **simmer,** cover,
   and cook until tender, 45 minutes to 1 hour.

3. Heat oil in large skillet over medium-high heat. Add onions, and **sauté** until soft, 3 to 5
   minutes. Add chopped chili peppers or 1 teaspoon ground red pepper, more or less to taste.
   Stir and sauté 1 minute to release flavor. Reduce heat to medium, add tomatoes and ground
   seed mixture. Stirring frequently, cook 5 to 7 minutes until tomatoes are soft.

4. Add tomato mixture and spinach to meat. Stir, cover, and cook until spinach is tender and
   flavor has developed, 12 to 15 minutes. Add salt and pepper to taste.

*To serve, the consistency should be thick enough to eat with the fingers of your right hand when
scooped up with stiff porridge* putu *(recipe page 77). It is also good alone or over rice.*

ꙮ Loz (Sweet Almond Balls with Pistachios)

Loz is a sweet treat delicacy to serve for the bride and groom's wedding feast.

Yield: 16 to 18 candies

2 cups ground almonds

½ cup confectioner's sugar, more as
needed

4 to 6 tablespoons orange blossom water
(available at international markets)

½ cup pistachio nuts, peeled, ground, more as
needed

Equipment: Medium mixing bowl, mixing spoon, pie pan, 1 package petit four paper cups

1. In mixing bowl, combine ground almonds, ½ cup confectioner's sugar, and just enough orange
   blossom water to form firm paste. Using clean hands, knead mixture until smooth. Set aside
   to rest about 10 minutes.

2. Place ½ cup confectioner's sugar and ground pistachios in pie pan, mix well, and set aside.

3. Pinch off walnut-size pieces of almond dough and, using palms of hand, roll into ball. Place in pie pan, and gently roll in pistachio and sugar mixture until evenly coated. Place in petit four paper cup and set aside. Continue making balls until all mixture has been used.

Serve immediately or store in airtight container and refrigerate. Serve as a sweet treat with tea or milk.

Chad

Chad, a landlocked country situated in north-central Africa, is bordered by Libya on the north, Sudan on the east, the Central African Republic and Cameroon on the south, and Nigeria and Niger on the east. It is a rural country that encompasses three different climatic zones. Nomadic pastoralists roam the northern Sahara desert region with their camels, goats, and sheep. The central region is home to seminomadic horsemen who herd cattle and sheep and still hunt with spears. The southern Sarh region, home to the Sara people, has the largest number of people, the most cities, and the best farming.

Chad, at the crossroads of African and Arab cultures, has over 200 ethnic groups. Those living in the upper two-thirds of the country are mostly Muslims. Elsewhere, the people of Chad primarily follow indigenous religious practices, except for urbanites who were converted to Christianity during the French colonial period, which ended in 1960 when independence was won.

Muslims in Chad marry within their clan, usually to first cousins; as specified in the Koran, men are limited to four wives. Men who instead follow traditional local practice sometimes have several dozen wives, guaranteeing a large number of children to support the father in his old age.

In Chad, when a girl is ready for marriage, she is initiated by female elders. These women tell her what to expect and help prepare her for the realities of married life. The girl learns secret codes and languages to help her communicate with other married women, should the need arise. A girl goes directly into marriage after a suitor shows interest in her, once he and his bride-price are accepted by the girl's father or a family elder.

When a girl's family agrees to marry her to a man from a different clan and the negotiations of the bride-price have been completed, a weeklong ceremony takes place in the settlement of the girl's family. Paying the bride-price actually cements the marriage; it is the same as a marriage certificate. What follows is a dancing, singing, and feasting celebration.

The bride misses the festivities, however, as she must stay in seclusion until she says goodbye to her family and friends and departs with her husband to his settlement. On the bride's arrival to her new home, her in-laws give her gifts, such as small animals. If her husband has other wives, they are there to welcome her into the family.

⚘ *Courgette avec Groundnuts* (Zucchini with Peanuts)

Every life-milestone celebration in Chad includes a feast. Among Muslims and other Chadians, whole roasted lamb (*méchoui*) (recipe page 27) is the centerpiece of the celebration. There are always dozens of vegetable dishes to go along with the meat.

Yield: serves 4 to 6

2 tablespoons vegetable oil

1 onion, **trimmed, finely chopped**

2 cloves garlic, trimmed, **minced**

3 to 4 zucchini (about 1½ to 2 pounds), sliced crosswise, **blanched**

1 tablespoon lemon juice

salt and pepper to taste

1½ cups **roasted** peanuts, **coarsely chopped**

Equipment: Large skillet with cover, mixing spoon, fork

Heat oil in large skillet over medium-high heat. Add onion and garlic, stir, and **sauté** until onion is soft, 3 to 5 minutes. Add zucchini and toss to mix. Reduce heat to medium, add lemon juice and salt and pepper to taste. Toss, cover, and cook until zucchini is tender, 7 to 12 minutes. Either mash zucchini mixture with a fork or serve chunky. Sprinkle with peanuts before serving.

Serve with tuo zaafi *(recipe page 33) or plain boiled rice.*

⚘ *Maize avec Épinards* (Corn with Spinach)

Some of the cooked vegetable dishes are as simple as this recipe.

Yield: serves 4

2 pounds fresh spinach, washed, **trimmed, coarsely chopped**

1 cup water

2 tablespoons vegetable oil

10-ounce package frozen corn kernels, thawed

2 onions, trimmed, **finely chopped**

ground red pepper to taste

salt and pepper to taste

Equipment: Large saucepan with cover, **colander**, large skillet with cover, mixing spoon

1. Put spinach in large saucepan, add water, and bring to boil. Reduce heat to **simmer**, cover, and cook 5 to 7 minutes, until tender. Drain in colander.

2. Heat oil in large skillet over medium-high heat. Add onions, stir, and **sauté** until soft, 3 to 5 minutes. Add corn, stir, and cook for 3 minutes. Reduce heat to medium. Squeeze spinach over sink to extract all water. Crumble dried spinach into skillet, and toss to mix. Add salt

and pepper to taste and ground red pepper to taste. Cover and cook for 7 to 12 minutes to heat through.

Serve vegetables either hot or at room temperature.

♟ *Broasheht* (Brochettes) (Grilled Meat on Skewer)

If roasted lamb, *méchoui* (recipe 27), is too expensive, cheaper cuts of meat would be made into *broashehts*. Roasting meat on skewers has always been a favorite among Africans. This recipe is popular not only in Chad but throughout most of Africa.

Note: This recipe takes 2 days.

CAUTION: GRILL OR BROILER IS USED.

Yield: serves 4

1 teaspoon **ground** paprika

1 teaspoon ground cinnamon

2 cloves garlic, **trimmed, minced**

salt and pepper to taste

ground red pepper to taste

2 tablespoons vinegar

2 pounds lean lamb, mutton, or beef, cut into 1½- to 2-inch cubes

2 onions, trimmed, quartered, with each quarter separated into 3 or 4 pieces

½ cup **finely chopped roasted** peanuts, for serving

4 cups rice (cooked according to directions on package), kept warm for serving

Equipment: Small bowl, mixing spoon, rubber spatula, large resealable plastic bag, 8 metal or wooden 8- or 10-inch skewers (if using wooden skewers, soak in water for at least 30 minutes before using so they don't burn), charcoal **grill** or broiler pan, metal tongs, oven mitts, serving platter

1. Put paprika, cinnamon, garlic, salt and pepper to taste, and ground red pepper to taste in small bowl, and stir in vinegar to make into paste. Using spatula, spread paste over inside of resealable plastic bag. Add meat, press out most of the air, and seal bag. Press on all sides of bag to massage paste into meat until evenly coated. Refrigerate for at least 6 hours or overnight.

CAUTION: ADULT SUPERVISION REQUIRED.

Prepare to grill or broil: Have an adult help prepare charcoal grill or preheat broiler.

2. Thread 4 meat cubes on a skewer, separating each chunk of meat with a piece of onion and ending with cube of meat on each end. Carefully squeeze meat and onion tightly together.

3. Place skewers side by side on prepared grill or broiler pan. Using metal tongs, turn to brown all sides, and cook to desired doneness, 15 to 20 minutes. Transfer to serving platter and sprinkle finely chopped nuts over meat before serving.

Serve skewered meat with cooked rice. Allow 2 skewers per person.

Democratic Republic of the Congo

In 1997, Zaire—once known as the Belgian Congo—was renamed the Democratic Republic of the Congo. The nation is surrounded by the Republic of Congo, the Central African Republic, South Sudan, Uganda, Rwanda, Burundi, Tanzania, Zambia, Angola, and the Atlantic Ocean.

Ruled by Belgium for many years, as the former name implies, the Democratic Republic of the Congo won its independence in 1960. Since its independence, the country has been dominated by dictators, particularly Joseph-Desiré Mobutu. It was Mobutu who renamed the country Zaire, and the new name was chosen after Mobutu was overthrown.

Seventy-five percent of the nation's people are Christians, mostly Roman Catholics. All life-cycle celebrations are a combination of Christian and traditional rituals. (See Protestant and Catholic Life-Cycle Rituals, page lxxiii, and African Life-Cycle Rituals, page lxvi.)

Urban women in the Democratic Republic of the Congo enjoy freedoms that women of marriageable age living in rural villages would not be permitted to have. Traditionally, parents choose a young woman's husband, arrange the marriage with his parents, and accept the dowry.

∳ *Pastelle* (Fried Fish and Vegetable Dumplings)

Fish are caught in the many rivers and lakes that run through the country. This dish would be prepared to serve guests at a wedding or to mourners at a funeral feast. *Pastelles* are usually deep fried in Africa; however, we suggest, for a healthier alternative, baking instead of deep frying.

Yield: serves 4 to 6

Filling:

water, as needed

2 (6 to 8 ounces each) boneless, skinless fish **fillets** (such as tilapia, cod, red snapper, or sea bass)

1 onion, **trimmed**, grated

½ cup parsley, trimmed, **finely chopped**

2 cloves garlic, trimmed, **minced**

2 tablespoons tomato paste

½ teaspoon red pepper, or to taste

salt and pepper to taste

all-purpose flour, as needed

1 tube prepackaged pizza dough (available at most supermarkets)

Equipment: Medium saucepan, fork, slotted spoon or **skimmer**, strainer, food processor or **blender**, rolling pin, pizza cutter or sharp knife, lightly greased or nonstick baking sheet, oven mitts, spatula

Preheat oven to 350°F.

1. Half fill medium saucepan with water. Bring to boil over medium-high heat, carefully add fish fillets, reduce to simmer and cook about 5 to 7 minutes, or until fish is opaque white and flakes easily when poked with fork.

2. Using slotted spoon or skimmer, remove fillets and place in strainer to drain. Discard water.

3. Prepare filling: In food processor or blender, **purée** cooked fish, onion, parsley, garlic, and tomato paste. Stir in red pepper and salt and pepper to taste. Set aside.

4. On lightly floured work surface, roll pizza dough out to ¼-inch thick using lightly floured rolling pin roll. Cut dough into about 4×4-inch squares using lightly floured pizza cutter or sharp knife.

5. Assemble Dumplings: Spoon about 2 to 3 tablespoons filling into center of each dough square. Dip finger in water and lightly brush around edge. Fold wrapper in half, enclosing filling. Pinch edges tightly together to seal. Repeat assembling dumplings, and place side by side on baking sheet. Continue until all dough squares are filled and folded.

6. Bake in oven for 8 to 10 minutes, or until golden on top. Carefully remove from oven. Using spatula, turn *pastelles* over, return to oven and continue baking 8 to 10 minutes or until golden on top. Carefully remove using oven mitts. Set aside to cool for 5 to 7 minutes.

Serve warm as a snack.

Equatorial Guinea and Gabon

Situated on the western coast of Africa, Equatorial Guinea and Gabon are covered almost entirely by a dense tropical rain forest. The two countries neighbor each other with Cameroon to the north and the Republic of Congo to the south of Gabon. The original inhabitants of Gabon were the Babinga, or Pygmies, who were in the area at least 7,000 years ago. Although it was first explored by the Porticoes, it eventually fell under French control. It became an independent country in 1960.

Nearly all Guineans and Gabonese are Bantu, whom Christian missionaries began converting during the 19th century. Today, most are either Roman Catholics or Protestants. They follow the Christian life-milestone events prescribed by their churches (see Protestant and Catholic Life-Cycle Rituals, page lxxiii); however, there is considerable influence from indigenous religions. (See African Life-Cycle Rituals, page lxvi.)

The majority of people live in small villages near the ocean or on the shores of the many rivers that run through the country. Fish is one of their most important foods, and *egusi* (or *eggussi*) (recipe page 65) and *boulettes de poisson* (recipe page 29) are favorite ways of preparing fish for feasts.

More French people now live in Gabon (and Cameroon) than during colonial times. The French have influenced not only the language but the food, especially the bread. French bread is eaten at every meal in Equatorial Guinea, Gabon, and Cameroon.

⚭ *Gâteau* (French Bread)

Instead of calling bread *pain* as the French do, people in this region of Africa call French bread *gâteau*, which in French actually means pastry or cake.

Yield: 2 loaves

4 cups all-purpose flour

2 teaspoons salt

1½ tablespoons sugar, divided

1¼ cups **lukewarm** water, divided

1 package active dry **yeast**

½ cup milk, **scalded** and cooled to lukewarm

1½ teaspoons solid shortening

Equipment: Flour **sifter**, large mixing bowl, small bowl, mixing spoon, damp kitchen towel, lightly floured work surface, knife, 9×12×2-inch baking pan, wax paper, scissors, pencil, ruler, greased baking sheet, dry kitchen towel, oven mitts, wire cake rack

1. **Sift** flour with salt and ½ tablespoon sugar into large mixing bowl.

2. In small bowl, sprinkle yeast over ¼ cup lukewarm water until dissolved and bubbly, 5 to 10 minutes. Add lukewarm milk, remaining 1 cup lukewarm water, shortening, and remaining 1 tablespoon sugar. Stir to dissolve.

3. Make a well (hole) in center of flour mixture, and pour in yeast mixture. Stir thoroughly to mix but do not **knead**. The dough will be soft. Cover with damp towel and set in warm place to rise to double in bulk, 1½ to 2 hours.

4. **Punch down** dough, and lightly knead in bowl. Transfer to lightly floured work surface, and cut in half with knife. Cover with damp towel.

   Fill baking pan halfway with water, and place in bottom of oven. (Steam from the pan of water ensures a crisp crust.)

Preheat oven to 400°F.

5. Cut wax paper 10×15 inches. Using pencil and ruler, mark a 9×12-inch rectangular pattern on dull side of wax paper. Place wax paper, shiny-side up, on work surface, and sprinkle lightly with flour. Place one piece of dough in center of pattern, and pat it out to size of pattern. Roll up dough, jelly roll–style, into a tight, 12-inch-long cylinder. It helps to pull up on the edge of wax paper to make the first few turns firm. Remove wax paper, lightly flour work surface, and continue to roll the cylinder back and forth, while pressing down, making it about 15 inches long. Using your hands, taper ends slightly. Repeat, making second loaf with remaining dough.

6. Place loaves side by side on greased baking sheet, leaving at least 2 inches between. Using scissors, cut 3 or 4 diagonal slits about ¼ inch deep across the tops. Cover with dry towel, set in warm place to rise to almost double in bulk, 20 to 30 minutes.

7. Bake in oven 15 minutes at 400°F, reduce heat to 350°F, and bake 30 minutes longer or until loaves are crisp and brown. Cool on wire cake rack.

Serve bread soon after it cools for best flavor and texture. To eat, break bread into chunks.

⚓ *Gâteau d'Huître* (Oyster Bread)

Gâteau d'Huître is ideal to serve for the wedding feast in Equatorial Guinea or Gabon.

Yield: serves 4 to 6

2 tomatoes, **trimmed, coarsely chopped**

5 cloves garlic, trimmed, **minced**

3 tablespoons olive oil

1 loaf French bread (recipe page 72) or store-bought, sliced into about 1-inch-thick slices

2 to 3 dozen oysters, **shucked**

½ cup parmesan cheese, grated

Equipment: Small bowl, mixing spoon, baking sheet, oven mitts

Preheat broiler.

1. Place tomatoes, garlic, and olive oil in small bowl, mix well, and set aside to **marinate**.

2. Place sliced bread side by side on baking sheet. Place 3 to 4 oysters on each bread slice. Spoon 1 tablespoon tomato mixture onto oysters, then sprinkle with parmesan cheese. Continue until all bread slices are covered.

3. Place in broiler, and cook about 2 to 3 minutes or until cheese is melted and golden. Carefully remove using oven mitts.

Serve warm as a starter for a wedding feast.

SOUTHERN AFRICA

The region of Southern Africa includes the following countries: Botswana, Lesotho, Namibia, South Africa, and Swaziland.

Botswana

Botswana, a landlocked country in southern Africa, is one of the world's most sparsely populated nations. About 90 percent of the Batswana people, as they are called, live along the country's eastern border, which it shares with South Africa and Zimbabwe. It shares the western border with Namibia.

Farming and herding have been the traditional means of subsistence; however, today that is changing. Since Botswana's independence in 1966, the population shift to urban areas has been overwhelming. Due to the country's high unemployment, many men have turned to South Africa for work in mines and on farms.

About 60 percent of the Batswana are Christians. However, indigenous religions and traditional beliefs remain important to all Batswana, even those who have become Christians. Traditional rituals are commonly combined with Christian rituals. (See Protestant and Catholic Life-Cycle Rituals, page lxxiii, and African Life-Cycle Rituals, page lxvi.)

Weddings among the San (Bushmen) of Botswana's Kalahari involve a considerable amount of ritual. Prior to the wedding day, the bride fasts in silence, and for four days she remains in a branch enclosure that is set up outside the village. At the end of the period of seclusion, the village women shave the heads of the bride and groom, who are then bathed and prepared for scarification. In this ceremony, they are cut simultaneously and their blood is intermingled as a symbol of their union. When the pattern of cuts has been completed on their bodies, a mixture of ashes and medicinal roots is rubbed into the cuts to ensure the formation of raised scars. Scarification is a way of announcing that the couple has gone through a purification ritual.

In Botswana's urban areas, a favorite way of celebrating a birth, a first communion, or a birthday is by having a *braii* (barbecue). A large amount of meat, usually goat, is spit-roasted for the occasion. For wealthier families, beef is the meat of choice. Stuffing yourself is a tribute to the host; it shows that you are aware he can afford the luxury of meat.

Beverages are usually drunk after the meal, not with it. In the cities and among men in the villages, beer and palm wine are favorite party drinks. In the villages, older men and women drink mild alcoholic home brews, either *bojalwa*, made from sorghum, or *kadi*, made from fermented roots and sugar.

Mealie-meal is the same as Lesotho's *putu* (recipe page 77)—a staple that is served at almost every meal. At tea time it is served thinned, while at other times it is thickened and served with sauce and/or *mopani*. *Mopani* are caterpillars that are cooked in hot ash for 15 minutes, boiled in saltwater, or sun-dried. Dried *mopani* are either deep-fried, roasted, eaten raw, or ground up.

ও *Seswaa* (Pounded Meat with Gravy)

Seswaa is a traditional Botswana recipe for a classic dish of stewed brisket. This hearty dish is ideal to nourish the soul after the scarification wedding ceremony.

Yield: serves 4 to 6

3½- to 4-pound beef brisket	water, as needed
1 onion, **trimmed, finely chopped**	2 tablespoons flour, more as needed
salt and pepper to taste	

Equipment: **Dutch oven** or **heavy-bottomed** saucepan with cover, large fork, mallet, medium saucepan, whisk, mixing spoon

1. Place meat and onion in Dutch oven or heavy-bottomed saucepan, and cover with water. Add salt and pepper to taste. Bring to boil over high heat, cover, reduce to simmer, and cook about 2½ to 3 hours or until meat is tender and cooked through. Add more water if necessary to prevent sticking.

2. Transfer brisket to clean work surface and, using mallet, pound until flaky. Reserve liquid to make gravy.

3. Prepare Gravy: Make **roux.** Place 2 tablespoons beef stock in saucepan, stir in flour, and whisk until smooth. Stirring constantly, add remaining beef stock. Simmer over medium-low heat or until mixture is thickened. Add salt and pepper to taste.

Serve brisket with putu *(recipe page 77) and gravy ladled over the top.*

Samosas Nama ya kgomo (Ground Beef Fritters)

Samosas made their way from India to Botswana by way of South Africa. They are a favorite finger food that is prepared for every celebration feast.

CAUTION: HOT OIL IS USED.

Yield: about 15 pieces

2 tablespoons vegetable oil, divided

½ pound lean **ground** pork

1 medium onion, **trimmed, finely chopped**

2 cloves garlic, trimmed, **minced**

1 medium potato, **parboiled**, peeled, finely **diced**

½ teaspoon ground red pepper, more or less to taste

¼ cup finely chopped fresh **coriander** leaves

salt and pepper to taste

15 frozen square egg roll wrappers, thawed (available in all Asian food stores and in the freezer section of most supermarkets)

vegetable oil, for **deep frying**

Equipment: Small skillet, mixing spoon, medium mixing bowl, work surface, knife, damp kitchen towel, large plate, **deep fryer**, deep fryer **thermometer** or wooden spoon, baking sheet, paper towels, wooden spoon, slotted metal spoon or metal tongs

1. Heat 1 tablespoon oil in small skillet over medium-high heat. Crumble in ground pork, stir, and **sauté** until browned, 3 to 5 minutes. Transfer pork to medium mixing bowl. Add remaining 1 tablespoon oil to small skillet, and heat over medium-high heat. Add onion and garlic, stir, and sauté until onion is soft, 3 to 5 minutes. Add garlic mixture to pork in medium mixing bowl. Add diced potato, ½ teaspoon ground red pepper, more or less to taste, coriander leaves, and salt and pepper to taste. Toss to mix well.

2. Using knife, cut thawed egg roll wrappers in half to make 3×6-inch strips. Work with one strip at a time, keeping the others covered with damp towel to prevent drying out.

3. Fill pastries: Place cup with water near work surface. Place 1 egg roll wrapper strip on work surface. Spoon 1 tablespoon meat mixture centered at one end of strip, about 2 inches up from bottom edge. Fold corner of bottom edge diagonally over filling to meet other side, forming a triangle. Moisten finger in cup of water and dab along 2 open edges to dampen. Press down on edges to seal in filling. Repeat making egg roll wrappers triangular packages. Place each package on large plate.

4. Prepare deep fryer: ***Caution: Adult supervision required.*** Place several layers of paper towels on baking sheet. Heat oil to 375°F on fryer thermometer, or oil is hot enough when small bubbles appear around wooden spoon handle when dipped in oil. Deep-fry in small batches, 3 or 4 at a time, until golden brown, 2 to 3 minutes. Remove with slotted metal spoon or metal tongs, and drain on paper towels.

To serve, place pastries on platter and eat while still warm for best flavor. Hot pepper sauce or ground red pepper is often sprinkled on the fritters. Have guests help themselves using only the fingers of the right hand. The left hand is used for personal grooming.

Lesotho

The tiny kingdom of Lesotho is totally surrounded by South Africa. With mainly natural borders, Lesotho is situated in rugged mountain terrain. The people call their country the "Kingdom in the Sky," since it claims to have the highest low-elevation point of any country in the world. The people are referred to as MoSotho (singular) and BaSotho (plural).

Cattle and horses are symbols of wealth in Lesotho. Goats are kept for slaughter, and angora goats and merino sheep provide most rural people with cash income from the mohair and wool. Flocks are tended by shepherd boys in their early teens, who are sent into the hills for a few years before returning to their villages as men to be given land of their own.

Most people in Lesotho are nominally Christian, primarily Roman Catholics. All life-milestone celebrations involve a combination of Christianity and indigenous beliefs. (See Protestant and Catholic Life-Cycle Rituals, page lxxiii, and African Life-Cycle Rituals, page lxvi.)

Newborns are baptized a few weeks after birth. Godmothers are selected for girls and godfathers for boys. After a church service, there is a family celebration, and gifts are brought for the newborn.

Lesotho Christians take great pride in their children's accomplishments, especially their first communion. The parents of children who make their first communion together share the expenses for the daylong communal feast and celebration.

At death, the BaSotho are traditionally buried in a sitting position, facing the rising sun, "ready to leap up when called." All burials are followed by a communal feast, which includes one or two cows slaughtered for the occasion.

⚱ *Afrikaanse Stoofschotel* (Vegetarian Curry)

Afrikaanse Stoofschotel is ideal to serve for the feast after a MoSotho's first communion.

Yield: serve 4 to 6

2 tablespoon vegetable oil

1 onion, **trimmed, finely chopped**

5 to 6 red potatoes, trimmed, quartered

2 teaspoons curry powder (store bought or homemade recipe page 88)

¾ cup water

½ head cabbage, trimmed, finely chopped

1 cup green beans fresh, trimmed or frozen (cooked according to directions on package)

14.5 ounces canned diced tomatoes

salt and pepper to taste

Equipment: Lrge saucepan, mixing spoon

1. Heat oil in saucepan over medium-high. **Sauté** onion and potatoes for 5 to 7 minutes, or until onions are soft and potatoes golden.

2. Stir in curry powder, mix well.

3. Stir in water, cabbage, green beans, and tomatoes, mix well. Cook 12 to 15 minutes or until potatoes are cooked through. Season with salt and pepper to taste.

Serve warm with putu *(recipe follows). Tear off small chunks, and use it to scoop up vegetables.*

⚱ *Putu* (Stiff Cornmeal Porridge)

A stiff porridge, eaten throughout Africa, is called *putu* in Lesotho. It is known as *nsima* in Zambia and Malawi, *ugali* in Kenya and Tanzania, *oshifima* in Namibia, and *mealie-meal* in South Africa. Like Italy's *polenta* and Romania's *mamaliga*, this porridge is eaten at every meal. It also can be made with milk instead of water.

Yield: serves 4 to 6

1 cup white **cornmeal**

1 cup milk

1 cup water

1 teaspoon salt

Equipment: Small bowl, mixing spoon, medium saucepan, greased serving platter

1. Put cornmeal into small bowl, and slowly stir in milk to make smooth paste.

2. Pour water into medium saucepan, add salt, and bring to boil over high heat. Stirring constantly, slowly add cornmeal paste and continue stirring for 2 or 4 minutes, until thickened.

Reduce heat to low, and stir frequently. Cook until mixture thickens, becomes stiff, and pulls away from sides of pan, 10 to 15 minutes. Remove from heat. Transfer to greased serving platter. Using greased or damp hands, shape into smooth round loaf. *Putu* becomes firm, like a loaf of bread, when it cools.

To eat, tear off a small chunk, and use it to scoop up stew and other foods or sauces.

Namibia

Namibia, located along the Atlantic coast of southern Africa, is bordered by Angola and Zambia on the north, Botswana on the east, and South Africa on the south. It gained independence in 1990. Namibia means "place of no people"; however' the country is hardly that. The population includes ten ethnic groups (four of which predominate), along with a large group of people of mixed ancestry and Afrikaners (whites with ties to South Africa). Many urban Namibians have adopted Western ways; however, in rural areas, traditional life-styles are still practiced.

Most Namibians profess Christianity, with the majority affiliated with the German Lutheran sect of Protestantism. (See Protestant and Catholic Life-Cycle Rituals, page lxxiii.) However, Church views on certain issues, especially on marriage, have been untenable for many Namibians. According to traditional beliefs, a man has the right to refuse to take as his wife any woman who is unable to get pregnant, although Christian churches consider premarital sex inappropriate. In actuality, many nominal Christians in Namibia have a church wedding only after the birth of the first child.

At puberty, women of the Himba ethnic group shave the front and top of their heads, leaving the hair in back long, which they braid with strands of plant fibers. After marriage, they take locks of hair from their brothers and their new husband and braid it in with their own. Their plaited hair is also plastered with a mixture of butter, ash, and ochre.

Every life-cycle celebration calls for a feast. Among the pastoral Herero and Himba ethnic groups, cattle—a form of wealth—are slaughtered only on very special occasions.

Potjie (Pork, Chicken, and Seafood Stew)

In Africa, this stew would be cooked in a three-legged pot placed over an open fire. *Potjie* is ideal to serve family and friends at a wedding celebration.

Yield: serves 8 to 10

¼ cup vegetable oil, more as needed

1 pound boneless pork, **cubed**

5 chicken thighs, halved

3 red bell peppers, **trimmed, seeded, coarsely chopped**

1 onion, trimmed, coarsely chopped

2 pounds skinless fish **fillets** (such as tilapia, cod, or sea bass) cut into 2-inch chunks

2 cups uncooked rice

4 cups chicken stock

1 teaspoon saffron

½ teaspoon red pepper or to taste

4 bay leaves

1 pound medium shrimp, peeled, **deveined**

2 cups green peas, frozen

salt and pepper to taste

For serving:

lemon wedges

Equipment: Crock Pot® (use according to manufacturer's directions), mixing spoon, fork, ladle

1. Heat ¼ cup oil in Crock Pot over high heat. Place pork and chicken in Crock Pot, and cook until lightly brown on all sides, about 10 to 12 minutes, stirring occasionally. Stir in bell pepper and onion, cook until soft, about 3 to 5 minutes. Cover and simmer 45 minutes to 1 hour, or until meat is almost cooked through. Add more oil if necessary to prevent sticking.

2. Add fish fillets, rice, chicken stock, saffron, red pepper, and bay leaves. Simmer 15 to 20 minutes. Add shrimp and peas, cook additional 5 to 10 minutes, or until rice is tender and fish is opaque white and flakes easily when poked with fork. Add salt and pepper to taste. Remove and discard bay leaves before serving.

Serve warm in individual bowls with lemon wedges.

⚘ *Um'bido* (Greens and Peanuts)

Groundnuts (peanuts) are plentiful in Namibia. For this recipe, the peanuts can be either boiled or **roasted**. If using roasted peanuts, simply sprinkle them over the cooked spinach or other greens before serving. This recipe is made with boiled peanuts.

Yield: serves 6

water, as needed

1 cup shelled, skinless peanuts

2 packages (10 ounces each) spinach or other greens, fresh or frozen (thawed)

2 tablespoons butter or margarine

salt and pepper to taste

Equipment: Medium saucepan with cover, mixing spoon, **colander**, serving bowl

1. Fill medium saucepan halfway with water, and bring to boil over high heat. Add shelled, skinless peanuts, and bring back to boil. Reduce heat to **simmer**, cover, and cook for 20 to 25 minutes, until soft. Add spinach or other greens and stir. Cover and cook 5 to 7 minutes, or until tender. Place colander in sink, and drain spinach mixture.

2. Transfer to serving bowl, toss with butter or margarine, and sprinkle with salt and pepper to taste.

Serve with putu *(recipe page 77).*

ꙮ *Kuli-Kuli* (also *Kulikuli*) (Peanut Patties)

Peanuts are an important food in Namibia. *Kuli-kuli* is often served with stews, sauces, and soups, or crumbled over boiled yams, **cassava**, and mashed plantains.

CAUTION: HOT OIL IS USED.

Yield: about 12 patties

1 pound shelled, **roasted** peanuts	**ground** red pepper to taste
¼ cup peanut oil, more or less as needed	peanut oil, for **deep-frying**
1 onion, **trimmed, finely chopped**	

Equipment: **Blender**, rubber spatula, medium bowl, medium skillet, slotted metal spoon, wax paper, work surface, **deep fryer**, paper towels, baking sheet, deep fryer **thermometer** or wooden spoon, napkin-lined breadbasket

1. Put nuts in blender and **blend**, switching blender on and off, until broken into small pieces. While blender is running, slowly **drizzle** just enough of ¼ cup oil through feed tube until mixture is a smooth paste. Transfer to medium bowl.

2. Heat 1 tablespoon oil in medium skillet over medium-high heat. Add onion and **sauté** until soft, 3 to 5 minutes. Stir in ground red pepper to taste and salt to taste. Add to ground peanuts in medium bowl. Gather into ball; mixture should hold together.

3. Divide dough into 12 equal balls, and flatten each into patty. Place on wax paper–covered work surface.

4. Prepare deep fryer: *Caution: Adult supervision required.* Place several layers of paper towels on baking sheet. Heat oil to 375°F on fryer thermometer, or oil is hot enough when small bubbles appear around a wooden spoon handle when it is dipped in the oil. Deep-fry in small batches, 3 or 4 at a time, until golden brown and crisp on both sides, 2 to 3 minutes. Remove with slotted metal spoon, and drain on paper towels.

Serve the patties in a napkin-lined breadbasket, and eat as you would biscuits. Kuli-kuli *keeps well in an airtight container for up to one week.*

South Africa

South Africa is on the southern tip of Africa and has coastlines on both the Atlantic and Indian Oceans. It shares borders with Namibia, Zimbabwe, Botswana, Mozambique, and Swaziland. It also contains the kingdom of Lesotho within its borders.

The people of South Africa are of diverse cultures and origins. Under the many years of apartheid (government-enforced racial segregation), South Africans were classified into four major groups: whites (Afrikaners of Dutch ancestry, along with people of English and French ancestry); blacks (regardless of ethnic group); coloureds (descendants of indigenous Africans who intermarried with the earliest European and Malay settlers); and Asians (descendants of Indians and Pakistanis brought to South Africa as indentured laborers). Apartheid was outlawed in 1994.

Most South Africans are Christians. The largest denomination in the country is the Dutch Reformed Church (DRC), or the *Nederduitse Gereformeerde Kerk,* which serves mainly Afrikaners. There are also more than 4,000 African indigenous churches that broke off from various missionary churches. These churches, run by and for blacks, are organized as the African Independent Churches (AIC). The AIC churches incorporate traditional local religious practices with Christian celebrations, especially for life-milestone events such as baptisms, weddings, and funerals.

Indigenous African religions are adhered to by large percentage of South Africans, mostly in rural areas. Many of those who adhere to traditional religions also have some contact with Christianity, and they often incorporate aspects of it into their indigenous religions.

Having marriages arranged by the families involved is an accepted practice throughout Africa. (See African Life-Cycle Rituals, page lxvi.) In South Africa, when a Zulu girl is ready for marriage (which can be as young as nine or 10 years of age), relatives of her suitor must pay *lobola* to her parents. A few years ago, it was the custom to pay the bride-price in cattle; now they pay cash.

The boy's father, mother, older sister or brother, and an uncle or two accompany him to meet his future in-laws. In anticipation of their arrival, the bride's family cleans, polishes, paints, and repairs until everything in the house and yard are clean and orderly. It is important for the bride-to-be to let her future in-laws know she helped with the work so they know she is worth all they have come to pay as *lobola.*

When the day arrives on which the two families are to meet, the dining table is covered with a freshly washed and ironed tablecloth and set with tableware brought out for important occasions. A sumptuous meal, easily the best meal of the year, is prepared. It usually consists of roast chicken, *borrie rys* (recipe page 85), pumpkin or squash casserole, green vegetables, **beetroot**, custard and jelly, assorted breads, cakes and pies such as *melk tert* (recipe page 86), soft drinks, and beer. Everyone is dressed in their best attire; however, only the bride's father and an uncle or male neighbor, acting as witnesses, sit at one end of the table opposite the prospective male in-laws. The bride-to-be, her mother, sisters, and female relatives do not eat with the guests—they are busy serving food and clearing away dirty dishes.

The future bride is forbidden to be present during *lobola* negotiations. One of the relatives is the go-between and takes over the meeting. A price is offered for the girl, which her father can accept or refuse. Discussion of the price may go back and forth until agreement is reached. When a deal has been struck, a verbal agreement is made in front of the witnesses, and the marriage is official. In the eyes of the community and the parents, the marriage is legitimate. *Lobola* is usually made in installments, and it is the custom for the *makoti* (bride) to live with her husband, at his parents' house, without shame or violating any taboos, until all the payments have been made. The couple then moves to their own hut. Zulu men can take as many wives as they wish as long as they can afford *lobola* for each one.

When an event involves feeding a large group, such as to pay *lobola*, to celebrate a christening dinner, or in connection with a funeral—or, when the wedding budget is lean—a *bredie* (a thick, flavorful meat and vegetable stew) might be prepared for the feast. The inexpensive cuts of meat used in the *bredie* go a long way to feed a crowd of people. Both the stew and the name are of Malay origin. (Malay laborers were brought to Cape Town in the 18th century by the Dutch during their many voyages to the East while trying to establish control of the Spice Trade.) Malay cooking is called "Cape Malay cuisine," and it is now popular throughout South Africa.

Among South African whites, most funerals follow Western-style Christian traditions. Usually a notice is placed in the local paper stating the date, time, and place of the funeral. Many people are cremated, in which case a service is held in the chapel at the crematorium. If there is a burial, there will be a service at a church, followed by a procession behind the hearse to the cemetery. Tea, drinks, or even a light meal may be served after the funeral at the home of the deceased's family.

Tribal African funerals follow very special rituals, with ancestors usually playing a major role. The funeral and mourning period can take days or even weeks to complete. Blacks living in South African cities often take leave from work to return to rural homeland areas to bury their relatives. Funerals are most often conducted according to indigenous traditions and tribal customs. Even among sophisticated Christian urbanites, an eldest son will carry out the ritual of sacrificing a bull at his father's funeral, in keeping with traditional practices.

♪ *Imbotyi Eluhlaza Bredie* (Green Bean and Lamb Stew)

Bredies are almost always made with the fattier cuts of lamb or mutton, which give the dish a rich flavor. A *bredie* is named for the main vegetable it is cooked with—tomatoes, green beans, cauliflower, or pumpkin. A famous bredie is *waterblommetjie*, made with a special water flower that grows wild in Cape Town ponds.

Yield: serves 4

2 tablespoons vegetable oil

1½ pounds boneless lamb shoulder, cut into bite-size chunks

1 cup onions, **trimmed, finely chopped**

2 cloves garlic, trimmed, **minced**

3 teaspoons ginger root trimmed, **grated**, or 1 teaspoon **ground** ginger

2 cups water

2 potatoes, peeled, cut into bite-size pieces

1 pound fresh string beans, **trimmed,** washed, cut crosswise into 1-inch lengths, or frozen cut green beans (thawed)

ground red pepper to taste

½ teaspoon ground thyme

salt and pepper to taste

Equipment: Large **heavy-bottomed** skillet or **Dutch oven**, slotted spoon, plate, mixing spoon, serving platter

1. Heat oil in large heavy-bottomed skillet or Dutch oven over medium-high heat. Add lamb and brown all sides, 7 to 12 minutes. Using slotted spoon, transfer to plate. Drain off and discard all but about 2 tablespoons fat. Add onions, garlic, and ginger root. Stirring constantly, cook over medium-high heat until onions are soft, 3 to 5 minutes. Return lamb to skillet with any liquid that has accumulated. Add water, bring to boil, and stir well. Reduce heat to **simmer**, cover, and cook 1 to 1½ hours, or until meat is tender.

2. Add potatoes, cover, and cook 10 minutes.

3. Add green beans, ground red pepper to taste, thyme, and salt and pepper to taste. Stir, cover, and cook for 20 minutes, or until meat and vegetables are tender.

To serve, mound on serving platter. Bredies *are traditionally served with hot boiled rice or* borrie rys *(recipe page 85).*

✂ *Boom Chakalaka* (Vegetarian Mixed Vegetables)

Boom Chakalaka can almost always be found at barbeques when families are negotiating the *lobola* price. It is served spooned over barbequed meat or served along with *Putu* (recipe page 77) as a side dish.

Yield: serves 6 to 8

3 tablespoons vegetable oil

2 **jalapeños, seeded, trimmed, minced**

2 onions, trimmed, **finely chopped**

2 bell peppers, trimmed, **seeded**, finely chopped

½ cup shredded carrot

3 cloves garlic, trimmed, minced

2 teaspoons curry powder, homemade (recipe page 88) or store bought

14.5 ounces canned diced tomatoes

½ cup shredded cabbage

14.5 ounces canned baked beans

¼ cup fresh **cilantro**

salt and pepper to taste

Equipment: Large saucepan, mixing spoon

1. In saucepan, heat oil over medium high heat. Add jalapeños, onions, bell pepper, carrot, garlic and curry powder, mix well. **Sauté** 3 to 5 minutes, or until onions are soft.

2. Stir in tomatoes and cabbage, bring to boil, reduce to simmer, and cook 5 to 7 minutes, or until cabbage is cooked through.

3. Stir in baked beans and cilantro, heat through over medium-low heat. Add salt and pepper to taste.

Serve warm or chilled over barbequed meat or with putu (recipe page 77).

¿ *Denningvleis* (Dried Fruit and Meat Curry)

Pinangkerrie (made with **tamarind** and the green leaves from an orange tree) and *denningvleis* are two very popular curry dishes often served at wedding feasts. They can easily be made in large quantities and heaped on platters. Guests help themselves from the platter, either using the fingers of the right hand, a fork, or a spoon. The left hand must never touch food; it is used only for personal grooming.

Yield: serves 6 to 8

1 cup dried apples

½ cup **pitted** prunes

½ cup seedless raisins

2 cups warm water

4 tablespoons vegetable oil, divided

1½ pounds boneless lean beef chuck, cut into 1-inch cubes

1 teaspoon salt

2 onions, **trimmed, finely chopped**

2 tablespoons curry powder (preferably Madras type) (available at all Asian food stores and some supermarkets)

3 tablespoons dark brown sugar, more or less to taste

2 tablespoons red wine vinegar

1 tablespoon strained fresh lemon juice

hot water, if necessary

For **garnish:**

½ cup salted peanuts, **coarsely chopped**

2 bananas

Equipment: Medium mixing bowl, mixing spoon, large **heavy-bottomed** saucepan with cover or **Dutch oven**, plate, slotted spoon, fork, large serving platter

1. Put dried apples, prunes, and raisins in medium mixing bowl. Add water and let soak for 1 hour, stirring occasionally.

2. Heat 2 tablespoons oil in large heavy-bottomed saucepan or Dutch oven over medium-high heat. Add cubes of meat, and sprinkle with salt. Stirring constantly, brown on all sides, 7 to 12 minutes. Using slotted spoon, transfer browned meat to plate.

3. Heat remaining 2 tablespoons oil in large saucepan or Dutch oven over medium-high heat. Add chopped onions, and **sauté** until soft, 3 to 5 minutes. Reduce heat to low, stir in curry powder, and return browned meat, including juices, to onion mixture. Add apples, prunes, and raisins (including their soaking water), 3 tablespoons brown sugar more or less to taste, vinegar, and lemon juice. Stir to mix well. Increase heat to high, bring to boil, and stir. Reduce heat to low, cover, and cook for 1 to 1½ hours, or until meat is fully cooked and easily pierced

with a fork. During cooking, if mixture seems too dry, stir in just enough hot water, if necessary, to keep mixture from sticking.

To serve, mound curry on large serving platter. For garnish, sprinkle curry mixture with coarsely chopped peanuts, and arrange peeled and sliced bananas over the top. Denningvleis *is traditionally served with* borrie rys *(recipe follows).*

Borrie Rys (Turmeric Rice, also Funeral Rice)

Borrie is the Afrikaans word for "turmeric" or "yellow." *Borrie rys* is customarily served with curry dishes or stew. Historically, this is known as "funeral rice" because it is often served at funeral feasts.

Yield: serves 4

2 cups water

1 tablespoon butter or margarine

1 cup long-grain rice

½ teaspoon turmeric

½ teaspoon salt

¼ teaspoon cinnamon

¼ cup seedless raisins

Equipment: Medium saucepan with cover, mixing spoon, fork, serving bowl

In medium saucepan, heat water and butter or margarine over high heat until water boils. Stir in rice, turmeric, salt, and cinnamon. Reduce heat to **simmer**, cover, and cook for 15 to 20 minutes, until rice is tender. Remove from heat, add raisins, and fluff with fork. Cover and let rest 10 minutes before serving for flavor to develop.

To serve, transfer to serving bowl to accompany denningvleis *(recipe page 84) or green bean* bredie.

Ovos Moles de Papaia (Papaya and Egg Pudding)

Eggs are used sparingly throughout Africa. While some Africans view eggs as taboo, others consider eggs a symbol of fertility. Therefore this dessert is ideal to serve for a wedding celebration, wishing the bride and groom many children in their future.

Yield: serves 4 to 6

1 **papaya, trimmed, seeded, coarsely chopped**

juice of 3 lemons or ¼ cup lemon juice

¼ cup water

2 cups sugar

1 teaspoon cinnamon

1 teaspoon ground clove

5 **egg yolks** (reserve egg whites for another use)

For **garnish**: prepared whipped topping

Equipment: Food processor or **blender**, rubber spatula, medium saucepan, mixing spoon, **candy thermometer**, large mixing bowl, electric mixer, 4 to 6 (4-ounce) **ramekins**

1. Place papaya, lemon juice, and water in food processor or blender, and **purée** on high for 30 seconds to 1 minute. Scrape down sides with rubber spatula, continue to **blend** until mixture is smooth.

2. Transfer purée to saucepan. Stir in sugar, cinnamon and clove. Stirring constantly, bring to boil over medium-high heat. Reduce to simmer, and continue cooking until mixture reaches 230°F on candy thermometer, stirring frequently to prevent sticking. Remove from heat, set aside.

3. Place egg yolks in large mixing bowl. Using electric mixer, beat yolks 2 to 3 minutes, or until slightly thick. Mixing constantly, slowly pour papaya mixture into yolks. Beat until smooth and thick, about 3 to 5 minutes.

4. Evenly transfer to individual ramekins. Cool to room temperature, and refrigerate for about 2 hours before serving. Dessert will thicken as it cools.

Serve pudding in individual ramekins with a dollop of whipped topping for dessert.

⚘ *Melk Tert* (Milk Pie)

All kinds of pies, both savory and sweet, are favored by South Africans. This *melk tart* is a classic recipe that all South Africans seem to love. It is included in the wedding banquet menus of several fine South African hotels.

Yield: serves 8

4½ tablespoons **cornstarch**

¾ cup sugar

¼ teaspoon salt

3½ cups milk

1 egg, beaten

½ teaspoon almond extract

½ teaspoon vanilla extract

1 (9-inch) frozen single-crust pie shell (baked according to directions on package)

For **garnish**: **cinnamon sugar**

Equipment: Small bowl, medium **heavy-bottomed** saucepan, whisk, cake knife

1. In small bowl, combine cornstarch, sugar, and salt.

2. Pour milk into medium heavy-bottomed saucepan, and whisk in egg and cornstarch mixture. Whisking constantly, cook over medium heat until thickened, 7 to 12 minutes. Do not boil. Reduce heat to low if necessary to prevent burning. Whisk in almond and vanilla extracts. Cool to lukewarm, and pour mixture into baked pie shell. Refrigerate until set, 3 to 4 hours. Before serving, sprinkle top with cinnamon sugar mixture.

To serve, cut in wedges, and serve as dessert.

Swaziland

The smallest country in the Southern Hemisphere, the kingdom of Swaziland is surrounded on three sides by South Africa and most of its eastern side borders by Mozambique.

Although nearly half the population of Swaziland belongs to the Zion Apostolic Church, many Swazi people include traditional indigenous practices with their Christian rituals and celebrations. (See Protestant and Catholic Life-Cycle Rituals, page lxxiii, and African Life-Cycle Rituals, page lxvi.) African Christian churches in Swaziland—and elsewhere in Africa—have been trying to stop polygamy and to discourage *lobola*, the bride-price practice. However, most African ethnic groups feel pride in their heritage and allegiance to the ways of their ancestors. Indeed, the payment of *lobola* validates the union of two people, legalizes marriage, and legitimates the children.

In traditional Swazi culture, a newborn remains nameless until he or she is three months old. The naming day is a big celebration, with everyone invited to view the ritual and take part in singing, dancing, and feasting. At three years of age, a baby is weaned and left in the care of siblings and grandparents while its mother works in the fields. At about age six, Swazi boys and girls are given a small cut in each ear lobe as their first test of bravery. From that time forward, they are expected to control their emotions in public.

Unlike many other traditional African societies, there are no special Swazi puberty ceremonies for boys. However, the Swazi royal family uses this period of passage from boyhood to manhood to encourage national unity. The Swazi nation is maintained by a system of age-related royal regiments (*libutfo*), which boys must join when they reach puberty. Boys from different clans have the same age mates through each advancement. The strong bonds that develop among the boys help decrease problems that might someday arise between clans, while promoting national pride and loyalty to the king.

When girls reach puberty, they take part in *umhlanga* in late August or early September—the exact date is selected by the royal astrologers. *Umhlanga* is a weeklong celebration for marriageable young women, who come from all over the kingdom to help repair the *indlunkulu* (great house) of the queen mother. After arriving, the girls spend a day resting, then set off in search of reeds, sometimes not returning for several days. *Umhlanga* is essentially a fertility celebration that gets its name from the large reeds gathered by the girls. On the sixth and seventh days, a reed dance is performed by the young women before the king, the queen mother, and important guests and onlookers. This dance is a showcase of potential wives for the king, who is encouraged to make a selection from the performing group. Afterward, there is always an elaborate feast for the dancers and spectators.

All wedding ceremonies include a grand feast, and, depending on the budget, cattle, goats, or sheep (recipe page 48) are roasted for the event. Along with the roasted meat, great quantities of food, such as *kurma* (recipe follows), *borrie rys* (recipe page 85) and *putu* (recipe page 77) are prepared for revelers.

Respect for both ancestors and the aged plays a large part in the complex structure of Swazi traditional society. Funerals are grand celebrations, and people come from miles around for the festivities. Cattle are usually slaughtered for the feast, which can go on for a week or more, depending upon the importance of the deceased. When the head-man of a village dies, he is buried at the entrance of the *sibaya*, a circular enclosure made of stacked reed stalks that is the center of community life. The *sibaya* is where the village's council of elders meets and where the best grain is stored.

At every meal, the Swazi people set aside a little food and pour a little home-brewed beer or sour milk onto the ground as an offering to the spirits of their ancestors

¿ Homemade Curry Powder

Curry dishes are commonplace in Swaziland, and several different kinds are often prepared for weddings and funeral feasts. The spices used in curries are always hand-ground for each dish. Grinding may be done with a mortar and pestle or by placing the spices on a hard surface and pounding them with a round rock. Every cook has her own blend of spices that varies with different types of food. The following is a mild curry recipe that can be made hotter by adding more dried red peppers to taste. For this recipe, use whole spices. Home-ground spices are not as finely pulverized as commercial blends, but they are fresher and therefore better.

1 whole dried red pepper, more if necessary	10 cumin seeds
6 cardamom pods	4 whole fennel seeds
1 stick cinnamon, broken into small pieces	10 **fenugreek** seeds
24 whole **coriander** seeds	5 whole white or black peppercorns
4 whole cloves	1 teaspoon **ground** turmeric

Equipment: **Mortar and pestle** or electric **blender** or nut grinder

Put cardamom pods, broken cinnamon stick, coriander, cloves, cumin, fennel, fenugreek, pep-percorns, turmeric, and 1 whole red pepper in the mortar. Using the pestle, pound as smooth as possible, or put in blender or nut grinder and **blend** or grind until smooth. If you want a more spicy curry powder, grind in more red peppers, one at a time, if necessary.

Note: For best flavor, use curry powder within three or four months of making it. Store spice mixture in tightly covered jar in cool, dark place.

¿ Kurma (Curried Chicken)

Curried chicken is a popular way to prepare fowl, and this is just one of a dozen or more variations. Curry dishes are generally included in life-cycle celebration feasts.

Yield: serves 4 to 6

2½ to 3 pounds chicken, cut into serving-size pieces

1 cup yogurt

2 tomatoes, **trimmed, coarsely chopped**

curry powder, homemade (recipe precedes) or commercial

1 tablespoon grated fresh ginger or 1 teaspoon **ground** ginger

1 clove garlic, trimmed, **minced**

2 tablespoons vegetable oil

2 onions, trimmed, finely sliced

1 cup water

Equipment: Paper towels, large mixing bowl, mixing spoon, small bowl, plastic food wrap, large skillet with cover or **Dutch oven**, serving bowl

1. Wash chicken pieces, and pat dry with paper towels. Put clean chicken pieces in large mixing bowl.

2. Put yogurt, tomato, curry powder, ginger, and garlic in small bowl, and stir to mix well. Pour yogurt mixture over chicken, and turn the pieces until they are well coated. Cover with plastic wrap and refrigerate for 3 to 4 hours to **marinate**.

3. Heat oil in large saucepan or Dutch oven over medium-high heat. Add onion and **sauté** until soft, 3 to 5 minutes. Stir in water and mix well. Add chicken pieces with **marinade**, and bring to boil. Reduce heat to **simmer**, cover, and cook for 45 minutes to 1 hour, or until chicken is tender. Test for **chicken doneness**.

To serve, transfer to serving bowl and serve with brêdes *(recipe page 104), putu (recipe page 77), and/or cooked rice.*

⚘ *Malva* (Apricot Pudding)

Malva is found throughout homes and restaurants in Southern Africa. It is a very popular dessert and an ideal ending to a wedding dinner or a funeral feast.

Yield: serves 4 to 6

Sauce:

1 cup heavy cream

½ cup butter

½ cup sugar

4 tablespoons hot water

Pudding:

1 cup flour

1 teaspoon baking soda

1 tablespoon butter

½ cup sugar

1 egg, beaten

3 tablespoons apricot jam

½ cup milk

Equipment: Medium saucepan, mixing spoon, medium mixing bowl, electric mixer or mixing bowl with mixing spoon, medium ovenproof baking dish with cover or foil, toothpick, oven mitts

1. Prepare sauce: In medium saucepan over medium-low heat combine cream, butter, sugar, and water, mix well. Continue cooking until butter is melted and sugar dissolved, about 5 to 7 minutes, stirring frequently. Keep warm.

Preheat oven to 350°F.

2. Prepare pudding: Combine flour and baking soda in medium mixing bowl, set aside.

3. Using electric mixer or mixing bowl with mixing spoon, combine butter and sugar, and beat until fluffy and smooth. Add beaten egg and apricot jam, mix well.

4. Alternating between flour mixture and milk, slowly add both to egg-jam mixture, mix well. Transfer to baking dish and cover with lid or foil. Bake in oven for 25 to 30 minutes, or until toothpick inserted in center comes out clean. Carefully remove from oven using oven mitts, remove cover and pour sauce over pudding.

Serve warm in individual bowls with dollop of ice cream.

EAST AFRICA

The region of East Africa includes the countries of Burundi, Djibouti, Eritrea, Ethiopia, Kenya, Madagascar, Malawi, Mozambique, Rwanda, Somalia, Tanzania, Uganda, Zambia, and Zimbabwe.

Burundi and Rwanda

Burundi and Rwanda are small and very similar nations in central Africa that border one another. The two landlocked nations are surrounded by the Democratic Republic of Congo, Uganda, and Tanzania.

In both, nearly every family lives in a self-contained compound, and the few urban areas are grouped around government centers. Both countries have three ethnic groups: the Hutu, the Tutsi, and the Twa (tropical forest foragers, sometimes called Pygmies). The Hutu make up the largest part of the population, while only about 15 percent of the people are Tutsi, and less than 1 percent are Twa. European missionaries arrived in the region around 1890, and today most people are Roman Catholics. In practice, almost all combine indigenous religions with Catholic rituals. (See Protestant and Catholic Life-Cycle Rituals, page lxxiii.)

When the Tutsi settled in the Rwanda and Burundi area several centuries ago, the Hutu were living there as well established farmers. The Tutsi were herders, to whom cattle owning meant wealth, prestige, and power. The Tutsi took control of the region, reducing the Hutu to serfdom through a contract known as *ubuhake*, an agreement whereby the Hutu would serve the Tutsi in exchange for protection and for the use but not the ownership of cattle.

Over time, there have been many intermarriages between the Tutsi and the Hutu, and the distinction between them has become one of class rather than of ethnicity. If you are wealthy, it is thought, you must be a Tutsi—even if you were born a Hutu. If, as a Tutsi, you became poor, you are looked down upon and called a Hutu.

Ever since the Tutsi's arrival, cattle have been a sign of wealth and prestige. For instance, before a wedding, the groom's family traditionally gives a cow to the bride's family. During the *gusaba*—the bride-price ceremony—the bride's family refers to her as *mutumwinka* ("You are exchanged for a cow"). The cow symbolizes the union between the two families.

Because of the importance of cattle, people associate *amata* (milk) with happiness, and because wealthy Tutsi and Hutu drank *ubuki* (an alcoholic beverage made from fermented honey), *ubuki* is associated with success and good fortune. Before long, the combination of milk and honey became sacred. All Rwandans greet friends at the New Year with *"Uzagire umwaka w'amata n'ubuki"* ("Have a year of milk and honey").

An important tradition at weddings is sharing a beverage, *ubuki* mixed with milk, from a washtub-sized bowl. After the bride and groom take the first sips, three or four people at a time take turns sipping the beverage through three-foot-long reed straws. The proportion of milk to *ubuki* varies, according to taste.

Kubandwa are puberty rites to initiate young boys, about 12 years old, into adulthood. The young Hutu and Tutsi male initiates are circumcised, then go through rigorous endurance exercises. On their return to their families, there is always a large communal feast with whole roasted bull, mutton, or lamb. After the puberty rites, men become *intore* (warriors) before they marry and settle down.

♪ *Muhogo Tamu* (Beef and Cassava Stew)

Cassava (also manioc) is a tuber that is a nutritious starch, like potatoes. It is used to thicken soups and stews. As African slaves traveled, cassava has traveled too; for instance, it is used by cooks in the West Indies and Brazil, where it is known as *farinhe de mandioca*.

CAUTION: Use care handling peppers. Wrap your hands in plastic wrap or slip them in plastic sandwich bag. While handling peppers, if you accidentally touch your eyes, rinse them out at once under cold running water.

Yield: serves 6

water, as needed

salt and pepper, as needed

1-pound **cassava**, peeled and cut into ½-inch cubes

¼ cup vegetable oil

1 onion, **trimmed, finely chopped**

1 teaspoon **ground** turmeric

1½ pounds lean beef, cut into ½-inch cubes

2 tomatoes, cut each into 6 wedges

1 cup coconut milk, homemade (recipe page 225), or canned (available at all Latin

American food stores and some supermarkets)

1 fresh green chili pepper, **seeded,** finely chopped, or ¼ teaspoon ground red pepper

3 tablespoons finely chopped fresh **cilantro,** or 1 tablespoon dried **coriander**

Equipment: Medium saucepan with cover, fork, **colander,** large skillet with cover, mixing spoon, small bowl, serving bowl

1. Fill medium saucepan ⅔ full with water, and add ½ teaspoon salt. Bring to boil over high heat, and add cassava cubes. Bring water back to boil. Reduce heat to **simmer,** cover, and cook until fork-tender but not mushy, 10 to 15 minutes. Drain in colander placed in the sink.

2. Heat oil in large skillet over medium-high heat. Add onion, stir, and **sauté** until soft, 3 to 5 minutes. Stir in turmeric, add beef, and toss to brown all sides, 7 to 12 minutes. Add tomatoes and 1 cup water, mix well. Bring to boil, and stir. Reduce heat to simmer, cover, and cook until beef is tender, 45 minutes to 1 hour.

3. In small bowl, combine coconut milk, finely chopped chili pepper or ground red pepper, and cilantro or coriander. Stir to mix well. Pour spicy coconut milk over beef in skillet. Add drained cassava, and toss to mix. Simmer for 10 to 15 minutes to heat through and for flavor to develop.

To serve, transfer to serving bowl and set on a cloth spread on the floor. After washing their hands, guests sit around the bowl, and each person eats from the section of bowl in front of them, using only the fingers of the right hand. The left hand must never touch food; it is used only for personal grooming.

Kosari (Bean Balls with Meat)

All celebrations call for great quantities of food. Fried beans, as in this recipe, are a favorite snack food. Platters of *kosari* are set out for guests, especially children, to munch on at weddings and other life-cycle celebrations. Omit the meat and one of the eggs to make vegetarian *kosari.*

CAUTION: HOT OIL IS USED.

Yield: serves 4

1½ cups dried **black-eyed peas**

½ cup warm water

2 eggs

½ teaspoon chili powder

salt and pepper to taste

2 onions, **trimmed,** grated

1 pound lean, **ground** beef

2 cups vegetable oil, for frying

Equipment: **Blender,** rubber spatula, medium mixing bowl, mixing spoon, paper towels, baking sheet, large **heavy-bottomed** skillet, wooden spoon or cooking **thermometer,** slotted spoon

1. In blender, grind dried peas, turning machine off and on, for about 1 minute to break up. With blender running, add warm water, a little at a time, through feed tube to make smooth paste, the consistency of a thick milk shake. Turn off machine once or twice, and scrape down sides of container using rubber spatula. Transfer to medium mixing bowl.

2. Add eggs, chili powder, grated onions, and salt and pepper to taste. Crumble in beef, and, using your hands, mix well.

3. Prepare to skillet-fry: **Caution: *Adult supervision required.*** Place several layers of paper towels on baking sheet. Heat oil in large heavy-bottomed skillet over medium-high heat. Oil is hot enough when small bubbles appear around a wooden spoon handle when it is dipped in the oil or when cooking thermometer registers 375°F.

4. Carefully drop tablespoonfuls of bean mixture, a few at a time, in oil and fry until browned on all sides, 2 to 3 minutes. Remove with slotted spoon, and drain on paper towels. Continue to fry in batches.

Serve warm or at room temperature. Use kosari *to scoop up stews or sauces or alone as a finger food snack.*

♪ Mango, Date, and Banana Crisp

This easy to prepare dish uses fresh fruits common throughout Rwanda. Upon returning home from the grueling puberty rituals, this refreshing yet sweet treat is ideal to replenish the young boys' spirits.

Yield: serves 4 to 6

¾ cup orange juice

1 teaspoon vanilla extract

½ cup all-purpose flour

½ cup rolled oats (oatmeal)

¾ cup brown sugar

½ teaspoon nutmeg

½ teaspoon cinnamon

½ teaspoon salt

6 tablespoons butter

4 ripe bananas, peeled, trimmed, cut into 1-inch slices

2 cups **pitted** dates, **coarsely chopped**

2 mangoes, **trimmed**, pitted, coarsely chopped

For serving: ice cream or whipped topping, as needed

Equipment: Small mixing bowl, mixing spoon, medium mixing bowl, medium ovenproof baking dish, oven mitts

Preheat oven to 375°F.

1. In small mixing bowl, combine orange juice and vanilla extract, mix well, set aside.

2. In medium mixing bowl, combine flour, rolled oats, brown sugar, nutmeg, cinnamon, and salt, mix well. Using clean hands, rub butter into mixture until small pea-size crumbs are formed. Set aside.

3. Place bananas, dates, and mangoes into baking dish. Pour orange juice mixture over fruit, gently tossing to evenly coat. Spoon oat-flour mixture over top of fruit, and bake in oven 15 to 20 minutes, or until golden on top. Carefully remove from oven using oven mitts.

Serve warm in individual bowls with a dollop of ice cream or whipped topping.

Djibouti, Ethiopia, and Eritrea

Djibouti, Ethiopia, and Eritrea are located in northeastern Africa. Djibouti is bordered by Eritrea to the north, Ethiopia to the southwest, and Somalia to the southeast. Ethiopia is completely landlocked, bordered by Sudan and South Sudan on the west, by Somalia and Djibouti on the east, by Kenya on the south, and by Eritrea on the northwest. Eritrea is located on the Red Sea coast and is bordered by Ethiopia and Djibouti on the south, and Sudan on the east and north.

Ethiopia has historic links to the Islamic cultures of the Middle East and to the ancient civilizations of the Mediterranean. Unlike other African countries (except Liberia), Ethiopia was never a European colony. Eritrea was a province of Ethiopia until it declared independence in 1993; however, the two countries are still closely connected, and the people are the same culturally.

Most Ethiopians and Eritreans adhere to one of the two main religions: Islam (See Islam and Islamic Life-Cycle Rituals, page lxxvi) and Christianity in the form of the Ethiopian Orthodox Christian Church. Others follow indigenous religions.

The Ethiopian Orthodox Church has close ties to the Coptic Church of Egypt, the head of which is the Patriarch of Cairo; thus, this Church differs in some ways from the Roman Catholic and Eastern Orthodox traditions. For Ethiopian Orthodox Christians, fasting, feasting, and worship are inseparable from daily life. Church services, accompanied by cymbals, the tolling of bells, and the chanting of rituals, often last throughout the night. All religious observances and life-milestone rituals are full of pageantry, with processions of beautifully robed clergy, some carrying *lalibela* (large filigree crucifixes) and others swinging pots of burning incense. Many priests carry ceremonial parasols of different colors and designs denoting their status in the Church; the parasol itself is symbolic of a link between heaven and earth.

Baptism at about three months of age is the first important event in an Ethiopian Christian's life. Usually, a great many infant baptisms take place on the same day. Infants are traditionally dressed in christening gowns worn by older siblings and cousins, often handed down from earlier generations. During the baptism ceremony, when the priest calls for those who will work together to raise the child in the way of the faithful, it is customary for a large number of family members and friends to come forward, signaling their commitment.

As part of the baptism ceremony, the priests, followed by the godparents carrying their godchildren, as along with family and friends, form a procession that circles the chapel and altar several times. Godparents give the baptized child a Coptic cross, blessed by the priest, for protection from the devil. The cross is suspended from a blue cotton cord called a *mateb*. Many Ethiopian Orthodox Christians wear these crosses around their necks throughout their lives.

After the baptism ceremony, there is always a party. A whole roasted bull, mutton, or lamb (recipe page 27) is the ideal centerpiece of a celebration feast, otherwise *tsebhi dereho* (recipe page 96) or other Ethiopian *wat* (stew) is prepared for the meal. Ethiopian Orthodox Christians slaughter animals in the tradition of the Old Testament by slitting the animal's throat.

First communion is the next important milestone for Christian boys and girls, and it too is full of pageantry and processions. Afterward, there is a celebration at home or in a rented hall. Grandmothers and aunts often spend days preparing the feast for this happy occasion.

Along with the Church-based rites, Ethiopian and Eritrean Christian weddings involve many regional traditions. An astrologer is usually consulted to set an auspicious wedding day and to counsel the couple concerning their compatibility. At one time, it was customary during the wedding ceremony to place an armed guard by the bridal couple in order to protect them from demons. Today, weddings for the masses are normally common law unions, accompanied by feasting late into the night. Weddings of the urban elite are celebrated by long and elaborate church ceremonies and processions. Wedding receptions include music, professional performers, dancing, and feasting, usually at a celebration hall or hotel ballroom.

Ethiopian Orthodox funerals are complex ceremonies that involve elaborate rites and long processions. The traditional period of mourning by the bereaved family is 40 days. The government has tried to discourage long periods of mourning, insisting that three days is sufficient time to grieve; however, traditional practices continue in many places.

Eating in Ethiopia involves many special rituals, from the washing of hands that precedes a formal dinner to the sipping from tiny cups of coffee served at the end of a meal. A traditional setting for a meal is around a gaily colored basket weave table called a *masob*. Before eating, soap, water, and a towel are brought to each diner to wash both hands. Only the right hand is used for eating; the left is considered unclean, even though it has been washed. Cutlery is not used in Ethiopia.

Ethiopians grow grapes for wine, which is the favorite beverage for celebrations. Other popular Ethiopian drinks are *talla* (a beer made from millet) and *tej* (an alcoholic drink made from fermented honey, similar to mead). Wine, *talla*, and *tej* flow freely at most celebrations.

Ethiopian Orthodox Christians have 160 fasting days a year, and additional days are designated for partial fasting, during which meat, eggs, milk, and other animal products are not eaten. Thus, Ethiopians have developed a variety of vegetarian dishes.

♪ *Telba* (Flaxseed Paste)

Telba is a healthy alternative to peanut butter and is eaten in much the same way, spread on *injera*. *Telba* is a quick, easy spread eaten to rejuvenate the body especially after a daylong Ethiopian wedding.

Yield: serves 2 to 4

1 cup flaxseed (available at International or Markets or health food stores)

¼ cup water, more as needed

1 tablespoon *berberé*, or to taste, homemade (recipe page 98) or store bought (available at International Markets)

2 tablespoons honey, or taste

For serving: **injera**, as needed (available at International Markets)

Equipment: Small skillet, spatula, nut or spice grinder, medium mixing bowl, whisk

1. Stirring occasionally, cook flaxseeds in skillet over medium-high heat 2 to 3 minutes, or until lightly toasted. Transfer to nut or spice grinder.

2. Pulverize seeds into fine powder. Transfer to mixing bowl.

3. Slowly **whisk** in ¼ cup water, adding more water if necessary to form smooth paste the consistency of peanut butter. Stir in 1 tablespoon *berberé* and 2 tablespoons honey or to taste, mix well.

Serve spread on injera *or toast for a healthy snack.*

♪ *Tsebhi Dereho* (Chicken in Red Pepper Paste)

Although many Muslim marriages in Ethiopia and Eritrea are arranged by parents (often between first cousins), educated urbanites sometimes select their own marriage partners. By tradition, every bride is expected to know how to cut a chicken into 12 pieces to make *tsebhi dereho*. The easiest way to cut a chicken into 12 pieces is to have it done by a butcher.

Yield: serves 6

¼ cup *berberé* (recipe page 98)

2½- to 3-pound chicken, cut into 12 pieces by butcher

juice of 2 lemons

salt to taste

½ cup butter or margarine

2 onions, **trimmed, finely chopped**

2 tablespoons tomato paste

4 **tomatoes, peeled**, chopped, or 16 ounces canned stewed tomatoes

2 cups water

2 teaspoons ginger root, **trimmed**, grated or 1 teaspoon **ground** ginger

6 whole hard-cooked eggs, peeled, for serving

Equipment: Paper towels, large bowl, large **heavy-bottomed** ovenproof skillet with cover or **Dutch oven**, mixing spoon, oven mitts, paring knife, large serving bowl

1. Prepare *berberé*. Keep covered and refrigerated until ready to use.

2. Rinse chicken pieces under cold running water, and pat dry with paper towels. Place in large bowl, and sprinkle all sides with lemon juice and salt to taste.

Preheat oven to 350°F.

3. Melt butter or margarine in large heavy-bottomed ovenproof skillet or Dutch oven over medium-high heat. Add onions, and **sauté** until soft, 3 to 5 minutes. Stir in ¼ cup prepared *berberé* and mix well. Add tomato paste, chopped fresh tomatoes or stewed tomatoes, water, and ginger, and stir well. Add chicken pieces and push down to cover with tomato mixture.

4. Bake in oven, covered, for 1 to 1½ hours until chicken is done. Test **chicken doneness**.

5. Using paring knife, make 4 or 5 small slits in 6 peeled, whole hard-cooked eggs.

To serve, transfer chicken pieces to large serving bowl. Arrange hard-cooked eggs around the chicken, and spoon tomato sauce over the top. Eat with h'mbasha *(recipe page 98) for sopping up sauce.*

⚘ *Mesir Wat* (Puréed Red Lentils)

Mesir wat provides a vegetarian option that can be served during partial days of fasting or as a side dish to round out any celebration feast.

Yield: serves 4 to 6

2 onions, **trimmed, coarsely chopped**

2 cloves garlic, trimmed, **minced**

2 teaspoons ginger root, trimmed, **grated**

¼ cup vegetable oil

1 teaspoon turmeric

2 tablespoons paprika

1 teaspoon cayenne pepper or to taste

1 pound red **lentils**

4 cups vegetable stock (available at most supermarkets), more as needed

salt and pepper to taste

Equipment: Food processor or **blender, Dutch oven** or **heavy-bottomed** saucepan with cover, mixing spoon

1. Place onions, garlic, and ginger in food processor or blender, and **purée** until smooth.

2. Heat oil in Dutch oven or heavy-bottomed saucepan over medium-high heat. Add onion-garlic purée, turmeric, paprika, and cayenne pepper. **Sauté** until soft and aromatic, about 5 to 7 minutes.

3. Stir-in lentils and vegetable stock. Bring to boil, cover, reduce to simmer and cook 35 to 40 minutes, or until lentils are cooked through and falling apart. Add more vegetable stock as needed to prevent sticking. Add salt and pepper to taste.

Serve warm with injera *for dipping.*

⚱ *Berberé* (Ethiopian Red Pepper Paste)

This is the basic recipe for hot pepper paste. There are countless other variations.

Yield: 1½ to 2 cups

1 teaspoon **ground** ginger	¼ teaspoon ground **allspice**
½ teaspoon ground black pepper	1 onion, **trimmed, finely chopped**
½ teaspoon ground **coriander** seeds	1 cup water, divided
½ teaspoon ground cardamom	8 tablespoons paprika
¼ teaspoon ground nutmeg	4 tablespoons chili powder
¼ teaspoon ground cloves	salt to taste
¼ teaspoon ground cinnamon	1 tablespoon vegetable oil

Equipment: Electric **blender**, rubber spatula, small saucepan, mixing spoon, 1-pint plastic or glass jar with cover

1. Put ground ginger, black pepper, coriander seeds, cardamom, nutmeg, cloves, cinnamon, allspice, and onion in blender. Add ¼ cup water and **blend** into smooth paste. Add little more water if paste is too thick. Turn off blender, once or twice and use rubber spatula to scrape down sides of bowl.

2. Put paprika and chili powder in small saucepan. Add blended mixture and remaining water and salt to taste, and stir until smooth. Cook over medium heat 5 to 7 minutes for flavor to develop. Do not boil. Remove from heat and cool to room temperature. Spoon paste into 1-pint plastic or glass jar. Carefully pour oil over surface of paste, and cover tightly.

Use with tsebhi dereho *(recipe precedes) or in other recipes calling for* berberé *or hot pepper sauce. Refrigerate for up to 5 months.*

⚱ *H'Mbasha* (Spiced Bread)

Ethiopians eat bread with every meal, and this is one of the most popular types.

Yield: 4 small loaves

1¼ cups **lukewarm** water	1 teaspoon salt
1 package dry active **yeast**	1 egg
1 teaspoon **ground fenugreek**	2 cups all-purpose flour
½ teaspoon ground **coriander** seeds	2 cups whole wheat flour
½ teaspoon ground **cardamom**	4 tablespoons warm melted butter or margarine

Equipment: Large mixing bowl, mixing spoon, lightly floured work surface, kitchen towel, fork or knife, large **heavy-bottomed** skillet with cover or griddle with cover (this could be a piece of foil or lid from large saucepan), metal tongs, **pastry brush**, napkin-lined breadbasket

1. Pour warm water into large mixing bowl and add yeast. Stir and let set for 5 to 10 minutes, until frothy.

2. Add ground fenugreek, coriander, cardamom, salt, and egg, and stir well. Add all-purpose and whole wheat flour, a little at a time, and use your hands to mix together. Transfer to lightly floured work surface, and **knead** until smooth, 7 to 10 minutes. Clean and lightly grease large mixing bowl. Place dough into bowl, and turn to grease all sides. Cover with towel, and keep in warm place to rise to double in bulk, 1 to 1½ hours.

3. Transfer dough to lightly floured work surface, **punch down** and divide into 4 pieces. Using your hands, lightly flatten each piece into round flat loaf, about ¼-inch thick. Using fork or knife, mark top of each loaf with crosshatch design. Cover loaves with towel.

4. Preheat heavy-bottomed skillet or griddle until drop of water sprinkled on surface sizzles away on contact. Place one or two loaves in dry skillet or griddle, and cover. Reduce heat to medium, and cook for 7 minutes. Turnover and continue cooking second side for another 7 minutes. Using metal tongs, remove from pan or griddle, and place on work surface. Using pastry brush, brush loaves with warm butter or margarine, place in napkin-lined breadbasket, and cover. Continue to cook remaining loaves the same way.

Serve either warm or at room temperature. Hold bread in your right hand, use your teeth to break off bite-size pieces. Never use your left hand. According to Muslim tradition, the left hand must never touch food; it is used only for personal grooming. The bread is used as a scoop to carry food from the bowl to your mouth.

Kenya

Kenya borders the Indian Ocean in East Africa. The equator runs through the middle of the country, which borders Somalia to the east, Ethiopia to the north, Tanzania to south, and South Sudan to the northwest. Kenya is home to more than 70 ethnic groups, although the differences between many of them have faded as Western cultural values filter into their lives.

The standard of living in major Kenyan cities ranks high compared with that of neighboring countries. Most city workers maintain connections with their extended families living in rural areas, and they leave the city periodically to help work on their families' farms. Even among urbanites who appear to have drifted away from ancestral traditions, tribal identity remains singularly important. When two Kenyans meet in the city, they almost always identify their tribes as they introduce themselves.

Most of Kenya's population is Christian: 40 percent are Protestants, and 30 percent are Roman Catholics. Most celebrate life passages by combining Christian rituals (see Protestant and Catholic Life-Cycle Rituals, page lxxiii) with the traditional customs of their tribes and local religions. A small percentage of Kenyans are Muslims, most of whom live along the coast. (See Islam and Islamic Life-Cycle Rituals, page lxxvi) Many others practice indigenous religions. (See African Life-Cycle Rituals, page lxvi.)

The pastoral Maasai, the best known of Kenya's tribal people, have managed to stay outside the mainstream of Kenya's development. They live a nomadic lifestyle, traveling throughout the year—mostly in the southern part of the country—to maintain their cattle herds. Among the Maasai, as for most ethnic groups in Kenya, circumcision remains as the main rite for boys passing into adulthood. The Maasai have a ceremony in which boys of about 14 years of age become warriors (*morans*). After circumcision, custom requires the group of boys to go out on their own, away from their people, and build a village (*manyatta*), where for eight years they must fend for themselves.

The Akamba people live in the eastern part of Kenya. Among the Akamba, youths of the same age, beginning at about 12, are grouped into an "age-set" (*rika*). They will stay together as a group and pass through the various stages of life until they die. As they become older, they gain seniority rights—especially young men but also, although to a lesser extent, young women. Young Akamba parents are known as "junior elders" and are responsible for the maintenance and upkeep of the village. Later in life, they go through a ceremony to become "medium elders" and, still later, "full elders," with the responsibility for death ceremonies and administering the law. The last stage of a person's life is that of "senior elder," with responsibility for the holy places.

The Swahili people, most of whom are Muslims, live along Kenya's coast. Today, Muslims in Kenya do not adhere to strict forms of Islam; instead, they are strongly committed to the education of women, who are also encouraged to participate in all levels of business.

The Turkana live in a remote, arid region in northwestern Kenya. Due to their isolation, the Turkana are probably the ethnic group in Kenya that is least influenced by the modern world. Like the Maasai, the Turkana are cattle herders, but unlike the Maasai, they have discontinued the practice of circumcision rituals for young boys. Turkana women wear a variety of beaded and metal adornments that identify stages in their lives. When a young Turkana girl is ready for marriage, she announces that fact by covering her body with a mixture of ochre (red or yellow pigment) and fat. When men are ready to find a mate, they cover part of their hair with mud, which is then painted blue and decorated with ostrich and other feathers. A set of rules and rituals bring the available individuals together.

For the marriage ceremonies of the Samburu people of Kenya, a couple shows their commitment to one another by crossing sticks. The sticks—given to the bride by the groom—are also used to brand his cattle, signifying that his wife and cattle are now his possessions.

Rendile women of the northern desert of Kenya wear their hair in a coxcomb made from mud, animal fat, and ochre to show that they have given birth to their first son. This hairstyle is worn until the boy is circumcised or until a close male relative dies, at which time the woman shaves her head. Wide arm bracelets are also worn by Rendile women to indicate their marriage status; to announce when a firstborn son has been circumcised, they add a wide band of bracelets above the elbow on their upper arms.

The Luo people live in western Kenya on the shores of Lake Victoria. Unlike most African tribes, the Luo do not circumcise adolescent boys during a coming of age ritual. Instead, several teeth are extracted from the boy's lower jaw. Although this has become a less common practice, many middle-aged and older Luo men are missing a few lower teeth from this ritual in their youth.

⚘ *Mtori* (Plantain and Beef Soup)

A dish that feeds a lot of people with little cost is *mtori*. Pots of *mtori* are commonly served along with *irio* at communal feasts in Kenya.

Yield: serves 4 to 6

2 to 3 pounds beef short ribs, cut into 3-inch lengths

8 cups water

2 teaspoons salt

3 ripe **plantains** (about 1½ pounds), peeled, cut into chunks

3 boiling potatoes (about 1 pound), peeled, quartered

2 onions, **trimmed**, peeled, **coarsely chopped**

1 tablespoon butter or margarine

Equipment: Large saucepan with cover or **Dutch oven**, mixing spoon, fork, slotted spoon or tongs, cutting board, sharp knife, ladle, electric **blender**, medium bowl, individual soup bowls

1. In large saucepan or Dutch oven, put short ribs, water, and salt. Bring to boil over high heat, and, using mixing spoon, skim off and discard foam that comes to surface. Reduce heat to **simmer,** cover, and cook for 1½ hours. Add plantains, potatoes, and onions. Stir, and continue to cook for 25 to 30 minutes, or until meat and potatoes are tender when poked with fork.

2. With slotted spoon or tongs, transfer meat to cutting board. Using sharp knife, remove bones, and cut away and discard fat and gristle. Cut meat into bite-size pieces.

3. Ladle potatoes, plantains, and liquid into electric blender. **Purée** in batches and pour into medium bowl. Return purée to large saucepan, and stir in pieces of meat and butter or margarine. Cook over medium heat to heat through, 5 to 7 minutes. Add salt to taste.

Serve hot in individual soup bowls. Although called a soup, this is actually a thick stew, and in Kenya it is served as a main course.

⚘ *Mukimo* (Vegetable Medley)

All ethnic and religious groups in Kenya have one thing in common: celebrations are communal, and great quantities of food must be prepared for feasts. *Mukimo* is a nourishing dish that can feed hundreds of people.

Yield: serves 8 to 10

1-pound bag frozen spinach (cooked according to directions on package)

½ pound frozen green beans (cooked according to directions on package)

1 onion, trimmed, **coarsely chopped, caramelized**

2 cloves garlic, trimmed, **minced**

1 cup sour cream, more as needed

1½ pounds potatoes, **trimmed**, cooked, mashed or instant mashed potatoes (cooked according to directions on package)

½ pound frozen corn (cooked according to directions on package)

salt and pepper to taste

Equipment: Food processor, large mixing bowl, large saucepan, mixing spoon

1. In batches, place spinach, green beans, caramelized onion, and garlic in food processor, **purée** until smooth, and transfer to large mixing bowl.

2. Place sour cream and mashed potatoes in mixing bowl with puréed spinach-green bean mixture. Using potato masher, mash until smooth, and mix well. Add more sour cream if needed.

3. Fold in corn, and add salt and pepper to taste.

4. Transfer to saucepan, and, stirring occasionally, heat through over medium-high heat.

Serve warm as a side dish with mtori (recipe page 101).

Madagascar

Madagascar is an island in the Indian Ocean off the southeastern coast of Africa. Most of the island's flora and fauna, as well as the sea creatures in the surrounding waters, are found nowhere else in the world. Even the people of Madagascar have distinctive customs and lifestyles that differ from those of other Africans.

The Malagasy people are descended primarily from Indonesian seafarers, black Africans, and Arabs. According to legend, Indonesians first arrived on the island a couple of thousand years ago, and after they took up residence, they acquired wives and slaves from the neighboring coast of Africa. Arabs came as traders and stayed.

Although one language is spoken in Madagascar, there are 18 recognized ethnic groups, each with its own customs, traditions, and territory. For centuries, rivalry has existed among them. Most groups are subsistence farmers, though some are herders who raise humpbacked *zebu* (cattle). About 40 percent of the Malagasy are Christian, divided almost equally between Protestants and Roman Catholics.

The Christian Malagasy have incorporated some of the customs and ideologies of Islam into their practices. Belief in *vintana* (fate or destiny), thought to have roots in Islamic cosmology (study of the universe), is incorporated into every facet of their lives. The date and time of a birth, circumcision, marriage, and burial are either good or bad, according to an individual's *vintana*. All auspicious occasions are planned around a person's *vintana*; for instance, the name of a newborn is chosen only after consulting an astrologer for a reading on the child's *vintana*.

Boys are circumcised at a very young age, and this is an occasion that is always accompanied by a huge feast with drinking and singing.

Among Malagasy pastoralist groups, *zebu* (cattle) are an extremely important item of prestige and wealth. Formerly, no young male passed to manhood until he had rustled someone's cattle and bragged about it. (This is now forbidden, however.) Still, even today, no self-respecting man can marry without his bride's price in cows. Even more important is for a man to possess cattle for slaughter at his funeral; it would bring disgrace to his family if he were to die without this property. The more bulls killed for a funeral, the greater a man's glory, proclaimed forever by horned skulls displayed on the stone walls of his tomb, along with elaborately carved drawings of his cattle. The greatest sacrifice is cattle, and only at funerals do these herders kill and eat their *zebu*. At lesser occasions, chickens, rice, honey, rum, sugar cane, or sweets are given in sacrificial ceremonies.

ꙮ *Varenga* (Shredded Beef)

In Madagascar, meat is eaten on only special occasions. *Varenga* is always eaten with mountains of *vary* (rice)—a way to make small quantities of meat go a long way. Served along with the main dish and *vary* are *brêdes* (recipe page 104) and a small bowl of *rano vola* (also called *ranon 'apango*), which is a rice broth made by simply adding boiling water to the residue left in the pot used to cook rice. Plenty of *mofo* (bread) is needed to sop up the juices.

Yield: serves 4 to 6

2 pounds lean boneless chuck steak, cut into 2-inch chunks	2 cloves garlic, **trimmed**, **minced**, or 1 teaspoon garlic granules
water, as needed	1 onion, trimmed, **finely chopped**
1 teaspoon salt	For serving: 4 to 6 cups cooked white rice, kept warm

Equipment: Medium saucepan with cover or **Dutch oven**, mixing spoon, fork, plate, serving platter

1. Place beef in medium saucepan or Dutch oven, and add water to cover by at least 1 inch. Add salt, garlic, and onion. Bring to boil over high heat, and stir. Reduce heat to **simmer**, cover, and cook for about 2 hours, or until meat is so tender you can easily shred it with your fingers. During cooking, add more hot water if necessary to keep meat well covered. To test doneness: Using fork, remove a piece of meat from the pan, put on plate and let cool enough to handle. Using your fingers, you should be able to easily shred the meat.

To serve, mound cooked rice on a serving platter, and spoon meat and pan juices on top. Serve with a basket of mofo.

℘ *Brêdes* (Boiled Greens)

The greens used for *brêdes* can be anything you can get from the garden or market, such as spinach, **chard** (also Swiss chard), **mustard greens, turnip** greens, **collard greens,** or **broccoli rabe** (also raab), or some combination. Spinach is used in this recipe.

Yield: serves 3 to 4

1 pound fresh spinach or other greens, rinsed, patted dry

2 cups water

salt and pepper to taste

Equipment: **Colander**, medium saucepan with cover, mixing spoon

Pour water into medium saucepan, and bring to boil over high heat. Add spinach and salt and pepper to taste. Reduce heat to **simmer,** cover, and cook until tender, 15 to 20 minutes.

Serve as a side dish or pour over vary *(rice).*

℘ *Koba Akondro* (Steamed Banana and Peanut Cakes)

In Madagascar, *koba akondro* would be made wrapped in banana leaves; however, we suggest using more readily available aluminum foil. *Koba akondro* is ideal to serve as a snack or dessert for a feast following the circumcision of a young boy.

Yield: serves 4 to 6

3 ripe bananas, peeled

¾ cup rice flour

¼ cup brown sugar

⅔ cup shelled peanuts, ground

½ teaspoon vanilla extract

3 tablespoons honey

Equipment: Medium mixing bowl, potato masher, large spoon, 4 to 6 (6×6-inch) pieces of nonstick aluminum foil, **steamer pan** or basket, metal tongs, baking sheet

1. Place bananas, rice flour, brown sugar, ground peanuts, vanilla extract, and honey in mixing bowl. Using potato masher, mash until mixture is smooth and thick paste is formed.

2. Spoon 2 to 3 tablespoons of mixture onto aluminum square. Wrap foil around mixture and secure, folding ends over seam, and press closed. Repeat until all of mixture is used and packages are made.

3. Stack packages in steamer basket or pan, and steam over high heat 25 to 30 minutes, or until cakes are firm. Using tongs remove packages, set side by side on baking sheet and cool to room temperature.

Serve as a sweet snack or as dessert at the end of a meal. Guests should open the koba akondro *and eat it right out of the aluminum foil.*

Mozambique

Mozambique is a long, narrow country on the southern coast of East Africa. It is bordered by the Indian Ocean on the east; by Tanzania on the north; by Malawi, Zambia, and Zimbabwe on the west; and by South Africa and Swaziland on the south.

A Portuguese colony until it gained independence in 1975, sharp cultural contrasts remain between the coastal cities, which were strongly influenced by Portuguese traders, and the interior of the country, where people follow ancient traditions and customs. Most Mozambicans are engaged in subsistence farming.

There are 10 major ethnic groups in Mozambique. The largest group is the Makua, living mostly in the north. Two-thirds of the population of Mozambique follows indigenous religions, about one-tenth are Muslims, and the rest are Christians, mostly Roman Catholics. Muslims and Christians generally blend local traditions with their religious celebrations. (See Islam and Islamic Life-Cycle Rituals, page lxxvi, and Protestant and Catholic Life-Cycle Rituals, page lxxiii.)

Traditional rituals are observed by most Mozambicans for life passages. At the time of a marriage, nothing is more important to the families of the bride and groom than negotiating *lobolo* (bride-price). The traditional payment is in the form of hoes—farming tools. Among the 10 to 15 hoes that are given as *lobolo*, there is a special marriage hoe, called a *beja*, that is not made to be used. It is carefully kept and passed along to the next generation, to be used again in the payment of a bride-price.

♟ *Camarão de Coco* (Coconut Shrimp)

Mozambique has an extensive coastline, and more than 50 rivers run through the country. Thus, it is only natural that fish and shellfish are important to the Mozambican diet. *Camarão de coco* is a wonderful way to fix shrimp for the *lobolo* meal or for a wedding feast.

Yield: serves 6

2 to 2½ pounds shrimp (48 to 54 shrimp), **peeled and deveined**

¼ cup butter or margarine, more if necessary

1 onion, **trimmed, finely chopped**

4 cloves garlic, trimmed, **minced**

2 tablespoons fresh parsley, finely chopped, or 3 teaspoons dried parsley flakes

½ teaspoon **ground** red pepper, more or less to taste

2 teaspoons ground cumin

3 peeled tomatoes, chopped or 12-ounce canned stewed tomatoes, chopped

salt and pepper to taste

2 cups coconut milk, homemade (recipe page 225), or canned

Equipment: **Colander**, large **heavy-bottomed** skillet, slotted spoon, medium bowl, mixing spoon

1. Put peeled and deveined shrimp in colander and rinse under cold running water. Drain well.

2. Melt ¼ cup butter or margarine in large heavy-bottomed skillet over medium-high heat. Add shrimp and tossing constantly, **sauté** until opaque pinkish-white, 3 to 5 minutes. Remove shrimp with slotted spoon and place in medium bowl. Add onion and garlic to same skillet, and add more butter or margarine, if necessary. Stir and sauté until onions are soft, 3 to 5 minutes. Add parsley, ½ teaspoon ground red pepper, more or less to taste, cumin, tomatoes, and salt and pepper to taste. Stir well, reduce heat to medium, and continue cooking for flavor to develop, 3 to 5 minutes. Stir in coconut milk, and **blend** well. Return shrimp to skillet, toss to mix, and cook 3 to 5 minutes to heat through.

Serve at once over rice.

⚘ *Masamba* (Spinach Cakes)

Masamba cakes are a great addition for any wedding celebration or funeral feast.

Yield: 8 cakes

1 pound frozen spinach (cooked according to directions on package)

1 cup macaroni (cooked according to directions on package), drained

2 eggs

1 cup plain **bread crumbs**, more as needed

2 cloves garlic, **trimmed**, **minced**

½ cup parmesan cheese

salt and pepper to taste

butter spray, as needed

Equipment: Medium mixing bowl, mixing spoon, greased or nonstick muffin tin, toothpick, oven mitts

Preheat oven to 400°F.

1. In mixing bowl, combine cooked spinach, cooked macaroni, eggs, bread crumbs, garlic, and parmesan cheese, mix well. Add salt and pepper to taste.

2. Evenly distribute spinach mixture into muffin tins. Sprinkle top of cakes with bread crumbs, coat crumbs with butter spray, and bake in oven 20 to 25 minutes, or until tops are golden and toothpick inserted in center comes out clean. Carefully remove using oven mitts, and set aside to cool 3 to 5 minutes. Remove cakes from muffin tin.

Serve warm with millet or as a side dish with a stew or soup.

⚘ Steamed Millet

Yield: serves 6

Millet or cornmeal porridge is served at every meal in Mozambique, much as potatoes or bread are served with meals in Western countries. A feast would be incomplete if one or the other were not on the menu. Millet is one of the most important grains in Africa. Buy millet at a health food store, and be sure to get hulled millet, not birdseed.

3½ cups water	½ cup boiling water
1 teaspoon salt	3 tablespoons butter or margarine
2 cups **millet**	

Equipment: Medium **heavy-bottomed** saucepan with cover, mixing spoon

1. Pour water into medium heavy-bottomed saucepan, and add salt and millet. Bring to boil over medium-high heat. Stir, reduce heat to **simmer**, cover, and cook for 20 minutes. After 20 minutes, stir to fluff millet, and taste it. (When fully cooked, millet has a texture similar to cooked white rice.) If it seems too dry, yet still has a little crunch, add ¼ cup boiling water, cover, and continue cooking 10 minutes more. Remove from heat, and stir in butter or margarine. Keep covered until ready to serve.

Serve millet as a side dish with fish, meat, or vegetables.

Somalia

Located on the shores of the Indian Ocean, on what is known as the Horn of Africa in the northeastern part of the continent, Somalia is bordered by Djibouti on the northwest, by Ethiopia on the west, and by Kenya on the southwest. It is the only African country where everyone speaks the same language and nearly everyone is of the same ethnicity: Somali.

There are two distinct groups of Somalis: nomads whose lives revolve around the seasonal movements of their herds and urbanites who live in the coastal towns and are involved in international trade.

For over a thousand years, Somalis have been Muslims, and life-cycle events are celebrated in accordance with Islam. (See, Islam and Islamic Life-Cycle Rituals, page lxxvi.) Somali Muslims also incorporate indigenous Somali customs with Islamic beliefs. For instance, ritual dances are done to placate evil forces, diseases, crop failures, marauding wild animals, and foreign invaders, while recreational dances celebrate happy events, including the coming of the rains, the harvest, marriages, and births.

In Somalia when a young man asks for a girl's hand in marriage, a promise of *meher*, or a payment, must be offered before the engagement is complete. Camels are the usual form of payment.

On the wedding day, a ceremony called the *Gelbis* is performed. The bride and groom gather with family and friends in front of a hut that has been constructed for this special occasion. The bride and groom are offered blessings, verses from the Koran are read, then they are taken to their new home and the celebration begins.

Meat is a luxury in Somalia, and when it is prepared for a meal, it means that something is being celebrated. The most elaborate celebration feasts are prepared for men who have returned from the *hajj* (pilgrimage to Mecca). For a Muslim man, this is considered the most important rite of passage in his lifetime, and he is given a hero's welcome when he returns home. The feasting and partying may continue nonstop for several days. *Kabab barreh*, whole roast lamb (recipe page 629) or roast goat, or often both, is typically prepared for the homecoming celebration.

⚖ *Huris Hilib* (Veal with Tomatoes)

Large assortments of other dishes are also prepared for the feast, *huris hilib* among them. This recipe uses veal, but it is equally good when made with chicken breasts or other kinds of lean, boneless meat.

Yield: serves 6

1 green pepper, **trimmed, seeded, coarsely chopped**	1 pound boneless lean veal or beef, cut into ½-inch cubes
3 potatoes, peeled and quartered	salt and pepper to taste
water, as needed	1 tomato, **peeled,** sliced, or 1 cup canned stewed tomatoes
2 tablespoons vegetable oil	
1 onion, **trimmed, finely chopped**	¼ cup **bread crumbs**
1 clove garlic, trimmed, **minced**	2 tablespoons butter or margarine

Equipment: Medium saucepan with cover, mixing spoon, food processor or potato masher, rubber spatula, large skillet, greased 8-inch baking pan, oven mitts

1. Put green pepper and potatoes in medium saucepan, and add just enough water to cover. Bring to boil over high heat. Reduce heat to **simmer**, cover, and cook until very tender, 20 to 25 minutes. Remove from heat, and allow to cool enough to handle.

2. Transfer potato mixture, including pan juices, to food processor, and **purée** until smooth and lump-free, about 1 minute, or mash with a potato masher.

   Note: *While processing, turn machine off once or twice, and scrape down sides of container with rubber spatula.*

Preheat oven to 350°F.

3. Heat oil in large skillet over medium-high heat. Add onions, garlic, and meat. Stir and **sauté** until meat is lightly browned, 12 to 15 minutes. Stir puréed potato mixture into meat mixture, and add salt and pepper to taste. Gently stir to mix. Transfer to greased 8-inch baking pan, and arrange tomato slices over top or cover with stewed tomatoes. Sprinkle with bread crumbs and salt and pepper to taste, and dot butter or margarine on top.

4. Bake in oven for 30 to 35 minutes, until top is lightly browned and mixture is bubbly.

To serve, place pan of huris hilib *on the table, and serve with side dish of cooked rice or millet.*

✎ *Skudahkharis* (Lamb and Rice)

To celebrate happy events—the birth of a son, a boy's circumcision, a man's return from Mecca, or a daughter's wedding—whole roasted lamb would be the first choice for the feast. Most Somalis can't afford such extravagance, so they might settle for a dish like this.

Yield: serves 4

4 tablespoons vegetable oil

1 pound lean lamb, cut into bite-size pieces

1 onion, **trimmed**, thinly sliced

1 clove garlic, trimmed, **minced**

2 tomatoes, finely chopped

1 teaspoon **ground** cumin

1 teaspoon ground cinnamon

½ teaspoon ground cloves

½ teaspoon ground cardamom

salt and pepper to taste

3 ounces (about ½ cup) canned tomato paste

2 cups raw white rice

4 cups boiling water

Equipment: Large **heavy-bottomed** saucepan with cover or **Dutch oven**, mixing spoon, large serving platter

1. Heat oil in large heavy-bottomed saucepan or Dutch oven over medium-high heat. Add meat, stir, and brown on all sides, 18 to 20 minutes. Add onions and garlic, stir, and **sauté** until onion is soft, 3 to 5 minutes. Stir in tomatoes, cumin, cinnamon, cloves, cardamom, salt and pepper to taste, and tomato paste. Stir to mix well, reduce heat to medium-low, and cook for 5 to 7 minutes for flavors to develop.

2. Slowly stir in rice and boiling water, and bring to boil over high heat. Reduce heat to **simmer**, cover, and cook for 18 to 20 minutes, until rice is done. Remove from heat and keep covered for 15 minutes before serving.

To serve, pile mixture on large serving platter, and place it on a cloth spread out on the floor or on a low table. Everyone uses only the fingers of their right hand to help themselves with each mouthful. According to Islamic tradition, the left hand must never touch food; it is used only for personal grooming.

✎ *Pear Sabayah* (Fruit Flat Bread)

Sabaya is traditional Somali flat bread served as a side with meat dishes, ideal for dipping. For a unique flavor, vegetables such as cabbage or cauliflower or fruit such as pears or pineapple can also be added to *Sabaya*. Pear *sabayah* is ideal to serve as a sweet treat during a wedding celebration.

Yield: serves 4 to 6

2 cups all purpose flour, more as needed

14.5 ounces canned pears, drained, mashed

⅓ cup sugar

½ teaspoon cinnamon

½ teaspoon salt

¾ cup warm water, more as needed

2 tablespoons vegetable oil, more as needed

Equipment: Medium mixing bowl, mixing spoon, rolling pin, cookie sheet, medium skillet, basting brush, spatula, paper towel–covered plate

1. In medium mixing bowl, combine flour, pears, sugar, cinnamon, salt, and water, mix well.

2. Knead dough until smooth, adding more flour if mixture is too sticky. Break off ping-pong-ball-size pieces of dough. Using palms of hands, roll into ball. Place on lightly floured work surface. Using lightly floured rolling pin, roll dough ball into ¼-inch thick disc. Set aside on cookie sheet. Continue until all discs are made.

3. Heat 2 tablespoons oil in skillet over low heat. Place *sabayas* in skillet, one at a time, and cook for 20 to 30 seconds. Using basting brush, brush disc lightly with oil. Continue turning and flipping until lightly golden on both sides. Remove from skillet, set on paper towel–covered plate to drain, and keep warm. Continue until all *sabayas* are cooked, adding oil as needed to prevent sticking.

Serve warm with stews for dipping or as a sweet treat.

Tanzania

Tanzania (the former nations of Tanganyika and Zanzibar) is a remarkable country. It contains Kilimanjaro, the highest mountain in Africa, and the continent's biggest lakes touch its borders to the north, west, and south. Along Tanzania's eastern border is the Indian Ocean; Uganda and Kenya are to the north; Burundi, Rwanda, and Congo are to the west; and Mozambique, Zambia, and Malawi are to the south. On its island of Zanzibar in the Indian Ocean, some of the world's finest spices and coffee are grown.

The population of Tanzania includes more than 120 ethnic groups. Centuries ago, Muslims came to Tanzania as spice traders from the East, and Christian traders came from Europe, primarily Portugal. Today, the Tanzanian population is almost equally split among Muslims, Christians, and those following indigenous religions.

The majority of Tanzanians live in rural areas. They live on the food they grow, often with no more than simple hoes to work their gardens. As in other African countries, the extended family traditionally feeds and cares for its members.

Muslims in Tanzania observe life's passages in accordance with Islam (see Islam and Islamic Life-Cycle Rituals, page lxxvi); however, practices and traditions are less conservative than in the Middle East. For instance, in Tanzania, women are allowed to receive an education and to work outside the home. Islamic modesty laws, too, are relatively moderate. Tanzanian Muslim women wear dress-length, loose black garments (*buibui*) and black head scarves that tie under the chin. Tanzanian Muslim men pray five times a day and look forward to making the *hajj* (pilgrimage) to Mecca. It is the most important rite of passage in a Muslim man's life.

Wedding traditions are important to Tanzanian Muslims. Parents arrange marriages, and the prospective groom's family pays a bride-price, which is refunded if all goes well. Men may have as many as four wives. A bride-price usually is paid only for the first wife.

After consummating a marriage, a *walima* (wedding reception) is given by the husband for friends and family to celebrate the auspicious occasion. Tanzanian Muslim men and women celebrate together at weddings and other festivities instead of partying in separate locations, as is done in many other Islamic countries.

If the family can afford it, roast lamb (recipe page 629) or goat are prepared for the wedding feast, along with many other dishes and assorted flat breads, such as *khobaz arabee* (recipe page 682) and *mkate wa ufute*, as well as large bowls of fruits and nuts.

₹ *Ndizi na Nyama* (Stewed Tomatoes with Bananas)

Many side dishes, such as this stew, are prepared for Muslim wedding feasts in Tanzania. *Ndizi na nyama* has an unusual combinations of flavors.

Yield: serves 6 to 8

2 tablespoons butter or margarine

1 onion, **trimmed, finely chopped**

2 tomatoes, **trimmed,** finely chopped, or 2 cups canned stewed tomatoes, finely chopped

8 bananas, peeled, cut crosswise into ½-inch pieces

1 cup **coconut milk**, homemade (recipe page 225), or canned (available at most supermarkets and all Latin American food stores)

½ teaspoon salt

½ teaspoon **ground** turmeric

1 teaspoon sugar, more or less to taste

Equipment: Medium saucepan with cover, mixing spoon

1. Melt butter or margarine in medium saucepan over medium-high heat. Add onions, stir, and sauté until soft, 3 to 5 minutes.

2. Add stewed tomatoes, bananas, coconut milk, salt, turmeric, and 1 teaspoon sugar, more or less to taste. Stir well and bring to boil. Reduce heat to **simmer**, cover, and cook 15 minutes.

Serve warm or at room temperature, as a side dish with meat.

₹ *Bata Iliyokaushwa* (Zanzibar Duck)

If roast lamb is too expensive for the wedding feast, other meat or fowl, sometimes both, are prepared for the celebration. Nutria (aquatic rodents) and *bata* (duck) are two favorites. This duck dish, using Zanzibar cloves, is popular throughout the East African coast. The recipe calls for dried whole red chili peppers; they are very hot, so use them cautiously.

Yield: serves 6

5- to 6-pound duck, fresh or frozen (thawed)

2 cups chicken broth

2 teaspoons **ground** cloves

dried whole red chili peppers to taste

2 tablespoons **cornstarch**

½ cup water

½ cup frozen orange juice concentrate, thawed

juice of 1 lime

1 green or red bell pepper, **trimmed, seeded, finely chopped**

salt and pepper to taste

For **garnish**: 2 oranges, cut into wedges

For serving: 6 to 8 cups cooked rice, kept warm

Equipment: Paper towels, work surface, sharp knife, large **heavy-bottomed** skillet, metal tongs, 12×9×2-inch baking pan, aluminum foil, serving platter

1. Rinse duck under cold running water, and wipe inside and out with paper towels. Place duck on work surface, and, using sharp knife, cut duck into serving-size pieces. Cut off any chunks of fat and set aside. Prick duck skin in several places with point of knife.

2. Finely chop about 2 tablespoons duck fat and put in large skillet. Heat over medium-low heat to **render**. Increase heat to medium-high, and add duck pieces. Fry on both sides, until golden brown, 10 to 15 minutes on each side. Fry in batches, and, using metal tongs, transfer duck pieces to baking pan.

Preheat oven to 350°F.

3. Pour off and discard any fat left in skillet. Pour chicken broth into skillet. Add ground cloves and dried red chili peppers to taste. Stir and bring to boil over medium-high heat.

4. In cup, combine cornstarch and water. Stir until smooth, and add to chicken broth mixture. Add orange juice, lime juice, bell pepper, and salt and pepper to taste. Stir until thickened, 3 to 5 minutes, and pour over duck in baking pan. Cover with foil.

5. Bake in oven for 1 hour. To test for doneness, pierce thigh of duck with point of a knife. The juice should trickle out a clear yellow. If juice is slightly pink, cook duck for another 15 to 20 minutes.

To serve, place the duck on a serving platter, and pour the sauce over it. Garnish with orange wedges and serve with rice.

⚘ *Achali ya papai bichi* (Green Papaya Chutney)

Achali ya papai bichi is eaten with meats and stews to enhance their flavor. This chutney is especially enjoyed for the wedding feast.

Yield: serves 6 to 8

2 tablespoons vegetable oil, more as needed

1 onion, **trimmed, finely chopped**

2 green **papayas**, trimmed, **seeded**, finely chopped (available at international markets)

1 teaspoon turmeric

1 teaspoon cumin

1 tablespoon ginger root, trimmed, grated

2 cloves garlic, trimmed, **minced**

1 habanera pepper, trimmed, minced

1 teaspoon sugar, more as needed

juice of 3 limes, or ½ cup lime juice

salt and pepper to taste

Equipment: Medium skillet, mixing spoon, airtight container

1. Heat 2 tablespoons oil in skillet over medium high-heat, stir in onion and green papaya chunks, **sauté** 3 to 5 minutes, or until onion is soft.

2. Stir in turmeric, cumin, ginger, habanera pepper, and sugar, and mix well. Stirring frequently, continue cooking additional 3 to 5 minutes or until papaya is tender. Remove from heat, stir in lime juice, and mix well. Add salt and pepper to taste.

3. Transfer to airtight container and refrigerate for up to 1 month.

Serve as garnish on meats, stews, or breads.

Uganda

Uganda, in eastern Africa, is bordered on the north by South Sudan, on the east by Kenya, on the west by the Democratic Republic of the Congo, and on the south by Tanzania and Rwanda. The country includes Lake Victoria, the second largest freshwater lake in the world, and the source of the great White Nile River. Few African countries are as well endowed as Uganda with water and fertile land, which makes subsistence comparatively easy for the large Ugandan population. Formerly a British colony, it became an independent nation in 1962.

Most Ugandans are Christians, almost equally divided between Protestants and Roman Catholics. (See Protestant and Catholic Life-Cycle Rituals, page lxxiii). The rest of the population is either Muslim (see Islam and Islamic Life-Cycle Rituals, page lxxvi) or followers of indigenous religions. (See African Life-Cycle Rituals, page lxvi). The Ugandan constitution guarantees religious freedom.

The Nile forms a natural dividing line that separates Uganda's south—home to the Bantu people, the country's largest ethnic group—from the north, where the Nilotes live. Nilotes are a group of related peoples who live near the source of the Nile. One of these groups, the Karamojong people, is notable for having tenaciously maintained their long-standing traditions; for instance, only recently have they begun wearing clothes. The Karamojong men tend their longhorn cattle, often singing and talking to them. Women are responsible for raising grain and other foods to supplement the basic diet of milk and blood from the cattle. Cattle are slaughtered only for feasts on special occasions.

Cattle represent wealth and prestige. Among the Karamojong—and all Ugandan herding groups—giving cattle to the bride's father in the bride-price negotiation is one of the most important parts of the marriage. It binds two families together, and all the relatives in both families are expected to help make the marriage work. Only after a marriage has been validated according to traditional beliefs will the couple arrange a church wedding. For Christian weddings, there is a church ceremony and a reception afterward.

Christian Ugandan men are permitted to have only one wife. Most adhere to this rule, although some marry only their first wife in church and then take another wife or perhaps several others in accordance with traditional African practice.

Death is marked by elaborate funeral rites. When someone in a community dies, everyone is expected to attend the funeral. A person who ignores a death is thought to harbor ill feelings toward the bereaved family and toward the community in general. A wake can last several days and involves singing, ritual dances, prayers, and feasting. Guests contribute to the expense of the food and drink. Mourners express their sorrow by emotional crying, shouting, and wailing. The dead are buried on land that belonged to them, not in cemeteries. The corpse is place in the ground, usually in a coffin, beside the main dwelling of the living compound.

Chickennat (Chicken in Peanut Sauce)

A little chicken or meat, combined with other ingredients, can go a long way to feed a hungry crowd at a wedding or funeral.

Yield: serves 4 to 6

2½ to 3 pounds whole chicken, cut into serving-size pieces

salt and pepper to taste

½ cup butter or margarine

2 cups water

2 onions, **trimmed, finely chopped**

1 cup peanut butter

2 **egg yolks**

For **garnish:** 1 tablespoon parsley, **coarsely chopped**

Equipment: Paper towels, large **heavy-bottomed** skillet with cover or **Dutch oven**, mixing spoon, metal tongs, plate, small bowl, whisk, large serving bowl

1. Rinse chicken under cold running water, and pat dry with paper towels. Sprinkle with salt and pepper to taste.

2. Melt butter or margarine in large heavy-bottomed skillet or Dutch oven over medium-high heat. Add chicken pieces and water, and sprinkle in finely chopped onions. Bring to boil. Reduce heat to **simmer**, cover, and cook for 45 minutes to 1 hour, or until chicken is tender. Test **chicken doneness**. Using metal tongs, remove chicken pieces and place on plate.

3. Put peanut butter in small bowl. Remove about ¾ cup chicken broth from pan and stir into peanut butter until well mixed. Stir egg yolks into peanut butter mixture. Whisking constantly, slowly add peanut mixture to remaining chicken broth. Return chicken pieces to skillet or Dutch oven, cover, and simmer to heat through, 7 to 12 minutes.

To serve, transfer to large serving bowl and sprinkle with parsley. Serve with rice, putu *(recipe page 77), or* matoke.

⚶ *Bufuke* (Mashed Sweet Potatoes with Beans and Onion Sauce)

Bufuke is a traditional vegetarian Ugandan dish. It is ideal to make in large quantities to serve to family and friends for a funeral feast.

Yield: serves 4 to 6

2 cups peanuts, shelled

14.5 ounces canned kidney beans, drained

16-ounce package **mung beans** (available at International Markets, cooked according to directions on package), drained

Sauce:

2 tablespoons vegetable oil

3 onions, **trimmed, finely chopped**

2 (14.5-ounce) canned stewed tomatoes, **coarsely chopped**

water, as needed

28 ounces canned sweet potatoes, drained

salt and pepper to taste

1 tablespoon butter or margarine, more as needed

1 cup vegetable broth (available at most supermarkets)

1 teaspoon, Cayenne pepper, or to taste

2 teaspoons flour, more as needed

1 cup coconut milk, homemade (recipe page 225), or canned

Equipment: Large saucepan, mixing spoon, potato masher, medium saucepan, small mixing bowl, whisk

1. Place peanuts, kidney beans, and cooked *mung* beans in large saucepan and cover with water. Bring to boil over medium-high heat, reduce to simmer 15 to 20 minutes.

2. Stir in drained sweet potatoes and salt and pepper to taste. Continue cooking 5 to 7 minutes, or until heated through. Remove from heat, add 1 tablespoon margarine or butter, and, using potato masher, mash all ingredients until smooth. Add more butter or margarine if necessary. Set aside, keep warm.

3. Prepare sauce: Heat 2 tablespoons oil in medium saucepan over medium-high heat. Add onions and **sauté** 3 to 5 minutes, or until soft. Stir in tomatoes, broth, and 1 teaspoon cayenne pepper or to taste, mix well. Bring to boil, reduce to simmer 5 to 7 minutes.

4. Place flour in small bowl, and **whisk** in coconut milk, a little at a time, mixing well to prevent clumping. Stir into onion-tomato mixture, mix well. Continue cooking 3 to 5 minutes, or until mixture is thickened, stirring frequently.

5. Transfer mashed peanut–bean mixture to serving bowl, and pour onion-tomato sauce over top.

Serve warm with flat bread for dipping.

Zambia

In south-central Africa, the landlocked nation of Zambia is surrounded by Angola, the Democratic Republic of the Congo, Tanzania, Malawi, Mozambique, Zimbabwe, Botswana, and Namibia. A British colony that was federated with Rhodesia at one time, Zambia became an independent country in 1964. Today the official language is English, which explains why many recipes have only English names.

Zambia has more than 70 ethnic groups—however, no single group is predominant. The majority of the population is Christian, most of whom are Roman Catholics.

The population of Zambia is divided almost equally between subsistence farmers and those who have left rural life to live in the modern cities. When Zambians move away from the farms that were passed down to them from previous generations, they give up their right to the land. They also give up kinship with the ethnic group of which they have been part. To take the place that kinship groups occupy in rural life, regional self-help societies have sprung up in cities to give people a place to turn in times of need.

Due to the high infant mortality rate, babies in Zambia are baptized soon after birth. Other than attending church for the ceremony, there is not much festivity. However, when children reach the age of nine or 10 and have their first communion, there is always a large communal celebration. Children by this time are on the road to a healthy life, and a celebration is in order.

When boys and girls reach puberty, they go through coming of age ceremonies. For boys, secret initiation ceremonies take them to a remote area to be circumcised and then to hunt and learn about the rituals and customs of their people. An important part of the girls' ceremony is instruction on being a wife and mother.

Before marriage, *lobola*—bride-price—is paid by a groom to the bride's father. Traditionally, *lobola* was paid in cattle, and, for those with no cattle, payment was made in the form of services performed by the groom. The payment is a form of insurance, meant to protect the bride from being badly treated by her husband. It can be returned to the husband's family if the wife finds cause to leave him, although that is rare.

Zambians do not ordinarily eat meat. Cattle are a form of wealth, and they are slaughtered only on important occasions such as weddings and funerals.

♩ Tigerfish with Mixed Greens

The Tigerfish, unique to Africa, are abundant throughout Zambia's rivers and lakes. The Tigerfish are similar to the South American piranha, which has razor sharp teeth and is an aggressive predator. During the coming of age rituals, young boys might be expected to catch, clean, and grill Tigerfish over an open fire. Forging for greens might be an added task assigned to the boys to complete the meal.

Yield: serves 4 to 6

2 tablespoons butter or margarine, more as needed

1 onion, **trimmed, finely chopped**

2 cloves garlic, trimmed, **minced**

14.5 ounces canned diced tomatoes

¼ pound kale, trimmed, **coarsely chopped**

¼ pound fresh spinach, trimmed, coarsely chopped

½ pound cabbage, trimmed, **cored**, finely chopped

4 to 6 (6 to 8 ounces *each*) skinless fish **fillets** (such as tilapia, sea bass, or red snapper)

juice of 1 lemon or 2 tablespoons lemon juice

For **garnish**:

¼ cup **slivered** almonds, more as needed

4 to 6 lemon wedges

Equipment: Medium saucepan with cover, mixing spoon, large skillet, spatula, fork, paper towel–covered baking sheet, large serving platter

1. Melt 2 tablespoons butter in saucepan over medium-high heat. Add onion and garlic, **sauté** 5 to 7 minutes or until soft. Stir in tomatoes, kale, spinach, and cabbage, and sauté additional 5 to 7 minutes or until cooked through. Set aside, cover, and keep warm.

2. Melt 2 tablespoons butter in skillet over medium-high heat. Add fish fillets, a few at a time, and cook on both sides, about 6 to 8 minutes, or until fish flakes easily when poked with fork. Transfer to paper towels to drain, keep warm. Continue cooking in batches until all fish are cooked through. Add more butter as needed to prevent sticking.

3. Prepare butter sauce: Melt 4 tablespoons butter in skillet over medium-low heat. Stir-in lemon juice, set aside.

4. Transfer onion-kale mixture to serving platter, place fish fillets side by side on top of onion-kale mixture. **Drizzle** butter sauce over top.

Serve warm with almonds sprinkled on top and garnished with lemon wedges.

♩ *Samp ye Dinawa* (Corn and Bean Mash)

Throughout the world, corn and beans are two crops commonly grown together. The beans return to the soil the nutrients taken out by the corn. Before harvesting, the corn is usually left on the stalk to dry. The hard kernels of either white or yellow corn are removed from the cob, pounded, and soaked for a couple of days in slaked lime or lye to break up the grain; the hull and germ are removed. What is left is sun dried and sold as **hominy**. When hominy is broken into fairly large pieces or is very coarsely ground, it's called "*samp*," or "pearl hominy." When finely ground, it's called "hominy grits" or simply "grits," a cereal beloved in the Southern United States. *Samp* is not easily available, and a good substitute for this recipe is canned hominy. *Samp ye dinawa* would be one of the many side dishes served with meat at a wedding feast or other life-cycle celebration.

Yield: serves 4 to 6

2 tablespoons vegetable oil

1 onion, **trimmed, finely chopped**

1 tomato, finely chopped

1 (14 ounces) canned **hominy**, drained (available at all supermarkets)

2 (14 ounces each) canned red beans

salt and pepper to taste

½ teaspoon **ground** red pepper, more or less to taste

Equipment: Large skillet with cover, mixing spoon

1. Heat oil in large skillet over medium-high heat. Add onion, stir, and **sauté** until soft, 3 to 5 minutes. Add tomatoes, stir, and cook until soft, 2 to 3 minutes. Add drained hominy, red beans with juice, salt and pepper to taste, and ½ teaspoon ground red pepper, more or less to taste.

2. Stir, reduce heat to **simmer**, cover, and cook for 12 to 15 minutes, to heat through and to blend flavors.

Serve as a side dish with meat.

♪ Lemon Grass Tea

Lemon grass grows throughout this region of Africa. Lemon grass tea is a popular refreshing drink for those who prefer something other than beer at celebration feasts.

Yield: serves 2

3 leaves of fresh **lemon grass**

2 cups boiling water

sugar to taste

Equipment: Teapot, spoon, strainer, cup

Put tea leaves in teapot and pour in boiling water. Leave to infuse for 3 minutes. If you wish to add sugar to taste, add it now. Stir and strain tea into cup.

Serve tea while hot, adding more sugar if necessary.

Zimbabwe

Zimbabwe is a landlocked country in south-central Africa surrounded by Botswana on the west, Mozambique on the east, South Africa on the south, and Zambia on the north. It was known as "Rhodesia" from 1895 to 1980. Today, the majority of the population is Christians, with the largest number belonging to the Roman Catholic Church. Most Zimbabweans combine local religions with Christianity. (See Protestant and Catholic Life-Cycle Rituals, page lxxiii, and African Life-Cycle Rituals, page lxvi.)

In Zimbabwe, indigenous religious beliefs about the spirits of ancestors are widely held. Ancestors, including recently deceased relatives, may speak to the living through human hosts. When these human hosts (or spirit mediums) enter a trance, they are thought to speak the words of the ancestor's spirit. The most important ancestors are great chiefs and storied warriors from centuries ago, and the mediums who are their living hosts hold a place of high status in society and are powerful and influential. The ancestor spirits are given attention and respect so that they will watch over and guard their descendants.

Weddings in Zimbabwe center around the bride-price. The Christian churches have discouraged bride-price; however, it is an ancient tradition that continues among all but the most sophisticated and educated urbanites. Two payments are involved. In years past, the *rutsambo* (the first payment) was simply a hoe (a garden tool)—but now it is usually a large cash payment, along with whatever else the future father-in-law requests. This might be anything from new clothes for his family to livestock. Once *rutsambo* is paid, the couple can live together as husband and wife. The second payment, *roora*, is usually delivered in installments; it may be cash or cattle. The husband is in no hurry to hand over the final payments until he is fully satisfied that his wife will fulfill all of her obligations.

When Zimbabwe President Robert Mugabe married in the early 1990s, the Roman Catholic Pope gave his blessing, well-wishers gave livestock, and dancers, dressed in animal skins, entertained the 6,000 guests. Wedding rings were exchanged, and the normally austere president sported red and white orchids on the lapel of his dark business suit. Among the wedding gifts were chickens, turkeys, and cattle. The Shona people gave pottery articles as part of the new bride's belongings.

The wedding feast included dozens of whole roasted steers (Zimbabwe is one of the world's great beef producers); game meat, such as crocodile, *kudu* (large antelope), and impala; caldrons of rice; bean stews; vegetable stews made with tomatoes; *courgettes* (zucchini); corn on the cob; mixed greens; and a large quantity of tropical fruits, such as papayas, mangos, and bananas. Most people drank beer or a nonalcoholic drink called *shandy*, made with ginger beer, a few drops of angostura bitters, and soda water. Some preferred *rock shandy* made with lemonade, soda water, and angostura bitters. Both drinks are served over ice.

✧ *Sadza ne Muriwo* (Vegetable Sauce with Cornmeal Porridge)

A wedding feast in Zimbabwe traditionally includes *sadza*—corn porridge—the same as *putu* (recipe page 77). When eaten with a sauce of vegetables or beans, it is called *sadza ne muriwo*.

Yield: serves 4

putu (recipe page 77)

2 tablespoons vegetable oil

1 onion, **trimmed, finely chopped**

3 tomatoes, finely chopped or 16 ounces canned stewed tomatoes

salt and pepper to taste

4 cups (about 1 pound) shredded cabbage

Equipment: Medium saucepan with cover, mixing spoon, serving bowl

1. Prepare *putu* (recipe page 77), and keep warm.

2. Heat oil in medium saucepan over medium-high heat. Add onion, stir, and **sauté** until soft, 3 to 5 minutes. Add finely chopped or stewed tomatoes, salt and pepper to taste, and shredded cabbage. Toss to mix, and bring to boil. Reduce heat to **simmer**, cover, and cook for 12 to 15 minutes, or until cabbage is tender.

Serve as a side dish with putu *in a separate serving bowl. To eat, take a handful of* putu *in your right hand, form it in a ball, and use it to scoop up a little vegetable mixture to put into your mouth. The left hand must never touch food; it is used only for personal grooming.*

❧ *Sebete se Halikiloeng with Morogo* (Liver with Creamed Spinach)

Sebete se halikiloeng with morogo is a satisfying dish to prepare and serve family and friends when they partake of the funeral feast. *Morogo*, grown throughout Africa, is a leafy green vegetable similar to spinach. We suggest using more readily available spinach.

Yield: serves 4 to 6

1 pound calves liver, cut into bite-size chunks

Morogo:

16-ounce bag fresh spinach

¼ cup water

2 tablespoon vegetable oil, more as needed

6 tablespoons heavy cream

2 tablespoons butter or margarine, more as needed

salt and pepper to taste

Equipment: Fork, large skillet with cover, large saucepan, mixing spoon

1. Place liver pieces on clean work surface, and, using fork, prick each piece several times.

2. Heat 2 tablespoons oil in skillet over medium-high heat. Add liver, and cook on all sides 10 to 15 minutes or until cooked through. Add more oil if necessary to prevent sticking. Remove from heat, cover, and keep warm.

3. Prepare morogo: Place spinach and water in saucepan, cook over medium-high heat 3 to 5 minutes, or until spinach is wilted.

4. Stir in heavy cream and 2 tablespoons butter or margarine, more as needed. Simmer until liquid is absorbed. Add salt and pepper to taste.

Serve warm in individual bowls with liver over morogo.

♪ *Dovi* (Beef Stew in Peanut Butter Sauce)

For Zimbabwean wedding and funeral feasts—to make sure there is plenty for everyone—dozens of side dishes, sauces, and stews are prepared to eat along with the roasted meat. One of the most popular stews is *dovi*.

Yield: serves 4 to 6

2 tablespoons vegetable oil

2 onions, **trimmed, finely chopped**

2 cloves garlic, trimmed, **minced**

2 green bell peppers, trimmed, **seeded,** chopped

2 pounds lean beef, **cubed**

4 tomatoes, chopped, or 16 ounces canned chopped tomatoes

2 cups water

½ cup smooth peanut butter

salt and pepper to taste

ground red pepper to taste

1 package (10 ounces) spinach or other greens, fresh or frozen (cooked according to directions on package), keep warm, for serving

Equipment: Large saucepan with cover or **Dutch oven**, mixing spoon, serving bowl

1. Heat oil in large saucepan or Dutch oven over medium-high heat. Add onions and garlic, stir, and **sauté** until onions are soft, 3 to 5 minutes. Add green pepper, cubed beef, fresh or canned tomatoes, and water. Bring to boil and stir. Reduce heat to **simmer**, cover, and cook until beef is tender, 35 to 45 minutes.

2. Thin peanut butter with about ½ cup hot liquid from pan until mixture has consistency of pancake batter. Stir in half peanut butter mixture to meat mixture. Add salt and pepper to taste and ground red pepper to taste. Continue to cook uncovered, until sauce thickens, 20 to 25 minutes.

3. Transfer cooked spinach or greens to serving bowl, and pour remaining half of peanut butter mixture over them.

Serve dovi *in one bowl and spinach or greens in another. The greens and meat stew are eaten together. Using the fingers of your right hand, take a little meat mixture and then greens at the same time, and pop into your mouth. The left hand must never touch food; it is used only for personal grooming.*

ASIA AND THE SOUTH PACIFIC

Russia

Kazakhstan

Mongolia

North Korea

Uzbekistan

Kyrgyzstan

Turkmenistan

Tajikistan

China

South Korea

Japan

Afghanistan

Pakistan

Nepal

Bhutan

Myanmar

Taiwan

India

Bangladesh

Laos

Philippines

Thailand

Vietnam

Cambodia

Sri Lanka

Malaysia

Brunei

Papua New Guinea

Singapore

Indonesia

Fiji

Pacific Ocean

Indian Ocean

Australia

New Zealand

N

2

Asia and the South Pacific

ASIA

Asia is a vast region of the world where many of the major religions of the modern world evolved. (See Religious Life-Cycle Rituals and Customs, page lxv.) From birth through death, most Asian cultures continue rituals and customs that have remained unchanged for centuries. Today, however, signs of change between ancient and modern ways appear everywhere. As the Asian nations and territories move into the future, they are plagued with such problems as scarce resources and exploding population growth.

In most Asian countries, rice is a symbol of life and fertility, and it figures strongly in many rituals. (The Western ritual of throwing rice at newlyweds, for example, is inherited from India.) Special rituals and prayers are said at the time rice is planted and again when it is harvested. In China. it is bad luck to overturn a bowl of rice and to have a bad experience might be referred to as "breaking one's rice bowl." In some Asian countries, rice is placed on the family altar and dedicated to the ancestors as a symbol of thanksgiving for a fruitful previous year and a desire for a successful coming year.

Afghanistan

Afghanistan is a mountainous country that is split from east to west by the Hindu Kush mountain range, which has peaks as high as 24,000 feet. It is bordered on the north by Turkmenistan, Tajikistan, and Uzbekistan; on the northeast by China; on the south and east by Pakistan; and on the west by Iran.

Afghanistan's population, consisting of hundreds of different ethnic groups, has one common bond: the Islamic religion. (See Islam and Islamic Life-Cycle Rituals, page lxxvi.) The majority of Afghans are Muslims. Currently, Afghanistan has undergone years of war and is working to rebuild after overthrowing the Taliban regime.

Family structure is often considered the backbone of Afghan society, and it is the custom, among both villagers and nomads, for several generations of family to live together. The head of the household is the oldest man, or patriarch. In the villages, families generally live in mud brick houses or in a walled compound containing several such houses. The same family structure is common among the nomads, except that black wool tents replace the mud brick structures.

In Afghanistan, as in other Islamic countries, the birth of a son is celebrated with festivities. An important event in a young boy's life is his circumcision, which takes place between the ages of five and 10. A feast is part of the circumcision celebration.

In Afghanistan, men and women attending a wedding celebrate in separate quarters or even different locations. In southeastern Afghanistan, the *pashai* (farmers) men often perform a traditional wedding dance, accompanied by musicians playing the *zuma* (oboe) and the *dûl* (doubleheaded drum), ancient instruments unique to the region. A whole lamb or two might be roasted for the wedding feast, or the male guests might be served *kebabs* (recipe page 48). Everything is put on the table at one time. Vegetable dishes are important at every meal. Bowls of *chaka* (recipe page 126) are set out to drizzle in soup, smear on bread, or pour over vegetables.

ৡ *Naan* (Afghan Teardrop-shaped Bread)

Great quantities of bread are usually eaten at each meal. Afghan *naan* is famous, and while the small breads (this recipe) are usually made at home, large breads, 16 to 18 inches long, are made in bakeries.

Yield: makes 6

4 cups all-purpose flour	1 teaspoon sugar
½ teaspoon salt	2 eggs
1 tablespoon baking powder	1 cup milk
¼ teaspoon baking soda	

Equipment: Large mixing bowl, mixing spoon, lightly floured work surface, 2 nonstick baking sheets, oven mitts, heatproof surface

1. Prepare dough: Put flour, salt, baking powder, baking soda, and sugar in large mixing bowl. Stir with a mixing spoon (or use your fingers) until well mixed. Make well (hole) in center of mixture, and drop in eggs, stirring them into flour. Slowly stir in milk, and stir constantly until all ingredients are well combined.

2. Transfer dough to lightly floured work surface. Sprinkle flour on hands, and work surface. **Knead** dough for about 10 minutes, or until it is smooth and can be gathered in a soft ball; sprinkle more flour on your hands and work surface as needed from time to time.

3. Lightly grease large mixing bowl, and place ball of dough inside, turning ball over to coat all sides. Cover bowl with plastic wrap, and let dough rest in warm, draft-free place for about 3 hours.

Preheat oven to 450°F.

Put 2 nonstick baking sheets into the oven to get them hot.

4. Prepare for baking: Divide dough into 6 equal portions. Lightly oil or butter your hands. Place one portion of dough on lightly floured work surface. Using your hand, flatten into teardrop shape, about 6 inches long by 3½ inches wide at base and tapered at top. Repeat making remaining portions of dough.

6. Using oven mitts, carefully remove preheated baking sheets from oven and place on heat-proof surface. Place breads side by side on pans, and bake in oven for 6 minutes, until firm to touch.

7. Remove from oven. Change oven temperature to broiler heat. Place pans, one at a time, on top rack under broiler to lightly brown tops of breads, 2 to 3 minutes.

Serve breads hot or at room temperature.

Khoresht-e Seib (Chicken Stew with Apples and Dried Fruit)

Circumcision is a special event for young boys in Afghanistan. The parents throw a large party on this day with feasting and celebration. *Khoresht-e Seib* is ideal to serve on this day.

Yield: serves 4 to 6

6 saffron threads

2½ cups hot water

2 tablespoons vegetable oil or *ghee* (available at international markets), more as needed

2 onions, **trimmed, finely chopped**

1 pound skinless, boneless chicken breast or thighs, cut into about 2-inch chunks

½ teaspoon cinnamon

juice of 1 lime or 2 tablespoons lime juice, more as needed

3 tablespoons brown sugar, more as needed

5 green cooking apples, trimmed, peeled, **cored, coarsely chopped**

1 cup **pitted**, dried tart cherries (available at most supermarkets or international markets)

salt and pepper to taste

For serving: 3 cups cooked rice (cooked according to directions on package)

Equipment: Small bowl, mixing spoon, large saucepan, large ovenproof baking dish with cover, large skillet, oven mitts

Preheat oven to 350°F.

1. In small bowl, stirring constantly, dissolve saffron in hot water, set aside.

2. Heat 2 tablespoons oil or *ghee* in saucepan over medium-high heat. Add onions and **sauté** 3 to 5 minutes, or until soft. Add chicken chunks, and sauté 12 to 15 minutes, or until golden brown on all sides. Add more oil or *ghee* if needed to prevent sticking.

3. Add saffron water, cinnamon, lime juice, and brown sugar, mix well. Transfer chicken mixture to ovenproof baking dish, set aside.

4. Heat 2 tablespoons oil in skillet over medium-high heat. Add apples and sauté 12 to 15 minutes or until golden on all sides, stirring frequently. Transfer to baking dish, arranging apples over chicken.

5. Sprinkle top with cherries, cover, and bake 25 to 30 minutes, or until chicken and apples are tender. Test **chicken doneness**. Carefully remove from oven using oven mitts.

6. Mixture should taste sweet and sour. Taste, and adjust flavor by adding lime juice or sugar if needed. Add salt and pepper to taste.

Serve warm over rice.

♪ *Chaka* (Afghan Yogurt Sauce)

At an Afghan feast, all the food is set out and eaten at the same time; there are no separate courses. The food is put out on low trays, and everyone sits around on the beautiful carpets that the Afghan craftsmen are famous for. Tea is the favorite drink.

If Afghanistan has a national dish, it is probably *chaka,* which is spread over everything they eat. A bowl of *chaka* is usually set out on the table.

Yield: about 1 cup

1 cup plain yogurt

3 cloves garlic, **trimmed, minced**

2 tablespoons **finely chopped** fresh mint, divided

salt to taste

Equipment: Small bowl, mixing spoon

Put yogurt into small bowl. Add garlic, 1 tablespoon chopped mint, and salt to taste. Stir to mix. Cover and refrigerate. Sprinkle the remaining 1 tablespoon of chopped mint on top.

To serve, place the bowl on the table. Each person can either add a dollop to their soup, use as a sauce for meat or fish dishes, or take as a dip for fresh vegetables.

♪ *Sheer Payra* (Cardamom Double Nut Fudge)

Sweets are welcomed for any social gatherings. A wedding celebration would not be complete without *sheer payra*. Cardamom is eaten to symbolize sweet joy for the years to come.

Yield: serves 8 to 10

⅔ cup milk	2 tablespoons butter
2 cups sugar	½ teaspoon ground cardamom
2 tablespoons light corn syrup	¼ cup pistachio nuts, **finely chopped**
¼ teaspoon salt	¼ cup walnuts, finely chopped

Equipment: Large saucepan, rubber spatula, **candy thermometer**, nonstick or greased medium baking pan

1. In saucepan over medium-high heat, add milk, sugar, corn syrup, and salt. Stirring constantly, cook 5 minutes, or until candy thermometer reads 240°F. Remove from heat, stir in butter, and let cool to 120°F.

2. Add cardamom, mix well. **Fold in** pistachios and walnuts. Transfer to baking pan, and use spatula to evenly spread over bottom. Let cool 1 hour, or until hardened. Cut into 1-inch squares.

Serve as a sweet treat for a wedding celebration or other joyous occasions.

Bangladesh

On the northern coast of the Bay of Bengal, Bangladesh is surrounded by India except for a small border with Myanmar (Burma). It is a low-lying land of many rivers.

The majority of people living in Bangladesh are Muslim, while the remaining population are mostly Hindu. Bangladesh struggles with overpopulation and a weak economy and is often inundated by tropical cyclones, monsoons, floods, and tidal waves. Many Bangladeshis live in rural areas, chiefly in small villages, and most Bangladeshis place importance on religion, prayer, family, and life-cycle celebrations. Among the Muslim majority, Islam dominates social, political, and religious life, and all life-cycle rituals are done according to Islamic law. (See Islam and Islamic Life-Cycle Rituals, page lxxvi.) The Hindus of Bangladesh follow many of the same rituals and customs as neighboring India. (See Hindu Life-cycle page lxxix.)

Both Muslim and Hindu Bangladeshis generally put great importance on having a male child. Only a son can continue the family line, and a Hindu son brings a dowry. Muslim men have traditionally followed the Persian system of paying a bride-price, but the Hindu dowry system is becoming popular among Muslims. Also, in the Hindu culture, only a son can perform the funeral rites that will ensure his father's soul safe passage into the afterlife.

Rice, the chief agricultural product of Bangladesh, and fish are the most popular foods for Bangladeshis, and tea is the most popular drink. (Alcoholic beverages are forbidden according to Islamic law.) Many different rice and fish dishes are served at wedding banquets, along with great quantities of sweets.

Both Muslim and Hindu parents choose their children's marriage partners. Muslims consult a religious person for an auspicious wedding day, and Hindus call upon an astrologer. Both Muslim and Hindu brides attend a *mehndi* ceremony before the wedding, in which henna is painted on their hands and feet.

☙ *Bhapa Chingri* (Steamed Shrimp with Mustard and Green Chilies)

Bhapa chingri is a tasty little dish served prior to the main course at a Hindi or Muslim wedding banquet.

Yield: serves 4 to 6

2 teaspoons yellow mustard powder

½ teaspoon **ground** turmeric

½ teaspoon cayenne pepper, or to taste

2 green Thai chilies, **trimmed, finely chopped**

¼ cup finely chopped onion

2 tablespoons olive oil

1 tablespoon water, more as needed

1pound medium-size shrimp, peeled, **deveined**

salt and pepper to taste

For serving:

2 to 3 cups white rice (cooked according to directions on package)

For **garnish:** ¼ cup shredded coconut

Equipment: Medium mixing bowl, mixing spoon, tongs, **steamer pan** or **basket** with cover

1. Place mustard powder, ground turmeric, cayenne pepper, chilies, onion, olive oil, and 1 tablespoon water in mixing bowl, mix well. Add shrimp, using tongs, toss to coat well. Add salt and pepper to taste.

2. Fill steamer pan ⅓ full with water. Bring water to boil over high heat.

3. Transfer shrimp mixture to steamer basket, and place over steamer pan. Cover and cook 8 to 10 minutes, or until shrimp are opaque white.

Serve warm over rice with coconut sprinkled on top.

☙ *Kedgeree* (Yellow Rice with Smoked Haddock or Fresh Fish)

Kedgeree is a Bangladeshi dish the English made popular while the region was under British colonial rule. For this *kedgeree* recipe, you can either add the *finnan haddie* after it is prepared according to the following recipe, or you can use more easily available fresh salmon, cod, or other firm skinless fish **fillets.** In India, yellow *kedgeree* is an ideal dish for occasions such as weddings. The eggs are symbolic of fertility, and the yellow turmeric symbolizes richness and good fortune.

Yield: serves 4 to 6

½ cup butter or margarine

1 pound fresh skinless fish **fillet**, cut into bite-size pieces

1 cup heavy cream

1 teaspoon **ground** turmeric

4 cups cooked rice (cooked according to directions on package)

4 hard-cooked eggs, shelled, chopped

¼ cup chopped parsley

salt and pepper to taste

For **garnish**: 1 lemon, cut into wedges

Equipment: Medium saucepan, mixing spoon, salad spoon and fork

1. Melt butter or margarine in medium saucepan over medium-high heat. Stir constantly, add fish chunks and **sauté** until **opaque** and cooked through, 3 to 5 minutes.

2. Stir in cream and turmeric. Cook until small bubbles appear around edge of pan. Reduce to **simmer**, add cooked rice, chopped eggs, parsley, and salt and pepper to taste. Gently toss to mix, using salad spoon and fork, and cook until heated through, 5 to 8 minutes.

To serve, pile kedgeree into a large serving bowl, and garnish with wedges of lemon around the edge. Sprinkle lemon juice on each serving.

✺ *Brindaboni* (Snow Peas and Sweet Potatoes)

Weddings are generally big, noisy affairs with great quantities of food. During traditional Muslim weddings, the women and men celebrate in separate quarters. At the Muslim wedding feast, *brindaboni* is a very popular dish, often served as one of many side dishes with roasted lamb or goat. When made with **snow peas**, sweet potatoes, and the unusual blend of spices, *brindaboni* becomes a very flavorful vegetarian dish for a Hindu wedding banquet.

Yield: serve 4 to 6

2 tablespoons vegetable oil

1 teaspoon **ground** cumin

1 teaspoon ground **coriander**

1 teaspoon ground turmeric

2 bay leaves

2 sweet potatoes, peeled, thinly sliced

½ pound **snow peas, trimmed**, sliced crosswise in half

Equipment: Large skillet with cover, wooden mixing spoon

1. Heat oil in large skillet over medium-high heat. Add cumin, coriander, turmeric, and bay leaves. Stir and cook for about 1 minute to develop the flavors. Add sweet potato slices, and toss to coat. Pour in water, and bring to a boil. Reduce heat to **simmer**, cover, and cook for 10 to 12 minutes, or until tender but not mushy.

2. Add snow peas, gently toss to mix, cover, and simmer for 3 to 5 minutes, or until heated through. Remove and discard bay leaves.

To serve, transfer to serving platter, and serve as a side dish with lamb, rice, and other vegetable dishes.

♪ *Shemai* (Sweet Vermicelli)

Sweets are an important part of joyous occasions in Bangladesh. A bowlful of *shemai* is the perfect ending to a wedding feast.

Yield: serves 4 to 6

8 tablespoons butter

2 cups fine vermicelli (available at Asian markets)

4 cups milk

3 tablespoons sugar

½ teaspoon cinnamon

½ cup raisins

¼ cup **slivered** almonds

1 pint heavy cream

Equipment: Medium saucepan, mixing spoon, serving bowl with cover or plastic wrap

1. Melt butter in saucepan over medium-low heat. Crumble in vermicelli, reduce heat to low, and, stirring constantly, cook 3 to 5 minutes, or until vermicelli is soft.

2. Stir in milk, and bring to boil over medium heat. Add sugar, cinnamon, raisins, and almonds, mix well. Reduce to low heat, and continue cooking 8 to 10 minutes, stirring frequently.

3. Stir in heavy cream, and continue cooking 3 to 5 minutes, or until heated through.

4. Remove from heat, transfer to serving bowl, cover, cool to room temperature, and refrigerate 30 minutes, or until ready to serve.

Serve chilled in individual bowls as a sweet treat at the end of a wedding celebration.

Bhutan

The Himalayan kingdom of Bhutan has been isolated for most of its history both by geography and by choice. The country transitioned to a constitutional monarchy in 2008, electing their leader the Druk Phuensum Tshogpa for the first time ever. Most Bhutanese are followers of Buddhism. (See Buddhism and Buddhist Life-Cycle Rituals, page lxxxii. Bhutan also has a minority population of Hindus.

Although more than a dozen native languages are spoken in this tiny country (which is only a little larger than Pennsylvania), English, the official working language, is taught in schools. Communities are clustered in fertile valleys around gigantic monasteries (*dzongs*), which can be four or five stories high. The *dzongs* are central to each town, and for centuries have served as administrative as well as religious centers. Community celebrations and festivals take place in and around the *dzong*.

Bhutan has no set rules about marriage, and polygamy is acceptable. Bhutanese Buddhists have no one ritual for weddings. Though an auspicious wedding date is usually selected by an astrologer, Bhutanese are not particularly rigid about the calendar, and they might latch on to one auspicious date, making the event several days long.

In Bhutan, marriages are traditionally prearranged by the couple's parents. Everyone in the community is generally expected to attend the wedding ceremony, which can be held in the home or in a Buddhist temple. The bride and groom wear new clothes; symbolic of a new beginning. An important part of wedding rituals is the white ceremonial scarf (*chata*). The person officiating puts a *chata* around the shoulders of the couple as they sit on meditation cushions. The meaning of marriage is then discussed: kindness, consideration, and affection toward each other. Many couples prepare an offering tray that contains items vital to life: a bowl with three fruits (usually a pear, apple, and orange); three jewels that represent the three jewels of Buddhism (the teacher [*Buddha*], teaching [*dharma*], and spiritual community [*sangha*]); burning incense (an offering to Buddha as well as a purifier); a piece of silk brocade cloth that represents a precious possession; two carefully folded *chatas* (one from each person, considered to be symbols of good luck); flowers; and an envelope with money. At the end of the service, the couple toast each other with fruit juice that has been provided for the occasion. As the newlyweds leave the temple, the guests shower them with rice (*chaamal*), symbolically sprinkling good wishes over them. Depending upon the family's wealth, a wedding feast may be provided for guests.

⚘ *Ema Datshi* (Fiery Chili Pepper and Cheese Stew)

Ema datshi is a national dish of Bhutan. Chillies are not a seasoning in Bhutan but rather a valuable vegetable. Therefore, traditional Bhutanese food is lavishly spiced with dried or fresh, red and green chillies. This is a spicy stew, and, although the Bhutanese would use the entire chili pepper, we suggest seeding the peppers. *Ema datshi* is often eaten with white or **red rice**. This dish is a must-have at any life cycle celebration in Bhutan.

Yield: serves 4 to 6

2 tablespoons vegetable oil	14.5 ounces canned diced tomatoes
1 onion, **trimmed,** thinly sliced	½ pound feta cheese, cubed
5 cloves garlic, trimmed, **minced**	For garnish: ½ cup **finely chopped cilantro**
½ pound chili peppers (**jalapeno** or Thai green peppers), trimmed, **seeded, julienned**	For serving: 2 to 3 cups rice (white or red rice, cooked according to directions on package)
4 cups water	

Equipment: Medium saucepan with cover, mixing spoon

1. Heat oil in saucepan over medium-high heat. Add onions and garlic, **sauté** 3 to 5 minutes, or until soft. Stir in chili peppers and water, mix well. Bring to boil over high heat, reduce to simmer 8 to 10 minutes.

2. Stir in tomatoes and cheese, simmer additional 4 to 6 minutes, or until mixture is heated through.

Serve warm over rice garnished with cilantro.

⚜ Masala (Spice Blend)

Masala can be a simple or very complex blend of spices, depending upon the cook and the dish being prepared. For this recipe, the blend is very simple.

Yield: serves 4

1 teaspoon poppy seeds

1 teaspoon **finely chopped** fresh ginger or **ground** ginger

1 tablespoon ground **coriander**

1 tablespoon **coarsely chopped** almonds

1 teaspoon ground cloves

Equipment: **Mortar and pestle**

Combine poppy seeds, finely chopped fresh ginger or ground ginger, ground coriander, coarsely chopped almonds, and ground cloves in mortar, and, using the pestle, press down on the spices to grind them together.

⚜ Paneer dhuai Kari (Fried Cheese with Yogurt Curry Sauce)

Use *paneer kari* immediately, or transfer to a small jar, cover tightly, and refrigerate to use in recipes calling for *masala*.

4 tablespoons vegetable oil, divided

paneer tikki (firm cheese) (recipe page 182), cut into ¼-inch squares

1 onion, **trimmed, finely chopped**

2 cloves garlic, trimmed, **minced**

½ teaspoon finely chopped fresh ginger or **ground** ginger

masala (recipe precedes)

3 tablespoons unsweetened **shredded** coconut, homemade or available at most supermarkets and Asian food stores

1 cup plain yogurt

½ cup water

salt and ground red pepper to taste

For **garnish**: 5 or 6 sprigs fresh mint, finely chopped

Equipment: Large skillet, slotted mixing spoon, plate

1. Heat 2 tablespoons oil in large skillet over medium-high heat. Add cheese cubes, in batches. Reduce heat to medium, and fry until golden, 10 to 12 minutes. Remove with slotted mixing spoon, and set on plate. Add remaining 2 tablespoons oil to skillet, and **sauté** onions over medium heat until soft and all sides are golden, 3 to 5 minutes. Add garlic, ginger, *masala*, and coconut. Reduce heat to low, stir constantly, and cook for about 2 minutes for flavors to develop.

2. Stir in yogurt and water to make smooth, creamy sauce. Add salt and ground red pepper to taste. Add fried cheese, and gently toss to coat. Cook until heated through, 3 to 5 minutes.

To serve, garnish with chopped fresh mint, and eat either hot or at room temperature. Use poppadums or other flatbread to scoop the cheese cubes out of the bowl.

Cambodia and Laos

Cambodia and neighboring Laos are located on the Indochinese peninsula of South East Asia, between Thailand and Vietnam. The people in both countries have suffered from many years of oppression and wars, which have left them mostly impoverished. As a result, the people, who are mostly farmers, can barely eke out a living. The majority of people in both countries follow the teachings of Buddha and celebrate life-cycle events accordingly. (See Buddhism and Buddhist Life-Cycle Rituals, page lxxxii.)

In Cambodia, it is customary for an engaged couple to exchange gifts. Among the gifts is a box of **betel nuts** from the future groom to his bride-to-be. When she accepts the betel nuts, it seals their commitment to marry. Once engaged, the groom accepts his responsibilities to his in-laws by taking a vow of servitude, known as *thvo bamro. Thvo bamro* can last from one month to two years, during which the groom works for his future in-laws. If he shows disrespect, complains, or fails to impress them, they can cancel the engagement.

Many city weddings follow Western customs, and couples choose their own partners. In the country, however, parents still choose their children's marriage partners. Each family appoints a marriage broker to investigate the other family and to make certain that their social and economic standing is good. Once the two families agree to the marriage, they consult an astrologer to select the wedding day, and exchange gifts, food, and plants.

The wedding ceremony takes place in the bride's home, where wedding rings and gifts are exchanged. The couple's wrists are tied together with red thread that has been soaked in holy water. The Buddhist priest delivers a sermon, and married guests pass around a candle to bless the newlyweds. After the ceremony, there is a grand feast with traditional music.

In Laos, the naming ceremony (*baci*) of a newborn baby is the first big event in a person's life. The celebration feast is held for family members, friends, and neighbors or the entire village, depending upon the family's wealth. During the celebration, money is tied to the baby's arm with red string. A Buddhist monk is asked to choose a name for the child, one that is astrologically correct for that child.

Boys go through a coming of age ceremony around the age of 13. Only close relatives are invited to the ceremony, which involves cutting the boy's hair. In some areas, a boy receives a tattoo to symbolize his manhood that is also supposed to ward off evil spirits.

In both Laos and Cambodia, the most important life-cycle event is the funeral. A Buddhist funeral is generally regarded as a festive occasion, since it represents the rebirth of the soul rather than the end of life. In both countries, the body can be cremated in an elaborate ceremony, depending upon the wealth of the family. After the body is washed and dressed, it is placed in a coffin. In Cambodia, the body is transported to a public crematorium to be burned. In Laos, the body is placed in a shelter in the garden or yard. The family holds a series of feasts and ceremonies before the body is taken to a cremation pyre on a river bank or to a field where it is washed, exposed to the sky, and then cremated. Family members traditionally show their grief by wearing white clothing and shaving their heads.

♘ Sweet and Sour Soup

Yield: serves 6 to 8

Rice is the mainstay of both the Laos and Cambodian diet, and no meal is complete unless rice is on the table. Soups are eaten with the meal.

2 quarts chicken broth

½ pound boneless chicken breasts or thighs, finely sliced

1 cup fresh pineapple, peeled, **cored, finely chopped**

1 tomato, **trimmed, coarsely chopped**

1½ cups zucchini, cut in half lengthwise and sliced crosswise ¼ inch thick

3 tablespoons white vinegar

3 tablespoons fish sauce (*nuoc mam*) *homemade* or available at Asian food stores

1 teaspoon sugar

½ pound headless medium **shrimp, peeled and deveined**

salt and pepper to taste

Equipment: Large saucepan, wooden mixing spoon

1. Pour chicken broth into large saucepan, add chicken, pineapple, tomato, zucchini, vinegar, fish sauce, and sugar. Bring to boil over medium-high heat. Stir, reduce heat to simmer, cover, and cook 1 hour.

2. Add shrimp, stir, and cook until shrimp are cooked through and **opaque** white. Add salt and pepper to taste.

To serve the soup, transfer to large serving bowl and have guests help themselves by pouring their serving into an individual bowl, which they pick up and drink. The shrimp and vegetables can be picked out of the bowl with the hand or a spoon.

♘ Mawk Mak Phet (Stuffed Chili Peppers)

Mawk mak phet is a quick, easy dish to prepare for any life cycle celebration feast. Banana leaves would be used in Cambodia or Laos; however, we suggest using more readily available aluminum foil.

Yield: serves 6 to 8

6 to 8 poblano peppers

3 to 4 (5 to 6 ounces *each*) skinless fish **fillets** (such as tilapia, red snapper, or sea bass)

water, as needed

½ cup white rice (cooked according to directions on package)

4 green onions, **trimmed, finely chopped**

2 cloves garlic, trimmed, **minced**

1 tablespoon fish sauce, homemade or available at Asian food stores

1 teaspoon ginger root, trimmed, **grated**

juice of 1 lemon or 1 tablespoon lemon juice

For serving: 6 to 8 lemon wedges

Equipment: Cutting board, sharp knife, medium saucepan, fork, slotted spoon or **skimmer**, **colander** or strainer, medium mixing bowl, mixing spoon, 6 to 8 (8×8-inch) aluminum foil squares, **steamer pan** or **basket**, metal tongs

1. Place poblano pepper on cutting board, and, using knife, slice each chili from stem to tip. (Be sure not to cut completely through pepper.) Remove and discard top, seeds, and membrane. Continue until all poblano peppers are trimmed and seeded. Set peppers aside.

2. Fill saucepan ½ full with water. Bring to boil over high heat. Carefully add fish fillets, and **poach** 4 to 7 minutes, or until fish is cooked through and flakes easily when poked with fork. Using slotted spoon or skimmer, remove fillets, and place in colander or strainer to drain. Discard cooking liquid. When fish is cool enough to handle, place in mixing bowl and flake with fork.

3. In mixing bowl, add cooked rice, onions, garlic, fish sauce, ginger root, and lemon juice to cooked fish, mix well.

4. Spoon mixture into poblano pepper, place pepper on aluminum square and roll up to seal securely. Continue until all peppers are stuffed and wrapped.

5. Fill steamer pan ⅓ full with water, and bring to boil over high heat. Place foil packages in steamer pan, and steam 20 to 25 minutes, or until peppers are tender and heated through. Add more water if necessary to prevent drying out. Use metal tongs to remove from steamer.

Serve each person a package with lemon for garnish. Each person will open foil and eat directly from package.

⚘ *Njum* (Bamboo Shoot Salad)

Njum is an easy to make Laotian salad that is more like a condiment. It is eaten with rice and meat dishes.

Yield: serves 4

2½ cups canned sliced bamboo shoots, drained, **blanched** (available at supermarkets)

1 clove garlic, **trimmed, minced**

1 tablespoon lime or lemon juice

1 tablespoon sugar

1 tablespoon fish sauce, homemade or available at Asian food stores

1 cup coconut milk, homemade (recipe page 225) or canned

3 green onions, **trimmed**, finely sliced

1 tablespoon **finely chopped** fresh basil

1 tablespoon finely chopped fresh mint

dried red pepper flakes, to taste

salt and pepper to taste

Equipment: Medium salad bowl, mixing spoon, small bowl, plastic food wrap

1. Put blanched bamboo shoots in medium salad bowl.
2. Prepare dressing: In small bowl, combine garlic, lime or lemon juice, sugar, fish sauce, and coconut milk. Pour dressing over bamboo shoots. Sprinkle green onions, basil, and mint over top, and toss to mix well. Cover with plastic wrap, and refrigerate until ready to serve.

To serve, put salad on table, and eat as a condiment with other dishes for the wedding feast.

China and Taiwan

The People's Republic of China in southern Asia has the largest population in the world. Taiwan, an island off the coast of China, was a Chinese province until 1895, when it was captured by Japan. Taiwan was returned to China in 1945, until nationalists, fleeing Communist rule in China, set up a separate government in Taiwan. Today, life-cycle events are still important in both countries, though many rituals are no longer performed or are done in moderation in mainland China, which is a Communist regime. Although officially atheist, China retains elements of its traditional religions—Confucianism, Taoism, and Buddhism

To most Chinese, food and friendship are inseparable, and any gathering without food is considered incomplete. Weddings, birthdays, funerals, holidays, and public ceremonies are celebrated with appropriate feasting. The more important the event, the more dishes are prepared for the occasion. The preparation of food holds special meaning; for instance, if fish is served, it is always the whole fish, including the head, to symbolize unity and togetherness. Red is the color of happiness, and many foods are colored red. Soups are usually served with a meal, and to serve shark fin soup is a symbol of status and wealth.

Noodles are a symbol of longevity, and they are served at all birthday celebrations, which are celebrated on New Year's Day, not the date of birth. The older the person is, the longer the noodles; sometimes they can reach 30 inches in length. In Northern China, on a woman's 66th birthday, her oldest daughter is expected to prepare 66 tiny dumplings for her mother. The dumplings can be stuffed with meat or other stuffings, such as *jien dui* (red bean paste), *buchu mandoo* (finely chopped vegetables), and *hom soi gok* (pork, shrimp, bamboo shoots, and mushrooms).

In Taiwan, traces of centuries-old Chinese wedding rituals are still included in modern-day weddings. The groom's *pinjin* ("bride's wealth") is often used by the bride-to-be to buy her trousseau, as well as furnishings for the home the newlyweds plan to share. In both mainland China and Taiwan, the wedding date is chosen from the Chinese almanac that coincides with the eighth month of *Zhong Qiu Jie*, the period of time in which the "moon is at its fullest and the flowers at their best." Cakes and sweets, such as peanut brittle or toffee, wrapped in red paper, are sent to friends and relatives to inform them of the forthcoming wedding.

An old ritual, performed more often in Taiwan than in mainland China, is the wedding tea ceremony held at the bride's future in-laws' home. According to traditional Chinese wedding rituals, the tea ceremony formalizes the marriage. All relatives from both families are expected to be present. During the ceremony, both the bridegroom and bride offer each parent a cup of tea; if, for instance, the future mother-in-law refuses to accept the cup of tea from her daughter-in-law-to-be, this means she refuses to accept her into the family.

In mainland China, funerals are family affairs, conducted by the eldest son. In Taiwan, the Taoist priest presides over the rituals. In both Taiwan and China, the body of the deceased is cremated. The casket is decorated with paper flowers, and paper money is burned with the body. After incense and ceremonial candles are burned, fireworks are shot off, which, according to tradition, intimidates evil spirits.

ৼ *Pei-ching-k'ao-ya* (Peking Duck)

The most important dish for special occasions in China or Taiwan is Peking duck. Not only the preparation but the serving and eating follow a set pattern.

Yield: serves 4 to 6

6 quarts water, more as needed

2 cups honey plus 1 to 2 tablespoons

10 thin slices peeled fresh ginger root, about 1 inch in diameter, or 2 tablespoons ground ginger

4½- to 6-pound **oven-ready** duck (if frozen, thaw according to directions on package)

¼ cup *hoisin* sauce (available at Asian food stores and most supermarkets)

1 tablespoon water

1 teaspoon sesame seed oil (available at Asian food stores)

2 teaspoons sugar

For serving: *po-ping* (Mandarin pancakes, recipe follows)

For **garnish:** 16 to 20 green onions, including green tops, trimmed, cut into 4-inch lengths

Equipment: 8- to 12-quart kettle, wooden mixing spoon, small plastic bag, **colander**, paper towels, kitchen string, oven mitts, large baking pan, sharp paring knife, large roasting pan with rack, work surface, **pastry brush**, medium bowl, small saucepan, small serving bowl, carving board, sharp meat knife, large serving platter

1. Prepare *po-ping*: Keep refrigerated until ready to serve.

2. Prepare ahead: Fill an 8- to 10-quart kettle ⅔ full with water; add 2 cups honey and ginger, mix well, and bring to boil over high heat.

3. Remove bag of innards from inside bird, put in plastic bag, and refrigerate for another use. Wash duck thoroughly under cold running water, and drain well in colander, about 10 minutes. Using paper towels, pat inside cavity and outside of duck until most excess water is removed. Skin on bird will no longer be shinny. Wrap middle of a 3- to 4-foot length of string around neck of duck and loop it under the wings. Make a handle of the string, extending above neck, by tying two ends together. String must be strong enough to hold bird without breaking.

4. *Note: Adult supervision required.* When water is at full boil, wearing oven mitts, hold duck by string handle and carefully lower it into boiling liquid. Dunk bird up and down 6 to 8 times, and then completely submerge bird in boiling liquid for 10 minutes. (The skin becomes very taut.)

5. Have colander ready in large roasting pan. Carefully remove duck from boiling liquid, and drain over sink. Place duck in colander to drain at least 30 minutes. Using wad of paper towels, wipe out duck cavity, and, with fresh paper towels, wipe off duck skin. Discard boiling liquid when it is cool enough to handle.

Preheat oven to 225°F.

6. Dry out duck: Remove and discard string. Place duck, breast side up, on rack set in large roasting pan and place in warm oven for 1 hour. Remove from oven. Lift rack and duck together from roasting pan, and set on work surface. Set roasting pan aside to use again. Allow duck to rest 30 minutes on rack, and then wipe out inside of duck with wad of paper towels. Use fresh paper towels to wipe off fat oozing from skin. Allow to rest 1 hour on rack, and repeat wiping duck inside and out several times. Using a pastry brush, coat duck's skin completely with 1 to 2 tablespoons honey.

7. While duck is drying out, make green onion brushes: Fill medium bowl with ice water. Using sharp paring knife, make 4 cuts 1-inch deep in each end of the green onions. Put onions in ice water so that cut ends will spread out and curl up. Refrigerate until ready to serve.

8. While duck is drying out, prepare sauce: In small saucepan, combine *hoisin* sauce, 1 tablespoon water, sesame seed oil, and sugar. Cook over medium heat, and stir until sugar dissolves, about 3 minutes. Reduce heat to low, and cook for 5 minutes more for flavor to develop. Cool to room temperature and transfer to small serving bowl.

Preheat oven to 450°F.

9. Return honey-coated duck on rack to roasting pan, set in hot oven to bake for 35 minutes, and then lower heat to 275°F and bake for 1 hour. Wearing oven mitts, remove from oven, turn duck breast-side down, and roast 1 hour longer. Skin becomes very dark and crisp. Remove from oven, and transfer duck to carving board. Allow to rest 20 minutes before carving.

10. Using sharp meat knife and your fingers, remove crisp skin from breast, sides and back of duck. Cut skin into serving-size pieces about 1×3 inches, and arrange slightly overlapping around edge of a serving platter. Cut wings and drumsticks from duck, and cut all meat away from breastbone and carcass, slicing it into strips about 1×3 inches, and pile in middle of serving platter.

To serve, heat foil-wrapped po-ping *in a 350°F oven for 5 to 10 minutes or until heated through. Unwrap* po-ping, *fold in half, and place on serving platter. Place bowl of hoisin sauce on plate, and surround with green onion brushes. All platters are placed in center of table. Traditionally, each guest spreads a* po-ping *flat on their plate, dips a green onion in sauce, and uses it as a brush to coat* po-ping *with sauce. The green onion is placed in the middle of* po-ping *with a piece of duck skin and a piece of duck meat on top.* Po-ping *is rolled up, enclosing the green onion, skin, and duck. The* po-ping *package is picked up and eaten with the fingers.*

Po-ping (Mandarin Pancakes)

Yield: about 24 pieces

2 cups **sifted** all-purpose flour   1 to 2 tablespoons sesame seed oil

¾ cup boiling water

Equipment: Large mixing bowl, wooden mixing spoon, damp towel, lightly floured work surface, rolling pin, 2½-inch cookie cutter or water glass, **pastry brush**, dry towel, **heavy-bottomed** 8-inch skillet, metal spatula, aluminum foil

1. Put flour in large mixing bowl, make a well (hole) in center, and pour in boiling water. Using wooden spoon, mix flour and water together until soft dough forms. Transfer to lightly floured work surface, and **knead** gently for 10 minutes or until smooth and **elastic**. Cover with damp towel, and allow to rest for 15 minutes.

2. On lightly floured work surface, roll dough to about ¼ inch thick. With 2½-inch cookie cutter or rim of glass, cut as many circles as possible from dough. Knead scraps together, roll out again, and cut more circles until you have about 24 pieces. Place circles side by side on work surface.

3. Using rolling pin, flatten each into 6-inch circle, rotating the circle so it keeps its round shape. With pastry brush, lightly brush one side of each circle with sesame seed oil. Cover with dry towel and continue until all circles are rolled out and brushed with oil.

4. Prepare to fry: Have a dry towel spread out on work surface. Place a heavy-bottomed 8-inch skillet over high heat for about 30 seconds. Reduce heat to medium, and cook pancakes, one at a time, in ungreased skillet. Using metal spatula, turn pancakes over when brown flecks appear on surface, about 1 minute on each side. Remove from skillet and place on towel to cool to room temperature. Cut piece of foil large enough to wrap around stack of pancakes. Wrap up pancakes and refrigerate until ready to serve.

Po-ping *are eaten with* pei-ching-k'ao-ya *(recipe precedes)*.

⚘ *Geung Nai* (Ginger Custard)

Geung Nai is a popular dessert in Hong Kong and in many parts of mainland China. *Geung nai* is ideal to serve at the end of any life cycle celebration as the ginger helps aid digestion and cleanses the palate.

Yield: Serves 4

2 eggs, beaten

4 tablespoons sugar

½ teaspoon salt

2 cups hot milk

2 tablespoons ginger extract, or to taste (available at international or Asian markets)

For serving: ¼ cup crystallized ginger (available at international markets)

Equipment: Medium mixing bowl, whisk, 4 (3-ounce each) small ramekins, **steamer pan** and **basket**, oven mitts, toothpick, plastic wrap

1. In mixing bowl, **whisk** together eggs, sugar, and salt until sugar is dissolved. Stirring constantly, add milk and ginger extract, mix well.

2. Transfer and evenly divide mixture into ramekins. Place ramekins into steamer basket.

3. Fill steamer pan ⅓ full with water, and bring to boil over high heat. Place steamer basket in pan, cover, and steam 20 to 25 minutes or until custards are firm and toothpick inserted in center comes out clean.

4. Remove steamer pan from heat, and cool custard to room temperature. Cover individual ramekins with plastic wrap and refrigerate 12 hours.

Serve individual ramekins at room temperature or chilled. Sprinkle crystallized ginger over top of each custard for the finale of a celebration feast.

India

India is the largest country of the subcontinent of south Asia. It is bordered by Bangladesh, Bhutan, Burma, China, Nepal, and Pakistan and has over 7,000 miles of coastline.

India's vast population, mostly Hindu, lives in a country of overwhelming diversity. To understand how Indians observe life-cycle events, it is necessary to know something about their country, their religion (see Hinduism and Hindu Life-Cycle Rituals, page lxxix), their lifestyles and habitats, and how they relate to one another.

India is divided into 25 states and seven union territories; each has its own culture, language, dress, religious rituals, arts and crafts, and food. Within each region, there are many different sects and branches of the Hindu religion, all following their own rituals and ceremonies. To add to the diversity, the Hindus were, for centuries, segregated by a very complicated caste system. The caste system doctrine states that each person is born to perform a specific job, marry a specific person, eat certain food, and have children who will continue the never changing cycle. In 1949, the Indian constitution abolished the caste system, making all men equal under the law; however, discrimination by caste continues to be an issue in modern India. For most Hindus, a totally casteless social system is contrary to their religious beliefs. The caste system was woven into every fiber of life, and to change this ancient religious practice seems to some an unattainable feat. In some rural areas, disobeying caste rules is still punished by death.

The most basic ceremonies for Hindus are those that involve the life cycle (*samskaras*). The *samskaras* include directions for carrying out the necessary rituals for each life-cycle event, for both high and low castes. These ancient ceremonies are often complex and minutely detailed; today they are not followed as closely in urban areas as they were in the past.

The haircutting ritual for baby boys is a very important occasion, and a feast is prepared for friends and relatives (see Hinduism and Hindu Life-Cycle Rituals, page lxxix). The most auspicious coming of age event for boys is the "thread ceremony" (see Hinduism and Hindu Life-Cycle Rituals, page lxxix), which includes a celebration feast for family and friends.

A coming of age ceremony for girls is still celebrated in some villages and tribal areas, signaling to the community that the girl is available for marriage. In the cities, the event may be marked by a change of dress; the girl may go from skirt or school uniform to Indian dress. The style of clothing she wears is restricted by region, religion, and caste.

The biggest and most important life-cycle celebration in India is the wedding. The majority of all Indians who marry have an arranged marriage, including university-educated, "foreign-returned" young men and women. (In some families, a young man or woman may exercise a right of veto after meeting the potential partner.) Wedding customs vary, even within a community; however, the arrangements are usually as extravagant as the bride's family can afford. It is not unusual for a father to go heavily into debt to give his daughter an expensive wedding, including the dowry, gifts to the groom's family, and a reception for hundreds of people or the whole village.

On the morning of the wedding, the bride arrives at the temple or wedding hall after having been elaborately dressed and adorned with makeup and jewels by her female relatives. The day before, she would have had intricate designs painted on her hands and legs with henna in the *mendhi* ceremony, a Muslim custom that Hindus have adopted. The bridal gown is usually a *sari*, beautifully decorated with gold brocade. Popular colors worn by brides are red for happiness, light green for purity and new life, and gold for wealth and good fortune.

Wedding receptions are elaborate affairs, and it is the sign of a gracious host and hostess to provide great quantities of betel leaf (*paan*), decorated with edible **silver leaf** (**vark**). *Paan* is a medicinal plant, whose leaves are often chewed in India, At one time, the preparation of *paan* after dinner was an elaborate ritual performed by the woman of the house. Today, many hostesses buy the *paan* already prepared.

In India, Hinduism influences every aspect of life. The rituals and customs extend not only to what food is cooked and how it is prepared but to how and where it is served. Meals are eaten in the kitchen; dining rooms are nonexistent. The person preparing the meal sits on the floor, as do those who eat it. Shoes are never worn in the kitchen, and before eating there is a ritual of hand and feet washing. In all classes of society, both urban and rural, food is eaten with the fingers of the right hand alone. The finger-and-bread-scoop method is acceptable; knives, forks, and spoons and men and women dining together are taboo at the traditional Hindu table. (Some urban families now eat at a table in the kitchen, occasionally using spoons.) In south India, banana leaves often replace the *thalis* (the trays food is eaten from). In many parts of India, even in the large cities, banana leaves are often used to serve hundreds of guests at a wedding banquet or reception. Meals generally consist of a great many dishes of different tastes, colors, and textures. The more important the occasion, then the more numerous and elaborate the foods will be that are served to guests.

Most Hindus do not eat meat or eat it only for special celebrations. Those who eat meat never eat beef or veal. In India, the cow, useful to every aspect of life, is sacred. Bullocks are the beasts of burden; they pull the plow, the waterwheel, and the wagon. Cow dung is burned for fuel, used for fertilizer and flooring, and plastered on the walls of houses. Cow's milk, curd, and buttermilk are essential nutrients. The cows are so revered, there is cow protection legislation; to kill a cow is considered the same as murdering a human being.

Ghee (Clarified Butter)

Hindus often use *ghee* in religious rituals. *Ghee* keeps well indefinitely, even when not refrigerated.

Yield: about 1 cup

1 pound unsalted butter or margarine

Equipment: Small saucepan, large spoon or **bulb baster**, small bowl with cover

1. In small saucepan, melt butter or margarine over very low heat, undisturbed, for 45 to 50 minutes, until it separates; solids on the bottom and clear oil (*ghee*) on the top. Do not let it brown.

2. The *ghee* on the top can be carefully spooned off or removed with a bulb baster into a small bowl. Either discard solids, or cover and refrigerate for another use. Allow *ghee* to cool to room temperature, cover, and refrigerate.

Serve ghee *over vegetables, spread it on bread, or use it in cooking instead of butter.*

⚭ *Chapatis* Indian Bread

Chapatis and phulkas (recipe follows), and *poppadums* (recipe page 180) are the popular breads of the region. They are used to scoop up food, making them indispensable to a meal. *Chapatis* are made on a *tawa*, a slightly concave, thin metal disc, 8 to 9 inches in diameter. The *tawa* is placed over an open fire.

Yield: 9 to 10 pieces

2 cups **atta** (**chapati flour**) (available at Indian and Middle Eastern food stores and some health food stores) or fine **ground** whole wheat flour

1 teaspoon salt

3 tablespoons *ghee*, homemade (recipe precedes) or available in a jar at Indian and Middle Eastern food stores), or vegetable oil

lukewarm water, as needed

Equipment: Work surface, kitchen towel, rolling pin, nonstick griddle, wide metal spatula, tongs, oven mitts

1. Mix flour and salt on work surface. Make a well (hole) in the center, and add *ghee* or oil. Using your fingers, mix until mixture resembles crumbs. Add ½ cup water, a little at a time, to make a pliable dough. Add more water, 1 tablespoon at a time, as needed. **Knead** the dough thoroughly for 8 to 10 minutes. Cover with a damp towel, and let rest for 2 hours.

2. Divide dough into 9 or 10 pieces, and roll them into balls. On floured work surface, roll out the balls, using a rolling pin, to a very thin disk about 8 to 9 inches across. Stack the completed disks, slightly overlapping on the work surface. Keep them covered with the damp towel.

3. Heat the griddle over medium heat. Place 1or 2 disks on the griddle, and grill for 2 or 3 minutes. Using the metal spatula, press down lightly until brown spots appear on the bottom side. Flip over and brown other side.

4. Just before serving, place *chapatis* under oven broiler or in toaster oven for about 1 minute, until they puff up in patches. Remove hot *chapatis* from oven with tongs. For safety, wear oven mitts.

Serve chapatis *as soon as they are cooked.*

⚭ *Phulkas* (Small Flatbreads)

Most people throughout the Indian subcontinent cook small 5-inch *tawas*.

Yield: 16 to 18 pieces

chapatis dough (recipe precedes)

Equipment: Lightly floured work surface, rolling pin, kitchen towel, nonstick griddle, metal spatula, oven mitts, aluminum foil

1. After *chapatis* dough has rested for 2 hours (*chapatis* recipe precedes), divide dough into 16 to 18 pieces, and roll into balls. On lightly floured work surface, using rolling pin, roll balls into very thin disks about 5 inches across. Stack completed disks, slightly overlapping, on work surface. Keep covered with damp towel.

2. Heat griddle over medium heat, and grill disks in batches. Using metal spatula, press down lightly until brown spots appear on the bottom side, and cook 2 to 3 minutes. Flip over and brown the other side, 2 to 3 minutes.

3. Just before serving, place *phulkas*, a few at a time, under oven broiler or in toaster oven for about 1 minute, until they puff up. Wrap in foil to keep warm while heating the remaining breads.

Serve phulkas as soon as they are cooked.

♦ Vegetable *Masala*

Since most Hindus are vegetarians, *vegetable masala* is an important dish at a Hindu wedding feast. Hindus also believe the red color from the tomatoes is a symbol of good luck and happiness.

Yield: serves 4 to 6

2 tablespoons **ghee** (homemade recipe page 142 or available at international markets), or vegetable oil, more as needed

1 onion, **trimmed, finely chopped**

3 cloves garlic, trimmed, **minced**

½ teaspoon turmeric

1 teaspoon mustard seeds

1 teaspoon ground cumin

1 tablespoon *masala* (homemade recipe, page 132, or available at international markets)

½ teaspoon cayenne pepper, or to taste

2 potatoes, peeled, cubed, **blanched**

1 cup baby carrots, **coarsely chopped,** blanched

10 fresh green beans, trimmed, coarsely chopped

14.5 ounces canned diced tomatoes

½ cup frozen green peas

salt and pepper to taste

For **garnish**: ½ cup finely chopped **cilantro** leaves

Equipment: Large skillet, mixing spoon

1. Heat 2 tablespoons *ghee* or oil in skillet over medium-high heat. Add onion and garlic, **sauté** 3 to 5 minutes, or until soft. Stir in turmeric, mustard seeds, cumin, *masala*, and cayenne pepper, mix well.

2. Stir in potatoes, carrots, green beans, green peas, and diced tomatoes, mix well. Sauté 7 to 10 minutes, or until potatoes are tender and cooked through. Add salt and pepper to taste.

Serve warm, garnished with cilantro.

✗ *Meeta Pilau* (Sweet Saffron Rice)

Sweets and rice hold a special place in India's social and religious life. Every joyous occasion or holiday, every arrival or departure, new baby or new job, promotion or award is celebrated with great quantities of sweets, many made with rice.

It is the belief that the Western practice of throwing rice at the wedding couple originated in India. During some Hindu ceremonies, the groom throws three handfuls of rice over the bride as a symbolic desire for many children. In other ceremonies, the bride and groom throw rice over each other. Sometimes the rice is colored to look like confetti.

Usually several different savory and sweet rice dishes are served for the same meal. This sweet rice dish is popular at wedding banquets. Its sweetness and yellow color are symbols of gold and good fortune.

Yield: serves 4 to 6

2½ cups water

salt, as needed

1 cup rice

3 tablespoons *ghee*, homemade (recipe page 142) or available in a jar at Indian and Middle Eastern food stores, or butter or margarine

¼ cup crushed cardamom seeds

¼ teaspoon **ground** cloves

¼ teaspoon ground cinnamon

1½ cups milk, more as needed

½ cup sugar

3 saffron threads (available at supermarkets) or ½ teaspoon ground turmeric

½ cup seedless raisins

For serving: ¼ cup **slivered** almonds

Equipment: Medium saucepan with cover, mixing spoon, **colander**, **heavy-bottomed** medium saucepan with cover, small saucepan, fork

1. Pour water into medium saucepan. Add ½ teaspoon salt, and bring to boil over high heat. Add rice, stir, reduce heat to **simmer**, cover, and cook for 6 minutes. Drain rice in colander.

2. In heavy-bottomed medium saucepan, heat *ghee* or melt butter or margarine over medium heat. Add drained rice, stir constantly, and cook for 2 to 3 minutes, until *ghee* is absorbed. Add cardamom, cloves, cinnamon, 1½ cups milk, and sugar. Stir frequently, bring to boil over medium-high heat, reduce heat to **simmer**, cover, and cook for 20 to 25 minutes, or until rice is tender and all the milk is absorbed. (If rice mixture gets too dry before rice is tender, stir in ¼ cup warm milk at a time to complete the cooking process.) Rice mixture should be creamy, not soupy or dry.

3. In small saucepan, heat ¼ cup milk over high heat until small bubbles appear around edge of pan. Remove from heat and add saffron or turmeric, stir, and set aside for 30 minutes. Using fork, stir the raisins and saffron or turmeric milk into rice.

To serve, transfer to serving dish, and sprinkle almonds over the top.

♻ *Badam Pistaz Barfi* (Almond and Pistachio Candy)

Yield: about 24 pieces

Panch armit, the "five immortal nectars"—sugar, milk, honey, yogurt, and *ghee*—are included in most Hindu life-cycle rituals and celebration feasts. This sweetmeat, made with three of the five immortal nectars, is served for life-cycle celebrations.

1 quart milk

1 cup granulated sugar

1 cup **ground** almonds

1 cup unsalted, **ground** pistachios

3 teaspoons *ghee*, homemade (recipe page 142) or available at Indian and Middle Eastern food stores, or unsalted butter or margarine, at room temperature

1 teaspoon almond extract

Equipment: **Heavy-bottomed** medium saucepan, wooden mixing spoon, buttered 8-inch square baking pan, metal spatula

1. Pour milk into heavy-bottomed medium saucepan, and bring to boil over high heat. Reduce heat to **simmer**, and using wooden mixing spoon, stir frequently and cook for 35 to 40 minutes, or until milk thickens to consistency of heavy cream. Stir sugar into milk and continue stirring for 10 minutes. Add ground almonds and pistachios, and continue stirring frequently 10 minutes longer. Stir in *ghee* or butter and almond extract. Continue stirring until mixture thickens to a solid mass and pulls away from sides of pan. Remove from heat, and quickly spread out in buttered 8-inch baking pan. Smooth top with metal spatula.

2. Let cool for about 30 minutes to the consistency fudge.

To serve, using a paring knife, cut into 24 small squares or diamond shapes.

Indonesia

Off the South East Asian coast, Indonesia is a sprawling archipelago consisting of nearly 13,700 islands. Only about half of the islands are inhabited, with diversified cultures existing in diversified living conditions ranging from Stone Age to high-tech.

As the fourth most populous country in the world, Indonesia is home to Arabs, Chinese, Pakistanis, Indians, Dutch and other Europeans, Polynesians, Eurasians, and the indigenous Indonesian peoples. Most Indonesians are Muslim, making Indonesia the largest Islamic country in the world. Hinduism, once a major religion, now exists mostly on Bali. A small percentage of the Indonesian population is Christian, with the majority Protestant. Most Indonesian Buddhists are of Chinese descent.

There can be a strong sense of nationalism among the different ethnic groups, and the population is encouraged to be Indonesian first and members of their *sukubangsa* (ethnic group) second. Generally, each ethnic group follows the life-cycle rituals of their particular religious traditions. (See Buddhism and Buddhist Life-Cycle Rituals, page lxxxii; Protestant and Catholic Life-Cycle Rituals, page lxxiii; Hinduism and

Hindu Life-Cycle Rituals, page lxxix; and Islam and Islamic Life-Cycle Rituals, page lxxvi.) However, it is not unusual for Indonesians to mix traditions and religions, forming new rituals and celebrations.

Many Indonesians observe a bathing ceremony for mothers-to-be; after the baby is born, there is another bathing ceremony. In Bali, the bathing ceremony is done at the third month; most other groups observe the *tujuh bulan* (seventh month) *selamatan*. A *selamatan* is a religious meal intended to assure harmony and good fortune. The seventh month is a time for other mothers with living children to give the mother-to-be emotional support. Infant mortality in Indonesia is very high, and so all the encouragement a soon-to-be mother can get is welcome. Elders always attend the *selamatan* to say the prayers. Everyone present partakes in a meal, which varies with each group. Usually, several rice dishes are served, among them *nasi uduk/gurth* (recipe follows), as well as *ikan mas* (carp), fried whole and eaten to give strength and endurance, and the shrimp dish, *sambal goreng udang* (recipe page 148). The rituals include scented or blessed water, special fresh fruit and flowers, and ceremonial cloth (*kain batik*) worn by the mother.

In Bali, children are thought to be reincarnated from their ancestors, and they are treated as holy until they are 210 days old (the length of a Balinese calendar year). The infant's feet touch the ground for the first time when he or she is three months old (the crawling stage is bypassed, as being too "animalistic"). The family celebration, when the infant first walks, is called *nyambutan* and includes a feast with great quantities of rice and a large variety of sweets.

₰ *Nasi Uduk/Gurih* (Rice in Coconut Milk)

This is a popular way to cook rice, and it is served at most family celebrations.

Yield: serves 6 to 8

1 pound rice, such as **basmati** or jasmine (available at Asian food stores and most supermarkets)

3½ cups coconut milk, homemade (recipe page 225) or canned

4-inch length of **lemongrass**, washed and **trimmed**

½ teaspoon salt

Equipment: Large saucepan with cover, wooden mixing spoon, fork

1. Place rice in large saucepan, add coconut milk, lemongrass, and salt. Bring to boil over medium-high heat. Stir rice, and **reduce** heat to simmer. Cover and cook until all moisture is absorbed, 18 to 20 minutes.

2. Remove and discard lemongrass. Cover, and let rice sit 5 to 10 minutes before serving. Fluff with fork before serving.

Serve rice with besengek daging (recipe follows).

❦ *Besengek Daging* (Beef in Coconut)

Besengek daging is an easy dish to prepare for any Muslim or Christian life-cycle celebration in Indonesia.

Yield: serves 4 to 6

3 pounds boneless beef tenderloin

water, as needed

2 tablespoons oil

1 onion, **trimmed, finely chopped**

1 teaspoon *trassi* (optional, available at Asian or international markets)

1 red chili pepper, trimmed, finely chopped

1 teaspoon **coriander**

½ teaspoon turmeric

½ teaspoon **tamarind** paste (available at international markets)

2 cups coconut milk, homemade (recipe page 225), or canned

2 teaspoons sugar

salt and pepper to taste

For serving: 4 to 6 cups cooked white rice

Equipment: **Dutch oven** or large stock pot, metal tongs, cutting board, sharp knife, large saucepan with cover, mixing spoon

1. Place meat in Dutch oven or stock pot, and cover with water. Bring to boil over high heat, cover, and reduce to simmer 45 minutes to 1 hour, or until tender and cooked through. Reserve 1 cup beef stock.

2. Using metal tongs, remove beef, and place on cutting board. Carefully cut into ¼-inch-thick slices. Set aside.

3. Heat 2 tablespoons oil in saucepan over medium-high heat. Add onion, and **sauté** 3 to 5 minutes, or until soft. Stir in *trassi*, chili pepper, coriander, turmeric, tamarind paste, and reserved beef stock, mix well. Simmer 5 to 7 minutes, or until heated through.

4. Stir in coconut milk, mix well. Add sliced beef, sugar and salt and pepper to taste. Continue cooking 3 to 5 minutes, or until sauce thickens.

Serve warm over rice.

❦ *Sambal Goreng Udang* (Shrimp in Spicy Sauce)

Seafood is plentiful in Indonesia, where this sweet and spicy dish is served with rice, peanuts, and fresh, thinly sliced vegetables.

Yield: serves 4

¼ cup vegetable oil

2 onions, **trimmed**, thinly sliced

1 clove garlic, trimmed, **minced**

1 pound medium **shrimp, peeled and deveined**

dried red pepper flakes, to taste

1 cup coconut milk, homemade (recipe page 225), or canned (available at Asian food stores and some supermarkets)

1 tomato, trimmed, **coarsely chopped**

1 green pepper, peeled, thinly sliced into rings

1 tablespoon packed brown sugar

salt and pepper to taste

Equipment: **Wok** or large skillet, mixing spoon

1. Heat oil in wok or large skillet over medium-high heat, add onion, garlic, and shrimp. Stir fry ingredients until shrimp turn **opaque white** and cooked through, 3 to 5 minutes. Add red pepper flakes, coconut milk, tomato, green pepper, brown sugar, and salt and pepper. Stir fry for about 5 minutes for flavors to **blend**. Remove from heat.

To serve, transfer to serving bowl. To eat sambal goreng udang, *spoon it over rice.*

Japan

Japan is a series of islands separated from the east coast of Asia by the Sea of Japan. Most Japanese are Shintoist or Buddhist, often blending different elements from both religions. In Japan, many life-cycle events, especially for children, are national celebrations. In the most popular, *Shichi-Go-San*, in November (see Shintoism and Shinto Life-Cycle Rituals, page lxxxiii) parents take children ages three, five, and seven to shrines to pray for their future. Another annual festival is Boys' Day (*Tango No Sekku*) on May 5. Symbolic items are displayed by parents in hopes that their sons will grow up healthy and strong. Warrior dolls (*Hina*), are displayed, iris leaves are placed under the eaves of homes to ward off evil, and large carp-shaped banners fly on poles over the houses where young boys live.

Girls' Day (*Hina Matsuri*) on March 3, is a national event honoring young girls. Traditionally, imperial court dolls, dressed in the costumes of ancient court ladies as well as peach blossoms, are displayed, and a sweet drink made with fermented rice, called *shirozake* is served.

Until the 1950s, Western-style courting or dating was not part of Japan's social scene, and arranged marriage was the custom throughout Japan. The Star Festival (*Tanabata*), a national event, was held on July 7 to celebrate the coming together of couples planning to marry.

From ancient times, *kagami-biraki* has been one of the essential Japanese wedding rituals to celebrate the beginning of a marriage. The rituals take place around the *butsudan* (the family shrine), found in many homes. The bride and groom break open a container of saké with a special mallet amidst cheers of congratulations from the guests. The saké is then served to all the guests.

The central feature of the Japanese wedding ceremony is the *sansankudo* (also *sakazukigoto*). Meaning "three-three nine times," *sansankudo* refers to a precise ritual of drinking saké. *Sansankudo* is an ancient custom (used in weddings as early as the Heian period [794–1185] and appearing in the 14th-century *Samurai Rules of Etiquette*) and is used in many Japanese functions to create or reinforce social bonds. As with all Japanese rituals, the *yuino,* the seating arrangement for *sansankudo,* is exceedingly precise and essential to the ritual itself. The drinking from the same cup is a symbolic agreement that the couple will share a lifetime of joy and sorrow. The Japanese regard three (*san*) as an extremely auspicious number; in earlier days, there were three people present at the wedding ritual, a fire was maintained for three nights, and three trays of food were served.

Most food served at the wedding feast is selected because of its symbolic connection to happiness, prosperity, long life, or hopes for many children. Sea bream (*tai*), kelp (*kombu*), and *sekihan* are essential to the traditional wedding feast and almost all other celebration feasts.

The wedding banquet can be simple or very artistic and formal (*kaiseki*). For the *kaiseki,* there can be as many as 15 different dishes, and each one is a work of art. For formal occasions, food must be pleasing to the eye as well as to the mouth. The *kaiseki* banquet follows a set order of courses: first appetizers, then a clear soup, then *sashimi* or *sushi* (recipes page 153). A grilled dish is followed by a boiled dish, a deep-fried dish, a steamed dish, and then salad. The meal ends with rice served with pickles and miso soup, which is garnished with such things as cooked shrimp, bean curd, chunks of cooked fish, button mushrooms, chicken, and pork meatballs. Several different garnishes are often added to each serving of miso. (Instant miso soup mix is available at all Asian food stores.) Prepare according to directions on package, and add garnishes of choice.

Origami is an ancient Japanese traditional art form. It is the folding of paper in beautiful, intricate ways to create elaborate objects such as birds, flowers, or other abstract designs. *Senbazuru,* the folding of 1,000 paper cranes, is considered a symbol of good luck and a long life. *Senbazuru* is an ideal gift to give a bride and groom at their wedding or to give to parents upon the birth of their child.

Hikicha Manju (also Kohaku Manju) (Red Bean Paste Buns)

Hikicha manju are served on auspicious occasions. The buns are eaten at banquets, or they are often given as gifts for the guests to take home at the end of a wedding feast.

Yield: 12 buns

½ cup sugar

¼ cup water

2¼ cups all-purpose flour

3½ teaspoons baking powder

¼ cup milk

2 tablespoons vegetable shortening

18 ounces canned sweetened red bean paste (about 1½ cups) (available at Asian food stores)

Equipment: Small saucepan, mixing spoon, **sifter**, lightly floured work surface, tablespoon, kitchen towel, wax paper, **steamer pan** or **wok** with **bamboo steamer basket**, oven mitts

1. In small saucepan, stir and dissolve sugar in water over low heat, about 30 seconds. Cool to room temperature.

2. Using flour sifter, **sift** flour and baking powder into mound on work surface. With your hands, make a well (hole) in center, and pour in sugar-water and milk. Using your fingers, mix liquids into flour mixture a little at a time, and mix in shortening. (If dough is too dry, add 1 tablespoon of water at a time, and if dough is too wet, sprinkle work surface and your hands lightly with flour.) Continue to **knead** for 12 to 15 minutes until dough becomes smooth and **elastic**. Cover dough with damp towel, and allow to rest for 1 hour.

3. Divide dough into 12 equal portions. Using your hands, roll each portion into a ball, and place on lightly floured work surface. Using your hands, flatten each ball into a 3½- to 4-inch disk. Spoon 1 tablespoon bean paste in center of disk. Wrap dough around filling and pinch edges tightly together to seal in filling. Rub bun lightly with oil. Repeat filling the buns.

4. Prepare to steam buns: Cut 12 squares of waxed paper, slightly larger than each bun, and rub each square lightly with oil. Set each bun, seam-side down, on wax paper square, and set about ¾ inch apart in steamer basket, allowing space to rise. The wax paper prevents buns from sticking to steamer basket. Don't crowd the steamer basket; it will be necessary to steam in batches.

5. To steam buns: Pour 4 cups water into lower pan of steamer pan or wok, and bring to boil over high heat. Place either perforated top pan with buns or bamboo steamer with buns over boiling water, cover, and steam for 15 to 20 minutes, until springy to touch and well risen. Wearing oven mitts, remove basket with buns. Remove buns from basket. Peel off wax paper, and place buns on wire rack. Continue steaming buns in batches. Add more water, and bring to boil, if necessary to continue steaming.

Serve immediately for best flavor and texture. Leftover buns can be refrigerated in covered container and reheated in a microwave oven or resteamed.

Tai No Tsumire Wan (Clear Broth with Porgy Dumplings)

The wedding feast will often include a broth (*tai no tsumire wan*), made with two meaningful ingredients: sea bream (*tai*) and kelp (*kombu*). When the broth is served to the bride and groom, the stems of the green garnish are made into a knotted ring to symbolize their union. Guests may have their garnish knotted, or chopped fresh parsley can be sprinkled over the soup to symbolize spreading good wishes for the couple. Sea bream is also known as porgy, a popular fish in Japan. Red snapper is very similar and makes a good substitute.

Yield: serves 6

1 pound skinless fish **fillets, coarsely chopped** (about 1 cup)

1 egg

1 teaspoon grated fresh ginger root or ½ teaspoon **ground** ginger

½ teaspoon salt

2 tablespoons all-purpose flour

6 cups *dashi*, homemade (recipe follows) or *katsuo dashi* (bonito broth) instant concentrate (available in 6.7-ounce bottles at Asian food markets). (Prepare according to directions on bottle—each serving: 1 teaspoon dashi concentrate to 1 cup hot water.)

2 to 6 fresh Japanese parsley stems (each about 6 inches long), **blanched**

For **garnish** (optional): 2 to 3 teaspoons **finely chopped** fresh parsley flakes

Equipment: Food processor, rubber spatula, 2 plates, medium saucepan, slotted spoon, plastic wrap, cup, scissors, ladle

1. Put fish in food processor, and process for about 10 seconds. Add egg, ginger, and salt, and process for 5 seconds. Use rubber spatula to scrape down sides of container. Sprinkle flour over fish mixture, and process for about 10 seconds into smooth paste. Transfer to plate. With wet hands, divide fish mixture into 6 portions, and form each into an oval dumpling. Repeat making dumplings, and place side by side on plate.

2. Fill medium saucepan ⅔ full of water, and bring to boil over high heat. Add dumplings, cook for about 2 minutes until they float to surface. Remove with slotted spoon, and place on plate. Cool to room temperature, and cover with plastic wrap. Refrigerate until serving time.

3. Prepare garnish: You will need either 2 or 6 stems of blanched fresh parsley, long enough to wrap around your finger and tie. Remove the tied ring from your finger and trim the ends with a scissors so that it will fit nicely in the soup cup. Place in cup of cold water until ready to serve. Repeat making rings.

4. Prepare to serve: Heat broth over medium-high heat until small bubbles appear around edge of pan (do not boil). Place a dumpling in each bowl, and ladle over hot soup. Garnish 2 bowls for bride and groom with knotted sprigs of parsley, and in remaining bowl either garnish with a knotted sprig and/or sprinkle with chopped fresh parsley flakes.

Serve the bride and groom first, then the parents of the bride and groom. It is customary to first pick out and eat the dumpling using chopsticks, then pick up the cup with both hands, to drink the broth.

⚜ *Dashi* (Basic Broth)

Yield: serves 6

6 cups water

1 piece (3-inch square) dried kelp (kombu) (available at Asian food stores)

½ cup (loosely packed) dried bonito flakes (*katsuo bushi*) (available at Asian food stores)

Equipment: Medium saucepan, metal tongs, mixing spoon, medium strainer, 1 or 2 coffee filters, medium bowl

1. In medium saucepan, bring the water and kelp almost to a boil (it should not actually boil) over medium-high heat. Remove pan from heat. Immediately remove kelp from water with metal tongs, discard kelp.

2. Sprinkle bonito flakes over the hot water, stir, and let stand undisturbed for 2 or 3 minutes, until bonito flakes sink to the bottom.

3. Line medium strainer with 1 or 2 coffee filters, and set over bowl. Strain liquid through filters, and discard filter contents.

Use for tai no tsumire wan (recipe precedes). Leftover broth can be cooled to room temperature, covered, and refrigerated for 2 to 3 days.

There are many different ways to assemble the *sushi*, and each is a work of art. Plating and garnishing are an important part of the total *sushi* experience. The color and shape of *sushi* must be appealing to the eye, and each piece is cut bite-size, easy to pop into the mouth. *Sushi* made without fish or meat is often included in the vegetarian meals after Buddhist wakes and funerals. When this recipe is made without fish, it is called *hana-zushi* (flowered rice). At banquets, *sushi* is eaten as an appetizer.

₰ *Nori-maki Sushi* (Vinegar Rice and Fish in Seaweed)

Sushi means vinegar-flavored rice. The vinegar-flavored rice is molded into small shapes and combined with a range of meat, fish, shrimp, or vegetable pieces either left raw, cooked, or smoked and garnished with condiments for dipping. This recipe is made with cooked fish.

Yield: serves 8 to 10

3 cups water

1 tablespoon vinegar

½ teaspoon salt

3 **coriander** seeds

6 strips (1×6-inches each) fresh, skin-on salmon **fillets**, about ½ inch thick (The skin will keep the fillets from falling apart.)

For **garnish**:

1 carrot

1 cucumber

For serving:

6 (7½×8½-inch) sheets *yaki nori* (toasted seaweed) (available at Asian food stores)

3 cups *sushi meshi* (*sushi* rice) (recipe follows)

12 spinach leaves, **trimmed** and **blanched**, patted dry with paper towels

shredded omelet (recipe page 155)

4 to 6 tablespoons Japanese soy sauce (available at all Asian food stores and some supermarkets)

1 or 2 tablespoons **wasabi** paste or powder (available at Asian food stores, prepared according to directions on package)

Equipment: Medium saucepan, slotted spatula, plate, baking sheet, oven mitts, plastic food wrap, work surface, kitchen string, **serrated knife**

1. Pour water into medium saucepan, add vinegar, salt, and coriander seeds. Bring to boil over high heat for 5 minutes. Reduce to **simmer**, add salmon strips, and **poach** gently for 4 minutes, or until fish is cooked through. (Fully cooked fish is **opaque white** and no longer translucent in the center.) Remove from liquid with a slotted spatula, and place on plate.

2. Spread sheets of seaweed, slightly overlapping, on baking sheet and slightly warm in 250°F oven for 5 to 8 minutes to enhance flavor.

3. To assemble: Place a 10- to 12-inch square of plastic wrap on work surface and place 1 sheet seaweed on top. Spread ⅙ of rice evenly on seaweed, leaving a 1-inch border on all sides. Pull or cut skin off salmon strip, and place fish on rice. Cover fish with 2 blanched spinach leaves. Sprinkle ⅙ of omelet over spinach. Using plastic wrap as a guide, carefully roll ingredients in sheet of seaweed, keeping the filling centered and making roll as tight as possible. Wrap string around plastic wrap and tie it in 3 places to hold it closed. Twist ends of plastic wrap closed. Repeat making rolls and refrigerate for at least 4 hours before serving.

4. Prepare for serving: Remove string and plastic wrap. Using serrated knife, cut rolls crosswise into slices about 1 inch thick. Arrange slices, cut-side up, on individual plates. Turn carrot and cucumber slices into flowers by cutting V-shaped notches around edge of each vegetable, and place on plate as garnish.

Serve with 2 dipping sauces: (1) a small dish of equal parts water and Japanese soy sauce; (2) a small dish of prepared wasabi paste.

⚘ *Sushi Meshi* (also *Sushi Rice*) (Japanese Vinegar-flavored Rice)

Yield: 3 cups

If using long grain rice instead of **short grain** rice for this recipe, use 2 cups of water instead of 1¾ cups.

1½ cups **short grain** rice (available at some supermarkets and Asian food stores)

1¾ cups water

2 tablespoons white vinegar

2 tablespoons sugar

Equipment: Medium saucepan with cover, kitchen towel, cup, Japanese wooden tub (*handai* or *sushi-oké*) or large bowl, Japanese wooden paddle (*shamoji*) or wooden mixing spoon, handheld fan (Japanese lacquered flat fan, *uchiwa*) or a piece of stiff cardboard or folded newspaper

1. Combine rice and water in medium saucepan, and bring to boil over high heat. Reduce heat to low, cover, and cook for 10 to 12 minutes, or until all the water is absorbed and rice is tender. Remove from heat, and remove pan cover. Place folded towel over pan of rice, set pan cover on top of towel, and let stand 15 minutes. The towel prevents moisture from dripping onto rice.

2. Pour vinegar into cup, and stir in sugar until it is dissolved. Transfer rice to wooden tub or large bowl. Rinse *shamoji* or wooden spoon under cold water, and use it to gently toss rice and at the same time fan the rice vigorously. (This combined tossing and fanning prevents the steam from condensing onto the rice.) While rice is still warm, toss it and sprinkle with vinegar, 2 tablespoons at a time, until well mixed.

The rice can be made several hours ahead and covered with a damp towel and plastic wrap; keep at room temperature. (Do not refrigerate, it will turn hard and crusty.)

Shredded Omelet

2 eggs	½ teaspoon salt
1 teaspoon cold water	1 teaspoon vegetable oil
½ teaspoon sugar	

Equipment: Small bowl, fork, medium skillet, metal pancake turner, work surface, **serrated knife**, large plate

1. Crack eggs into small bowl. Add water, sugar, and salt; using fork, beat well.

2. Heat oil in skillet over medium-high heat. Add egg mixture, and swirl to cover bottom of pan evenly and thinly. Cook until set, about 1 minute, turn and cook briefly on other side until firm. Transfer omelet to work surface. When cool enough to handle, roll egg into a cylinder and cut crosswise into very thin strands. Separate strands on large plate to prevent them from sticking together.

Use with nori-maki sushi *(recipe page 153).*

ChiChi Dango Mochi (Sweet, Chewy Cake)

When celebrating the national Boys' or Girls' Day in Japan, *chichi dango mochi*, a soft and chewy dessert, is ideal to prepare for family and friends. The addition of the red food coloring symbolizes good fortunes for years to come.

Yield: 36 to 48 pieces

1 pound glutinous rice flour (available at international or Asian markets)	1 teaspoon vanilla extract
	14.5 ounces coconut milk, homemade (recipe page 225), or canned
2½ cups sugar	
1 teaspoon baking powder	½ teaspoon red food coloring
2 cups water	1 cup confectioner's sugar, more as needed

Equipment: Medium mixing bowl, mixing spoon, large mixing bowl, whisk, greased or non-stick medium ovenproof baking dish, foil, toothpick, oven mitts, pie pan, 36 to 48 petit four paper cups

Preheat oven 350°F.

1. In medium mixing bowl, combine rice flour, sugar, and baking powder, mix well. Set aside.

2. In large bowl, **whisk** together water, vanilla extract, coconut milk, and red food coloring. Slowly add rice flour mixture, mix well.

3. Transfer to baking to dish, cover with foil, and bake 45 minutes to 1 hour, or when toothpick inserted in center comes out clean. Carefully remove from oven using oven mitts, set aside to cool.

4. Place 1cup confectioner's sugar in pie pan, set aside.

5. Using sharp knife, cut cake into 1- to 1½-inch squares. Remove squares one at a time from pan, and roll in confectioner's sugar to coat all sides. Place in petit four paper cups. Continue until all pieces have been coated in sugar. Add more confectioner's sugar if necessary.

Serve as a sweet treat, or transfer to airtight container and refrigerate until ready to eat.

Kazakhstan

Located at the crossroads of Europe and Asia, Kazakhstan is the second largest state of the former Soviet Union after Russia. It extends from the Caspian Sea in the west to China in the east and is bordered on the north by Russia and shares its southern border with all of the other Central Asian states, except Tajikistan.

More than a hundred different national groups make their home in Kazakhstan; even though the largest group is the Kazakhs, European Slavs actually outnumber Kazakhs if counted together. These demographics are changing rapidly, however, because Europeans have been leaving Kazakhstan and because the Kazakhs have a much higher birth rate. Once a nomadic people, the Kazakhs were forced, under Communism, to settle in collective state-run farms or small villages. Historically, the Kazakhs have been Muslim and have returned to Muslim practices, including life-cycle rituals, since independence in 1991. (See Islam and Islamic Life-Cycle Rituals, page lxxvi.)

Because of the long Russian presence, Kazakhs combine Russian cooking with local foods, especially in urban areas. For a wedding celebration, for example, they may have the *zakuska* table with *baklazhannaya ikra* (recipe page 508), sliced onions sprinkled with vinegar and sugar, and boiled mushrooms with yogurt. The feast might also include *kartofel'naya zapekanka* (recipe page 509) and *stolichnyi salat* (recipe page 507). Large loaves of unleavened bread are eaten along with Russian black bread. Bread is torn into chunks and eaten with each mouthful of food.

Nothing is better for the celebration feast than *plov* (rice pilaf), prepared with mutton, beef, or *kazy* (horse meat) and enriched with fruits and nuts. When the family can afford it, a whole lamb is slaughtered and roasted over an open spit for the wedding feast. The lamb is accompanied by side dishes of noodles and smoked sausages made of *kazy*, a Kazakh specialty. *Alma-ata plov* (a pilaf) (recipe follows) is prepared when family and friends gather for the circumcision celebration.

⚜ *Alma-Ata Plov* (Pilaf with Meat and Fruit)

Alma-ata plov (a pilaf) is prepared when family and friends gather for the circumcision celebration.

Yield: serves 6

6 tablespoons vegetable oil, more or less as needed

1 pound lean lamb or beef, **cubed**

2 onions, thinly sliced

2 carrots, **trimmed** and **julienned**

10 or 12 dried apricots, **coarsely chopped**

½ cup seedless raisins

1 cooking apple, **cored** and coarsely chopped

2 cups long grain rice

4 cups chicken broth

salt and pepper to taste

For **garnish**: ½ cup **slivered** almonds, **blanched** and **roasted**

Equipment: Large skillet, mixing spoon, slotted spoon, large ovenproof casserole with cover, oven mitts, medium saucepan

Preheat oven to 350°F.

1. Heat 2 tablespoons oil in large skillet over medium-high heat. Add meat cubes and **sauté**, stirring constantly, for 6 to 8 minutes, or until well browned. Add remaining 2 tablespoons oil if necessary to prevent sticking. Using slotted spoon, transfer meat to large ovenproof casserole.

2. Heat 2 tablespoons oil in same large skillet over medium-high heat. Add onions and sauté until soft, 3 to 5 minutes. Add carrots, apricots, raisins, apple, and rice. Stir to coat rice with oil, and cook for 2 minutes. Add 1 tablespoon oil, if necessary. Pour rice mixture over meat in casserole.

3. Pour chicken broth into medium saucepan, and bring to boil over high heat. Pour hot broth over rice mixture in casserole, and add salt and pepper to taste.

4. Bake in oven, covered, for 40 to 50 minutes, or until rice is tender. Using oven mitts, carefully uncover casserole and taste for doneness. Return to oven to cook uncovered for 10 to 15 minutes to brown top. Sprinkle roasted almonds over the top.

Serve alma-ata plov *from the casserole with* churek *(recipe page 441) for sopping.*

⚜ *Shalgam* (Pan-Fried Turnip Balls)

Shalgam is a tasty starter to a wedding feast celebration. Turnips are a hearty root vegetable popular throughout the countryside and villages of Kazakhstan.

Yield: serves 4 to 6

2 pounds **turnips, trimmed**, quartered

water, as needed

2 tablespoons vegetable oil, more as needed

2 onions, trimmed, **finely chopped**

1 egg, beaten

½ cup **lentils** (cooked according to directions on package), drained

2 teaspoons cayenne pepper, or to taste

1 teaspoon **allspice**

salt and pepper to taste

2 cups plain **bread crumbs**, more as needed

Equipment: Large saucepan, strainer or colander, medium skillet, mixing spoon, food processor or **blender**, medium mixing bowl, pie pan, paper towel covered baking sheet, medium saucepan, slotted spoon

1. Place turnips in saucepan, cover with water, and bring to boil over high heat. Reduce to simmer 10 to 15 minutes, or until tender and cooked through. Transfer to colander or strainer to drain. When cool enough to handle, squeeze additional water from turnips. Set aside.

2. Heat 2 tablespoons oil in medium skillet over medium-high heat, add onions, reduce to medium-low, and **sauté** 10 to 15 minutes, or until onions are **caramelized**. Stir frequently and add more oil if needed to prevent sticking.

3. Transfer to blender or food processor and add turnips. **Blend** until pulverized. Transfer onion-turnip mixture to medium mixing bowl.

4. Add egg, cooked lentils, cayenne pepper, allspice, and salt and pepper to taste. Using clean hands, **knead** until mixture is smooth and mixed well. Set aside.

5. Place 2 cups bread crumbs in pie pan. Set aside.

6. Pinch off ping-pong-ball-size pieces of dough, and, using palms of hands, roll into ball. Place in pie pan, and roll to coat in bread crumbs. Set on baking sheet. Continue until all mixture is used, adding more bread crumbs if needed.

7. Heat ½ cup oil in medium saucepan over medium-high heat. Add a few balls one at a time, and cook 5 to 7 minutes, or until golden on all sides. Add more oil if necessary to prevent sticking. Remove, using slotted spoon, and place on paper towel–covered baking sheet to drain.

Serve warm as an appetizer for any life-cycle celebration feast in Kazakhstan.

All important life events such as weddings and other special occasions are celebrated with a traditional feast called *dastarkhan* (literally "tablecloth," "festive table"). At a wedding party, it was once traditional for kinsmen of the bride and groom to be served *kuiryk-bauyr*—boiled meat thinly sliced and served with sour milk and salted broth. Those served then dabbed the sour milk on their faces. The women who served would sing, "We ate *kuiryk-bauyr* and became kinsmen" as they distributed the food because the *kuiryk-bauyr* meal celebrated oath taking and commitment. This custom is apparently not practiced any longer.

The *dastarkhan* features meat and lots of it. In particular, horse meat specially bred to be tender and fat is the most desirable and hence also the most expensive, followed by lamb or mutton and beef. The festive table is usually decorated with dishes of sweet and savory fritters, nuts, and dried fruits. The feast begins with various drinks of fermented milks such as *kumyss* (mare's milk), *shubat* (camel's milk), and *airan* (cow's milk yogurt), followed by tea with milk or cream. The tea is served by women and young ladies, and they are carefully attentive, pouring only a little tea into the special teacups called *pialas*. Filling a *piala* (handle-less teacup) to the brim signals to the guest that it is time to leave. The frequency of filling the *piala* denotes the utmost hospitality that a Kazakh host can offer a guest.

With the tea are served savory herb-stuffed fritters called *gutap* (recipe follows), raisins, and salty snacks from milk products such as *irimshik* and *kurt*. Fried wheat flour pastries called *baursak* are also frequently served. Of these, *domalak baursak* (recipe page 163), which has cottage cheese or sour cream, is considered the best for celebrations. After these come smoked and aged meats and dried sausages, made of choice parts of horse meat, such as *kazy*, *shuzhuk*, or, more often, mutton. Then comes the *pièce de résistance*—*beshbarmak*—tender horse meat or mutton, boiled and served with broad flat noodles that resemble lasagna, together with sliced onions. The broth in which the meat has been cooked is served in a separate bowl as soup and is called *sorpa*. For dessert, there may come fried crisp fritters dipped in or drizzled with honey syrup, fresh fruits such as melon, watermelon, peaches, apricots, or grapes (all locally grown and of fine flavor), and more tea.

Gutap (Herb-filled Fritters)

Gutap are fritters stuffed with different herbs. They are usually served before the main meat dish, *beshbarmak*, during the celebratory feast known as *dastarkhan*.

Yield: 10 servings

Dough:

1½ cups flour, plus more for rolling out

½ teaspoon salt

2 tablespoons butter, at room temperature

⅔ cup warm water

Green herb filling:

¼ cup fresh dill, minced

¼cup fresh parsley, minced

2 to 3 garlic cloves, minced

½ cup spring onions (scallions), finely chopped

1 teaspoon salt

1 teaspoon black pepper

2 tablespoons melted butter

½ cup cold butter, **diced**

Equipment: Large mixing bowl, mixing spoon, plastic wrap, rolling pin, **pastry brush**, clean kitchen towel, small and large saucepans, large frying pan, wire rack, whisk

1. In a large bowl, combine the flour, salt, and butter.

2. Make a well (hole) in the center of the flour mixture. Gradually pour in the water, stirring in the surrounding flour until all comes together into a dough that no longer sticks to the sides of the bowl.

3. On a floured surface, knead the dough until smooth, about 5 to 7 minutes. Let rest at room temperature for 30 minutes to 1 hour, covered with plastic wrap. 4. Prepare green herb filling: In a bowl, combine the dill, parsley, garlic, spring onions, salt, and pepper.

5. On a lightly floured surface, roll out the dough to a rectangle ¼-inch thick. Brush the surface of the dough with the melted butter. Fold the dough in half, then fold again in half, making a total of four layers. With a rolling pin, press the four layers and roll out as thinly as possible to a large rectangle.

6. Cut the dough into 2-inch-square pieces. Take one dough square, place a teaspoonful of herb filling and a piece of butter in the center. Fold one edge of the square to the opposite edge, covering the filling. Press the edges firmly to seal. Keep the rest of the dough squares (that you are not working with) covered with a clean kitchen towel to prevent them from drying.

   Continue filling the dough squares until all the filling and dough are used up.

7. In a deep frying pan over medium heat, heat 2 inches of oil to 350°F. Add the squares a few at a time so as not to crowd the pan and lower the temperature of the frying oil.

   Deep-fry until golden on both sides, about 4 minutes. Drain on a wire rack to allow excess oil to drip.

Serve with sour cream sauce (recipe follows).

⚘ Sour Cream Sauce

Yield: about 1 cup

2 tablespoons butter

1 small onion, finely chopped

1 teaspoon flour

salt and pepper to taste

¼ cup sour cream

¼ cup milk, if needed

1 teaspoon vinegar

Equipment: Small saucepan, wooden mixing spoon, whisk

1. In a small saucepan over low heat, melt the butter and stir in the onion. Stir-fry until aromatic and softened but not browned.

2. Whisk in the flour, salt, and pepper.

3. Gradually whisk in the sour cream, until a smooth paste is formed.

4. Add the milk little by little, if necessary, to thin out the sauce if it is getting too thick.

Adjust the seasoning, and add more salt if needed.

5. Stir in the lemon juice.

⚘ *Beshbarmak* (Festive Meat Stew)

Beshbarmak means "five fingers," referring to the traditional way of eating this celebratory dish. Nowadays, however, it is more common to eat it with knife and fork. Also often called "*besh*" for short, it is the most well-known of Kazakh dishes and is regarded as the Kazakh national dish. The most desirable meat for *beshbarmak* is horse, which in Kazakhstan is specially bred for tenderness. It is said that the fat from the finest horse meat tastes similar to duck fat. The carrots and potatoes are additions that other regions add to their *beshbarmak*.

Yield: 4 to 6 servings

2½ to 3 pounds meaty ribs of horse meat or lamb or mutton shoulder or beef brisket (or a mixture of different cuts from the same animal)

3 teaspoons **kosher salt**, or to taste

2 cloves garlic, finely minced

1 teaspoon freshly ground black pepper

Sauce:

3 tablespoons horse fat (from cooking the horse sausage) or oil

2 onions, sliced into half rings

3 cups meat broth (from cooking the marinated meat)

½ cup fresh dill, finely chopped, plus more for garnish

½ cup fresh parsley, finely chopped, plus more for garnish

1 pound fresh *kazy* (horse meat sausage) or lamb sausage (*merguez*) or beef sausage

2 bay leaves

1 onion, sliced into half rings

3 carrots, peeled but left whole (optional)

4 potatoes, peeled but left whole (optional)

salt and pepper to taste

Noodles (as an alternative to making your own noodles: 1 pound of lasagna noodles or about 1 pound packaged *zhaima* noodles made specifically for use in *beshbarmak*):

3 cups flour

½ teaspoon salt

1 large egg, well beaten

½ cup meat broth (from cooking the marinated meat)

Equipment: Large bowl, 2 deep saucepans with cover, frying pan or shallow saucepan with cover, large serving platter or individual serving plates

Note: Needs to be prepared a day ahead.

1. A day before *beshbarmak* is to be served, marinate the meat (except the sausage). Rub the meat thoroughly with the salt, garlic, and pepper, place in a bowl covered with plastic wrap for at least 4 hours or, better still, overnight.

2. The following morning, prick the sausage in several places so that it does not burst during cooking.

3. Place in a saucepan with water to cover, set it at medium heat, and cook slowly, covered, for about 2 to 3 hours, or until tender. Lamb or beef sausage, which is not as wide in diameter as horse sausage, will require less cooking time.

4. Turn off the heat, and let the sausage cool in the water. Skim off the fat on the surface, and use for cooking the sauce, or refrigerate to use for other dishes. The cooking water will be very salty and can be discarded. Keep the sausage warm until needed.

5. In another saucepan, put in the marinated meat, cover with cold water, and bring to a boil.

6. As soon as the water comes to a rolling boil, turn off the heat, and quickly rinse the meat of any scum that has formed on the surface.

7. Return the meat to the washed saucepan, cover with cold water (at least 12 cups), and bring again to a boil. (Changing the cooking water makes for a clearer broth and better taste but is not absolutely necessary.)

   Skim off all froth and scum from the broth.

8. Turn down the heat to low, and keep the meat simmering for 2 to 2½ hours, until fork-tender. Top up the water as needed to keep the meat covered. Adjust the seasoning, adding salt and pepper if necessary. Leave the meat in the cooking broth.

9. Prepare the noodles: In a bowl, combine the flour and salt. Make a well (hole) in the center of the flour mixture, and add the egg and the broth.

10. Gradually mix in the flour, until all comes together into a dough that does not stick to the sides of the bowl. Knead the dough for 5 to 8 minutes until smooth and pliable.

    Cover with plastic wrap or clean kitchen towel, and let rest at room temperature for 30 minutes to 1 hour.

11. On a lightly floured surface, divide the dough into two. Roll out one portion as thinly as you can make it without the dough tearing. Cut into 2 inches wide by 4 inches long noodles (rather like lasagna). Leave the noodles in one layer on the floured surface to dry. Make sure they do not touch; otherwise they will stick to one another.

12. Roll out and cut the other piece of dough in the same manner.

13. Slice the sausage into ¼-inch-thick pieces, and keep warm.

14. Slice the other pieces of meat into smaller portions, also ¼ inch thick, and keep warm.

15. Add the bay leaves and onions to the broth.

16. Warm up the serving platter or individual plates.

17. Add the carrots and potatoes, and cook for 10 to 15 minutes, or until tender. Remove from the broth, slice into bite-size pieces, and keep warm until ready to serve.

    Cook the noodles in the broth, or in a separate pan in salted water, about 4 minutes. If using store-bought dry noodles, allow 6 minutes for cooking (or as directed on package).

    Shortly before serving, prepare the sauce.

Sauce:

18. In a shallow saucepan, heat the fat or oil over medium heat. Stir in the onions, season with salt and pepper, then add the broth, and let the onions cook, covered, until translucent. The onions may be left raw, if a sharper tasting sauce is preferred.

    Turn off the heat, and stir in the dill and parsley.

19. Prepare the serving platter: brush the bottom of the warmed platter with a tablespoonful of horse fat or oil.

20. Place the noodles in one layer, then the meat, mixing the sausage and the meats, and onions. Top with the onion sauce, and garnish with more dill and parsley. Alternatively, plate individual servings in the same manner.

Serve the hot broth in small bowls for each person.

₡ *Domalak Baursak* (Sour Cream Doughnuts)

Baursak is a generic name for puffy pastries that resemble doughnuts. They can be made savory or sweet, but they are most often served as accompaniments to a meat dish and are thus more frequently salty. The basic *baursak* dough does not need to have sour cream, but for special occasions, sour cream or cottage cheese is added to the dough to make it richer and tastier. As well, there is one other step to making *domalak baursak* that marks it as a special occasion dish: it needs to be boiled first before being fried.

Baursak is also made for the memorial meal called *as beru* that is served one year after the death of family members. The *as beru* meal is held to remember the life of the departed family member, as well as to mark the end of mourning. It is believed that the scent of *baursaki* as they fry and puff up in hot oil rises up to reach the spirits in heaven.

Yield: 12 to 15 pieces

2 cups sour cream or cottage cheese	8 cups water
1 cup flour	¼ to—½ cup flour for rolling
3 eggs, beaten	oil for deep-frying
1 tablespoon butter, melted	1 cup sour cream
1 tablespoon sugar	1 cup sugar
¼ teaspoon salt	

Equipment: Food processor, rolling pin, large saucepan, frying pan, sieve, wire rack or paper towels, serving dish

1. In a food processor, process sour cream or cottage cheese until smooth. Add flour, egg, butter, sugar, and salt to make a stiff dough. Remove dough and knead for 7 to 10 minutes until smooth and **elastic**.

2. On a lightly floured surface, roll dough out into a cylinder about ½ inch in diameter. Cut into slices 4 inches long.

3. Bring water to a simmer in a large saucepan. Add fritters, a few at a time, and cook for 2 to 3 minutes after they float. Drain thoroughly on a sieve, and allow to drip dry.

4. Heat oil to 360°F. Roll drained fritters in flour, and slip into hot oil a few at a time.

   Fry to a golden brown, and drain on a wire rack or paper towels.

To serve, arrange on a serving dish, and spoon sour cream over fritters. Sprinkle with sugar.

Korea

Korea has been divided into two countries since 1948: North Korea (the Democratic People's Republic of Korea) and South Korea (Republic of Korea). The majority of South Koreans are Christian or Buddhist; often the ideas and rituals of these religions are mixed with shamanism (the belief that the spirits of nature inhabit both living and nonliving things).

South Korea is the only country in the world where intraclan marriages are banned. According to Confucian scholars, the ban originated in China thousands of years ago, and its purpose was to prevent birth defects due to the marriage of close relatives.

Giving birth to a son is considered a great event in the life of a Korean woman. Because of its importance, women offer prayers and follow rituals in the hopes of giving birth to a boy. Often, offerings are made for 100 days to Taoist shrines, to Buddhist shrines, and to various things in nature, such as rocks, trees, streams, and mountains. The grandmother spirit, *samshin halmoni*, is the main spirit involved with childbirth. Her shrine is kept inside the house and is represented by a piece of folded paper or clean straw hung in one corner of the room. The spirit traditionally guides the child in its growth and well-being throughout its young life. Seaweed soup and rice are offered to the grandmother spirit morning and evening for one week, and the same foods are eaten by the new mother.

In Korea, a baby's 100th day (*paegil*), its first birthday (*ortol*), and an adult's 60th birthday (*hwangap*) are all very special life-cycle celebrations. The 100th-day party marks the baby's survival of a critical period in infancy. Gifts are given to the baby, and offerings of food are made to the grandmother spirit. Family and friends celebrate with wine, rice cakes, and a grand feast. The first birthday celebration is enjoyed in much the same way but is regarded as a more important event. As guests leave the celebration, the child's parents give them each a package of rice cakes. Sharing their rice cakes is a symbol of good health and happiness for the child.

Koreans traditionally use the Chinese lunar calendar, which is based on 60-year cycles—when people reach their 60th year, the cycle returns to the year of their birth. For the *hwangap* (60th birthday), the family usually throws a lavish party, and loved ones visit to honor the celebrant. Rituals involve bowing and drinking wine to honor the celebrant, while traditional Korean music plays throughout the festivities. Rice cakes and fresh fruit are part of the feast.

In Korea, wedding rituals (*shingei*) follow rules set down by Confucius in his book of rites. There are two types of marriage: love marriage (*yonae*) and arranged marriage (*chungmae*). The favorite season for marrying in Korea is in the fall, after the harvest moon, and the date is based on the couple's horoscopes. A fun betrothal event is the prearranged delivery of a large box of gifts for the bride. The box (*ham* or *hahm*) is usually delivered by friends of the groom. It contains an assortment of items: fabric for the traditional Korean dress (*banbok*), jewelry, and some symbolic items, such as stalks of ripened **millet**, which represent a wish for many children. As the group comes within earshot of the house, the deliverers begin shouting, "*Hahm* for sale!" Family members toss the group money, and the box is given to the bride in exchange for food and drink.

In Korea, the betrothal is an important part of the nuptials. The families of the couple gather in the bride's family home to meet and eat. According to ancient traditions, the couple is seated at the head of a long table, with the bride-to-be's family sitting down one side and the groom's family seated across from them. After each family member is formally introduced, the meal is served.

The traditional wedding ceremony is held in the bride's home. Most brides wear Western-style wedding dresses, though some prefer to wear the traditional Korean dress (*banbok*), which has a long full skirt (*chima*) made of silk. The wedding ceremony begins with an exchange of bows and drinks. The bride and groom face one another across a table filled with objects symbolic of many aspects of the life they are about to begin together. This ceremony is followed by another called the *pyebaek*, which is the bride's first greeting to her husband's family. It is at this time that the bride presents the groom's family with their gifts.

An altar is set up, and on it are placed items of Korean symbolism, such as a wooden or live goose, which symbolizes fidelity. The groom, while holding the goose, may *kowtow* ("bow low") to his bride as a display of his sincerity and faithfulness. Other altar items include *otsuka* (symbolic shapes and figures woven from straw), dried pheasant, a gourd bottle of rice wine tied in blue and red thread, rice cakes, chestnuts, dates, and fruits.

The groom's kinfolk, after being bowed to, receive a cup of "bride's wine" (also called "cup of the wine of mutual joy") and small portions of pheasant. The in-laws pelt the bride on the long white sleeves of her wedding gown with dates and chestnuts, wishing her good fortune as a mother. On leaving, they may discreetly deposit *kowtow* money for the bride in a white envelope on a tray.

♪ *Kook Soo* (Noodle Soup with Meatballs)

The Korean wedding banquet known as "noodle banquet" (*kook soo sang*) is much less formal and elaborate than other Asian wedding feasts. The banquet gets its name from the noodle soup (*kook soo*) served with the meal. Noodles represent a wish for a long and happy life.

Yield: serves 6

8 ounces **ground** beef

1 small onion, **finely chopped**

1 teaspoon **sesame seeds**

½ teaspoon ground ginger

salt and pepper to taste

½ cup all-purpose flour

1 egg, beaten

2 tablespoons vegetable oil, more as needed

8-ounce package thin egg noodles (cooked according to directions on package and drained) (available at Asian food stores and most supermarkets)

1 teaspoon sesame oil

6 cups canned beef broth

1 clove garlic, finely chopped

2 green onions, finely sliced

3 tablespoons soy sauce, more or less to taste

1 teaspoon rice vinegar

ground red pepper, to taste

Equipment: Large mixing bowl, 2 small shallow bowls, large skillet, slotted spoon, large serving bowl with cover or tureen (covered casserole dish), mixing spoon, large saucepan

1. Prepare meatballs: In large mixing bowl, combine ground beef, onion, sesame seeds, ginger, and salt and pepper to taste. Using your hands, mix well. Form into tiny ¾-inch meatballs (makes about 20).

2. Prepare to pan-fry: Put flour in one small shallow bowl and beaten egg in another small shallow bowl. Heat 2 tablespoons oil in large skillet over medium heat. Dip each meatball in flour, shake off excess, then dip in egg mixture, and put in skillet. Fry a few meatballs at a time for 5 to 7 minutes until cooked through and browned on all sides. Using slotted spoon, transfer to large serving bowl or tureen. Continue frying meatballs, adding more oil as needed.

3. Sprinkle cooked, drained noodles with sesame oil to prevent them from sticking together, and add to serving container with meatballs. Cover to keep warm.

4. In a large saucepan, bring beef broth to boil over medium-high heat. Add garlic, green onions, soy sauce, rice vinegar, ground red pepper to taste, and salt and pepper to taste. Reduce heat to **simmer** for 5 to 7 minutes for flavor to develop. Pour over noodle mixture in serving container, stir, and cover.

To serve, set soup on the table with a ladle and small bowls for portioning out individual serving. In Korea, soup is eaten with the meal, not first as an appetizer as in Western cultures.

♪ *Daikon Kimchi* (Pickled Radishes)

Note: This recipe takes over 2 days.

Kimchi is so much a part of Korean life that it is considered a national treasure by the South Korean government. Many different types of *kimchi* are prepared for the wedding feast. The ultimate *kimchi* for special celebration feasts is *possam kimchi*. It is very complicated, and added to the vegetables are such items as octopus, salted shrimp juice, and oysters. The following *kimchi* is made with easily available ingredients. Daikon radishes are long white tubular radishes popular in many Asian countries.

Yield: serves 8 to 10

2 pounds *daikon* radishes (available at Asian food stores and some supermarkets), peeled and cut into 1-inch cubes

1 tablespoon **kosher salt**

3 tablespoons dried red pepper flakes

3 cloves garlic, **finely chopped**

1 tablespoon rice vinegar

1 tablespoon soy sauce

1 tablespoon **sesame seeds**

½ teaspoon salt

½ teaspoon sugar

Equipment: **Colander**, large mixing bowl, 2-quart food container with tight-fitting lid

1. Put cubed daikon radishes in colander set in sink, and sprinkle with kosher salt. Toss to mix well, and let drain for 5 minutes. Using your hands, squeeze out excess water. Transfer radishes to large mixing bowl. Add red pepper flakes, garlic, rice vinegar, soy sauce, sesame seeds, regular salt, and sugar. Toss to mix well.

2. Transfer to 2-quart container. Cover loosely with lid so that, as the *kimchi* ferments, the gas can escape. Leave at room temperature overnight or up to 2 days for flavor to develop. Cover leftovers tightly with lid, and refrigerate up to one week.

To serve, put kimchi in a small serving bowl. To eat, take a little kimchi with each bite of food.

Dduk Boki (Korean Rice Cakes)

Dduk Boki is a favorite dish throughout Korea. It is a quick, easy, and ideal to serve at a wedding feast or at a baby's first birthday celebration.

Yield: serves 4 to 6

Sauce:

2 tablespoons chili pepper paste, or to taste (available at international or Asian markets)

1 teaspoon rice vinegar (available at most supermarkets)

2 tablespoons vegetable oil, more as needed

2 cloves garlic, trimmed, **minced**

4 tablespoons soy sauce

1 tablespoon ginger root, **trimmed, grated**

1 teaspoon sugar

1 pound package *dduk* (rice cake sticks), fresh or frozen (cooked according to directions on package) (available at international markets), drained, cut into about 2- to 3-inch-long sticks

salt and pepper to taste

For **garnish**:

½ cup roasted **sesame seeds**

½ cup green onions, trimmed, **finely chopped**

Equipment: Medium mixing bowl, mixing spoon, large skillet, tongs

1. Prepare sauce: In mixing bowl, combine chili pepper paste, soy sauce, ginger, sugar, and vinegar, mix well. Set aside.

2. Prepare rice cakes: Heat 2 tablespoons oil in skillet over medium-high heat. Add garlic, and **sauté** 1 to 2 minutes. Add rice cake sticks, and sauté 3 to 4 minutes or until golden on all sides. Add more oil if needed to prevent sticking.

3. Stir in chili pepper sauce, cook 2 to 3 minutes, or until heated through. Add salt and pepper to taste.

Serve warm, garnished with sesame seeds and green onions as a starter for the wedding feast or birthday celebration.

Kyrgyzstan

Kyrgyzstan is a highly mountainous country located in the eastern part of Central Asia. It is bordered by China on the east and shares borders with Tajikistan, Uzbekistan, and Kazakhstan.

Like other Central Asian Republics, the majority of people living in Kyrgyzstan are Muslim. (See Islam and Islamic Life-Cycle Rituals, page lxxvi.) Under Communism, religious practices were officially discouraged. Since gaining independence in 1991, the Kyrgyz Muslims have been free to observe the life-cycle customs of Islam. In addition to the Muslim population, Kyrgyzstan still has a large Russian minority, particularly in the cities, and these Russians celebrate the life-cycle rituals of the Russian Orthodox Church. (See Eastern or Orthodox Church Life-Cycle Rituals, page lxxv).

The food of Kyrgyzstan is simple and hearty, similar to neighboring countries. Rice, noodles, or potatoes and both yeast and flat breads are eaten at almost every meal. For special occasions and life-cycle feasts, mutton, beef, or goat are added to the pot. Pigs are raised in the region, but the pork is eaten only by the Christian or Chinese foreigners who live in the country. Other dishes served at a celebration feast are *kartophelnye piroshki z baraninoy, baklazhannaya ikra* (recipe page 508), and *salat* (recipe page 169), along with assorted cheeses and breads.

In Muslim countries, salads are not eaten as a separate course, but rather all food is placed on the table and eaten at the same time.

⚘ *Besh Barmak* (Meat with Noodles and Vegetables)

The Kyrgyzstan people are frugal, and nothing is wasted. *Besh barmak* is usually made with horsemeat; however we suggest using more readily available beef or lamb. *Besh barmak* is inexpensive, making it perfect for serving a large group of family and friends at a wedding celebration feast.

Yield: serves 4 to 6

2 tablespoons vegetable oil, more as needed	4 carrots, trimmed, coarsely chopped
4 onions, **trimmed, coarsely chopped**	salt and pepper to taste
4 cloves garlic, trimmed, **minced**	1-pound package egg noodles
4 pounds mutton or beef	For **garnish**: ½ cup chives
water, as needed	

Equipment: **Dutch oven** or large stock pot with cover, mixing spoon, tongs, cutting board, slotted spoon, medium mixing bowl, strainer or **colander**, sharp knife

1. Heat 2 tablespoons oil in Dutch oven or large stock pot over medium-high heat. Add onions and garlic, and **sauté** 3 to 5 minutes, or until soft. Add meat and cook 15 to 20 minutes, or until brown on all sides, using tongs to turn frequently. Add more oil if needed to prevent sticking.

2. Add water to cover carrots and salt and pepper to taste. Bring to boil over high heat, cover, reduce to simmer, and cook about 2½ to 3 hours or until meat is cooked through and falling off bone. Add more water if necessary to prevent sticking.

3. Using tongs, remove meat and place on cutting board to rest. Using slotted spoon, transfer vegetables to mixing bowl, set aside, keep warm. Reserve liquid.

4. Return reserved liquid to boil over high heat. Add noodles, and cook according to directions on package. When tender, remove, using slotted spoon, and place in strainer or colander to drain. Set aside, keep warm. Reserve liquid.

5. Using sharp knife, carefully slice meat from bone into serving-size pieces.

6. Place about a cup of noodles on individual plates, top with sliced meat and vegetables.

Serve warm garnished with chives. Pour reserved broth into small bowls, and serve as a clear soup.

⚘ *Salat* (Tomato, Cucumber, and Yogurt Salad)

In Muslim countries, salads are not eaten as a separate course, but rather all food is placed on the table and eaten at the same time.

Yield: serves 4

2 large tomatoes, sliced ¼ inch thick	¼ cup virgin olive oil
2 small cucumbers, thinly sliced diagonally	salt and pepper to taste
1 red onion, thinly sliced	¾ cup plain yogurt

Equipment: Medium serving platter, spoon, plastic food wrap

1. Arrange tomato and cucumber slices alternately, slightly overlapping on medium serving platter. Separate onions into rings and spread over top. Sprinkle with oil and salt and pepper. Cover with plastic wrap, and let stand at room temperature for about 2 hours for flavors to develop.

2. Prepare to serve: Uncover and spoon dollops of yogurt over the vegetables.

Serve at room temperature as a salad.

♪ *Chai iz Revenya* (Rhubarb Tea)

Tea is the favorite beverage in Kyrgyzstan, especially when it is made with rhubarb as in this recipe.

Yield: serves 4 to 6

2 cups frozen rhubarb, thawed and chopped, or 2 cups fresh rhubarb, **trimmed** and chopped	6 cups water
	sugar to taste

For **garnish**:

4 to 6 fresh mint leaves

1 lemon, cut in 4 to 6 wedges

Equipment: Medium saucepan, mixing spoon, strainer, widemouthed pitcher, spoon, beverage glasses

1. Put rhubarb and water into medium saucepan, and bring to boil over medium-high heat. Reduce heat to **simmer**, and cover. Stirring occasionally, cook until rhubarb is mushy and fully cooked, 30 to 40 minutes.

2. Strain rhubarb liquid into widemouthed pitcher. Using back of spoon, press on residue in strainer to release all liquid. While liquid is hot, stir in sugar to taste. Cool to room temperature, and refrigerate. Discard rhubarb residue or cover and refrigerate for another use.

To serve, pour rhubarb liquid over ice cubes in glasses, and garnish with wedge of lemon and sprig of mint.

Malaysia and Singapore

Malaysia consists of a narrow peninsula located south of Thailand in southeastern Asia and the northern part of the island of Borneo.

Malaysia's population is among the most varied in East Asia, consisting of Malays, Chinese, Indians, and indigenous groups known as *bumiputra*, or "sons of the soil." Indigenous tribes have their own languages and religions, although many have become Muslim or Christian. Many Chinese and Indians in Malaysia are descendants of workers brought by the British to work on the rubber plantations or in tin factories. Malaysian life-cycle events vary according to the country of origin and religious preference.

Singapore is a small group of islands located between Malaysia and Indonesia, and Singapore City, its capital, is one of the world's busiest ports. Singapore is an ethnically diverse country where Buddhists, Hindus, Muslims, and some Christians live side by side. The largest portion of Singapore's population is Chinese, followed by Malay, then Indian. As in Malaysia, life-cycle events of the people of Singapore vary according to the country of origin and religious preference.

Some Malay women can be very superstitious and keep themselves and their newborn infant protected from bad weather and evil spirits at all times. According to this custom, the baby must not be exposed to wind and cold, nor must it be praised for fear of attracting jealous spirits. The baby's head is ceremonially shaved 40 days after birth, at the end of the mother's confinement. After this ceremony, family and friends gather to view the baby, which can be a simple or elaborate affair depending upon family superstitions. If there is a feast, several rice dishes similar to the Indonesian *nasi uduk/ gurih* (see recipe page 147) and/or the more elaborate Malaysian *nasi kuning lengkap* (see recipe follows) might be served.

In both Malaysia and Singapore, wedding ceremonies are conducted according to religious preference. After the traditional ceremony, if the family can afford it, a big showy wedding reception with plenty of beautifully presented food is a current trend. It's not unusual for families to invite several hundred people to a hotel or restaurant to share the joy of their son's or daughter's marriage. Modern-day receptions are often a blending of the best of several cultures and include plenty of toasts, merrymaking, drinking and eating, picture taking, and even the newlywed couple performing a karaoke duet.

Rice is fundamental to the existence of the Malays, and they believe it to possess an essential life force. For a Malay, rice is synonymous with food, and its presence is what distinguishes a meal. Therefore, ceremonials that mark every stage of life from birth through coming of age, marriage, and death involve a symbolic meal of rice.

Nasi Kuning Lengkap (Yellow Rice in Cone-shape)

Rising like a golden mountain, yellow rice, made into a cone shape, is the centerpiece of the banquet table. An Indonesian cone mold is available at some Asian food stores, or a conical-shaped strainer, about 8½ inches deep, available at most kitchenware stores, can also be used. Or make a mold using cardboard that can be cut and formed into a cone shape about 8 inches tall and about 8 or 10 inches across at the base. Line the cardboard cone with foil, and spray the inside with vegetable cooking spray. Set the prepared mold, point end-down, in a container like a deep bowl or pitcher, so that it can be filled easily without tipping over.

Yield: serves 8

3 tablespoons vegetable oil, divided

1 cup onions, **finely chopped**

2 cloves garlic, finely chopped

6 cups fresh coconut milk made from 6 cups **coarsely chopped** coconut and 6 cups hot water (recipe page 225) or 6 cups canned

coconut milk (available at some supermarkets and most Asian food stores)

2 pieces **lemon grass**, each **trimmed** to 4 inches long

4 teaspoons **ground** turmeric

1 tablespoon salt

3 cups long grain rice

For **garnish**:

3 hot, red chili peppers

12 to 15 romaine lettuce leaves, trimmed, washed, and separated

2 cucumbers, cut crosswise into ¼-inch-thick slices

8 hard-cooked eggs, peeled

2 eggs, lightly beaten and prepared per instructions

½ cup finely chopped celery leaves

Equipment: Large saucepan, mixing spoon, prepared cone-shaped mold (see introduction), thread, small skillet, wide metal spatula

Note: Use care when handling peppers. Wrap your hands in plastic wrap, or cover them with plastic sandwich bag. If you accidentally touch your eyes, rinse them out at once under cold running water.

1. Heat 2 tablespoons oil in large saucepan over medium-high heat, add onion and garlic, stir, and **sauté** 3 to 5 minutes until soft. Add coconut milk, lemon grass, turmeric, salt, and rice. Stir and cook until small bubbles appear around edge of pan. (Do not let milk boil.) Reduce heat to **simmer**, cover, and cook 20 to 25 minutes, until rice is tender. Remove from heat and keep covered until all the liquid is absorbed. Remove and discard lemon grass.

2. Fill greased cone-shaped mold with cooked rice, packing it firmly. Cover opening with foil, and refrigerate overnight to firm.

3. Unmold rice onto the center of a large round serving platter. Tie stems of 3 peppers together with thread. Place the tied ends at the very top and spread the peppers to cascade over the rice. Place lettuce leaves around base of rice. Arrange sliced cucumbers and quartered hard-cooked eggs on lettuce.

4. Heat remaining 1 tablespoon oil in small skillet over medium-high heat. Add lightly beaten eggs, and cook undisturbed for 1 minute, or until bottom is lightly browned. Using wide metal spatula, turn egg over, and cook 1 minute more. Slide it onto a plate, and cut into strips about ¼-inch wide. Decorate the rice cone by scattering strips of egg over the surface. Sprinkle with celery leaves.

To serve, place in the center of the banquet table as the centerpiece. Some side dishes served with the rice are *rempah* (recipe page 174), and others can be purchased at Asian food stores, such as *atjar kuning* (yellow pickles) and *rempejek* (peanut wafers).

♪ *Curry Laksa* (Curried Seafood and Coconut Soup)

Any life-cycle celebration is enhanced by serving *curry laksa*.

Yield: serves 4 to 6

Rempah paste:

20 **shallots, trimmed, minced**

10 cloves garlic, trimmed, minced

1 tablespoon crushed red pepper, or to taste

2 red chilies, trimmed, minced

2 teaspoons *belcan* or shrimp paste (available at international or Asian markets)

6 candlenuts (available at international or Asian markets)

3 tablespoons curry powder, homemade (recipe page 88) or store-bought

2 tablespoons vegetable oil, more as needed

3 stalks **lemon grass**, trimmed

3 sprigs curry leaves (available at international or Asian markets)

1 quart chicken stock

2 (14.5 ounces *each*) canned coconut milk, or homemade (recipe page 225)

1 pound package firm tofu, cut into 2-inch cubes

12 fresh scallops

12 large shrimp, peeled, **deveined**

For serving: 2½ cups vermicelli noodles (cooked according to directions on package)

For **garnish**:

2 cups bean sprouts, trimmed, **blanched**, more as needed

3 **hard-cooked** eggs, peeled, halved

Equipment: **Mortar and pestle** or food processor or **blender**, spatula, **Dutch oven** or large stock pot, mixing spoon

1. Prepare *rempah* paste: Place shallots, garlic, crushed red pepper, red chilies, *belcan*, candlenuts, and curry powder in mortar and pestle, food processor, or blender, and grind into paste. Set aside.

2. Heat 2 tablespoons oil in Dutch oven or stock pot over medium-high heat. Add *rempah* paste, lemon grass, and curry leaves, **sauté** for 2 to 3 minutes, or until aromatic. Add more oil if necessary.

3. Stir in stock and bring to boil, reduce to simmer 10 to 15 minutes.

4. Stir in coconut milk, tofu, scallops, and shrimp. Return to boil over high heat, reduce to simmer, and, stirring constantly to prevent curdling, cook 5 to 7 minutes, or until shrimp and scallops are opaque white and cooked through. Add salt and pepper to taste. Remove and discard curry leaves and lemon grass stalk.

Serve warm in individual bowls over vermicelli noodles, garnished bean sprouts, and hard-cooked egg.

♪ *Rempah* (Coconut-Beef Patties)

This is one of many side dishes served with rice.

Yield: about 20 pieces

1 pound **ground** beef	1 clove **finely chopped** garlic
4 cups **coconut**, finely grated	¼ teaspoon ground cumin
1 egg	salt and pepper to taste
2 teaspoons ground **coriander**	2 to 3 cups vegetable oil, for frying

Equipment: Baking sheet, paper towels, food processor, rubber spatula, large **heavy-bottomed** skillet, wide metal spatula, oven mitts

Preheat oven to lowest setting.

1. Line baking sheet with several layers of paper towels. Set aside.

2. Combine beef, grated coconut, egg, coriander, garlic, cumin, and salt and pepper to taste in food processor. Process until mixture is blended, smooth and fluffy, about 3 minutes.

   Note: While processing, turn machine off once or twice, and scrape down sides of container with a rubber spatula.

3. For each patty, scoop up about ¼ cup of mixture with your hands, and pat into a round disk about 2 inches in diameter and ½ inch thick.

4. Heat oil in large heavy-bottomed skillet over medium-high heat. Add patties a few at a time, and fry for about 5 minutes on each side until browned and cooked through. Transfer cooked patties to drain on paper towel–covered baking sheet, and place in oven to keep warm while cooking remaining patties.

To serve, arrange meat patties on platter, and serve with nasi kuning lengkap *(recipe page 171).*

Mongolia

Mongolia, a mountainous country located in central Asia, is bordered by Russia to the north and China to the south. The Mongol people endure challenging weather throughout the year with cold, harsh winters and hot, parched summers. Their will and determination to survive have given them great strength and perseverance. The majority of Mongol people are nomadic and practice Tibetan Buddhism or Shamanism. (See Buddhism and Buddhist Life-cycle Rituals and Shamanism Life Cycles and traditions, page lxxxii.)

Traditionally, if a Mongolian man wishes to marry, he asks a matchmaker to send gifts of tea, sugar, and a white handkerchief symbolizing harmony and prosperity to his future bride-to-be. The bridegroom also sends cattle, sheep, or other livestock to the bride's family. If the gifts are accepted by the girl's family, this symbolizes acceptance of the marriage. Gifts should total to nine or be divided by nine as this is an auspicious number in Mongolian culture. Weddings are time of joyous celebration with lots of food, dancing, singing, and music. The festive occasions usually lasts two to three days.

⚘ *Buuz* (Steamed Meat Dumplings)

When families gather for a festive wedding reception, *Buuz* is perfect to have on the menu.

Yield: serves 4 to 6

2 tablespoons vegetable oil, more as needed

1 onion, **trimmed, finely chopped**

3 cloves garlic, trimmed, **minced**

1 pound ground mutton or beef

salt and pepper to taste

1 package wonton skins (available at most supermarkets or international markets)

Equipment: Large skillet, mixing spoon, **pastry brush**, baking sheet, **steamer pan** or **basket**, tongs, serving platter

1. Prepare filling: Heat 2 tablespoons oil in skillet over medium-high heat. Add onion and garlic, and **sauté** until soft about 3 to 5 minutes. Crumble in meat, and cook 10 to 12 minutes, or until browned and cooked through. Add more oil if necessary to prevent sticking. Remove from heat, set aside.

2. Prepare dumplings: One at a time, place wonton skins on clean work surface. Spoon about 1 tablespoon meat mixture in center. Using clean, wet finger, moisten edges of wonton skin. Make a pouch by bringing opposite edges of wonton skin together over meat mixture. Pinch together to seal. Set aside on baking sheet. Continue until all wrappers are filled and mixture is used.

3. Fill steamer pan ⅓ full with water and bring to boil over high heat. Transfer dumplings to steamer basket, place in steamer pan, cover and steam 12 to 15 minutes, or until cooked through. Carefully remove dumplings from steamer using tongs, and place on serving platter, keep warm. Continue steaming in batches. If necessary, add more water to steamer to prevent drying out.

Serve warm as a starter for a wedding celebration feast.

Myanmar (Burma)

Myanmar, located in South East Asia and bordered by Thailand, China, India, and Bangladesh, is made up of many different cultures. It is customary in Myanmar for people to live in communities and compounds with others of the same ethnic heritage. Most Burmese are Buddhists. (See Buddhism and Buddhist Life-Cycle Rituals, page lxxxii.)

Among Buddhists, the occasion for a feast may be a christening, a birthday, a Buddhist initiation or ear-piercing ceremony, a wedding or wedding anniversary, or a celebration held in honor of deceased parents. A feast can take place in one's home or in a monastery and usually includes offerings of food and other items to the monks.

Almost all Burmese eat with their fingers. Both soup and salad are served with the main dishes, not as separate courses. Appetizers and desserts are reserved for ceremonial occasions. Otherwise, the final course is tea, without milk or sugar, and fresh fruit.

In Myanmar, birth is an auspicious occasion in every family, and before the child is born, the expectant mother is closely guided by astrology. Each day of the week is designated by a different animal and is significant to the infant's horoscope. After the baby is born, the mother receives many gifts and good wishes from family and friends.

The month of *Tabodwe* (usually falling near February) is not only the time to celebrate the rice harvest but also the time that young boys of seven years or more enter a monastery for a brief time and devote themselves to prayer. At the same time, young girls participate in a formal ear-piercing ceremony called *shinpyu*. The foods served at a *shinpyu* ceremony vary, depending upon the wealth of the celebrants. The more wealthy enjoy a meal that can consist of as many as four meat and four fish and shellfish dishes, plus vegetable soup and rice. A middle-class family will sit down to fewer dishes, and the poor honor the day with a meal of rice and pickled vegetables.

Myanmar marriages involve only the mutual consent of the two parties concerned. Living and eating together is enough to constitute marriage, and traditionally the marriage is valid if neighbors recognize it as such. However, if desired, weddings can be as elaborate as the couple's wishes and the parents' financial position can make them. The simplest wedding is held at the home of the bride-to-be. Parents of both parties and relatives are present along with a gathering of elders. The bride and groom sit together on a smooth mat as they pay obeisance to parents and the "triple gems": the Buddha, the *dharma* (also *dhamma*, which means "truth" or "law"), and the *sangha* (which refers to Buddhist monks).

The marriage ceremony is performed by a master of ceremonies dressed like a Brahmin (a Hindu of priestly caste). During the ceremony, the hands of the bride and groom are tied with a silk scarf and dipped in a silver bowl of water. This ritual signifies that they are now joined together as one. At the end of the ceremony, silver coins and paper confetti are showered on guests as symbols of wealth and hopes for many children for the newlyweds. The refreshments served after the ceremony can range from simple tea with cakes to an extensive buffet laden with beautifully garnished delicacies.

According to Buddhist beliefs, death is accepted as just one stage in the endless cycle of existence. (See Buddhism and Buddhist Life-Cycle Rituals, page lxxxii.) The body of the deceased remains behind while the soul moves on to a new rebirth. No formal periods of mourning are designated by the Buddhist religion. On the day a person dies, a monk from the family's monastery is brought to the home of the deceased. Family members make a feast offering to the monastery. The deceased is bathed and fully dressed in favorite garments. Candles, incense sticks, water, and token offerings of food are placed at his or her head. An earthen water pot is placed under the bed on which the body is laid.

At the funeral, the height of each family member is measured with string. The lengths of string are then put into the coffin as a reminder to the deceased of his or her earthly family. A coin, 25 *pya* (about 4 cents), is placed in the mouth of the deceased. This is used as payment to the navigator guiding the soul across to the land of the dead. The water pot is then broken. At this time, the grieving family is expected to show their emotions, loudly wailing (crying is considered healthy and cathartic for the mourners).

A weeklong wake then takes place to appease the spirit of the dead, who according to legend, stays in the house for up to a week after its demise. Doors and windows are kept open to make it easy for the spirit of death to exit the premises. A week later, monks are again invited to the house to pray and to remind the spirit of the deceased that it is no longer a member of the household and must go on its way.

⚖ *Weta Hin* (Curried Pork)

In rural areas, curry is served only on special occasions. Each person is served boiled rice, and a little food is taken from each accompanying dish to eat with it.

Yield: serves 4

1 onion, **finely chopped**

5 cloves garlic, finely chopped

1 tablespoon finely chopped ginger root

1 teaspoon **ground** turmeric

½ teaspoon dried red pepper flakes

2 tablespoons vegetable oil

2 pounds boneless lean pork shoulder, cut into 2-inch cubes

1 teaspoon sesame oil (available at Asian food stores)

16-ounce can of whole tomatoes, drained

1 stalk fresh **lemon grass**, finely chopped (available at Asian food stores)

1 tablespoon fish sauce (*nuoc mam*) (available at Asian food stores)

cooked rice, kept warm for serving

Equipment: Electric **blender**, rubber spatula, **Dutch oven** or large saucepan with cover

1. Put onion, garlic, ginger root, turmeric, and red pepper flakes in blender. Cover and **blend** until smooth, about 1 minute.

   Note: While blending, turn machine off once or twice, and scrape down sides of container with rubber spatula.

2. Heat vegetable oil in Dutch oven or large saucepan over medium-high heat. Add cubed pork, blended onion mixture, sesame oil, tomatoes, lemon grass, and fish sauce. Using a fork,

break up tomatoes. Bring to boil and stir. Reduce heat to **simmer**, cover, and cook until meat is tender, about 1½ hours.

To serve, transfer cooked rice to serving bowl, and either cover with weta hin *or serve it in separate bowls.*

¿ *Ohn-No-Kauk-Swe* (Burmese Chicken Coconut Soup)

Ohn-No-Kauk-Swe is a classic chicken soup with a unique Burmese twist of coconut milk with spices. It is a welcome addition to serve at any life-cycle celebration in Myanmar.

Yield: serves 4 to 6

2 onions, **trimmed, finely chopped**, divided

1 tablespoon ginger root, trimmed, **grated**

4 cloves garlic, trimmed, **minced**

1 chili pepper, trimmed, finely chopped

5 cups chicken stock, divided

2 tablespoons all-purpose flour

2 tablespoons vegetable oil, more as needed

4 to 6 chicken breasts or thighs, cut into 1-inch cubes

½ teaspoon cayenne pepper or to taste

2 teaspoons paprika

½ teaspoon turmeric

14.5-ounces coconut milk, homemade (recipe page 225), or canned

For serving:

2 cups vermicelli noodles (available at most supermarkets) (cooked according to directions on package)

4 green onions, trimmed, finely chopped

2 tablespoons **cilantro**, trimmed, finely chopped

4 to 6 lime wedges

Equipment: Food processor or **blender**, medium mixing bowl, whisk, **Dutch oven** or large stock pot, mixing spoon, **strainer**, small bowl

1. Place ½ chopped onions, ginger root, garlic, chili pepper, and ½ cup stock in food processor or blender and **purée**, set aside.

2. Place flour in mixing bowl, and slowly **whisk** in 1 cup stock. Set aside.

3. Heat 2 tablespoons oil in Dutch oven or stock pot over medium-high heat. Add remaining chopped onion, and **sauté** 3 to 5 minutes or until soft. Add chicken, and sauté 10 to 12 minutes or until golden on all sides. Add more oil if necessary to prevent sticking.

4. Reduce heat to medium-low, and stir in onion-ginger purée, cayenne pepper, paprika, and turmeric, mix well.

5. Pour flour mixture through strainer into Dutch oven or stock pot with chicken, mix well. Add remaining 3½ cups stock, mix well. Bring to boil over high heat, reduce to simmer 15 to 20 minutes, or until chicken is tender and cooked through. Test **chicken doneness**.

6. **Temper** coconut milk in small bowl with 1 cup liquid from cooked chicken soup. Stir into chicken soup, mix well. Stirring frequently, continue cooking 5 to 7 minutes, or until heated through.

Serve warm in individual bowls over vermicelli. Garnish with green onions, cilantro, and lime wedges.

♨ *Thorebut Htamin* (Buttered Rice with Raisins and Cashew Nuts)

The number of dishes is important (more is better), so it is not unusual for several rice dishes to be served at the same meal.

Yield: serves 4

2 cups rice

4 cups water

¼ teaspoon salt

1 cup butter or margarine, cut into small pieces (about the size of walnuts)

1 cup golden raisins

1 cup **roasted** cashew nuts

Equipment: Medium saucepan with cover, mixing spoon

1. Put rice in saucepan. Add water, salt, and butter or margarine. Bring to a boil over medium-high heat, and stir. Reduce heat to **simmer**, cover, and cook 20 for minutes. Remove from heat, keep covered for 5 minutes.

2. Add raisins and cashews, and stir to mix thoroughly. Let stand, covered, 15 minutes for flavor to develop before serving.

To serve, transfer to serving bowl, and serve with weta hin *(recipe page 177).*

Nepal

The tiny, landlocked country of Nepal is located on the southern slopes of the Himalayan mountains between India on the south and the Tibetan region of China on the north. Nepal is home to numerous ethnic groups, each with its own language, customs and culture. Most Nepalese are Hindus, the official religion of Nepal.

The Hindus, along with the country's Buddhist minority, have, over the centuries, interwoven many of their rituals with local traditions of animism (the belief that all things have a soul) and shamanism (sorcery or magic). This blending has formed many unusual and complex religious practices. In ceremonies performed by the Hindu temple priest (*pujaari*), the Buddhist monk (*lama*), or the village shaman (*jhaakri*), some form of worship (*pujaa*) will focus on all things in nature. Rites of passage, especially funerals, and curing ceremonies are interwoven with animists' and shamans' concerns for placating local spirits and natural forces. Cows are sacred to Hindus and are protected and not eaten. Even trees are given offerings of flowers and colored rice by the people of Nepal.

Hindus have a very important ceremony for boys of the higher castes (see Hinduism and Hindu Life-Cycle Rituals, page lxxix), known as the "thread ceremony." During the ritual, the young men receive a sacred "thread" (a three-strand rope or cord), which symbolizes their transition into manhood and officially welcomes them into their religion. In Nepal, the thread ceremony (*janal purniama*) is held during the month of *Saaun* (July–August). Men wear the thread, which is looped over the left shoulder and tied under the right arm, for the rest of their lives, changing it only if it is damaged or defiled.

Among most Nepalese, marriages are prearranged by parents. The wedding ceremony usually takes place on an auspicious date selected by an astrologer. Most weddings are held in midwinter, especially during January and February, well after the harvest and before the spring planting. Wedding ceremonies vary with each ethnic group, and some can be very complicated affairs, lasting up to a week. Very important to all celebrations are the groups of professional musicians referred to as "wedding bands," who travel around the country providing music for weddings. At different stages of the ceremony, the wedding procession, led by a wedding band, moves back and forth between the bride's and groom's houses.

Among the upper Hindu castes, the weddings are loud, musical affairs accompanied by much drumming and horn blowing as the bride's and groom's parties travel to and from each other's villages, sometimes over a period of several days. Solemn rituals, with aspects of the Hindu fire ceremony (see Hinduism and Hindu Life-Cycle Rituals, page lxxix), take place in the evening, usually at the home of the bride's parents. Food is important to wedding celebrations, and there is often more than one great feast, depending upon the family's wealth. In Nepal, as in a number of other Asian countries, red is a happy color and worn for weddings (white is the color for funerals and mourning). During the ceremony, to denote marriage, women have the traditional Hindu application of vermilion (red dye) applied in the parting of their hair.

⚗ *Poppadums* (Bean or Lentil Flatbread (Wafers))

Bread, an important staple, is eaten at every Nepalese meal. Life-cycle celebration feasts include several different breads, among them *poppadums*. *Poppadums* are crisp, paper-thin flatbreads about 6 inches in diameter, made from beans or lentils. They are sold in dried form in Asian and Indian food stores and are either roasted, grilled, or fried at home. Traditionally *poppadums* are deep-fried at 375°F for about 1 minute, until puffed and crisp, then drained on paper towels. They are easier to prepare, delicious, and fat-free when baked in a toaster oven. They are done when they turn puffy, brown, and crisp. They can also be baked in a conventional oven (directions follow).

Yield: Depends on package size.

1 package *poppadums* (available at most
Asian, Indian, and Middle Eastern food
stores)

Equipment: Kitchen towel, nonstick baking sheet, tongs or metal spatula, oven mitts

1. Separate the *poppadums* from the package, and keep covered with damp towel until ready to bake.

Preheat oven to 350°F.

2. To bake in batches: Place 2 or 3 flatbreads side by side on nonstick baking sheet, and bake for 4 to 6 minutes on each side, or until puffed, brown around the edges, and crisp. Use tongs or metal spatula to turn over.

To serve, stack in a napkin-lined basket to keep warm. Break the breads into manageable pieces, and use each piece to transport food to your mouth.

⚘ *Aalu Achaar* (Nepalese Potato Salad)

In Nepal, an endless array of dishes are prepared for the sacred "thread ceremony" feast, and *aalu achaar* would be included.
Roasted sesame seeds are available in Asian or international markets.

Yield: serves 4 to 6

½ cup roasted black **sesame seeds** (*iri goma*) (available at Asian or international markets)

3 green chili peppers, or to taste, **trimmed, seeded, finely chopped**

1teaspoon turmeric

1 teaspoon cayenne pepper

4 tablespoon vegetable oil

juice of 2 lemons or 3 tablespoons lemon juice

4 to 6 medium-sized potatoes, boiled, peeled, cut into 1-inch cubes

salt and pepper to taste

For **garnish**: 4 tablespoons **minced cilantro**

Equipment: Medium skillet, wooden spatula, nut grinder or **mortar and pestle**, salad bowl, mixing spoon, salad fork and spoon, plastic wrap

1. Place roasted sesame seeds in nut grinder or mortar and pestle. Grind into powder and transfer to salad bowl.

2. Add chili peppers, turmeric, cayenne pepper, vegetable oil, and lemon juice, mix well.

3. Add potatoes, and, using salad fork and spoon, toss to mix well. Add salt and pepper to taste. Cover with plastic wrap, and refrigerator for 1 hour or until ready to serve.

Serve chilled as a side dish garnished with cilantro.

ℰ *Rasgulla* (Cheese Balls in Syrup)

Yield: serves 10 to 12

Most Hindu, Buddhist, and Muslim life-cycle celebrations, with the exception of funerals, include great quantities of sweets. Throughout the Indian subcontinent, candy making is a family tradition passed from one generation to another. *Halvais* (candy makers) sell their specialties in bazaars and small shops. *Rasgulla* are a popular sweet treat made with *paneer* (recipe follows).

paneer tikki (firm cheese) (recipe follows)

½ teaspoon crushed cardamom seeds

1 tablespoon farina (available at most supermarkets and Middle Eastern food stores)

2 cups sugar

1¾ cups water

1 tablespoon **rosewater** (available at Middle Eastern food stores and pharmacies)

Equipment: Food processor, rubber spatula, medium bowl, mixing spoon, wax paper, baking sheet, medium saucepan, **candy thermometer**, slotted spoon, raised-edge serving dish

1. Put firm cheese in food processor. Add cardamom and farina, and process until smooth, about 1 minute. Using spatula, scrape cheese mixture down from sides of bowl, and process for 30 seconds more. Transfer cheese mixture to medium bowl. Using clean hands, form cheese mixture into walnut-size balls, and place on wax paper–covered baking sheet.

2. Put sugar into medium saucepan, add water, stir, and bring to a boil over medium-high heat. Stir, reduce heat to medium, and cook until syrup forms a thread when a little is lifted on a spoon or the syrup registers 230° to 240°F on a candy thermometer. Reduce heat to low.

3. Gently drop cheese balls, a few at a time, in syrup, and **simmer** 8 to 10 minutes, or until balls are puffy. Carefully lift balls out of syrup with slotted spoon, and place in raised-edge serving dish. Pour remaining syrup over the balls and sprinkle with rosewater.

Serve warm or at room temperature. Nepalese eat by dipping the fingers of the right hand into the bowl and scooping out a cheese ball; a spoon would be more helpful.

ℰ *Paneer Cheena* (Soft) and *Paneer Tikki* (Firm) (Indian Cheeses)

Paneer (Indian cheese) is easy to make and is eaten throughout the Indian subcontinent. When the cheese is soft and fresh, it is called *paneer cheena*, and when it is firm, it is called *paneer tikki*. The soft cheese is used in desserts and some savory dishes. The firm cheese is cut into wedges, and even when heated, it keeps its firmness rather than melting. Firm cheese is used for *rasgulla* (recipe precedes).

5 cups milk

juice of 2 lemons

Equipment: **Noncorrosive** medium saucepan with cover, wooden mixing spoon, **colander**, 3 layers of cheesecloth about 14 inches square, large bowl, heavy-duty rubber band

1. Heat milk in medium saucepan over medium-high heat until small bubbles form around the edge of the pan. Cook 2 to 3 minutes, stirring with wooden mixing spoon to prevent a film from forming on the top. Remove from heat, and stir in lemon juice. Cover, and let stand until milk separates, about 1 minute.

2. Place a colander lined with the layered cheesecloth over a large bowl. When the thick white curd separates from the pale greenish whey, pour it into the cheesecloth-lined colander. Gather the edges of the cheesecloth together to make a pouch, and gently squeeze out the whey. (Discard the whey, or cover and refrigerate for another use. In Nepal and many other countries, the whey is considered a healthy, refreshing drink. It is also used as a soup stock instead of water.) Wrap a heavy-duty rubber band around the top of the pouch, and hang over the sink faucet so that the bag contents will drain into the sink.

3. For a soft cheese (*paneer cheena*), remove from bag in 1 hour. For a firm, dry cheese (*paneer cheena*), drain overnight. Use for making *rasgulla* (recipe precedes).

Both the soft and firm cheeses are used in cooking or simply sprinkled with assorted spices, such as turmeric, mint, ground red pepper or cumin, and eaten with bread.

Pakistan

Pakistan, located between Afghanistan and India, consists of four regions containing not only differences in climate and terrain but in lifestyle, language, and dress. Pakistani peoples are identified by their region; for instance, those living in the Baluchistan region are known as Balochi, and those in the Sindh region are known as Sindhi. However, despite many regional differences, the majority of the Pakistani population have a strong unifying sense of being Pakistani. Most Pakistanis are Muslim; however, a small portion of the population is Hindu.

After centuries of living in close proximity, the Hindus and Muslims of Pakistan have adopted many of each others' rites and customs. Muslim Pakistanis, for instance, have adopted the dowry system, the shaving off of a newborn's hair, and burning incense at holy places, while many Hindu brides perform the Muslim *mehndi* (henna) ceremony.

The birth of a male heir is generally a happy event. The father rushes off to buy candy, packed in colorful boxes, which he distributes to relatives and friends to announce the birth. In return for receiving the *luddus*, family and friends give money to the child. Also a favorite infant gift is a sacred charm (*ta'weez*), given to protect the child against all evil.

Sweets, such as *badam pistaz barfi* (recipe page 146), hold an important place in life-cycle rituals. They can be given as an offering to the gods and goddesses by the Hindus or as a gesture of goodwill and friendship. The art of making candies is a family business passed down from one generation to the next. Every village, no matter how small, will have a *halwai* (a sweetmeat seller).

The most important life-cycle event for Pakistani Muslim boys is circumcision, which usually takes place when the boy is between the ages of five and six. Traditionally in rural areas, circumcision is performed by the local barber, who also prepares the feast following the circumcision (the barber prepares feasts for other life-cycle occasions as well). Those in urban areas are likely to arrange a party at home, while in the countryside the whole village attends. The child, dressed in fancy clothes specially made for this occasion, receives small gifts of money from the guests.

The extended family, with many relatives living together or nearby, is a source of strength for most Pakistani, and most seldom marry outside their clan. It is common and acceptable among Muslim families in Pakistan for first cousins or even an uncle and a niece to marry. Marriage is considered more of a bond between families than a personal undertaking, and it is not unusual for families to arrange marriages for their yet-to-be-born children. Quite often the couple to be married meet for the first time on their wedding day; however, in urban areas today, once an engagement is formally announced, the couple may date, usually accompanied by a chaperone.

According to tradition, the bride's family is expected to pay for the largest and most expensive wedding feast they can afford. Marriage ceremonies often last for three days, during which time the father of the bride must feed and accommodate hundreds of guests. He not only buys the wedding clothes for the groom and the groom's parents and siblings but is expected to give expensive gifts of clothing and jewelry to senior in-laws.

In Pakistan, most of the ceremonies associated with a marriage are not Muslim but traditional to the Indian subcontinent. In a traditional celebration, the bride remains in seclusion for two weeks prior to the wedding, while her family and friends prepare for the big event. The formal coming together of the families unfolds in two stages. The first day, the bride remains home while her family visits the groom's house; the next day, the groom remains home while his family visits the bride's house, where the *mehndi* ceremony takes place. In the *mehndi*, a symbolic expression of joy, the groom's sister or mother applies henna to the hands and feet of the bride-to-be.

A few days before the wedding celebration, the legal aspects of the marriage, such as signing dowry documents, takes place in a Muslim civil ceremony (*nikah*). The wedding (*shadi*) is a lavish celebration with invited guests, great quantities of food, traditional dancers, and musical entertainment. In Pakistan, popular music known as *qaw-wali* is often played at weddings. The newlyweds remain formally seated throughout the festivities and then leave to eat in a secluded area apart from the guests. At some point during the festivities, the couple departs the wedding reception for the groom's house.

A day or two after the wedding, the groom's parents hold the *walima*, a reception honoring the married couple. The seated bride and groom greet throngs who come to pay their respects and partake in a lavish feast. In rural villages, the barber traditionally prepares the *walima* feast.

The height of Pakistani hospitality is to offer a fine *paan* to guests after dinner. For weddings, hundreds of *paan* are prepared and decorated with edible **silver leaf** (*vark*). They are decoratively placed on the buffet table where guests can help themselves.

The more important the celebration, the more elaborate the menu, and the more dishes and accompaniments are served. Great quantities of rice are always included, either plainly boiled or cooked with other ingredients, such as the *murgh biryani* (recipe page 187).

Aaloo Keema (Spicy Ground Beef with Potatoes)

Pakistanis love meat, and *aaloo keema* is a hearty, simple meal ideal for a boy's circumcision celebration feast.

Yield: serves 4 to 6

6 whole peppercorns

6 whole cloves

½ teaspoon ground cumin

1 teaspoon **coriander**

½ teaspoon turmeric

1 teaspoon cayenne pepper or to taste

1 teaspoon ginger paste (available at international markets)

1 teaspoon garlic paste (available at international markets)

2 tablespoons oil, more as needed

1 onion, **trimmed, finely chopped**

4 cloves garlic, trimmed, **minced**

1 pound ground beef

14.5 ounces canned diced tomatoes

2 potatoes, trimmed, peeled, **cubed**

2 cups water, more as needed

1 teaspoon *masala*, homemade (recipe page 132) or store bought

2 green chilies, trimmed, finely chopped

2 tablespoons **cilantro**, trimmed, finely chopped

3 green onions, trimmed, finely chopped

For **garnish**: 4 to 6 lime wedges

Equipment: Small bowl, mixing spoon, **Dutch oven** or large sauce pan with cover

1. Place peppercorns, cloves, cumin, coriander, turmeric, cayenne pepper, ginger paste, and garlic paste in small bowl, mix well, set aside.

2. Heat 2 tablespoons oil in Dutch oven or saucepan over medium-high heat. Add onions and garlic, **sauté** 3 to 5 minutes, or until soft. Crumble in meat, and cook 10 to 12 minutes or until browned, stirring frequently.

3. Stir in spice mixture into meat, mix well.

4. Stir in tomatoes, potatoes, and water, bring to boil, cover, and reduce to simmer, 12 to 15 minutes, or until potatoes are tender and cooked through. Add more water if necessary to prevent sticking.

5. Stir in in *masala*, green chilies, cilantro, and green onions, mix well. Cook additional 3 to 5 minutes, or until heated through.

Serve warm with naan *(recipe 124) for dipping and garnished with lime wedges.*

🌿 *Kimochdun* (Almond and Apricot Bread)

A wedding feast includes assorted Indian breads (*chapatis* and *phulkas*) (recipes page 143), as well as this very delicious Pakistani bread made with locally grown almonds and apricots.

Yield: 1 loaf

1 package active dry **yeast**	2 tablespoons butter, at room temperature
1 teaspoon sugar	2 tablespoons honey
1 cup **lukewarm** water	1 tablespoon salt
4 cups all-purpose flour, divided, more if needed	2 cups whole wheat flour
1 cup **scalded** milk	1 cup dried apricots, quartered, with skin on
	whole almonds (about 3 ounces)

Equipment: Medium mixing bowl, wooden mixing spoon, plastic wrap, large mixing bowl, kitchen towel, measuring cup, lightly floured work surface, rolling pin, greased 10- to 12-inch round baking pan 2 to 3 inches deep, paring knife, oven mitts

1. Make the **yeast** sponge: In medium mixing bowl, dissolve yeast in warm water. Add sugar, and, using a mixing spoon, beat in 2 cups of all-purpose flour to make a smooth batter. Cover with plastic wrap, and let rise in a warm place until double in bulk, about 1 hour.

2. Make the dough: In large mixing bowl, pour the hot milk over the butter, honey, and salt, stir to melt butter, and cool to lukewarm. Add the yeast sponge and stir in remaining 2 cups of all-purpose flour and 2 cups of whole wheat flour, ½ cup at a time, until soft dough forms. Transfer to a lightly floured work surface, and **knead** until smooth and **elastic**, 8 to 10 minutes. If dough is sticky, knead in additional all-purpose flour, 1 tablespoon at a time.

3. Rinse and dry large mixing bowl, and lightly grease sides and bottom. Place the dough in the greased bowl, and turn it so that the entire surface of the dough is lightly greased. Cover with towel, and let rise in a warm place until double in bulk, about 1to 1½ hours. To test if doubled in bulk: poke fingers into dough; if the dent remains, the dough is ready. Uncover and gently punch dough down and knead on lightly floured work surface for 3 minutes until smooth.

Preheat oven to 350°F.

4. Using the heels of your hands, flatten dough out until it is 1 inch thick. Sprinkle the apricots and almonds over the dough, and roll up jellyroll fashion. Shape the dough into a ball, and gently knead in the apricots and nuts to distribute them throughout the dough.

Transfer dough to prepared baking pan, and press out to fit in the pan. Cover lightly with dry towel, set in warm place to double in bulk, 45 minutes to 1 hour. Transfer dough to greased baking pan. Using a paring knife, cut a ½-inch-deep X, centered, on the surface of the dough.

5. Bake in oven for 35 to 45 minutes, until light golden brown and bread sounds hollow when tapped.

To serve kimochdun *as they do in Pakistan, cut it into wedges and serve warm.*

♗ *Murgh Biryani* (Chicken Pilaf)

There are many different ways of making *biryani*. *Biryani* is usually served at weddings and other life-cycle family celebrations, as it is a dish easy to prepare for a large group of people. *Murgh biryani*, a specialty of the Shindh region, is popular all over the country. The Shindh region is where the famous rich and nutty-flavored **basmati rice** is grown. (Basmati rice is available at all supermarkets.) The secret to a good *biryani* is for the chicken and the rice to be partially cooked before combining and cooking further.

Yield: serves 4 to 6

1 cup water	salt to taste
2 cups **basmati** or other long-grain rice, soaked in cold water for 1 hour and drained	1 cup yogurt
	1 cup *masala* (recipe page 132)
ghee, homemade (recipe page 142) or available in a jar at Indian and Middle Eastern food stores, or unsalted butter, divided, as needed	1 teaspoon ground cinnamon
	6 to 8 serving-size chicken pieces
	2 cups chicken broth

For **garnish**:

2 onions, thinly sliced	1 cup sliced almonds, **roasted**
	2 hard-cooked eggs, quartered

Equipment: Medium saucepan with cover, wooden mixing spoon, large mixing bowl, plastic food wrap, large buttered casserole with cover, tongs, oven mitts

1. **Parboil** rice: Pour water into medium saucepan, add rice, 2 tablespoons of *ghee* or butter or margarine, and salt, stir with wooden spoon, and bring to a boil over high heat. Reduce heat to **simmer**, cover, and cook for 5 minutes. Remove from heat, keep covered, and set aside.

2. Put yogurt in large mixing bowl. Using a mixing spoon, stir in *masala* and cinnamon. Add salt to taste, and stir until well mixed. Cover with plastic wrap and refrigerate.

3. Heat 7 tablespoons of *ghee* or butter or margarine in large skillet over medium-high heat. Add chicken pieces, and fry in batches for 5 to 7 minutes, until golden brown on each side. (The chicken will finish cooking in the oven.) Turn chicken pieces with tongs. When all the

chicken pieces are browned, add to yogurt mixture and coat well. Cover with plastic food wrap, and refrigerate for 2 hours, turning chicken pieces frequently.

Preheat oven to 350°F.

4. Spread half of the rice over the bottom of a large buttered casserole and place chicken pieces on top. Pour the yogurt mixture over the chicken, and cover with the remaining rice and smooth top with back of spoon. Pour the chicken broth over the rice. Cover the casserole, and bake in the oven for 40 minutes. Uncover the casserole and continue cooking until all the liquid has been absorbed, 15 to 20 minutes.

6. For garnish: Heat 3 tablespoons *ghee*, butter, or margarine in medium skillet, over medium-high heat. Add sliced onions and fry until soft and golden, 3 to 5 minutes.

To serve, heap the biryani *on a serving platter, and sprinkle with fried onions and roasted, sliced almonds for garnish. Place hard-cooked egg wedges decoratively over the* biryani.

♨ *Sai Gosht* (Spinach with Meat)

Sai gosht, a specialty from the Sindh region, is now a favorite throughout Pakistan. Although a special red spinach called *kulfa* is used for this dish in Pakistan, any variety of spinach will do. This is one of the many dishes prepared for life-cycle celebrations.

Yield: serves 6 to 8

½ cup *ghee*, homemade (recipe page 142) or available in a jar at Indian and Middle Eastern food stores, or butter or margarine

2 onions, **finely chopped**

4 cloves garlic, finely chopped

1½ tablespoons *masala* (recipe page 132) or *garam masala* (available at Middle Eastern and Indian food stores)

2 pounds lean boneless lamb, cut into 1-inch cubes

2 pounds fresh spinach, washed, drained, and chopped, or 2 boxes frozen chopped spinach, thawed, drained, and squeezed to remove excess water

salt to taste

1 cup yogurt

Equipment: Large saucepan with cover, mixing spoon,

1. Heat *ghee* or melt butter or margarine in large saucepan over medium heat. Add onions and garlic, and **sauté** for 2 to 3 minutes until soft. Add the *masala* or *garam masala*, stir, and cook for 2 minutes. Add the meat, and stir to coat. Cover and cook 20 minutes, stirring frequently.

2. Add the spinach and salt to taste to the meat mixture, stir, and cook for 2 minutes. Reduce heat to **simmer**, stir in the yogurt, cover, and cook until meat is tender, 30 to 45 minutes. Stir occasionally to prevent sticking.

To serve, transfer meat mixture to large serving platter.

♪ *Besan Ke Ladoo* (Sweet Nut Balls)

Besan ke ladoo are popular throughout Pakistan and are a special treat to serve for any life-cycle celebration, especially when decorated with silver leaf. Large platters would be placed on tables for guests to help themselves.

Yield: serves 6 to 8

1 cup *ghee*, homemade (recipe page 142) or available in a jar at Indian and Middle Eastern food stores, or melted unsalted butter

2 cups chickpea flour (available at international or Asian markets)

1½ cups sugar

2 teaspoons ground cardamom

3 tablespoons **slivered** almonds

3 tablespoons pistachios, **finely chopped**

For **garnish: silver leaf** (available at international or Middle Eastern markets)

Equipment: Medium saucepan, mixing spoon, medium mixing bowl, serving platter

1. Place *ghee* or melted butter and chickpea flour in saucepan, and heat over medium-low. Stir constantly to prevent lumps from forming. Cook about 7 to 10 minutes, or until mixture becomes strongly aromatic. Remove from heat, and set aside until cooled to warm. Transfer to mixing bowl.

2. Stir in sugar, cardamom, almonds, and pistachios. Using clean hands, **knead** well.

3. Pinch off ping-pong-ball-size pieces of dough, and, using palms of hands, roll into balls. Set aside on serving platter. Continue making balls until all dough has been used.

4. Tear off pieces of silver leaf and randomly decorate tops of balls.

Serve as a sweet treat for any joyous life cycle celebration.

Philippines

The Philippines consists of a group of over 7,000 islands in the South China Sea, located south of Taiwan and east of mainland Asia.

For many centuries, the indigenous people of the Philippines have shared their islands with people who migrated from Europe, the Middle East, China, Malaysia, and the United States. The Spanish, however, have perhaps made the strongest cultural impact on the Filipino people. The Spanish not only brought Catholicism and Spanish customs, food, dress, and language to the Philippines, but in the 19th century, a Spanish decree required all natives, regardless of ancestry, to acquire a Spanish surname.

The majority of Filipinos are Roman Catholic; the remaining are Christian Protestant, Muslim, and Buddhist. For Filipino Catholic families, the church is the center of life, and almost every *barrios* (town) has a church or chapel. Besides serving as a call to mass, church bells announce baptisms, weddings, and funerals. (See Protestant and Catholic Life-Cycle Rituals, page lxxiii.)

Filipinos generally follow the custom that every relative, no matter how far removed, is recognized as a family member, forming a close kin group. The first important life-cycle event among the Catholic Filipino population is the infant's baptism, which often brings together this extended family. For such a festive occasion, the family might serve chicken dishes, such as *rellenong manok* (recipe follows), or pork, such as *puerco horneado* (see recipe page 589), and several rice and bean dishes. An important part of the happy celebration is a sweet table covered with cakes, cookies, puddings such as *dulce de leche* (see recipe page 563), and candies such as *turrón* (see Spanish recipe page 438). In Filipino Catholic tradition, godparents are selected who will oversee the rearing of the child if the parents are no longer able to do so and to act as a source of guidance for the child, often extending into adulthood. This is called *compadrazco*, and it assures the child a secure future.

When Filipino boys reach puberty, they are usually circumcised. In the cities, circumcisions are often done in hospitals by doctors. However, in the countryside, the traditional method is still being performed. Small groups of boys are taken to a remote area, where they bath in a river prior to the circumcision ceremony. They are given guava leaves to chew on, which are later placed on the wound as a medicinal antiseptic.

The marriage ceremony for Filipino Catholics takes place in the church. The wedding rituals of the veil, candle, and cord observed by traditional Filipino families were introduced in the early 18th century by Spanish missionaries. The godparents of both the bride and groom, as primary sponsors, are usually looked upon as honored guests. Couples who are special relatives or friends of the bride and groom are selected to be the veil sponsors, candle sponsors, and cord sponsors for their wedding. The six sponsors and the godparents stand at the altar front as the bride and groom kneel during the mass. The veil ceremony symbolizes the unity of the two families into one by placing a veil over the groom's shoulders and the bride's head. For the candle ceremony, which symbolizes enlightenment and God's presence in the ceremony, the candle sponsors light the candle at the altar and puts it out before the end of the ceremony. The cord ceremony concludes the rituals when the *yugal* (nuptial tie—a cord made out of silk threads, flowers, coins, or beads) is loosely entwined in a figure eight around the necks of both the bride and groom. The cord is a symbolic reminder of the mutual responsibility the couple will carry throughout the marriage. At the end of the ceremonies, sponsors sign the wedding papers as witnesses, and they are expected to make small donations to the church.

The wedding reception usually includes great quantities of food and drink, music, and dancing. A fun tradition is the "money dance" when relatives and friends pin money on the newlyweds, covering them from head to toe.

The centerpiece of many wedding feasts is the *lechón*, a grilled or spit-roasted whole suckling pig, and/or *rellenong manok* (recipe follows).

Food plays an important part in Filipino life not only in times of joy but also in times of sorrow. Wakes, which honor the life of the deceased person, often take on the air of a *fiesta* (celebration), with relatives and friends coming from far and near to attend. Great quantities of food and drink are served. The *novena* (Roman Catholic nine days of prayers) is held after the funeral, and death anniversaries are celebrated with a mass or a visit to the grave.

Rellenong Manok (Stuffed Chicken)

This recipe for *rellenong manok* is of Spanish origin. It has been adopted by the Filipinos, who often serve it at weddings. Adding the hard-cooked eggs to the stuffing is symbolic of life and fertility.

Note: Each time before and after handling raw chicken, wash work surface, utensils, and your hands with soapy water, and rinse well.

Yield: serves 4 to 6

4½- to 6-pound whole chicken (Have butcher **bone** chicken, leaving wings and legs intact.)

¼ cup soy sauce

1 tablespoon vegetable oil

1½ cups onion, **finely chopped**

4 cloves garlic, finely chopped

1 pound lean Spanish or Italian pork sausage (not in casing)

½ pound **ground** lean pork

3 cups **cubed** white bread

½ cup grated cheddar cheese

3 **egg whites**

½ cup seedless raisins

salt and pepper to taste

4 hard-cooked eggs, peeled

6 tablespoons sweet pickle relish

½ cup melted butter

Equipment: Paper towels, work surface, large bowl, plastic food wrap, large skillet, mixing spoon, large mixing bowl, 12×9×2½-inch baking pan fitted with wire rack, 3 or 4 metal **truss** pins or skewers, kitchen string, **bulb baster**, aluminum foil, meat **thermometer**, **pastry brush**, oven mitts

1. Since chicken is **boned**, the packet with liver and gizzard are already removed from cavity. Rinse chicken under cold running water, drain, and pat dry with paper towels. Place chicken on work surface. Using your hands, rub soy sauce over skin and in cavity of chicken. Place chicken in large bowl, cover with plastic wrap, and refrigerate until ready to stuff.

2. Prepare stuffing: Heat oil in large skillet over medium-high heat. Add onions and garlic, stir and **sauté** until soft, 3 to 5 minutes. Reduce heat to medium, crumble in pork sausage and ground pork. Stirring constantly, **sauté** until meat is browned, 7 to 12 minutes. Transfer to

large mixing bowl, and let cool to room temperature. Using your hands, combine cubed bread, cheese, egg whites, raisins, and salt and pepper to taste. Cover with plastic wrap and refrigerate for 2 to 3 hours.

Note: The stuffing must be thoroughly chilled before filling cavity of chicken.

Preheat oven to 325°F.

3. Stuff chicken: Place bird, breast-side up, on rack in baking pan. Fill neck cavity with about ½ cup of stuffing, and close by fastening neck skin to back with metal truss pin or skewer. Spread half of remaining stuffing over bottom of cavity. Place peeled hard-cooked eggs, end to end, inside of cavity on top of stuffing, running length of bird. Sprinkle eggs with pickle relish, add remaining stuffing over and around eggs. Keep stuffing loosely packed, don't press it down.

4. Close opening: Insert truss pins or skewers into skin on either side of opening. Place them, one above the other, about ½ inch apart. Wrap string around pins or skewers, and lace opening shut, like lacing a boot. Draw sides of opening tightly together and knot string. Use string to tie legs together so chicken holds its shape during baking. Using pastry brush, cover chicken with melted butter. Insert meat thermometer into meatiest part of chicken. Combine remaining melted butter and soy sauce; use it to **baste** chicken with bulb baster or spoon.

5. Bake in oven for 2 to 2½ hours, basting frequently with soy sauce mixture. If chicken browns too quickly, cover loosely with sheet of foil.

6. Test for **doneness**: Chicken is done when thermometer registers 185°F. You can also test for doneness by piercing chicken thigh with tip of knife; if juices trickle out clear, chicken is done. If juices are pinkish, roast another 15 to 20 minutes. Allow chicken to rest 10 to 15 minutes for easier carving.

To serve, since chicken is boned, slice it in half lengthwise, and lay each half cut-side down. Cut off drumsticks. Slice each half crosswise into thick pieces so everyone gets some egg.

⚘ *Bihon* (Filipino Longevity Noodles)

Pancit bihon (also *bigon*, rice stick noodles) are Filipino longevity noodles. Most people in Asian countries eat long noodles that symbolize long life and prosperity at life-cycle celebrations. Rice stick noodles come in 8- or 16-ounce packages. They are available either in a white and fairly straight form or light tan and crinkly. Rice stick noodles are precooked when you buy them. They need only to be rehydrated, not boiled. Allow 1 to 2 ounces dried noodles per person.

Yield: serves 4 to 6

8 ounces rice stick noodles, either white or tan (available at Asian food stores)

hot water, as needed

3 tablespoons vegetable oil, divided

2 onions, **finely chopped**

6 cloves garlic, finely chopped

3 carrots, **trimmed**, finely chopped

3 cups finely sliced **bok choy** (Chinese cabbage), including green tops (available at Asian food stores and most supermarkets)

4 or 5 cooked chicken thighs, cut into bite-size pieces

For **garnish**:

3 green onions, trimmed and finely sliced crosswise at an angle

2 cups oyster sauce (available at Asian food stores)

2 teaspoons curry powder, more or less to taste

1 teaspoon red chili paste, more or less to taste (available at Asian markets)

2 hard-cooked eggs, peeled and sliced

Equipment: Large bowl, **colander**, **wok**, or large skillet, mixing spoon, metal tongs

1. Put rice stick noodles in large bowl. To reconstitute: Soak white noodles in warm water for 10 to 20 minutes to soften, or soak the light tan rice sticks in very hot water for 30 to 40 minutes to soften. Drain in colander, and sprinkle with 1 tablespoon oil to keep them from sticking together. Set aside

2. Heat wok or large skillet over high heat, add remaining 2 tablespoons oil and swirl to coat pan. Add finely chopped onions and garlic. Stir and **sauté** until onions are soft, 3 to 5 minutes. Add carrots, **bok choy**, and pieces of cooked chicken thighs, and toss to mix. Reduce heat to medium, cover, and cook 7 to 12 minutes for flavor to develop. Remove from heat and keep covered.

3. In small bowl, combine oyster sauce, 2 teaspoons curry powder (more or less to taste), and 1 teaspoon red chili paste, more or less to taste. Stir into chicken mixture. Cook and stir chicken mixture over medium-high heat to heat through, 5 to 7 minutes. Remove from heat. Add softened noodles, and, using tongs, toss to mix and coat with sauce.

To serve, divide into individual soup bowls. Garnish each serving with a sprinkle of green onions, and place 2 or 3 slices of hard-cooked eggs on top.

♪ *Brazo de Mercedes* (Custard Cream–Filled Sponge Cake)

All guests, from the officiating priest to the youngest child, line up at the sweets table to enjoy *brazo de mercedes*.

Yield: serves 6 to 8

10 **eggs, separated**

½ teaspoon cream of tartar

¾ cup sugar

butter-flavored cooking spray

14 ounces canned condensed milk

1 teaspoon vanilla extract

¼ cup confectioner's sugar, more as needed

Equipment: Medium mixing bowl, whisk or electric mixer, 2 same-size baking sheets, wax paper, spatula, toothpick, oven mitts, medium saucepan, mixing spoon, serving platter

Preheat oven to 350°F.

1. Prepare meringue: Place egg whites and cream of tartar in medium mixing bowl, and, using whisk or electric mixer, **whisk** until soft peaks form. Gradually whisk in sugar, and continue mixing until well blended.

2. Place wax paper on baking sheet, and coat with butter-flavored cooking spray.

3. Pour meringue onto wax paper–covered baking sheet, and, using spatula, spread out evenly. Bake 20 to 25 minutes, or until meringue is golden brown and toothpick inserted in center comes out clean. Using oven mitts, carefully remove and set aside to cool.

4. Prepare filling: stirring constantly, heat egg yolks and condensed milk in saucepan over medium-high heat 4 to 6 minutes, or until mixture thickens. Stir in vanilla extract, mix well, remove from heat and set aside.

5. Sprinkle cooled meringue with ¼ cup confectioner's sugar, adding more if needed.

6. Cover meringue with sheet of wax paper, then invert 2nd baking sheet over top. Carefully flip meringue onto inverted baking sheet. Remove original baking sheet and wax paper.

7. Spread filling evenly over meringue. Gently roll up long side of meringue, encasing filling. Transfer to serving platter.

To serve, cut into individual slices at any Filipino life-cycle celebration.

Sri Lanka

An island in the Indian Ocean, Sri Lanka is a multiethnic, multireligious, and multi-linguistic country, where for centuries, the four major world religions have been firmly established among several ethnic groups. The largest ethnic group, the Sinhalese, make up about three-quarters of the population. Other significant ethnic groups are the Tamils, most of whom are Hindus, the Moors of Arabic ancestry, and the Burghers (which means "town dwellers"). The Burghers are mostly Christian and are descendants of Portuguese, Dutch, and British colonists.

Distinctions between the Buddhists, Hindus, Muslims, and Christians in Sri Lanka are not always clear-cut. Sri Lankans have been mixing and borrowing religious rituals and symbols from one another for generations. For example, most Sinhalese are Buddhists, yet they follow the stratified caste system of the Hindus. It is not unusual to see Sri Lankan Muslims wearing the *thali*, a symbolic marriage necklace of Tamil Hindus. Because of Sri Lanka's diverse population, life-cycle rituals vary not only by racial and religious differences but by intermarriage, mixed heritage, region, or whether one is a villager or urban dweller.

In Sri Lanka, the anticipated birth of a baby is regarded as an exciting event that families look forward to with great enthusiasm. When the baby is born, it is customary for visiting family and friends to bring gifts for the infant.

Among the Sinhalese and Tamil, the first important event in the baby's life comes at around eight months old, when, for the first time, the baby is given solid food (usually boiled rice with milk). For Hindus, the first mouthful of solid food is such an important occasion, it is fed to the baby in the *kovil* (the Hindu temple). Whenever decisions have to be made concerning the child, the family consults an astrologer, which they do when the child reaches the age of two years. The astrologer chooses an auspicious hour for the child to be given its first lesson by a scholarly relative, head schoolmaster, or temple monk.

A Sir Lankan girl is eligible for marriage when she reaches puberty, and the family celebrates her coming of age. Followers of traditional Tamil and Sinhalese rituals keep the young girl in seclusion for about 16 days. It is considered bad luck for the girl to look upon a male, even her own brother, during her seclusion. Again an astrologer is consulted, and an auspicious date for the "coming out" ritual is selected. A *dboby* (washerwoman) comes to the house to prepare the girl; all jewelry and clothes the girl was wearing when she started her first menstruation are discarded by the *dboby*. The *dboby* then bathes the girl by pouring water over her from a clay pot. To complete the bath ritual, the *dboby* smashes the pot on the ground. Once the girl comes out of seclusion, the family throws a big party in her honor where she receives gifts, often jewelry and cash. Many families today are ignoring the rituals and opting for just the celebration party.

Most marriages in Sri Lanka are arranged. At one time, a marriage broker, the *magul kapuwa*, brought eligible people together. Today, the marriage broker has been replaced by a go-between, which might be an aunt, colleague, parent, or friend. The go-between usually consults with an astrologer throughout the entire marriage negotiation process. Horoscopes come in the form of a chart written on paper, or an *ola* (a scroll made of a cured piece of talipot palm leaf). Good and bad periods of each person's life are listed on these charts. When a marriage is proposed, the horoscopes of both the man and the woman are compared, and if more than half of 20 "conditions" are favorable, the nuptial arrangements continue.

For Sinhalese Buddhists, the astrologer first decides whether the couple's birth dates are compatible, then he or she charts an auspicious time for every step of the ceremony. The couple marries in a decorative house-like structure called a *poruwa*. It is usually up to the bride's maternal uncle to arrange the ritual proceedings.

Dowries are a part of the arranged marriage, and the bride's parents must come forth with property, cash, jewelry, and a house for the groom. A Tamil custom allows the groom's family to take part of the dowry and add it to the dowry they are preparing for their own daughter. It is up to the go-between not only to ask for a substantial dowry from the bride's parents but also to do the proposing.

Weddings are often lavish celebrations, especially among those living in cities, taking place in a wedding hall or hotel. Brides are generally beautifully dressed in rich silks embroidered with gold thread. Tamils can either have the marriage ceremony in a temple and the reception elsewhere, or, if the wedding ceremony and reception take place in a hotel, a priest comes to perform the marriage rituals before the guests. Muslims have an evening celebration, which can be very elaborate, in the bride's home or in a hotel. Most Christian Burghers prefer church ceremonies, followed by the reception in either a hotel or the bride's family's home.

A charming ritual performed during the Tamil marriage ceremony is when the little fingers of the bride and groom are tied to each other with gold thread, and water from a silver urn is poured over the knot to symbolize sharing. Adding to the happy occasion, a chorus of girls sing *jayamangala gatha* (songs of good wishes and celebration).

Following the wedding celebration, the tradition is for a Tamil bridal couple to spend the wedding night at the groom's family home. The following day, they are visited by the bride's parents and other family members. If the couple take a honeymoon journey, the groom's parents welcome them back with a homecoming party.

The rituals for the dead in Sri Lanka vary according to religious beliefs. Hindus and Buddhists cremate their dead. According to the *Koran* (Islamic holy book), Muslims must bury their dead within 24 hours. Muslim mourners carry their dead to the cemetery on a covered stretcher and place them in the ground without a coffin. Most Christians prefer the traditional coffin burial for their deceased, though cremation has become common. In Sri Lanka, a paper *stupa* (Buddhist monument) may be placed on the cremation pyre, and at intervals after the funeral, meals are offered to monks in honor of the departed.

Rice is the most important food in Sri Lanka. Rice curries made with cooked vegetables in coconut milk are popular and are included in life-cycle celebration feasts.

Kadhi (Yogurt Sauce)

Yogurt, popular throughout the world, is an important ingredient in Sri Lankan cooking. This typical yogurt sauce is used to spoon over raw, boiled, or steamed vegetables or to use as a dip for chips or Indian flat breads, such as *chapatis* or *poppadums* (recipe page 143).

Yield: 2 cups

½ teaspoon **ground** turmeric	red pepper flakes, to taste (optional)
½ teaspoon ground mustard seeds	1 tablespoon vegetable oil
1 teaspoon ground cumin	2 cloves garlic, **finely chopped**
1 teaspoon ground **coriander**	2 cups plain yogurt

Equipment: Small skillet, mixing spoon, small bowl with cover, rubber spatula

1. In small skillet over medium heat, add turmeric, mustard seeds, cumin, coriander and red pepper flakes. Stir constantly, and cook until mustard seeds begin to pop, about 1 minute.

2. Add oil and garlic, stir, and **sauté** until garlic is soft, about 2 minutes. Stir in yogurt, and cook to heat through, 2 to 3 minutes. Cool to room temperature, transfer to small bowl, cover, and refrigerate for up to 5 days.

Serve kadhi *as a dip or as a sauce over vegetables.*

⚱ *Samosa* (Vegetarian Pastries)

Samosa are favorite savory filled pastries that definitely would be prepared for life-cycle celebration feasts. This is a vegetarian treat.

Yield: 20 pieces

2 cloves garlic, **finely chopped**

½ teaspoon **ground** ginger

½ teaspoon ground turmeric

½ teaspoon ground **coriander**

½ teaspoon ground cumin

3 tablespoons vegetable oil, divided

1 onion, finely chopped

1 carrot, **trimmed**, finely chopped

1 potato, peeled, finely chopped

½ teaspoon salt

½ cup water

½ cup fresh or frozen green peas

juice of 1 lemon

2 sprigs fresh coriander (also called **cilantro**), finely chopped, or 1 tablespoon ground dried coriander leaves

5 sheets (14×18-inch) **filo** (also phyllo) pastry (available in 1-pound boxes in the freezer section of supermarkets)

½ cup melted butter or margarine

Equipment: Mixing spoon, medium skillet with cover, work surface, knife, ruler, damp kitchen towel, 2 cups, **pastry brush**, baking sheet, oven mitts

1. In cup, mix garlic, ginger, turmeric, coriander, and cumin with 1 tablespoon of oil and stir until mixture forms a paste.

2. Prepare filling: Heat remaining 2 tablespoons of oil in medium skillet over medium-high heat. Add finely chopped onion, and **sauté** until soft, 2 to 4 minutes. Reduce heat to medium, stir in spice paste, and cook 1 minute. Add finely chopped carrot and potato, salt, and water. Stir, cover, and cook for 12 to 15 minutes, or until potato is tender. Stir in peas, lemon juice, and coriander. If mixture seems watery, cook uncovered for 5 to 10 minutes to **reduce**.

3. Cut pastries: On work surface, neatly stack the 5 sheets filo. Using a sharp knife and a ruler, mark the 18-inch length into 4 equal strips, each 4½inches wide. Cut through the 5 sheets; you will have 20 strips of filo, each 4½×14 inches. Keep covered with damp towel, and work with one strip at a time.

Preheat oven to 375°F.

4. Fill pastries: Have ready a cup with melted butter and a pastry brush. Put one strip of filo on work surface, lightly brush with melted butter or margarine, and place a tablespoon of

filling at one end, 2 inches up from bottom edge. Fold a corner of the bottom edge diagonally over the filling to meet the other side, forming a triangle (two edges are 4½ inches long and folded diagonal side is about 6 inches long). Press edges together to seal in filling. Repeat folding the pastry strip up and over (like folding a flag) to make a small triangular package with the filling wrapped inside. Brush with melted butter, gently press edges to seal package, and place on baking sheet. Repeat assembling, and place about 1 inch apart on baking sheet.

5. Bake in oven for 12 to 15 minutes, or until golden, puffy, and crisp.

Serve either warm or at room temperature.

⚘ *Gowa Mallum* (Curry Cabbage Salad)

A delicious addition to the buffet table at a Sri Lankan wedding reception is *gowa mallum*.

Yield: serves 4 to 6

2 teaspoons mustard

1 teaspoon Maldive fish (available at international markets)

½ cup **shredded** coconut

1 green chili, **trimmed, finely chopped**

1 head cabbage, trimmed, **cored**, shredded, or 1 pound package shredded cabbage

2 tablespoons olive or vegetable oil

1 onion, trimmed, finely chopped

2 cloves garlic, trimmed, **minced**

¼ cup curry leaves (available at international markets)

For **garnish**:

¼ cup raisins

¼ cup **slivered** almonds

4 to 6 lime wedges

Equipment: Medium mixing bowl, mixing spoon, salad fork and spoon, large skillet with cover, serving bowl

1. Place mustard, Maldive fish, shredded coconut, and green chili in mixing bowl, mix well.

2. Add cabbage, and, using salad fork and spoon, toss to mix well. Set aside.

3. Heat oil in skillet over medium-high heat. Add onions, garlic, and curry leaves, and **sauté** 3 to 5 minutes, or until onions are soft. Stir in cabbage mixture, cover, and cook 5 to 7 minutes, or until cabbage is soft. Remove from heat, and set aside to cool to room temperature.

4. Remove and discard curry leaves before serving. Transfer to serving bowl, and add salt and pepper to taste.

Serve at room temperate sprinkled with raisins and almonds and garnished with lime wedges.

Tajikistan

Sometimes referred to as the "Rooftop of the World" because of its rugged mountainous terrain, Tajikistan is the southernmost of the Central Asian countries. It is the poorest and most underdeveloped of the former Soviet republics. The difficult terrain and harsh weather, along with constant threats of earthquakes, make this a difficult place to live.

Despite the years of official atheism under the Soviet regime, virtually all Tajiks are Muslims and celebrate life-cycle events according to Islamic traditions, which have been revived since independence in 1991. (See Islam and Islamic Life-Cycle Rituals, page lxxvi.)

☙ *Sambusa* (Meat Pies)

Sambusa is a meat pie with a flaky crust that is usually baked in a traditional oven called *"tandyr"* but these days in a modern oven in urban areas. It shares a common origin with *samsa* from neighboring Uzbekistan (and linguistically is a distant relative of the vegetarian *samosa* of India). Tajik *sambusas* and Uzbek *samsas* are usually stuffed with meat (lamb or mutton, beef, or chicken—never pork) and onions or with pumpkin, potatoes, or carrots. There are also sweet *sambusas* filled with fruit preserves. Among local connoisseurs, the mark of a high-quality savory *sambusa*, similarly as for *samsa*, is a good quantity of fat in the filling, such that it should spurt out as a diner bites into the pie. The ideal fat is *dumba*, the fat melted down from the tail of a special breed of sheep known as "fat-tailed sheep." *Sambusas* are very popular as a party food and are usually served at festivities and life-cycle celebrations with tea.

Yield: about 40 pies

Dough

4 cups flour, plus more for rolling out	1 cup water, plus more as needed
½ teaspoon salt	½ cup vegetable oil
1 egg, well beaten	

Filling:	¼ pound mutton or lamb fat, finely chopped
2 pounds mutton or lamb, minced	salt and pepper to taste
1½ pounds onions, finely chopped	

Eggwash and garnish:	2 tablespoons water
1 egg, well beaten	2 to 3 tablespoons a mix of black or white **sesame seeds** and nigella seeds

Equipment: Large mixing bowl, mixing spoon, plastic wrap, rolling pin, baking tray or cookie sheet, **pastry brush**, oven mitts

Preheat oven to 375 F.

1. Prepare the dough: in a large bowl, combine the flour and salt. Make a well (hole) in the center, and add the egg and water. Mix in the flour gradually until all come together into a

pliable dough. The dough must be neither too hard nor too soft, adjust the consistency by adding a bit more water or flour. Knead the dough for 8 to 10 minutes until smooth and elastic. Cover with plastic wrap, and let rest for at least 30 minutes.

2. Meanwhile, prepare the filling. In a large bowl, mix the meat, onions, fat, salt, and pepper until well combined. Set aside until needed.

3. On a lightly floured surface, divide the dough into two. Roll out one dough ball to as thin a sheet as possible. Keep the other ball wrapped so as not to dry out. Brush the sheet with oil.

4. Beginning with the longest side, roll up the sheet into a tight cylinder. Roll out the cylinder into a thin sheet one more time. Brush the sheet with oil, and roll up again into a tight cylinder. Slice the cylinder into 2-inch wide pieces. Roll each piece into a disk ¼ inch thick in the center and thinning toward the edges. Place tablespoon of filling in the center. Fold over one-third of the dough disk toward the center over the filling.

   Fold over the other thirds of the dough disk toward the center, so that all meet at the center with a slight overlap. Press the edges firmly together into seams to enclose the filling to end up with a pyramid, whose three seams radiate from the center of the filled *sambusa*.

5. Place the filled *sambusa* seam-side down on a greased baking tray or cookie sheet.

   Roll out the other dough pieces, fill, and seal in the same manner.

6. Place the filled *sambusas* with 1 inch of space between them on the baking tray.

   In a bowl, mix well the egg and water. Brush the surface of the *sambusas*, and sprinkle with a few sesame or nigella seeds.

7. Bake for 30 to 40 minutes, or until the *sambusa* crusts are golden brown.

   Sambusas *are usually accompanied by tea.*

¿ *Palov* (Tajik Pilaf)

As in Uzbekistan where no special occasion is without the national dish *plov*, *palov* is the celebratory food in Tajikistan and the national dish. It is inevitably served at weddings, funerals, and other significant family events and special occasions. It is also called *osh*. There are subtle distinctions between other regions' rice dishes and Tajik *palov*. Tajiks flavor with spices such as cumin, coriander, pepper, and sometimes with star anise and saffron, as well as with fresh herbs such as basil, dill, parsley, mint, chives, and sorrel. Quinces may also be included in a Tajik *palov*, and quail eggs, pistachios, dried apricots, or fresh pomegranate arils used for garnish, depending on the region and the personal inclination of the cook. *Palov* is eaten with a fresh salad of tomatoes, onions, cucumbers dressed with dill, salt, and fresh lemon juice, as well as freshly baked round bread called "*naan/non.*"

Just before a wedding ceremony, a festive *palov*, called *oshi nahor*, is served early in the morning, between five and nine, in separate parties for relatives and friends at the family homes of the bride and groom. The *oshi nahor* is usually cooked by a hired male specialist chef called an "*oshpaz.*" The *oshpaz* organizes the buying and preparation of the huge quantities of ingredients required for parties of up to a few hundred diners, as well as for coordinating the cooking.

Traditional wedding feasts once lasted for several days; however, a recent marriage austerity law limits wedding feasts to one day in order to ensure that people do not impoverish themselves or get into too much debt,

Yield: about 10 servings

3 pounds **short grain** rice

2 cups lamb fat (from fat-tailed sheep) or sunflower oil

3 pounds lamb shortribs or 2 pounds boneless lamb shoulder or beef shoulder or ribs, cut into large cubes

3 large onions, sliced into half rings

3 pounds carrots, peeled and sliced into thick **julienne** strips

2 fat heads whole garlic, unpeeled

2 cups dried chickpeas, soaked overnight

1 cup dried barberries, soaked at least 1 hour

3 quinces, peeled, **cored**, and sliced into cubes

1 tablespoon **coriander** seed

1 tablespoon cumin seed

8 cups meat broth or water

salt and pepper to taste

2 pomegranates for garnish

Equipment: **Heavy-bottomed** wok or Dutch oven, pot for soaking rice, **colander**, stirring spoon

1. Wash the rice very well, changing the water several times until the water runs clear. Soak the rice with water to cover for at least 1 hour.

2. In a heavy-bottomed large wok or Dutch oven, heat the oil over medium heat, and brown the meat.

3. Add the onions and stir-fry until softened, then add the carrots, stirring the mixture until caramelized.

4. Add the garlic heads, chickpeas, barberries, quinces, coriander, and cumin.

5. Add 8 cups broth or water, and bring to a boil.

6. Add salt and pepper, making it saltier than usual because the taste will be diluted once the rice is cooked.

7. Drain the rice, and add to wok in one layer. Do not mix.

8. Add more broth or water to go above the level of the rice by an inch. Cook the mixture until the water has been absorbed to the level of the rice. Poke a few holes through the rice, cover the pan with a heavy lid or bowl. Turn down the heat to its lowest setting, and let the rice cook for 45 minutes to 1 hour, or until cooked through.

9. Turn off the heat, and let the rice rest, covered, for about 15 to 20 minutes.

To serve, mound the rice on a large platter, surround with the meat, chickpeas, barberries, and quinces, and top with the garlic heads. Garnish with pomegranate arils.

Bulgur Plov (Bulgur Pilaf)

Pilafs, such as this recipe *for bulgur plov*, are popular throughout the Central Asian republics and can accompany the main dish in life-cycle and other feasts.

Yield: serves 4 to 6

2 tablespoons butter or margarine

1 onion, chopped

1¼ cups **bulgur** (available at most supermarkets and health food stores)

1¾ cups water or chicken broth

salt to taste

Equipment: Medium saucepan with cover, mixing spoon, kitchen towel

1. In medium saucepan, melt butter or margarine over medium-high heat. Add onion, stir, and **sauté** until soft, 3 to 5 minutes. Add bulgur, and, stirring constantly, cook for 3 minutes. Add water, chicken broth, and salt to taste. Bring to boil and stir. Reduce heat to **simmer**, cover, and cook, stirring occasionally, until bulgur is tender, 20 to 25 minutes.

2. Remove from heat, remove cover, and stretch a towel over the pan. Replace cover over the towel, and set aside for 10 to 15 minutes until serving time. (The towel absorbs moisture from the steam and keeps it from dropping into the bulgur pilaf.)

Serve plov *with* piti *and* salat *(recipe page 169).*

♗ *Osh Plov* (Lamb and Carrot Stew)

A traditional Tajikistan dish, *osh plov* is a hearty, filling meal perfect for a winter wedding.

Yield: serves 6 to 8

3 cups water, more as needed

1 teaspoon salt, more as needed

2 cups rice (such as **basmati**, Thai, or brown)

6 tablespoons vegetable oil, more as needed

3 onions, **trimmed**, finely sliced

1½ pounds lamb shoulder, cut into bite-size pieces

4 carrots, trimmed, **julienned**

1 teaspoon crushed red pepper flakes

1 teaspoon cumin

1 teaspoon **coriander**

1 whole bulb garlic

pepper to taste

For serving: *naan*, homemade (recipe page 124) or available at international markets

Equipment: Medium mixing bowl, **Dutch oven** or large stock pot with cover, mixing spoon, strainer

1. Place 3 cups water and salt in mixing bowl, add rice, and set aside to soak for 30 minutes.

2. Heat 6 tablespoons oil in Dutch oven or large stock pot over medium-high heat. Add onions, and fry 3 to 5 minutes, or until golden. Add lamb and fry 12 to 15 minutes, or until golden on all sides. Add more oil if necessary to prevent sticking.

3. Stir in carrots, red pepper, cumin, coriander, and 2 cups water, and mix well. Reduce heat to medium-low, cover and cook about 5 to 7 minutes, or until carrots soften.

4. Drain rice through strainer, and stir into meat mixture, mix well. Add garlic bulb and 1½ cups water, bring to boil, cover, and reduce to simmer 30 to 35 minutes, or until rice is tender and cooked through. Add more water if necessary to prevent sticking. Add salt and pepper to taste. Remove and discard garlic bulb.

Serve warm on a large platter using naan *to scoop up handfuls of meat, rice, and vegetables. Only the right hand should be used for eating as the left hand is used for grooming purposes.*

Thailand

Thailand is located in South East Asia, southeast of Myanmar (Burma). The majority of all Thais are Buddhist (see Buddhism and Buddhist Life-Cycle Rituals, page lxxxii); however, elements of Hinduism and other beliefs are often blended with Buddhist belief. Mystics, mediums, and astrologers are often consulted by members of every social and economic class.

In rural areas, many people believe the spirit *phi* is responsible for babies. A few days before the infant's birth, food offerings are left out to appease the *phi* spirit in hopes of the child's safe delivery. The infant, for the first month of birth, is not considered a family member. At the end of 30 days, the family holds a special rite to accept the child into the family. Baby boys are often given names that mean "strength" or "honor," while girls are named for feminine qualities, such as "beauty" and "purity," or after flowers, plants, and fruits.

Astrology is taken seriously in Thailand, especially when selecting a prospective marriage partner. Most Thai marriages take place in an even-numbered lunar month. This is because weddings involve two people, therefore the wedding months should be multiples of two, the best being the second, fourth, sixth, and eighth.

As many as nine Buddhist monks can officiate at a traditional Thai wedding. Prior to the ceremony, the groom's family and guests carry platters of symbolic food to the bride's home. When the groom arrives at precisely 9:09 a.m. (a time considered auspicious and lucky by many Thais), the platters are presented to the bride's family.

Before the groom and his family are able to enter the bride's home, they must pass "toll gates" or gold chains held by guests of the bride. The bride groom must give the gate holders money in order to pass. He then enters the bride's home, and the money is blessed by either a Buddhist monk or an elder family member from the bride's side.

After the money is blessed, the couple kneels inside a semicircle: both the bride and groom wear headdresses of looped white yarn called *mongkols*. The two *mongkols* are joined by a string to symbolize the uniting of the man and woman as husband and wife. Monks place a white cord (*sai sin*) around the area where the couple is kneeling, marking it off as a sacred zone. A half hour of chanting and blessings follow, and the senior monk, using a sprig of Chinese gooseberry, sprinkles the couple with holy water. Later at the wedding reception, guests take turns pouring purified water over the joined hands of the bride and groom.

Thai Buddhists believe in an afterlife and reincarnation. Funerals are looked upon as celebrations, and beautifully designed structures are built for the cremation and are burnt along with the body, three to seven days after death.

Ethnic minorities, such as Muslims and nearly all hill tribal groups, bury their dead rather than cremate them. Village funerals can be very elaborate, with everyone taking part in the activities. Some tribes dress in gaily decorated costumes that are worn only during funerals. Water buffalo and cattle are slaughtered, and the meat divided among either the clan of the deceased or the entire village.

The Thai words for rice and food are synonymous. Rice represents life and is revered as such. To cook rice in the Thai manner, choose a long grain variety of polished white rice. Rice is soaked overnight, then drained and steamed. This takes longer than cooking it directly in the water, but it gives a very fluffy and grainy result. It must be served as soon as it is cooked; it will go hard and dry if left to stand.

A Thai meal is based on rice, but the number and variety of dishes served with rice is limited only by the chef's time, imagination, patience, and budget. It is customary to have soup, two or more *kaengs* (dishes with sauces), and as many *krueng kieng* (side dishes) as possible. Other than the rice, which is served hot, food is generally served at room temperature.

Some Thais eat mostly with spoon and fork, while many eat with their fingers. Everything is served at once, and diners choose according to individual taste, combining each dish separately with a little rice.

⚘ *Kao Hom Moo* (Thai Pork and Fragrant Rice)

Meat is the highlight of most Thai meals and always served on special occasions. This is a festive way of preparing pork.

Note: Use care when handling peppers. Wrap your hands in plastic wrap, or cover them with plastic sandwich bag. If you accidentally touch your eyes, rinse them out at once under cold running water.

Yield: serves 10 to 12

12 cups cooked rice (cooked according to directions on package), at room temperature

1½ cups carrots, **trimmed, finely chopped**

1½ cups green onions, trimmed, thinly sliced

3 tablespoons fresh **cilantro**, finely chopped

4 cloves garlic, finely chopped

2 **jalapeño** peppers, trimmed, **seeded,** finely chopped

10 tablespoons *nam pla* (fish sauce) or soy sauce, more or less to taste, divided (fish sauce is available at Asian food stores)

4 tablespoons lime juice, divided

2 tablespoons sugar

6 pounds boneless pork loin (have butcher **butterfly** meat and pound into ½-inch-thick rectangular piece suitable for stuffing)

1½ cups brown sugar, firmly packed

1 cup water

For serving: *Nam tua* peanut sauce (recipe follows)

Equipment: Large mixing bowl, mixing spoon, work surface, kitchen string, paring knife, large roasting pan with wire rack, plastic food wrap, small bowl, **bulb baster**, meat **thermometer**, oven mitts

Preheat oven to 325°F.

1. In large mixing bowl, combine rice, carrots, green onions, cilantro, garlic, jalapeños, 8 tablespoons fish sauce or soy sauce (more or less to taste), 2 tablespoons lime juice, and sugar. Stir to mix well.

2. Place prepared pork loin, cut-side up, on work surface. Spread about half rice mixture onto surface of meat and roll up, jelly roll fashion, to enclose rice filling. Using string, tie roast in 3 or 4 places to secure filling. Place fat-side up on wire rack in roasting pan. Cover remaining rice mixture with plastic wrap and refrigerate until ready to serve.

3. In a small bowl, combine brown sugar, remaining 2 tablespoons lime juice, remaining 2 tablespoons fish sauce or soy sauce, and water. Stir to mix well. Spread over pork. Insert meat thermometer in center of meat.

4. Roast in oven until meat thermometer reaches 160°F, 2½ to 3 hours. Using bulb baster, **baste** frequently to moisten meat. Let stand 20 minutes before carving.

5. Remove rice from refrigerator, and let sit at room temperature at least 1 hour before serving.

To serve, cut pork into ¼-inch thick slices. Mound reserved rice in the center of a large serving platter. Surround rice with slightly overlapping slices of pork. Serve with bowl of peanut sauce (recipe follows) to spoon over each serving.

ꙮ *Nam tua* (Peanut Sauce)

Yield: about 3 cups

1 cup crunchy peanut butter

1 cup plain low-fat yogurt

¼ cup green onions, chopped

¼ cup lemon juice

¼ cup honey

2 tablespoons soy sauce

1 teaspoon **ground** ginger

½ teaspoon ground red pepper

Equipment: Medium mixing bowl, mixing spoon

In a medium bowl, combine peanut butter, yogurt, onion, lemon juice, honey, soy sauce, ginger, and red pepper. Stir until smooth.

To serve, put sauce in small bowl. To eat, each person spoons sauce over a serving of pork.

⚘ Ma Ho (Pork and Pineapple)

The literal translation of this appetizer, *ma ho*, is "galloping horses." It is often served at wedding banquets. The combination of fruit and meat gives interesting contrast in both color and texture.

Yield: serves 6 to 8

1 tablespoon vegetable oil

4 cloves garlic, **finely chopped**

1 pound lean **ground** pork

1 to 2 **jalapeño** peppers, **trimmed, seeded,** finely chopped

2 tablespoons sugar

½ cup dry roasted peanuts, finely chopped

1 head leaf lettuce, separated, washed, drained well

For serving: 16-ounce can of sliced pineapple, drained

For **garnish**: fresh mint or **coriander** leaves

Equipment: **Wok** or large skillet, mixing spoon

1. Heat oil in wok or large skillet over medium-high heat. Stir-fry garlic until soft, 3 to 5 minutes. Crumble in pork, and stir-fry until browned, 5 to 7 minutes. Add peppers and sugar, and stir-fry for 2 minutes. Add peanuts, stir in thoroughly, and remove from heat.

2. Dry lettuce leaves by gently patting with paper towels and arrange them decoratively on a serving platter. Place a well drained pineapple slice on each leaf. Mound spoonfuls of meat mixture equally in the center of each slice of pineapple.

To serve as an appetizer, chill for about 1 hour before serving. Garnish with sprigs of either fresh mint or coriander leaves. To eat, pick up the lettuce leaf, and wrap it around the pineapple-meat mixture.

⚘ Khanom Tuay Fu (Thai Rice Flour Muffins)

Khanom tuay fu is a light fluffy dessert that the groom's family prepares and presents to the bride and her family on their wedding day. The muffins symbolize the love shared by the newlyweds for years to come. In Thailand, a different food coloring is added to each batch, giving a colorful touch to the presentation. Popular colors are pink, green, yellow, orange, and white.

Yield: serves 6 to 8

1 cup rice flour (available at international or Asian markets)

1 package quick rising **yeast** (activated according to directions on package)

½ cup **rosewater** (available at international markets)

1 cup sugar

1 teaspoon baking soda

food coloring of your choice (optional)

Equipment: Medium mixing bowl, mixing spoon, clean kitchen towel, 1 to 2 dozen round petit four paper cups, **steamer pan or basket**, toothpick, serving platter, plastic cover

1. Place rice flour in mixing bowl, and stir in activated yeast, adding just enough rosewater to moisten, mix well.

2. Stir in sugar, remaining rosewater, and baking soda, mix well.

3. Add food coloring if desired, mix well. Cover and place mixture in warm place for 1 to 2 hours, or until bubbles begin to form (mixture will be thick yet fluid).

4. Fill petit four cups: Carefully fold batter, and fill each petit four cup about ¾ full. Place filled cups in steamer basket. Continue until all batter is used.

5. Fill steamer pan ⅓ full with water, bring to boil, place steamer basket in pan, cover and steam 10 to 15 minutes, or until toothpick inserted in center of muffin comes out clean.

6. Remove muffins from steamer, and place on serving platter, cover and place in refrigerator 45 minutes or until ready to serve.

Serve chilled as a treat for the wedding celebration feast.

Turkmenistan

Located in the southwestern part of Central Asia, Turkmenistan is bordered on the south by Iran and Afghanistan. The Caspian Sea forms the western border, and Kazakhstan and Uzbekistan are to the north. It is a dry country dominated by the Kara Kum Desert, one of the largest sand deserts in the world.

Most Turkmen are Sunni Muslims who speak various dialects of the Turkmen language. Since the breakup of the Soviet empire, the Turmen are free to follow the customs of Islam, including celebrating life-cycle events.

Central Asians are fond of very sweet pastries and candies, usually made with nuts. Sweet candies are reserved for special occasions, such as *Lailat al-Qadr*, the so-called Night of Power, a celebration for children who have learned all 114 chapters of the Koran, the Islamic holy book, and when boys are circumcised. (See Islam and Islamic Life-Cycle Rituals, page lxxvi.)

Lamb Chektyrma (Lamb Soup)

Lamb chektyrm is a simple, yet classic soup popular throughout Turkmenistan. The addition of saffron and mint provides a different flavor that is welcomed at a wedding celebration feast.

Yield: serves 4 to 6

¼ teaspoon saffron

2 tablespoons hot water, more as needed

2 tablespoons vegetable oil, more as needed

2 pounds lamb, cut into bite-size chunks

4 onions, **trimmed, finely chopped**

14.5 ounces canned stewed tomatoes, finely chopped

5 cloves garlic, trimmed, **minced**

2 cups spinach, trimmed, finely chopped

2 teaspoons parsley, trimmed, finely chopped

½ teaspoon dry mint

1 tablespoon paprika

salt and pepper to taste

Equipment: Cup, spoon, **Dutch oven** or large stock pot with cover, mixing spoon

1. Place saffron in cup, and stir in 2 tablespoons hot water, mix well to dissolve saffron threads. Set aside.

2. Heat 2 tablespoons oil in Dutch oven or stock pot over medium-high heat. Add meat, and, stirring frequently, cook 12 to 15 minutes, or until browned on all sides. Add more oil if necessary to prevent sticking.

3. Add onions and garlic, and **sauté** until soft about 3 to 5 minutes.

4. Add 5 cups water, bring to boil over high heat, cover and reduce to simmer 1 to 1½ hours, until meat is tender and cooked through.

5. Stir in saffron water, tomatoes, spinach, parsley, mint, and paprika, and continue cooking 15 to 20 minutes, or until heated through. Add salt and pepper to taste.

Serve warm in individual bowls with crusty bread for dipping.

⸙ *Sladkoye Pyechenye Iz Gryetskikh Orekhov* (Walnut Brittle)

Central Asians are fond of very sweet pastries and candies, usually made with nuts. Sweet candies are reserved for special occasions, such as *Lailat al-Qadr*, the Night of Power, and circumcisions.

Yield: serves 6

1 cup sugar

1 teaspoon **ground** cinnamon

1 cup walnuts, **coarsely chopped**

Equipment: Baking sheet, aluminum foil, medium skillet, wooden mixing spoon, knife, candy dish

1. Cover baking sheet with foil, and, using your hand, coat with butter. Set aside.

2. Melt sugar in medium skillet over medium heat. When sugar turns golden brown, reduce heat to low. Stir in cinnamon and nuts, and cook about 2 minutes.

3. Transfer to foil-covered baking sheet, and spread out to cool to room temperature. When cool enough to handle, break or cut with knife into bite-size pieces.

To serve, arrange pieces in a candy dish. Store in airtight container.

Uzbekistan

Located right in the middle of the Central Asia region, Uzbekistan is bordered by Kazakhstan on the north and Turkmenistan on the south. It also shares borders with Afghanistan, Tajikistan, and Kyrgyzstan. As with the other Central Asian countries, the Uzbeks are primarily Muslims, and while religion was officially discouraged during the Soviet period, independence in 1991 has left Uzbeks to celebrate life-style events according to Islamic traditions. (See Islam and Islamic Life-Cycle Rituals, page lxxvi.)

ℓ *Qovurma Chuchvara* (Fried Meat Pies)

Qovurma chuchvara are small savory pies, filled with meat, that can be held in the hand. They are rather like Chinese fried wontons, but unlike wontons, they cannot be made with pork. Lamb, beef, or chicken are the usual meats used for filling. Unlike regular *chuchvara*, which are boiled, *qovurma chuchvara* are fried and thus make excellent finger food or snacks and are popularly made for parties and family celebrations, in particular for weddings, in Uzbekistan.

Yield: about 60 pieces

4½ cups flour, plus more for rolling out	2 onions, very finely chopped
1 teaspoon salt	½ teaspoon salt
2 eggs, well beaten	½ pound ground lamb, beef, or chicken
¼ cup water, plus more if necessary	½ teaspoon ground cumin
¼ cup butter	oil for deep frying

Equipment: Large mixing bowl, mixing spoon, plastic wrap, rolling pin, 2-inch- or 3-inch-diameter round cookie cutter, frying pan, 2 baking trays or cookie sheets

1. Prepare the dough: In a large bowl, combine the flour and salt. Make a well (hole) in the center of the flour mixture, and stir in the eggs and water. Gradually mix in the flour toward the well until the mixture forms a soft, pliable dough. Add a bit more water if the dough is too stiff or a bit more flour if too runny.

2. On a lightly floured surface, knead the dough until smooth and **elastic**, about 8 minutes.

   Cover with plastic wrap, and let rest for at least 30 minutes to 1 hour.

3. While dough is resting, prepare the filling. In a frying pan, melt the butter over medium heat. Stir in the onions, and cook until softened. Add salt and cumin, then add the meat. Stir and cook the meat until it changes color. Turn off heat and let the meat cool.

4. Prepare the pie crusts: Divide the dough into 3 to make it easier to roll out.

   Roll each piece into a large rectangle, as thinly as possible. Keep the other dough pieces covered while working so as not to dry out.

5. Cut out 2- to 3-inch-diameter disks. Place a teaspoonful of filling in the center of the dough disk. Press the dough edges firmly together to seal the disk into a crescent form. If needed, moisten the dough lightly with water. Bring the ends of the crescent together to form a circle, press firmly. Continue filling and sealing the rest of the dough disks in a similar manner.

   Note: Adult supervision required during deep-frying.

6. In a deep-frying pan, heat enough oil (about 2 inches) for frying to 360°F.

   Fry the *chuchvara* in small batches, so as not to lower the temperature of the oil.

   Fry until golden brown. Drain on a wire rack to let excess oil drip.

Serve with suzma *(yogurt sauce).*

Palov, or *plov*, the Central Asian term for pilaf, is the quintessential dish for special celebrations, especially weddings. Although there are hundreds of variants of *palov*, there is one that is most popularly made for weddings, *tuy palovi*. There is an apocryphal story told about this dish. There once was a prince who fell in love with a beautiful young lady. Unfortunately, the lady came from a poor family and thus was considered an unsuitable bride for the prince. Unable to marry his beloved, the prince fell ill and refused to eat. The great doctor Avicenna (Ibn Sinna) was called, and he recommended that the prince make efforts to connect lovers and feed them *palov osh*. (Both *palov* and *osh* are terms used for rice.) *Palov osh* is also an acronym for the seven ingredients that are necessary to make the dish: P (*piyoz*, "onions"), A (*ayoz*, "carrots"), L (*lahm*, "meat"), O (*oliyo*, "oil," "fat"), V (*veet*, "salt"), O (*ob*, "water"), SH (*sholi*, "rice").

The ideal fat for use in *palov* (and other Uzbek celebratory foods) is *dumba*, the fat rendered (melted down) from fat-tailed sheep. *Palov*, especially for weddings and big events, is cooked in a huge cauldron (*kazan*), which is shaped like a wok without a handle. The quantities required for such large gatherings are enormous and need a lot of effort to stir and mix, hence it is usually men who cook *palov* for festivities. *Palov* is usually served with a salad of diced tomatoes and onions, with a sprinkling of chili.

ʭ *Tuy Palovi* (Wedding Palov)

Yield: about 12 servings

¾ cup **rendered** *dumba* fat or oil

4 pounds lamb shoulder, boneless leg of lamb, or beef stewing meat, **cubed**

2 large onions, finely chopped

3 pounds carrots, peeled and sliced into fat matchsticks

3 cups meat broth or water

2 cups prepared chickpeas (canned and drained are fine, though for best flavor, soak dried chickpeas overnight)

2 whole fat garlic heads, unpeeled

1 cup sultana (golden) raisins

½ cup dried barberries (*zereshk*, available in Middle Eastern food shops, optional)

1 tablespoon salt, or to taste

1 tablespoon **coriander** seeds, ground

2 tablespoons turmeric

1 tablespoon cumin seeds, ground

2 pounds long grain rice

Equipment: *Kazan* or large **heavy-bottomed** saucepan or Dutch oven with cover, large bowl, mixing spoon, oven mitts, large serving platter

1. In a *kazan* or large heavy-bottomed saucepan or Dutch oven, heat half of the fat or oil over medium heat. Brown the meat on all sides, then transfer the meat and any juices to a bowl, and set aside until needed.

2. Add the rest of the fat or oil, then add the onions, and stir-fry until golden and softened. Stir in the carrots, and after 10 to 15 minutes, when the carrots have softened, return the meat together with all the meat juices and fat.

3. Stir in the chickpeas, garlic heads, raisins, barberries, salt, coriander, turmeric, and cumin.

4. Add the broth, bring to a boil, then turn down heat to its lowest setting, and let everything simmer for 1 hour, or until the chickpeas are tender.

5. Remove the garlic heads, and set aside as garnish. Check the seasoning, and add salt if needed. The seasoning needs to be saltier than usual to flavor the rice.

6. Add the rice carefully to lie in one layer over the carrots. Do not stir.

7. Carefully so as not to disturb the layer of rice, add enough water to cover the rice by 1 inch.

8. Turn up the heat to medium-high, and let the rice cook until the water is fully absorbed. Now turn down the heat to its lowest setting, and stir, but only to mix the top portion of the rice. Cover the pan.

9. After 15 minutes, check the rice, it should be soft and fully cooked. If not, mix just the top portion of the rice again, replace the cover, and cook for a further 5 minutes. Do not open the pan again, turn off the heat, and allow the rice to rest undisturbed until it is ready to be served.

10. Just before serving, carefully mix everything, and mound the rice, along with carrots and chickpeas, raisins, and barberries, on a warmed serving platter. Distribute the meat cubes all over the mound, and top with the reserved garlic heads.

♉ *Tashkent Non* (Uzbek Bread)

Tashkent non is a staple bread served with most meals in Uzbekistan. To celebrate special occasions such as a wedding, bright food coloring is painted on to enhance the visual appearance of the bread. A *chekich*, a wooden handle with metal spikes, is used in Uzbekistan to stamp the center of bread and keep it from rising. However, since most people do not have this tool, we suggest using a more readily available fork.

Yield: serves 4 to 6

1 package quick rising **yeast** (activated according to directions on package)

2 cups water

2 teaspoons salt

1 cup whole wheat flour

3½ cups unbleached all-purpose flour, more as needed

1 tablespoon vegetable oil, more as needed

1 tablespoon fennel seeds (available at international markets)

For serving:

honey, as needed

butter, as needed

Equipment: Medium mixing bowl, mixing spoon, damp kitchen towel, baking stone or baking sheet, fork, **pastry brush**

1. Place activated yeast, water, and salt in mixing bowl, mix well.

2. Stir in whole wheat flour, mix well.

3. Gradually stir in 3½ cups unbleached all-purpose flour, a little at a time, until soft dough is formed. Turn dough out onto clean work surface, and, using clean, lightly floured hands, **knead** until smooth.

4. Return to bowl, cover with damp kitchen towel, and set aside in warm place to rise for about 2 hours or until doubled in size.

5. On lightly floured work surface with lightly floured hands, evenly divide dough into 4 to 6 balls. Cover and let rise 20 to 25 minutes.

Preheat oven to 425°F.

6. Place dough balls onto baking stone or baking sheet, and, using clean hands, press fist into center of each ball. Using fork, lightly pierce center of dough, making a 2-inch round pattern. Using pastry brush, oil tops of dough balls. Continue until all dough balls are punched, pierced, and brushed with oil. Sprinkle fennel flower seeds over top of each ball, and bake in oven 12 to 15 minutes, or until tops are golden.

Serve warm with butter or honey.

ꙅ *Tort iz Sushyonykh Fruktov I Orekhov* (Dried Fruit and Nut Tart)

The fertile region surrounding Uzbekistan is famous for fruit and nut orchards. Dried fruit and nuts are used in everything from soups to candy. This easy to make tart is one of the many desserts served for religious holidays, family gatherings, and life-cycle celebrations.

Yield: serves 10 to 12

tart pastry (recipe follows)

1 cup apple juice, divided

1 cup honey, divided

18 dried apricots or peaches, or combination

1 teaspoon grated orange rind

3 eggs

1 teaspoon vanilla extract

2 tablespoons melted butter

1 cup whole almonds

1 cup chopped walnuts

For **garnish**: 2 cups whipped cream or whipped topping

cinnamon sugar, to taste

Equipment: Small saucepan, wooden mixing spoon, medium mixing bowl, whisk, rubber spatula, lightly greased 10-inch springform pan, oven mitts, knife

1. Prepare *tart pastry* (recipe follows), and refrigerate.

2. Prepare fruit: Pour ½ cup apple juice and ½ cup honey into small saucepan. Stir and bring to boil over medium-high heat. Add dried fruit and orange rind, and reduce heat to low. Cook for 20 to 25 minutes, stirring frequently, until fruit is soft and puffed. Remove from heat, and cool to room temperature.

3. Prepare topping: Put eggs in medium mixing bowl, and, using a whisk, beat in the remaining ½ cup apple juice, ½ cup honey, vanilla, and melted butter. Using rubber spatula, **fold in** whole almonds, chopped walnuts, and dried fruit mixture.

Preheat oven to 350°F.

4. Assemble: Unwrap pastry, and place in lightly greased 10-inch springform pan. Using your hand, press pastry evenly over bottom and about ¾ inch up sides of pan. Spread egg mixture evenly over pastry.

5. Bake in oven 40 to 50 minutes, or until crust is golden brown. Cool to room temperature before removing sides of springform pan.

To serve, cut into wedges, and serve with dollop of whipped cream or whipped topping, sprinkled with cinnamon sugar.

⸎ Tart Pastry

1¼ cups all-purpose flour

¼ cup sugar

½ cup cold unsalted butter, cut into small pieces

¼ teaspoon salt

1 egg yolk

Equipment: Food processor, lightly floured work surface, plastic wrap

1. Prepare crust: Put flour, sugar, butter, and salt in bowl of food processor. Process until mixture resembles bread crumbs. Drop egg yolk through feed tube, and process until pastry dough pulls away from sides of container and forms ball, about 30 seconds. Remove from container, and transfer to lightly floured work surface.

Note: While processing, turn machine off once or twice, and scrape down sides of container with rubber spatula.

2. Form pastry dough into ball, and press to about ½-inch flat. Wrap in plastic wrap and refrigerate for 30 minutes.

Use with tort iz sushyonykh fruktov i orekhov *(recipe precedes).*

Vietnam

Vietnam is located in South East Asia just south of China. The religion most Vietnamese embrace is referred to as *Tam Giao*, the "triple religion," or "Vietnamese Buddhism." It combines elements of Buddhism, Confucianism, and Taoism with ancestor worship. In the countryside, animist belief (everything has a soul) is added to *Tam Giao*. About 10 percent of the Vietnamese population are Roman Catholics.

With such a variety of religion in Vietnam, there are no shortages of life-cycle celebrations. Significant events in life, birth, marriage, and death were once marked by elaborate ceremonies. After the war years in the late 20th century, ceremonies became simpler under Communist rule, however lately, there has been a return to more elaborate rituals, especially for weddings and funerals.

The Vietnamese family is likely to have a small party when a baby is one month old. After the first year, birthdays are not celebrated on the date of birth; instead, all birthdays are celebrated on *Tet*, the first day of the New Year.

Traditionally, a family asked the help of a matchmaker to choose a marriage partner for their son or daughter. Today, couples generally select their own mates and usually consult fortune-tellers to see if they are compatible and to choose an auspicious day for the wedding. The wedding ceremony itself consists of two parts. On the first day, the groom, with his parents and a small group of family members and friends, goes to the bride-to-be's home to seek permission to marry her. Often, the groom presents the traditional offering of **betel nuts** to the bride's family.

On the second day, there is a celebration after the bride and groom have performed ancient rituals at an altar set up for the occasion. At this ceremony, held at the groom's house, the "guardian god of marriage" is traditionally asked to bless and protect the couple. Three tiny cups are filled with rice wine and placed on the altar. The elder who leads the ceremony bows before the altar, takes a sip from one of the cups, and passes it to the groom. The groom takes a sip, then passes the cup to the bride, who also sips from it. The groom then takes a piece of ginger and rubs it in salt, and both bride and groom eat a little of it to signify their lasting love. Only then are they ready to exchange wedding rings and drink the remaining two cups of wine. Once the solemnities are over, it is time for a feast with family and friends.

Wedding banquets are a group affair. The food, such as rice, is placed on the table in large bowls; guests then fill their individual bowls with rice. Using chopsticks, they pick out pieces of fish, meat, and vegetables from other large bowls and add it to the rice.

Pork or beef is eaten at weddings and other auspicious occasions. Larger animals, such as water buffalo, are prepared and eaten when someone dies. Funerals are elaborate affairs. To ensure a comfortable afterlife, the family provides colorful paper model houses, "spirit money," and other necessities to be burned along with the body. Relatives take turns guarding the coffin during the night. Traditionally, a coin is placed in the mouth of the deceased for luck, and a bowl of rice is left in the coffin. In some parts of Vietnam, a knife is rested on the stomach of the dead person to ward off evil spirits.

Exhumation is a common practice in Vietnam. Three years after burial, the family exhumes the body from the grave site and collects the bones. The bones are cleaned and placed in a smaller earthen coffin for reburial. A photograph of the dead is usually placed on the family altar at home and sometimes also in a temple. Offerings of food or burning incense are made to the spirit of the deceased on special occasions or on the death anniversary.

ё *Cha-Gio* (Pork Rolls)

CAUTION: HOT OIL IS USED.

Yield: serves 8

vegetable oil, as needed

2 cloves garlic

½ pound lean **ground** pork

¼ pound shrimp, cooked, peeled, **coarsely chopped**

4 green onions, **trimmed, finely chopped**

½ cup daikon radish (available at Asian food stores and some supermarkets)

2 tablespoons Vietnamese fish sauce (*nuoc mam*) (available at Asian food stores)

2 ounces *sai fun* (cellophane) noodles, soaked in warm water 15 minutes and drained well (available at Asian food stores)

8 (10-inch square) lumpia wrappers, frozen (available at Asian food stores)

Equipment: **Wok** or large skillet, wooden mixing spoon, work surface, **deep fryer** (see Glossary for tips on making a deep fryer), paper towels, baking sheet, **deep fryer thermometer**, slotted spoon or metal tongs

1. Heat 2 tablespoons of oil in wok or large skillet over medium-high heat. Add garlic and stir for about 30 seconds. Crumble in pork, and stir-fry for 3 minutes. Add shrimp, green onions, radish, fish sauce, and drained noodles. Stir-fry for 2 to 3 minutes for flavors to develop. Remove from heat, and cool to room temperature.

2. Spread lumpia wrappers on work surface, and spoon equal amounts of pork mixture in the center of each. Roll up to completely enclose filling. Seal the end flap with a dab of water.

3. Prepare deep fryer: *Caution: Adult supervision required.* Have several layers of paper towels ready on a baking sheet. Heat oil to 375°F on fryer thermometer (or oil is hot enough when small bubbles appear around a wooden spoon handle when it is dipped in the oil). Deep-fry 2 or 3 at a time, until golden brown, 3 to 5 minutes. Remove with slotted metal spoon or metal tongs, and drain on paper towels.

To serve, each person receives a cha-gio. *It is usually cut diagonally in 3 or 4 pieces and set on a plate. It is eaten with Vietnamese dipping sauce (recipe follows). Before each bite, dip the* cha-gio *in dipping sauce.*

ᨇ *Nuoc Cham* (Vietnamese Dipping Sauce)

Yield: about 2½ cups

½ cup Vietnamese fish sauce (*nuoc mam*) (available at Asian food stores)

2 tablespoons rice wine vinegar (available at Asian food stores)

2 teaspoons sugar

1 cup water

¼ cup grated carrots

1 clove garlic, **finely chopped**

juice of ½ lime

ground red pepper, to taste

Equipment: Small bowl with cover, mixing spoon

Put fish sauce, rice wine vinegar, water, grated carrots, garlic, juice of ½ lime, and ground red pepper to taste into small bowl, stir well. Cover and refrigerate until ready to serve.

To serve, spoon a little into individual small dipping containers. Each person has an individual dish of dipping sauce.

ᨇ *Che Dau Trang* (Rice Pudding with Black-eyed Peas)

Che Dau Trang is a memorable dish for children and adults alike at the *Tet* celebration.

Yield: serves 4 to 6

Coconut sauce:

¼ cup half-and-half

2 teaspoons **cornstarch**

14.5-ounces coconut milk, homemade (recipe page 225), or canned

3 teaspoons sugar, more as needed

1 cup glutinous sweet rice (prepared according to directions on package) (available at international or Asian markets)

14.5-ounce can **black-eyed peas**, drained

For **garnish**:

¼ cup toasted **sesame seeds**, more as needed

Equipment: Cup, spoon, small saucepan, mixing spoon, medium mixing bowl, plastic wrap, individual serving bowls

1. Make slurry: In cup, combine half-and-half and cornstarch, mix well. Set aside.

2. Make coconut sauce: In saucepan, bring coconut milk to simmer over medium-low heat. Stir in slurry and 3 teaspoons sugar, mix well. Continue cooking 3 to 5 minutes, or until sauce is thickened. Set aside.

3. In mixing bowl, combine cooked glutinous rice, black-eyed peas, and ½ cup sugar, mix well. Cover, cool to room temperature, then refrigerate for 1 hour or until ready to eat.

Serve warm or chilled in individual bowls with coconut sauce drizzled over top. Sprinkle with sesame seeds.

THE SOUTH PACIFIC

The South Pacific area typically includes the countries of Australia, New Zealand, Fiji, Papua New Guinea, and the smaller islands of Polynesia, Melanesia, and Micronesia.

Australia

Australia, the sixth largest country (in land mass) and smallest continent in the world, is south of Papua New Guinea and Indonesia in the Indian Ocean. Most of the Australian population is clustered in towns and cities along the southeastern seaboard, between the cities of Adelaide and Brisbane. The vast inland regions of Australia, which are sparsely populated, are known as the *bush* and the *outback*. The outback encompasses nearly four-fifths of Australia's total area. Very few people live in this extremely flat and barren territory. The Australians who call the outback home live an isolated existence either in one-street towns or on the dusty plains. The bush, less desolate, has more wildlife and boasts a little rain.

Australia's original settlers, the Aborigines, arrived on the continent some 40,000 years ago. The next settlers, the British, came in the 18th and 19th centuries, many of whom were convicts sent to Australia when it was a penal colony. Australia was also settled by Germans, Chinese, Italians, and Greeks. Today, Australia is a multicultural country, with immigrants of many races, nationalities, and religions. The Eurasian population celebrates life-cycle events according to the religion, rituals, and festivities of their homeland. It is not unusual to have a combination of Italian, Greek, and Asian dishes served at the same banquet.

Many immigrants are forming new rituals, blending Australian customs with their traditional rites. For instance, some Asian couples have two wedding ceremonies: one Buddhist and one civil. The bride often makes several dress changes, wearing both traditional and Western wedding attire during the daylong celebration.

The Aborigines in Australia live between two worlds: one with their traditional customs and the other with modern Western culture. Many of the younger generations of Aborigines have moved from their tribal lands to join the Australian mainstream. Tribal

Aborigines carry on the traditions of their ancestors, and social gatherings (*corroborees*) involve a great deal of singing and dancing and storytelling. Music is very important to Aboriginal culture and is used during sacred ceremonies to communicate with spirits.

Life-cycle rituals for Aborigine boys begin when they are about eight years old. At that time they go through very complex circumcision rituals followed by a celebration feast for the whole clan. When boys reach 12 or 13, they are sent to live in the bush for a few months and to fend for themselves. These "boy-to-manhood" rituals take more than a year to complete, and at the end of them, there is always a big ceremony and feast. Once into manhood, the young men take part in a *kunapipi* ceremony—fertility rites to prepare them for marriage.

The Aboriginal ceremonial feasts include what is called "bush tucker" (survival food). Crocodile, goanna (monitor lizard), kangaroo, possum, fatty muttonbird, and the witchetty grub (insect larvae that feed on the wood of the eucalyptus trees) are prized by Aborigines as good "tucker." Witchetty grubs (from the Aboriginal *witjuti*, the name of roots in which the grubs are often found) are eaten either live and raw, or cooked, and are now considered a gourmet delicacy in Australia. Canned grub soup is available in some Australian supermarkets, and it can also be purchased over the Internet. Crocodile and kangaroo meat has become quite commonplace in most meat markets in Australia. Along with these meats, endless seeds, ferns, berries, and fruits are part of the Aboriginal banquet fare.

Along Australia's eastern seaboard, the majority of the population lives in middle-class suburban homes, many of which have a barbie (barbecue) and garden. During their summer (our winter), the barbecue pit is the center of many social events. ("Barbie" can also mean barbecue party.)

For Australians living in the outback, planning a life-cycle happening, such as a birthday, anniversary party, or wedding or funeral, can be no easy task. Guests often must travel great distances to attend and usually plan to spend the night. Invitations are often issued over a radio transceiver or CB (a radio that receives and transmits) or satellite phones, since many remote areas cannot support cell phone coverage or landline telephones. Fruits, vegetables, and other foodstuffs must come by way of "mail lorry" (mail truck) over dirt roads or by "goods train" (freight train). In the most remote areas of the outback, such as along the barren Nullarbor Plain, a train referred to as the "Tea and Sugar" arrives in isolated communities once a week, and families of railroad workers and nearby cattle and sheep stations (ranches) come to do their weekly shopping for groceries and other sundries.

⚘ *Emu Kofta* (Meatballs)

Emus are a large, fluffy, flightless bird, native to Australia. They are an important source of meat, leather, and oil for the Aborigines. When young boys are sent into the bush and are required to fend for themselves, they learn how to hunt, skin, and prepare emu.

Emu meat is lean, low in fat, and considered a healthy alternative to traditional red meat. We suggest using more readily available ground meat, such as lean beef, lamb, or turkey.

Yield: serves 4 to 6

1 onion, **trimmed, finely chopped**

2 cups parsley, trimmed, finely chopped

1 tablespoon dried mint

2 tablespoons peppercorns

2½ pounds lean ground meat

salt to taste

For serving: *chaka* sauce (recipe page 126)

Equipment: Food processor or **blender**, large mixing bowl, plastic wrap, baking sheet, oven mitts, toothpicks

1. Place onion, parsley, dried mint, and peppercorns in food processor or blender, and **purée** until smooth. Transfer to large mixing bowl.

2. Crumble in meat, and, using clean hands, mix well. Add salt to taste. Cover with plastic wrap, and place in refrigerator 1 to 2 hours or until ready to bake.

Preheat oven to 375°F.

3. Remove mixture from refrigerator. Using clean hands, pinch off walnut-size pieces of mixture, and roll in palms of hands to form balls, and set on baking sheet. Continue until all mixture is used.

4. Bake in oven 15 to 20 minutes, or until cooked through. Carefully remove from oven using oven mitts, and place toothpick in center of each ball.

Serve warm as a starter dish with chaka *for dipping (recipe page 126).*

Puftaloons (Steak and Mushroom Pie)

Casseroles and large meat pies are favorites at large Australian family get-togethers and social gatherings. The old English classic, steak and kidney pie, which came with the early settlers, is being replaced by this more healthful recipe.

Yield: serves 6

1½ pounds lean top round steak, cut into 1-inch cubes

¼ cup all-purpose **flour**

salt and pepper to taste

½ teaspoon **ground** nutmeg

2 tablespoons vegetable oil, divided, more as needed

4 tablespoons butter or margarine, divided, more as needed

2 onions, thinly sliced

2 cups sliced fresh white mushrooms (approximately 7 ounces)

2 tablespoons fresh parsley, **finely chopped**

1 cup canned beef broth

¼ cup canned tomato paste

egg wash

½ box (1 sheet) frozen **puff pastry sheets**, thawed (available in most supermarkets)

Equipment: Medium mixing bowl, cup, large skillet, mixing spoon, large mixing bowl, buttered 9-inch deep-dish pie pan, lightly floured work surface, lightly floured rolling pin, knife, scissors, **pastry brush**, aluminum foil, oven mitts

1. Place meat cubes in medium mixing bowl. In cup, mix flour, nutmeg, and salt and pepper to taste. Sprinkle nutmeg mixture over the meat, and, using clean hands, toss to coat. Set aside.

2. Heat 1 tablespoon oil and 2 tablespoons butter or margarine in large skillet over medium-high heat. Add onions and mushrooms. Stirring frequently, **sauté** until soft, 4 to 5 minutes. Using mixing spoon, transfer to large mixing bowl.

3. Place skillet back on the heat without cleaning, and add 1 more tablespoon oil and 2 tablespoons butter or margarine. Heat over medium-high heat. Add meat cubes (a few at a time), and toss to lightly brown meat on all sides, 4 to 5 minutes. Add to onion and mushroom mixture. Continue sautéing until all the meat is browned. Add more oil and butter or margarine, as needed.

4. Add chopped parsley, beef broth, and tomato paste to meat mixture. Toss to mix, and transfer to buttered deep-dish pie pan. Cool to room temperature, and refrigerate for 1 hour.

Preheat oven to 400°F.

5. Place pastry sheet on lightly floured work surface, and, using lightly floured rolling pin, roll out pastry to about 10 inches square. Lay pastry over meat mixture, and press down around the rim of the pie pan. Using a knife, trim off the overhang, and save the pastry scraps. Using a knife, cut a 2-inch-long crisscross, in the center of the pastry. Curl back the edges in the middle of the X to make a decorative vent for steam to escape. Cut the pastry scraps with the scissors into leaves, stars, or confetti-like shapes, and scatter them over the top. Using a pastry brush, brush top of pastry well with egg wash. (If the pastry is rough-looking, that's fine; it makes a more interesting-looking pie.)

6. Place pie in oven, and bake for 15 to 20 minutes, or until top is golden brown. Reduce the oven heat to 350°F, and place a piece of foil over the pie to prevent the top from getting too brown. Continue baking for 15 to 20 minutes more. Using oven mitts, remove from oven.

Serve the pie while still warm, cutting the top into wedges and spooning out the meat filling.

⚮ Sticky Toffee-Date Pudding

No Australian meal is complete unless desserts, called "afters" (because they are eaten "after" the meal), are brought to the table and served with a "cuppa" (a cup of tea). An old favorite "after" served at life-cycle parties is stick toffee-date pudding.

Yield: serves 4 to 6

Toffee sauce:

1 cup brown sugar

1 cup whipping cream

1 teaspoon vanilla extract

2 tablespoons butter

Pudding:

1 cup **pitted** dates, **finely chopped**

1½ cups water

1 teaspoon baking soda

6 tablespoons butter, room temperature

1¼ cups brown sugar

3 eggs

2 cups all-purpose flour

1½ teaspoons vanilla extract

For serving:

whipped topping or ice cream

Equipment: Medium saucepan, mixing spoon, small saucepan, electric mixer or large mixing bowl with mixing spoon, greased or nonstick **springform** pan, toothpick, oven mitts

Preheat oven to 350°F.

1. Prepare toffee sauce: Place sugar, 1 cup whipping cream, vanilla extract, and butter in medium saucepan. Bring to boil over medium-high heat, reduce to simmer 3 to 5 minutes, or until sugar is dissolved, stirring frequently. Set aside, keep warm.

2. Prepare pudding: Place dates in small saucepan, and add water. Bring to boil over medium-high heat, reduce to simmer, and cook 3 to 5 minutes, or until dates are soft. Remove from heat, stir in baking soda, mix well, and set aside.

3. Place butter and brown sugar in electric mixer or mixing bowl, mix well. Add eggs one at time, mix well.

4. Gradually stir in flour, vanilla extract, and date mixture, and mix well.

5. Transfer to springform pan, and bake 35 to 40 minutes, or until toothpick inserted in center comes out clean.

6. Carefully remove springform pan from oven using oven mitts, and set aside to cool 10 to 12 minutes. Carefully remove sides of springform, and place pudding on serving platter.

To serve, cut into individual servings with toffee sauce poured over top. Add a dollop of whipped topping or ice cream for an extra treat.

⚜ *Macadamia Bickies* (Twice-Baked Macadamia Nut Cookies)

Another favorite treat is *bickies* (biscuits or cookies), especially when made with macadamia nuts. Indigenous to Australia, macadamia nuts were "bush tucker" food for the Aborigines long before the Europeans discovered them in the 1820s. They were originally called "bush nuts," "Queensland nuts," or "bauple nuts."

Yield: about 90 pieces

3 eggs

¾ cup sugar

1 cup oil

1 teaspoon vanilla extract

1 cup **coarsely chopped** macadamia nuts

1 cup chocolate chips

2 cups all-purpose flour	¼ teaspoon salt
1½ teaspoons baking powder	1½ cups corn flakes

Equipment: Large mixing bowl, wooden mixing spoon, small bowl, rubber spatula, plastic wrap, greased baking sheet, aluminum foil, vegetable oil spray, lightly floured work surface, oven mitts, **serrated knife**

Note: Mix ingredients with a mixing spoon; do not use an electric mixer or food processor.

Preheat oven to 350°F.

1. Put eggs in large mixing bowl. Add sugar and oil, and stir well using a wooden mixing spoon. Stir in vanilla extract, nuts, and chocolate chips until well mixed. Put flour, baking powder, and salt in small bowl, and stir together. Add flour mixture a little at a time, stirring after each addition. Using rubber spatula, stir in corn flakes. Cover bowl with plastic wrap, and refrigerate overnight.

2. Prepare to bake: Cover baking sheet with piece of foil, and grease foil with vegetable oil spray. Divide dough into 3 balls. Using clean hands, roll one ball into the shape of a rope 1 inch wide and about 15 inches long on lightly floured work surface. Repeat, making 2 more ropes, and place them side by side, with space between them to allow for rising, on foil–covered baking sheet. Bake in oven until golden, 25 to 30 minutes.

3. Using oven mitts, remove from oven, and allow to rest 10 minutes. Using a serrated knife, slice each log diagonally across into ½-inch-thick slices. Lay the slices side by side, with cut side on the baking sheet. Bake in the oven 3 to 5 minutes to lightly toast. Cool to room temperature.

Serve as a sweet treat at birthday parties or on the dessert buffet table for other life-cycle celebrations. These cookies freeze well; store in a resealable plastic freezer bag.

Fiji

Fiji is a group of more than 300 islands located in the Pacific Ocean northeast of Australia. The population is made up of Fijians who are descendants of Polynesians, Melanesians, and Indians, who are descendants of indentured laborers recruited over a century ago. The Indian population has increased more quickly than the native population, and there are now more Indians living on Fiji than indigenous peoples.

The majority of the indigenous Fijians are Christian. Christianity was brought to Fiji by Methodist missionaries, and superstitions, astrology beliefs, and nature events have been interwoven into their religion. Many native Fijians live in small villages centered around a Methodist church and mission schools.

Indians are not allowed to own land in Fiji (only native Fijians and the government can own land), which has added to the tension between Fijians and Indians. There is no social mixing and almost no intermarriage between the two groups. Fiji Indians have their own villages with their own places of worship and their own schools, and they prepare dishes from their Indian homeland. (See India and the subcontinent recipes pages 140 to 146.)

Indians introduced fire walking to Fiji. The indigenous Fijians adopted the ritual, except that they walk on heated stones instead of hot embers. Wedding celebrations now often call for a display of fire walkers.

Kava, a nonalcoholic drink made from the crushed root of a pepper plant, is a ceremonial drink among Fijians. It is served from a *bilo* (coconut cup). Onlookers perform ritual clapping, clapping once before the *kava* is drunk and three times after it is swallowed. *Kava* might be enjoyed at any auspicious occasion, such as a child being born, a boat being completed, a roof being raised, a child returning home, and the like.

The first important event in a Christian Fijian child's life is his or her christening. Feasts are prepared by Fijians for this celebratory occasion. Among native Fijians, a wedding or funeral is a community affair and also involves feasting. A flotilla of boats often brings neighboring communities to the celebration. A *tambua*, a ceremonial object of respect made of the polished tooth of the sperm whale, is often given at births, presented to distinguished guests, given to show sympathy at funerals, or given when a contract or agreement is entered into. It is customary for a groom to present a tooth to the father of the bride, prior to the wedding.

⚶ *Kokoda* (Chilled Fish with Coconut Cream)

In Fiji, *kokoda* is a favorite dish to serve at the beginning of any life-cycle celebration feast.

Yield: serves 4 to 6

3 (4- to 6-ounce) skinless fish **fillets** (such as tilapia, mahi-mahi, halibut, or cod), cut into bite-size pieces

juice of 5 limes or 1 cup bottled lime juice

½ cup white vinegar

2 tablespoons ginger root, **trimmed, grated**

1 cup coconut cream (recipe page 225)

1 onion, trimmed, **minced**

1 green chili, trimmed, **seeded, finely chopped**

salt and pepper to taste

For serving:

4 to 6 Bibb lettuce leaves

2 tomatoes, trimmed, finely chopped, for garnish

½ cup **shredded** coconut, for garnish

Equipment: Large glass mixing bowl, mixing spoon, plastic wrap, **strainer** or **colander**, individual plates

1. Place fish, lime juice, vinegar and ginger in mixing bowl, and, using mixing spoon, mix well. Cover with plastic wrap, and refrigerate 6 to 7 hours, mixing 2 to 3 times to evenly coat. Fish will become **opaque** white.

2. Remove fish from refrigerator, transfer to strainer or colander, drain and discard excess lime and vinegar juice. Return fish to mixing bowl.

3. Stir in coconut cream, onion, and green chili, mix well. Add salt and pepper to taste.

Serve chilled on individual plates with 2 to 3 tablespoons fish mixture spooned over each lettuce leaf. Garnish with tomatoes and shredded coconut as a starter to a meal.

⚘ Shrimp Palusami (Shrimp in Coconut Cream)

Feasts center around the suckling pig (recipe page 243), which is baked in a pit over heated stones covered with palm fronds and banana leaves. Baked with the suckling pig are chunks of plantains, sweet potato, peeled breadfruit, taro root, and fish and shrimp wrapped in large leaves. In Fiji, shrimp *palusami* would be wrapped in leaves. For this recipe, we're wrapping the shrimp in foil.

Yield: serves 4

6 large cabbage leaves, washed and well drained, divided

2 to 3 pounds medium **shrimp**, chopped, shelled, **peeled and deveined**

1 cup **finely chopped** onion

salt and pepper to taste

1 cup coconut cream, homemade (recipe follows) or canned (available at Asian food stores and some supermarkets)

water, as needed

Equipment: Medium mixing bowl, mixing spoon, 4 (8½×10-inch) rectangles of aluminum foil, oven mitts, 9- to 10-inch square baking dish

Preheat oven to 350°F.

1. Finely chop 2 cabbage leaves, and place in medium mixing bowl. Add chopped shrimp, onion, salt and pepper, and coconut cream, and stir well.

2. Place 4 sheets of foil side by side on work surface, and set one of the 4 remaining whole cabbage leaves on top of each. Spoon equal amounts of shrimp mixture in the center of each leaf. Fold the leaves over the filling. Wrap and seal each stuffed leaf in foil. Arrange packages in baking dish, add about 1½ inches of water in bottom.

3. Bake in oven for 1 hour, until shrimp are fully cooked. Check shrimp **doneness**; they should be opaque pinkish-white when done.

To serve, each person gets one package as an appetizer during the wedding feast. The contents of the package are eaten by tearing open the foil.

⚘ Fresh Coconut for Grating

Note: When buying a fresh coconut, make sure that it has no cracks and that it contains liquid. Shake it, and if you do not hear swishing liquid, select another. When making coconut milk and cream, it is not necessary to remove the brown inner skin before you grate coconut meat.

Yield: about 3 to 4 cups grated coconut

1 ripe coconut (at least 2 pounds)

Equipment: Ice pick or metal skewer, kitchen towel, hard surface, oven mitts, hammer, food processor fitted with coarse grating attachment

1. *Caution: Adult help required*: Have an adult pierce the "eyes" of the coconut with an ice pick or metal skewer. Drain liquid, discard or save for another use.

2. Wrap coconut in towel and place on hard surface. Protect your hands with oven mitts, and crack coconut open with hammer. Break into pieces small enough to fit in feed tube of food processor, for grating.

3. In food processor fitted with coarse **grater**, grate coconut pulp, about 4 minutes. (You should have about 4 cups loosely packed coconut pulp.)

Use grated coconut to make lolo *(coconut milk) or coconut cream (recipe follows) or pack in air-tight container and freeze.*

ℰ *Lolo* (Coconut Milk)

Yield: about 2 cups

2 cups grated fresh coconut, homemade (recipe precedes) or unsweetened, grated coconut (available canned or frozen at Asian food stores or most supermarkets)

2 cups boiling water, more if necessary

Equipment: Electric **blender** or food processor, strainer, double-thickness cheesecloth or cotton napkin, small bowl, spoon

1. In blender or food processor, mix coconut and 2 cups boiling water for 2 minutes; let cool for 30 minutes.

2. Line a strainer with double-thickness dampened cheesecloth or napkin and set over small bowl. Pour coconut mixture into the cloth, a little at a time, making sure all liquid drains through cloth. Once all liquid has drained, pick up the four edges of cloth, and twist it tightly to release as much coconut milk as possible into the small bowl. Discard coconut in cloth.

This process makes thick coconut milk. For thinner coconut milk, add a little more water until you reach desired consistency.

ℰ *Coconut Cream*

Yield: about 1 cup

1 cup heavy cream

2 cups grated fresh coconut, homemade (recipe precedes) or unsweetened, grated coconut (available, canned or frozen at Asian food stores and most supermarkets)

Equipment: Small saucepan, electric **blender** or food processor, strainer, double-thickness cheesecloth or cotton napkin, small bowl, spoon

1. In small saucepan, heat cream until small bubbles appear around edges of pan.
2. In blender or food processor, mix coconut and heated cream for about 2 minutes. Allow to cool for 30 minutes.
3. Line strainer with double-thickness dampened cheesecloth or napkin, and set over small bowl. Pour coconut mixture into cloth, a little at a time, making sure all liquid has drained through the cloth. Pick up four edges of cloth, and twist tightly to release as much liquid as possible. Discard coconut in the cloth.

New Zealand

New Zealand, about 1,200 miles southeast of Australia, consists of two islands, North Island and South Island, which are separated by the Cook Strait. The greatest concentration of people live on North Island. The descendants of Europeans, primarily from the British Isles, are generally city dwellers and belong to the Anglican Church.

The indigenous people, the Maoris, live in settlements in remote regions of the country. Most Maoris combine traditional Maori beliefs with Christianity. The ancestors of the Maoris migrated centuries ago to New Zealand, which they called *Aoteuroa* ("the long white cloud"). They came by seagoing canoes from islands somewhere in the mid-Pacific and developed a unique culture, considered one of the most advanced in all of Polynesia.

According to Maori tradition, the land is sacred, and it must be cared for and protected. The people get from the land not only their food but also their identity; the cycle of birth and death springs from Mother Earth. At a Maori's birth, the father or a Maori priest recites a ritual prayer (*karakia*) to bestow supernatural powers on the child, especially if it is the firstborn. After the ceremony, a feast is held for everyone in the community.

New Zealand has some 40 different Maori groups. Many Maoris have fused the Western language and way of life (referred to as *pakena*) with their own. Traditional Maori social activities take place at the communal ceremonial gathering site (*marae*). The *marae* includes the meeting house, dining hall, utility buildings, and sometimes a church. There are about a thousand *marae* throughout New Zealand where only the Maori language is spoken and Maori food is eaten. This is where all meetings, ceremonial gatherings (*hui*), and such special events as weddings and funerals take place.

At the *marae* compound, everything is communal, from gathering the food to sharing it in the dining hall. The men prepare the *hangi*, an earth oven, which is a pit filled with fire-heated stones that can cook hundreds of pounds of mutton, pork, beef, chicken, eel, cabbage, and *kumara* (sweet potatoes) at one time. Women do most of the food preparation, table setting, and cleanup work, with the help of the children. Men are called upon to bake bread leavened with homemade potato yeast. (A bread with similar flavor but different texture can be made with mashed potatoes and active dry yeast). Potato bread (recipe follows) is prepared for all life-cycle celebrations.

Weddings are often planned for Easter or Christmas holidays, and many relatives gather to share in the celebration. Most brides wear the *pakeha* (Western-style) wedding attire. Vows are spoken in Maori, and the rite takes place in either the church or the meeting house, followed by speeches, singing, dancing, and feasting in the *marae* dining hall. Kinfolk bring their harvest of sweet potatoes, cabbages, seaweed, seafood, and assorted meats to be cooked in the *hangi*. A crew of women serve the food buffet-style to the throngs who attend the celebration.

The Maori rituals of death (*tangihanga*) are elaborate and long. The death rites take place in the meeting house where families spend three days and nights together, making speeches about the deceased, paying tribute to the ancestors, reciting ancient tales, expressing their grief and beliefs in chants, and singing Maori songs around the casket. Mourning is public; according to Maori traditions, the deceased belongs to the tribe, not to the individual family. Contributions of food, cash, and personal help are given by mourners for such ceremonial gatherings. On the third day of the funeral ritual, after a church service, the grave is dug by the men in the family, and the deceased is buried with cherished personal belongings. The rituals end with a cleansing rite followed by a celebration feast.

⚘ *Maori Potato Bread*

Potatoes are not native to New Zealand and were probably introduced to the Maoris by Christian missionaries in the early 19th century, who also probably showed the Maoris how to make the leavening agent for making bread. In this potato bread recipe, freshly mashed potatoes and dry active yeast are used to speed up the procedure.

Note: This recipe takes two days.

Yield: 1 round loaf (about 8 inches)

2 cups mashed potatoes leftovers or prepared instant

2 cups **lukewarm** water

1 package active dry **yeast**

7 cups bread flour, divided, more or less as needed

2 teaspoons salt

2 teaspoons sugar

½ cup **cornmeal**

1 teaspoon cornstarch

½ cup cold water

Equipment: Large mixing bowl, wooden mixing spoon, plastic wrap, lightly floured work surface, kitchen towel, baking sheet, sharp knife, 8-inch square baking pan, small pan, heat-proof surface, **pastry brush**, oven mitts, wire cake rack

1. Prepare yeast sponge: Put mashed potatoes in large mixing bowl, add lukewarm water, yeast, and 4 cups flour, and stirring gently, mix ingredients. Cover with plastic wrap and allow to stand in warm place for 6 to 8 hours or overnight. The sponge is ready to use when it is very thick and bubbly.

2. Uncover the yeast sponge, and sprinkle in salt and sugar. Using wooden mixing spoon, carefully **fold in** 2½ cups flour. Do not stir, as stirring will toughen the dough. Using your hands, continue slowly folding in flour, ½ cup at a time, until dough is no longer sticky and can be formed into a ball. Transfer to lightly floured work surface, and **knead** until smooth and **elastic**, 5 to 8 minutes. Grease large mixing bowl, and place dough in bowl, turning to grease all sides. Cover with towel, and let rise in a warm place until doubled in bulk, 1½ to 2 hours.

3. **Punch down** dough with your fist. Transfer to lightly floured work surface, and shape into round loaf. Sprinkle loaf with cornmeal, and place on baking sheet. Cover with towel, and let rise for 1½ to 2 hours, until almost double in size. Using a sharp knife, make a crisscross slash, about ¼-inch deep on top center of loaf.

Preheat oven to 375°F.

4. Fill an 8-inch-square baking pan with about ½ inch water, and place on bottom of oven. (This helps the bread form a nice crust.)

5. In small saucepan, dissolve cornstarch in cold water, and bring to a boil over high heat. Cool slightly, and, using pastry brush, coat top and sides of loaf with cornstarch mixture.

6. Bake bread in oven for 30 to 35 minutes, or until loaf is golden brown. Using oven mitts, remove from oven. Remove loaf from baking sheet, and invert on wire rack to cool to warm.

Serve the bread fresh from the oven while still slightly warm for best flavor.

Grapefruit, Kiwi, and Watercress Salad

Kiwi fruit is cultivated in New Zealand, and most New Zealanders seem to have a variety of fruit trees growing in their backyard. This salad made with easily available fruit would probably be included in the birthday or anniversary dinner menu.

Yield: serves 6

4 fresh grapefruit, peeled, **pith** removed and sectioned or two jars (26 ounces each) grapefruit sections (available in the refrigerated section of most supermarkets)

3 **kiwis**

2 tablespoons lemon juice

1 tablespoon cider vinegar

3 tablespoons vegetable oil

2 teaspoons honey

salt and pepper to taste

1 bunch fresh **watercress**, rinsed, patted dry, **trimmed**

For **garnish**: **cinnamon sugar**, to taste

Equipment: Strainer, medium bowl, knife, work surface, small bowls with cover, pint jar with tight-fitting lid, medium serving platter

1. Drain grapefruit sections in strainer placed over a medium bowl. Cover and refrigerate grapefruit juice for another use.

2. Peel kiwi, and, on work surface, slice crosswise into ¼-inch thick slices. Put slices in small bowl, cover, and refrigerate until ready to assemble.

3. Prepare dressing: In pint jar, combine lemon juice and vinegar. Add oil, honey, and salt and pepper to taste. Cover jar tightly and shake to mix. Refrigerate until ready to use.

4. Assemble: Arrange watercress in a ring around edge of medium serving platter. Fill in center with well drained grapefruit sections. Place the kiwi slices on the top center of the grapefruit. Slightly overlap the kiwi slices in a decorative pattern. Do not completely cover the grapefruit. Cover with plastic wrap and refrigerate until ready to serve.

*To serve, uncover salad. Shake dressing in jar, and **drizzle** over fruit. Sprinkle with cinnamon sugar to taste, for garnish.*

⚜ *Afghan Biscuits* (Chocolate Cornflake Cookies)

Afghan biscuits are the perfect treat to serve at a children's birthday celebration for everyone to enjoy.

Yield: 1 to 2 dozen

¾ cup butter

½ cup sugar

1¼ cup flour

¼ cup cocoa

2 cups unsweetened cornflakes

1 container chocolate icing (available at most supermarkets)

½ cup walnuts or **slivered** almonds, **finely chopped**, more as needed

Equipment: Electric mixer or medium mixing bowl with mixing spoon, tablespoon, nonstick or greased baking sheet, oven mitts, spatula

Preheat oven to 350°F.

1. Using electric mixer or mixing bowl with mixing spoon, combine butter and sugar until light and fluffy. Gradually add flour and cocoa, mix well. **Fold** cornflakes into mixture.

2. Spoon heaping spoonfuls of mixture onto baking sheet and press together, about 1½ to 2 inches apart, and bake in oven about 10 to 15 minutes. Carefully remove from oven using oven mitts, and set aside to cool.

3. When cookies are cool, using spatula, spread icing over top of cookies, and then sprinkle with walnuts. Continue until all cookies are iced and sprinkled.

Serve as a special treat.

Papua New Guinea

Papua New Guinea (PNG) lies about 90 miles northeast of Australia and includes the eastern half of the island of New Guinea and hundreds of neighboring islands. Plagued with frequent mud slides, earthquakes, volcanic eruptions, and drought, the islanders are no strangers to natural disasters. In recent years, a *tsunami* (a huge ocean wave produced by an underwater earthquake) did devastating damage and took many lives.

For better than 100 years, PNG has been a destination for Christian missionaries, who have had a strong influence on the native people. PNG is a Christian country, according to its constitution. Christian New Guineans combine Christianity with traditional beliefs; magic and sorcery remain powerful influences throughout their lives.

The indigenous population of PNG consists of several hundred groups or societies, each with their own language or dialect, customs, and traditions. Mainly due to the country's rugged, often impassable terrain, many clans live a near Stone Age existence, isolated not only from the rest of the world but from one another. Though modernization has begun in the country, for the vast majority of native peoples living in small villages, their way of life and social structure remain unchanged. The social structure is generally small, based on family, clan, or tribe. Loyalty and obligation to the extended family are an important part of life.

Contrasts abound in this land where the only form of communication between some villages is talking drums, while in other parts of PNG, people converse via a high-tech microwave telephone system. Coastal villages consist of thatch-roofed houses, usually built on stilts, a school, and a *haus tambaran* ("spirit house," also known as the men's ceremonial house). Most coastal villagers earn a living from the sea (fishers, coral divers, canoe builders, net makers, etc.) or by farming. Highlanders live in similar villages, except their huts cling to the sides of mountains, and people forage from the forests or work on coconut and coffee plantations. Coffee, the nation's most profitable crop, grows well in the highland altitudes.

When young boys pass into adulthood, they are taken to the *haus tambaran,* which is the meeting place for the secret men's society and off-limits to women. Among some groups, the boys undergo a grueling initiation into manhood. Scarification is one of the acts performed on the boys. Mask and statue carvings, body painting with mud and ash, and the sacred flute are all used in the boy-to-manhood rituals. When the initiation is completed, there is usually a great celebration (*sing-sing*).

Endless life-cycle customs and rituals can be found in PNG. Some groups have a food exchange ceremony honoring recently deceased elders. The clan comes together, each member bringing quantities of food to share at the festive occasion.

Like other life-cycle celebrations, weddings are communal, and the entire village might take part in the preparations and celebration. The husband-to-be customarily pays a bride-price to the family of his future wife. Since the pig is a prized possession and a form of wealth, the bride's price is often paid with a pig or two plus a little cash.

Funerals are usually momentous occasions, and the rituals are very complex. Each clan has its own funerary traditions, which might include internment, cremation, or burial at sea. Some clans sink the body in the sea or set it adrift. Ancestral worship and spirit beliefs are usually part of death rituals. Among some groups, the secret men's societies make *dukduks* (ritual costumes) or carve *malangans* (masks or totemic figures) to honor the dead. ("*Malangan*" refers to the carvings as well as a complex system of spiritual ideas, rites, and beliefs.)

Eating pork is reserved for important celebration feasts. For the people who can afford it, every important life-cycle celebration means the roasting of a whole suckling pig. The pig is roasted in a *mumu*, a traditional underground oven. A pit is dug, fire-heated stones are placed in the bottom, and meat and vegetables are wrapped in herbs and leaves and placed on the stones. The pit is then sealed with palm fronds, banana leaves, and branches, and the contents are roasted and steamed.

Celebrations are almost always communal, and it is not unusual for many weddings to take place on the same day. On such occasions the roasting pit can be several hundred yards long and filled with hundreds of whole pigs.

Vuaka Vavi Ena Lova (Roast Suckling Pig)

Baked in the pit with the pigs are chunks of plantains, sweet potato (*kaukau*), peeled **breadfruit, taro root,** and fish, each separately wrapped in banana leaves. Also wrapped in leaves and baked in the pit is *pota*, a mixture of chicken and salt pork. This recipe for roast suckling pig is adapted for the kitchen oven.

Yield: serves 14 to 20

6 tablespoons dark brown sugar

1 cup Chinese soy sauce

6 cloves garlic, **finely chopped**

For **garnish**:

6 ripe **plantains**, cut crosswise into 2-inch chunks

12-pound suckling pig (weighed when dressed), rinsed and patted dry with paper towels

6 tablespoons vegetable oil

1cup butter or margarine, divided

2 pounds sweet potatoes, boiled to done, yet firm (not mushy), peeled and cut crosswise into 2-inch chunks

1 lemon or large lime

Equipment: Small saucepan, mixing spoon, paper towels, small bowl with cover, large plastic bag (about 24×30 inches), kitchen string, large roasting pan with rack, aluminum foil, **bulb baster,** oven mitts, large skillet with cover, large saucepan with cover

1. Prepare **marinade**: Put the brown sugar and soy sauce in a small saucepan, and over medium heat, stir to dissolve the sugar, 1 to 2 minutes. Remove from heat, stir in the garlic, and cool to room temperature. Using a crumpled wad of paper towel, dab the pig inside and out with half the soy sauce mixture. Slip the pig into a large plastic bag, seal, and refrigerate for 4 to 6 hours to absorb the marinade. Transfer remaining marinade to small bowl, cover, and refrigerate to use for basting the pig during roasting.

Preheat oven to 450°F.

2. Prepare pig to roast: Using string, tie the pig's legs. To do this, bend the back legs in a crouching position and tie them together, under the pig. Tie the front legs straight out in front. Place the pig upright on rack, in large roasting pan. Make a lemon-size wad of foil, and place it in the pig's mouth to keep it open. Cover the ears and tail with foil to prevent burning.

3. Mix remaining marinade with oil. Using a wad of paper towel, dab it all over the pig.

4. Roast pig: Roast at 450°F for 30 minutes, and then reduce heat to 325°F for 4½ to 5 hours (allow 30 minutes for each pound), or until cooked through and registers 165° to 175°F on meat thermometer. Using a bulb baster, **baste** frequently with marinade. If necessary, make more marinade.

5. Prepare garnishes: 30 minutes before serving, melt ½ cup butter or margarine in large skillet over medium-high heat. Add plantain chunks and fry, tossing frequently, until golden, 15 to 20 minutes. Cover and keep on low heat. Melt remaining ½ cup butter or margarine in large saucepan over medium-high heat. Add sweet potatoes, reduce heat to medium and fry, carefully turning the pieces, until they are golden, 15 to 20 minutes. Cover and keep on low heat.

To serve, transfer the pig to large platter or tray. Remove the foil from ears and tail. Replace the foil in the mouth with whole lemon or lime. Arrange plantain and sweet potato chunks around the pig and serve as the centerpiece for the wedding feast.

Canned fish and bully beef, shipped from Australia, and mutton flaps, the belly portions of sheep, from New Zealand are very popular and often are included in the wedding feast or other life cycle sing.

⚘ *Kumara Bake* (Sweet Potato Pumpkin Casserole)

Kumara, also known as sweet potato, is popular throughout the South Pacific. *Kumara* is a mainstay of the Guinean diet, and *Kumara Bake* would be found at many life-cycle celebrations.

Yield: serves 6 to 8

1½ pounds sweet potatoes, **trimmed**, peeled, quartered

4 potatoes, trimmed, peeled, quartered

water, as needed

4 slices bacon, **finely chopped**

1 onion, trimmed, finely chopped

2 cloves garlic, trimmed, **minced**

1 tablespoon cayenne pepper, or to taste

1 tablespoon turmeric

1 cup chives, trimmed, finely chopped

14.5 ounces canned pumpkin

2½ cups heavy cream

1 cup milk

14.5 ounces canned stewed tomatoes, finely chopped

3 **hard-cooked** eggs, finely chopped

salt and pepper to taste

1 cup **bread crumbs**, more as needed

1 cup cheddar cheese, **grated**, more as needed

Equipment: Large saucepan or stock pot, slotted spoon, **strainer** or **colander**, large greased or nonstick ovenproof baking dish, medium saucepan, mixing spoon, oven mitts

Preheat oven to 350°F.

1. Place sweet potatoes and potatoes in large saucepan or stock pot, and add water to cover. Bring to boil over high heat, reduce to simmer, and cook 6 to 8 minutes or until **parboiled**. Using slotted spoon, transfer to strainer or colander to drain. Spoon into baking dish, set aside.

2. Cook bacon in medium saucepan over medium-high heat 3 to 4 minutes, or until fat is rendered. Stir in onions and garlic, **sauté** 3 to 5 minutes, or until soft. Stirring frequently, add cayenne pepper, turmeric and chives, mix well. Remove from heat.

3. Stir pumpkin, heavy cream, milk, tomatoes, and boiled eggs into bacon-onion mixture, mix until well blended. Add salt and pepper to taste.

4. Add pumpkin mixture to sweet potato mixture, mix well. Sprinkle bread crumbs over top, and then add cheese to cover. Bake in oven 20 to 25 minutes, or until potatoes are tender. Carefully remove from oven using oven mitts.

Serve as a side dish at a life-cycle celebration feast.

CARIBBEAN

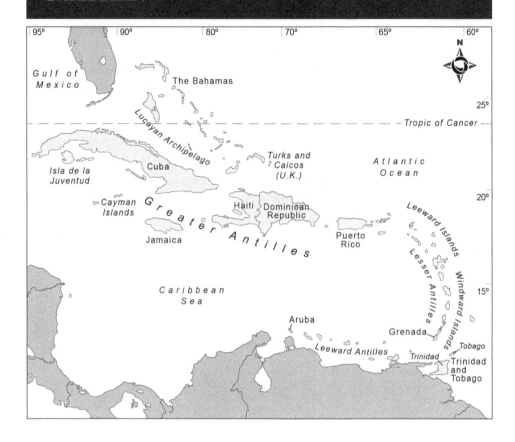

3

The Caribbean

The Caribbean islands are located in the Caribbean Sea, which stretches from Venezuela in the south to the area between Florida and Mexico in the north. The popular image of the Caribbean is that it is a land of tropical breezes, palm trees, blue skies, gentle seas, and lush green vegetation and that all islands are alike. Behind this stereotyped image of island paradises are unique islands with marked differences in peoples and geography, ranging from tropical to arid semidesert islands.

The original inhabitants, Arawak Indians and Caribs (they gave the region its name), disappeared after the arrival of Europeans, mostly through disease and war. Nearly everyone who calls the islands "home" are transplants. Caribbean traditions, customs, and food arrived with the explorers, conquerors, settlers, slaves, and indentured workers from Europe, Africa, India, Asia, and Latin America.

The majority of the Caribbean people are at least partially descended from African slaves. The remainder includes direct descendants of European colonists and the East Indians brought to the islands as indentured laborers when slavery was abolished in the 19th century. The Chinese also immigrated to the area in search of economic opportunities.

Black Wedding Cake (Caribbean Fruitcake)

All of these ethnic groups have adapted the life-cycle traditions and foods of their homelands to conditions of the islands, creating new traditions and foods that spread throughout the Caribbean. A perfect example is the black wedding cake. It is a version of the English fruitcake; however, it is made with ingredients native to the tropical islands.

This cake is called "black cake" because of its dark brown color. In the tropics, burnt sugar syrup is added to make the cake even darker. Burnt sugar syrup (available at Caribbean food stores and some supermarkets) is a thin, black, bitter liquid. It is also added to meat and fish stews to enrich the color. Burnt sugar syrup is not essential to the taste of this recipe; however, it adds to the presentation. Black wedding cake is also known as "bride's cake" and "Christmas cake."

Note: This recipe takes more than one day.

Yield: serves 35 to 45

5 cups chopped mixed **candied fruit: papaya,** pineapple, cherries, apricots, or **citron** (1¼ cups each or any combination)

1½ cups seedless raisins (9-ounce container equals 1½ cups)

1½ cups chopped dates (9-ounce container equals 1½ cups)

2 cups chopped nuts (walnuts or pecans)

7½ cups all-purpose flour, divided

1 teaspoon salt

6 teaspoons baking powder

1 teaspoon ground cinnamon

1½ teaspoons ground **allspice**

½ teaspoon ground cloves

½ teaspoon ground nutmeg

14 eggs, lightly beaten

2 cups unsalted butter, melted

1½ cups warm water

2 tablespoons burnt **sugar syrup** (optional)

3½ cups dark brown sugar

½ cup rum for misting (optional)

4 to 5 (8 ounces each) tubes **almond paste,** for assembling (available at all supermarkets)

1 to 2 tablespoons water (optional)

butter cream icing (recipe follows), for frosting

Equipment: 3 springform pans (each a different size: 6, 9, 12 inches), aluminum foil, 3 **cake circle boards** (each a different size: 6, 9, 12 inches), 2 large mixing bowls, flour sifter, electric mixer or mixing spoon, rubber spatula, oven mitts, toothpick, wire cake rack, small spray bottle (optional), medium bowl, 2 baking sheets, **icing spatula** or dinner knife, large round serving tray or platter, 10 (4- to 6-inch) skewers, small cutting pliers, pitcher of warm water, paper towels

1. Prepare springform pans: Cut a piece of foil large enough to cover one side of each cake circle board and fit smoothly over the edges. Open the side ring latch on each springform. Remove the metal pan bottom, and replace it with a circle board of the same size. Place the cake board, foil-side up, in the side ring, then close and tighten the side ring latch around it to secure the bottom in place. Repeat assembling all three pans. Butter the sides and the foil-covered bottom of each pan and sprinkle with flour, shake out excess, and set pans aside.

Preheat oven to 275°F.

2. Put candied fruit, raisins, dates, and nuts in a large mixing bowl. Add 1½ cups flour, and using your hands, toss to coat fruit mixture.

3. Sift remaining 6 cups flour, salt, baking powder, cinnamon, allspice, cloves, and nutmeg into the remaining large mixing bowl. Add lightly beaten eggs, melted butter, burnt sugar syrup

(optional), and brown sugar into flour mixture. Using an electric mixer or mixing spoon, beat until batter is smooth, 3 to 5 minutes. Fill each springform pan about ⅔ full with batter.

4. Bake cakes in oven for 2½ to 3 hours, or until toothpick inserted in center of each comes out clean and cakes pull away from sides of pans. Using oven mitts, remove from oven, and place on wire rack. Let cakes cool for 1 hour before removing sides of pans.

5. Remove sides of springform pans, but keep cakes on the cake boards. (The boards support the cakes.) Set the cakes on the wire rack to cool for at least 2 hours before continuing. When cakes are cool to the touch, carefully turn topside-down on work surface. Remove the cake boards, and if the foil sticks to the cake, carefully peel it off, and recover the circle boards with a new piece of foil. Place the cake board, foil-side up on the work surface, then slide the topside-down cake onto it. The bottom of the cake, which has a smooth flat surface and sharp corners, is now the top; repeat with all 3 cakes.

6. Wrap each cake in foil, and refrigerate overnight or up to a week for flavor to develop. Lightly mist the top and sides of cakes with rum from a spray bottle two or three times during the week to enhance the flavor (optional).

Preheat oven to 250°F.

7. Prepare to coat cakes with almond paste: Remove almond paste from packages and put in medium bowl. Allow paste to sit at room temperature for at least 2 hours, and mix well. If almond paste seems too stiff to spread, beat in 1 to 2 tablespoons water.

8. Set cakes on baking sheets. Using icing spatula or dinner knife, spread a thin layer of almond paste over the top and sides of each cake. Place in oven for 20 to 30 minutes to dry almond paste. Cool cakes to room temperature before icing them.

9. Assemble 3-tier cake: Set largest (12-inch) cake on large round serving tray or platter. Poke one skewer in the center and space the other four skewers equally apart, in a 4-inch radius from the center skewer. Using small cutting pliers, cut the exposed tops off of the 5 skewers so they are even with the top of the cake. (The skewers give added support when the other cakes are place on top.) Center the 9-inch cake on top of the trimmed skewers. Poke 1 skewer in the center of the 9-inch cake, and space the other four skewers equally apart in a 2-inch radius from the center. Cut the skewers even with the top of the cake as before, and center the 6-inch cake on top.

10. Prepare 2 batches butter cream icing (recipe follows).

11. Frost cakes with icing: Prepare a pitcher of warm water and paper towels to keep icing tool clean as you work. Keep surface around cake clean by covering with paper towels. Start icing from the top (6-inch) cake layer and work down the other two tiers. Smooth icing and place completed 3-tier cake in cool dry place until ready to serve.

To serve, decorate the cake with flowers of your choice, and place cake in the center of the buffet or cake table. Set cake plates, dessert forks, napkins, and a silver cake knife and serving spatula next to the cake. Arrange to have a family member or dear friend cut the cake after the bride and groom take the first slice.

✦ *Butter Cream Icing*

Two batches of this butter cream icing are needed to cover the wedding cake.

Yield: 9 cups

½ cup butter

½ cup solid vegetable shortening

8 cups confectioners' sugar, sifted, more if
necessary

½ cup heavy cream, more if necessary

1 tablespoon vanilla extract

Equipment: Large mixing bowl, electric mixer or mixing spoon, rubber spatula

Put butter and shortening into large mixing bowl, and, using an electric mixer or mixing spoon, beat until creamy. Beating constantly, add confectioners' sugar, a little at a time, alternately with ½ cup cream. If mixture seems too stiff, add a little more cream, ½ tablespoon at a time, to make icing a spreadable consistency. If too runny, add confectioners' sugar, 1 tablespoon at a time, to thicken. Beat in vanilla extract.

Use for black wedding cake (recipe precedes), or cover and refrigerate for another use. Use within 1 week.

Bahamas

The Commonwealth of the Bahamas is made up of more than 750 islands and cayes in the North Atlantic Ocean about 50 miles off the east coast of Florida. Only about 30 of the islands and cayes are inhabited. While not geographically part of the Caribbean, the Bahamas border the Caribbean Sea, and the Bahamians have many social and historical ties to the rest of the region.

The original inhabitants of the Bahamas were the Arawak Indians, who were wiped out by disease when Europeans arrived. The Bahamas became a British colony, and large numbers of African slaves were brought to the islands. Today the majority of the population is of African descent.

The islands became an independent country in 1973; however, legacy of British colonialism remains. The official language of the Bahamas is English, and the majority of the people are Christians, split fairly evenly among Baptists, Anglicans, and Roman Catholics. Bahamians generally celebrate the life-cycle events prescribed by their branch of Christianity. (See Protestant and Catholic Life-Cycle Rituals, page lxxiii.)

Weddings are community celebrations, and the bride, if the budget allows, wears a long white wedding dress with veil. Most ceremonies are held in a church, followed by a reception of small sandwiches, cake, and punch in the church social hall or the home of the bride's parents. Or guests are invited to the reception at a restaurant or hotel.

Traditionally, two cakes are prepared, one for the bride and one for the groom. The bride's cake is called "silver wedding cake." It is a three-tiered fruitcake (see recipe for black wedding cake, page 235), covered with edible **silver leaf**, symbolizing prosperity. The groom's cake (recipe follows) is pound cake often covered with edible gold leaf, symbolizing his authority as head of the family. The cakes are covered with butter cream icing (recipe page 238) and allowed to dry for a day or two before decorating with gold or silver leaf.

Fresh English ivy and tiny pink rose buds are usually added as decorations on the wedding cake. A cedar seedling is placed on top of the cake, and, according to tradition, the newlyweds plant the seedling together at their future homestead. The decorative cakes are not cut at the reception but later when the bride's parents give a party in their home honoring the newlyweds. Many families save the top layer of the wedding cake and serve it at the christening of their first child.

❧ *Groom's Gold Wedding Cake* (Sand Torte)

The groom's cake is a basic pound cake calling for all significant ingredients—flour, sugar, butter, and eggs—to be of the same weight. A similar cake called "and torte" is also popular.

Yield: serves 10 to 12

1 cup flour	**6 eggs, separated**
1 cup **cornstarch**	2 tablespoons vanilla or rum extract
2 teaspoons baking powder	For **garnish**: butter cream icing (recipe page 238)
1 cup unsalted butter, at room temperature	
1 cup sugar	**Gold leaf** (available at some Middle East and Indian food stores)

Equipment: Flour **sifter**, medium mixing bowl, large mixing bowl, mixing spoon or electric mixer, rubber spatula, buttered 9-inch tube pan, oven mitts, toothpick, knife, wire cake rack, serving platter, **icing spatula** or dinner knife, small artist's paintbrush or feather (optional), serving platter

Preheat oven to 350°F.

1. **Sift** flour, cornstarch, and baking powder in medium mixing bowl.

2. Put butter and sugar in large mixing bowl, and, using mixing spoon or electric mixer, beat until light and fluffy, 2 to 4 minutes. Add egg yolks, 2 at a time, beating well after each addition. Add sifted flour mixture, a little at a time, beating well after each addition. Beat in vanilla or rum extract.

3. Put egg whites into clean, dry, medium mixing bowl, and, using clean, dry electric mixer or mixing spoon, beat until soft peaks form. **Fold in** whites with batter, using rubber spatula. Transfer batter to buttered 9-inch tube pan.

4. Bake in oven for 45 to 50 minutes, or until toothpick inserted in centers comes out clean. Cool cake in pan for 10 minutes. Run knife around side of pan and flip onto wire cake rack.

5. Prepare butter cream icing (recipe page 238).

6. Assemble cake: Place cake on serving platter. Beginning at the top, cover cake with icing, using icing spatula or dinner knife. Decorate cake with greenery, such as English ivy, placed around the base and in the center hole of the cake. Continue to decorate with gold leaf, simply lay the small pieces on the icing with your fingers, they should stick by themselves. A small artist's paint brush or feather can be helpful to spread each piece.

⚶ *Calalou* (Crab Stew with Okra and Greens)

The comfort food of the Caribbean is *calalou* (also *callaloo* or *callilu*). Dasheen leaves, a variety of **taro root** grown in the Southern United States, or spinach can be used for this recipe if *calalou* leaves are not available.

Yield: serves 6

2-ounce slice salt pork, diced, or 4 tablespoons butter or margarine

2 onions, sliced

2 cloves garlic, **finely chopped**

½ pound **dasheen** leaves or spinach, washed and chopped

salt and pepper to taste

1 potato, peeled, **diced**

½ pound okra, **trimmed**, sliced crosswise into 3 pieces

6 cups chicken broth

½ pound cooked crabmeat, fresh, canned, or frozen (available at most fish markets and supermarkets)

ground red pepper to taste

6 cups cooked white rice, for serving

Equipment: Large saucepan with cover, mixing spoon

1. In large saucepan over medium heat, **render** chopped salt pork until fat is released, about 5 minutes, or if not using salt pork, melt butter or margarine.

2. Increase heat to medium-high, and add onions and garlic. Stir and **sauté** until onions are soft, 3 to 5 minutes. Add dasheen or spinach and ½ teaspoon salt. Cover, and cook until greens are limp, 1 to 2 minutes. Add potato, okra, and chicken broth and stir. Reduce heat to **simmer**, cover, and cook 20 to 25 minutes, or until potato and okra are tender. Add crabmeat, salt and pepper to taste and ground red pepper to taste. Stir, cover, and cook until crabmeat is heated through, 5 to 7 minutes.

Serve as a main dish over cooked rice with a basket of floats.

⚜ Conch Fritters

Conch, readily available throughout the Caribbean, is a mainstay for many Bahamians. Conch Fritters, a quick and easy dish, are a perfect snack for any life-cycle celebration. We suggest using lobster meat if unable to find conch.

Yield: serves 4 to 6

2 cups conch meat, **trimmed, finely chopped** (available at seafood or international markets)

3 cloves garlic, trimmed, **minced**

1 red bell pepper, trimmed, finely chopped

2 celery ribs, trimmed, finely chopped

1 onion, trimmed, finely chopped

1 tomato, trimmed, **seeded**, finely chopped

1 cup heavy cream

2 tablespoons vegetable oil, more as needed

2 eggs, beaten

2 cups flour

4 teaspoons baking powder

water, as needed

1 teaspoon cayenne pepper, or to taste

salt and pepper to taste

CAUTION: *HOT OIL IS USED.*

Equipment: Large mixing bowl, mixing spoon, **deep fryer** (used according to manufacturer's directions) or medium **heavy-bottomed** saucepan and deep fryer thermometer or wooden spoon, slotted spoon or **skimmer,** baking sheet with several layers of paper towels

1. Place chopped conch, bell pepper, celery, tomato, heavy cream, 2 tablespoons vegetable oil, eggs, flour, and baking powder in mixing bowl, mix well. A little at a time, add just enough water until mixture is smooth and lump-free and holds together.

2. Add cayenne pepper and salt and pepper to taste, mix well.

3. Prepare to deep fry: *Caution: Adult supervision is required.* Fill deep fryer with oil according to manufacturer's directions, or fill medium heavy-bottomed saucepan with about 3 inches of vegetable oil. Heat oil to reach 375°F on deep fryer thermometer, or place handle of wooden spoon in oil; if small bubbles appear around surface, oil is ready for frying.

4. Carefully drop spoonfuls of conch mixture into hot oil. Fry 3 to 4 conch fritters at a time for 5 to 7 minutes, or until golden on all sides. Remove using slotted spoon or skimmer, and set aside on paper towels to drain. Continue frying in batches.

Serve warm as a starter for any life-cycle celebration.

⚜ Plantain Bisque

Plantains are plentiful throughout the Caribbean islands. Plantain bisque is an inexpensive yet nutritious dish to serve for the starter at a wedding feast.

Yield: serves 4 to 6

4 to 6 **plantains, trimmed**, peeled, **coarsely chopped** (4 cups required)

water, as needed

½ pound bacon, **finely chopped**

1 onion, trimmed, **minced**

2 cloves garlic, trimmed, minced

4 cups vegetable broth or beef stock

1 cup heavy cream

salt and pepper to taste

For **garnish**: ½ cup chives

Equipment: Medium saucepan, fork, **strainer** or **colander**, medium mixing bowl, potato masher, large saucepan with cover, mixing spoon

1. Place plantains in medium saucepan, and add water to cover. Bring to boil over high heat, reduce to simmer, and cook 20 to 25 minutes, or until plantains are tender when poked with fork. Transfer to strainer or colander, drain and discard water.

2. Place plantains in mixing bowl, and, using potato masher, mash until smooth. Set aside.

3. Heat bacon in large saucepan over medium-high heat. When fat is rendered, add onions and garlic, and **sauté** 3 to 5 minutes or until soft.

4. Add mashed plantains and broth, mix well. Bring to boil over high heat, cover, and reduce to simmer 20 to 25 minutes, or until mixture is thickened. Stir frequently.

5. Stir in heavy cream, and add salt and pepper to taste, mix well. Cook over medium-low until heated through about 4 to 6 minutes.

Serve warm in individual soup bowls, garnished with chives sprinkled over top.

Cuba

Cuba is the largest island in the West Indies and sits just 90 miles south of Florida. It was one of the first islands visited by Columbus, and as with other Caribbean islands, the indigenous population of Arawak Indians was wiped out by disease soon after European contact. Cuba became a Spanish colony, and the Arawak Indians were replaced by African slaves brought by the Spaniards to work on the sugar and tobacco plantations. With the help of the United States, Cuba broke from Spain in 1899, though the Spanish influence remained in language and religion, which was predominantly Roman Catholic.

Although Cuba was nominally independent, it was greatly influenced by the United States until a revolution led by Fidel Castro established a new regime in 1959. Initially, relations between the United States and Cuba remained friendly after Castro's take-over; however, by 1961, the United States broke off relations with Cuba, and Castro formed an alliance with the Soviet Union. Castro embraced the Communist philosophy of his new partner, and, even with the fall of Communism in Europe, Cuba remains a Communist society.

Today, Cuba is a multiracial society with a population of mainly Spanish and African origins. The largest organized religion is the Roman Catholic Church, although Cuba's Communist regime is officially atheist. After Pope John Paul's visit in 1997, there has been a resurgence of Catholic rituals and observances among the people. (See Protestant and Catholic Life-Cycle Rituals, page lxxiii.) Most Catholic life-cycle celebrations are once again being observed but not on the same grand scale of the pre-Fidel Castro days.

One of these observances is baptism. Shortly after birth, babies are baptized so that, if they die, they can become *angelitos* (little angels) and go to heaven. Children are usually named after a saint on whose day they are born, along with the name of either parent and/or a favorite relative, living or dead.

Among the rural Catholic families, when the baby is 40 days old, the mother and *compadres* (godparents) take it to church to hear *missa* (mass). This is called *sacamisa* and commemorates the presentation of the Infant Jesus in the Temple by the Virgin Mary. It is customary, following the *sacamisa*, for the parents to invite the godparents for a feast meal, which, depending upon the budget, can be a grand *fiesta* (celebration) with music, singing, and dancing. The poor, who cannot afford the cost of a special *missa*, can bring their baby to any scheduled *missa* and join in the celebration.

In the rural areas of Cuba, marriages take place at an early age, depending upon regional customs. The girls are usually about 15 and the boys are 17 or 18. Civil weddings have been more common under Communism; however, since the Pope's visit, more Cuban couples are being married in the Catholic Church. Most young people like the pageantry of the church wedding; however, it is expensive, and only a select group can afford it.

For the most elegant Cuban wedding, the *lechoncito asado* (recipe follows) is the centerpiece of the wedding feast table, and *bolo de frutas* (fruitcake) is the traditional Cuban wedding cake, which is the same or similar to Caribbean black wedding cake (recipe page 235).

⚘ *Lechoncito Asado* (Cuban Suckling Pig)

Cubans love roast suckling pig. See directions to buy, prepare, roast, and carve (page 243). When budget allows, it is the centerpiece of the *sacamisa*, baptism, confirmation, or wedding celebration banquet. The expert who prepares the pig holds the distinguished title of *la lechonera* (suckling pig master).

Yield: serves 8 to 12

10- to 15-pound **oven-ready** suckling pig (available at butcher shops and most supermarkets special order)

¼ cup vegetable oil

2 tablespoons salt and pepper

For serving: *mojo criollo* (recipe follows)

For **garnish**:

1 whole lemon or lime

4 large onions, **trimmed**, sliced across and separated into rings

Equipment: Paper towels, **pastry brush**, aluminum foil, large shallow roasting pan with wire rack, meat **thermometer**, oven mitts, serving platter

Preheat oven to 350°F.

1. Follow directions in Papua New Guinea section (page 231) for more details on how to prepare and roast suckling pig.

2. Oil and season pig: Using pastry brush, cover pig all over with oil. Sprinkle salt and pepper in the inside cavity and over skin.

3. Roast the pig undisturbed in oven for 2½ to 4 hours (depending upon weight—allow 30 to 35 minutes per pound roasting time), remove foil from ears and tail, and continue roasting for 30 minutes more. Test for **doneness**: Meat is done when meat thermometer registers 175° to 180°F and thigh joints move easily in their sockets.

4. Transfer to serving platter and replace the foil in the mouth with a lemon or lime. Arrange raw onion rings around the pig. Let the pig rest for at least 20 minutes for easier carving.

Serve pig with side dish of mojo criollo *to spoon over the slices. The onions are eaten with the pig.* Roasted potatoes, riz créole *(recipe page 254),* piononos *(recipe page 245), and* calalou *(recipe page 240) would also be on the wedding menu.*

৬ *Mojo Criollo* (Cuban Pork Sauce)

Mojo criollo is the classic Cuban sauce for roasted *lechôn* (pig). It is also sometimes made with sour Seville oranges (*naranjas agrias*) mixed with fatty pork. This recipe uses easily available ingredients and is an excellent sauce for most pork dishes.

Yield: about 3 cups

3 cloves garlic, **finely chopped**

½ cup frozen lime juice concentrate, thawed

1 cup frozen orange juice concentrate, thawed

2 cups water

2 tablespoons vegetable oil

1 tablespoon ground cumin

1 tablespoon ground oregano

salt and pepper to taste

Equipment: 1-quart glass jar with lid, small saucepan, spoon, small serving bowl

1. Put garlic, lime and orange juice concentrates, water, oil, cumin, oregano, and salt and pepper to taste in quart jar. Tightly cover jar with lid, and shake well. Refrigerate at least 4 hours for flavor to develop, shaking occasionally.

2. Pour juice mixture into small saucepan, and, over medium-high heat, cook until heated through, 2 to 3 minutes.

To serve put into small bowl, and spoon over each serving of suckling pig.

☙ *Piononos* (Stuffed Plantains)

A wonderful side dish with the pork is *piononos*, which uses plantains. Plantains can be prepared dozens of ways, but this recipe is more elegant than most. It is a popular party dish throughout the Caribbean and Latin America.

Yield: serves 4 to 6

2 or 3 large ripe **plantains**

2¼ cups vegetable oil, divided

¼ pound hot spicy bulk sausage meat, such as *chorizo*

1 pound lean ground meat (pork or beef or combination)

1 cup onion, **finely chopped**

2 cloves garlic, finely chopped

1 green bell pepper, seeded, finely chopped

3 **tomatoes, peeled**, finely chopped

2 tablespoons **cornstarch**

½ cup water

salt and pepper to taste

1 cup grated cheddar cheese

Equipment: Baking sheet, paper towels, knife, large skillet, slotted metal spatula, work surface, greased standard muffin pan (12 cups *each* 2¾ inch wide), oven mitts, large ovenproof serving platter, toothpicks

1. Prepare plantains: Have ready paper towel–covered baking sheet. Using a knife, **trim** ends off each plantain, and slice lengthwise into 3 or 4 strips, depending upon their size. Remove and discard peelings.

2. Heat ¼ cup oil in large skillet over medium-high heat, and fry plantains, a few at a time, 2 to 3 minutes on each side, until golden. Remove with slotted metal spatula, and drain on paper towels. Remove and discard oil left in skillet.

3. Prepare stuffing: Crumble sausage and ground meat into skillet. Over medium-high heat, fry until cooked through, 3 to 5 minutes. Reduce heat to medium and add onions, garlic, green pepper, and tomatoes. Tossing frequently, cook until onions and pepper are soft, 5 to 7 minutes. Stir cornstarch into ½ cup water until smooth, and stir into meat mixture. Add salt and pepper to taste, and cook until sauce thickens and meat mixture holds together, 3 to 5 minutes.

Preheat oven to 350°F.

4. Assemble: Place greased muffin pan on work surface. Line the sides of each muffin cup with a plantain slice, overlapping the ends to cover the whole side of the cup. Fill the center of each muffin cup with meat mixture. Pack down meat mixture, and smooth the top even with the plantain. Repeat filling muffin cups using all the meat mixture.

5. Bake in oven 30 to 35 minutes, or until meat is browned. Remove from oven, sprinkle each patty generously with grated cheese, and return to oven to melt, 3 to 5 minutes. Allow to rest in pan for 10 minutes before removing from muffin cups. Transfer to serving platter, and, if necessary to prevent plantains from unwrapping, poke a toothpick through overlapping ends.

Serve as a side dish with lechoncito asado *(recipe page 243) and cooked black beans with sour cream and chopped onions.*

♪ *Picadillo* (Cuban Beef Hash)

Picadillo is an inexpensive and easy to prepare dish that is ideal to serve at any Cuban life-cycle celebration.

Yield: serves 4 to 6

2 tablespoons vegetable oil, more as needed

1 onion, **trimmed, finely chopped**

4 cloves garlic, trimmed, **minced**

1 green bell pepper, trimmed, finely chopped

2½ pounds lean ground beef

28 ounces canned tomato sauce

½ cup stuffed green olives, reserve liquid

½ teaspoon ground clove

½ teaspoon ground cumin

¼ teaspoons ground cinnamon

2 tablespoons Adobo seasoning (available at most supermarkets and international markets)

¼ cup capers

½ cup raisins

salt and pepper to taste

Equipment: **Dutch oven** or **heavy-bottomed** skillet with cover, mixing spoon

1. Heat 2 tablespoons oil over medium-high heat in Dutch oven or heavy-bottomed skillet. Add onion, garlic, and bell pepper, and **sauté** until soft, about 3 to 5 minutes. Crumble in ground beef, and cook 8 to 10 minutes, or until cooked through.

2. Stir in tomato sauce, olives, ½ cup reserved olive juice, clove, cumin, cinnamon, Adobo seasoning, capers, and raisins. Mix well. Bring to boil over high heat, cover, reduce to simmer 25 to 30 minutes. Stir occasionally.

Serve warm over rice.

Dominican Republic

The Dominican Republic shares the eastern two-thirds of the island of Hispaniola with Haiti. The subtropical Hispaniola sits to the south and east of Cuba.

Hispaniola was one of the first islands visited by Columbus, and the Dominican Republic has been heavily influenced by Spain. Roman Catholicism is the official religion, and all life-cycle events are celebrated according to the Church. (See Protestant and Catholic Life-Cycle Rituals, page lxxiii.) The Dominican people, who are mostly mulatto, that is, of mixed black and white ancestry, also speak Spanish, which is the official language.

The Catholic Church plays such an important role in Dominican life that even the secular life-cycle event of a high school graduation involves several visits to the church.

The day begins when students, each accompanied by his or her godfather (*compadrazgo*), meet on the school grounds. Together, they march proudly to the church where mass is held honoring the godfathers and blessing the students. Afterwards, the students and godfathers march back to the school for the graduation ceremony. Godfathers are included in the daylong activities, even attending the many parties for classmates. The following Sunday, after church, each family has a celebration dinner for friends and relatives.

The Catholic Church takes on an even greater role in weddings, which must take place in a church to be recognized officially. In Cibao, the most Spanish part of the country, traditions reflect the strict Spanish rules of courting, betrothal, and marriage. Young girls are chaperoned during the courting, and the boys are expected to ask permission to marry from the girl's parents.

On hot days in the Dominican Republic—and that's most of the time—this easy to make juice cooler can satisfy most kids having a name day or birthday party. *Frio-frio* (*frio* means "cold" in Spanish) are also called "snow cones" or "snowballs." They are made by pouring a dollop of fruit syrup over a paper cupful of crushed ice. The fastest way of making fruit syrups is by mixing thawed, but not diluted, frozen fruit juice concentrates with **simple syrup**. Stick a straw into the crushed ice, and sip the cool liquid through the straw.

❧ *Chivo Picante* (Spicy Goat Meat)

Chivo picante originates from the Northwestern region of the Dominican Republic, where there is a large population of goats. The goats feed on wild oregano, and it is believed this gives their meat its unusual flavor. This simple yet tasty dish will serve many and is perfect to serve friends and family at a high school graduation celebration.

Yield: serves 6 to 8

4 pounds goat meat, trimmed, cut into bite-size pieces (available at Latin American or International markets)

juice of 2 lemons or 4 tablespoons lemon juice

1 red onion, **trimmed**, quartered

4 cloves garlic, trimmed, **minced**

1 teaspoon oregano, fresh or dried

2 tablespoons vinegar

2 tablespoon vegetable oil

2 tablespoons sugar, more as needed

1 cup water, more as needed

14.5 ounces canned stewed tomatoes, **coarsely chopped**

2 **jalapeños**, trimmed, **finely chopped**

8 ounces canned tomato sauce

salt and pepper to taste

For serving: 6 to 8 cups cooked rice

Equipment: Large mixing bowl, **Dutch oven** or **heavy-bottomed** saucepan with cover, mixing spoon, fork

1. Place goat meat, lemon juice, onion, garlic, oregano, and vinegar in mixing bowl, mix well. Set aside.

2. Heat 2 tablespoons oil over medium-high heat, add 2 tablespoons sugar, and, stirring constantly, cook until browned about 3 to 4 minutes.

3. Stir in meat mixture, and add 1 cup water, bring to boil over high heat, cover, reduce to simmer 30 to 35 minutes, or until meat is tender when poked with fork. Add more water if necessary to prevent sticking.

4. Stir in tomatoes, jalapeños, and tomato sauce, mix well. Adjust sugar to taste. Add salt and pepper to taste. Cook 6 to 10 minutes, or until heated through.

Serve warm over rice.

℥ *Frituras de Ñame* (Fried Yam Cakes)

Traditionally, *frituras de ñame* are made with **yams**, not sweet potatoes. Since genuine yams are not readily available, sweet potatoes are a good substitute. Fried yam cakes are often served with the *bacalaitos* for a wedding buffet.

Yield: about 20 pieces

1 pound fresh yams or sweet potatoes, peeled

1 onion, quartered

1 tablespoon melted butter

2 egg yolks

1 tablespoon fresh parsley, **finely chopped**, or 2 teaspoons dried parsley flakes

salt and pepper to taste

¼ cup vegetable oil, divided

Equipment: Food processor with grating attachment, rubber spatula, medium mixing bowl, paper towels, baking sheet, large **heavy-bottomed** skillet, tablespoon, slotted metal spatula

1. Using food processor fitted with grating attachment, grate yams or sweet potatoes and onion into container. Add melted butter, egg yolks, parsley, and salt and pepper to taste. Process until smooth and mixture comes away from sides of container. Transfer mixture to medium mixing bowl.

   Note: While processing, turn machine off once or twice, and scrape down sides of container with rubber spatula.

2. Prepare to fry: *Caution: Adult supervision required.* Place several layers of paper towels on baking sheet. Heat half the oil in large heavy-bottomed skillet over medium-high heat. Use about 1 tablespoon yam mixture to make each cake, and place cakes in heavy-bottomed skillet. Using back of spoon, flatten cakes slightly. Fry in small batches, leaving space between each cake. Fry for 2 to 3 minutes each side, or until golden and crisp around the edges. Using slotted metal spatula, remove cakes and drain on paper towels. Keep in warm place while frying remaining cakes.

Serve cakes, while they are still warm, as a side dish with pudding and souse (recipe page 264).

♪ *Pan Dulce de Harina de Maíz* (Sweet Corn Bread)

All celebrations, depending upon the budget, will have either pork, beef, goat, chicken, or pigeons as a main dish, with a large assortments of candies and cakes. The centerpiece of a Dominican wedding is the Caribbean black wedding cake (recipe page 235).

Pan dulce de harina de maíz is often included in the sweet assortment.

Yield: 2 loaves

1½ cups (8-ounces) mixed **candied fruit, finely chopped**

4¼ cups all-purpose flour, divided

3 cups yellow **cornmeal**

1 tablespoons baking powder

½ teaspoon ground cinnamon,

½ teaspoon nutmeg

½ teaspoon cloves

½ cup coconut milk, homemade (recipe page 225), or canned (available at most supermarkets and all Latin American food stores)

½ cup milk

6 tablespoons solid vegetable shortening, at room temperature

6 tablespoons butter or margarine, at room temperature

¼ cup sugar

4 eggs

2 cups finely grated unsweetened **coconut**, fresh, canned, or frozen

1 teaspoon fresh lime rind, finely grated

Equipment: Small bowl, flour **sifter**, medium mixing bowl, 12-ounce cup, large mixing bowl, electric mixer or whisk, rubber spatula, 2 buttered and floured 7×4×3-inch loaf pans, toothpick, oven mitts, knife, wire cake rack, serving platter

Preheat oven to 400°F.

1. Place candied fruit in small bowl, sprinkle with ¼ cup flour, and toss to coat evenly.

2. **Sift** remaining 4 cups flour, cornmeal, baking powder, cinnamon, nutmeg, and cloves into medium mixing bowl. Combine coconut milk and regular milk in cup, and set aside.

3. In large mixing bowl, combine solid vegetable shortening and butter or margarine. Using electric mixer or whisk, beat until light and fluffy, 1 to 2 minutes. Beat in sugar and eggs, one at a time, beating well after each addition. Beating constantly, alternate adding flour mixture, 1 cup at a time, and ¼ cup milk mixture, beating well after each addition. Continue to beat until batter is smooth, 1 to 2 minutes. Using rubber spatula, **fold in** mixed candied fruit mixture, grated coconut, and fresh lime rind. Pour batter equally into the 2 prepared loaf pans.

4. Bake in oven for 35 to 45 minutes, or until toothpick inserted in the center comes out clean and the tops are golden brown. Using oven mitts, remove from oven, and let cool in pans for about 5 minutes. To remove loaves from pan, run a knife around the inside edges and flip onto wire cake rack to cool completely.

To serve, slice the loaves crosswise, and arrange the pieces decoratively on a serving platter.

Grenada

Grenada, part of the Windward Islands, is about 100 miles north of Venezuela. The overwhelming majority of Grenada's population is of African descent with small communities of East Indians brought to the island as indentured workers and a few descendants of early European settlers.

Grenada was originally colonized by France, which is reflected in the fact that more than half of the population is Roman Catholic. British forces invaded the island in 1762, and today English is the official language, and the Church of England has the largest Protestant following on the island. Members of both religions celebrate the life-cycle events prescribed by their churches. (See Protestant and Catholic Life-Cycle Rituals, page lxxiii.)

Religion is at the heart of all celebrations. Christenings, adult baptisms, weddings, and funerals are all celebrated with a Caribbean flare, using the foods native to the island, especially spices.

In fact, Grenada, known as the "isle of spice," grows about 40 percent of the world's supply of nutmeg and mace. Nutmeg is the seed of the nutmeg tree, and mace is the bright red membrane that covers the nutmeg seed. A wonderful fruit dish using nutmeg is *matrimony* (recipe page 260).

♟ Cold Cream of Breadfruit Soup

Yield: serves 6

In the hot, humid Caribbean, a cold soup is a welcome addition to the wedding buffet. Put the soup in a tureen or punch bowl, and provide a ladle and small cups. The guests can serve themselves and drink the soup from the cup.

4 tablespoons butter or margarine

1 cup onions, **finely chopped**

2 cloves garlic, finely chopped, or 1 teaspoon garlic granules

2 cups fresh **breadfruit**, peeled, **cored, coarsely chopped, blanched** for 2 minutes, and drained, or 4 slices canned breadfruit, drained and coarsely chopped (available at

most supermarkets and all Latin American food stores)

4 cups chicken broth

1 cup half-and-half

salt and pepper to taste

For **garnish**: 1 tablespoon fresh parsley, finely chopped

Equipment: Medium **heavy-bottomed** saucepan, mixing spoon, medium mixing bowl, food processor, ladle, tureen or punch bowl, individual soup bowls

1. Melt butter or margarine in medium heavy-bottomed saucepan over medium-high heat. Add onions and garlic, and, stirring constantly, **sauté** for 3 to 5 minutes, or until soft and transparent. Stir in chopped breadfruit, pour in chicken broth, and bring to a boil. Stir,

reduce heat to **simmer**, cover, and cook for 20 to 25 minutes, or until breadfruit can easily be mashed against the side of the pan using the back of the spoon. Remove from heat, remove cover, and allow to cool to warm.

2. Ladle half of the breadfruit mixture into the food processor, and pour in ½ cup of half-and-half. Process for about 1 minute, or until smooth. Pour into medium mixing bowl. Ladle remaining breadfruit mixture into processor, and add the remaining half-and-half. Process 1 minute or until smooth, pour into bowl with first batch, and add salt and pepper to taste. Cover and refrigerate until ready to serve.

Note: While processing, turn machine off once or twice, and scrape down sides of container with rubber spatula.

To serve, pour into either a tureen or individual soup bowls. Sprinkle with parsley flakes for garnish.

♪ Roasted Pork with Black Bean–Corn Salad

This dish makes a festive and complete meal for any life-cycle celebration in Grenada.

Yield: serves 6 to 8

Black bean–corn salad:

16 ounces canned black beans, rinsed, drained

10-ounce package frozen corn kernels, thawed, drained

7½ ounces canned hearts of palm, drained cut into ¼-inch rounds

2 tomatoes, **trimmed, seeded, finely chopped**

1 red onion, trimmed, finely chopped

½ cup fresh **cilantro**, finely chopped

¼ cup olive oil

juice of 2 limes or 4 tablespoons lime juice

1 teaspoon **coriander**

Roasted pork sauce:

1½ cups orange juice

¼ cup **shallots, minced**

3 tablespoons light brown sugar

2 tablespoons ginger root, trimmed, peeled, **grated**

2 bay leaves

½ teaspoon **allspice**

salt and pepper to taste

Roasted pork:

3 shallots, trimmed, finely chopped

¾ teaspoon ground **allspice**

¾ teaspoon ground ginger

4 tablespoons olive oil

3-pound pork tenderloins

water, as needed

For serving:

1 pound fresh spinach, trimmed, washed, drained

2 avocados, trimmed, **pitted**, sliced

For **garnish**: ¼ cup fresh parsley, trimmed, finely chopped

Equipment: Medium salad bowl, mixing spoon, plastic wrap, medium saucepan, small bowl, roasting pan, meat thermometer, oven mitts, cutting board, sharp knife, large serving platter

1. Prepare black bean–corn salad: Place black beans, thawed corn, hearts of palm, tomatoes, onion, cilantro, ¼ cup olive oil, lime juice, and coriander in salad bowl, mix well. Cover with plastic wrap and refrigerate until ready to use.

2. Prepare pork roast sauce: Place orange juice, shallots, brown sugar, grated ginger, bay leaves, and allspice in medium saucepan. Over medium-high heat, bring to simmer 8 to 10 minutes, or until mixture becomes slightly thick and syrupy. Remove heat, cover, and set aside.

Preheat oven to 500°F.

3. Prepare roasted pork: In small bowl, combine shallots, allspice, ginger, and 4 tablespoons oil, mix well. Place meat in roasting pan, and rub shallot mixture into meat. Pour 1 cup water into roasting pan.

4. Roast in oven about 25 to 30 minutes, or until meat is browned on all sides. Add more water, as needed to prevent drying out.

5. Reduce oven heat to 350°F. Return meat to oven, and cook additional 30 to 35 minutes or until internal temperature reads 150°F when thermometer is placed in thickest part of meat. Add more water as needed to prevent drying out.

6. Carefully remove meat from oven using oven mitts. Place on cutting board, and let rest 5 to 10 minutes. Using sharp knife, cut into ¾-inch- to 1-inch-thick slices.

7. Prepare serving platter: Spread a layer of spinach over serving platter. Mound black bean–corn salad in center of platter. Surround salad with slightly overlapping slices pork and avocado.

8. Remove and discard bay leaves from roasted pork sauce. **Drizzle** sauce over pork and avocado slices. Sprinkle parsley over top.

Serve at room temperature for any life-cycle occasion.

✑ Guava Pie

The fruit **guava** comes in many varieties, ranging in smell and flavor from sweet to offensive. Canned guava is recommended for this recipe.

Yield: serves 8 to 10

16 ounces canned **guavas**, drained (available at Latin American food stores and most supermarkets)

2 to 3 tablespoons sugar

½ teaspoon ground nutmeg

juice of ½ lime

2 egg whites

2 (9-inch) unbaked pie crusts, homemade, or frozen (thawed)

For serving: whipped heavy cream

Equipment: Food processor, rubber spatula, medium mixing bowl, small mixing bowl, electric mixer or **whisk**, 9-inch pie pan, lightly floured work surface, ruler, paring knife, fork, oven mitts

Preheat oven to 400°F.

1. **Purée** canned, drained guava and 2 tablespoons sugar in food processor, about 1 minute. Taste for desired sweetness; if necessary, add remaining 1 tablespoon sugar and process 6 seconds to make sweeter. Transfer to medium mixing bowl, and, using rubber spatula, stir in nutmeg and lime.

   Note: *While processing, turn machine off once or twice, and scrape down sides of container with rubber spatula.*

2. Put egg whites into small mixing bowl, and, using an electric mixer or whisk, beat until stiff peaks form. Using rubber spatula, **fold in** egg whites with guava mixture. Pour into unbaked pie crust, and smooth top with rubber spatula.

3. Place second crust on lightly floured work surface. Using a ruler and paring knife, cut ½-inch-wide strips out of the crust, and lay them across the pie in a lattice (crisscross) pattern. Press the ends of fork into the edge of pie crust to make a ridged, sealed border around the outer edge of the pie pan.

4. Bake in oven for 20 to 25 minutes, or until pie is lightly browned and filling is bubbly. Using oven mitts, remove pie from oven, and cool to warm.

Serve guava pie at room temperature with a dollop of whipped cream on each serving. Serve guava pie with coffee or tea after a baptism, christening, or funeral.

Haiti

Haiti occupies the western third of the island Hispanolia, which is also home to the Dominican Republic. Hispanolia is a subtropical island that lies to the south and east of Cuba.

Haiti experienced a devastating earthquake in January 2010, leaving millions homeless and living in ruins. With conditions in Haiti as they are, there is no reason to indulge in elaborate life-cycle celebrations. Today, weddings, births and funerals are simple family affairs.

The majority of Haiti's population consists of peasant farmers, descendants of African slaves, brought to the island to work on the French-owned plantations. After an uprising and bitter struggle, the former slaves defeated Napoleon's forces and drove all the whites off the island. The former slaves gave the new nation the old Indian name "Haiti" (high hills), and on January 1, 1804, the republic of Haiti declared its independence. French, the official language of Haiti, is spoken by only 10 percent of the people; most Haitians speak Créole, a pidgin language.

While under French control, the African *vodun* (voodoo) was widely practiced by the slaves even though it was outlawed by the French. After the defeat of the French, voodoo resurfaced, and it is now accepted as a vital part of Haitian culture.

Most Haitians profess Catholicism and celebrate the traditional life-cycle events prescribed by the Church (see Protestant and Catholic Life-Cycle Rituals, page lxxiii); however, they also retain their voodoo practices. For almost 300 years, the Haitians have blended the two together. For example, the use of candles, bells, crosses, prayers, and making the sign of the cross, elements of the Catholic Church, are used along with African dances, drumming, and the worship of ancestral spirits.

⚘ *Riz Créole* (Creole Rice)

The birth of the firstborn son is a joyous addition to the family because he will carry on the family name and inherit the family farm. Most Haitians turn to the Catholic Church for the infant's christening, which is generally a colorful and noisy affair. The christening garments are traditionally handed down from past generations. After the ceremony, a celebration feast is held, usually in the church social hall The christening feast will include *griots de porc* (recipe page 256), *extra-rich hominy grits* (recipe page 255), *riz Créole* (recipe follows), *pain Haïtien* (recipe page 255), and *matrimony* (recipe page 260. Cookies, coffee, and cold beverages complete the menu.

Yield: serves 4

2 tablespoons butter or margarine	½ teaspoon ground turmeric
¼ cup green onions, **finely chopped**	½ teaspoon paprika
½ red bell pepper, **trimmed**, seeded, and finely chopped	salt and pepper to taste
	2 cups water
1 tomato, finely chopped	1 cup long grain rice

Equipment: Medium saucepan with cover, mixing spoon, serving bowl

Melt butter or margarine in medium saucepan over medium-high heat. Add finely chopped green onions, red bell pepper, tomato, turmeric, paprika, and salt and pepper to taste. Stirring constantly, **sauté** for 2 to 3 minutes for flavors to develop. Add water and rice, and bring to a boil. Stir, reduce heat to **simmer**, cover, and cook for 15 to 20 minutes, until rice is tender. Remove from heat. Let stand covered for 5 minutes.

To serve, transfer to serving bowl, and serve warm as a side dish with *griots de porc* (recipe page 256).

ৼ *Extra-Rich Hominy Grits*

Yield: serves 8

4 cups water

½ teaspoon salt

1½ cups coarsely ground quick-to-cook **hominy grits** (also called "grits") (available at all supermarkets)

½ cup whole milk or half-and-half

4 tablespoons butter or margarine

¾ cup shredded cheddar cheese

Equipment: Medium saucepan with cover, mixing spoon, serving bowl

1. Pour water in medium saucepan, add salt, and bring to boil over high heat. Add grits, and cook for 2 minutes, stirring constantly to prevent lumping. Reduce heat to medium-low, cover, and cook for 10 to 12 minutes, stirring occasionally.

2. Stir in milk or half-and-half and butter or margarine, and continue stirring until mixture is smooth and creamy. Add cheese and stir until completely melted.

To serve, pour into a serving bowl, and serve as a side dish with one of the many Caribbean meat dishes in this section.

ৼ *Pain Haïtien* (Haitian Bread)

One of France's more positive legacies in Haiti is bread, which Haitians love and eat in great quantities. Most Haitians, especially farmers, don't have ovens in their kitchens but have outside clay-dome ovens in their yard where they bake their beloved *pain* with and without yeast. When made with yeast, as in this recipe, the bread has a lighter and more tender texture.

Yield: 24 pieces

2 packages dry yeast

1½ cups **lukewarm** water

¼ cup honey

2 tablespoons vegetable oil

1 teaspoon salt

1 teaspoon ground nutmeg

4½ cups bread flour or all-purpose flour, divided

For **glaze**:

½ teaspoon freeze-dried instant coffee granules

2 tablespoons milk

Equipment: Large mixing bowl, mixing spoon, lightly floured work surface, lightly greased medium mixing bowl, clean kitchen towel, greased baking sheet, long knife, 4-ounce cup, **pastry brush**, oven mitts, breadbasket, cloth napkin

1. Add yeast to lukewarm water in large mixing bowl, and stir to dissolve. Stir in honey, oil, salt, nutmeg, and 2 cups flour. Beat until very smooth, about 1 minute. Gradually add just

enough of remaining 2½ cups flour to make a stiff dough that is no longer sticky. Transfer to lightly floured work surface. **Knead** until smooth, 5 to 8 minutes.

2. Put dough in lightly greased medium mixing bowl, and turn to grease all sides. Cover with towel, and set in warm place to rise to double in bulk, 45 minutes to 1 hour. Dough is ready if indentation remains in it when gently poked with your finger.

3. **Punch down** dough with fist. Transfer to greased baking sheet, spread dough out evenly to cover bottom of pan, and smooth top of dough. Using the back side of a long knife, mark off 24 pieces in the dough by making 4 equally spaced marks in the dough, the length of the pan, and 6 across, marking off 24 pieces total. Cut down into dough only halfway, not through to the bottom. Cover with towel, and let rise in warm place until double in bulk, about 30 minutes.

Preheat oven to 350°F.

4. In cup, dissolve instant coffee granules in milk. Using pastry brush, brush top of dough with coffee mixture to give it a glaze. Bake in oven until golden brown, 30 to 35 minutes.

Serve fresh from the oven, break bread apart, and place in bread basket. Cover with napkin to keep warm.

⚜ *Griots de Porc* (Marinated Spicy Pork)

Pork is reserved for special occasions, such as baptisms and wedding feasts. It is quite expensive, especially since the Haitian pig population was wiped out by swine fever a number of years ago. This recipe can be made with beef or goat instead of pork.

CAUTION: Use care when handling peppers. Wrap your hands in plastic wrap or slip them in plastic sandwich bags when handling peppers. Do not touch your eyes while handling peppers. If you accidentally touch your eyes, rinse them under cold running water at once.

Yield: serves 6

1 onion, **finely chopped**

1 teaspoon dried thyme

¾ cup orange juice

¼ cup lemon juice

1 hot chili pepper (**jalapeño**), seeded and finely chopped, or ½ teaspoon ground red pepper

2 cloves garlic, finely chopped

3 pounds lean pork shoulder, cut into 2-inch cubes

water, as needed

1 tablespoon **cornstarch**

For serving: 6 cups cooked white rice

Equipment: Large resealable plastic bag, large saucepan with cover, slotted mixing spoon, medium bowl, **bulb baster** or large spoon, **whisk**

1. Prepare marinade: Put onion, thyme, orange juice, lemon juice, finely chopped pepper or ground red pepper, and garlic into large plastic resealable bag. Seal bag tightly and shake to mix. Open bag, add meat, seal tightly, and shake to coat. Refrigerate overnight.

2. Put meat and marinade into large saucepan, and add water to cover. Bring to boil over high heat, reduce heat to **simmer**, cover, and cook until tender, about 1 hour.

3. Using slotted mixing spoon, transfer meat to medium bowl. Using bulb baster or large spoon, skim off and discard fat from marinade. Reheat marinade in saucepan over high heat, and bring to boil, stirring occasionally. Reduce heat to simmer, and, stirring frequently, cook, uncovered, until **reduced** by half, 15 to 20 minutes.

4. Stir cornstarch into ½ cup water until smooth. Whisk cornstarch mixture into reduced marinade, and continue whisking until thickened, 2 to 3 minutes. Reduce heat to low.

5. Return meat to thickened sauce, and toss to coat. Increase heat to simmer, cover, and cook to heat through, 5 to 7 minutes.

Serve over rice with plenty of pain Haïtien *(recipe page 255). Stuffed plantains (recipe page 245) are traditionally served with this dish.*

Jamaica

An island in the West Indies, Jamaica is 90 miles south of Cuba and 100 miles east of Haiti. Originally colonized by Spain, Jamaica fell under British control in 1655 and did not become independent until 1962. Today, Jamaica is a multiracial society of Africans, East Indians, Scots, Chinese, and English.

The majority of the population is Christian and celebrates life-cycle events in accordance with the Christian traditions. (See Protestant and Catholic Life-Cycle Rituals, page lxxiii.) In addition to these Western religious traditions, Jamaica is also the birthplace of the *Rastafarian* religion, which has attracted many followers among Jamaicans of African descent. The aim of the "Rastas," as they are called, is to restore dignity and pride to the black race and to recreate the African way of life without the technology of the West, which in Rasta terminology is called Babylon.

Rasta men are easily noticed because of their "dreadlocks," braided strands of hair allowed to grow, often below the waist. The role of Rasta women is controversial, and although men enhance the status of women by giving them the title "queen," the belief is that women are subordinate to men. Most Rasta men are known to be good fathers and take pride in caring for their children.

Rasta weddings are happy occasions, and all attendees are free to do their own thing. There is no special person officiating, nor is there a special ceremony. Rasta marriages are common-law; however to be legal in Jamaica, couples must register at the office of records.

⚘ *Stuffed Cho-cho* (**Stuffed Chayote**)

In Jamaica, *cho-cho*, a tropical squash, is often served with *souse*. Elsewhere *cho-cho* is known as **chayote,** mirliton, or its French name *christophene*. A dish known as "pudding and souse" (recipe page 264) is prepared for special occasions throughout the Caribbean. Jamaicans eat souse without the pudding for life-cycle celebrations. Souse is the same as headcheese, which is available in the deli section of supermarkets or butcher shops. Hot **Scotch bonnet** peppers, native to Jamaica, **garnish** the platter and are eaten with the *souse*.

Yield: serves 4

2 chayotes (about 1 pound each) (available at all Latin American food stores and most supermarkets)

8 tablespoons butter or margarine, divided

1 large onion, **finely chopped**

½ cup grated Parmesan cheese, divided

salt and pepper to taste

Equipment: Large saucepan, paring knife, tablespoon, medium bowl, paper towels, large **heavy-bottomed** skillet, mixing spoon, greased baking sheet, oven mitts, serving platter

1. Put whole chayotes into large saucepan, and cover generously with water. Bring to boil over high heat, and reduce heat to **simmer** for 30 minutes, until tender. To test doneness, poke chayotes with a paring knife. If knife goes in easily, they are done. Drain and rinse chayotes under cold water to cool. When cool enough to handle, slice in half, lengthwise, and remove and discard seeds.

2. Using a tablespoon and paring knife, carefully scoop out the pulp, leaving about ¼-inch thick boat-like shells. Put pulp into medium bowl. Set the chayote shells upside down on several layers of paper towels to drain. **Coarsely chop** the scooped-out pulp.

3. In large heavy-bottomed skillet, melt 4 tablespoons butter or margarine over medium-high heat. Add onion and **sauté**, stirring frequently, until soft but not brown, 2 to 3 minutes. Add the chopped chayote, ¼ cup grated cheese, and salt and pepper to taste. Stirring frequently, reduce heat to medium-low, and cook until most of the liquid has cooked off and the mixture is the consistency of mashed potatoes, 5 to 10 minutes.

Preheat oven to 350°F.

4. Fill the 4 chayote shells equally with onion mixture. Place the filled shells side by side on greased baking sheet. Dot the top of each with remaining 4 tablespoons butter or margarine, and sprinkle with remaining ¼ cup grated cheese.

5. Bake in oven for 25 to 30 minutes, or until tops are lightly browned.

To serve, transfer to a serving platter. Eat cho-cho while still warm.

⚘ **Lentils, Vegetables, and Greens in Coconut Milk**

Rastafarians are dedicated to keeping their bodies pure and clean; therefore they are known vegans. This recipe would be perfect for any Rastafarian life-cycle celebration. It is ideal for them to serve their family and friends.

Yield: serves 4 to 6

2 tablespoons vegetable oil, more as needed

1 onion, **trimmed, finely chopped**

4 cloves garlic, trimmed, **minced**

2 summer squash, trimmed, **coarsely chopped**

1 eggplant, trimmed, peeled, cut into 1-inch cubes

3 carrots, trimmed, thinly sliced

½ pound broccoli **florets**, trimmed, finely chopped

14.5 ounces canned sweet potatoes, drained

1 **jalapeño,** trimmed, minced

1 cup **lentils**, rinsed, drained (cook according to directions on package)

14.5 ounces coconut milk, homemade (recipe page 225), or canned, more as needed

1 pound fresh baby spinach, rinsed, drained

salt and pepper to taste

Equipment: **Dutch oven** or **heavy-bottomed** saucepan, mixing spoon

1. Heat 2 tablespoons oil in Dutch oven or heavy-bottomed skillet over medium-high heat. Add onions and garlic, and **sauté** until soft, about 3 to 5 minutes. Add more oil if needed to prevent sticking.

2. Stir in squash, eggplant, carrots, broccoli, sweet potatoes, jalapeño, and coconut milk. Cook 12 to 15 minutes, or until vegetables are tender and cooked through. Add more coconut milk if mixture seems dry.

3. Stir in spinach and cook additional 3 to 5 minutes, or until wilted. Add salt and pepper to taste.

Serve warm over rice.

⚘ Vegetarian Pasta

Rastafarians find interesting and varied ways to eat vegetables. This is a simple vegetarian dish with veggies, beans for protein, and spices to enhance flavor. It is ideal to serve at any Rastafarian life-cycle celebration.

Yield: serves 4 to 6

2 tablespoons olive oil, more as needed

1 onion, **trimmed, finely chopped**

2 cloves garlic, trimmed, **minced**

1 yellow bell pepper, trimmed, **julienned**

1 red bell pepper, trimmed, julienned

14.5 ounces canned black beans, rinsed, drained

2 tomatoes, trimmed, finely chopped

1 pound frozen broccoli (cooked according to direction on package)

¼ cup minced fresh basil or 1 teaspoon dried basil

2 teaspoons fresh oregano or ½ teaspoon dried oregano

salt and pepper to taste

1 pound fettuccine (prepared according to directions on package), keep warm

Equipment: Large skillet, mixing spoon, tongs

1. Heat 2 tablespoons oil in large skillet over medium-high heat. Add onion, garlic, yellow bell pepper, and red bell pepper, and **sauté** until soft, about 5 to 7 minutes.

2. Stir in in black beans, tomatoes, and broccoli, and cook additional 2 to 3 minutes, or until heated through. Stir in basil, oregano, and salt and pepper to taste.

3. Add fettuccine to vegetable mixture, and, using tongs, mix well. Add more oil if mixture seems dry.

Serve warm.

⚘ Matrimony (Fresh Fruit Medley)

Fresh fruit is very abundant on the Caribbean islands, and *matrimony* is a nice dessert at the end of a heavy birthday or wedding feast. How the dish got its name is a mystery, but it's perfect to serve at a wedding reception.

Yield: serves 6

8 **carambolas**, ends **trimmed** and sliced ¼-inch thick crosswise

3 large oranges, peeled and **segmented**

1 (14-ounce) can sweetened condensed milk, or 1½ cups whipped cream

1 teaspoon ground nutmeg

Equipment: Medium glass or ceramic serving bowl, mixing spoon, plastic food wrap, serving spoon, small dessert bowls

1. Put carambolas and oranges in a medium glass or ceramic serving bowl, and toss to mix. Cover bowl with plastic wrap and refrigerate.

2. At serving time: Add sweetened condensed milk or whipped cream, sprinkle with nutmeg, and toss to mix.

To serve, place bowl of matrimony on the dessert table with a serving spoon. Provide small dessert bowls and spoons for guests so that they can help themselves. Eat with a slice of pan dulce de harina de maíz *(recipe page 249).*

Puerto Rico

Puerto Rico is an island in the Caribbean Sea, located east of the Dominican Republic. It is a semiautonomous commonwealth that has been under the protection of the United States since the Spanish-American War of 1898. Most Puerto Ricans are of Spanish descent; however, after decades of intermarriage, racial lines are practically nonexistent. Puerto Rico is officially a bilingual country (English and Spanish), but island-born Puerto Ricans prefer to speak Spanish to one another as a matter of cultural pride.

The majority of the Puerto Ricans are Roman Catholics. Most life-cycle events, from christening the newborn infant to the burial of an elder, are celebrated according to the Catholic Church. (See Protestant and Catholic Life-Cycle Rituals, page lxxiii.) The rituals are similar to other Latin American countries except among descendants of slaves who were brought from West Africa to Puerto Rico in the 1500s. People of African descent often combine African rituals and voodoo with Catholic traditions; the worship of African gods with Catholic saints is not uncommon. Spiritualism (*espiritismo*) and witchcraft (*brujeria*) are very much alive in Puerto Rico. It is common practice among all islanders, not only those of African descent, to consult *curanderos* (healers) and *espiritistas* (spiritualists) about love and marriage, health, childbirth, revenge, wealth, and death.

✧ *Ponque* (Puerto Rican Pound Cake)

Ponque is a moist cake often served at joyous occasions such as birthdays or weddings. This sweet treat is enjoyed by adults and children alike.

Yield: serves 6 to 8

1 cup butter	1 cup milk
½ cup vegetable oil	1 teaspoon coconut extract
5 eggs	1 teaspoon rum-flavored extract
3 cups sugar	1 teaspoon butter-flavored extract
3 cups all-purpose flour	1 teaspoon lemon extract
½ teaspoon baking powder	1 teaspoon vanilla extract
½ teaspoon salt	

Glaze:	
½ cup water	1 teaspoon rum-flavored extract
1 cup sugar	1 teaspoon butter-flavored extract
1 teaspoon coconut extract	1 teaspoon vanilla extract
	1 teaspoon almond extract

Equipment: Electric mixer or mixing bowl and mixing spoon, spatula, greased or nonstick Bundt or tube pan, toothpick, oven mitts, large round serving platter, small saucepan, spoon

Preheat oven to 325°F.

1. Combine butter, oil, and sugar in electric mixer or mixing bowl with mixing spoon, mix until fluffy and well blended. Add eggs, one at a time, beating well between each addition.

2. Gradually stir in flour and milk, alternating between two. (Start and end with flour.)

3. Stir-in coconut extract, rum extract, butter extract, lemon extract, and vanilla extract, and mix well.

4. Using spatula, transfer batter to Bundt or tube pan. Bake 1½ to 2 hours or until toothpick inserted in center comes out clean. Carefully remove from oven using oven mitts, and set aside to cool 5 to 10 minutes. Turn cake out onto serving platter.

5. Prepare glaze: In small saucepan, bring water, sugar, coconut extract, rum extract, vanilla extract, and almond extract to boil over high heat, reduce to simmer 5 to 7 minutes, or until sugar is dissolved. Stir constantly.

6. Spoon glaze mixture over top of cake, and set aside to cool.

Serve cut into individual slices with milk, tea, or coffee.

₡ *Sopa de Pollo* (Puerto Rican Chicken Soup)

Sopa de Pollo, a comforting and nutritious soup, would be served to warm the hearts and souls of family and friends who gather at the home for a funeral. Throughout the evening, everyone would help themselves to a bowl of *sopa de pollo* with *tostones* (twice-fried green plantains) and hot chocolate or coffee, while mourners tell stories of the deceased.

Yield: serves 8 to 10

1 (4- to 5-pound) chicken, cut into serving-size pieces

2 potatoes, **trimmed**, peeled, **cubed**

1 onion, trimmed, **finely chopped**

2 ribs celery, trimmed, finely chopped

2 carrots, trimmed, finely chopped

4 cloves garlic, trimmed, **minced**

8 sprigs **cilantro**, trimmed, rinsed, finely chopped

1 teaspoon oregano

2½ quarts water, more as needed

1 cup brown rice

salt and pepper to taste

Equipment: **Dutch oven** or large stock pot with cover, mixing spoon

1. Place chicken, potatoes, carrots, celery, onion, garlic, cilantro, and oregano in Dutch oven or stock pot, and add 2½ quarts water. Bring to boil over high heat, cover, and reduce to simmer, 20 to 25 minutes. Add more water if necessary.

2. Stir in rice, and continue cooking 45 to 50 minutes, or until chicken is tender and cooked through, adding more water if necessary. Test chicken **doneness**. Add salt and pepper to taste.

Serve warm in individual soup bowls with warm tostones.

₡ *Pepinos en Salsa de Naranja* (Stewed Cucumbers in Orange Sauce)

One of the many side dishes, besides beans and rice, would probably be this unusual Puerto Rican recipe of cucumbers and orange juice.

Yield: serves 4

3 cucumbers, each about 8 inches long	3 tablespoons butter or margarine
½ teaspoon salt, more as needed	½ teaspoon white pepper
1 tablespoon **cornstarch**	1 teaspoon grated orange rind
1¼ cups fresh orange juice, strained	

Equipment: Vegetable peeler, knife, work surface, teaspoon, medium saucepan, **colander**, cup, medium skillet, medium deep serving dish

1. Peel cucumbers, and cut in half lengthwise. Using a teaspoon, scrape out and discard seeds. Cut cucumbers halves crosswise into ½-inch slices.

2. Fill medium saucepan halfway with water, add ½ teaspoon salt, and bring to boil over medium-high heat. Drop cucumber pieces into boiling water, reduce heat to **simmer**, and cook for 5 minutes. Drain in colander placed in sink.

3. Put cornstarch in cup, and stir in ¼ cup orange juice to make **slurry**. Melt butter or margarine in medium skillet over medium-low heat. Add remaining 1 cup orange juice, and, when small bubbles appear around edge of pan, stir in slurry. Stirring constantly, increase heat to medium, and cook until mixture thickens, 2 to 3 minutes. Add white pepper and grated orange rind. Add cucumber, and toss to coat and heat through, 3 to 5 minutes.

To serve, transfer to serving bowl as a side vegetable with asopao de pollo *(a Puerto Rican chicken and rice stew),* Pepinos en salsa de naranja *is also a great side dish with pork.*

Trinidad and Tobago

Trinidad and its tiny neighbor Tobago, just 20 miles to the northeast, sit just off the coast of Venezuela. Both islands have warm and humid climates typical of the tropics. The islands were united as a single British colony in 1888 and gained full independence in 1962.

Most citizens are descendants of African slaves and East Indian indentured servants. The East Indians were originally brought in to resolve the labor shortage created by the emancipation of the African slaves in 1833.

The blacks and East Indians retain distinct social patterns, with different diets, religions, cultural traditions, and lifestyles. Most blacks are Roman Catholics, a remnant of the Spanish conquest of the region, and follow the life-cycle traditions of their Church. (See Protestant and Catholic Life-Cycle Rituals, page lxxiii.) The East Indians are Hindu or Muslim. (See Hinduism and Hindu Life-Cycle Rituals, page lxxix, and Islam and Islamic Life-Cycle Rituals, page lxxvi.)

Most Hindu East Indians living in the Caribbean follow, as much as possible, the religious traditions of their homeland, often adding their own touches of drama and color. For example, altars are covered with hibiscus and other native flowers, prayer beads and lamps are decorated with seashells, and Hindu priests often call worshipers to prayer by blowing on a conch shell.

◊ *Pudding and Souse* (Blood Sausage with Lime-Marinated Pork)

The Roman Catholics have also added local flavor to their life-cycle celebrations. Guests at celebrations, whether a christening party, birthday, wedding, or funeral feast, expect meat and certain special occasion dishes, such as pudding and souse. Pudding refers to the blood or "black" sausage, and souse is lime-marinated meat, usually made with a whole pig's head and feet or similar parts of goats, sheep, or beef. Souse is also known as "headcheese," although it is not a cheese. Both blood sausage and headcheese are available in the deli section of most supermarkets and butcher shops. For serving, allow one or two slices for each per person. See step 4 in instructions on cooking the blood sausage before serving it. Headcheese requires no cooking. Arrange the slices, slightly overlapping, on a serving platter. It is best to buy the blood sausage, but you can make the *souse*.

One or two salads, several breads, such as banana bread, and iced drinks are served along with pudding and souse.

Yield: serves 4 to 6

4 pounds fresh pork jowls, tails, feet, or ears, in any combination

1 onion, peeled and quartered

3 teaspoons salt, divided

1½ cups fresh lime juice

1 tablespoon oil

For serving: 1 to 1½ pounds commercially made blood sausage (pudding), cut crosswise into ¼-inch thick circles

For **garnish:**

1 cucumber, **trimmed,** sliced crosswise

1 bunch **watercress** or Italian flat-leaf parsley

½ teaspoon liquid hot sauce, more or less to taste

Equipment: Large **heavy-bottomed** saucepan with cover or **Dutch oven**, mixing spoon, knife, metal tongs, large bowl, metal strainer, medium bowl, plastic food wrap, heavy-bottomed skillet, large serving bowl, large serving platter

1. Wash pork thoroughly under cold running water, and place in large heavy-bottomed saucepan or Dutch oven. Add enough water to cover the pork by at least 2 inches. Add onion and 2 teaspoons salt, and bring to boil over high heat. Skim off and discard the particles and foam that form on the surface. Reduce heat to **simmer,** cover, and cook 30 minutes. Remove cover, and cook 1½ hours longer. The pork pieces are done when they can be easily pierced with a knife. Using metal tongs, transfer pork pieces to a large bowl until cool enough to handle. Continue simmering the liquid until it is **reduced** to about 2 cups, 45 minutes to 1 hour.

2. Remove and discard bones, fat, gristle, and skin from meat. Cut or pull the meat apart into bite-size pieces. Sprinkle with remaining 1 teaspoon salt and lime juice. Toss to coat.

3. Place a metal strainer over a medium bowl, strain the cooking liquid, and discard residue left in strainer. Pour the strained liquid over the meat, stir, and set aside to cool. Transfer the meat mixture to a serving bowl, cover with plastic wrap, and refrigerate overnight to set.

4. At serving time: Heat 1 tablespoon vegetable oil in heavy-bottomed skillet or on griddle over medium-high heat. **Sauté** blood sausage slices, a few at a time, until lightly browned, 3 to 5 minutes on each side.

5. To serve, spoon chunks of souse onto a serving platter and garnish with cucumber slices and watercress or parsley. **Drizzle** the souse with liquid hot sauce or serve it on the side. Arrange the blood sausage slices attractively around the souse.

Serve at room temperature. The pudding and souse are eaten as finger food at a life-cycle celebration.

⚘ Stuffed Breadfruit

Breadfruit is popular throughout the Caribbean, and Trinidad and Tobago are no exception. Stuffed breadfruit is an excellent addition to any life-cycle celebration in Trinidad or Tobago.

Yield: serves 6 to 8

1 **breadfruit,** peeled, **parboiled,** cooled (available at international markets)

2 tablespoons vegetable oil, more as needed

1 onion, **trimmed, finely chopped**

2 cups finely chopped green onion

14.5 ounces canned diced, tomatoes, drained

¾ pound lean ground beef

¼ pound ground ham

1 tablespoons red pepper flakes, or to taste

salt and pepper to taste

water, as needed

Equipment: Cutting board, sharp knife, large skillet, mixing spoon, roasting pan, oven mitts

Preheat oven to 375°F.

1. Place breadfruit on cutting board, and, using sharp knife, carefully remove and discard core and 8 to 10 tablespoons of pulp. Trim just enough pulp off bottom side of breadfruit so that it stands upright. Set aside.

2. Heat 2 tablespoons oil in skillet over medium-high heat. Add onions, garlic, and scallions, and **sauté** 3 to 5 minutes or until soft.

3. Crumble in ground beef and ground ham. Cook 12 to 15 minutes, or until meat is cooked through, stirring frequently.

4. Stir in tomatoes, mix well. Add crushed red pepper, salt and pepper to taste.

5. Stand breadfruit upright in roasting pan, and fill with meat mixture. Add just enough water to cover bottom of roasting pan. Bake in oven 50 minutes to 1 hour, or until breadfruit is

tender and mixture is heated through. Add more water if necessary to prevent drying out. Carefully remove from oven using oven mitts. Let stand 5 to 10 minutes before serving.

Serve warm with breadfruit cut into individual slices and with meat mixture spooned over top.

♂ *Papaya, Coconut, and Sweet Yam Pudding*

This pudding is a delicious combination of tropic flavors.

Yield: serves 4

1 cup half-and-half

3 tablespoons butter or margarine

1 cup raw yam or sweet potato, peeled and grated

½ cup ripe **papaya**, mashed

3 eggs

4 tablespoons light brown sugar

¼ teaspoon salt

¼ teaspoon ground nutmeg

¼ teaspoon ground cinnamon

1 teaspoon vanilla extract

1 teaspoon grated lemon **zest**

½ teaspoon coconut extract

4 tablespoons canned grated coconut in heavy syrup (available at Asian food stores)

For **garnish**: whipped cream

Equipment: Medium saucepan, wooden mixing spoon, fork or **whisk**, small bowl, buttered 6-inch soufflé dish or buttered ovenproof casserole, oven mitts, wire cake rack, knife, individual dessert dishes

Preheat oven to 300°F.

1. Put cream and butter or margarine in medium saucepan, and cook over medium-high heat until small bubbles appear around the edge of the pan. Reduce heat to low, add grated yam or sweet potato, and stir. Cook until potato is soft, 3 to 5 minutes. Stir in mashed papaya, and remove from heat. Set aside.

2. Using fork or whisk, beat eggs in a small bowl. Beat in the brown sugar, salt, nutmeg, cinnamon, vanilla, lemon zest, and coconut extract. **Fold in** egg mixture and grated coconut (including the coconut syrup) with cream mixture. Pour into buttered soufflé dish or buttered ovenproof casserole.

3. Bake in oven for 1¾, to 2 hours or until knife inserted in the center of pudding comes out clean. Remove from oven, and set on wire rack to cool.

To serve, spoon pudding while still warm into individual dishes, and add dollop of whipped cream to each serving.

4

Europe

The majority of people living in Europe are Christians, with 76 percent of the population identifying themselves as Christians (see Protestant and Catholic Life-Cycle Rituals, page lxxiii), although most countries have sizable Muslim and, to a lesser extent, Jewish communities. Roman Catholics, who comprise the largest single Christian group with about 48 percent of the European population, live mainly in Spain, Portugal, Italy, Ireland, Belgium, southern Germany, Hungary, and Poland. The Eastern Orthodox Church is the second major Christian group in Europe with 34 percent of the population. It has a strong following in Eastern Europe, primarily in Russia, Georgia, Greece, Bulgaria, Romania, and the republics of the former Yugoslavia, except for Slovenia, which is mostly Roman Catholic. In third place with 19 percent of the population is Protestantism, which is surprising, considering that the Reformation arose in Europe. The greatest concentration of Protestant Christians is found in Northern and Central Europe—England, Scotland, northern Germany, the Netherlands, and the Scandinavian countries. Although Christianity has been said to be the major unifying force in Europe, the Reformation in the 16th century and the Age of Enlightenment in the 18th century ushered in agnosticism and atheism, and from the 19th century onward, there has been an increasing interest in Buddhism and other Eastern religions. There is an increasing trend toward secularism among contemporary Europeans, and recent surveys show a decline in church attendance and membership. The importance of religion in daily life is lowest among the Scandinavian countries and highest in the Southern European countries, in particular where there have been civil wars along religious lines and ongoing interreligious conflict, such as Kosovo and Bosnia and Herzegovina. At the same time and rather paradoxically, there is a revival of interest among nominal Christians in traditional European beliefs, such as Wicca and Druidism, as well as in age-old Eastern faiths such as Zen Buddhism and Hinduism. There is as well a rise in contemporary trends, such as New Age and neopaganism (Rodnovery and similar nature-based beliefs), that amalgamate an eclectic mix from ancient European and Eastern faiths, such that a type of syncretism and religious pluralism is becoming widespread. Nevertheless, there is still a considerable number of Europeans for whom it is important that major life-cycle events, such as weddings and funerals, be celebrated according to their inherited family beliefs.

Throughout the Christian world, many countries, cities, and towns, as well as parishes, dioceses, and ecclesiastical provinces, have their particular patron saints, many of whom are unknown outside the country or local area. The custom of giving children the names of Christian saints dates from the first millennium. By the 13th century, this custom had spread across the continent of Europe. Today, when Christian parents are more likely to choose their children's names without regard to past traditions, the older European Christian churches strongly recommend that if the chosen first name is not of Christian origin or significance, then a saint's name should be bestowed at baptism as a middle name.

In Roman Catholic countries, the custom has been to celebrate the feast day of the saint whose name the person received at baptism instead of or in addition to the person's birthday. This so-called baptismal saint is considered a special personal patron all through life. Children are made familiar with the history and legend of "their own" saint. They are inspired by his or her life and feel protected and bonded with their patron saint.

All Christian churches have rituals and customs for every stage of life, from the crib to the grave. Although the basic rituals of each Christian group remain much the same across Europe, how the rituals are celebrated varies from country to country, from region to region within a country, and between the urban and rural populations of a country or region.

After Christianity, Islam is the religion with the second largest number of adherents in Europe. Historically, Islam has been present in Eastern Europe since the seventh century, in the area that is now Dagestan, and from there spread throughout the Northern Caucasus region. To this day, the North Caucasus (which is still a part of the Russian Federation), comprising seven autonomous republics (Dagestan, Chechnya, Ingushetia, Karachay-Cherkessia, Kabardino-Balkaria, Stavropol-Krai, and Adygea), two Volga republics (Tatarstan and Bashkortostan), as well as the Crimea Peninsula and the Astrakhan Oblast, are predominantly Muslim. More recently, in the late 20th and early 21st centuries, non-European Muslims have been migrating to Europe. Germany and France have the largest populations of migrant Muslims, followed by the Scandinavian countries and Great Britain. With the right of freedom to worship in Western European countries, Muslims have built mosques for regular worship, as well as for educating the younger generations born in Europe in the Islamic faith and languages (such as Turkish in Germany).

THE BRITISH ISLES

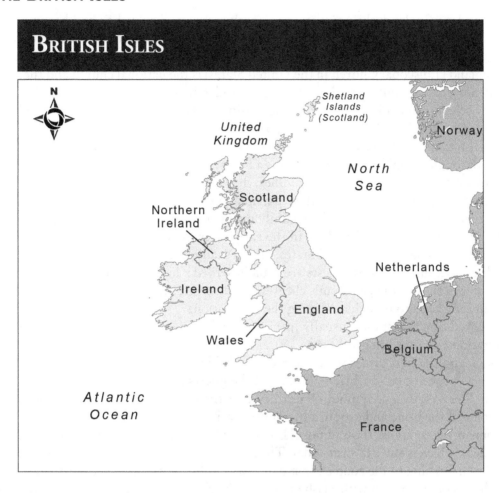

A constitutional monarchy comprising England, Scotland, Wales, and Northern Ireland, the United Kingdom (UK) is located on an archipelago (i.e., a cluster of islands) that is separated from northwestern Europe by the English Channel, the North Sea, and the narrow Straits of Dover. Great Britain, the largest of the British Isles, contains the main constituent parts of the United Kingdom—England in the south, Scotland in the north, and Wales in the west. The United Kingdom also encompasses Northern Ireland, the northeastern corner of Ireland, the second largest of the British Isles; the small Isles of Man and Wight; and the Shetlands, Orkneys, and Hebrides, island chains off Great Britain. Although the term "Great Britain" is sometimes employed to refer to the United Kingdom, the name "England" should never be used to describe the UK as a whole, for England is only one part of the modern united monarchy.

England

In modern England, the population is largely urban and suburban and has in recent years become more ethnically diverse, with many persons of Asian and African descent living in London, the capital, and in the other large cities of the country. The Church of England (Episcopal Church in the United States) is the national church and the largest denomination, but virtually all major world religions can be found in the UK. People celebrate most life-cycle events according to their particular religion. (See Protestant and Catholic Life-Cycle Rituals, page lxxiii.)

English families often come together to share a home-cooked meal, especially on Sunday. Although the midday Sunday meal is a hearty feast, it is called "lunch." Even when children marry and have their own families, they often return with their children for the weekly Sunday lunch reunion at their parents' home. This tradition is especially practiced in farming communities where family members usually live close to one another.

English weddings are often held in the early afternoon. Wedding rehearsal dinners, which are popular in the United States, are virtually unheard of in England. After an English wedding ceremony, guests are usually served a hearty sit-down dinner or buffet. Later in the evening, cold cuts, cheeses, condiments, salads, and assorted breads are set out for guests to munch on during the celebration.

The wedding reception is usually in a rented hall, hotel, inn, or family home. In past generations, the wedding cake was a simple wheat cake or bread-like biscuit. It was broken, and the first pieces were eaten by the bride and groom. The remainder of the cake was broken over the bride's head, and the guests gathered up the crumbs and ate them. The cake was a symbol of fertility and the earth's abundance. It supposedly guaranteed the bride and groom a life of prosperity and many children.

For many generations, the traditional English wedding cake has been the fruitcake (recipe page 273), which is still a favorite today. The top tier, called the "christening cake," is saved for the christening of the couple's first child. When the top is used for a christening, it is usually decorated on top with a crib or cradle. The christening is a joyous occasion and is usually followed with a large party at either a rented hall or the family home.

The English usually end formal and informal dinners and buffets with a *cheese board*, an assortment of cheeses with crackers served with coffee and port (sweet wine). Sometimes a light savory course is served after dessert. This course generally consists of such simple dishes as stuffed mushrooms (recipe follows), spiced prawns (recipe page 271), or Welsh rarebit (recipe page 292). Most savories make excellent appetizers.

♪ *Brandy Butter Stuffed Mushrooms on Toast*

Yield: serves 4 to 6

½ cup butter or margarine, more as needed
1 clove garlic, **finely chopped**

1 **shallot**, finely chopped
2 teaspoons parsley, finely chopped

1 teaspoon brandy-flavored extract or 1 tablespoon brandy

1 cup **bread crumbs**

salt and pepper to taste

16 fresh medium mushrooms, stems removed, rinsed, and dried with towel

½ cup shredded Swiss cheese

4 slices bread, crusts removed

Equipment: Medium skillet, mixing spoon, 9-inch pie pan, plastic food wrap, oven mitts, serving platter or individual appetizer plates

1. Prepare brandy butter: Melt ½ cup butter or margarine in medium skillet, over medium heat. Add garlic and shallot, stir, and sauté until soft, about 1 minute. Remove from heat, add parsley, brandy extract or brandy, bread crumbs, salt, and pepper, and stir to mix well.

2. Stuff mushrooms: Using your hands, rub outside of each mushroom cap with butter or margarine, and place side by side, bottom-side up in pie pan. Fill caps equally with brandy butter and sprinkle each with shredded cheese. Cover with plastic wrap, and refrigerate until serving time. Add salt and pepper to taste.

Preheat oven to 350°F.

3. At serving time: Bake in oven for 10 to 12 minutes, or until mushrooms are just tender and cheese is melted. Toast bread, and cut each slice diagonally to form 2 triangular pieces. Set on a serving platter or individual plates. Set 2 mushrooms on each piece of toast, and spoon pan drippings over each serving.

Serve warm as an appetizer or savory (after-dinner item). It is best to use a fork and knife to eat this dish.

⚶ *Spiced Prawns* (Spiced Shrimp)

Spiced prawns is another popular English appetizer or savory that is elegant and easy to make.

Yield: serves 4

2 tablespoons butter or margarine

2 tablespoons all-purpose flour

1 cup milk

½ teaspoon curry powder

1½ cups (about ½ pound) small shrimp, cooked, and **peeled and deveined**

salt and pepper to taste

4 slices white toast, crusts removed and buttered on one side

For **garnish:** 2 tablespoons grated Parmesan cheese

Equipment: **Heavy-bottomed** medium skillet, whisk, mixing spoon, medium bowl with cover, greased baking sheet, oven mitts, metal spatula, individual appetizer plates

1. Prepare sauce: Melt 2 tablespoons butter or margarine in heavy-bottomed medium skillet over medium-high heat. Remove from heat, and whisk in flour until smooth. Reduce heat to

medium, and return skillet to heat. Whisking constantly, slowly add milk until sauce is smooth and thickened. Stir in curry powder. Remove from heat and let cool to room temperature.

2. Using mixing spoon, **fold in** shrimp. Add salt and pepper to taste. At this point, the shrimp mixture can be transferred to medium bowl, covered, and refrigerated until serving time.

At serving time, preheat broiler.

3. Place toast, buttered side up, on greased baking sheet. Divide shrimp mixture equally on each slice of toast, and sprinkle with grated cheese. Broil until golden brown and bubbly, 3 to 5 minutes. Remove from baking sheet using metal spatula and place on individual appetizer plates.

Serve at once while still hot. Forks and knives are needed for eating spiced shrimp.

Tea is more than just a warming, stimulating liquid to the English. Drinking tea is a ritual that has been part of English life since about 1700. The English drink tea at all hours of the day, beginning first thing in the morning. A designated "tea" can be prepared for many different occasions: afternoon tea, funeral tea, high tea, and Christmas tea, to mention a few. "Tea" is also the name of a meal. In rural areas, where the heartiest meal is at midday, the lighter evening meal is called "high tea" (also "meat tea"). In the cities, where dinner is served late in the evening, "tea" is an afternoon snack. Afternoon tea should be a relaxing and pleasant break from work and the pressures of the day.

Traditional fare for afternoon tea includes bread and butter; a special bread, such as scones; biscuits (cookies); a selection of cakes; and two or three different thin sandwiches. Fresh fruit, cookies, and nut candies are also welcome. A children's tea or nursery tea is usually a simple affair. The menu might include tiny sandwiches spread with butter, jam, honey, or mashed banana; gingerbread; or some kind of cake served with *cambric tea*, which is warm milk with sugar to which a drop or two of tea is added.

An English funeral usually includes a funeral tea prepared by the widow or other family members of the deceased. Besides tea, assorted sandwiches, cakes, biscuits (cookies), and candies are provided; alcoholic beverages are also usually available for the mourners.

Whether in times of stress and sorrow or in moments of joy, the English turn almost automatically to their favorite beverage. Tea is a great comforter; it relaxes people and encourages friendship. To drink tea English-style, some people prefer to pour the desired amount of milk in the cup before adding the tea, while others add the milk after the tea is in the cup. A debate raged for months in *The Times of London* whether to add milk before or after the tea is added to the cup. Opinions were divided, although everyone agreed that one should never add hot milk to the tea.

✿ English Tea

boiling water	1 teaspoon tea leaves for each cup to be served and 1 teaspoon for the pot (**Note:** *The best tea is made with loose black tea leaves.*)
For serving:	sugar
cold milk	

Equipment: Tea kettle, teapot, tea cozy (this is an insulated cloth cover for the teapot) or thick kitchen towel, tea strainer

1. Add a little boiling water to the teapot, swirl the water to warm the pot, and pour it out.
2. Put proper amount of tea leaves in the pot; add 1 cup boiling water for each serving. Put the lid on, and cover the teapot with a tea cozy or a thick towel. Let the tea brew for 5 minutes before serving.
3. Pour tea through a strainer into the cup.

Serve tea with something to munch on, preferably something sweet.

The traditional English wedding cake takes more than a month to prepare. The fruit-cake can be rich, such as the black wedding cake of the Caribbean (recipe page 235), or it can be made according to the following recipe. To make a three-**tiered wedding cake**—a 10-inch bottom layer, an 8-inch middle layer, and a 6-inch top layer—requires three batches of this recipe. *Note: It is easier to make the recipe three times than trying to triple it.* After making the three batches, distribute the batter among the three prepared cake pans.

✿ English Fruitcake

Yield: 8-inch cake

3 cups seedless golden raisins	¾ cup butter or margarine
2 cups seedless raisins	grated rind of ½ lemon or orange
2 cups chopped mixed **candied fruits**	¾ cup dark brown sugar
1 cup **slivered** almonds	4 eggs, beaten
2 cups all-purpose flour	2 tablespoons brandy or rum or 1 tablespoon frozen orange juice concentrate
½ teaspoon salt	
½ teaspoon ground cinnamon	For **garnish: marzipan** (available at all supermarkets)
½ teaspoon ground nutmeg	

Equipment: Buttered 8-inch springform pan, scissors, parchment paper, small bowl, flour **sifter**, medium mixing bowl, large mixing bowl, electric mixer, mixing spoon, rubber spatula, spray bottle with misting nozzle, oven mitts, aluminum foil, toothpick, wire cake rack, large plastic bag, work surface, rolling pin

Prepare baking pan: Cut parchment paper to fit bottom of buttered 8-inch springform pan, place in pan, and lightly butter top surface of paper.

Preheat oven to 350°F.

1. Put golden raisins, raisins, chopped mixed candied fruit, and almonds in small bowl.

2. **Sift** flour, salt, cinnamon, and nutmeg into medium mixing bowl. Scoop out 1 cup flour mixture and sprinkle over mixed fruit mixture. Toss well until fruit mixture is thoroughly coated with flour.

3. In large mixing bowl, beat butter or margarine, using electric mixer or mixing spoon, until creamy, 1 to 3 minutes. Add lemon or orange rind and brown sugar, continue beating until well mixed. Beat in eggs, one at a time, beating well after each addition, and continue beating for 1 minute. Using rubber spatula, **fold in** about ½ cup flour mixture and floured fruit mixture, and mix well. Stir in remaining flour mixture, brandy, rum, or orange juice concentrate until well blended. Pour cake mixture into prepared pan and smooth top. Using spray bottle filled with water, spray air about 12 inches above pan to lightly mist surface of cake. *Note: The little amount of steam from the misting prevents the top of the cake from forming a hard crust during the long baking.*

4. Bake at 350°F for 1 hour. Reduce heat to 325°F and cover top of cake with foil. Bake 1 hour longer, or until toothpick inserted in center comes out clean. Cool cake in pan for 30 minutes, release side ring, and turn cake upside down on wire cake rack to cool completely. Remove pan bottom and peel paper from bottom of cake.

5. To age fruit cake: Put about ½ cup brandy or rum in spray bottle, and lightly mist cake all over. Put cake in large plastic bag and seal to make airtight. At least once a week, for one month, unwrap and spray cake with brandy or rum. Rewrap each time for flavor to develop.

Continued:

6. After one month, cover cake with marzipan (instructions follow), or wrap in plastic wrap and refrigerate or freeze to use at another time.

*Note: The top surface of fruitcakes is seldom smooth, so it is a good idea to turn the cake upside down before covering with **marzipan**.*

℘ Marzipan Topping for Fruitcake

1 cup smooth apricot jam

2 to 3 (8 ounces each) tubes **marzipan** (available at all supermarkets)

granulated sugar, as needed

fruitcake (recipe precedes)

Equipment: Small saucepan, mixing spoon, work surface, rolling pin, **pastry brush**, dinner knife

1. Put apricot jam in small saucepan and warm over medium-low heat until melted, 3 to 5 minutes.

2. Sprinkle work surface and rolling pin with granulated sugar to prevent sticking.

   Using rolling pin, roll 1 tube marzipan into a circle about ⅛ inch thick. Use 8-inch spring-form pan bottom as a pattern, place it on top of rolled-out marzipan to get exact cake size. Cut out marzipan circle with a knife.

3. Brush cake surface with melted apricot jam. Place marzipan circle on top of jam and carefully press in place.

4. Sprinkle work surface and rolling pin again with granulated sugar. Roll remaining marzipan in a strip, the length and width to completely cover sides of cake. Use the side ring of the springform pan for a pattern. It may be easier to work with shorter lengths to wrap around the cake then pinch them together.

5. With wet fingers, pinch the top and side edges of the marzipan together. Smooth over all seams with wet dinner knife. Cover with plastic wrap and refrigerate for 2 or 3 days for marzipan to dry and harden.

   Continued:

6. Cover prepared fruitcake with whipped icing (recipe follows).

   Cover the English wedding cake with whipped icing.

₰ Whipped Icing

Yield: 3 to 4 cups

prepared fruitcake (recipe page 273), covered with **marzipan** (recipe page 274)

4 tablespoons all-purpose flour

1 cup milk

½ cup: solid shortening, at room temperature

½ cup unsalted butter, at room temperature

1 cup granulated sugar

1 teaspoon vanilla extract

Equipment: 8-inch **cake board**, medium **double boiler**, whisk, large mixing bowl, electric mixer, rubber spatula, serving tray, wax paper, **icing spatula**

1. Place prepared fruitcake on cake board.

2. Fill bottom pan of double boiler halfway with water, and bring to boil over high heat. Put flour in top pan of double boiler, and whisk in milk until lump-free. Set over boiling water, mixing frequently, and cook until thickened, 12 to 15 minutes. Cool to room temperature.

3. Put solid shortening and butter in large mixing bowl, and, using electric mixer, beat until creamy. Beating constantly, add sugar, a little at a time, and continue beating for 3 to 5 minutes, until light and fluffy.

4. Beating constantly, slowly add cooled flour mixture and beat for 3 to 5 minutes more. Add vanilla extract and beat 1 minute more.

5. Icing the fruitcake: Place prepared cake on serving tray. To keep tray clean, cover with wax paper that is easy to remove after icing cake. Spread icing over top of cake with icing spatula. Work down over the sides until cake is completely covered.

To serve, allow cake to firm 3 or 4 hours. Today, decorating cakes, especially wedding cakes, with fresh flowers and greenery, especially English ivy, is very popular. Simply have the flowers and greenery cascade over the cake in a natural way.

When someone wants special individualized candies or treats to commemorate a life-cycle event, *rout biscuits*, a form of **marzipan**, are often tinted with food coloring and made into the desired shapes. In the following recipe, instructions are given for making heart-shaped designs, popular for weddings.

♣ *English Rout Biscuits* (English Marzipan)

Yield: makes 25 to 30 pieces

8-ounce package **almond paste** (*Look for almond paste that does not contain glucose or syrups, as it may be too soft to shape.*)

¼ cup butter or margarine

1½ to 2 cups confectioners' sugar, **sifted**

1 tablespoon rum or orange juice

2 teaspoons corn syrup

For **garnish**:

food coloring (*For richer-colored **marzipan**, use paste food coloring instead of the liquid form.*)

walnut halves, as needed (optional)

granulated sugar (optional)

Equipment: Medium mixing bowl, electric mixer, work surface, baking sheet or tray, heart-shaped candy molds (optional), 1-inch heart-shaped cookie cutter (optional)

1. Crumble almond paste into medium mixing bowl. Add butter or margarine. Beat with an electric mixer on medium speed until combined. Add 1 cup sifted confectioners' sugar, rum or orange juice, and corn syrup. Beat until thoroughly combined.

2. Shape mixture into a ball. Transfer to work surface and **knead** in as much of the remaining confectioners' sugar as needed until mixture is firm enough to hold its shape and forms a flexible paste for modeling consistency.

3. Divide into small portions to make into various shapes and colors, and place on baking sheet to firm.

The following are just a few suggestions for decorating the biscuits—or use your own creative talents:

For *walnut bonbons*: Tint marzipan to desired color by adding a few drops of food coloring to mixture and, using your hands, **blend** in. Roll colored marzipan into

½-inch balls. Stick half a walnut on either side, press lightly together on baking sheet or tray, and set aside to firm.

For preparing heart shapes: Color portion of marzipan pink with food coloring and follow one of these two different methods: (1) Using heart-shaped candy molds, press marzipan into heart-shaped molds; allow to set overnight on baking sheet or tray. Remove by inverting filled molds on work surface, causing candies to fall out. (2) Use a 1-inch heart-shaped cookie cutter: Sprinkle work surface with granulated sugar. Place each 1-inch ball of marzipan on the sugar, and, using your hands, flatten it into a disk slightly larger than the 1-inch cookie cutter. Cut each disk with the 1-inch heart-shaped cookie cutter. Place on baking sheet or tray and allow to firm up overnight.

For a baby shower, shape biscuits into rattles, cribs, tiny teddy bears, or babies. For birthdays, shape into numbers or flowers to put on the cake. *Rout biscuits* can be shaped into fruits, bugs, worms, or small animals and used as edible cake decorations.

Serve decorative *rout biscuits* with English tea (recipe page 273).

Funerals in England are undergoing changes in practice, with a trend toward "green" (i.e., ecological) coffins made of recycled or natural materials, such as cartons or basketry, that will eventually break down underground. Burial in these green coffins in a forest or as part of a tree-planting ritual is gaining in popularity. The traditional practice of holding a funeral feast of a cold meal, usually featuring a cold ham and pease pudding, has declined in urban areas, though may be observed in the countryside by those interested in preserving or reviving age-old traditions. It was once considered a shame not to be able to be "buried with ham."

Roast Glazed Ham

Yield: about 30 servings

13-pound smoked ham, bone-in

3 to 5 tablespoons English (sharp) prepared mustard

5 tablespoons demerara (natural brown) sugar

about 3 tablespoons whole cloves

Equipment: Large stockpot or picnic cooler box for soaking ham, foil, oven mitts, spatula, serving tray

Depending on how salty the ham is, it may need presoaking to remove most but not all of its saltiness.

1. Place the ham in a large pot or a picnic cooler, and cover with cold water and leave overnight. If the ham is very salty, it may be necessary to change the water at least once.

2. Take the ham and place it on a roasting pan lined with two generous sheets of foil—one crosswise and one lengthwise—both sheets large enough to cover the ham loosely so that air can circulate over the ham while it is roasting.

3. Bake in a preheated 325°F oven, for 4 hours 20 minutes (at 20 minutes per pound).

4. Half an hour before the end of roasting time, remove the ham from the oven.

   Turn up the oven to 425°F.

5. Slice the skin off both sides of the ham, leaving as much fat as possible. Score the fat by shallowly slicing diagonally crosswise and lengthwise all over to create a diamond pattern, and insert a clove in the center of each diamond. Using a spatula, spread mustard all over the surface. Sprinkle the sugar all over, and put the ham in the middle or lower rack of the oven.

6. Roast for 30 minutes more, or until the ham is well glazed and golden.

   Allow the ham to cool thoroughly before setting it on a large tray for serving.

Best served with Cumberland sauce (recipe follows).

♪ Cumberland Sauce

This is a classic English sauce served cold. It is traditionally served with preserved cooked meats such as ham or gammon, roasted game such as venison and pheasant, and also pork or other meat pies.

Yield: 1 small bowl of sauce

1 lemon	¼ cup port or red wine
1 orange	1 tablespoon English mustard powder
5 tablespoons good-quality redcurrant jelly (with a high fruit content)	1 teaspoon powdered ginger

Equipment: Vegetable peeler, small saucepan, oven mitts, small serving bowl

1. Peel the lemon and orange as thinly as possible, taking care not to include any of the white pith. Squeeze the juice and reserve.

2. Slice the peel into fine slivers, about ½ inch in length. Place the peel in a small saucepan covered with water and bring to a boil to remove most of their bitterness. Drain well.

3. Place the jelly in a small saucepan with the port over low heat to melt. Take off the heat.

4. Whisk the mustard and ginger with half the lemon juice and all of the orange juice. Stir in the mustard mixture and the drained peel into the melted jelly.

5. You may add more lemon juice if the sauce is too sweet for your taste. Transfer to a serving bowl.

Ireland

Ireland, the second largest of the British Isles, lies west of Great Britain across the Irish Sea. Ireland is divided into two countries, the Republic of Ireland, which makes up more than 80 percent of the island, and Northern Ireland, which is part of the United Kingdom. Most of the people in the Irish Republic are Roman Catholic, while the majority of the people in Northern Ireland are Protestant. Most Irish life-cycle events center around the dominant Church in the region. (See Protestant and Catholic Life-Cycle Rituals, page lxxiii.)

January pudding is an old Irish dessert many mothers and grandmothers enjoyed when they were little children. To keep traditions alive, they often prepare it as a special treat for their children or grandchildren on a birthday or name-day celebration.

☙ January Pudding

Yield: serves 6 to 8

½ cup unsalted butter, at room temperature

½ cup brown sugar

2 eggs, lightly beaten

2 heaping tablespoons raspberry jam

1 cup all-purpose flour

½ teaspoon baking soda

For serving: raspberry jam sauce (recipe follows)

Equipment: Medium mixing bowl, electric mixer or mixing spoon, flour **sifter**, small bowl, rubber spatula, buttered **steamed pudding mold** (1-quart size) with cover or 1-quart stainless mixing bowl, scissors, wax paper, aluminum foil, kitchen string, **steamer pan**, oven mitts, serving plate

1. Put butter and brown sugar in medium mixing bowl, and, using electric mixer or mixing spoon, beat until light and fluffy, 1 to 2 minutes. Beat in eggs and raspberry jam.

2. **Sift** flour and baking soda into small bowl. Using rubber spatula, fold the flour mixture into the egg mixture. Spoon the batter into buttered pudding mold or buttered 1-quart stainless mixing bowl. Cut a piece of wax paper to fit over the top of the mold or bowl and butter one side of it. Place the circle of wax paper, buttered-side down, on top of the pudding batter. If using the mold, close the cover. If using the bowl, cut a piece of foil large enough to cover the top and at least 2 inches down the sides of the bowl. Place foil over the top of bowl and press firmly against the sides. Tie foil in place with string just under the ledge of the bowl.

3. Place mold or bowl on rack in the steamer pan. Fill steamer pan with boiling water to reach about two-thirds up the sides of the pudding container. Bring to boil over high heat, and cover the steamer pan. Reduce heat to **simmer** and cook for 2 hours. From time to time, check water level. Add more boiling water when level drops below halfway up the sides of the pudding container.

4. While pudding is cooking, prepare raspberry jam sauce (recipe follows).

5. Using oven mitts, remove mold from the water and place on heatproof surface. Remove the cover and wax paper. Let the pudding cool for 30 minutes before removing from mold or bowl. To remove pudding from mold or bowl, place the serving plate upside down over top

of pudding container. Holding both firmly together, flip plate and mold or bowl together so pudding drops onto plate. Carefully lift off empty container.

To serve, cut the warm pudding into wedges. Put raspberry jam sauce in a small bowl to spoon over each serving.

ᨆ *Raspberry Jam Sauce*

Yield: serves 6 to 8

½ cup raspberry jam   juice of 1 lemon

¼ cup water

Equipment: Small saucepan, mixing spoon, small serving bowl, serving spoon

Put raspberry jam, water, and lemon juice into small saucepan. Stir and heat over low heat until heated through and well blended, 2 to 3 minutes.

To serve, pour into small serving bowl. Serve as sauce for January pudding (recipe precedes).

Traditionally, Catholic weddings take place in the church following a long engagement. New Year's Day is considered the luckiest day of the year to be married. If the wedding is held in the country, the reception is most likely to be at the bride's family home or a pub (i.e., a public house or bar where food is also served). In the cities, the reception would probably be in an inn or hotel ballroom. The traditional Irish wedding cake is a fruitcake, similar to the English wedding cake (recipe page 273).

Mead is the drink for celebrating a wedding, the birth of a child, a birthday, a retirement, an engagement, a promotion, or some other occasion to make merry. It is also drunk in memory of a departed friend or family member or shared with other mourners during a wake.

The traditional Irish wake for the dead, with several nights of drinking, reminiscing, and storytelling, is now only a remembrance of Ireland past. The Catholic Church has discouraged it in recent years because it had become too social, too expensive, and the butt of too many jokes. The present procedure is to hold the wake for only one night at home before it is taken to the church for a brief rosary service (a Roman Catholic devotion) on the second evening. The funeral occurs on the following morning.

During the long wake-keeping time of the past, relatives and neighbors sat with the casket. Because shame attached to any person who fell asleep, a kettle of soup or stew was kept simmering on the stove so that the all-night mourners could revive themselves when the need arose.

Dried peas are popular in rural Ireland, where, until the 20th century, few fresh vegetables beyond potatoes, onions, cabbage, and carrots were available. Pea and ham soup could keep mourners nourished during a wake.

⚘ *Pea and Ham Soup*

Yield: serves 8

4 slices bacon, **coarsely chopped**

2 onions, chopped

9 cups water

2¼ cups (about 1 pound) dried green split peas

1½ to 2 pounds smoked ham hocks, cut into 2- or 3-inch lengths

1 bay leaf

½ pound cooked ham, cut into bite-size chunks

salt and pepper to taste

milk, if needed

Equipment: Large skillet, mixing spoons, large saucepan with cover or **Dutch oven**, ladle, large soup bowls

1. **Render** bacon in large skillet over medium-low heat, 3 to 5 minutes. Add onions, increase heat to medium-high, and **sauté** until soft, 3 to 5 minutes.

2. Transfer sautéed onions and pan drippings to large saucepan or Dutch oven. Add water, split peas, ham hocks, and bay leaf. Bring to boil over medium-high heat, stir, and reduce heat to **simmer**. Cover and cook for 1½ to 2 hours, until peas are soft yet tender. Add ham and salt and pepper to taste, cover, and continue to simmer for 30 minutes. If soup is too thick, add a little milk to thin. Bring the soup to simmer and heat through; do not boil. Remove and discard bay leaf.

To serve, ladle into large soup bowls and serve with soda bread (recipe follows).

Many Irish women still make soda bread every day. There is no waiting for it to rise, nor does it require extensive kneading. The less handling of the dough, the better the bread will be. It is important to use buttermilk when making soda bread because its reaction with baking soda helps the bread rise. If buttermilk is not available, substitute either sour milk or sour cream. You can make sour milk or sour cream by adding one tablespoon of white vinegar to each cup of fresh milk or heavy cream.

⚘ Soda Bread

Yield: 2 loaves

4 cups cake flour

¼ teaspoon salt

2 tablespoons baking soda

1½ teaspoons cream of tartar

¼ cup sugar

1 tablespoon caraway seeds

3 tablespoons raisins

¼ cup solid vegetable shortening

1¼ cups buttermilk

Equipment: Flour **sifter**, large mixing bowl, **pastry blender** (optional), lightly floured work surface, lightly floured baking sheet, sharp paring knife, oven mitts, wire cake rack, napkin-lined breadbasket

Preheat oven to 400°F.

1. **Sift** flour, salt, baking soda, cream of tartar, and sugar into a large mixing bowl. Using your fingers or pastry blender, rub in shortening until mixture resembles coarse meal. Add raisins, caraway seeds, and buttermilk, and, using your hands, mix the dough until it holds together.

2. Transfer to lightly floured work surface, **knead** for 20 seconds, and divide dough in half. Use your hands to shape each piece into a round loaf. Place each loaf on lightly floured baking sheet with at least a 3-inch space between the loaves. Using paring knife, cut a deep X in top of each loaf and sprinkle lightly with flour.

3. Bake for 30 to 35 minutes, until lightly browned and firm. Test for **bread doneness**. Transfer to wire cake rack to cool.

Serve while warm from the oven, and place loaves in napkin-lined breadbasket. Serve with pea and ham soup (recipe page 281) or Dublin coddle (recipe follows).

Dublin coddle is a filling and nourishing stew traditionally served to restore one's health after too much partying, especially on Saturday night.

Dublin Coddle (Dublin Stew or Sausage and Potato Stew)

Yield: serves 6 to 8

1 cup all-purpose flour

2 pounds pork sausage, cut into 2- or 3-inch pieces

4 slices bacon, coarsely chopped

2 onions, sliced

2 cloves garlic

2 carrots, thickly sliced

4 potatoes, thickly sliced

9 cups water or apple cider

salt and pepper to taste

For **garnish**: 1 tablespoon chopped fresh parsley or 1 teaspoon dried parsley flakes

Equipment: Pie pan, large skillet, slotted spoon, plate, large saucepan with cover or **Dutch oven**, deep plates or soup bowls

1. Put flour in pie pan. Dip each piece of sausage in the flour to coat.

2. **Render** bacon in large skillet over medium-low heat, 3 to 5 minutes. Increase heat to medium-high, add flour-coated sausage pieces, and fry on all sides until browned, 5 to 7 minutes. Using slotted spoon, remove sausage from skillet and place on plate. Add onions and garlic to skillet, and sauté until soft, 3 to 5 minutes.

3. Put sausage, onion mixture, pan drippings, carrots, and potatoes in large saucepan or Dutch oven. Add water or apple cider and salt and pepper to taste. Bring to boil over high heat, and reduce heat to **simmer**. Cover and cook for 1 hour. Garnish with parsley.

To serve, spoon into deep plates or soup bowls, and serve together with soda bread.

Many Irish cakes, bread, and tarts are made with fruit. Kerry cake is easy to make and an Irish favorite.

ℰ *Kerry Cake* (Apple Cake)

Yield: serves 9 to 12

¾ cup butter or margarine	1 ½ cups cake flour, **sifted**
½ cup granulated sugar	¼ teaspoon salt
3 eggs	1½ teaspoon baking powder
grated rind of 1 lemon	1 teaspoon ground cinnamon
3 apples, pared, **cored**, and **diced**	For **garnish**: confectioners' sugar

Equipment: Large mixing bowl, electric mixer, mixing spoon, flour **sifter**, medium mixing bowl, rubber spatula, greased 8- or 9-inch square or round cake pan, oven mitts, toothpick, wire cake rack

Preheat oven to 350°F.

1. In large mixing bowl, using an electric mixer, beat butter with sugar until creamy. Add eggs, one at a time, beating well after each addition. Using a mixing spoon, stir in lemon rind and diced apples.

2. **Sift** flour, salt, baking powder, and cinnamon into medium mixing bowl. Using mixing spoon or rubber spatula, **fold in** flour mixture with egg mixture, a little at a time, and **blend** well. Pour into greased 8- or 9-inch square or round cake pan.

3. Bake in oven for 30 to 35 minutes, until golden, and when toothpick inserted in center comes out clean. Cool on wire cake rack. While still warm, sprinkle top with confectioners' sugar.

Serve, slightly warm, cut into squares or, if made in a round pan, cut in wedges.

Scotland

Scotland, one of the constituent parts of the United Kingdom, occupies the northern third of the island of Great Britain. Originally, the clan, a group of related families with one head (*laird*), was an important fighting force and the foundation of Scottish society. Over time, the solidarity of clan lineage has developed into a strong point of Scottish national pride. In Scotland, many important family events, such as births, christenings, weddings, and burials, have their origins in ancient Celtic rituals that predate Christianity.

Childbirth and the first few months of a newborn's life in particular were traditionally considered precarious to both the mother's and the baby's life, so that many *saining* (protective) practices arose to safeguard their lives and to confer blessings on the new baby. Until the new mother was *kirked* ("churched," i.e., gone to attend church services), she was to stay indoors and refrain from all but the most essential tasks. The baby was often given lay baptism (*baistidh breith*—"birth baptism"), in case it did not live long enough to be properly baptized in church. There was also a custom of hanging red coral beads on the infant's neck to guard against the evil eye. Another practice to ward off the evil eye was to spit three times into the infant's face: this spitting custom recalls similar traditional practices in Eastern Europe. On the way to church on the day of baptism, it was customary to hand a christening piece—two buttered biscuits or soda scone sandwiched with a silver coin—to the first person met by the person (usually not the mother) holding the infant. This was meant to ward off evil spirits. This custom survives to this day in some parts of Scotland with a variation—the piece is given after the christening on the way out of the church, and also it takes the form of bread and cheese to those who visit a newly baptized infant.

To soothe teething infants, a teething bannock (also called "teething plaster" because of the widespread belief in its efficacy) was given for the child to play with, and when it broke, a small piece was given to the child to suck on, and the rest was shared among the family in the hope that they would take away some of the discomfort with them. This practice was believed to banish subsequent teething problems. A wedding bannock (*bonnach bainnse*), made by a happily married and wise woman (a "wise matron") on a bride's wedding day, was broken over the bride's head as she entered her new home after the ceremony. This custom was to ensure a prosperous and fertile marriage.

❧ Oatmeal Bannock

Yield: 4 farls (portions) or 1 bannock

¾ cup flour, plus more for rolling out

½ cup fine oatmeal or oat flakes

1 teaspoon baking powder

¼ teaspoon baking soda

pinch of salt

1 teaspoon sugar

2 tablespoons butter or thick cream

¼ cup buttermilk or yogurt

additional butter for greasing

Equipment: Food processor, baking tray or cookie sheet, mixing bowl and spoon, oven mitts

Preheat oven to 400°F.

1. If using oat flakes, grind to a fine meal in a food processor.

2. Grease the baking tray and sprinkle it evenly with flour. Set aside.

3. In a mixing bowl, combine the flour, fine oatmeal, baking powder, baking soda, salt, and sugar. Mix well. Rub in the butter, or stir in the cream. Add the buttermilk and mix well until the mixture forms a soft dough.

4. Turn dough onto a well floured surface and lightly knead for about 5 minutes. Shape the dough into a round loaf, ¾ inch thick. Cut into 4 and place well apart on the prepared baking tray. (These individual portions are called farls.) Alternatively, keep whole.

5. Bake in a preheated 400°F oven for 15 to 20 minutes, or until pale golden. An uncut bannock may need an additional 8 to 10 minutes of baking time.

The favorite time of year for weddings in Scotland is between the November term day (*Martinmas*, on November 11) and the New Year. Many old customs and rituals are still observed at Scottish weddings. Blackening of the bride and also the groom (depending on the region) is an old tradition that is still practiced in some parts of Scotland today, in particular the area around Aberdeenshire. Days or weeks before the actual wedding, friends of the bride and groom "abduct" them and douse them with buckets of soot or feathers or foul-smelling liquids. The origin of this custom may lie in the belief that doing so will repel evil spirits and ensure good fortune for the marriage. Another reason may be that, having undergone public humiliation and being seen at their most unflattering, the couple will be able to withstand any future unpleasantness that comes their way.

The Luckenbooth is a traditional betrothal gift or love token with the motif of two hearts and a crown, often with a thistle (the symbol of Scotland), made into a pendant, brooch, or ring. Its name comes from the locked booths in which they were sold in Edinburgh. It was also believed to protect nursing mothers from having their milk stolen or their newborn infants harmed by evil spirits.

The Scottish wedding celebration is a joyous and sometimes riotous affair—a grand excuse for feasting, drinking, and merrymaking. This practice is in direct contrast to the harshness and frugality that characterized Scottish life during various periods in the past. In the 16th century, for instance, a law was passed restricting extravagant eating because of food shortages, although exemptions were granted for certain feast days and special celebrations.

Scottish weddings are usually held in a church, most Scots being members of the national church or of another Protestant denomination. A small number of Scottish weddings are held in hotel ballrooms, at home, or in a castle rented for the occasion. Whether the wedding food is just a light repast or a full dinner, shortbread is sure to be on the menu. The following recipe is called "Petticoat Tails" for the frilly-looking border around the edge of the shortbread.

₡ *Petticoat Tails* (Scottish Shortbread)

Yield: 8 to 12 pieces

1¼ cups all-purpose flour

3 tablespoons **cornstarch**

¼ cup sugar, more as needed

½ cup chilled butter or margarine, cut into small pieces

Equipment: Large mixing bowl, lightly greased 8- or 9-inch springform pan, fork, oven mitts, knife, serving platter

Preheat oven to 325°F.

1. In large mixing bowl, combine flour, cornstarch, ¼ cup sugar, and butter or margarine. Using your hands, rub mixture together until it is crumbly. Form into a ball (it is still crumbly) and transfer to springform pan. Using your fingers, press dough to evenly cover bottom of pan and pat smooth. Press into dough with back of fork to make decorative border, about 1 inch wide all around the edge.

2. Bake in oven for 35 to 40 minutes, until golden brown. Remove from oven and, while still warm, sprinkle with 1 tablespoon sugar, and cut into 8 to 12 wedges. Cool to room temperature and remove sides of pan.

To serve, decoratively place wedges on serving platter. Eat as a cookie.

Scottish salmon is a prized food fish around the world. Few Scottish wedding receptions would be complete unless poached whole salmon is on the buffet table. Traditionally, whole fish is cooked with the head on in a special poaching kettle. The following recipe is an easy way to get the same end result.

₡ *Poached Salmon*

Yield: serves 10 to 12

butter or margarine, as needed

6- to 8-pound **oven-ready** whole salmon with head and tail attached (available at most supermarkets and all fish markets)

For cold **garnish:**

lettuce leaves, as needed

5 to 6 hard-cooked eggs, shelled and cut in half

10 to 12 tomato slices

½ cup chicken broth

salt and pepper to taste

For **garnish:** fresh parsley as needed

10 to 12 lemon wedges

For serving: prepared Hollandaise sauce or mayonnaise (*Hollandaise sauce mix is available at all supermarkets; prepare according to directions on package.*)

Equipment: Aluminum foil, scissors, paring knife, large roasting pan or baking sheet, oven mitts, meat thermometer, small bowl, large serving platter, kitchen towel, small serving bowl

Preheat oven to 350°F.

1. Using scissors, cut foil large enough to generously enclose fish and place on work surface. Rub butter or margarine thickly over foil, and set fish in the center. Using paring knife, make 3 or 4 diagonal slits, 2 to 3 inches long, in fish skin. (The skin shrinks during cooking; cutting slits keeps fish from curling up.) Bring ends of foil together above the fish so juices can't leak out. Pour chicken broth over the fish, and sprinkle with salt and pepper to taste. Pinch ends of foil together so there is airspace above the fish (about an inch or two of air). This allows room for steam to collect during cooking. Place in roasting pan or on baking sheet.

2. Bake in oven for 1½ to 2 hours, depending on size. (Fish is done when meat thermometer registers 145°F when inserted in the thickest part of the flesh, or when fish flakes easily when poked with a fork.) If fish is to be served warm, do not open foil for 10 minutes. If fish is to be served cold, cool to room temperature before removing foil.

3. Open foil and drain fish juices into small bowl. Slide fish onto serving platter. Using paring knife, peel off skin only from top of fish. Leave head and tail intact, and discard skin.

4. If serving fish warm, pour fish juices over fish, and garnish with parsley and lemon wedges. Serve with small bowl of Hollandaise sauce to spoon over each serving.

5. If serving fish cold, place lettuce leaves around cooled fish. Garnish with parsley, lemon wedges, sliced hard-cooked eggs, and sliced tomatoes. Pour fish juices over fish. Serve with small bowl of mayonnaise to spoon over each serving.

Serve fish, either warm or cold, with thinly sliced dark bread and butter.

The Scottish wedding feast usually includes some sort of game dish, usually partridge or quail, but if there is no hunter in the family, *howtowdie* (roast chicken) (recipe follows) will do just fine. Traditionally, the bird is stuffed with *skirlie* (recipe follows). For this recipe, *skirlie* is made as a dressing or side dish and baked in a casserole.

⸖ *Howtowdie* (Roast Chicken)

Yield: serves 6

3- to 4-pound chicken, **oven-ready**	2 cups hot water, more as needed
6 onions, quartered	salt and pepper to taste
½ cup melted butter or margarine	For serving: *skirlie* (recipe follows)

Equipment: Shallow roasting pan, **pastry brush**, oven mitts, paring knife, carving board, **bulb baster** or mixing spoon, small saucepan, whisk, strainer, serving bowl, serving platter

Preheat oven to 375°F.

1. Place chicken, breast side up, in shallow roasting pan. Arrange onions around chicken. Brush chicken and onions with melted butter or margarine. Add 2 cups hot water to roasting pan.

2. Roast in oven for 1 to 1¼ hours. Test for **doneness**: Pierce thickest part of chicken with knife, if juices trickle out clear, not pinkish in color, the chicken is done. Transfer chicken to carving board, and let rest 15 minutes before slicing. Using bulb baster or mixing spoon, skim off and discard most fat from pan juices.

3. Prepare gravy: For each cup of pan juices, combine 2 tablespoons flour with ½ cup water to form a paste, and quickly whisk to prevent lumping. In small saucepan, cook and whisk over medium heat until gravy thickens. Add salt and pepper to taste, and strain gravy into serving bowl.

To serve, place the chicken pieces in the center of the serving platter and surround with onion wedges. Each person gets a piece of chicken, a wedge of onion, a spoonful of skirlie (recipe to follow), and a **drizzle** *of gravy.*

⚜ *Skirlie* **(Oat Dressing)**

Yield: serves 6

1 cup butter or margarine, divided	½ teaspoon ground **coriander**
1 onion, **finely chopped**	¼ teaspoon ground nutmeg
1 cup regular oats	1½ cups chicken broth
½ teaspoon: salt and pepper	

Equipment: Large skillet, mixing spoon, buttered medium ovenproof casserole with cover, oven mitts

Preheat oven to 350°F.

1. Melt ½ cup butter or margarine in large skillet over medium-high heat. Add onion, **sauté**, and stir until soft, 2 to 3 minutes. Stir in oats, salt and pepper, coriander, and nutmeg. Reduce heat to **simmer**, stir, and cook until oats are golden brown, 3 to 5 minutes. Transfer to buttered medium ovenproof casserole, and pour over 1 cup chicken broth. Dot top with remaining ½ cup butter.

2. Cover casserole and bake in oven for 40 to 45 minutes. Remove cover, add remaining ½ cup chicken broth, and bake, uncovered for 15 to 25 minutes more, until golden.

Continue with *howtowdie* (recipe precedes).

⚜ *Cranachan* **(Scottish Berry Cream)**

Cranachan is a traditional dessert that features the best of local Scottish products—in other words, single malt whiskey, as well as berries, cream, and oatmeal. It is often served as a special dessert—as a finale to a celebratory meal, either for a birthday or other family occasion or gathering.

Yield: serves 4

6 tablespoons oatmeal

2½ cups double cream

6 tablespoons honey

3 tablespoons single malt whiskey (any other whiskey, such as blended or bourbon, will not do)

3 cups fresh raspberries, strawberries, blueberries, or other berries in season

Equipment: Heavy-bottomed skillet, oven mitts, wire whisk or hand or stand mixer, 4 dessert glasses for serving

1. In a skillet, dry toast oatmeal until golden brown.
2. Whip cream to soft peaks. Stir in honey and whiskey, and mix well.
3. Set aside for each glass 6 raspberries or 2 strawberries, sliced, as garnish.
4. Fold oatmeal and remaining berries into cream, crushing a few berries to release color.
5. Place 3 whole raspberries or strawberry slices at the bottom of each glass. Add cream mixture. Garnish each glass with the reserved fruits.

Serve with shortbread.

The Dundee cake is one the most popular cakes to grace the Scottish tea table, especially for christening and birthday celebrations. Neighbors often bring Dundee cakes to feed mourners at a wake.

Dundee Cake (Light Fruitcake)

Yield: serves 10–14

1 cup butter or margarine, at room temperature

1 cup sugar

4 eggs

2½ cups cake flour, divided

1 teaspoon baking powder

½ teaspoon salt

3 tablespoons lemon juice

½ cup seedless raisins, **finely chopped**

½ cup dried currants, finely chopped (available at most supermarkets)

½ cup **glacé cherries**, finely chopped (available at most supermarkets)

grated rind of 1 lemon

2 tablespoons grated orange rind

1¼ cups sliced almonds

Equipment: Large mixing bowl, electric mixer, rubber spatula, mixing spoon, flour **sifter**, medium mixing bowl, small bowl, greased 10×5×3-inch loaf pan, oven mitts, toothpick, wire cake rack, aluminum foil, serving plate

1. Put butter and sugar into large mixing bowl, and using electric mixer, beat until fluffy, about 2 minutes. Using rubber spatula, scrape down sides of bowl. Beat in eggs, one at a time, until well mixed.

    Ten minutes before baking, preheat oven to 325°F.

2. **Sift** 2¼ cups flour, baking powder, and salt into medium mixing bowl. With electric mixer on low speed, add flour mixture, a little at a time, alternately with lemon juice, and beat until smooth.

3. In small bowl, mix raisins, currants, glacé cherries, lemon and orange rinds, and sliced almonds. Add remaining ¼ cup flour and toss to coat. Using mixing spoon or rubber spatula, **fold in** raisin mixture with batter. Transfer to greased loaf pan.

4. Bake in oven for 1 to 1½ hours or until toothpick inserted in middle comes out clean. Using oven mitts, remove from oven, allow to cool 15 minutes in loaf pan, and turn out on wire rack to cool completely. Wrap in foil to keep fresh and allow 2 or 3 days for flavors to develop before eating.

To serve, cut into ¼- to ½-inch slices and place, slightly overlapping, on serving plate. Wrapped in foil, Dundee cake freezes well for up to one month.

Old-fashioned wakes are still held in many parts of Scotland, although how the wake is celebrated varies with each region. After the deceased is buried, mourners go to the home of a family member for tea and sandwiches or a home-cooked meal. Most urbanites prefer to take the mourners to a hotel for a prearranged sit-down dinner.

Wales

Wales, the two-pronged western peninsula of the island of Great Britain, is the third major component of the United Kingdom. The Welsh, like the Scots, are of Celtic origin. The majority of Welsh people are Protestants, mainly Methodists, and they follow life-cycle celebrations according to their church. (See Protestant and Catholic Life-Cycle Rituals, page lxxiii.) The Methodist religion grew out of the Anglican Church (Church of England) and became popular among the Welsh.

Welsh weddings are often short and simple and need not take place in church. Castles, hotels, and wedding halls are often rented for the occasion. Breads, often filled with currants or other dried fruit, are basic to Welsh meals and are usually included in wedding and other Welsh life-cycle feasts.

❦ *Bara Brith* (Speckled Bread)

Note: This recipe takes 24 hours.

2 cups chopped mixed **candied fruit**	1 cup hot tea
1 cup brown sugar	4 cups **self-rising flour**

¼ teaspoon salt

¼ cup butter or margarine

1 egg, well beaten

Equipment: Small bowl with cover, mixing spoon, large mixing bowl, **pastry blender** (optional), greased 9×5×3-inch loaf pan, oven mitts, wire rack

1. Put chopped mixed candied fruit and brown sugar into small bowl, stir, and pour over hot tea. Cover and let stand at room temperature overnight. (Do not refrigerate.)

Preheat oven to 350°F.

2. **Sift** flour with salt into large mixing bowl. Add butter or margarine and, using a pastry blender or your fingers, work butter or margarine into flour. Make a well (hole) in the center of flour, add egg and candied fruit mixture. Using mixing spoon, stir to mix well. Transfer to greased loaf pan.

3. Bake in oven for 1½ to 2 hours, or until toothpick inserted in center comes out clean. Cool bread in pan for 30 minutes, then transfer to wire cake rack to cool to room temperature.

To serve, cut in slices and serve with fruit and cheeses. This is a popular bread to serve with afternoon tea or at a bridal shower.

The Welsh love freshwater fish, especially when cooked or served with bacon. Such dishes are often served for baptism lunches after church or as part of the buffet table at the wedding receptions.

⚘ *Brythyll a Chig Moch* (Trout with Bacon)

Yield: serves 6

12 slices bacon

6 **oven-ready** whole trout (10 to 12 ounces each)

2 tablespoons fresh parsley flakes or 1 tablespoon dried parsley flakes

salt and pepper to taste

Equipment: Paper towels, baking sheet, large skillet, metal spatula or metal tongs, shallow roasting pan, aluminum foil, oven mitts, fork

1. Have ready several layers of paper towels on baking sheet. Fry bacon in large skillet over medium-high heat, until soft and **rendered**, but not crisp, 3 to 5 minutes on each side. Transfer bacon to paper towels to drain. Lay bacon strips side by side in shallow baking pan. Save rendered bacon fat.

Preheat oven to 350°F.

2. Rinse fish under cold running water and pat dry with paper towels. Using pastry brush, brush skin and inside of fish with rendered bacon fat. Sprinkle inside of fish with parsley flakes and salt and pepper to taste. Place fish on top of bacon in shallow baking pan. Cover with foil.

3. Bake in oven for 15 minutes, uncover, and continue to bake for 10 to 12 minutes more or until fish flakes apart easily when poked with a fork.

Serve as the first course at a wedding feast or as the main dish for a baptism luncheon. Allow one whole fish and two slices bacon for each serving.

In the past, appetizers were known in the British Isles as "fore bits" because they were eaten before the main meal. An old tradition among English aristocrats was to have a savory dish served after dessert at formal banquets. The savory was referred to as "rear bits" because it was served at the end, or rear, of the meal. Some food historians believe the word "rarebit" could have been a form of the phrase "rear bits" since rarebit was often served as an after-dinner savory.

⚄ *Caws Pobi* (Welsh Rarebit; also Welsh Rabbit)

Yield: serves 4

1½ tablespoons butter	1 teaspoon prepared mustard
1 cup sharp cheddar cheese, grated	ground red pepper to taste
2 tablespoons milk	4 to 6 slices hot toasted white bread, buttered on one side for serving

Equipment: **Double boiler**, mixing spoon, baking sheet, oven mitts

1. Fill bottom pan of double boiler halfway with water, and bring to boil over high heat. Set the other pan over the pan with boiling water, add butter, and melt. Reduce heat to **simmer**, and add cheese, stirring occasionally until melted. Stir in milk, mustard, and ground red pepper to taste, and mix well.

Preheat broiler or toaster oven.

2. At serving time, place slices of toast, butter-side up, on baking pan. Spoon cheese mixture onto the toast. Place under the broiler or in a toaster oven to lightly brown, 3 to 5 minutes.

Serve immediately while hot. To serve as a savory or "rarebit" after the wedding feast, cut in half and **garnish** *with a sprig of parsley.*

Leeks, the national emblem of Wales, are often eaten on the feast day of Wales's patron saint, St. David. *Tatws rhost* (oven-fried potatoes) are a favorite old Welsh recipe and often served along with *brythyll a chig moch* (recipe precedes) at a baptism luncheon.

⚄ *Tatws Rhost* (Oven-Fried Potatoes)

Yield: serves 6

4 leeks, trimmed, white part only	6 potatoes, peeled and thinly sliced
8 slices bacon, **coarsely chopped**	

6 green onions, with tops, trimmed and chopped

½ cup water

salt and pepper to taste

Equipment: Knife, work surface, **colander**, large skillet, mixing spoon, greased 9×13×2-inch baking pan, aluminum foil, oven mitts, serving platter

Preheat oven to 400°F.

1. Slice leeks on work surface, transfer to colander, and rinse carefully under cold running water to remove any sand particles. Drain well.

2. Fry bacon in large skillet over medium-low heat until **rendered**, 3 to 5 minutes. Add leeks, stir, and sauté for 3 to 5 minutes, until leeks are soft, not browned.

3. Arrange potato slices in greased baking pan. Spoon over bacon, leeks, and pan drippings. Pour water over potatoes, sprinkle with green onions, and add salt and pepper to taste. Cover with foil.

4. Bake in oven for 35 minutes. Uncover and bake until potatoes are tender and bacon is crispy but not burned, 15 to 20 minutes.

To serve, transfer to serving platter and serve hot.

In the past, most Welsh homes did not have ovens. For name-day, baptism, and wedding celebrations, sweet cakes and biscuits were usually made on the griddle. The following recipe for *ffrois* (Welsh crepes) is typical of griddle-style desserts.

ꬒ *Ffrois* (Welsh Crepes)

Yield: serves 4 to 6

6 tablespoons dried currants

1 cup all-purpose flour

¼ teaspoon salt

3 eggs

1¾ cups milk

vegetable oil, as needed, for pan frying

For **garnish**: confectioners' sugar

Equipment: Large cup, large mixing bowl, electric mixer or whisk, kitchen towel, paper towels, work surface, **heavy-bottomed** 6- or 8-inch skillet

1. Put dried currants in cup, cover with water to soak for 10 minutes, and drain well.

2. Put flour, salt, eggs, and milk in large mixing bowl, and, using electric mixer or whisk, beat until smooth, 2 to 3 minutes.

3. To pan fry: Have ready paper towels spread out on work surface. Using a paper towel dipped in oil, lightly grease bottom and sides of heavy-bottomed 6- or 8-inch skillet.

4. Heat skillet over medium-high heat until hot, about 1 minute. Add ¼ cup batter and swirl in pan to completely coat bottom of pan with thin layer of batter. Quickly add a little more batter, if necessary, to cover bottom of pan. When edges pull away from sides of pan and surface

turns dull, slide crepe onto towel to remove from skillet, 2 to 3 minutes. Return crepe to skillet, bottom-side up, and quickly fry second side, about 1 minute. Remove from skillet and place on towel. Repeat making crepes, greasing skillet each time before adding batter and adjusting heat as necessary if skillet becomes too hot. Slightly overlap crepes on towel.

5. To assemble: Sprinkle each crepe with ½ teaspoon currants and confectioners' sugar, and roll the crepe around the currants. Or you can stack the sprinkled crepes in layers and cut into wedges, like a cake.

Serve stacked cakes with candles for a birthday or name-day party. Serve rolled crepes on a serving platter for a dessert table at tea time or as dessert at a wedding banquet.

✂ *Crempog Hufen* Cream Pancakes

Cream pancakes are made as an extra-special luxurious treat for birthdays, and they may even be served to the celebrant on a tray in bed.

Yield: 4 to 6 servings

1 cup flour	4 yolks
¼ teaspoon salt	2 cups thick cream
4 small eggs	

Equipment: Mixing bowl and spoon, electric mixer or whisk, **heavy-bottomed** skillet

1. In a bowl, combine the flour and salt. Make a well (hole) in the center, and add the eggs, yolks, and cream. Mix together, for about 3 minutes, until smooth.

2. Cook on a heavy-bottomed skillet and serve, following instructions for *ffrois* (recipe precedes).

NORTHERN EUROPE

Northern Europe includes the Baltic States of Estonia, Latvia, and Lithuania, as well as the Scandinavian countries of Denmark, Finland, Iceland, Norway, and Sweden.

Baltic States

The three Baltic nations—Lithuania, Latvia, and Estonia—are all bordered by Russia and Belarus on the east and the Baltic Sea on the west. After years of being under the control of the Soviet Union, the three Baltic countries became independent in 1991, several months before the Soviet empire formally dissolved. Today, all three nations are working toward establishing economic, political, and cultural stability.

Estonia

The northernmost of the three Baltic republics, Estonia is linked with neighboring Finland, just 50 miles to the north across the Gulf of Finland. Like the Finns, most

NORTHERN EUROPE

Estonians belong to the Lutheran Church. All life-cycle events are celebrated according to their religion. (See Protestant and Catholic Life-Cycle Rituals, page lxxiii.)

Even though the various Christian groups have their own traditions for funerals, including Estonians, some traditions are fairly similar. If the funeral is for a young wife, she is often buried in her wedding dress. Women in mourning wear black or dark clothes, while men usually wear a black ribbon on the lapel of their coats. Coffins are built of wood and have six sides and are narrow at the foot end. Estonians have preserved the tradition of kissing the dead as a way of saying the last goodbye.

In Estonia, mourners sing hymns every evening, followed by prayers for dead relatives from the past three generations. After each evening's prayers, a special meal is served, prepared by the best cook of the neighborhood. If the family has a pig, it is killed and eaten on this occasion.

A new tradition that has developed, in both villages and cities, is throwing flowers into the grave. Funerals usually last three days in villages and two at the most in cities. After the burial, mourners are invited to the funeral repast at the home of the deceased if it is in the countryside or possibly to a restaurant if it is in the city.

Before eating, a toast is given in memory of the deceased; wine or brandy is the chosen beverage. Usually the meal begins with assorted appetizers, similar to the Russian *zakuska* table. Breads, such as *saldskabmaize* (recipe page 299), and rolls, *ūdens kliņģeri* (recipe page 298), are also served. If a pig is prepared, it is accompanied by many side dishes, including *kugelis* (recipe page 303).

Beets and potatoes are probably the most important vegetables in Eastern European cooking. In Estonia, no meal would be complete if it didn't have more than one potato or beet dish on the table. *Rossol'ye*, a hearty appetizer salad (recipe follows), is an Estonian specialty.

⚘ *Rossol'ye* (Potato Salad)

Yield: serves 8 to 10

2 cups sour cream

1 tablespoon prepared horseradish

2 tablespoons prepared mustard

2 teaspoons sugar

salt and pepper to taste

1 cup canned pickled **beets**, drained, chopped

2 apples, peeled, **cored**, **cubed**

6 new potatoes, boiled, peeled, cubed

2 Polish or kosher dill pickles, drained, cubed (available at all supermarkets)

½ cup drained pickled **herring**, cut into bite-size pieces (available in refrigerated section of most supermarkets)

½ pound lean cooked beef or ham, chopped

For **garnish**:

8 lettuce leaves

4 hard-cooked eggs, peeled, chopped

Equipment: Medium mixing bowl with cover, mixing spoon, large mixing bowl, salad tools, plastic food wrap, large salad bowl, small serving bowl

1. Prepare dressing: Put sour cream into medium mixing bowl. Add horseradish, mustard, and sugar, and stir. Add salt and pepper to taste. Stir, cover, and refrigerate.

2. In large mixing bowl, combine chopped pickled beets, apples, potatoes, pickles, herring, and beef or ham. Toss carefully with salad tools. Cover with plastic wrap, and refrigerate until ready to serve.

3. At serving time: Line large salad bowl with lettuce leaves. Uncover salad mixture, and pour over half of the prepared sour cream dressing. Using salad tools, toss to mix. Transfer to prepared salad bowl. Sprinkle with chopped hard-cooked eggs, for garnish.

Serve remaining sour cream dressing in a separate small serving bowl to spoon over. Serve rossol'ye *as a first course on the appetizer table. Rossol'ye is eaten with bread and butter.*

Many life-cycle feasts end with *pannkoogid*, a plate-size pancake eaten for dessert.

❦ *Pannkoogid* (Dessert Pancakes with Fruit Marmalade)

Yield: serves 6

3 eggs, well beaten	2 teaspoons vanilla extract, divided
1½ cups milk	2 tablespoons melted butter or margarine
1 cup all-purpose **flour**	butter or margarine, as needed for frying
½ teaspoon salt	
For serving:	confectioners' sugar to taste
1 cup sour cream	2 cups raspberry, blueberry, or lingonberry marmalade

Equipment: Large mixing bowl or electric **blender**, whisk or mixing spoon, plastic food wrap, kitchen towel, work surface, **heavy-bottomed** nonstick 8- or 9-inch skillet, baking sheet, oven mitts, small bowl, small serving bowl

1. In large mixing bowl or electric blender, combine eggs and milk. Add flour, salt, 1 teaspoon vanilla extract, and melted butter or margarine. **Blend** or beat 1 to 2 minutes, until smooth. Cover with plastic wrap, and refrigerate for 1 to 2 hours. (The batter will be thin.)

Preheat oven to warm.

2. Prepare to fry: Spread a kitchen towel out on work surface. Melt 1 tablespoon butter or margarine in heavy-bottomed nonstick 8- or 9-inch skillet over medium-high heat, and swirl in pan to coat. Remove from heat, and pour in ½ cup batter, tilting pan to spread evenly over bottom. Return to heat, and fry 2 to 3 minutes, until golden brown and dull on top. Remove from heat and flip onto kitchen towel. Return pancake, bottom-side up, to skillet, and fry second side for about 1 minute. Transfer pancakes to baking sheet, and keep in warm oven until ready to serve. Repeat making pancakes, using all the batter. Add butter or margarine, 1 tablespoon at a time, to recoat pan, as needed.

3. In small bowl, mix sour cream with remaining 1 teaspoon vanilla extract and confectioners' sugar to taste.

Serve each pancake flat on the guest's dinner plate. Put marmalade in small serving dish. Eat the pancake by putting a spoonful of marmalade on the surface, folding over, and cutting into bite-size pieces. Add a dollop of sweetened sour cream.

Latvia

Latvia, traditionally known as the "workshop of the Baltic," is the middle country of the Baltics. The majority of Latvians belong to the Lutheran Church, although a large Roman Catholic population resides in the country. People of both religions follow the life-cycle traditions of their respective churches. (See Protestant and Catholic Life-Cycle Rituals, page lxxiii.) Latvians, or Letts as they are called, represent only about half of the population; Russians, Belarusians, Ukrainians, and Poles make up the rest.

In Latvia, for weddings, baptisms, name day celebrations, or funeral meals, most people set the food out and let people help themselves buffet-style. In Eastern Europe, people in neighboring countries share many of the same recipes, all adding their own special touches or ingredients. For example, sometimes a dish will be called "Russian-style," "Minsk-style," or "Romanian-style." Such dishes as Belarus-style *kolbasa z kapustov* (recipe page 450) and Ukraine-style *zulynez gribnoy* (recipe page 515) have crossed borders. The Lithuanian jellied pork called *košeliena* or *šaltiena* appears on Latvian buffet tables as *galerts*. To complete the bountiful buffet, plenty of bread is prepared; *ūdens kliņģeri* and *saldskabmaize* (recipe follows) are among the assortment.

¿ *Ūdens Kliņģeri [Kliņģeri]* (Pretzel Rolls)

Yield: 10 or 12 pieces

1½ cups **lukewarm** water	3 tablespoons salt, divided
3 teaspoons dark brown sugar, divided	4 cups all-purpose **flour**
1 package active dry **yeast**	½ cup **cornmeal**, for baking

Equipment: Large mixing bowl, mixing spoon, kitchen towel, lightly floured work surface, knife, wax paper, greased baking sheet, metal spatula, large saucepan, slotted spoon, wire cake rack, oven mitts

1. Pour lukewarm water into large mixing bowl. Stir in 1½ teaspoons dark brown sugar and sprinkle with yeast. Let set until bubbly, 5 to 10 minutes. Stir in remaining 1½ teaspoons sugar and 1 tablespoon salt. Gradually add flour, 1 cup at a time, and use your hands to mix dough until flour is well incorporated.

2. **Knead** dough in the bowl until smooth, about 5 to 7 minutes. The dough should be shiny. Cover with towel, and set in warm place to rise to double in bulk, about 1 hour.

3. Transfer dough to lightly floured work surface, and divide into 10 or 12 equal pieces.

4. Form into pretzel-shaped rolls: Place piece of wax paper on work surface. Between the palms of your hands, roll a piece of dough into a thin rope about 8 inches long. Loop ends over each other to make into a pretzel-shape. To keep pretzel from coming apart, dampen ends with water and pinch them in place. Place on wax paper, and repeat making pretzel-shaped rolls. Leave them set until they begin to rise, about 10 minutes.

Preheat oven to 425°F.

Lightly sprinkle cornmeal on greased baking sheet.

5. Fill large saucepan ⅔ full with water. Add remaining 2 teaspoons salt, and bring to boil over high heat. Carefully add rolls, a few at a time, and boil on one side for 2 minutes. Turn over, and boil on second side for 1½ minutes. They should become firm and puff up. Carefully

remove with slotted spoon, and drain on wire cake rack for 1 minute. Place on prepared baking sheet.

6. Bake in oven for 12 minutes. Using oven mitts, remove pan from oven. Using metal spatula, turn rolls over, return to oven, and bake 7 to 10 minutes more, until golden brown. Transfer to wire cake rack to cool.

Serve with soup or appetizers at the life-cycle celebration. Mothers often hang an ūdens kliņģeri *on a string, and use it for their baby's teething ring.*

Breads prepared for Catholic life-cycle celebrations are always blessed by the priest. Baking breads and cakes is an important part of wedding preparation rituals in all Eastern European countries.

¿ *Saldskabmaize* (Sweet-sour Bread)

Note: This recipe takes 10 to 12 hours.

Yield: 1 loaf

4 cups **sifted** all-purpose **flour**, divided

1¼ cups warm water (about 200°F)

1 package active dry **yeast**

1 teaspoon sugar

3 tablespoons **lukewarm** milk

1 teaspoon salt

2 to 3 teaspoons caraway seeds

Equipment: Large metal mixing bowl, kitchen towel, wooden mixing spoon, electric mixer (optional), cup, small spoon, floured work surface, plastic food wrap, greased baking sheet, small spray bottle, oven mitts

1. Rinse large metal mixing bowl under hot water to warm, and wipe dry with towel. Put 2 cups flour into warm bowl, and gradually stir in the warm water. Cover with towel, and let stand 10 minutes.

2. Using wooden spoon or electric mixer, beat flour mixture for 3 to 5 minutes, until cooled to room temperature. Cover with towel, and leave in a warm place overnight or for 10 to 12 hours for flavor to develop.

3. In cup, sprinkle yeast and sugar over lukewarm milk. Stir and set aside in warm place for 5 to 10 minutes until **frothy**.

4. Using a wooden spoon, stir yeast mixture into flour mixture. Add remaining 2 cups flour, salt, and caraway seeds. Using your hands, mix well. Transfer to floured work surface and **knead**, sprinkling flour on work surface and your hands, until dough is no longer sticky. Clean and grease large mixing bowl or use new large mixing bowl. Form dough into a ball, and place in greased large mixing bowl. Turn dough to grease all sides. Cover with plastic wrap, and leave in warm place to rise to double in bulk, 1 to 1½ hours.

Preheat oven to 400°F.

5. Transfer dough to lightly floured work surface, **punch down** and knead until smooth and **elastic**, 5 to 10 minutes. Shape into rectangular loaf about 10 inches long. Place on greased baking sheet, and, using a spray bottle filled with cold water, lightly spray air around the loaf, but not directly on the loaf.

6. Bake in oven for 45 minutes to 1 hour, until golden brown and sounds hollow when tapped on the bottom. Test **bread doneness**.

To serve, break into chunks. Throughout most of Eastern Europe, it is considered bad luck to cut bread with a knife at weddings. The superstition holds that to cut the wedding loaf is to sever the marriage.

Lithuania

Lithuania, the most westerly Baltic republic, is also the largest in area and population. Most Lithuanians live in urban areas, and the majority belong to the Roman Catholic Church. All life-cycle celebrations center on the Church. (See Protestant and Catholic Life-Cycle Rituals, page lxxiii.)

Most Lithuanian children are baptized, and then they have their first communion around age 12, followed by confirmation at age 14 or 15, according to Church doctrine. Names can be chosen from the Lithuanian Name Day Calendar, which lists as many as four to five names for each day. The names come from varied sources: Lithuanian mythology (the names of ancient gods and goddesses, for example), Lithuanian and general European history (war heroes, kings, queens), classical literature, and a few made-up names that expressed the parents' wishes for their child, such as "Hope of the Nation" (*Viltautas*). Nevertheless, the custom of celebrating name days is not really prevalent. Birthdays may be celebrated with a party, and friends and family give the celebrant a present. At work, colleagues may greet a celebrating co-worker on the working day nearest his or her birthday.

Secular life-cycle celebrations include the first day of the first (at age 7) and last years (at age 18) of school, at which parents' participation is important. The final year of secondary school features a very important celebration, *Šimtadienis*, which marks 100 days before the final exams. *Šimtadienis* is a significant tradition celebrated throughout the country and is an important rite of passage for young people. The custom is for 11th-grade students and staff to take charge of organizing the event for the graduating class. For the students, this is their first opportunity to shoulder responsibility for a major event. There is usually a varied program, including speeches and presentations from the staff as well as from the students, with musical performances and literary and sometimes dramatic contributions as well. In the evening *Šimtadienis* is capped by a party at a hired venue for the graduating class, with no parents or teachers invited. Students usually get dressed up, and, for many, this is their first time to wear formal clothes, wear high heels and makeup (for the girls), ties (for the boys), and to drink alcohol. The party features food, of course, as well as music and dancing, and usually ends close to, if not at dawn.

Many of the old wedding traditions are being revived, although they are somewhat modified or simplified. Years ago, every wedding began with a matchmaker responsible for getting the families together. After the match was set, the families would get together to discuss the dowry. For the dowry, parents provided daughters with one or more chests made of wood from trees inhabited by storks in the belief they would bring good luck and lots of babies. The chests became known as "hope chests"; girls kept jewelry, letters, money, clothing for her future first-born, candles, medicinal herbs and linens, blankets, and personal clothing she made for married life. The number, size, and beauty of her dowry chests were the indication of the bride's wealth, taste, and qualities as a future wife and mother.

When dowry carriers came to take the chests away to the groom's home, relatives of the bride sat on them and pretended they were unwilling to give them away. To make it look like the bride had more possessions, stones were sometimes put inside the chests to make them heavier.

Today, weddings are simpler, but many of the traditions have survived in modified form. Dowries are mostly symbolic, and the ritual of sending dowry carriers adds to the merriment of the wedding celebration. Weddings used to be four days long, but now two days is the customary length.

On the morning of the wedding day, the bride says good-bye to her parents and siblings. After the ceremony in the church or registrar's office (for non-Catholics), it is customary for the matchmaker, if one was used, and bridegroom's friends to drive the wedding car. From the back seat, the newlyweds throw candy to children along the way. Somewhere on the car route, friends and relatives of the bride often block the road with a rope of flowers. Those in the car have to buy their passage with candy and bottles of brandy or wine.

When the wedding party arrives at the home of the bride's parents, the newlyweds are greeted at the threshold with a loaf of bread sprinkled with salt and wine glasses of pure water, symbols for a rich full life and good fortune.

✿ *Svočios Karvojus* (Wedding Cake)

This wedding cake, also called *karvojus* for short, has a significant role during the wedding ceremony. A piece of it is given to guests to take home after the wedding feast. Although it is called "cake," it is more of a very rich yeast round loaf. It is simply decorated with a dough braid all along the bottom, baked at the same time as the loaf. Stems of rue and flowers, as well as baked dough stars and birds, are inserted into mounded circles on top of the loaf.

Dough:

1½ cups milk

4 tablespoons fresh **yeast**

2 cups sugar

3 pounds flour

10 **egg yolks**

2 cups butter

1 teaspoon salt

3 cups raisins

3 teaspoons vanilla extract

oil or butter, for greasing

Decor:

2 cups flour

⅔ cup water

Icing:

1 cup milk

3 cups powdered sugar

Equipment: Large mixing bowls, electric mixer with dough paddle attachment, **pastry brush**, oven mitts

1. Prepare dough: In a large bowl, put warm milk, and add yeast combined with half of the sugar and 1 pound flour. **Blend** well, and let rest in a warm place until risen.

2. In a large mixer bowl, with mixer at medium speed, beat egg yolks until lemon-colored and fluffy. Mix in melted butter.

3. Detach beater whisk and attach dough paddle or hook. At low speed, mix the 2 pounds of flour and salt, and the yeast mixture until all comes together into a dough.

4. Remove dough from the mixer, and, with floured hands, knead on a lightly floured work surface until small blisters form.

5. Add raisins, continuing to knead them in until well combined.

6. Place dough into a well greased large bowl, turn it all so that all surfaces are greased.

   Cover with a clean kitchen towel or plastic wrap, and let rise in a warm place until doubled in volume, about 1 to 2 hours.

7. Take ⅔ of the dough, shape into a round bun, and place on a greased and floured baking sheet. Divide remaining dough into three, and roll out into cylinders long enough to go around the bottom of the round bun.

8. Make a three-strand braid. Lightly brush surface of the braid and the bottom of the bun with water, and affix the braid.

9. At the very top center (summit) of the bun, take a floured glass rim, and press into the dough rather deeply, about 1 to 1½ inches deep, to create a circle. Surrounding the summit, make more circles all around the surface of the bun. These circles will become mounds for inserting decorations.

10. Insert lengths of disposable chopsticks or other ovenproof sticks of similar size in the middle of the circles. (Once the bun is baked, the decorations, fresh flowers, and fresh rue will be inserted into the cavities thus formed or directly on the sticks.)

11. Set the baking sheet with the braid-decorated bun in a warm place to rise for another 45 minutes to 1 hour.

12. Bake in the bottom rack of a preheated 400°F oven for about 1 hour, or until the loaf is golden brown and sounds hollow when tapped underneath. Allow to cool thoroughly.

13. Prepare the decorations. In a bowl, place the flour, and gradually add water to make a stiff dough. You may not need all the water, so add it gradually.

14. Knead until smooth and pliable, then roll out on a lightly floured work surface to ½ -inch thickness.

15. Cut out with cookie cutters, or shape with your fingers: stars, crescent moons, birds, flowers, according to your fancy. Place on a greased baking sheet and bake in a preheated 300°F oven for 15 to 20 minutes, or until just golden. Allow to cool, then brush with icing.

16. While waiting for the decorations to cool, prepare the icing. In a bowl, place the icing sugar; gradually whisk in milk to make icing with the consistency of light cream. You may not need all the milk, so gradually add it in.

17. Brush loaf with the icing, leaving the sticks in place. Remove the sticks once icing has set. Brush baked decorations with icing.

18. In the cavities made by the sticks or on the sticks themselves, insert the baked dough decorations such as stars, half moons, and birds.

19. Just prior to the wedding feast, set the decorated bun on a serving platter, and insert stems of fresh rue and flowers in several cavities on the bun.

Roast whole suckling pig (recipe page 243) is the preferred meat for a Lithuanian wedding celebration. If it's more than the family can afford, stuffed cabbage (recipe page 474), assorted soups and stews, and vegetable dishes, such as this well-loved *kugelis* (a dish adopted from German cuisine), are served for all celebration meals.

⚲ *Kugelis* (Potato Pudding)

Yield: serves 8 to 10

8 slices bacon, **finely chopped**	5 ounces canned evaporated milk
8 **potatoes** for grating	6 eggs, beaten
1 onion, peeled	salt and pepper to taste

Equipment: Medium skillet, mixing spoon, food processor fitted with **grater** attachment or hand grater, rubber spatula, large mixing bowl, well buttered 9×13×2-inch baking pan, oven mitts, knife

Preheat oven to 425°F.

1. Fry chopped bacon in medium skillet over medium-high heat. Stir and fry until crisp, 3 to 5 minutes. Remove from heat.

2. Using food processor with grater attachment or hand grater, grate potatoes and onion. Drain off and discard excess liquid from potato mixture, and transfer to large mixing bowl. Add fried bacon with pan drippings, milk, eggs, and salt and pepper to taste. Beat to mix well. Transfer to well buttered baking pan, and spread smooth.

   Note: While processing, turn machine off once or twice, and scrape down sides of container with rubber spatula.

3. Bake in oven 30 minutes. Reduce heat to 375°F, and cook for 30 to 40 minutes more, or until pudding is set and top is golden brown

Serve from baking pan while still warm, and cut into serving-size pieces.

⚘ Košeliena or Šaltiena (Jellied Pork)

A favorite dish of Lithuanians is jellied pork, which they call either *košeliena* or *šaltiena*. It is served at almost all celebration feasts. The same dish is called *"galerts"* in Latvia.

Yield: about 10 to 12 servings

3 pounds pork hock or knuckle (halved or quartered)

1 pound chicken legs

1 tablespoon coarse (kosher) salt

10 to 52 peppercorns

3 bay leaves

3 stalks celery, cut in half

3 carrots, peeled and cut in half crosswise

2 large onions, peeled and left whole

1 cup parsley, finely chopped

1 cup spring onions, sliced finely crosswise

ground white pepper

1 tablespoon (or more to taste) vinegar (optional)

For **garnish**: 2 hard-cooked eggs, sliced

Equipment: Large stockpot, strainer or sieve, serving dishes, oven mitts

1. Clean the pig's hock/knuckle and chicken legs thoroughly; singe them if there are any remaining hairs. Rinse well and place in stockpot, fully covered with cold water, and bring to a boil. Boil for 5 minutes, then pour off the water, and rinse everything well.

2. Clean the stockpot, add the pork hock and chicken legs, and add cold water to cover. Bring to a boil, and assiduously remove all scum that rises. This will help keep the broth and resulting aspic clear. Add salt, peppercorns, bay leaves, celery, carrots, and onions.

3. Simmer gently for 4 hours, or until the meat is tender. Take out chicken after 1 hour, and reserve.

4. Pass stock through a sieve, and, once it has cooled down, refrigerate it. The stock will jell.

   Remove the layer of fat from the surface of the jellied stock. Be sure to remove all traces of fat, as this will cloud the aspic. The peppercorns, bay leaves, celery, onions, and most of the carrots can be discarded. If you wish, keep a carrot piece or two for garnish. Remove and discard the bones.

5. Dice, as neatly as you can, the pork and chicken meat and skin. Discard any fatty bits. Dice one or two carrot pieces and mix in. Alternatively, slice the carrot/s into thin disks and reserve.

   Add parsley, and mix everything gently so as not to squash the carrots.

6. Lay at the bottom of 3 or 4 shallow bowls, or one shallow serving dish, some carrot disks (if using), spring onions, and egg slices. Distribute the diced meat and skin among the bowls or serving dish. Refrigerate until ready to be filled with stock.

7. Bring degreased stock to a boil, and continue cooking until it has boiled down to about 2 to 3 cups. Taste, and add salt and pepper if needed. Add vinegar to sharpen the flavor, if you wish.

8. Ladle stock over the meat mixture. Refrigerate overnight until the aspic (jellied stock) is set.

   Cut into neat squares or wedges, and serve with lemon slices, horseradish, and a splash of vinegar or mustard.

To serve, dark Lithuanian rye bread spread with butter goes very well with this.

Bread is an indispensable part of every meal, and Lithuanians have hundreds of bread recipes. *Bulvinis ragaisis* is a favorite that is taken to the church to be blessed by the priest on many life-cycle occasions.

⚘ *Bulvinis Ragaisis* (Potato Bread)

Yield: 1 loaf

¼ cup **lukewarm** water	3 to 3½ cups all-purpose **flour**
1 package active dry **yeast**	2 teaspoons salt
½ teaspoon sugar	1 egg, beaten
¾ cup lukewarm milk	2 tablespoons sour cream
1 medium baking **potato**, peeled and grated	For **garnish: egg wash**

Equipment: 2 small bowls, wooden mixing spoon, large mixing bowl, kitchen towel, lightly floured work surface, buttered 9×5×3-inch loaf pan, **pastry brush**, oven mitts, wire cake rack, napkin-lined breadbasket

1. In first small bowl, sprinkle lukewarm water with yeast and sugar. Stir, let stand 5 to 10 minutes, until bubbly and doubled in volume. Pour milk into second small bowl, and stir in grated potato.

2. In large mixing bowl, stir to combine 3 cups flour and salt. Make a well (hole) in the center, and pour in yeast mixture and potato mixture. Stir to mix well. Stir in egg and sour cream until well mixed. Using mixing spoon, beat flour with liquid until dough forms into a ball, 3 to 5 minutes. Transfer to lightly floured work surface, and **knead**, adding up to ½ cup more flour if necessary to make a smooth, nonsticky dough. Clean and grease large mixing bowl,

place the dough in, and turn to coat all sides. Cover with towel, and let rise in warm place until double in bulk, 1 to 1½ hours.

3. Gently **punch down** dough to release air, and put in buttered loaf pan. Cover with towel and set in warm place to rise to double in bulk again, about 1 hour.

Preheat oven to 375°F.

4. Using pastry brush, brush loaf with egg wash, and bake in oven for 35 to 40 minutes, or until loaf has a hollow sound when tapped on the bottom. Test bread for **doneness**. Flip loaf onto wire cake rack to cool.

Serve in napkin-lined breadbasket with other breads and rolls.

৬ *Kolacky* (Filled Cream Cheese and Butter Cookies)

Kolacky cookies are made throughout Lithuania, Poland, and neighboring countries for festive occasions. They often make an appearance at a wedding cookie table. The traditional filling is poppy seed (recipe follows). They may be filled with apricot (recipe follows) as well.

Yield: 30 to 32 cookies

2 cups flour, plus more for rolling out dough	¾ cup cream cheese
½ tsp salt	1 teaspoon vanilla extract
1 cup butter	icing sugar, for sprinkling (optional)

Equipment: Mixing bowls, electric mixer, rolling pin, parchment paper, cookie sheet, oven mitts, medium saucepan, wooden spoon, food processor

1. Prepare the cookie dough: Combine the flour and salt in a bowl, and set aside.

2. In a larger bowl or the bowl of an electric mixer, cream the butter and cream cheese with vanilla extract until smooth and fluffy. Stir in the flour, and knead into a smooth dough.

   Wrap in plastic wrap, and chill several hours, preferably overnight. While the dough is chilling, prepare the fillings.

3. Prepare the poppy seed filling (recipe follows). 4. Prepare the apricot filling.

4. Assemble the cookies: Roll out the chilled dough on a lightly floured surface into a rectangle ¼ inch thick.

5. Cut out cookies with a 2-inch round cookie cutter.

6. Place on a parchment paper–lined cookie sheet, and create a cavity in each one with your thumb or teaspoon.

7. Fill the cavities with a teaspoonful of filling, either poppy seed or apricot. Bake the filled cookies in a preheated 350°F for 15 to 20 minutes, or until pale golden.

8. Holding the parchment paper edges, transfer the cookies to a cake rack to cool.

   Sprinkle with icing sugar, if desired.

Store in an airtight tin.

❦ *Poppy Seed Filling*

Yield: enough to fill 30 cookies

1 cup finely ground poppy seeds

½ cup honey

¾ cup milk

1 tablespoon lemon juice

¼ cup sugar

¼ teaspoon salt

1 teaspoon vanilla extract

Equipment: Medium saucepan, wooden spoon

1. Place poppy seeds in a medium saucepan, and add the honey, milk, lemon juice, sugar, and salt.

2. Over medium heat, bring to a boil, then reduce heat and simmer, stirring continuously for 15 to 20 minutes, or until thickened. It is done when a wooden spoon dragged through the mixture leaves a trail at the bottom of the pan. Allow to cool, then stir in vanilla.

Use as directed for kolacky *cookies (recipe precedes). This filling can be made up to two days ahead. Store covered in the refrigerator until needed.*

❦ *Apricot Filling*

Yield: enough to fill 30 cookies

1 cup dried apricots, rinsed

1½ cups water

⅓ cup sugar, or ¼ cup honey plus 2 tablespoons sugar

1 tablespoon lemon juice

1 tablespoon butter

Equipment: Electric mixer, medium saucepan, food processor, wooden spoon

1. Put the apricots in a saucepan, and cover with water.

   Heat to boiling over medium heat, and let stand until well plumped. Let cool.

2. Purée apricots in a food processor.

3. Place the apricot purée and lemon juice in a saucepan, add sugar, and allow to simmer for 15 to 20 minutes, or until thickened. It is done when a wooden spoon dragged through the mixture leaves a trail at the bottom of the pan. Allow to cool, then stir in butter.

Use as directed for kolacky *cookies (recipe precedes).*

Scandinavia

Scandinavia is a region of northern Europe that includes the countries of Norway, Sweden, Denmark, Finland, and the island country of Iceland. It is a cold area with long, dark winters and short summers. Most Scandinavians have the same or similar life-cycle celebrations because the majority of the people belong to the Lutheran Church. (See Protestant and Catholic Life-Cycle Rituals, page lxxiii.)

Over time, rituals, customs, and foods have crossed the borders of Scandinavia. While the customs and foods are similar throughout these countries, each country has its own names for these things. For example, a popular cake the Norwegians call "*kransekake*" is called "*kransekage*" (recipe page 309) by the Danes and "*kranskaka*" by the Swedes. The name means "wreath cake," and it is a pyramid of baked cookie rings, each layer a little smaller than the previous one. This festive pastry is drizzled with butter icing (*smjörkrem*) (recipe page 324) and decorated with miniature trinkets, flags, flowers, or greenery appropriate to the celebration—weddings, anniversaries, landmark birthdays, and even national holidays.

Although the recipe for this wreath cake is similar throughout Scandinavia, each country has its own traditions for serving it. When it is made for a wedding in Finland, for example, a bottle of champagne is placed in the center of a large round serving tray, and the baked rings are stacked to completely cover the bottle. The cake is eaten by breaking off the rings and serving pieces to guests. When the champagne bottle is exposed, it is opened, and everyone drinks a toast to the bride and groom.

The Scandinavians use a special set of pans to make the *kransekage*. The pans consist of ring-shaped grooves in graduating sizes. The pans are available at kitchenware and bakery supply stores, but they are a little expensive. The following instructions for the preparation of the **cake boards** can be used instead of purchasing the special pans needed for making the cookie rings used in *kransekage*.

Cardboard cake boards cut into circles are called **cake circles,** and they can be used for making the 18 cookie rings for the *kransekage*. The rings range in size from 12 inches in diameter for the bottom cookie to 3½ inches at the top. The cake circles are available at most craft and hobby shops and kitchenware and bakery supply stores in packages of 12 (either 12, 10, 8, or 6 inches).

ℰ *Cake Circles for Kransekage*

Equipment: Eighteen 12-inch **cake circles**, a compass with a pencil, scissors or a sharp pallet knife, dark permanent marker, heavy-duty aluminum foil

1. Using the compass and pencil, mark off the boards that need to be trimmed smaller. Each board will be ½-inch smaller than the last. As you are measuring each cake board, using marker, write the number of each cake circle in the center of the board, with the size of each board under the number. The sizes of the boards are as follows: #1 (12 inches), #2 (11½ inches), #3 (11 inches), #4 (10½ inches), #5 (10 inches), #6 (9½ inches), #7 (9 inches), #8 (8½ inches), #9 (8 inches), #10 (7½ inches), #11 (7 inches), #12 (6½ inches), #13 (6 inches), #14 (5½ inches), #15 (5 inches), #16 (4½ inches), #17 (4 inches), and #18 (3½ inches). Stack the boards in numerical order.

2. Cut the cake boards to size, using the scissors or pallet knife. Keep the boards in numerical order.

3. Cover the unnumbered side of the boards with foil, leaving the numbers visible on the other side. Directions to cover the board with foil are in the glossary under cake boards (cake circles). Keep the boards stacked in numerical order, and begin making the *kransekage*.

If you are using a standard-size food processor, you will need to process this dough recipe in two batches to make an 18-layer *kransekage*.

Ɛ̌ *Kransekage* (also *Kransekake* or *Kranskaka*) (Wreath Cake; Scandinavian Wedding Cake)

Yield: serves 25 to 35

1 pound (2 cups) unsalted butter, at room temperature

2 cups confectioners' sugar, **sifted**

2 cups (16 ounces) **almond paste**

2 whole eggs

2 egg yolks

2 teaspoons almond extract

5 cups all-purpose **flour, sifted**

nonstick cooking spray

For assembling: *butter icing*
   (recipe page 324)

Equipment: Food processor, rubber spatula, mixing spoon, medium mixing bowl, plastic wrap, 18 prepared **cake circles** (instructions precede), lightly floured work surface, wide spatula, 2 baking sheets, oven mitts, wire cake rack, large tray or serving platter with at least a 14-inch flat surface, **pastry bag** with fine writing tip

1. Put 1 cup butter and 1 cup confectioners' sugar in food processor, and process until creamy and well mixed, 30 seconds. Continue to process on medium speed. Break 1 cup almond paste into small pieces, and add through the feed tube a few pieces at a time. Process until mixture is smooth. Add 1 egg, 1 egg yolk, and 1 teaspoon almond extract. Process until well mixed. Add 2½ cups flour, a little at a time, and process until thoroughly mixed, 3 to 4 minutes. Do not overprocess.

Note: While processing, turn machine off once or twice, and scrape down sides of container with rubber spatula.

2. Transfer dough to medium mixing bowl. If dough seems too soft to roll between the palms of your hands, cover with plastic wrap and refrigerate for about 1 hour to firm up.

3. Cover cake boards: Lightly coat foil side of 1 cake board with nonstick cooking spray. Work only with the amount of dough you can easily handle at one time. Using your hands, roll it into a 1-inch thick rope on lightly floured work surface. Place the rope along the outer edge of the foil-covered board. Continue making short lengths of rope, and join them together into a smooth ring inside the outer ring. Using your hand or wide spatula, press gently to flatten the dough to about ¼ inch thick, tapering down at the edge so dough does not hang over the edge of the cake board. (The inside edge of the cookie rings can be uneven because

they will not show.) Continue covering the remaining cake boards with dough rings. As each board is finished, lightly cover with plastic wrap and refrigerate until ready to bake.

Preheat oven to 350°F.

4. Prepare to bake: Remove cake boards from refrigerator as needed. Arrange covered cake boards about 1 inch apart on baking sheets. Only remove the cake boards being used, and keep the others refrigerated.

Note: If using the kransekage *pans, directions come with the pans, or use the following directions. Coat pans with nonstick cooking spray. Spoon dough into a large pastry bag fitted with a plain ½-inch tip. (Don't use a larger tip, or the cookie rings may expand too much.) Pipe dough out in a long rope into the ring-shaped grooves of the pans. Press rope ends or any breaks in the dough together to form smooth, unbroken rings.*

5. Bake cookie-covered cake boards in batches in oven until lightly golden, 30 to 40 minutes. Remove from baking sheets and place on wire cake rack to cool, about 30 minutes. With cookie rings still on cake boards, carefully flip cookie onto wire cake rack to set, 1 hour. Wrap in plastic wrap, and refrigerate for at least 4 hours or overnight to firm up. Do not remove the boards until ready to assemble. The numbers on the back of the cake boards make it easy to stack in proper order.

6. Prepare butter icing.

7. To assemble: Beginning with cake board #1, transfer cake board to tray or serving platter. Keeping the cookie ring attached to the cake board, dab the bottom side of the board with icing to make it stick to the tray or platter. Carefully remove the cookie ring from cake board #2, taking care not to break it. Turn the cookie ring over, and spread icing on the bottom to act as glue. Set ring #2 on top of ring #1. Repeat icing and stacking cookie rings in numbered sequence. If necessary, dab extra icing under a ring to keep the layers level. If any rings break, use a dab of icing to glue them back together as you stack them.

8. Decorate *kransekage*: Spoon icing in a pastry bag fitted with a fine writing tip. Make icing loops, dots, or any design you like. If icing seems too thick to pass through writing tip, add a little water to thin before filling pastry bag.

To serve, let the kransekage *stand for at least 1 hour, until the icing sets. Add the decorations of your choice. To assemble at a later date: Freeze individual rings, wrapped in plastic wrap or foil for up to one month. When ready to use, unwrap and thaw before assembling.*

Denmark

The country of Denmark, sharing a border with Germany on the south, consists of a peninsula and small island in the Baltic Sea. It is the smallest of the Scandinavian countries, and even though it lacks many natural resources, Denmark has a strong economy and industry. The Danes are admired worldwide for their education and science, craftsmanship and culture, industry and commerce.

Most Danes belong to the Lutheran Church and observe all life-cycle celebrations according to the Christian doctrine. (See Protestant and Catholic Life-Cycle Rituals, page lxxiii.) The christening of a newborn is an important day for most Danish families. Family, relatives, and friends come before the minister for the solemn ceremony of introducing the infant to the Lutheran faith. Traditionally, the infant wears a christening gown that has been in the family for many generations. Afterwards, a family dinner is served with a cake honoring the newly baptized child.

The Danes celebrate many life-cycle events with generous feasts, setting out platters, bowls, and trays of food. The Danish *smørrebrød* (literally, "bread and butter") is world famous. Open-faced sandwiches, made from a choice of hundreds of local delicacies, are prepared for the feast, along with *fyldt svinemørbrad* (recipe follows) and *frikadeller med citronsovs* (recipe page 312), assorted cheeses, fresh fruits, and marvelous puddings. If it is a wedding, the *kransekage* (recipe page 309) will be the centerpiece on the buffet table. Whatever the occasion, the Dane's favorite beverages are beer and fruit juices.

Throughout Scandinavia but particularly in Denmark, pork is served on special occasions. The Danes are very fond of combining dried fruits with meat, as is the case in the following recipe, *fyldt svinemørbrad*, a wonderful dish to serve at a christening dinner or a wedding banquet. In Sweden, a similar dish is called *fläskkarre*.

Fyldt Svinemørbrad (Danish Pork Tenderloins)

Yield: serves 6 to 8

2 pork loins (¾ to 1 pound each), **butterflied** by the butcher lengthwise

salt and pepper to taste

3 cooking apples, **finely chopped**

12 **pitted** prunes, soaked in 2 cups hot water for 1 hour and drained

2 cups water, more as needed

2 tablespoons all-purpose **flour**

Equipment: Work surface, kitchen string, knife, shallow roasting pan with rack, oven mitts, meat thermometer (optional), cutting board, aluminum foil, metal spatula, medium saucepan, measuring cup, small mixing bowl, small spoon, whisk, small serving bowl

Preheat oven to 325°F.

1. Place the loins, cut-side up, on work surface. Sprinkle with salt and pepper to taste. Place half of the chopped apples and 6 prunes down the center of each tenderloin. Roll up each loin, jelly-roll style, and tie with string to securely close. Place them side by side, seam-side down, on rack in shallow roasting pan. Pour 2 cups water into the bottom of the pan to catch the fat drippings. If necessary, to prevent drying out, add more water, 1 cup at a time, to keep the same 2-cup water level during the baking.

2. Bake in oven for 1½ to 1¾ hours, or until meat thermometer registers 160°F. Remove from oven, and transfer meat to cutting board. Cover with foil to keep warm until ready to serve.

3. Prepare gravy: Remove rack from roasting pan. Scrape up brown bits of pan drippings with metal spatula from the bottom of the roasting pan. Put pan drippings in measuring cup. There should be about 2 cups, if not add more water. Transfer drippings to medium saucepan. Bring to boil over medium-high heat. In small mixing bowl, stir together ¼ cup water with flour to make a smooth paste. Pour flour mixture into the pan drippings, and whisk until thickened, 3 to 5 minutes. Add salt and pepper to taste and cook 1 minute longer.

To serve, remove string and slice meat crosswise into 1- or 2-inch thick slices. Serve gravy in a small serving bowl, and spoon a little gravy over each serving.

A popular appetizer at a Danish wedding banquet is *frikadeller med citronsovs.*

✄ *Frikadeller med Citronsovs* (Danish Meatballs with Lemon Sauce)

Yield: 25 to 30 pieces

½ pound **ground** veal	½ cup water
½ pound ground lean pork	salt and pepper to taste
½ cup fine dry white **bread crumbs**	1 bay leaf
2 tablespoons grated onion	*citronsovs*, for serving (recipe follows)
½ cup light cream	

Equipment: Medium mixing bowl, wax paper, baking sheet, large shallow saucepan, slotted metal spoon, medium baking pan, serving bowl or **chafing dish**

1. Put veal, pork, bread crumbs, and grated onion in medium mixing bowl. Using your hands, mix well. Add light cream, water, and salt and pepper to taste. Continue to mix with your hands until mixture holds together and comes away from sides of bowl.

2. Form meatballs: Dampen your hands and roll about 1 tablespoon of mixture into a walnut-sized ball. Place on wax paper–covered baking sheet. Dampen your hands each time, and continue to make meatballs, using up all the meat mixture.

3. **Poach** meatballs: Fill large shallow saucepan with at least 2 inches of water. Add bay leaf and ½ teaspoon salt. Bring to boil over high heat. Reduce heat to **simmer**, and drop in a few meatballs at a time, don't crowd the pan. Poach meatballs for 4 to 5 minutes. Remove with slotted metal spoon and drain over the pan. Place in medium baking pan. Continue poaching all the meatballs.

4. The cooked meatballs can be served immediately or covered and refrigerated to be served later. To serve later, reheat meatballs in boiling water for 1 to 2 minutes, or place in the oven or microwave until heated through, 2 to 5 minutes.

To serve, transfer meatballs to a serving bowl or chafing dish, and pour citronsovs *(recipe follows) over them.*

Citronsovs can be used over fish or other meat dishes. This sauce is what makes *frikadeller* distinctly Danish, setting it apart from Sweden's *kjottboller* (meatballs).

⚜ *Citronsovs* (Danish Lemon Sauce)

Yield: about 2½ cups

2 tablespoons unsalted butter

2 tablespoons all-purpose **flour**

1½ cups chicken broth

½ cup light cream

juice of ½ lemon

salt and white pepper to taste

2 egg yolks

¼ cup heavy cream

Equipment: Medium saucepan, whisk, mixing spoon

1. Melt butter in medium saucepan over low heat. Whisk in flour to make a smooth paste. Increase heat to medium. Whisking constantly, slowly add chicken broth, then light cream. Continue whisking until mixture is smooth and glossy and the consistency of heavy cream. Stir in lemon juice and salt and white pepper to taste. Turn heat to low.

2. Stir egg yolks with heavy cream in cup until well mixed. Stir about ¼ cup butter mixture into egg mixture, to **temper**. Whisking butter mixture constantly, return egg mixture to the pan. Increase heat to medium, and whisk constantly until sauce thickens to consistency of heavy cream. Do not let it boil, or it will curdle and become inedible.

Use with frikadeller *(recipe precedes).*

Beets are a favorite vegetable in all Scandinavian countries. *Syltede rødbeder* is served as one of the little dishes on the *smørrebrød*.

⚜ *Syltede Rødbeder* (Danish Pickled Beets)

Note: This recipe takes 8 or more hours.

Yield: serves 4 to 6

14 ounces canned sliced **beets**, drained

¾ cup white or cider vinegar

½ cup water

2 to 3 tablespoons sugar

salt and pepper to taste

2 teaspoons caraway seed

Equipment: Medium bowl with cover, small saucepan, mixing spoon, serving dish

1. Put drained beets into medium bowl.

2. Prepare pickling juice: Put vinegar, water, and 2 tablespoons sugar into small saucepan. Bring to boil over high heat, and cook for 2 minutes. Taste to adjust the sweetness, adding the remaining 1 tablespoon sugar if necessary.

3. Pour pickling juice over beets. **Fold in** salt and pepper to taste and caraway seeds. Cool to room temperature. Cover and refrigerate for at least 8 hours.

To serve, drain beets, and transfer to serving dish. The beets can be kept covered and refrigerated for up to 2 weeks. Syltede rødbeder *is served cold.*

Finland

Situated in the northeastern tip of Europe, Finland is a land of pristine lakes (over 60,000) and thick forests of dark pine and silver birch. It is bordered by Sweden on the east, Norway on the north, Russia on the east, and the Gulf of Finland and the Baltic Sea on the south. Over 93 percent of the population are Finnish, about 5 percent are Swedish, and the remainder are comprised of Russians, Estonians, Roma (gypsy), and Sámi. Interestingly, despite Swedes comprising a mere 5 percent of the population, Swedish is an official language, that is, with the same standing as Finnish. This is due in part because of a long history of Swedish rule and also because a good amount of Finnish literature was and still is written in Swedish.

Much like the other Scandinavians, the majority of Finns belong to the Lutheran Church and follow the life-cycle traditions of the Church. (See Protestant and Catholic Life-Cycle Rituals, page lxxiii.) There is also a small group (1.1 percent of the population) of adherents of the Orthodox Christian faith. Although these events are similar to those celebrated in other Christian countries, the Finns add their own distinctive touches.

One of those touches involves weddings and the summer solstice, the longest day of year, on June 21. In Finland, the summer solstice is called Midsummer Day. Celebrations begin on Midsummer Eve and end on the eve of the Feast of St. John the Baptist, June 23. The customs and rituals attached to the three-day festival, especially when it comes to marriage, blend Christian symbolism with ancient pagan beliefs.

In Finland, more couples marry during the Midsummer celebration than at any other time of the year. On the morning of the wedding, it is the tradition for the bride and her girlfriends to congregate in the sauna. (Most Finnish homes have saunas, a steam or dry heat bath, usually in a room or cabinet.) A traditional custom was to cut the bride's hair very short in front of her friends, and everyone present would sob crocodile tears to show their sorrow. This haircut represented her loss as a single woman. After the haircut, the bride would put on the *tzepy*, the traditional headdress worn by married women. The *tzepy* is a close-fitting cap, with either a hard or soft crown, and it is trimmed with lace and embroidery. The traditional bridal sauna ritual has been modernized as part of a bachelorette party, with the sauna decorated with flowers and birch branches.

In Helsinki, thousands of people gather to watch a solemn ceremony in which a newly married couple, chosen to represent all the men and women married that day in

Finland, is rowed across the water to a small island. On the island, a huge tower has been built of fir trees and the hulls of old boats, and together the bride and groom set it ablaze. The tradition symbolizes hope for a bright future for all of the newlyweds and a request for eternal light and warmth from the sun.

During the Midsummer celebrations, eating, music, singing, dancing, swimming, and sitting in the sauna are all important elements of the festivities. Traditionally, Finns participate in a Midsummer sauna and then enjoy a lavish feast. The table is usually decorated with birch branches and flower garlands. The menu includes assorted herring and other fish dishes, cheeses, both smoked and fresh fish, shellfish and meats, wild mushrooms, assorted berries, and melon dishes. No Midsummer meal is complete unless there are assorted cakes such as *kermakakku* (recipe page 318) and breads, among them *pulla* (recipe page 316).

In addition to weddings and the Midsummer Day events, the birth of a child is an exciting event for Finns. When the mother and baby return home, friends and relatives come to visit, and they bring gifts for the infant and a covered dish or baked goods for the family.

One to three months after the baby's birth, a christening ceremony is held in the church, followed by a family celebration at home or in a restaurant. According to tradition, the infant will wear the christening dress that has been worn by other family members. This may include the baby's mother or father and siblings whose names are embroidered on the garment.

Together with the Swedes, Finns celebrate name day more frequently than other Scandinavian countries, such as Denmark or Norway. The Finnish name day calendar, unlike the Catholic name day calendar, does not list only Catholic saints' names. The Finnish name day calendar lists pre-Christian names, Catholic names, Swedish names, and also Russian names. In addition, contemporary names are added as well, and the criterion for inclusion is for 500 people to have been given the name. There are currently 848 names in the Finnish name day calendar. It continues to be a popular publication, with a press run of over 14 million calendars annually: quite impressive for a country with a population of just over 5.5 million. The calendar is revised every 5 years. Name day used to be celebrated with more pomp: A name day tree was set up by the celebrant with the expectation that family and friends would leave presents under it. A decorated pole was once erected in the yard as well. Nowadays, name day is celebrated with less fanfare with coffee and cake.

Besides the Finnish name day calendar, there is also a Swedish name day calendar, and the criterion for inclusion is for only 50 people to have the same name. The indigenous Sámi (Lapp) also have their own name day calendar, and the Orthodox Christian minority also have an Orthodox name day calendar with Orthodox saints' names. (Interestingly, there are as well official name day calendars for dogs, cats, and even horses.)

A contemporary trend among newly married Finnish couples is to choose a totally different surname from their previous ones to demonstrate their start of a new life and family. This was made possible by a law passed in the 1990s that allowed men and women to choose their own surname. However, about 80 percent of Finnish women have adopted their husband's family name or combine their maiden name and their husband's family name with a hyphen.

Another unique tradition the Finnish people have developed is a distinctive style of hospitality known as coffee table entertaining. For an occasion, such as a birthday, name day, anniversary, wedding, christening, and funeral, it is an old custom to serve guests seven items from the coffee table. The assortment always includes a bread, such as *pulla* (recipe follows), or if it's a name day party, it would be *hieno nimipäivärinkilä* (recipe page 317). Usually two cakes and four kinds of cookies round out the seven items. The Finnish people are great coffee drinkers, and with each piece of pastry, they have another cup of coffee.

Precise rules govern coffee table etiquette regarding what is eaten and in what order. A bread is eaten with the first cup of coffee. The second cup of coffee is sipped along with *kermakakku* (recipe page 318) and cookies. A rich and gooey cake is always eaten last along with the third cup of coffee.

⚶ *Pulla* (Cardamom Bread)

Yield: 2 loaves

1 package active dry **yeast**

¼ cup **lukewarm** water

1 cup canned evaporated milk

½ cup sugar, more as needed

½ teaspoon salt

½ teaspoon **ground** cardamom

2 eggs, slightly beaten

4 to 4½ cups all-purpose **flour**

¼ cup melted butter or margarine

For **garnish**:

egg wash (made with milk)

¼ cup sliced almonds

sugar, as needed

Equipment: Large mixing bowl, mixing spoon, kitchen towel, lightly floured work surface, greased baking sheet, **pastry brush**, oven mitts, wire cake rack, bread knife, serving platter or breadbasket

1. Dissolve yeast in lukewarm water in large mixing bowl. Stir in evaporated milk, ½ cup sugar, salt, cardamom, 2 eggs, and 2 cups flour. Beat in melted butter until mixture is smooth and glossy. Stir in enough of the remaining, 2 to 2½ cups flour, ½ cup at a time, to make dough easy to handle. Cover with towel, and let rest for 15 minutes.

2. Turn dough out onto lightly floured work surface. **Knead** until smooth and **elastic**, 8 to 10 minutes. Wash, dry, and grease large mixing bowl. Place dough in bowl, and turn to grease

all sides. Cover with kitchen towel, and let rise in warm place to double in bulk, about 1 hour. **Punch down** dough. Cover and let rise for the second time until double in bulk, about 1 hour. Dough is ready if impression remains when poked with your finger.

3. Divide dough in half. Divide each half into 3 parts. On lightly floured work surface, roll each part into a rope, 1 inch thick. Braid 3 ropes together to make straight loaf. Pinch ends of braided dough together, and fold the pinched ends under the braid. Repeat braiding with remaining three ropes. Place each braided loaf on lightly greased baking sheet. Cover with towel, and let rise to double in bulk, 30 to 45 minutes.

Preheat oven to 375°F.

4. Brush loaves with egg wash, and sprinkle with almonds and sugar to taste. Put breads in oven, and bake until lightly browned, 20 to 25 minutes. Test **bread doneness**. When done, cool on wire cake rack.

To serve, slice and place on platter or in breadbasket. Set on the coffee table. Munch on a slice of pulla *while sipping on the first robust cup of brew.*

Hieno nimipäivärinkilä is made with *pulla* dough (recipe precedes) and shaped into a ring instead of a braid. Cookies are usually stacked in the center of the ring, and birthday candles are poked around the top.

ᕯ *Hieno Nimipäivärinkilä* (Fancy Name Day Sweet Bread)

Yield: 1 large loaf

pulla dough (recipe precedes)

For **garnish:**   ½ cup chopped or sliced almonds

egg wash   12 sugar cubes

Equipment: Lightly greased large cookie sheet or lightly greased 12- to 16-inch pizza pan, **pastry brush**, small plastic resealable bag, hammer, oven mitts, wire cake rack, large serving tray, bread knife

1. Prepare *pulla* dough: Follow steps 1 to 3 of preceding recipe.

2. After *pulla* dough has risen the second time and an impression remains when poked with your finger, turn dough out onto lightly floured work surface. Form into a rope 24 to 27 inches long, and pinch the ends together to form into an oval or circular ring. Place on lightly greased cookie sheet or lightly greased 12- to 16-inch pizza pan. Let rise to double in bulk, 30 to 45 minutes.

Preheat oven to 400°F.

3. Using pastry brush, brush dough with egg wash, and sprinkle with sliced almonds. Put sugar cubes in small plastic bag. Coarsely crush the cubes by gently tapping the bag with a hammer. Sprinkle the crushed sugar over the bread.

4. Bake in oven for 20 to 25 minutes, or until lightly browned and sounds hollow when tapped on the bottom. Cool on wire cake rack before serving.

To serve, place the uncut bread ring on a large serving tray, and place on the coffee table. Provide a bread knife for slicing.

A Midsummer tradition, baking a "silent cake," is supposed to foretell the future. According to custom, several unmarried women get together to bake a cake without talking. They each take a small piece of the baked cake and sleep with it under their pillow to dream of the man in their future. The *kermakakku* (recipe follows), a popular name day and birthday cake, can easily be baked without speaking.

Kermakakku (Cream Pound Cake)

Yield: serves 12

1 cup heavy cream

2 eggs

1 teaspoon vanilla

1 ½ cups all-purpose **flour**

1 cup granulated sugar

2 teaspoons baking powder

½ teaspoon salt

For **garnish**: confectioners' sugar

Equipment: Large mixing bowl, electric mixer, rubber spatula, small bowl, **sifter**, medium mixing bowl, greased 9-cup **Bundt pan**, oven mitts, serving platter, cake knife

Chill large mixing bowl in freezer at least 1 hour.

Preheat oven to 350°F.

1. Pour heavy cream into chilled large mixing bowl and using electric mixer, beat until stiff peaks form, 3 to 5 minutes.

2. In small bowl, beat eggs and vanilla until light and fluffy. Using the rubber spatula, **fold in** egg mixture with whipped cream.

3. **Sift** flour, granulated sugar, and baking powder into medium mixing bowl. Using rubber spatula, **fold in** flour mixture with whipped cream mixture. Pour batter into greased Bundt pan.

4. Bake in oven until cake pulls away from sides of pan, 50 to 60 minutes. Cool in pan 10 minutes. Flip onto wire cake rack, and let cool completely.

To serve, set upright on serving platter, and sprinkle with confectioners' sugar. Cut into wedges at serving time.

Ankanrintaa Riista Kastikkeessa (Duck in Game Sauce)

Game such as elk, deer, and rabbit abound in Finnish forests and woodlands, as well as wild ducks in the numerous clear lakes. They are rarely to be found served in restaurants, however, being made and eaten mostly at home. Game is usually accompanied by the wild mushrooms and berries that are eagerly gathered in the forest undergrowth. The following recipe is typical of contemporary dishes created in Finland that showcase the high-quality products that are available, as well as the bountiful game and wild berries and fungi gathered from the wild. Cloudberry vodka and other wild berry–flavored vodkas are now being made by several Finnish companies. The subtle flavor of cloudberries with which the vodka is infused will add a distinct Finnish touch to the sauce. If not available, it is fine to use red wine. And, similarly, the cloudberry jelly, which may be difficult to obtain, can be substituted with rowan or red currant or crab apple jelly.

Yield: 4 servings

2 to 2½ pounds mallard breasts

½ teaspoon salt

8 black peppercorns, roughly crushed

12 juniper berries, roughly crushed

½ cup unsweetened (natural) apple juice

3 tablespoons butter

2 cups cleaned chanterelles, or other wild mushroom, such as porcini, sliced into bite-size pieces

½ cup cloudberry vodka or red wine

1½ cups thick cream

1 tablespoon flour

2 tablespoons cloudberry jelly, or rowan or red currant or crab apple jelly

1 teaspoon mustard

1 teaspoon (or more to taste) lemon juice

For **garnish**: 2 tablespoons parsley, chopped

Equipment: **Heavy-bottomed** skillet, small skillet with cover, whisk, warmed holding dish, aluminum foil, 4 warmed dinner plates, oven mitts

1. Make several small, shallow incisions all over the skin of the duck breasts. Rub the skin and flesh with salt, pepper, and juniper, making sure some of the seasoning gets inside the incisions.

   Let the duck breasts stand at room temperature for about 1 hour.

2. Place the duck breasts skin-side down on a cold heavy-bottomed skillet. Turn on the stove at low heat. Allow the duck breast to cook slowly and gently, pressing down on them from time to time so as to better render the fat.

3. Turn the breasts after about half of the fat has melted, and the skin is a beautiful golden brown and has become crisp.

4. Pour off the excess fat from the skillet. (The duck fat will keep well in a covered jar in the refrigerator and is good for cooking potatoes.)

5. Add the apple juice and turn up the heat to medium for 5 to 6 minutes.

6. Ideally, the breasts should still be quite pink, but cook them a bit further according to your personal preference. (Too long cooking will turn them dry and leathery, however.)

7. Remove the duck breasts from the pan, and transfer to a warmed holding dish, with a sheet of foil loosely tented over them to keep them warm.

8. Set aside the skillet with the juices from cooking the duck breasts. The juices will be needed again later.

9. In another, smaller skillet, melt the butter over medium heat. When the butter is hot, turn down the heat to low, add the mushrooms and let them cook gently, covered, for 20 minutes. (The slow cooking ensures that any microorganisms in the wild mushrooms are no longer harmful.) Turn off the heat.

10. Heat the cooking juices from the duck in the first skillet over medium heat.

11. Pour in the cloudberry vodka (or red wine, if using) to deglaze the pan, loosening all the bits at the bottom of the pan with a wooden spoon.

12. Whisk in the cream and the flour, then stir in the mushrooms, and lower the heat. Continue to stir the sauce until it is thoroughly heated. Do not allow it to boil.

13. Stir in the cloudberry jelly (or other jelly, if using) and mustard.

14. Adjust the seasoning, adding more salt if needed, or lemon juice if a little sharpness is needed. Turn off the heat, and keep warm while you slice the duck breasts.

Spoon the sauce onto warmed plates, lay the duck breasts on top with mushrooms alongside, and sprinkle with parsley.

Iceland

Iceland is often considered one of the Scandinavian countries even though it is an island in the North Atlantic sitting some 600 miles to the west of Europe. Iceland is known as the "land of fire and ice." The fire refers to the numerous volcanoes that cover vast areas with molten lava and the thousands of geysers erupting steaming water; at the other extreme of the landscape are ice fields and glaciers. The steaming hot water spewing out of geysers is harnessed and piped into homes in Reykjavik, Iceland's capital city. Greenhouses heated by the *hver* (hot springs) are able to grow bananas, oranges, and pineapples.

The first settlers arriving about 900 CE were Norwegian Vikings, exiled from their mother country. They were seafaring people, and today their descendants have the most modern fleet of fishing boats and fish processing plants in the world. Ninety-four percent of the current Icelandic population is predominantly descended from Norse and Celts. There is a foreign population of about 6 percent.

Most Icelanders belong to the Evangelical Lutheran Church, the state religion, and celebrate life-cycle events according to their religion. (See Protestant and Catholic Life-Cycle Rituals, page lxxiii.)

Newborns are baptized at around six months of age, and a family dinner follows. Many babies are born out of wedlock since numerous couples do not marry until they can afford their own apartment or home. They often live together, and perhaps have a child or two, before marrying. When the couple does decide to marry, the children walk down the aisle with them and take part in the ceremony. Weddings follow Western traditions—a white wedding dress with veil for the bride, business suit for the groom; the ceremony is usually in church. The wedding cake could be *kransekage* (recipe page 309) or the English wedding fruitcake (recipe page 273) or the basic white cake with white icing.

Funerals are similar to those in the United States, and the body is buried or cremated. After the burial, a meal is served for mourners, usually a *smørrebrød* table at the family home. Food is prepared, and covered dishes are brought in by neighbors and friends. While others go to the funeral, the neighbors and friends stay to help set up the feast. Pots of coffee and alcoholic beverages are made ready for the bereaved family and hungry mourners on their return.

The main course of a celebration feast is usually lamb or pork or both and a variety of fish dishes. Because of Iceland's seafaring tradition, fish is a mainstay of Icelandic cooking and is processed and cooked in every way imaginable. At a celebration feast, a great variety of fish dishes are served. *Fiskbudingur* (recipe follows) might be one of the selections.

⚘ *Fiskbudingur* (Fish Soufflé)

Yield: serves 6 to 8

10 tablespoons butter or margarine, divided

8 tablespoons dry **bread crumbs**, divided

1 pound skinless fish **fillets** (such as cod or haddock)

water, as needed

½ cup all-purpose **flour, sifted**

1 cup milk

salt and white pepper to taste

6 eggs, separated

Equipment: 1½- to 2-quart ovenproof casserole or soufflé dish, 2 medium saucepans, fork, **colander**, small bowl, whisk, large mixing bowl, rubber spatula, medium mixing bowl, electric mixer (optional), oven mitts, serving spoon

1. Prepare ovenproof casserole or soufflé dish: Coat bottom and sides with 2 tablespoons butter or margarine, and sprinkle 3 to 4 tablespoons bread crumbs over bottom and sides to cover well. Shake out excess.

Preheat oven to 375°F.

2. Put fish in medium saucepan, and cover with water. Bring to boil over high heat. Reduce heat to **simmer**, and cook for 5 to 7 minutes, until fish flakes easily when poked with fork. Place colander in sink, and drain fish. Cool enough to handle, break fish into bite-size pieces, and put in small bowl.

3. Melt remaining 8 tablespoons butter or margarine in second medium saucepan over medium heat. Remove from heat, and whisk in flour until smooth. Return to medium heat. Whisking constantly, slowly add milk, and **blend** well. Cook, whisking constantly until very thick,

5 to 7 minutes. Add salt and white pepper to taste. Transfer milk mixture to large mixing bowl, and set aside to cool to warm.

4. Using whisk, beat egg yolks together. Add beaten eggs to milk mixture and mix well. Using rubber spatula, **fold in** fish pieces.

5. Put egg whites in medium mixing bowl. Using electric mixer, beat egg whites until stiff, 2 to 3 minutes. Using rubber spatula, fold egg whites into milk mixture. Transfer to prepared casserole or soufflé dish, and sprinkle remaining 4 to 5 tablespoons bread crumbs over top.

6. Bake in oven for 45 to 55 minutes, until golden brown and set.

To serve, set baking container on the table with serving spoon. Fiskbudingur *can be eaten either warm or cold. Serve with boiled potatoes and* agurkesalat *(recipe follows).*

Cold leftover soufflé can be cut into 1-inch thick slices, sautéed in butter, and served for breakfast.

Sheep are an important part of Icelandic farming, and every part of the animal is eaten at celebrations. Lamb spareribs are very popular and often eaten at weddings and other life-cycle celebrations. They are every bit as delicious as those from the pig; this recipe can be made with either.

ᘓ *Golden Glazed Lamb Spareribs*

Yield: serves 4

3 pounds lean lamb spareribs (breast of lamb)	½ teaspoon ground cinnamon
1 cup peach preserves	½ teaspoon ground **allspice**
½ cup pineapple juice	1 teaspoon salt
½ teaspoon **ground coriander**	1 orange, peeled and sliced

Equipment: Large shallow roasting pan with rack, small bowl, mixing spoon, oven mitts, heatproof surface, **pastry brush**, large knife

Preheat oven to 325°F.

1. Place slabs of ribs on rack in large shallow roasting pan. Bake in oven for 1 to 1½ hours.

2. In small bowl, stir together peach preserves, pineapple juice, coriander, cinnamon, allspice, and salt. Using oven mitts, remove lamb from oven, and place on heatproof surface. Using pastry brush, brush ribs generously with peach mixture to **glaze** meat. Arrange orange slices on the ribs. Return to oven and bake 35 to 45 minutes longer, or until tender. Let meat rest at least 10 minutes before cutting ribs apart.

Serve as one of the many dishes on the buffet table. Ribs are best eaten with the fingers, so provide plenty of napkins.

Iceland was under Danish rule until fairly recently (1944), and so it is only natural the cooking in Iceland reflects Danish influences. The Danish *smørrebrød* (literally, "bread and butter") table is the preferred way to entertain at home for birthday, anniversary, or baptism celebrations or to feed mourners after a funeral. Open-faced sandwiches are made from hundreds of local delicacies. The open-faced sandwiches can be any size and made of just about anything. In Danish, the fixings are called "*paalaeg*," literally "something laid on" the bread.

The bread for open-faced sandwiches is rye or pumpernickel, and it is heavily spread with butter before adding the *paalaeg*. The sandwiches should be decoratively arranged so that they are inviting to eat. Cold cuts and sausages, cheeses, all sorts of herring and smoked fish, eel, shrimp and vegetables, hard-cooked eggs, and pickles are used for making *paalaeg*. Other standard items on the *smørrebrød* table are *syltede rødbeder* (recipe page 313) and *agurkesalat (recipe follows)*.

⚬ *Agurkesalat* (Pickled Cucumber Salad)

Yield: serves 4

2 or 3 cucumbers (6 to 8 inches long), washed, patted dry

1 cup white vinegar

1 tablespoon sugar

2 tablespoons chopped fresh dill or 1 teaspoon dried dill

salt and white pepper to taste

Equipment: Fork, paring knife, small bowl with cover, small saucepan, mixing spoon

1. Score cucumber skin lengthwise with fork. With paring knife, cut them crosswise in thin slices, and put into small bowl.

2. Pour vinegar into small saucepan, and add sugar. Bring to boil over high heat, stir to dissolve sugar, and remove from heat. Cool to room temperature. Pour vinegar mixture over cucumber slices. Sprinkle with dill and salt and white pepper to taste. Toss to mix, cover, and refrigerate for 2 to 3 hours for flavor to develop.

Serve in a small bowl as a salad or use as garnish on open-faced sandwiches.

⚬ *Bruntérta* (Chocolate Spice Cake)

This chocolate cake, scented and flavored with cinnamon and cloves, is popular for birthdays. The amount of cloves may be decreased, if you wish.

Yield: 8 to 10 servings

4 cups flour

3 teaspoons cinnamon

2 teaspoons ground cloves, or to taste

2 teaspoons baking powder

½ teaspoon baking soda

¼ teaspoon salt

2 tablespoons unsweetened cocoa powder

1 cup butter

1¼ cups sugar	1 teaspoon vanilla extract
2 eggs	¾ cup milk

Equipment: Mixing bowl, stand electric mixer, three 8-inch baking pans, rubber spatula, oven mitts, cake rack, serving platter or tray, parchment paper, metal spatula, prechilled piping bag with decorative tip

1. Ten minutes before baking, preheat the oven to 350°F.

2. Line three 8-inch baking pans with parchment paper. Leave a 2-inch margin above the sides of the pan to facilitate releasing the cakes when done. Set the pans aside.

3. In a large bowl, combine the flour, cinnamon, cloves, baking powder, baking soda, salt, and cocoa powder.

4. In the bowl of an electric mixer, cream the butter and sugar at medium speed until lemon-colored and fluffy.

5. Add the eggs and vanilla, and continue to mix well, until the mixture falls into ribbons when the beaters are raised.

Note: *While processing, turn machine off once or twice, and scrape down sides of container with rubber spatula.*

6. Decrease the speed, and add the flour mixture in three portions, alternating with half the milk. The batter should be fairly thick. Divide the batter among three parchment-covered 8-inch baking pans.

7. Bake at 350°F for 20 to 25 minutes, or until cake tests done (a toothpick inserted in the center should come out clean and dry).

8. Let cool in the pan for 5 minutes, then transfer the cakes with the aid of the parchment paper edges to a cake rack to cool.

9. When cakes are completely cool, prepare the butter icing (recipe follows).

10. Place a tablespoon of icing in the center of the serving platter, and put one cake layer bottom-side up on it. (Tuck narrow sheets of parchment paper under the bottom of the cake to catch any spills during icing. These can be removed just prior to serving.)

11. Spread a quarter portion of the icing evenly on the cake. Top with another layer of cake, bottom-side up, spread similarly with another quarter portion of the icing. Place the last layer of cake, right-side up, and spread it and the sides with the icing. Alternatively, put the icing into a prechilled piping bag with a decorative tip, and use it for covering the layers and decorating the top and sides.

ꝕ *Smjörkrem* (Butter Icing)

This is a versatile icing for use with the chocolate spice cake (recipe precedes). It can be flavored with rum or orange liqueur or almond flavoring, depending on personal preference. The original Icelandic recipe uses raw egg yolks, but they can be left out. The cream serves to make the icing smoother.

Yield: enough to cover 3 layers of cake

1 cup butter, softened

2 to 2½ cups (to taste) icing sugar

2 **egg yolks** (optional)

1 teaspoon vanilla or other flavoring, such as rum

2 to 3 tablespoons cream

Equipment: Electric mixer, mixer bowl, metal spatula for spreading icing

1. Put the butter and 2 cups icing sugar in the mixer bowl. Mix at medium speed until icing is homogeneous and fluffy.

2. Add the vanilla or your chosen flavoring, then mix in the cream briefly until thoroughly incorporated and the icing is smooth.

3. Spread icing with a metal spatula or put into a prechilled piping bag with decorative tip.

♪ *Vínarterta* (Multilayer Cake with Prune Filling)

Vínarterta is a cake often made for festive occasions. It consists of 5 to 7 layers of cardamom-flavored shortbread sandwiched with a prune filling. Rhubarb is also often used to make the filling.

Yield: 8 to 10 servings

Shortbread layers:

4 cups all-purpose flour

1 teaspoon baking powder

¼ teaspoon salt

1 cup butter

1½ cups sugar

2 eggs

3 tablespoons cream

1 teaspoon vanilla extract

1 teaspoon cardamom seeds, finely ground, or 1 teaspoon cardamom powder

Prune filling:

3 cups **pitted** prunes

1 cup water

1 teaspoon vanilla

1 tablespoon lemon juice (optional)

Butter cream icing:

½ cup butter, softened

2½ cups icing sugar

2 tablespoons cream

Equipment: Medium and large mixing bowls, mixer with dough paddle attachment, rubber spatula, metal spatula, medium saucepan, food processor, mixing spoon, oven mitts

1. Prepare the shortbread: In a bowl, combine the flour, baking powder, and salt.

2. In the bowl of a stand mixer, cream the butter at medium speed, and gradually add the sugar until well mixed. Add the eggs one at a time, beating well after each addition, until the mixture is light and fluffy. Add the cream, vanilla, and cardamom.

3. Now replace the beaters with a dough paddle attachment. With the mixer at low speed, gradually add the flour until everything comes together into a dough.

4. Remove the dough from the mixer, and with floured hands, knead the dough lightly and smooth into a ball. Wrap in plastic wrap, and chill for one hour.

5. Divide the chilled dough into 7 parts. Ten minutes before baking, preheat the oven to 375°F.

   Using an 8-inch cake pan as a template, cut out 7 parchment paper circles on which to bake the layers.

6. Roll out the dough one at a time on a lightly floured parchment paper circle, to ¼ inch thickness, and cut to size. Add the cutout pieces to add to the rest of the dough. Place as many dough circles as will fit on one baking sheet.

7. Bake in the preheated oven for 10 to 12 minutes, or until just beginning to turn golden at the bottom edge.

8. Repeat with the remaining layers. Set aside on a wire cake rack to cool.

9. Prepare the prune filling: Put the prunes in a saucepan with water, and cook over medium heat until softened.

10. Allow to cool, then put into food processor to **blend** until smooth.

11. Stir in the vanilla. You may wish to brighten the flavor of the filling by adding lemon juice.

12. Put a layer of cake on a serving platter lined on the outer margins with parchment paper to catch any drips. The paper can be removed before serving.

13. Spread about ⅓ cup of filling on each layer of cake. Continue spreading the filling until all but the top layer is filled.

14. Wrap the cake in plastic wrap, and store in a cool place overnight or up to two days to allow the layers to absorb the filling.

15. Prepare the butter cream icing. In a medium bowl, with a mixer, beat the butter and sugar at medium speed until smooth. Add the cream and mix just until incorporated. Spread on the top and sides of the cake.

Serve vínarterta at room temperature. Slice with a sharp knife into fairly narrow pieces, about 2 inches by 1 inch. This cake keeps well in the refrigerator for about 2 weeks (if it has not been completely eaten before then). It also stores well in the freezer (about 3 months) and thaws rapidly.

Norway

Norway is a mountainous country that is bordered by the North Sea on the southwest, Sweden on the east, Finland and Russia on the northeast, and the Barents Sea on the north. Its long coastline, 1,700 miles, has many islands and fjords or narrow sea inlets. Thanks in part to the discovery of large oil and gas reserves in the North Sea, Norway is one of the world's richest countries.

The majority of Norwegians are Lutheran and follow the life-cycle events prescribed by the Lutheran Church. (See Protestant and Catholic Life-Cycle Rituals, page lxxiii.) In recent years, though, Norway has become home to increasing numbers of immigrants. The government has opened the country to foreign workers and the asylum seekers from various parts of the world. Complete religious freedom is assured them, even though the state religion is the Evangelical Lutheran Church.

Name days are a Catholic Christian tradition that Norway adopted when it was first Christianized. But when Norway and the other Scandinavian countries converted to Protestantism, celebrating name days according to the Catholic Christian calendar was relegated to folk tradition. In 1988, a new Norwegian name calendar was published with two names for each day, following the popularity of a similar calendar published in Sweden. The names on the new name calendar were a mixture of old and new—some were chosen from the old Norwegian name calendar, some from famous personages' names (kings, queens, famous Norwegians), and from the most popular names given to children born between 1900 and 1988. A revised version of the modern name calendar was published in 1995 and added the most popular names given to children born between 1988 and 1995. The name calendar is revised regularly, and the names contained therein are valid to a certain date. And with the Norwegian predilection for partying and having fun, there is now a renewed interest in celebrating name day. (There is a long-standing restriction as to the kind of names that are given to children. Names that are traditionally surnames are not permitted for use as first names.)

In Norway, urbanites have more sedate Western-type weddings, while country weddings are more colorful and raucous. Often the traditional country wedding is a three-day celebration with a big meal served each day. Traditionally, wedding invitations were given out by a designated person, the *bedamann* (the bidding man). Wedding guests are limited to family and close friends. Bride and groom traditionally wore their regional *bunads*, the clothing unique to a certain region. These days, brides may choose to wear a white gown, as is the common practice in the Western world, or opt for a *bunad*. Wedding guests may also opt to wear a *bunad*, as it is widely recognized nationally as formal wear and often worn for weddings, baptisms, and confirmations, as well as Norwegian Constitution Day and other public events.

A traditional bridal headdress was a metal (silver or gold) crown with bangles that tinkled as the bride walked, alluding to the old belief that the sound scared away evil spirits that may be tempted to harm her on her wedding day. A Bible or psalm book was once carried by a bride in her purse as part of her wedding attire. At the end of the ceremony, fir trees were planted by wedding guests on either side of the door of the newlywed's home in anticipation of children to come.

The wedding party and guests begin eating about mid-afternoon and continue celebrating far into the night with plenty of singing and dancing and all-round good fun. Roasted pig, home-cured ham, smoked pork and sausages, *dyresteg* (venison or reindeer roast, recipe page 331), Norwegian sauerkraut with caraway seeds, cauliflower, sweet peas and carrots, and an assortment of cakes and puddings are some of the foods prepared for these meals. After the ceremony, there is a reception with food and drink, usually a three-course dinner served to each guest, or guests help themselves to a *koldtbord* (buffet table). Before the festivities can begin, however, usually everyone joins in singing some songs. Several people will have prepared their own lyrics appropriate to the occasion, sung to familiar tunes, and everyone else is expected to join in from song sheets distributed to the guests. Then there are several toasts, each one introduced by a toastmaster. There is an accepted order for the people who wish to toast the new couple: the father of the bride, followed by the groom, then the bride, the maid of honor, best man, groom's father, bride's mother, groom's mother, grandparents, godparents, and then other family members and friends. The last speech is a formal thank you for the meal. There may be games throughout the festivities as well.

Besides the wedding cake, there are usually several more cakes at the sweets table. Family and friends often bring these to the wedding reception, among which are *bløtkake* (cream layer cake) (recipe page 332) and *marsipankake* (marzipan cake) (recipe page 333), both traditional celebratory cakes. After the meal, dancing follows, and the festivities may go on till the morning. Before the festivities end, there is another meal, usually a lighter one, of soup and bread, sandwiches, or sausages.

Wedding cakes are often regional, such as the labor-intensive *brudlaupskling*. This cake is made of dozens of pancake-like layers, cooked on an iron griddle and smeared with butter and a mixture of cheese, heavy cream, and syrup. Each layer is then folded and cut into small, square cakes. The easier to make *kransekage* (recipe page 309) is preferred by many couples.

The first big meal for country weddings is held after the church nuptials, when guests are treated to a late night feast beginning with nourishing *spinatsuppe* (recipe page 329), sour cream porridge called *rømmegrøt* (recipe page 329), and a concoction called *dravle*, made of curds and whey sweetened with syrup. As a show of community unity, everyone drinks from a communal bowl filled with beer.

In the morning, guests refresh themselves with coffee and cakes. The party continues through the second day and night, and on the third day things start to wind down and slowly life returns to normal.

⚜ *Spinatsuppe* (Spinach Soup)

Yield: serves 4 to 6

2 pounds fresh spinach, washed, drained, **coarsely chopped**, or 2 (16-ounce) packages of frozen chopped spinach, thawed, drained

2 quarts chicken broth

3 tablespoons butter or margarine

2 tablespoons all-purpose **flour**

1 teaspoon salt

¼ teaspoon **ground** nutmeg

¼ teaspoon ground white pepper

For **garnish:** 2 hard-cooked eggs, sliced

Equipment: Large saucepan, mixing spoon, food processor, ladle, small **heavy-bottomed** saucepan, medium saucepan with cover, whisk, individual soup bowls

1. Put spinach in large saucepan and add chicken broth. Bring to a boil over high heat, and stir. Reduce heat to **simmer**, and cook for 8 to 10 minutes, until spinach is well cooked. Remove from heat, and set aside to cool to warm.

2. **Purée** spinach mixture in two batches to avoid overfilling processor. Ladle half the spinach mixture into food processor and purée until smooth and lump-free. Repeat with second batch. Pour both batches into medium saucepan.

3. In small heavy-bottomed saucepan, melt butter or margarine over medium-low heat. Remove pan from heat, and whisk in flour. Return pan to heat, and continue whisking until mixture is smooth. Whisk in 1 ladle of puréed spinach mixture to butter mixture. Pour back into medium saucepan with the rest of the puréed spinach mixture in it. Cook over medium-high heat until small bubbles appear around edge of pan. Reduce heat to low. Add salt, nutmeg, and white pepper. Stir, cover, and cook 5 minutes.

To serve, ladle into individual soup bowls, and **garnish** *each serving with a few slices of hard-cooked egg.*

At country weddings, the dish most anticipated by the guests is *rømmegrøt* (recipe follows). According to tradition, the bride's mother is supposed to make it for the groom and serve it to him on their wedding night. *Rømmegrøt* is considered the national dish of Norway and is often eaten as the evening meal.

Norwegians use cultured heavy cream (somewhat akin to English clotted cream or Balkan *kaymak*) to make *rømmegrøt*. You can make your own by adding buttermilk to heavy cream (smetana recipe page 450). Allow two or three days for the *rømmegrøt* to develop before adding to the *rømmegrøt* recipe. A good substitute for Norwegian sour cream is **crème fraîche.**

⚜ *Rømmegrøt* (Sour Cream Porridge)

Rømmegrøt is a traditional dish that was once an indispensable element at every special occasion and life-cycle event. It is the Norwegian comfort food par excellence. It was given to a new mother to provide comfort and nutrition immediately after delivery. It would make its appearance at the wedding reception, carried by the bride to serve the groom, the first meal she would serve him. It was also a dish shared among mourners at a funeral. Proper sour cream is essential for this dish. Traditional accompaniments were slices of smoked meat and flat bread.

Yield: 6 to 8 servings

4 cups sour cream (European-style, at least 35 percent fat with no thickeners or additives); if not available, substitute 4 cups heavy cream, plus 2 tablespoons lemon juice

1½ cups flour

2 cups full fat milk

¾ teaspoon salt

For serving:

sugar

cinnamon

melted butter

Equipment: Medium **heavy-bottomed** saucepan, medium saucepan or milk pan, mixing spoon, whisk, small bowl, ladle, serving bowls

1. First prepare the alternative sour cream if proper European-style sour cream is not available. The simplest way is to add the lemon juice to heavy cream, and let it stand for 20 to 30 minutes, or until it coagulates. The resulting curdled mixture can then be used as sour cream.

2. In a heavy-bottomed medium saucepan, put the sour cream to simmer over low heat.

3. In a smaller saucepan, put the milk to warm up over low heat, ready to bring to a boil when needed.

4. After the sour cream has been simmering for ¼ hour, slowly add about ⅓ of the flour while constantly stirring to avoid lumps. It may help prevent lumps to put the flour in a sieve or sifter, and whisk it in constantly as it is being sieved or sifted over the simmering cream.

5. Continue to simmer the porridge until butterfat rises. Skim off or pour off the butterfat to a separate bowl. Reserve this butterfat for serving. Do not be concerned if there is not enough butterfat to skim off, simply add melted butter for serving.

6. Let the milk in the other saucepan come to a boil.

7. Gradually sift or sieve in the rest of the flour to the porridge, whisking constantly as you do so.

8. Gradually whisk in the milk until the porridge reaches the desired consistency—neither too solid nor too runny. The porridge will also thicken further as it cools down.

9. Add the salt and continue to simmer for another 10 minutes, or until you can no longer detect a raw flour taste to the porridge.

10. Remove from the heat, and ladle into serving bowls.

11. Spoon over the reserved butterfat (if any) or melted butter. Top with sugar and cinnamon, and serve at once.

Traditionally, this porridge was served with flat bread and cured meats.

Roasted venison (or reindeer) is often included in the Norwegian wedding feast. If you don't have a hunter in the family, your butcher can often special-order a venison roast from his purveyor.

✉ Dyresteg (Roasted Venison)

Yield: serves 6 to 8

4 to 6 pounds boneless haunch of venison or reindeer

3 tablespoons butter or margarine, at room temperature

salt and pepper to taste

2 to 3 cups canned beef broth

1 tablespoon **flour**

1 tablespoon red currant or raspberry jelly

½ cup sour cream

Equipment: Kitchen string, paring knife, shallow roasting pan with rack, oven mitts, heat-proof surface, **bulb baster** or large spoon, meat thermometer (optional), baking sheet, aluminum foil, measuring cup, small **heavy-bottomed** saucepan, whisk, serving platter, small serving bowl

Preheat oven to 475°F.

1. Tie roast up neatly at ½-inch intervals with string so it will hold its shape while cooking. Using your hand, spread the softened butter evenly over the meat. Place the roast on a rack in a shallow roasting pan.

2. Bake roast in hot oven to **sear** for 20 minutes, or until browned.

Reduce heat to 375°F.

3. Using oven mitts, remove roast from oven, and place on heatproof surface. Sprinkle the roast with salt and pepper to taste. Carefully pour 2 cups beef broth into the bottom of the roasting pan and return to oven. Allow about 20 minutes per pound. Cook 1¼ to 1½ hours for rare, 1¾ to 2 hours for well done. During the baking, use the bulb baster or large spoon to **baste** about every 30 minutes, adding more beef broth if the pan gets dry. To test doneness for meat, insert meat thermometer into thickest part of the roast; it should register about 160°F for medium doneness and about 170°F for well done.

4. Remove roast from oven, and transfer to baking sheet. Pour pan juices into measuring cup, cover roast with foil, and return to turned-off oven to keep warm while making sauce.

5. Prepare sauce: Skim and discard the fat from the pan juices. Add water, if necessary, to make 1 cup of liquid. In small heavy-bottomed saucepan, melt butter over medium-low heat. Pull pan off heat, and whisk in flour. Return pan to heat, and continue whisking until mixture is smooth. Whisk in pan juices, and increase heat to medium. Whisk until mixture thickens, 3 to 5 minutes. Remove from heat. Whisk in jelly, sour cream, and salt and pepper to taste.

To serve, remove the strings from the roast, thinly slice the meat, and place on serving platter. Pass the sauce separately in a small serving bowl. Spoon sauce over each serving.

₡ *Bløtkake* (Cream Layer Cake)

This cake makes its appearance at most celebrations, especially on birthdays. It is then called *"geburdsdagkake"* or just *"bursdagkake"* (birthday cake). The fruits served with it are usually strawberries, blueberries, raspberries, blackberries—or whatever fresh fruits suit your or the birthday celebrant's fancy, such as kiwifruit. The cake may even have different fruits on each layer. The juice for brushing on the cake as well may be orange or pear or apple—whatever combines best with the chosen fruits and the maker's personal preference. The cake is cut with a small circle in the middle, which is reserved for the birthday celebrant to have for breakfast the following morning after his or her birthday. The rest of the cake is sliced in pieces radiating from the hole in the center.

Yield: about 8 servings

Cake batter:

Butter for greasing baking pan(s)

¾ cup flour, plus more for sprinkling on baking pan(s)

1 heaping tablespoon **cornstarch** or potato flour

1¼ teaspoon baking powder

¼ teaspoon salt

4 eggs, separated

1 cup sugar

1 teaspoon vanilla

3 tablespoons cold water

Filling and frosting:

4 cups heavy whipping cream

1 tablespoon sugar

1 cup strawberry, raspberry, or other fruit preserve (good-quality, high-fruit-content is best)

3 to 4 cups fresh berries or fruit of your choice—strawberries, blueberries, blackberries, raspberries, or kiwifruit slices

Equipment: Electric mixer, mixing bowls, mixing spoon, rubber spatula, three 8-inch round cake pans, parchment paper, oven mitts

1. Prepare the cake pans: Butter the pans, and sprinkle evenly with flour. Shake off any excess. Alternatively, line the pans with parchment paper.

2. In a large mixing bowl, combine the flour, cornstarch, baking powder, and salt. Set aside.

3. In a medium bowl, whip the egg whites to soft peaks. Gradually add ½ of the sugar while continuing to whip until stiff peaks form.

4. In a small bowl, beat well the egg yolks with vanilla and ½ cup sugar until light and fluffy and falls into ribbons when the beater is raised. Stir in cold water.

5. Make a well (hole) in the center of the flour mixture, and mix in the yolk mixture until well combined. Gently fold in the flour and yolk mixture into the stiffly beaten egg whites, just until combined. Spoon the batter into the prepared pans.

6. Bake in a *cold* oven set to 350°F for 25 to 30 minutes, or until cake test done (insert a toothpick or wood skewer in the center, and if it comes out dry, the cake is done). Allow

the cakes to rest in the pan(s) for 10 to 15 minutes, then allow to cool thoroughly on a cake rack.

7. When the cakes are cool, you can begin to fill and frost them. Wash and dry well the chosen fruits. Slice those that will be placed on the layers, and leave whole those that will decorate the topmost layer.

8. Place the first cake bottom-side up on the serving platter. Place a border of parchment paper all around under the margins of the cake. They will catch any spills, and once the cake is decorated, they can be taken out to leave a neat finish around the cake.

9. Whip the cream with the sugar until soft peaks form.

10. Sprinkle 2 to 3 tablespoons of orange juice evenly on the cake, then spread with a thin layer of strawberry preserve. Spread a generous layer of whipped cream. Over this, lay pieces of cut fruits.

11. Lay another cake on top of the first cake, again bottom-side up. Sprinkle with orange juice as before, spread with strawberry preserve, then with whipped cream. Lay the pieces of cut fruits.

    For the topmost layer, place the last cake right-side up over the two filled ones, sprinkle with orange juice, but do not spread with preserve unless you want a pink-topped cake.

12. Now spread the remainder of the whipped cream over the sides and top of the cake. Alternatively, transfer the cream to a piping bag with a decorative tip, and pipe cream all over.

13. Arrange the reserved whole berries on top. Use your creativity to create patterns, taking advantage of the different colors of the fruits you have chosen. Perhaps divide the space into quarters, with the larger strawberries delineating the borders, and the smaller raspberries inside filling the spaces. And maybe add some blackberries to add contrasting color. It is best to refrigerate the cake overnight before serving to allow the layers to settle and absorb the fillings.

14. When ready to serve, cut out a hole in the center of the cake (like the "core" of a pineapple) so that the resulting piece is a cylinder. Keep the cylinder in the refrigerator for the celebrant to eat for breakfast the following day. Cut the other servings radiating from the hole in the center.

It is best to store any uneaten portions in the refrigerator.

♔ *Marsipankake* (Marzipan Cake)

Together with *bløtkake* (recipe precedes), *marsipankake* is another cake that makes a predictable appearance at celebrations. It is made from a similar type of sponge cake base as is used with *bløtkake*, but it is a little bit richer, as it uses 6 eggs instead of 4. You may opt to use the same sponge cake recipe and procedure as in the *bløtkake* recipe.

Yield: about 8 servings

1 cup flour	¼ teaspoon salt
1½ teaspoons baking powder	6 eggs

1 cup sugar

1 teaspoon vanilla extract

1 tablespoon lemon juice

Filling and decoration:

1 cup raspberry preserves (or ½ cup raspberry, ½ cup apricot preserves)

1½ cups heavy whipping cream

3 tablespoons icing sugar, plus more for rolling out the **marzipan**

½ cup chopped walnuts or toasted almond flakes

1 ripe banana, sliced and sprinkled with lemon juice to prevent the slices browning (or other fruit of your choice)

1 pound prepared marzipan

For cake decoration:

colored sprinkles

fresh edible flowers

molded marzipan leaves or flowers

Equipment: Electric mixer, medium and large mixing bowls, mixing spoon, rubber or metal spatula for spreading, 9- or 10-inch round springform cake pan, rolling pin, oven mitts

1. Prepare the cake pan: Butter the bottom and sides, and sprinkle evenly with flour. Shake out the excess.

Preheat oven to 350°F.

2. In a medium bowl, combine the flour, baking powder, and salt.

3. In a large mixing bowl, using the electric mixer at medium speed, beat the eggs with the sugar and vanilla until light and fluffy, and the mixture falls from the beater in smooth ribbon-like strands.

4. Lower the mixer speed, stir in the flour mixture and the lemon juice, and mix well until homogeneous.

5. Spoon into the prepared springform pan, and place in the middle rack of the oven.

6. Bake for 25 to 30 minutes, or until the cake tests done (insert a wooden skewer or toothpick in the center of the cake; if it comes out dry, without any batter sticking to it, the cake is done). Remove the cake from the oven, but let it stand for 10 to 15 minutes to allow it to cool down slightly before taking if off the pan. Leave on a cake rack to cool completely.

7. When the cake is cool, prepare the filling. With the mixer, whip the cream and icing sugar to soft peaks. Slice the cake crosswise into 3 even layers. Lay the bottom-most layer first on a parchment-covered serving platter. Spread it with a generous layer of raspberry preserves, followed by a thin layer of cream. Lay the middle cake layer over, and spread it with a generous layer of apricot preserves. Sprinkle half of the nuts over it, then spread a thin layer of cream, followed by another sprinkling of nuts. Lay the topmost layer over, spread with a layer of raspberry preserves, then distribute the banana slices over it. Spread the remaining cream in a thin layer over the banana slices and over the sides.

8. Dust a clean kitchen towel with icing sugar, and roll the marzipan out to a size slightly larger than the cake. Use the towel or the rolling pin to carry the marzipan closer to the cake, and position the marzipan over the cake. Press it gently in place, and tuck the edges under the

cake, or else cut off the excess, flush with the cake bottom. Use any cutoff bits as decoration, fashioning them into leaves or flowers.

9. Refrigerate overnight to allow the flavors to meld and the cake to settle before serving.

As with *bløtkake* (recipe page 332), if this cake is intended for a birthday, cut out a circle from the center of the cake going all the way down, so that you have a cylinder-shaped slice of cake. Store this cylinder in the refrigerator, covered, for the celebrant to have for breakfast the following morning. Slice the cake radially from the hole in the center.

Store any leftover cake in the refrigerator.

Sweden

Sweden is a country dominated by rivers and over 100,000 lakes, which make up nearly a third of the total land area. It is bordered by Norway on the west, Finland on the northeast, and the Baltic Sea on the southwest.

The Swedish people enjoy the highest standard of living in Europe. An overwhelming majority of the population belongs to the Evangelical Lutheran Church, the state religion, and follow life-cycle events prescribed by the Church. (See Protestant and Catholic Life-Cycle Rituals, page lxxiii.) Despite the presence of a state religion, Sweden has complete religious freedom, making it a secure haven for the many Muslims, Jews, Hindus, and Buddhists who live there. They each follow life-cycle celebrations according to their religion.

Besides the traditional Christian life-cycle celebrations, the Swedes celebrate the birth of a baby and birthdays. Most Swedish babies are christened, and the parents usually have their immediate family and godparents to a small Sunday dinner after the church service, forgoing large christening parties. The custom of baby showers is not practiced, as gifts for newborn children are not given until after the birth.

Name days (*namnsdagar*; *namnsdag*, singular) were celebrated in Sweden once it became wholly Christianized, sometime after the 15th century. The names referred to Catholic Christian saints' feast days for each day of the year and were printed on calendars. The Swedish traditional name day calendar was valid for a certain time period. Its validity expired in 1901. In 1972, a contemporary name day calendar published by a printer roused renewed public interest in name days. Finally in 2001, a workgroup from the Swedish Academy of Sciences, published a modern name day calendar with two names for each day. The contemporary calendar is intended to be updated every 15 years. It is customary to give a card or a little present on someone's name day, especially for a child.

Birthdays for children (and the not so young as well) start with breakfast in bed with the family singing "Happy Birthday to You" and bringing presents to the celebrant. The presents (usually) are not opened until breakfast has been eaten. A child's birthday (*kalas*) is celebrated with young friends who bring gifts and stay to play games and eat home-baked cake. Older celebrants may bring a cake to work or invite friends around for drinks. For milestone birthdays, at 30, 40, and onward, many celebrants hold a big party where toasts and speeches from family and friends, songs, and games are the order of the day.

A special day for children, usually in their early teens, is their confirmation in the Church of Sweden. It is followed by a family celebration with cake and gifts. Confirmation used to mark the coming of age, usually at age 14 or 15. In the last century, after confirmation, one could go to work or leave home. These days, religious confirmation is not as widely practiced as it once was, and nonreligious confirmation has taken its place among nonobservant Swedes. Nonreligious or secular confirmation study groups for 14- to 15-year-olds were initiated by the Humanists (*Humanisterna*) in the 1990s. These were replaced by weeklong *humanistik konfirmation* (humanist confirmation) camps, where topics such as human rights, racism, love, equality, and gender roles, as well as topics raised by the participants themselves, are discussed. At the end of the camp, a confirmation ceremony is held where the participants demonstrate to the assembled parents what they have learned.

Although funerals are generally life-cycle events in most Christian countries, they are handled differently in Sweden, where they are a celebration of the continuity of life. Upon hearing the news of a death, neighbors and friends pitch in to provide the family of the deceased with platters, bowls, and baskets of food. On the 1st of November, departed members of the family are remembered with wreaths and candles lit at their grave sites.

Wedding ceremonies are held mostly in the church, followed by a dinner and dancing afterwards. In the countryside, weddings are community affairs in both the preparation and the celebration. In the urban areas, as in other European cities, the celebration often includes champagne, flowers, and the traditional bridal waltz to start the dancing.

For many Swedes, the wedding events begin before the actual ceremony. Prior to the wedding, it is customary for friends of the bride to surprise her with a hen night (*möhippa*) and for the groom's friends to surprise him with stag night (*svensexa*); both are rowdy affairs with practical jokes and lots of beer drinking.

On the Sunday before the wedding, the couple may have a *lysning*. The *lysning* is an afternoon party, after church, with a light meal and drinks. The couple receives presents from the guests at this afternoon party, not at the wedding. An old tradition is for the bride's mother to give the bride a gold coin to be worn inside the right shoe, and for the bride's father to give her a silver coin for the left shoe. It was believed that doing so meant the bride would not go without money during her wedded life.

On the day of the wedding, the bride's family traditionally welcomes the guests to the church. During the service, the bride and groom walk up the aisle together. Couples exchange two rings at their engagement, so at the official ceremony, the bride usually receives a second gold band. At the end of the service, the couple generally exits the church first. They stand just outside the entrance to receive good wishes and congratulations from departing guests.

The reception is usually held at a community hall or restaurant. According to Swedish tradition, a bridal arch of flowers designates the place of honor in the banquet hall. The arch is like a canopy of flowers, either fresh or dried, that frames the seated newlywed couple as they eat. During the festive meal, it is customary for guests to raise their glasses many times to toast (*skål*) the newlyweds.

The buffet table is the most important form of entertaining in Sweden, including at wedding celebrations. The formal buffet (*kalas*) is not the same as the better known *smörgåsbord*, which is really a sandwich buffet. (*Smör* refers to "butter" and *bord* is "bread.") Whether the buffet is *kalas* or *smörgåsbord* depends upon the budget. For both types of buffet, the centerpiece is often a decorated pig's head or perhaps a whole suckling pig (recipe page 425). Herring dishes are generally served in several forms— pickled, jellied, baked, smoked, and poached; other prepared foods include assorted pork and beef dishes, often reindeer meat (recipe page 331); breads; potatoes; cheeses; salads; and cakes. These dishes are laid out onto a long table or several tables for self-service. Important eating etiquette is to never pile lots of food on the plate at one time; it is eaten in several courses. The standard order of eating is to start with the fish, move on to the meat and then to the hot dishes, and finish with cheeses. Guests usually take a break before turning to the desserts with coffee. Separate plates are provided, and guests are offered a fresh plate each time they go to the buffet. It is considered rude and bad luck to take the last bit of food in the serving dish.

As with wedding traditions throughout the world, cakes are often part of the celebration. An unusual regional wedding cake called *spettekaka* is so complicated that only commercial bakers can make it. It is made by beating sugar and scores of eggs for hours on end. The concoction is baked by drizzling batter onto a rotating spit in front of an open fire. The batter clings to the spit as it rotates, and the finished cake ends up about 12 inches wide at the base and about 2 feet tall. A popular Swedish wedding cake that is much easier to make is the *kranskaka* (recipe page 308).

The following recipe for pea soup with pork, *ärter med fläsk*, is typical of the types of dishes that would be served on the buffet table.

Ärter med Fläsk (Pea Soup with Pork)

Yield: 6

1 pound (2 cups) yellow split peas

8 cups water

1 pound lean salt pork in one piece

2 onions, **finely chopped**

1 whole onion, peeled and studded with 4 cloves

½ teaspoon **ground** marjoram

1 teaspoon salt, more or less to taste

Equipment: Medium saucepan, mixing spoon, cutting board, meat knife, serving dish, tureen or covered casserole dish, ladle, soup spoons, soup bowls

1. Put yellow peas in medium saucepan, add water, salt pork, chopped onions, clove-studded onion, and marjoram. Bring to boil over high heat. Stir, reduce heat to **simmer**, cover, and cook until peas are tender, 1 to 1½ hours. Remove and set aside the clove studded onion and salt pork.

2. Transfer pork to cutting board. Slice the pork into individual serving pieces, and place them on a serving dish. Pour the hot soup into a tureen or casserole dish, and cover it to keep warm.

Serve pea soup with plenty of crusty bread for dunking and sopping. Place soup on the kalas *or* smörgåsbord *table with soup bowls and soup spoons next to it. Each person ladles soup in a bowl and eats it with a spoon.*

Fresh salmon is one of Sweden's favorite foods. Fresh salmon marinated in dill (*gravlax*, or, to give it its full name, *gravad lax*), served cold with mustard sauce, is traditionally on the *kalas* and *smörgåsbord* table.

⚮ *Gravlax* (Dill-cured Salmon)

Yield: 6 to 8 servings

2 pounds fresh salmon, middle portion, cleaned and scaled, backbone and small bones removed

3 tablespoons sugar

¼ cup kosher (coarse) salt

2 tablespoons white peppercorns, coarsely ground

½ to ⅔ cup fresh dill, chopped coarsely

For **garnish**: 1 lemon, thinly sliced

Equipment: Kitchen knife, glass or earthenware dish, wooden board or heavy dish, some full tin cans for weighing down the salmon during the curing period, aluminum foil

1. Cut the salmon in half to make two fillets with the skin on. Make several incisions on the skin side so that the flavors can seep in.

2. Mix well the salt, sugar, and pepper, and rub all over the salmon flesh and skin. Place a third of the dill at the bottom of a glass dish.

3. Lay a fillet, skin side down. Sprinkle another third of the dill on the flesh side of the fillet.

   Lay the remaining fillet over and sprinkle with the rest of the dill. Cover the fillets with foil and place a cutting board or flat plate on top.

4. Weigh the board or plate with something heavy—tin cans, for example, distributed evenly.

   Refrigerate for 24 to 48 hours, turning the fish a few times, making sure to spoon the marinade thoroughly over both sides of each fillet.

5. Remove the fillets from the marinade, and scrape off the seasonings and dill. Pat the fillets dry, and slice finely on the diagonal, leaving behind the skin and the dark flesh close to it, which can be discarded.

Garnish with lemon slices, and serve with mustard and dill sauce (recipe follows).

⚜ Swedish Mustard and Dill Sauce

Yield: about 1½ cups

4 tablespoons Swedish or mild mustard

2 tablespoons Dijon mustard

2 tablespoon sugar

2 tablespoons wine vinegar

1 cup oil (not olive)

salt and pepper to taste

3 tablespoons fresh dill, **finely chopped**

Equipment: Small mixing bowl with cover, whisk, small serving bowl

1. Whisk mustard, sugar, and vinegar in small mixing bowl. Whisking vigorously, add the oil in a slow, thin stream. The sauce will thicken rapidly, but continue to whisk until all the oil is incorporated. Whisk in the salt and pepper and finely chopped dill.

2. Cover and refrigerate.

To serve, transfer to small serving bowl, and place beside the gravlax on the buffet table.

⚜ Aprikoser och Plommonspackad Fläskkarré (Pork Tenderloin with Apricots and Apples)

Pork is a well loved meat all over Scandinavia, and one of the most popular ways to cook and eat it is roasted and stuffed with dried fruits. The following recipe for *fläskkarré* (pork tenderloin) is similar to the Danish *fyldt svinemørbrad* (recipe page 311), which is roasted with the popular Scandinavian filling of prunes and apples. This recipe uses dried apricots combined with prunes. It is served with the aromatic root vegetables that accompany the meat in the roasting pan and a cream sauce. Fresh green peas and applesauce make good side dishes for *fläskkarré*.

Yield: Serves 6 to 8

4- to 5-pound pork loin, boneless, in one piece

16 dried apricots

8 prunes

1 cup water

2 tart apples, peeled, **cored**, quartered

2 tablespoons oil

3 tablespoons butter

2 onions, peeled, quartered

2 carrots, peeled, cut into large pieces	2 cups broth or white wine
2 parsnips, peeled, cut into large pieces	2 bay leaves
	2 cups double (thick) cream
salt and pepper	For **garnish**: ½ cup chopped parsley

Equipment: Saucepan, paper towels, wooden spoon, basting spoon, **heavy-bottomed** roasting pan, oven mitts, aluminum foil, serving tray, serving bowl

1. Ask the butcher to tie the loin at 1-inch intervals and to create a pocket through the middle so that the apricot and prune stuffing can be inserted.

2. In a saucepan, place the apricots and prunes with water, and bring to a boil over medium heat. Turn off the heat, and let the dried fruits sit in the water until well plumped. Take out the fruits, drain, and pat dry.

3. With the handle of a wooden spoon, season the pocket with salt and pepper. Insert 8 apricots and 8 prunes into the pocket, making sure they are tightly packed. Salt and pepper the loin all over.

4. Ten minutes before using, preheat the oven to 350°F.

5. In a roasting pan over medium heat, melt the butter and oil. When the oil and butter are hot, add the loin, and brown it evenly on all sides, around 15 to 20 minutes.

6. Add the onions, carrots, parsnips, apples, the remaining 8 apricots, and bay leaves. Stir to coat them with the butter and oil.

7. Add the broth or wine, if using, and let it come to a simmer. Turn off the heat.

8. Place the roasting pan in the oven, and allow to roast for 1½ to 2 hours. **Baste** the meat and vegetables with the liquid in the pan from time to time.

9. Check that the meat is tender, then remove it to a warmed serving dish, and cover it loosely with a tent of foil to keep warm while you prepare the sauce. Transfer the vegetables and fruits to a serving bowl, and keep them warm.

10. Strain the juices left in the roasting pan, and pour into a small saucepan. Whisk in the cream, and allow to cook over medium heat until it begins to simmer. Adjust the seasoning, and add salt and pepper if needed.

11. Spoon some sauce over the loin, and keep some in a sauce bowl for serving. Sprinkle the loin and vegetables with parsley.

Serve at once, with applesauce and green peas.

Hundreds of different sandwich combinations have evolved with an eye for their aesthetic appearance as well as taste and for display at the *smörgåsbord*. *Vårsörgåsar* are finger sandwiches that can be whipped up in no time for a birthday party or to add to the buffet table at other celebrations.

♪ *Vårsörgåsar* (Spring Sandwiches)

Yield: 24 pieces

12 slices day-old white bread

10 anchovy **fillets, finely chopped**, or 1 tube anchovy paste

4 tablespoons butter or margarine, at room temperature

2 tablespoons prepared mustard

4 hard-cooked eggs, peeled **coarsely chopped**

¼ cup fresh dill or fresh parsley, finely chopped

2 tablespoons vegetable oil

2 tablespoons butter or margarine

Equipment: Work surface, **serrated knife**, food processor, rubber spatula, small mixing bowl, plastic food wrap, paper towels, baking sheet, large skillet, metal spatula, serving platter

1. Stack bread slices on work surface and using serrated knife, trim off crusts.

2. Put anchovies, butter or margarine, mustard, coarsely chopped hard-cooked eggs, and dill or parsley in food processor. Process until smooth, about 1 minute. Transfer to small mixing bowl.

Note: While processing, turn machine off once or twice, and scrape down sides of container with rubber spatula.

3. Thickly spread egg mixture onto 6 slices of bread. Top each slice with a remaining slice of bread, and lightly press them together. If not using right away, wrap each sandwich in plastic wrap and refrigerate up to 3 days or freeze up to 2 weeks. Defrost frozen sandwiches before frying.

4. Prepare to fry: Place several layers of paper towels on baking sheet. Heat oil, and melt 2 tablespoons butter or margarine in large skillet over medium heat. Add the sandwiches, 1 or 2 at a time. Fry each sandwich for 2 to 3 minutes on each side, until golden brown and crisp. Drain on paper towels. Cut each diagonally, from corner to corner, into 4 triangular pieces.

To serve, stack the finger sandwiches on a serving platter and place on the buffet table.

Herring is the favorite fish in the Scandinavian countries, and the buffet table often has several different herring dishes. This dish is made up of bits of food always available in most Swedish kitchens. The name "save the family" refers to the vital role herring has played in the Scandinavian diet. When times were hard, a family could always beg, borrow, or fish for a little herring. It was tasty, nourishing, and plentiful and saved many families from starvation.

✻ *Familjens Räddning* ("Save the Family" Herring Platter)

Yield: serves 2

2 to 4 lettuce leaves, washed and patted dry

4 to 6 pieces pickled **herring**, drained (available at all supermarkets)

1 small cucumber, peeled, finely sliced

½ cup pickled **beets**, homemade (recipe page 313), or canned

2 hard-cooked eggs, each cut into 4 or 6 wedges

½ cup sour cream

For **garnish**: 2 tablespoons parsley, **finely chopped**

Equipment: Large round dinner plate, mixing spoon

Cover the large dinner plate decoratively with 2 to 4 lettuce leaves. Mound the herring in the center, and surround with a ring of cucumber slices. Next make a ring of pickled beets. Border the plate with a sunburst of egg wedges. **Drizzle** with sour cream, and sprinkle with parsley flakes, for garnish.

To serve, place the herring plate on the buffet table. This is wonderful nibbling food to leisurely enjoy with rye or pumpernickel bread and butter.

WESTERN EUROPE

Western Europe includes the following countries: Austria, Belgium, France, Germany, the Netherlands, and Switzerland.

Austria

For more than 600 years, until the end of World War I in 1918, Austria was the heart of a powerful empire—the Austro-Hungarian Empire—that included Hungary and Czechoslovakia and stretched from southern Poland to the Adriatic. Its capital, Vienna, was one of the most exciting cities in Europe—an international center of great music and fine cuisine.

Although present-day Austria is only a tiny remnant of the old Austro-Hungarian Empire, its geographic position on the southeastern approach to Western Europe and on the north-south routes between Germany and Italy gave it great strategic importance during World War II and the Cold War.

Most Austrians are of German descent, and the majority belong to the Roman Catholic Church, celebrating most life-cycle events according to the Church's rites and traditions. (See Protestant and Catholic Life-Cycle Rituals, page lxxiii.)

To Austrians, eating is serious business, and great care is taken to provide the finest fare for life-cycle celebrations. Austrian christenings, first communions, weddings, wedding anniversaries, and funerals are usually memorable events. Austrians eat not only well but often. The day begins with coffee, milk, and wonderful rolls. *Gabelfrühstück* (fork breakfast) is a hearty midmorning meal. The big meal of the day is at noon and usually includes soup, meat, vegetables, potatoes, and rich dessert. Celebration feasts usually take place at the midday meal and often expand the menu to include fish or the much prized venison from the Austrian Alps. Late afternoon is the time for *jause*, a coffee and dessert break, and evening supper is usually light, often just soup, salad, and bread. A pastry or cake, for which Austria is world famous, is usually eaten as a bedtime snack.

Austrian cooking has been enriched by neighboring influences—paprika dishes from Hungary; dumplings from Germany; and pasta, tomato cookery, and schnitzel (which started out as *piccata alla Milanese*) from Italy. The Turks, who besieged Vienna twice, get credit for Austria's heavenly coffees: *melange* (coffee with milk), *melange mit schlag* (coffee with milk and whipped cream), *Wiener eiskaffee* (Viennese iced coffee) (recipe page 347), and *mokka* (black coffee). Whatever the dish, in Austrian kitchens it has been refined, enriched, and generally improved, thus assuming a new, uniquely Austrian character.

A typical Austrian celebration meal begins with *vorspeise* (appetizer), *suppe* (soup), *hauptspeise* (main course), and *beilagen* (several raw and cooked side dishes). Also included are either *kuchen* or *torte* (cake) or *mehlspeise* (any baked specialty made with flour). A warm or cold after-meal sweet treat, *nachspeise*, is served during the dancing part of the celebration. With a fine meal, Austrian adults favor drinking beer, wine, or *sekt* (sparkling wine). Children drink fruit-flavored waters and wine spritzers (wine mixed with sparking water).

♨ *Gailtaler Hochzeitsuppe* (Gailtal Valley Wedding Soup)

The Gailtal Valley is in the southernmost province of Austria, called Carinthia. This soup is traditionally served at weddings, church events, and other special occasions; hence the name Wedding Soup. It is also called Church Day soup, as it is often served for the Sunday meal. This soup is served at the beginning of the wedding feast.

Yield: 4 servings

1 pound vegetables for soup (carrots, leeks, celeriac root or celery stalks, parsnips, parsley), washed well

½ pound beef shoulder

½ pound lamb shoulder

6 cups water

1 pound chicken parts for soup (legs, backs)

5 peppercorns

2 to 3 whole cloves

1 stick cinnamon

12 saffron strands

1 teaspoon dried basil

pinch of anise powder

pinch of ginger powder

2 egg yolks

½ cup thick cream

1 tablespoon flour

¼ cup dry white wine

salt and pepper to taste

Equipment: Vegetable peeler, large saucepan, bowls, oven mitts

1. Peel carrots, parsnips, and celeriac; cut off and discard the roots and coarse green leaves from leeks. Trim off ends of parsley stems and celery stalks. Slice all vegetables into large pieces, about 3 inches long.

2. In a large saucepan, put vegetables together with beef and lamb. Cover with water.

   Over low heat, simmer for about 1½ hours, skimming assiduously any foam that arises.

3. After 1 hour, add chicken, peppercorns, cloves, cinnamon, saffron, basil, anise, and ginger, and continue cooking until assorted meats are tender.

4. Remove meat and half the vegetables, and set aside to cool. Pass broth and remaining half of the vegetables through a fine sieve.

5. Beat egg yolks with cream and flour, stir into broth.

6. Slice cooled meats and vegetables, set aside into small, neat, bite-size pieces, and add to broth.

7. Reheat broth to just under boiling point. Do not let it come to a boil.

Season with salt, pepper, and white wine, and serve at once.

Perhaps the most famous Austrian dish is *schnitzel* (a word meaning "little cut" of meat). The beloved Austrian delicacy *Wiener schnitzel* is enjoyed at many life-cycle celebrations. If made with chicken instead of veal, the dish is called *backhendl* and when made with pork, *schweinsschnitzel*.

To make Wiener schnitzel, choose top-quality veal from the center of the rump. Have butcher slice it ¼ inch thick and trim all fat. Allow about 4 to 6 ounces per person. Have the butcher pound each slice as thin as possible (about ⅛ inch), making them oven-ready, or you can do it yourself (instructions follow). Follow the same directions if making schnitzel with chicken breast or boneless pork cutlet.

♪ *Wiener Schnitzel* (Viennese Veal Cutlets)

Yield: serves 6

6 (4 to 6 ounces each) veal slices

½ cup milk

3 eggs

salt and pepper to taste

1 cup all-purpose flour, for dredging

1 cup **bread crumbs**

6 tablespoons butter or margarine, more as needed

6 lemon slices, for garnish

1 tablespoons parsley, finely chopped

Equipment: Plate, plastic food wrap, wooden chopping block, wooden **meat mallet** or small **heavy-bottomed** skillet, paring knife or scissors, 3 pie pans, fork, baking sheet, large **heavy-bottomed** skillet, metal spatula, serving platter

1. Prepare and pound cutlets: Place a 10- or 12-inch sheet of plastic wrap on a wooden chopping block. Place a cutlet on top, and cover with another sheet of plastic wrap. Using either a wooden mallet or bottom surface of a small heavy-bottomed skillet, carefully flatten cutlet to about ⅛ inch thick. Remove plastic wrap. Using a paring knife or scissors, make small vertical cuts (about ½ inch deep and 1 inch apart) all around edges of the cutlet to keep it from curling up as it fries. Repeat preparing cutlets, and stack on a plate.

2. Prepare pans for breading cutlets: In first pie pan, put all the flour. In second pie pan, put milk, eggs, and salt and pepper to taste, and, using a fork, beat to mix well. In third pie pan, put bread crumbs.

3. Bread the cutlets: Dredge cutlet in flour, coat both sides, and shake off excess. Dip in the egg mixture, coat both sides, and shake off excess. Coat both sides with bread crumbs. Press bread crumbs on to the cutlet with your hands. Place breaded cutlet on a baking sheet covered with plastic wrap. Repeat, breading remaining cutlets, and place side by side on a baking sheet with a sheet of plastic wrap between layers.

4. Melt 6 tablespoons butter or margarine in a large skillet over medium-high heat. Fry one or two cutlets at a time, do not crowd the pan. Fry for 3 to 5 minutes on each side until golden brown and crisp. Using tongs, carefully transfer cutlet to serving platter, and keep warm,

but do not cover or breading will get soggy. Continue frying cutlets, adding more butter or margarine when needed to prevent sticking.

To serve, place a slice of lemon on top of each cutlet, and sprinkle with parsley. Boiled potatoes and spätzle (recipe follows) are served with the cutlets.

Spätzle is one of Austria's comfort foods. *Spätzle*, tiny dumplings, are included in the menu for christening feasts, weddings, and funerals. Almost every household has a *spätzle* maker, which looks something like a flat shredder. It is placed over a pot of boiling water and a flat sliding box filled with noodle dough is pushed back and forth along runners at the sides of the grater. The noodle dough is forced through the holes to form teardrop-shaped dumplings, which cook in seconds. A good substitute is a colander; push the dough mixture through the colander holes with a rubber spatula. The dough mixture separates into small teardrop shapes as it drops into the boiling water.

Spätzle (Tiny Dumplings)

Yield: serves 4

Water, as needed

salt and pepper to taste

2 eggs

1½ cups all-purpose flour, more if necessary

¼ teaspoon baking powder

½ cup milk

¼ teaspoon ground nutmeg

2 cups ice cubes

vegetable oil, as needed

½ cup butter or margarine

½ cup onions, finely chopped

For **garnish**:

2 tablespoons grated Parmesan cheese, more as needed

1 tablespoon chopped fresh parsley, or 2 teaspoons dried parsley flakes

Equipment: Large saucepan, food processor or large mixing bowl, mixing spoon, large bowl, *spätzle* maker or **colander**, rubber spatula, strainer or slotted spoon, large skillet, 2 forks, serving bowl

1. Prepare dumpling dough: Fill a large saucepan ⅔ full with water, add 1 teaspoon salt, and bring to a boil over high heat. While water is heating, put eggs, 1½ cups flour, baking powder, milk, and nutmeg in a food processor or large bowl. Process or beat with a mixing spoon until well mixed. If mixture is sticky, add a little more flour, ½ tablespoon at a time, until smooth.

2. Prepare to cook: Fill a large bowl halfway with water, add ice cubes, and place near the stove. Fill *spätzle* maker or colander with egg and flour mixture (dumpling dough). Cooking in batches, press about half the dumpling dough through the spätzle maker into boiling water, or, using a rubber spatula, push through the holes of a colander. Boil dumplings for 2 to 3

minutes, or until they swell and rise to the surface, stirring often to prevent sticking together. Using a strainer or slotted spoon, remove the dumplings, and transfer them to the bowl of ice water to stop the cooking action. Cook remaining dough. When all the dumplings are cold, drain thoroughly, and sprinkle with just enough oil to prevent them from sticking together.

3. At serving time, prepare sauce: Melt butter or margarine in a large skillet over medium-high heat. Add onions, and sauté for 2 to 3 minutes, or until soft. Add dumplings, and, using 2 forks, toss to heat through, about 3 to 4 minutes. Transfer to a serving bowl, and sprinkle with 2 tablespoons grated cheese and parsley.

Serve with extra cheese to sprinkle over dumplings. Spätzle *makes a great side dish with* Wiener schnitzel.

Austrians consider a meal incomplete unless it ends with dessert. Cakes and pastries are the crowning glory of Viennese cuisine. Traditionally, pastry is eaten with a cup of coffee.

♫ *Wiener Eiskaffee* (Viennese Iced Coffee)

Yield: serves 1

1 scoop rich vanilla ice cream, softened

1 cup strong black coffee

2 tablespoons prepared whipped cream

For **garnish**: confectioners' sugar

Equipment: Tall heatproof glass, spoon

1. Place the ice cream in a tall heatproof glass, and fill with coffee. Put a dollop of whipped cream on top, and sprinkle with confectioners' sugar.

To serve, stir as you drink the coffee.

Belgium

Located in northwestern Europe between the Netherlands on the north and France on the south, Belgium contains two major linguistic groups—French-speaking Walloons in the south and the Flemish-speaking Flemings in the north. A German-speaking minority lives close to the eastern border with Germany. Each region has its own separate educational administration, and children are taught their regional language.

Belgium is predominantly Roman Catholic, and religion plays an important part in the nation's culture. The country has many Catholic schools where children get religious instruction along with their regular studies. Belgium is the last country in northern Europe to have a Catholic monarch, and most national holidays are still based on religious occasions, particularly Christmas and Easter. The people traditionally turn to the Catholic Church for important life-cycle events. (See Protestant and Catholic Life-Cycle Rituals, page lxxiii.)

Although church attendance is low, most Belgians see to it that their children are baptized, make first communion, and go to Sunday school. Baptisms are conducted according to Catholic ritual, and the ceremony is usually followed by a family dinner, either at home or at a local restaurant. The big occasion for most children is when they make their first communion at age 12. This life-cycle event marks the child's passing into young adulthood. The celebration usually includes a big family party with plenty of sweets, and children receive gifts from relatives and friends.

Belgian endive is originally from Belgium where it is called *whitloof* (white leaf) due to its delicate whitish-green color. The color is a result of the vegetable being grown in complete darkness to prevent it turning deep green; the endive also turns bitter if it is exposed to light.

₰ *Whitloof Farci au Fromage* (Belgian Endive with Ham in Cheese Sauce)

Yield: 6 or 8

water, as needed

salt and pepper, as needed

6 or 8 fresh Belgian endives

6 or 8 boiled ham slices

1 cup dry white wine or chicken broth

1 cup milk

2 tablespoons butter or margarine

¼ pound Gruyère or Emmental cheese, **coarsely chopped** (available in refrigerated section of most supermarkets)

¼ teaspoon nutmeg

Equipment: Medium saucepan, **colander**, 1 or 2 buttered 8- or 9-inch-square baking pan, small **heavy-bottomed** saucepan, mixing spoon, oven mitts

Preheat broiler.

1. **Blanch** endives: Fill medium saucepan halfway with water, add 2 teaspoons salt, and bring to boil over high heat. Add endives, and continue to boil for 3 minutes. Drain endives in colander until cool enough to handle.

2. Wrap a slice of boiled ham around each endive and place seam-side down in buttered 8- or 9-inch baking pan, do not stack. Place remaining endive in a single layer on second baking pan.

3. Pour white wine or chicken broth into small heavy-bottomed saucepan. Add milk and butter or margarine. Bring to boil over medium-high heat, stir to melt butter or margarine. Reduce heat to medium-low, add cheese, and stir to melt cheese and thicken sauce. Stir in nutmeg and salt and pepper to taste. Pour cheese sauce over wrapped endives in baking pan.

4. Place in oven under broiler for 12 to 18 minutes, or until heated through, and sauce is bubbly and lightly browned.

Serve as the first course for the wedding reception luncheon. Each person is served a ham-wrapped endive.

Southern Belgium grows particularly fine asparagus, which is a favorite vegetable throughout the country. The following easy to prepare dish would be served for a family celebration dinner.

⚜ *Asperges de Malines* (Asparagus with Egg Sauce)

Yield: serves 4

2 hard-cooked eggs, **coarsely chopped**   ¾ cup melted butter, cooled

1 tablespoon fresh parsley, finely chopped   2½ to 3 pounds fresh asparagus

salt and pepper to taste

Equipment: Small bowl with cover, fork, paring knife or vegetable peeler, large saucepan, metal tongs, spoon, large serving platter

1. In small bowl, mash chopped hard-cooked eggs with fork. Add parsley and salt and pepper to taste, and stir to mix well. Stirring constantly, slowly pour in melted butter in a thin stream. Cover and set aside.

2. Using paring knife or vegetable peeler, trim off tough fibrous bottom part of each asparagus spear. Wash under cold running water.

3. Fill large saucepan ⅔ full with water and bring to boil over high heat. Add 2 tablespoons salt and asparagus, and boil for 8 to 10 minutes (depending upon thickness of spears), or until tender. Do not overcook. Using tongs, transfer asparagus to large serving platter, and arrange neatly so that all lay in same direction. Carefully spoon sauce in a ribbon across the middle of asparagus.

Serve asparagus while still warm as a side dish.

The Walloons have many of the same life-cycle customs as neighboring France (see France page 352). Some Belgian brides prefer *coûque de visé*, a sugar crusted egg-rich bread for the wedding celebration feasts in place of *pain de marriage* (recipe page 355). *Coûque de visé* is the same as French brioche, except the French do not add the coarsely crushed sugar cubes or rock candy crystals.

Special brioche pans are available at kitchenware stores. They range in size from 4 to 9½ inches in diameter. For this recipe, you can use either an 8-inch brioche pan or 8-inch springform pan that is at least 4 inches deep.

The original recipe for *coûque de visé* calls for homemade rock candy crystals that take at least one to two weeks to crystallize. In this recipe, you can substitute crushed sugar cubes or commercial rock candy crystals.

☙ *Coûque de Visé* (also French Brioche) (Belgian Egg Bread)

Note: This recipe takes 24 hours.

Yield: 1 loaf

6 tablespoons coarsely crushed sugar cubes or rock candy crystals, homemade or commercial (available at candy stores or some supermarkets)

1 package active dry **yeast**

3 teaspoons sugar, divided

3 tablespoons **lukewarm** water

½ cup milk

½ cup butter or margarine, at room temperature

½ teaspoon salt

3 cups **sifted** all-purpose flour

2 eggs, beaten

For **garnish: egg wash**

Equipment: Small bowl, small spoon, small saucepan, **candy thermometer** (optional), greased large mixing bowl, mixing spoon, lightly floured work surface, greased plastic food wrap, 8-inch greased brioche or 8-inch springform pan, **pastry brush**, oven mitts, aluminum foil (optional), wire cake rack

1. If adding homemade rock candy crystals, prepare at least 1 to 2 weeks ahead.

2. In small bowl, dissolve yeast and ½ teaspoon sugar in lukewarm water, and let stand until foamy, 5 to 10 minutes.

3. Bring milk to boil in small saucepan over medium-high heat. Add butter or margarine, remaining 2½ teaspoons sugar, and salt, and stir until dissolved. Remove from heat, and set aside to cool to lukewarm.

4. Put 1¾ cups flour in large mixing bowl. Add beaten eggs, yeast mixture, and milk mixture, beat until well mixed and smooth. Beating constantly, add remaining 1¼ cups flour, a little at a time, to form soft dough. Transfer to lightly floured work surface, and knead until smooth and satiny, about 3 to 5 minutes. Shape dough into a ball, and put into greased large mixing bowl, and turn dough to grease all sides. Grease one side of plastic food wrap and place, greased-side down, over bowl of dough. Leave dough in warm place to rise to double in bulk, 1½ to 2 hours.

5. Transfer dough to lightly floured work surface, punch down, and knead for 3 to 5 minutes. Knead half the crushed sugar cubes or crushed rock candy crystals into the dough. Shape into a ball, place in greased large bowl, and turn dough to grease all sides. Cover with greased plastic wrap, and refrigerate overnight.

6. Next morning, remove dough from refrigerator, and bring to room temperature, about 1 hour. Pull off a piece of dough about the size of an egg. Shape remaining dough into a ball and place in 8-inch greased brioche or springform pan. Using your finger, poke a hole about 1 inch deep into the top center of loaf. Form the egg-size piece of dough into a light bulb shape, and set small bottom end into the hole, making a top knob on the loaf. Cover with greased plastic wrap, and leave in warm place to rise until double in bulk, 1 to 1½ hours.

Preheat oven to 375°F.

7. Using pastry brush, gently brush loaf with egg wash, and sprinkle with remaining 2 tablespoons crushed sugar cubes or crushed rock candy crystals.

8. Bake in oven for 40 to 45 minutes, or until golden brown. If top knob of dough looks like it might be getting too brown, cover it with small piece of foil. Test **bread doneness**, and adjust cooking time accordingly. Using oven mitts, remove from baking pan, and cool on wire cake rack.

Serve this bread on the day it is baked for best flavor and texture.

₵ *Rijsttaart* (Rice Tart)

Rijsttaart, literally "rice tart" is a traditional tart (single crust pie) most famously made in the city of Verviers, once renowned for its wool textile industry, in the province of Liege. Historically, rice was a very costly food item in Europe because it had to be imported at great expense from far-off countries. Hence, it was reserved for special occasions, such as Christmas and other special occasions, such as birthdays. From Verviers, this tart filled with a rich and creamy rice pudding has spread throughout Belgium, and it is now one of the most loved of Belgian desserts. A ready-made unbaked 9-inch pie crust can be used, instead of making one from scratch.

Pie crust:	¾ cup butter or shortening, diced
2 cups all-purpose flour	½ cup ice-cold water
1 teaspoon salt	

Filling:	4 large **egg yolks** or 2 large eggs
1½ cups cooked pudding rice (**short grain** rice, such as the type used for risotto)	¼ teaspoon salt
	1 teaspoon vanilla extract
½ cup sugar	½ tablespoon grated lemon rind
1 cup milk	¼ teaspoon grated mace or nutmeg, optional
1 cup heavy cream	For **garnish**: confectioners' sugar

Equipment: Medium mixing bowl, wire **pastry blender** or food processor, plastic wrap, 9-inch pie pan or tart pan, oven mitts, wire rack

1. Prepare crust: In a bowl, combine flour and salt until well mixed. Cut into flour mixture with a wire pastry blender, or rub in lightly with your fingers, the butter or shortening until mixture resembles coarse crumbs. Sprinkle ice-cold water evenly over flour- butter mixture, a little at a time, until all particles are moistened and are beginning to clump together. With floured hands, bring moistened particles together into a ball, and knead briefly to smooth

surface. (Alternatively, place all ingredients for pastry in a food processor, and pulse until mixture comes together. Remove from food processor with floured hands, and shape into a ball.) Cover with plastic wrap, and leave to rest, refrigerated, for 30 minutes.

2. On a lightly floured surface, roll out dough to ⅛-inch thickness, and place on a 9-inch pie or tart pan. Crimp edges with a fork or with your fingers into a rope pattern, if desired, if using a pie pan. If using a tart pan, simply trim pastry edges flush with the rim. Prick surface of pastry lightly with a fork, and set aside in a cool place or refrigerate while you make the filling.

3. Prepare filling: In a saucepan over medium heat, place cooked rice, milk, and sugar. Simmer until milk is completely absorbed, stirring frequently to prevent sticking. Set aside to cool for 15 to 20 minutes.

4. Ten minutes before baking, preheat oven to 350°F.

5. Stir in cream, egg yolks or whole eggs, salt, vanilla extract, lemon rind, and mace or nutmeg (if using) to cooled rice mixture, and spoon into prepared pastry.

6. Bake in the middle rack of preheated oven for 25 to 35 minutes, or until filling is set and golden. Allow to cool thoroughly on a wire rack before serving.

Garnish with confectioners' sugar, if desired.

France

France, the largest country in Western Europe, has long been a world leader in both fashion and food. In a sense, Paris, the French capital, became the world capital of good eating because of the French Revolution that began in 1789. Ignited in part by the excessive social and economic privileges enjoyed by the nobility, the Revolution, in its most violent phase in the early 1790s, led to death on the guillotine for many French aristocrats. With their livelihoods gone, many fine chefs who had been in noble service went to Paris and opened restaurants specializing in what they knew best, haute cuisine. Thus, in the last two centuries, other countries have come to look to France for inspiration in what to eat.

The majority of French are Roman Catholic, and most life-cycle celebrations are conducted according to the Catholic Church. Protestantism in France began in the 16th century with the Reformation. The Huguenots are perhaps the most famous of French Protestant groups, who were followers of Calvinist teachings, and they were concentrated in northern France. While they were briefly allowed to practice their religion by the Edict of Nantes, King Louis XIV revoked their privileges, and they ended up being persecuted. Many Huguenots fled to England and to the then English colonies in America. By 1789, however, with the Declaration of the Rights of Man and of the Citizen, they regained their freedom to worship. Today, in the 21st century, Huguenots have survived in communities in the Cévennes, Alsace, England, and Australia. Protestants in France number around 1 million adherents, or over 2 percent of the total French population. With the efforts of the Evangelical Protestants, their number is said to be increasing, in contrast to the trend in other Western European countries. (See Protestant and Catholic Life-Cycle Rituals, page lxxiii.) Additionally, France has a small Jewish minority and one of the largest Muslim immigrant communities in Europe, mostly from former French colonies in North Africa.

A family's financial and social status determines how they will celebrate life-cycle events and whether the celebration will be haute cuisine or cuisine bourgeoisie. Haute cuisine is refined, elegant French cooking, prepared by highly trained cooks, called "chefs." Weddings or other special occasions serving haute cuisine are always spectacular and expensive events. On the other hand, cuisine bourgeoisie—French country cooking—includes many classic dishes that are hearty and well within the budget of most French couples, such as *poulet Marengo* (recipe page 359).

Most French life-cycle celebrations are followed by a celebratory meal. After a baptismal ceremony, for instance, the family group either goes to a restaurant or holds a family dinner at home. French church weddings, which are generally held in the morning, are usually followed by a brunch or luncheon reception that takes place in the bride's family home or in a wedding hall, restaurant, or hotel banquet room. At the reception, it is customary for newlyweds to toast using a *coupe de marriage* filled with champagne. This special two-handled cup is often a family heirloom that has been passed down through generations.

Hors d'oeuvres (appetizers) are part of all celebration feasts regardless of social status. Hors d'oeuvres are eaten anytime and anywhere, from a simple farmer's lunch to an affluent wedding or birthday celebration. The farmer's or working person's hors d'oeuvres might be simple platters of sliced fresh tomatoes drizzled with olive oil and a sprinkle of parsley, or anchovy fillets on slices of toast, or sausage with assorted cheeses served with freshly baked bread. When haute cuisine is followed, formally attired waiters present the hors d'oeuvres on silver trays. The selection would be *pâtés* (the word means "pie," but they are a loaf made of a mixture of meat, seafood, or vegetables), *les crudités* (decoratively cut assorted raw vegetables, such as tiny baby carrots, celery hearts, and radishes), and expensive lobster or filled pastries, such as the following recipe for *chausson aux champignons* (mushroom pastries).

⚘ *Chausson aux Champignons* (Mushroom Pastries)

Yield: serves 8 to 10

¼ cup butter

2 cups fresh mushrooms, finely chopped

1 onion, finely chopped

2 cloves garlic, finely chopped or 1 teaspoon garlic granules

4½-ounce can deviled ham (available at all supermarkets)

salt and pepper to taste

nutmeg cheese pastry (recipe follows)

Equipment: Large skillet, wooden mixing spoon, medium mixing bowl, teaspoon, cup of water, lightly greased baking sheet, fork, oven mitts, large serving platter

1. Melt butter in a large skillet over medium-high heat. Add finely chopped mushrooms, onion, and garlic. Stirring frequently, sauté for 3 to 5 minutes, or until onion is soft and mushrooms are golden. Remove from heat. Transfer to a medium mixing bowl. Stir in deviled ham and salt and pepper to taste.

2. Prepare nutmeg cheese pastry (recipe follows).

   Ten minutes before baking, preheat oven to 425°F.

3. Assemble: Place a heaping teaspoonful of mushroom mixture in the center of a pastry circle. Lightly moisten your finger with water, and brush it along the edge of the pastry circle. Fold pastry shell over the mushroom mixture to encase the filling, making pastry into a half moon. Press the edges of the pastry shell together to firmly seal in the mushroom mixture. Place on a lightly greased baking sheet. Prick the pastries 2 or 3 times with a fork to allow steam to escape while cooking.

4. Bake in preheated oven for 10 to 15 minutes, or until golden.

To serve, place warm pastries on a large serving platter. To eat pastries, pick one up from the tray with your fingers. Cocktail napkins should be provided for guests.

℧ *Pâtisserie Fromage avec Muscade* (Nutmeg Cheese Pastry)

Yield: 20 to 24 pieces

2 cups all-purpose flour	½ teaspoon ground nutmeg
½ cup grated cheddar cheese	¾ cup vegetable shortening
¼ teaspoon salt	¼ cup water

Equipment: Large mixing bowl, **pastry blender**, or 2 forks (optional), plastic food wrap, lightly floured work surface, rolling pin, 3- or 4-inch round cookie cutter, clean kitchen towel

1. Put the flour, cheese, salt, and nutmeg in large mixing bowl. Using a pastry blender, cut in shortening until the mixture is crumbly. Add water, a little at a time, and, using your hands, mix until smooth dough forms. Form into a ball, flatten to a 1-inch-thick disk, wrap in plastic wrap, and refrigerate for 30 minutes.

2. On a lightly floured work surface, using a rolling pin, roll the pastry out to ⅛-inch thickness. Using a 3- or 4-inch cookie cutter, cut out 20 to 24 circles. Stack, slightly overlapping, on work surface and cover with a towel.

Use in making chausson aux champignons, or pastries can be refrigerated overnight in an airtight container or frozen for up to 1 month. Thaw before using.

Pain de marriage (wedding bread) is wrapped in a napkin and taken to church to be blessed by the priest. The bread is then taken to the wedding breakfast, where the bride and groom cut it together and share the first slice. The sharing of bread symbolizes their unity as husband and wife. Some couples have brioche (rich egg bread) baked for their wedding bread. Brioche is the same as Belgium's *coûque de visé* (recipe page 350), except that the Belgians, unlike the French, add crushed sugar cubes or rock candy crystals.

⚜ *Pain de Marriage* (Wedding Bread)

Yield: 1 large loaf

1½ cups all-purpose flour	2 eggs
1 cup rye flour	½ cup honey
2 tablespoons baking powder	½ cup orange juice
½ teaspoon baking soda	1 cup melted butter or margarine
1 teaspoon salt	1 teaspoon almond extract
½ teaspoon ground cardamom	1 tablespoon grated orange peel
½ teaspoon black pepper	1 cup chopped or sliced almonds

Equipment: Flour sifter, medium bowl, large mixing bowl, electric mixer, mixing spoon or rubber spatula, greased 9×5-inch loaf pan, oven mitts, toothpick, wire cake rack

Ten minutes before baking, preheat oven to 350°F.

1. Sift all-purpose flour, rye flour, baking powder, baking soda, salt, cardamom, and black pepper into medium bowl.

2. In a large mixing bowl, beat eggs, using an electric mixer, until thick and yellow, about 2 to 3 minutes. Beating constantly, add honey, orange juice, melted butter or margarine, almond extract, and orange peel. Beat until well mixed, 1 to 2 minutes. Using a mixing spoon or rubber spatula, fold in the flour mixture, 1 cup at a time, blending well after each addition. Fold in the almonds. Pour batter into a lightly greased 9×5-inch loaf pan.

3. Bake in preheated oven for 45 to 50 minutes, or until toothpick inserted in the center comes out clean. Allow to cool for 10 minutes before turning onto wire cake rack.

Serve bread either warm or cold. After the bride and groom slice the bread, it is shared with grandparents, parents, and the wedding party. Each guest then gets a slice.

The first decorated wedding cakes were really wedding breads with icing on them.

During the 17th century, French pastry chefs created the forerunners of today's elaborate tiered wedding cakes. The cake was heavily spiced, much like the English wedding cake, and coated with marzipan, similar to the Caribbean black wedding cake (recipe page 235).

In France, the *croquembouche* (meaning "crisp in mouth") not only is a great wedding cake but is also made for other auspicious occasions, such as birthdays, saints' days, and anniversaries. The *croquembouche* is an assembly project of tiny custard-filled cream puffs. Traditionally, the cream puffs are dipped in sugar syrup, which hardens and "glues" them together as they are stacked.

⚘ Croquembouche (Celebration Cake of Cream Puffs)

This recipe is much easier to make than traditional *croquembouche*; the cream puffs hang off toothpicks around a foil-covered, cone-shaped piece of Styrofoam. Prepare the cone first and have everything ready to assemble. The decorations can be anything you like. Some ideas are listed as garnishes in the recipe.

Yield: 30 to 40

Choux à la crème (recipe follows)

2 (8 ounces each) butter cream icing, homemade (recipe page 238), or canned (available at all supermarkets)

For **garnish**: Candied cherries, fresh strawberries, or fresh or dried flowers

Equipment: 18-inch cone-shaped Styrofoam (available at craft and hobby stores), **serrated knife**, aluminum foil, double-sided mounting tape (available at all supermarkets or office supply stores), large round tray or platter, toothpicks, paring knife, rubber spatula or mixing spoon, **pastry bag** fitted with ¼-inch plain tip, 1 or 2 baking sheets

1. Prepare Styrofoam: Using a serrated knife, cut off about 5 inches from the top pointed end of the cone. Completely cover Styrofoam cone with foil, tucking it under the bottom about 1 inch. Attach several strips of double-sided mounting tape to large round tray or platter, set the cone on top, and press down to secure. Cover surface of the cone with toothpicks, spaced about 1 inch apart and sticking out halfway.

2. Prepare choux pastry (cream puff pastry): To make a larger *croquembouche*, you will need to make 3 or 4 batches of choux pastry.

3. Prepare the cream filling or vanilla pudding mix, according to directions on package. (Keep refrigerated until ready to use.)

4. Assemble: Open cans of butter cream icing, and, using small knife, put a thick dab of icing on the flat bottom side of each cream puff, and press onto toothpicks around the bottom of the cone. Complete each row, fitting cream puffs close together and working toward the top.

   Continue to decorate the *croquembouche* by poking candied cherries, fresh strawberries, or fresh or dried flowers into spaces between the cream puffs. At the top, put a small bouquet of flowers, ribbons, or decorations of your choice.

Choux à la crème are pastry shells that puff up during baking, and then they are filled with a small amount of pudding-like mixture after they are baked. *Choux* is the pastry, and *la crème* is the filling (recipe follows). First we will make and bake the pastry.

♪ *Choux à la Crème* (Cream Puffs)

Yield: 3 to 4 dozen

1 cup water	4 eggs, at room temperature
½ teaspoon salt	**egg wash**
½ cup unsalted butter	French cream filling (recipe follows) or 1 to
1 cup bread flour or all-purpose flour, **sifted**	2 boxes vanilla pudding mix (available at all supermarkets)

Equipment: Medium **heavy-bottomed** saucepan, wooden mixing spoon, medium mixing bowl, 1 or 2 baking sheets, parchment paper, teaspoon or **pastry bag** fitted with ¼-inch plain tip, **pastry brush**, wire cake rack

Ten minutes before baking, preheat the oven to 400°F.

1. Prepare choux pastry: Heat water and salt in a medium heavy-bottomed saucepan over medium-high heat. Stir until butter melts and mixture comes to a boil, remove from heat. Add flour all at once, and beat briskly with a wooden spoon for 2 or 3 minutes until mixture pulls away from the sides of the pan. Return pan to heat for about 30 seconds, beating vigorously to dry out the pastry dough. Cool for 5 minutes. Beat in eggs, one at a time, beating briskly after each addition until mixture is glossy and very smooth. After eggs are added, continue to beat for 3 minutes more. The mixture should cling to the sides of the pan and to the mixing spoon.

2. Prepare to bake: Line baking sheets with parchment paper. Make choux pastry the size of walnut shells. (The balls puff up as they bake.) If using a spoon, make small mounds, and leave a 2-inch space between each. For more uniform results, pipe choux dough through the pastry bag. Fill pastry bag fitted with ¼-inch tip. Hold the bag with the tip almost touching the parchment paper. Do not move the tip as you gently squeeze the bag from the top. Allow the desired amount of dough to bubble up around the tip of the pastry bag and quickly lift the bag to finish making the ball. The small point formed when you lift the tip can be pressed down with a moistened finger. Repeat making the pastries, spacing them 2 inches apart on baking sheets. Brush each choux pastry lightly with egg wash.

3. Bake in the preheated hot oven for 15 minutes. Reduce heat to 325°F, and bake 20 to 25 minutes longer, until firm and golden brown. Remove from the oven, and transfer pastries to a wire cake rack to cool.

4. Prepare the French cream filling. Keep covered and refrigerated until ready to use.

5. Fill the choux pastries: Using a paring knife, make a ½-inch slit in the side of each pastry. Uncover and stir French cream filling, or, if using prepared pudding mix, do the same. Using a rubber spatula or mixing spoon, fill the pastry bag fitted with a ¼-inch plain tip with the cream filling. Squeeze about 1 teaspoonful of filling into each slit. Place the filled shells side by side on the baking sheet.

Unfilled baked choux pastries can be refrigerated up to 1 week in an airtight container or frozen for about 1 month. Place the filled choux in a 275°F oven for 3 to 5 minutes to crisp and freshen.

⚘ *French Cream Filling*

Yield: about 2 cups

½ cup sugar

2 tablespoons **cornstarch**

¼ cup **sifted** all-purpose flour

¼ teaspoon salt

2 **egg yolks**, slightly beaten

¼ cup milk, at room temperature

2 cups **lukewarm** half-and-half

1 tablespoon unsalted butter

1 teaspoon vanilla or almond extract

Equipment: Medium **heavy-bottomed** saucepan, mixing spoon, small bowl, plastic food wrap

1. In a medium heavy-bottomed saucepan, mix the sugar, cornstarch, flour, and salt. In a small bowl, mix the egg yolks with cool milk, and stir into the sugar mixture until smooth. Continue to stir, adding warm light cream to sugar mixture, a little at a time, until well mixed.

2. Cook over medium heat, stirring constantly, until thickened, 8 to 10 minutes. Reduce heat to low, and stir constantly for 5 minutes. Remove from heat, and stir in butter to dissolve. Cool to room temperature, stirring frequently to keep smooth consistency and to prevent crust from forming on top. When cool, stir in vanilla or almond extract. When finished mixing, lay plastic wrap directly onto the top of mixture to prevent a film from forming. You must refrigerate for 3 or 4 hours before using.

Traditionally, French weddings are morning affairs requiring a brunch or lunch-type menu. A large platter of *beignets soufflés* set out for hungry guests is a welcome treat. The *beignets soufflés* offer a way of using up any puff pastry dough that might be left over from making the *croquembouche*.

⚘ *Beignets Soufflés* (Deep-Fried Puff Pastry, also Fritters)

CAUTION: HOT OIL IS USED.

Yield: serves 6 to 10

puff pastry dough (step 1 only, recipe page 357)

vegetable oil, for deep-frying

For **garnish**: granulated sugar

For serving: assorted fruit jams or marmalades

Equipment: Teaspoon, wax paper, baking sheet, **deep fryer** (see glossary for tips on making a deep fryer), deep fryer thermometer or wooden spoon, paper towels, baking sheet, metal tongs or slotted metal spoon

1. Prepare puff pastry dough.

2. Divide dough into heaping teaspoonfuls on wax paper–covered baking sheet.

3. Prepare to deep-fry: ***Caution: Adult supervision required.*** Heat oil to 375°F on deep fryer thermometer or until small bubbles appear around a wooden spoon handle when it is dipped

in the oil. Have ready several layers of paper towels on baking sheet. Fry pastries, a few at a time, carefully turning with metal tongs or slotted metal spoon to brown all sides, about 3 minutes. Transfer to paper towels to drain. Keep warm until ready to serve. Continue frying in batches.

4. Sprinkle beignets generously with sugar, for garnish.

Serve at once while still warm with side dishes of assorted fruit jams or marmalades.

According to legend, on the night of June 14, 1800, after defeating Austrian troops at Marengo in Italy, Napoleon wanted to celebrate with a fine dinner. However, his Swiss chef, Dunand, had lost his food wagons during the battle, so he was forced to scrounge for whatever he could find in the vicinity. Coming up with a few chickens, eggs, tomatoes, olive oil, and garlic, he concocted what became a bourgeoisie classic—*poulet Marengo*. The dish is perfect for a French wedding luncheon when garnished with heart-shaped **croûtes** and eggs, the symbol of fertility. Today, a few more ingredients, such as mushrooms, are added to make the recipe more interesting.

⚘ *Poulet Marengo* (Chicken Marengo-style)

Yield: serves 4 to 6

1 tablespoon vegetable oil

10 tablespoons butter or margarine, divided

2½- to 3½-pound roasting chicken, cut into serving-size pieces

3 cloves garlic, finely chopped

2 cups mushrooms, fresh or canned (drained), sliced

2 **tomatoes, peeled**, seeded, and finely chopped

1 tablespoon tomato paste

1½ cups canned beef broth

salt and pepper to taste

4 to 6 slices white bread, for garnish

4 to 6 eggs, for garnish

2 tablespoons finely chopped parsley, for garnish

Equipment: Large **heavy-bottomed** saucepan with cover or Dutch oven, metal tongs, baking pan, mixing spoon, work surface, paring knife or heart-shaped cookie cutters, large skillet with cover, metal spatula, paper towels, saucer

Preheat oven to 250°F.

1. Heat oil and 4 tablespoons butter or margarine in large heavy-bottomed saucepan or Dutch oven over medium-high heat. Add chicken pieces and fry, in batches, until golden brown on both sides, 5 to 7 minutes on each side. Remove chicken with metal tongs, leaving the juices in the saucepan, put in baking pan, and keep warm while frying remaining pieces.

2. Stir garlic into juices left over in saucepan or Dutch oven used to fry chicken. Add mushroom, tomatoes, tomato paste, beef broth, and salt and pepper to taste, and stir well. Return

fried chicken pieces to saucepan or Dutch oven, cover, and cook over medium heat for 45 to 50 minutes, or until tender and cooked through. Test for **chicken doneness**.

3. Prepare **croûtes**: Place bread slices on work surface, and, using paring knife or heart-shaped cookie cutter, cut each slice into a heart shape. Melt 4 tablespoons butter or margarine in large skillet over medium-high heat. Add heart-shaped bread slices and fry until golden brown, 2 to 3 minutes on each side. Remove with metal spatula and drain on paper towels.

4. Just before serving, melt remaining 2 tablespoons butter or margarine in large skillet over medium heat. Break eggs, one at a time, into a saucer, and transfer to skillet. **Baste** eggs, cover, and cook until whites are set and yolks are done, 3 to 5 minutes.

To serve, arrange the chicken pieces on a large platter and spoon sauce over top. Place the croûtes around the edge of the platter with the pointed ends facing out. Arrange fried eggs either between or on each heart-shaped croûte. Sprinkle with parsley and serve at once.

❦ *Torte de Pistache Praliné* (Pistachio Praline Torte)

This pistachio praline torte is a festive cake, rather similar to the French cake called *Succès*, popularized by the renowned confectioner, André Le Notre. Nut-based tortes like this are often served for birthdays and other special family occasions or gatherings. This recipe can be varied through the use of other nuts, such as almonds, pecans, macadamias, or even cashews. This torte needs to mellow for 24 hours before serving.

Yield: 8 to 10 servings

1¼ cups sugar	⅓ cup brandy or rum
2 cups unsalted pistachio nuts, finely ground	1 teaspoon lemon juice
6 egg whites	¼ cup water
1 tablespoon vanilla extract	1 cup unsalted pistachio nuts, chopped
3 tablespoons confectioners' sugar	For **garnish**: confectioners' sugar for sprinkling
1¼ cups unsalted butter	

Equipment: Parchment paper, pencil, mixing bowls from small to large, electric mixer, piping bag with decorative tip, cookie sheet or shallow baking tray, food processor or nut grinder

1. Prepare 3 sheets of parchment paper. With a dark pencil, draw a 9-inch circle in the middle of each of the sheets. The drawn circles serve as a template for the torte layers. Set aside.

2. In a small bowl, combine ½ cup sugar with 2 cups finely ground pistachio nuts. Set aside.

3. With scrupulously clean beaters in an equally scrupulously clean bowl, beat egg whites to soft peaks. While continuing to beat, gradually add ¼ cup sugar and vanilla, and continue beating until egg whites form stiff peaks. Gently fold in the sugar and finely ground pistachio nut mixture, mixing just until homogeneous. Spoon egg white and pistachio nut mixture into a piping bag.

4. Place a parchment sheet on a baking tray or cookie sheet, with the drawn template facing the cookie sheet. Using a plain decorative tip, pipe in spirals within the circle drawn on the reverse side of the parchment sheet. Prepare only one meringue layer at a time. Keep meringue and nut mixture chilled while waiting for each layer to be baked.

Sprinkle meringue disks with confectioners' sugar (place the sugar in a fine strainer, and tap it with a spoon so that the sugar exits in a fine even stream without any lumps).

5. Place baking tray in the middle rack of a preheated 300°F oven, and immediately turn down the temperature to 250°F. Let the meringue bake for 35 to 40 minutes, or until golden and crisp. Lift parchment paper with the baked meringue disk, and set on a wire rack to cool.

Continue with the rest of the meringue and nut batter.

6. Make pistachio nut praline. In a saucepan, combine ½ cup sugar, lemon juice, water, and chopped pistachios over low-medium heat. Simmer until sugar caramelizes and thickens. Quickly pour the thick syrupy mixture onto a buttered cookie sheet and allow to cool undisturbed.

7. With a metal spatula, release the praline (the solidified pistachio and caramel mixture). The praline will splinter. Place splinters and other fine bits in a food processor and pulse to a fine powder.

8. In a mixer bowl, cream butter, and gradually add the pistachio praline powder until mixture is homogeneous. Stir in brandy or rum.

9. Release the cooled pistachio meringue layers from parchment paper.

10. Place a tablespoon of pistachio praline buttercream in the middle of your serving plate.

11. Place one meringue disk on the buttercream (this prevents it from moving while being filled), and, using a piping bag, pipe half of the praline buttercream on it. Top with the other meringue disk, and pipe the remaining half of the praline buttercream. Set the last meringue disk on the buttercream. It is usually left bare of the praline buttercream, but if desired, reserve a bit of the filling to spread on it.

12. Refrigerate the torte for 24 hours to allow the flavors to meld and develop before serving.

Sprinkle torte all over with confectioners' sugar just before serving.

Germany

Located in the heart of Europe, Germany became a unified state only in 1871. The country experienced hardship and defeat in both World Wars and was divided into Communist East Germany and democratic West Germany from 1945 until 1990. Although reunification has created some economic difficulties, Germany at the end of the 20th century is one of the wealthiest and most industrialized nations of Europe. The German population is almost equally split between Roman Catholics and Protestants, with the great majority of the latter being Lutherans. Most Germans turn to their church when conducting celebrations surrounding baptisms, first communions, weddings, funerals, and important religious holidays. (See Protestant and Catholic Life-Cycle Rituals, page lxxiii.) There is a substantial ethnic Turkish community, of which the first generation came as *Gastarbeiter* (guest workers) in the 1960s, as well as an increasing number of refugees from beleaguered states in Africa and the Middle East. Germans of Turkish origin and migrants from the Middle East are predominantly followers of Islam. (See Islam and Islamic Life-Cycle Rituals, page lxxvi.)

In the state of North Rhine-Westphalia, the birth of a child is usually announced to the neighborhood with a set of baby clothes (for the appropriate gender) hanging from a line just above the house door, with or without a paper or cardboard stork attached to the line. As with its neighboring country Netherlands, the 50th birthday is a significant milestone and is usually celebrated with a whole-day party, sometimes at a rented hall. Family and friends will often create skits that depict certain events of the celebrant's life or regale the guests with humorous anecdotes, self-written poems, and songs. From then onward, every decade's birthday is marked with a special celebration.

A wedding is called *Hochzeit* (high time), a term that aptly describes the importance of this event in the lives of the bride and groom and their families. Each region in Germany has its own traditions. One is *Polterabend* (rumble night), which takes place a day or a week before the wedding ceremony. Family and friends of the bride and groom collect a mass of breakable items—vases, tiles, plates, cups made of glass, ceramic, or earthenware—that will make a great deal of noise. These are broken at the entry to the bride's house, to the accompaniment of food and drinks. The shards are believed to bring good luck. Another is kidnapping the bride (*Die Enführte Braut*). At some point during the dancing at the wedding reception, the bridesmaids, best man, and other friends take the willing bride to a favorite pub of the couple. After a round of drinks, they go on to the next hangout. The groom has to pay the ransom—that is, the tab run up by the kidnapping party. Prior notice, of course, is given to the pub owners. There is also a tradition of the newlyweds drinking from a bridal chalice (*Der Hochzeitbecher*)—two cups made of glass or ceramic connected by a hinge. It takes considerable skill to drink at the same time from the chalice without spilling a drop. To do so ensures long-lasting happiness and good fortune. One tradition in the Rhine region is to give the newlyweds money but not as it is or enclosed in envelopes. Guests use their imagination and time to create interesting objects, such as a multitiered wedding cake, a bird, or a miniature house—all ingeniously fashioned out of money bills.

In Germany, the *Verlobung* (engagement) is as binding as the wedding. It is often announced in the local paper, or an engagement notice is mailed to friends and relatives. After learning the good news, friends can casually drop in to congratulate the family, or the bride-to-be's family may plan a *Verlobungsfeier* (engagement feast). Such guests often enjoy a simple late morning repast of punch with cheese and crackers. Many parents also prepare a cold buffet that includes assorted salads, cold meats, poached fish (such as Scottish salmon, recipe page 286), and assorted breads. The *Verlobungsfeier* often takes place in the bride's family home or a restaurant. The party is generally an elegant sit-down dinner followed by speeches praising the upcoming marriage. A German wedding reception of traditional fare can take place at a local restaurant, inn, or hotel or at the home of the bride's parents. Guests are usually provided with mountains of food and plenty to drink, with choices varying according to region and season. Meat is almost always served—wild game or fowl are the most popular, followed by suckling pig (recipe page 425) and veal or beef. *Tafelspitz* (the summit of the table) is a popular main dish for weddings and special occasions. For the finale, a *Baumkuchen* is a luxurious choice for dessert because the preparation of this elaborate cake, with 15 to 20 thin layers, requires much effort and considerable expense. *Baumkuchen* is a cake that is difficult, if not impossible, to produce at home. The dancing at a wedding party often lasts till the early hours of the morning, and, to lift flagging spirits, chilled tiny glasses of schnapps (*Jägermeister* is a favorite, or Limoncello) are circulated. And to signal the wrapping up of the party, one final dish is served: often a nourishing and warming soup, such as beef goulash (*Rindegulaschsuppe*), to restore guests before they make their way home.

⚘ *Westfälische Hochzeitsuppe* (Westphalian Wedding Soup)

The wedding feast usually features a soup as the first course, and it is known as "wedding soup" (*Hochzeitsuppe*). Each region has its own version of this soup. It is also commonly made for a Sunday meal. The recipe that follows is one that is traditionally made in the region of Westphalia. This is a clear soup, and great care is made to keep it as clear as possible by sieving the stock several times. The garnishes should not crowd the tureen or the individual bowls—less is more in this instance, as the main attraction is the clarity of the soup.

Yield: 6 to 8 servings

Stock

2 pounds beef shank (bone-in)

2 pounds whole chicken for soup, quartered

½ pound beef round in one piece

1 stalk lovage, halved

Garnish:

½ pound white asparagus, sliced into bite-size pieces

Dumplings:

½ cup water

¼ head celeriac, peeled and sliced into chunks, or 2 stalks celery, halved

1 leek, halved

8 cups water

4 egg whites, beaten

½ pound cauliflower, divided into small **florets**

¾ cup carrots, peeled and sliced into disks

1 cup fresh parsley, minced

¼ cup butter, melted

3 tablespoons fine **semolina**

1 egg, beaten

1 pinch salt

Egg garnish:

2 eggs

½ cup milk

1 pinch salt

1 pinch freshly ground nutmeg

1 pinch freshly ground nutmeg

1 tablespoon butter for greasing

4 cups water

Equipment: Large stockpot, small saucepan, sieve, large and small bowls, covered bowl, **double boiler**, 3 ramekins or custard cups, foil, soup tureen, ladle, oven mitts

1. Make the stock: Into a large stockpot, place beef shank, add cold water, and simmer over low heat for 1 hour. Do not let it come to a boil, else the flavor of the soup will be affected by bitter essences being extracted from the bones.

2. Remove beef shank and set it aside. Pass stock through a sieve into a large bowl, and return to cleaned stockpot.

3. Add chicken, and simmer for 1 hour over low heat. Skim any foam that rises. Thirty minutes before the hour is up, add stock vegetables. Remove chicken and vegetables, and set aside.

4. Add beaten egg whites to the simmering stock to absorb all impurities. Turn off heat, and pass stock through a sieve once more. Season stock with salt.

5. Slice the choice parts of meat from the shank and chicken into small neat pieces. Reserve.

6. Prepare vegetable garnishes: Take 2 cups of stock from stockpot, and place into a small saucepan. Over gentle heat, cook the asparagus, cauliflower, and carrots separately, until they are bite-tender. Reserve the vegetables. Sieve stock, and return to stockpot.

7. Prepare the egg garnish: Mix well eggs, milk, salt, and nutmeg. Pour into buttered ramekins to fill them halfway. Cover ramekins with foil, and set them on the top half of a double boiler. Fill the bottom half of the double boiler with water, and set at medium heat. Allow to steam until egg mixture is set, about 20 minutes. Leave ramekins to cool. Unmold the egg garnishes, slice into neat bite-size pieces, and reserve.

8. Prepare dumplings: Mix well water, melted butter, and egg. Stir in semolina, salt, and nutmeg, and leave to rest for 10 minutes to let semolina absorb the liquids. Form into tiny balls.

9. In a large saucepan, put 6 cups of water to boil over medium heat. Add dumplings, without crowding the pan. Cook for 10 to 15 minutes, or until dumplings rise to the surface. Remove pan from heat. Add one cup of cold water to the pan, and let dumplings rest for 10 minutes. They will have doubled in size. Drain and keep them in a covered bowl to stay warm.

10. Just before serving, assemble garnishes and dumplings. Add the sliced meat pieces, vegetable garnishes, and egg garnish to the stock. Over medium heat, bring soup to just under boiling point. Do not let it come to a boil. Put dumplings at the bottom of the serving

tureen, and ladle the soup and garnishes over. If serving individually, put 3 dumplings per bowl and distribute vegetable and egg garnishes evenly.

Sprinkle with minced parsley, and serve at once.

Sauerbraten (marinated pot roast) is a classic German meat dish. For flavors to fully develop, begin this recipe three days before serving. Classic *Sauerbraten* in the Rhine region is usually made of horsemeat, from horses especially bred for the table.

⚜ *Sauerbraten* (Marinated Pot Roast)

Note: This recipe takes three days.

Yield: serves 6 to 8

3 to 4 pounds beef, rolled rump roast, boneless chuck, or top round	4 black peppercorns
	1 teaspoon salt
5 cups water, more as needed	4 tablespoons vegetable oil
2 cups red wine vinegar	8 gingersnaps, crumbled (available in cookie aisle at all supermarkets)
2 onions, finely sliced	
2 bay leaves	2 tablespoons brown sugar
6 whole cloves	3 tablespoons all-purpose flour

Equipment: Fork, large plastic, glass, or ceramic bowl with cover, medium saucepan, mixing spoon, paper towels, strainer, small bowl, large saucepan with cover or Dutch oven, metal tongs, large baking pan, 3- or 4-cup-size measuring cup, **bulb baster** or mixing spoon, large skillet, whisk, chopping block, meat knife, small sauce bowl

1. Prick beef roast all over with fork, and place in large plastic, glass, or ceramic bowl. Set aside.

2. Prepare marinade: Pour 5 cups water, and wine vinegar into medium saucepan. Add onions, bay leaves, cloves, peppercorns, and salt. Bring to boil over high heat, stir, and remove from heat. Cool to warm, and pour over meat. Add more cold water, if necessary, to completely cover meat. Cover and refrigerate for 3 days, turning meat daily.

3. On serving day: Remove meat from marinade, pat dry with paper towels. Strain and save marinade in small bowl.

4. Heat oil in large saucepan or Dutch oven over medium-high heat. Add meat and brown on all sides, 25 to 30 minutes. Add marinade, bring to boil, reduce heat to simmer, cover, and cook 1½ hours. Turn meat, cover, and simmer 1 to 1½ hours longer, or until tender. Transfer meat to large baking pan and keep warm. Pour pan drippings into 3- or 4-cup measuring cup. Skim off grease, using bulb baster or spoon. Allow meat to rest 15 to 20 minutes before slicing.

5. Prepare gravy: Add water to pan drippings if necessary, to make 2½ cups of liquid for gravy, pour into large skillet. Or, if you have more than 2½ cups pan drippings, transfer excess to

covered container, and refrigerate or freeze for another use. Bring liquid to boil over medium-high heat. Stir in crumbled gingersnaps and brown sugar until well mixed, and reduce heat to simmer.

6. Make slurry: Stir flour into ½ cup water to make smooth paste. Whisk slurry into gingersnap mixture and continue to whisk until smooth and thickened, 3 to 5 minutes.

To serve, slice meat on chopping block, using meat knife. Place slices, slightly overlapping, on serving platter, drizzle about ½ cup gravy on slices, and pour remaining gravy into sauce bowl to spoon over each serving.

Sauerbraten is usually served with plain boiled potatoes and horseradish (recipe follows). Just a touch of horseradish is eaten with each bite of the meat. Horseradish is one of the favorite German condiments; it is served with everything from sandwiches to banquet meats.

₡ **Homemade Horseradish**

Yield: about 2 cups

½ pound fresh horseradish, washed, peeled, and chopped (available at most supermarkets)

½ cup: white vinegar

½ cup water

1½ teaspoons sugar, more if necessary

Equipment: Electric **blender**, mixing spoon, rubber spatula, 1-pint jar with cover

1. Put chopped horseradish, vinegar, water, and 1½ teaspoons sugar in blender, and **blend** on high until finely ground. Turn off machine once or twice, use rubber spatula to scrape down sides of container. Adjust seasoning, adding a little more sugar if necessary. Transfer to pint jar, cover tightly, and refrigerate.

Serve horseradish as a condiment, as a dip with meat or seafood, or in sauce recipes.

In Germany, funerals are simple. In the Catholic tradition, requiem mass and burial are followed by a *Beerdigungsfeier* (funeral feast). Secular (nonreligious) funerals and cremations are increasingly being practiced. For nonreligious Germans, family members of the deceased are responsible for preparing the program for a *Beerdigungsfeier*. Often this includes the songs and type of music, as well as poetry, favored by the deceased. Family and friends are usually given time to share their memories of the deceased during the gathering. When cremation has been chosen instead of burial, the wishes of the deceased are respected as to where to scatter the ashes. Scattering ashes over a body of water requires special permission from the local environment authorities. Burial in a forest (in officially and specifically designated areas) is also gaining in popularity, in particular among the ecologically minded. If the funeral is in the countryside, the feast is usually given in the home of the deceased; in the city, the feast is often held in a local restaurant. The noontime menu could include *Sauerbraten* (recipe precedes) with boiled potatoes and *Erbspüree* (recipe follows). Open sandwiches on *Brötchen* (round bread rolls) filled with cheese or ham and a streusel cake (*Streuselkuchen*) are most commonly served for a funeral meal. (For a similar cake to *Streuselkuchen*, see the recipe for Mennonite *mango platz*, pp. 568.)

⚶ *Erbspüree* (Stewed Yellow Peas)

Yield: serves 4 to 6

6 slices lean bacon, diced

1 onion, finely chopped

1 cup each: carrots and celery, finely chopped

2 leeks, finely chopped, rinsed, drained

2 cups dried yellow peas

6 cups water

¼ teaspoon ground marjoram

salt and pepper to taste

Equipment: Large skillet, slotted spoon, paper towels, plate, large saucepan with cover or Dutch oven, mixing spoon, serving bowl

1. Fry bacon in large skillet over medium heat to render, 3 to 5 minutes. Using slotted spoon, remove bacon pieces, and transfer to paper towel–covered plate to drain. Add onion to skillet, and stir to coat with bacon fat. Increase heat to medium-high, and sauté until soft, 3 to 5 minutes. Set aside.

2. Put carrots, celery, leeks, and dried peas into large saucepan or Dutch oven. Add water, bring to boil over high heat, and stir. Reduce heat to simmer, cover, and cook for 35 to 45 minutes, until peas are soft yet tender and have absorbed all the liquid. Stir occasionally to prevent sticking. Stir in marjoram and salt and pepper to taste.

To serve, transfer cooked peas to serving bowl, and sprinkle with bacon. Serve hot as a side dish with Sauerbraten *(recipe page 365).*

Germany's culinary history is identified with sweet and savory breads of all sizes and shapes. For religious holidays, such breads were baked in a variety of shapes, from rings, hearts, and animals, to saints, especially St. Nick. *Kugelhopf* is the traditional name-day sweet bread.

⚶ *Kugelhopf* (also *Bundt Kuchen*) (Sweet Bread)

Yield: serves 8 to 10

1 package active dry **yeast**

1 cup **lukewarm** milk

3 cups all-purpose flour, divided

½ cup butter, at room temperature

1 cup sugar

4 eggs

¼ teaspoon salt

zest of 1 lemon

½ teaspoon ground nutmeg	½ cup sliced almonds, **blanched**
1 cup seedless raisins, soaked in warm water for 10 minutes and drained	For **garnish**: confectioners' sugar

Equipment: Small mixing bowl, mixing spoon, kitchen towel, large mixing bowl, electric mixer, rubber spatula, greased **Bundt pan**, oven mitts, wire cake rack, serving platter

1. Make yeast sponge: In small mixing bowl, dissolve yeast in lukewarm milk, 5 to 10 minutes, until bubbly. Stir in 1 cup flour, cover with towel, and let rise in warm place until double in bulk and spongy looking, about 1 hour.

2. In large mixing bowl, using electric mixer or mixing spoon, beat butter until creamy. Add sugar and eggs, one at a time, beating well after each addition. Add salt, lemon rind, and nutmeg, and beat to mix well. Use rubber spatula to scrape down sides of bowl.

3. Using mixing spoon or rubber spatula, gently stir in yeast sponge, remaining 2 cups flour, and drained raisins. Mix well. Sprinkle bottom of Bundt pan with almonds, add dough, and spread evenly in pan. Cover with towel, and let rise in warm place until almost double in bulk, ¾ to 1 hour.

Preheat oven to 350°F.

4. Bake in oven for 45 minutes to 1 hour, until golden brown. Wearing oven mitts, remove from oven. Flip pan to remove bread, and place on wire cake rack to cool. While still warm, sprinkle with confectioners' sugar.

To serve, slice in wedges, and place on serving platter.

The Netherlands

Wedged into the northwestern corner of Europe between Belgium and Germany, and lying across the English Channel from Great Britain, the Netherlands is a small, flat, low-lying country that has for centuries faced the threats of inundation by the North Sea and invasion by more powerful European neighbors. Both threats became reality in the 20th century. The Netherlands was invaded by Nazi Germany in 1940 and occupied until 1945. In 1953, a great flood cost many Dutch lives; to prevent the recurrence of such a tragedy, the Dutch built the Delta Project, a storm-surge barrier of massive dams and dikes that took 33 years to complete.

The Netherlands has a Catholic majority, living mainly in the southern part of the country and an almost equal number of people who claim no religious affiliation. Dutch Protestants are divided into several groups, with the largest being the Dutch Reformed Church. In the Netherlands, church and state are separate, and everyone is guaranteed religious freedom by the constitution. Life-cycle celebrations are either secular or according to religious beliefs. (See Protestant and Catholic Life-Cycle Rituals, page lxxiii.) A very old custom, especially in the country, is for families to dress their newborn in christening clothes and show the child to relatives and friends. The baby is again dressed in christening clothes at about five to seven months for his or her baptism, which is usually followed by a family dinner. Friends drop in with gifts for the baby during the afternoon, and enjoy a light repast of sweets, cakes, and candy with either hot or cold beverages, depending upon the weather.

The birth of a baby is celebrated by eating a rusk spread with sugar-coated aniseeds called *"Beschuit met muisjes"* (rusk with little mice). The sugar-coated aniseeds are called "little mice" because of the aniseed stem that sticks out like a tail from each one. The rusk is spread with butter, and white and blue *muisjes* are sprinkled on top for a boy and white and pink for a girl. Everyone is offered these celebratory rusks to eat when they visit the new baby. Children will bring some to share with their school-mates when a sibling is born. The birth of a child in the Royal Family is celebrated with rusks sprinkled with white and orange *muisjse*. *Muisjes* may also be spread on buttered bread for breakfast. The use of aniseed stems from its property of stimulating lactation in new mothers and as a symbol of fertility. *Beschuit met muisjes* is usually accompanied by a tiny glass of *Kandeel*, a warm drink that resembles eggnog (see recipe page 370). Birthdays are celebrated more elaborately in the Netherlands than in any other country in Europe, for the Dutch do not have name days. Most homes prominently display a calendar listing each family member's birthday. On the morning of someone's birthday, family members come into the bedroom with gifts and candy and sing a birthday song. Later in the day or in the evening, friends and relatives come with presents. Reaching the age of 50 is an important milestone, and the Dutch usually call this event "seeing Abraham" (for a male) and "seeing Sarah" for a female, in reference to the Biblical passage John 8:57: "You are not yet fifty years old and you have seen Abraham." Fifty years and every decade thereafter is called a "crown year" (*Kroonjaar*), and birthdays on these years are celebrated with typical Dutch humor. In the workplace, colleagues will decorate the celebrant's office with balloons and streamers and often, in the spirit of a good-natured prank, an effigy of the celebrant in a Zimmer frame. The 60th year is called "seeing Isaac or Rebekah"; the 70th, "seeing Jacob or Rachel"; the 80th, "seeing Joseph or Asenath"; the 90th, "seeing Ephraim"; and finally the 100th, "seeing Methuselah." On a person's 100th birthday, the mayor of the town delivers a congratulatory letter from the King or Queen.

A Dutch birthday celebration does not have one birthday cake but a variety of cakes, cookies, and other sweet treats. Adult guests drink *Kandeel*. The beverage is generally made with white wine, but apple cider also works well. Nowadays, *Kandeel* is more often bought ready-made and is served with ladyfinger biscuits or cinnamon biscuits. To celebrate a newborn, *Kandeel* is served with *Beschuit met muisjes*.

ॐ *Kandeel* (Spiced Celebratory Wine)

Yield: serves 4 to 6

4 eggs	juice of 1 lemon
1 cup sugar	1 quart dry white wine or apple cider
1 teaspoon lemon zest	1 stick cinnamon

Equipment: Medium mixing bowl, whisk, medium saucepan, individual beverage cups

1. In medium mixing bowl, using whisk, beat eggs with sugar until light and fluffy. Add the lemon rind and lemon juice.

2. Pour dry white wine or apple cider into medium saucepan, and whisk in egg mixture. Beating constantly, heat over medium heat until bubbles appear around the edge of pan. Add cinnamon stick, and simmer for 3 minutes, stirring frequently. Remove cinnamon stick before serving.

Serve warm, in individual cups.

Dutch couples often have a civil ceremony at city hall that is then followed by a wedding ceremony in their church. The wedding is followed by a reception at the bride's parents' home, a restaurant, an inn, or a hotel ballroom, depending upon budget. Many Dutch entertain with the *rijsttaffel* (rice table) of Indonesian origin. For 300 years, Indonesia, formerly known as the Netherlands East Indies, was a colony under Dutch control. Many Dutch settlers in the spice-rich colony had leisure and money and employed many Indonesian servants. They turned *rijsttaffel*, the simple indigenous style of eating, into an ostentatious display of food and a form of entertainment. Often anywhere from 10 to 100 white-coated servants formed a procession bringing one dish after another to diners during the three- or four-hour meal. To Indonesians, *rijsttaffel* simply meant rice meal, not rice table. Because many Indonesians subsisted on rice and fish, with a little meat or chicken for special occasions, they resented the wasteful display of food by the Dutch settlers. Since the Dutch left the country, Indonesians say there are no rice tables, but there is rice on every table.

Today in the Netherlands, the *rijsttaffel* remains a popular form of entertaining. The presentations are much simpler than in past years; there are usually no servants, and the hot and cold dishes vary with each Dutch chef or hostess. For instance, in the Netherlands, unlike in Indonesia, bread is served with the *rijsttaffel*, and it is not unusual for Dutch Jews, on the Sabbath and some religious feasts, to serve the kosher meal *rijsttaffel*-style. At weddings, this hearty feast is followed by the Western-style tiered wedding cake, champagne, and dancing.

A sweet table is usually provided at Dutch baptisms, birthdays, and weddings. *Roomborstplaat* (brown sugar candy) is an old Dutch recipe that mothers and grandmothers have been making for their children for many years.

✿ *Roomborstplaat* (Brown Sugar Candy)

Yield: 20 to 24 pieces

1½ cups granulated sugar

1½ cups dark brown sugar

½ teaspoon salt

½ teaspoon cream of tartar

1 cup milk

¼ cup butter or margarine, at room temperature, more as needed

1 teaspoon vanilla extract

2½ cups **coarsely chopped** walnuts

Equipment: Medium **heavy-bottomed** saucepan, wooden mixing spoon, **candy thermometer** (optional), baking sheet, wax paper

1. Put granulated sugar, brown sugar, salt, cream of tartar, and milk into medium heavy-bottomed saucepan. Stir and cook over medium heat until sugars dissolve, 3 to 5 minutes. Continue to cook until candy thermometer registers 236° to 238°F, 12 to 15 minutes. Remove from heat and cool to 220°F about 10 to 20 minutes. Stir in ¼ cup butter or margarine, vanilla extract, and walnuts. Using wooden mixing spoon, beat until creamy, 2 to 3 minutes.

2. Cover baking sheet with wax paper, and lightly coat surface of wax paper with about 1 tablespoon butter or margarine. While still soft, drop spoonfuls of candy batter onto wax paper about 1 inch apart from each other. Cool to room temperature.

Serve the same day for best flavor, but the candy may be stored in airtight container, with wax paper between layers, for several days.

In the Netherlands, when fresh fruits are not in season or are too expensive, many cooks turn to dried fruits. A compote is fruit cooked in syrup; it is often served along with the cake and cookies at an afternoon birthday party.

✿ *Gedroogde Abrikozen* (Apricot Compote)

Note: This recipe takes 24 hours.

Yield: serves 6

1½ cups water

½ cup sugar

3 cups dried apricot halves, soaked according to directions on package, drained

3-inch stick of cinnamon

3 or 4 whole cloves

½ cup toasted sliced almonds

For serving: 1 cup prepared whipped cream

Equipment: Medium saucepan with cover, mixing spoon, medium bowl with cover

1. Pour water into medium saucepan, and bring to boil over medium-high heat. Stir in sugar to dissolve. Add drained apricots, cinnamon stick, and cloves, and bring to a boil. Stir, reduce heat to simmer, cover, and cook for 20 to 25 minutes, or until apricots are tender. Stir in almonds and cool to room temperature.

2. Transfer apricot mixture to medium bowl, cover, and refrigerate at least 24 hours for flavor to develop. Remove and discard cinnamon stick and cloves.

Serve in individual dessert dishes, and top each serving with whipped cream.

Eggs, especially when hard-cooked, are a popular snack food or appetizer in most countries. The Dutch make *gehaktnestjes*, which are similar to the Scotch eggs of Scotland. *Gehaktnestjes* are easy to make and always a welcome treat.

♪ *Gehaktnestjes* (Meatball Nests)

Yield: serves 6

1 pound bulk seasoned pork sausage or finely ground beef

6 hard-cooked eggs, peeled

1 cup all-purpose flour

1 cup **bread crumbs**

2 raw eggs

3 tablespoons water

2 cups vegetable oil

Equipment: Work surface, small bowl, fork, 2 pie pans, large plate, plastic food wrap, paper towels, baking sheet, large **heavy-bottomed** skillet, wooden spoon, slotted spoon, serving platter

1. On work surface, divide sausage or beef into 6 equal portions. Flatten a portion in your hand, and place a peeled hard-cooked egg in the center. Wrap sausage or beef completely around the egg to encase it, and pat smooth. Repeat this process to encase all the eggs with sausage or beef.

2. Put raw eggs in small bowl, add water, and beat well with fork. Put flour in one pie pan and bread crumbs in the other. Dip an encased hard-cooked egg in flour to coat completely, and shake off excess. Cover encased egg with beaten eggs, and roll it in bread crumbs to make a thick coating. Repeat coating for remaining encased hard-cooked eggs. Place on plate, cover with plastic wrap, and refrigerate for 1 hour to firm.

3. Prepare to skillet-fry: *Caution: Adult supervision required.* Have ready several layers of paper towels on baking sheet. Pour oil in large heavy-bottomed skillet, and heat over medium-high heat. Oil is hot enough when small bubbles appear around a wooden spoon handle when it is dipped in the oil. Carefully put prepared hard-cooked eggs into oil, and fry on all sides until golden brown, 5 to 7 minutes. Remove with slotted spoon, and drain on paper towels.

To serve, cool the eggs to warm before cutting in half lengthwise. Arrange on serving platter, with cut-side up. Serve warm or cold as an appetizer or light snack.

Switzerland

Situated in the middle of Europe, Switzerland has survived as an independent nation for more than 700 years. The Swiss remained neutral during both world wars and have become known for helping victims of wars. The International Red Cross was founded in Switzerland in the mid-1800s. Switzerland is greatly influenced by the neighboring countries of Italy, France, Germany, and Austria. Many cultures, customs, and foods have spilled over the borders, making the various regions of Switzerland different from one another even in language and religion. The tastes of the 23 cantons (states) can easily be divided along their linguistic lines. The Swiss Germans have their own dialect; the Swiss living along the French border have a different dialect known as *Les Suisses Romandes*, and *Graubunden Romansh* is the name given to the language spoken by the Swiss living along the Austrian and Italian borders.

The Swiss population is almost equally divided between Protestants and Roman Catholics, and all life-cycle celebrations are conducted according to the religious tradition of the region. (See Protestant and Catholic Life-Cycle Rituals, page lxxiii.)

In Switzerland, many traditions have grown out of cheese and cheese making. One such ancient tradition among the cheese-making families is to set aside, upon the birth of a child, a great wheel of cheese. It is marked with the baby's name, birth date, and other vital statistics. The cheese is eaten only during the person's life-cycle celebrations, such as christening, graduation, promotions, new jobs, betrothal, wedding, and anniversaries. The last of the cheese would be eaten, as a final tribute, by mourners at the individual's funeral.

This following recipe, originally from the French region of Switzerland, is popular all over the country. It is often prepared for a wedding banquet.

Tomates au Fromage (Stuffed Tomatoes with Cheese)

Yield: serves 4 to 6

4 to 6 **tomatoes, peeled**

salt and pepper to taste

3 **shallots,** finely chopped

1 cup grated cheese (preferably half Parmesan and half Gruyère)

(available in the deli section of all supermarkets)

½ cup **fresh white bread crumbs**

4 to 6 tablespoons melted butter

Equipment: Paring knife, teaspoon or **melon baller**, small bowl with cover, greased 8- or 9-inch square or round baking pan, small bowl, oven mitts, serving platter

Ten minutes before needed, preheat oven to 375°F.

1. Using a paring knife, cut about 1 inch off the top of each tomato. Using a teaspoon or melon baller, scoop out about 3 teaspoons from inside the tomato shell. Put the scooped out tomato flesh and cutoff tops of the tomato in a small bowl, cover, and refrigerate for another use. Set the tomatoes, cut-side up, in an 8- or 9-inch square or round greased baking pan. Sprinkle each tomato with salt and pepper and chopped shallots.

2. Mix the cheese and bread crumbs in a small bowl. Fill each tomato equally with the bread crumb mixture. Carefully spread 1 tablespoon of melted butter over the top of each stuffed tomato.

3. Bake in a preheated oven for 10 to 12 minutes, or until the cheese is melted and the tomatoes are tender but still hold their shape.

To serve, transfer to a serving platter, and eat while still warm.

With all the rich dairy products in Switzerland, it is no surprise that some Swiss pastries and desserts have become world famous. In Switzerland, most children have both a birthday and name day celebration with cake and ice cream; the following recipe for *Aargauer rüebli torte* (carrot cake) is a favorite for these celebrations.

ℰ *Aargauer Rüebli Torte* (Carrot Cake)

Yield: serves 10 to 12

1 tablespoon butter	1 teaspoon ground ginger
1 cup dried **bread crumbs**, divided	1 teaspoon ground baking powder
¾ cup grated raw carrots	6 large eggs, separated
1½ cups ground almonds	1¼ cups sugar
½ teaspoon ground mace	1 tablespoon lemon zest
½ teaspoon ground cinnamon	3 tablespoons lemon juice

For **garnish**:

confectioners' sugar icing (recipe follows)

mixed chopped **candied fruits** (available at all supermarkets)

Equipment: 8-inch springform pan, wax paper or parchment paper, pencil, scissors, mixing spoon, medium bowl, small bowl, 2 large mixing bowls, electric mixer or whisk, rubber spatula, oven mitts, toothpick, wire cake rack, dinner knife or **icing spatula**, airtight storage container

1. Place springform pan on a sheet of wax paper or parchment paper, use a pencil to trace around the bottom and cut out with scissors. Butter the interior sides of the spring-form pan, and coat with ¼ cup dried bread crumbs. Shake out the excess bread crumbs. Place the wax paper circle on the bottom of the pan, butter, and sprinkle with bread crumbs.

   Ten minutes before baking, preheat oven to 350°F.

2. In a medium bowl, mix the grated raw carrots and ground almonds.

3. In a small bowl, mix the remaining ¾ cup bread crumbs with mace, cinnamon, ginger, and baking powder. Transfer the breadcrumb mixture to the carrot mixture, and stir to mix well.

4. In a large mixing bowl, using an electric mixer or whisk, beat the egg yolks until thick and lemon-colored, about 3 to 5 minutes. Beating constantly, add the sugar, grated lemon peel, and lemon juice, a little at a time. Using a rubber spatula, fold in the carrot mixture.

5. Put the egg whites into a second large mixing bowl, and, using clean, dry electric mixer beaters or whisk, beat the whites until stiff, about 2 to 3 minutes. Using a rubber spatula, fold the egg whites into the carrot mixture. Transfer to the prepared 8-inch spring-form pan.

6. Bake in the preheated oven for 1 hour, or until a toothpick or wooden skewer inserted in the center of the cake comes out without any crumbs. Release the sides of the pan, and place the cake still on the bottom part of the spring-form pan, on a wire cake rack to cool to room temperature.

7. Prepare confectioners' sugar icing.

8. Frost the cake: Using a dinner knife or icing spatula, spread the confectioners' sugar icing over the top and sides of the cake. Sprinkle the top with mixed chopped candied fruits to garnish.

To serve, cut in wedges. Store in an airtight container. The cake flavor improves on the second day.

♭ Confectioners' Sugar Icing

Yield: about 1 cup

1 cup confectioners' sugar, **sifted**

1 tablespoon water

½ teaspoon vanilla extract

Equipment: Medium bowl, mixing spoon

In a medium bowl, mix the confectioners' sugar with water until smooth. Stir in the vanilla extract, and mix well.

Use to ice Aargauer rüebli torte *(recipe precedes).*

The one thing the different cultural and linguistic regions of Switzerland have in common is a passion for salads, cheese, wine, and excellent breads. Breaded *Berne oder emmentaler zopf* (rich egg bread from Berne) is similar to Jewish challah (recipe page 670).

Swiss chocolate is the finest in the world, and the Swiss consume about 23 pounds of it per person, per year. They are, without question, the chocolate-eating champions of the world. It's impossible to set up a celebration buffet table without one of Switzerland's famous chocolate cakes.

♭ Praline Schokoladentorte (Praline Chocolate Cake)

Praline chocolate cake is a rich and sumptuous cake that is often made for birthdays and other special family occasions.

Yield: 10 to 12 servings

4 ounces unsweetened chocolate, 65 to 70 percent cocoa content

¼ cup butter

5 egg yolks

⅔ cup sugar

¼ teaspoon salt

1 tablespoon vanilla extract

7 egg whites

½ cup **sifted** all-purpose flour

¼ cup sifted **cornstarch**

1½ cups **toasted nuts** of your choice— almond flakes, unsalted pistachios, unsalted macadamias

1 cup heavy cream

confectioners' sugar to taste

½ teaspoon unflavored gelatin

4 tablespoons rum or fruit **liqueur** of your choice

2 tablespoons sugar

4 tablespoons hot water

½ cup apricot jam, melted and passed through a fine strainer

Equipment: 10-inch round or square cake pan, preferably springform, small and large mixing bowls, saucepan, mixer, wooden mixing spoon, wooden skewer/ toothpick, knife, **pastry brush**, serving plate, fine strainer

Ten minutes before baking, preheat oven to 350°F.

1. Butter a 10-inch round or square cake pan, preferably springform. Sprinkle with flour, and tip the pan from side to side to get an even coating throughout. Discard excess flour. Set cake pan aside.

2. In a small bowl, combine sifted flour and sifted cornstarch, and set aside.

3. In a saucepan, place butter and chocolate over low heat until melted. Set aside until thoroughly cool.

4. With scrupulously clean beaters and mixing bowl, beat egg whites to stiff peaks.

5. In another mixing bowl, combine egg yolks, ⅔ cup sugar, salt, and vanilla. Beat egg yolk mixture well with the beaters used previously for the egg whites (no need to wash), until light colored and creamy. Beat in reserved and cooled chocolate mixture.

6. With a mixing spoon, gently fold in half the stiffly beaten egg whites, just until well mixed, into the chocolate and yolk mixture.

7. Spoon in the remaining stiffly beaten egg whites and sift (again) the flour and cornstarch mixture over them. Gently fold, just until mixture is homogeneous, and spoon into prepared baking pan.

8. Bake in the middle rack of preheated oven for 30 to 35 minutes, or until done. Insert a wooden skewer or toothpick in the center of the cake, and if it comes out without any crumbs sticking to it, the cake is done.

9. Remove cake from oven, and let it cool for 10 minutes in the pan. Release the side of the springform (if using) or unmold the cake (if using a regular cake pan) and let it cool completely on a wire rack.

10. Prepare praline (nut cream) filling. Toast nuts on an ungreased baking tray at 350°F for 8 to 10 minutes, or just until golden. Keep an eye on the nuts, as they scorch very quickly. Allow to cool, then process ⅔ of the nuts in a food processor until very fine. Melt gelatin in ¼ cup of water in a steamer or double boiler (or as directed on the packet). Allow to cool.

11. In mixer bowl, Beat cream to soft peaks, then, while continuing to beat, add gelatin little by little, until cream is stiff. Take care not to overbeat; otherwise it will turn to butter. Gently stir in the confectioners' sugar to taste, followed by the ground nuts.

12. Make rum syrup: In a small bowl, dissolve sugar in hot water. Stir in rum.

13. Cut cake into two even layers. Place a spoonful of nut cream filling in the center of the cake serving plate, and set the bottom layer of cake on it (this stops the cake from moving around while being filled). Brush half the rum syrup over the bottom layer, and evenly spread ¾ of cream filling on it. The remaining nut cream filling will be used for the top layer. Place the top layer over the filling, and moisten it with the rest of the rum syrup. Brush the strained apricot jam over the entire surface of the cake (top and exposed sides). Spread the reserved nut cream filling over the top layer, and sprinkle the remaining ⅓ of the toasted nuts evenly over the filling.

14. Dust the whole cake with confectioners' sugar (put confectioners' sugar in a fine strainer, and tap it to release the sugar evenly without any lumps).

Let cake stand for at least 3 hours, ideally overnight, to allow flavors to meld and fully develop before serving.

SOUTHERN EUROPE

Southern Europe includes the countries of Albania, Bosnia and Herzegovina, Croatia, Greece, Italy, Kosovo, Macedonia, Montenegro, Portugal, Serbia, Slovenia, and Spain.

Albania

Albania is a small mountainous country in the Balkan Peninsula of Southeastern Europe. It lies where the Adriatic Sea narrows to meet the Ionian Sea, just across the heel of Italy. The country is referred to as Shqipëria (The Land of the Eagles), the people, as Shqiptarë (Children of the Eagles), and the language, Shqip. Its neighbors are Montenegro and Kosovo to the north, Greece to the south, and the Former Yugoslav Republic (FYR) of Macedonia to the east. Culturally, Albanians comprise two major ethnic groups: northern Ghegs and southern Tosks. The Ghegs and Tosks are found not only within Albania but in neighboring countries as well.

For over 2,000 years, the region that includes what is now Albania experienced Greek, Roman, and then Ottoman Turkish domination. Christianity came quite early into Albania, between the first and second centuries CE, creating two major Christian

SOUTHERN EUROPE

sects—Albanian Orthodox and Roman Catholic. Later, close to four centuries of Ottoman Turkish rule brought Islam. At the end of World War I, Albania fell under Communist rule, and all religious activity was outlawed until the 1990s, when the ban on religion was lifted, and churches and mosques were reopened.

The Albanian Constitution provides for religious freedom. There is no official state religion declared, although Muslim holidays are universally celebrated because of long-standing historical observance. Almost 59 percent of Albanians declare themselves Muslim, but there are no outward signs of this, and most are not observant. Women do not wear headscarves or burqas. Albanian Muslims are mostly nondenominational (that is, neither Sunni nor Shia adherents), but the Bektashi Sufi Order, a mystical Islamic sect, has its headquarters in Tirana, the capital of Albania. Albanian Muslims are not as rigid about following Islamic modesty laws as other Muslim countries, but they do follow the dietary restrictions on not eating pork. Drinking alcohol, however, is not forbidden; to the contrary, no life event can be properly celebrated without it. About 17 percent of the population are Christian (Albanian Orthodox and Catholic), though this percentage is disputed by the Albanian Orthodox and Catholic Church, claiming that the number of Christian adherents is closer to 24 percent. The remainder is divided among Protestants, other Christian sects, atheists or agnostics, and a small number of Jews. For most life-cycle celebrations, Albania's Orthodox, Roman Catholic,

Protestant, and other Christian sects, as well as Jewish and other minorities, follow the traditional rituals of their churches. (See Eastern or Orthodox Church Life-Cycle Rituals, page lxxv, and Protestant and Catholic Life-Cycle Rituals, page lxxiii.)

Traditionally marriages were arranged between families, usually by the parents or through an intermediary familiar with the groom's and bride's families. Most contemporary weddings are nonreligious, due to most Albanians' religious nonobservance, as well as a high incidence of interfaith marriages. Traditional wedding celebrations used to begin a whole week before the day of the wedding ritual itself (*jav e-nuses*). Separate groom and bride parties were held on different days of that week, with the bride being given gifts and sweets and guests given glazed almond favors called *kufeta*. The bride is expected to bring a dowry, called *paja*, of gifts for the groom's family, household linen, nightclothes, and furniture. The groom reciprocates with a dowry called *dhunti* consisting of jewelry, gold, and clothes for the bride. An old rural tradition at Christian weddings is for the bride to display extreme grief and sorrow upon departing the family home. Amid tears and wailing, the bride, dressed in her wedding finery, bids her family goodbye. Anything less would be an insult to her parents.

The difficult transition from Communist rule has brought many hardships, including food shortages and high unemployment, and immediately following the transition, celebrations tended to be more modest and mostly family affairs. With an improvement in economic conditions, however, there is a return to more elaborate celebrations, and events such as the birth of a baby or a wedding are often celebrated with great enthusiasm by the whole community.

The proximity of other Balkan countries, including Greece and Italy, as well as shared histories, has naturally influenced Albanian culture. Nowhere is this mutual cultural intermingling more evident than in the sphere of celebratory foods, most of whose origins can be traced to Ottoman Turkish or Greek culinary traditions (for example, candy-glazed almonds called *kufeta*).

Albanian food is simple and hearty, and all life event celebrations feature a preponderance of meat dishes washed down with copious alcoholic drinks called *raki*, distilled from grapes or other fruits, and variously flavored with juniper, mulberry, pear, or nuts—and weddings are no exception. They offer the best opportunity for the most elaborate feast that the families can afford. Muslim weddings and other celebrations call for a whole roasted lamb, when the budget allows, or a lamb stew made with mutton liver, entrails (intestines), or ground lamb patties. Feasts usually begin with hot and cold appetizers known as *mézé*. Hot *mézé* may include fried foods (*fërgesa*), skewered grilled foods (*qebab*), as well as spit-roasted *kordhëza* or *kukrec* (internal organs of lamb or mutton), and savory pastries filled with various meats, vegetables, and/or cheese. Assorted stuffed vegetables and grape leaves are a usual feature. Cold *mézé* may include salads of fresh or grilled marinated vegetables, small fish such as sardines and other seafood, pickles, and cheese dishes. The main dish usually is a whole roast lamb or a hearty lamb stew with the entrails (internal organs) or ground lamb patties. Desserts are an assortment of rich pastries with honey and nuts, often enclosed in layers of fine pastry and bathed in syrup, such as *baklava, ravani, halva,* and *kadaif*—the culinary legacy of five centuries of Ottoman Turkish rule. *Kabuni,* which is simply cooked rice, becomes transformed into a dessert and a favorite party dish when sweetened with **cinnamon sugar** and raisins and sprinkled with walnuts or almonds. One or two different bean dishes may also be prepared for a celebration feast. Albanian feasts often include extra sweet pastries and desserts. Greek- and Middle Eastern–influenced pastries are favorite endings to Muslim circumcision feasts and Christian baptism celebrations.

The day after the wedding, the bride's family may visit her, bringing sweets (*me peme*). And a week later, their friends and other relatives may also visit: This custom is known as "first visit" (*te pare*). In some rural communities, throughout the first month of marriage, the bride wears her best clothes and expects visits from the couple's friends and relatives.

⚘ *Shendetlie* (Honey and Walnut Cake)

Shendetlie is a special dessert that was once made exclusively for important occasions and holidays. Made with honey and butter and walnuts, it was regarded as a high-energy, health-giving food, suitable for children as well, owing perhaps to the association with the word *shën-det,* meaning "health."

Yield: about 25 to 30 pieces

2 cups flour	4 tablespoons honey
1 teaspoon baking powder	1 cup butter, melted
¼ teaspoon baking soda	2 cups finely chopped walnuts
¼ teaspoon salt	1 egg yolk, beaten, for brushing
5 eggs	1 tablespoon water
¾ cup sugar	

Syrup:

¾ cup sugar	2 cups water
2 tablespoons honey (preferably orange blossom honey)	1 teaspoon lemon juice
	5 cloves
	zest of 1 orange

Equipment: Mixing bowls, flour **sifter**, **whisk**, hand or stand mixer (optional), 12×8-inch baking pan, oven mitts, parchment paper, fork, **pastry brush**, small saucepan, knife

1. Prepare baking pan: Line with two layers of parchment paper, letting the top of the parchment sheets extend to about an inch beyond the baking pan. Butter the parchment paper, and dredge with flour.

2. In a bowl, sift flour, baking powder, baking soda, and salt.

3. In another bowl, beat eggs and sugar until well combined. Stir in honey and melted butter, and mix thoroughly. Add flour mixture and nuts, blending well, until mixture forms a dough. The resulting dough will be quite stiff, unlike a regular cake batter.

4. Spoon into prepared baking pan, and level the surface. Use a fork to lightly score lines on the dough surface. Mix egg yolk with the water to make an egg wash, and brush it over the cake.

5. Bake in preheated oven at 300°F for 40 minutes. Because of the high sugar and honey content, watch carefully that the cake does not get scorched. Let cake cool completely in the pan.

6. Prepare syrup: In a saucepan, place sugar, honey, water, lemon juice, cloves, and orange zest. Let simmer for about 10 minutes, until sugar is completely dissolved.

7. Meanwhile, cut cake, still in the pan, into squares. Spoon hot syrup over cold cake, and allow to stand 4 to 5 hours, or, better yet, overnight before serving.

Kadaif (Shredded Phyllo Pastries)

Kadaif are sweets made with phyllo pastry so finely shredded as to resemble very thin noodles. *Kadaif* is known by various names all throughout the Balkans, Greece, Turkey, and the Middle East (wherever the Ottoman Turkish rule and earlier Persian Empire had been)—*knafeh, knafa, kataifi.* The finished pastries and the shredded phyllo dough are both called by the same name.

There are two ways of making the sweets: one is by enclosing the nut and sugar filling between two layers of the phyllo dough. The other is by enclosing the filling within strips of the pastry, to make individual rolls easier for serving and eating. The rolls are more decorative and thus more appropriate for a celebratory occasion. This recipe gives both methods.

Yield: about 24 servings

1 pound *kadaif* (shredded **phyllo** pastry available in Middle Eastern food shops or specialty stores)

2½ cups chopped walnuts (reserve ½ cup for decoration)

Syrup:

2 cups sugar

1½ cups water

½ cup crushed graham crackers

2 tablespoons cognac or brandy or other **liqueur** (optional)

2 tablespoons sugar

1 cup butter, melted

1 lemon, cut into thin slices

1 stick cinnamon

1 teaspoon vanilla essence

Equipment: Oven mitts, mixing bowl, mixing spoon, clean kitchen towels, 12×8-inch baking tray, cookie sheet or shallow baking tray, small saucepan, spoon, ladle

1. Prepare filling: In a bowl, mix 2 cups of chopped walnuts, graham crackers, cognac, and sugar.

2. Take *kadaif* pastry, and spread it on a clean, dry working surface to loosen the strands. Have ready a clean kitchen towel or two to cover the pastry dough while you are working on the individual rolls to prevent the whole from drying out.

Layered version:

1. Have ready two baking trays, one 12×8-inch, the other a larger, shallow one (or a cookie sheet). Butter the smaller tray.

2. On the larger tray, place phyllo pastry dough and pour half the melted butter over, using your fingers to evenly cover all the strands.

3. Divide pastry dough into two; place ½ at the bottom of the small baking tray.

   Spread filling over this layer. Top with the remaining half of pastry dough. **Drizzle** the rest of the butter over.

4. Bake in preheated oven at 280°F for 1½ hours, or until just barely golden. Remove from oven and allow to cool.

5. Once thoroughly cooled, pour syrup over the pastry, and allow to rest overnight, until all the syrup has been absorbed. Slice into 3-inch squares for serving.

Rolled version:

1. Have ready a buttered 12×8-inch baking pan. Carefully separate a 3-inch-wide portion of the phyllo pastry dough. Cover the rest with a damp towel.

2. With the short end of the separated phyllo dough closest to you, fold it over so that you have a doubled-up section of about 4 to 5 inches at the beginning of this portion of phyllo dough.

3. Place a tablespoon of filling in the middle of this doubled-up section. Start rolling up the pastry to secure the filling and prevent it from spilling out. Continue rolling to the end of the separated portion of phyllo dough. Lay the finished roll, seam-side down on the prepared baking pan. Continue with the rest of the filling and phyllo dough. Drizzle melted butter over.

4. Bake in preheated 280°F oven for 1½ hours, or until just barely golden. Allow to cool.

   When thoroughly cooled, pour syrup over the rolls, and sprinkle with the reserved walnuts.

   Allow to rest overnight, until all the syrup has been absorbed.

Syrup:

1. In a pan, place all the ingredients for syrup, except vanilla. Allow to simmer until the sugar is dissolved.

2. Remove cinnamon stick and lemon slices, pressing syrup off with a spoon.

3. When syrup has cooled down to lukewarm, add vanilla, and pour over the cooled sweets.

♦ *Kurabie* (Butter-Yogurt Cookies)

Kurabie are Albanian variants of similar nut-based cookies, called *ghraybeh* (Lebanonese recipe page 685), *kourabiedes* in Greek, as well as assorted other variants of the name, that were and still are enjoyed throughout what was once the Ottoman Turkish empire. They often make an appearance at special occasions and celebrations, when half or all of the flour is replaced by grated almonds, walnuts, hazelnuts, or other nuts.

Yield: 24 cookies

2½ cups flour (or 1¼ cups flour and 1¼ cups finely grated or powdered walnuts, almonds, or hazelnuts)

1 teaspoon baking powder

¼ teaspoon baking soda

¼ teaspoon salt

½ cup butter

½ cup plus 2 tablespoons sugar

2 eggs

1 tablespoon vanilla extract and/or grated rind of 1 large lemon

¼ to ½ cup thick yogurt

1 egg yolk, beaten

confectioners' sugar

Equipment: Oven mitts, measuring cups and spoons, mixing bowls and spoons, hand or stand mixer (optional), cookie sheet or shallow baking tray, parchment paper, **pastry brush**

1. Preheat oven to 375°F. Line cookie sheet with parchment.

2. In a bowl, sift flour; combine with baking powder, baking soda, and salt.

3. In a large bowl, cream butter and sugar until very light. Add eggs, vanilla, and yogurt, and **blend** until well mixed. Stir in flour mixture to make a soft dough. Chill for 2 hours.

4. Shape dough into walnut-sized balls, form them into ovals, and place them evenly spaced on prepared cookie sheet. Brush balls with the egg yolk. Sprinkle with confectioners' sugar.

5. Bake for 10 to 15 minutes. Do not let the cookies brown.

Store in an airtight tin.

Within three days after a child is born, sweet fritters, covered in sugar or dipped in syrup and called *petulla*, are prepared by the family to be distributed to relatives and friends. A party is held on the third day after birth, when friends and family bring gifts as well as *petulla* for the baby. Orthodox Albanians will wait until the child is baptized before holding this celebration. The name of the child, for those of the Orthodox faith, is chosen by the godparents. Birthdays are not celebrated by Orthodox families. Rather, name days are celebrated: a name day is the feast day of the saint after whom a child is named. Greetings on this day are "Happy name day" and "To good health and long life." To celebrate a name day, pastries, fruit preserves, coffee, a fermented milk drink called *kos*, and *raki* (grape and other fruit- or herb-flavored liqueur) are served. The first haircut and the first nail cutting are additional events that are marked by celebrations. Circumcision, on a boy's reaching his preteens, is celebrated with a feast that would include assorted stuffed vegetables and stuffed grape leaves.

In Albania, it is widely believed that the good have an easy death, while bad people, a difficult one. Funerals take place on the same day or the next after the death. Female (and rarely male) relatives will wail, tear, or cut their hair, wear clothing inside out, or even scratch their faces during mourning. There is a tradition in southern Albania of funeral singing, led by a female mourner (often someone who does this for a living) and joined by a chorus. Mourning continues for forty days. After the funeral, a banquet is organized by the dead person's family for all the mourners. After an Orthodox Christian burial service, mourners are given a piece of bread (*pogaca*) and a glass of *raki*. Mourners spill a bit of the *raki* on the ground, saying, "For the peaceful rest of your soul," and then proceed to drink the rest. A memorial feast for all the departed in a family takes place in spring, during which slices of bread topped with boiled wheat grains, called *collivi*, are shared by all family members. A place is reserved at the table for the dead.

⚭ *Liptao* (Cheese Spread)

Liptao is the Albanian version of the original Hungarian regional cheese spread called *Liptó*, named after the northern Slovakian region, once part of the Austro-Hungarian Empire, called Liptov. This cheese spread is usually included in an assortment of cold *mézé*, accompanied by fruit-flavored brandy called *raki*.

Yield: serves 4

5 tablespoons virgin olive oil

2 onions, **finely chopped**

5 cloves garlic, finely chopped

1 pound cottage cheese or drained yogurt

2 tablespoons chopped pimento (available in jars at all supermarkets)

salt and pepper to taste

Suggested **garnish**es: 4 sliced dill pickles, 6 or 8 stuffed green olives, sliced carrots and celery, 4 or 6 slices rye or pumpernickel bread, 2 or 3 hard-cooked eggs, quartered

Equipment: Large skillet, mixing spoon, shallow serving bowl

Heat oil in large skillet over medium-high heat, add onion and garlic, stir, and **sauté** until onion is soft, 3 to 5 minutes. Reduce heat to medium, add cottage cheese or drained yogurt, and stir to mix. Add pimento and salt and pepper to taste, heat through, and remove from heat.

To serve, transfer to a shallow serving bowl, and decoratively arrange the garnishes around the liptao*: sliced dill pickles, green olives* (ulinje)*, carrot and celery slices, assorted breads, and quartered hard-cooked eggs. Use garnishes to scoop up the* liptao*. Cover and refrigerate leftover* liptao *for up to 1 week.*

When *quofte me mente* are made into small balls, they are a favorite hot *mézé* at wedding banquets.

♪ *Quofte Me Mente* (Minted Meatballs)

Caution: Hot oil is used.

Yield: serves 4 to 6

1 pound lean ground lamb or beef	1 teaspoon ground cinnamon
2 eggs, lightly beaten	salt and pepper to taste
1cup stale **bread crumbs**	vegetable oil, for **deep-frying**
2 tablespoons chopped fresh mint or 1 teaspoon dried mint flakes	

Equipment: Medium mixing bowl, mixing spoon, 2 baking sheets, wax paper or parchment paper, work surface, **deep fryer** (see glossary for tips on making one), fryer thermometer (optional), paper towels, wooden spoon, metal tongs or **slotted spoon**

1. In medium bowl, combine ground meat, eggs, bread crumbs, mint, cinnamon, and salt and pepper to taste. Using a mixing spoon or hands, stir to mix well. Let mixture stand for 10 minutes.

2. Cover 1 baking sheet with wax paper or parchment paper, and place on work surface. Using your hands, roll small amounts of meat into walnut-size balls, and place side by side on the wax paper.

3. Prepare to deep-fry: *Caution: Adult supervision required.* Have ready several layers of paper towels on another baking sheet. Heat oil to 375°F on a fryer thermometer or until small bubbles appear around a wooden spoon handle when it is dipped in the oil.

4. Fry meatballs, a few at a time, carefully turning with metal tongs or slotted metal spoon to brown all sides, about 3 minutes per meatball. Transfer to paper towels to drain. Keep warm until ready to serve. Continue frying in batches.

To serve, arrange meatballs on a serving platter. Guests eat the meatballs by picking them up with their fingers.

Bosnia and Herzegovina

Bosnia and Herzegovina is a multiethnic, multireligious state located in Southeastern Europe. To the north and west, it is bounded by Croatia, to the east by Serbia, and to the south by Montenegro. Bosnia is mostly mountainous and Herzegovina mostly flatland. The population consists of Muslims and Christians (Catholic and Eastern Orthodox). This division also follows ethnic lines: Bosniak Muslims, ethnic Croat Catholics, and ethnic Serb Eastern Orthodox Christians. (The designation "ethnic

Croat" and "ethnic Serb" is to distinguish Bosnian citizens who claim their ethnicity as Croat or Serb from the citizens of neighboring countries of Croatia or Serbia.)

Bosnia and Herzegovina, as separate regions, were formerly part of Yugoslavia. A destructive civil war that started in 1992 finally ended in 1995, resulting in the establishment of the Federation of Bosnia and Herzegovina (also known as the Bosniak-Croat Federation) consisting of 51 percent of the territory and 63 percent of the population. The remaining 49 percent of the territory was allocated to the ethnic Serb-ruled Republika Srpska. The Herzegovina region, which has been populated traditionally by a majority of ethnic Croats in the west and ethnic Serbs in the east, was split into two cantons—West Herzegovina and Herzegovina-Neretva. These two cantons are included in the 10 similarly autonomously governed cantons within the Federation of Bosnia and Herzegovina. The Federation and Republic together are regarded as a single state (Bosnia and Herzegovina) for diplomatic, fiscal, and foreign policy matters. Life cycle celebrations follow the traditions of the three predominant religions. (See Islam and Islamic Life-Cycle Rituals, page lxxvi; Protestant and Catholic Life-Cycle Rituals, page lxxiii; Eastern or Orthodox Church Life-Cycle Rituals, page lxxv.)

For Eastern Orthodox Bosnians (ethnic Serbs), choosing a name for a child is the responsibility of the child's godfather (*kum*) and godmother (*kuma*). Chosen by the child's parents for their good qualities or among their close friends, the *kum/kuma* will continue to play an important role throughout the child's life. They become part of the family and are expected to be present at all the child's significant events, such as birthdays, graduations, and marriage. One privilege of a godparent on his or her godchild's first birthday is to cut a lock of the child's hair and keep it.

Prior to the civil war in the 1990s, intermarriage among the different ethnic groups was more prevalent, comprising about 40 percent of all registered marriages. Wedding ceremonies once reflected the ethnic mix, incorporating customs from the groom's and bride's ethnic origins. A throwback from centuries of Islamic rule in the Balkan region is the tradition of the bride's parents presenting the new couple with a dowry rug—a handwoven *kilim* or hand-knotted carpet with the couple's initials and their wedding date. This custom disappeared in the 1990s. Brides usually wear white and are accompanied by bridesmaids. In common with other special occasions, guests are served an abundance of food and drink.

A Muslim wedding starts at the bride's house, with family and friends gathered to help the bride get ready. Then the groom, accompanied by family and friends, comes to fetch the bride. The groom's family and friends are served food and drink; meanwhile, the bridesmaids decorate the cars with flowers and bows. The bridesmaids also pin flowers on the guests' clothes and receive money as they do so. As the bride leaves her house, the men sing a song called "*Ilahija*." Candies are thrown into the air, fireworks are set off, and everyone drives to the town hall for the marriage to be officially registered, the cars honking the whole way to indicate a wedding party in progress. After the bride and groom have signed the registry book, all proceed to the mosque or the groom's house where the imam performs a ceremony and blesses the new couple with appropriate verses from the Koran.

Before the bride and groom enter the groom's house for the ceremony, she has to hold a Koran together with a loaf of bread she has baked herself. Then the bride and groom eat honey from the same spoon or drink something from the same cup. In certain areas of Bosnia, the bride enters the house by ducking under the groom's outstretched arm. At the conclusion of the religious ceremony, guests may sing a song for the newly married couple. The wedding party is usually held at a restaurant or rented hall, with dancing and much food and drink. The bride serves coffee to the guests, with a bridesmaid on hand with a basket to receive money. Cutting and serving the wedding cake is the final event, with the couple smearing each other with cream.

Eastern Orthodox funeral ceremonies are elaborate events. At the cemetery, a meal of assorted salads and roast meats is served to honor the deceased. The same types of food are also served a year later when the gravestone is set on the grave. Christians and Muslims customarily wear black while mourning family members.

Food in Bosnia reflects influences from its Balkan neighbors as well as Middle Eastern and Turkish cuisine. Although many religious and ethnic differences divide Bosnia and its other Balkan neighbors, food serves as a unifying thread. Slow-cooked vegetable soups and stews, with meat added whenever the budget allows, are favored dishes. Christian celebration feasts call for lamb or *prebranac peceno prase* (roasted suckling pig with baked lima beans, recipe page 425); Muslim feasts traditionally serve roast lamb or goat (recipe page 629). Fruits and vegetables, as well as breads and pastries doused in honey, are prepared much the same way in every Balkan kitchen—only the name of the dish changes depending on the language of the householder.

Soups, a favorite beginning to a Bosniak meal, are hearty and thick and are included in most life-cycle celebration feasts. The combination of vegetables depends upon the season, the cook, or (at a wedding feast) the preferences of the bride and groom. Soup is always eaten with bread.

For Christians in Bosnia and Herzegovina, baptism is the most important event in a child's life. The church baptismal service is usually followed by a celebratory feast, either at home or in a restaurant. If the celebration is at home, the family puts the *bosanski lonac* (Bosnian meat pot, recipe follows) in the oven to cook slowly. In some villages, the sealed container is taken to the baker who bakes it for the family.

❧ *Bosanski Lonac* (Bosnian Meat Pot)

Yield: serves 6

1 cup shredded cabbage

3 potatoes, peeled and **cubed**

salt and pepper to taste

2½ pounds pork, beef, or lamb, or any combination, **cubed**

8 cloves garlic, peeled

1 cup water

2 cups canned stewed tomatoes, divided

1 cup pearl onions, peeled, fresh, frozen, or canned (drained)

1 cup **diced** carrots

1 cup diced celery

3 sprigs fresh parsley, finely chopped, or 2 teaspoons dried parsley flakes

Equipment: Greased medium heatproof earthenware casserole with cover or **Dutch oven**, heavy-duty aluminum foil, oven mitts, trivet

Preheat oven to 325°F.

1. Spread shredded cabbage over the bottom of a greased medium heatproof earthenware casserole or Dutch oven. Layer potatoes over the cabbage, and sprinkle with salt and pepper to taste. Add meat, whole garlic cloves, water, and 1 cup stewed tomatoes. Add onions, carrots, celery, and remaining 1 cup stewed tomatoes. Sprinkle with salt and pepper to taste and parsley flakes. Cover and seal with heavy-duty foil so no steam can escape while cooking.

2. Cook in preheated oven for 3½ hours. Using oven mitts, carefully remove the casserole from the oven. Allow to rest 15 minutes before serving.

To serve, take the pot to the table, and place on a trivet. Using oven mitts, remove foil and lid in front of the guests, releasing all the appetizing aromas.

⚬ *Podvarak* (Baked Sauerkraut)

Cabbage is a staple in most European kitchens, especially when made into sauerkraut. The following unusual but simple recipe would be served as a side dish with *bsanski lonac*. After much eating and drinking at a wedding celebration, sauerkraut juice, considered a digestive aid, is often consumed to calm the stomach.

Yield: serves 6 to 8

4 cups (2 pounds) canned sauerkraut

3 tablespoons bacon drippings or vegetable oil

2 onions, **finely chopped**

2 tart apples, peeled, **cored, diced**

½ cup brown sugar

1 potato, peeled and grated

salt and pepper to taste

1 cup sour cream

6 ounces canned tomato paste

Equipment: Strainer, medium bowl, mixing spoon, large skillet, 2 forks, greased medium casserole or baking pan, oven mitts

Preheat oven to 350°F.

1. Drain sauerkraut in a strainer, discard the juice, or cover and refrigerate juice for another use. Rinse sauerkraut under cold running water, press out the water with your hands, and transfer to a medium bowl.

2. Heat bacon drippings or oil in a large skillet over medium-high heat. Add onions and apples, stir, and **sauté** until soft, 3 to 5 minutes. Separate sauerkraut with your hands as you add it to onion mixture so that it doesn't form lumps. Reduce heat to **simmer**. Add brown sugar, grated potato, and salt and pepper to taste. Using 2 forks, toss to mix. Cover and cook for 10 minutes to allow the flavors to blend.

3. In a small bowl, mix sour cream and tomato paste. Transfer sauerkraut mixture to a greased medium casserole or baking pan. Pour sour cream and tomato paste mixture over the top of the sauerkraut, and toss to mix.

4. Bake in preheated oven for 30 to 40 minutes, or until golden and bubbly.

To serve, put the casserole or baking pan on the table, and serve as a side dish with Bosanski lonac.

⚘ *Bosanska Baklava* (Bosnian Baklava)

No celebration in Bosnia (and as well in the neighboring countries) is complete without *baklava*. *Baklava* is a syrup-drenched, nut-filled pastry that has made its way from its original home in Ottoman Turkey (and its earlier home in Persia) to spread throughout the Middle East, Greece, and the Balkans—in fact, wherever the earlier Persian Empire and later Ottoman Turkish Empire extended. Each country has its own variant on the nuts used for filling, taking advantage of the nuts most commonly grown in the region. In Bosnia, walnuts are preferred, and the syrup used for soaking the finished pastries contains lemon slices to add a tangy scent and flavor. With the butter and nuts and syrup, these are extremely rich pastries, so they are best cut into small pieces. One or at most two would be sufficient for a serving.

Yield: 1 tray of pastries

Syrup:	water to cover
1 pound sugar	2 unwaxed lemons, sliced thinly crosswise

Pastry and filling:	½ cup sugar
1 pound **phyllo** pastry	1 cup butter
1 pound walnuts (⅔ pound ground, ⅓ pound chopped)	½ cup neutral-tasting oil (corn or sunflower)

Equipment: Small saucepan, oven mitts, 12×10-inch baking pan, medium bowl

1. First prepare syrup: In a small saucepan, put sugar and add water to cover the sugar by an inch. Bring mixture to a boil, then lower heat to allow the mixture to simmer for about 15 minutes. The resulting syrup should not be too thick—it should be a thin syrup. Remove syrup from the heat, and allow it to cool slightly. Then add lemon slices, and set aside syrup to cool completely. Transfer to a bowl. The syrup must be cold when poured over the *baklava*.

2. Next, prepare the pastries. Butter well a 12×10-inch baking pan. Ten minutes before baking, preheat oven to 320°F.

3. In a small pan, melt butter over low heat, taking care not to let it brown. Turn off heat, and mix in oil. Use the butter-oil mixture at once while still warm.

4. Lay 3 sheets of phyllo pastry at the bottom of the pan. Brush each sheet well with the butter-oil mixture. Cover unused phyllo pastry sheets with a clean moist kitchen towel so that they do not dry out. Reserve three sheets for the topmost layer. Lay 2 sheets of phyllo, brush each one with the butter-oil mixture, and sprinkle with some coarsely chopped walnuts. Continue laying 2 sheets of phyllo, brushing each one with the butter-oil mixture, and alternately sprinkling with chopped walnuts and ground walnuts, until the phyllo and nut filling are used up. Top with the reserved 3 sheets. Brush the top 2 with the butter-oil mixture, but leave the topmost sheet as is.

5. With a sharp knife, cut through the layers for small individual serving pieces—either squares (1½×1½-inch) or diamonds. Bake in preheated oven until the *baklava* is golden brown, about an hour.

6. Remove from oven and at once pour cold syrup over, especially along the cut lines.

Leave the pastries to rest, and thoroughly absorb the syrup for 24 hours before serving.

Šape (Bear Paws)

Šape are butter and nut cookies that are similar to shortbread. They are traditionally made in Church households for feasts or special occasions, such as birthdays, weddings, and christenings, as well as Christmas. Their name is derived from their shape, like a bear paw (*šapa*, singular), owing to the traditional cookie molds used for baking them.

Yield: about 30 cookies

½ cup ground walnuts	1 teaspoon vanilla essence
2½ cups all-purpose flour	grated **zest** of 1 unwaxed lemon
1 teaspoon baking powder	1 large egg, beaten
¼ teaspoon salt	About 2 to 3 tablespoons milk (if necessary)
¾ cup butter	¼ cup butter, melted, for greasing cookie molds
¾ cup sugar	
	2 cups confectioners' sugar

Equipment: 2 mixing bowls, measuring cups and spoons, mixing spoon, hand or stand mixer (optional), cookie molds or Madeleine baking pan, cookie sheet, oven, oven mitts

1. In a large bowl, combine flour, walnuts, baking powder, and salt.

2. In another bowl, beat butter with sugar until light and fluffy. Stir in vanilla and lemon zest. Mix in egg, followed by flour mixture. The resulting dough will be crumbly.

Add about 2 to 3 tablespoons of milk to enable dough to hold its shape.

3. Brush cookie molds or Madeleine baking pan with melted butter. Fill molds with dough about ⅔ full.

4. Place filled molds on a cookie sheet, and bake at 350°F for about 15 minutes, or until golden. Allow cookies to rest for a couple of minutes, then unmold and sprinkle generously with confectioners' sugar.

These will keep for about a week in an airtight tin.

Croatia

Formerly part of Yugoslavia, Croatia declared its independence in 1991, although it was not until the end of an interethnic war in 1995 that it became a truly sovereign country. It is bordered on the north by Slovenia and Hungary, on the east by Bosnia and Herzegovina as well as Serbia, and on the south by Montenegro. Its coastline, on the west, faces the Adriatic Sea. The population is 90 percent Croatian, and the rest are Serbs, Bosniaks, Slovenes, Hungarians, Roma (gypsy), and other ethnic groups. Catholic Christian adherents comprise 86 percent and Orthodox Christians 4 percent; the remaining 10 percent are Muslim and other faiths.

Life-cycle celebrations follow the rituals of the Catholic and Orthodox Christian Churches (see Protestant and Catholic Christian Life-cycle rituals, page lxxiii; Eastern or Orthodox Church Life-cycle rituals, page lxxv): births, marriages, and funerals are major events. Immediately after the birth of a child, the father and his friends have a celebratory party over two days, even while the mother and child are still at the hospital. Once the newborn is brought home, relatives and friends come to visit in a custom called *babine*. They usually bring a present for the baby of money and an article of infant clothing (usually a bodysuit) and disposable diapers, as well as something for the household— usually coffee and cookies. And when gazing at the newborn, it is customary to spit while commenting that the baby is worthless (*ništatinevaljaš!*)—a holdover from ancient superstition—to distract any evil spirits hanging about from harming the baby.

Very few traditional wedding customs have survived to modern times. One of them is the bridegroom's father presenting an apple inserted with coins to ask for a girl's hand, though nowadays the groom would do it himself. Following this, the groom's mother would make a visit called *kolač*, this time bringing a *pogača*, a round loaf of bread, for the girl and others to share. Once the girl agreed to the proposal, their intended wedding is registered with the parish priest, who then announces the event to the church congregation. This traditional custom called *napovidi* (notices) is still observed today. Before a funeral, mourners pay their respects at a wake. After a funeral, a feast called *sedmina* (one-seventh) is held for all the mourners.

The celebratory foods served at special occasions reflect some commonalities with neighboring countries: Mediterranean influences are evident in the use of olive oil, and a variety of cooked vegetable dishes reflect Ottoman Turkish culinary tradition. Most celebrations feature roast or grilled meat, either pork or lamb. An elaborate beef stew, called *pašticada*, or more precisely *Dalmatinska pašticada* (recipe follows) because it originates from the region of Dalmatia, is often served at weddings and other special occasions.

♧ *Dalmatinska Pašticada* (Dalmatian Braised Beef)

Yield: about 10 servings

Note: This recipe takes 2 days' preparation.

2 pounds of beef round or topside, or other stewing beef in one piece, or veal leg

½ cup **diced** smoked bacon

2 large onions

1 root parsley (also known as "Hamburg parsley"); if not available, substitute 1 bunch parsley

3 carrots

1 cup celeriac root; if not available, 2 stalks celery

4 cloves of garlic, finely chopped

¼ cup tomato concentrate

1 cup olive oil

¾ cup cider vinegar

2 whole cloves, or ¼ teaspoon powdered cloves

6 dried seedless prunes

6 dried figs

2 apples, peeled, **cored**, quartered

3 cups red wine

2 tablespoons mustard

3 bay leaves

3 rosemary sprigs, each about 4 inches long

bunch fresh thyme

salt and pepper to taste

Equipment: Large bowl or deep tray, large **heavy-bottomed** saucepan with lid, oven mitts, kitchen tongs, serving platter, serving bowl for sauce

1. The day before, lard the meat: Insert the tip of a knife at various points throughout the meat, and insert the diced bacon. Salt and pepper it, then spread with a marinade of mustard, oil, and vinegar, and leave it to rest overnight in a large bowl, covered with plastic wrap in the refrigerator.

2. The following morning, peel and chop onions, carrots, root parsley, and celeriac, and set aside.

3. Remove meat from its marinade. Do not wash the bowl or dispose of any marinade remaining.

4. Heat 3 tablespoons of oil in a large saucepan, and brown meat quickly on all sides. Return the meat to its marinating bowl. In the same oil (add more if needed), sauté onions and garlic until softened, then stir in carrots, root parsley, and celeriac. Pour in wine and remaining marinade, cloves, bay leaves, rosemary, and thyme. Add meat, and leave to simmer gently for 2 hours. Top up with more wine, if necessary. Some prefer to add the Croatian sweet wine Prošek at this point.

5. Midway during cooking, stir in tomato concentrate, diluted with some of the cooking liquids, the prunes, figs, and apples. Check seasoning, and add salt and pepper if needed.

6. When meat is tender, remove it, slice into individual serving pieces, and lay them on a warmed serving platter. Discard bay leaves, and any visible rosemary and thyme twigs.

Puree the stewing vegetables with remaining braising liquid. Reheat and pour some over the sliced meat; serve the rest of the sauce in a bowl.

Dalmatinska pašticada *is best served with pasta or gnocchi.*

ᨊ *Medimurska Gibanica* (Medimurje-style Gibanica)

Medimurska gibanica is a festive layer cake with alternating fillings of poppy seed, walnuts, cream cheese, and apple, topped with sour cream. It is often served at important occasions and family celebrations.

Yield: about 12 servings

Pastry:

½ pound **phyllo** pastry, fresh or frozen and thawed

½ cup butter, melted in heated ¼ cup milk

Poppy-seed filling:

1 cup ground poppy seeds

¾ cup milk, heated to boiling

4 tablespoons sugar

½ teaspoon vanilla

2 tablespoons rum or rum flavoring

grated rind of ½ lemon

2 **egg whites**, beaten to stiff peaks

1. Combine poppy seeds, milk, sugar, vanilla, rum, and lemon rind. Gently fold in egg whites. Set aside.

Cheese filling:

8 ounces cottage cheese or cream cheese

3 **egg yolks**

1 teaspoon vanilla

grated rind of 1 lemon

2 tablespoons lemon juice

¼ teaspoon salt

¼ cup raisins

2 egg whites

½ cup sugar

1. Combine cheese, yolks, vanilla, lemon rind and juice, salt, and raisins and mix well. Beat egg whites to soft peaks; gradually add the sugar, continuing to beat until peaks are stiff but still glossy. Set aside.

Walnut filling:

1 cup finely chopped walnuts

2 tablespoons sugar

½ teaspoon cinnamon

1. Combine nuts, sugar, and cinnamon. Set aside.

Apple filling:

1 pound apples, peeled, **cored**, and grated

¼ cup raisins

2 tablespoons powdered sugar

1 teaspoon cinnamon

1. Combine apples, raisins, sugar, and cinnamon, and let stand until apple juices run.

Topping:

3 cups sour cream mixed well with 2 well
  beaten **egg yolks**, 1 beaten **egg white**, and
  2 tablespoons sugar

confectioners' sugar for sprinkling

Equipment: Mixing bowl, mixing spoon, wire **whisk**, hand or stand mixer (optional), bowls to hold fillings and toppings, clean kitchen towel, 9-inch square baking pan, oven mitts, **pastry brush**

1. Preheat oven to 350°F. Butter a 9-inch square baking pan. Cover unused phyllo pastry under a kitchen towel to prevent drying.

2. Lay 3 sheets of phyllo in the baking pan. Brush each sheet thoroughly with the milk-butter mixture. Spread the poppy seed filling evenly over the phyllo pastry. Over the poppy seed layer, place 3 sheets of phyllo, brush each sheet thoroughly with the milk-butter mixture, and spread the cheese filling evenly.

3. Over the cheese layer, place another 3 sheets of phyllo, brush each sheet thoroughly with the milk-butter mixture, and spread the walnut filling evenly. Over this, lay a further 3 sheets of phyllo, brush each sheet thoroughly with the milk-butter mixture, and spread the apple filling evenly. Pour the apple juice over the apples. Lay the top layer of 3 sheets of phyllo, brushing each sheet with the milk-butter mixture, and pour all the remaining milk-butter mixture over.

4. Bake for 30 minutes, then remove the cake from the oven and quickly pour over the sour cream topping. Return the cake to the oven and continue baking until the topping is golden, about 15 minutes more. Let the cake cool to room temperature, then refrigerate for 4 hours or overnight.

Sprinkle with powdered sugar, and cut into squares to serve.

Greece

Located along the Mediterranean Sea in the southeastern corner of Europe, Greece has a recorded history that spans more than 2,500 years of struggles and accomplishments. Much of what we take for granted today in Western science, architecture, art, medicine, and theater has its origins in ancient Greece.

Most life-cycle events revolve around the Greek Orthodox Church. (See Eastern or Orthodox Church Life-Cycle Rituals, page lxxv.) Although freedom of religion is extended to all, Greece recognizes the Eastern Orthodox Church as its "prevailing" religion. Among the younger generation, secularism is on the rise, as in most other European nations. Nonetheless, important life-cycle events such as marriage and funerals are still celebrated according to rites of the Greek Orthodox Church. Besides tradition and inherited beliefs, there is another reason for the Greeks to maintain their adherence to the Greek Orthodox Church. Throughout almost four centuries of Turkish domination of Greece under the Ottoman Empire (from the fall of Constantinople in 1453 to independence in 1821), the Greek Orthodox Church was the most important unifying factor for the Greeks, and their belief and observance of Greek Orthodox festivals preserved their ethnic identity and kept their hope alive that they would one day become independent and overthrow the Turkish invaders.

Most Greek celebrations, such as births, baptisms, and weddings, include roasted lamb and special breads decorated to commemorate the occasion and often blessed by a priest.

Frozen bread dough can be used to make a decorative loaf. While still frozen, cut off a piece of dough to shape or cut into flowers, leaves and vines, or birds and religious symbols. (You might want to buy two packages of frozen dough, one to make into the loaf and one for the decorative pieces.) Follow the instructions on the package to thaw and prepare. Be sure to shape the loaf before adding the decorative pieces of dough. Brush the reverse side of the decorative pieces lightly with water or **egg wash** to make them stick to the loaf. The loaf needs to rise according to the directions on the package. To give the decorations a shiny finish, brush their surface with egg wash before baking.

Besides lamb and breads, a traditional Greek menu can include vegetables—stuffed (recipe page 640) or baked into pies (recipe page 645) and casseroles (recipe page 494)—as well as dishes of olives and pickles, tubs of *feta* (a crumbly white cheese), and bottles of *retsina* (a Greek apéritif) and ouzo (a Greek **liqueur**).

At the birth of a baby, relatives and friends come to pay their respects with gifts and money, and *kafés ellínikós* (Greek coffee) and a table of sweets are usually set out for the visitors. *Pasteli* (recipe follows), another favorite treat for guests, are small, wrapped candies traditionally given out at the baptism.

⚱ *Pasteli* (Sesame Seed and Honey Sweets)

Yield: 25 to 35 pieces

1½ cups honey

¾ cup water

3 cups **sesame seeds**

½ cup **blanched** almonds, finely ground

1 teaspoon grated orange rind (orange zest)

Equipment: Medium saucepan, wooden mixing spoon, **candy thermometer** (optional), aluminum foil, cookie sheet, large knife, pitcher, clear plastic food wrap

1. Put honey and water in medium saucepan. Stirring constantly, cook over medium-high heat until mixture reaches firm ball stage, or 250°F on candy thermometer (see **sugar syrup** in Glossary of Food Terms). Remove from heat, and add sesame seeds, almonds, and orange zest.

2. Cover a cookie sheet with aluminum foil, and spread sesame mixture about ¼ inch thick on nonstick cookie sheet. While still slightly warm, cut the candy into squares using a large knife. To keep candy from sticking, dip knife into pitcher of hot water, shaking off any excess, before making each cut. When cool, wrap each individual square in plastic wrap.

Store in covered container. Serve at a name day party, or set out dishes of pasteli *at a wedding.*

Baptism is the first important life-cycle event in a Greek child's life. After the Greek Orthodox service, relatives, friends, and neighbors gather for the christening feast. The traditional celebration includes plenty of food and drink, and the singing and dancing often continue well after the infant guest of honor has been put to bed.

Almonds, grapes, and honey, among the world's earliest cultivated foods, are usually included in Greek religious ceremonies for christenings, weddings, and memorial services. For instance, after the christening ceremony, godparents offer guests pouches of Jordan coated almonds known as *ta koufeta* (recipe follows), either as the guests leave the church or later at the reception that follows. The custom of offering these candy-coated nuts symbolizes a sweet life for the infant, with blue Jordan almonds in blue netting pouches for boys and pink Jordan almonds in pink netting for girls. At weddings, white Jordan almonds in white netting are passed out to the guests as they leave the church or reception.

The tradition of sugar-glazed almonds (*ta kouféta*) as favors harks back to the honey-dipped almonds offered to newlyweds by the priest in the early days of the Greek Orthodox Christian Church. The *ta kouféta*, placed on the ceremonial tray together with the wedding crowns (*stefana*, also *stephana*) worn by both bride and groom and later presented to guests, have symbolic significance. White denotes purity. The almond's egg shape symbolizes fertility and the new life opening up for the newlyweds. The almond's hardness denotes the endurance of marriage, and its sweetness, the sweet joys of future life.

⚜ *Kouféta* (Jordan Almond Pouches)

Yield: about 28 pouches

2 pounds (about 144 pieces) Jordan candy-
    coated almonds (available at candy stores
    and Middle Eastern food stores)

Equipment: Pink, blue, or white netting, cut into 6- or 8-inch squares or circles (8-inch circles of netting are available in assorted colors at most handicraft shops), 28 feet of narrow, pink, blue, or white satin ribbon cut into 12-inch lengths, scissors

Put 5 Jordan almonds in the center of a square or circle of netting. Enclose the almonds in the netting, and twist the unfilled portion of the netting around the almonds to form a pouch. Wrap a ribbon around the twisted area, tie tightly, and make a pretty bow. Repeat as necessary.

To serve, arrange all the pouches in a basket or on a silver tray, and offer one to each guest.

Instead of celebrating birthdays, Greek children often celebrate their name days. (See Eastern or Orthodox Church Life-Cycle Rituals, page lxxv.) The name day party includes a festive meal with plenty of sweets for gift-bearing relatives and friends. Even without an invitation, adults will drop in on friends on their name day and offer their greetings, often bringing a small present. The celebrant will usually have pastries, sweets, and savory appetizers on hand to offer well-wishers.

When a couple is engaged and the wedding details have all been arranged, in rural areas (now less observed in the cities) the engagement rings are blessed by a priest, who then places the rings on the affianced pair's left ring fingers. The priest then says the blessings *Kala Stephana* (Good Wedding Crowns, meaning "To a beautiful wedding") and *I Ora I Kali* (The Time, the Good, meaning in essence, "Your marriage comes at a good time"). Another prewedding custom is that of *Krevati,* an age-old tradition involving the bride's single friends who get together to prepare and adorn the marriage bed. The families of the bride and groom and close friends gather around the bed and sing traditional songs while it is being made. It is customary for the groom not to immediately approve of the group's efforts and to disarrange the sheets (as many as three times) to the merriment of everyone assembled. Once the groom approves, then rice, flowers, and other decorations are sprinkled on the bed. Each guest is offered the opportunity to throw decorations from a basket circulated by a friend or family member. It is also customary to lay money in coins or bills. These offerings symbolize wishes of fertility, beauty, and prosperity for the couple's future life. A young child is then made to sit briefly on the decorated bed—a boy or girl, depending on which the couple wishes as their firstborn.

Amygthalota (Almond Cookies)

These almond cookies are made not only for weddings and baptisms but for all celebratory occasions. They are intended to be eaten during the festivities, as well as presented to departing guests as favors, elegantly enclosed in tulle fabric and tied with colored ribbon or lace. A variant of these cookies, shaped into pears, is traditional to the island of Hydra—pear *amygthalota* (recipe follows).

Yield: about 24 cookies

1½ cups finely ground **blanched** almonds

¾ cup icing sugar

1 tablespoon orange blossom water

1 tablespoon lemon juice

3 **egg whites**	24 whole blanched almonds
pinch of salt	

Equipment: Mixing bowls, mixing spoon, wire whisk, hand or stand mixer (optional), piping bag with star nozzle, oven mitts, baking tray or cookie sheet, parchment paper

1. In a bowl, mix well the ground almonds, icing sugar, orange blossom water, and lemon juice.

2. In a separate bowl or in a hand or stand mixer, beat egg whites with salt until stiff peaks form. Gently fold the ground almond mixture into the beaten egg whites, being careful not to deflate them.

Preheat the oven to 350°F.

3. Line a baking sheet with parchment paper. Add the almond mixture to a piping bag fitted with a star tip. Pipe the almond mixture into 24 small rings or rosettes, laying a blanched almond on each. Bake for 15 to 20 minutes, or until just turning golden at the bottom. Allow cookies to cool, and then store in an airtight tin.

The cookies will keep for a couple of days.

⚜ *Pear Amygthalota* (Pear-shaped Almond Cookies)

These almond cookies, shaped into pears, are a traditional celebratory pastry made on the island of Hydra. They can also be formed into crescents, rings, or other cookie shapes. Unlike the previous *amygthalota* recipe, these are made with semolina.

Yield: about 25 to 30 cookies

3 cups finely ground **blanched** almonds	25 to 30 whole cloves
½ cup icing sugar	Butter, for greasing hands
½ cup fine **semolina** (cream of wheat)	1 cup icing sugar for sprinkling
3 **egg whites**, beaten to a light froth	¼ cup additional orange blossom water for brushing
2 tablespoons orange blossom water	

Equipment: Mixing bowls, mixing spoon, wire whisk, hand or stand mixer (optional), oven mitts, baking tray or cookie sheet, parchment paper, **pastry brush**

1. In a bowl or in hand or stand mixer, mix to a smooth, workable dough the ground almonds, icing sugar, semolina, egg whites, and 2 tablespoons of orange blossom water. The dough should be firm enough to be formed into shapes. Add a bit of extra semolina if the dough is too sticky.

Preheat oven to 325°F.

2. Line a shallow baking tray or cookie sheet with parchment paper.

With buttered fingers, take walnut-sized pieces of dough, and shape into 25 small pears.

Stick a clove, flower bud downward, at the top of each pear for the "stem." Lay pears on prepared baking tray. Bake in the middle rack of the preheated oven for 15 minutes, or until pastries are just lightly colored.

3. As soon as they are out of the oven, brush the pears with orange blossom water. Put the remaining icing sugar in a sieve and sprinkle over the pears. Allow this first coating to dry.

Brush the pears one more time with orange blossom water, and sprinkle over additional icing sugar.

Store in airtight tins, and use within a couple of days.

The Greek wedding celebration is full of rituals and symbolism. The bride and groom exchange double rings and sip wine from a single golden goblet. Crowns of orange blossoms, called *stefana* (also *stephana*), joined together by ribbons, are crossed over the heads of the couple three times. The crowns symbolize the bride and groom's elevation to king and queen of the home they will share. Wearing their still joined crowns and holding tall, lit candles, the couple follows the priest around the altar three times. This practice is referred to as the ceremonial wedding "dance," and it symbolically represents life as a continuous circle. According to tradition, the crowns are carefully preserved by the couple. When one of them dies, the crowns are buried with the body.

A member of the wedding party usually offers guests *kouféta* (Jordan Almond Pouches) recipe page 396) as the guests leave the church after the wedding or as they arrive at the reception that follows. Because the wedding feast is a very important event for most Greeks, the main dish is usually spit-roasted lamb, the principal meat served for special occasions in Greece. However, the wedding feast is traditionally an elaborate affair, and an endless array of other dishes are usually also included.

When the festivities are over, the bridal couple goes to the groom's family home. On their arrival, the groom's mother gives the bride a glass of honey mixed with water. The daughter-in-law sips this mixture so that, from this day forward, her words will sound as sweet as honey. The mother-in-law smears the overhead door frame with honey so that strife will never enter the couple's married life. A **pomegranate** is smashed on the threshold, its abundant seeds symbolizing future offspring. The couple may also share a quince to ensure that their life together will be as sweet as the taste of this fruit. The bittersweet taste of the quince also reminds them that they have taken each other "for better, for worse, the bitter with the sweet." Because Greece consists of a mountainous mainland and numerous islands scattered throughout the Aegean and Mediterranean Seas, many Greek rituals vary from region to region and from island to island.

A memorial (*mnemósinon*) and a memorial meal (*makaria*) follow a Greek burial service (cremation is forbidden by the Greek Orthodox Church). The *mnemósinon* and *makaria* are repeated at 40 days, six months, one year, and three years after the death. The following fried fish recipe (*psari savoro*) is traditionally prepared for these feasts.

The rosemary sauce served with this dish has a special significance because the herb rosemary symbolizes remembrance.

℧ *Psari Savoro* (Fried Fish with Rosemary Sauce)

Yield: 4 servings

rosemary sauce (recipe follows)

4 fish **fillets** (about 6 to 8 ounces each); cod, tilapia, or catfish are good choices

½ cup all-purpose flour for **dredging**

salt and pepper to taste

2 to 4 tablespoons olive oil, for frying

Equipment: Large pan, mixing spoon, wax paper–covered baking sheet, large skillet, metal spatula, serving platter

1. Prepare rosemary sauce, and keep warm.
2. Put flour and salt and pepper to taste in pie pan, and stir to mix. Coat both sides of fish with flour mixture, and shake off excess. Place floured fish fillets on wax paper–covered baking sheet.
3. Heat 2 tablespoons oil in skillet over medium-high heat. Add fish fillets and fry until browned on both sides, 3 to 5 minutes each side. Using metal spatula, remove fish from skillet, and place on serving platter.

To serve, spoon rosemary sauce over the fillets. Serve warm or at room temperature.

℧ *Saltsa Savoro* (Rosemary Sauce)

Yield: 1½ cups

½ cup olive oil

1 garlic clove, **finely chopped**

3 tablespoons all-purpose flour

¼ cup white vinegar

1 tablespoon tomato paste

2 cups water

2 sprigs fresh rosemary or 1 teaspoon dried rosemary

salt and pepper to taste

Equipment: Medium skillet, mixing spoon, small bowl

1. Heat olive oil in medium skillet over medium-high heat. Add garlic, stir, and fry for 1 minute. Remove from heat.
2. In small bowl, combine flour, vinegar, tomato paste, and water until smooth and lump-free. Return skillet with garlic oil in it to medium-high heat, and stir in flour mixture. Stirring constantly, bring to a boil, and reduce heat to **simmer**. Add rosemary, and stir until sauce thickens, 2 to 3 minutes. Add salt and pepper to taste. Keep warm.

Serve with psari savoro *(recipe precedes).*

Kólliva (also *kóliva*, *kólyva*) is the traditional memorial offering of sweet boiled wheat for the first-year anniversary (*mnemósinon*) of a departed family member. All other deceased family members are also included in the memorial service, and their names are listed and presented to the officiating priest well before the service begins. *Kólliva* is not simply a recipe. The entire process of its making constitutes an offering of love and remembrance. As such, making *kólliva* requires a quiet house, full awareness, and concentration (no watching television while making it), loving attention to every detail, and the prayer "Lord, Jesus Christ, have mercy on your servant" uttered at every step of its preparation. Every family has its own recipe for *kólliva*: Honey may be substituted for the sugar, as it prevents the wheat from drying out. Minced fresh parsley may also be added to the mixture for added color, and pomegranate seeds may also be used for a decorative edging.

After first being blessed by the priest, the *kólliva* is shared with parishioners attending the *mnemósinon*. Eating *kólliva* is a symbolic reminder that the dead are not forgotten.

♪ *Kólliva* (Memorial Wheat)

Preparing *kólliva* takes two or three days; one day to soak the wheat, and one or two days to dry the wheat and prepare the presentation. When the ritual decorations are omitted, the dish is called *varvara*.

Note: This recipe takes 2 or 3 days.

Yield: serves 20 to 25

1¼ cups unpeeled whole **wheat berries** (sold in health food stores), soaked overnight in water

½ cup **sesame seeds, toasted**

½ cup chopped walnuts

½ cup seedless raisins

½ cup granulated sugar or honey

½ tablespoon ground cumin

1½ teaspoon ground cinnamon, divided

½ cup graham cracker crumbs

1 cup confectioners' sugar, more if necessary

cinnamon sugar, as needed

For **garnish**:

20 to 30 white Jordan almonds (available at candy and specialty food stores)

20 to 30 walnut halves

arils (seeds) of 1 **pomegranate**, optional

Equipment: Large saucepan with cover, mixing spoon, **colander**, work surface, paper towels, clean pillow case, baking sheet, oven mitts, metal spatula, **mortar and pestle** or electric **blender**, large mixing bowl, 10- to 14-inch-long oval or rectangular serving tray, wax paper, flour **sifter**, 8½×11-inch paper, pencil, scissors

Note: This recipe takes 24 hours.

1. Prepare grain: Put presoaked, drained wheat in large saucepan, and cover with water, at least 3 inches above the kernels. Bring to boil over high heat, reduce heat to **simmer**, and cover, stirring occasionally to prevent sticking. During cooking, keep the water level high, adding more hot water when necessary. Cook 1 to 1½ hours, or until kernels begin to break open and are tender. Remove from heat. Drain thoroughly through colander placed in sink. Rinse kernels under warm running water, and allow to drain well for an hour.

Preheat oven to 225°F.

2. Cover work surface with several layers of paper towels, and spread out kernels. Pat dry with additional paper towels. Transfer kernels to clean pillow case, roll up pillow case, and squeeze to release any water. Transfer to baking sheet, and using your hands, spread out the kernels so that they are not stacked on top of one another.

3. Place in oven for 4 to 5 hours until kernels are completely dried. Turn frequently with spatula.

4. Crush toasted sesame seeds, using mortar and pestle or in blender, until pulverized, set aside.

5. In large mixing bowl, combine dried kernels, ground sesame seeds, chopped walnuts, raisins, granulated sugar or honey, cumin, and ½ teaspoon cinnamon. Using your hands, toss to mix well.

6. Prepare for serving: Cover an oval or rectangular serving tray with wax paper. Using your hands, make wheat mixture into a 1-inch-thick oval shape. Sprinkle graham cracker crumbs evenly over the mixture. **Sift** a ¼-inch-thick layer of confectioners' sugar over the surface. Wrap a piece of wax paper around your hand and press down on the confectioners' sugar to make the top smooth and compact.

7. Add ritual decorations: To make a stencil in the shape of a cross, use a piece of paper about as large as the top of the *kólliva*. Fold the paper in half lengthwise and with a pencil, draw half of a cross that will cover the desired length. Cut out the half of a cross. Open the paper and center the cutout cross on top of the *kólliva*. Sprinkle remaining 1 teaspoon ground cinnamon over the cutout to stencil the cross shape over the powdered sugar. Carefully remove and discard paper.

8. Using scissors, cut raisins in half. On the left side of the cross, press the raisin pieces into the confectioners' sugar to form the initials of the deceased. On the right side of the cross, form the raisin pieces into the letters IC XC NIKA (this means "Jesus Conquers"). The literal meaning of the letters is as follows: IC means "Jesus Christ," XC means "Nazarene," and NIKA means "King of the Jews." Make a decorative border using the Jordan almonds, walnut halves, and pomegranate seeds, if desired. Lightly sprinkle with cinnamon sugar.

To serve: The priest should be notified several days in advance that you are bringing the kólliva *for the memorial service. Along with the* kólliva, *an envelope containing a donation and the name of the deceased should be brought to the church about an hour before the services begin. The* psalti *(the cantor or chosen church singer of liturgical music) places it on the sacramental table, between two tall candles* (lambathes), *each tied with a black ribbon, signifying death. The candles are lit when the memorial service begins. At the end of the service, an altar boy carries the tray to the back of the church, where the* kólliva *is spooned into little plastic cups and given to the parishioners as they leave the church.*

Italy

Italy, the boot-shaped peninsula that extends into the Mediterranean from Central Europe, has given the world some of its finest architecture, art, literature, and music, particularly opera. Italy is also the world's largest wine producer. The majority of Italians are Roman Catholic, and most life-cycle events are observed according to Catholic traditions. (See Protestant and Catholic Life-Cycle Rituals, page lxxiii.)

Unsurprisingly for a country in which the Vatican—the seat of the Pope—is located, Roman Catholic religious events such as baptism, first communion, and confirmation are significant family celebrations. A newborn child is usually christened within the first year at a special baptism mass, followed by a party for the extended family and close friends. The preferred venue customarily was at home, mostly in consideration of the baby's comfort, with most of the food offerings homemade, especially the baptism cake (it was considered bad luck to purchase one). Nowadays, most families opt for a restaurant or rented venue. Traditionally, firstborn children were named after their paternal grandparents, and the second-born after their maternal grandparents. There are exceptions, however, such as someone born on Christmas who would be named Natale or Natalia, the birthday of the son of God taking precedence over family considerations. In addition, a child would often receive a patron saint's name as a second name. First communion is the next significant religious event for Catholic children between the ages of seven and 10, followed a few years later, usually by age 14, by confirmation.

Italian celebrations are loaded with symbolism, such as the giving of *bomboniera* as a memento to guests at baptisms and wedding celebrations. The *bomboniera* can be small elaborate ceramic or painted wooden boxes or simply netting (tulle) or lace fabric tied like a pouch and filled with three Jordan almonds representing the Holy Trinity or five representing the five letters in the Italian word *amore* (love). *Confetti* are not tiny bits of paper but rather candy-coated nuts. When made with netting and filled with *confetti*, the custom of giving *bomboniera* is exactly the same custom as the Greek *kou-féta* (recipe page 396). The Italians also use white netting for weddings and pink or blue for the birth of girls or boys.

Italians are very family-oriented, and life cycle celebrations are always an excellent opportunity to assemble the extended family. Unlike in the United States where children's birthday parties are exclusively for children, in Italy, besides the celebrant's friends and their parents, all the family's adult relatives and often friends and neighbors are invited as well. Organized games are not a usual feature of children's birthday parties in Italy. As with other family celebrations, the focus is on a great variety of food. Mini pizzas, home-baked cookies and cakes, mini bagel-shaped breads filled with ham and cheese (*tarallini*) are on offer, as are the universally ubiquitous potato chips, lollipops, ice cream, and soft drinks. Once the birthday celebrant has shared his or her cake with all, the children usually go outdoors in the garden to play (if held at home), and the adults continue to chat, eat, and drink. Nowadays, especially in urban areas where outdoor play space in private homes is limited, more and more families are opting to hold birthday parties at a pizzeria or other local venue.

In common with all other Italian family celebrations where food is the focal point, a wedding offers the greatest opportunity for the most elaborate feasting. Traditionally in small towns in Southern Italy, two banquets were held: the first hosted by the groom's family, the second a week later by the bride's. One other interesting tradition from Southern Italy is formal prenuptial agreements: even in traditional farming communities, notarized contracts listed each partner's economic contribution (in land or material goods) to the union. Modern times and pragmatic financial considerations have limited wedding receptions to a single celebration. Northern Italians tend to have more restrained, intimate celebrations limited to family and closest friends, whereas Southern Italians tend to invite more people and spare no expense for a grand event. Dwindling religious observance (as well as the rise of second marriages because of divorce) has made civil rather than religious weddings common. (The Catholic Church does not sanction a religious wedding for a divorced person.) It has also become fashionable to hold weddings at unconventional or outdoor venues, such as a mountain or a beach.

Sunday is the ideal day to be wed as it is believed to bring lasting happiness. Some months, such as May (a month devoted to the Virgin Mary) and August (regarded an unlucky month that invites illness), and the 40-day period of Lent are considered inauspicious. As in other countries, it is customary for the bride to wear something old, something new, something borrowed, and something blue. Anything of gold was not to be worn by the bride, other than the wedding ring. The traditional color for a wedding dress was green in some regions, symbolizing fertility; in Tuscany, it was black, though white has now become the accepted color for a (first) wedding dress. A traditional Venetian bride would have worn a second-best wedding dress for the ceremony, reserving the best to dance in at the reception. Meanwhile for the groom, it was traditional to carry a piece of iron, to ward off bad luck and the "evil eye." Yet another deterrent of bad luck was an intentional tear in the bridal veil. It was also customary for the groom to present the bride with her bouquet (though she can choose the arrangement), as his last gift to his girlfriend before she becomes his wife. A large bow is usually stretched atop the entrance to a Catholic church to indicate that a wedding is to take place. After most ceremonies, traditionally the newlyweds shattered a glass, and the number of shards indicated the number of years of married bliss they would enjoy.

An Italian wedding party features, as expected, great quantities of *nutrimento* (food), which is the focal point of the festivities—usually starting with sweet liqueurs or stronger alcoholic drinks, then two or three *primi piatti* (first courses), which may be pasta with different sauces, a wedding soup, or special breads such as ring-shaped *taralli* or *crescentine in tigelle* (English muffin–type breads decoratively embossed) served with Parma ham and assorted cheeses. A traditional main course was a whole roast baby pig (*porchetta*) or lamb (*abacchio*). The centerpiece of a wedding reception is a dessert table of fresh fruits, cakes, and various celebratory cookies—*cenci* fritters shaped into bows, braids, twists, or other shapes and coated with icing sugar, *tarallini* "bracelets" made with dried fruits, *bocconotti* tartlets filled with grape jam or chopped almonds and chocolate, and flower-shaped *cantrelli*.

The newly married couple start a circle or line dance called "tarantella," inviting guests to join in. The dance ends at the dessert table, where the dancers and other guests take a cookie. Guests take home sugared almonds, called *confetti*, usually in odd numbers of 3, 5, or 7 wrapped in tulle, together with keepsakes, called *bomboniere*, usually a small decorative or useful item. Nowadays, it has become popular to choose handcrafted ethnic goods to benefit some charitable organization.

♪ *Zuppa di Nozze* (Wedding Soup)

Wedding soup is popular in southern Italy where **escarole**, a slightly bitter green leafy vegetable is the traditional ingredient; spinach is a good substitute. The meatballs for wedding soup can be made ahead of time and refrigerated for up to two days or frozen for up to one month.

Yield: serves 8

1 egg

1 pound lean ground meat (combination beef and veal is recommended)

½ cup **fresh white bread crumbs**

2 tablespoons flat-leaf (Italian) parsley, finely chopped

1½ teaspoons grated lemon rind

1 teaspoon grated nutmeg

½ teaspoon salt

8 cups canned beef broth

3 cups escarole leaves, washed, drained, chopped into bite-size pieces

For serving: grated Parmesan cheese, as needed

Equipment: Large mixing bowl, **whisk** or fork, baking sheet, oven mitts, medium storage container with cover, large saucepan with cover, mixing spoon, ladle, individual soup bowls

1. Prepare the meatballs: Put the egg in a large mixing bowl, and, using a whisk or fork, beat lightly. Add the ground meat, bread crumbs, parsley, lemon rind, nutmeg, and salt. Using clean hands, mix everything together for 2 to 3 minutes.

2. Using wet hands, form the meat mixture into marble-size balls. Keep your hands moistened while making meatballs, and set them in a single layer on baking sheet. Cover loosely with plastic wrap, and refrigerate for 1 hour to allow the balls to become firm.

   Ten minutes before needed, preheat the oven to 350°F.

3. Bake in the oven for 15 to 20 minutes, or until browned on the outside and no pink is showing on the inside when cut open. Cool to room temperature, transfer to a medium container, cover, and refrigerate until ready to serve.

4. Prepare the soup: Put beef broth in a large saucepan, and bring to a boil over high heat. Add the escarole, stir, and bring to a boil. Reduce heat to medium-high, cover, and cook 5 minutes more until the escarole is tender. Add the meatballs and **simmer**, uncovered, for 5 to 7 minutes or until the meatballs are heated through.

To serve, put 2 or 3 meatballs in each soup bowl, and ladle the escarole broth over them. Pass grated cheese for sprinkling.

Italians have different cookies specially baked for almost every occasion and celebration. For wedding receptions, large trays of *biscotti di nozze* (recipe follows) are set out for guests to munch on.

⚘ *Biscotti di Nozze* (Wedding Cookies)

Yield: about 100 pieces

6 eggs, beaten	½ teaspoon salt
1¼ cups sugar	½ teaspoon ground anise
¾ cup vegetable oil	5 to 6 cups all-purpose flour
5 teaspoons baking powder	For **garnish**: confectioners' sugar, as needed

Equipment: Electric mixer or **whisk**, large mixing bowl, lightly floured work surface, rolling pin, ruler, pizza cutter or paring knife, 2 or 3 cookie sheets, oven mitts, wire cake rack, serving platter

Ten minutes before baking, preheat the oven to 350°F.

1. Using an electric mixer or whisk, beat the eggs until **frothy**. Add the sugar, oil, baking powder, salt, and ground anise, beating well after each addition. Beat in 2 cups flour, a little at a time, until a soft dough forms. Using your hands, continue adding just enough of the remaining 3 to 4 cups flour, a little at a time, to make a nonsticky, stiff dough. **Knead** until smooth and satiny, about 3 to 5 minutes. Transfer to a lightly floured work surface. Using a lightly floured rolling pin, roll into a large rectangle about ½ inch thick. Using a ruler and pizza cutter or paring knife, cut the dough into 2-inch long and ¾-inch wide strips, and place the pieces on a cookie sheet.

2. Bake in the middle rack of the preheated oven for 8 to 10 minutes, until golden brown. Transfer to a wire cake rack, and, while still warm, sprinkle with confectioners' sugar.

To serve, arrange the cookies on a serving platter, and set on the buffet table at the wedding reception. Wedding cookies can also be used for the *torta di biscotti*.

⚜ *Tarallini Dolci* (Sweet Pastry Rings)

These lemon-glazed rings were once made exclusively for weddings in the town of Guadalfiera.

Yield: 12 pieces

Dough:

1½ cups flour (plus more for rolling the dough)

1 teaspoon baking powder

3 eggs

3 tablespoons olive oil

3 tablespoons sugar

Frosting:

1½ cups powdered (confectioner's) sugar

1 tablespoon (or more) lemon juice

Equipment: Small and large mixing bowls, clean moistened cloth or kitchen towel, large saucepan, sharp knife, baking tray or cookie sheet, oven mitts

1. Into a large bowl, sift the flour and baking powder together.

2. In a smaller bowl, **blend** well the eggs, oil, and sugar. Make a well (hole) in the flour, pour in the egg mixture, and mix all into a soft dough. Let rest, covered with a moist clean cloth or kitchen towel, for 30 minutes.

3. Divide the dough into 12 equal pieces. Take a piece of dough one at a time, and, on a lightly floured surface, roll it out with lightly floured hands to a 5-inch cylinder. Cover the other pieces with a moist cloth to keep them from getting dry. Join the end pieces of the cylinder together to form a ring. Place the finished ring on a cloth-covered tray. Continue making rings with the rest of the dough.

4. Cook the rings: Fill a large, deep saucepan halfway with water, and bring to a boil over high heat. Drop the rings, three at a time, into the boiling water. As soon as they float up (in about 30 seconds or less), remove them to the cloth-covered tray to dry thoroughly. Continue boiling the rest, and let all dry completely.

5. Lightly score the rings in the middle with a very sharp knife, so that the cut runs all the way from one end to the other.

   Ten minutes before baking, preheat the oven to 400°F.

6. Bake the rings: Transfer the dried rings to a parchment-covered baking tray. Bake for 5 minutes, then lower the heat to 350°F, and bake for a further 5 minutes, or until golden. Transfer the rings to a rack, and allow to cool completely.

7. Frost the rings. In a small bowl, place the icing sugar, and add the lemon juice. Mix until smooth, adding more lemon juice if necessary for an easily spreadable consistency. Brush the

tops of the *tarallini* with frosting. When the frosting is dry, *tarallini* can be stored in the refrigerator, covered with plastic wrap.

Serve the tarallini at room temperature.

Baptism parties share with all other special occasions—such as weddings and saints' feast days—a vast diversity of celebratory cookies and pastries made with nuts, such as *amaretti* cookies and *bocconotti* tartlets. Another aspect common to family celebrations, again featuring nuts, in particular the almond, is *bomboniere*—keepsakes accompanied by sugared almonds wrapped in tulle (*confetti*).

Amaretti (sing., *amaretto*) are almond-flavored cookies, of which the most famous are those that have been continuously made by the Lazzaroni family since the end of the 1800s in Saronno, a town near Milan, in northern Italy. The story goes that the Saronno *amaretti* date from the 1700s, when a young couple baked a batch with the only ingredients they had in the house, in honor of a Cardinal's surprise visit to the town. The Cardinal was so delighted with the cookies that he blessed them with a long and fruitful marriage.

Traditionally *amaretti* and similar cookies were made by country folk only for special family celebrations—baptism, wedding, first communion, and confirmation. Nowadays they are made more frequently or bought as sweet accompaniments for coffee or weekend snacks. Almonds—with their slightly bitter skins and sweet white kernels—are said to represent the bitter-sweet aspects of marriage. The following recipe is adapted from a traditional one from the region of Molise, 250 kilometers southeast of Rome.

♪ *Amaretti Tradizionale* (Traditional Almond Cookies)

Yield: about 20 pieces

1½ tablespoons all-purpose flour

1 teaspoon baking powder

¼ teaspoon baking soda

1½ tablespoons cocoa powder

1 pound raw (unroasted) almonds, with their skins, finely ground

2 eggs

1 tablespoon bitter almond extract

8 ounces sugar

¼ cup icing sugar

Equipment: Bowls, wire whisk, baking tray or cookie sheet, parchment paper, oven mitts, varicolored tissue for wrapping (from craft or bakery supply shops), ruler, scissors, serving bowl or basket

1. In a bowl, mix well the flour, baking powder, cocoa, and ground almonds.

2. In another bowl, beat the eggs until frothy with the almond extract, and mix in the sugar. Add the egg mixture to the flour mixture, and mix well to form a dough. Cover with plastic wrap, and let the dough rest in the refrigerator for an hour.

Ten minutes before baking, preheat the oven to 350°F.

3. From the dough, form small balls about 1 inch in diameter. Roll the balls in icing sugar, press them slightly to flatten their tops, then lay them on a parchment-lined baking tray, well spaced as they will spread slightly during baking.

   Bake in the middle rack of the preheated oven for 10 to 12 minutes. Transfer *amaretti* to a rack to cool.

4. When thoroughly cool, they can be wrapped in assorted colored tissue. Using ruler and pencil, mark off ten 4-inch squares on the assorted colors of waxed tissue. Using scissors, cut out the squares. Place two cookies in a square of tissue with bottoms touching, and wrap tissue around them like a pouch. Twist tissue just above the cookies to secure.

To serve, place the wrapped cookies in a bowl or basket, and set out for guests to help themselves.

According to tradition, in some parts of Italy and Sicily, children are given gifts of toys and sweets on All Souls' Day, November 2. Legend has it that the dead leave their tombs on the night between All Saints' Day, November 1, and All Souls' Day to pilfer the best pastry shops and toy stores for sweets and toys for their descendants. When the children awake on November 2, they search for the hidden goodies and shout with joy and thanks to their dead ancestors when they find them.

It was once traditional to serve chicken soup for funerals. It was made of chicken broth with small pieces of chicken or, in the past, when chicken was considered a luxury, beaten eggs were stirred into the soup.

Italians eat *fave dei morte* (tiny cookies shaped to look like fava beans) on All Souls' Day. Fava beans and chestnuts were symbols of the dead in ancient Greece and Rome. In some parts of Italy, All Souls' Day is celebrated with village festivals at which people eat huge bowls of fava bean soup, along with roasted chestnuts, to celebrate the memory of their dead ancestors.

Fave dei Morte (Dead Men's Beans)

Yield: about 24 "beans"

1 cup ground almonds, **blanched**	¾ cup sugar
¾ cup all-purpose flour	grated rind of 1 lemon
1 teaspoon ground cinnamon	1 egg, beaten
¼ cup butter or margarine, cut into small pieces and chilled	

Equipment: Food processor, rubber spatula, greased cookie sheet, oven mitts, wire cake rack, serving plate

Ten minutes before baking, preheat the oven to 350°F.

1. In a food processor, combine the ground almonds, flour, and cinnamon, and pulse to mix, about 2 to 3 seconds. Add the butter and pulse until mixture resembles coarse crumbs, about 1 minute. Add the sugar, lemon rind, and egg, and process to form a smooth dough, about 1 minute.

   Note: While processing, turn machine off once or twice, and scrape down sides of container with rubber spatula.

2. Transfer the dough to a medium mixing bowl, and pinch off walnut-size pieces. Shape each into an oval, resembling the shape of fava beans. Place on a greased cookie sheet about 1 inch apart.

3. Bake in the preheated oven for 15 to 20 minutes, or until lightly browned. Transfer to a wire cake rack to cool.

To serve, arrange decoratively on a serving plate. Eat in memory of an ancestor.

Kosovo

Kosovo declared its independence unilaterally from Serbia in 2008. It is a landlocked country, hemmed in by Serbia to north and east, Montenegro and Albania to west and southwest respectively, and Macedonia to the southeast. About 90 percent of the population are Kosovars of Albanian descent, mostly from the Gheg ethnic group. The remaining 10 percent are Serbs, Bosniaks, Turks, Roma (gypsy), and other ethnic groups. Kosovars are predominantly Muslim (95 percent), with the rest following the Orthodox Christian and other Christian denominations (Catholic, Protestant). Life-cycle celebrations tend to be similar to those practiced in Albania, as well as in neighboring Balkan countries. (See Islam and Islamic Life-Cycle Rituals, page lxxvi; Eastern Orthodox Church Life-Cycle Rituals, page lxxv; and Protestant and Catholic Life-Cycle Rituals, page lxxiii.)

Marriage is the most significant life event for Kosovars. Traditional wedding rituals have similar elements to those of neighboring countries. An intermediary, usually a married man of good social standing and moral character, is sent by a young man's family with a marriage proposal to the girl's family. The girl's family does not reply immediately, taking time to gather more information about the young man and his character and financial standing, as well as that of his family. If the girl's family finds the young man and his family acceptable, then they invite the intermediary to commence preparations for the engagement. Traditionally, the wedding ceremony would take place a year after the engagement in order to allow the bride to prepare her dowry, which includes making clothing for her and the groom, future children, and as well a shroud for her to be buried in. At the very least, the groom's family needed a month to make the preparations for the wedding ceremony itself.

Traditional Kosovar Islamic weddings took place over three days hosted at the groom's family house. The second day was for the ceremony itself, and the third was for leave-taking by the invited guests. Nowadays, wedding feasts are held at restaurants or other large halls, and young couples make the arrangements for the wedding themselves.

A traditional wedding feast usually began with the preparation of *qyshkek*, a dish of sweetened boiled cracked whole wheat. The wheat was cleaned three days before the wedding day, in a ritual that involved spreading the whole wheat grains on low tables for young girls and old women of the extended family and neighborhood to look through. This traditional wheat-cleaning ritual would be accompanied by singing and dancing to traditional music with tambourines. Once the wheat was cleaned, it was cracked, to reduce the amount of time needed for cooking. Other dishes for a wedding feast would be a lamb or veal stew with vegetables (*ferges*), savory pies made with phyllo pastry (*byrek*), buttermilk, yogurt, assorted goat's and sheep's cheeses, pickled vegetables and fresh vegetable salads, and sweets such as *halva* and rice pudding. One pastry that is usually made by friends of the groom's family who live along the route taken as the bride and dowry are transported to the groom's house is *llokuma*.

Llokuma (Puffed Pastries)

Llokuma are savory fried pastries made for special occasions, such as weddings and the birth of a child. They are best eaten freshly made, dipped into a garlicky yogurt sauce. The origin for these *llokuma* can be traced to similar puffed pastries or doughnuts called *luqmat el qadi* in Arabic and are no doubt related linguistically and culinarily to the Greek fried pastries called *loukoumades*.

Yield: about 30 pieces

3½ cups all-purpose flour, plus more for
  rolling out

1½ teaspoons baking soda

½ teaspoon salt (or to taste)

1 cup plain unflavored yogurt

2 eggs

½ cup sparkling (mineral) water

oil for frying

Equipment: Small and large mixing bowls, mixing spoon, wire **whisk**, knife, frying pan, **skimmer**, cake rack, tray, serving tray

1. In a large bowl, combine 3½ cups flour, ½ teaspoon of baking soda, and salt.

2. In a smaller bowl, whisk the eggs to a froth, then add the yogurt, the remaining teaspoon of baking soda, and the sparkling water.

3. Make a well (hole) in the center of the flour mixture, and pour in the egg mixture. Mix together until the mixture forms a dough. Taste a bit of the dough, and, if necessary, add more salt. The consistency of the dough should be neither too soft nor too hard—add a bit more sparkling water if too hard, a bit more flour if too soft. Place dough on a well floured surface. Knead the dough briefly until smooth and **elastic**, about 5 minutes. Roll out to

¼-inch thickness, and cut out with a knife or cookie cutter into small rectangles, approximately 1×2 inches.

4. Fry in about 1 inch of oil, without crowding the pan, to a golden brown on both sides. Drain and serve at once with garlic and yogurt sauce (recipe follows).

ℰ *Salcë me Hudhër* (Garlic and Yogurt Sauce)

This sauce is often served with *llokuma* and other fried dishes.

Yield: 1 cup

1 cup thick unflavored yogurt

2 tablespoons olive oil

4 cloves garlic, finely minced

salt and pepper to taste

For **garnish**: fresh parsley or fresh mint, chopped (optional)

Equipment: Medium bowl, mixing spoon, plastic wrap, serving bowl

1. In a bowl, mix well the yogurt, oil, and garlic until well combined. Add salt and pepper to taste.

2. Transfer the mixture to a serving bowl. Leave to rest, covered with plastic wrap in the refrigerator, for at least 1 hour before serving to allow the flavors to meld.

Garnish with herbs as desired.

Macedonia

Macedonia—or to give it its full name, the Former Yugoslav Republic of Macedonia—is landlocked by Kosovo and Serbia to the north, Bulgaria to the east, Albania to the west, and Greece to the south. There is an ongoing dispute with Greece about its chosen name Macedonia because the northern region of Greece is also called Macedonia. The population comprises Orthodox Christian (Slavic) Macedonians, Aromanians (Vlahs), and Serbs, as well as Muslim Albanians, Roma (gypsy), and Turks. There is a minority of Catholics, Protestants, and adherents of other faiths. Life-cycle celebrations are celebrated according to the traditions of the major religions. (See Islam and Islamic Life-Cycle Rituals, page lxxvi; Eastern or Orthodox Church Life-Cycle Rituals, page lxxv.) Relations are fragile between the Muslim ethnic groups (25 percent) and the 65 percent Christian majority. Macedonian national culture is largely based on Macedonian Christian (Eastern) Orthodox practices.

The birth of a son is regarded as a significant family event, and infants are normally baptized before their first birthday. New mothers traditionally did not go outside the house until 40 days had passed since delivery. As with neighboring countries that adhere to Orthodox Christian traditions, name days are more significant than birthdays.

Macedonians are given two names: a Christian name that is given after a saint or some-one in the family and a second name that reflects the parents' hopes and wishes, such as Zdravko (Healthy) or Spase (Saved). The tradition is to hold open house on a person's name day—on the day commemorating a saint after whom a person is named—and family and friends are all welcome to partake of food and drinks. There are name days of historically and culturally significant saints, and those days are declared national holidays. As well, villages celebrate the name day of their patron saint as a community: Everyone gets the day off work, and people visit one another's houses and have open house.

Marriage traditions have much in common with neighboring countries. In the old days, marriages were usually arranged by the parents. A go-between, not related by blood to the groom—variously called *strojnik* (for Muslims) or *pobratim*—would visit the intended bride's house with the proposal. If the father consented, the engagement was set, and preparations for the wedding were organized. The traditional role of the *pobratim* included dressing the groom on the wedding day and fetching the bride and extended to guiding the groom as to how to behave as a married man. These days, *pobratimi* are usually the groom's brothers or, if he has none, then a close male married relative. Nowadays, *pobratimi* mainly have a ceremonial role, as couples marry for love and arrange their wedding themselves.

Memorial services for departed family members are observed on the ninth day, 40th day, six months, a year, and three years after death. At the gravesite, family mem-bers usually share bread, cheese, olives, and wine and light candles in remembrance.

Sweet foods are traditionally served during special occasions such as births, wed-dings, and funerals. In common with other Balkan countries, Macedonian cooking reflects the long history of Ottoman rule, and syrup-drenched *baklava* and nut-based sweets are popular.

✑ *Turta* (First Tooth Cake)

This cake is made to celebrate a child's first tooth. It is usually made at double the quantity of ingredients, so as to have plenty to go around when relatives visit. The usual presents are coins and rice, to represent wishes for the child's teeth to be strong, healthy, and white.

Yield: about 12 servings

4 cups flour	¼ teaspoon salt
2 teaspoons baking powder	1 tablespoon vanilla essence
¼ teaspoon baking soda	½ cup ground walnuts
grated **zest** of 1 large lemon	2 large eggs, beaten
2 cups sugar	

½ cup light olive oil, plus more for greasing baking pan

½ cup unflavored yogurt

For **garnish**: icing sugar

Equipment: Large mixing bowl, small bowl, hand or stand mixer (optional), mixing spoon, 10-inch-diameter deep cake pan, oven mitts, cake rack, wooden skewer for testing cake

Preheat oven to 350°F.

1. Grease baking pan with oil.

2. In a large bowl or mixer bowl, put flour, baking powder, baking soda, lemon zest, sugar, salt, vanilla, and walnuts. Combine well. Make a well (hole) in the center, and add beaten eggs, followed by oil and yogurt. Mix well until mixture is homogeneous.

3. Spoon into prepared baking pan, and bake for 30 to 45 minutes, or until golden, and a wooden skewer inserted in the center of the cake comes out clean. Leave to cool on a rack. When completely cooled, unmold from pan, and sprinkle generously with icing sugar.

ὅ *Pogacha* (Round Loaf)

Pogacha is the classic Macedonian celebratory round loaf, of which there are many varieties. Since bread is eaten at every meal, special breads such as *pogacha* are baked and blessed by the priest for christenings and weddings. Adding eggs to the dough makes the bread special. The Macedonian rich egg bread *pogacha* is similar to other culture's enriched breads, such as Jewish *challah* (recipe page 670). For weddings, the *pogacha* is braided, like the *challah*, but the ends are brought together into a wreath. This particular *pogacha* is made with eggs, yogurt, and white cheese.

Yield: 1 loaf

1 cup yogurt at room temperature

1 teaspoon sugar

2 teaspoons active fresh yeast

3 eggs (2 for dough, 1 for **egg wash**)

½ cup oil

½ teaspoon salt

4 cups flour, plus more for rolling out

1 cup white cheese (feta or similar), crumbled or chopped

½ cup butter, melted, plus more for greasing cake pan

¼ cup **sesame seeds**

Equipment: Mixing bowls, mixing spoon, stand mixer with dough hook attachment, **pastry brush**, 12-inch round cake pan, oven mitts

1. Prepare the yeast: In a medium bowl, put the yogurt and sugar. Mix well, then stir in the yeast. Leave to rest in a warm, draft-free place for about 10 to 15 minutes, or until frothy.

2. In the bowl of a stand mixer fitted with a dough hook, pour in the yeast mixture, followed by 2 eggs, oil, and salt. Start mixing at low speed until all is combined. Add the flour, and mix at medium speed until the mixture forms a dough. Mix for 5 to 7 minutes until dough is smooth and **elastic** and does not stick to your fingers or the bowl. Remove the dough and

transfer to a well buttered bowl, turn the dough so that all surfaces are coated with the butter, cover with plastic wrap, and let rise in a warm place until doubled in volume, about 1 to 1½ hours.

Punch down the risen dough, and roll out to a thickness of ¼ inch on a well floured surface.

Brush the surface of dough with butter and sprinkle with cheese. Roll the dough to enclose the cheese filling.

3. Cut the roll into slices about 2 inches long. Place the slices, cut side up, in the buttered cake pan. Cover with plastic wrap, and let rise until doubled, about 45 minutes.

4. Ten minutes prior to baking, preheat oven to 375°F.

5. Prepare the egg wash: Beat the egg with a tablespoon of water. Carefully brush the surface of the risen rolls with egg wash, and sprinkle with sesame seeds. Place in the oven to bake. Reduce heat to 350°F after 15 minutes, and continue baking for another 15 to 20 minutes, or until the bread is golden and sounds hollow when tapped.

ꙮ *Gurabii* (Walnut-filled Pastries)

These pastries are usually served with coffee, or on their own at special occasions. Like other nut-based pastries made throughout the region, such as *kourabiedes* in Greece, and *kurabie* in Albania, *gurabii* reflect the influence of centuries of the Ottoman Turkish Empire on celebratory food in the region.

Yield: 25 to 30 cookies

4 cups flour, plus more for rolling out

1 tablespoon baking powder

¼ teaspoon baking soda

¼ teaspoon salt

½ cup sugar

1 cup light olive oil or any neutral flavored oil

1 cup white wine

½ cup finely chopped walnuts

1 teaspoon (or more to taste) cinnamon

1 cup icing sugar

1 tablespoon vanilla sugar (or 1 teaspoon vanilla essence)

Equipment: Small and large mixing bowls, mixing spoon, cookie sheet, oven mitts, rolling pin, 2-inch cookie cutter, teaspoon

1. Prepare pastry dough: Combine flour, baking powder, baking soda, salt, and half the sugar in a large mixing bowl, and make a well (hole) in the center. Pour in oil and wine into the well, and stir until well combined.

2. With floured hands, bring mixture together to form a dough. The dough should be soft but not sticky. Add a bit more flour if necessary. Knead dough on a well floured surface until soft and **elastic**. Roll out to ¼-inch (or less) thickness, and cut out circles with a 2-inch cookie cutter or floured glass rim.

3. Prepare filling: in a bowl, mix walnuts with cinnamon and the remaining sugar.

   Fill a pastry circle with a teaspoon of walnut filling. Bring the edges together to form a half-moon, and firmly crimp the edges with a fork or with fingers to seal. Place the filled pastries on a buttered cookie sheet, and bake in a preheated 350°F oven for 20 to 25 minutes, or until the pastries are pale golden.

4. Remove from the oven, and roll in icing sugar mixed with vanilla sugar or vanilla essence.

Stored in an airtight tin, gurabii *will last a week or more, if they remain uneaten that long.*

Montenegro

Montenegro is a west Balkan country that was once part of the former Yugoslav Republic but regained its independence in 2006. To the northwest, it is bounded by Bosnia and Herzegovina, to the northeast by Serbia, to the east by Kosovo, and to the southeast by Albania. Its southwest coast faces the Adriatic Sea. Its population is multiethnic: comprised of 45 percent Montenegrins, 28 percent Serbs, and the remaining 25+ percent distributed among Bosniaks, Albanians, and Croats. The majority of Montenegrins and Serbs follow the Orthodox Christian tradition. Montenegrin Bosniaks and most of the resident Albanians adhere to Islam. About 30 percent of Montenegrin Albanians, together with Montenegrin Croats, are Catholics. Life-cycle celebrations follow the traditions of these religious denominations. See Eastern or Orthodox Church Life-Cycle Rituals, page lxxv; Islam and Islamic Culture Life-Cycle Rituals, page lxxvi; Protestant and Catholic Life-Cycle Rituals, page lxxiii.

As with neighboring Balkan countries, the significant life-cycle celebrations are associated with birth, marriage, and death. Montenegrin Orthodox Christian cultural traditions share common elements with Serbian Orthodox traditions (see Serbia, page 424); nevertheless, a Montenegro Orthodox Church has been recently established to create a distinct identity for Montenegrin Orthodox Christians. A Montenegrin wedding tradition was established as law during King Nicola's reign (1910–1918): newlyweds would plant an olive tree to symbolize their union. Funerals are elaborate affairs, accompanied by a meal of roasted meats and salads at the cemetery. A similar commemorative meal takes place on the first anniversary of the death. Montenegrins consider one's presence at funerals more important than at weddings: They believe that one can be forgiven for not attending a wedding but not for missing a funeral.

Weddings and other life-cycle events are celebrated with copious amounts of food and drink. The cuisine of Montenegro reflects influences from Turkey (from its centuries-long history of Ottoman Turkish rule) in common with its Balkan neighbors, Mediterranean influences from Greece and Italy, and as well elements of Austro-Hungarian cuisine. Roast or grilled meats, lamb or veal stews, stuffed kale rolls, and sweets are common offerings at feasts. Celebrations are toasted with local wines and brandies (*rakija*) distilled from local fruits: plum brandy (*šljivovica*), apple brandy (*jabukovača*), or pear brandy (*kruškovača*).

⚝ *Japraci* (Stuffed Kale Rolls)

In Montenegro, a local variety of kale called *raštan* is the leaf of choice for enclosing a filling of fresh and preserved meat and rice. A substitute may be a dark, noncurly kale variety known as *cavolo nero* or *nero di Toscana*.

Yield: 12–15 servings

2 pounds kale (*nero di Toscana* or *cavolo nero* variety) or collards, well washed

3 tablespoons olive oil

1 large onion, finely chopped

1 pound beef or veal, **diced**

¼ pound smoked pork loin or smoked bacon, diced, or ¼ pound air-dried ham

(Prosciutto, Serrano ham, or similar), chopped

¼ pound dry pork sausage, diced

3 ounces rice, rinsed and well drained

salt and pepper to taste

2 tablespoons parsley, minced

juice of 1 lemon

1 cup or more yogurt for serving

Equipment: Large **heavy-bottomed** pot or saucepan with lid, oven mitts, tongs, large bowls, tablespoon, 2 large flat plates or trays, toothpicks, a plate to fit inside the large saucepan to cover wrapped rolls, serving bowl

1. Prepare the leaves and rice-and-meat filling: Trim tough ribs of the kale level with the leaf surface. **Blanch** leaves in a large pot of boiling water to soften for a couple of minutes. Remove leaves with tongs, and plunge at once into a bowl of cold water to arrest cooking (thus preserving their color). Drain leaves thoroughly, and stack on a large plate or tray.

2. Sort through the kale leaves, and reserve the best looking whole ones for wrapping.

   Set aside the smaller or imperfect leaves for lining the saucepan in which the rolls will be cooked.

3. In a large, deep heavy-bottomed saucepan, heat olive oil over medium heat. Stir in chopped onion, and sauté until softened. Add beef or veal, smoked pork loin, sausage, and rice. Season with pepper, and cook until the beef changes color. Remove from heat and allow to cool.

4. When rice and meat mixture is cool enough to handle, stir in parsley, taste, add salt if needed, and transfer mixture to a large bowl. (There is no need to wash the saucepan—it will be used to cook the wrapped rolls.)

5. Fill and wrap the leaves. Assemble on a table the bowl of cooled filling, tablespoon, large plate or tray to wrap the leaves on, the drained leaves, and the large saucepan. Place a layer of small or imperfect leaves at the bottom of the saucepan. On this bottom layer will be placed the filled and wrapped rolls.

6. Begin wrapping: Lay a whole leaf face up on the plate or tray (the base of the leaf closest to you and the top away from you). Place about 1 to 2 tablespoons of filling (depending on the size of the leaf) at the base of the leaf. Roll the base of the leaf over the filling and away from you to enclose the filling once. Bring the left side of the leaf snugly across the filling, followed by the right side. Proceed to roll tightly away from you until the leaf completely encloses the filling. Fasten the ends with a toothpick, if necessary. Place the wrapped roll seam-side down on top of the layer of leaves in the saucepan. Continue with wrapping and filling the rest of the leaves, placing the rolls snugly against one another in neat layers. Place subsequent rolls atop the first layer, packing them in snugly. When all the leaves and filling have been used up, lay any remaining leaves over the rolls to cover them, and place a plate, face down, over them to keep them from being dislodged during cooking.

7. Cook the rolls: Gently pour lightly salted hot water mixed with lemon juice to a level just below the topmost rolls. Simmer slowly over very low heat for about 2 hours. Allow to cool down in the pan for at least 30 minutes before serving.

These are best served topped with yogurt. These stuffed kale rolls also taste good, if not better, the day after, when they have mellowed and the flavors have melded. Refrigerate once the rolls have cooled to room temperature.

Portugal

As in neighboring Spain, the majority of Portuguese consider themselves Roman Catholic, although less than a fifth (19 percent) are regular churchgoers and receive the sacraments. Nonetheless, a larger percentage than regular churchgoers still observe the life-cycle celebrations that center around Catholic Church rituals: baptisms, first communions, weddings, and funerals. Since the Inquisition, non-Catholics have not been allowed to a large degree to live in Portugal, much less to practice their religion. However, in the 19th century with the arrival of British families engaged in the wine trade (mainly port), the Church of England (Anglicans) and other Protestant denominations, such as the Methodists, Presbyterians, Baptists, and Congregationalists entered the country. When the constitutional monarchy was established in 1834, religious toleration, albeit in a limited fashion, was granted to the adherents of the Church of England, and eventually a chapel was permitted to be built in Lisbon. Four years later, another Anglican chapel was built. At the same time as the Anglicans were allowed to worship in Portugal, a breakaway Catholic sect was being formed by Catholic priests and regular churchgoers who did not accept the infallibility of the Pope. This was the Lusitanian Catholic Apostolic Evangelical Church. Another successful Protestant sect is the Pentecostals. To date, there are about 50,000 to 60,000 Protestants (Anglicans and other denominations) in Portugal, or less than 1 percent of the Portuguese population. (See Protestant and Catholic Life-Cycle Rituals page lxxiii).

Traditionally a child's saint's day was celebrated in addition to his or her birthday. A saint's day, otherwise known as name day, celebrates the saint after whom a child is named or with the same name as the child celebrant. Roman Catholic calendars list one or more saints' names for each day of the year, and it used to be customary to choose a child's name accordingly. In contrast to Spain, a first communion is more religion-oriented in Portugal: The cake would be adorned with a Bible or cross or rosary beads made from marzipan. A girl, upon turning 15, would be feted with a *Quinzeañera*—a party to celebrate her coming of age as a young woman. This is an elaborate event, often at a restaurant, with the celebrant outfitted in grand style and all her friends invited, as well as the extended family.

Traditional weddings used to take place over a whole week, though nowadays these have become greatly curtailed. The wedding feast itself (and similar big feasts) is called *o copo de agua* (the glass of water—rather tongue-in-cheek, as these feasts feature a great deal more than water). In rural Portugal, the day might begin with breakfast at the groom's house, where a stew, such as a goat meat *chanfana* (or other regional specialty) would be served with *arroz cabidela*, a traditional dish for weddings made with chicken, duck, or rabbit meat (including the blood), bread, cheeses, and other cold meats. After the repast, guests and the groom proceed to the church to await the bride. It is considered a bad omen if the bride and groom see each other before the ceremony. Portuguese weddings are noted for their gargantuan feasts: varied appetizers preceding a multicourse meal, followed by a pause for dancing, and then different buffet tables set up with seafood, cheeses, fresh fruits, and other delicacies. As a finale, an entire roast pig often appears with soup—usually a *caldo verde* (green soup). All these celebratory dishes are liberally accompanied by excellent Portuguese red and white wines, beer, and other drinks. Desserts are diverse and feature Portuguese confectionery rich in eggs and milk, in addition to a wedding cake that may have a filling of traditional egg custard, served with sparkling wine or port—both of these are also Portuguese specialties. On leaving, guests would be served more food for the road: cold cuts, fruits, confectionery, assorted nibbles. It is not unknown for a wedding event to last from one morning until the wee hours of the next.

ꙮ *Biscoitos de Casamento* (Wedding Cookies)

It is customary in Portugal to provide wedding guests with cookies decoratively wrapped as party favors. The following is a traditional recipe, meant to be shaped into circles or hearts and decorated with piped icing and/or the initials of the bride and groom. The original recipe is meant to be deep fried, but, for convenience and even results, baking is preferable.

Yield: about 30 to 35 cookies

4 cups flour

¼ teaspoon salt

½ cup butter, softened

1 teaspoon vanilla extract

2 heaping tablespoons brown sugar	For dusting: vanilla-flavored sugar
3 eggs	For piping: colored icing (optional)

Equipment: Flour **sifter**, mixing bowls and spoon, food processor (optional), plastic wrap, cookie sheets, parchment paper, oven mitts

Ten minutes before baking, preheat oven to 325°F.

1. Sift flour with salt, and set aside.

2. In a large bowl, mix well softened butter, vanilla extract, sugar, and eggs. Add flour, and mix well to form a dough. (If using a food processor, process dough ingredients just until everything comes together. Remove dough.) Form dough into a smooth ball, knead quickly but lightly, enfold in plastic wrap, and let it rest in the refrigerator for an hour.

3. Roll out on a lightly floured surface to ¼-inch thickness, and cut out hearts or circles with a cookie cutter.

4. Place cookies evenly spaced on parchment-lined cookie sheets. Bake in the middle rack of preheated oven for 8 to 10 minutes, or until just golden at the bottom edges. Do not allow the cookies to brown. Sprinkle cookies with vanilla-flavored sugar.

Alternatively, decorate cookies with piped icing (for example, on heart-shaped cookies, draw a tuxedo in black and white icing or a bridal dress and necklace drawn in white icing).

Wrap a few cookies in transparent colored paper, and tie the package with colored ribbon.

Codfish, both fresh and salted, is a popular Portuguese food. Cooks speak lovingly of cod as *o fiel amigo* (the faithful friend). They claim 365 ways to cook it, one for each day of the year. Salt codfish cakes are often on the appetizer menu for most celebration feasts. Portuguese salt codfish cakes (*bolinhos de bacalhau*) are quite similar to Dominican Republic *bacalaitos*.

If Portugal has a national soup, it has to be *caldo verde*. This green soup, a specialty of the northern region, is a favorite in even the most sophisticated Lisbon homes. It is often served for the family celebration meal after a church christening ceremony.

♪ *Caldo Verde* (Green Soup)

Yield: serves 6 to 8

3 tablespoons olive oil	1 pound greens: kale, spinach, or **collard** greens, or combination, fresh, rinsed, trimmed, or frozen (thawed)
3 cloves garlic, **finely chopped**	
8 cups water	½ pound sausage (either Portuguese *linguiça* or *chouriço* or Polish *kielbasa*), sliced in ½-inch pieces
2 potatoes, peeled and shredded	
	salt and pepper to taste

Equipment: Large saucepan with cover or **Dutch oven**, mixing spoon, potato masher, individual soup bowls

1. Heat oil in a large saucepan with cover or Dutch oven over medium-high heat, add garlic, **sauté**, and stir until soft, 2 to 3 minutes. Add water and potatoes, and bring to a boil over high heat. Reduce heat to **simmer**, cover, and cook for 15 to 20 minutes, or until potatoes are soft. Using a potato masher, mash the potatoes so that the liquid becomes creamy.

2. Add greens, sausage, and salt and pepper to taste to creamed potato mixture, and stir. Bring to a boil over medium-high heat, stir, then reduce heat to simmer, cover, and cook until greens are done, 15 to 20 minutes.

Serve in soup bowls with plenty of bread for dipping.

Meat is always the centerpiece of a Portuguese celebration feast. It can be kid (young tender goat), lamb, pork, or, if the budget allows, beef. Pot roast is called *alcatra*, which comes from *alcatre*, the Portuguese word for rump, the preferred cut of meat for pot roast, which is a style of cooking, not a cut of meat. Boneless rump, heel of round, and Boston cut are good cuts of beef to use in this recipe.

Alcatra (Portuguese Pot Roast)

Yield: serves 6 to 8

4 tablespoons olive oil

4 to 5 pounds **oven-ready, boned**, rolled beef rump

1 onion, chopped

3 cloves garlic, **finely chopped**

1 carrot, trimmed and chopped

2 red bell peppers, trimmed, seeded, and chopped

6 fresh **cilantro** leaves or 1 tablespoon ground **coriander**

4 cups dry red wine or chicken broth, more if needed

1 bay leaf

salt and pepper to taste

5 potatoes, peeled and thickly sliced

2 strips bacon, chopped

For **garnish**: 2 tablespoons fresh chopped parsley

For gravy: flour, as needed water, as needed

Equipment: Large roasting pan with cover, metal tongs, plate, mixing spoon, oven mitts, **bulb baster** (optional), carving board, medium skillet, **whisk**, strainer, sauce bowl, meat knife, medium serving bowl, serving platter

1. Heat the oil in a large roasting pan over medium-high heat. Add the meat, and brown on all sides, about 7 to 12 minutes. Remove the meat with metal tongs, and set on a plate. Add the onions, garlic, carrot, red bell peppers, and cilantro or coriander to roasting pan. Stir and **sauté** until onions are soft, 3 to 5 minutes. Return meat to roasting pan, and pour wine or

chicken broth over it. Add bay leaf and salt and pepper to taste. Bring to a boil, reduce heat to **simmer**, cover, and cook for 20 minutes.

Ten minutes before baking, preheat oven to 375°F.

2. Put roasting pan in preheated oven and bake, covered for 1½ hours, basting occasionally. Using oven mitts, remove tray from oven, add potatoes, and sprinkle them with chopped bacon. Cover and bake for 45 minutes more. Reduce oven temperature to 325°F, and using a bulb baster or mixing spoon, **baste** the meat and potatoes. Bake, uncovered, for 30 minutes more, until meat and potatoes are fork-tender and browned. Add more wine or chicken broth, when necessary so the bottom of the pan is generously covered with pan juices and the meat doesn't dry out.

3. Remove potatoes from roasting pan, put into a medium serving bowl, and keep warm. Transfer meat to a carving board, and let rest for 20 minutes before slicing. Using a bulb baster or mixing spoon, skim off and discard most of the fat from the pan juices. Transfer the pan juices to a medium skillet. Discard bay leaf.

4. Prepare gravy: For each cup of pan juices, combine 2 tablespoons flour with ½ cup water to form a slurry, and quickly whisk in to prevent lumping. Cook and whisk over medium heat until gravy thickens, 3 to 5 minutes. Add salt and pepper to taste. Strain into a sauce bowl.

To serve, slice meat across the grain, using a meat knife. Place sliced meat on a warmed serving platter, and surround with potatoes. Serve with gravy to spoon over each serving.

All special occasions and all religious holidays call for special breads. Some holidays are created around bread, such as the yearly *Festa dos Tabuleiros* in the city of Tomar. Girls are adorned with headdresses made of loaves of bread stacked more than five feet high. *Massa sovada* are special rolls prepared for christenings, weddings, and anniversaries. They are eaten throughout the meal, with the soup or the main course or at the end of the meal.

⚘ *Massa Sovada* (Sweet Bread Buns)

Yield: 12 rolls

1 package active dry **yeast**	1 egg
¼ cup water at room temperature (70°F)	1 cup milk or half-and-half
5 tablespoons sugar, divided	3½ to 3¾ cups all-purpose flour
1 teaspoon salt	For **garnish: egg wash**
2 tablespoons melted butter or margarine	

Equipment: Large mixing bowl, wooden mixing spoon, rubber spatula, lightly floured work surface, lightly buttered 9×13-inch baking pan, clean kitchen towel, **pastry brush**, oven mitts, napkin-lined breadbasket

1. In a large mixing bowl, sprinkle the yeast over water. Let yeast stand until dissolved, about 3 to 5 minutes. Using a wooden mixing spoon, stir in 3 tablespoons sugar, salt, melted butter

or margarine, egg, and milk or half-and-half, and mix well. Stir in 3½ cups flour to form a smooth dough.

2. Scrape dough onto a lightly floured work surface. Sprinkle flour over the dough, and **knead** until dough is no longer sticky but smooth and elastic, about 8 to 10 minutes. Shape the dough into 12 equal balls and place, evenly spaced, on a lightly buttered 9×13-inch baking pan. Cover with a towel, and place in a warm place to rise until double in bulk, 45 minutes to 1 hour.

Ten minutes before baking, preheat oven to 350°F.

3. Brush egg wash over the tops of the rolls, and sprinkle with remaining 2 tablespoons of sugar. Bake in the middle rack of preheated oven for 25 to 30 minutes, or until golden brown.

To serve, separate the rolls and transfer to a napkin-lined breadbasket.

Portuguese nuns in the Catholic convents are famous for making wonderful pastries, candies, cookies, preserves, and elaborate wedding cakes. For christenings, name-day celebrations, and weddings, the nuns sell little pastry creations, such as the delightfully named *orelhas de abade* (abbot's ears), *papos de anjo* (angel's breasts), and the following recipe, *barrigas de freiras* (nuns' bellies). Many of the dishes prepared by the nuns are made with simple ingredients used in this recipe.

⚘ *Barrigas de Freiras* (Nuns' Bellies)

Yield: serves 4

¾ cup water

1 cup sugar

2 tablespoons unsalted butter

4 cups fresh white **bread crumbs**, best made from French or Italian bread

8 **egg yolks**, beaten

For **garnish**:

ground cinnamon

slivered almonds

Equipment: Medium **heavy-bottomed** saucepan, wooden mixing spoon, **candy thermometer** (optional), serving dish

1. Pour water into a medium heavy-bottomed saucepan, add sugar, and stir to dissolve. Bring to a boil over medium-high heat, stirring frequently. Reduce heat to **simmer**, and cook until mixture thickens to a syrup and reaches soft ball stage or 234° to 236°F on a candy thermometer (see **sugar syrup** in Glossary of Food Terms). Remove from heat, and stir in butter until melted. Add bread crumbs and stir well to mix.

2. Return syrup mixture to low heat, and stir in egg yolks, one at a time, beating well after each addition. Continue cooking over low heat, stirring constantly until syrup thickens, 5 to 10 minutes. Do not increase heat. Transfer to a serving dish, and sprinkle with ground cinnamon and toasted almonds.

Serve this dessert in very small portions because it is extremely sweet. It will be enjoyed best with a cup of tea or coffee at the end of a meal.

Serbia

Serbia is a west Balkan country that was once part of Yugoslavia. In 1989, Yugoslavia broke up along ethnic lines, resulting in a protracted civil war that eventually led to the independent state of Serbia in 2006. Serbia is bounded on the north by Hungary, on the east by Romania and Bulgaria, on the west by Croatia and Bosnia and Herzegovina, and on the south by Montenegro, Kosovo, and Macedonia. The Serbian population is predominantly ethnic Serbs, with a minority of Hungarians, Bulgarians, Roma (gypsy), and other ethnic groups. Around 90 percent of Serbians are adherents of the Serbian Orthodox Church. The rest are Catholics, Protestants, or followers of other faiths. While 40 percent of Serbians admit that religion does not play an important part of their daily life, nevertheless life cycle events such as baptism, marriage, and funeral rites are widely celebrated according to the Serbian Orthodox tradition (see Eastern or Orthodox Church Life-Cycle Rituals, page lxxv). Each ethnic group in Serbia observes life-cycle celebrations according to their professed religion. (See Protestant and Catholic Life-Cycle Rituals, page lxxiii, and Islam and Islamic Life-Cycle Rituals, page lxxvi.)

When a Serbian child is baptized, the priest cuts three locks of hair from the child's head, as an offering to God. These are preserved in wax, and will either be given to the mother or to the child's godparents for safekeeping.

Serbian Orthodox weddings are noted for the prewedding tradition known as *skup*. Early on the morning of the wedding, family and close friends gather at the bride's house as she gets ready, and the groom formally asks for the hand of the bride. The bride's brother tries to test the groom's commitment by presenting "fake" brides, and, together with the groom's brother or best man, they go through "negotiations" for how much the groom is prepared to "pay" for the real bride. Throughout this stage of the *skup*, the bride is supposed to stay out of sight. The so-called payment and bargaining are all in good fun, to evoke much laughter and merriment among the guests, and do not involve serious exchanges of money or goods. *Skup* is accompanied by much drinking of the potent local *rakija*, often a light meal or snacks to go with the drinks, music, singing, and dancing. As the bride leaves the house, she is often serenaded with traditional songs.

Thereafter, all proceed to the church for the wedding ceremony in a cavalcade of cars decorated with Serbian flags waving and with horns honking all the way. The ceremony itself is solemn, following the traditions of the Serbian Orthodox Church. After rings are exchanged, the bride and groom are crowned to signify that they are king and queen of their kingdom, the home that they will soon establish. Coins rather than rice are thrown as the newlyweds leave the church, which children enjoy scrambling for. At the reception, a traditional ring dance, called the *kolo*, begins the festivities. As with all Serbian important celebrations, there is an abundance of food and drink, especially of *rakija*, the local alcoholic drink.

Serbians remember their family members who have departed with a memorial mass 40 days after their death and again after one year. At this memorial event, called *parastos*, a sweet dish of boiled wheat grains flavored with nuts and spices, called *koljivo*, is served.

Serbian food, like that of its Balkan neighbors, reflects the influences of Turkish cuisine, stemming from its history of close to four centuries of Ottoman rule. There are also obvious borrowings from neighboring countries, in particular from the rich tradition of Austro-Hungarian cuisine, in particular in pastry and confectionery. Food at wedding banquets may include traditional cookies homemade by family and friends, as well as stuffed cabbage rolls (*sarme*, singular *sarma*), cheese pastries, and nut-filled pastries.

If the wedding is in winter, Serbs roast a 50- or 60-pound hog for the reception; if it's in the summer, lamb is the preferred meat. The roasting is done outdoors, snow or sunshine, nonstop, day and night, for perhaps 20 to 30 hours. Even children take turns working the hand crank that rotates the pig over the fire for even roasting. The *razhan* (rod or spit), which is rammed through the length of the animal, rests on steel tripods on either side of the fire. A drip pan is usually employed to catch the pig grease. Toward the end of the roasting, loaves of bread are set in the pan to absorb the drippings. This dripping-soaked bread is a delicacy that is served with the meat. *Prebanac* (lima beans, recipe follows) is almost always served with the roast pig.

⚜ *Peceno Prase* (Roast Suckling Pig)

Yield: 10 to 12

CAUTION: *ADULT SUPERVISION REQUIRED.*

10- to 15-pound **oven-ready** suckling pig

kosher salt to taste

1 lemon

1 cup vegetable oil

12-ounce bottle light beer or 1½ cups apple cider

For **garnish**: small apple

Equipment: Aluminum foil, large roasting pan with rack, **bulb baster** or large mixing spoon

Preheat oven to 400°F.

1. Rub inside of pig with kosher salt. Wrap a lemon with foil, and place in the mouth of the pig to keep the mouth open during baking. Set the pig in an upright position on the rack in the roasting pan. Rub oil over the entire outside of pig. Cover ears and tail with foil to prevent burning.

2. Bake pig in oven for about 5 hours, basting frequently with beer or apple cider and pan drippings, using bulb baster or large mixing spoon.

Serve the roast pig at room temperature with prebanac *(recipe follows)*, pogacha *(recipe page 414), and salad.*

⚜ Prebanac (Baked Lima Beans)

Note: This recipe takes 24 hours.

Yield: serves 6 to 8

4 cups large dried lima beans	4 red onions, **finely chopped**
2 bay leaves	2 tablespoons paprika
1 cup vegetable oil	salt and pepper to taste

Equipment: Large bowl, **colander**, large saucepan with cover, mixing spoon, greased **Dutch oven** or greased large ovenproof casserole, oven mitts

1. Soak the beans overnight in water. When ready to cook, drain the beans in colander. Transfer the beans to a large saucepan, and add water to reach at least 2 inches above the top of the beans. Add bay leaves, bring to a boil over high heat, and stir. Reduce heat to **simmer**, cover, and cook for 1½ hours, or until soft. Remove and discard the bay leaves.

2. Heat the oil in a large skillet over medium-high heat. Add the onions, and **sauté** until soft, about 3 to 5 minutes. Sprinkle in the paprika and salt and pepper to taste, and stir to mix well. Add the onions and pan drippings to the cooked beans, and stir. Transfer the beans to a greased Dutch oven or greased large ovenproof casserole.

Ten minutes before baking, preheat the oven to 350°F.

3. Bake the beans for 35 to 45 minutes, or until the top is golden brown.

To serve, put the pot or casserole of beans on the table and serve warm with peceno prase.

⚜ Koljivo (Serbian Memorial Wheat)

Koljivo is a dish of sweetened and spiced whole wheat grains, prepared in memory of a departed family member. It is shared among the congregation at a Serbian Orthodox memorial mass. The same dish, with the minor variation of grinding half of the wheat grains, is served for *Krsna Slava*, the feast day of a Serbian family's patron saint. The Slava tradition is unique to Serbian Orthodox adherents. It commemorates a family's chosen saint (Slava) by inviting family and friends to the home and serving a celebratory meal. Slava is a syncretic reconciliation of Orthodox Christian and pre-Christian Slavic pagan practices. The family's celebration of Slava often dates back several generations. *Koljivo* and a round bread loaf called "*Slava kolac*" are important elements of the Slava celebratory meal.

Yield: about 12 to 15 servings

½ pound hulled wheat grains (also known as **wheat berries**)

½ pound ground walnuts

zest of 1 lemon, finely grated

½ pound (or more to taste) confectioners' sugar

¼ teaspoon ground cloves

⅓ tablespoon (or more to taste) nutmeg or cinnamon

splash of rum, brandy, or nut-flavored **liqueur** (optional)

For decorating:

additional confectioners' sugar

whole or **slivered** almonds and raisins

Equipment: Large **heavy-bottomed** saucepan, **colander**, measuring spoons, large mixing bowl, wooden spoon, food processor, **grater**

1. In a heavy-bottomed saucepan, place wheat and wash well. Cover with 2 to 3 inches of water above the grains, and let soak overnight.

2. The following morning, drain wheat, wash again, and cover with fresh water up to 2 to 3 inches above the grains, and bring to a boil.

3. Turn down heat, and simmer until tender but not mushy. Depending on the type of wheat grain, this may take anywhere from 1 to about 2 to 2 ½ hours or more.

4. Transfer wheat to a sieve or colander, leaving grains to thoroughly drain for an hour or more. Spread wheat in one layer on a clean cloth or tablecloth, and cover with another clean cloth. Let wheat rest for another 30 minutes to 1 hour. (If intended to be used for Slava, grind half of the wheat in a food processor.)

5. Transfer to a large mixing bowl, and combine with walnuts, lemon zest, sugar, cloves, and nutmeg. Taste and add more sugar or spices as necessary. Add your chosen flavoring liqueur.

To serve, spoon into a deep serving bowl, preferably glass, and smooth the top. Sprinkle with confectioners' sugar, and decorate with almonds and raisins to form a cross.
Each family member or guest is served a spoonful each.

♀ *Svadbarski Kupus* (Wedding Cabbage)

Svadbarski kupus is a hearty dish of layers of pickled cabbage (sauerkraut) alternating with layers of smoked pork and several kinds of meat. After more than 4 hours of slow cooking in a traditional deep clay pot, what emerges is melt-in-the-mouth cabbage steeped in the aromatic and smoky essences of the meats and spices. True to its name, it is a celebratory dish served at weddings, special family occasions, and other important events.

Yield: about 12 to 15 servings

2 whole heads of sauerkraut, about 3 to 4 pounds each

3 tablespoons lard

½ pound meaty smoked bacon with rind or Canadian bacon

½ pound smoked short ribs of pork (bone-in), cut into 2-inch pieces

½ pound pork shoulder or belly, **cubed**

½ pound stewing beef, cubed

½ pound stewing mutton or lamb, cubed

2 large onions, chopped

3 large tomatoes, chopped

1 head garlic, chopped finely

6 bay leaves

6 tablespoons sweet paprika

freshly ground black pepper

2 to 3 (or more to taste) fresh whole hot chilli peppers, or 1 teaspoon cayenne pepper

salt to taste

Equipment: Deep earthenware casserole or Dutch oven, oven mitts

1. Reserve 6 to 8 large whole leaves from the sauerkraut, and slice the rest into 4- to 5-inch pieces. The whole leaves will be used to line the bottom and top of the casserole.

2. Grease bottom and sides of a deep earthenware casserole or Dutch oven with lard. Put a layer of whole sauerkraut leaves, 3 or 4, enough to cover the bottom of the casserole. The idea is to have 3 or more layers of alternating meat, vegetables, and seasoning. Distribute part of the bacon and short ribs, followed by a good layer of sliced sauerkraut. Distribute part of the pork, beef, and mutton over the sauerkraut. Sprinkle some of the onions, tomatoes, and garlic.

3. Follow with seasoning: Take 2 bay leaves and tear them into halves or thirds, and scatter them. Sprinkle 1 to 2 tablespoons of paprika, three or four grinds of black pepper, and chilli peppers or cayenne to taste.

4. Build the subsequent layers in similar fashion: a layer of bacon and short ribs, a layer of sauerkraut, a layer of pork, beef, and mutton, then a layer of onions, tomatoes, and garlic and seasoning spices. Continue until all the ingredients are used up.

5. Press down firmly on the layers and cover with the remaining whole leaves of sauerkraut. Add enough water to come up to about ⅓ of the casserole (the sauerkraut will also give off their own liquid); cover the casserole with its lid. Bring to a boil over medium heat, then turn down heat to allow everything to simmer slowly for 4 to 5 hours, until cabbage is meltingly tender and most of the liquid has evaporated, leaving only a small amount of flavorsome broth. Check the level of liquid midway, and add a cup or so of water to ensure that the dish is not drying out and sticking to the casserole. (This dish is not meant to be soupy, however.)

To serve, ensure that each serving has a good helping of meat, together with the cabbage.

Slovenia

Slovenia was part of Yugoslavia until its independence in 1991. It is located in south Central Europe. To the north it is bounded by Austria, to the east by Hungary, to the south by Croatia, and to the west by Italy. Slovenes comprise 83 percent of the population, with Serbs, Croats, Bosniaks, and other ethnic groups as minorities. About 60 percent of the population are Catholic Christians, 3 percent are Orthodox or other

Christian denomination, and 2 percent are Muslim. Life-cycle celebrations in general follow the Catholic and Orthodox Christian rituals (page lxxiii and lxxv, respectively), as well as Islam and Islamic rituals (page lxxvi).

Life-cycle celebrations in Slovenia share some common elements with the other countries that once formed part of Yugoslavia. Name days (in the local language called *"god"*) are celebrated in addition to birthdays. For those who do not have a particular saint's day to celebrate as their name day, they may choose to celebrate their name day on the first day of November, which is All Saints' Day. This is also the day when all departed family members are remembered. People go to clean up their relative's graves, light candles, and place fresh flowers or, according to contemporary practice, artificial flowers.

Slovenian wedding day traditions involve several tests for the groom. Depending on the region, these tests may involve feats of strength—carrying hay bales, mowing grass, or sawing a log—or tests of skill, such as playing a musical instrument, or singing. There may be an obstacle (*šranga*) set up along the path on his way to fetch his bride. This usually involved a roadblock with a log. There, a group of men would be waiting with musicians, fortified with plenty of drink. The groom had a choice to pay up with a certain sum of money or to saw the log. The money would be set aside for the couple to set up house. Once the money had been handed over or the log sawn, all would then proceed to the church for the ceremony. This would be followed by a festive meal with plenty of food and drink, music (traditional and contemporary), and dancing. There is also a custom of messing up the newlyweds' room so that they would need to tidy up before being able to go to sleep.

On Bled Island are 99 steps leading up to the chapel, a popular venue for weddings. If a groom carries his bride up those steps, it is believed to bring good fortune to both.

⚇ *Vinska Omleta* (Omelet in Wine)

This is a dish once served to new mothers to help them quickly regain their strength and for added nourishment.

Yield: 2 servings

4 eggs

2 tablespoons grated Parmesan cheese

salt and pepper to taste

4 tablespoons butter

1 cup (or more) white wine

Equipment: Mixing bowl, wire **whisk**, **heavy-bottomed** skillet or omelet pan, oven mitts,

1. Beat the eggs with the cheese, salt, and pepper.

2. Over medium heat, melt the butter in a skillet. Pour in the eggs, and cook until the bottom is golden. Turn the omelet over and cook for another 3 or more minutes, or until golden.

3. Add the wine, cover, and cook for 1 to 2 minutes or until hot.

Serve at once.

♪ *Orehova Potica* (Walnut Potica)

Potica is a classic Slovenian pastry and is sure to grace the table at special occasions and family celebrations. *Potica* with walnut filling is the most popular of all.

Yield: about 12 servings

Yeast starter:

2 teaspoons active dry **yeast**

¼ cup **lukewarm** milk

1 tablespoon sugar

Dough:

4 cups flour, plus more for rolling out the dough

½ cup sugar

1 teaspoon salt

grated rind of 1 lemon

2 **egg yolks**, beaten (reserve the whites for the filling)

½ cup butter, melted, plus more for greasing bowl and baking pan

½ cup whole milk or cream

1 teaspoon vanilla extract

1 tablespoon rum or rum essence

Walnut filling:

3 cups finely ground walnuts

½ cup sugar

¼ cup honey

¼ cup cream

¼ cup melted butter

1 teaspoon cinnamon

1 teaspoon vanilla

½ to 1 cup raisins (optional)

2 **egg whites**, beaten stiff

Egg wash:

1 egg, well beaten, with 2 tablespoons milk

Equipment: Electric mixer with dough paddle attachment, medium and large bowls, clean tablecloth, clean kitchen towel, rubber spatula, plastic wrap, **pastry brush**, 12-inch round baking pan or baking tray, oven mitts

1. Prepare dough: In a medium bowl, combine milk and sugar, and stir in yeast. Leave to rest in a warm place for about 15 minutes until frothy.

2. In a large bowl, combine flour, sugar, salt, and lemon rind. Make a well (hole) in the center, and add yeast mixture, followed by egg yolks, melted butter, milk, vanilla extract, and rum. Use a mixer with dough paddle attachment at low speed for 1 to 2 minutes until thoroughly combined, then increase speed to medium until dough is smooth and no longer sticks to the sides of the bowl. Turn out onto a lightly floured work surface, and knead for about 5 to 7 minutes until dough is **elastic**.

3. Place dough in a buttered bowl, turn to coat all sides with butter, then cover with plastic wrap, and let rise in a warm, draft-free place until doubled in volume, about an hour.

4. Prepare walnut filling: In a bowl, combine ground walnuts, sugar, honey, cream, butter, cinnamon, vanilla, and raisins, if using. Fold in egg whites, and set aside until ready to use.

5. Punch dough down, and roll out on a lightly floured tablecloth to a rectangle of about ¼-inch thickness. Spread dough evenly with the filling, using a rubber spatula. Starting at the dough's long side, use the tablecloth as an aid to moving and rolling the filled dough as firmly as possible. Pinch edges to seal.

6. Transfer filled roll to a well buttered round cake pan, or alternatively slice into two and place side by side on a buttered baking sheet. Pinch the cut edges to seal. Cover with plastic wrap or a clean kitchen towel, and let rise in a warm place until nearly doubled in volume, about 30 to 45 minutes.

6. Bake in preheated 350°F oven for 30 to 35 minutes, or until golden. About 10 minutes before the baking time is up, brush with egg wash.

Let roll cool thoroughly before slicing into individual pieces.

Spain

Spain has been linked for centuries to the cultures of both Europe and North Africa. Earlier settlements by Celts, Phoenicians, Greeks, Romans, and Visigoths, including five different waves of North African Berber rule from 711, until the *Reconquista* (Reconquest) by King Ferdinand and Queen Isabella in 1492, have influenced Spanish culture. The third wave of Berber rule, from 929 to 1086, established the Caliphate of Cordoba. This period is noted as the Golden Age of Moorish culture, when mathematics, medicine and other sciences, astronomy, navigation, music, arts and crafts, and architecture flourished, attracting scholars and craftspeople from all over to settle, including Jews. Agriculture, horticulture, and gastronomy also flourished with the cultivation of rice, oranges, and other fruits and vegetables brought in through trade with Asia and the Middle East.

Eight centuries of Moorish rule have left their imprint on Spanish culture, beginning with language: words prefixed by "al" (such as "algebra") and place names prefixed by "ben." The cuisine is no exception: Moorish and Jewish influences are evident in dishes that combine meat and fruits, in the use of olive oil rather than lard in pastry, in sweets created from ground nuts and eggs without leavening, and in diverse dishes featuring eggplant.

Five extensive mountain ranges divide and, before modern transport and infrastructure, isolated the country's regions. Further contributing to regional diversity are the different climatic conditions and the different ecological and agricultural systems—the interior deserts, the temperate northwest, the cool Mediterranean coast, the subtropical southern regions. There are 17 autonomous regions in all, with four major distinctive languages—Castellano or Spanish, Catalan, Valencian, Galician (as well as their regional dialects, all of which share a common Roman Latin origin), and Basque, which does not and is unrelated to any other world language. These autonomous regions have retained their own distinctive traditions and cuisine.

Largely due to the Reconquista and as a symbol of national unity, Roman Catholic Christianity has defined Spanish life and cultural traditions since 1492. However, in common with other countries today, Spain is undergoing secularization. Although over 80 percent of Spanish people identify themselves as Catholic, only 30 percent of those actually attend mass. The majority go to church only for weddings, baptisms, or first communions. Secularization has also affected wedding rituals: since the early 2000s, the preference is for civil marriages rather than church ceremonies. The trend toward secularization is not uniform across the country, however. The most practicing Catholics are found in Murcia and the Canary Islands, while those with the least are in Catalonia and the Basque Country (perhaps not surprising in light of strong separatist movements there). Nowadays, mainly as a result of immigration from Morocco, Latin America, and other countries, Spain has a multicultural minority: 2 percent of the population is comprised of Muslims, Protestants, Orthodox Christians, Jews, Buddhists, Bahais, and Mormons. (See Protestant and Catholic Life-Cycle Rituals, page lxxiii.)

First communion is an important event in Spain, and families will spend heavily for the finest clothes and an elaborate celebration for their children. Traditionally, several parents would join together and share expenses for the first communion celebration in a *merendero* (small restaurant). They would each invite their relatives and friends to the celebration, which involved singing, dancing, and feasting on *cocido* (meat stew), Spain's national dish. Each cook, village, and region makes it differently, but the classic one-pot recipe, *cocido Madrileño,* is from Madrid (recipe page 436).

Nowadays, first communion celebrations are more individually oriented, and celebratory foods and decorations are themed according to the celebrant's preferences and hobbies. Whether celebrated at home or in a restaurant, there will be a central table featuring a decorative centerpiece: a miniature tree (*arbolito de chucherías*) created out of assorted sweets in the celebrant's favorite color(s) and a first communion cake. For a boy, the cake may feature a banner of the celebrant's favorite football team. In the past, first communion cakes were more religion-oriented, with a rosary, cross, or Bible piped on the icing. These days, first communion cakes may frequently feature a little doll made of marzipan to represent the celebrant. The celebrant's favorite foods are usually served, and there is an abundance of candies, chocolate, marshmallows, and other sweets that children adore. The types of food served depends on the time of the celebration, as well as the season. Most first communion celebrations are held in May and June, when the weather is pleasant; the cold of winter has passed, and the stifling heat of summer has not set in. A typical celebration food for a buffet or as an accompaniment to drinks that is popular with both children and adults is *empanadillas de jamon y queso* (recipe page 434), small crescent-shaped hand pies filled with ham and cheese.

Spanish weddings are usually celebrated with a grand feast. In the cities, it is usually at a restaurant, hotel, or country inn. In the country, the feast may be at the groom's parents' house or at an inn. Wealthy Spanish families often have the reception in one of the many beautifully restored castles or monasteries called *paradores* (literally, halting places) that can be found in every region of the country.

Some wedding traditions are familiar to Americans, such as the bride wearing something old, something new, something borrowed, something blue—symbolizing, respectively, the continuity of life, the hope for a bright future, the bonds of friendship, and fidelity. The wearing of the *mantilla*, a traditional part of Spanish attire, is making a comeback, replacing the bride's wedding veil. The old custom of the groom presenting the bride with 13 coins, called *arras*, as his commitment of financial support has now been replaced by the bride and groom's mutual exchange of coins to symbolize their joint commitment for their livelihood. The wedding ring (*allianza*) is worn on the right hand's ring finger.

Traditional Spanish weddings feature no bridesmaids, best man, or maid of honor, although through the influence of modern communications media, some weddings are beginning to include bridesmaids. During the banquet, the *padrino* (godfather, usually the father of the bride) and *madrina* (godmother, usually the mother of the groom) or the bride and groom themselves circulate among the guests, handing out *detalles* (favors), such as gifts of perfume or small bottles of wine. The guests, in return, give envelopes containing money. A modern practice is to provide a bank account number with the wedding invitation. In some places, the traditional custom of cutting the groom's tie and auctioning it off is still practiced. At the end of the ceremony, the bride and groom are showered with rice or flower petals.

Great quantities of food and wine are important to the success of all Spanish celebrations, particularly in weddings. Depending upon the region and the budget, the menu can include roasted kid (young goat) or suckling pig (recipe page 425); seafood, such as mussels, shrimp, and fish, especially eel; and meat stews (*cocidos*). The celebration meal also often includes *tapas* (appetizers) and a variety of side dishes, cheeses, and breads, such as *pan mistura* (recipe page 437). The *tapas* can be simply bowls of salted almonds, olives, pickled vegetables, hard-cooked eggs with a sauce such as *all-i-oli* (recipe page 434), *banderillas* (recipe follows), or platters of thinly sliced ham. Fresh fruit is eaten at the end of a meal, while a variety of sweet pastries, cakes, and candies are always available to eat during the celebration.

This following recipe is one of the many *tapas* dishes. Most ingredients are available in the deli section of supermarkets.

Banderillas (Miniature Kebabs)

Yield: serves 6

12 to 18 **pitted** black olives

12 to 18 pitted green olives

10-ounce jar **marinated** artichoke hearts (available in all supermarkets)

12 *each*: cooked shrimp and cooked scallops (available in the seafood section of all supermarkets)

6 ½-inch cubes boiled ham

6 pieces cooked sausage, cut in ½-inch slices

12 ½-inch cubes cheese

1 cup *all-i-oli*, for serving (recipe follows)

Equipment: 12 6-inch wooden skewers, serving platter

1. Thread any combination of ingredients on wooden skewers.

2. Prepare *all-i-oli* and put in small serving bowl.

Serve kebabs on a serving platter with a side dish of all-i-oli as a sauce to spoon over or use as dip.

✄ *All-i-oli* (Garlic and Olive Oil Sauce)

This sauce is literally garlic (*all*) and (*i*) oil (*oli*) in the Catalan language. It is made *only* with garlic, oil, and salt and is not to be confused with garlic mayonnaise, which is made with raw egg yolk. In most restaurants in Catalonia and Valencia provinces, *all-i-oli* in a small bowl is usually brought to the table together with another bowl of sieved fresh ripe tomatoes mixed with olive oil, to be eaten with slices of fresh bread, as an appetizer, while waiting for the rest of the food to come.

Yield: about 1 cup

4 cloves garlic, **finely chopped**

½ teaspoon salt

¼ cup extra virgin olive oil

Equipment: **Mortar and pestle**, electric **blender**, rubber spatula, spoon, small bowl with cover, small jar with cover

1. Put garlic and salt in a mortar, and, with the pestle, pound to a smooth purée. Slowly add oil drop by drop, adding the next only when the previous drop has been fully incorporated. The result will be a thick white emulsion, like mayonnaise. If the mixture does not thicken or thins after having become thick, scoop it out from the mortar. Then add a teaspoon of bread crumbs into the mortar, pound until fine, and proceed to add the mixture drop by drop.

2. Alternatively, in a blender, **blend** all ingredients on high until smooth, and there are no visible garlic pieces.

Serve all-i-oli *in a small bowl. Any leftover* all-i-oli *can be stored in a covered jar and refrigerated.*

✄ *Empanadillas de Jamón y Queso* (Ham and Cheese Hand Pies)

These savory crescent-shaped hand pies please children and adults alike and are a popular item at buffet tables for first communion, parties, and other family gatherings. They are simple and quick to make, especially with ready-made pie crust, and they freeze well. They can be made well ahead of time, stored in the freezer, and reheated at 400°F for 7 to 10 minutes just prior to the event. Alternative fillings are blanched spinach with sharp white cheese made of goat's or sheep's milk or roast tomato and onion purée mashed with tuna or anchovy.

Yield: 6 to 8 pastries

Olive oil pastry (or substitute 9-inch ready-made pie crust pastry):

2 cups unbleached flour, or half whole wheat, half regular flour

½ teaspoon salt

½ teaspoon baking powder

½ cup olive oil

1 egg

4 tablespoons cold water

Equipment: Mixing bowls, mixing fork, electric mixer or food processor, wooden spoon, rolling pin, cookie cutter or drinking glass, **pastry brush**, baking tray or cookie sheet, parchment paper, oven mitts

1. To prepare pastry: In a bowl, mix well the flour, baking powder, and salt. Make a well (hole) in the center, and pour in the olive oil, egg, and water. Mix well with a fork until well combined. With floured hands, take dough, and knead gently until smooth, about 3 to 5 minutes. Form into a ball, wrap in cling film, and refrigerate for 1 hour.

2. Alternatively, use a food processor: Place all the ingredients in processor bowl. Process only until the ingredients come together. With floured hands, remove from processor, knead, and shape the dough until smooth. If using ready-made pie pastry, keep it refrigerated until needed. While dough is resting, prepare the filling.)

Ham and cheese filling:

1 cup ham (serrano, prosciutto, or similar), diced

1 cup cheese (cheddar, goat's cheese), **diced** or shredded

2 tablespoons cream cheese, softened

In a bowl, mix thoroughly the ham, cheese, and cream cheese.

Egg wash:

1 egg, beaten, mixed with 1 tablespoon water

Ten minutes before baking, preheat the oven to 375°F.

1. Assemble pastries: Remove dough or ready-made pie crust pastry from the refrigerator; roll out to ⅛ inch on a lightly floured surface. With a 3½-inch or 4-inch cookie cutter (or a floured glass rim), cut out circles. Cover pastry circles with a clean, moistened kitchen towel until ready to be filled. Take one pastry circle, and place a teaspoonful of filling in the center.

   Fold pastry over to cover the filling. Seal edges of the pastry with a brush lightly dipped in egg wash. Crimp pastry edges firmly with the tines of a fork, or with your fingers for a braided cord effect. Place assembled pastry on a cookie sheet lined with parchment. Continue with the rest of the pastry and filling, spacing the pastries equally on the tray. Brush the tops of the pastries with remaining egg wash.

2. Bake for 20 to 25 minutes, or until pastries are golden.

Serve warm. These are also good cold.

Despite regional differences, Spaniards have several things in common—their religion, the use of *sofrito* (a preliminary cooking step of frying garlic, onions, and tomatoes), and *cocido* (one-pot stew). There are as many ways of making *cocido* as there are cooks in Spain. The way it is served remains constant—the broth is strained and served as a soup for the first course, while the vegetables are served separately, often before the meat and chicken, which are served as the third course.

⚜ *Cocido Madrileño* (Madrid Stew)

Yield: serves 6

½ pound piece bacon or salt pork

1½ pounds *chorizo* or Italian sausage

water, as needed

2 pound piece eye of round or sirloin tip of beef

2½ to 3 pounds frying chicken, cut into serving-size pieces

3 cloves garlic, **finely chopped**

2 onions, thinly sliced

4 **leeks**, white part only, sliced

4 carrots, sliced

6 small new potatoes, scrubbed

1 cup drained, canned *garbanzos* (also called chickpeas)

16 ounces canned chopped tomatoes (with liquid)

salt and pepper to taste

1 cup uncooked small noodles (shells, bows, or elbow macaroni)

Equipment: Medium saucepan, slotted spoon, large saucepan with cover or **Dutch oven**, mixing spoon or **skimmer**, tongs, cutting board, meat knife and fork, strainer, large serving platter, serving bowl, individual soup bowls

1. Put bacon or salt pork and sausage in a medium saucepan, and cover with water. Bring to a boil over high heat, and cook for 10 minutes. Drain bacon or salt pork and sausage, and discard the liquid. Set aside the sausage.

2. Put drained bacon or salt pork in a large saucepan or Dutch oven. Add beef, chicken, garlic, and 3 quarts (12 cups) water. Bring to a boil over high heat. Using a mixing spoon or skimmer, skim off and discard any foam that rises. Reduce the heat to **simmer**, cover, and cook for 1 to 1½ hours, or until beef is tender and chicken is done. (See glossary for tips on **chicken doneness**.)

3. Add onions, leeks, carrots, potatoes, *garbanzos*, tomatoes, drained sausage, and salt and pepper to taste. Bring to a boil over high heat, reduce heat to simmer, and cover. Cook for 20 to 25 minutes, or until potatoes are tender.

4. Using a slotted spoon or tongs, remove bacon or salt pork and beef, and place them on a cutting board. Place chicken pieces on a large serving platter, and keep warm. Using a meat knife and fork, cut beef and bacon or salt pork into serving-size slices, place on the platter with the chicken, and keep warm. Using a slotted spoon, remove vegetables from broth,

place in a serving bowl, and keep warm. Set a strainer over a medium saucepan and strain the broth. Spoon any residue in the strainer over the vegetables.

5. Cook broth over medium-high heat, bring to a boil, and reduce heat to simmer. Add the noodles, stir, and cook for 6 or 7 minutes, or until tender.

To serve, ladle into individual soup bowls for the first course. After eating the soup, guests help themselves to vegetables and then the meats. Serve with plenty of bread.

Every Spanish meal includes bread, and *pan mistura* (recipe follows) is a type of bread that is both delicious and nourishing.

Pan Mistura (Spanish Corn Bread)

Yield: 1 loaf

1 package dried active yeast

1½ cups **lukewarm** water

2¾ cups all-purpose flour

1½ cups yellow **cornmeal**

1½ teaspoons salt

Equipment: Small bowl, mixing spoon, large greased mixing bowl, lightly floured work surface, plastic food wrap, paring knife, greased baking sheet, clean kitchen towel, oven mitts, wire cake rack

1. In a small bowl, dissolve the yeast in lukewarm water until bubbly, 5 to 10 minutes.

2. In a large mixing bowl, mix the flour, cornmeal, and salt. Make a well (hole) in the center of the flour mixture, and pour in the yeast mixture. Stir the flour into yeast mixture to make a soft dough. Transfer the dough to a lightly floured work surface and **knead** for 7 to 9 minutes, or until smooth. Place the dough in a greased large mixing bowl, and turn to coat all sides of the dough with grease. Grease one side of a sheet of plastic wrap, and place with the greased side down over the bowl of dough. Let rise in a warm place until double in bulk, 1 to 1½ hours.

3. Transfer the risen dough to a lightly floured work surface, **punch down,** and knead again for 7 to 9 minutes. Shape the dough into a flattened disk about 6 inches wide. Cut an X on top, and place on a greased baking sheet. Cover the loaf with a towel and leave in a warm place to rise again until almost double in bulk, 45 minutes to 1 hour.

Ten minutes before baking, preheat the oven to 450°F.

4. Bake in the middle rack of the oven for 15 minutes, then reduce heat to 350°F, and bake for 20 minutes more. Test for bread **doneness**. Remove from the oven, and cool on wire cake rack.

Serve bread while slightly warm from the oven with cocido Madrileño *(recipe page 436).*

In Spain, candy and other sweets are prepared for special occasions and holidays.

♪ *Turrón* (Candy Nougats)

Yield: serves 8 to 10

1 tablespoon confectioners' sugar

1 tablespoon **cornstarch**

1¼ cups sugar

10 tablespoons honey, divided

2 tablespoons milk

3 tablespoons **almond paste**

1 pound sliced or whole almonds, **blanched**

Equipment: Small strainer, aluminum foil, baking sheet, medium **heavy-bottomed** saucepan, wooden mixing spoon, **serrated knife**, pitcher, small candy dish

1. Put confectioners' sugar and cornstarch in a small strainer, and sprinkle lightly over a foil-covered baking sheet. Set aside.

2. Put sugar and 8 tablespoons honey in a medium heavy-bottomed saucepan. Stirring constantly, cook over medium heat until the sugar melts and the mixture is golden, about 3 to 5 minutes. Stir in the remaining 2 tablespoons of honey and milk, and, using your hand, crumble in the almond paste. Remove from heat, and beat with a wooden mixing spoon until smooth. Pour a ½-inch-thick layer of the mixture onto prepared foil-covered baking sheet. Smooth the top of candy mixture. Using a serrated knife dipped in a pitcher of warm water, cut the candy into 1-inch squares.

To serve, stack candy squares on a small dish to eat as a sweet snack.

In the Basque country in northern Spain (including a part of it in France), it was once traditional for a new mother to celebrate her baby's birth with a party as soon as she had recovered her strength. This celebratory feast was called *Atzolorras*. Women in the neighborhood would be invited, and each would bring a chicken or other fowl as a present. A variety of food and drink—diverse salads, roast chicken, apple cider, sweet wine—would be served, and the feasting, laughing, and dancing would continue until late at night. This was a party exclusively for women, and the only male allowed to be present was a musician, usually an accordionist, and he was also responsible for fetching and taking the rather tipsy participants home (in those days, by cart). Although the tradition of *Atzolorras* is now rarely celebrated, there is a traditional Basque cake, known as *Gâteau Basque* (in the French part of Basque country) or *Pastel Vasco*, that is a must at all Basque celebrations and special events.

♪ *Pastel Vasco* (also *Gâteau Basque*) (Basque Pie)

The name *pastel* (in Spanish) or *gâteau* (in French) means "cake," but this confection is a pie. (The French terminology used in this recipe comes from its use by French Basques.) The filling can be either cream or cherry preserve, or both, with the fruit preserve between the cream filling. If using cherry preserves, choose a very good-quality one, that is, with 60 percent or more fruit content; 2 cups is sufficient.

Yield: 6 to 8 servings

1½ cups flour	¼ teaspoon almond extract
1 teaspoon baking powder	2 eggs
¼ teaspoon salt	1 cup ground almonds
½ cup sugar	1 egg, beaten for assembly and finishing egg wash
½ cup butter	

Equipment: Flour **sifter**, food processor, rolling pin, mixing bowl, milk pan or small saucepan, **heavy-bottomed** medium saucepan, oven mitts

1. Sift flour, baking powder, and salt.

2. In a food processor, process sugar, butter, and almond extract until light and creamy. Add eggs, one at a time; then add flour mixture and almonds. Process just until mixture comes together into a dough. Remove dough from the processor, enclose in plastic wrap, and chill for 2 hours.

3. Meanwhile prepare custard cream filling (recipe follows).

   Ten minutes before baking, preheat oven to 325°F.

4. Assemble cake: Divide dough into 2 parts, making the larger piece about ⅔ of the dough. Roll out the larger piece on a lightly floured surface to a disk about ⅛-inch thick; use to cover the bottom and sides of a 9-inch pie plate or flan dish. Prick the bottom crust in several places with a fork to prevent it from bubbling while baking. Spread filling evenly over bottom crust. Brush the exposed portion of the bottom crust with beaten egg.

5. For the top crust, roll out the smaller piece of dough enough to cover the pie pan with an overhang of about 1 inch. Brush undersides of the overhang with beaten egg, and position the top crust over the filling. Press the edges of the top crust and bottom crust together, and crimp with a fork all around the edges, or with your fingers, into a scalloped edge to firmly seal. Brush top crust with remaining egg wash. With the tines of a fork, lightly score top crust with three to four bars, evenly spaced. Turn the pie, and score another set of bars perpendicular to the previous ones. Make a small hole in the center of the top crust for steam to escape.

6. Bake in the middle rack of preheated oven for 35 to 45 minutes or until pastry is golden brown.

Let cool completely before serving.

৬ *Crème Patissière* (Custard Cream Filling)

2 cups milk	½ cup sugar
1 3-inch stick cinnamon	3 eggs or 4 **egg yolks**

¼ cup flour   zest of 1 lemon or 1 orange

pinch salt

Equipment: Medium **heavy-bottomed** saucepan, milk pan, wooden mixing spoon

1. In a saucepan or milk pan over low heat, warm milk with cinnamon until it starts to simmer. Turn off heat, and leave cinnamon to infuse for 15 to 20 minutes.

2. In another heavy-bottomed pan, blend sugar, eggs, flour, and salt. Slowly whisk in warm milk, stirring constantly until there are no lumps. Cook at very low heat, stirring until mixture thickens and starts to throw off a bubble or two. Turn off heat at once, continuing to stir to prevent a crust from forming. Mix in grated lemon rind.

Leave to cool completely before using. Use in pastel vasco.

EASTERN EUROPE

Eastern Europe includes Armenia, Azerbaijan, Belarus, Bulgaria, the Czech Republic, Slovakia, Georgia, Hungary, Moldova, Poland, Romania, Russia, and Ukraine.

Armenia

Situated in the Transcaucasian region between the Black and Caspian Seas, Armenia is surrounded by Turkey, Iran, and the other Transcaucasian nations, Georgia and Azerbaijan.

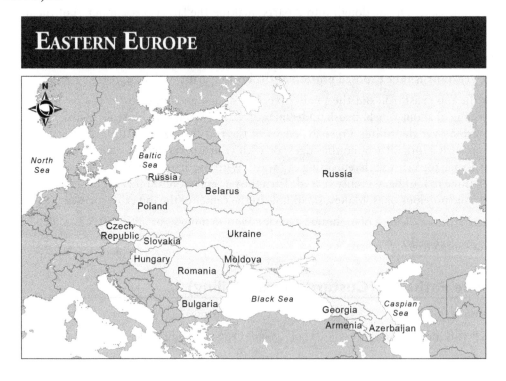

EASTERN EUROPE

Armenia was the first country in the world to establish Christianity as its official religion in 301 CE. It is the smallest of the former Soviet republics, and gained its independence in 1991 when the Soviet Union was dissolved. The Armenian population is predominantly ethnic Armenian (98 percent), with a minority (1 percent) of Yezidis and other groups. Yezidis are an ethno-religious group who speak Kurdish and practice a syncretic religion that combines Zoroastrian, Christian, Islamic, and Judaic elements. After years of Communist oppression, most citizens are openly showing loyalty to their Church in the years since independence in 1991. Almost all babies born in Armenia are baptized by the Armenian Apostolic Church. Other life-cycle events are similar to those celebrated by the Eastern Orthodox Churches. (See Eastern or Orthodox Church Life-Cycle Rituals, page lxxv.)

Bread is eaten with every meal, and special breads are baked for religious holidays. Great quantities of bread are prepared for life-cycle celebration feasts.

Churek **(Armenian Flat Bread with Sesame Seeds)**

Yield: about 10 pieces

1 package active dry **yeast**	½ cup melted butter or margarine
3 teaspoons sugar, divided	1 teaspoon salt
2½ cups **lukewarm** water, divided	2 to 3 tablespoons **sesame seeds**
6 cups all-purpose **flour**	

Equipment: Small bowl, mixing spoon, large mixing bowl, kitchen towel, lightly floured work surface, lightly floured rolling pin, nonstick baking sheet, spray bottle, oven mitts, wide metal spatula, wire cake rack, napkin-lined breadbasket

1. Sprinkle yeast and 1 teaspoon sugar into ½ cup lukewarm water in a small bowl. Let stand 5 minutes, and then stir to dissolve yeast completely. Set the yeast mixture in a warm, draft-free place (such as an unlighted oven) for 5 to 10 minutes, or until almost doubled in volume.

2. Put flour into large mixing bowl and make well (hole) in center. Pour in yeast mixture, remaining 2 cups lukewarm water, melted butter, remaining 2 teaspoons sugar, and salt. Using a mixing spoon, beat flour into water mixture until soft, spongy dough is formed, 3 to 5 minutes. Cover with towel and set in warm, draft-free place until double in bulk.

Preheat oven to 350°F.

3. Place dough on lightly floured work surface and divide into 10 equal pieces. Shape into balls, and, using lightly floured rolling pin, roll each ball into a disk, as thin as possible (less than ¼ inch). Place 2 or 3 disks on nonstick baking sheet. Using spray bottle filled with cold water, lightly mist each disk with water, and sprinkle with sesame seeds.

4. Bake in oven for 20 to 25 minutes until the loaves are golden brown. Allow to firm up for 10 minutes before transferring to wire cake rack with wide metal spatula. Continue baking remaining loaves in batches.

To serve, place churek in napkin-lined breadbasket, and spread with butter or margarine. This bread keeps well for several days, at room temperature, when wrapped in foil.

Wheat berries are eaten to celebrate religious holidays, the harvest, and at funerals. A baby's first tooth is celebrated with *agra hadig*; *agra* means "tooth," and *hadig* refers to the celebratory dish of wheat berries and fruits. Normally this event takes place when the child is about a year old. It is not simply a celebration of a tooth emerging but rather an opportunity to discern a probable pattern to the child's future. On this occasion, the mother sits the infant upright on a chair or on the floor and places five items in front of him or her. The first item that the child picks up is believed to foretell the child's future. But before the child can make a selection, its head is covered with a scarf or veil, and a bit of the *hadig* is sprinkled on it to invoke fruitfulness. The objects are a book, knife, scissors, hammer, and coin.

If the child picks up a book, then he or she is destined for life as a scholar, a member of the clergy, or a career in the teaching profession. If a knife, then a future as a surgeon or physician. If scissors, then a career connected with sewing or tailoring. If a hammer, then a future connected to the building profession or construction. If a coin, then the child will be wealthy or be successful in banking or finance.

If *agra hadig* is held during the daytime, then the guests are mostly female relatives and friends, and the celebratory meal will consist of sweet foods. If the event is held in the evening, men will be included as well, and the festive table will include a more elaborate banquet featuring savory as well as sweet dishes.

⚶ *Hadig* (Wheat Berries with Pomegranate and Raisins)

Yield: serves 4

2 cups water

1 cup **wheat berries**

¼ teaspoon salt

½ cup sugar

1 teaspoon **ground** cinnamon or 1 cinnamon stick

seeds of 1 **pomegranate**

1 cup seedless golden raisins

½ cup of any or a mix of the following: washed and chopped dried apricots, dried cranberries

For **garnish**: ¼ cup sliced almonds

Equipment: Medium **heavy-bottomed** saucepan with cover, wooden mixing spoon, strainer, medium bowl, serving bowl

1. Bring water to boil over high heat in medium heavy-bottomed saucepan. Slowly stir in wheat berries and salt. Reduce heat to **simmer**, cover, and cook just until the skins begin to burst but not until mushy, 30 to 40 minutes. Remove from heat, and pour into strainer to drain.

2. Transfer to medium bowl. Stir in the sugar and, cinnamon, and ¾ of the pomegranate, and raisins, and other dried fruits.

Serve warm or at room temperature. Spoon hadig *into a china serving bowl, and smooth top. Garnish with almonds and remaining fruits. Eat as dessert.*

An Armenian child observes three sacraments simultaneously when it is christened: baptism, communion, and Christmation (confirmation) in the Armenian Apostolic Church tradition. Usually the christening is performed in church, unless the child's life is in danger, and the child is then urgently christened at home. A dish that is traditionally served for christening is *hassa*. *Hassa* is eaten with a small spoon very carefully—because of its powdery consistency. Otherwise, if ingested without due care, one risks inhaling the powder, making the eater cough.

⚜ *Hassa* (Traditional Armenian Christening Dish)

The ingredients for this dish can be found in most stores that stock Middle Eastern foods. Adjust the amount of spices to personal taste.

Yield: about 30 (very small) servings

1 pound unsalted, roasted dried chickpeas

⅓ pound sugar-glazed chickpeas (reserve ¼ cup for decoration)

⅓ pound sugar-glazed almonds (reserve ¼ cup for decoration)

¼ pound sugar-glazed fennel seeds

¼ teaspoon nutmeg

½ teaspoon cinnamon

½ teaspoon ground anise seed

½ teaspoon ground fennel seed

¼ teaspoon ground cardamom

½ cup powdered sugar

Equipment: **Blender** or food processor, large bowl, mixing spoon, serving bowl

1. Grind chickpeas to a fine powder in a blender or food processor. Sift and regrind any coarse pieces. Transfer to a large bowl.

2. Add remaining ingredients to the powdered chick peas, and mix thoroughly.

3. Taste mixture, and adjust spicing and sweetness to personal taste.

4. Transfer to a glass (preferably) serving bowl. Decorate the top with the reserved chickpeas and almonds.

Serve as dessert.

⚜ *Harsness Abour* (Bride's Soup)

This recipe is based on a traditional soup that may once have been served by a new bride to her new husband or made by a mother-in-law to serve to her new daughter-in-law.

Yield: 4 to 5 servings

3 tablespoons olive oil

1 large onion, chopped

8 cups beef or lamb broth

½ cup rice

½ pound ground lamb

1 pound very ripe tomatoes, chopped

salt and pepper to taste

1 tablespoon dried mint, crushed

2 tablespoons lemon juice

Equipment: **Heavy-bottomed** saucepan, **blender** or food processor, rubber spatula, wooden spoon, oven mitts

1. In a heavy-bottomed saucepan over medium heat, warm the olive oil and add the onion. Stir and cook slowly until golden brown. Remove half of it, and reserve until needed.

2. Add the tomatoes to the pan, add salt and pepper. Stir and cover the pan, and let the tomatoes cook until very soft.

3. Turn off the heat, and purée the tomato mixture in a blender or food processor. Return the puréed tomato mixture to the saucepan, and add the broth, rice, and lamb.

4. Bring to a boil, then reduce the heat to low, and let everything simmer until the rice is cooked.

5. Taste the soup, and add salt and pepper if necessary. Stir in the reserved onions and the mint.

Just before serving, stir in the lemon juice.

⚘ *Haskanoush* (Sweet Wheat Pastries)

This is a traditional pastry made in Western Armenia for festive family events and special occasions. It was so treasured that families passed on the recipe from one generation to the next. The pastry is made to resemble a spike of wheat grains, hence the name *hask*, meaning "wheat," and *anoush*, "sweet." To reproduce the design of a wheat spike, the surface of the pastry is snipped in three parallel rows with tiny scissors.

Yield: about 35 pastries

Dough:

1 cup butter, melted

1 cup milk at room temperature, plus more if needed

2 eggs at room temperature, well beaten

3½ to 4 cups flour, plus more for rolling

¼ teaspoon salt

1 teaspoon powdered *mahleb* (also *mahlab*, the kernels of wild cherry pits, available in most Middle Eastern food shops), or almond essence

Nut filling:

3 cups walnuts, finely chopped

4 tablespoons sugar

1 tablespoon cinnamon

⅛ teaspoon powdered cloves

2 **egg whites**, beaten to soft peaks

Syrup:

2 cups sugar

1 cup water

2 tablespoons lemon juice

½ teaspoon orange blossom water

½ teaspoon **rosewater** (optional)

Equipment: Mixing bowl, mixing spoon, stand mixer with dough paddle attachment, rubber spatula, baking tray or cookie sheet, plastic wrap, clean kitchen towel, oven mitts, small saucepan, rolling pin, sharp fine-tipped small scissors, parchment paper, wire rack

1. In a bowl, mix butter, milk, and eggs until well combined.

2. Combine in the large bowl of a stand mixer with dough paddle attachment, the 3½ cups flour, salt, and *mahleb*. At low speed, gradually pour the butter mixture into the flour mixture.

   Increase the speed to medium, and mix until the mixture forms a dough and no longer sticks to the sides of the bowl. The consistency of the dough should be neither too soft nor hard—about the consistency of an earlobe. Add a bit more flour or milk, if necessary. Let dough rest, covered with plastic wrap, for half an hour. Meanwhile prepare nut filling and syrup.

3. Prepare the nut filling: In a bowl, mix all the ingredients, and reserve until ready for use.

4. Prepare the syrup: In a small saucepan over medium heat, bring sugar and water to a boil. Stir in lemon juice, reduce heat, and allow syrup to simmer for about 5 minutes. Turn off heat and allow to cool.

5. Once completely cool, stir in the orange-blossom water and rosewater. Set aside until ready to use.

6. Assembly: Have ready sharp scissors with small, fine-tipped blades, and line 2 to 3 baking trays or cookie sheets with parchment paper. If you have only one baking tray or cookie sheet, the pastries can be baked on the same tray, sequentially. Have ready also a small bowl of water and a pastry brush.

7. Take the dough, and, with your hands, make 2-inch balls.

8. With a rolling pin, roll a ball into a disk about 4 to 5 inches in diameter. Keep the other balls covered with a clean kitchen towel to prevent them drying out.

9. Place a teaspoonful of filling in the center of the disk. Spread it to form a straight line at the center, but keep the edges free of filling.

10. Fold the edge of the disk nearest you toward the middle to enclose the filling. Continue to roll to the end of the disk.

11. Brush lightly the seams with water, and press firmly to seal. Similarly brush the ends of the roll lightly with water, and press them firmly to seal, tapering them to a point.

12. Lay the filled roll, seam-side down on the parchment-lined baking tray. Continue to roll, and fill the rest of the disks in the same manner.

13. Place filled rolls about 1 inch apart on baking tray. When all the rolls have been filled, they can be decorated.

14. With fine-tipped scissors, make a series of snips lengthwise along the roll, with a narrow space in between each snip. Stop snipping well before the tapered ends. Make two more

rows, narrowly spaced, parallel to the first row. The snips will resemble rows of little chevrons or scales.

Preheat oven to 350°F.

15. Bake rolls for 15 to 20 minutes, or until just turning golden.

While rolls are fresh out of the oven, quickly dip each one into the cool syrup, and allow to drain on a wire rack.

Azerbaijan

Although Azerbaijan is considered a Transcaucasian country like Georgia and Armenia, it is different is some key ways. The most important of these differences is that it is a Muslim state, and most Azerbaijanis, like neighboring Iranians, belong to the Shi'ite branch of Islam. Most of the Muslim people of the former Soviet Union belong to the Sunni branch of Islam. Even before independence in 1991, the Muslim mosques, which had closed since the 1930s, were reopened in the mid-1980s. Today Muslim traditions are being restored, and life-cycle events are celebrated according to the Islamic tradition. (See Islam and Islamic Life-Cycle Rituals, page lxxvi.)

Plov, or *ash*, is the Azeri word for "pilaf," the most popularly made celebratory dish for family events and all special occasions. Of all the different varieties of *plov*, *fisinjan plov*, made with meatballs of chicken or lamb, and cooked in a sweet and sour sauce is considered the most delicious. The sauce is made from chopped walnuts and the sour-sweetness comes from pomegranate syrup (*narsharab*). Apparently it was (and in some places still is) the custom to drop a red-hot horseshoe into the sauce to achieve the desired dark color. And to ensure an even darker result, a nail-studded pomegranate was often cooked in the sauce as well. The horseshoe and nails are, of course, retrieved just before serving. (This ancient use of horseshoes and nails in cooking was perhaps a way of introducing iron into the diet, before iron supplements in the form of tablets became more widely available.)

⚜ *Fisinjan Plov* (Pilaf and Meatballs with Pomegranate Sauce)

Plov takes pride of place as the centerpiece for a feast on a large serving platter, and it is usually surrounded by a variety of garnishes in separate bowls. A delicacy called *qazmaq* is sliced in small pieces as a garnish for the rice or is served in a separate bowl or plate. *Qazmaq* is the crisp buttery crust that forms on the *lavash*—the thin unleavened sheet of bread laid at the bottom of the rice cooking pan. The *plov* is garnished with pomegranate arils and walnut halves.

Yield: 4 servings

Meatballs:

1 pound ground lamb or beef

salt and pepper to taste

½ teaspoon cinnamon

4 tablespoons melted butter or *ghee* (clarified butter) homemade (recipe page 142)

1 large onion, sliced into fine half rings

1 cup chopped walnuts

3 tablespoons pomegranate syrup (*narsharab*, available in most Middle Eastern food shops), or more to taste

2 cups meat broth (or water)

2 cups long grain or **basmati rice**

salt, as needed

4 cups water for soaking rice

12 cups water for cooking rice

1¼ cups melted unsalted butter (or clarified butter), for greasing pan and drizzling over rice, plus more as needed

½ teaspoon saffron threads (or about 15 to 20 threads)

1 *lavash* (thin unleavened bread sheet) for *qazmaq*

1 large **pomegranate**, peeled and separated into arils

1 cup roasted walnut halves

Equipment: Medium and large bowls, skillet, **colander**, **heavy-bottomed** saucepan with cover, clean kitchen towel, small glass, large serving platter or tray, serving bowl for the meatballs, serving plate for the *qazmaq*

1. Make meatballs: In a bowl, mix the lamb or beef with salt, pepper, and cinnamon. Moisten your hands with water, and shape meat mixture into 2-inch balls.

2. Heat 4 tablespoons of butter in a skillet, and, over medium heat, brown meatballs on all sides. Transfer meatballs to a bowl, and set them aside until needed.

3. In the same skillet over medium heat, add a tablespoon or two more of butter if necessary, and fry onion slices until soft and just turning golden. Stir in walnuts and pomegranate syrup, followed by the reserved meatballs, and finally the meat broth. Bring to a boil, then reduce heat, and let meatballs and sauce simmer for about 45 minutes, or until meatballs are cooked through.

4. Adjust seasoning, and add salt and pepper, or more pomegranate syrup if needed. The sauce should be a balance of sweet and sour. Turn off heat.

5. While sauce is simmering, wash the rice and rinse thoroughly until the rinse water is completely clear of starch. Soak washed rice with 4 cups very hot water and 1 tablespoon of salt. After 1 hour, drain the rice.

6. Bring 12 cups of water and 1 tablespoon salt to a boil over medium-high heat. Add rice, stir, and allow to cook for 10 to 15 minutes, or just until al dente. The rice should not be completely soft; there should be a bit of hardness left in the middle.

7. Meanwhile put saffron threads in a small glass. Pour in 2 to 3 tablespoons of boiling water. Let the saffron threads infuse the water until it is yellow-orange.

8. Drain rice, and rinse with warm water.

9. Take a heavy-bottomed saucepan with a cover, and spread the bottom and a little up the sides with softened butter.

10. Lay 1 sheet of *lavash* flat on the bottom of the pan. Spoon in a quarter of the rice, and drizzle with 2 to 3 tablespoons of butter. Cover with another quarter of the rice, and

likewise drizzle with butter. Spread another layer of rice, drizzled with butter. Top with remaining rice, and drizzle with remaining butter. Poke holes through the rice, and slowly drizzle the saffron water all over the top. Lay a clean kitchen towel over the top of the saucepan, to absorb the steam that will rise from the rice. Cover saucepan.

11. Cook at low heat for 40 to 45 minutes. Check from time to time that the *lavash* at the bottom is not scorching. Best to place a heat diffuser under the saucepan to prevent scorching. Turn off heat.

To serve, reheat meatballs, and place in a serving bowl. With a large spoon, mound the rice on a large serving platter, distributing the saffron-colored rice and the white rice more or less equally. Slice the qazmaq *(the lavash at the bottom of the pan) into triangles or whatever shape you prefer, and place on a separate plate, or make a decorative border of it around the rice mound. Scatter the pomegranate arils and walnut halves all around the rice. Place the heated meatballs in their serving bowl (its bottom wiped clean) either at the summit of the rice, or alongside the rice on the serving platter.*

ℰ *Badambura* (Almond-filled Pastries)

These pastries are usually made for the New Year, *Nowruz*, but are also made for festive occasions and important family events throughout the year. The pastry is a multilayered rich and pliable yeast dough, which is rolled into fine, almost translucent sheets, and rolled together to be cut into small pieces. The pieces are shaped into oval "boats" by pressing with the thumb on the cut side, filled with a sweet almond filling, then sealed and baked. The multiple concentric layered crust of these pastries is very attractive.

Yield: 24 pieces

Yeast starter:

⅓ cup warm milk, plus more for adjusting consistency of dough

1 tablespoon sugar

1 tablespoon flour

1 teaspoon active dry **yeast**

Dough:

4 ½ to 5 cups flour, plus more for rolling out

1 egg, at room temperature

1 egg yolk, at room temperature

1 teaspoon vanilla

1 tablespoon sugar

¼ teaspoon salt

1 cup warm melted butter

1 cup full-fat Greek-type, unsweetened yogurt, at room temperature

Filling:

1 pound peeled **blanched** almonds, finely ground

1 pound sugar

1 teaspoon cardamom seeds, finely ground

1 teaspoon vanilla extract

For assembly and finish:

1 cup melted butter or clarified butter (*ghee*) homemade (recipe page 142)

1 cup powdered (icing) sugar

Equipment: Small and large mixing bowls, electric mixer with dough paddle attachment or mixing spoon, baking tray or cookie sheet, sieve, oven mitts, wire cake rack

1. Prepare the yeast starter: Combine the warm milk, sugar, and flour in the bowl of a stand mixer with dough paddle attachment. Stir in the yeast, and leave for 10 to 15 minutes until frothy.

2. Into the yeast mixture, at low speed, mix in 3 cups of the flour until well incorporated. Gradually add the egg, egg yolk, vanilla, salt, sugar, melted butter, yogurt, and 1½ cups of flour. Continue mixing until all come together as a dough that no longer sticks to your hands or the sides of the bowl. If needed, adjust the consistency of the dough by adding a bit more flour if too sticky or a bit of warm milk if too hard and dry.

3. Transfer the dough to a greased bowl, cover with plastic wrap, and leave to rise in a warm place, without a cold draft, for about 1 hour, or until risen.

4. Meanwhile prepare the filling: in a small bowl, mix well the finely ground almonds, sugar, vanilla, and cardamom. Set aside until ready to use.

5. Take the dough and deflate, and divide into 8 equal pieces. Roll each into a ball. Take 1 dough ball, roll out on a lightly floured surface to a thin sheet, as thin as possible. Keep the other balls covered while doing this so that they do not dry out. Thoroughly brush the dough sheet, from edge to edge, with melted butter. Roll out another dough ball, as thin as the first, and lay it on the first one, stretching it with your fingers if necessary so that the sheets are aligned.

   Repeat with the other remaining dough balls, brushing them thoroughly with butter, and aligning them.

6. Now begin rolling the sheets tightly, beginning at one edge. If any yeast bubbles have formed on the sheets, use a knife point to pierce and deflate them. Even out the diameter of the roll by pressing your fingers along its length.

7. Cut the long roll crosswise into 24 slices, each 1½ inches wide. Stand all the slices on their cut side. Take the loose end of the slice, and press it down with your thumb to shape the slice into an oval "boat" that will receive the filling. Fill each boat with 2 teaspoons of filling, pressing down with the spoon and your fingers. Press the edges tightly together into a seam to enclose the filling. Lay the filled pastry seam-side down on a parchment-lined cookie tray or baking sheet.

8. Repeat shaping the slices into boats and filling them in the same manner. Space them well apart on the baking sheet.

   Ten minutes before baking, preheat the oven to 300°F.

9. Bake in the middle rack of a preheated oven for 10 to 15 minutes, or just until the bottom edges are turning golden. The tops should still be pale. Transfer to a wire cake rack to cool.

Put powdered sugar in a small sieve, and tap sieve over the pastries just before serving.

Belarus

One of the former Soviet Republics, Belarus is small country in the northern part of Eastern Europe. It is bordered on the east by Russia, on the south by Ukraine, and on the west by Poland, Latvia, and Lithuania. It is often referred to as "White Russia," which is a translation of the Russian name, *Belorussia*. Despite its recent independence, Belarus maintains many ties with Russia, and approximately 13 percent of the Belarus population is Russian.

Most Belarusians belong to the Eastern Orthodox Church, although a great many Roman Catholics (nearly 15 percent) live in the country. The basic life-cycle rituals are similar for all Christians in Eastern Europe and Russia. (See Eastern or Orthodox Church Life-Cycle Rituals, page lxxv.) The same or similar foods are served at celebration feasts, especially bread. Bread, blessed by the priest, is the center of religious and life-cycle rituals. Preparing the food and baking the bread, as it has been done for generations, is an important part of the total observance.

Smetana (sour cream) is used liberally in Eastern European cooking. It is difficult to imagine cooking in this region without it. Homemade sour cream has a richer flavor than the commercial product, and it will not clump when added to hot soups.

Smetana (Homemade Sour Cream)

Note: *This recipe takes over 24 hours.*

Yield: about 4 cups

4 cups heavy cream   2 tablespoons buttermilk

Equipment: Medium glass bowl, mixing spoon, plastic food wrap

1. Pour heavy cream into medium glass bowl, and stir in buttermilk. Cover with plastic wrap and let stand for 24 hours in warm place to develop.

2. Uncover and stir to **blend**. Cover with plastic wrap and refrigerate.

To serve, use in recipes calling for sour cream, or use as a sauce.

Sausage and cabbage are often called the "comfort foods" of Eastern Europe. This traditional recipe, made with both ingredients, would be served as an appetizer or side dish on the banquet table in a wealthy home. Most everyone else eats it as the main dish with side dishes of *kartofel'naya zapekanka* (recipe page 509), *zulynez gribnoy* (recipe page 515), and *stolichnyi salat* (recipe page 507).

Kolbasa z Kapustov (Sausage and Cabbage)

Yield: serves 4 to 6

1 pound lean kielbasa (Polish sausage) or   1 onion, **finely chopped**
   other lean smoked pork sausage, cut across
   into 1-inch pieces (available at all
   supermarkets)

1 pound head cabbage, **shredded**, or 16-ounce package shredded cabbage (available at most supermarkets)

½ teaspoon salt

2 cups canned beef broth

3 tablespoons dark brown sugar

1 tablespoon **cornstarch**

2 tablespoons water

juice of 1 lemon

Equipment: Medium saucepan with cover or **Dutch oven**, mixing spoon, small bowl

1. Put sausage pieces into medium saucepan or Dutch oven, over medium-high heat. **Sauté**, tossing constantly, until browned on all sides, 5 to 7 minutes. Add chopped onions and stir. Cook for 3 to 5 minutes to soften. Add shredded cabbage and salt. Reduce heat to medium, cover, and cook for 5 to 7 minutes to wilt cabbage. Add beef broth, increase heat to medium-high, and bring to boil. Reduce heat to **simmer**, cover, and cook for 35 to 45 minutes.

2. Stir brown sugar and cornstarch with water in small bowl until smooth. Stir brown sugar mixture into cabbage mixture, and add lemon juice. Stirring frequently, simmer, uncovered, for 15 to 20 minutes to thicken.

Serve hot as a side dish or main course with plenty of bread to soak up juices.

Dziady is a memorial feast of pre-Christian origins that is celebrated to honor the dead in Belarus. (Similar traditions are celebrated in neighboring countries: in Lithuania it is called *Ilges*; in Latvia, *Velines*, in the Ukraine, *Didova Subota*; and in Denmark, *Sialuda*.) *Dziady* means "grandfathers" and traditionally was celebrated in spring and autumn with ritual meals and libations, intended for the living and the dead. These days it is celebrated on November 2. In 1988, the custom of celebrating *Dziady* was revived to commemorate the memory of victims of Soviet repression, estimated at over 200,000. There is an annual march in Karapaty, Belarus on *Dziady*.

It was traditional to prepare for *Dziady* by personal cleansing and bathing and cleaning the house thoroughly. In the bathroom, a bucket of clean water was left for the ancestors to clean themselves, and a new broom was left for them as well. Once all was in readiness, the householder or father opened all the doors and lit a candle, invoking the ancestors to come in and be welcome. For the feast, there would be an odd number of courses but never fewer than five, and they included meat as well as hot dishes. The dishes would be those that did not need to be cut at the table—only spoons were used, and these would be left unused on the table for some time to allow the ancestors to use them. Before the next course was served, some of the previous course was placed on a plate and left on the window sill. On this day, beggars would be invited, or food would be taken to them. Throughout the meal, the conversation focused on the family's ancestors, beginning with the oldest or most illustrious that anyone could remember—who they were, what they were noted for, their accomplishments, and character traits, and so on. Finally, the most recently deceased family members were also honored and their achievements and character discussed. The family's ancestors' teachings and sayings were repeated and talked about so that they could be passed on to the younger generation to remember.

The other commemorative day for ancestors is *Radonitsa* (Ancestor Veneration Day), which is observed as a national holiday on the second Tuesday after Orthodox Easter. On this day, families visit the graves of their departed family members and share traditional foods such as *kutia* (honey-flavored grains) and *kulichi* (a sweet bread). Painted Easter eggs, sweets, and candles are left on the graves.

Weddings traditionally took place in the autumn, after most of the agricultural work for the year was finished and the harvest was in, so that there was an ample amount of culinary ingredients that could be prepared for the wedding feast. An ancient Belarusian custom during the wedding ceremony is the use of ceremonial towels. These are not ordinary wiping towels but rather woven and richly embroidered by hand, customarily by the bride herself, and often passed down through several generations. The ceremonial towels have symbolic meaning during the wedding ceremony. The bride and groom stand on a *padnozhnik* towel (step-on towel). The Belarusian bride drags this towel behind her as she walks around the altar, and this walk symbolizes a path for her unmarried friends to follow, in other words, into matrimony. In the past, the bride's family also prepared gift towels to be given to the main members groom's family as symbols of the bond created between two families.

Belarusian dishes share a common tradition with Lithuanian and Polish cuisine, as a result of Belarusia's historical past as part of Lithuania and later the Lithuanian-Polish Commonwealth. As a result of political upheavals followed by Soviet rule, there was little interest in traditional Belarusian cuisine, and not many recipes for old festive dishes have survived. A salient example is this "recipe" for the classic holiday dish known as *piačysta*. The ingredients are given as "beef, boar meat, sucking pig, veal fillet, hare, goose and turkey-hen," but no proportions are given for any of them or what parts of the meat are needed. The instructions are no clearer: "It may be braised, fried or boiled, taken from the stock and placed in hot oven for some time. Put the meat in a deep frying-pan, add the salt and dust with spices, onion and garlic. Pour over with some boiled water, then transfer to a hot oven."

♻ *Mačanka* (Pork Stew in Sour Cream)

Mačanka is a popular offering in Belarusian restaurants, whose origin is said to be the 18th-century meat sauce called *veraščaka*. It is usually served with pancakes.

Yield: 4 servings

2 tablespoons oil

1 large onion, sliced finely

2 pounds meaty short ribs

1 tablespoon flour

1 cup water or meat stock

1 cup sour cream, plus more if needed

salt and pepper to taste

1 tablespoon mustard

3 bay leaves

Equipment: **Heavy-bottomed** saucepan, oven mitts, whisk, earthenware or glass baking dish with cover

1. In a heavy-bottomed saucepan over medium heat, warm the oil, and when hot, stir-fry the onion slices until well browned. Set the onions aside.

2. Add a bit more oil to the pan, if necessary, and brown the short ribs over medium heat. Transfer the ribs to a baking dish with cover.

3. Turn down the heat to low under the saucepan. Whisk in the flour to absorb the remaining oil and cooking juices, then gradually add water and whisk to form a smooth paste. Stir in the sour cream and bay leaves, season with salt and pepper. Turn off the heat, and pour the sour cream mixture over the ribs in the baking dish.

Preheat oven to 350°F.

4. Mix in the reserved onions, cover, and bake in preheated oven for 45 minutes to 1 hour, until the meat is tender. From time to time, check the level of liquid in the baking dish, and add more water or sour cream if needed.

This dish is traditionally served with pancakes.

♪ *Pierniki* (Honey-glazed Poppy Seed Cookies)

This is a traditional poppy seed cookie made for festive family events. After baking, it is glazed with honey or icing sugar mixed with crushed poppy seeds.

Yield: about 24 cookies

1 cup butter

2 tablespoons sugar

2 egg yolks

¼ cup sour cream (or more as needed)

2 cups flour (or more as needed)

¼ teaspoon salt

½ cup poppy seeds

Equipment: Mixing bowl, mixing spoon, food processor (optional), plastic wrap, rolling pin, cookie sheet or baking tray, oven mitts, **heavy-bottomed** saucepan

1. In a bowl, cream butter and sugar until lemon-colored and fluffy. Mix in egg yolks thoroughly, followed by sour cream. Mix in flour and salt, then poppy seeds, until all are well combined to form a dough. If dough is a bit dry, add more sour cream gradually, by the spoonful. If conversely the dough is too soft, add a bit more flour. Adjust with sour cream or flour until the consistency of the dough is like that of an ear lobe—soft and pliable—and no longer tacky. These steps can be done in a food processor, processing the ingredients only until the point when the mixture comes together into a dough.

2. Shape dough between your hands into a smooth ball. Cover dough with plastic wrap, and refrigerate for 30 minutes for easier handling.

   Ten minutes before baking, preheat oven to 375°F.

3. On a lightly floured surface, roll out dough to ¼-inch thickness. Cut with cookie cooker dusted with flour. Place cookies about an inch apart on a greased and floured cookie sheet.

   Bake in the middle rack of preheated oven for 12 to 15 minutes, or until just turning golden.

   Allow to cool on wire cake rack.

When completely cooled, glaze cookies with honey-poppy seed glaze or sprinkle with sugar-poppy seed mixture (recipes follow).

Honey-poppy Seed Glaze

   Yield: enough to coat 24 cookies

⅔ cup honey   ½ cup water

⅓ cup sugar   ½ cup poppy seeds, crushed

   Equipment: Small saucepan, tongs, wire rack, airtight container

1. In a small saucepan, combine honey, sugar, and water. Let mixture come to a boil for about 5 minutes. Turn off heat, allow to cool slightly.

2. Using tongs, dip *pierniki* cookies into warm syrup. Lay glazed cookies on a wire rack, and sprinkle with poppy seeds.

Store cookies, when dry, in an airtight container.

Sugar-poppy Seed Mixture

   Yield: enough to coat 24 cookies

1½ cups icing sugar   ½ cup poppy seeds, crushed

   Equipment: Mixing bowl, shallow baking tray, airtight container

1. In a bowl, mix icing sugar with poppy seeds.

2. Lay *pierniki* cookies on a baking tray. Sprinkle with sugar and poppy seed mixture.

   Turn cookies over so that the other side gets coated as well.

Store the cookies in an airtight container.

Bulgaria

Situated in the heart of the Balkan Peninsula, Bulgaria borders the Black Sea on the east, Romania to the north, Serbia and Macedonia to the west, and Greece and Turkey to the south. Due to the mountainous terrain, most of the population work and live in urban areas.

Bulgaria is particularly identified with yogurt, which was discovered by ancient Bulgarians. In 1908, the Russian microbiologist Ilya Metchnikoff isolated the lactic acid microbes in yogurt. He found that the microbes were the prime factor in promoting the unusual longevity found in some regions of Bulgaria, where it was claimed that a daily diet of natural yogurt containing **acidophilus** aided digestion and promoted good health and long life. Metchnikoff, who won the Nobel Prize in medicine for his discoveries, named the microbes *Bacillus bulgaricus*, in honor of the Bulgarian octogenarians that he studied.

After 40 years of religious restrictions imposed by the Communists, Bulgaria acquired freedom of worship in the late 1980s. Today, more than 90 percent of the people have returned to the Bulgarian Orthodox Church. (See Eastern or Orthodox Church Life-Cycle Rituals, page lxxv.) Bulgaria also has sizable Muslim and Roman Catholic communities, as well as a Jewish minority with just over 1,000 members. The synagogue in Sofia is considered one of the largest in Eastern Europe, and, before World War II, the Jewish population of Bulgaria numbered about 48,000. Most of those who survived the Holocaust have emigrated to Israel since the end of World War II. Each group follows the life-cycle customs and rituals of its church. (See Islam and Islamic Life-Cycle Rituals, page lxxvi, and Protestant and Catholic Life-Cycle Rituals, page lxxiii.)

In spring, specifically on Lazarus Sunday, in north central Bulgaria, there is a coming of age event called *Lazarouvane*. On this day, girls of marriageable age wear traditional dress and carry baskets with flowers and willow wreaths with flowers on their heads. They visit all the houses, singing songs for health, for those who work on the land such as shepherds and plowmen, and for the rebirth of life in spring. In the village square, there is dancing to the traditional circle dance known as *horo* in celebration of youth. The girls throw their wreaths from a bridge to the river below, and the one whose wreath goes farthest is said to be the first to be married among the group.

Since the end of Communist rule, more Bulgarian weddings are being performed in churches. As in neighboring countries with Eastern Orthodox traditions, the wedding negotiations and organization of the festivities are undertaken with the assistance of godparents or witnesses (*kumove*; *kumova*, singular). The *kumove* (usually a couple who are best friends of the groom, acting as best man and maid of honor) become part of the family and are expected to make a substantial gift to the new couple. They may later on become godparents to the offspring of the newlyweds. Traditionally, the first task of a witness is to be the prospective groom's emissary to the bride's father to ask for her hand. If the father agreed, he would then ask his daughter three times if she also agreed to marry. If she replied "yes" three times, then this signaled the start of the pre-engagement period. Ascertaining the prospective bride's agreement to marriage is a custom unique to Bulgaria.

Other wedding customs are unique to Bulgaria, foremost of them being the color red to be worn by the bride on her veil—either the veil itself or some small item attached to it, such as a red ribbon or red beads. This is believed to protect her against adversity throughout married life. Another is for the bride to carry a clove of garlic in a handkerchief, again as a talisman against evil spirits. The wedding dress itself is not supposed to be washed until the first anniversary has passed or until the first child is born.

The long and solemn Bulgarian Orthodox wedding rituals are usually followed by a festive Bulgarian wedding meal, which is today often held at a restaurant and is traditionally paid for by the groom's family. Big or small, wedding receptions are usually noisy, exciting events with much music and dancing. Dancing includes traditional Bulgarian dances beginning with the witnesses (*kumove*) in the dance called *kumova rachenista*. In this dance, there are lead dancers who carry gifts, which the best man and maid of honor (the *kumove* or witnesses) may receive only in exchange for money or by dancing themselves. The bride and groom may even be called upon to dance for their wedding cake. After the wedding ceremony, the groom's mother serves the new couple a round loaf of bread called "*blaga pitka.*" Traditionally, the first piece offered to the newlyweds is salty, to signify the trials that the couple will face. The "salt" may include spices such as paprika or fenugreek or savory, or a mixture of these and other spices called *sharena sol*. The second piece is dipped in honey to signify the joys of married life. Another ritual involves breaking another loaf over the newlyweds' heads or having them pull the loaf apart, and the one who ends up with the bigger piece gets to play a larger role in decision making in the marriage. Who gets to be the one "to wear the pants in the family" is determined by yet another curious traditional custom: the one who steps on the other's foot first.

Favorite beverages for wedding receptions are *boza*, made from fermented grain, and *mastika*, a grape brandy, and *slivovitza*, a strong plum brandy, which are both used for making the wedding toast.

The Bulgarian wedding table might include suckling pig (recipe page 425) for Christian celebrations and spit-roasted lamb (recipe page 629) for Muslims. Wedding dishes enjoyed by all Bulgarians, regardless of religion, include *rengha*, smoked herring (recipe page 457); *sarmi*, cabbage rolls or stuffed grape leaves; *agneski drebulijki*, shish kebab; *shopska salata*, cucumber salad (recipe page 457); and breads (*pitka*) of all sizes, shapes, and grains.

Bulgarian food incorporates many dishes from neighboring Balkan countries' and Turkish cuisines, in particular a predilection for lamb and cooked vegetables. It is well-known for its strong flavors and extensive use of seasoning spices such as fenugreek (*sminduh*), savory (*chubritza*), paprika, thyme, lovage, and garlic or other garlic-tasting herbs, such as honey garlic (called *samardala*). For instance, the appetizer *rengha* (recipe follows) has a particularly distinctive taste. *Rengha* on toast is best eaten with a dab of yogurt or with the refreshing, nonalcoholic yogurt drink, *ayran*. A favorite beverage throughout the Balkans and Middle East, *ayran* is made simply by mixing equal amounts of yogurt and water in a glass of ice plus salt to taste.

ꙍ *Rengha* (Smoked Herring Fillets, also Kippered Herring)

Yield: serves 4

3½-ounce canned smoked **herring** fillets (also Kipper Snacks) (available at all supermarkets)

juice from ½ of a lemon

3 tablespoons virgin olive oil

3 slices white bread, for serving

For **garnish**: 2 teaspoons minced fresh parsley or 1 teaspoon dried parsley flakes

For serving: ½ cup yogurt

Equipment: Knife, small bowl with cover, spoon, toaster, small side dish, small serving plate

1. Cut smoked herring into 1- to 2-inch pieces, and put into small bowl. Sprinkle pieces with lemon juice and oil, and stir to coat. Cover, and **marinate** for several hours or overnight.

2. At serving time, toast bread slices, **trim** off crusts, and cut each into 4 square pieces.

To serve, mound herring in center of small serving plate, sprinkle with parsley, and surround with toast squares. Serve with a side dish of yogurt. To eat, put 1 or 2 pieces of herring on the toast, and add a dab of yogurt.

ꙍ *Shopska Salata* (Cucumber Salad)

Yield: serves 4

2 cloves garlic, **finely chopped**

1 cup shelled walnuts

2 tablespoons vinegar

½ cup virgin olive oil

salt and pepper to taste

1 or 2 cucumbers, peeled and finely chopped

2 lettuce leaves, washed and drained

Equipment: Electric **blender**, rubber spatula, small bowl with cover, shallow serving bowl

1. Prepare walnut sauce: Put garlic, walnuts, and vinegar in blender. Cover, and **blend** on high speed for about 12 seconds. Run at slow speed, and slowly pour oil through feed hole in cover until blended, about 10 seconds. Transfer to small bowl, and add salt and pepper to taste. Cover and refrigerate.

2. At serving time, line shallow serving bowl with lettuce leaves, spoon chopped cucumber on top, and **drizzle** with walnut sauce.

Serve with basket of crackers or as a relish or topping with lamb or suckling pig.

ꙍ *Torta Garash* (Garash Torte)

This rich chocolate torte is a popular offering in Bulgarian cafes and is usually made to celebrate special family occasions, such as birthdays and other significant events.

Yield: 12 to 15 servings

6 **egg yolks**	2 cups finely ground walnuts
⅔ cup sugar	butter for greasing pans
6 **egg whites**	

Ganache filling:	8 ounces semisweet chocolate, chopped
1 cup heavy whipping cream	¾ cup finely chopped walnuts for decoration

Chocolate glaze:	4 tablespoons butter
6 ounces semisweet chocolate, chopped	2 tablespoons light corn syrup

Equipment: Mixing bowls and spoon, wire **whisk**, hand or stand mixer (optional), 2 8-inch springform cake pans, parchment paper, wooden skewer, small **heavy-bottomed** saucepan, **double boiler**, oven mitts, spatula, serving dish or tray

1. Line 2 8-inch springform pans with parchment, and butter them well. Sprinkle evenly with flour and set aside.

Preheat oven to 350°F.

2. In a bowl, thoroughly mix egg yolks and sugar.

3. In another bowl, whip egg whites to semistiff peaks. (Do not overwhip, or the cake will be dry.) Gently fold the finely ground walnuts into the egg whites, followed by the egg yolk mixture, just until homogeneous. Spoon batter into prepared pans, and bake for 20 to 25 minutes, or until toothpick or wooden skewer used as cake tester comes out clean. Cool cakes on a rack, and slice each cake in half.

4. While cakes are baking, prepare ganache filling. In a small saucepan over low heat, bring cream to just under boiling point (when steam starts to rise but before bubbles form).

   Add chocolate all at once, turn off heat, and let it melt on its own without stirring (this prevents the ganache from getting a grainy texture).

5. After 10 minutes, mix ganache until the chocolate is thoroughly incorporated into the cream. Let ganache cool to room temperature.

6. Just before use, whip ganache by hand or with a mixer at medium speed for 2 to 4 minutes, or until fluffy.

8. Prepare strips of parchment paper to protect the serving dish while filling or glazing the cake. Lay the parchment strips between the bottom layer of the cake and the edge of the serving dish.

9. Assemble cake: Set aside about ⅓ of the ganache for covering the sides. Put a tablespoon of filling in the center of your serving dish to keep the cake in place during filling. Lay one cake layer, and, using a spatula, spread it with filling. Continue with the remaining three layers, spreading the filling as with the first layer. Use reserved filling to cover the sides of the stacked layers. Refrigerate the assembled cake to allow the filling to set.

10. When the cake is thoroughly cold, prepare the glaze. In a double boiler, melt chocolate with butter and corn syrup, and mix thoroughly. Take cake out of the refrigerator, and pour glaze over the cake, allowing it to drip down to completely cover the sides.

11. Let glaze rest until stable, then sprinkle the finely ground walnuts all around the margin of the topmost layer and the upper third of the sides.

Remove the parchment strips before serving.

♍ Apple and Walnut Banitsa

Banitsa (also spelled *banitza*) is usually a savory dish made of phyllo pastry and a white cheese and yogurt filling, traditionally served for breakfast. They are filled with charms or good luck wishes wrapped in foil for Christmas and New Year. However, there are also sweet *banitsa* that are prepared as snacks or desserts for special occasions and that are then also known as *shtrudel* (a throwback to culinary influences from the Austro-Hungarian Empire).

Yield: 25 to 30 pieces

3 apples, peeled, **cored**, roughly grated	1 teaspoon (or more to taste) cinnamon
2 tablespoons lemon juice	½ cup bread crumbs
2 cups chopped walnuts	1 cup butter, melted
1 cup sugar	1 package (about a pound) **phyllo** pastry

Equipment: Oven mitts, mixing bowls and spoon, **pastry brush**, 12×8-inch baking dish, clean kitchen towel, knife

Ten minutes before baking, preheat oven to 350°F.

1. Butter a 12×8-inch baking dish.

2. In a bowl, **blend** well the apples with lemon juice to prevent browning. Add walnuts, sugar, cinnamon, and bread crumbs, and mix well.

3. On a clean kitchen towel, lay 2 sheets of phyllo, and brush each with melted butter. Lay another two sheets, and brush each with melted butter. Place 3 to 5 spoonfuls of the apple-walnut mixture along the long edge of the phyllo sheet, close to the edge. Roll over the phyllo to cover the filling, lifting the towel with your fingers to facilitate rolling. Place the filled roll seam-side down on the baking dish. Repeat with the rest of the phyllo and filling; brush rolls with butter.

4. Bake for 20 to 25 minutes, or until golden.

Slice into 2½- to 3-inch pieces for serving.

Czech Republic and Slovakia

In 1993, after years of internal ethnic rivalry, the Central European nation of Czechoslovakia split into two independent states—the Czech Republic and Slovakia. The division, initiated by the Slovaks, was amiable. Although most Czechs regretted the separation, the Czech Republic, with its recently approved short name Czechia, has become the most stable former Communist state in Europe and one with the lowest rate of unemployment. The area that is now the Czech Republic had been part of the Austro-Hungarian Empire for many centuries. Surrounded as it is by Magyar, Slavic, and Germanic cultures, it is not surprising that the cultural traditions of the Czech Republic have been influenced by all three of its neighbors. The population of the Czech Republic is predominantly Slavic. Many citizens from the less developed Slovak Republic have moved west to the Czech Republic where they can find greater economic and cultural opportunities. Thousands of mixed marriages have occurred between the Czech and Slovak peoples, and the two groups have made progress in resolving their differences.

In a recent survey, 72 percent of the population of Czechia declared themselves as without any religious affiliation, and the remaining 26 percent identified themselves as Christians, of which 21 percent are Roman Catholic, 4 percent are other Christian, and 1 percent are Eastern Orthodox. Although historically Czechs were largely followers of the reform movement against Catholicism led by Jan Huss in the 15th century, the population was forced to convert to Catholicism under Habsburg rule, and today the Protestant denominations, such as the Czechoslovakian Hussite Church, Evangelical Church of Czech Brethren, the Silesian Evangelical Church of the Augsburg Confession, and the Moravian Church, constitute a 1 percent minority among Czech Christians. There is a small community of Vietnamese, numbering just over 6,000, with their own Buddhist temple in Varnsdorf, the first Buddhist temple to be constructed in the country. Additionally, there are enough Korean Buddhists to worship at 10 Korean Buddhist temples, mainly in Prague and Brno. Ethnic Czechs tend to practice Tibetan Buddhism. There is a small Muslim minority of about 4,000 immigrants. In addition, the ancient Slavic pagan religion Rodnovery has a small following, as has Wicca.

In striking contrast, in neighboring Slovakia, only 24 percent were atheists or not affiliated to any religion. The remaining 76 percent declared themselves Christian: with 66 percent Catholic (62 percent Roman Catholic and 4 percent Slovak Greek Catholic). Protestants in the Reformed Christian Church and Evangelical Church of the Slovak Augsburg Convention, as well as the Evangelical Methodist Church, account for 9 percent. The Czech and Slovak Orthodox Church constitute 0.9 percent, and Jehovah's Witnesses represent 0.3 percent. Other religions, such as Islam and Judaism, constitute another 0.5 percent. There are also a small Slovakian pagan group called Krug Peruna and a few followers of neopaganism.

Czech and Slovak adherents of Christian faiths observe most life-cycle celebrations according to their religion. (See Protestant and Catholic Life-Cycle Rituals, page lxxiii.) As in many Christian countries, baptism is a special family event. After a baptism, many urban Czechs and Slovaks prefer dining in a restaurant, while relatives in the country prefer to hold their baptism celebration meal at home. The national dish for both Czechs and Slovaks, whether urban or rural, is *knedlo, zelo a vepro* (dumplings, sauerkraut, and roast pork).

ৠ *Sauerkraut* (Fermented Cabbage)

Yield: serves 6 to 8

2 pounds finely shredded cabbage	2 teaspoons **kosher salt**

Equipment: Work surface, clean kitchen towel, large saucepan, 1 quart mason jar with 2-part dome lid, oven mitts, metal tongs

1. Sterilize the jar: Prepare a clean work surface, and cover with a clean towel. Fill a large saucepan ¾ full with water. Bring to a boil over high heat, then lay the jar on its side in the water, add the 2-part dome lid, and boil for 5 minutes. Wearing oven mitts and using metal tongs, carefully remove the jar from the water, discard the water, and place upside down to drain on a clean, dry towel. Remove the 2-part dome lid, and place as well on the towel.

2. Tightly pack the jar halfway with shredded cabbage, pressing strongly down if necessary. Add 1 teaspoon salt. Tightly pack the remaining cabbage, filling up to the shoulder of the jar. Add the remaining 1 teaspoon salt. Add cold water up to the rim of the jar. Set the lid loosely on top of the jar.

3. Let the cabbage stand at room temperature for 9 days, adding more cold water each day as the water level drops. Screw the lid on tightly, and refrigerate until ready to serve.

Serve the sauerkraut as a side dish or condiment or to make knedliki a zeli *(recipe follows).*

ৠ *Jepová's Knedliki a Zeli* (Dumplings, Sauerkraut, and Roast Pork)

Yield: serves 6 to 8

2 pounds sauerkraut, homemade (recipe precedes) or 32 ounces canned sauerkraut	1 teaspoon paprika
2 cups water, more as needed	½ cup vegetable oil
3½- to 4½-pound **oven-ready boned** pork roast	3 cloves garlic, **finely chopped**
salt and pepper to taste	7.5-ounce tube ready-to-bake homestyle or buttermilk biscuits, for dumplings (available in refrigerated section of all supermarkets)

Equipment: **Colander**, large roasting pan with cover, large skillet, mixing spoon, metal tongs, **meat thermometer (optional)**, **bulb baster** or mixing spoon, oven mitts, medium saucepan, scissors, slotted spoon, medium bowl, serving platter

1. Drain the sauerkraut in a colander and rinse under cold water. Spread the drained sauerkraut over the bottom of a large roasting pan, and add 2 cups water.

Preheat oven to 325°F.

2. Rub the pork roast with salt and pepper and paprika.

3. Heat the oil in a large skillet over medium-high heat. Add the garlic, stir, and **sauté** 1 to 2 minutes to release flavor. Add the pork roast to brown on all sides, about 5 to 7 minutes. Using metal tongs, put the browned pork roast on top of the sauerkraut in a roasting pan, and pour the pan drippings from the skillet over the top.

4. Bake, covered, in the preheated oven for 2¼ to 3 hours (allow 35 to 45 minutes baking time per pound). Check for doneness: When a meat thermometer inserted into the center of the meat registers 175° to 185°F, the roast is well done. Using a bulb baster or spoon, **baste** the pan drippings over the meat once or twice during baking. Remove from the oven, and allow the meat to rest about 20 minutes before slicing.

5. Prepare the dumplings: Fill a medium saucepan halfway with water, add 1 teaspoon salt, and bring to a boil over high heat. Open the tube of ready-to-bake biscuits, and separate the biscuits. Using scissors, cut each biscuit in half and drop into boiling water. Cook in batches, if necessary to avoid crowding the pan. Reduce to a rolling boil, turning over once or twice. Cook for about 10 minutes, or until the dumplings come to the surface, and then cook for 3 to 5 minutes longer. Taste for doneness, and adjust the cooking time accordingly (when dumplings are light and airy and no longer taste doughy, they are done). Remove with a slotted spoon, and place in a medium bowl.

To serve, place meat slices in the center of a serving platter, surround with sauerkraut, and spoon dumplings over the meat. Serve at once.

In the past, names were chosen according to a calendar of Catholic saints' names, and any unusual names or any not listed on it had to be approved by a special office. This restriction has since been relaxed. Name days (*svatek* or *jmeniny*) used to be celebrated more commonly in the past, but celebrating birthdays has become more popular nowadays.

The Czechs have many traditional wedding customs. One tradition is for the bride to wear a wreath of rosemary made by her bridesmaids, as a symbol of love, loyalty, and wisdom. Before the wedding reception, a plate would be broken for the newlyweds to sweep up together.

After a Czech or Slovak funeral, a small reception for mourners, with food and beverages, is held at the house of the deceased. After a final farewell toast to the deceased, everyone eats a light meal that usually includes a fruit dumpling called *ovocné knedlíky* (recipe follows), bread such as *houska*, and cheeses, fruits, and cakes with brandy, as well as schnapps (an alcoholic beverage, usually a fruit liqueur) and hot tea.

⚜ *Ovocné Knedlíky* (Fruit Dumplings)

Yield: serves 6

1 tablespoon butter

½ cup cottage cheese

1 egg yolk

salt, as needed

4 tablespoons milk

1 cup all-purpose flour, **sifted**

12 fresh, **pitted** plums, apricots, peach halves, or prunes

6 teaspoons **cinnamon sugar**

¼ cup melted butter

For **garnish**: granulated sugar

Equipment: Food processor, rubber spatula, large mixing bowl, plastic food wrap, lightly floured rolling pin, lightly floured work surface, knife, large saucepan with cover, slotted spoon, serving bowl

1. Put the butter, cottage cheese, egg yolk, ½ teaspoon salt, and milk in a food processor.

   While the processor is running, add the flour through the feed tube. Pulse until the flour mixture leaves the sides of the container, about 1 minute. Transfer to a large mixing bowl, cover with plastic wrap, and let rest for 30 minutes.

   Note: While processing, turn machine off once or twice, and scrape down sides of container with rubber spatula.

2. Using a lightly floured rolling pin, roll the dough on a lightly floured work surface into a 9×12-inch rectangle, about ¼ inch thick. Using a knife, cut into 12 pieces, each 3 inches square. Place the pitted fruit in the center of each square, and sprinkle with ½ teaspoon cinnamon sugar. Wrap the dough around the fruit, forming it into a ball.

3. Fill a large saucepan halfway with water. Add 1 teaspoon salt for each quart of water, and bring to a boil over high heat. Drop the dumplings into boiling water, a few at a time. Cover and cook about 8 to 10 minutes, or when the dumplings rise to the top. Reduce the heat to **simmer**, and cook for 3 to 5 minutes longer. Use a slotted spoon to remove the dumplings, and drain them well. Taste a dumpling, and adjust cooking time for doneness. When done, put into a serving bowl, pour melted butter over, and sprinkle with sugar.

Serve hot as dessert.

⚜ *Koláče* (Czech Sweet Buns)

Koláče (also *kolachy* and *kolache*) are sweet round buns or rolls made of yeast dough and filled with various fruits, poppy seeds, or nuts. Occasionally, they may be topped with crumbs or streusel. The origin of *koláče* is the Czech word for cake, *kolac* or *kolacek*, which comes from the word *ƙolo*, meaning circle, a reference to the circle dance performed at traditional Slavic weddings. *Koláče* may have been part of early wedding feasts as dessert. Nowadays, they are made not only for weddings but for all family celebrations and gatherings, as well as for important occasions. They also make special treats to go with coffee.

Yield: about 30 rolls

2 cups milk	4½ tablespoons dry yeast
½ cup sugar	5 to 6 cups all-purpose flour
2 eggs, beaten	apricot or poppy seed filling
½ cup butter	Finishing glaze: 3 tablespoons sugar dissolved in ¼ cup hot water or ¼ cup melted butter
1 teaspoon salt	

Apricot filling:	¼ cup sugar
½ pound dried apricots	1 tablespoon lemon juice
hot water to cover	2 teaspoons butter
Poppy seed filling:	¼ teaspoon salt
1 cup ground poppy seeds	1 teaspoon vanilla
1½ cups milk	Streusel topping:
½ cup sugar	½ cup all-purpose flour
3 tablespoons butter	¼ cup butter
2 tablespoons all-purpose flour	½ cup sugar

Equipment: Small and medium saucepans, small and large mixing bowls, **pastry brush**, cookie sheet or baking tray, parchment paper, oven mitts

1. Prepare dough: In a medium saucepan, **scald milk** (heat until small bubbles form around the edges of the pan) over low heat, remove from heat, and let cool for 10 minutes. Then add sugar, eggs, butter, and salt, and beat thoroughly. Cool mixture to a little warmer than room temperature, and pour into a large bowl. Sprinkle yeast over warm milk mixture, and leave in a warm, draft-free place for 15 minutes until mixture is frothy.

2. Gradually mix in 5 cups flour and, if necessary, the remaining cup of flour, and mix to a very soft dough. Brush surface of the dough with a light coating of oil, then cover with a damp towel, and leave again in a warm, draft-free place until doubled in size, about 1 to 1½ hours.

3. While the dough is rising, prepare the poppy seed filling and/or the apricot filling. In a small saucepan over low heat, combine poppy seeds, milk, sugar, butter, flour, and salt. Bring to a boil, then reduce heat, and allow mixture to simmer for half an hour, stirring intermittently. Set aside, and let mixture cool thoroughly before using.

4. To make apricot filling, place apricots in a medium saucepan and cover with hot water. Simmer for 20 minutes, or until tender.

5. Drain and process apricots until smooth in a food processor or blender with the sugar and lemon juice. Transfer to a pan, add butter, and simmer again until butter melts. Set aside to cool before use.

Fillings can be made ahead and refrigerated, well covered, for up to 3 to 4 days.

6. Take the risen dough, and shape into walnut-sized balls. Place balls 2 inches apart on baking sheets lined with parchment paper. Cover with damp cloth or clean kitchen towel, and let rise in a warm, draft-free place until doubled in volume, about 1 hour.

7. While balls are rising, make streusel. In a small bowl, combine flour, sugar, and salt. Cut or rub in ¼ cup of butter until mixture resembles rough crumbs. Set aside.

8. Dip your thumb in flour, and make a cavity in the center of each ball. Fill the balls with chosen filling, then sprinkle with streusel, if desired, and bake at 350°F for 15 to 20 minutes, or until golden on top.

9. Remove from oven, and, while still hot, brush with the finishing sugar and hot water glaze or with melted butter.

These rolls freeze well. Thaw and reheat in a moderate oven (not the microwave) briefly before serving.

Laskonky (Slovakian Hazelnut Meringue Cookies)

Laskonky are festive cookies made of finely ground nuts, usually hazelnuts, and stiffly beaten egg whites (meringue), baked until crisp, then sandwiched with a cream filling. They are rather similar to the Parisian meringue pastries called "*macarons,*" which have become very popular. The traditional way of making them in Slovakia is to whip the egg whites over hot water. The procedure below does away with the hot water process.

Yield: 10 to 12 sandwiched cookies

1 cup confectioners' (powdered or icing) sugar

⅔ cup finely ground hazelnuts, walnuts, or almonds

2 large **egg whites** at room temperature

½ teaspoon cream of tartar (optional)

5 tablespoons granulated sugar

Caramel nut cream filling:

⅔ cup sugar

½ cup double cream

2 tablespoons butter, **diced**

2 yolks, well beaten

⅓ cup finely ground hazelnuts, walnuts, or almonds

1 teaspoon vanilla extract

1 teaspoon instant coffee (optional)

Equipment: Baking trays, parchment paper, small and large bowls, electric mixer, piping bag with round tip smaller than ½-inch diameter, small saucepans, oven mitts

1. Line two baking trays or cookie sheets with parchment paper. Set aside.

2. In a small bowl, combine powdered sugar and nuts.

3. In a large, scrupulously clean bowl, place egg whites and cream of tartar, and, with equally scrupulously clean beaters, whip egg whites to soft peaks. (If the bowl and beaters have the slightest bit of fat, such as egg yolk, on them, the egg whites will not whip successfully.) Start adding granulated sugar gradually until the egg whites form stiff peaks. Gently fold in the powdered sugar and nut mixture, just until homogeneous. Do not overmix, or the air beaten into the egg whites will be lost.

4. Spoon the egg white and nut mixture into a piping bag with a plain round tip smaller than ½ inch. Pipe 1-inch diameter disks or slightly larger ovals (the classic *laskonky* shape), spaced about 3 inches apart, directly onto the parchment (the meringue disks will spread during baking). Take the baking sheet with the meringue disks on them in both hands, and rap sharply on the counter to let any air bubbles out.

Heat oven to 350°F.

5. Place baking sheet in the middle rack of the oven, and immediately reduce oven temperature to 300°F. Bake for 15 to 17 minutes, or until set and crisp. Continue to bake a bit longer if they are still soft, but do not allow them to color. Remove meringues from the oven, still on the parchment paper, and let them cool on a wire rack.

6. Meanwhile, prepare filling: In a small saucepan over low heat, heat cream to just under boiling point (small bubbles will be appearing occasionally at the edges of the pan). Stir cream and set aside.

7. Make caramel: In a small sauce pan over medium heat, melt sugar until it turns golden brown and gives off a caramel aroma. Reduce heat to low, and whisk in the warm cream, egg yolks, and nuts. Be careful of the hot steam rising as you whisk in the cream. Continue whisking until the mixture thickens. Stir in instant coffee granules, and turn off heat. Let caramel and nut cream mixture cool completely, then stir in vanilla extract, and chill thoroughly.

8. Assembly: Release meringues from parchment paper. Spread a generous layer of caramel and nut cream filling on the bottom side (flat side) of one meringue disk. Top with another disk, right side (mounded side) up. Continue filling the remaining disks. Let *laskonky* stand for a few hours, or overnight, to allow flavors to fully develop and meld before serving.

Georgia

Mountainous Georgia is the westernmost country of the Transcaucasian region between the Black and Caspian Seas. Bounded on the west by the Black Sea, Georgia shares borders with Russia, Turkey, Armenia, and Azerbaijan.

Despite the difficult years under Soviet rule, most Georgians refused to leave their homeland, and today more than 90 percent of Georgians still live in Georgia. The

Georgians are very proud of their national traditions and the traditions of the Georgian Orthodox Church. The Orthodox life-cycle events—baptisms, communions, name days, weddings, and funerals—are important family celebrations centering around a lavish feast at home.

Ritual celebrations, great and small, take place around the *supra* (food-laden table), an important part of Georgian culture. For life-cycle celebrations, except for the most casual, a *tamada* (toastmaster) oversees the proceedings at the *supra*. The *tamada* is always a man, more often an elder who knows most people present. He guides the party through a series of toasts, each followed by a downing of wine. A *merikipe* (server) is selected to make sure no one is holding an empty wine glass. Wine is not simply a drink to accompany food but a part of the ritual—to welcome the newborn, to say farewell to the dead, and to impart good wishes to newlyweds.

Supra, or banquets, come in two categories: celebratory banquets and mourning banquets. The celebratory banquets (*lkhinis suprebi*) are those that mark happy life-cycle events such as births, baptisms, birthdays, and weddings. The mourning banquets (*ch'rinis suprebi*), in contrast, are for funerals and are held three times after a death: immediately after death, 40 days after, and at the first year anniversary.

The toasts at a mourning banquet are distinct in style and content from those made at a celebration banquet. The *tamada* (the toastmaster) first raises a toast to the deceased to wish him or her eternal well-being and peace, followed by toasts to the memory of the relatives that predeceased him or her. All the dead patrilineal relatives, from the oldest to the youngest generation, are named and toasted. Then come the toasts to the living relatives of the deceased—from the extended family members to the closest family of the deceased.

The total number of toasts at a mourning *supra* must be an odd number. The number of spoonfuls of ritual dishes, such as *k'olio* and *shilaplavi*, passed from hand to hand by the *tamada*'s assistants, must likewise be an odd number. The ritual dishes at a mourning supra include traditional Georgian dishes, as well as those borrowed from other traditions such as *k'olio* and *shilaplavi*. *K'olio* is a sweet porridge of whole wheat grains with almonds and raisins that calls to mind the *kolliva* or *kolyvo* eaten at memorial services in other countries that follow Eastern Orthodox Christian practices. *Shilaplavi* is a savory spicy *pilaf* or *plov* based on lamb or mutton. Another traditional dish served at funeral meals is *buglama*. The word "*buglama*" is from the Turkish language and means "steamed." Although as a festive dish, *buglama* is usually served with a variety of vegetables; for a funeral banquet, it is served in its most simple form—boiled beef or lamb or mutton, flavored with garlic and dill.

Walnuts, a specialty of Armenia and Georgia, are added to everything, from soup to candied nuts. This recipe for *satsivi*, made with walnuts, is a typical meat dish served frequently at the *supra* for life-cycle and holiday feasts.

✻ *Satsivi* (Chicken with Spicy Walnut Sauce)

Yield: serves 6

4 tablespoons vegetable oil, divided

6 boneless, skinless chicken breasts

1 cup chicken broth

1 onion, **finely chopped**

1 cup walnuts, finely chopped

1 cup unsweetened **pomegranate** juice
(available at Middle East food stores)

1 cup water

1 teaspoon **ground** cinnamon

salt and pepper to taste

¼ teaspoon ground **coriander**

¼ teaspoon ground **allspice**

Equipment: Large skillet with cover, metal spatula, medium skillet, mixing spoon, slotted spoon, serving platter

1. Heat 2 tablespoons oil in large skillet over medium-high heat. Add chicken breasts, and **sauté** on each side for about 5 to 7 minutes, until lightly browned. Add chicken broth, and reduce heat to **simmer.** Cover and cook for 15 to 20 minutes.

2. Prepare walnut sauce: Heat remaining 2 tablespoons oil in medium skillet over medium-high heat. Add onion, stir, and sauté until soft. Stir in walnuts, pomegranate juice, water, cinnamon, salt and pepper to taste, coriander, and allspice. Stirring frequently, bring to boil. Pour walnut mixture over chicken breasts in large skillet. Cover and simmer for 20 to 25 minutes until chicken is fully cooked. Check **chicken doneness.**

3. Using slotted spoon, transfer chicken breasts to serving platter, and keep warm. Continue to simmer walnut mixture in large skillet. Stirring occasionally, cook until thickened, 10 to 15 minutes. Spoon sauce over chicken.

Serve with bulgur plov *(recipe page 201) and* churek *(recipe page 441).*

✻ *Korkoti* (Wheat Berries with Honey and Nuts)

Wheat berries hold a special place in Eastern European Christian life-cycle rituals. In Georgia, very sweet and chewy *korkoti* is traditionally made in celebration of a baby's first tooth.

Yield: serves 4

3 cups water

1 cup **wheat berries**

¼ teaspoon salt

¼ cup sugar

¼ cup honey

½ cup finely **ground** walnuts

Equipment: Medium **heavy-bottomed** saucepan with cover, wooden mixing spoon, strainer, medium bowl, small serving dish

1. Bring water to boil over high heat in medium heavy-bottomed saucepan. Gradually stir in wheat berries and salt. Reduce heat to **simmer,** cover, and cook for 30 to 40 minutes, or just

until the skins begin to burst but not until mushy. Remove from heat, and pour into strainer to drain.

2. Transfer to medium bowl, and while still warm, stir in the sugar, honey, and nuts.

Serve warm or at room temperature. Korkoti *is put in a small serving dish and eaten with a spoon.*

℘ *Pelamushi* (Grape and Cornmeal Squares)

Georgia is famous for growing wonderful grapes, and, besides the ubiquitous wine, celebrations generally include a dish or two made from grapes. *Pelamushi* is an unusual combination of two simple ingredients—cornmeal and grape juice.

Yield: about 30 pieces

1½ cups fine white **cornmeal**   2 cups water

3 cups frozen grape juice concentrate, thawed

Equipment: Food processor, rubber spatula, medium saucepan, mixing spoon, 8-inch baking pan, sharp knife, serving platter

Note: *While processing, turn machine off once or twice, and scrape down sides of container with rubber spatula.*

1. Put cornmeal in food processor, and process to flour consistency, 2 to 3 minutes.

2. Pour thawed grape juice concentrate and water into medium saucepan. Stir and bring to boil over medium-high heat. Reduce heat to **simmer**. Slowly stir in processed cornmeal, and continue stirring until well mixed. Reduce heat to low, and, stirring frequently to prevent sticking, cook for 15 minutes, until thickened and cornmeal is cooked. Rinse 8-inch baking pan with cold water, and pour in cornmeal mixture. Smooth top with rubber spatula. Cool to room temperature.

To serve, cut into 2-inch squares or diamonds, using a knife rinsed under cold running water. Arrange pieces on a serving platter. Eat as dessert or as snack with cup of chai *(tea).*

Stuffed vegetable dishes called *tolma* (recipe follows) are popular as festive offerings for family events and special occasions throughout Georgia. The usual vegetables are grape leaves, tomatoes, eggplants, zucchini, and sweet peppers. There is, however, one fruit—the quince, noted for its extraordinary scent, that needs cooking before it can be eaten as it is mouth-puckeringly astringent when raw—that is often used for stuffing at its peak season in autumn. It is often roasted together with lamb.

℘ *Komshis Tolma* (Stuffed Quinces)

In this recipe, quince is slowly braised in a broth flavored with dried apricots, onion, and garlic.

Yield: 6 servings

1 pound lamb shoulder, boneless, ground	6 quinces
2 tablespoons fresh tarragon, finely chopped	2 tablespoons butter
2 tablespoons fresh dill, finely chopped	2 large garlic cloves, finely chopped
¼ teaspoons ground **coriander**	1 large onion, finely chopped
¼ teaspoon ground cinnamon	4 cups beef broth, plus more as necessary
½ teaspoon salt	
¼ teaspoon freshly ground black pepper	1 cup dried apricots, washed and **diced**
½ cup cooked rice	For **garnish**: 1 tablespoon fresh tarragon, finely chopped

Equipment: Skillet, small and large bowls, clean kitchen towel, large **heavy-bottomed** saucepan with cover

1. In a skillet over medium heat, brown lamb, then mix in tarragon, dill, coriander, cinnamon, salt and pepper, and rice. Transfer to a bowl until needed.

2. With a dry kitchen towel, rub fuzz from quinces, then wash them thoroughly. From the stem end, cut off a slice about 1-inch thick and set the slices aside. If there are still stems, retain them. These slices will be the "lids" of the stuffed quinces. With a knife, remove core and surrounding pulp, leaving a 1-inch-thick shell and the quince bottom intact. Finely chop the pulp, and discard seeds and core.

3. In the same skillet used for the lamb, melt butter over medium heat, stir in garlic and onions, and cook until aromatic and softened. Remove half the mixture to a small bowl, and set aside until needed.

4. Stir in chopped quince pieces, reduce heat to low, and cook until soft, about 15 to 20 minutes. Add quince mixture to meat mixture. Taste, and adjust the seasoning, adding salt and pepper if needed. Fill the quince shells, and cover each with the sliced-off tops.

5. In a heavy-bottomed saucepan, pour in beef broth, add reserved garlic and onion mixture, and season with salt and pepper. Place the stuffed quince shells upright, and scatter dried apricots around. Cover pan, and allow to simmer gently for 45 minutes, or until quinces are tender. Top up with more broth if level goes lower than an inch around the quinces.

Serve quinces with broth, onions, garlic, and apricots. Sprinkle with fresh tarragon leaves as garnish.

The Ossetians are a distinct ethnic group who speak an Eastern Iranian language and follow Eastern Orthodox Christian traditions. They live in an area divided into North Ossetia (in a region that belongs to Russia) and South Ossetia, an area that has historically been part of Georgia. Since 1990 and the South Ossetian War between Georgia and Russia, South Ossetia declared itself a republic independent of Georgia but is unrecognized by most countries.

♬ *Fydzhin* (Ossetian Meat Pie)

This pie, in particular with its decorative braided border, is served at festive family events.

Yield: about 8 servings

2 pounds mixed beef and pork, minced

1 large onion, finely chopped

5 cloves garlic, minced

1 small sweet red pepper, **diced**

1 small hot chili pepper, minced (optional)

salt and black pepper to taste

1 cup beef broth

Dough:

3 pounds ready-made yeast dough (available frozen or chilled from most supermarkets)

butter for greasing baking pan, plus more for gilding (spreading on the baked pie)

2 egg yolks, well beaten, mixed with 2 tablespoons milk

Equipment: Large bowl, rolling pin, 10-inch diameter by (at least) 4-inch-deep ovenproof casserole dish or pie pan, small bowl for egg wash, **pastry brush**, oven mitts

1. Prepare dough: If frozen, let it thaw overnight in the refrigerator. On the day of preparation itself, leave the thawed/refrigerated dough at room temperature while you prepare the filling.

   In a large bowl, combine meat, onions, garlic, red pepper, salt, and freshly ground black pepper. Add ⅔ cup beef broth, and mix in thoroughly. Cover with plastic wrap, and set aside until ready to use.

2. Butter the casserole dish or pie pan. Prepare crust. Take ⅓ of the dough (about 1 pound), and set it aside, covered to prevent it drying out. This will be used for decorative braiding.

3. Divide the remaining dough into two, the larger one about ⅔ of the dough, and the smaller about ⅓. Roll out the larger piece to fit the 10-inch ovenproof casserole dish or pie pan as a bottom crust. Spoon filling into the crust, and smooth the top.

3. Take the smaller piece, and roll it out to fit as a top crust to cover the casserole dish or pie pan. Cut out a hole, about 1 inch in diameter, in the center of the top crust. Cut out four equidistant slits between the central hole and the rim of the crust. Using pastry brush, brush edges of the top and bottom crust with egg wash, and press firmly to seal.

4. Divide the reserved dough into three equal pieces. On a lightly floured surface, shape into rods long enough to encircle the top of the casserole dish or pie pan. Braid the rods and press into place, using egg wash to "glue" the braid to the top crust. Brush the top crust and surface of the braid with remaining egg wash.

5. Bake in preheated 400°F oven for 20 minutes, then pour in remaining beef broth through the central hole. Reduce the heat to 350°F, and continue to bake for 30 to 40 minutes more, or until pastry is golden.

6. Remove pie from oven, and brush surface with butter.

Serve immediately.

Hungary

Hungary, a small landlocked country in central Europe, is bordered on the east by Romania, the north by Slovakia, the west by Austria, and the south by Croatia and Serbia. Hungary is predominantly Roman Catholic with a large Protestant minority and a small Jewish minority. At the beginning of the 20th century, Jews constituted almost 5 percent of the total Hungarian population and almost a quarter of the population of the capital, Budapest. After the Holocaust and World War II, the surviving Jewish population in Budapest numbered fewer than 100,000. Although there are fewer than 20,000 Jews left at present in the country, the Jews in Hungary today nevertheless comprise the largest Jewish community in Eastern Europe, outside of the Soviet Union. In Budapest alone, there are 20 active synagogues.

From the end of World War II to the 1970s, Hungary's Communist government strictly controlled religion. However, at the end of the 1970s, relations between the Hungarian government and the Roman Catholic Church improved. Today, Hungarians observe most religious life-cycle celebrations according to their church. (See Protestant and Catholic Life-Cycle Rituals, page lxxiii, and Jewish Life-Cycle Rituals, page lxviii.) The eating habits and customs, including traditional clothing, of Hungarians belonging to different Christian denominations differ. The Church, in the past, discouraged intermarriage between them. The Church was in charge of recording births, baptisms, weddings, and deaths until the State took over this responsibility.

During childbirth, traditionally the father could be present only once the child was born, and if the child was a boy, he was given to the father to hold. Horsemen took their newly born children to the stable and sat them on a horse in order to ensure that he would love horses. Children's names followed certain conventions: The first son took on the name of the father; the first daughter, the name of the mother. Subsequent children then got their grandparents' names. Protestants customarily took their children's names from the Bible (Daniel, Rachel, etc.).

A child was usually baptized 2 to 3 days after birth, taken to church by the godmother (chosen by the child's parents beforehand) and traditionally carried by the midwife. After the ritual, a feast was held for family members, godparents, the midwife, and other intimate friends of the family. Traditional foods at a baptism feast included a milk loaf (*kalács*) and large pretzels.

For Catholic children's first communion (*első áldozás*), traditionally the church would be decorated with flowers and green wreaths. Girls received a wreath, and boys would receive a flower to pin on their chests, and there were gifts from godparents. When Protestant children underwent confirmation (*konfirmalás*), the clergyman was given small gifts, such as flowers or colored eggs, to thank him for teaching the children.

Customs associated with life-cycle celebrations, especially weddings, vary from region to region and from city to village. A man's coat, called *szűr*, was traditionally used to announce his intention to ask for a bride. He would leave his *szűr*, as if by accident, in a girl's house, and if it was hung outside the following day, he would know that his suit has been rejected. If, however, it was not, then he could let his best men (a group of his married friends) ask for the girl's hand. The principal best man (*első vőfély*) was in charge of organizing the wedding, issuing the invitations, and serving as master of ceremonies during the wedding festivities, as well as ensuring that everyone had food and drink. The principal best man also took charge of the music, ensuring that the traditional wedding songs were performed throughout the meal. These included wine songs, toasts, and humorous and entertaining songs.

In the old days, the handkerchiefs intended to be given as presents to the groom and important guests would have been made and embroidered by hand by the young girl and her mother. The groom's wedding shirt was traditionally made at the bride's house and carried to the groom's house on the wedding day. The same shirt would be preserved for his funeral. The traditional bridal apron, often richly decorated with hand embroidery, and part of the wedding dress, was carefully stored to be used to cover sick children for quicker healing.

The wedding feast, as with other life-cycle celebrations, was marked with generous amounts of food and drink before and after the ceremony. In the past, appetizers (*elöételek*) were served only in the dining halls of the aristocracy, not by the peasants. Appetizer dishes would not be eaten first by most Hungarians but with the meal. Traditional wedding feast dishes include wedding soup (*húsleves*) from pork or beef broth with fancy-shaped pasta, such as snails (*csiga*), diamonds, or strawberry leaves. Another is a porridge made from spelt, buckwheat, or millet grains, cooked in meat stock, seasoned with salt and pepper, and topped with onions fried in lard and a pretzel for the last course at a wedding. As it signals the end of the wedding, it is known as "farewell porridge" (*kitolókása*). Among the Hungarian community in Transylvania (Romania), a cake shaped like a chimney, called *kürtőskalács*, is popular at weddings and other special occasions. *Kalács* made in the shape of windows or keys were once traditionally given as gifts to the wedding party. The officiating priest at the wedding would also get a doughnut-shaped *kalács* with a filled bottle of wine in the middle as a present.

The following cheese spread recipe would be used on bread or eaten with fruit at the end of the meal. It is from the north Hungarian region of *Liptó*. Neighboring Austrians make a popular substitute called "*liptauer*" (available at all supermarkets), which many people think is Hungarian, but it is not. When the recipe combines authentic *Liptó* cheese with butter, it is called *körözött júhtúró*. The Austrians make a similar mixture, and call it "*liptauer garniert*," and Albanians have their own version, which they call "*liptao*" (see recipe page 384).

⚘ *Körözött Júhtúró* (Liptauer Cheese Spread)

Note: This recipe takes 24 hours.

Yield: about 2½ cups

1 cup *Liptó* (sheep's milk cheese, available at most cheese shops and some specialty food stores) or gorgonzola

1 cup butter or cream cheese, at room temperature

2 tablespoons anchovy paste (available at all supermarkets)

2 teaspoons prepared mustard

4 tablespoons grated onion

2 teaspoons caraway seeds

1 tablespoon Hungarian paprika

Equipment: Food processor, rubber spatula, small bowl with cover

1. Combine large-curd cottage cheese or *Liptó* cheese and butter or cream cheese in food processor. Add anchovy paste, prepared mustard, grated onion, caraway seeds, and paprika. Process for about 1 minute, until smooth.

Note: While processing, turn machine off once or twice, and scrape down sides of container with rubber spatula.

2. Transfer cheese spread to small bowl, cover, and refrigerate for at least 24 hours for flavors to develop.

Serve as spread for bread or crackers or as a dip for raw vegetables such as carrot, celery, and zucchini sticks.

Although stuffed cabbage is prepared in all Balkan countries, few recipes are better than the *töltött kaposzta* made in Hungary (or so Hungarians proudly claim). Cabbage, whether as little stuffed cabbages for appetizers or as whole heads filled with ground meat, is prepared for most Hungarian life-cycle celebrations.

⚘ *Töltött Kaposzta* (Stuffed Cabbage)

Yield: serves 8

water, as needed

salt and pepper, as needed and to taste

1 large green cabbage

¾ pound *each*, ground beef and pork

1 onion, **finely chopped**

1 egg

1 cup raw white rice

3 cups canned stewed tomatoes with juice

2 cups water

For serving:

1 tablespoon Hungarian paprika

1 cup sour cream

Equipment: Paring knife, work surface, large **heavy-bottomed** saucepan with cover, oven mitts, metal tongs, large pan, medium bowl, large mixing bowl, large serving bowl, small side dish

1. Prepare the cabbage: Using a paring knife, cut out and discard the core at the bottom of the cabbage. Fill a large saucepan more than halfway with water, add 1 teaspoon salt, and bring to a boil over high heat. Reduce the heat to **simmer,** then add the whole cabbage with its head facing down. **Blanch** the cabbage until the leaves soften, about 4 to 5 minutes. Use metal tongs to press down on the cabbage to keep it submerged in water. Using oven mitts and metal tongs, lift the cabbage out and transfer to a large pan. When cool enough to handle, carefully peel the cabbage leaves off, leaving them whole. Place the cabbage in a medium bowl. If the leaves become difficult to peel off, put the cabbage back into boiling water for 3 or 4 minutes until you have 8 to 10 separated leaves. Cut out and discard any tough, fibrous veins at the bottom end of each leaf. (The leaves should be soft and flexible.) Discard the water in the large saucepan. Chop the small leaves from the center of the cabbage, and spread over the bottom of a large saucepan.

2. Prepare the stuffing: Put the beef, pork, onion, egg, salt and pepper to taste, and raw rice in a large mixing bowl. Using your hands, mix thoroughly.

3. Stuff the cabbage leaves: Place a cabbage leaf on the work surface with the leafy top edge toward the center of the table or counter. Place 2 or 3 tablespoons of meat mixture in the center of the leaf. Fold over the sides to cover the filling, and roll up, beginning at the bottom edge of the leaf. Place the stuffed cabbage, seam-side down, on top of small cabbage leaves at the bottom of the large saucepan. Repeat stuffing the cabbage leaves until all the meat mixture is used. If there are extra leaves, coarsely chop them, and spread over the top of the cabbage rolls. Any remaining meat mixture can be sprinkled over the cabbage rolls. Pour the stewed tomatoes and water over the top of the stuffed cabbage rolls.

4. Bring to a boil over high heat, then reduce heat to simmer, cover, and cook for 1½ hours.

5. To serve: Transfer cabbage rolls to a serving bowl. Pour the cooking liquid into a small bowl, and stir in paprika and sour cream to make a sauce to **drizzle** over the cabbage rolls.

Serve cabbage rolls as an appetizer or main course at a wedding banquet. Serve plenty of Macedonian pogacha *(recipe page 414) for sopping up the juices and Romanian* tocana cartofi *(recipe page 495).*

The word "*kalács*" comes from the Slavic *kolo,* meaning "circle." *Kalács* is a sweet cake, plain or stuffed with raisins, **candied fruit**, and nuts, made of yeast dough. A specially shaped *kalács* can be made for weddings, holidays, name days, and other life-cycle events. *Somodi kalács,* once made only for weddings, is a cinnamon-flavored yeast cake rolled out in thin layers similar to a strudel and baked in an earthenware mold with a center tube (like an angel cake baking pan).

Somodi Kalács (Somodi Cake)

This cake was once made exclusively for weddings. The high-protein flour used enables the dough to be stretched to gossamer thinness.

Yield: 8 to 10 servings

4 to 4½ cups high protein (bread) flour, plus more for rolling out the dough	1¼ cups sugar
1¼ cups warm milk	1 tablespoon (or more to taste) cinnamon
2 teaspoons active dry **yeast**	1 cup sultana raisins
1 cup butter, melted, plus more for greasing	1 teaspoon salt
	2 large eggs

Equipment: Electric mixer with dough hook attachment, measuring cups and spoons, medium and large bowls, mixing spoon, rolling pin, clean tablecloth, **pastry brush**, angel cake or **Bundt pan**, oven mitts

1. Prepare yeast mixture: Place ¼ cup warm milk into a medium bowl. Mix in 2 tablespoons flour, 1 tablespoon sugar, and yeast. Let mixture rest in a warm place for 10 minutes until frothy.

2. In a large bowl, put 4 cups of flour and salt. Make a well (hole) in the center, and add the yeast mixture, 1 egg and 1 egg white, and ¾ cup milk. Using an electric mixer with dough paddle attachment, mix at low speed until all is incorporated. Increase speed to medium for 5 to 7 minutes, until smooth and **elastic**. The dough should no longer stick to the sides of the bowl or your fingers.

3. Check consistency of the dough. The consistency depends on the quality of the flour used, but the finished dough should be soft, pliable, and no longer tacky—the consistency of an earlobe (a traditional European way of describing dough consistency). If too soft, add a bit more flour, starting with ¼ cup. Restart the mixer, and check again. If too hard, add a bit more milk, starting with ¼ cup.

4. Add ¾ cup melted butter, and restart the mixer, until all the butter is thoroughly incorporated and dough is smooth again. Remove dough to a well buttered large bowl for rising. Cover with plastic wrap, and leave in a warm place until doubled, about 1 to 1 ½ hours.

5. Deflate dough, and set in the middle of a clean, well floured tablecloth. Roll out to as large a rectangle as possible and as thin as you can make it (almost transparent, without creating holes in the dough). If holes appear, simply patch them from remaining dough. Brush all over, all the way to the edges, with melted butter, then sprinkle evenly with cinnamon sugar. Fold the left and right sides of the dough to meet in the center. Brush all over with melted butter, and sprinkle with cinnamon sugar, followed by raisins. Now fold the top and bottom sides of the dough to meet in the center. Brush all over again with melted butter, sprinkle with cinnamon sugar and raisins. Finally, roll up, starting from the side nearest you, as tightly as you can. Press the ends to prevent the filling from spilling out.

6. Fit the rolled-up dough into a well buttered angel cake pan. Join the two ends of the roll to form a ring. Cover with a clean kitchen towel or plastic wrap, and leave to rise in a warm place until doubled in volume, about 45 minutes. Brush the risen ring with yolk glaze (the remaining yolk thinned with 1 to 2 teaspoons water).

Ten minutes before baking, preheat oven to 350°F.

7. Bake in the middle rack of the oven for 30 minutes, or until golden brown and sounds hollow when tapped.

8. Remove from oven, and cool thoroughly on a wire rack, then slice to serve.

If desired, the kalács *can be decorated with a glaze and topped with nuts and cherries. Follow the instructions for decorating the braided* ostor kalács *(recipe follows).*

⚘ Ostor Kalács (Braided Coffeecake)

For funeral feasts, woven or braided *kalács* cakes signify the hair sacrifice placed on a fresh grave. Among some groups, *kalács* is baked in the shape of a small ring and placed on the arm of a stillborn baby, so the infant will have something to nibble on and play with when arriving in the hereafter.

Yield: 1 large loaf

1 cup milk

½ cup butter or margarine

1 package dry yeast

½ cup sugar

2 eggs, beaten

4 to 5½ cups all-purpose flour

½ teaspoon salt

1 cup confectioners' sugar, for icing, more as needed

3 teaspoons water, for icing, more as needed

8 to 12 candied cherries

For **garnish**:

8 to 12 walnut halves

Equipment: Small saucepan, mixing spoon, flour **sifter**, large mixing bowl, lightly floured work surface, clean kitchen towel, greased baking sheet or large pizza pan, oven mitts, toothpick, wire cake rack, dinner knife or **icing spatula**, **pastry brush**

1. Warm milk in a small saucepan with butter until melted, then cool to lukewarm. Sprinkle yeast on top, and leave for 10 to 15 minutes, or until dissolved and frothy. Stir in sugar and eggs.

2. **Sift** flour and salt into a large mixing bowl. Make a well (hole) in the flour mixture, then add yeast mixture, and stir to form a smooth dough. Mix dough with your hands until dough pulls away from the sides of the bowl. Transfer to a lightly floured work surface. **Knead** for 5 minutes or until dough is smooth and **elastic**. Transfer dough to a large mixing bowl, greased with butter, and turn to coat all sides of the dough with the butter. Cover with towel and set in warm, draft-free place to rise until double in bulk, about 1 to 1½ hours.

3. Take risen dough and knead lightly in the bowl to deflate air bubbles. Pull the sides of the dough to the center, turn the dough over, and cover with towel. Let the dough rise again for 30 minutes to 1 hour.

4. Transfer dough to a lightly floured work surface. Divide into 3 equal parts to form into ropes about 14 inches long. Pinch 3 ropes together at one end and start braiding. When done,

pinch together the loose ends of the braid to stop it unraveling. Transfer the braid to a greased baking sheet or large pizza pan, and join the ends to form a ring. Cover lightly with a towel, and let rise a third time in a warm, draft-free place for 30 to 40 minutes, or until almost double in bulk.

Ten minutes before baking, preheat oven to 400°F.

5. Bake in the preheated oven for 25 to 35 minutes, or until golden brown and toothpick inserted in the center comes out clean. Remove from the oven, and transfer to a wire cake rack to cool.

6. Decorate cake while still warm: Put 1 cup confectioners' sugar into a small bowl, and stir in 3 tablespoons water to make a soft icing. Adjust the icing consistency accordingly, using a little more confectioners' sugar or water. Using a dinner knife or icing spatula, spread icing over the top of the warm *kalács*. Garnish with walnuts and cherries, and lightly brush them with icing.

To serve, place on the table as the centerpiece of a celebratory feast. A candle can be set into the center of the ring. To eat, cut into 2-inch-thick slices.

Moldova

Moldova is in the most southwesterly corner of the former Soviet Union. It gained its independence in 1991, but Russian forces remain in the region of Transnistria. The tiny country is sandwiched between Ukraine to the northeast and Romania to the west. Moldova is a multiethnic country, with a predominantly (76 percent) Moldovan population and significant minorities of Ukrainians (8 percent) and Russians (6 percent). Other minorities are Gagauz, a Turkish-speaking group (4 percent), Romanians, Bulgarians, and other ethnic groups. The Moldavians share a common heritage and language with their Romanian neighbors. The official language is Romanian (though patriots prefer to call it "Moldovan"—which is virtually the same language). Over 93 percent of Moldovans declare themselves to be Orthodox Christian. The Moldovan Orthodox Church has ties to the Romanian, Bessarabian, and Russian Orthodox Churches.

Life-cycle celebrations, in accordance with the custom of the Orthodox Christian Church, begin with the baptism of newborns. (See Eastern or Orthodox Christian Church Life-Cycle Rituals, page lxxv.) The parents select three couples to act as sponsors for their infant and to participate in the baptism rituals. One of the sponsors' more interesting tasks comes after the baby has been dipped in a basin of water (the font) and returned to its mother's arms. Each of the three couples in turn go through the motions of spitting three times over their shoulders. The spitting signifies the baptized baby was purged of the devil. After the baby is dressed in new clothes, they join the congregation, carrying icons and banners from the church, and they parade around the church grounds or through the village with other worshippers. The singing and chanting procession is led by two or three men ringing a large bell, which they carry suspended from poles. The baptism is announced by the revelers, and a celebration feast follows.

Moldova shares many similarities with its neighbors Romania and Ukraine, particularly with regard to cuisine, which reflects diverse influences from Turkish as well as other Eastern European countries' food traditions. Baked, boiled, or fried dumplings or filled pastries are staples of a life-cycle celebration. They are eaten as appetizers, in soup, as the main meal, or filled with jam or fruit for dessert. The following recipe for *kartophelnye vareniky* (stuffed potato dumplings) is a typical dish served.

⚘ *Kartophelnye Vareniky* (Stuffed Potato Dumplings)

Yield: 18 to 20 pieces

18 to 20 **pitted** prunes, soaked in warm water for 10 minutes and drained

½ cup walnuts, **finely chopped**

¾ cup sugar, divided

3½ cups mashed potatoes, cooled to room temperature

1 egg, beaten

salt to taste

½ cup all-purpose **flour**, more if necessary

1 tablespoon **cornstarch**

1 cup butter or margarine

1½ cups **bread crumbs**

For serving: 1 cup sour cream

Equipment: Work surface, knife, small bowl with cover, mixing spoon, food processor, rubber spatula, lightly floured work surface, damp kitchen towel, lightly floured rolling pin, large saucepan, slotted spoon, large heatproof platter, small saucepan, small serving bowl

1. Prepare filling: On work surface, finely chop prunes, and place in small bowl. Add finely chopped walnuts and ¼ cup sugar. Stir, cover, and refrigerate.

2. Prepare dough: Put mashed potatoes in food processor, add egg, salt, ½ cup flour, and cornstarch. Pulse and process until mixture pulls away from sides of container and forms a ball, 1 to 2 minutes.

   Note: While processing, turn machine off once or twice, and scrape down sides of container with rubber spatula.

3. Transfer to lightly floured work surface, and **knead** until smooth, 3 to 5 minutes. If dough is sticky, add a little more flour. Using lightly floured rolling pin, roll dough ¼ inch thick. Using knife, cut into 2½-inch squares. Place squares slightly overlapping on work surface, and cover with damp towel to prevent drying out.

4. Assemble dumplings: Place a heaping teaspoon prune filling in center of each dough square. Enclose filling in dough, and shape into a ball. Repeat making dumplings, using up all the dough.

5. Fill large saucepan halfway with water, add ½ teaspoon salt, and bring to boil over high heat. Drop dumplings, a few at a time, in boiling water. When water comes back to boil, reduce

heat to **simmer**, and cook for 15 to 20 minutes, or until dough is cooked. (It should taste tender and airy when done.) Using slotted spoon, transfer dumplings to large heatproof platter, and keep warm.

6. Prepare topping: Melt butter in small saucepan over medium heat. Add bread crumbs, stir to coat, and heat through, 3 to 5 minutes.

To serve, spoon breadcrumb mixture over dumplings, sprinkle with remaining ½ cup sugar, and serve at once. Serve with small serving bowl of sour cream to spoon over dumplings.

Many recipes from neighboring regions have crossed into Moldova. The banquet feast might include *zulynez gribnoy* listed in the Ukrainian section (recipe page 515) and *kolbasa z kapustov* described in the Belarus chapter (recipe page 450), eaten along with the potato dumplings.

♨ *Poale-n Brâu Moldovenesti* (Moldovan Cheese Pastries)

These pastries are also known as *brânzoaicele* and are so much identified with Moldova that some have called it the "national pastry." Traditionally they were made during winter and just before Lent. Their name, which is literally "hem in belt," is said to refer to the ancient practice of country women raising the hem of their skirt and tucking it into their belt while working, so as not to impede their movements.

Yield: 12 pastries

Dough:

1 cup **lukewarm** milk

2 teaspoons active dry **yeast**

⅓ cup sugar

4 to 4½ cups flour, plus more for rolling out the dough

2 eggs

¼ cup butter, plus more for greasing

¼ teaspoon salt

grated **zest** of 1 orange

1 cup powdered sugar or 3 to 5 tablespoons vanilla sugar, to finish

Cheese filling:

1½ cups cottage cheese, well drained

⅔ cup sugar

2 eggs

2 tablespoons **semolina**

grated zest of 1 orange

½ cup raisins

¼ teaspoon salt

egg wash: 1 egg yolk plus 2 tablespoons milk

vanilla sugar

Note: Vanilla sugar needs to mature for two weeks before using. If you wish to make your own, instead of buying prepackaged vanilla sugar (which can be expensive outside of Europe), take 1 or 2 vanilla beans, place them in a small glass jar with an airtight lid, and cover with about a cupful or two of sugar. Keep the jar in a dark place for about 2 weeks to allow the vanilla beans to properly infuse the sugar. As the sugar gets depleted, keep adding more sugar to the jar. The vanilla beans will continue to be effective at infusing sugar for years.

Equipment: Mixing bowl, wooden spoon, electric mixer with dough paddle attachment, rolling pin, baking tray or cookie sheet, plastic wrap, parchment paper, **pastry brush**, airtight jar for making vanilla sugar

1. Prepare dough: In large mixing bowl (or a mixer with dough paddle attachment), put warm milk and 1 tablespoon sugar. Stir in yeast, and leave mixture to rest in a warm place until frothy, about 10 to 15 minutes.

2. Mix in flour (at low speed in mixer), and, when thoroughly combined with the yeast mixture, gradually add remaining sugar, salt, eggs, orange peel, and softened butter. Continue to mix until butter is completely incorporated, and all comes together into a dough that no longer sticks to the sides of the bowl.

3. Remove dough from bowl, and knead on a lightly floured surface until dough becomes smooth and **elastic**, about 5 to 7 minutes.

4. Transfer dough to a greased bowl, turn it around so that the rest of the dough gets greased as well. Cover dough with plastic wrap, and let it rest in a warm place for about 2 hours, or until doubled in volume.

5. Meanwhile prepare filling. In a bowl, combine cottage cheese, orange zest, eggs, raisins, semolina, and salt until smooth. Cover with plastic wrap, and keep refrigerated until needed.

6. Assemble pastry: Deflate risen dough, and roll out on a lightly floured surface to a large rectangle of about ⅛-inch thickness. Cut into square pieces, each measuring about 4 inches. Place a heaping teaspoonful of filling in the center of each square. Pinch firmly together the opposite sides of the square to seal and enclose the filling. Continue filling the remaining squares.

7. Place filled squares well apart on baking tray or cookie sheet lined with parchment paper.

    Let squares rest, covered with a clean kitchen towel, in a warm place until almost doubled in volume, about 1 hour.

Preheat oven to 400°F.

8. Brush carefully the risen squares with egg wash, and bake for 15 to 20 minutes, or until golden. Remove baked squares from oven to cool on a wire rack.

When thoroughly cool, sprinkle with powdered sugar or vanilla sugar (recipe for making it yourself precedes).

⚘ *Cozonac Moldovenesc* (Moldovan Rich Yeast Cake)

This sweet festive loaf is well-known, if not notorious, for being extraordinarily rich, as it includes 10 egg yolks. However, this quantity of yolks contributes to the good keeping qualities of this yeast cake. The usual filling is a mixture similar to that used for Italian *panettone*, of raisins, nuts, and candied peel, with the addition of cocoa powder, but an alternative filling is given here of walnut and honey cream.

Yield: 1 loaf 12 inches by 6 inches (10 to 12 servings)

1 to 1½ cups milk, warm

½ cup sugar

2 teaspoons active dry **yeast**

4 to 4½ cups high-gluten (bread) flour

¼ cup butter, melted

10 medium **egg yolks**

1 teaspoon vanilla essence

grated **zest** from 1 lemon

¼ teaspoon salt

¼ cup buttermilk, yogurt, or sour cream

¼ cup oil

For filling: a mixture of nuts, raisins, cocoa powder, and candied citrus peel, the proportions according to personal preference, or walnut honey cream filling (recipe follows)

Equipment: Small bowls, large mixing bowl, mixing spoon, electric mixer with dough paddle attachment, oven mitts, loaf pan 12 by 6 inches (at least 6 inches deep), **pastry brush**

1. Prepare dough: In a small bowl, place ¼ cup warm milk, 1 tablespoon sugar, and stir in yeast. Let rise in a warm place until frothy, about 10 to 15 minutes.

2. In the mixing bowl of a mixer with dough paddle attachment, place flour. Make a well (hole) in the center of the flour, and mix in yeast mixture at low speed until well incorporated. Mix in gradually the remaining sugar, ¾ cup milk, and melted butter. Gradually increase speed to medium, and add yolks one by one, vanilla, lemon zest, salt, and buttermilk, until all comes together into a dough and leaves the sides of the bowl. Add oil, and start gently kneading it into the dough. At this point, the consistency of the dough should be neither too hard nor too soft. It should be the consistency of an earlobe—soft, pliable, and no longer tacky. Add a bit more flour or milk to attain this consistency, if necessary. Continue to work dough in the mixer for at least 1 hour until it is smooth and starts to form bubbles as yeast begins to work.

3. Turn off mixer, remove dough, and knead it on a lightly floured work surface for 10 to 15 more minutes until thoroughly smooth and **elastic**. The bubbles will become more uniform at this point. Place dough in a greased bowl, flip dough, cover with plastic wrap, and let rest in a warm place until doubled in volume, about 2 hours.

4. Prepare loaf pan: Line pan with parchment paper to extend about 2 inches above the sides. Butter well the bottom and sides of the parchment paper, and sprinkle evenly with flour. Set prepared pan aside until needed.

5. Deflate dough, and divide into two equal pieces. Roll dough to the dimensions of loaf pan and about 1 inch thick. Spread with half the nut filling (recipe follows), leaving the margins free of the filling. Seal the ends and edges to prevent filling from spilling out. Roll and fill the other piece of dough in the same manner.

6. Put filled rolls side by side and twist them, pinching the ends firmly to seal. Place twisted roll inside loaf pan, and set in a warm place to rise until it reaches about ½ to 1 inch above the sides of the loaf pan, about 1 to 1½ hours. Do not let it to rise beyond that, or the dough may overflow. Gently brush with egg yolk mixed with remaining milk. Sprinkle with sugar, if desired.

Preheat oven to 350°F.

7. Place in the middle rack of oven, and bake for 45 to 50 minutes, or until the loaf is golden and sounds hollow when tapped.

8. Remove from oven, leave in the pan for 15 minutes, then transfer, still in the parchment paper, to a wire rack to cool thoroughly in a place free from drafts.

Once completely cool, the loaf can be sliced neatly; otherwise, it has a tendency to tear.

Nut Filling

Yield: enough filling for 1 loaf cake

⅓ to ½ cup light cream (or more if necessary)

2 tablespoons honey

½ cup sugar

1 to 2 tablespoons unsweetened cocoa powder (or more if you wish a darker filling)

2 tablespoons rum or rum essence

Equipment: **Heavy-bottomed** small saucepan, wooden spoon or whisk for stirring, rubber spatula, oven mitts

1. In a heavy-bottomed small saucepan over low heat, warm the cream, honey, and sugar, stirring until the sugar is dissolved.

2. Stir in the cocoa. The filling should be opaque at this point. If at all translucent, add a bit more cream as necessary.

3. Turn off the heat, and allow the filling to cool. Just before using, stir in the rum.

Use to fill the rolls in cozonac moldovenesc *(recipe precedes).*

Poland

Located in northeastern Europe, Poland is bordered by Germany on the west, by the Czech Republic and Slovakia on the south, by Belarus and Ukraine on the east, and by the Baltic Sea on the north. From the 18th century to the end of World War I, Poland was controlled by Russia. An independent republic between the World Wars, Poland was invaded by Nazi Germany in 1939, an act that began World War II. Poland was a Communist state under the domination of the Soviet Union from 1945 until 1989, when Communist rule ended. Most Poles are Roman Catholic with strong attachments to church and family. Most life-cycle celebrations are conducted according to the Roman Catholic Church. (See Protestant and Catholic Life-Cycle Rituals, page lxxiii.)

As in other countries with predominant Catholic Christian populations, name day (*imieniny*) is celebrated and is often considered more important than a birthday, particularly by more senior celebrants, perhaps because they do not wish to be reminded of their age. All calendars are printed with name days, which are the feast days of Catholic saints.

Departed family members used to be remembered on the Slavic pagan festival of *Dziady*, which was celebrated twice a year, in spring and autumn. With the coming of Christianity, November 2 was dedicated to celebrating *Zaduszki* (Day of Prayers for the Dead) following All Souls' Day on November 1. Graves were cleaned and tidied, candles lit, and flowers arranged, and a priest would be asked to bless the grave with holy water and prayers. Likewise, the family home was cleaned and prepared to welcome returning souls. A window or door would be left open, and a chair drawn closer to the fire. A comb, basin, and towel would also be left on a bench for the dead souls to wash and tidy themselves. The table would be set with a commemorative meal, and it was not cleared until the following morning to ensure that returning souls were not disturbed. A special bread was also baked and left at the grave or given to the poor.

Poles believe the success of a marriage depends on the lavishness of the hospitality and the gaiety of the wedding celebration. It's not unusual for Polish weddings to go nonstop for three or four days, and invited guests often take off work to attend. Many old Polish customs are brought to life with music and dancing. The *czepek* (money dance) has a long history; it allows guests to pay money for the privilege of dancing with the bride. The money is looked upon as a wedding gift to the couple. When the groom pays for the privilege of a dance with his new wife, it is a signal to the guests that the wedding couple are exiting the festivities. The dancing and feasting continues, with more food and drink, after they depart. The late night repast is usually pastries and fruit. Decorated wedding bread and wedding cake are both prepared for Polish weddings, depending upon the region, village, city, or family preference. The first Polish wedding breads date back to the 13th century. This was a sweet bread made with yeast. Called *korowaj*, it comes from the Polish word for circle. The baking of the wedding bread is important, with special rules and procedures. The godmother of the bride is responsible for baking the bread with the help of selected women. Clumps of dough are shaped into birds, flowers and ivy, chickens, and other barnyard animals. The wedding bread is similar to Ukrainian wedding bread and *krendel* (recipe page 512). The first pieces of wedding bread are cut for the bride and groom, then for parents and grandparents, next for the attendants and all the guests, including children. The sharing of bread is a symbol of abundance and goodwill. Wedding feasts are considered the grandest of family celebrations, and no expense is spared to give guests the very best and the most food the family can afford. Today, the Polish wedding feast begins with *zakaski* (small bites or appetizers). The tradition probably originated centuries ago with the aristocracy. The *zakaski* generally included pickles, pickled herring, *salatka z piklowanymi jajkami* (recipe follows), smoked meats and sausages with mustard and horseradish (recipe page 366), sauerkraut (recipe page 461), cheeses, *piroshki* (recipe page 486), and *pierogi* (recipe page 487), baskets of hearty breads and rolls, and bowls of nuts, figs, and raisins. Bowls of *smetana*, either homemade (recipe page 450) or commercial, are usually provided for guests to spoon over dumplings. *Zakaski*, either hot or cold, are supposed to stimulate the eye and thus whet the appetite, so it is important to make the presentations as attractive as possible.

Salatka z Piklowanymi Jajkami (Polish Salad with Pickled Eggs)

Yield: serves 6

pickled eggs (recipe follows)

¼ cup virgin olive oil

2 tablespoons lemon juice

salt and pepper to taste

1 head romaine lettuce, rinsed, drained, torn into bite-size pieces

1 red onion, thinly sliced and separated into rings

Equipment: Small bowl, **whisk**, medium salad bowl, salad tools, individual salad plates

1. Prepare pickled eggs.

2. Prepare dressing: Pour oil into small bowl, whisk in lemon juice and salt and pepper to taste, and set aside.

3. Assemble salad: Put lettuce and onions into medium salad bowl. Whisk oil dressing, **drizzle** over salad mixture, and toss to coat. Cut pickled eggs into wedges, and arrange on top of the salad.

Serve as zakaski *with salad plates for guests to help themselves. Provide plenty of bread.*

Pickled Eggs

Yield: serves 6

2 (14 to 16 ounces each) cans **beets** with juice
water, as needed

¾ cup vinegar

1 cup sugar

2 bay leaves

10 whole cloves

6 hard-cooked eggs, peeled

Equipment: 2-cup-size measuring cup, small container with cover, small saucepan, mixing spoon, large plastic resealable bag

1. Drain beet juice from cans of beets, and pour into 2-cup-size measuring cup. Put beets in small container, cover, and refrigerate for another use. Add water to the beet juice, if necessary to make 2 cups of liquid, and pour into small saucepan. Add vinegar, sugar, bay leaves, and cloves. Bring to boil over medium-high heat, and stir to dissolve sugar. Reduce heat to **simmer**, and cook 5 minutes. Cool to warm.

2. Put peeled, whole hard-cooked eggs into large plastic resealable bag, and pour in warm beet juice mixture. Close bag securely, and refrigerate for at least 12 hours for flavor and color to

develop. Turn bag once or twice to make sure all eggs are developing color from the beet juice mixture.

Use with salatka z piklowanymi jajkami *(recipe precedes), or put drained eggs in a bowl and eat as a snack. Pickled eggs keep well for 1 week if covered and refrigerated.*

⚜ *Piroshki* (Filled Pastries)

There are many fillings for *piroshki*, such as cottage cheese, finely chopped hard-cooked eggs, mashed potatoes, and cooked fish. Any leftover vegetables or meat can be finely chopped and used as filling.

Yield: about 3 dozen

beef filling (recipe follows)	2 eggs, beaten
3½ cups all-purpose flour	3 tablespoons sour cream
½ teaspoon salt	**egg wash**
¾ butter or margarine	

Equipment: Food processor, rubber spatula, lightly floured work surface, plastic food wrap, lightly floured rolling pin, 2- to 2½-inch cookie cutter or water glass, **pastry brush,** fork, lightly greased baking sheet, oven mitts, wire cake rack

1. Prepare beef filling.

   Note: While processing, turn machine off once or twice, and scrape down sides of container with rubber spatula.

2. Put flour, salt, and butter or margarine in food processor, and pulse until mixture resembles fine crumbs, about ½ minute. Add beaten eggs and sour cream, and pulse to mix about 1 minute, until mixture pulls away from sides of container and forms a ball. Transfer to lightly floured work surface, and **knead** 1 to 2 minutes until smooth and satiny. Divide dough into 2 pieces, and shape each into ½-inch-thick disk. Cover each disk of dough separately in plastic wrap, and refrigerate 30 minutes.

3. Work with one piece of dough at a time, and keep the other refrigerated. On lightly floured work surface, roll dough with lightly floured rolling pin to about ¼ inch thick. Use 2- to 2½-inch cookie cutter or rim of water glass to cut out circles in the dough. Sprinkle lightly with flour, stack, and cover with plastic wrap. (It's easier to roll dough very thin when pieces are small.) Using lightly floured rolling pin, roll each circle into a thinner 3-inch circle. Lightly sprinkle the circles with flour, stack, and cover with plastic wrap.

   Preheat oven to 400°F.

4. Fill pastry circles: Place 1 tablespoonful of filling in center of each circle, and brush edges with egg wash. Fold dough over into a half circle, encasing filling, and press edges together

with a fork. Poke the top of each 2 or 3 times with fork to make vent holes in pastries. Place on lightly greased baking sheet, and brush tops with egg wash.

5. Bake in oven for 15 to 20 minutes, until golden brown. Remove from oven and transfer pastries to wire cake rack to cool.

6. While first batch is baking, repeat process with remaining dough in refrigerator.

Serve at room temperature with soup, or set out on the zakaski *table as a light snack.*

♔ *Beef Filling for Piroshki*

Yield: about 3 cups

2 tablespoons butter or margarine

1 onion, **finely chopped**

1 clove garlic, finely chopped

1½ pounds ground lean beef

salt and pepper to taste

Equipment: Large skillet, mixing spoon

1. Melt butter or margarine in large skillet over medium-high heat. Add onion and garlic, stir, and **sauté** until onion is soft, 2 to 3 minutes. Crumble ground meat into skillet, stir, and cook until browned, 5 to 10 minutes. Add salt and pepper to taste.

Use with piroshki *(recipe precedes).*

Dumplings of all sizes and shapes, with savory and sweet fillings, are probably the most popular finger food in Eastern Europe. It would be hard to find a wedding feast that did not provide great quantities of dumplings for guests to munch on.

♔ *Pierogi* (Boiled Filled Pockets)

Yield: serves 6 to 8

cheese filling (recipe follows)

4 cups all-purpose flour

1 teaspoon salt

5 eggs, well beaten

1 teaspoon water, more if needed

egg wash

1 cup melted butter or margarine, for **garnish**

4 tablespoons dry **bread crumbs**, for garnish

Equipment: Food processor, rubber spatula, large mixing bowl, plastic food wrap, lightly floured rolling pin, lightly floured work surface, 2- to 2½-inch cookie cutter or water glass, tablespoon, dinner fork, wax paper, baking sheet, large saucepan, slotted spoon

1. Prepare cheese filling.

2. Place flour, salt, and eggs in food processor, and pulse until mixture is very coarse and grainy; it should not form a ball. The mixture should pack easily when a small amount is pressed together in the palm of your hand. If mixture is too dry and doesn't hold together, add water, 1 teaspoon at a time, to reach correct consistency. If it gets too wet, add a little more flour. Transfer dough to large mixing bowl, and form into a ball. Cover with plastic wrap, and let rest for 10 minutes.

   Note: While processing, turn machine off once or twice, and scrape down sides of container with rubber spatula.

3. Divide dough into 3 equal pieces. Work with one piece at a time, keeping the others covered with plastic wrap. Using lightly floured rolling pin, roll dough as thin as possible on lightly floured work surface. Using 2- to 2½-inch cookie cutter or rim of water glass, cut out circles. Sprinkle lightly with flour, stack, and cover with plastic wrap. (It's easier to roll dough very thin when pieces are small.) Using lightly floured rolling pin, roll each 2- or 2½-inch circle into a 3-inch circle by rolling it thinner. Sprinkle lightly with flour, stack, and cover with plastic wrap. Repeat cutting pastry circles with remaining dough.

4. Fill pastries: Place 1 tablespoon filling in center of each circle. Using finger, brush edges with egg wash, and fold dough over into a half circle to encase filling. Press edges of circle together, and seal using fork. Place side by side on wax paper–covered baking sheet.

5. Fill large saucepan ⅔ full with water, add 2 teaspoons salt, and bring to boil over high heat. Add dumplings, a few at a time, so that they don't stick together. Cook 7 to 10 minutes, until tender. To test doneness, taste a dumpling, adjust cooking time accordingly. When done, remove with slotted spoon, and place in serving bowl. **Drizzle** each batch with melted butter or margarine to prevent sticking together, and keep warm. Before serving, sprinkle with bread crumbs.

Serve dumplings as a side dish or as a zakaski *(appetizer).*

¿ Cheese Filling for Pierogi

Yield: about 2½ cups

2 cups ricotta or cream cheese, at room temperature

4 tablespoons seedless raisins

1 egg

4 teaspoons sugar

Equipment: Medium mixing bowl, mixing spoon

Put ricotta or cream cheese, raisins, egg, and sugar into medium mixing bowl, and stir to mix well.

Use as filling for pierogi *(recipe precedes).*

Kielbasa (Polish sausage), is the most traditional food at Polish weddings. Everyone expects it and loves it, especially when it is cooked with purple cabbage. This delicious sausage dish can be served as an appetizer or side dish.

✤ *Kielbasa z Kapustoy* (Sausage with Cabbage)

Yield: serves 4 to 6

2 tablespoons butter or margarine

1- to 1½-pound head purple cabbage, shredded

2 cups canned beef broth

salt and pepper to taste

2 tablespoons dark brown sugar

1 tablespoon **cornstarch**

½ cup lemon juice

1 pound *kielbasa* or other smoked sausage, thinly sliced

Equipment: Large saucepan with cover, mixing spoon, small bowl, serving bowl

1. Melt butter or margarine in large saucepan over medium-high heat. Add cabbage, stir, reduce heat to **simmer**, and cook for 5 minutes. Add beef broth, stir, cover, and simmer 45 minutes.

2. In small bowl, stir dark brown sugar, cornstarch, and lemon juice with ½ cup cooking liquid from saucepan. Add brown sugar mixture to cabbage mixture, and stir until thickened, 3 to 5 minutes. Add sausage, stir, cover, and simmer 30 minutes.

To serve, transfer to serving bowl, and serve with thick slices of bread.

Today in Poland, many couples are having smaller weddings with family and a few close friends.

✤ *Piernik* (Gingerbread Cake)

In the days when spices were very rare and thus prohibitively costly, using so many of them in cooking was a display of great wealth, as well as a sign of the importance of the occasion. *Piernik* uses quite a number of spices and was made exclusively for special occasions and celebrations, such as Christmas. It was even believed that such a liberal amount of spices conferred magical attributes to *piernik*, such as stimulating children to learn to read. The *piernik* dough needs to mature for 4 to 6 weeks to develop its full flavor before being baked. (Because of the amount of honey and sugar contained in the dough, it does not ferment or spoil during this time.) Once baked, it is filled with plum or other jam and again allowed to mature and soften for 3 to 4 days, before receiving a decorative coating of chocolate glaze and further decorations. With the amount of time and effort lavished in the making of it, this is truly a cake for the most special of occasions.

Yield: 10 to 12 servings

Gingerbread dough:

¾ cup honey

1 cup butter

⅔ cup sugar

3½ cups flour (plus more for rolling out)

½ teaspoon salt

2 teaspoons ground cinnamon

1 teaspoon ground cloves

1 teaspoon ground ginger

⅔ teaspoon ground cardamom

⅔ teaspoon ground **allspice**

⅔ teaspoon ground nutmeg

½ teaspoon ground star anise

⅓ teaspoon ground black pepper

1½ teaspoons baking soda

¼ cup milk

2 eggs

Filling and decoration:

1 cup good-quality (that is, with a high fruit content) plum or apricot jam

¼ cup butter

8 ounces dark chocolate (or, depending on personal preference, milk chocolate), chopped

marzipan figures and other cake decoration, according to personal taste

Equipment: Small **heavy-bottomed** saucepan, glass or stoneware mixing bowl, small bowl, mixing spoon, electric hand mixer, clean kitchen towels, kitchen twine, 9-inchsquare baking pans (preferably 3, but if only 1 is available, then bake the cakes sequentially), parchment paper, metal spatula

1. In saucepan, melt honey, butter, and sugar over low heat until sugar is completely dissolved. Set aside to cool.

2. Once honey mixture has cooled, combine flour, salt, and spices in a large glass or stoneware mixing bowl.

3. In a small bowl, dissolve baking soda in milk. Beat in the eggs. Make a well (hole) in the center of the flour mixture, and pour in honey mixture, followed by the milk mixture. Mix well, until thoroughly combined. The resulting dough should be firm but not sticky. Add more flour or milk if needed to adjust the consistency. Cover bowl with a clean towel, and tie it securely around with kitchen twine. Let dough mature in the refrigerator. The honey and sugar content will prevent the dough from spoiling. To prevent other smells in the refrigerator from being absorbed by the dough, put the towel-wrapped bowl inside a loose paper bag.

4. A week before the cake is needed, remove dough from the refrigerator, and prepare it for baking. Line baking pan(s) with parchment paper extending an inch or more beyond pan. (It is easier to lift the cake from the pan using the parchment paper, especially if only 1 baking pan is available.) Divide dough into 3, and roll out on a floured surface to fit baking pan, with a thickness of about ½ inch.

5. Bake in a preheated 325°F for 15 to 20 minutes until golden brown, and tests done (if a wooden skewer or toothpick inserted in the middle comes out dry). Remove from cake pan (using the parchment paper edges to lift it out), then leave to cool, still on the parchment paper, on a cake rack.

6. Once cakes are cool, warm plum or apricot jam over low heat in a saucepan.

7. Place 1 cake on a tray, and spread evenly with half the jam, leaving an inch margin bare all around the edges. This is to prevent the jam leaking out from the layers when pressed down.

Top with another cake, and spread evenly with remaining jam. Cover the jam with the last cake. Cover the filled cake with parchment paper on all sides, and place a cutting board over the cake to weigh it down. Over the cutting board, rest a few heavy books. Leave the cake to rest somewhere cool but not in the refrigerator, for 3 to 4 days. This is to allow the cake to become soft and develop more flavor.

8. Once cake has softened, it can be decorated. In a saucepan, melt butter over low heat. Off the heat, add chopped chocolate. After a couple of minutes, stir the chocolate but wait until it has thickened slightly to start glazing. Pour chocolate glaze in the center of the top layer. Smooth the chocolate glaze over edges and the sides, using a metal spatula. Decorate with marzipan figures or other garnishes, and leave to set.

Store in a cool place (not the refrigerator), wrapped loosely in parchment paper or a clean kitchen towel.

Romania

Bordered on the east by Moldova and the Black Sea, on the north by Ukraine, on the west by Hungary and Serbia, and on the south by Bulgaria, Romania was under Communist rule from the end of World War II until late 1989. The majority of Romanians belong to the Romanian Orthodox Church. (See Eastern or Orthodox Church Life-Cycle Rituals, page lxxv.) Roman Catholics comprise the largest minority group. (See Protestant and Catholic Life-Cycle Rituals, page lxxiii.) Jews in Romania today number just over 3,000, after hundreds of thousands were killed during the Holocaust. After World War II, most of the Romanian Jews who had survived (about 300,000) began to emigrate to Israel. (The ninth largest Jewish Hasidic community and dynasty was founded by a rabbi from Klausenberg, Romania.) Around 90 percent of the population are ethnic Romanians; about 8 percent are Hungarian, and the rest are Roma (gypsy), German, and ethnic groups from neighboring countries.

For the majority of Romanians, life-cycle celebrations follow the traditions of the Romanian Orthodox Church—name days are celebrated in addition to birthdays. Often a person will celebrate a name day several times a year: for example, if several saints have the name Stefan (Stephen), then all those days are name days for a boy named Stefan, or he can choose which of the St. Stefan's days he would prefer to celebrate. Celebrations for a name day (*Ziua Onomastica* or *Ziua Numelui*) are usually hosted in a simple manner by the celebrant at home with a light meal or snacks and drinks. Guests may bring homemade cakes or savory food or drinks as presents. When a child is baptized, the parents choose godparents who will take on an important function during the ceremony, as well as a significant role throughout the child's life. The godparents carry the child to church, as well as dry and dress her or him after the ceremony. A year after baptism, a party is held to celebrate the child's first haircut, *a lua motul*, usually on the child's name day. On this occasion, the godparents have the privilege of cutting the first lock. (In the past, a cake was broken over the child's head after the haircut.) Then, a tray of assorted items is set before the child—a pen, coin, flower, book, and so on, and whichever item the child picks up is believed to augur the type of life or profession she or he will lead. If a flower, then the child will be well liked, as flowers are. If a pen, the child will become a writer; if a coin, then she or he will be rich. This is an event shared with relatives and friends with food, music, and dancing until late at night.

Romanian Orthodox funerals are usually held two or three days after death but never on a Sunday or on Holy Saturday. One Romanian funeral custom is for mourners to carry horseshoe-shaped funeral wreaths to the church and thereafter to lay them atop the covered grave. Towels are a significant ritual item and are worn by pallbearers around their arms. (In the past, these ritual towels were handwoven and beautifully decorated with embroidery and were given as presents to all mourners.) The burial may be followed by a light repast at a restaurant or the bereaved family's home or, in a few instances, by the distribution of individual wrapped packages of food and drink to all mourners. Forty days after the funeral, mourners gather around the grave to share a memorial meal.

Under the Communist regime, religious observances were strongly discouraged, and most Romanian weddings were civil services conducted at the local mayor's office. Since the end of Communism, couples have been returning to the tradition of elaborate church weddings.

Romanian weddings, which usually occur on Sunday, are the focus of many traditions and rituals involving food and drink. The cooks know exactly when to bring out the food, and special "cupbearers" are charged with maintaining a steady flow of drinks to the guests. *Țuică*, a plum brandy, is the main drink at weddings. The day before the wedding, a large loaf of bread is baked especially for the wedding ceremony and blessed by the priest. To complete the ceremony, the bride and groom, sharing the same plate and spoon, take bites out of the wedding loaf, while friends sprinkle them with water and grains of corn. Sprinkling the couple with these basics of life is a symbolic ritual that blesses them and wishes them a joyful life together.

The Székely people, a predominantly Hungarian group living in the Transylvania region of Romania, have wedding customs that differ from those practiced in other parts of either Romania or Hungary. Székely wedding couples traditionally have the *menyasszonykalácsfa*, a bridal cake tree also called a "life tree" or "*életfa*." Everything placed on the *prémes* (furry twigs) of the tree symbolically expresses a good wish for the couple. The unusual name—furry twigs—probably comes from the elaborate items decorating the tree, which are copies of the embroidered decoration on the bride's wedding dress.

Preparing the *menyasszonykalácsfa* begins with selecting branches of the right size and shape, a task always performed by the men. The important thing is to select a sturdy central branch with many branches going upward. The men clean the branches and remove the bark. The women then prepare the dough, the *csöröge* (recipe follows) to cover the branches, or the branches are dipped into thick pancake batter (*palacsinta appareil*). With either coating, the branches are put into the oven to bake. (It might be best to work with smaller branches that can fit in the oven. After the branches are baked, **florist wire** can be used to wire them together.)

A large cake serves as the base of the tree. (Setting the branch in a block of Styrofoam covered with foil would make a more secure base. Conceal the foil with sheet cake, then frost.) Adults and children have a hand in making decorations, which can be crafted from colored ribbons; small fresh fruits, such as cherries, plums, apricots, or grapes; or cookie dough cut into the shapes of birds, frogs, flowers, leaves, and butterflies and then baked and hung from the tree. A pouch is often hung on the tree and filled with money intended for the bride.

The finished *menyasszonykalácsfa* is brought to the bride's house on the morning of the marriage, together with all the wedding gifts. Along with the large decorated tree, a lucky bride may receive as many as 15 or 20 extra decorated *prémes* (furry branches). The *prémes* are carried as symbols of good fortune in a procession to the new home of the newlyweds. At the end of the wedding dinner, guests break off twigs and eat the crusty coating. The bride usually sets aside the prettiest *prémes,* which she keeps for many years. The following pastry dough recipe can be used to coat the *prémes* or can be made into cookies to be placed around the *menyasszonykalácsfa* or hung from the branches of the tree.

♫ Csöröge (Cookie Pastry Dough for Covering Branches)

The name for this pastry dough, *csöröge,* echoes the name of contemporary Turkish pastries called *cörek*. Besides their use for covering tree branches for the decorative *menyasszonykalácsfa* tree, this dough can be formed with cookie cutters into cookies.

Yield: about 16 cookies or enough to cover a branch about the size of 1 or 2 coat hangers

Prepare tree branches for covering (see preceding directions)

1 cup all-purpose flour	1 tablespoon sour cream
4 egg yolks	¼ teaspoon salt
½ teaspoon sugar	For **garnish**: confectioners' sugar
1 teaspoon rum extract	

Equipment: Food processor, rubber spatula, lightly floured work surface, lightly floured rolling pin, knife or cookie cutter of desired shapes, baking sheet, oven mitts, serving platter (if making cookies)

1. Put flour, egg yolks, sugar, rum extract, sour cream, and salt into a food processor. Process just until mixture comes together into a dough and pulls away from sides of container. With a rubber spatula, scrape dough away from food processor container, and shape into a smooth ball. Transfer to a lightly floured work surface, and **knead** into a firm dough, 3 to 5 minutes. Let dough rest for 15 minutes.

   Note: While processing, turn machine off once or twice, and scrape down sides of container with rubber spatula.

   Preheat oven to 350°F.

2. Using a lightly floured rolling pin, roll dough about ⅛ inch thick.

3. Make *prémes*: Place prepared branches on work surface. Cut dough into 1½-inch strips and wrap around branches, completely covering them (like wrapping with bandages), and place on baking sheet.

4. Make cookies: Using cookie cutters, cut dough into desired shapes, and place on baking sheet. If they are to be hung from the *menyasszonykalácsfa*, punch a hole in each cookie.

5. Bake in preheated oven for 25 to 35 minutes, or until golden. Carefully remove from oven and allow to cool to room temperature.

6. If you made cookies, sprinkle with confectioners' sugar.

The prémes *would be fun to make for birthday or anniversary celebrations. The cookies can be wired onto the branches or placed on a serving platter.*

The national dish of Romania is *ghiveci*, a medley of vegetables cooked in a special casserole dish called *guvens*. *Ghiveci* is traditionally made with whatever vegetables are available. Meat is often cooked with the vegetables, especially for baptism and wedding feasts.

♪ *Ghiveci* (Medley of Vegetables Casserole)

Yield: serves 6 to 8

water, as needed

2 potatoes, peeled, **cubed**

2 carrots, trimmed, sliced

2 celery ribs, trimmed, sliced

2 cups **cauliflowerets**, fresh or frozen (thawed)

½ pound green beans, trimmed, cut into 1-inch pieces, or frozen (thawed) cut beans

2 tablespoons vegetable oil

2 onions, **finely chopped**

2 cloves garlic

4 tomatoes, chopped

salt and pepper to taste

1 teaspoon dried thyme leaves

1 zucchini, trimmed, sliced

1 green bell pepper, trimmed, seeded, chopped

Equipment: Large saucepan with cover, **colander**, large skillet with cover, mixing spoon, greased medium casserole with cover or baking pan with cover, oven mitts

Preheat oven to 350°F.

1. Fill large saucepan with 1 to 2 inches water, add potatoes, carrots, celery, cauliflower, and green beans. Bring to boil over high heat, then reduce heat to **simmer**, cover, and cook for 10 minutes. Remove from heat, and drain in a colander. Discard liquid, or cool, cover, and refrigerate the liquid for another use.

2. Heat oil in a large skillet over medium-high heat, and add onions and garlic. Stir and **sauté** until soft, about 3 to 5 minutes. Add tomatoes, salt and pepper to taste, and thyme. Stir, then reduce heat to simmer, cover, and cook 5 minutes for flavors to develop. Remove from heat and keep covered.

3. Spread potato mixture over the bottom of a greased medium casserole or baking pan. Add salt and pepper to taste, and spread half the tomato mixture on top of the potato mixture. Layer zucchini slices and chopped green pepper over the tomato mixture. Top zucchini and green pepper layer with the remaining tomato mixture.

4. Bake in preheated oven, covered, for 50 to 60 minutes, or until vegetables are tender.

Serve the casserole along with bors de pui *(recipe follows) and* tocana cartofi *(recipe follows). Be sure there is plenty of rye and pumpernickel bread on the table.*

Potatoes are a much loved Romanian vegetable. *Tocana cartofi* is a favorite way of preparing them.

⚮ *Tocana Cartofi* (Creamed Potatoes)

Yield: serves 6

2 tablespoons vegetable oil

2 tablespoons flour

1 tablespoon paprika

2 cups canned beef broth

6 potatoes (2½ to 3 pounds), peeled, **cubed**

½ cup heavy cream

salt and pepper to taste

Equipment: Large **heavy-bottomed** skillet with cover, mixing spoon, serving bowl

1. Heat oil in large heavy-bottomed skillet over medium heat, stir in flour until smooth. Slide skillet off heat, and slowly stir in beef broth until smooth. Stir in paprika until well mixed. Return to heat, and stir constantly until thickened, 3 to 5 minutes.

2. Add potatoes, toss to coat, and cover. Cook for 20 to 25 minutes, until tender. Add cream, gently toss, cover, and cook for 5 minutes.

To serve, put into serving bowl to eat with bors de pui *(recipe follows).*

The following dish is typical of Romanian cooking, simple but full of flavor. Sauerkraut juice is often added instead of lemon juice to sharpen the flavor of food.

♪ *Bors de Pui* (Poached Chicken)

Yield: serves 6

3 to 4 pounds chicken, cut into serving pieces

4 cups water

4 onions, chopped

1 celery rib, sliced

2 leeks, white part only, well washed, sliced

1 carrot, trimmed, sliced

salt and pepper to taste

2 cups sauerkraut juice or juice from 2 lemons mixed with 2 cups water

3 egg yolks

1 cup sour cream

For **garnish**: 1 tablespoon fresh or dried dill, or tarragon leaves

Equipment: Large **heavy-bottomed** saucepan with cover or **Dutch oven**, mixing spoon

1. Put chicken into a large heavy-bottomed saucepan or Dutch oven. Add water, onions, celery, leeks, carrot, and salt and pepper to taste. Bring to boil over high heat, then reduce heat to **simmer**, and cover. Cook for 45 minutes, or until the chicken is tender. Add sauerkraut juice or lemon juice mixture, stir, then increase heat to medium-high, and bring to a boil. Remove from the heat.

2. Beat egg yolks with sour cream. **Temper** the egg and sour cream mixture by stirring in ½ cup chicken broth. Return to the pan with the chicken mixture, and stir to mix through.

To serve, transfer to a serving bowl, and sprinkle with dill or tarragon. Serve with side dishes of tocana cartofi *and* ghiveci.

Dessert is often *fructa crude* (fresh fruit). A bowl of apples, plums, peaches, and pears is put on the table with small plates and special fruit knives for peeling the fruit. Peeling and eating fresh fruit is an art in Romanian culture. Using the fruit knife, one can carefully peel the fruit from the bottom, working up and round, keeping the peel in one long snake-like coil. To eat the fruit, cut into bite-size pieces, never put the whole fruit in your mouth; that's considered crude and bad manners.

♪ *Savarina* (Savarin Cakes)

For birthdays and other special occasions, a popular celebratory treat is *savarina*—a syrup-drenched cake filled with whipped cream. They are usually bought from bakeries to be taken home for the birthday celebrant to share with family.

Yield: 12 cakes

Dough:

½ cup warm milk

1 tablespoon sugar

1 packet dry or fresh **yeast**

2 cups flour

¼ teaspoon salt

3 eggs, beaten

Syrup:

2 cups water

1 cup sugar

Filling:

2 cups heavy whipping cream

2 tablespoons sugar

For **garnish**:

5 to 6 tablespoons good-quality (60 percent fruit content) Morello cherry jam or blueberry jam

⅓ cup butter, melted

2 tablespoons butter, melted, for greasing

¼ cup rum or 3 tablespoons rum essence

zest from 1 lemon or orange, thinly sliced

1 teaspoon vanilla extract

2 teaspoons grated lemon or orange zest

12 candied or fresh cherries

Equipment: Mixing bowls and spoons, wire **whisk**, electric mixer (optional), clean kitchen towel, small saucepan, 12-cup cupcake pan, cupcake liners, knife, cake rack, small tray, **pastry bag** and star tip, oven mitts

1. Prepare dough: In a small bowl, put milk and sugar, and stir in yeast. Let yeast mixture rest in a warm, draft-free place for about 10 minutes, until frothy.

2. In a large bowl or a stand mixer bowl, combine flour and salt, mixing well. Stir in yeast mixture, followed by eggs and butter, and mix well until a homogeneous dough is formed. With floured hands, shape dough into a smooth ball. Butter the bowl, and return the dough ball, turning it so that all surfaces are covered with a thin layer of butter. Cover bowl with a damp clean kitchen towel, and let rest in a warm place until doubled in volume, about 45 minutes.

3. Prepare syrup: In a saucepan, let water and sugar come to a boil until sugar has completely dissolved. Turn off heat, add zest slices, and let the syrup to cool to room temperature. Just before use, take out zest slices, and stir in rum.

4. Prepare a 12-cup cupcake baking pan. Butter 12 cupcake liners, and use to line the baking pan.

   On a floured work surface, place risen dough, deflate, and divide it into 12 pieces. Shape dough pieces into balls, and place them in the baking pan. Let rise in a warm place, covered with a damp kitchen towel until almost doubled in volume, from 30 minutes to 1 hour.

   Ten minutes before baking, preheat oven to 350°F.

5. Bake the *savarinas* for 20 to 25 minutes, or until golden brown. Remove cakes from the oven, and let them rest until completely cool.

6. Turn the cakes upside down, and slice them crosswise about a quarter of the way from the top (the flat side) to make "lids." Immerse cakes into the syrup for 1 to 2 minutes, until they

have absorbed the syrup. Place syrup-drenched cakes on a cake rack to drain, with a tray beneath to catch the drips.

7. Prepare cream filling: In a mixer bowl, start whipping cream at low speed. When it has begun to thicken, add sugar, zest, and vanilla, and continue whipping until stiff.

8. Transfer to a pastry bag fitted with a star tip. Pipe cream to fill the bottom half of each cake. Top cakes with their lids, and put a heaping spoonful of jam in the center of the lids. Top with cherries.

Refrigerate cakes for an hour or more before serving.

Russia

Despite the loss of the newly independent Soviet republics, Russia (or its long-form name, the Russian Federation) is still the largest country in the world, stretching from the Baltic Sea in the west to the Pacific Ocean in the east. Although ethnic Russians form a large majority of the population, people of around 200 other nationalities and ethnic groups can be found throughout Russia. Many of these groups have their own life-cycle celebrations and rituals, but for the purposes of this book, the focus will be on celebrations of the Russian Orthodox Church.

In 1988, the Russian Orthodox Church, the largest Eastern Orthodox Church in the world, celebrated 1,000 years of Christianity in Russia. Once the state religion of Russia, the Russian Orthodox Church, along with all religions, suffered under the antireligious policies of Communism.

Starting with the reforms of Mikhail Gorbachev (*glasnost*) in 1985 and continuing with the fall of the Communist empire in 1991, the restrictions against religious freedom have been slowly fading away. Under the current Russian government, Christian holidays are once again official state holidays. In addition, the christening of children is on the rise, religious funerals are more common, and church weddings are becoming fashionable. (See Eastern or Orthodox Church Life-Cycle Rituals, page lxxv.)

Despite the prohibition on religious practices during the Communist period, baptisms nevertheless took place in secret. From the late 1980s, baptism started being practiced openly again. The first step in baptism is choosing a saint's name or a Church name. Special name day calendars list the names of Russian Orthodox Christian saints' names, although not everyone who is baptized these days has a saint's name. There is no hard-and-fast rule: Usually the name chosen is one that appears as close as possible to the child's birthdate. That saint then becomes the child's guardian saint. Godparents are chosen, and they are responsible for carrying the child during the baptism. The baby wears two sets of clothes: one worn before the ceremony, all white, and another after being anointed with oil, dipped into the water, and dried with a white towel. The baby is then changed into a baptismal gown with a cross, and most often it is one that has been worn by preceding siblings or passed down in the family. After the baptism, there is a celebratory feast for all the family and friends. The celebration of name days (*imeniny*), which in the pre-Communist period was common and of greater significance than birthdays, fell into disuse during the Communist era and is only now beginning to arouse interest. Celebrants receive greeting cards or flowers. First communion and confirmation follow when the child is between 12 and 14.

Birthdays are celebrated either on the day itself or on the following weekend if it occurs on a working day. It is never celebrated before, as it is considered bad luck to do so. Birthday greetings as well are never made before the actual date. It is the birthday celebrant, if an adult, who prepares the food for a birthday party or pays for the meal if it is held at a restaurant. School-age celebrants get a small present, such as a pencil or notebook, from their teacher. A popular birthday cake is Napoleon.

♪ *Napoleon Cake*

This is easily the most commonly made birthday or celebration cake in Russia. Although it is called a "Napoleon cake," the pastry does not resemble the classic French Napoleon cake, which uses *mille feuille* (puff pastry). The filling as well is uniquely Russian—with condensed milk and butter.

Yield: 12 to 15 servings

Note: The cake is best made 2 or 3 days before it is needed to allow the filling to stabilize.

Pastry:

4 cups flour

½ teaspoon salt

1 cup butter, cut into small cubes

1 egg, beaten

2 tablespoons lemon juice

½ cup ice cold water

Butter cream filling:

1¼ cups butter at room temperature

14-ounce can sweetened condensed milk

1 teaspoon vanilla extract (optional)

Equipment: Small bowl, mixing bowl, food processor, rubber spatula, rolling pin, baking sheet, oven mitts, parchment paper, pencil, 9-inch diameter plate as template for drawing circles on parchment paper, wire rack for keeping layers from puffing during baking, metal spatula for spreading filling, cake plate or serving platter

1. In a bowl, combine flour, salt, and sugar. Rub in butter until mixture resembles cornmeal. Make a well (hole) in the center of the mixture.

2. Mix thoroughly in a small bowl the egg, lemon juice, and water, and pour into the well in flour mixture. Gradually mix flour mixture into the liquids until all come together to form a dough. Alternatively, these steps can be done in a food processor, as follows: Pulse the flour and salt, then add the butter until the mixture resembles cornmeal. Mix egg, lemon juice, and

water, and gradually add to the flour mixture in the processor. Pulse until everything just comes together.

The next steps are the same for the hand-mixed dough as for the food processor–mixed dough.

3. With floured hands, take dough out of the bowl, and knead briefly on a floured surface to form a ball. Divide ball into 7 pieces, place into a bowl, cover with plastic wrap, and refrigerate for an hour.

4. Prepare 8 baking parchment sheets. On 7 of them, draw (with a pencil) a 9-inch diameter circle in the center. This will serve as your guide or template for rolling out the dough disks (which when baked will be the cake layers). Lay the 8th parchment sheet on top of the dough when rolling it out. It will be used for all 7 dough disks. The dough will not touch the drawn circle, as it will be rolled out on the reverse side.

5. Place 1 dough ball centered on the drawn circle on the reverse side of a parchment sheet. Cover with a full parchment sheet, and with a rolling pin, roll out to about ¼ inch beyond the edge of the drawn circle. Trim the dough disk to the drawn circle, but keep the trimmings which will also be baked for decor. Continue rolling out the remaining 6 dough balls. Holding the edges of the parchment paper, transfer two (or three if you have a large baking sheet) of the rolled-out dough disks to a baking sheet. No need to grease the baking sheet as the parchment will prevent sticking.

Ten minutes before needed, preheat oven to 400°F.

6. Prick dough disk all over with a fork, and invert a buttered and floured wire rack directly on top to keep them from puffing up during baking. Add dough trimmings to bake along the sides of the baking sheet.

7. Bake in the *lowermost* rack of the oven for 15 to 20 minutes, or until pale golden. Remove the wire rack that you've placed over the cakes during the final 5 minutes of baking so that the pastry disk can bake through. Transfer baked disks to cool on a wire cake rack.

8. Continue baking the remaining dough disks and trimmings.

9. When all the disks have cooled to room temperature, prepare cream filling.

10. Prepare butter cream filling: In mixer bowl, beat butter, and gradually add condensed milk, until half has been incorporated.

11. Taste. If sweet enough for your taste, then the rest of the condensed milk can be kept for some other use. Note that the cake layers are not sweetened, so the filling has to be just a bit sweeter. If the filling is not sweet enough, keep adding a bit more of the condensed milk, little by little, to reach the desired level of sweetness.

12. Stir in vanilla extract during the final stage of beating.

Assembly:

13. In the center of your cake plate or serving platter, place a dab of filling, then place a cake layer over it. This will stop the cake from sliding around. Take some strips of parchment paper and tuck them under the first cake layer to catch any spilled filling. Remove the paper strips before serving.

14. Place about ¼ cup of filling in the center of the first layer, and spread it to within an inch of the edge. You want to keep this space bare for the filling to spread out once all the layers are packed. Continue stacking the layers and filling them. Spread the remaining filling to cover the top and sides of the cake.

15. Take the baked trimmings, put them into a clean paper or plastic bag, and crush them coarsely with a rolling pin. Reserve.

16. Refrigerate the filled cake, covered loosely, overnight or, better still, for 2 days to allow the cake layers to absorb all the cream and for the flavors to meld. If the filling starts to run, just spoon it all back to the top and sides of the cake. The filling will firm up with refrigeration. Once the filling has stopped running, add the decoration. Sprinkle the crushed trimmings all over the top and sides of the cake. Remove parchment paper strips just before serving. Slice with a warmed knife (dip knife in hot water and wipe dry) for neat cuts.

Serve with milk for children or with tea or coffee for adults.

♪ *Kulebyaka* (Multilayered Savory Pie)

Kulebyaka is a traditional Russian celebratory dish. From the outside, it resembles nothing more than an elaborately decorated loaf of bread, but once sliced, it reveals its glory—several layers of assorted fillings. The fillings, which may be as few as two or as many as seven, are varied: chopped meat with onions, salmon, mushrooms, cabbage, and maybe even rice. For a grand, truly festive and complicated *kulebyaka*, the different fillings are kept distinct from one another by a layer of crêpes. The pie crust that encloses the fillings is usually a rich yeast dough, like that for a brioche, though it may also be made from puff pastry. *Kulebyaka* is usually served before the main course in a sit-down festive dinner but can also appear as one of several dishes, if not the centerpiece, in a celebratory buffet. *Kulebyaka* has crossed borders and has become incorporated into French cuisine as *coulibiac*, brought over by Russian émigrés. (See also the Ukrainian version, Koulibiac, page 514.)

Yield: 10 to 12 servings

Pastry:	4 to 5 cups flour, plus more for rolling out
½ cup warm water	1 teaspoon salt
1 tablespoon sugar	¾ cup butter, melted
2½ teaspoons active dry **yeast**	4 eggs, beaten

Equipment: Small bowls, large mixing bowl, electric mixer with dough paddle attachment, rubber spatula

1. Prepare dough: In a small bowl, put warm water, and stir in sugar. Stir in yeast, and leave in a warm place for about 10 to 15 minutes, until frothy.

2. In a large mixer bowl, put 4 cups flour, and combine with salt. Make a well (hole) in the center of the flour mixture, and pour in yeast mixture. With the dough paddle attachment

on the mixer, start mixing the flour and yeast mixture at low speed. Add eggs, and mix until fully incorporated. Add butter, and mix until everything comes together into a dough. You may need to mix in more flour if dough is a bit runny at this point. Or, conversely, if the dough is too hard, mix in a bit of warm (not hot) water. The consistency should be soft, pliable, and no longer tacky. With floured hands, transfer dough to a floured surface.

3. Knead dough, for about 5 to 7 minutes, until it is smooth and **elastic**. Grease a bowl with oil, put dough in, turn it over so that the other surfaces get oiled as well, and cover with plastic film. Let rest in a warm place until doubled in volume, about 1 to 1½ hours.

4. Deflate dough, knead it again briefly, return to the oiled bowl, flip the dough, cover, and let it rest again until well risen, about 45 minutes to 1 hour.

5. Meanwhile prepare the crêpes that will enclose the filling inside the pie.

Crêpes:

Yield: approximately 12 pieces

½ cup flour	4 eggs, well beaten
1 tablespoon sugar	1 ½ cups milk
½ teaspoon salt	2 to 3 tablespoons oil for greasing the pan and plate

Equipment: Bowl, whisk, crêpe pan or shallow skillet, oil brush, ¼ cup measure, crêpe turner, parchment paper, oiled plate, oven mitts

6. In a bowl, combine flour, sugar, and salt. Make a well (hole) in the center, and pour in eggs.

Whisk until well combined, then gradually whisk in milk until batter is the consistency of thin cream. You may not need all the milk, so add it slowly.

7. Over low-medium heat, place a crêpe pan or shallow skillet. Brush a bit of oil over the surface. When skillet is hot, place about ¼ cup batter, and quickly swirl it around by tilting the pan so that it spreads in an even thin layer. Tip any extra batter back into the bowl. Cook for about a minute until little bubbles appear on its surface and the bottom is pale golden.

Flip the crêpe, and cook the other side briefly. Transfer the crêpe to an oiled plate.

8. Continue cooking the rest of the batter, and stack the crêpes, with parchment paper in between so that they do not stick to each other.

9. Prepare the fillings.

Salmon filling:

Yield: 1 layer of filling

2 pounds skinless salmon **fillets**	¼ cup fresh dill
salt and pepper to taste	¼ cup butter, melted
¼ cup white wine	

Equipment: Aluminum foil, **double boiler**, fork, oven mitts

10. Place salmon fillets on a sheet of foil, long enough and wide enough to wrap them in. Add salt and pepper to taste, and pour white wine over. Fold over foil to enclose the salmon.

    Place in the upper half of a double boiler. Cover. Fill bottom pan halfway with warm water, and bring water to a boil. Allow salmon to steam for 20 minutes, or until it flakes easily when tested with a fork.

11. When completely cool, lift the foil-wrapped salmon out with tongs, remove any small bones, and slice the fish into bite-size pieces. Sprinkle fish with dill, and gently stir in melted butter. Taste, and add salt and pepper if needed. Transfer to a bowl, and allow to cool.

12. Prepare the cabbage filling.

Cabbage filling:

   Yield: 1 layer of filling

½ head medium green cabbage, **cored**, finely shredded

1 tablespoon salt

2 tablespoons butter

2 hard-cooked eggs, chopped finely

salt and pepper to taste

Equipment: **Colander**, sauté pan, oven mitts, clean kitchen cloth/towel

13. Place cabbage in a colander, and sprinkle with salt, mixing it in well into the cabbage with your hands. This is to soften the cabbage as well as get rid of excess moisture. After about 15 to 20 minutes, rinse cabbage thoroughly with cold water, place in a clean kitchen cloth or towel, and wring well to absorb all moisture.

14. Heat a sauté pan over medium heat, melt the butter, and add cabbage. Stir-fry cabbage for about 4 to 5 minutes. Turn off heat, let cabbage cool, and mix in the eggs. Transfer to a bowl. Check seasoning, and, if needed, add salt and pepper to taste.

15. Prepare the mushroom filling.

Mushroom filling:

   Yield: 1 layer of filling

2 tablespoons butter

1 tablespoon oil

1 fat garlic clove, finely minced

1 onion, peeled and finely chopped

½ pound white champignon mushrooms, thinly sliced

1 cup cooked rice

salt and pepper to taste

¼ cup fresh parsley, chopped

Equipment: Sauté pan, oven mitts, bowl

16. In a sauté pan over medium heat, warm butter and oil. When hot, stir in garlic and onion, and fry until aromatic, 2 to 3 minutes. Add mushrooms, and stir-fry until mushrooms have

become a bit limp, about 5 minutes. Stir in rice to absorb the juices given off by the mushrooms, and cook for another 2 to 3 minutes.

17. Turn off heat. Add salt and pepper to taste. Stir in the parsley. Transfer to a bowl, and allow to cool.

18. Prepare the egg wash.

Egg wash:

Yield: enough to gild 1 kulebyaka

2 egg yolks, well beaten   4 tablespoons milk

Equipment: Bowl, whisk, **pastry brush**, aluminum foil made into small tubes as steam vents

18. In a small bowl, mix the yolks with the milk. Set aside until needed.

Assembly:

19. Deflate dough, and reserve about a fistful for decoration.

20. On a lightly floured surface, roll out dough to a large rectangle, ¼ inch in thickness.

    With the long side closest to you, lay three crêpes along the middle of the rectangle (they may overlap if need be); leave bare a border of about 1 inch along the short sides of the rectangle. Place salmon flakes in a neat, even layer along the center of the crêpes. Lay another three crêpes over the salmon, and place the cabbage filling in an even layer. Lay another three crêpes over the cabbage, and place the mushroom filling in an even layer. Cover the mushrooms with the remaining crêpes.

21. Fold over one long side of the rectangle toward the center to enclose all the fillings. Fold over the other side to overlap the first. Brush the edges with egg wash, and pinch the edges firmly to seal.

22. Fold over the short sides of the rectangle, brush the edges with egg wash, and firmly press down to seal. Remember that the top of the *kulebyaka* will become the bottom, so the sealed seams should be on top.

23. Transfer *kulebyaka* to a well buttered baking sheet, seam side down. Let it rest for about 30 to 40 minutes to enable dough to rise a little.

    Ten minutes before baking, preheat oven to 375°F.

24. Meanwhile, prepare the decorations. Roll out the reserved dough to ⅛-inch thickness. Cut out or mold with your fingers leaves, petals, stems, twigs, whatever you fancy. Traditional decoration design included branches molded from dough. Brush the egg wash all over the surface of the (still unbaked) *kulebyaka*. Fix decorations in place, and brush the surface of the decorations with egg wash.

25. Make three equidistant holes along the top of the *kulebyaka* (you may incorporate this in your design), and insert small foil tubes to ensure they stay open during baking. The holes will enable steam to escape, so that the *kulebyaka* does not burst during baking.

26. Bake in preheated oven for 40 to 45 minutes, or until nicely browned. Leave to rest for 15 to 20 minutes, to allow the contents to settle. Remove the foil tubes before serving. Slice individual servings with a sharp knife.

Serve hot or at room temperature.

Marriage practices vary considerably among the nationalities and between urban and rural areas. Country weddings usually follow old traditional Russian *usviats* (wedding rituals). They are a three-day marathon, Friday through Monday, with breaks for sleep and work.

In the cities, civil ceremonies usually take place in a municipal "wedding palace." A member of the local council quickly performs the rite and pronounces the couple husband and wife, while family and friends look on. Many couples find the civil ceremonies sterile and cold and hold a church service after the civil ceremony with candlelight and vestments, chanting and incense, and organ music.

In the Soviet era, it was customary for Moscow newlyweds to take a crêpe paper–draped taxi to the Lenin Mausoleum in route to their reception. On arrival, wedding couples were ushered to the front of the line, where according to tradition, the bride tossed her flowers on Lenin's casket for good luck. In other Soviet cities, couples went to the tomb of the war heroes for this ritual. Communism is dead, but the flower tossing lives on.

After the ceremony the wedding guests usually pile into vehicles, and, with horns blaring, they form a procession to the bride's parents' house. Relatives bundle up the belongings of the bride in a sheet and carry them back to the procession. This symbolizes the bride's move to her new home.

The groom's parents wait for the wedding party at the entrance of their house with symbolic offerings. Outside the entrance to the house, a wooden bowl of salt and a freshly baked loaf of beautifully decorated bread, Russian symbols for good luck, will have been set out on a table. The bread is sliced by the host and dipped in the salt. He offers it to the newlyweds and says, "*Khleb da sol'*," literally translated as "bread and salt" but meaning, "Good luck and have a wonderfully rich, full life."

Before entering the house, the newlyweds each raise a glass of vodka, drink half, and fling the rest over their shoulder. When the groom smashes his glass on the ground, it signals the beginning of the festivities. The party generally lasts late into the night with plenty to eat and drink.

An important phase of the celebration is the *nadel* (gift-giving) ritual, held on the second day. Well-wishers bring gifts to the newlyweds and cheer and applaud as the gifts are opened. A special wedding bread called *karavai* is traditionally served at the *nadel*.

The baking of the *karavai* is the responsibility of the bride's godmother. She supervises the work of the *karavainitsy* ("wedding loaf women"), her female helpers. The *karavai* is a round white loaf decorated with pine cones, flowers, leaves, and images of children, birds, and animals made out of dough. The decorations are symbols of good health, wealth, happiness, and many children.

༞ *Karavai* (Wedding Loaf)

Yield: 1 decorated loaf

2 or 3 packages frozen bread dough   **egg wash**

flour, for work surface

Equipment: Work surface, cookie cutters (any shapes), large baking sheet, pizza pan, or roasting pan

1. Follow the directions on the package to prepare the dough for baking. Shape the dough into a loaf or wreath.

2. Decorate uncooked dough with pieces of dough in various shapes. You can use cookie cutter shapes, or mold the dough into shapes as if working with clay. Remember to allow room for the dough to rise. Brush the decorated loaf with egg wash to make the bread shiny. The bread can be baked on a large baking sheet, pizza pan, or roasting pan.

The bride's friends may also bake sweet *klubtsy*, a pastry in the form of intertwined rings, while the groom's party brings *baranki*, ring-shaped rolls. The breads symbolize the joining together of two people.

Great quantities of food and drink are important to the success of the wedding. The beverages are milk, soda, seltzer, hot tea, and *kvass* (a cold beer-like beverage made from black bread and honey). Vodka is also very popular.

A wedding feast would be unthinkable without the *zakouska* (appetizer) table. Dozens of *zakouski* (little dishes) are prepared for nibbling. The variety of *zakouski* is endless, with many items readily available from the delicatessen section of a supermarket. A variety of flavors, colors, and textures are important.

༞ *Zakouska* Table (Appetizer Table)

pickled **herring** in wine sauce and in sour cream

sauerkraut sprinkled with caraway seeds

assorted cheeses

green and black olives

pickled hot peppers, pickled **beets**, pickled mushrooms (*selenyia gribi*), pickled green tomatoes

anchovy on sliced hard-cooked egg (*kilki croutyia yaitza*)

assorted cold cuts

mustard, horseradish, butter or margarine, sour cream

assorted breads and rolls

Equipment: Cloth tablecloth, serving platters and bowls, serving forks, spoons and knives, napkins, appetizer plates and flatware

1. Cover the dinner table with a freshly pressed tablecloth. Place a centerpiece on the table. (Fresh flowers and candles are always lovely.) Place salt and pepper shakers on the table. Fill

the appropriate platters and serving bowls with the food. Always include the proper serving utensil for each item. Bread and rolls look nice in a basket lined with a napkin. Place appetizer plates, napkins, and eating utensils on the table or on the sideboard.

2. Easy to prepare *zakouski* include such dishes as freshly boiled new potatoes tossed with dill and seasoned with salt and pepper, devilled eggs, sliced cucumber sprinkled with salt and mixed with sour cream, and *stolichnyi salat*.

Many salads are called Russian salad, but *stolichnyi salat* shows the Russian flare for an unusual mix of ingredients.

⚘ *Stolichnyi Salat* (Russian Salad)

Yield: serves 8 to 10

4 potatoes, washed

1 orange, peeled, **pith** removed, and cut into bite-size pieces

½ pound cooked chicken, cut into bite-size pieces

2 apples, **cored**, cut into bite-size pieces

2 carrots, peeled, **trimmed**, cut into circles about ¼ inch thick

1 cup frozen peas, thawed

2 green onions, trimmed and thinly sliced crosswise

3 hard-cooked **egg yolks**

3 tablespoons olive oil, divided

3 tablespoons white wine vinegar, divided

1 cup mayonnaise, divided

1 cup sour cream, divided

salt and pepper to taste

For **garnish**: sprigs of fresh parsley

Equipment: Medium saucepan, fork, tablespoon, work surface, paring knife, large mixing bowl, plastic food wrap, mixing spoon, small mixing bowl with cover, serving platter

1. Put potatoes in medium saucepan, and cover generously with water. Bring to boil over high heat. Reduce heat to **simmer**, and cook for 20 to 30 minutes, or until just tender when poked with a fork. Remove potatoes from water, and cool to warm. Using paring knife, peel, place on work surface, and cut into ½-inch chunks. Put potatoes in large mixing bowl, and add orange, chicken, apples, carrots, peas, and green onions. Toss to mix.

2. Prepare salad dressing: In a small mixing bowl, mash hard-cooked egg yolks using back of fork. Stir in 2 tablespoons olive oil to make a smooth paste. Stir in 2 tablespoons vinegar, ½ cup of mayonnaise, and ½ cup sour cream. Add salt and pepper to taste. Stir dressing, pour over potato mixture, and toss to mix well. Cover with plastic wrap, and refrigerate until ready to serve.

3. Prepare garnish dressing: In small mixing bowl, mix remaining 1 tablespoon olive oil, 1 tablespoon vinegar, ½ cup mayonnaise, and ½ cup sour cream. Add salt and pepper to taste. Cover, and refrigerate until ready to serve.

4. At serving time, transfer salad mixture to serving platter. Stir prepared dressing, and pour over salad. Garnish with sprigs of fresh parsley.

To serve, place on table with other zakuski *on the* zakouska *table.*

Russians who are often unable to afford fish roe caviar have come up with an affordable substitute, *baklazhannaya ikra* (eggplant caviar), often referred to as "poor man's" caviar.

₹ *Baklazhannaya Ikra* (Eggplant Caviar)

Yield: serves 6 to 10

1½ to 2 pounds large eggplant	4 cloves garlic, finely chopped
2 tablespoons olive oil	3 **tomatoes, peeled,** finely chopped
2 onions, **finely chopped**	1 tablespoon honey
1 green pepper, **trimmed,** finely chopped	juice of 1 lemon
	salt and pepper to taste

Equipment: Baking sheet, oven mitts, paring knife, small bowl, medium skillet, mixing spoon, food processor, rubber spatula, medium serving bowl with cover

Preheat oven to 375°F.

1. Put eggplant on baking sheet, and bake in oven until tender, 35 to 45 minutes. Remove from oven, and set pan aside to cool. After baking, the eggplant skin easily peels off using paring knife. Put the eggplant insides in a small bowl. Discard skin.

2. Heat 2 tablespoons oil in medium skillet over medium-high heat. Add onions, green pepper, and garlic, and stir. **Sauté** until soft, 3 to 5 minutes. Add eggplant and tomatoes, stir, and bring to boil. Reduce heat to **simmer,** cover, and cook 30 minutes, stirring occasionally. Stirring frequently, remove cover, and continue to simmer for 15 to 20 minutes, until most of the liquid is evaporated and mixture has thickened. Let cool enough to handle, and transfer to food processor container.

   Note: *While processing, turn machine off once or twice, and scrape down sides of container with rubber spatula.*

3. Add honey, lemon juice, and salt and pepper to taste. Process until smooth, about 1 minute. Transfer to medium serving bowl, cover, and refrigerate for about 4 hours for flavors to develop.

Serve eggplant caviar on the zakouska *table. It can be spread on crackers or bread or used as dip for raw vegetables, such as carrot, celery, cucumber, and zucchini.*

Russians love potatoes so much they call them *vtoroi khleb* (the second bread). A potato dish is almost always prepared for the wedding feast, and a favorite way to fix them is in the *zapekanka* (casserole) (recipe follows).

✿ *Kartofel'naya Zapekanka* (Casserole of Mashed Potatoes)

Yield: serves 4 to 6

2 pounds potatoes, peeled and quartered	salt to taste
water, as needed	2 eggs, lightly beaten
5 tablespoons butter or margarine, divided	2 tablespoons vegetable oil
1 cup milk	3 onions, thinly sliced
	½ cup sour cream

Equipment: Medium saucepan, **colander**, large mixing bowl, potato masher or electric mixer, mixing spoon, large skillet, greased 2-quart casserole, oven mitts

1. Put potatoes in medium saucepan, and cover generously with water. Bring to boil over high heat. Reduce heat to **simmer**, and cook until tender, 15 to 20 minutes. Drain potatoes in colander. Transfer to large mixing bowl. Add 3 tablespoons butter or margarine, milk, and salt to taste. Using potato masher or electric mixer, mash until smooth. Beat in eggs.

2. Heat oil and remaining 2 tablespoons butter or margarine in large skillet over medium-high heat. Add onions, stir, and **sauté** until soft, 3 to 5 minutes.

Preheat oven to 350°F.

3. Assemble: Place half the mashed potatoes in greased casserole, and smooth top. Spread onions over potatoes, and cover with remaining mashed potatoes. Spread sour cream over the top.

4. Bake in oven for 30 minutes, or until top is lightly browned.

To serve, place the casserole on the table, and have guests help themselves.

Ukraine

Ukraine is the second largest country in Europe after Russia and is blessed with mineral and agricultural wealth. Located north of the Black Sea, Ukraine shares borders with Moldova, Romania, Hungary, Slovakia, Poland, and Belarus. As with other former Soviet republics, a large Russian population remains in Ukraine, about 22 percent. Since 2014, the Crimean region of the Ukraine has been taken over by Russia, leading to an ongoing political crisis.

Although most Ukrainians belong to the Orthodox Church, the Church itself has split into several factions with the removal of Russian power. These differences notwithstanding, Ukrainians celebrate life-cycle rituals in much the same way as their Orthodox brethren. (See Eastern or Orthodox Church Life-Cycle Rituals, page lxxv.)

Since the fall of Communism and Ukrainian independence in 1991, interest in observing the old religious rituals and traditions is undergoing a revival—baptism, first communion, confirmation, wedding ceremonies, and funeral rites. More and more couples are exchanging vows in the various branches of the Orthodox Church, though first they must have the mandatory civil ceremony at the Palace of Rituals (a fancy name for the government marriage bureau).

It was a tradition for new mothers to go to church for a cleansing ritual 40 days after birth, with cleansing prayers said over her. Often it was also then that the child was baptized. For baptism, parents usually choose a godfather (*kum*) and godmother (*kuma*), who are responsible for guiding the child throughout his or her life. At the baptismal font, traditionally honey and milk were added for girl infants to grow up to be beautiful; the roots of the herb elecampane were added for boy infants to grow up with robust health, or an axe was placed nearby for the boy to become a skilled worker. Those who were present at the christening usually dropped a penny into the font for good luck. Ritual haircutting (the first haircut) occurred on or after the child's first birthday.

Name day is an Orthodox Christian tradition of choosing a saint to be a child's guardian. The saint was chosen as one whose name was listed on the Orthodox name day calendar on the day nearest to the child's birthdate. Name day used to be more faithfully celebrated in pre-Communist times, when people would go and light a candle in church on their guardian saint's feast day. During the Communist period when religious observance was totally prohibited, the custom of celebrating name day was generally abandoned. Nowadays, interest in the custom is being renewed. Friends and family usually send cards bearing well-wishes or small presents and gather together for a small celebration with cakes and other sweets and coffee or tea.

As in Russia, birthdays are celebrated on the day itself or after. It is considered bad luck to celebrate it or to greet a celebrant before the actual birthday. During a birthday party, family and friends take quite some time to express to the celebrant their heartfelt greetings, not only "Happy Birthday" but also for good health, happiness, joy, success in the workplace, a satisfying career, and other well-meant wishes covering all aspects of the celebrant's life. When giving flowers to a birthday celebrant, Ukrainians ensure that they are an odd number (3, 5, 7, etc.). Even-numbered flower bouquets are reserved for the dead.

Ukrainians observe Orthodox Christian traditional funeral customs. After the funeral, a meal is shared with all the mourners. A memorial meal is shared on the ninth and 40th days and then again at six and 12 months after the funeral. *Kolyvo*—cooked wheat or barley mixed with honey—is customarily carried before the coffin in the funeral procession. Afterwards, it is shared among the mourners as the first course of the funeral meal.

A traditional custom after the funeral meal was to put a glass of *horilka* (vodka) and a piece of bread on the windowsill for the deceased. Over the nine days following death, it was commonly believed that the dead returned home. The day after the funeral, a luncheon "to wake up the dead" was brought to the grave. This luncheon officially ended the funeral and marked the beginning of memorial observance.

The schedule of observance of memorial services is based on the belief that the soul of the deceased left the body on the third day and the spirit on the ninth day, and on the 49th day the body ceased its earthly existence.

Provody is a yearly remembrance rite that is still faithfully observed on the first Sunday after Easter. Families gather at ancestral graves to remember their departed loved ones. The observance of *provody* in Ukraine most likely predates Christianity, as a celebration of spring and the renewal of life and nature, but has been incorporated into Orthodox Christian belief to represent Christ's victory over death. Another day of remembrance for the dead is on *Didova Subota* (Grandfathers' Saturday), on the 49th day after Easter, or the day before Whitsun. On this day, families take food to the graves of loved ones, as well as bringing food to the poor and the aged. Bread, honey, and other sweet foods are brought to church to be blessed and afterwards given to the poor. Among the Hutsuls, a sheep- and cow-herding subethnic Ukrainian group in the Carpathian region, it is still the custom to bring the first dairy products of the year on *Didova Subota* to be blessed in church. Afterwards, they are given to the poor.

When visiting the grave of a family member, relatives leave a small shot glass of vodka (*horilka*) on the tombstone or the grave. At the Christmas Eve meal, the deceased are once again remembered. A sheaf of wheat, called "*did*" or "*didukh* (great ancestor), personifies the family's dead members and is set at the place of honor (under Orthodox Christian icons). Straw is scattered under the table and on the table itself, over which the tablecloth is laid. After the meal, three spoonfuls of every dish are placed on a plate with a spoon for the family's dead ancestors.

Bread plays a significant role not only as food but also as a sacred object and divine symbol in Ukrainian folk tradition. (It is perhaps fitting that the Ukraine has, in the past, been named the breadbasket of Russia when it was part of the Soviet Union; nowadays, it has become known as the breadbasket of Europe.) Not only for the farmers who cultivated wheat but also for the majority of Ukrainians, bread was considered a holy gift from God. As such, all important family events were and continue to be graced with special breads for the occasion. Bread is present to invoke good fortune and blessings during the birth of a child, the wedding ceremony, the move to a new home, and the start of a new undertaking, as well as at funerals.

The main ritual wedding bread is *korovai*. It is made of a special, rich dough. The *korovai* is round and lavishly decorated with little flags and figurines from nature—such as the sun, moon, birds, butterflies, leaves, flowers—all fashioned from bread dough. It was prepared by (traditionally, happily married) women at the new home of the affianced couple. Throughout the *korovai*'s preparation, traditional wedding songs were sung. Usually *korovai* is sweet tasting, almost like cake, and often so enormous and heavy with embellishment that it takes a couple of strong attendants to carry one into the wedding hall. The *korovai* is used by the priest to bless the bride and groom before the wedding ceremony, and it is displayed in a prominent place during the wedding. Upon arrival at her new home, the bride is greeted with the *korovai*. After the ceremony, the *korovai* is meant to be served to all the guests. A piece of the *korovai* is often kept by the bride and eaten on the birth of her first child.

Thawed, frozen dough can be used to make *korovai*. To give it a sweet, cake-like taste, **glaze** or sprinkle the bread with confectioners' sugar mixed in a little water after it is baked. Buy two or more loaves for the bread itself (follow directions on the package) and an extra loaf or two to make the decorations. Working with the dough to make the decorations is like working with clay, except you need to allow the dough to rise after finishing the different shapes (follow rising and baking directions on the package). Cookie cutters can also be used to make the decorations. Flatten dough on a lightly floured work surface, and cut out the desired shapes, allowing the dough to rise. To decorate the loaf, touch the backside of each decoration with a dab of water and then gently attach it to the loaf of bread before baking in the oven. Or the decorations can be baked separately on a cookie sheet and attached to the baked bread with toothpicks, wooden skewers, or **florist wire**.

Kalach (also written as *kolach*) is the bread for funerals and memorial days, as well as for Christmas. *Pyrohy* and the much smaller *pyrizhky* are pies stuffed with various fillings—meat, cheese, peas, cabbage, mushrooms, fruits, or poppy seeds. They are customarily made for family celebrations and other festive events. It was an old custom to give *pyrohy* to beggars at the entrance to a church so that they could offer prayers to the dead.

As more and more couples exchange vows in the various branches of the Orthodox Church, village weddings are simple civil ceremonies followed by a colorful procession to the church. The wedding celebration then often goes on for two or three days. The ideal menu for a village wedding feast includes assorted appetizers (recipe page 506), great loaves of different breads, mountains of both savory and sweet filled pastries and dumplings (recipes pages 486 and 516), roasted suckling pig (recipe page 425), *koulibiac* (recipe page 514), cakes, cookies (recipe page 516), and nuts. Most urbanites have shorter receptions, with fewer people, less food, and pork roast or *kotlety pojarski* replaces suckling pig.

♪ *Krendel* (Sweet Bread)

Krendel, a very popular sweet bread in many of the countries of the former Soviet Union, is made into a pretzel or figure eight shape as the centerpiece for birthdays and name day celebrations. Double or triple the recipe if it is being used for a large, decorative wedding loaf.

Yield: 1 loaf

3 tablespoons **lukewarm** water1 package dry **yeast**

½ cup sugar, divided

3 cups all-purpose **flour**, divided, plus more for surfaces

½ teaspoon salt

¼ cup cold butter or margarine, **coarsely chopped**

2 eggs, lightly beaten

½ cup light cream

egg wash

For **garnish**: confectioners' sugar

Equipment: Small bowl, mixing spoon, flour **sifter**, large mixing bowl, work surface, kitchen towel, greased baking sheet, **pastry brush**, oven mitts, wire cake rack, cloth napkin

1. Pour lukewarm water into small bowl, sprinkle in yeast and 1 teaspoon sugar. Leave for 10 minutes until frothy.

2. **Sift** 2 cups flour, salt, and remaining ½ cup sugar into large mixing bowl. Using your hands, work cold butter into flour mixture until it becomes crumbly. Add beaten eggs, and stir well. Add cream and yeast mixture, and stir to mix. If dough is sticky, add flour, ½ cup at a time, until smooth. Form dough into a ball. Transfer to well floured work surface, and, using lightly floured hands, **knead** for 5 minutes, or until smooth and **elastic**. Form into ball, place in lightly greased bowl, and turn to grease all sides. Cover with towel, and let rise to double in bulk, 1 to 1½ hours.

Preheat oven to 350°F.

3. Shape into loaf: **Punch down** dough, and on lightly floured work surface, shape into long rope, about 2 inches thick. Place dough on greased baking sheet, and shape into whatever shape you like. Cover with towel, and let rise in a warm place until double in bulk, 30 to 45 minutes. Using pastry brush, brush top of dough with egg wash.

4. Bake in oven for 30 to 35 minutes, or until golden. Using oven mitts, remove from oven, and transfer to wire cake rack. While warm, sprinkle with confectioners' sugar.

To serve sweet bread, cut into slices, or place on a cloth napkin and have guests break off a chunk. Spread with butter or jam.

The centerpiece for a wedding banquet is frequently the *koulibiac* (**poached** salmon baked in puff pastry). It can be prepared simply, shaped as a large rectangle or in a more decorative shape like a large, round-bodied fish, resembling an angelfish.

To make the pattern for fish-shaped pastry you need 9×15-inch paper, 9-inch round dinner plate, pencil, and scissors. Lay the dinner plate upside down in the center of the paper, and trace around it with a pencil. Draw the fish tail on one side of the circle and the head on the opposite side of the circle, making the overall fish length about 15 inches. Using scissors, cut out the fish pattern. The fish-shaped presentation is worth the little extra effort. Directions for both pastry shapes are given in the recipe. Follow step 3 if making the rectangular shape and step 4 if the fish shaped is being attempted.

℥ *Koulibiac* (also *Coulibiac*) (Salmon in Puff Pastry)

Yield: serves 10 to 12

2 pounds fresh skinless salmon **fillet**, about 1 inch thick

2 cups chicken broth

water, as needed

1 bay leaf

4 tablespoons butter or margarine

1 onion, **finely chopped**

2½ cups (about 1 pound) mushrooms, finely sliced

1 cup long grain rice (cooked according to directions on package)

juice of 1 lemon

3 tablespoons parsley, finely chopped

salt and pepper to taste

flour, for surfaces

1½ packages (total of 3 sheets) frozen **puff pastry**, thawed, unwrapped

4 hard-cooked eggs, shelled, chopped

egg wash

Equipment: Large skillet with cover, fork, wide metal spatula, 9-inch round dinner plate, large skillet, mixing spoon, large mixing bowl, lightly floured work surface, paring knife, lightly floured rolling pin, baking sheet, 9×15-inch paper, plate, pencil, and scissors, damp kitchen towel, **pastry brush**, oven mitts

1. Put salmon fillet in large skillet, and add chicken broth and enough water to cover. Add bay leaf, and bring to boil over high heat. Reduce heat to **simmer**, cover, and cook 20 minutes, or until the fish flakes easily when poked with fork. Remove from heat. Using wide metal spatula, remove fish from pan, and set on large plate to cool. Discard liquid, or cover and refrigerate for another use. When fish is cool enough to handle, using your fingers, flake into large chunks. Feel for small bones in fillets as you flake and discard.

2. Prepare filling: Melt butter or margarine in large skillet over medium-high heat. Add onions, stir, and cook until soft, 3 to 5 minutes. Add mushrooms, and reduce heat to medium. Stirring frequently, cook 10 to 15 minutes until mushrooms soften and are fully cooked. Transfer to large mixing bowl. Add the cooked rice, lemon juice, parsley, and salt and pepper to taste. Toss gently to mix.

3. Prepare rectangular pastry: On lightly floured work surface, unfold 3 pastry sheets, and cut 1 sheet in half with paring knife. Overlap matching edges of a full sheet and half sheet by 1 inch, and lightly dab between them with a moistened finger. Press moistened sheets

together so that they stick to each other. Using lightly floured rolling pin, roll out to 10×16 inches. Repeat with second whole pastry sheet and second half sheet. To transfer pastry to baking sheet, carefully fold over 3 or 4 times (to keep from tearing) and unfold on baking sheet. Repeat folding over second pastry, but do not remove from work surface. Cover with damp towel until ready to assemble.

4. Prepare fish-shaped pastry: Place the fish pattern on top of 10×16-inch pastry sheet and cut around it with paring knife. Sprinkle lightly with flour. Carefully fold over 3 or 4 times, and unfold in baking sheet. Repeat folding over second pastry, but do not remove from work surface. Cover with damp towel until ready to use.

5. Save pastry scraps to decorate top pastry. Use scraps to cut out an eye, thick fish lips, and fins. Using scissors, cut little ½-inch nips (>>>) facing in the same direction, over top pastry to resemble fish scales. When pastry bakes, the nips puff up.

Preheat oven to 400°F.

6. To assemble: Cover bottom pastry (on baking sheet) with half the rice mixture, and stay about 1 inch inside the edges. Cover rice with salmon chunks and chopped eggs. Top with remaining rice, piled high in the middle. Using pastry brush, lightly brush water around 1-inch edge of bottom pastry. Unfold second pastry over the filling, line up the edges, and press together. Using your fingers or the back of fork, press down on edges to seal pastry together. After pastry is assembled, decorate with cutout pieces. Lightly dab the backside of each cutout with water to make it stick. Brush pastry and decorative pieces with egg wash. Using knife, cut 3 or 4 vent slits in top pastry to let steam escape when cooked.

7. Bake in oven for 25 to 35 minutes, or until golden brown. Using oven mitts, remove from oven, and allow to rest 10 minutes before cutting.

To serve, place the whole, uncut koulibiac *as the centerpiece on the buffet or dinner table so that everyone can enjoy the beautiful presentation. Serve warm or at room temperature with a side dish of sour cream* (smetana) *to spoon over each serving.*

Life-cycle celebration feasts almost always include two very popular Ukrainian foods, mushrooms and sour cream, as in the following recipe.

✣ *Zulynez Gribnoy* (Baked Mushrooms in Sour Cream)

Yield: serves 6

4 tablespoons butter or margarine

1 onion, **finely chopped**

2½ cups (about 1 pound) sliced fresh mushrooms

1 tablespoon all-purpose **flour**

½ cup milk

1 cup sour cream

salt and pepper to taste

½ cup **bread crumbs**   ½ cup shredded mozzarella cheese

Equipment: Large skillet, mixing spoon, buttered shallow 8-inch baking pan, 2 small bowls, oven mitts

1. Melt butter in skillet over medium-high heat. Add onions, and **sauté** until soft, 3 to 5 minutes. Add mushrooms, and reduce heat to medium. Stir and cook until soft, 10 to 15 minutes. Remove from heat. Transfer to buttered shallow baking pan.

Preheat oven to 350°F.

2. In small bowl, stir flour into milk until smooth. Stir in sour cream and salt and pepper to taste. Spoon over mushrooms and **fold in**. In second small bowl, mix bread crumbs and shredded cheese. Sprinkle bread crumb mixture over top mushrooms.

3. Bake in oven for 20 to 30 minutes until top is golden brown.

Serve warm or at room temperature as an appetizer or as a side dish.

Sweets are always popular, and assorted cakes, pastries, and cookies are typical of Ukrainian life-cycle celebrations.

Paliushky (Walnut Finger Cookies)

Yield: about 40 pieces

½ cup butter or margarine   1 egg yolk

2½ tablespoons solid vegetable shortening   2 tablespoons sour cream

1 cup confectioners' sugar, divided, more if   **zest** of 1 lemon, **grated**
necessary
                                              ½ cup walnuts, chopped
¼ teaspoon salt
                                              2 cups all-purpose **flour**

Equipment: Medium mixing bowl, electric mixer, wooden mixing spoon, rubber spatula, plastic food wrap, lightly greased cookie sheet, oven mitts, metal spatula, wire cake rack, small bowl, serving platter

1. In medium mixing bowl, using an electric mixer or wooden mixing spoon, beat butter or margarine and vegetable shortening until light and fluffy. Beat in ½ cup confectioners' sugar, salt, egg yolk, sour cream, and lemon zest, beating well after each addition. Using wooden mixing spoon or rubber spatula, **fold in** walnuts and flour. Cover bowl with plastic wrap, and refrigerate for 1½ to 2 hours until firm.

Preheat oven to 350°F.

2. Shape cookies: Using your hands, pull off about 3 tablespoons dough at a time, and shape into a round rope about 2½ inches long and ½ inch thick. Continue making cookies, and space them about 1 inch apart on lightly greased cookie sheet.

3. Bake in oven for 10 to 12 minutes, or until brown around the edges. Using oven mitts, remove baking sheet from oven. Let stand about 3 minutes to firm up before using metal spatula to transfer to wire cake rack to cool enough to handle.

4. Roll warm cookies, one at a time, into small bowl with remaining ½ cup confectioners' sugar. Return to wire cake rack to cool completely. Add more confectioners' sugar if necessary.

To serve, stack paliushky *on serving platter. Store in airtight container for up to 1 week.*

CENTRAL AND SOUTH AMERICA

Gulf of Mexico

Mexico

Belize

Guatemala
El Salvador
Honduras
Nicaragua
Costa Rica
Panama

Galapagos
Islands

Ecuador

Caribbean
Sea

Colombia

Venezuela

Guyana
Suriname
French Guiana

Atlantic
Ocean

N

Peru

Brazil

Bolivia

Pacific
Ocean

Chile

Paraguay

Uruguay

Argentina

Atlantic
Ocean

Falkland
Islands
(U.K.)

5

Latin America

CENTRAL AMERICA

The Central American region of Latin America includes the countries of Belize, Costa Rica, El Salvador, Guatemala, Honduras, Mexico, Nicaragua, and Panama.

Belize

Belize is a country in Central America, located southeast of Mexico and east of Guatemala, facing the Caribbean Sea. Its area is slightly smaller than Massachusetts. It was a British colony, previously known as the British Honduras, until it gained full independence in 1981. It is noted for having the world's second largest coral reef and as the only country in Latin America to have English as its official language. Its climate is tropical, with hot and humid weather. There are low mountains in the southern part of the country, but the terrain consists mostly of flat plains. Over half of the land area is forested, and Belize is famous for its timber. Tourism is the main economic activity, followed by exports of tropical agricultural products, such as bananas, sugar, cacao, and citrus; marine products such as shrimp and fish; and oil.

Belize has a diverse multiethnic population, as a result of its centuries-long history as a Spanish and then later a British colony. Over 80 percent of the population is of mixed European ancestry, from a mixture of Mexican Spanish and Maya (who are known as *mestizos*, 53 percent) or descendants of the earliest British colonial settlers and African slaves (known as Creoles, 26 percent). The political and economic elites come from these two major ethnic groups. The rest of the population includes Mopan, Kekchi, and Yucatec Maya (11 percent), Garinagu or Garifuna (descendants of Africans and Carib and Arawak Indians, 6 percent), and Mennonites and other whites, 5 percent. Minority ethnic groups comprise the remainder: Asians, such as East Indians, Chinese, and Middle Easterners (Lebanese). English is the official language, and over half of the Belizean population speak English as their first language. With the influx of Central Americans from Guatemala, Honduras, and El Salvador, Spanish is gradually supplanting English as the first language of Belizeans in certain districts. A minority also speak several Mayan dialects, Garifuna, and Low German (Plautdietsch) as their first language.

The majority of Belizeans are Christians, either adherents of Catholicism or Protestantism, who observe the life-cycle celebrations of each denomination accordingly (see Protestant and Catholic Life-Cycle Rituals, page lxxiii). The Anglican Church was once the predominant religious institution in Belize, catering to the needs of British colonists. The Anglicans also established primary and secondary schools, besides parish churches, and these were the traditional centers of community life. Other Protestant evangelical religious groups, such as the Scottish Presbyterians, Methodists, Baptists, Seventh-Day Adventists, also have adherents in Belize. Other Christian churches include the Quakers, Mormons, Jehovah's Witnesses, and other marginal Christian denominations.

Other religions with adherents, to a minor extent, are Hinduism, Judaism, Baha'i, and Islam. Among the Garifuna, Rastafarianism is practiced. Syncretism, that is, a mix of indigenous religious practices and traditions with Catholic rituals and beliefs, is common to Mayan, Creole, and Garifuna groups, most of whom have converted to Catholicism or other Christian denominations. Nominally Catholic Garifuna continue to observe their *dugu* ritual, and nominally Catholic Creoles tend to believe in *obeah-myalism* or witchcraft.

Belize is home to several groups of Mennonites. Mennonites are a group of Anabaptists, who believe that baptism should be done only when a person has reached adulthood, not at infancy. Certain groups of Mennonites, in common with the Amish (another similar group of Anabaptists), reject the use of modern technology, such as electricity and motor cars. (There are progressive Mennonites who do not mind using electricity or cars.) The aim of the majority of Mennonites who have settled in Belize is to create a peaceful community where they can live a simple Christian life, free of the influences of modern fashions and trends. They do not listen to music or dance, and they do not drink any alcohol. They dress modestly, the women in traditional long-sleeved cotton dresses, and the men in overalls. They farm organically, raising vegetables and animals for food, and produce cheese and other dairy products that they sell to the local community. The government of Belize granted the Mennonites freedom to practice their religion, freedom from military conscription (Mennonites believe in pacifism and nonviolence), freedom from land taxes, and freedom to establish their own schools and banks and to carry out their businesses without government intervention.

The Mennonites in Belize comprise Plautdietsch-speaking and Pennsylvania German–speaking groups. Both groups include descendants of Mennonites who had been invited to settle in Russia by Catherine the Great in the 1760s, mainly to utilize their agricultural skills in developing the area that is now the Ukraine. Their economic success in farming the Ukraine led to their persecution during the Russian Revolution of 1917 and subsequent wars, prompting migration to Canada and the United States. When the United States government wanted to enroll them into the Social Security program, and the Canadian government instituted universal education in English, many migrated to Mexico. And when conditions in Mexico became intolerable because of the drug wars and other government policy issues, they decided to move somewhere else more amenable to their way of life, and they chose to migrate to Belize.

The Mennonite communities in Belize are located in Upper Barton Creek and Lower Barton Creek, Blue Creek, Little Belize, Progresso, Springfield, Pine Hill, Shipyard, and Spanish Lookout. The Upper and Lower Barton Creek colonies were established in the late 1950s and early 1970s. Some members of these groups have since settled in Mennonite colonies elsewhere in Latin America, such as Bolivia and Paraguay. Besides Plautdietsch and Pennsylvania German, they speak English and Spanish.

Belize Mennonite communities grow potatoes, cabbage, beans, tomatoes, watermelons, carrots, peanuts, sweet peppers, and coriander (cilantro), and these products have become diversified and have enhanced the available food in Belize. The Mennonites also produce cattle and raise cereal grains for fodder, as well as produce milk and cheese. They have engineering workshops for making and repairing their farming machinery and equipment, as well as carpentry workshops for making wooden furniture. The Spanish Lookout colony is the most progressive Mennonite community; it practices an evangelical form of Mennonite Christianity, with services in Spanish and English, as well as in the Garifuna language. The Belize Evangelical Mennonite Church has had success in converting Creoles, Garifuna, Maya, and *mestizo* Belizeans. The Evangelical Mennonites have established 39 elementary schools and two secondary schools for their own communities. In contrast to the more conservative Mennonites, progressive Mennonites use mobile telephones and motor cars, and they have established a supermarket, as well as a car workshop business.

The indigenous Garifuna (even those who have converted to Christianity) often practice a funerary ceremony called *adugurahani*, or *dugu* for short, which has elements of spirit possession. *Adugurahani* means "Feasting the Dead," and it is a ritual to honor the spirits of a family's dead ancestors. It is also akin to a family reunion as it seeks to bring together all the members of a family—the living as well as the dead. Its additional purpose is as a therapeutic or curative ceremony by calling on deceased ancestors to help heal family members who have become ill or who have met with misfortunes and accidents. It is believed that illness and accidents are caused by the resentment of the family's dead ancestors, who feel that they are being neglected or forgotten by the younger (and living) generation.

The *dugu* takes place over two to four days and often goes on for as long as two weeks. Family members and friends of the sick or unlucky person(s) gather to drum and sing, calling ancestral spirits to the ceremony. A Garifuna priest or shaman, called *Buyai* (also called *Buyei*), leads the ceremony and organizes the entire event, from the venue to the food, the types and colors of clothing to be worn, the kinds of sacrifices necessary, and the duration of the ritual. When the *Buyai* decides that the ancestral spirits have arrived, the sick person can be fed and is sprinkled with rum. Other guests are also sprinkled with rum, and they may also experience spirit possession during the ritual. The rest of the food and alcohol is sacrificed (by sinking them in the sea or burying them in the ground). At the end of the *dugu* ritual, the *Buyai* deems the ill person on the road to recovery, and the unlucky person freed from his or her run of bad luck.

Holding a *dugu* festival requires a considerable outlay of resources, and the preparatory stages often begin two years before the event. If there is no temple (*dabuyaba*), one has to be built, according to certain specifications (facing east, with doors to north and south, the west end closed and allocated for the *Buyai*'s inner sanctum and the family's private space). A kitchen and sheds for the pigs and chickens to be raised for food for the festivities are also constructed. All buildings are made of local, natural materials, with thatched roofs and dirt floors. Two sets of clothing per person for both sides of the family (the maternal and paternal) have to be made of specific design and pattern, all on the *Buyai*'s instructions.

The *Buyai* functions as both priest and healer, and he is often assisted by another *Buyai*, a messenger, cooks, musicians such as drummers and *sisira* players (gourd shakers), and singers. The ceremony itself is a syncretistic mix of indigenous Garifuna and Catholic ritual, with holy water being sprinkled throughout the temple. The central feast for the ancestors, besides including meat from the locally raised pigs and chickens, often includes fresh fish and seafood gathered by a group of people assigned to this task. Everything used for gathering food from the sea is blessed at a Catholic mass held in the temple. The fish and seafood collectors are accompanied to their boats with drumming. The same drumming also accompanies the seafood collectors as they bring their catch back to the temple and kitchen.

A long banquet table is laid for the ancestors inside the temple. Food for the ancestors is left for some time to give them time to eat. Thereafter, everyone takes some food from the table and spreads it on banana leaves on the ground. Not all the food is meant to be eaten—some is buried in the ground or dropped into the sea, as sacrifices to the ancestral spirits. Everyone present is enjoined to eat and join in the ancestral feast. Throughout, drumming and dancing are going on in the temple, while at the same time a Catholic mass is celebrated at the temple each morning.

≬ *Hudut*

Hudut is a traditional Garifuna dish of two separate parts: a fish stew with a spiced coconut broth and its accompaniment of mashed plantains, called *fufu*. *Hudut* may be one of the dishes served during a *dugu* ritual. The fish stew is quite similar to the Creole dish called *sere*. In Honduras, this same Garifuna fish soup, with the addition of chunks of potato or **cassava** (also called *yuca*) is called *sopa de pescado*, and the mashed plantain that accompanies it is called *machuca*.

Yield: 6 servings

6 medium-sized whole fresh snapper, bream, or mackerel, or 6 pounds **fillet**, skin-on

juice of 2 lemons or 3 limes

salt and freshly ground black pepper to taste

oil, for frying

4 tablespoons coconut or other oil

3 onions, finely chopped

4 cloves garlic, finely chopped

½ teaspoon powdered cumin (optional)

1 tablespoon ground annatto seeds

3 whole habanero chili peppers

10 tender, young okra pods, sliced into 1-inch lengths (optional)

6 sprigs culantro or 1 bunch **cilantro**, chopped

6 sprigs thyme

6 sprigs oregano or basil

7 cups coconut milk, homemade (recipe page 225), or canned

Equipment: Frying pan, deep large saucepan, food processor, small bowl, oven mitts

1. Prepare fish: Remove scales, gills, and intestines (you may request the fishmonger to do this). Wash well. Make several crosswise slits along the body.

2. Rub into the slits lemon or lime juice, salt, and pepper. Let stand for 10 to 15 minutes, then pat dry.

3. In a frying pan, pour enough oil for frying (about ½ inch depth), and heat over medium heat. Fry fish until golden on both sides, leaving enough space between each fish (do not crowd the pan). Drain and set aside.

4. In a heavy-bottomed saucepan over medium heat, add coconut oil, and sauté onions and garlic until onions are softened. Stir in coconut milk, add cumin, if using, and Habanero chilis, and reduce heat to low to cook coconut milk gently. Stir from time to time to make sure the coconut milk is not sticking to the pan.

5. When the coconut milk starts to boil, take ¼ cup into a small bowl, and add the annatto seeds. Let seeds **steep** for 15 to 20 minutes until the coconut milk has turned orange. Rub seeds with your fingers to extract as much color. Add colored coconut milk to pan, and stir.

6. Take 1 cup of coconut milk, and add to the mashed plantains. Stir in okra, if using, and reserved fried fish. Stir in culantro, thyme, and oregano or basil. Let okra cook for 10

minutes, until tender but still slightly crisp. Turn off heat. Place fish into individual serving bowls, surrounded by okra and coconut milk.

7. Place *fufu* alongside the fish, if the serving bowl is large enough, or on a separate plate. Hudut *is usually eaten with the fingers.*

⚗ Fufu

Yield: serves 6 to 8

4 green **plantains**, peeled and left whole

2 ripe plantains, peeled and left whole

salt to taste

Equipment: Deep large saucepan, food processor, small bowl, oven mitts

1. In a deep saucepan, add water halfway, and let it come to a boil over high heat.

2. Add green plantains, and, after 5 minutes, add ripe plantains. When plantains are tender (about 20 minutes), transfer them to a food processor. Add salt, and process until plantains are thoroughly mashed. Add a cup of coconut milk from the stew (*hudut* recipe precedes). Process briefly to incorporate the coconut milk.

3. Shape *fufu* into fist-sized ovals.

Serve together in the same bowl as the fish stew or on a separate plate.

⚗ Darasa (Banana and Coconut Dish)

Darasa is a banana and coconut dish wrapped in banana leaves and steamed. It is often made for family celebrations and special occasions. The banana leaves add their unique scent to the dish, but if banana leaves are not available, parchment paper can be used.

Yield: 12 pieces

10 semiripe bananas

⅔ cup coconut milk, homemade (recipe page 225), or canned, or more as needed

juice and grated rind of 1 orange

juice and grated rind of 1 lime

½ teaspoon salt, or to taste

freshly ground black pepper to taste

12 sheets 9-inch-square fresh banana leaves or parchment

12 sheets aluminum foil

Equipment: Large mixing bowl, wooden mixing spoon, **double boiler** or 8-quart saucepan with steamer basket or **colander**, tongs, oven mitts

1. Into a large bowl, grate bananas. Add coconut milk, juice, and rind of the orange and lime, salt, and pepper, and stir well to combine. Pass banana leaves, if using, through boiling water to make them flexible.

2. Place about ⅔ cup of the banana mixture in the center of a banana leaf or parchment paper. Fold the sides over to form a neat packet. Enclose the packets in aluminum foil and seal firmly.

3. In a large double boiler or 8-quart saucepan fitted with a steamer or colander, put water halfway, and bring to a boil over medium heat. Place foil-wrapped packets in the upper pan of double boiler or steamer. Cover, and allow to cook for about 20 to 25 minutes, or until banana mixture is firm. (Test one to make sure.)

Allow to cool for 15 minutes before serving.

Costa Rica

Costa Rica is a small country in Central America between Panama to the south and Nicaragua to the north. Its eastern coastline faces the Caribbean Sea, and its western coastline faces the North Pacific Ocean. Its area is slightly smaller than West Virginia. When Columbus arrived in 1502, over 25,000 Indians lived in the area, but they were wiped out by European diseases and conquest. Costa Rica remained under Spanish control until it joined the United Provinces of Central America in 1823. This federation was short-lived, and Costa Rica gained full independence in 1838. In 1949, Costa Rica became the first country to abolish its armed forces. The Costa Rican economy is based on ecotourism and exports of agricultural produce, including bananas, sugar, coffee, and beef. Its high standard of living provides citizens with universal access to education, social benefits, healthcare, electricity, and sanitation. Hence Costa Ricans enjoy the lowest rates of infant mortality and longest life expectancy at birth in Latin America.

Over 83 percent of the population of Costa Rica is comprised of people of European descent and *mestizos* (mixed Spanish and Indian). Indigenous Indians account for a mere 2.4 percent, mulattos account for almost 7 percent, and the rest are blacks.

Costa Rica is the only country in the Americas with an official state religion, the Roman Catholic Church, but its constitution provides for freedom of religion. The majority of Costa Ricans (over 70 percent) claim to be adherents of the Roman Catholic Church and celebrate the life-cycle events prescribed by the Church. (See Protestant and Catholic Life-Cycle Rituals, page lxxiii.) Nevertheless, of these, only 44 percent declared themselves to be actively practicing their faith. About 14 percent of Costa Ricans are Evangelical Christians, or *evangelicos*, as Protestants are referred to in Latin America. The Protestant denominations represented include Methodists, Lutherans, Baptists, and Episcopalians. The Church of Jesus Christ of Latter-Day Saints (the Mormons) have a strong presence in Costa Rica with over 35,000 adherents, and the temple in San Jose serves as a regional worship center for surrounding countries (Nicaragua, Panama, Honduras) as well. There is also a thriving Jewish community in Costa Rica, and many important posts in the Costa Rican government have been previously filled by those of the Jewish faith. Of the non-Christian faiths, Buddhism has the largest following of around 100,000 members. Additionally, Jehovah's Witnesses, the Unification Church, Taoism, Hinduism, Islam, Hare Krishna, Scientology, paganism, and Wicca have marginal presences in the country.

Indigenous Indian communities comprise several ethnic groups: Cabecares, Bri, Huetares, Terrabas (also known as Teribes), Borucas (also Bruncas), Gutatusos/Malekus, Chorotegas, and Guaymís (more correctly known as Ngäbes, akin to the same group found in Panama). Each ethnic group has or had its own language, social traditions, indigenous medicinal practices, and religious beliefs. However, through centuries of persecution, not many indigenous populations survive today, let alone to have preserved their traditions. The Cabecares or Cabecar Indians (also known as the Chirippo) are more fortunate than most; because of their remote location in the Cordillera mountains, they are the least affected by outside influences, and hence have retained their original language, Cabecar, which they speak in addition to Spanish. Notwithstanding the conversion to Christianity of 95 percent of the community (predominantly Roman Catholic, 14 percent Protestant), they have also kept their traditional religious belief in Sibo, whom they consider the Creator of the Universe and Supreme God. Their myths and legends are preserved in writing, in both the Cabecar language and Spanish.

The Bri Bri (also Bribri) are another isolated community who live in the mountains and reservations of southern Costa Rica. There are also Bri Bri living in northern Panama. The Bri Bri have a matrilineal society: Only women can own and inherit land and prepare the sacred cacao drink served during their rituals. The Bri Bri, as well as other indigenous Indians in Costa Rica and Panama, regard the cacao tree (whose fruits are the source of chocolate) to be sacred. In their mythology, the cacao tree originally was a woman turned by the God Sibo into a tree. Hence, the wood of the cacao tree is never used for firewood, and a special drink made of the cacao is prepared and served only by women at all rituals and special occasions, including girls' rites of passage, such as the first menstruation. Bri Bri men are given specific roles by their clan; these include acting as shaman (*awa*) and as *oko*, a special role for dealing with the dead, such as touching the remains, singing funeral songs, and preparing food to be eaten at funerals.

The first important life-cycle celebration among Roman Catholics, in Costa Rica as well as elsewhere in Latin America, is the *bautismo* or *bautizo* (baptism), which takes place when the baby is six to eight weeks old. After the church service, everyone goes to the home of the parents to partake in a buffet. The buffet most often includes two salads, *arroz con pollo* (recipe follows), and a favorite cake from Nicaragua, *pastel de tres leches*. A dessert made with corn, *tamal de elote* (recipe follows), is another traditional dish served. In most Latin American countries, corn, a symbol of motherhood, is an important food at life-cycle celebrations.

Among Roman Catholics, first communion is another family event celebrated with a family feast. The celebration goes on all afternoon when young friends gather for cake (called *queque* in Costa Rica) and ice cream, games, and other entertainment, such as smashing the *piñata*.

For weddings, most couples marry in church. The bride's parents are hosts for the occasion, which can include a party before and after the wedding day. For up to three days, guests have a good time eating, drinking, and dancing. When the newlyweds leave for their honeymoon, guests finally go home.

Wedding cakes are either the same in Costa Rica as they are in the United States, or they can be the famous black wedding cake (recipe page 235) of the Caribbean. The wedding cakes are usually very grand and elaborately decorated with the traditional wedding couple dolls on top.

⚉ *Arroz con Pollo* (Chicken and Rice)

The traditional feast dish is *arroz con pollo*. It can be prepared in various ways, but this favorite is easy and delicious.

Yield: serves 6 to 8

3 cups white rice

1 onion, **finely chopped**

1 green bell pepper, **trimmed** and finely chopped

2½ to 3 pounds chicken, cut into serving-size pieces

4 cups water

½ cup carrots, finely chopped and **blanched**

½ cup string beans, sliced and blanched

½ cup raisins

½ cup frozen peas, thawed

½ cup **pitted** green olives, sliced

2 tablespoons vegetable oil

salt and pepper to taste

Equipment: Large ovenproof saucepan with cover, oven mitts, serving bowl

Preheat oven to 350°F.

1. Sprinkle rice, onion, and bell pepper over bottom of large ovenproof saucepan. Set chicken pieces on top and add water. Cover saucepan. Place in oven and bake for 45 minutes to 1 hour.

2. Before the last 10 minutes of baking, using oven mitts, remove from oven, and uncover. Sprinkle in carrots, string beans, raisins, peas, and sliced green olives. Cover and return to oven to heat through and finish the remaining 10 minutes of baking. Test for **doneness** of chicken.

To serve, transfer mixture to serving bowl and serve as main meal for the family baptism party.

⚉ *Tamal de Elote* (Corn Pudding)

This cake-like dessert with corn is unusual and delicious.

Yield: serves 8 to 10

12 ounces canned condensed milk

6 cups canned whole kernel corn, drained

3 eggs

1 cup melted butter or margarine

1 teaspoon ground cinnamon

whipped cream (optional)

Equipment: Electric **blender**, rubber spatula, greased 8-inch square cake pan, toothpick, oven mitts

Preheat oven to 350°F.

1. Combine condensed milk, corn, eggs, melted butter or margarine, and cinnamon in blender. **Blend** for 3 minutes, or until smooth. Using rubber spatula, transfer mixture to greased cake pan.

2. Bake in oven for 45 to 50 minutes, or until a toothpick inserted in center comes out clean.

Serve as a dessert at room temperature for best flavor. Some people add a dollop of whipped cream to each serving.

ᘔ *Cajeta de Leche* (Milk Fudge)

Candy is served at most life-cycle celebrations, and this easy fudge is a Costa Rican specialty.

Yield: about 15 balls

12 ounces canned condensed milk	1½ tablespoons butter or margarine
1 cup powdered milk	For **garnish**: sliced almonds, macadamia nuts, or small pieces of **candied fruit**

Equipment: Large mixing bowl, wooden mixing spoon, candy-size or mini paper cupcake cups, baking sheet, paring knife, small serving dish

1. In large mixing bowl, combine condensed milk, powdered milk, and butter or margarine. Stir until smooth.

2. Separate candy-size or mini paper cupcake cups onto baking sheet. Using your hands, form mixture into 1-inch balls, and set each in a paper cup. With a knife, cut a cross on the top of each ball. In the center of the cross, place either a slice of almond, macadamia nut, or small piece of candied fruit.

To serve, arrange the candies, in paper cups, on a serving dish. Traditionally the balls were placed on lemon leaves to absorb the lemon flavor.

ᘔ *Queque Batido de Vainilla* (Vanilla Cake)

This is a classic cake for birthdays and other important occasions. It can be filled with the pastry cream included in this recipe, or with *dulce de leche* (recipe on page 563).

Yield: 10 servings

Cake:	1 teaspoon baking powder
1½ cups flour	1 cup butter, softened

| 1 cup sugar | 5 eggs |
| 1 teaspoon vanilla | ½ cup milk |

Pastry cream:	2 tablespoons butter
4 tablespoons **cornstarch**	1 teaspoon vanilla essence
4 cups milk	Cream frosting:
1 can (14 ounces) sweetened condensed milk	2 cups whipping cream
	¼ cup icing sugar

4 **egg yolks**, well beaten

Equipment: Mixing bowls, stand or hand mixer, mixing spoon, 2 8-inch layer cake pans, wooden skewer, oven mitts, wire rack, saucepan, rubber spatula, piping bag and decorative tips

Preheat oven at 325°F.

1. Butter and flour the cake pans, set aside.

2. Prepare cake batter. In a bowl, combine flour and baking powder, and sift. Set aside.

3. In another bowl, beat at medium speed the butter and sugar until fluffy and pale-colored. Mix in vanilla, then eggs, one at a time, adding the next only when the previous one has been thoroughly incorporated. Reduce mixer speed, and gradually add flour and baking powder mixture, followed by milk. Mix only until the mixture is homogeneous. Do not overbeat. Spoon into prepared baking pans.

4. Bake for about 25 to 30 minutes, or until done. A wooden skewer inserted into the center should come out clean when cake is done. Remove from oven, let cool in pans for 10 minutes, then unmold to cool completely on a wire rack, covered by a clean, dry kitchen towel.

5. Prepare pastry cream: In a saucepan, place cornstarch and gradually whisk in milk to form a smooth paste. Continue whisking while adding the remaining milk to ensure that no lumps form. Whisk in condensed milk until mixture is smooth.

6. Turn on heat to medium, and cook, whisking continuously until small bubbles form on the edges of the pan. Reduce heat to low, then gradually whisk in yolks, continuing to whisk until mixture thickens. Immediately turn off heat, and whisk in butter and vanilla. Let pastry cream cool thoroughly before using.

7. Assemble cake: Split cakes horizontally to make 4 even layers. Spread pastry cream evenly between layers.

8. Prepare cream frosting: in a bowl, whip cream to soft peaks. Gradually add icing sugar, and continue to whip until cream stands in stiff peaks. Do not overbeat, or cream will turn to butter. Using a piping bag with decorative tip, cover sides and top of the cake evenly with whipped cream frosting.

Serve decorated with edible sprinkles, glitter, and the like.

El Salvador

El Salvador is the smallest of the Central American countries and the only one without an Atlantic coastline, although its western coast faces the North Pacific Ocean. It is bordered by Honduras on the north and east and by Guatemala on the west. Its area is similar to that of New Jersey.

The original inhabitants were Pipil Indians, descendants of Aztecs. Spain conquered the area in 1525 and remained in control until 1821, when El Salvador joined the United Provinces of Central America, which lasted until 1838.

Today, the majority (86 percent) of the population are *mestizos* (mixed Indian and Spanish parentage), with about 13 percent white; indigenous Indians and other ethnic groups comprise less than 0.8 percent. Fifty percent belong to the Roman Catholic Church and follow life-cycle events according to Church doctrine. Protestant adherents account for 36 percent, and the remaining 14 percent belong to other religions or have no religious affiliation. (See Protestant and Catholic Life-Cycle Rituals, page lxxiii.) Of the Protestant denominations, Anglicans, Lutherans, and Baptists are represented. The Church of Latter-Day Saints (Mormons) also has adherents in El Salvador. There is a small community of Sephardic Jews who fled Spain during the Inquisition, as well as German Jews who left Europe just before World War II. The Jewish community maintains a synagogue in El Salvador. There is also a small Muslim community.

Major family events—birth and baptism, marriage, and death—are usually celebrated in church. A religious marriage connotes social status. Most El Salvadorian couples would prefer a large church wedding, but the expense involved is prohibitive.

Almost every El Salvadoran meal includes beans and rice, but for special occasions, sweet potato dishes, especially when made extra sweet, are symbolic of a sweeter life.

✇ *Los Camotes* (Candied Sweet Potatoes)

Yield: serves 6

6 cups water

4 cups sugar

4 cups dark brown sugar

3 teaspoons ground cinnamon

6 whole cloves

6 sweet potatoes, peeled and quartered

½ cup melted butter or margarine

Equipment: Medium saucepan, mixing spoon, buttered 12×10×2½-inch baking pan, aluminum foil, oven mitts, serving bowl

1. Combine water, granulated sugar, cinnamon, cloves, and brown sugar in a medium saucepan. Stirring constantly, bring to a rolling boil over medium-high heat until the sugar dissolves. Reduce heat at once to low, and cook for 2 hours until the sauce thickens.

Preheat oven to 350°F.

2. Put quartered sweet potatoes in a single layer in buttered baking pan. Brush the potatoes with melted butter or margarine, and cover with foil.

3. Bake in the preheated oven for 40 to 50 minutes, or until tender. Keep warm.

To serve, transfer sweet potatoes to a serving bowl, and cover with thick sugar sauce.

Pupusas originated in El Salvador and are now found in other Latin American countries. Whenever a family gathering or party is held, expect to eat *pupusas*. They are filled with cheese (*pupusas de queso*), refried beans (*pupusas de frijoles refritos*), or fried pork (*pupusas de chicharrón*). To make *pupusas de frijoles refritos*, instead of the cheese, use refried beans (available in the Mexican food section of most supermarkets or all Latin American food stores).

♪ *Pupusas de Queso* (Salvadoran Cheese Pies)

Yield: makes 4

2 cups hot water

1 teaspoon salt

4 cups *masa harina* (available in the Mexican food section of most supermarkets or all Latin American food stores)

½ cup shredded cheese or refried beans (available in the Mexican food section of most supermarkets or all Latin American food stores)

4 tablespoons vegetable oil, more if necessary

Equipment: Large mixing bowl, mixing spoon, wax paper, work surface, large skillet, metal spatula, paper towels, serving plate

1. Pour hot water into a large mixing bowl, add salt, and *masa harina*, and stir well. Divide the mixture into 8 equal-size balls (a little larger than golf-ball-size), and place on wax paper–covered work surface.

2. Pat each ball into a disk about ¼ inch thick and 2½ inches across. Place on wax paper, and pile about 1 heaping teaspoon shredded cheese or refried beans on top of 4 disks, staying well within the edges. Cover with the remaining 4 disks, and press edges together to seal in the cheese or beans.

3. Heat 4 tablespoons oil in large skillet over medium-high heat. Fry *pupusas*, in batches, for 3 to 5 minutes on each side, until golden brown. Drain on paper towels.

To serve, stack pupusas *on a serving plate. Eat with your fingers.*

When a girl reaches the age of 15 in most Latin American countries, her birthday is usually celebrated in a more lavish manner than usual (depending on the family's circumstances) in a tradition known as *quinceañera* (literally, 15th year). El Salvador is no exception, and the *quinceañera*, or *quince* for short, is also known as *fiesta de rosa* (pink party), as customarily the celebrant wore a pink dress or ball gown. The pink theme may extend to all aspects of the party, including the celebration cake and the knife to slice it with. These days pink is no longer the only color theme, and girls are free to choose their favorite color. The *quinceañera* celebrates the transition of a girl to a young woman, and she may be dressed as a princess in a formal ball gown, with an entourage of equally formally dressed girlfriends and their escorts. The presents that she receives from family and friends are usually jewelry such as a ring, bracelet, necklace, or makeup and accessories. Before the celebration party held in the evening with a banquet for family and friends featuring the celebrant's and family's favorite foods and live or DJ music and dancing, there is as well a religious aspect to the *quinceañera*. The celebrant is presented to the church community at a thanksgiving mass, usually in the early afternoon. The celebrant may also have undergone religious training provided by the church for months prior to the event. The religious training may not be all about Catholic catechism but may also touch upon chastity and relationships with boys, as well as discussions about future life and livelihoods.

✿ *Refresco de Ensalada* (Fruit Salad Drink)

This is an unusual drink, as it is really a mix of several fruits—a fruit salad—whose juices are meant for drinking. You may substitute whatever fruit is in season or according to your preference: plums, strawberries, grapes, as long as they are cut into very small pieces, like tiny dice. There are tropical fruits that are commonly used in El Salvador for this refreshing drink and which may not be easily available outside the country. These are the aromatic sweet-sour cashew fruit, known as *marañon* in El Salvador and the *mamey colorado* (*Pouteria sapota*), a sweet fruit with reddish-brown flesh and a central shiny seed with a faint cinnamon flavor. *Refresco de ensalada* (*ensalada*) is a popular drink and is often served at parties and get-togethers. For the optional syrup, use sugar, honey, stevia, or other sweetener.

Yield: 6 to 8 servings

juice of 1 lemon

3 apples, a mix of green-skinned and red-skinned varieties

1 large pineapple, or 1 20-ounce can pineapple slices in 100 percent pineapple juice

1 ready-to-eat (ripe) mango

2 nectarines or peaches

4 oranges

10 cups cold water

¼ teaspoon salt (optional)

1 bunch **watercress** or half a head iceberg lettuce, finely chopped

syrup from ½ cup sugar (or ¼ cup honey or 1 teaspoon) and 1 cup water (optional)

Equipment: Large glass bowl or pitcher for serving, serving ladle

1. Wash fruits very well, and wipe dry.

2. Into the serving bowl, put lemon juice.

3. Slice and core apples, and dice. Stir diced apples into lemon juice to prevent them turning brown.

4. Peel pineapple, making sure to extract the "eyes," which can cause itching on the tongue. Cut off and discard the leaves and core. Dice the flesh. If using the canned pineapple, dice the slices. Add diced fruit and juice to the serving bowl.

5. Peel mango, slice off the two "cheeks" (the halves surrounding the pit) as close to the pit as possible. Dice and add to serving bowl. Cut along the perimeter of the pit, and dice the flesh. Add to serving bowl. Discard pit.

6. Dice nectarines or peaches. Peel 2 oranges, and dice the flesh. Add diced nectarines and oranges to serving bowl. Juice remaining oranges, and add to diced fruits in serving bowl.

7. Add chopped watercress or lettuce. Stir in cold water. Taste, and if you feel it lacks sweetness, make a light syrup.

8. In a small saucepan, put sugar (or honey) and water over low heat. Simmer until sugar dissolves. Let cool, then add to the *ensalada*.

9. Cover with plastic wrap, and allow to chill for 4 hours or, ideally, overnight.

Guests drink the juice first and eat fruits with a spoon.

Guatemala

The northernmost Central American country, Guatemala is one of the most populated countries in Central America. It is bordered by Mexico on the north and by Belize, Honduras, and El Salvador on the east. Its western coast faces the North Pacific Ocean, and it has access to the Gulf of Honduras and the Caribbean Sea on the east. Its area is slightly smaller than Pennsylvania.

Guatemala, once part of the Mayan empire, was conquered by Spaniards in the 16th century. It remained under Spanish control until the 19th century when Guatemala joined the short-lived United Provinces of Central America. A republic was established in 1839 after this federation collapsed.

Over half (almost 60 percent) the population are people of Spanish heritage—people of European descent and *mestizos* (mixed Spanish and Indian)—and the remaining 40 percent are indigenous Indians. Although the official language is Spanish, there are 23 officially recognized indigenous languages, among them Quiche, Garifuna, and Cakchiquel.

Most people belong to the Roman Catholic Church and follow its life-cycle traditions. Well over a third of Guatemalans have converted to Protestantism. (See Protestant and Catholic Life-Cycle Rituals, page lxxiii.) In the aftermath of the 1975 earthquake, many Guatemalans converted in appreciation for the help they received from Protestant relief agencies. The lack of hierarchy and spontaneous expressions of faith among Protestants have also been factors in their conversion. There is also a

Jewish and Muslim presence in Guatemala. Many of the indigenous Indians combine native traditions with Catholicism. Among Western Highland Mayas, there is a syncretic veneration of Maximón or San Simón, a cigar-smoking, alcohol-swilling idol. Other Maya continue to follow their ancient traditions in rituals and ceremonies called *costumbre* (also ancestral beliefs), which are held in caves, on mountain or volcanic peaks, and at archaeological sites. The sites are often decorated with candles, flowers, and often include offerings of sacrificed chickens or other small animals. Since the 1990s, there has been a move to bring Mayan ancestral beliefs (*costumbre*) into the open and publicize them in various media.

One Guatemalan life-cycle celebration that occurs outside the confines of religion is the coming of age ceremony at age 10. The 10th birthday is celebrated with a community party, much like Christian confirmations or Jewish bar mitzvahs. The parents explain what adulthood means and the responsibilities that all young adults have to their family and community. The villagers slaughter pigs for the party. Everyone has a good time eating, drinking, and dancing.

In Guatemala, especially for Mayan families, mother and child are given special care for the first 40 days after birth. As soon as the child is born, animals are slaughtered for feasting and thanksgiving. Several ceremonies are performed to ward off the evil eye and to ensure that mother and child do not become ill or cursed. The first birthday for a Mayan child is typically celebrated with a grand feast held at a large venue with many children and guests from the community. There are bags of goodies for the invited children and one or more *piñatas*.

Guatemalan girls at the age of 15 have a celebration similar to that in other Latin American countries but on a less opulent scale. They get a pretty dress to wear, a present of jewelry such as a ring from their parents, as well as a doll, to represent the last toy she will receive because from this year onward she is considered an adult with no more need for toys. If the family can afford it, a ballroom is rented for the occasion, where the celebrant dances a waltz with her father and later with an escort. A Guatemalan custom is to have 14 children aged 1 to 14 at the party, to represent the years that the celebrant has experienced. Guatemalan boys are beginning to gain equal opportunities to have a party on their 15th birthday, although not on the same scale as girls' celebrations.

It is also a custom in Guatemala to visit the home of the birthday celebrant early in the morning and rouse him or her with loud music or fireworks, thus letting the entire neighborhood know of the event. Another custom is to push celebrants while they are taking a bite of cake, so that they get cake all over the face. This is all done in lighthearted fun. Typical foods served at a birthday party are tamales, usually filled with chicken and eaten with a sauce of roasted peppers, tomatoes, and sesame seeds, and birthday cake. Not all birthday parties will feature a *piñata*, as it is rather pricey.

ஃ *Pepían* (Beef in Pumpkin Seed and Sesame Seed Sauce)

Pepían is a classic Guatemalan dish whose origin is pre-Hispanic. It was traditionally prepared for religious rituals and to celebrate important events. In contemporary times, it has become a popular dish for family gatherings and celebrations. Together with *plátanos en mole* (recipe follows), this ancient dish has been declared part of the intangible cultural heritage of the country (*Patrimonio Intangible Cultural de la Nación*). The dish uses several kinds of peppers, not all of them hot and spicy. Each chili contributes its own unique taste, and the interaction of these different chilis adds a complex flavor to this traditional dish. Chili peppers can usually be bought at Latin American food shops or online. The *guaque* chili, also known as *huaque* or *guajillo*, is the dried form of the *mirasol* chili and, of these three, is the hottest and spiciest. *Guaque* chili peppers are a common ingredient in Guatemalan and Mexican cuisine. The *pasilla* chili, also known as *pasa* (dried) chili, is the dried form of the *chilaca* chili and has an earthy flavor. The *ancho* chili (literally, wide) is the dried form of the *poblano* chili and has a fruity flavor.

Yield: 4 to 5 servings

2½ to 3 pounds meaty beef ribs

8 cups beef broth

1 bunch green onions

1 large tomato, quartered

5 sprigs **cilantro**, left whole

Salt to taste

2 cups green beans, sliced into 2-inch lengths

5 potatoes, peeled and **cubed**

2 *guaque* chili peppers

6 *ancho* chili peppers

2 *pasilla* chili peppers

2 cinnamon sticks

1½ cups green pumpkin seeds (*pepitoria*)

1½ cup **sesame seeds**

5 tomatoes, halved

3 *tomatillos* (*miltomate*), dehusked, halved

1 red sweet pepper, quartered

4 garlic cloves, unpeeled

2 corn tortillas, soaked in water to cover

Equipment: Large saucepan with cover, skillet or **heavy-bottomed** frying pan, medium bowl for soaking tortillas, baking tray, **blender**, fine-meshed sieve, oven mitts

1. In saucepan over medium heat, place ribs, beef broth, green onions, tomato, cilantro, and salt to taste. Bring to a boil, skim the froth, and reduce heat to let meat simmer until almost tender, about 40 minutes.

2. When a fork can easily pierce the meat, add green beans and potatoes.

3. While meat is simmering, in a skillet, toast the chili peppers (removing their seeds), cinnamon, green pumpkin seeds, and sesame seeds, placing them on the skillet without mixing them.

4. Place tomatoes, tomatillos, and sweet red pepper skin-side up on a baking tray. Add garlic cloves. Brush all with oil on all sides, and grill until the skins of the tomatoes, tomatillos, and sweet pepper are blistered. Allow to cool.

5. In a blender, grind to a paste the toasted pumpkin seeds and sesame seeds, adding a few spoonfuls of water to facilitate grinding. When the pumpkin and sesame seed paste is smooth, add toasted chili peppers, tomatoes, *tomatillos*, sweet pepper, soaked tortillas (squeezed to remove excess water), and **blend** until smooth. Pass blended mixture through a fine sieve, and combine with the meat, green beans, and potatoes in saucepan.

6. Let *pepían* simmer until thoroughly hot and broth has thickened to the consistency of thick gravy. Add a bit of water if it is too thick. Taste, and adjust the seasoning, adding more salt if needed.

Serve with rice.

⚜ Arroz Guatemalteco (Guatemala-style Rice)

All banquets in Guatemala include a variety of side dishes, such as this popular rice dish.

Yield: serves 4 to 6

2 tablespoons vegetable oil	½ cup sweet peas
1 cup rice	2 cups water
1 cup mixed vegetables (carrots, celery, and sweet red bell peppers), **finely chopped**	salt and pepper to taste

Equipment: Large **heavy-bottomed** skillet with cover, mixing spoon,

1. Heat oil in large heavy-bottomed skillet over medium-high heat. Add rice and mixed vegetables, stir, and **sauté** for 3 to 5 minutes to coat rice with oil.

2. Add water, stir, and bring to boil. Reduce to low, cover, and cook for 20 minutes, until rice is tender. Add peas and salt and pepper to taste. Stir to mix well.

⚜ Plátanos en Mole (Plantains in Sweet Mole Sauce)

Plátanos en mole, also known as *mole de plátano* (plantain *mole*) is a traditional Guatemalan dessert. Unlike the more widely known *mole* sauce of Mexico, which is savory, the *mole* sauce for this dessert is sweet and uniquely Guatemalan. In 2007, in recognition of its uniqueness, *plátanos en mole* was officially designated an intangible part of the nation's cultural heritage (*Patrimonio Cultural Intangible de la Nación*). It is a very popular dessert, often made at home, but also makes its appearance at family gatherings and festivities.

Yield: 6 servings

6 ripe **plantains**	½ cup plus 4 teaspoons **sesame seeds**
oil, for frying	½ cup green pumpkin seeds (*pepitoria*)
1 dried *guaque* chili pepper or 1 *guajillo* chili pepper, or any chili pepper	2 cinnamon sticks

5 very ripe tomatoes, chopped, or ½ cup thick tomato purée

2 *champurrada* (traditional Guatemalan cookies for dunking in hot chocolate) or other plain cookies, crumbled

6 **pitted** prunes, chopped

3 tablespoons *achiote* oil (optional)

1 cup good-quality unsweetened dark chocolate, or 1 cup pure unsweetened cocoa powder and ¼ cup butter

2 tablespoons sugar, more to taste

salt

Equipment: Medium frying pan, shallow saucepan, **blender**, small saucepan, small covered storage jar, oven mitts

1. Peel and slice the plantains diagonally crosswise, as much as possible in equal widths so that they cook evenly.

2. In a medium frying pan over medium heat, pour oil to about ¼-inch depth, and put plantain slices to fry until golden brown on both sides. Do not crowd pan. Drain on paper towels.

3. Meanwhile, in a skillet over low heat, in separate places, put chili pepper, sesame seeds, green squash seeds, and cinnamon sticks to dry-fry until aromatic, about 5 minutes.

4. Take out 4 teaspoons of the dry-fried sesame and reserve for garnish.

5. Put the remaining dry-fried ingredients into a blender, adding ¼ cup water to facilitate blending. Add tomatoes or tomato purée, cookies, and prunes. **Blend** all until smooth.

6. In a shallow saucepan over medium heat, warm *achiote* oil, and stir in the blended mixture. When mixture starts to simmer, add chocolate, sugar, and salt, stirring until chocolate is completely incorporated into the sauce. Taste and adjust the seasoning.

7. Add fried plantains, and simmer until plantains are heated through. Allow to cool thoroughly before serving. Transfer to a serving dish, and scatter reserved sesame seeds on top.

Honduras

The second largest country in Central America, Honduras has a relatively long Caribbean coastline (400 miles) and a short Pacific coastline (40 miles). It is bordered by Nicaragua on the southeast, El Salvador on the south, and Guatemala to the west. Its area is slightly larger than Tennessee.

At one time, the region was part of the Mayan empire, and descendants of this ancient civilization live in Honduras today. Explored by Columbus on his last voyage in 1502, Honduras remained under Spanish control until 1821, when it joined a federation of Central American states. In 1838, Honduras seceded from the federation and became independent.

The majority (90 percent) of Hondurans are of European descent or *mestizos* (mixed Spanish and Indian), although the descendants of the Maya and some other Indian groups make up a small percentage (7 percent) of the population. A group of people living on the Honduras islands in the Caribbean and along the Caribbean coast of Honduras are referred to as "black Caribs" and comprise 2 percent of the population. There is additionally a white minority of 1 percent. Although most black Caribs are Catholic, they add many African customs and rituals to life-cycle celebrations. Most *mestizo* and white Hondurans are Catholic and celebrate life-cycle events according to the doctrines of the Church. (See Protestant and Catholic Life-Cycle Rituals, page lxxiii.) In a recent survey on religious affiliation, 47 percent of Hondurans declared themselves to be Catholic, 36 percent as Protestant, and the remaining 17 percent gave no reply or "other." Protestant groups are a fast-growing minority in the country, and missionaries have helped attract members with social service programs. Along the Mosquito Coast, the Moravians and Anglicans have a considerable following. Other denominations such as Jehovah's Witnesses, Episcopalian, Lutheran, Mennonite, and The Church of Jesus Christ of Latter-Day Saints (Mormons) are also represented. There is a small Jewish community, with a synagogue in Tegucigalpa and another in San Pedro Sula. A Muslim minority has a mosque in San Pedro Sula.

Two important childhood rites in the Catholic Church are baptism and communion. Catholic children are baptized at a few months of age, and usually a party is held after the church ceremony. Relatives and close friends are usually invited to the baptism and party. The first communion is held when children are seven years old. Girls are dressed like little brides in a long white dress, usually of satin, and a head veil. A family dinner is held after the service when the child receives presents from family and friends.

The *piñata*, which has become a common feature of contemporary birthday parties, was not so common in previous times. For many poor families, a *piñata* was not affordable. If a child wanted a *piñata* for his or her birthday, it was often instead of a birthday cake and soft drinks. Most of the time, in the countryside, it was fashioned out of a clay pot, covered with colored paper, and filled with mangoes, sugar cane, or other fruits in season, instead of the candies and other goodies that fill them today.

Funerals are sad occasions, especially if a child dies. The child is referred to as *angelito* (little angel). The funeral procession traditionally walks to the cemetery and is led by the priest and several small children carrying flowers to lay on the grave. After the burial, the mourners go to the home of the deceased for a meal of soup, beans, and tortillas. If the family can afford it, meat is added to whatever is being served.

The foods of Honduras are similar to those in other Central American countries. Maize (corn) and frijoles (beans) are the staples. *Nacatamales* (large corn cakes stuffed with vegetables and meat) are favorites.

Bananas are a major export of Honduras, and *pan de banano* is a favorite treat, often served as dessert for life-cycle celebrations.

✥ *Pan de Banano* (Banana Bread)

Yield: 1 loaf

½ cup butter or margarine, at room temperature

½ cup sugar

1 pound ripe bananas (about 2 or 3), peeled and mashed

½ teaspoon salt

1 teaspoon ground cinnamon

1 tablespoon lemon juice

1 egg, well beaten

1½ cups all-purpose flour

2 teaspoons baking powder

Equipment: Large mixing bowl, electric mixer or whisk, medium bowl, flour **sifter**, rubber spatula, greased 9×5-inch loaf pan, oven mitts, toothpick, knife, small dessert bowls, serving spoon

Preheat oven to 350°F.

1. Put butter or margarine and sugar into large mixing bowl, and, using electric mixer or whisk, beat until light and fluffy. Add mashed bananas, salt, cinnamon, lemon juice, and egg, and beat well.

2. In medium bowl, **sift** flour with baking powder. Using rubber spatula, **fold in** flour, a little at a time, with banana mixture. Transfer batter to prepared loaf pan.

3. Bake in oven for 45 to 50 minutes, until toothpick inserted in center comes out clean.

*To serve as bread, cut into slices and serve with honey. To serve as dessert, put slices in small bowls with a **drizzle** of cream over each serving.*

To satisfy a sweet tooth, desserts are made from unexpected ingredients, such as this simple dessert made with cheese.

✥ *Dulce de Queso* (Sweet Cheese)

Yield: serves 4 to 6

1 pound mozzarella cheese, at room temperature

2 cups dark brown sugar

1 cup water

2 teaspoons ground cinnamon

Equipment: Sharp knife, shallow 8-inch-square or round baking pan, small saucepan, mixing spoon

1. Using a sharp knife, cut cheese into ¼-inch strips, and lay them in a shallow 8-inch-square or round baking pan.

2. In a small saucepan, combine brown sugar, water, and cinnamon. Bring to a boil over medium-high heat, stirring constantly to dissolve sugar. Reduce heat to **simmer** for 5 minutes without stirring. Pour brown sugar mixture over the cheese.

Serve immediately either by spooning a serving over pan de banano *(recipe precedes) or simply by spooning a helping into a bowl to eat as dessert.*

⚶ *Tarta de Cumpleaños* (Birthday Cake)

This is a popular cake often made for birthdays in Honduras. It is commonly served with a meringue icing.

Yield: 8 to 10 servings

4¼ cups flour, plus extra for sprinkling on cake pan

4 teaspoons baking powder

¼ teaspoon salt

1½ cups butter, plus extra for greasing cake pan

2 cups sugar

4 eggs

4 yolks (set the whites aside for meringue icing, recipe follows)

1 teaspoon vanilla extract

½ teaspoon almond extract (optional)

1 cup milk

Equipment: 12-inch round cake pan, mixing bowls, **sifter**, mixer, rubber spatula, oven mitts, wire rack, saucepan, **candy thermometer**

Preheat oven at 350°F.

1. Butter and flour cake pan. Set aside.

2. In a bowl, combine flour, baking powder, and salt. Sift and set aside.

3. In another mixing bowl, place butter and sugar, and beat at medium speed until light-colored and fluffy. Add eggs and egg yolks, one at a time, beating well after each addition. Mix in the vanilla extract and almond extract (if using). Reduce speed to low. Mix in flour, followed by milk, mixing only until mixture is homogeneous.

4. Transfer to prepared baking pan. Bake in preheated oven for 45 to 50 minutes, or until golden and tests done. A wooden skewer or toothpick inserted in the center should come out clean. Remove cake from oven. Let cool in pan for 10 minutes, then unmold and allow to cool completely on a wire rack. Split cake into two or three even layers, and frost with meringue icing.

⚶ *Merengue* (Meringue Icing)

This is the usual icing for covering the birthday cake. It comes out a glossy white. A few drops of food coloring can be added, if desired. If different colors are desired, divide the meringue into several bowls, and dye each bowl individually.

Yield: enough to ice 1 12-inch-diameter cake

¼ teaspoon cream of tartar

4 **egg whites** (set aside from cake recipe)

2 tablespoons icing sugar

2 cups sugar

½ cup water

¼ teaspoon salt

1 teaspoon vanilla extract

½ teaspoon almond extract (optional)

food coloring (optional)

Equipment: Large bowl, mixer, small saucepan, **candy thermometer** (optional), oven mitts, metal or rubber spatula

1. In mixing bowl, place cream of tartar and egg whites, and beat with mixer at high speed until foamy. Add the icing sugar, and continue to beat until soft peaks form. Turn off mixer.

2. In a saucepan, combine sugar, water, and salt, and cook over medium heat, stirring until sugar dissolves. Bring to a boil, and cook without stirring for 2 minutes, or until it registers at 236°F on a candy thermometer.

Note: Next step involves pouring hot sugar syrup. Adult supervision is required.

3. Turn on mixer at low speed, then pour hot syrup in a fine stream over the egg whites, while continuing to beat. Once all the syrup has been poured, increase mixer speed to high, and beat until stiff peaks form. Stir in vanilla and almond extract (if using), and food coloring (if using).

Use to frost between the layers and top and sides of tarta de cumpleaños.

Mexico

About one-fifth the size of the United States, Mexico is bordered on the south by Belize and Guatemala and on the north by the United States. The wealthy Aztec empire, which was conquered by the Spanish in the 16th century, was just the latest in a series of empires that included the Mayans and Toltecs. Under Spanish control, Mexico expanded beyond its current boundaries and controlled most of the Southwestern United States. Some of the oldest settlements in the United States were founded in the 16th century by Spaniards. Mexico won its independence in 1821 after a long struggle with Spain.

Mexico is a country of extreme contrasts, from deserts to jungles, and from modern skyscrapers in Mexico City to remote Indian villages in the mountain regions. The vast majority of Mexicans are *mestizo*, a mixture of Spanish and Indian people. But whether they live in the guarded, walled mansions of the wealthy, the tin-roofed hovels of the city slums, or the one-room, thatched adobe shacks of small subsistence farmers, Mexicans have one thing in common, their religion. The Roman Catholic Church dominates every facet of life, and life-cycle events are celebrated in accordance with its teachings. (See Protestant and Catholic Life-Cycle Rituals, page lxxiii.)

Besides Church-prescribed life-cycle events, Mexicans celebrate the *Quinceañera*, an important celebration for girls when they reach 15 years of age. When the family can afford it, a big party is held with dancing, cake, and ice cream or an elaborate dinner, as well as lots of presents for the birthday girl.

Catholic weddings take place in church. If the couple can afford it, they have a lengthy nuptial Mass. The bride wears a white gown with a veil, and the groom dons a tuxedo. Catholic weddings in Mexico are full of special rituals, such as the *lazo*, a huge rosary that is placed around the shoulders of the bride and groom as they are kneeling at the altar while the priest prays over them. They are also presented symbolic gifts during the ceremony—coins (silver or gold), a Bible, and a rosary. These are handed to the couple by *padrinos* (sponsors), who are usually two special people (not godparents) the couple have chosen. The coins symbolize prosperity. The Bible and rosary signify keeping the Catholic faith in their home.

When a child is 40 days old, he or she may be presented to God and to the church in a celebration called *Las Presentaciones*. Traditionally, girls were presented at the age of three, but nowadays, girl babies may also be presented at 40 days. The celebration is intended to ask God to protect the child and to give thanks for a safe childbirth (especially in developing countries where infants' and delivering mothers' mortality rates are high). This is an established Mexican tradition that has also spread to South American countries. This Catholic tradition originates from the presentation of the baby Jesus, at the age of three, at the Temple and of Mary, his mother. This is a separate tradition from baptism. During Sunday mass at the church, the officiating priest calls the names of the children to be presented. Those who are 40 days old are carried by their godparents (*padrinos*), and those who are three years old are led by the hand, accompanied by their parents and godparents to the front of the church and presented to the congregation. The ritual begins with marking the child with the sign of the cross, followed by anointment with the oil of catechumens, and, finally, the consecration of the child to the Virgin Mary. This ritual is also a prelude to baptism. Nowadays, most families choose to celebrate the baptism of their child without the introductory presentation.

The child is dressed in festive clothes—for a girl of three, usually a fancy gown, and for a boy, a formal suit. Following the presentation mass at the church, there is usually a feast with family and friends. The child is given presents ranging from rosaries to jewelry, clothes, and money.

☽ *Mole de Guajolote* (Turkey in Mole Sauce)

Mole (pronounced **mo'**-lay) is the specialty of the town of Puebla, renowned in Mexico for its unique cuisine that merges the best of indigenous Mexican cooking with Spanish and French and other foreign elements. *Mole* is the supreme celebration dish in Puebla and its most famous dish, whose fame has spread even beyond the borders of Mexico. *Mole*'s complex flavor derives from several kinds of chilis, not all fiery hot, diverse herbs and spices, and long, patient preparation and cooking. It is *the* dish for all important occasions and family events, such as the presentation at the church (*las presentaciones*), first communion, baptism, and a wedding.

At a first communion for a girl in Puebla, chicken *mole*, rather than turkey, was served, including other Puebla specialties, such as *patitas de cerdo a la vinegreta* (vinegar-marinated pork legs), *arroz con tomate y verdura* (rice with tomatoes and vegetables), *frijoles refritos* (refried beans), or *chicharron en salsa verde* (pork crackling with green sauce). For adults, the drinks served were locally brewed beer, rum, and mineral water. For children, the drinks were natural fruit juices.

There is no one definitive way of making mole—every cook prepares mole sauce according to personal taste. The long preparation involves frying and grinding the herbs and spices separately and melding them all together to simmer into a rich, thick sauce, redolent with spices. Serve this with white rice and for drinks, *agua de jamaica* (a drink made of the dried flowers of *Hibiscus sabdariffa*, the same flowers in hibiscus tea) or some other natural fruit juice. Drinking this with a cola drink is not advised, as the flavors of the spices and herbs in the sauce would clash with the cola flavor.

Yield: 8 to 10 servings

1 8-pound turkey, or 2 4-pound chickens, cut into serving pieces

2 *chipotle* chilis (these and the other chilis are available in Latin American food shops or online)

6 *mulatto* chilis

6 *ancho* chilis

4 *pasilla* chilis

about 1½ cups lard, or ½ cup lard and 1 cup vegetable oil

1 teaspoon aniseed

4 tablespoons **sesame seeds**

½ teaspoon whole cloves

4 black peppercorns

1 stick cinnamon, crushed into pieces

1 teaspoon whole **coriander**

1 teaspoon thyme

1 teaspoon marjoram

3 bay leaves

½ cup **blanched** almonds

½ cup raw peanuts

¼ cup pumpkin seeds (*pepitas*)

¼ cup raisins

2 large onions, about 2 cups, finely chopped

1 head garlic, peeled and finely chopped

3 *tomatillos*, dehusked, washed, chopped (available at Latin American food shops)

2 large tomatoes, chopped

⅓ cup **cilantro**

2 slices bread or corn tortillas

2 ounces unsweetened chocolate

stock from cooking the turkey

salt to taste

Equipment: Large saucepan with cover, large **heavy-bottomed** saucepan with cover or Dutch oven, large frying pan or skillet, medium heavy-bottomed frying pan or cast-iron skillet, fine sieve or strainer, spice grinder or food processor or **blender**, large casserole for serving, oven mitts

1. Prepare turkey: In large saucepan with cover, place turkey pieces with salted water to cover. Bring to a boil over medium heat, skim off all froth; lower heat to let turkey simmer for 1 hour, or until tender. Drain, but reserve stock for later use. Let pieces air-dry, or wipe dry with paper towels.

2. In large frying pan or skillet, heat 1 cup of lard over medium heat, and fry turkey pieces in batches until golden brown on all sides. If preferred, debone at this time, taking care to leave neat pieces. Place fried turkey in a casserole that can be brought to the table. Set aside.

   CAUTION: Use care when handling peppers. Do not touch your eyes while handling peppers. If you accidentally touch your eyes, rinse them under cold running water at once.

3. Prepare spice mixture. Wash the chilis, remove stems, and set seeds aside. Tear the chilis into pieces, and set aside.

4. In heavy-bottomed medium frying pan or cast-iron skillet over low heat, dry-toast sesame seeds until aromatic. Be careful not to burn them. Set aside 2 tablespoons for garnish.

5. In the same frying pan over low heat, add reserved chili seeds, aniseed, peppercorns, cloves, cinnamon pieces, and coriander seeds, and dry-toast until slightly browned and aromatic, about 2 to 3 minutes.

6. Place 2 teaspoons of the toasted sesame seeds and remaining toasted spices, thyme, marjoram, and bay leaves into a spice grinder or food processor. Grind until finely pulverized. Pass ground spices through a fine sieve, and discard any remaining large pieces. Place ground spices into a large bowl.

7. Prepare chili purée: In the same frying pan or skillet used previously, heat 3 tablespoons of lard over medium heat. Fry the chili pieces separately, each lot for a few seconds, until slightly darkened. Do not allow them to burn. Place chilis in a bowl, and cover with hot water. Let the chilis soak for about ½ hour.

8. Purée ⅓ of the chilis, ½ cup of their soaking liquid, and ½ cup stock in a blender or food processor. Pass purée through a fine sieve, pressing to get as much purée as possible; discard larger, unpuréed pieces. Set chili purée aside.

9. Return skillet to stove over low heat, add 3 tablespoons lard, and fry separately the almonds, peanuts, pumpkin seeds, and raisins until golden, a minute or less for each. Keep a watchful eye so that the raisins and nuts do not scorch. Add toasted nuts and raisins to the spice bowl.

10. In the same skillet, add a tablespoon of lard if needed, and fry the bread or tortillas until golden. Break into small pieces, and add to the spice bowl.

11. In the same skillet, over medium heat, add 3 tablespoons lard. Stir-fry the onions and garlic until brown and aromatic. Add onions and garlic to the spice bowl.

12. In the same skillet, heat 2 tablespoons lard over medium heat. Add the remaining ⅔ of the chili purée, tomatoes, and *tomatillos*, and cook for about 10 to 15 minutes, or until completely softened. Add the chili purée, tomatoes, and *tomatillos* to the spice bowl.

13. Transfer the contents of the spice bowl to a blender or food processor. Add the cilantro. **Blend** or process to a purée. Pass through a fine sieve, and discard the larger pieces.

14. In a heavy-bottomed saucepan or Dutch oven over medium high heat, heat 3 tablespoons lard, and add the reserved chili purée. Cook, stirring constantly, until thickened, about 10 to 15 minutes.

15. Add the spice mixture, bring to a boil, then reduce heat to let the whole simmer for about 30 minutes, stirring frequently to avoid the mixture sticking to the pan. Stir in the chocolate, then 4 cups of stock. Allow to simmer for 1 hour, or until mole has thickened to the consistency of heavy cream. Season with salt.

16. Pour the mole over the reserved fried turkey in the casserole. Allow to cook, covered, over low heat, until the turkey is heated through and the sauce has thickened further. Stir from time to time to make sure the sauce is not sticking to the pan. Taste and adjust the salt to your taste.

To serve, sprinkle with reserved sesame seeds.

Champurrado is a traditional drink prepared for new mothers to enhance their milk supply and to boost their energy after giving birth. It is also most popularly made during the Christmas season (*Las Posadas*) and the Day of the Dead (*Dia de los Muertos*). *Champurrado* is also drunk for breakfast or as an afternoon snack during the cold season and eaten with *churros* (rod-shaped fritters).

🐚 *Champurrado* (Hot Chocolate Drink)

Champurrado is a hot chocolate drink, thickened with *masa harina* (the alkaline-treated dried corn flour used to make corn tortillas) and flavored with cinnamon and occasionally anise, nutmeg, orange zest, or vanilla. Mexican chocolate is usually flavored with cinnamon and sugar and is sold as disks or bars. A substitute is unsweetened (dark) chocolate. *Piloncillo*, also called *panela,* is unrefined cane sugar; its color ranges from pale to dark brown. *Masa harina* is not the same as cornmeal; if it is not available, grind up corn tortillas in a food processor until finely powdered as a substitute.

Yield: 4 to 6 servings

4 cups milk

2 sticks cinnamon

4 ounces Mexican chocolate (disks or bars)

3 ounces unrefined brown sugar (*piloncillo* or *panela*), or to taste

½ cup *masa harina* or 1 cup fresh *masa* dough (both available at Hispanic food shops)

2 cups water

grated **zest** of 1 orange or 1 teaspoon vanilla or 1 teaspoon freshly grated nutmeg, or 1 star anise (optional)

Equipment: Medium saucepan, mixing bowl, metal whisk, oven mitts

1. In medium saucepan over low heat, warm milk with cinnamon, chocolate, and sugar until tiny bubbles appear. Turn off heat, cover pan, and allow flavors to infuse the milk for about 30 minutes.

2. In a bowl, place the *masa harina,* and, little by little add water, whisking continuously to avoid creating lumps. Continue adding water until the *masa harina* is completely moistened and forms a lump-free paste. Whisk in the rest of the water for a smooth slurry.

3. Return saucepan with milk and chocolate mixture to the stove at low heat. Gradually whisk in the *masa harina* slurry to thoroughly combine with the milk and chocolate mixture. Let simmer for 10 to 15 minutes, until *masa* is cooked and the *champurrado*'s consistency is like gravy. Adjust consistency to your preference by adding more milk or water. Taste, and add more sugar to taste, if needed.

4. Just before serving, sprinkle grated orange zest, or stir in vanilla, or freshly grated nutmeg, or a star anise, if desired.

Serve in cups or, as is traditional in Mexico, in glazed thick-walled stoneware mugs. Be careful to drink champurrado *slowly, as the* masa harina *keeps the heat, and the drink may be scaldingly hot right after being poured.*

Food plays an important role in life-cycle celebrations, and this cake is served on all special occasions—engagement parties, weddings, baptisms, first communions, and birthdays.

♪ *Torta del Cielo* (Heavenly Cake)

8 ounces almonds, **blanched**	10 **eggs, separated**
1¼ cups sugar, divided	¼ teaspoon salt
½ cup cake flour	1 teaspoon vanilla extract
1 teaspoon baking powder	For **garnish**: confectioners' sugar (optional)

Equipment: Pencil, scissors, parchment paper, 10-inch springform pan, food processor or **blender**, rubber spatula, 2 medium bowls, flour **sifter**, mixing spoon, large mixing bowl, electric mixer or egg beater, oven mitts, toothpick, wire cake rack, serving platter

1. Prepare pan: Using pencil and scissors, cut parchment paper to fit bottom of 10-inch springform pan. Oil pan bottom, not the sides, then set paper in place. and lightly oil the top surface of the paper.

Preheat oven to 325°F.

2. Finely grind almonds with ¼ cup sugar in food processor or blender. Transfer to medium bowl. **Sift** cake flour and baking powder into nut mixture, and stir thoroughly with mixing spoon.

Note: *While processing, turn machine off once or twice and scrape down sides of container with rubber spatula.*

3. In large mixing bowl, using electric mixer or egg beater, beat egg whites with salt until mixture forms stiff peaks.

4. Using electric mixer or egg beater, beat egg yolks in second medium bowl until **frothy**. Add vanilla and remaining 1 cup sugar a little at a time, and beat for 2 to 3 minutes, or until

mixture becomes thickened and lemon-colored and forms a ribbon when beaters are lifted from the bowl. Using rubber spatula, **fold** nut mixture into egg yolk mixture, then fold in whites. Pour into prepared springform pan, and smooth top.

5. Bake in oven for 50 to 60 minutes, or until toothpick inserted in center comes out clean. Place on wire rack to cool for 1 to 2 hours. Release sides of pan, flip cake onto wire rack, remove pan bottom, and peel off paper.

To serve, transfer cake to serving platter, and dust top with confectioners' sugar. The cake can also be frosted with butter icing (recipe page 324) or whipped cream.

Happy occasions, such as baptisms and christenings, call for plenty of sweets. *Yemitas* are perfect for the sweet table because they are made with eggs, the Mexican symbol for life.

Yemitas (Egg Yolk Candies)

Yield: 25 to 30 pieces

1 quart heavy cream	12 **egg yolks**
¼ teaspoon baking soda	1½ teaspoons **ground** cinnamon
2½ cups sugar	For **garnish:** 1 cup **cinnamon sugar**

Equipment: Large **heavy-bottomed** saucepan, wooden mixing spoon, medium mixing bowl, whisk, **candy thermometer** (optional), baking sheet, 25 to 30 candy-size or mini cupcake paper cups

1. Pour heavy cream into large heavy-bottomed saucepan and add baking soda. Stirring constantly, bring to boil over medium-high heat. Remove from heat to prevent boiling over, 3 to 5 minutes. When foam subsides, return to heat, bring back to boil, and then quickly remove from heat. Cool to warm, add sugar, and stirring constantly, return to medium heat, and cook until mixture thickens, 20 to 30 minutes.

   Note: *Mixture is sufficiently thickened if you can see the bottom of pan when mixture is separated with a spoon. Cool to room temperature.*

2. Put egg yolks in medium mixing bowl, and use whisk to beat in ground cinnamon. Beat yolk mixture into cooled cream mixture. Return to medium heat, and stir constantly until mixture reaches hard ball stage (see **sugar syrup** in Glossary of Food Terms), or 250° to 266°F on candy thermometer. Remove from heat, and cool to warm.

3. Using a wooden mixing spoon, beat mixture until it reaches a very thick, fudge-like consistency, 10 to 15 minutes. Using your hands, shape into marble-size balls. Put cinnamon sugar in small shallow bowl. Roll balls in cinnamon sugar to coat well. Place side by side on baking sheet until set.

To serve, put each ball in a candy-size or mini cupcake paper cup.

Little tacos are a favorite snack at family gatherings or as an **appetizer** at other celebrations.

♪ *Taquitos* (Little Tacos)

CAUTION: HOT OIL IS USED.

Yield: serves 10 to 12

48 small (3-inch-diameter) tortillas (available at Latin American food stores and most supermarkets)

2 to 3 cups vegetable oil

2 cups lettuce, shredded, for serving

12 ounces canned refried beans, for serving

1 pound lean pork, beef brisket, or chicken, cooked and shredded, for serving

1 pound mozzarella or Monterey Jack cheese, shredded, for serving

Equipment: Paper towels, baking sheet, large **heavy-bottomed** skillet or **Dutch oven**, fryer **thermometer** or wooden spoon, metal tongs, large ovenproof serving platter, oven mitts

1. Prepare to skillet-fry: *Caution: Adult supervision required.* Place several layers of paper towels on baking sheet. In heavy-bottomed skillet or Dutch oven, heat oil to 375°F on fryer thermometer, or until small bubbles appear around a wooden spoon handle when it is dipped into the oil. Fry tacos in small batches, 2 or 3 at a time, until golden and crisp, 1 to 2 minutes. Remove with metal tongs, and drain on paper towel–covered baking sheet.

   Preheat broiler.

2. Prepare to assemble: Place tacos side by side on large ovenproof serving platter. Sprinkle each with a little shredded lettuce. Add about 1 teaspoon fried beans, cover with shredded meat or chicken, and top with 1 or 2 teaspoons shredded cheese. Place under broiler for 1 to 2 minutes to melt cheese.

Serve immediately, so that tacos are nice and hot.

Nicaragua

Nicaragua is the largest Central American country, but it is also the most sparsely populated. Its eastern coast faces the Caribbean Sea, and its western coast faces the North Pacific Ocean. Nicaragua lies between Honduras to the north and Costa Rica to the south. In area, Nicaragua is slightly larger than Pennsylvania. Its climate is tropical, with cooler areas in the central interior highlands. There are many active volcanoes along the Pacific coastal plain. The geography of the Pacific side of the country is dominated by two large lakes, Nicaragua and Managua. The name "Nicaragua" comes from *Nicarao*, the largest indigenous settlement when the Spanish colonists arrived, and *agua* from the two lakes. First settled by the Spanish in 1522, Nicaragua finally gained its independence in 1838. Nicaragua is the poorest country in Central America, notwithstanding its exports of manufactured textiles, coffee, bananas, beef, and gold.

The majority (about 69 percent) of people living in Nicaragua are *mestizos* (mixed Spanish and Indian). The remaining population comprises mostly pure Spaniards (17 percent), blacks (9 percent), and indigenous Indians (5 percent), whose ancestors lived in the area before the Spaniards arrived 400 years ago. Just over 70 percent of Nicaraguans are Catholic, and about 15 percent are Protestant. Of the Protestant denominations, Moravians comprise 2 percent, and Episcopalians comprise less than 1 percent. In addition, there are minorities of Jehovah's Witnesses, Jews, Muslims, The Church of Jesus Christ of Latter-Day Saints (Mormons), the Church of Scientology, Baha'i, and Mennonite adherents.

The indigenous Sumu and Miskito ethnic groups live along the Caribbean Coast of Nicaragua, and, as a result of evangelical missions in the 19th century by Moravian Protestants and Catholics, they have become Protestant and Catholic adherents. In the Sumu native religion, natural forces such as the sun, moon, and wind are worshipped. The Sumu sun god was called Mapapak. Additionally, traditional Sumu belief involved spirits called *walasa*, *nawah*, and *diwalah*, who were capable of helping or harming people, to the point of causing death. Despite their conversion to Christianity, Sumu indigenous beliefs have been preserved by shamans (*sukia*), who function as spiritual advisers, priests, exorcists, and healers. The Miskito indigenous religion centered on moon worship. The Miskito additionally believed in omens and evil spirits (*lasas*). Although the Sumu and Miskito celebrate life-cycle events, such as birth, marriage, and death, with Christian ceremonies, courtship customs follow traditional ways: The prospective groom offers gifts, which include food and firewood, to his intended bride's family. As a result of isolation and lack of resources for a continuous Christian pastoral presence, in actual practice, Miskito Christians have mixed Catholic and Moravian Protestant rituals, as well as indigenous Miskito concepts of divine spirits. Miskito funeral traditions include an indigenous memorial ceremony on the first year after death, called "*Sikro*."

Among the Catholics, religious holidays and life-cycle celebrations are observed according to Church doctrine. (See Protestant and Catholic Life-Cycle Rituals, page lxxiii.) Birthdays or name days, baptisms, communions, weddings, and funerals are celebrated with a feast, complete with drinking, especially the popular celebration drink *pinollo*, made from cocoa beans.

Sopa de Chayote (Chayote Soup)

Many celebration feasts begin with soup, such as *sopa de chayote*. When even a little meat or chicken is added to a dish, it becomes a special festive treat.

Yield: serves 6

2 large **chayotes**, peeled and sliced (available at all Latin-American food stores and many supermarkets)

water, as needed

salt and pepper to taste

2 tablespoons butter or margarine	1 tablespoon all-purpose flour
1 onion, **finely chopped**	4 cups chicken broth
1 clove garlic, finely chopped	For serving: 1 cup cooked and shredded chicken breast

Equipment: Large saucepan, slotted spoon, food processor, rubber spatula, mixing spoon, medium saucepan with cover, measuring cup, ladle, individual soup bowls

1. Put chayotes in large saucepan, and cover generously with water. Add salt to taste, and bring to boil over medium-high heat. Reduce heat to **simmer**, cover, and cook until tender, 15 to 20 minutes.

2. When tender, using slotted spoon, transfer chayotes to food processor. Measure 2 cups cooking liquid in measuring cup, add to chayote, and process until smooth. Discard any remaining cooking liquid.

Note: While processing, turn machine off once or twice, and scrape down sides of container with rubber spatula.

3. Melt butter or margarine in medium saucepan over medium-high heat. Add onion and garlic, stir, and **sauté** until onion is soft, 3 to 5 minutes. Reduce heat to medium, stir in flour, and cook, stirring constantly, for 1 minute. Stir in chicken broth until mixture is smooth.

4. Stir processed chayote mixture into chicken broth. Add salt and pepper to taste. Add chicken, stir, cover, and cook until heated through, 5 to 7 minutes.

To serve, ladle into individual soup bowls. Eat as the first course for a confirmation party or wedding reception.

Most life-cycle meals include *nacatamales*, plate-size tamales, that are considered the national dish of Nicaragua. In Nicaragua, *nacatamales* are wrapped in banana leaves that have been simmered in boiling water for about 10 minutes to soften. The banana leaves are placed on cooking parchment, wrapped tightly, and tied with string. This recipe uses foil for each package instead.

❦ *Nacatamales* (Nicaraguan Tamales)

Yield: serves 12

2 cups distilled white vinegar, divided	½ cup lime juice
3 tablespoons paprika	3 pounds **boned** pork shoulder or butt, cut into 1×2-inch chunks
1½ teaspoons dried oregano leaves	
3 cloves garlic, **finely chopped**	2½ cups long grain rice
1 teaspoon ground cumin	*masa* (recipe follows)
1 cup orange juice	

2½ pounds (about 6) potatoes, peeled and sliced crosswise into ¼-inch thick circles, each circle cut in half

12 canned hot yellow chili peppers, drained (available at all Latin American food stores and some supermarkets)

12 **pitted** prunes

72 (2 cups) small pimiento-stuffed, Spanish-style olives

¾ cup seedless raisins

salt and pepper to taste

3 cups fresh mint leaves, lightly packed, rinsed, and drained

2 large onions, **trimmed**, *each* sliced into 6 ¼-inch-thick circles

2 green bell peppers, trimmed, seeded, *each* sliced into 6 ¼-inch thick rings

2 large tomatoes, trimmed, *each* sliced into 6 ¼-inch thick circles

Equipment: Small bowl, mixing spoon, large resealable plastic bag, medium bowl, strainer, 12 pieces (12×18 inches each) aluminum foil, work surface, large saucepan with cover, heatproof plate, slotted metal spoon or metal tongs, plate

1. Prepare marinade: In small bowl, combine ½ cup vinegar, paprika, oregano, garlic, and cumin. Stir to mix well. Transfer paprika mixture to large resealable plastic bag, and add remaining 1½ cups vinegar, orange juice, and lime juice. Close bag and shake to mix well. Add meat chunks, close bag, and shake to coat meat with marinade. Refrigerate overnight. Turn bag several times to coat meat well.

2. Soak rice: Put rice in medium bowl, cover with water by 1 inch, and set aside to soak at least 8 hours or overnight. Drain in strainer.

3. Prepare *masa*.

4. Prepare to assemble: Put 1 piece foil on work surface. Spoon ¾ cup *masa* onto center of foil. Pat to flatten slightly. Poke 1 chili pepper, 1 prune, and 6 olives into the *masa*, and cover with ¼ cup rice. Top with 1 tablespoon raisins. Place 5 or 6 potato slices around edge of *masa*. Sprinkle with salt and pepper to taste.

5. Using slotted spoon or tongs, divide marinated pork into 12 equal portions. Set portions on baking sheet. Place one portion of meat on top of rice, and spoon 1 tablespoon marinade onto meat. Discard remaining marinade. Place 3 or 4 mint leaves on meat. Stack 1 slice *each* of onion, bell pepper, and tomato on top of each mint leaf.

6. Carefully enclose filling, fold foil edges together to seal in the ingredients, and make the tamale wrap waterproof. Repeat assembling remaining tamale wraps.

7. Stack tamale wraps in large saucepan. Put a heatproof plate on top to keep tamale wraps from floating. Fill pan with enough water to cover tamale wraps. Bring water to boil over medium-high heat, and cook for 45 minutes. Add more hot water, when necessary, to keep water covering tamale wraps. Reduce heat to **simmer**, cover pan, and cook for 1 hour more. Check water level frequently, adding more when necessary to keep the tamale wraps covered.

8. Remove tamale wraps with slotted metal spoon or metal tongs, and drain well.

To serve, place each nacatamal *on a plate, with the seam-side up. Guests get a packaged tamale wrap, which they open and eat while the contents are still warm.*

♪ *Masa* for Nacatamales

Yield: serves 12

1¾ pounds russet potatoes, peeled, quartered, boiled until tender, 15 to 90 minutes

1 cup vegetable oil

2 onions, **trimmed**, finely chopped

6 cloves garlic, **finely chopped**

4 cups corn *tortilla* flour (also called dehydrated *masa* flour) (available at Latin American food stores and most supermarkets)

2 cups beef broth or water

salt and pepper to taste

Equipment: Potato masher, large skillet, mixing spoon, food processor, medium bowl, rubber spatula, large bowl

1. Drain potatoes and mash, using potato masher.

2. Heat oil in large skillet over medium-high heat. Add onions and garlic, stir, and reduce heat to medium. Fry, stirring frequently, until onions are very brown, 20 to 30 minutes.

Note: While processing, turn machine off once or twice, and scrape down sides of container with rubber spatula.

3. Put mashed potatoes in food processor, add fried onion mixture, pan drippings, *tortilla* flour, and beef broth or water. Add salt and pepper to taste. Process until well mixed, 1 to 2 minutes. Transfer to medium bowl.

Use for nacatamales.

♪ *Torta de Chocolate para Cumpleaños* (Chocolate Birthday Cake)

This is a cake popularly made for birthdays, as its name implies.

Yield: 8 to 10 servings

3 cups flour

3 tablespoons cocoa powder

pinch salt

1½ teaspoons baking powder

¼ teaspoon baking soda

2 cups butter

1½ cups sugar

4 eggs

1 teaspoon vanilla extract

1¼ cups yogurt

Equipment: **Sifter**, large bowl, mixing bowl, mixing spoon, electric mixer, rubber spatula, 10-inch springform cake pan, wooden skewer or toothpick, wire rack, oven mitts

Preheat oven to 325°F. In large bowl.

1. Butter and flour springform cake pan, and set aside. Combine flour, baking powder, baking soda, cocoa powder, and salt. Sift and set aside.

2. In mixer bowl, place butter and sugar, and beat at medium speed until light-colored and creamy. Add eggs one at a time, beating well after each addition, until the mixture is smooth. Add vanilla and yogurt. Reduce speed to low, and add flour mixture. Mix batter only until homogeneous.

3. Using rubber spatula, transfer cake batter to prepared baking pan, and bake in preheated oven for 40 to 45 minutes, or until it tests done. A wooden skewer or toothpick inserted in the center of the cake should come out clean.

4. Remove from oven, and let cool in pan for 10 minutes. Release cake, and allow to cool completely on wire rack, covered with a clean, dry kitchen towel.

5. Split the cake into 2 equal layers, and spread with the celebrant's favorite filling or frosting.

If desired, the cake can be covered with marshmallow fondant (recipe follows) and decorated as desired.

Fondant de Nubes (Marshmallow Fondant)

Yield: enough to frost a 2-layer cake

8 ounces mini marshmallows

3 tablespoons water, or more as needed

4 cups icing sugar, **sifted**

¼ cup solid vegetable shortening for greasing

Equipment: Microwave-safe bowl, wooden spoon or rubber spatula, electric mixer with kneading hook, plastic wrap

1. Grease a microwave-safe bowl, and place the marshmallows and water in it.

   Microwave on medium-high for 30 seconds. Stir with a greased wooden spoon or greased spatula. Continue to microwave for another 30 seconds, or until melted.

2. Transfer the mixture into the greased bowl of a stand mixer fitted with a greased kneading hook. Add ¾ of the icing sugar, and knead it into the marshmallow mixture. Knead the mixture until smooth and no longer sticky. If the fondant seems too dry, add water, a teaspoon at a time. Continue kneading until the fondant is smooth and **elastic**, about 6 to 8 minutes.

3. With greased hands, remove the fondant from the mixer bowl, and shape into a ball. Grease the kneaded fondant on all sides, enclose in plastic wrap, and store in a resealable bag in the refrigerator overnight before using.

4. Sprinkle your work surface and rolling pin with icing sugar. If you wish to color the fondant, do so now, with a few drops in the middle of the flattened ball. Knead the color in until it is incorporated evenly, and roll out the fondant to ⅛ inch.

Use fondant to cover cakes, petit fours, cupcakes, or, when flavoring is added, as filling for handmade chocolate candies.

Panama

The southernmost country of Central America, Panama is the narrowest point between North and South America, which is why the isthmus was chosen for the Panama Canal that links the Pacific and Atlantic Oceans. Panama is bounded on the north by Costa Rica and on the south by Colombia. Panama has a tropical climate with a rugged, mountainous terrain. Its area is smaller than South Carolina.

After European contact, Panama became a center for shipments to Central and South America. When Colombia revolted against Spain, Panama joined the Greater Republic of Colombia, which included Venezuela, Colombia, and Ecuador, but unlike Venezuela and Ecuador, Panama was unable to break away from Colombia. After Colombia refused to grant a lease to the United States for the building of the canal, Panama broke from Colombia with the support of the United States.

Because of Panama's position as an isthmus between two continents, Panama has a diverse population. About 65 percent of Panamanians are *mestizos*, part Spanish and part indigenous Amerindian. Several indigenous Indian groups constitute over 12 percent of the population, including the Ngäbe (8 percent), Buglé (<1 percent) (these two are often lumped together incorrectly as Guaymí), Kuna (also Cuna, 2.4 percent), Embera (<1 percent), Wounaan, Naso Tjerdi (Teribe), and Bri Bri. Over 15 percent of the population includes many blacks and mulattos whose ancestors came from the West Indies to work on the Panama Canal, and about 7 percent are people of European (white) descent.

The Panamanian Constitution provides for freedom of religion. The majority of Panamanians (75 percent to 85 percent) adhere to the Roman Catholic Church and follow the life-cycle traditions of the Church. (See Protestant and Catholic Life-Cycle Rituals, page lxxiii.) The remaining 15 percent to 25 percent of Panamanians adhere to Protestantism and other religions, such as Baha'i, Judaism, Islam, Buddhism, Hinduism, and Rastafarianism. About 10 percent of the Ngäbe and Buglé are Baha'i adherents, and the Kuna practice their indigenous religion, Ibeorgun. The Ngäbe have their own native religion, Matamata. Other Christian denominations include The Church of Jesus Christ of Latter-Day Saints (Mormons), whose Panamanian members number around 40,000, Jehovah's Witnesses, Baptists, Episcopalians, Methodists, and Lutherans. The majority of Protestants are from the black communities, as well as expatriates.

Baptism (*bautismo*, also *bautizo*) for infants is an important Roman Catholic Christian ritual in Panama. Although among urban Panamanians, secularism is on the rise, nevertheless the majority still wish to have their children baptized. Baptism requires the child to have godparents (*padrinos*)—a *padrino* (godfather) and *madrina* (godmother)—and for parents, selecting the appropriate godparents for this relationship, called *compadrazgo*, is crucial. Godparents are chosen for their financial and social status, as well as moral standing. They must be well respected in the community and serve as role models for the child as he or she grows up. They may be called upon to help support the expenses toward the child's upbringing, clothes, or books, or education. If the parents pass away, the godparents are expected to support the child, even toward a university education. Even when the child is grown, the relationship (*compadrazgo*) that links the godchild's family and the godparents continues to play a role, in referrals for jobs, for instance. After baptism, a toast (*brindis*) is often shared with all the attending family and relatives. There is also the custom of throwing *bolo*, traditionally coins but these days chocolate coins, in the air for young guests to pick up. The *bolo* symbolizes prosperity, in the hope that the newly baptized child will not want for anything as he or she grows up. It is considered an honor to be asked to serve as a godparent and to refuse to do so is considered an insult.

Children's birthday parties in Panama are commonly held at school. They will often feature snacks, a birthday cake, occasionally a *piñata*, and bags of goodies, locally called "*canastitas.*" Every children's party, whether held at home or elsewhere, will have *canastitas* for every child guest to bring home. Most invitations will have suggestions for the kind of present for the child. "*Lluvia de sobres*" is a euphemism for money in envelopes. "*Talla* x" refers to the clothing size of the child ("x" being the desired size). It is rare for invitations to include toys as desired birthday presents. Games are a feature of birthday parties and are usually led by a hired entertainer. Parents are often asked to participate in the birthday games as well.

Los quince años (15 years) is an opulent celebration for girls on their 15th birthday. It is often an extravaganza, quite similar to a wedding, except there is no bridegroom, and most upper middle and elite classes in Panama hold it for their daughters. Some give their daughters a choice of a trip to Europe or a *quince años* party, and a number of families give their daughters both. The day itself begins with a mass in church, with blessings and special prayers by the priest for the girl's health and future life and success. Later that evening, either at home or at a rented venue in a hotel or restaurant, the party takes place. It begins with a dance by the celebrant's court comprising 14 pairs of the celebrant's female and male friends, all dressed in formal clothes—tuxedos for the boys and elegant ball gowns for the girls. This dance heralds the grand entrance of the *quinceañera* (the celebrant) with two escorts, her relatives or close friends. The celebrant is usually dressed in a white ball gown, almost like a bridal dress, except without a train and veil. Thereafter, a toast (*brindis*) is proposed, with speeches from her family and closest relatives and friends and presentations of presents, usually an item of jewelry, such as a diamond ring and her first high-heeled shoes from her parents. A sumptuous dinner follows, and dancing to a live band or DJ goes on until the early hours of the morning. The cutting of the cake, which is also akin to a wedding cake but with 14 figurines representing the celebrant's court, instead of a bride and groom, occurs the following day at the house of the celebrant, surrounded by her female friends. The presents are all opened and admired, with some being put away into a hope chest to be preserved for the celebrant's eventual wedding. The cost of holding such an extravaganza is exorbitant, and many families save up for years or even go into debt for the event.

A wake (*velorio*) is traditionally observed when a person dies. This usually takes place at home (or at a funeral home in urban areas), where the deceased is on display in a coffin, and mourners visit the home to pray. A *novena* (a nine-day cycle of prayers) takes place over the nine days following the death, as well as the first month after the death and the first year anniversary. In the countryside, professionals (most commonly women), called "*rezadoras*" (from *rezo*, meaning "prayer"), are usually requested or hired to perform the novena prayers. The cycle of prayers is believed to keep the soul of the departed from suffering and to ask for the forgiveness of his or her sins. For 40 days after death, in addition to the novena prayers, a lamp was kept burning in the home altar in memory of the dead. In urban areas, general religious faith and observance among Catholics are on the decline, and the nine-day cycle of prayers is not as meticulously performed for the dead as in earlier days.

Panama's indigenous communities have their own life-cycle celebrations based on indigenous rituals, not on Catholic or other Christian traditions, and these traditions have survived the European conquest. Most of the seven indigenous communities live in Eastern Panama, in particular the Darien region. The Kuna (also spelled Cuna), the second most numerous indigenous group with a population of over 65,000, are matrilineal, which means that the women own the land and the husband comes to live with the wife's family after a wedding. The Kuna celebrate a girl's coming into puberty with a three-day ritual called *inna-nega*. Depending upon the wealth of the family, several hundred people may attend. The three-day celebration can cost the family years of savings. The occasion is one of great importance to the Cuna since the girl is now of childbearing age. During the ceremony, she is given a permanent name, and her hair is cut. Following the ceremony, a feast is held for family and friends, which might include either *arroz con pollo* (see Costa Rican recipe page 527) or *pebellón caraqueño* (recipe follows) and side dishes of black beans (canned, cooked according to directions on can, available at all supermarkets); hard-cooked eggs, a symbol of fruitfulness, and plantains, such as *piononos* (see Cuban recipe page 245).

On the first two days of the *inna-nega* festival, the community's women prepare and serve food and drink, while the indigenous priests (*kantules*) occupy a ritual house and chant stories that detail the history of the Kuna community. On the third day, all the women join the men, and the celebrant is given her permanent, adult name, and her hair is cut. The women will all wear the same *mola* on their dresses or blouses, one for the front and a different one for the back. The *mola* is an artisanal textile art unique to the Kuna: it consists of meticulously appliquéd colorful fabric in abstract patterns on a black background. The *mola* is designed and made in secret, way before the *inna-nega* ceremony, and, as often happens, the design is much admired and thereafter copied by the rest of the community.

In the countryside, a boy will receive his own machete at the age of seven or eight, indicating that he is old enough to help gather food for the table or earn a livelihood to help his family. For the Ngäbe and Buglé indigenous groups, when a boy reaches the age of puberty, he participates in a coming of age ritual called *"guro."* Only males may participate in this ritual. A group of men take the young man into the jungle where he undergoes physical feats that challenge his endurance and resilience. Throughout the endurance testing, elders carry out ceremonial chanting.

Regardless of ethnic or religious background, a wedding celebration is a grand affair in Panama. It calls for *pebellón caraqueño* (recipe follows), a dish made with flank steak, a meat Latin Americans hold in high esteem for its fine flavor. The dish is especially popular for weddings because hard-cooked eggs, as a symbol of fertility, are added to it.

୬ *Pebellón Caraqueño* (Steak with Rice, Black Beans, and Plantains)

Yield: serves 6

1½ pounds flank steak, cut into 2 or 3 pieces

5 cups canned beef broth

1 onion, **finely chopped**

1 clove garlic, finely chopped

2 **tomatoes, peeled** and chopped

For serving:

4 cups canned black beans, drained

salt to taste

2 tablespoons olive oil

6 cups cooked rice (cooked according to directions on package), kept warm for serving

6 hard-cooked eggs, peeled and quartered

3 **plantains** or regular bananas, fried (recipe follows)

Equipment: Large saucepan with cover, fork, mixing spoon, **colander**, food storage container with cover, large mixing bowl, large skillet, large platter

1. Put meat in large saucepan, add beef broth, and bring to boil over medium-high heat. Reduce heat to **simmer**, cover, and cook 1½ to 2 hours, until fork tender. Allow meat to cool in the broth. Drain broth in colander over food storage container, cover, and refrigerate for another use. Shred the meat with your fingers. In large mixing bowl, combine the meat with onion, garlic, and tomatoes. Add salt to taste.

2. Heat olive oil in skillet over medium-high heat. Add shredded meat mixture, stir, and **sauté** until onion is cooked and mixture is very dry, 7 to 12 minutes.

3. Fry plantains or bananas.

To serve, put rice in center of large platter, and heap the meat mixture on top. Arrange quartered hard-cooked eggs on top of meat. Surround the rice with black beans, and decorate the edge of the platter with fried plantains or bananas.

♀ Fried Plantains or Bananas

Yield: serves 4 to 6

3 **plantains** or regular bananas   4 tablespoons vegetable oil

Equipment: Paring knife, large skillet, slotted spoon

1. Peel plantains, and cut in half lengthwise, then cut crosswise into thirds. If using bananas, peel and cut into thirds.

2. Heat oil in large skillet over medium-high heat, and fry plantains or bananas until golden brown on both sides, 3 to 5 minutes.

Use for pebellón caraqueño *(recipe precedes).*

♀ *Arroz con Pollo Estilo Panameño* (Panamanian-style Rice and Chicken)

Arroz con pollo is a dish that is encountered throughout all of Latin America. The name may be the same, but each country's version of *arroz con pollo* is different. Each country has its own unique way of preparing this dish, adding its own distinctive variations. Panamanian-style *arroz con pollo* is distinguished by the addition of green olives, capers, and green peas. In Panama, *arroz con pollo* is a celebratory dish, often made for birthdays and other special occasions, family events, and holidays.

Yield: 8 servings

3 pounds chicken breast or backs, including skin and bone

5 tablespoons achiote seeds (available at Latin American food shops or online)

2 onions, peeled and chopped

2 stalks celery, chopped

5 culantro leaves (also called *recao*, *Eringium foetidum*; if culantro is not available, substitute 1 cup **cilantro**)

2 red sweet peppers, sliced into fine strips

5 cups water

4 tablespoons oil

4 cloves garlic, minced

4 bay leaves

½ cup tomato paste or 1 cup tomato sauce

4 cups rice, washed and drained

2 cups frozen green peas

1 small jar capers

1 small jar green **pitted** olives

1 jar pickled red peppers (*morrones*)

salt and pepper to taste

Equipment: Large stockpot, large **heavy-bottomed** saucepan or Dutch oven, sieve, oven mitts

1. In large stockpot, put chicken breasts, achiote seeds, half of the onions, celery, culantro, and red peppers. Add water. Cook over medium-high heat until it comes to a boil. Skim all froth and scum that rise. Reduce heat and simmer for 20 to 25 minutes, until chicken is no longer pink.

2. Remove skin and bones from chicken, and slice meat into cubes. Salt and pepper chicken cubes on all sides, and set aside. Pass chicken stock through a sieve, and discard the vegetables used to flavor the stock, pressing down well to extract as much flavor as possible. Set stock aside.

3. In a heavy-bottomed saucepan or Dutch oven over medium heat, warm oil and fry the remaining chopped onions and garlic, stirring frequently until onions and garlic are aromatic. Stir in chicken and bay leaves, and allow to cook for 5 to 7 minutes. Stir in rice and tomato paste.

4. Pour over the reserved chicken broth, and add water, if needed, so that the broth covers the chicken and rice by1 inch. Stir to distribute tomato paste into broth. Cover pan, turn up heat to high, and let it come to a boil; taste, and add salt if necessary.

5. Turn down heat to medium-low, add olives, capers, and pickled sweet peppers on top. Do not stir. Let cook until liquid is totally absorbed.

6. Turn off heat, cover, and let the *arroz con pollo* stand for 10 to 15 minutes.

Just before serving, mix in the olives, capers, and pickled red peppers, and mound on a large serving plate or individual plates.

SOUTH AMERICA

South America includes the countries of Argentina, Bolivia, Brazil, Chile, Colombia, Ecuador, French Guiana, Guyana, Paraguay, Peru, Suriname, Uruguay, and Venezuela.

Argentina

Situated in the southern half of Latin America, Argentina is bordered by Chile on the west, Bolivia and Paraguay on the north, and Uruguay and Brazil on the east, although the Atlantic coastline forms most of the eastern border. Argentina is the second largest country in Latin America in both population and area (Brazil is first). Its area is just slightly less than a third of that of the United States.

Argentina was colonized by Spain in the 16th century and remained under Spanish control until 1810, when Argentina declared its independence after Spain was defeated by Napoleon. Argentina's population is comprised predominantly of Europeans or mixed Europeans (*mestizos,* people of mixed Indian and European origins), with just 2.4 percent of Amerindian origin and 0.4 percent of African origin. Besides the Spanish, the Italians have had a profound influence on the country, and people of Italian descent make up a fairly large portion of the population.

More than 90 percent of the population are nominally Roman Catholic, though less than 20 percent profess to be active observants. By law, the president and vice president of the country must be Roman Catholic, but the constitution guarantees religious freedom for all. Less than 10 percent are Protestant adherents, and just over 2 percent belong to The Church of Jesus Christ of Latter-Day Saints (Mormons) and Jehovah's Witnesses.

Argentina has the largest Muslim community (mostly due to immigration from Lebanon and Syria), as well as the largest mosque, in Latin America, numbering around 400,000 to half a million adherents, about 1 percent to 2 percent of the total population. (Former President Carlos Menem, elected in 1989, was born of Syrian Muslim parents but converted to Catholicism to qualify for the presidency. His legacy to Argentine Muslims is the construction of the King Fahd Islamic Culture Center, the largest mosque in Latin America.) There is also a Jewish community in Argentina, with between 180,000 to 230,000 members. It is the largest Jewish community in Latin America. There are also Greek, Russian, and Syrian Orthodox communities. Additionally, there is a strong Mennonite presence. The first Mennonites began coming to Argentina in 1917, and in 1943 North American Mennonite missionaries began work with indigenous Indians. The biggest waves of Mennonite immigration occurred from 1986 to 2014. Mennonites from Mexico (who had migrated from Canada and the United States) established four new colonies: the first, La Nueva Esperanza, in 1986 near Guatraché, La Pampa province, the second colony in Pampa de los Guanacos, Santiago del Estero province, founded in 1995, the third, Colonia del Norte, founded in 2004 near the city of Santiago del Estero, and the fourth, founded in 2014 near Villa Mercedes, San Luis Province.

There are 35 different groups of indigenous Amerindians in Argentina, whose population totals around 600,000. The three largest groups are the Mapuche (population at just over 200,000), Toba (population just over 125,000), and Guarani (population around 105,000). The Northwest region of Argentina has the highest percentage of Catholics. Catholic observance there shows many syncretistic influences, due to the high percentage of indigenous communities. In the northwestern provinces of Salta and Jujuy, nominally Catholic indigenous Colla also practice traditional forms of worship. Religious festivals in the Northwest often show a combination of indigenous Andean ceremonies with Catholic icons.

Most Catholic Porteños (the inhabitants of Buenos Aires) rarely go to church; when they do, it is on major feast days such as Christmas, Easter, or a particular saint's day. Nevertheless, for most Argentinians, baptism, communion, and weddings are celebrated according to the Roman Catholic Church. (See Protestant and Catholic Life-Cycle Rituals, page lxxiii.) Babies are baptized at a few weeks old, and first communion is celebrated around the ages of seven or eight. Weddings are generally held in a church.

As is the custom in many Catholic nations, a funeral feast is held after the burial. Depending upon the region and wealth of the bereaved family, the funeral feast almost always includes meat, usually beef. Among the people living in the Pampas (the cattle-raising region of Argentina), several cattle are slaughtered for the occasion and cooked over an open fire, an *asado* (barbecue, recipe follows). Part of the ritual to honor the departed soul involves the beverage *mate*. Before the feasting begins, mourners take a turn to sip *maté* through a *bombilla* (metal straw). Everyone uses the same *bombilla*, and it is an insult to the bereaved family if anyone refuses.

For family gatherings and other celebratory occasions such as birthdays, baptisms, and first communions, Argentinians usually make an *asado*. An *asado* is an extravaganza of grilling an assortment of beef meat and meat products, as well as internal organs. These include short ribs, flank and skirt steaks, ribeye steaks, blood sausages and coiled sausages, offal such as kidneys and intestines. The offerings also include provolone cheese and vegetables, also for cooking on the grill. A designated grill chef for the day orchestrates the cooking masterfully, from making the fire (itself a true test of skill), to ensuring that the meat and other items are cooked just right. Other people are designated to make the salad, usually a simple one of tomatoes, onions, and lettuce, as well as sauces such as *chimichurri* or *salsa criolla*.

⚘ *Asado* (Argentinean Mixed Grill)

The amount of meat and meat products is usually calculated based on just over a pound per person. The selection usually includes:

1 rack of beef short ribs

thin flank steak (*matambre*)

thick flank steak (*vacío*)

skirt steak (*entraña*)

chorizo sausages

blood sausages (*morcillas*)

coiled sausages

kidneys (*riñones*), washed and marinated in vinegar, then rinsed well

other offal (*achuras*), such as sweetbreads or organs from the thymus gland and pancreas (*molleja*), small intestines (*chinchulines*, or *chinchu* for short), and the large intestines (*tripa gorda*), washed and marinated in vinegar, then rinsed well

provolone cheese (*provoleta*)

Vegetables for grilling:

onions, peeled, sliced in half

potatoes, left whole

sweet peppers, sliced in half or left whole

Accompaniments:

salad of lettuce, tomatoes, and onions, dressed with vinaigrette at the last minute

potato salad

Other accompaniments:

French bread (baguette)

French fries

chimichurri sauce

creole sauce (*salsa criolla*)

1. The first steps are to clean the grill and to light a fire. No chemical fire starter is used to start the fire, only paper and kindling. Using chemicals is frowned upon and demonstrates lack of skill on the part of the grill chef. Either firewood or charcoal or a mix of both is used, as long

as the firewood is not too thick, otherwise it will take too long to become embers. Painted wood is not good for firewood, as it will give off noxious fumes. Once the fire has died down to glowing embers, grilling begins. The grill is set between 6 to 12 inches above the embers, depending on their heat.

2. All of the meat is placed at the same time on the grill. Both sides of the meat are seared first at high heat to seal the juice in, before being seasoned with coarse salt. The cooking should be slow and at even heat. Thinner cuts will cook in less time, and thicker cuts will take longer.

   The ribs are placed with the bones facing the embers. To ensure that there will be enough embers for grilling, a fire is kept burning alongside on the left side of the grill so that there is a ready supply of embers.

3. To test if the meat is ready, do not pierce the meat, or the juices will escape, and the meat will be dry. Press the meat surface with grilling tongs: If the surface is too soft and yielding, it is still raw. If the surface is elastic (yields slightly), it is cooked *a punto* (medium). If the surface is firm, then the meat is well done.

4. The sausages, offal, and provolone cheese do not require too much cooking time and are served first. The sausages are either opened and spread on bread or placed whole on bread.

   Next come the ribs and other parts with bone. Ribs take an hour and a half to cook. The steaks are served last.

Alfajores, an Argentine tradition served at first communion parties, are cake-like cookies filled with creamy caramel-flavored *dulce de leche*.

Alfajores Santafecinos (Frosted Caramel-filled Cookies)

Yield: about 20 cookies

2 cups *dulce de leche* (recipe follows)

1 cup all-purpose flour

½ teaspoon salt

3 egg yolks

1 teaspoon melted butter

1 cup confectioners' sugar, more if necessary

½ cup heavy cream, more if necessary

Equipment: Large mixing bowl, mixing spoon, lightly floured work surface, lightly floured rolling pin, 2-inch cookie cutter or water glass, 1 or 2 lightly greased cookie sheets, oven mitts, metal spatula, wire cake rack, small bowl, **pastry brush**, serving tray

1. Prepare *dulce de leche*: Cover and refrigerate until ready to use.

2. Put flour and salt in large mixing bowl. Make well (hole) in the center, and drop in the egg yolks and melted butter. Using your fingers, mix the ingredients together to form into a ball

of dough. Transfer dough to lightly floured work surface, and **knead** vigorously for 10 minutes, or until smooth and **elastic**. Let dough rest for 10 minutes.

Preheat oven to 350°F.

3. On lightly floured work surface, roll dough to about ⅛ inch thick with lightly floured rolling pin. Using 2-inch cookie cutter or the rim of a glass, cut out as many circles as you can from the dough. Gather the scraps together, and form them into another ball. Roll dough out again, and cut into circles as with other dough. Repeat until all the dough has been used. Place the circles 1 inch apart on 1 or 2 lightly greased cookie sheets.

4. Bake in oven for 10 minutes, or until the cookies are lightly browned. Using a metal spatula, transfer cookies to a wire rack to cool.

5. Prepare icing: Put 1 cup confectioners' sugar into small bowl, stir in ½ cup heavy cream, a little at a time, and **blend** well. The icing should coat the spoon lightly. If it seems thin, add a few spoonfuls of confectioners' sugar; if it is too thick, add a little more cream.

6. Using a pastry brush, coat the tops of half the cookies with a thin layer of icing, and let dry for 10 minutes.

7. Spread a thick layer of *dulce de leche* on the remaining cookies. Place the cookies on top of each other like a sandwich, with *dulce de leche* in the center and icing on top.

To serve, stack alfajores santafecinos *on a tray and serve as sweet treats at baptism celebrations and first communion parties.*

Dulce de leche is popular not only in Argentina but throughout Latin America. It is eaten as a dessert and even used as a spread on bread. *Dulce de leche* is also called *natillas piuranas*, *manjar blanco*, and *leche quemada*.

⚘ *Dulce de Leche* (Caramel-flavored Milk Pudding)

Yield: about 4 cups

15 ounces canned condensed milk

3 cups whole milk

½ teaspoon baking soda

1 cup dark brown sugar

¼ cup water

Equipment: Small saucepan, wooden mixing spoon, medium **heavy-bottomed** saucepan

1. In small saucepan, stirring constantly, bring condensed milk, whole milk, and baking soda to a boil over high heat, and immediately remove pan from heat.

2. Put sugar and water into medium heavy-bottomed saucepan, and cook over low heat, stirring constantly, until the sugar dissolves. Stir in hot milk mixture and cook over very low heat for 1 to 1½ hours, stirring occasionally. The mixture becomes a thick amber-colored pudding when done.

Use with alfajores santafecinos *(recipe precedes), or serve as dessert.*

⚮ *Pasta Frola* (Argentinian Linzertorte)

This Argentinian adaptation of linzertorte is a pie often made for birthdays and other celebrations. The most common fillings are quince paste (*membrillo*) and guava paste. *Dulce de leche* (recipe precedes) and *dulce de batata* (sweet potato spread) are also well loved fillings.

1¼ cups flour

1 cup finely ground almonds

1 teaspoon baking powder

¾ ¾cup butter

½½cup sugar

¼ teaspoon salt

1 teaspoon vanilla

1 teaspoon grated lemon **zest** (optional)

2 eggs, beaten

2½ to 3 cups *dulce de leche* (recipe precedes, or available at Latin American food shops or online)

1 egg yolk beaten with 1 tablespoon water for egg wash

For **garnish**: icing sugar

1. In a bowl, combine the flour, ground almonds, and baking powder.
2. In a mixing bowl, cream the butter and sugar until light-colored and fluffy. Mix in salt, vanilla, and lemon zest. Mix in the eggs and the flour and almond mixture to make a soft dough. Chill, covered, for 2 hours.

   Ten minutes before baking, preheat oven to 350°F.
3. Divide the dough into two parts: ⅓ and ⅔ of the dough. Roll out the larger piece to cover the bottom and sides of a pie pan, with a bit extra for the overhang. Spread generously with the *dulce de leche*, reserving a bit for later. Roll out the remaining dough to ⅛-inch thickness. Cut equal strips, about ½ to ⅔-inch wide, using a decorative pastry cutter, or leave it plain-edged. Cover the filling with the strips in a lattice pattern. Brush the crust overhang with egg wash. Press lightly to seal the top strips to the overhang.
4. Bake in a preheated oven for 30 to 40 minutes, or until the pastry is golden.

   Allow to cool, then top up the spaces between the lettuce with the reserved *dulce de leche*.

Just before serving, sprinkle with icing sugar.

⚮ *Blaettertorte* (Napoleon Cake)

Blaettertorte means "cake of leaves" or "sheets: (*blaetter*), and, true to its name, this celebratory cake consists of several sheets or layers of cake, and between the layers is a filling of vanilla custard pudding. This cake is usually made for a special occasion, such as a birthday or some other important event. *Blaettertorte* is a cake popular among the Canadian Mennonites, most of whom have migrated to found colonies in Mexico and subsequently Argentina.

Yield: 10 to 12 servings

Cake:

3 cups flour

3 tablespoons **cornstarch**

3 teaspoons baking powder

¼ teaspoon salt

¾ cup butter, at room temperature

1 cup sugar

Vanilla custard filling:

5 tablespoons sugar

5 tablespoons flour

5 tablespoons cornstarch

5 cups milk

3 large eggs, at room temperature, well beaten

3 tablespoons milk

5 **egg yolks**, well beaten

1 tablespoon butter

2 teaspoons vanilla extract

1 cup thick cream for whipping

Equipment: Small, medium, and large mixing bowls, mixing spoon, 3 cookie sheets or shallow baking trays, parchment paper, oven mitts

1. In a medium bowl, combine well the flour, cornstarch, baking powder, and salt. Set aside.

2. In a large bowl, beat the butter and sugar together until the mixture is light and creamy, and the sugar is well incorporated into the butter. Add the well beaten eggs and the milk, beating them well into the butter mixture. Gradually mix in the flour mixture to form a dough. Knead the dough briefly on a lightly floured surface, until smooth, and form into a log. Enclose the log in plastic wrap, and refrigerate for at least 2 hours.

3. Prepare the vanilla custard filling: In a small mixing bowl, combine well the sugar, flour, and cornstarch, and whisk in ¼ cup of the milk, making sure no lumps form. Keep whisking until the mixture is smooth. Add the well beaten egg yolks, and when they are completely incorporated, gradually add ¾ cup milk, mixing well.

4. In a saucepan, place the remaining 4 cups of milk and heat at a low temperature just until small bubbles form on the sides of the pan. Add the flour and egg mixture, whisking continuously until it comes to a boil. Keep whisking until the custard is smooth, and immediately turn off heat. Stir in the butter and the vanilla extract.

5. Let the custard cool completely, at room temperature, occasionally giving it a stir so that a skin does not form on the surface.

6. Once thoroughly cool, the custard can be covered with a sheet of plastic wrap and refrigerated until ready to use.

7. Prepare the cake layers. Prepare 11 sheets of parchment paper, each large enough to generously hold a 9-inch circle of cake dough.

8. Prepare 10 template sheets: On one side of each parchment sheet, draw with a dark pencil a circle, 9 inches in diameter. You will be using the other side of the sheet, so the dough will not touch the pencil drawing.

9. Take the dough log out of the refrigerator, and divide into 10 equal pieces. Take one piece of dough and place it on the reverse side of the template sheet, in the middle of circle. Using a rolling pin, roll the dough out between the two parchment sheets to just beyond the 9-inch circle. With a knife or pizza cutter, trim the excess dough (those that extend beyond the drawn circle), and set aside. These will also be baked later.

10. Remove the top parchment sheet, prick the dough layer all over with a fork, and place the bottom parchment sheet with the rolled out dough on it on a cookie sheet or baking tray.

   Bake in the center rack of a preheated 350°F oven for 6 to 7 minutes, or until a golden brown. Transfer the baked layer, still on the parchment paper, to a wire rack to cool completely.

   While waiting for one layer to bake, roll out the next layer so that it is ready to go into the oven as soon as the previous one is baked. Repeat the process with the rest of the dough.

11. Take the dough trimmings, and place them on the top parchment sheet (the same one used to roll out all the previous layers). Place on a cookie sheet, and bake for 4 to 5 minutes, or until golden brown. Remove the sheet to a wire rack to cool completely.

12. Assemble the cake: In a large mixing bowl, whip the cream until soft peaks form. Then gently fold in the chilled vanilla custard, mixing well for about a minute at low speed until the filling is smooth.

13. In the middle of your serving plate, place a tablespoon or two of filling, and place one cake layer on it. This prevents the cake from sliding around during assembly. Spread evenly about ¾ to 1 cup of filling on each cake layer. Cover the top and sides of the cake as well. Crush the trimmings and sprinkle them on the top and sides of the cake.

13. Cover with plastic wrap, and refrigerate for at least 10 hours or ideally for 24 hours until the filling is completely absorbed by the cake layers.

This cake is very rich, so make your slices a bit thinner than usual.

Bolivia

Mountainous, landlocked Bolivia is located in the heart of South America, surrounded by Brazil, Chile, Peru, Paraguay, and Argentina. When the Spanish arrived in the 16th century, most of Bolivia was controlled by the Inca Empire. After the Spanish defeated the Incas, the native population was enslaved, mainly in pursuit of the mineral wealth that made Bolivia famous. By the time of Bolivian independence in 1825, the mineral wealth was largely exhausted. Much of Bolivian history since its independence from Spain has been dominated by disastrous wars fought in an attempt to gain access to the sea.

Over half the population of Bolivia lives on a high plateau (average altitude over 12,000) between two chains of the Andes. The remoteness of this high plain protected the native population from European diseases that wiped out other Indians in Latin America, and today Indians make up more than 50 percent of the population. The next largest group are *mestizos* (mixed Indian and Spanish). The Roman Catholic Church dominates Bolivian life. Most *mestizos* and Indians combine ancient Inca and other Indian beliefs with Christian practices in their life-cycle ceremonies. (See Protestant and Catholic Life-Cycle Rituals, page lxxiii.)

Bolivia is host to the largest population of Mennonites in Latin America, in total over 70,000 members living in 25 colonies. Most of them have migrated from Canada, the United States, Argentina, Paraguay, and Mexico, after having lived there for a number of years, but because of recent changes in government or local policies, some Mennonite communities found that their special privileges had been rescinded. In Bolivia, the Mennonites have been given special privileges by the government—the freedom from being conscripted into Bolivian military service, the right to set up their own schools, and freedom from certain taxes.

Mennonites are a sect of Anabaptists (from the Greek *ana*, meaning "again")—Christians who believe that baptism should occur only in adulthood so that the person being baptized truly understands the tenets of that particular faith. (The Amish are also an Anabaptist sect that branched out later from the Mennonites because they believed in stricter observance.) Some Mennonites use electricity and cars, but most of those who chose to settle in Latin America eschew electricity (they use solar energy mainly) and use horse-drawn wagons for personal travel, as well as to transport goods that they buy or sell. In keeping with their wish to be as removed as possible from the influences of the outside world, the majority of the Mennonite colonies in Latin America are self-sufficient agricultural settlements, raising vegetables and domestic animals, such as cows and chickens, for their own food. Their contact with the surrounding non-Mennonite communities is limited to selling their agricultural produce, which includes milk and cheese, and selling basic farm tools and machinery of their own manufacture, as well as providing repair services for farm machinery. They may also but very rarely purchase from the local shops any items that they cannot raise or manufacture themselves. Their modest dress—long dresses with long sleeves and caps for women and overalls with long-sleeved shirts for men, even in the tropical heat of Latin America—sets them apart and makes them conspicuous when they venture outside of their communities.

Mennonite life-cycle celebrations, like their lifestyle, are simple and plain. Baptism occurs only upon the onset of adulthood. Birthdays are celebrated at home, usually with a homemade cake. A Mennonite wedding usually takes place at home, most commonly in the bride's family home, although in contemporary times, there are some communities where a wedding may take place in church. In keeping with the Mennonite preference for simplicity, every element of a wedding is kept as plain, simple, and as free of ostentation as possible. The bride's dress, in common with most Western brides, will be white, but most often is homemade and modest. The bride carries a Bible together with a simple posy of flowers. Often only the bride and groom are present at the ceremony, without bridesmaids or best men. A church elder or pastor usually officiates at the simple religious ceremony, and most often the entire community is present. The reception is also simple, most often a dinner and a cake. There is no dancing, nor is alcohol served.

When a Mennonite dies, he or she is washed and dressed in plain clothes and commonly placed in a simple wooden coffin, either open or closed, for viewing at home. It is rare for a deceased Mennonite to be embalmed. Friends and relatives will visit for two days to view the deceased and comfort the mourning family. Burial is commonly on the third day after the death. Flowers, as well as eulogies praising the deceased, are considered unnecessary and a vanity, but hymns will be sung. If the cemetery is too distant from the family home, the coffin is transported in a horse-drawn hearse, and mourners walk or also ride in horse-drawn buggies. The grave will have been dug by hand, and a blessing is pronounced over the grave. A simple stone tablet with the deceased's birth and death dates are all that will mark a Mennonite grave. After the burial, all the mourners share a meal prepared or brought by the church community at the home of the deceased.

♨ *Mango Platz* (Mennonite Crumb Cake with Mango)

Platz is a Mennonite cake often made for a large gathering or to bring as a potluck offering, for example for a funeral meal. The name is short for the Ukrainian dessert called *platsok.* It is also similar to contemporary German streusel cakes. *Platz* features a shallow cake base on top of which are placed whatever fruit is in season or even a mixture of several fruits. The fruit layer is covered with a rich streusel topping, that is, a loose crumbly mixture of flour, sugar, and butter. Mangoes are not a traditional fruit used in Mennonite *platz* cakes. The usual fruits are plums, apples, apricots, and nectarines. In Uruguay and other Latin American countries where Mennonites have settled, local and plentiful tropical fruits, such as mangoes, are often used in *platz.*

Yield: about 10 to 12 servings

2 cups flour

2½ teaspoons baking powder

¼ teaspoon salt

½ cup butter or shortening, softened

½ cup sugar

½ teaspoon vanilla extract

2 eggs, well beaten

⅔ cup milk

2½ to 3 cups **cubed** or sliced ripe mango (flesh from 3 mangoes, each weighing about 12 ounces)

Streusel or crumb topping:

1¼ cups flour, plus a bit more for preparing the baking pan

¾ cup sugar

½ cup butter, plus more for greasing the baking pan

1 teaspoon vanilla extract

Equipment: Mixing bowl; mixing spoon; 9×13 inch baking pan, 2 inches deep, or jelly roll pan, oven mitts

1. Prepare the baking pan: Grease a 9×13 inch baking pan or jelly roll pan, and sprinkle with an even coating of flour. Tap out the excess flour, and set aside.

2. In a medium mixing bowl, combine the flour, baking powder, and salt until well mixed.

3. In a larger bowl, beat the butter and sugar together until light and creamy. Stir in the vanilla, and mix in the eggs and milk. Gradually add the flour mixture, mixing well until just incorporated. Spoon the batter into the prepared baking pan. Gently smooth the surface, and distribute the mango cubes or slices evenly over the batter.

4. Prepare the crumb (streusel) topping: In a bowl, combine the flour and sugar, and mix in well the vanilla extract. Lightly rub in the butter until the mixture forms little lumps. The lumps do not have to be uniform. Scatter the crumbs evenly all over the mango layer.

5. Bake in a preheated 350°F oven for 25 to 30 minutes, or until golden brown, and a wooden skewer or toothpick inserted in the center comes out clean.

To serve, slice into square pieces.

Marriage is the most significant event in a person's life. In particular for Roman Catholics, every stage of the courtship, betrothal, and the wedding ceremony includes set rituals with music, chanting, or singing and folk dances. Godparents [*compadres*, or *padrino* (godfather) and *madrina* (godmother)] for the wedding ceremony are held in high esteem and are selected with great care by both Indian and Hispanic cultures. The godparents participate in the marriage ceremony and are given gifts by the bride and groom.

Cooked cabbage is a hearty, filling dish that goes well with meat or chicken pies. It would be served at a birthday party or other life-cycle celebrations.

✑ *Guiso de Repollo* (Cabbage in Sauce)

Yield: serves 4

3 tablespoons vegetable oil	1 tablespoon tomato sauce
1 onion, **finely chopped**	salt and pepper to taste
3 tomatoes, chopped	1 pound green or white cabbage, finely shredded, **blanched**, drained
dried red pepper flakes to taste	
	4 potatoes, peeled, cooked, and quartered

Equipment: Large skillet, mixing spoon, serving bowl

1. Heat oil in large skillet over medium-high heat, add onion, and sauté 3 to 5 minutes, until soft. Reduce heat to medium, and add tomatoes and dried red pepper flakes to taste. Stir and cook for 5 minutes for flavors to develop.

2. Stir in tomato sauce, and **blend** well. Add salt and pepper to taste.

3. **Fold in** blanched and drained cabbage and cooked potatoes. Continue to cook until heated through, 10 to 15 minutes. Add more salt and pepper if desired.

To serve, transfer to serving bowl, and serve hot or at room temperature as a side dish.

Among the Aymara and Quechua ethnic groups in Bolivia, the first haircut (*rutucha*) is a momentous event and is celebrated accordingly. In Aymara and Quechua culture, the hair is regarded as valuable, and thus cut hair is never just thrown away with the trash. Additionally, it is believed that hair can be used in witchcraft for performing spells, and it is thus kept from getting into the hands of malicious people. The first tuft of hair severed during the *rutucha* ceremony is believed to have curative properties and is sometimes added to an infusion. The *rutucha* party is also the first time that a child is presented formally to the wider community.

The sponsor, called *padrino* (godfather) or *madrina* (godmother), is chosen by the parents with care, usually a person of good moral, social, and economic standing, in the hope that the child will grow up to be like him or her. A foreign person, i.e., non-Aymara or non-Quechua, may be invited to be the sponsor in the hope that the child will not be exposed to discrimination. The sponsor is responsible for organizing the party, and the parents take care of the food, drinks, such as *chicha* and *coca* leaf tea. Usually the *rutucha* takes place in late afternoon at the parents' house.

The *rutucha* begins with the father of the child saying a few welcoming words and then calling on the sponsor and guests to the highlight of the party—the *kichacar* (to bloom), in other words, the haircutting. The guests are invited to snip a few strands of hair from among the tangled areas and enclose these in money in a traditional colorful handwoven fabric called "*aguayo*." However, most of the hair is left for the sponsor and the parents to cut. Half of the head, the left, is allocated for the sponsor; the other half, the right, is left for the parents. Once all the hair has been cut, the money is counted, and the sponsor tops up the total sum so that it is a round number. The money received during the *rutucha* is set aside for the expenses of raising the child.

ꙮ *Chicha Morada* (Purple Corn Juice)

Chicha is a generic name given to fermented and nonfermented drinks, usually made from corn, in Latin America. In Bolivia, besides corn, peanuts, plantains, bananas, **cassava**, and amaranth can also be used to make *chicha*, depending on the region. Life-cycle celebrations and important occasions are celebrated with fermented *chicha*.

Yield: about 20 cups

4 ears of purple corn	2 whole cloves
½ tablespoon aniseed	1 cinnamon stick

peel from a pineapple or from a mandarin orange or 5 pieces of quince (peel and flesh)

5 quarts water

sugar to taste

Equipment: 5-quart saucepan, large sterilized glass jars, fine sieve or cheesecloth, oven mitts

1. Scrape the kernels from the corn, and place in a large saucepan with the aniseed, cinnamon, and cloves. Simmer over low heat until the corn kernels begin to burst.

2. Turn off the heat, and let cool in the pan. When thoroughly cool, transfer to large sterilized glass jars or other large containers. Add the pineapple peels or mandarin orange peel or quinces.

3. Cover well, and leave for a day or two to ferment.

4. Strain through a fine sieve or cheesecloth, chill well, and add sugar to taste before serving.

♪ *Ají de Lengua* (Beef Tongue in Chilli Pepper Sauce)

For family celebrations, such as birthdays, *ají de lengua* (also *picante de lengua*, beef tongue in pepper sauce) is often served. A *piñata* filled with sweets and small presents may also be a feature at birthday parties. Although not originally Bolivian but rather a Mexican tradition, a *piñata* has now been adopted as a birthday party feature in many other countries in South America (and in other parts of the world as well).

Yield: 8 to 10 servings

1 fresh beef tongue

1 pound Bolivian fresh white cheese (substitute halloumi or mozzarella)

8 large potatoes, peeled and quartered

1 pound reconstituted and peeled *tunta* (white freeze-dried potatoes, also known as white *chuño*, substitute whole medium potatoes, one per serving)

Pepper sauce condiments:

4 yellow chili peppers (known as *locoto*), substitute 4 sweet yellow peppers plus 1 or more hot chili peppers to taste

salt, as needed

Fresh salsa:

1 onion, finely sliced

2 large tomatoes, finely sliced

2 onions, finely chopped

1 cup parsley, finely chopped

1 teaspoon oregano, crumbled

2 large **tomatoes, peeled** and finely chopped

2 cups frozen peas

1 teaspoon black pepper, freshly ground

1½ teaspoons cumin powder

4 cloves of garlic, 2 left unpeeled

salt to taste

2 tablespoons olive oil

Equipment: Pressure cooker, baking tray, **mortar and pestle** or food processor, **colander, double boiler,** mixing bowl, oven mitts.

Note: Adult supervision required for proper use of pressure cooker.

1. Prepare the tongue for cooking: Cut off the top part of the tongue and discard. Wash the tongue well.

2. Place in a pressure cooker with 6 cups boiling water with salt to taste, ½ teaspoon of black pepper, ¾ teaspoon cumin, and 2 peeled garlic cloves. Allow to cook for about an hour and a half. The meat should be thoroughly tender.

3. Once the pressure cooker has been depressurized, remove the tongue and check it for tenderness by slicing into the tip. If thoroughly tender, peel off the outer membrane and slice diagonally into individual serving pieces. Set the broth aside.

4. Prepare the pepper and garlic purée for the spicy sauce. Place the yellow peppers and 2 unpeeled garlic cloves on a tray under a broiler for 10 to 15 minutes until the skin on the peppers is well blistered and the garlic is aromatic. Allow to cool, and peel the peppers and garlic. Purée the peeled peppers and garlic with the hot chili pepper(s) (if not using *locoto* peppers) by pounding in a mortar and pestle or in a food processor. Set aside.

5. Prepare the fresh salsa: In a bowl, mix the finely sliced onion and tomatoes, salt and oil, and cover with plastic wrap. Keep refrigerated until needed.

6. In a frying pan over medium heat, heat the oil, and sauté the onions until softened. Add the parsley, oregano, chopped tomatoes, frozen peas, yellow pepper and garlic purée, and ½ cup of the stock from tenderizing the tongue. Add salt to taste.

7. Add the tongue, and let it simmer for 10 to 15 minutes, or until the peas are done, to absorb the flavors of the sauce. Add more stock if the sauce is too thick.

8. In a separate saucepan, boil the potatoes in salty water, for about 20 to 25 minutes, or until tender. Drain the potatoes through a colander, and set aside.

9. Make a cavity in the soaked and peeled *tuntas*, and tuck in a slice of cheese. Cook over steam in a double boiler until tender.

Note: If tuntas *are not available, add an extra potato per serving. Slit the extra potato as soon as it is boiled, and tuck in a slice of cheese. Keep the potatoes warm until ready to serve.*

To serve, on each plate, place one or two slices of tongue, spoon over the spicy sauce, and place the potatoes and tuntas *alongside. Add a tablespoon or more of the fresh salsa.*

Brazil

Brazil, South America's largest country, takes up nearly half the continent and shares a border with every other South American country except Chile and Ecuador. One of its most important features is the Amazon River basin, which drains more than a third of country.

Unlike other Latin American countries whose recent histories were dominated by Spain, Brazil was conquered and populated by the Portuguese, who began settling in Brazil in the 16th century. Although Brazil declared independence in the 19th century, the Portuguese influence is still strong. Portuguese is the official language, while Spanish is spoken in the border areas because Brazil shares borders with 10 Latin American countries. Other languages spoken are German, Italian, Japanese, English, and Amerindian languages.

About 65 percent of Brazilians are Roman Catholics, and about 22 percent are Protestant. The life-cycle traditions prescribed by the Christian churches are celebrated. (See Protestant and Catholic Life-Cycle Rituals, page lxxiii.)

Beyond language and religion, though, Brazil is a land of different regions and people. About 48 percent of Brazilians are white, and another 43 percent are mixed white and black. Blacks make up close to 8 percent, Asians just over 1 percent, and indigenous groups make up less than 1 percent of the population. The extremely diversified population is a result of geographic diversity and over 400 years of Africans, Europeans, and Indians melding, creating a complicated racial melting pot.

Of the life-cycle events, children's birthdays are similar to those in the United States. Adults often have a small family gathering, followed by a larger party to celebrate the event. In Brazil, friendships are important, and to fail to attend a close friend's birthday party is taken as an insult and often severs the relationship.

Weddings generally begin with the couple signing civil documents in a small home ceremony attended by the immediate family, and it is followed by the religious ceremony in a church. After the Mass, if the family can afford it, a large reception is held at a hotel or club, complete with music, singing, and dancing.

For funerals, families usually bury their dead within 24 hours. The body, dressed in black, lies in state in a coffin at the family home. During an all-night vigil, mourners drink and have a light repast while they hover around the casket, speaking only pleasantries about the deceased. At a designated hour, the hearse, carrying the coffin, leads a procession to the church, where a requiem is offered. In small towns, the body is buried in the church's private cemetery, in the large cities, the procession moves to a large public cemetery. Masses are held in memory of the deceased after seven days, 30 days, and again after one year.

Eating is one of the great pleasures in Brazil, and all life-cycle celebrations call for plenty of food. Bread, rolls, and other pastries are prepared for almost every celebration.

No party or celebration in Brazil takes place without *brigadeiros*. Whether it is a birthday party at home, or at school, or at the office, a wedding, a baby shower, or an engagement party, there are sure to be *brigadeiros*. *Brigadeiros* are usually eaten after the birthday cake. The name *"brigadeiro"* comes from the sweets made and distributed by lady campaigners for a brigadier who ran for the presidency of Brazil in 1945. Despite the delicious sweets, the brigadier lost, but his name left its mark on these sweets.

❦ *Brigadeiros* (Brazilian Chocolate Truffles)

In its most basic form, it can even be made in a cup and eaten with a spoon. But the most popular way of serving it is in fluted mini cupcake paper cases. In addition to the standard chocolate or rainbow-colored sprinkles, *brigadeiros* can come coated with chopped nuts, such as pistachio, almond, or walnut. The *brigadeiro* mixture can also be used as a filling for cakes.

Yield: 25 servings

1 can (14 ounces) sweetened condensed milk

8 tablespoons unsweetened cocoa powder

1 tablespoon butter, plus more for rolling

1 tablespoon vanilla essence

chocolate sprinkles, chopped nuts, rainbow-colored sprinkles

mini cupcake paper cases

Equipment: **Heavy-bottomed** saucepan, wooden spoon, oven mitts

1. In a heavy-bottomed saucepan over medium-low heat, cook the milk, cocoa, and butter while constantly stirring, for about 10 to 15 minutes, or until very thick.

2. When the mixture leaves the sides of the pan, and a wooden spoon leaves a trail through the mixture when drawn across it, it is done.

3. Allow to cool, stir in vanilla, then chill thoroughly for 1 hour or more.

4. With buttered hands, shape tablespoonfuls of the mixture into balls. Roll the balls in sprinkles or nuts to coat them completely, then place in paper cases. Keep chilled until ready to serve.

❦ *Beizinhos de Coco* (Coconut Kisses)

Made in the same way as *brigadeiros*, these coconut-based sweets are usually paired with chocolate *brigadeiros* at celebration tables.

Yield: 25 pieces

1 can (14 ounces) sweetened condensed milk

½ cup fresh grated coconut, plus more for coating

1 tablespoon butter, plus more for rolling

mini cupcake paper cases

Equipment: **Heavy-bottomed** saucepan, wooden spoon, oven mitts

1. In a heavy-bottomed pan over medium-low heat, cook the milk, coconut, and butter while constantly stirring, for about 10 to 15 minutes, or until very thick.

2. When the mixture leaves the sides of the pan, and a wooden spoon leaves a trail through the mixture when drawn across it, it is done.

3. Allow to cool, then chill thoroughly for 1 hour or more.

4. With buttered hands, shape tablespoonfuls of the mixture into balls. Roll the balls in coconut to coat them completely, then place on paper cases. Keep chilled until ready to serve.

The following dish is unusual in that it combines chicken with shrimp and peanuts. It might be served at a family first communion dinner.

⚖ *Xinxim de Galinha* (Chicken with Shrimp and Peanut Sauce)

Yield: serves 6

3½ to 4 pounds chicken, cut into serving pieces

4 tablespoons lime or lemon juice

2 cloves garlic, **finely chopped**

salt and pepper to taste

2 tablespoons olive oil

1 onion, grated

1 cup dried shrimp, finely ground (available at all Asian and Latin American food stores)

½ cup dry roasted peanuts, ground

dried red pepper flakes to taste

1 cup chicken broth

¼ cup palm oil (*dendê*) (available at all Latin American food stores)

Equipment: Large bowl, mixing spoon, large **heavy-bottomed** skillet with cover

1. **Marinate** the chicken: Put the chicken pieces in large bowl, and sprinkle with lime or lemon juice, garlic, and salt and pepper to taste. Refrigerate to marinate for about 1 hour, turning the mixture often to coat well.

2. Heat oil in large heavy-bottomed skillet over medium-high heat. Add the onion, shrimp, peanuts, and dried pepper flakes to taste, stir, and **sauté** for 5 minutes to allow flavor to develop. Add the chicken pieces with the marinade juice and chicken broth to the skillet, and reduce heat to **simmer**. Cover, and allow to cook until chicken is tender, 45 to 50 minutes. Test for **chicken doneness**.

3. Add palm oil. Adjust seasoning, adding more salt and pepper if desired. Cook for 3 to 5 minutes longer, turning chicken to coat both sides.

Serve with white rice and farofa de azeite de dendê *(recipe follows).*

A Brazilian meal would not be complete without some form of **cassava** or **manioc** meal. It is put into a *farinheira*, a sort of shaker, and sprinkled on meat, poultry, and vegetables at the table. Or it is made into a *farofa*, which is more elaborate. It is put into a bowl and spooned over the main course of almost every meal.

⚖ *Farofa de Azeite de Dendê* (Cassava Meal with Palm Oil)

Yield: serves 6 to 8

2 cups **cassava** (manioc) meal (available at all Latin American food stores)

4 tablespoons palm oil (*dendê*) (available at all Latin American food stores)

Equipment: Large **heavy-bottomed** skillet, wooden mixing spoon, serving bowl

1. In a large heavy-bottomed skillet over low heat, toast cassava meal until it begins to turn very pale tan, 15 to 20 minutes. Stir frequently so that the meal does not burn.

2. Stir in palm oil, and cook until it is well blended and the mixture is bright yellow.

To serve, transfer to serving bowl. To eat, spoon a desired amount over each serving of xinxim de galinha *(recipe precedes) or with any meat or other poultry dish.*

Chile

Chile is a long, narrow country on the western coast of South America between the Andes Mountains and the Pacific Ocean. Originally under the control of the Inca and Mapuche tribes, thousands of Indians were converted to Catholicism during the Spanish conquest, around the 16th century. Chile remained under Spanish control until it won its independence in 1818. Since the 1980s, Chile has been steadily developing its economy and from the 1990s has benefitted from a democratically elected government. It is now one of the most politically and economically stable and progressive countries in South America.

Almost 90 percent of Chile's population are either descendants of the Spanish invaders or people of mixed lineage (*mestizo*), both Indian and Spanish. The Mapuche ethnic group comprises just over 9 percent of the population, and the rest belong to diverse indigenous ethnic groups, such as the Aymara (less than 1 percent) and other indigenous and unspecified groups, such as the Quechua, Colla, Diaguita, Kawesgar, Yagan, Rapa Nui, and Likan Antai.

In a recent survey, just over 70 percent of the population identified themselves as Christian, with 58 percent as Roman Catholic adherents and just over 14 percent as Protestant. About 4 percent are adherents of various religious denominations, such as Jehovah's Witnesses. The remaining 24 percent declared themselves as agnostics (those who believe in a supreme being or a god without any specific name), as atheists (those who do not believe in the existence of such a supernatural being), or as not aligned with any organized religion or faith. Fewer than 30 percent of Chileans feel that religion is an important aspect of their lives.

Among the indigenous ethnic groups, over half (65 percent) declared themselves as Roman Catholic, just under 30 percent identified themselves as Protestant, and the remaining 6 percent identified their religious affiliation as "other." The Mapuche, who comprise over 85 percent of all of Chile's indigenous inhabitants, practice a syncretistic (mixed) form of Christian observance; that is, while being nominally Catholic or Protestant, they continue to follow the dictates of their indigenous spiritual leaders, called *longkos* or *machis*, especially in matters related to illness and well-being, and observe traditional indigenous rituals. Additionally, there are Jewish communities and synagogues in several towns, and there are Muslim adherents and mosques in three locations.

Several Protestant denominations are represented in Chile. These are the Lutherans, Anglicans, Methodists, Presbyterians, Seventh-Day Adventists, Pentecostals, and others. The Lutherans arrived with the wave of German immigration in the early 19th century. The Church of Jesus Christ of Latter-Day Saints (Mormons) has a significant following of over 120,000 members. Other faiths with adherents in Chile are the Baha'i religion, Buddhism, and Hinduism.

Although the Roman Catholic Church enjoys special privileges, there is separation of church and state, and freedom to practice non-Catholic religions at home and to set up non-Catholic schools has been guaranteed to all citizens since a special law passed in 1865. Life-cycle events are celebrated according to the religious or spiritual beliefs of the families concerned. (See Protestant and Catholic Life-Cycle Rituals, page lxxiii, and Judaism and Jewish Life-Cycle Rituals, page lxviii, and Islam and Islamic Life-Cycle Rituals, page lxxvi.)

Baptisms are a particularly important life-cycle event in Chile, especially for Roman Catholics. As in many other Latin American countries, the godparents ([*compadres*, also *padrino* [godfather] and *madrina* [godmother]) play an important role in the lives of their godchildren. First of all, they are chosen on the basis of their economic, professional, and moral standing and whether they would be good role models for the child. In case the child's parents die or cannot provide for their child, the godparents are expected to step in and provide support. For the baptismal church service, first communion, and wedding of a godchild, godparents are involved in the rituals and take responsibility for some of (if not most of, or all) the expenses of the events. After the mass, the parents and godparents invite family and friends to the festive meal, which can be in the home, a restaurant, or a hall.

Marriage takes place usually when couples are in their early to midtwenties, though the age varies by region. In the larger cities, couples are free to date and marry whomever they like. Most Chileans have two weddings: a civil one at a government registry office with a gathering of a few close friends and a more elaborate ceremony in church with a larger group of invitees. For the latter, there is usually a celebratory dinner and dancing afterward until the morning, when breakfast will also be served. Because church weddings can be very expensive, more and more couples are having a small civil ceremony. It is also possible to have a church ceremony first, and register it within eight days.

The waters off the coast of Chile are known for the plentiful fish and seafood, and often both are included in the wedding feast. *Congrio* are very large, bottom-feeding fish found in Chilean waters. They are considered the finest of all fish according to Chilean fish lovers and deserve to be better known and appreciated. Chilean *congrio* are fish that belong to the same family as cod; they are called "cusk-eels" but are not actually eels because they have ventral fins, which eels do not have. Two types of cusk-eels are used for this dish: the pink (*dorado*) and the red (*colorado*). Substitute any white, dense- or firm-fleshed fish, such as cod, haddock, or pollock, for this recipe.

⚓ *Congrio en Fuente de Barro* (Cusk-eel with Tomatoes and Onions)

Yield: serves 4 to 6

2 pounds **fillets** of cod or other white firm-fleshed fish, such as haddock or pollock

salt and pepper to taste

juice of 1 lemon

1 teaspoon ground paprika

4 to 6 tablespoons butter or margarine

6 onions, **finely chopped**

6 tomatoes, chopped

4 slices firm white bread, pan fried in butter or margarine

1 cup milk

For **garnish:**

2 hard-cooked eggs, sliced

1 tablespoon parsley, chopped

Equipment: Large skillet, mixing spoon, buttered medium ovenproof casserole with cover, oven mitts

1. Sprinkle fish fillets with salt and pepper, lemon juice, and paprika. Set aside.
2. Melt 4 tablespoons butter or margarine in large skillet over medium-high heat. Add onions, stir, and **sauté** until soft, 3 to 5 minutes. Add remaining 2 tablespoons butter or margarine, and reduce heat to medium. Add tomatoes, stir, and sauté for 5 minutes longer.

Preheat oven to 350°F.

3. Layer half tomato mixture in buttered casserole, cover tomatoes with fish, and add layer of fried bread. Spread remaining tomato mixture over top of fried bread. Arrange sliced hard-cooked eggs over tomato mixture, and pour milk over the top.
4. Cover and bake in oven for 30 minutes, or until fish flakes easily when poked with a fork.

Serve from casserole dish for a lovely, satisfying, full-flavored dish.

Throughout Latin America, avocados are a favorite food. For a special occasion, avocados are stuffed and served as an appetizer.

⚓ *Aquacates Rellenos* (Stuffed Avocados)

Yield: serves 6

3 large avocados

juice of 1 lemon

1 cup chopped, cooked ham

3 hard-cooked eggs, chopped

1 cup commercial mayonnaise

salt and pepper to taste

For **garnish:** iceberg lettuce, shredded, for **garnish**

Equipment: Sharp knife, medium bowl, mixing spoon, six salad plates

1. Cut avocados in half, and remove and discard pit. Sprinkle the cut sides of the avocados with lemon juice, and set aside.

2. In medium bowl, combine ham and chopped hard-cooked eggs. Fold in mayonnaise and salt and pepper to taste.

3. Make a bed of shredded lettuce on each of six salad plates. Place an avocado half, cut side up, on each plate. Spoon equal amounts of ham mixture over each of the 6 avocados.

Serve as the first course for a wedding reception or family dinner.

Birthdays are celebrated in Chile by singing the birthday song to the celebrant and giving presents: toys, games, books, stuffed animals, if the celebrant is a child; if an adult, flowers, books, perfume, or after-shave lotion, a clothing accessory such as a scarf, a ring or bracelet or other small jewelry. After singing the birthday song, if friends and family and other well-wishers are feeling energetic, four people each take one limb of the celebrant and toss him or her in the air, the number of times corresponding to the celebrant's age. Sometimes a surprise party is held at home, and party decorations normally include balloons, banners, and flowers. For a young child's birthday party, party games will be organized for the little guests, and entertainment may be laid on, such as a clown or puppet show, as well as party favors for the guests to take home. However, the most important marker for Chilean birthdays, similar to those in other countries, is a birthday cake, usually baked by family members, or bought, in the flavor preferred by the celebrant, with candles to be blown out by the celebrant.

Most children and adults in Chile, when asked what kind of cake they prefer for their birthday, will undoubtedly say *torta de piña* (pineapple cake). This quintessential and well loved Chilean birthday cake is made of layers of sponge cake filled with pineapple and frosted with whipped cream. The next most popular cake requested for birthdays is *Selva Negra* (Black Forest cake).

℘ *Torta de Piña* (Pineapple Cake)

Yield: 10 to 15 servings

Cake dough:

8 medium eggs, separated

1½ cups (12 ounces) sugar

2 cups (8 ounces) flour, combined well with 2 teaspoons baking powder

2 to 3 tablespoons butter and 2 to 3 tablespoons flour for greasing cake pans

Filling:

1 large fresh ripe pineapple, peeled, or 1 16-ounce can pineapple in its own juice

1 cup natural pineapple juice (only if using fresh pineapple)

3 tablespoons rum, brandy, or whisky

1 15-ounce can condensed milk

grated **zest** from 2 lemons

juice from 2 lemons

sugar to taste

Frosting:

2 cups heavy cream for whipping

½ cup icing or powdered sugar

Equipment: Large mixing bowl, electric mixer, 2 10-inch round cake pans, parchment paper or aluminum foil, oven mitts, wire rack, piping bag with decorative tips, spatula, **pastry brush**

1. Prepare the cake. Butter the cake pans and sprinkle flour over the pan, tapping the pans to distribute the flour in an even layer. Discard the excess flour.

2. Place the egg whites in the mixing bowl of a mixer, and at medium speed, beat to stiff peak stage. Gradually add the sugar, a little at a time, then the yolks, one at a time, until all the yolks are incorporated. Reduce the speed to low, then add the flour and baking powder mixture, and gently mix for just two minutes more. Do not overmix or the air beaten into the egg whites will be lost. Transfer into 2 10-inch round baking pans.

3. Bake in the middle rack of a preheated 350°F oven for 30 to 35 minutes, or until golden. Insert a wooden skewer in the middle of the cake, and, if it comes out clean, the cake is done.

   If the two pans do not fit side by side in the oven, place one on a lower rack, and switch pans at the end of 20 minutes.

4. Leave to cool for 10 minutes in the pan, then remove and allow to cool thoroughly on a wire rack, covered with a clean, dry kitchen towel.

5. Prepare the filling. If using fresh pineapple, discard the central hard core, and slice the pineapple into bite-size pieces. Reserve a few for decorating the cake at the end.

6. Slice the canned pineapple into bite-size pieces. Reserve a few for decorating the cake at the end.

7. In a bowl, mix the pineapple juice with rum. In another bowl, mix the condensed milk with the grated lemon zest and lemon juice. Taste both mixtures, and add sugar as needed.

8. Assemble the cake. Slice each cake in half crosswise to make four layers. Place one layer, crust side down on a large serving plate. Surround the bottom of the cake with sheets of parchment or aluminum foil to keep the plate clean during assembly. Brush the first layer with the juice mixture, followed by the condensed milk and lemon juice mixture. Distribute half of the pineapple pieces. Place another layer of cake over, brush with the juice mixture, followed by the condensed milk mixture. Place another layer of cake, brush with the juice mixture, followed by the condensed milk mixture. Distribute the remaining pineapple pieces. Place the last layer of cake, brush with the juice mixture, and the condensed milk mixture.

9. In a clean, dry bowl, whip the cream to soft peaks. Gradually add the icing sugar, and continue to whip to stiff peak stage. Do not overwhip, or the cream will turn to butter. Transfer the whipped cream to a piping bag with a decorative tip.

10. Cover the cake all over with an even layer of whipped cream, reserving some for making rosettes on the top layer. Decorate the cake with your chosen cake decoration, such as edible glitter or sprinkles, and the reserved pineapple pieces and rosettes of whipped cream.

Unlike Chile's other indigenous groups, the Rapa Nui originate from Polynesia and are believed to have arrived on Easter Island sometime in the year 1000 CE, or as early as 400 CE, or as late as the 1600s (researchers are divided on these dates). They are Chile's most remarkable and resilient indigenous population who have survived and preserved their culture throughout over 1000 years of hardship, mostly inflicted by European explorers and missionaries. At the end of the 19th century, only 111 people had survived Western-introduced diseases, forced deportation as slave labor, and internal conflicts. Today, the Rapa Nui ethnic community number over 3,000. The Rapa Nui have a rich store of traditional life-cycle celebrations and practices, beginning with the birth ritual that involves the severing of the umbilical cord. During childhood, the first haircut and the first wearing of a loincloth would have been celebrated. At the age of eight, children's legs were tattooed. Upon reaching puberty, both boys and girls participated in what would be called "survival training" today—they were taken to an island to live for several months. Although these activities were called "rituals" and "ceremonies," they constituted in reality a school for imparting Rapa Nui traditional knowledge. Included in the "curriculum" were games of physical prowess and the art of war. There they were taught useful skills, according to their individual talents, such as tattooing (a demanding body art form and sign of adulthood among Polynesian men and women), writing, stone carving, woodworking, and other crafts.

Umu is the Rapa Nui traditional way of cooking food in an underground or earth oven, also called a "firepit." In Chile, it is called *curanto*, from an indigenous Mapuche term.

For very special celebrations and ceremonies for important life-cycle events, such as a wedding, the birth of a child, a housewarming, or to honor the dead, as well as the feast days of certain Catholic saints, such as Saint Peter, special *umus* are prepared. An *umu tahu* is made at the start of the festivity or ceremony, and, at the end, to give thanks for the success of the festivities and ceremony, an *umu hatu* is made.

These two ceremonial *umu* involve the collective efforts of a whole community, and preparation for these special feasts often begins a year in advance. The yearlong planning provides enough time to raise enough root crops, such as true yams (*Dioscorea alata*), sweet potatoes, and taro, as well as bananas, pigs, and chickens, for the celebratory feasts to feed 500 people or more.

To make an *umu tahu*, a large cavity is dug in the earth, its dimensions according to the number of people to be served and the amount of food to be cooked.

The cavity is lined on the sides and bottom with rectangular volcanic stones, carved to fit. The lining is usually assembled from odd numbers of stones. On the bottom stones, a bonfire is lit with firewood, and sometimes dried leaves, branches, and other vegetable material. Above and surrounding the fire, smaller stones of more or less equal size are placed to contain the fire, as well as to enable them to heat up.

While the fire is being prepared, the ingredients for the feast are washed, and some are wrapped in banana leaves. Besides pork, poultry, root crops, and other vegetables and fruits, the most desirable seafood, such as lobster, swordfish, and mahi are also included in a ceremonial *umu*. Other fish and seafood that are cooked in an *umu*, depending on the season, are groupers (*kopuku*), flagtails (*mahore*), octopus (*heke*), and sea urchins (*titeve*).

Once the stones are red-hot, they are removed to one side with special sticks, and the cavity is lined with fresh banana leaves. The food is then introduced in layers. Each layer is separated by banana leaves and red-hot stones. First come beef, pork, and chicken, wrapped in banana leaves. Next come the root crops: sweet potatoes (*kumara*), taro, yams (*uhi*), and **cassava**. These are followed by layers of fish, shellfish, and edible seaweed, also wrapped in banana leaves. A sweet dish of grated or mashed bananas (*po'e*) is wrapped in banana leaves and placed in the very top layer. Lastly, a layer of leaves and galvanized iron roofing is placed over the *umu* cavity, then a thick layer of soil is laid over this, in order to conserve the heat. *Umu* cooking takes a long time, from 2 to 3 hours, depending on the quantity of food.

The whole process of creating the *umu tahu*, from assembling the volcanic stones and leaves for the fire pit and preparing the ingredients, to the cooking, often lasts 6 hours. Throughout this time, the assembled guests and hosts socialize and sing. The same procedure is repeated for *umu hatu*, the closing ceremonial feast. The feast is served on banana leaves.

Po'e (Banana and Coconut Sweet)

Traditionally, this dish would be wrapped in banana leaves and cooked in an underground oven, the *umu*. This is a contemporary and more convenient way of preparing this traditional Rapa Nui sweet.

Yield: 8 to 10 servings

2 pounds ripe bananas, mashed or grated

½ pound pumpkin, **cassava**, taro, or yam (*Dioscorea alata*), peeled, grated

2 pounds flour, **sifted**, or more as needed

½ pound sugar, or to taste

2 pounds fresh grated coconut

2 cups coconut oil or any neutral-tasting oil

butter for greasing cake pan

Equipment: Large mixing bowl, wooden mixing spoon, 12×8-inch cake pan, oven mitts

Preheat oven to

1. In a large bowl, combine the bananas and pumpkin. Gradually add the flour and sugar, followed by half of the grated coconut. Make a well into the mixture, and stir in the oil, mixing

in the flour mixture starting from the center outward. The resulting batter should not be too runny. Add more flour as needed.

2. Transfer the batter to the prepared pan, and bake in preheated oven for 40 to 45 minutes, or until it tests done. A wooden skewer or toothpick inserted in the center should come out dry. Allow to cool.

To serve, slice the cake into individual serving pieces. Top each slice with the remaining half of grated coconut.

Chile's indigenous Quechua people remember and honor their ancestors on the first three days of November, which in the Roman Catholic calendar is the festival of All Saints' (*Todos Los Santos*). Throughout the three days, ritual tables are set with enormous quantities of celebratory food, and the personal effects of departed ancestors are displayed. The Quechua honor their dead with songs and prayers for a day and a night, and all their clothing is washed before burial. A year after death, the community's traditional spiritual leader and healer, the *yatiri*, leads in a community-wide final farewell. In a more extensive manner, another of Chile's indigenous groups, the Atacameños (who live in the Atacama Desert) have a four-phase funeral ritual. Beginning with the day of death itself, the family prays and sings for their departed family member for a day and night in the ritual called "*cóflar*." Then the deceased is dressed, and his or her customary sash is exchanged for one especially made for funerals. All the surviving family members are cleansed by the *yatiri* at the same time that all the deceased clothes are washed. On the first anniversary of the death, a ceremony called "The End of the Year" is officiated by the *yatiri* so that all the family members can bid a final goodbye.

Colombia

Located on the northwest corner of South America, Colombia is the only country on the continent to have coastlines on both the Atlantic and Pacific Oceans. It is bordered by Panama on the northwest, on the east by Venezuela and Brazil, and on the southwest by Peru and Ecuador.

At the time that the Spanish conquered the area in the 16th century, there was a highly developed economy (based on gold and emerald mining) and an advanced society established by the indigenous Muisca Indians in the Colombian highlands. The capital name Bogotá comes from the Muisca word *Bacatá*. Archaeological and historical research shows that Bacatá was the capital of a well developed society. (A volcano on Io, one of the moons of the planet Jupiter, is named after the Muisca god Bochica.) The Tairona ethnic group was another similarly developed society at the time of the Spanish conquest. Colombia remained under Spanish control until 1824, when the country joined with Venezuela, Ecuador, and Panama to form the Republic of Greater Colombia. Venezuela and Ecuador formed their own countries soon after, and Panama declared its independence in 1903 when Colombia refused to ratify the lease granting the United States rights to dig the Panama Canal.

Currently, Colombia's population is a diverse group, including *mestizos* (mixed Spanish and Indian) and people of Spanish descent (84 percent), Afro-Colombian (including mixed white and black, black, mixed black and Indian), comprising 10 percent, and indigenous groups 3.4 percent. Altogether, there are between 100 to 102 different indigenous Indian groups living in 33 regions in Colombia, from the highlands to the lowlands. A recent population survey shows over 1 million who identified themselves as indigenous Indians. Of these, the Muisca number 14,000. The Wayuu, who live on the Caribbean coast of Colombia, close to the border with Venezuela, comprise the largest ethnic group, with over 140,000 people, about one-fifth of Colombia's ethnic population.

The Catholic Church was the official religion until 1991 when the Colombian Constitution was revised to provide equal treatment to all religions. The Catholic Church still has the most adherents, about 70 percent of Colombians, although only 25 percent are active observants. Protestantism, especially the Pentecostal denominations, is gaining ground, with nearly 17 percent adherents. Other religions with minor membership (less than 3 percent of the total population) include indigenous religions, Baha'i, Jehovah's Witnesses, Seventh-Day Adventist Church, Islam, Judaism, Hare Krishna, Buddhism, Taoism, Mormonism, Hinduism, Rastafarianism, and the Orthodox Christian Church. Just over 8 percent of the population claim to be agnostics or atheists.

Religious holidays and life-cycle events are observed according to people's religious affiliations. (See Religious Life-Cycle Rituals and Customs, page lxv.)

In small villages and remote areas of the country, babies at risk of dying (usually those born prematurely) are often baptized by a traditional midwife (*partera*). The baptism means the baby dies a Christian.

The Wayuu indigenous religion centers on belief in *Maleiwa* (God), the creator of the Wayuu people and everything. Girls at the age of puberty, or as soon as they begin menstruating, undergo seclusion and training for some months, and sometimes up to two years. During this time, their hair is shaved, and they are taught how to sew, cook, and weave, and learn about pregnancy and birth control. They are also put on a vegetarian diet (*jaguapi*) and are obliged to bathe frequently. Marriages are usually arranged, sometimes as early as age 11 for girls.

For Catholics, after baptism and first communion, confirmation is usual for young people between 12 and 15 years old. Confirmation takes a long time since the young people must study the Bible and make a commitment to the Catholic faith. For the confirmation ritual, the children make a circle around the Bishop as he puts a cross of holy oil on the forehead of each person and taps his hand on the cheek. The oil is a symbol that Christ lives and will forever be with the young person from that moment on. Tapping the cheek is a signal to wake up to the light of a new life through Jesus

Christ. After the church service, families and friends of the confirmed children often join together to celebrate the happy occasion. This can be a dinner party in a restaurant or in someone's home. Today, more and more families are opting for the more relaxing, less expensive outdoor gathering. After eating a picnic feast, parents lounge while the children play.

As for foods for life-cycle celebrations, the most important events call for meat on the table. In the cities, especially Bogotá, *sobrebarriga Bogotana* is prepared for baptisms, first communions, confirmations, and wedding feasts.

⚜ *Sobrebarriga Bogotana* (Flank Steak, Bogotá-Style)

Yield: serves 4 to 6

2 pounds flank steak with fat left on

1 onion, **finely chopped**

2 cloves garlic, finely chopped

2 tomatoes, chopped

2 or 3 parsley sprigs

½ teaspoon ground thyme

1 bay leaf

salt and pepper to taste

6 cups canned beef broth

2 tablespoons butter or margarine, at room temperature

1 cup **fresh bread crumbs**

Equipment: Large saucepan with cover, mixing spoon, fork, metal tongs or meat fork, paper towels, broiler pan with rack, small skillet, mixing spoon, oven mitts, meat fork and knife, strainer, serving bowl, serving platter

1. Put meat in large saucepan, add beef broth, onion, garlic, tomatoes, parsley, thyme, bay leaf, and salt and pepper to taste. Bring to boil over medium-high heat. Reduce heat to **simmer**, cover, and cook for 2 to 2½ hours, until fork tender.

Preheat oven to 350°F.

2. Lift out meat with metal tongs or meat fork, and pat dry with paper towels. Place meat, fat-side up, on rack of broiler pan. Save cooking liquid.

3. Melt butter or margarine in small skillet, add bread crumbs, and stir to coat well. Spoon buttered crumbs thickly onto surface of meat. Place in oven for 15 to 20 minutes until crumb coating is golden brown. Allow to rest for 20 minutes before cutting into ¼-inch-thick slices and arranging on platter.

4. Reheat cooking liquid over medium heat. Strain into serving bowl, and serve as gravy to spoon over meat.

Serve with papas chorreadas *(recipe follows) and salad.*

This marvelously rich potato dish goes well with flank steak. For the less fortunate, this recipe is often the main dish for life-cycle celebrations.

⚘ *Papas Chorreadas* (Potatoes with Cheese and Onion Sauce)

Yield: serves 6

6 potatoes, scrubbed

2 tablespoons butter or margarine

1 onion, **finely chopped**

2 **tomatoes, peeled** and chopped

salt and pepper to taste

½ cup heavy cream

1 cup shredded Swiss or Monterey Jack cheese

Equipment: Large saucepan, knife, large skillet, mixing spoon, serving bowl

1. Peel and quarter potatoes, and put into large saucepan. Cover generously with water, and bring to boil over medium-high heat. Reduce heat to **simmer**, cover, and cook until very tender, 25 to 30 minutes. Drain and keep warm in serving bowl.

2. Melt butter or margarine in large skillet over medium-high heat. Add onion, stir, and **sauté** until soft, 3 to 5 minutes. Add tomatoes and salt and pepper to taste, and cook, stirring frequently, 5 to 7 minutes. Stir in heavy cream and cheese, until cheese is melted.

To serve, pour cheese and onion sauce over potatoes, and eat while warm.

In many parts of Colombia, especially in the western part of the country, in particular along the South Pacific Coast, no celebration—birthday, wedding, engagement, confirmation, baptism, first communion—is complete without *torta negra* (black cake), a rich, dark fruitcake heady with rum and sweet wine. A notable difference between Colombian black cake and Caribbean black cake is the presence of candied papaya and/or candied figs in the Colombian version. Even children's parties are celebrated with *torta negra*, and even the smallest children learn to enjoy eating this special cake. The two-week maceration period of the fruits in rum and wine is enough to evaporate the alcohol.

⚘ *Torta Negra Colombiana* (Colombian Black Cake)

2 cups **pitted** prunes

4 cups mixed dried fruit—raisins, candied figs (*brevas caladas*), candied **papaya** (*papaya calada*)

½ cup rum

1 cup sweet red wine or Moscatel

3⅓ cups flour

¼ teaspoon salt

1 teaspoon baking powder

¼ teaspoon baking soda

1 teaspoon cinnamon

½ teaspoon nutmeg

½ teaspoon cloves or **allspice**

2 cups butter, softened

1¾ cups sugar

4 large eggs, at room temperature, separated

1 tablespoon vanilla extract

3 or more tablespoons burnt sugar coloring (also called "baker's caramel" [*dulce quemado*], available at Latin American and Caribbean food shops or online)

Note: This recipe takes 2 or more weeks.

1. At least 2 weeks before baking, in a glass jar with cover, place the prunes and dried fruit with half of the rum and half of the wine. Cover, and let the jar stand undisturbed in a cool, dark place to slowly macerate.

2. In a bowl, mix together the flour, salt, baking powder, baking soda, cinnamon, nutmeg, and cloves or allspice.

3. In the bowl of with an electric mixer, mix at medium speed the butter with the sugar until creamy and light-colored. Add the yolks one by one, mixing thoroughly after each addition. Stir in vanilla. Turn off the mixer. Add the flour and spice mixture, and turn on the mixer on low. Mix for 1 minute, and scrape down the sides of the bowl. Add the burnt sugar coloring, and mix for 1 minute more.

4. Remove the bowl from the mixer, and fold in the macerated fruits, scraping all liquids. Transfer contents to a bowl and set aside. Clean and dry the mixer bowl and beaters thoroughly.

5. At medium speed, mix the egg whites until foamy. Add the remaining sugar, and continue beating to soft peaks. Fold gently and lightly into the batter. Transfer to the prepared pan, and bake in a preheated 325°F oven for 1½ to 2 hours, or until a wooden skewer inserted in the center of the cake comes out clean. Remove cake from the oven, and let cool for 10 minutes in the pan. Unmold, using the parchment overhang to remove the cake, and let cool thoroughly on a wire rack.

6. Ice with butter icing frosting (recipe page 324), and decorate with chosen cake decoration.

Among the Wayuu ethnic community who live along the Caribbean seacoast, life-cycle events and important occasions are celebrated with goat dishes, in common with other island countries in the Caribbean Sea. The most renowned of these festive dishes is *friche*. This is often accompanied by *yaja*, an *arepa* made of corn, and a drink called *yajaushi*, made from goat's or cow's milk mixed with corn, salt, and sugar. For celebrations, the Wayuu also make a potent alcoholic drink called *chirrinchi*, from *panela*, the unrefined sugar extracted from sugar cane juice, fermented for several weeks.

ᕊ *Friche* (Wayuu-style Goat Stew)

Yield: about 10 servings

2 cups goat's blood (if not available, chicken blood can be substituted, or as an alternative, goat, chicken, or rabbit livers can be liquefied in a blender with a little water)

3 pounds boneless goat meat (shoulder, ribs, leg) or lamb, **diced**

juice of 4 to 5 large lemons

salt and freshly ground black pepper to taste

1 cup oil, or more as needed, for frying

1 pound goat or lamb offal (heart, liver, lungs, etc.), washed, well drained, patted dry, diced

3 onions, minced   1 large green sweet pepper, diced

half a head of garlic, minced

Note: If using fresh blood from a goat just recently slaughtered, it must be immediately mixed with salt to prevent it from coagulating and then allowed to cool, preferably in the refrigerator, while preparing the rest of the ingredients.

1. In a large bowl, combine the lemon juice, salt, and pepper, and immerse the goat's meat in it. Rub the juice into all the meat surfaces, and leave the meat to marinate for 20 to 30 minutes.

2. While meat is marinating, fill a deep saucepan halfway with water, and when it comes to a boil, add the liver, heart, lungs, and other offal. Lower the heat to a simmer, and parboil for about 10 to 15 minutes until the offal changes color and are halfway cooked. Drain the offal on a colander, and set aside.

3. Heat the oil in a large deep skillet or large shallow saucepan over medium heat. Brown the goat meat, frying in batches so that the pan is not crowded. Drain and set aside.

4. Fry the offal next until brown. Drain and set aside.

5. In the remaining oil (add some if insufficient), brown the onions and garlic over medium heat until aromatic. Stir in the diced green pepper, and return the fried meat and offal to the pan.

   Mix well and cook for 5 minutes.

6. Stir in the blood, lower the heat, and let the stew cook gently for 30 minutes. Stir the stew from time to time to prevent it from sticking to the pan. Taste and adjust the seasoning.

Serve with corn arepas *(see recipe page 622) or boiled cassava.*

Ecuador

The name "Ecuador" means equator in Spanish, which is appropriate since the equator runs through the center of this country in the northwestern part of South America. The Pacific coastline forms one border, and Columbia and Peru the others.

By the time the Spanish arrived in the 16th century, the Inca Empire had absorbed and conquered the Kingdom of Quito, which had flourished around 1000 CE. Spain ruled the area until 1824, when, after a 14-year struggle, Ecuador joined Venezuela, Columbia, and Panama in a confederacy known as Greater Columbia. This union fell apart in 1830, and Ecuador became independent.

Today, the population is made up of *mestizos* (mixed Spanish and Indian), Indians, and people of Spanish descent. Almost all Ecuadorians are Roman Catholics and celebrate life-cycle events prescribed by the Church, with certain local touches added. (See Protestant and Catholic Life-Cycle Rituals, page lxxiii.)

When Andean Indians marry, they combine old local customs with those of the Catholic Church. On the night prior to the wedding day, *las cosas de mediano* (wedding food) is carried by the groom to the home of his bride. The food usually includes cooked guinea pigs and *pollo en salsa de huevos* (recipe page 592), baskets of bread, ears of corn, peeled potatoes with sauce, hard-cooked eggs, and bottles of rum. The two fathers say a blessing over the bride and groom, and then they bless the food.

Catholic weddings must always be held in a church. However, because of the cost of a church ceremony, it is not uncommon for *mestizos* to have a less expensive civil ceremony with a *maestro de ceremonias de boda* (master of ceremonies) officiating. Most couples will add a few Catholic rituals to their civil ceremony. A ritual popular among most Hispanic Catholics is draping the long rosary over the shoulders of the kneeling bride and groom. In a church, the godparents perform the ritual, but in some Indian communities, the *maestro* places the rosary around the newlyweds. After the placement of the rosary, more blessings are bestowed upon the couple, they exchange rings, and they declare their undying devotion to one another.

Most Ecuadorians live on soups and thick stews of beans and corn with other vegetables. For special happy occasions, such as a baptism or wedding, the least expensive and most available meat is *cuy* (guinea pig); it would be used in this recipe. We suggest using regular pork instead.

♪ *Puerco Horneado* (Ecuador Pork Roast)

Yield: serves 4 to 6

2¾- to 3-pound **oven-ready** pork loin, **boned**, rolled, and tied (available at most butcher shops and supermarkets)

½ teaspoon salt, more as needed, divided

3 cloves garlic, **finely chopped**, or 1 teaspoon garlic granules

1 teaspoon ground marjoram, divided

3 fresh basil leaves, finely chopped, or 1 teaspoon crushed basil

1 teaspoon ground cumin, divided

½ teaspoon ground red pepper, more or less to taste

3 cups boiling water, more if needed

2 tablespoons all-purpose flour

1 tablespoon wine vinegar

3 tablespoons cold water

1 teaspoon dried parsley flakes

Equipment: Small bowl, mixing spoon, plastic food wrap, medium roasting pan with wire rack, oven mitts, meat thermometer (optional), **bulb baster** or mixing spoon, small serving bowl, spoon, meat knife

1. In small bowl, combine ½ teaspoon salt, garlic, ½ teaspoon marjoram, basil, ½ teaspoon cumin, and ½ teaspoon ground red pepper, more or less to taste. Rub mixture on meat. Wrap meat in plastic wrap, and refrigerate for 8 hours or overnight.

Preheat oven to 450°F.

2. Remove plastic wrap and place meat on rack in roasting pan. Bake in oven until browned, 10 to 15 minutes. Using oven mitts, remove from oven.

Reduce oven to 350°

3. Insert meat thermometer into center of meat if using one. Pour 3 cups boiling water around meat, and return to oven to bake, basting frequently with bulb baster or mixing spoon. Add more water if needed, bake until thermometer registers 170°F, or for about 1 to 1½ hours. Remove from oven, and allow to rest for 10 minutes before slicing.

4. Prepare sauce: Measure 2 cups greaseless pan drippings into a small saucepan. Whisk in flour, vinegar, 3 tablespoons water, remaining ½ teaspoon marjoram, basil, and remaining ½ teaspoon cumin. Cook, whisking constantly over medium-high heat until sauce thickens, 3 to 5 minutes. Stir in parsley flakes.

To serve, cut roast into ½-inch-thick slices. Put gravy in small serving bowl, and spoon over meat. Serve with medley of vegetables, such as squash, corn, and tomatoes.

⚭ *Torta de Novia* (Bride's Cake)

This is a classic Ecuadorian bridal cake, richly flavored with fruits, nuts, and spices—quite similar to a fruit cake. The recipe for the cake dough needs to be doubled to make 3 layers of 12 inches, 10 inches, and 6 inches in diameter. The quantities of ingredients for the doubled recipe are beyond the capacity of home mixers and bowls, so prepare only one batch of cake dough at a time. First make the largest cake for the bottom layer of 12 inches in diameter.

Yield when doubled for all 3 layers: about 80 pieces, each 1 by 2 inches

Cake dough:

5½ cups flour, **sifted**, plus a bit for sprinkling over greased cake liners

1 tablespoon baking powder

½ teaspoon ground cinnamon

½ teaspoon grated nutmeg

¼ teaspoon powdered cloves

1 tablespoon instant coffee

1½ tablespoons sugar

½ cup hot water

Orange syrup:

1 cup sugar

⅔ cup water

Almond butter cream icing:

4 cups soft butter

2 cups butter, softened, plus extra for greasing

3½ cups powdered (icing or confectioners') sugar

¼ cup brandy or rum

7 large eggs

½ cup **candied fruits** (apricot, pineapple, figs), chopped

½ cup candied cherries, halved

½ cup ground walnuts

½ cup **blanched** almonds, toasted and ground

1 tablespoon orange **liqueur**

½ cup apricot jam, strained (passed through a fine sieve)

12 cups icing sugar, sifted

2 teaspoons almond essence

1 cup blanched almond flakes

selection of cake decorations: edible flowers, ribbons, edible "pearls," etc.

Equipment: 3 round cake pans 12, 10, and 6 inches in diameter by 3 to 3½ inches deep, parchment paper, stand or handheld mixer, large and small mixing bowls, fine-meshed sieve, wooden skewer, **pastry brush**, cake decorator piping tubes, oven mitts

1. Prepare the cake pans: They should be between 3 and 3½ inches deep and with diameters of 12, 10, and 6 inches. Line them with a double layer of parchment paper, greasing the layers and in between layers with butter. Dust the buttered layers with flour, and tip out the excess flour. Set aside.

2. In a mixing bowl, combine well the flour, baking powder, cinnamon, nutmeg, and cloves. Set aside.

3. In a small bowl, combine the instant coffee and sugar. Stir in hot water until the coffee and sugar are dissolved. Set aside to cool.

   Ten minutes before baking, preheat oven to 325°F.

4. In a stand mixer, beat the butter at medium speed with sugar until light and fluffy. Gradually add the brandy or rum, then the eggs, one at a time, beating well until the mixture is smooth before adding the next egg. At low speed, add the flour in three batches, followed by the coffee mixture in two batches. Turn off the mixer, and fold in the fruits and nuts with a large wooden spoon. Spoon the batter into the 12-inch pan, and bake in the center rack of preheated oven for about 1 hour and 45 minutes, or until golden and risen. A wooden skewer inserted in the center should come out clean.

5. While the cake is baking, prepare the orange syrup. In a small saucepan at low heat, dissolve the sugar in the water until the sugar is dissolved. Allow the syrup to simmer for 5 minutes. Set aside to cool. Once cool, stir in the orange liqueur. Set aside.

6. Once the cake is out of the oven, let it cool for 30 minutes in the pan. Use a wooden skewer to poke holes all over the cake, all the way to the bottom. Pour the syrup over the cake, letting it soak thoroughly before adding more. Brush the cake with the strained apricot jam.

   Leave the cake to cool completely. Once thoroughly cool, it can be iced.

7. To make the second and third layers of the cake, prepare another batch of the cake dough and orange syrup, as given previously. Divide the cake dough into the prepared 10-inch and 6-inch pans, filling each pan about ⅔ full.

8. Bake both cakes together in the middle rack of preheated oven. If there is not enough space for both, place one on the rack below, and switch the cakes around after 30 minutes.

9. Bake the 6-inch cake for 1 hour, or until golden and well risen. Bake the 10-inch cake for 1 hour and 15 minutes, or until golden and well risen. Insert a wooden skewer in the center of each cake to test, and the skewer should come out clean when the cake is done.

   Cool the cakes, pour over the orange syrup, and brush with strained apricot jam, as before.

10. Prepare the butter cream icing. In an electric mixer bowl, put the butter and beat at medium speed until pale. Gradually add the icing sugar, a little at a time, beating well after each

addition until the mixture is smooth. Spread over the stacked cake layers. Use cake decorating tubes with the buttercream icing to pipe your choice of patterns all over the cake layers.

Distribute the almonds throughout, and place your chosen pieces of additional cake decor.

The following recipe is a typical chicken dish in Ecuador where eggs are used often because they are a sign of fertility, good for wedding celebrations.

♷ *Pollo en Salsa de Huevos* (Chicken in Egg Sauce)

Yield: serves 4 to 6

¼ cup vegetable oil

3½- to 4-pound chicken, cut into serving pieces

1 large onion, **finely chopped**

1 clove garlic, finely chopped

1 tablespoon dry mustard

salt and pepper to taste

2 cups chicken broth

6 hard-cooked eggs, finely chopped

Equipment: **Dutch oven** or large **heavy-bottomed** skillet, mixing spoon, metal tongs, baking sheet, oven mitts, serving platter

1. Heat oil in Dutch oven or large heavy-bottomed skillet over medium-high heat. **Sauté** chicken pieces, in batches, until golden on both sides, 7 to 12 minutes. Using metal tongs, transfer to baking sheet until all chicken pieces are cooked.

2. Sauté onions and garlic in the oil left over in Dutch oven or large skillet until onions are soft, 3 to 5 minutes. Reduce heat to medium, and stir in dry mustard and salt and pepper to taste.

3. Return chicken pieces to skillet or Dutch oven. Pour chicken broth over chicken, and bring to boil over medium-high heat. Reduce heat to **simmer**, cover, and cook for 45 to 55 minutes, until chicken is done. Test **chicken doneness.**

4. Transfer chicken to serving platter, and keep warm. Increase heat to medium-high under sauce in Dutch oven or large skillet. Stir in chopped eggs and cook just long enough to slightly thicken the sauce, 3 to 5 minutes.

To serve, pour sauce over chicken. This dish is usually served with a side dish of rice or potatoes.

Guyana

Guyana is located on the northeast coast of South America, just above the equator. It is east of Venezuela, west of Suriname, and north of Brazil.

Unlike most of Latin America, Guyana was not colonized by the Spanish or the Portuguese. France, Britain, and the Netherlands all established settlements in the area, but the majority of settlements were Dutch. The British took control of the region in 1831, and as a result, Guyana is the only English-speaking nation in South America and has close ties to other former British colonies in the Caribbean. In 1966, Guyana achieved independence.

In 1834, slavery was outlawed, and to fill the labor shortage on sugarcane plantations, Hindu workers were brought from India as indentured workers. People of East Indian descent now make up 40 percent of the population, and those of African descent, about 30 percent. Twenty percent are mixed, and the remaining 10 percent are indigenous Amerindians. A minority of less than 1 percent are made up of Portuguese and other white, as well as Chinese, inhabitants. Guyana's indigenous groups consist of Arawak, Macushi, Wapishana, Patamuna, Akawaio, Carib, Warrau, Waiwai, and Arekuna Amerindians. Additionally, Atorad, Trio, and Taruma Indians have settled in Guyana from neighboring countries.

In contrast to its Latin neighbors, in Guyana, Protestantism is predominant. Denominations such as the Pentecostal Church, Seventh-Day Adventists, Anglicans, and Methodists have 35 percent of the population as adherents. Hindu followers account for 25 percent of the Guyanese population, and Catholics, 7 percent. Other Christian sects account for 20 percent. Islam has about 7 percent adherents, Jehovah's Witnesses, about 1 percent, and Rastafarianism, less than 1 percent.

The East Indians live in close-knit communities and follow the traditional Hindu rituals and ceremonies of their homeland. (See India, page 140, and Hinduism and Hindu Life-Cycle Rituals, page lxxix.)

When a Hindu dies, the body is cremated three days later. It is customary for the family to hold a memorial ceremony for the deceased, and relatives, friends, and villagers are expected to attend. The Hindu ceremony (*puja*) is held to help remember the soul of the deceased. An altar is made of a small banana tree and garlands of tropical flowers set on a mud base. The Hindu priest (*pundit*) lights fires in tiny clay bowls (*deyas*) and also lights sandalwood incense sticks. The priest then puts a round, white finger marking, called *tikkas*, on everyone's forehead. He chants *mantras* (repeated prayers) and makes food offerings to the sacred fire on the altar.

A male relative of the deceased also sits on the altar with the priest. He makes offerings of milk, rice, and *ghee* (recipe page 142) to the sacred fire. Both men wear white ritual garments (*kurtas*).

After the priest finishes the *puja*, everyone present partakes of the feast. The meal consists of *rotis* (recipe follows), a curry dish, rice, pumpkin, bhindi with coconut. Mourners sit on floor mats, and the meal that has been placed on banana leaves is eaten with their fingers.

Roti is one of several Indian flatbreads. Hindus in Guyana add coconut to the *roti* recipe, making it unusual.

⚘ *Roti* (Flatbread with Coconut)

Yield: about 12 loaves

1 cup finely shredded coconut (available at East Indian food stores or Asian food stores and some supermarkets), or place shredded coconut in blender until finely ground

2¼ cups **self-rising flour**

1 to 1¼ cups cold water

vegetable oil, for pan frying

Equipment: Medium mixing bowl, mixing spoon, lightly floured work surface, clean kitchen towel, large **heavy-bottomed** skillet or griddle, **pastry brush**, wide metal spatula, plate

1. In medium mixing bowl, combine coconut and flour. Add water, a little at a time, stirring constantly until dough is soft, smooth, and pulls away from sides of bowl. Transfer dough to lightly floured work surface. Cover with towel for 30 minutes.

2. Divide dough into 12 equal balls. Using your hands, flatten each ball into thin circles, about 5-inches across, on lightly floured work surface. Place finished *rotis* on work surface, and keep covered with towel until ready to fry.

3. Heat large heavy-bottomed skillet or griddle over medium-high heat. Using pastry brush, brush griddle or skillet with oil. Cook breads in batches until both sides are golden, about 2 minutes on each side. Remove from griddle or skillet with wide metal spatula, and transfer to plate to keep warm while cooking remaining loaves. Add more oil, when necessary to keep bread from sticking to skillet.

Serve rotis *while still warm for best flavor.* Rotis *are used to scoop food from the plate to one's mouth.*

⚘ *Guyanese Pepperpot*

Guyanese pepperpot (also spelled pepper pot) is regarded as the national dish of Guyana, and it is distinguished by the use of cassareep, a dark brown syrup boiled down from **cassava** juice. The cassava that is used for cassareep is normally toxic, but when thoroughly and properly cooked, it poses no danger. The juice is extracted from fresh cassava tubers and boiled down through long hours of cooking, until it becomes thick and the edible flavoring known as "cassareep." Credit for discovering the process of making this extraordinary syrup goes to the black Carib Indians, also known as the Garifuna. The flavor of cassareep is bittersweet, almost akin to blackstrap molasses, except with its own inimitable aroma from the various spices used in its making—among them cinnamon, cloves, and others kept a trade secret. Cassareep is also well-known for its antiseptic properties, such that it acts as a preservative, and in the days before refrigeration, cassareep kept this stew from spoiling for days or even weeks and months, as long as it was brought to a boil daily. Guyanese pepperpot is usually made for Christmas, but it is also made for special occasions and important events. Some Guyanese cooks substitute oxtail or venison or other game meat, such as labba, for the pig's feet. The labba is a Guyanese wild animal that lives in the forest, and its main food is fruits and nuts. It is also known as *paca* or *gibnut* and is much appreciated by Guyanese for its tender, succulent meat. Pepperpot is best when a mixture of different meats is used. Lamb or mutton or even goat (young kid) can be also be used.

Yield: 8 to 10 servings

2 to 3 pig's trotters or 1 oxtail, or a mixture, cleaned, cut into large pieces

1 pound stewing beef or lamb or young goat meat, **cubed**

1 pound boneless shoulder or belly pork, cubed

3 tablespoons oil

2 large onions, chopped

4 to 5 cloves garlic, peeled, crushed

2 chili peppers (or to taste, preferably local wiri, or other hot chili pepper)

½ cup cassareep (available from some stores selling Caribbean or West Indian foods)

2 pieces, about 4 to 5 inches, cinnamon sticks

1 heaping tablespoon unrefined sugar (*panela*), or palm sugar or dark brown sugar

salt and freshly ground black pepper to taste

2 to 3 sprigs basil

1 bunch fresh thyme

water, as needed

Equipment: Large saucepan with cover, **skimmer**, oven mitts

1. In a large saucepan, put the pig's trotters or oxtail, cover with water, and bring to a boil over medium-high heat. As soon as it comes to a boil, start skimming off the froth that forms at the surface. Lower the heat, and keep the pan simmering until the feet are half-cooked. Test by inserting a fork; it should go in halfway through without too much resistance. Turn off the heat. Discard the water, and set the feet aside.

2. In the cleaned and dried saucepan, heat the oil over medium heat. Sauté the onions until they are softened and golden brown. Stir in the garlic, and continue to sauté until the onions and garlic are aromatic. Stir in the beef and pork, and increase the heat to medium-high. Keep stirring until the meat cubes are browned on both sides, about 7 to 10 minutes. Stir in the chili peppers, cassareep, cinnamon sticks, unrefined sugar, salt and pepper to taste, and thyme, mixing the condiments thoroughly with the meat.

3. Add the reserved pig's feet and enough water to come up to just below the level of the meat. Let the pan come to a boil, covered. Reduce the heat to let the pan simmer for an hour, or until the meat is very tender.

4. Fifteen minutes before turning off the heat, stir in the basil. Taste and adjust seasoning, adding more salt and pepper if needed.

Serve (ideally, reheated to a boil the following day to allow the flavors to meld) with thick slices of homemade white bread, or plain white rice, or boiled cassava cubes, or roti, with a side dish of cooked greens, such as callaloo.

♪ **Black Cake**

Black cake is a dark fruit cake that is commonly prepared in Guyana and other Caribbean countries for the Christmas season. However, it is also always present on the table on special occasions and important family gatherings, such as milestone birthdays and, most especially, weddings. It is prepared at least 2 months before the event, so that the cake has time to properly mature and absorb its numerous rum "baths." For a wedding or a milestone birthday, black cake is covered with a layer of marzipan (first brushed with an apricot or other fruit glaze so that the marzipan adheres to the cake), then covered with a layer of royal icing. The cake is then decorated with appropriate decorations, such as edible glitter or sparkles.

Yield: about 20 servings

Fruit:

1¼ cup currants

1¼ cup **pitted** prunes

1¼ cup raisins

½ cup candied cherries

⅓ cup candied lemon peel

⅓cup candied orange peel

1 cup **blanched** almond flakes

2 cups rum or port wine

Cake batter:

2 cups flour

1 teaspoon baking powder

½ teaspoon baking soda

¼ tsp salt

½ teaspoon cinnamon

½ teaspoon nutmeg

½ teaspoon ground mace

½ teaspoon ground cloves or **allspice**

1 cup butter

⅔ cup brown sugar

1 teaspoon vanilla essence

5 eggs

2 tablespoons caramel coloring, or more as needed, homemade (see directions in recipe) or available at Caribbean food shops

¼ cup rum

1 bottle of dark rum for pouring over cake

Caramel coloring:

½ cup sugar

2 tablespoons water

Equipment: Food mill or food processor, large glass jar with cover, small **heavy-bottomed** saucepan, 10×4-inch-deep springform pan (or 12×3-inch-deep springform pan for a slightly thinner cake that will bake a bit faster), parchment paper, mixing bowl, electric mixer, oven mitts, wooden skewer or toothpick, clean and dry kitchen towel, aluminum foil

Note: This recipe takes 2 or more weeks.

1. Prepare the dried fruits and nuts. Wash well and pat dry. Chop finely in a food mill or food processor. Transfer finely chopped mixture to a glass jar. Pour over 2 cups of rum or port wine, mix well, cover, and allow to macerate for at least 2 weeks in a cool, dark place.

2. Prepare the caramel coloring: In a small heavy-bottomed saucepan over low heat, place ½ cup of sugar, and let it caramelize slowly. The sugar will turn into a transparent syrup that rapidly takes on an amber, then a brown color. Keep a close watch on the pan, turning and moving the pan as necessary, so that caramelization occurs evenly throughout. When the syrup is dark brown and very thick, add water. Be careful, as the addition of water will cause the pan to sputter.

Allow the mixture to simmer just until the caramel and water are thoroughly combined. Set aside until needed.

3. Prepare the cake batter: First, grease and line a 10-inch round springform baking pan with a double layer of parchment paper. Make the parchment liner extend an inch above the cake pan (this prevents the cake surface from browning too rapidly, and keeps the cake bottom from scorching while baking). Set aside.

Ten minutes before baking, preheat oven to 275°F.

4. In a bowl, combine the flour, baking powder, baking soda, salt, cinnamon, nutmeg, mace, and cloves. Mix until homogeneous and set aside.

5. In a large mixing bowl over medium speed, mix the butter and sugar until fluffy and pale-colored. Stir in the vanilla extract. Add the eggs one at a time, mixing well until the previous one is incorporated before adding the next. With a wooden spoon, stir in the fruits together with any remaining macerating liquid, and mix well. Add the flour and spice mixture, and mix until the batter is smooth. Stir in the caramel coloring, adding more as needed to get a very dark color, and stir in the rum.

6. Transfer the batter to the prepared cake pan. Bake for 2 to 2½ hours, or until done. (If using a larger cake pan, start testing just before 2 hours have passed.) A wooden skewer or tooth-pick inserted in the center of the cake should come out clean when cake is done.

7. Remove from the oven, pierce the surface all over with the skewer or toothpick, and slowly dribble in about ½ cup of rum over the cake. Once the rum is absorbed, gradually dribble over another ½ cup, or as much as the cake will absorb.

9. Wrap the cake in parchment paper, then in a clean, dry kitchen towel, and lastly in foil. Moisten the cake with about a half cup of rum weekly, replacing the covering well, so that the cake does not dry out.

To serve, cover with a layer of marzipan (recipe page 274), and frost with royal icing.

Kanki (Steamed Coconut and Cornmeal Parcels)

Kanki is an Afro-Guyanese dish, often made in the rural areas of Guyana. It is principally made around the time surrounding Guyanese Emancipation Day (August 1), a holiday that commemorates the abolition of slavery in Guyana and the other British colonies in the Caribbean on the same day in 1834. *Kanki* is also made for important family events and other special occasions.

Yield: about 15 to 20 pieces

4 cups fresh or frozen unsweetened grated coconut, or grated flesh from 1 large fresh, mature coconut (Green or unripe coconuts will not have the desired consistency for this dish.)

1 pound fine yellow **cornmeal** (not *masa harina*)

½ cup brown, unrefined sugar (*panela*), palm sugar, or white sugar, or more to taste

½ cup raisins

¼ cup butter or margarine, melted

½ teaspoon nutmeg

½ teaspoon freshly ground black pepper

1 teaspoon vanilla extract or almond extract

2 cups coconut milk (not coconut juice) or full-fat milk, or as needed

15 to 20 sheets, 8 by 8 inches, cut from fresh banana leaves or aluminum foil, for wrapping

kitchen twine, for tying

Equipment: Large mixing bowl, **double boiler** or steamer or large saucepan with steaming basket, tongs, oven mitts

1. Prepare the wrapping: Pass the cut-up banana leaves through very hot water, or soak them for a few minutes until they are pliable. Pat them dry, or leave them to air-dry while you prepare the rest of the ingredients.

2. Prepare the *kanki* filling: In a large bowl, combine the grated coconut, cornmeal, brown or white sugar, raisins, melted butter, nutmeg, black pepper, and vanilla until they are well mixed. Gradually stir in the coconut milk, adding only enough until the mixture is moist but still holds its shape. (It should not be dripping wet like a slurry.) You may not need all of the 2 cups, or you may need a bit more. Supplement with regular milk if you do not have enough coconut milk.

   Taste, and add more sugar if needed.

3. Place 2 tablespoons of the coconut and cornmeal mixture in the center of the banana sheet or foil. Fold over the sides to loosely enclose the mixture in a neat parcel. The *kanki* will need space to expand as it cooks. Tie the parcel with kitchen twine if using banana leaf.

4. In a double boiler or large saucepan with a steaming basket, bring 4 cups of water to a boil over medium-high heat. Place the parcels in the top pan of the double boiler, or in the steaming basket, and let them steam for 40 to 45 minutes, or until done. Test one to make sure.

The kanki *can be eaten warm or at room temperature.*

Paraguay

Paraguay is a landlocked country centrally located in South America between Bolivia, Brazil, and Argentina. Its area is just slightly smaller than California. Guarani-speaking Indians were the original inhabitants of the region, and Guarani is the most often used language after Spanish. Spanish explorers penetrated the region in the

16th century, and Jesuits set up settlements in the next century. Paraguay revolted against Spanish rule in 1811 and declared itself a republic. Since independence, Paraguay has been troubled by wars and dictatorships, and internal strife has left Paraguay less developed than many of its South American neighbors.

The majority (95 percent) of the population are *mestizo* (part Spanish, part Indian), and of these, about 90 percent are Roman Catholic. About 6 percent of the population are Protestant. Life-cycle celebrations are celebrated according to the traditions of the Catholic Church and Protestant denominations (see Protestant and Catholic Life-Cycle Rituals, page lxxiii). There is a small minority of Mennonites. At birth, babies are baptized, but the first religious ceremony children actively participate in is first communion. Around seven years old, children make their first confession to the priest to cleanse them in preparation for receiving their first communion.

When the child is baptized, the family observes the happy occasion with a meal for relatives and friends. The celebration begins when everyone relaxes and takes a sip of the *yerba maté* as it is passed around. The meal is preceded by large bowls or baskets of freshly baked *sopa Paraguaya* (recipe page 603), set out for guests to munch on while eating their thick soup of either *so'o-yosopy* (recipe page 602) or *caldo de zapallo tierno* (recipe page 603). Along with the filling soup, there are always beans and rice and perhaps a chicken dish, such as *arroz con pollo* (recipe page 558 or 527). For the first communion, no special celebration is observed, other than a family dinner.

Celebrating a child's birthday in Paraguay in days gone by, especially during the winter, usually meant a cup of hot chocolate with cookies, a birthday cake, a piñata filled with candy and sweets for the invited guests to take home, and decorations crafted by the celebrant's mother with the help of other family members and other siblings. The cookies became more elaborate as economic conditions improved and were replaced by pastries, such as *pasta frola* (Argentinian *linzertorte*, see recipe page 564), pancakes filled with jam or *dulce de leche* (recipe page 563), *alfajor* cookies (recipe page 562). The milk chocolate drink made way for bottled soft drinks and juices. Older celebrants used to be thumped (gently or strongly) on their backs after the birthday song was sung. Another tradition was for the invited guests to bring eggs and flour, ostensibly to make a cake, but the eggs were broken and flour sprinkled over the head of the celebrant as a prank.

Nowadays, parents have more money but less time to prepare these delicacies or to host parties at home, and it has become common to hire a catering service or party venue for children's birthday parties, where miniature sandwiches, tiny pizzas, small hamburgers with French fries, and hotdogs are served. These party venues and party planning services additionally offer various activities to entertain the young guests. There are all sorts of play equipment, such as trampolines, inflatable castles, rally simulators, and the like. For preteen and teenage girls, a spa day ending in a *karaoke* session has become popular, with the participants getting facials, nail care, and having makeup applied, followed by a singing competition. Sleepover parties have also become popular, especially among those aged 8 to 12, with children bringing their own sleeping bags, and often entertainment is provided, such as a clown or magician.

♪ *Chocolate de Cumpleaños* (Birthday Chocolate Drink)

Yield: 6 servings

6 teaspoons **cornstarch**

6 cups milk

6 tablespoons sugar

6 tablespoons cocoa powder

Optional flavorings: grated orange **zest**, a teaspoon of vanilla, a teaspoon of cinnamon, grated mace or nutmeg

Equipment: Mixing bowl, medium saucepan, wire whisk, oven mitts

1. In a mixing bowl, place the cornstarch and whisk in 3 cups of the cold milk until the cornstarch is fully combined with the milk.

2. In a medium saucepan over medium heat, place the chocolate and sugar, and whisk in the rest of the milk, little by little, to form a smooth paste without lumps. Gradually whisk in the rest of the milk, followed by the milk and cornstarch mixture. Alternatively, place all the ingredients in a blender, and **blend** until smooth. Then transfer to a saucepan to cook until done.

3. Whisk continuously to avoid the chocolate sticking to the pan. Let the chocolate mixture come to a boil.

4. Turn off the heat, and ladle the chocolate into cups. Top each cup with one of the following optional flavorings: choose from grated orange zest, a teaspoon of vanilla, a sprinkling of powdered cinnamon or nutmeg or mace.

Serve with the birthday cake or cookies.

♪ *Torta de Cumpleaños con Crema de Coco* (Birthday Cake with Coconut Cream Filling)

This layer cake, with a sponge cake base and coconut cream filling, is popular for birthdays and other family celebrations.

Yield: 10 to 12 servings

Sponge cake:

10 medium eggs, separated

¾ cup sugar

Syrup:

1 cup water

1 teaspoon vanilla extract

1 cup **self-rising flour**

¼ cup sugar

Coconut cream filling:	¼ cup icing sugar
2 cups heavy cream for whipping	2 cups freshly grated coconut
Dulce de leche filling:	2 pounds *dulce de leche* homemade (recipe page 563), or available at Latin American food shops
Optional Cake Decoration:	Fresh fruit in season, cake glitter, edible sprinkles, and other decorations

Equipment: Mixing bowl, stand or hand mixer, rubber spatula, mixing spoon, 2 10-inch round baking pans, wooden skewer for testing, parchment paper or aluminum foil, large platter for serving, oven mitts, clean kitchen towel

1. Butter and flour 2 10-inch baking pans. Set aside.

   Ten minutes before baking, preheat oven to 350°F.

2. In a mixing bowl, using a stand or hand mixer, beat the egg whites to soft peaks. Gradually add the sugar, the yolks, one by one, and the vanilla, while continuing to beat until all is thoroughly combined. Turn off the mixer, and gently fold in the flour until well combined.

3. Divide the batter equally into the baking pans, and bake in the middle rack of preheated oven for about 30 to 40 minutes, or until golden. A wooden skewer inserted in the center of the cakes should come out clean. If both pans do not fit on the same rack, put them on different racks, and switch the pans after 20 minutes.

4. Remove the cakes, and allow to cool in the pan for 10 minutes. Unmold cakes onto a wire rack to allow them to cool thoroughly.

5. When cool, split each cake into 2 even layers. Cover with a clean, dry kitchen towel.

6. Prepare the syrup: In a small saucepan over medium heat, place the water and sugar, and cook until the sugar is dissolved. Let cool.

7. Prepare the coconut cream: In a well chilled mixing bowl and using well chilled beaters, whip the cream to soft peaks. Add the icing sugar, and continue to whip until the cream is stiff.

8. Assemble the cake: Place one cake layer, crust-side down, on a large serving platter. Surround the cake with parchment paper or aluminum foil to catch any drips and to keep the platter clean. Brush syrup over the cake. Spread with a generous layer of *dulce de leche*. Top with another layer of cake, brush with syrup, and spread with a layer of whipped cream, and distribute some grated coconut over it. Set the third cake layer, brush with syrup, and spread with the remaining *dulce de leche*. Set the final cake layer on it, and brush with syrup. Spread the remaining whipped cream over the top and sides of the cake, and distribute the remaining grated coconut over the cake top and sides.

Decorate the cake with fresh fruits in season, such as strawberries, kiwis, or cherries and/or cake glitter, according to preference.

As in much of Latin America, when a girl reaches 15 years of age in Paraguay, she takes part in a *quinceañera*, a party to introduce her into womanhood. The party can be quite expensive, and families often go heavily in debt to give their daughter a beautiful *quineañera*.

Wedding ceremonies take place in a church, followed by a *fiesta* either in a local hall or the bride's home. Musicians are plentiful in Paraguay, and small ensembles of three or four are easily available for weddings and other life-cycle celebrations. Many people prefer traditional folk music played on the Paraguayan harp and guitars over the modern music of today.

Funerals are solemn affairs and accompanied by specific songs and chants. The family holds a wake, in which the body is laid out, either in the home or church. After 24 hours, the body is carried to the cemetery by a hearse or on the shoulders of male family members and friends. A funeral feast is held at the home of the deceased after the burial.

Many Paraguayans speak two languages, Spanish and Guarani. *So'o-yosopy* is the Guarani name for *sopa de carne* (beef soup). A superstition in Paraguay holds that if anyone who doesn't enjoy cooking is in the kitchen while *so'o-yosopy* is cooking on the stove, the soup will separate and spoil.

So'O-Yosopy (Beef Soup)

Yield: serves 6

2 pounds lean ground beef

8 cups water, divided

2 tablespoons vegetable oil

2 onions, **finely chopped**

1 green bell pepper, **trimmed**, seeded, finely chopped

4 **tomatoes, peeled**, chopped

½ cup white rice

For serving: grated Parmesan cheese

Equipment: Food processor, rubber spatula, large skillet, mixing spoon, large saucepan with cover, ladle, individual soup bowls

1. Put the ground meat in food processor, add 1 cup water, and process until mashed and smooth, 2 to 3 minutes. Set aside.

   Note: While processing, turn machine off once or twice, and scrape down sides of container with rubber spatula.

2. Heat the oil in large skillet over medium-high heat. Add the onions and peppers, stir, and **sauté** until soft, 3 to 5 minutes. Reduce heat to medium, add the tomatoes, stir, and cook until the mixture is thick and well blended, 5 to 7 minutes. Cool slightly.

3. Transfer the mashed beef and its juices to a large saucepan. Stir in the sautéed onion mixture. Add the remaining 7 cups water, stir, and bring to a boil over medium-high heat. Reduce heat to a **simmer**, add the rice, and stir. Cover and cook until the rice is tender, 20 to 25 minutes.

To serve, ladle into individual soup bowls, and sprinkle each serving with Parmesan cheese.

In Paraguay, *yerba maté* is known as Paraguayan tea, a popular ceremonial drink. It is made from *yerba* leaves that are dried in an outdoor oven and pounded into a powder that is mixed with water. It is traditionally drunk from a *maté*, a vessel made from a vegetable gourd or cow horn, and sipped through a *bombilla*, a sort of metal or wooden drinking straw with a filter. The drink can be either hot or cold. On social occasions, such as a wedding, the silver-trimmed *maté* is passed around, and everyone has a sip from the same silver *bombilla*.

Soups are very popular in Paraguay and are served at most life-cycle parties. *Caldo de zapallo tierno* (recipe follows) is easy to make and inexpensive. When a large crowd is expected at a first communion party, a large batch of zucchini soup can feed them cheaply.

⚘ *Caldo de Zapallo Tierno* (Zucchini Soup)

Yield: serves 6

2 tablespoons vegetable oil	1 pound zucchini, grated
1 onion, **finely chopped**	salt and pepper to taste
1 clove garlic, finely chopped	1 egg
5 cups chicken broth	For **garnish**: 3 tablespoons grated Parmesan cheese
3 tablespoons raw rice	1 tablespoon parsley, finely chopped

Equipment: Large saucepan with cover, mixing spoon, small bowl, whisk, ladle, individual soup bowls

1. Heat the oil in a large saucepan over medium-high heat, and add the onions and garlic. Stir and **sauté** until the onions are soft, 3 to 5 minutes. Add the chicken broth and rice, and reduce heat to a **simmer**. Stir, cover, and cook for 10 minutes. Add the zucchini, stir, and continue to simmer until the zucchini is very tender, about 10 to 15 minutes. Add salt and pepper to taste.

2. Just before serving, beat the egg with cheese and parsley in a small bowl, and whisk into the soup.

To serve, ladle the soup into individual soup bowls to eat as the first course at a family dinner.

The following recipe is called "soup" (*sopa*), but it is really a wonderful, hearty corn bread made with two kinds of cheese. It is traditionally served with *so'o-yosopy* (recipe precedes).

⚘ *Sopa Paraguaya* (Paraguayan Corn Bread)

Yield: serves 6 to 8

8 tablespoons butter or margarine, at room temperature, divided	2 onions, **finely chopped**
	½ pound cottage cheese

2 cups **cornmeal**	1 teaspoon salt
½ pound Münster cheese, grated	1 cup milk
16 ounces canned cream-style corn	**6 eggs, separated**

Equipment: Large skillet, food processor, rubber spatula, large mixing bowl, medium mixing bowl, **whisk,** greased and floured 10×13×2½-inch baking pan, oven mitts, toothpick

1. Heat 4 tablespoons butter or margarine in a large skillet over medium-high heat. Add the onions, and **sauté** until soft, 3 to 5 minutes. Remove from heat, and set aside.

2. In food processor, combine the remaining 4 tablespoons butter or margarine and cottage cheese, and process until thoroughly blended, about 1 minute. Add the grated Münster cheese, onions, cornmeal, cream-style corn, salt, milk, and egg yolks. Process for about 1 minute to mix thoroughly but still retaining some texture. Transfer to a large mixing bowl.

Note: While processing, turn machine off once or twice, and scrape down sides of container with rubber spatula.

Preheat oven to 375°F.

3. In a medium mixing bowl, using a whisk, beat the egg whites until soft peaks form. Using a rubber spatula, **fold** the egg whites, a little at a time, into the cornmeal mixture. Pour the batter into the prepared 10×13×2½-inch baking pan.

4. Bake in the preheated oven for 45 to 55 minutes, or until toothpick inserted into center comes out clean.

To serve, cut into squares while still warm, and keep covered with a cloth napkin to maintain freshness and warmth. Serve at once.

Peru

Peru is on the west coast of South America, bordered on the north by Colombia and Ecuador, on the east by Brazil and Bolivia, and on the south by Chile. It is a land of cold and rugged mountain regions, vast deserts, hot, humid plains, and jungles. Its area is just slightly smaller than Alaska.

Peru was once part of the Inca Empire until the Incas were conquered by the Spaniard Francisco Pizarro in 1533. Spain remained in control until 1824, making Peru a vice royalty, the seat of government.

Although 81 percent of Peruvians are Roman Catholics, about 13 percent are Protestants, and most follow all life-cycle rituals according to traditions of both churches (see Protestant and Catholic Life-Cycle Rituals, page lxxiii). The people are as varied as the land. They range from wealthy white descendants of Spanish landowners (15 percent of the population) to pure-blooded Indians (45 percent) following the same customs and rituals practiced by their Incan ancestors. Another 37 percent are mixed European and Amerindian (*mestizos*). Most Incan descendants live in isolated mountain regions.

In the Amazon region of Peru, other Indians live the same prehistoric lifestyle their ancestors did thousands of years ago. Most Indians, though, except for the most isolated tribes, combine Catholic rituals with their traditional practices. Due to the high percentage of Amerindians in the population, two indigenous languages, Quechua and Aymara, are official languages together with Spanish.

Traditional wedding customs are gradually changing, especially in urban areas. Couples are mostly free to select their own marriage partner. In the past, marrying without parent approval was unacceptable. For a marriage to be legal, the law requires a civil service at city hall. All Catholic weddings are held in a church a few days after the civil ceremony.

It is customary for the wedding reception to follow the religious church ceremony. Depending upon the family's wealth, the reception can be a grand affair in a hotel ballroom or a small family supper. Or it can be a gathering of friends and relatives for a *pachamanca*. The word means "earth oven," referring to an ancient way of cooking food over heated stones, like a pit barbecue. The centerpiece of the feast is either *lechoncito asado* (suckling pig, see Cuban recipe page 243) or *cabrito* (kid goat). Baked in the pit along with the pig and/or goat are *cuy* (guinea pig), chickens, and other meats depending upon the number of guests and budget. Both sweet and white potatoes, ears of corn, and other vegetables, as well as tamales, are cooked along with the meat. After the pit is filled with the food, it is sealed with earth, and the top is decorated with flowers and greenery. The cooking begins early in the morning, and by late afternoon, when guests begin arriving, the food is almost ready to eat. The guests work up an appetite singing and dancing and entertaining the newlyweds.

Ocopa is a rich sauce, based on nuts and fresh farmer's cheese. It is originally made with dried yellow chili peppers called *aji amarillo* and an herb related to the marigold, *huacatay* (*Tagetes minuta*). This dish comes from the southern Peruvian city of Arequipa. *Ocopa* is often served with boiled potatoes, hard-cooked eggs, roast meats, shrimps, or any dish that would benefit from a tasty sauce. Usually peanuts are used, but other nuts, such as walnuts, are commonly used. Pecans, almonds, or pistachios, depending on personal preference, may also be substituted. Fresh farmer's cheese in Peru is tangy, and the nearest approximation in flavor is possibly either a mix of cream cheese and feta or soft goat's cheese.

⚜ *Ocopa Arequipeña* (Arequipa-style Nut Sauce)

Yield: serves 6

6 waxy potatoes (such as Yukon Gold), peeled, quartered	salt and pepper to taste
water, as needed	1 cup finely chopped onions
	⅓ cup olive oil

12 raw walnuts, finely ground, or ¼ cup finely ground peanuts

2 cloves garlic, finely chopped

3 to 10 dried *ají amarillo*, or to taste (available from Latin supermarkets)

3 sprigs *huacatay* (dried *huacatay* may be available from Latin

For **garnish**:

½ cup black olives, **pitted**

supermarkets), or substitute ⅓ cup fresh **cilantro**

½ pound fresh farmer's cheese, or goat's cheese, or 3 ounces cream cheese and 1 ounce feta cheese

soda crackers, as needed

For serving: slices of fresh farmer's cheese or any mild cheese

6 hard-cooked eggs, sliced in half or quarters

lettuce leaves

Equipment: Medium saucepan, **colander**, skillet, food processor, rubber spatula, large mixing bowl

1. Put the potatoes in a medium saucepan, and cover generously with water. Add ½ teaspoon salt, and bring the water to a boil. Reduce heat to **simmer** until potatoes are tender. Drain in colander and set aside.

2. In a skillet, dry-toast the *ají amarillo* until they turn dark and fragrant. Remove from heat, and soak in hot water to cover for 10 to 15 minutes. Drain the peppers, but keep the soaking liquid.

3. Put the nuts, onions, garlic, *ají amarillo*, a few spoonfuls of the soaking liquid, and *huacatay* in the food processor. Process about 1 minute. Gradually add the oil, and pulse, until the mixture is smooth. If the mixture is too runny, add a couple of soda crackers, and process until thickened. Taste, and add salt if needed.

Note: *While processing, turn machine off once or twice, and scrape down sides of container with rubber spatula.*

4. Put some lettuce leaves on individual serving plates, and arrange the potatoes on them. Pour the *ocopa* sauce over the potatoes.

To serve, garnish with the sliced black olives and hard-cooked egg.

The nuns in Latin American countries are known for making delicious candies and pastries. The tradition was brought by the first nuns who arrived from Spain around 1600. The nuns sell the cakes and *dulces* (sweets) to support charity schools for girls. In Lima, the capital of Peru, it is considered good luck for a bride to have her wedding cake made by the nuns. The recipe that follows for a cake made with fillings of pineapple and caramelized, sweetened condensed milk is a typical Peruvian treat. The recipe can easily be doubled or tripled to serve more people.

◌ *Alfajor de Huaura* (Peruvian Pineapple Layer Cake)

Yield: serves 10

2 (15 ounces each) cans sweetened condensed milk, for filling

2 teaspoons vanilla extract, divided

3 eggs

1 cup granulated sugar

½ cup water

¾ cup all-purpose flour

1 teaspoon baking powder

½ teaspoon salt

confectioners' sugar, as needed

16 ounces canned crushed pineapple, well drained

1 sweet potato, baked, peeled, mashed

½ cup sugar

Equipment: Deep saucepan, can opener, rubber spatula, small bowl with cover, small saucepan, aluminum foil, mixing spoon, 15½×10½×1-inch jelly roll pan, medium mixing bowl, electric mixer (optional), small bowl, oven mitts, toothpick, paring knife, clean kitchen towel, work surface, serving platter, cake knife

1. Prepare the caramelized milk filling: Place 2 unopened cans sweetened condensed milk in a deep saucepan, cover generously with water, and bring water to a boil. Reduce heat to simmer and cook for 3 hours. (The sweetened condensed milk thickens to a caramel-like substance when heated in the can.) Remove cans from water, and allow to cool enough to handle. Open the cans, and transfer the caramelized milk to a bowl. Add 1 teaspoon vanilla extract, and stir well. Cover, and refrigerate until ready to use.

2. Prepare the pineapple filling: Put mashed sweet potato, drained crushed pineapple, and ½ cup sugar, more or less to taste, in small saucepan. Stir, and heat through over medium heat for flavor to develop, 5 to 7 minutes. Cool to room temperature, cover with foil, and refrigerate until ready to use.

3. Prepare the baking pan: Line a jelly roll pan with a piece of foil and generously grease with butter or margarine. Set aside.

Preheat the oven to 350°F.

4. Prepare the cake: Put eggs in a medium mixing bowl, and using an electric mixer or mixing spoon, beat until thick and light yellow, 3 to 5 minutes. Beating constantly, add granulated sugar, a little at a time. Beat in water and vanilla extract until well mixed.

5. In a small bowl, mix flour, baking powder, and salt. Add flour mixture to egg mixture, a little at a time, and beat just until smooth. Pour batter into prepared jelly roll pan, and smooth out, using rubber spatula.

6. Bake in the middle rack of a preheated oven until a toothpick inserted in the center comes out clean, about 12 to 15 minutes. Immediately loosen cake from the sides of the pan by running a paring knife around the edge of the cake.

7. Place clean towel on work surface, and sprinkle generously with confectioners' sugar. Carefully flip cake over onto towel, and remove and discard foil. Using paring knife, trim edges of cake, if necessary, to make them even and smooth.

8. Assemble the cake: Cut the cake into 4 rectangles, 10½×3¾ inches each. Lay one rectangle flat on a serving platter. Spread a layer of filling, and top with another rectangle of cake, leaving top and sides of the cake plain. Sprinkle confectioners' sugar over the top and sides of the cake.

To serve, cut cake into slices about 1 inch thick.

In Peru, as in Bolivia, the first haircut is an important rite of passage among the Quechua and Aymara ethnic groups. The haircutting ceremony in Peru, called *rutuchiku*, as well as that in Bolivia (where it is known as *rutucha*), is believed to originate from similar haircutting rituals for the Inca nobility. In Peru, *rutuchiku* used to be performed at the ages of five or six. Nowadays, the ritual is performed after the first year. The *rutuchiku*, as well as marking the first haircutting and first nail cutting, is also a naming ceremony, and the child is given his or her permanent name. Before this ceremony, the child has a temporary or infant name. The *rutuchiku* also is the time when the child comes into property of his or her own: animals, such as llamas, guinea pigs, and sometimes land, given as presents by relatives and/or guests.

The parents of the child usually approach would-be sponsors by inviting them for a drink of *aguardiente* (local brandy) with or without a meal, and broach the matter when sufficient drinking has proceeded. The sponsors—*padrino* (godfather) and *madrina* (godmother)—are responsible for hosting the haircutting party at his or her house, as well as for inviting their relatives and friends. The *padrino* and *madrina* are chosen according to their moral, social, and economic standing, in order to serve as good role models for the child. The guests of the sponsors arrive early and are served brandy while waiting for the child and his or her family and their guests. The ceremony usually begins at nine in the evening. The parents of the child bring food, drinks (brandy and beer), cigarettes, and coca leaves, and they are accompanied by their relatives and friends. The parents also present a ceremonial gift to the sponsors, consisting of two cooked chickens and two *cuyes* (guinea pigs), with *humitas* (corn dumplings), potatoes, and a bottle of *aguardiente* (local brandy), all specially wrapped. As soon as the child's parents and relatives and friends arrive, formal greetings between the two sets of guests ensue, with exchanges of kisses, and brandy is served to everyone. Then the child's family and relatives serve the food they have brought to the sponsors' guests, most usually a *pachamanca* (traditional underground oven–cooked meal) of *humitas* (corn dumplings wrapped in corn husks) and potatoes, and sometimes various meats. Only when the sponsors' guests have eaten and drunk their fill do the child's relatives and friends eat. After the meal, the ceremony can begin.

A blanket, newly woven for the occasion, is laid on the floor. The child is also dressed in newly woven clothes. On the blanket are two plates, a pair of scissors adorned with red and white ribbons, *aguardiente*, a napkin of coca leaves, cigarettes and matches. Each guest is given three coca leaves by the child's parents, which are placed in a bowl, at the same time that the guest confers three wishes for the child's future. Once all the guests have given their blessings, the *padrino* or *madrina* starts with the first snip. With the first tuft of hair snipped, the *padrino* or *madrina* lay an amount of money in one of the plates. One of the guests is designated secretary, to take note of the amounts of money or other goods, sometimes animals and land, that each person has contributed or promised. This meticulous accounting has a purpose. When it is time for other guests' children to have their own haircutting rituals, their generosity will be reciprocated. There is a certain amount of competition among the contributors, especially when they have imbibed quite a lot of brandy. It is not unusual for the child to receive a cow or land, in addition to blankets, clothing, and silver goods.

The haircutting proceeds in a leisurely manner, with the sponsors calling a break for coca chewing or cigarette smoking or brandy drinking during the proceedings. Only those called upon by the sponsors can participate in the haircutting. In other parts of Peru, the sponsor also sprinkles quinoa over the child's head in the form of a cross before the haircutting. The excess quinoa is sprinkled over the coca leaves. Once all the hair and nails have been cut and placed in the same bowl as the coca leaves and quinoa grains, the bowl is given to the sponsors, who will then bury the contents in the ground as an offering to Pachamama, the Earth Mother.

Pachamanca (Earth Oven Celebration Meal)

Pachamanca (earth oven celebration meal) is usually reserved for very special celebrations and occasions because of the long process of preparing the underground oven. However, once the food has been put inside to cook, there is no need for intermittent attention until the two- or three-hour cooking time is up. A specific person is designated to open the *pachamanca* when the food is done, and he or she is called the "godfather" or "godmother" of the *pachamanca*.

The traditional method of cooking a *pachamanca* is given here for reference. A contemporary method then follows for cooking in an oven and steamer.

Because *pachamanca* is typically made in a hole in the ground, a good replacement meal is *humita dulce* or *humita salada*. (*Humitas* [sweet or savory] are one component of the pachamanca, but can also stand on their own.)

Traditional method:

Yield: about 20 servings

2 legs of lamb

20 pieces pork ribs

4 chickens, each cut into 6 large serving pieces

6 guinea pigs specially raised for food, or substitute Cornish hens

20 *humitas* (also *humintas*, corn dumplings)

20 potatoes, peeled and, if large, quartered; if small, leave whole

20 sweet potatoes, peeled and sliced into large chunks

20 oca tubers, peeled

10 cups lima beans

10 corn cobs, cut in half

10 **plantains**, unpeeled, sliced in half

1 to 3 chili peppers, or to taste

salt and freshly ground black pepper to taste

2 pounds fresh white cheese, or substitute halloumi, mozzarella, or white soft goat's cheese

Optional: a few fresh leaves of the chili pepper plant, some sprigs of fresh *huacatay* (*Tagetes minuta*), or fresh sage leaves

good quantity of banana leaves for wrapping food items and covering the *pachamanca*

enough jute sacks to cover the top of the *pachamanca*

2 or more dense, heavy fabric sheets for final covering of the *pachamanca*

Equipment: Digging shovel, fireplace tongs, firewood, flat stones1. Make a hole in the ground where you want to prepare the *pachamanca*.

2. Light a wood fire near where the *pachamanca* will be prepared, and heat a good quantity of stones (preferably flat).

3. Once the stones are very hot, using fireplace tongs, carefully transfer the stones to make a bed in the bottom of the hole.

4. Lay the food items in layers: First put the sweet potatoes, potatoes, oca tubers, all wrapped in banana leaves. Over them lay hot stones, with some space between each stone.

   On the second layer, place the meats seasoned with salt, pepper, garlic, and *ají panca* to taste (optional, paprika). The most commonly used meats are lamb, pork, kid, and chicken.

   Optionally, lay on the meat leaves of the chili pepper plant, *huacatay*, and sage for flavor.

   Place a larger number of hot stones as the meats take longer to cook.

5. On top place the *humitas*, beans, guinea pigs, cheese, bananas, and corn. Cover this layer likewise with banana leaves and then some jute sacks or other dense fabric. Cover with another thick, heavy fabric to keep the heat in. Finally, seal the *pachamanca* with dry soil. It is customary to put a cross on top that will be removed by the person responsible for opening the *pachamanca*—the "godfather" of the *pachamanca*.

6. Cooking time is usually between 2 and 3 hours.

Steamer or double boiler method:

Use the same ingredients as for the traditional method or those that follow.

Yield: about 20 servings

humita dulce

humita salasa

4 pounds boneless lamb cubes

4 pounds pork chops or meaty ribs

4 pounds chicken pieces, a mix of breasts, backs, legs

olive or other vegetable oil, for greasing

20 potatoes, peeled and quartered if large; if medium, leave whole

15 sweet potatoes, peeled and sliced in large chunks

2 pounds lima beans, shelled

Marinade for the lamb:

10 cloves garlic, finely grated

1 to 2 sprigs *huacatay* (*Tagetes minuta*), finely chopped

Marinade for the pork:

5 tablespoons *ají panca* paste (available at Latin American food shops or online as *pasta de ají panca*)

10 cloves garlic, finely grated

Marinade for the chicken:

3 teaspoons yellow chili pepper paste (available at Latin American food shops or online as *pasta de ají amarillo*)

few sprigs *huacatay* (*Tagetes minuta*)

few sprigs *chincho* (*Tagetes elliptica*)

1 to 2 sprigs *chincho* (*Tagetes elliptica*), finely chopped

2 tablespoons ground cumin

salt and freshly ground black pepper to taste

½ cup oil

2 tablespoons oregano, crumbled

½ cup white vinegar

1 tablespoon ground cumin

salt and freshly ground black pepper to taste

½ cup oil

salt and freshly ground black pepper to taste

Equipment: Food processor, 3 large mixing bowls, 2 baking trays, plastic wrap, Dutch oven (or enamel-lined saucepan or **heavy-bottomed** saucepan), oven mitts

1. Prepare the sweet *humitas* (recipe follows).

2. Prepare the savory *humitas* (recipe follows).

3. In 3 separate bowls, mix the marinades for the various meats.

   Mix in the meats, and leave to marinade for at least 30 minutes, covered with plastic wrap.

   Divide the different meats into 4 portions, and wrap each portion separately in aluminum foil. Set the wrapped packets aside until needed.

4. Divide the potatoes, sweet potatoes, and lima beans into 4 portions. Place a sprig or two of *huacatay* and *chincho* over the vegetables. Wrap each in aluminum foil, and set aside.

Preheat oven to 350°F.

5. Cooking: Place the meat packets on the middle rack of preheated oven. Place the potato and sweet potato packets below them.

6. Bake for 1 hour, or until the lamb is tender, the pork and chicken are done, and the potatoes and sweet potatoes are tender. Keep the meat and potato packets warm until ready to serve.

7. Add water halfway up the bottom part of a steamer or double boiler. Bring to a boil over medium-high heat.

8. Lay the *humitas* in overlapping rows, and place the lima bean packets over them. Strew a couple of *huacatay* and *chincho* sprigs over the top, and cover. The lima beans will be done in about 15 to 20 minutes. Remove them to a covered container, and keep warm.

5. The *humitas* will be done in about 45 minutes, but take out one first and check. Once the *humitas* are done, turn off the heat, but leave the *humitas* in the steamer to keep warm until ready to serve.

To serve, each diner's plate gets portions of the meat, potatoes, sweet potatoes, lima beans, and sweet and savory humitas. *Alternatively, place the meat and vegetables and dumplings in large platters, and diners help themselves from the platters.*

⚘ *Humita Dulce* (Sweet Corn Dumplings)

Yield: enough for the *pachamanca* meal

kernels from 8 cobs of sweet corn, scraped off the cobs with a knife

2 tablespoons butter, melted

¼ cup heavy cream

2 eggs, beaten

1 cup raisins

½ cup sugar, or to taste

1 tablespoon ground cinnamon

about 1 cup **cornmeal**

corn husks or aluminum foil for wrapping

Equipment: Knife, food processor, rubber spatula, corn husks or aluminum foil

Note: *While processing, turn machine off once or twice, and scrape down sides of container with rubber spatula.*

1. Combine the corn kernels, butter, cream, eggs, raisins, sugar, and cinnamon in a food processor. Process until the kernels are finely chopped. If the mixture is runny, add only enough cornmeal to make a light paste of the mixture.

2. Take 2 cornhusks, and lay a tablespoon of the mixture in the middle. Alternatively, wrap the mixture securely in aluminum foil. Fold over to enclose the mixture, and tie firmly with strips of cornhusk.

Use with pachamanca *(recipe precedes).*

⚘ *Humita Salada* (Savory Corn Dumplings)

Yield: enough for the *pachamanca* meal

kernels from 8 sweet corn cobs, scraped off the cobs with a knife

2 tablespoons butter, melted

1 cup grated or crumbled fresh white cheese, farmer's cheese, or mozzarella

salt to taste

2 eggs, beaten

¼ cup heavy cream

about 1 cup **cornmeal**

corn husks or aluminum foil for wrapping

Equipment: Knife, food processor, rubber spatula, corn husks or aluminum foil

1. Combine the corn kernels, butter, cream, eggs, cheese, and salt in a food processor. Process until the kernels are finely chopped. If the mixture is runny, add just enough cornmeal to make a light paste of the mixture.

2. As with the sweet *humitas*, take 2 cornhusks, and lay a tablespoon of the mixture in the middle. Tie firmly with strips of cornhusk. Alternatively, wrap the mixture securely in aluminum foil.

Use with pachamanca *(recipe page 609).*

Uruguay

South America's smallest country, Uruguay, is situated on the east coast of South America, south of Brazil and east of Argentina. Unlike other South American countries, it has no rainforests, swamps, jungles, or deserts. It is a pleasant country of grasslands and an attractive coastal region.

Uruguay was originally colonized by the Portuguese in 1680, but it was seized by Spain by 1778. Uruguay broke from Spain in 1811 but was taken over by the Portuguese from Brazil. Finally, independence was won with the help of Argentina in 1825. By the time of independence, only about 500 native Indians remained. In 1831, all the men of the indigenous Charrua tribe were killed by the Uruguayan army in the Massacre of Salsipuedes, and the remaining 300 women and children were forced to work as household slaves and servants in Spanish Uruguayan homes. Today Uruguay is the only South American country without an indigenous Indian population, although a recent population survey shows 2.4 percent of Uruguayans claiming indigenous Indian descent.

Over 95 percent of the people are descendants of Spanish immigrants or of mixed races—*mestizos*, part Spanish and part Indian, or part African and part Spanish. The remaining 4 percent are black. Uruguayans are the most secular of all Latin Americans; religion is not an important part of daily life, as it is in most Latin countries. Just under 50 percent of Uruguayans are Roman Catholics, and about 11 percent are Protestant. Over 20 percent believe in God but without a religion. About 17 percent professed to being either agnostic or atheist. Other religions with members in Uruguay are Judaism, Islam, Baha'i, Jehovah's Witnesses, Hinduism, and Buddhism.

There are four Mennonite colonies in Uruguay, the first three established between 1948 and 1952. To date, there are about 1,500 baptized members in the country spread among 23 congregations, most of whom are converts from the general Uruguayan population. The actual number of Mennonites (children below the age of 16 to 18) is greater because only adults are baptized and registered as Mennonites. The colonies are noted for being mostly self-sufficient in food, raising a variety of agricultural produce as well as dairy products. They also supply the surrounding towns with their produce.

Most life-cycle events are connected to Christian traditions (See Protestant and Catholic Life-Cycle Rituals, page lxxiii), but marriage can take place outside of a church, and in some remote parts of the country, there are no churches.

An Uruguayan custom, also practiced in several other South American countries, is the drinking of *yerba maté*. The herbal tea is mixed in a *maté*, or gourd, and sipped through a *bombilla* (metal or silver straw). The tea is believed to have magical powers, and the Indians used it in religious ceremonies. Today, at the end of a wedding, everyone sips *yerba maté* through the same *bombilla* to show respect and unity to the newlyweds. To refuse to take a sip is an insult to everyone present.

All throughout Latin America, *albóndigas* (meatballs) are popular and one of the many dishes served for a wedding, family gathering after a baptism, or birthday party. They are easy to make, and everyone seems to love them. Each country has its own special way of making them.

♭ *Albóndigas* (Meatballs Uruguay-style)

Yield: serves 4 to 6

8 tablespoons vegetable oil, divided

2 onions, **finely chopped,** divided

1 tomato, **peeled** and chopped

1 teaspoon ground red pepper, more or less to taste

1 teaspoon sugar

salt and pepper to taste

1 pound veal, finely ground

1 cup **fresh bread crumbs**

4 tablespoons grated Parmesan cheese

¼ cup seedless raisins

½ teaspoon grated nutmeg

2 eggs

2 cups canned beef broth

2 cups dry red wine

1 bay leaf

Equipment: Large skillet, mixing spoon, large mixing bowl, shallow bowl, slotted spoon, large saucepan, large serving bowl

1. Heat 4 tablespoons oil in large skillet over medium-high heat. Add 1 chopped onion, stir, and **sauté** 3 to 5 minutes, until soft. Add tomato, 1 teaspoon ground red pepper, more or less to taste, sugar, and salt and pepper to taste. Reduce heat to medium, and, stirring frequently, cook until mixture thickens and is quite dry, 3 to 5 minutes. Set aside to cool to room temperature.

2. In large mixing bowl, combine veal, bread crumbs, Parmesan cheese, raisins, nutmeg, and cooled tomato mixture. Add eggs, and mix thoroughly. Form mixture into 2-inch balls.

3. Put flour in shallow bowl. Roll meatballs in flour to coat all sides, and shake off excess.

4. Heat remaining 4 tablespoons oil in large skillet over medium-high heat. Fry meatballs in batches until lightly browned on all sides, about 12 to 15 minutes. When they are done, lift them out with slotted spoon and set aside.

5. In large saucepan, sauté remaining chopped onion for 3 to 5 minutes until soft. Add beef broth, wine, and bay leaf. Stir and reduce heat to **simmer**, 5 to 7 minutes for flavor to develop. Add meatballs, cover, and cook over low heat until fully cooked, 30 to 40 minutes.

To serve, spoon meatballs into large serving bowl, and pour sauce over them. Serve with bread for sopping up the sauce.

Meat is always served on special occasions. This recipe is rather unusual and a favorite in Uruguay.

Lomo de Cerdo a la Caucana (Pork Loin Baked in Milk)

Yield: serves 4 to 6

4 tablespoons butter or margarine	4 cups milk
2 pounds boneless pork loin or **boned** pork shoulder	¼ cup lemon juice
	salt and pepper to taste

Equipment: Large skillet, metal tongs, medium roasting pan, medium bowl, meat thermometer (optional), **bulb baster** or mixing spoon, oven mitts, slotted spoon, small serving bowl

Preheat oven to 325°F.

1. Melt butter or margarine in large skillet over medium high heat, add pork, and lightly brown all sides, about 12 to 15 minutes. Using metal tongs, transfer to medium roasting pan.

2. In medium bowl, mix milk and lemon juice. (The milk will curdle from the lemon juice.) Pour curdled milk mixture over pork. Sprinkle with salt and pepper to taste. Insert meat thermometer into middle of roast, if using one.

3. Bake in oven for 2 to 2½ hours, until tender, basting frequently with bulb baster or mixing spoon. Meat thermometer should register 170°F when done.

4. Using oven mitts, remove meat from oven, and keep warm. Using slotted spoon, remove and discard fat from the milk sauce in roasting pan. Carefully transfer sauce to medium saucepan. Cook over medium-high heat until **reduced** to about half and thickened, 7 to 12 minutes.

To serve, pour sauce into small bowl, and serve separately. Slice the meat, and serve hot with rice or potatoes.

Birthdays of older children between eight and 12 years old in urban areas, such as the capital Montevideo, are popularly celebrated with sleepovers, either at home, at a hotel, or a hired venue coordinated by party organizers that offer this kind of service. Locally called *pijamadas* (pajama parties), the sleepover parties usually last for about 12 hours, beginning at 9:30 p.m. and ending after breakfast at 9:30 a.m. the following morning. The party starts with various activities, such as a trampoline, an inflatable castle, wall climbing, or swimming, depending on the range of play equipment and facilities at the venue. Dinner and the birthday cake then follow. Next come less strenuous activities—such as a treasure hunt. For those who are unable to go to sleep and wish to go on partying, videos of popular children's movies may be shown. Throughout these activities, there are one or two adults who keep an eye on the children to make sure that they are safe. The adults usually stay awake the entire time. The children bring their own sleeping bags. Breakfast the following morning is usually a chocolate drink, juice, and *alfajores*.

ꙮ *Timbales de Arroz con Atún y Alcaparras* (Molded Rice with Tuna and Capers)

A popular dish for celebrations is *timbales de arroz con atún y alcaparras* (molded rice with tuna and capers).

Yield: 6 servings

2 cups cooked plain rice

4 teaspoons parsley or chives, minced

1 teaspoon garlic powder

grated **zest** from 1 lemon

salt and pepper to taste

2 cans tuna in olive oil, drained and mashed

2 hard-cooked eggs, finely chopped

1 sweet red pepper, finely chopped

½ cup green olives, finely chopped

6 pickled baby onions, finely chopped

6 pickled gherkins, finely chopped

½ cup pickled capers

½ cup mayonnaise or thick yogurt, more as needed

1 tablespoon catsup, more as needed

1 teaspoon lemon juice, or to taste

oil for greasing molds

For **garnish**: choose from finely minced chives or parsley, sliced olives, whole pickled baby onions, slices of pickled gherkins, whole capers

Equipment: 2 large mixing bowls, 6 metal ring molds, serving plates

1. In a mixing bowl, combine the rice, parsley or chives, garlic powder, and grated lemon zest. Add salt and pepper to taste. Chill, covered, until ready to use.

2. In another mixing bowl, combine the mashed tuna, hard-cooked eggs, sweet red pepper, olives, baby onions, gherkins, and capers. Add mayonnaise or yogurt to bind the tuna mixture. Add just enough catsup to tint the mixture a delicate pink. Taste, and add lemon juice to perk up the flavor. Chill well, covered, for an hour or more before molding.

3. To assemble: Grease the ring molds, and set on the serving plates. Put a uniform layer of rice, about 1 inch thick, at the bottom. Press gently to compact the layer so that the rice grains will not separate when unmolded. Place a uniform layer of the tuna mixture next, the same thickness as the rice layer, and press evenly. Top with the same thickness of rice, again

compressing the layer to ensure it does not fall apart when unmolded. Top with chives or parley. Twist the ring molds to release the timbales, and surround the timbales with an assortment of the other garnishes, artfully arranged.

⚘ *Postre Chajá* (Chajá Cake)

Postre chajá is an elaborate cake that was created in a confectionery shop in the department of Paysandú in Western Uruguay in the 1920s. It has since spread to other regions of Uruguay. It is essentially a layered sponge cake filled with *dulce de leche*, whipped cream, crisp meringue, and canned peaches. *Postre chajá* (literally, *chajá* dessert) is named after the bird *chajá* (*Chauna torquata*, or southern screamer), found near waterways in Uruguay and neighboring countries. The cake's soft and fluffy texture is reminiscent of the *chajá* bird's fluffy feathers. It is a special cake often made for celebrations and important events.

Yield: 10 servings

Sponge cake:

5 large eggs at room temperature

2 cups sugar

2 cups cake flour, **sifted**, plus extra for cake mold

butter, for greasing

Meringue:

3 **egg whites** at room temperature

2 cups icing (confectioners') sugar

Filling:

16-ounce can sliced peaches in light syrup

2 cups heavy cream

2 cups *dulce de leche* homemade (recipe page 563), or available at Latin American food shops

Equipment: Stand or hand electric mixer, mixing bowls, 8-inch springform cake pan, baking tray or cookie sheet, parchment paper, pencil for drawing, rubber and metal spatulas, oven mitts, wire rack for cooling cake, piping bag with plain and decorative tips, **pastry brush**

Preheat the oven to 375°F.

1. Prepare the sponge cake. Butter an 8-inch springform cake pan, and sprinkle with 1 tablespoon flour. Shake the pan to distribute the flour in an even layer. Discard the excess.

2. In a mixer at medium speed, beat the eggs and sugar until fluffy and pale-colored.

   Turn the speed down to low, and gradually add the flour, mixing only until combined.

   Transfer the batter to the prepared cake pan, and bake in the center rack of preheated oven for 15 minutes.

3. Lower the oven temperature to 350°F, and bake for another 15 minutes, or until golden. Insert a wooden skewer in the center of the cake, and if it comes out dry, the cake is done.

   Transfer the cake to a wire rack to cool, but let it stand for 10 minutes before unmolding.

4. Unmold the cake to let it cool completely.

5. Prepare the meringue. Draw, with a pencil on a sheet of baking parchment, a circle with the same diameter as the cake pan. Line a cookie sheet or baking tray with the parchment, drawn-side down.

Preheat the oven to 200°F.

6. In the mixing bowl of a stand mixer, beat the egg whites to soft peaks. Gradually add the icing sugar and continue beating to stiff-peak stage. Transfer the meringue to a piping bag with a plain tip. Using the drawn circle on the reverse as a guide, pipe the meringue in concentric rings to make a disc with the same diameter as the cake. With the rest of the meringue in the piping bag, pipe smaller discs on the remaining space on the baking tray. These do not have to be of equal sizes, as they will be broken up later when the cake is assembled.

7. Bake the meringue discs for 2 hours, or until very dry. Increase the oven temperature to 220°F, and continue to bake the meringues for 15 minutes, so that they take on a bit of color.

8. Prepare the cream frosting. Have the cream, mixing bowl, and beaters well chilled before whipping. Whip the cream to soft peaks, and gradually add icing sugar until the cream is fully whipped. Take care not to overbeat, or the cream will turn to butter. Transfer the whipped cream to a piping bag with a decorative tip.

9. Assemble the cake: Reserve enough peach slices to cover the top of the cake. Set aside in the refrigerator until needed. Slice the remaining slices into small cubes, and set aside.

Slice the cake into three even layers, with the aid of toothpicks to measure off the height of the layers and a length of thread passed through the cake to slice each layer.

9. On a large serving plate, set the bottom layer of the cake. Brush it thoroughly with the syrup from the peaches. Spread evenly with *dulce de leche*. Next, lay the middle layer of the cake. Brush with the peach syrup, and cover with a generous layer of whipped cream. Place a layer of peach cubes over the cream. Set the meringue disc over the peach cubes, press gently and lightly (so as not to crack the fragile meringue), and spread with a layer of cream, and a layer of peach cubes. Place the topmost cake layer, press gently to make the layers even, and brush with the remaining peach syrup. Spread cream over the cake top and sides, leaving a bit for the final decor. Crumble the small meringue discs, and stick them to the sides of the cake. Lay the reserved peach slices in a nice pattern on the top of the cake. Pipe a decorative border to surround the peaches. Chill at least 4 hours before serving.

Venezuela

Occupying most of the northern coast of South America, Venezuela is bordered by Colombia on the west, Guyana on the east, and Brazil on the south. Originally inhabited by the Arawak and Carib Indians, Venezuela was one of the first sites of European contact on the continent, explored by Columbus on his third voyage in 1498. Venezuela remained under Spanish control until the 19th century when it joined with Colombia and Ecuador to form the Greater Republic of Colombia, which lasted until 1830.

Today, Venezuela is one of the most prosperous countries in South America. The population consists of several different ethnic groups, including *mestizos* (mixed

Spanish and Indians), Europeans, Africans, and Indians, but they are unified by their language, Spanish, and their religion, Roman Catholicism. Venezuelans generally follow the life-cycle traditions of the Catholic Church. (See Protestant and Catholic Life-Cycle Rituals, page lxxiii.)

Venezuelans commonly celebrate a birthday by singing the local version of the universal "Happy Birthday to You" song, followed by *"Ay que noche tan preciosa,"* a song composed in 1953 by Luis Cruz for his girlfriend at the time. The song was later popularized in the 1960s and 1970s and has since become a standard element of birthday celebrations throughout the country.

¡Ay! que noche tan preciosa, es la noche de tu día, todo lleno de alegría en esta fecha natal.

Tus más íntimos amigos esta noche te acompañan, te saludan y desean un mundo de felicidad.

Yo por mi parte deseo lleno de luz este día, todo lleno de alegría en esta fecha natal.

Y que esta luna plateada, brille su luz para ti, y ruego a Dios porque pases un cumpleaños feliz.

Oh, what a precious night, it is the night of your day, all is full of pleasantness on this the date of your birth.

Your closest friends will be with you tonight, they will wish you health and a world of happiness.

Me, for my part, I wish that today be full of light, all full of happiness on this the date of your birth.

And may this silver moon shine its light for you, and I pray to God that you have a happy birthday.

The lyrics of the "Happy Birthday" song in Venezuela, sung to the same melody as in the United States and most other countries, are, *"Cumpleaños feliz, te deseamos a ti, cumpleaños* [name], *cumpleaños feliz"* ("Happy birthday, we wish you, birthday [name], happy birthday"). After the singing, the celebrant blows out the candles on the birthday cake and receives hugs from everyone around. If the birthday celebrant is of school age, he or she would receive the *sala* or *paliza*—gentle blows on the back and arms, but this custom is apparently dying out. The celebrant often receives small presents or flowers from close friends and relatives.

♪ *Torta de Auyama* (Squash Cake)

One of the cakes that Venezuelans are very fond of and often make at home is squash cake, *torta de auyama* (also spelled *ahuyama*). Although it is called a cake, its consistency is more of a pudding and is usually served as dessert when families gather for a special event or to celebrate a birthday. *Torta de auyama* is rather unusual as it marries the sweetness of squash with the saltiness of hard cheese. Pumpkin may also be used instead of winter squash.

Yield: 8 to 10 servings

4 pounds winter squash, preferably a variety without too many fibers, such as acorn or butternut squash (this will yield, depending on the squash, about 3½ to 4 cups puréed flesh), or 4 cups ready-to-use mashed pumpkin

3 tablespoons butter, plus extra for greasing baking pan

½ pound hard yellow cheese, grated

6 eggs

1 cup sugar, plus ¼ cup for making caramel

1 teaspoon vanilla extract

2 cups whole milk

2 cups **self-rising flour**

½ cup raisins

For serving (optional): whipped cream

Equipment: Steamer or **double boiler** or microwave, food mill or food processor, rubber spatula, 9- to 10-inch round baking pan, oven mitts

1. Butter and flour the baking pan, and set aside.

2. Prepare the squash: Wash well, and remove the seeds and all traces of seed membranes, but do not peel. Slice into large pieces, and steam in a steamer or double boiler until tender, about 25 minutes. Alternatively, place in a glass covered dish and microwave until tender, about 10 to 15 minutes, depending on the power of your appliance. Scoop out the flesh, and discard the peel. Mash the flesh in a food mill or food processor until smooth and no lumps remain. Combine with the butter and cheese. Set aside.

Preheat oven to 325°F.

3. In a large mixing bowl, beat the eggs and sugar with a mixer at medium speed until light-colored and fluffy. Stir in the vanilla. Reduce the mixer speed to low, and add the mashed squash mixture and the milk, mixing until the batter is smooth.

4. Take a spoonful of the flour, and mix with the raisins (this is so that the raisins do not sink to the bottom of the baking pan). Add raisins to the batter. Mix in the flour, a cup at a time, and mix only until all is combined.

5. Transfer to the prepared baking pan, and bake on the middle rack of preheated oven for 1 hour, or until golden. If a wooden skewer is inserted in the center, it will come with just a bit of moisture; this is fine as long as the batter has solidified as this is more of a pudding than a cake.

6. Let the cake cool in the pan. When thoroughly cool, chill the cake for at least 2 hours, ideally overnight.

To serve, unmold the cake onto a serving plate, and serve with whipped cream, if desired.

One of the unique Latin American life-cycle events is also celebrated in Venezuela. When girls turn 15, they have a *quinceañera*, or a special 15th birthday party. The ritual, a form of debutante's or "coming out" ball, announces that the birthday girl is now a woman and ready to join the social world. The expense of the party varies according to the family's wealth. Families are known to go into debt for years to pay off the expense of a *quinceañera* party.

Weddings in Venezuela are often grand affairs. When families can afford it, they invite thousands of people and spare no expense to give their daughter a beautiful send-off. It is considered good luck for the bride and groom to sneak away from the wedding reception shortly after it begins without anyone seeing them leave.

A Venezuelan wedding feast would probably begin with bowls of *caviar criollo* (recipe follows) that they spread on *arepas* (recipe page 622) and a soup such as *sopa de chayote* (see recipe 549), as well as several salads. Beef is popular throughout South America, and the tender, lean and economical flank steak (*sobrebarriga*) is a special favorite. The highlight of the wedding reception is the table laden with sweets—the wedding cake; puddings, such as *dulce de leche* (see Argentina recipe page 563); and fresh fruits and assorted candies, such as *cajeta de leche* (recipe page 528).

Although *pabellón caraqueño* is well liked throughout South America, some Venezuelans think of it as their national dish. The way the plantains, black beans, rice, and meat are placed on the platter is said to resemble a striped flag (*pabellón*), similar to the Venezuelan flag. A simpler dish made with black beans is this recipe for *caviar criollo*. *Criollo* means "Creole," which is a person originally of Spanish ancestry born in the New World and looked upon as a native Venezuelan.

⚱ *Caviar Criollo* (Creole Caviar)

Yield: serves 6

1 cup dried black beans	dried red chili flakes to taste
water, as needed	3 cloves garlic, **finely chopped**
5 tablespoons olive oil	2 teaspoons ground cumin
1 onion, **coarsely chopped**	salt to taste

Equipment: Medium saucepan with cover, mixing spoon, large skillet, strainer, small serving bowl

1. Put beans in medium saucepan, and cover generously with water. Bring to boil over medium-high heat. Reduce heat to **simmer**, cover, and cook about 1 hour, or until tender. Drain well in strainer.

2. Heat 2 tablespoons oil in large skillet over medium-high heat, and add onion. Stir and **sauté** until soft, 3 to 5 minutes. Add red pepper flakes to taste, garlic, and cumin. Stir, and cook for 2 minutes. Add drained beans, remaining 3 tablespoons oil, and salt to taste. Stir and cook to heat through.

To serve, transfer to small serving bowl, and serve as a side dish with chicken or grilled beef.

Venezuelans love cocktail nibbles and when *cachapas de jojoto* are made small and wrapped around a piece of cheese, they become an ideal appetizer. These pancakes are often eaten instead of bread at a dinner party.

⚘ *Cachapas de Jojoto* (Corn Pancakes)

Yield: makes about 12

1½ cups corn kernels, if frozen thaw thoroughly

½ cup heavy cream

1 egg

3 tablespoons all-purpose flour

¼ teaspoon sugar

½ teaspoon salt

2 tablespoons melted butter or margarine

vegetable oil, as needed for frying

½ pound *queso blanco*, Münster, or Monterey Jack cheese, cut into 12 pieces about ¼×1½ inches, for serving

Equipment: Electric **blender**, rubber spatula, large **heavy-bottomed** skillet, metal spatula, baking sheet, paring knife, cloth napkin or serving platter

1. Put corn kernels, cream, egg, flour, sugar, salt, and melted butter or margarine into blender. Cover and **blend** until smooth, 1 to 2 minutes. Turn off blender once or twice, and use rubber spatula to scrape down sides of container.

2. Heat 2 tablespoons oil in large heavy-bottomed skillet over medium-high heat. For each pancake, spoon out 2 tablespoons batter to make them about 1½ inches in diameter. Don't crowd the pan. Cook in batches until lightly browned, 3 to 5 minutes each side, turning once using metal spatula. Keep on baking sheet in warm oven.

To serve as bread substitute, wrap in a napkin, and serve warm. To serve as an appetizer, wrap each pancake around a piece of cheese, and arrange them on a platter. Serve at once while still warm.

Arepas are a type of corn bread made from specially processed flour from pre-cooked corn. It is not the same as the Mexican flour called *masa*. *Arepas* flour is available at Latin American food stores.

⚘ *Arepas* (Venezuelan Corn Bread)

Yield: makes 8 to 10

2 cups *arepas* **corn flour**

1 teaspoon salt

2 cups water, more or less as needed

oil, for frying

Equipment: Large mixing bowl, mixing spoon, large **heavy-bottomed** griddle or skillet, metal spatula, baking sheet, oven mitts

1. Put flour and salt into large mixing bowl, and stir in about 2 cups water, a little at a time, to make a stiff dough. Let the dough rest for 5 minutes, then form into 8 to 10 balls flattened slightly to 3 inches across and about ½ inch thick.

Preheat oven to 350°F.

2. Prepare to fry: Put baking sheet into the preheated oven. Spread about ½ tablespoon oil over large heavy-bottomed griddle or skillet to lightly coat surface. Over medium heat, cook breads, in batches, 5 minutes per side. Transfer to baking sheet in oven, and continue to bake for 20 to 30 minutes, turning them with spatula 2 or 3 times during baking to lightly to brown all sides.

To serve, eat the bread warm, split it open, and spread butter or margarine on both sides. Some people pull out and discard the inside dough with their fingers and butter the remaining crispy crust.

MIDDLE EAST

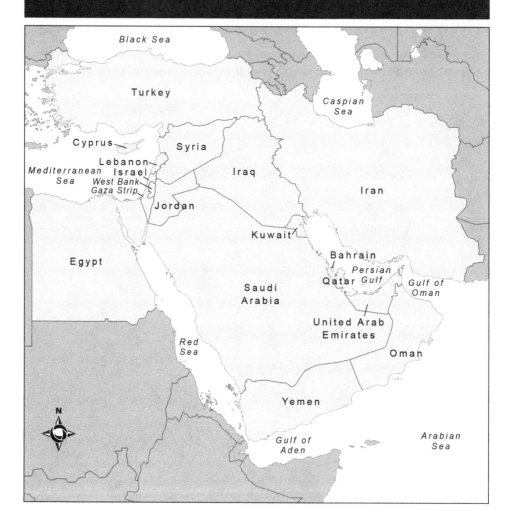

6

The Middle East

The "Middle East" was first used as a term in 1902 to refer to the area between Arabia and India, that is, the region between the Near East (the Ottoman Empire and the Balkans) and the Far East (China, Japan, and the other countries of East Asia). The modern definition of the Middle East encompasses the region that includes Bahrain, Cyprus, Egypt, Iran, Iraq, Israel, Jordan, Kuwait, Lebanon, Oman, Qatar, Saudi Arabia, Syria, Turkey, United Arab Emirates, and Yemen. The world's oldest civilizations arose between two major river basins in this region—the Tigris and Euphrates, also called Mesopotamia, and the Nile. The entire area between the Tigris and Euphrates Rivers is called the Fertile Crescent. In Mesopotamia, the rivers flow down from their source in the mountains of what is now eastern Turkey through modern-day Syria, Iran, Iraq, and Kuwait, finally emptying into the Persian Gulf. The Nile flows from Lake Victoria in modern-day Uganda and Lake Tana in Ethiopia through South Sudan, Sudan, and Egypt, emptying into the Mediterranean Sea. Some of the earliest writing systems and cultures, empires, major wars, and religions were born in this region.

Islam was a major factor in unifying most of the countries in this region. Belief in Islam among the predominantly Muslim countries of the Middle East is divided among several denominations. The two major denominations are Sunni and Shia, and their acrimonious split happened in 632 CE after the death of the prophet Muhammad, based primarily on each side's recognition of the rightful successor to Muhammad. The conflict between Sunni and Shia Islam continues to this day: The Wahhabi school of Islam in Saudi Arabia actually considers the Shia sect as not legitimately Islamic. Besides these major denominations, minor sects have branched out from these, and they also affect the interpretation of Islamic law (sharia) and level of observance among Muslim countries. At one end are the more or less tolerant countries such as Turkey and Jordan. At the other end are the repressive countries such as Iran and Saudi Arabia.

Islam is not the only religion in the Middle East, however. Judaism and Christianity are well represented, as are Baha'i, the Druze religion, Yazidism, Zoroastrianism, Yarsanism, Mandaeism, and Shabakism.

The modern discovery of oil has brought about a radical change and another dimension of differentiation in the region. Vast crude oil resources discovered in Saudi Arabia, Iran, Iraq, and United Arab Emirates have dramatically changed their economies within recent decades, and most of the population enjoy enhanced standards of living, while others, such as Yemen, count among the poorest and least developed countries in the world.

The languages spoken in the region are diverse. They include Arabic and its many derivative dialects. Bedouins and Berbers, for instance, speak their own version of Arabic, which is nowhere near the literary Arabic of the Quran. Hebrew, Persian, Turkish, and Kurdish are the other major languages. English and French are also spoken among the educated classes. Due to the migration of many Jews from the Diaspora to Israel, as well as the presence of various Christian monasteries, diverse international languages are spoken besides English and French: German and its medieval version of Yiddish, modern Spanish and Ladino (or medieval Spanish), Romanian, Greek, Armenian, Russian, Ethiopian (several regional dialects), Italian, Bulgarian, Hindi (from Indian Jews), and many, many more.

Despite vast cultural, political, and geographical differences that set each Middle East country apart from the other, there are many similarities when it comes to the foods prepared for life-cycle celebration feasts. The two major culinary influences on food in the Middle East is their shared history as part of the Persian Sassanid Empire of the 7th and 8th centuries, and later of the Turkish Ottoman Empire for almost 400 years from the 16th to the early part of the 20th century. The Ottoman Empire and its cuisine were in their heyday in the 17th and 18th centuries, and many of the royal dishes cooked in the royal kitchens must have found their way, through dissemination by palace servants and others, to the wider world outside. Among those foods are *baklava* and *konafa,* which are widely prepared and eaten today, all throughout the Middle East and elsewhere that was under the Ottoman Empire, such as the Balkan region and Greece.

The most iconic celebratory food throughout the Middle East is lamb. For Muslims, it is not a celebration feast unless there is lamb and unleavened wheat bread. In the Middle East, sheep and wheat date back thousands of years to when they were both domesticated to become humankind's first controlled food supplies. The sheep and goat (as well as the camel) are the animals that are most adapted for survival in the desert-like conditions of most countries in the Middle East. By eating the grass and weeds that humans could not digest, the sheep turned into nourishing meat.

Harvesting wild wheat became valuable to humans because it increased food supplies, and it could be stored for a long time.

The favorite Middle East vegetable is eggplant, and yogurt is the preferred form of milk. There is a widespread religious taboo for both Muslims and Jews against eating any meat from pigs.

For both Muslims and Jews, the rituals of feasting include not only what food can be eaten but how it is processed, purchased, stored, prepared, and cooked, in addition to the rituals and etiquette of eating. Devout, religiously observant Jews say a prayer over bread, and there are eating procedures, prayers, and rituals for every occasion. Muslims likewise pray over food, and the rituals carry over into the etiquette of eating.

Muslims traditionally eat with the thumb, forefinger and middle finger of the right hand. The left hand is considered unclean. To eat with one finger is considered a sign of hatred, to eat with two shows pride, three is in accord with the Prophet Mohammed, while to eat with four or five fingers is a sign of gluttony.

Notwithstanding the passion for lamb, the mainstays of most meals are vegetables, pulses, and fruit. Tomatoes have been adopted wholeheartedly in the Middle East and feature on almost every menu, as do cucumbers and aubergines. Chickpeas, lentils, and sesame are also important, and sesame is made into both savory dishes, such as *tahina* sauce, and sweets such as varieties of *halva*. Fruit, notably dates, figs, pomegranates, and lemons, are served in various combinations to sweeten and enhance celebratory as well as daily foods. The traditional sweeteners for confectionery include honey, date syrup, and sugar syrup, often flavored with spices and orange-blossom water, as well as rosewater.

ARABIAN PENINSULA

The Arabian Peninsula includes the countries of Bahrain, Kuwait, Oman, Qatar, Saudi Arabia, the United Arab Emirates (UAE), and Yemen. Most people living in the Arabian Peninsula are Muslims. The non-Muslims are usually indentured workers from India, Pakistan, Bangladesh, and Sri Lanka, brought by wealthy landowners to Oman, Qatar, and United Arab Emirates. There is also a small Christian community in Kuwait, UAE, and other countries, predominantly Catholics from the Philippines, who work in various professions in technical and industrial, as well as domestic capacities.

All Muslim life-cycle celebrations are according to their religion. (See Islam and Islamic Life-Cycle Rituals, page lxxvi.)

Roast meat, in particular goat and lamb (or occasionally young camel), is *the* celebratory dish in Arab culture. Whether it is an occasion for rejoicing, such as a wedding, or for mourning, roast lamb or goat is part of the feast. Lamb or goat is usually slow-cooked, over an open fire or in an underground oven, for hours until the meat is so tender that it almost falls off the bone. At that point, it is also more convenient to eat, as traditional dining is accomplished with only the fingers of the right hand. Slow-roasted meat dishes are usually accompanied by rice, flavored with spices, and often colored yellow with turmeric or red with tomato paste. The names of the dishes vary, depending on their origin, but, with better communication and transportation networks and the spread of dishes from one country to another, the distinction between these dishes is becoming blurred. For instance, *shuwa* (recipe page 633) is typically made in Oman and the UAE. *Quozi* (also *qozi*, *qoozi*, and sometimes *ghozi*) is a similar slow-roasted lamb dish, originally from Iraq, which is stuffed and roasted. It is served with rice made colorful with diverse dried fruits and nuts. In Saudi Arabia and Yemen, a similar dish of roast lamb wrapped in foil and cooked over an open fire is *madfoon*. In Jordan, Syria, and Palestine, a closely related style of cooking is *zarb*. *Haneeth* is a roast lamb dish, originally from Yemen, that is made for weddings and other important occasions. It has become popularized throughout the Arabian Peninsula. *Haneeth* is cooked suspended over the fire in an underground clay oven called a *tandoor* or *tabun*.

Bahrain

Bahrain is an archipelago (group of islands) in the Persian Gulf and the Gulf of Bahrain. It lies east of Saudi Arabia. Since the Middle East economic boom in the 1970s, Bahrain has done much to elevate the standard of living for its people by improving health care, education, and housing. Most of the population are urbanites, living in cities where ancient mosques and modern glass skyscrapers share the skyline and where donkey carts and Rolls-Royce cars share the roads. Bahrain has one of the most modern communication systems in the world and is well established as a center in banking and commerce.

The majority of Bahraini are Muslims, and all life-cycle events are observed according to their religion. (See Islam and Islamic Life-Cycle Rituals, page lxxvi.)

At one time, motherhood was the sole aim of the Muslim woman's life. Today, girls are getting a full education and finding jobs in government and business. In Bahrain, women have a great many rights and privileges, but when it comes to family and children, they prefer to follow the strict Islamic traditions. While many Bahraini women are not completely veiled, most still prefer a head covering when in public. They dress modestly, preferring long-sleeved garments, even in the summertime.

The Middle Eastern families who adhere to ancient Muslim traditions follow rigid religious guidelines. When a Muslim woman marries, her loyalty is to the family she was born into. She is always a member of her father's family. For this reason, she does not change her name when she marries. A woman's children are members of her husband's family. Her wealth passes to her children upon her death and thus out of her father's family and into that of her husband. The ideal marriage, then, is between the children of two brothers. Muslims are aware of the genetic problems of such marriages, but this has not yet altered the practice.

Circumcision for boys at about seven or eight is a universal custom throughout Islam. In Bahrain, circumcisions are a family celebration, and the father often shoots off fireworks to celebrate the event. There is always a great feast, and for the firstborn son, whole roasted lamb is prepared.

In Arab countries, a whole kid (baby goat) or lamb is roasted on a spit for feast days and weddings. The meat is presented on a huge tray, surrounded by large quantities of rice, and garnished with peeled, hard-cooked eggs.

If you are going to roast whole baby lamb, be sure your oven is large enough to accommodate it. Otherwise, have the butcher cut it up, or you may grill it outdoors, or pay to have it baked in a larger commercial oven at a local bakery or restaurant.

⚡ *Kabab Barreh* (Roasted Whole Baby Lamb)

Yield: serves about 12

1 **oven-ready** 14- to 18-pound baby lamb

2 cups onions, **finely chopped**

salt and pepper to taste

2 tablespoons **ground coriander**

1 cup melted **rendered** butter
(recipe page 650) or melted butter or margarine

For serving:

10 to 12 cups cooked white rice

10 to 12 hard-cooked eggs, peeled

Equipment: Paper towels, medium bowl, mixing spoon, **pastry brush**, large roasting pan, aluminum foil, oven mitts, meat thermometer, **bulb baster**, large serving tray

Preheat oven to 325°F.

1. Rinse lamb inside and out under running water, and wipe dry with paper towels.

1. In medium bowl, mix chopped onions, salt and pepper to taste, coriander, and melted rendered butter or melted butter or margarine. Using pastry brush or your hands, rub the lamb inside and out with onion mixture. Place lamb in large roasting pan. If either end of the lamb overhangs the pan, make a shield of foil under the overhanging part to channel the drippings into the roasting pan.

2. Roast lamb in oven for 7 to 9 hours, or until meat is browned and very tender. **Baste** frequently with pan drippings using bulb baster or spoon. To keep from getting too dark, cover loosely with foil for the last hour or so of cooking. Meat thermometer inserted in thickest part of thigh should register 165°F for well-done meat. (Allow 30 to 35 minutes per pound.)

To serve, place the whole lamb on a large serving tray, and surround with rice. Decoratively arrange the peeled hard-cooked eggs on top of the rice.

♪ *Machboos* (Bahraini Spiced Braised Chicken and Rice)

Machboos (also *makbus*) is a dish of meat, vegetables, assorted spices, and rice that is made all over the Arabian Peninsula. *Machboos* is frequently served with a topping of onions and nuts called "*hashwa*" for celebrations. It originated in Saudi Arabia as the dish *kabsa*. The distinctive flavor of *machboos* is due to the use of dried limes (*loomi*) and the spice blend *baharat*. *Baharat* means "spice," and in its basic form, it is a mixture of black pepper, cumin, coriander, cardamom, nutmeg, and other spices, but there are as many variants of *baharat* as there are cooks in the region. Dried limes are a favorite seasoning for fish, especially in the Gulf countries, but are also used for meat dishes. Dried limes are a product of Oman. They come in brown and black and are hence often called "black limes"; their color is the result of having been boiled in salt and then sun-dried. To use them, they have to be pierced or broken into pieces. The meat for *machboos* can be chicken (recipe follows), beef, lamb, camel, kid (young goat), or it can be any firm-fleshed fish.

Yield: 5 servings

3 tablespoons olive or other vegetable oil

1 whole chicken, about 5 pounds, cut into serving-size pieces

2 tablespoons butter or *ghee*, homemade (recipe page 142)

2 large onions, finely chopped

1 tablespoon fresh ginger, finely chopped

6 cloves garlic, finely chopped

1 to 2 hot chili peppers (or to taste), seeds removed, sliced finely

1 tablespoon *baharat* (see recipe page 665)

1 teaspoon turmeric

1 teaspoon salt, or to taste

2 large tomatoes, finely chopped

3 dried limes, pierced through with a knife in several places

5 green cardamom pods

¼ teaspoon ground cloves

1 stick cinnamon

4 cups chicken stock or water

3 cups **basmati rice** (soaked for 20 minutes, then washed and rinsed well)

½ cup **cilantro**, chopped

⅓ cup fresh parsley, chopped

hashwa (topping)

2 tablespoons oil

1 large onion, finely sliced

3 cloves garlic, minced

2 tablespoons ginger, minced

1 tablespoon *baharat* (see recipe page 665)

1 cup **blanched** almond flakes or **pine nuts**

¼ cup sultana raisins

rosewater for sprinkling (optional)

Equipment: **Heavy-bottomed** saucepan or Dutch oven, oven mitts, bowls, large serving platter or tray

1. In heavy-bottomed saucepan or Dutch oven over medium heat, heat oil, and brown chicken pieces on both sides. Transfer to a bowl.

2. To remaining oil in the pan, add butter or *ghee*, and, when hot, add onions, stirring constantly until golden. Stir in garlic, ginger, chili pepper, *baharat*, and turmeric. Add chicken pieces, salt, tomatoes, dried limes, cardamom, cloves, cinnamon, and chicken stock or water. Bring to a boil, then reduce heat to let everything simmer, covered, for 40 to 45 minutes, or until chicken is tender.

3. Stir in rice, cilantro, and parsley. Add more stock or water, if necessary, to come up to 1 inch above the rice.

4. Raise heat to bring pan to a boil, then reduce heat, and let everything simmer, covered, for 15 to 20 minutes until all stock has been absorbed, and rice is done.

5. While rice is cooking, prepare the *hashwa*: In a frying pan or skillet over medium heat, fry the onion in oil until golden brown. Set aside.

6. In the remaining oil in the pan, sauté garlic and ginger until aromatic. Stir in *baharat*, almonds or pine nuts, and raisins, and sauté until almonds are golden.

7. Turn off heat. Combine reserved onions with the almond and raisin mixture.

To serve, arrange the rice and chicken mixed together on a large serving platter or tray, or, alternatively, mound the rice and arrange chicken pieces on top. Sprinkle the hashwa *over the rice and chicken. Sprinkle a few drops of rose water over all.*

Muhallabieh is a favorite rice pudding prepared for boys after their circumcision. It is soothing and easy to digest. This pudding is traditionally served to visitors and guests at the birth of a son. It is said that a family will serve it on the birth of a daughter only if she is the fifth child, after having had four sons.

✿ *Muhallabieh* (Rice Pudding)

Yield: serves 4 to 6

2 cups uncooked **basmati rice**

1 cup water, or ¾ cup orange juice and ¼ cup water

1 quart milk

¾ cup sugar

For **garnish**: ½ cup chopped pistachio nuts

Equipment: Electric **blender** (optional), rubber spatula, medium bowl, mixing spoon, medium saucepan, individual serving bowls

1. Put uncooked rice in blender, and **blend** until pulverized. Transfer pulverized rice to medium bowl, add 1 cup water or ¾ cup orange juice and ¼ cup water mixture, and stir to make a paste.

2. Put milk in medium saucepan, and bring to boil over medium-high heat. Slowly stir in rice mixture and sugar. Reduce heat to simmer, and, stirring frequently, cook until thickened, 45 minutes to 1 hour.

3. Pour into individual serving bowls, and allow to cool to room temperature and refrigerate.

To serve, garnish each serving with chopped pistachio.

Kuwait, Oman, Qatar, and the United Arab Emirates

Kuwait is bordered on the north and west by Iraq and to the south by Saudi Arabia, with the Persian Gulf to the west. The city of Kuwait is one of international banks, high-rise buildings, and air-conditioned homes. These days most men wear jeans or business suits, and women wear Western outfits like jeans or miniskirts underneath their robe-like *aba*.

Marriage is arranged by the parents in a very meaningful way. Marriage to a cousin is preferred, and marriage to a first cousin is considered to be the best possible match. The families know each other, and the bride and groom would have met as children. Marriage outside of the clan is a last resort. Instead, a young woman might wait for an opportunity to become a cousin's second wife rather than marry out of the clan. Men are free to take up to four wives.

The degree to which women are consulted on their choice of husband varies with each family. A young person who marries without parental consent is expelled from the family and hence from the clan. A young girl brings wealth with her bride-price to her family in marrying, and she knows her value in that sense.

In Islamic marriages in Kuwait, the couple must sign a contract before the marriage, and the woman can specify what is acceptable for her in the marriage. She can limit the number of additional wives her husband may take, and she can also have a large divorce settlement fee written into the contract, thereby making it less likely for her husband to divorce her.

The trend in Kuwait in recent years among the middle and upper classes has been for ostentatious wedding parties, a sharp contrast with the age-old practice of simple celebrations. The trend is a result of influence from Western media and the massive financial influx from oil profits. Guests usually number around 700 to 800, and it is not unusual for a family to send out 1,000 invitations. Preferences are for fresh flowers flown in from Holland, famous singers hired for the entertainment, and for the bride's and groom's chairs to be decorated with gold bars and fresh roses flown in especially for the occasion. Gifts for guests are usually brand-name perfumes, and the most honored guests are provided with expensive cutlery to eat with.

Oman is bounded by the Gulf of Oman and the Arabian Sea to the north, east, and southeast and to the west by Yemen, Saudi Arabia, and the United Arab Emirates. Oman was an extremely poor country until the discovery of oil in 1960s. Regardless of the new wealth and modernization in the cities, the people continue to follow the traditional lifestyle according to conservative Islamic values.

Among Muslims, there is great strength in the family unit. Families are very large, including two or three generations, uncles, several aunts for each uncle, and assorted cousins. In traditional families, they all live together in a compound with several mud brick houses around an open courtyard.

Sometimes the birth of the firstborn son means so much to the family that the parents may become known by the child's name. They are addressed as *abu* (father of) or *umm* (mother of), followed with the name of the child. Friends and family show a sign of respect and recognition of the couple's good fortune in having a son when they address them in this way.

While men and women are traditionally segregated outside the home, some work together in industry and government offices. In Oman, women have entered the professions, and some even hold jobs on the police force.

Shuwa (Spiced Roast Lamb)

This is a classic celebration dish made in Oman and the United Arab Emirates. *Shuwa* is prepared for all special occasions, such as the last day of Eid, as well as important life-cycle celebrations. It is a dish communally prepared and eaten by an entire village or clan. Young goat (kid) is most often used to make this dish. Omanis prepare this with a very liberal amount of hot chili peppers—sometimes as many as 25 to 30. Adjust the amount of peppers to the level of heat that diners can take. *Shuwa* is traditionally wrapped in dried banana or date palm leaves and placed inside jute sacks, before being cooked in an underground oven, but it can just as easily be prepared in a regular oven.

Yield: 6 to 8 servings

CAUTION: Wrap your hands in plastic wrap, or slip them in plastic sandwich bags when handling peppers. Do not touch your eyes while handling peppers. If you accidentally touch your eyes, rinse them under cold running water at once.

1 head garlic, peeled, finely minced2 teaspoons freshly ground black pepper

2 teaspoons ground cumin

2 teaspoons ground **coriander**

2 teaspoons turmeric

1 teaspoon ground cloves

1 teaspoon ground cardamom

Spiced rice:

3 tablespoons oil

2 teaspoons whole cumin seeds

5 cardamom pods

4 cloves

1 stick cinnamon

1 to 5 dried red hot chili peppers (according to level of heat desired), chopped

¼ cup olive oil

½ cup vinegar

juice of 2 lemons

7 to 8 pounds lamb chunks, bone-in, or leg of lamb

3 star anise

4 bay leaves

6 cups **basmati rice**

6 cups water, or more as needed

salt and freshly ground black pepper to taste

Equipment: Large bowl, roasting tray, **heavy-bottomed** saucepan with cover or Dutch oven, oven mitts, large serving plates or trays, parchment paper, kitchen twine, aluminum foil

Ten minutes before using oven, preheat oven to 250°F.

1. Prepare lamb: In large bowl, combine garlic, black pepper, cumin, coriander, turmeric, cloves, cardamom, chili pepper, olive oil, vinegar, and lemon juice until well mixed.

2. Mix well with the lamb, or, if using a whole leg, make ½-inch-deep incisions all over lamb, and insert spice mixture into the incisions. Cover, and allow to marinate overnight, refrigerated.

3. Cut parchment paper into 12-inch-square pieces. Divide meat into 6 to 8 portions, and place on banana leaves or parchment paper. Add all marinating juices and spices.

   Wrap parchment paper securely to enclose the meat, using kitchen twine if necessary. Enclose parchment-wrapped parcels in foil, and seal well. Place wrapped parcels in roasting tray. If using a whole leg, line the roasting tray with parchment paper before laying the leg. Cover leg with more parchment paper, and seal roasting tray with aluminum foil.

4. Place roasting tray in the center of preheated oven for 3 hours (for the parcels) and for 3½ to 4 hours for the whole leg. The meat should be very tender and almost falling off the bone.

5. Prepare rice: Wash rice three times, until the rinse water is no longer milky. Soak in water to cover for 30 minutes. Drain and allow to air-dry.

6. Heat oil over medium heat in a heavy-bottomed saucepan with cover or Dutch oven. Stir-fry whole spices for a few minutes until aromatic. Add water, and, when it boils, add rice. The water should cover the rice by 1 inch. Add more boiling water as needed. Season with salt and pepper. Cover pan, and let it come to the boil. Reduce heat to lowest possible temperature, and let rice cook gently for 15 to 20 minutes.

7. Discard bay leaves, cinnamon, and star anise.

Serve rice on large serving platters, with roast lamb pieces on top.

Qatar lies on a peninsula, bounded to the north and east by the Persian Gulf, to the west by the Gulf of Bahrain, and to the south by Saudi Arabia. Since Sheik Hamad bin Khalifa Al-Thani took power in this sleepy country, he is slowly changing Qatar's image as the region's most backward state. In a Muslim country were women have traditionally been homebodies, the young sheik leader has been hiring women to fill government jobs.

Qatar is struggling to modernize while retaining strict Islamic traditions. In the cities, traditional Arab and modern dress coexist. Many women wear long-sleeved, floor-length, Western-style dresses to work. Some may add the *hijab*, the traditional black headscarf. The young men prefer to wear jeans and T-shirts, while the older men prefer the long white *dishdasha* robe, the national dress of Qatar.

Most Qatari, including the working women, believe life-cycle rituals should follow strict Islamic law and traditions. There are separate schools for girls, socializing without a chaperone is forbidden, and most marriages are arranged.

The religious part of a marriage takes place in the bride's family home. While the couple are in different rooms, a *mutawa* (holy man) asks the couple if they will take each other as husband and wife. The bride and groom sign the contract and are legally married though they will not join each other as man and wife until after the wedding ceremony.

✿ *Esh Asaraya* (Cream Cheese Dessert)

Esh asaraya (also *aysh al saraya*) translates to "bread of the sultan's harem." It is a very rich bread pudding or dessert made with cream cheese and is often served for family celebrations.

1 cup sugar

½ cup water

grated rind and juice of 1 lemon

1 cup hot water

8 pieces of toasted crustless white bread, broken into fine crumbs

1 cup cream cheese, softened

1 cup whipping cream

2 teaspoons orange-blossom water or **rosewater**

For **garnish**:

½ cup pistachios, chopped

½ cup almonds, chopped

Equipment: Medium saucepan, 4 glass dessert dishes

1. Make caramel syrup: In saucepan over medium heat, bring to a boil the sugar, water, and lemon juice. Leave to simmer until thickened and golden brown. Turn off heat.

   (The hot syrup will continue cooking in the hot pan and will turn darker. Do not overcook, or the syrup will scorch and taste bitter.)

2. Leave syrup to cool in saucepan, and when thoroughly cool, add 1 cup hot water.

3. Return the saucepan to cook over low heat until the caramel is completely dissolved. Stir in bread crumbs, and let them absorb all the syrup. Turn off heat, and let bread crumb mixture cool.

4. Stir in lemon rind, and divide the mixture among 4 dessert dishes.

5. Whip cream to soft peaks, and combine with cream cheese. Stir in orange-blossom or rosewater.

Spoon cream cheese mixture over the bread crumbs, sprinkle with pistachios and almonds, and leave to chill for at least 1 hour before serving.

The United Arab Emirates (UAE) are seven Arab states that gained their independence from the United Kingdom in 1971. The country is bounded by the Persian Gulf on the north and east, by Oman to the southeast, and by Saudi Arabia to the west. In a relatively short time, the UAE has gone from a little known desert country to an international business and vacation destination with five-star hotels. In recent years, the discovery of oil has brought wealth and a new way of life to the small population. Today the UAE is a federation of seven Arab states or emirates. Each emirate is named after its main town or city and is controlled politically and economically by its sheikh. *Emir* or *sheikh* means "prince."

The Arabs of the UAE usually have large families with one or two wives and numerous children. They have a strong alliance to all of their kin, and the extended family often lives together in a compound with adjoining houses.

The people of the UAE not only eat three meals a day, but they also eat two other small meals called *fualah*. Traditionally, one *fualah* is between breakfast and lunch, and the other is between lunch and dinner. The *fualah* also becomes a ritualistic meal when there is an important event to celebrate or the need for a religious gathering. The morning *fualah* is a good time to view the newborn son, while the late afternoon *fualah* is the best time to celebrate the circumcision of a boy or a wedding. The food served includes a variety of fruits, sweets, nuts, and *kahve* (recipe page 643). Perfumes and incense are also passed around as part of the ritual. Incense is placed in burners, lit, and fanned until it is burning well enough to produce wafts of smoke.

Saudi Arabia

Saudi Arabia is located in the Arabian Peninsula, bordered by Jordan and Iraq to the north, the Persian Gulf and the United Arab Emirates to the east, Oman and Yemen to the south, and the Red Sea to the west. In Saudi Arabia, Islam is not just a religion that can be separated from daily life and government, it is the framework for both secular and spiritual life. Every facet of life is governed by the Islamic religion. (See Islam and Islamic Life-Cycle Rituals, page lxxvi.) In their private lives, the two most important family celebrations are the birth of a child, especially a boy, and weddings.

The holy city of Mecca where every Muslim man expects to make the *hajj* (pilgrimage) is in Saudi Arabia. The *hajj* to Mecca is without question the most important rite of passage any Muslim can experience. Regardless of where they live, family and friends always have a big feast to celebrate a person's *hajj* to Mecca upon the return home.

Saudis may give a boy as many as four names: his own name, his father's and grandfather's names, and a tribal or family name.

After kindergarten girls are not allowed to go to school with boys. In later life they are not allowed to work with men, to drive cars, or to appear in public without being fully shrouded. The socially preferred role for Saudi women is to be in the home. If women or girls want to work, it should be in medicine, education, or social work. They then should work only with female patients, students, and clients.

The long black outer cloak worn by women is the *abaaya*, and they are not permitted out of their house without it.

The long, white garment worn by men is a *thobe*. The subtle style differences and the fabric quality are signs of wealth. The traditional cloth that is worn on the head was originally used to shield the face and neck from wind and sandstorms. Now, however, it is highly fashionable for men to wear it with even Western-style business suits. The traditional men's dress is required for school, in the mosque during prayer, and at wedding celebrations.

When Saudis die, they must be buried within 24 hours. There are no elaborate funeral services, nor are there cemeteries with monuments, even for very important people. A plain, small name plate is all one sees at a grave site.

A young woman almost always accepts the man her parents have chosen as her husband. Often the paternal or maternal grandmother plays an important role in the selection of a prospective mate. Her wedding is the most important day in the life of a Saudi woman, and it is an elaborate celebration. Wedding expenses can sometimes be exorbitant, but the cost is shared by both the groom and family of the bride.

At wedding celebrations, held in the evening at the home of the bride or in a hotel, male and female guests do not mix. The men never see the bride, since it is unacceptable for an unveiled Saudi woman to be seen by men who are not her close relatives.

Wedding photos, a new innovation, are taken only by female photographers and are never publicly displayed. The bride and groom make a formal appearance among the women guests to receive their congratulations. Male and female guests bring with them appropriate wedding presents for the newlyweds.

All meals, including the wedding feast, are eaten while sitting on the floor. There are no eating utensils since everyone eats with the fingers of the right hand. The left hand must never touch food, as it is used only for personal grooming. The soles of the feet are considered unclean, and it is offensive to point them at another person. It is also impolite to stare at other people while they are eating. Looking down at your own plate instead is considered good manners. (However, Saudis who have been educated or who have traveled to the West may prefer to sit on chairs and use silverware rather than sit on rugs and use their right hands to eat.)

Offering a large variety of food in great quantities is considered good manners. So is setting out the food on elegant silver platters on beautiful tablecloths, which have been decorated with bowls of fresh fruit and flowers. This lavish hospitality shows the generosity of the host and hostess.

The main dish of a wedding feast is likely to be whole roasted stuffed lamb (recipe follows) or kid. The pieces of meat are piled on huge serving platters and surrounded by mounds of rice. The platters of food are often so big and heavy that it takes two servants to carry them to the male guests, who sit cross-legged on the rugs in the dining room.

The bride, along with her women wedding guests, eats apart from the men. Their feast is often as elaborate as that served to the men. In some households, the women must first serve the men before they can eat, which is often the leftovers.

The beverages are raisin tea, made with water in which raisins have been soaked; lemonade; "Saudi champagne" (a nonalcoholic carbonated fruit drink); and Arabic coffee flavored with cardamom. In Saudi Arabia, alcoholic beverages are forbidden.

When the meal is over, the guests rinse their fingers in bowls of perfumed water brought to them by servants. Tea and coffee are served at the end of the feast, never with the food. Feasts can last far into the night.

Kharoof Mahshi (Roast Stuffed Lamb or Kid)

Feasts for important family events or special occasions, such as a wedding, almost always include a large platter with flavored rice and roast meat, whether lamb or kid or chicken. *Kharoof mahshi* features a whole kid or lamb, stuffed with spiced rice. It is considered the Saudi national dish and is ever present at most major life-cycle events. It is served on a large platter surrounded with eggs, to be shared among several diners. In traditional dining style, there are no individual place settings; rather, each diner eats from the portion of the platter directly in front of him or her, using only the right hand.

Yield: 10 to 12 servings

3 teaspoons salt

½ teaspoon freshly ground black pepper

2 tablespoons **cilantro**, minced

1 teaspoon candied ginger, minced

2 large onions, minced

whole lamb or kid, about 14 pounds, rinsed inside and out, patted dry

4 cups cooked rice

2 cups pistachio nuts, **coarsely chopped**

1 cup almonds, coarsely chopped

1½ cups sultana raisins

1 cup clarified or regular butter, melted

12 flat breads or pita, for lining the serving platter

For **garnish**:

12 hard-cooked eggs, sliced in half

1 cup toasted almond flakes or slivers or pistachio nut halves

¼ cup flat-leaf parsley, chopped

¼ cup cilantro, chopped

12 medium tomatoes, sliced in half

Equipment: Medium and large mixing bowls, large needle and kitchen thread or small metal skewers, baking pan large enough to hold lamb or kid, basting brush, oven mitts, large serving platter

Preheat oven to 300°F.

1. Prepare lamb: In a bowl, mix salt, pepper, cilantro, and ginger with a quarter of the onion. Rub lamb thoroughly inside and outside with this mixture. Mix rice with pistachio nuts, almonds, raisins, and the remaining onions. Stuff the lamb cavity with rice mixture. Sew the opening shut, or seal with small metal skewers.

2. Place lamb on a grid in a large baking pan. Brush thoroughly with clarified butter, and roast in preheated oven until meat is very tender and well browned, about 4½ hours. **Baste** frequently with pan drippings.

3. Bring to the table whole on a large platter for presentation to the assembled guests, and once the whole lamb has been appreciated, take it back to the kitchen for cutting into serving-size pieces.

Serve on platter lined with a layer of flat breads; place rice over bread and the meat portions equally distributed on top. Surround rice with eggs and tomatoes. Sprinkle almonds or pistachios, parsley, and cilantro all over rice and pieces of meat.

Fruit is eaten throughout the meal and also at the end. This is just one of many fruit dishes that will be set out for guests during a wedding feast.

⚭ *Munkaczina* (Zesty Orange Salad)

Yield: serves 6

3 large oranges, peeled, thinly sliced

2 onions, **trimmed**, thinly sliced

3 tablespoons vegetable oil

3 tablespoons wine vinegar

ground red pepper to taste

salt to taste

12 ripe black olives, **pitted** and sliced

Equipment: Medium serving platter with raised lip, 8-ounce cup, mixing spoon

1. Arrange orange and onion slices, alternately, slightly overlapping in medium serving platter.

2. In cup, combine oil, vinegar, ground red pepper and salt. Stir, and pour over orange and onion slices. Let salad **marinate** for 1 hour at room temperature. Sprinkle with sliced black olives before serving.

Serve as one of the side dishes with lamb or goat for a wedding feast.

Yemen

Yemen is located in the southwest corner of the Arabian Peninsula and is bounded on the north by Saudi Arabia, on the east by Oman, on the south by the Arabian Sea and the Gulf of Aden, and on the west by the Red Sea. Except for the language, which is

Arabic, and the fact that most people are Muslims, there are great cultural differences among the regional groups in Yemen. The people living in the coastal lowland are racially and culturally influenced by the neighboring African countries (Eritrea and Dijbouti) just across the strait of Bab el Mandeb. The people living in the cities and towns scattered over the rugged terrain of the mountains and valleys of Northern Yemen live by strict Islamic laws.

On occasions of family feasts, female relatives and friends gather in the kitchen to help with the food preparations. Their job is to prepare and serve food to the men, who always eat separately from the women.

Boys and girls have different role models. Girls are taught to be subservient while still very young, and boys learn to be aggressive and decisive. Girls are kept at home with the women and small children. They do not have the freedom to come and go as boys do.

In the past, young boys were not considered culturally to have gone through an adolescent stage. As soon as they reached puberty they were accepted as adults, eligible for marriage and expected to help protect and provide for the family. Young women could be married after their menstruation began and have children while they were not yet grown themselves. This is slowly changing, but only in the cities where education is making the difference.

Appetizers are an important part of every family celebration feast, and among the most popular throughout the Mediterranean region and the Middle East are stuffed grape leaves. In Greece, they are called *dolmas*, in Turkey, *yalanci dolma*, and in Libya, *abrak*. In Egypt, 1 tablespoon dry mint leaves are added to the meat mixture, and it is called "*wara enab mahshi.*" In Armenia, ground lamb, added along with rice, is called "*misov derevapatat.*" In Yemen, stuffed grape leaves are called "*yab-ra.*"

Yab-Ra (Stuffed Grape Leaves)

Yield: about 6 dozen

16-ounce jar grape leaves (available at Middle Eastern food stores and some supermarkets)

1 pound chopped lean beef or lamb

½ cup long grain rice, uncooked

3 cloves garlic, **finely chopped**

salt and pepper to taste

½ cup lemon juice

3 cups chicken broth

Equipment: **Colander**, large mixing bowl, mixing spoon, work surface, paring knife, large saucepan with cover, heatproof dinner plate (slightly smaller than saucepan), serving platter

1. Prepare grape leaves: Remove leaves from jar, and carefully separate them. Grape leaves are packed in a brine or salty solution, so it is necessary to rinse them under cold running water. Stack leaves in a colander to drain. Set aside about 6 or 8 leaves to line bottom of saucepan.

2. Prepare filling: Combine chopped beef or lamb, rice, and garlic in large mixing bowl. Using clean hands, mix well and add salt and pepper to taste.

3. On work surface, spread out one grape leaf, with the dull-side up and stem end facing you. Using paring knife, cut off stem before stuffing leaf. Place about 1 teaspoon of the filling on the center of the leaf. (For larger leaves, use a little more.) Start to roll up the leaf from end where stem was. Tuck in the sides of the leaves to enclose the filling. Continue rolling, making little packages each about ¾ inch thick and about 2 inches wide. Place stuffed leaves seam-side down on work surface. Repeat until all the leaves are filled.

4. Line bottom of large saucepan with 6 to 8 grape leaves. Place stuffed leaves on top and pack them close together, with seam sides down. When first layer is complete, make a second layer, packing the stuffed leaves close together. Continue building layers until all the stuffed leaves are in the saucepan.

5. It is necessary to weigh down the stuffed grape leaves as they cook. Do this by placing a heatproof dinner plate, a little smaller than the diameter of the pot, upside down, on top of the stuffed leaves.

6. Add lemon juice and broth or water. Bring to a boil over high heat. Reduce heat to simmer, cover saucepan, and cook for 45 minutes. Remove from heat, and cool to room temperature before removing from pan. Stuffed grape leaves keep well in covered container, refrigerated, for at least four days.

To serve as an appetizer, arrange stuffed grape leaves on serving platter. To eat, pick up with your fingers, and pop into your mouth.

❦ *Mozat Bellaban* (Braised Lamb Shanks in Yogurt Sauce)

Mozat bellaban is a popular way of preparing lamb in Kuwait. Several different types of lamb dishes are traditionally served at weddings in Kuwait.

Yield: serves 6

6 lean lamb shanks	½ teaspoon peppercorns
¾ cup vegetable oil, divided	2 quarts plain yogurt
water, as needed	**2 egg yolks**
1 onion, quartered	¼ cup **sifted cornstarch**
1 carrot, peeled and chopped	½ cup chopped fresh mint
2 bay leaves	For **garnish**: 6 peeled hard-cooked eggs
4 cloves	

Equipment: Large **heavy-bottomed** skillet, metal tongs, large saucepan with cover or **Dutch oven**, medium enameled or stainless saucepan, small skillet, whisk, serving spoon, serving platter

1. Heat ¼ cup oil in large heavy-bottomed skillet over medium-high heat. Brown lamb shanks well on all sides, 7 to 12 minutes. When browned, transfer to large saucepan or Dutch oven, and add water to cover. Add onion, carrot, bay leaves, cloves, and peppercorns. Bring to boil over high heat. Reduce heat to simmer, cover, and cook for 30 to 45 minutes, or until done.

2. Prepare yogurt sauce: While shanks are cooking, mix yogurt, egg yolks, cornstarch, and salt in medium enameled or stainless saucepan. Whisking constantly, bring to boil over medium heat. Reduce to low, and, stirring frequently, cook for 5 to 7 minutes until thickened.

3. At serving time, heat remaining ½ cup oil in small skillet over medium-high heat. Add garlic and chopped mint, and stir constantly, until garlic is soft, 3 to 5 minutes. Remove from heat.

To serve, place braised lamb shanks on large serving platter, spoon over hot yogurt sauce, and top with garlic mixture. Decorate with wedges of hard-cooked eggs, and serve with rice and flat bread.

⚘ *Maghrebia* (Meat Stew with Couscous)

Couscous is popular throughout North Africa and the Middle East. It would be one of the 30 or 40 dishes prepared for the wedding feast.

Yield: serves 6 to 8

1 pound lamb or lean beef, cut into hearty chunks

1 bay leaf

1 teaspoon **ground** cinnamon

2 teaspoons salt

¼ teaspoon pepper

water, as needed

3 pounds chicken, cut into serving-size pieces

10 onions, peeled

6 carrots, peeled, **coarsely chopped**

1½ cups canned chickpeas (garbanzo beans)

10-ounce package frozen green peas, thawed

2 boxes (5.8 ounces each) **couscous** (available at all supermarkets)

¼ cup parsley, **finely chopped** for **garnish**

Equipment: Large saucepan or **Dutch oven**, mixing spoon, large shallow serving platter, tongs, slotted metal spoon, large serving bowl, ladle, individual soup bowls

1. Place meat, bay leaf, cinnamon, salt, pepper, and 3 cups water in large saucepan or Dutch oven. Bring to boil over medium-high heat. Reduce to simmer, cover, and cook for 45 minutes.

2. Add chicken pieces, onions, carrots, chickpeas, and green peas. Add enough water to cover chicken and vegetables. Bring to boil over high heat. Reduce heat to simmer, cover, and cook for 40 to 50 minutes, until chicken and meat are very tender.

3. Prepare couscous according to directions on package, and keep warm.

4. Place warm couscous on large shallow serving platter. Make a well (hole) in the center, and, using tongs and slotted spoon, arrange meat, chicken, and vegetables in the center of the couscous. Sprinkle with parsley.

To serve, pour broth into a large serving bowl with ladle. Each person is given an individual soup bowl for the broth, which they drink.

The ceremonial serving of coffee to guests expresses the importance of hospitality throughout the Middle East. Coffee is always freshly made, and often the beans are roasted and ground each day. Sugar is always added to the coffee while it cooks, so different brews must be served to please those who like different degrees of sweetness. In Saudi Arabia, a cardamom seed is added to the pot while the coffee is brewing. The special long-handled pot for preparing coffee is called a *kanaka*.

Coffee was discovered in Ethiopia about 1,000 years ago, and for many years the world's supply was shipped from the port of Yemen.

⚷ *Kahve* (Middle East Coffee)

Yield: serves 4

2 cups water

4 teaspoons sugar, more or less to taste

4 teaspoons coffee, freshly ground to powder consistency or espresso grind (available at supermarkets and specialty coffee stores)

Equipment: Kanaka or small saucepan, teaspoon, 4 small cups (such as demitasse, Turkish coffee, or tea cups)

1. Put water in *kanaka* or small saucepan, and bring to boil over high heat.

2. Stir in 4 teaspoons sugar (1 teaspoon per serving gives average sweetness). Top the water with powdered ground coffee or espresso grind so that it floats on the water. Bring water again to boil, remove from the heat, and let the froth that has risen die down. Repeat boiling process once more. Bring to a boil, and stir coffee well into the water, trying not to lose the froth.

3. Pour at once into small cups, swirling the pot slightly as you pour so that a little froth is included in each cup.

Serve at once, the grounds will settle at the bottom of the cup and should not be drunk. Drink the coffee black as they do in Yemen. The coffee is served with pastries, such as tamriah *(recipe page 667).*

Cyprus

Cyprus, an island in the Mediterranean Sea, is located to the south of Turkey and to the east of Syria. Approximately 80 percent of people in Cyprus are of Greek origin, and most of the remaining are of Turkish origin. The Greeks follow the Greek Orthodox life-cycle rituals (see Eastern or Orthodox Church Life-Cycle Rituals, page lxxv); see also discussion of Greek weddings (page 399). The Turks, who are Muslims, follow the life-cycle rituals according to their religion. (See Islam and Islamic Life-Cycle Rituals, page lxxvi.)

In the Greek communities, many traditions have grown around the village wedding ceremony. Everyone in the town is invited to the celebration, often lasting three days. One unusual custom is the Filling the Mattress. The village women take bedding, blessed by the priest, to the reception, and each holds an edge as they dance and sing. They then sew the covering to a mat, which they stuff and sew up. This is placed on the wedding bed.

The night before the wedding, the groom is shaved by the best man in front of his friends to symbolize his giving up bachelorhood. A lovely local custom is the blessing of the bride by her father before she walks down the aisle.

Within the Greek Orthodox Church, the duties of the best man and bridesmaid are spelled out in detail. Following the ceremony, they are expected to give financial assistance and even physical protection in times of crisis. They may later become godparents of the couple's first child, thereby entering into a virtual blood relationship because their children are legally prohibited from marrying their godchildren.

On the day of the wedding, guests are invited into the new home immediately following the ceremony, and the best man pours each a glass of brandy and offers a piece of traditional seed cake. Then the feasting and celebrating really begin with music provided by a band composed of an accordion, violin, and drums. Often the *aulos*, the shepherd's flute, and the *bouzouki*, a stringed guitar-like instrument, are included.

After a traditional wedding, the young couple start the dancing, and during this time paper money is pinned to their clothes until the garments are completely covered. The party goes into high gear when groups of men challenge each other dancing the lively *pidiktos*, the ancient leaping dance performed only by men.

Over a two- or three-day period, the musicians lead the revelers as they move to and from the homes of different relatives and to the village square where dancing, singing, and feasting continue until everyone is exhausted.

Among Turkish Cypriot communities, much of the wedding tradition is dictated by the presiding Muslim holy man of the village. In prominent families a *mullah*, or religious leader of high rank, may come from the Turkey mainland for the final blessing.

On special days, such as a religious holiday or birthday, an elaborate feast is prepared. The feast may include spit-roasted whole lamb (recipe page 629) or mutton or goat roasted in the beehive clay ovens set out in the yard. Assorted breads and vegetables are served with the meat. This wonderful casserole-type pie is included in the feast. The spinach filling can also be used for making little individual pastries. To make pastries, assemble according to *bureks* (recipe page 646).

ꝰ *Tirópeta Tou Spetioú* (Family-style Spinach Pie)

Yield: serves 12 to 14

6 tablespoons extra virgin olive oil

2 onions, **finely chopped**

2 packages (10 ounces each) frozen chopped
  spinach, thawed and drained

1 pound feta cheese (available in dairy section
  of all supermarkets)

1½ cups cottage cheese, drained

6 eggs, well beaten

salt and pepper to taste

1 cup (½ pound) melted butter or margarine,
  more if needed

20 sheets **phyllo** (available in freezer section
  of all supermarkets), thawed according to
  directions on package

Equipment: Large skillet, mixing spoon, large mixing bowl, potato masher or fork, rubber spatula, damp kitchen towel, **pastry brush**, buttered 9×12×2-inch baking pan, sharp knife, oven mitts

1. Heat olive oil in large skillet over medium-high heat. Add onions, stir, and **sauté** until soft, 3 to 5 minutes. Squeeze spinach to remove and discard liquid. Break up spinach clumps with your hands as you add it to onions. Stir well, reduce heat to simmer, and cook until liquid evaporates, 3 to 5 minutes. Remove from heat.

2. In large mixing bowl, mash feta cheese with cottage cheese, using potato masher or back of fork. Stir in eggs and salt and pepper to taste. Using rubber spatula, **fold in** spinach mixture.

Preheat oven to 350°F.

3. Assemble pie: While working with one sheet phyllo, keep remaining sheets covered with damp towel. Butter the top sheet of phyllo with melted butter or margarine and lay in buttered 9×12-inch baking pan. Continue to brush each sheet, and place it on top of the last, covering the bottom layer of baking pan with 10 sheets of phyllo.

4. Spoon spinach filling on top of the layer of phyllo in baking pan, and spread smooth with rubber spatula. Brush a sheet of phyllo with melted butter, and place over the spinach mixture. Repeat layering all the remaining sheets of phyllo, brushing each first with melted butter. Roll or push edges of phyllo down all around the pan to hold in mixture. Brush top and edges completely with melted butter. Lightly score top into pieces (3 lengthwise cuts and 4 or 6 across) with a sharp knife. (This will guide you when cutting after baking.)

5. Bake in oven 35 to 40 minutes, until golden brown. Using oven mitts, remove from oven, and let rest 10 minutes before cutting into pieces.

Serve hot or at room temperature. Put on the buffet table, and have guests help themselves.

Afelia is a Greek dish (Muslims do not eat pork), which would be served at a baptism or name day dinner along with *tirópeta tou spetioú* and salad.

⚘ *Afelia* (Pork with Coriander)

Yield: serves 4 to 6

1 tablespoon vegetable oil

2 pounds lean boneless pork shoulder, cut into 1-inch chunks

1 cup dry white wine

1 tablespoon **ground coriander**

salt and pepper to taste

4 cups chicken broth

1 pound **new potatoes**, cut in quarters

2 cups sliced mushrooms

Equipment: Large saucepan with cover or **Dutch oven**, mixing spoon, serving bowl

1. Heat oil in large saucepan or Dutch oven over medium-high heat. Add pork, stir, and brown on all sides, 7 to 10 minutes. Reduce heat to medium. Add wine, coriander, and salt and pepper to taste, and stir to mix well. Cook for 10 minutes for flavors to develop and sauce to **reduce**.

2. Add chicken broth, new potatoes, and mushrooms. Increase heat to medium-high, and bring to boil. Stir, reduce heat to simmer, cover, and cook 20 to 25 minutes, or until potatoes are tender.

To serve, transfer to serving bowl and serve with khobaz arabee *(recipe page 682).*

Bureks are popular throughout the Mediterranean and Middle East. Both Greek and Turk Cypriots prepare great quantities for family gatherings because they're easy to make and delicious. They can be made with different fillings and served on the *mezze* (appetizer) table for wedding receptions.

⚘ *Bureks* (Turkish Pastries)

Yield: 36 pieces

1 cup (8 ounces) cream cheese, at room temperature

1 egg, lightly beaten

1 tablespoon chopped parsley

salt and pepper to taste

2 sheets **phyllo**, thawed according to directions on package

½ cup (¼ pound) butter or margarine, melted

Equipment: Medium mixing bowl, mixing spoon, work surface, sharp knife, ruler, damp kitchen towel, **pastry brush**, buttered cookie sheet, oven mitts, serving plate

1. Prepare filling: In medium mixing bowl, beat cream cheese, egg, and parsley with mixing spoon until well mixed. Add salt and pepper to taste.

2. Cut phyllo: Stack 2 phyllo sheets on work surface, and, using sharp knife and ruler, cut the 18-inch length phyllo across into 6 3-inch-wide strips. Cut each strip into 3 equal pieces. (Each piece will be almost square.) Keep stack of 36 pieces of phyllo under damp towel.

Preheat oven to 350°F.

3. Assemble pastries one at a time, keeping others covered with damp towel. Place one piece of phyllo parallel with edge of table. Place 1 teaspoon cream cheese mixture on the phyllo about halfway between one edge and the center. Roll the cream cheese in the phyllo, leaving the two sides open. (As they bake, the cheese spreads out toward the two open ends.) Place on buttered cookie sheet, seam-side down. Brush with melted butter. Continue to fill and roll remaining phyllo pieces, and place them close together on cookie sheet. Brush tops with melted butter.

4. Bake in oven for 10 to 12 minutes or until lightly browned.

To serve, arrange on a serving plate so they are easy to pick up. Serve warm or cold as a finger snack.

❦ *Pastitsia* (Almond Cookies)

In Cyprus, as in Greece, almonds are always present in various forms at celebratory occasions, such as engagements, weddings, parties, the birth of a baby, baptisms, birthday or name days, and other important family events. *Pastitsia* are almond cookies, rather similar to *amygthalota* (almond cookies, recipe page 397) made in Greece. *Pastitsia* are often given as favors (*kerastika*) to invited guests to celebrate a birthday or baptism.

Yield: 40 cookies

2 pounds **slivered blanched** almonds	**4 egg whites**
1½ cups sugar	grated **zest** of 2 large oranges
½ cup powdered sugar	1 teaspoon almond essence

Equipment: Food processor, parchment paper, teaspoon, baking tray/cookie sheet, oven mitts

Ten minutes before baking, preheat oven to 325°F.

1. In food processor, coarsely chop 1 cup of the almonds, take out, and reserve for use later.

2. Add remaining almonds, sugar, and powdered sugar, and process to a fine powder. Add zest, almond extract and egg whites, and quickly mix to a paste.

3. Take teaspoonfuls of the **almond paste**, and shape into cylinders. Roll cylinders in the reserved coarsely chopped almonds and shape into crescents. Lay crescents on a parchment paper–lined baking tray.

4. Bake in preheated oven for 10 to 12 minutes, or until just lightly touched with gold. Do not let them brown. Gently transfer the baked crescents, still on the parchment, to a wire rack to cool.

Store in an airtight container.

Egypt

Egypt is located in the northeast corner of Africa. It is bordered on the west by Libya, on the south by Sudan, on the east by Israel and the Red Sea, and on the north by the Mediterranean. Although Egypt is considered an Arab nation, and most Egyptians are Arabs, they are proud of their own unique history and culture, which they consider different from the rest of the Arab world.

Egypt has a large rural population known as *fellahin*. The name is from the Arabic word *falaha*, which means "to labor" or "till the earth." Egypt also has a sizable Bedouin population. They are desert nomads who travel from one oasis to the next with their flocks.

Islamic beliefs and traditions form a common bond that unites most Egyptians, and all life-cycle events are according to their religion. (See Islam and Islamic Life-Cycle Rituals, page lxxvi.)

In the cities, the people have a modern lifestyle often influenced by the Western world. About 10 percent of the population, mostly urbanites, belong to the Coptic Christian Church. They are descended from ancient Egyptians who converted to Christianity in the second or third century. Many Copts have a small cross tattooed on their wrists. Copts follow life-cycle events according to their religion. (See Eastern or Orthodox Church Life-Cycle Rituals, page lxxv.)

In the cities, Muslim baby boys are circumcised at birth, by a doctor, before they leave the hospital. In the countryside, families usually have the traditional circumcision done before the child is five years old. Circumcision is a very important event in a boy's life, and there is always a celebration feast. On the day of circumcision, it is customary for the boy to ride around the village on a horse followed by family and friends. Some of the men carry guns, which they fire in the air to announce the happy event.

Egyptian women are not required legally to wear veils or traditional Muslim clothing. They can vote, attend school, own property, drive cars, and enjoy the same privileges as men. They probably enjoy more legal equality than women of other Arabic countries, and the government is encouraging women to take a more active role in city and national affairs.

In the cities, young people can meet at work, in clubs, at social gatherings, and through friends. After a couple meets and dates, if they decide to marry, the boy should ask the girl's parents for permission. If everyone is agreeable, there is an engagement party, which may be either small or elaborate. It is customary for the bride's parents to give a dowry, usually money, to the groom.

Most Muslim and all Christian brides living in the cities wear the Western-style long white wedding dress with a veil. Urban Egyptians seem to favor grand wedding receptions held in a hotel ballroom with music, dancing, and great quantities of food and drink. In rural areas, it is the parents' responsibility to arrange the marriage of their children. The choices of mate is always made within the village, and often matches are made between cousins or other relations. Traditionally in the country, newlyweds live with the groom's family. The young bride is subordinate to her husband and her mother-in-law, but when she has children, her status rises.

In Egypt, wedding ceremonies are very simple civil contracts rather than religious ones. All that is needed is the signing of a formal contract between the groom and the bride's male guardian, who is usually her father, but it could also be a brother or uncle. The contract is signed in front of witnesses. To make the marriage more "official," the wedding party visits the office of *Al Mazoun* (government witness). He oversees a special contract that guarantees a payment to the wife in the event of a divorce.

The wedding feast begins with *mezze* (appetizers), and the assortment includes black olives (*zeitoun*), plates of white sheep's cheese (*gebna beida*), turnips and cucumber pickles (*torshi*), small boiled shrimp (*gambari*), fried smelts (*bissaria*), and Egyptian-style eggplant (*bedingane masri*) (recipe page 652).

⚘ *Torshi Left* (Pickled Turnips)

Torshi means "pickle," and *left* means "turnip." These pickled turnips start out white but get dyed pink by the addition of **beetroot** slices. These and the following pickled cucumbers would be part of the appetizers (*mezze*) for a celebratory meal.

Yield: 2 pounds of pickles

2 pounds small, firm white **turnips**	4 tablespoons pickling (coarse) salt
1 fresh, raw **beetroot**	3 cups water
handful of celery leaves	1 cup white vinegar
2 cloves garlic	

Equipment: Vegetable peeler, large glass jar with tight-fitting lid washed very well and sterilized, small saucepan

1. Wash turnips and beetroot well, and peel. Slice into half-moons about ½ inch thick. In sterilized glass jar, place turnip and beetroot slices in alternating layers, distributing celery leaves and garlic equally among the layers.

2. In saucepan, place salt, water, and vinegar over medium heat until solution boils.

3. Pour over turnips and beetroot. Add more boiling water if the solution does not fully cover the vegetables.

4. Close jar and store in a warm place. The pickles should be ready in a week. Once opened, refrigerate.

Eat within a few weeks after making.

⚘ *Torshi Khiar* (Pickled Cucumbers)

Much like pickled turnips (recipe precedes), these pickled cucumbers would be included among the appetizers (*mezze*) for a celebratory meal.

Yield: 2 pounds pickles

2 pounds small, firm pickling cucumbers	5 to 6 whole **coriander** seed
2 cloves garlic	4 tablespoons pickling (coarse) salt
handful of celery leaves or a bunch of dill	3 cups water
1 tablespoon of dill seed	½ cup white vinegar
6 to 10 black peppercorns or mustard seeds	

Equipment: Large glass jar with tight-fitting lid, well washed and sterilized; small saucepan

1. Wash cucumbers well, and place in sterilized glass jar.

2. Distribute garlic, celery or dill, dill seed, black peppercorns, and coriander seed equally among the cucumbers.

3. In saucepan over medium heat, bring to a boil the salt, water, and white vinegar. Pour the boiling solution over cucumbers. Add more hot water if the solution does fully cover the cucumbers.

4. Place in warm place to mature. The cucumbers should be ready to eat in 7 to 10 days. Refrigerate after opening.

These cucumber pickles, similarly with the turnip pickles, will not keep beyond a few weeks.

In countries where most people do not have refrigeration, it is necessary to render or clarify butter to prevent it from turning rancid. Rendered butter keeps for months without refrigeration.

☙ *Samnah Baladi* (Rendered Butter)

Rendered butter is also known as "clarified butter" or "*ghee.*"

1 pound unsalted butter	4 tablespoons coarse **bulgur**, or all-purpose **flour**

Equipment: Small saucepan, large spoon, small container with cover

1. Melt butter in small saucepan over low heat. Add bulgur or flour, and cook on low heat until butter separates (clarified butter rises to the top and solids go to the bottom after about 5 to 7 minutes). Remove from heat, and cool to room temperature.

2. Carefully skim off the clear rendered butter and put into small container. Rendered butter keeps for many months even without refrigeration. Either discard residue, or refrigerate and use in soup.

Use over vegetables or in recipes calling for rendered butter. Among Bedouin, rendered butter is poured over rice for flavoring.

There are four ways to drink coffee in Egypt: *mazbootah* is with one teaspoon of sugar; *areehah* has less sugar than *mazbootah*; *ziadah* has more sugar than *mazbootah*; and *saddah* is with no sugar at all (i.e., black). Sugarless bitter coffee (*saddah*) is served at wakes as a sign of deep grief. Drinking it is a show of sympathy for the bereaved. The cups used for serving coffee at a funeral should be plain because a floral or other joyful motif would not be in keeping with the somber mood of the occasion. Egyptian coffee (*ahwa*) is brewed in a similar manner to *kahve* (recipe page 643). When making *ahwa*, a cardamom seed is added to the *kanaka* or metal coffee pot. *Ahwa* is served very hot, in small cups (*finjaan*) or small glasses.

Serving great quantities of food at a banquet is a sign of a hospitable host and hostess. The meal must end with fresh fruit to refresh the mouth and cleanse the palate.

⚘ *Al Burtugal Wal Zabib al Mutabal* (Spiced Oranges)

Fresh orange slices sprinkled with cinnamon is a light and refreshing dish to end a rich meal.

Yield: 6 to 8 servings

½ cup sugar

1 cup water

½ cup sultana (golden) raisins

2 cinnamon sticks, each about 3 inches long

½ teaspoon allspice berries

2 tablespoons candied ginger, finely chopped

zest from 2 lemons, in fine slices (Ensure there is no white **pith**.)

juice from 1 lemon

6 large oranges

1 **pomegranate**, for garnish

For **garnish**: 1 teaspoon cinnamon powder

Equipment: Small saucepan, glass serving bowl or platter, peeler or paring knife, plastic wrap

1. In saucepan over low heat, combine the sugar, water, raisins, cinnamon sticks, allspice berries, and ginger. Simmer gently for 15 to 20 minutes to allow the spices to fully infuse the water and until the syrup is slightly thickened. Turn off heat, let cool to room temperature, and stir in the lemon zest and juice.

2. Transfer to a glass bowl for serving.

3. Peel oranges, trimming off all the white pith. Slice oranges crosswise into ½-inch-thick slices. Cut slices into bite-size pieces, and combine with cooled syrup in the bowl. Chill, covered with plastic wrap, for at least 4 hours, or preferably overnight. Before serving, discard lemon zest.

4. Peel the pomegranate, and separate the arils (seeds), discarding all the white pith. Scatter the pomegranate arils over the spiced oranges.

Sprinkle cinnamon powder over all, and serve.

Eggplants have been grown in the Middle East for more than 1,500 years. In the Middle East, eggplants come in a variety of shapes and colors. Some are slim and long. Others are oval, about the size of a small apple, and white, resembling large eggs (hence the name). The most commonly used are the large purple or purple-streaked varieties similar to those used in the United States. When buying eggplant, whatever its size or shape, look for uniform color and a firm, smooth skin. Arabs say they have over a thousand ways to cook eggplant. It's not unusual to find eggplant prepared several different ways for an Arabian wedding feast. The following dish, *bedingane masri* is served as an appetizer. *Bedingane* (also *badengane*) means "eggplant."

Bedingane Masri (Egyptian-style Eggplant)

Yield: serves 8 to 12

2 eggplants (about 1 pound each), **trimmed,** stems discarded, and cut crosswise into ½-inch-thick disks

extra virgin olive oil, as needed

2 tomatoes, trimmed, **finely chopped**

1 onion, finely chopped

3 tablespoons fresh parsley, finely chopped

1 clove garlic, finely chopped

3 tablespoons red wine vinegar

salt and pepper to taste

Equipment: **Pastry brush,** 2 baking sheets, oven mitts, medium bowl, mixing spoon, serving platter

Preheat oven to 425°F.

1. Using pastry brush, brush both sides of eggplant slices with olive oil, and place side by side on baking sheets.

2. Bake in oven for 20 to 25 minutes, or until browned and tender. Cool to room temperature.

3. Prepare tomato dressing: In medium bowl, combine chopped tomatoes, onion, parsley, garlic, red wine vinegar, and ¼ cup olive oil. Using mixing spoon, stir to mix.

4. Arrange eggplant slices in single layer on serving platter, and spoon tomato dressing evenly over each slice. Add salt and pepper to taste.

Serve at room temperature for best flavor.

One week after the birth of a child, many Egyptian families, Coptic Christian and Moslem alike, invite relatives and friends to see the newborn; this is called *Sebou,* the Seven-Day Party. The guests bring gifts for the child, usually in sets of seven—seven pairs of socks or seven shirts—because the number seven is regarded as fortuitous. For baby girls, gold jewelry such as earrings, bracelets, and necklaces are the usual gifts. Prayer rolls encased in silver or gold with precious stones are pinned to the baby's clothes or near the bed to protect against evil spirits. On *Sebou*, the baby is given a bath and dressed in new clothes. Salt is sprinkled around the mother and throughout the house to keep the evil eye away. The baby is carried throughout the house in a specially decorated crib, while other family members holding candles follow. The mother than carefully steps over the baby seven times without touching him or her, while the older women present create sufficient noise for the baby to hear. A feast with a whole sheep or lamb usually follows, prepared by the mother and female relatives, and sweet favors of cookies and sweets are distributed to the guests. In the past, the *Sebou* was also an occasion for naming the newborn child, as well as for circumcision for boys and ear piercing for girls. A traditional drink served during *Sebou* is made from the peeled dried roots of the plant *moghat* (*Glossostemon bruguieri* or *Dombeya arabica*). The plant is found throughout Egypt, Iran, Iraq, Yemen, Saudi Arabia, Turkey, and Morocco and is commonly used in Egyptian traditional medicine. *Moghat* is also believed to stimulate the production of breast milk.

✒ *Moghat* (Seventh-day Feast Drink)

Yield: 5 cups

5 tablespoons clarified butter (*ghee*) homemade (recipe page 142)

5 tablespoons *moghat* powder (*Glossostemon bruguieri* dried root powder, available at Middle Eastern food shops)

5 cups hot water

5 teaspoons sugar (or to taste)

Equipment: Saucepan, whisk, small cups

1. Over low-medium heat in a saucepan, warm the butter, and whisk in the *moghat* powder until golden.
2. Whisk in the hot water, then the sugar. The *moghat* will thicken as it cooks. Add more water if needed, so that the *moghat* is liquid enough to drink. Taste the *moghat*, and add more sugar to your taste.

Pour into small cups to serve.

Fatta is originally a Nubian (southern Egypt) celebratory dish, which has since been adopted throughout Egypt for serving at weddings, to celebrate a first pregnancy, and other special occasions with a large number of invited guests. The name *fatta* means "crumbs" because one version of this dish is to break the toasted pita bread into crumb-like pieces. Usually a lamb is specially slaughtered to prepare *fatta*. It is eaten by Christians and Muslims alike to break a major fast. The potherb *molokhia* (also *molokheya* [*Corchorus olitorius*]) may also be added to *fatta* to give the broth a silky, viscous finish that is much appreciated by *molokhia* fans.

⚘ *Fatta* (Lamb and Rice Soup)

Yield: 10 to 12 servings

2 pounds boneless lamb, sliced into small cubes

2 large onions, finely chopped

Salt and freshly ground black pepper to taste

1 cinnamon stick

2 bay leaves

4 cardamom pods

10 cups water

½ pound fresh or frozen *molokhia* leaves, sliced into small pieces (available from Middle Eastern food shops), optional

1½ cups rice, washed and drained

3 cups water

8 tablespoons clarified butter (*ghee*) homemade (recipe page 142)

¼ teaspoon salt

8 fat garlic cloves, peeled and finely chopped

¼ cup vinegar

2 whole pita bread, sliced in half crosswise, and toasted until crisp

For **garnish**: ½ cup parsley, finely chopped

Equipment: Large stockpot with cover, skillet, medium saucepan with cover, ladle, large casserole or soup tureen for serving

1. Prepare broth: Place lamb cubes, onions, salt, pepper, cinnamon stick, cardamom, and bay leaves into stock pot. Add water, cover, and bring to a boil over medium heat. Skim off all froth, reduce heat to low, and let meat simmer until tender. Remove meat from the broth, and allow to thoroughly drain on a sieve until needed. If using *molokhia*, add its leaves to the broth, and cook until tender, about 10 to 15 minutes. Taste broth, and adjust the salt, if needed. Keep broth hot, or reheat it just before serving.

2. In skillet over medium heat, warm 3 tablespoons clarified butter, and fry the drained meat for 5 to 7 minutes until slightly crisped on the surface. Transfer meat to a bowl.

3. In the same skillet, add 3 more tablespoons of clarified butter, and over low heat, sauté garlic until pale golden. Do not let garlic turn brown, or it will taste bitter. Turn off heat, and stir in the vinegar.

4. Meanwhile, in a separate pan with cover, put rice with water, ¼ teaspoon salt, and 2 tablespoons *ghee*. Bring to boil over medium heat, then reduce heat, and let rice cook until done, about 20 minutes.

5. Assembly: On the bottom of a large, warmed casserole, place 2 slices of toasted pita bread.

   Sprinkle with half of the sautéed garlic and vinegar mixture, and put half of the cooked rice in one layer. Gently ladle very hot broth over to moisten the rice and bread, without disturbing the layer. Top with the remaining toasted pita bread, and add the rest of the rice in one layer. Top with the fried meat and the rest of the garlic-vinegar mixture. Gently ladle more hot broth over the top, and sprinkle with parsley.

Serve at once, steaming hot.

🎜 *Basbousa bil Laban Zabadi* (Semolina Cake with Yogurt)

Basbousa is a cake that is often made as dessert for family gatherings and celebrations.

Yield: 10 to 12 servings

Syrup:

1 cup sugar

½ cup water

Cake batter:

2 cups **semolina** (or replace ½ cup with finely ground almonds)

¼ cup sugar

¼ cup flour

1 teaspoon baking powder

rind (in large slices) and juice of 1 lemon

1 tablespoon orange-blossom water or **rosewater**

¼ teaspoon baking soda

2 eggs, beaten

½ cup butter

½ cup thick yogurt or sour cream

15 to 20 whole almonds, skinned and **blanched**

Equipment: Small saucepan, large mixing bowl, mixing spoon, 9-inch round or 9×12-inch rectangular baking pan, oven mitts

1. First prepare the syrup because it should be cold when poured over the hot cake.

2. In a small saucepan over medium heat, put sugar, water, lemon rind, and juice to boil.

   Simmer for 10 to 15 minutes, or until thickened. Allow to cool to room temperature, then discard the lemon rind, and stir in the orange-blossom water or rosewater. Refrigerate, covered, while preparing the batter for the cake.

   Ten minutes before baking, preheat oven to 350°F.

3. Butter a 9-inch round or 9×12-inch rectangular baking pan. In a large mixing bowl, combine and mix well the semolina, sugar, flour, baking powder, and soda. Stir in the vanilla, eggs, butter, and yogurt, mixing well after each addition, until the batter is homogeneous. The batter should be moist but still hold its shape

4. Spoon the batter evenly into the prepared baking pan, and let it rest for 20 minutes. Score the mixture into squares or diagonally into lozenges (diamonds). Place an almond in the center of each square or lozenge.

5. Bake for 25 to 30 minutes, or until golden, the top springs back when pressed.

   Remove the cake from the oven, and immediately pour the cold syrup over it.

Let the cake cool thoroughly before serving.

Iran

Iran is bordered on the north by Armenia, Azerbaijan, Turkmenistan, and the Caspian Sea, and on the east by Afghanistan and Pakistan. To the south and southwest are the Indian Ocean and the Persian Gulf. The west and northwest borders are shared with Iraq and Turkey. The population comprises many different ethnic and cultural groups who generally share one common bond—they are almost all Muslims. (See Islam and Islamic Life-Cycle Rituals, page lxxvi.) Indigenous Persians (also known as Iranians) comprise the largest ethnic group. Other sizable ethnic groups are Turks, Kurds, and Arabs.

In the 1930s, women were given the right to vote and were freed from wearing the *chador*, a long black cloth that is draped over the head and body but does not cover the face. In 1979, however, the women voted for the Islamic restrictions limiting their freedom and then chose to wear the *chador*. During the 1990s, the enforcement of some of the modesty law restrictions have relaxed.

A number of customs are associated with childbirth in Iran. On the seventh month of pregnancy, seven sets of clothing (including bibs, socks, hats, blankets, etc.) were prepared by the prospective mother's family, seven being considered as auspicious in ancient Zoroastrian belief. These items were placed in a chest, and sweets, candies, and coins were inserted between the different items. Traditionally, cloth diapers and other necessities (soap, cleansing materials, sugar) were also included. The prospective father's family, in turn, prepared a feast, featuring a whole lamb or calf or several chickens, for all the relatives and friends.

On the sixth day after birth, baby girls traditionally had their ears pierced. Baby boys would be circumcised on odd-numbered days—3, 5, 7, 9, but if they were weak or if there was no one to perform the circumcision, it was postponed for the boy's seventh or ninth year. It was traditional to name a baby on the sixth night, and it was celebrated with a feast. Dishes during the baby naming feast would include *sheehandaz*, *ghormeh sabzi*, and *shereen polow*. At this feast, the new mother would eat rice for the first time since giving birth.

If the parents' wish for a boy child had been fulfilled, a sheep would be slaughtered on the seventh day. This celebration is called *aghigeh*. During the feast, entertainers or musical performers would be invited. Puppet shows were also a popular entertainment, especially for circumcision celebrations.

On the seventh day after giving birth to a girl or on the tenth for a boy, mother and baby would be bathed, traditionally at a public bathhouse, accompanied by female relatives. Before leaving the house, the mother would have a Quran held over her head and the baby's, and lucky charms were placed around her neck to protect her and the baby from the evil eye. At the bathhouse, the mother and baby and guests would be welcomed by the staff with incense, singing, and drums. The mother would be pampered thoroughly with henna and special hair treatments, facials, and honey body massages. Her relatives would have brought all kinds of celebratory food, sweets, fruits, and sherbets. According to age-old tradition, at the end of the bath celebration, the mother would be given a dish of two soft-boiled eggs and a sweet called *ghaout* to enjoy and have blessed clay applied to her forehead and another incense session before heading back home. More feasting would continue at home, for a special meal called *Valimeh*, typically with lamb dishes, with more family and friends, and, often, entertainment. Guests bring gifts for the baby, such as clothes and toys, while close relatives often bring something made of gold. The next celebration for the new baby and mother would be on the fortieth day, with another ceremonial bath.

✿ Shereen Polow (also *Javaher Polow*) (Sweet Rice, also Jeweled Rice)

Iranian celebratory banquets typically offer a variety of rice dishes, and many have symbolic meaning. In this elaborate dish, the colorful vegetables, fruits, and nuts added to the rice resemble jewels, and so it is often also called "*javaher polow*" (jeweled rice). This dish is made for very special occasions and family events, such as weddings and the birth of a child. The ingredients provide a range of colors—orange from carrots, orange peel, and the costly spice saffron; green from pistachio kernels; creamy white from blanched almonds; golden brown from the sultana raisins and dry-fried almonds, and ruby red from barberries. The crystallized sugar provides sparkle. The luxurious spice saffron is used twice in this dish—in liquid form, first to color the rice and lend its exotic flavor, and then to add scent to the mixture of cardamom, cinnamon, pistachio, and dried roses.

Yield: 8 servings

4 cups good-quality **basmati rice** (available at all supermarkets)

water, as needed

salt, as needed

25 to 30 threads saffron

3 oranges

5 carrots, peeled and sliced into 1½-inch long by ¼-inch wide **julienne** strips

sugar, as needed

½ cup unsalted pistachio kernels

½ cup **blanched** almond slivers

½ cup seedless golden raisins (sultanas) or dried currants

⅓ cup dried barberries, picked clean of stems and other debris, washed, thoroughly dried (available at Middle Eastern food shops; substitute dried unsweetened cranberries or fresh **pomegranate**)

3 tablespoons rock candy or crystallized sugar

1 cup olive or other vegetable oil

½ cup clarified butter (*ghee*) homemade (recipe page 142), or store bought

Equipment: Small and large mixing bowls, vegetable peeler, plastic food wrap, paring knife, **mortar and pestle**, small saucepan, small frying pan, mixing spoon, strainer, 4-quart **heavy-bottomed** saucepan with cover or Dutch oven, oven mitts, large serving dish

1. Wash rice 3 times in cool water until the rinse water is no longer milky white. Place washed rice in a mixing bowl, cover with cold water, and add 2 tablespoons salt. Let soak for at least

3 hours, to a maximum of 6 hours. The salty soaking enables the rice to swell up properly without losing its shape during the long cooking time.

2. Meanwhile with the vegetable peeler, remove rind from oranges, taking care not to include the white **pith**. Cut rind into fine slivers with a paring knife. Put the rind slivers in a small saucepan, cover with cold water, and allow to boil (to remove the rind's bitterness). Strain and rinse the orange rind well, return to saucepan, and cover with fresh cold water. Reboil two more times, and strain and rinse as before. Set orange rind slivers aside. Wrap orange pulp in plastic wrap, and refrigerate for another use.

3. Place pistachio kernels in boiling water for 5 to 8 minutes to make it easier to ease the kernels from their skins. Continue to soak the skinned kernels in the same hot water for 20 minutes, or until soft enough to slice readily into slivers. Set aside two teaspoons of the pistachio slivers and place into a bowl for garnishes.

4. In small frying pan over low heat, dry-fry 2 teaspoons of the almond slivers until golden. Keep a watchful eye on them so that they don't get scorched and become bitter. Put the golden almonds in the bowl for garnishes. Take 2 teaspoons of the blanched (unfried) almonds, and add to the bowl of garnishes. Set the remaining blanched almonds aside.

5. In the same frying pan, over low heat, warm two tablespoons of oil, and fry the drained barberries for 1 to 2 minutes, or until they turn a bright red. Do not overcook them as they burn quickly and will turn bitter. Turn off heat, and add barberries to the bowl of garnishes.

6. Soak golden raisins or dried currants in warm water for 15 minutes. Add 2 teaspoons of raisins to the bowl of garnishes, and set the rest aside.

7. In a small saucepan, combine 2 tablespoons sugar and 1/3 cup water in small saucepan. Cook over medium heat, without stirring, until the sugar dissolves. Stir in drained orange rind slivers, the remaining pistachio kernels, and the rest of the almonds. Reduce heat, and let mixture simmer for 8 minutes. Remove from heat, and set aside. Drain through strainer, and reserve the syrup.

8. In a mortar, crush saffron threads with 1/4 teaspoon sugar to a fine powder. Transfer to a small bowl, and infuse the pulverized saffron with 5 teaspoons hot water. The saffron will tint the water a bright orange. Set aside saffron water until needed.

9. After 2 hours of soaking, drain rice in a strainer, and rinse with cold water. Fill a 4-quart heavy-bottomed saucepan or Dutch oven 2/3 with water, and bring to a boil over medium-high heat. Add drained rice and 2 teaspoons salt. Bring back to a rolling boil, and cook uncovered for 2 to 3 minutes to partially cook the rice. The rice should be tender on the outside but still firm in the center. Drain rice in a strainer, and rinse with lukewarm running water. Return rice to the mixing bowl.

10. To a heavy-bottomed saucepan or Dutch oven, add 1/2 cup oil and 2 tablespoons water.

    Using fingers or a spoon, lightly sprinkle a 1-inch layer of rice to cover the bottom of the pan. This bottom layer will become brown and crisp and is known as *tahdig*, a very desirable part of Iranian rice dishes.

11. Over the rice sprinkle some carrots, orange rind, nuts, raisins, and 1 to 2 teaspoons of the spice mix (recipe follows). Make another layer of rice, and again sprinkle carrots, orange rind, nuts, raisins, and the spice mix. Continue making layers, with the final layer being rice.

12. Mix the reserved syrup (used for the orange rind) and the saffron water, and pour on top of the rice. With the handle of a wooden spoon, make 3 to 4 holes through the layers, all the way to the bottom of the pan. Cover the lid of the saucepan or Dutch oven with a clean kitchen towel.

13. Cook rice at medium-high heat for 2 to 3 minutes, or until you see steam issuing strongly from the holes in the rice. Cover the saucepan, and reduce heat to the lowest possible, and let the rice cook slowly for 30 minutes. It can remain thus, cooking at low heat for another hour, if necessary.

14. To serve, place the whole pot, still with its cover, into a sink with a few inches of water. This will enable steam to rise from the bottom of the pot and make it easier to loosen the bottom layer of crisp *tahdig*. Gently scoop out the rice onto a warmed serving platter, mixing the layered contents as you do so, to form a finely shaped mound. Do not disturb the bottom layer of *tahdig*.

Sprinkle the reserved bowl of garnishes over, and sprinkle the barberries as well ("the jewels").

Crush the crystallized sugar, and scatter them on top, to add sparkle to the "jewels."

Drizzle clarified butter over all. Finally, take the bottom layer of crisped, well browned rice (*tahdig*), cut or break into pieces, and serve on a separate plate. *Tahdig* is a delicacy that is much appreciated, and often it does not reach the table but is eagerly divided amongst those in the kitchen.

⚘ *Spice Mix for Shereen Polow*

15 saffron threads

⅓ cup unsalted pistachio nut kernels, finely chopped

4 tablespoons dried rose buds or petals, chopped

2 teaspoons finely crushed cardamom seeds (discard the pods)

2 tablespoons powdered cinnamon

In a **mortar and pestle**, pound the saffron threads to a fine powder. Mix the saffron with the pistachios and the rest of the spices.

Store in a small airtight container until needed.

Unmarried children live with their parents or relatives until married, and when they do marry, it is usually arranged by their parents. If a son or daughter doesn't approve of the selected mate, parents seldom, if ever, force the union.

The most important part of Muslim weddings is the *agd* (legal ceremony), where the contract is agreed upon and signed. In Muslim countries with stricter modesty laws, the groom and bride are separated by a door, and the holy man sits with the groom while marrying the couple. In Iran, segregated weddings were reinstituted in 1979, but before that time, the couple were together in the same room.

The holy man, chosen by the groom, reads the marriage contract and recites the traditional prayers. During the *agd*, which traditionally takes place in the home of the bride, only female relatives and friends are allowed, and they take part in several symbolic formalities. Today, some couples have their *agd* in the private rooms of a hotel or marriage hall. The husband cannot join his wife until later at the *arusi* (reception) for women only. She is not allowed to mingle with the male guests at any time.

Traditionally after the *agd*, an *arusi* for men only takes place on the same night at the groom's home or hotel ballroom. Usually a convoy of buses and cars carries the noisy and cheering family members and friends to the *arusi*. According to strict Islamic law, at no time are men and women allowed to be together in the same room for any part of the wedding celebration.

The *arusi* is a grand celebration with feasting far into the night. The meal includes dozens of *mezze* (appetizers). Some appetizers have symbolic meaning: A platter of feta cheese, fresh herbs, and bread is served to bring happiness and prosperity; bowls of hard-cooked eggs in the shell and baskets with walnuts and almonds in the shell symbolize fertility. A bowl of honey is set out for a sweet future. The table is adorned with fresh flowers and herbs, all significant to the couple's future. The feast includes whole roasted lamb (recipe page 629) and 40 or 50 different dishes, candies, and desserts. Other *mezze* include bowls of olives and raw vegetables such as radishes, slices of cucumber, and *sebzi panier*.

❧ *Sebzi Panier* (Cheese and Herb Appetizer)

Yield: serves 5

5 slices rye or whole wheat bread	10 walnut halves
10 slices goat cheese or Greek feta cheese	10 leaves of fresh **coriander** or basil

Equipment: Bread knife, work surface, large serving tray, 3 medium serving bowls

1. Using a serrated knife, cut each slice of bread lengthwise and crosswise into 4 equal pieces. (You will have 20 small pieces of bread.)

Place the cheese, walnuts, and herb leaves in separate bowls, and place them on the serving tray. Arrange the slices of bread around the bowls on the tray. Place the tray on the dining table.

To serve, guests help themselves by sandwiching the ingredients between two pieces of bread. First place a slice of cheese on a piece of bread, and top it with a walnut half and a leaf of coriander or basil. Hold it in the fingers of your right hand to eat.

The Iranian meal is not served as a sequence of fixed courses. Instead, all the food is spread out at one time on the tablecloth-covered floor. *Bessara* is eaten as a dip with raw vegetables or with pieces of flat bread.

⚘ *Bessara* (Fava Bean Purée)

Yield: serves 6 to 8

16 ounces canned fava beans (available at all supermarkets)

2 cloves garlic, **finely chopped**, divided

2 green onions (including green tops), **trimmed**, finely chopped

1 tablespoon fresh **cilantro**, chopped

1 teaspoon crushed dried mint

1 teaspoon **ground** cumin seed

salt and pepper to taste

ground red pepper to taste (optional)

1 tablespoon extra virgin olive oil, more as needed

For serving:

1 onion, sliced into rings

2 lemons, cut in wedges

Equipment: Electric **blender** (optional), rubber spatula, small bowl with cover, small skillet, mixing spoon

1. Put beans with juice in blender, add 1 clove chopped garlic, and **blend** until smooth.

   Note: While processing, turn machine off once or twice, and scrape down sides of container with rubber spatula.

2. Transfer to small bowl. Add green onions, cilantro, mint, cumin seed, and salt and pepper to taste, and stir to mix well. Stir in ground red pepper to taste if desired. Cover and refrigerate.

3. Heat 1 tablespoon olive oil in small skillet over medium-high heat. Add onion and fry until browned and crisp, 5 to 7 minutes.

To serve, sprinkle top of fava bean purée with fried onions and drizzle lightly with olive oil. Serve with lemon wedges and extra ground red pepper so that diners can season it to suit their tastes. Serve with bite-size wedges of flat bread or crackers and raw vegetables.

Sweet desserts as we know them in the Western world are never eaten at the end of an Iranian meal. Only fresh fruit is acceptable at the end of a meal. Any combination of fruit can be used in *paludeh* (also *faloodeh*).

⚘ *Paludeh (Faloodeh)* (Persian Fruit Medley)

Yield: serves 4

1 cup strawberries, stemmed and sliced

2 ripe peaches, peeled and sliced

½ cantaloupe or honeydew (or combination), **cubed** and peeled granulated sugar to taste

1 tablespoon **rosewater** (available at Middle Eastern food stores and pharmacies)

Equipment: Medium serving bowl with cover, mixing spoon

1. Combine strawberries, peaches, and melon cubes in serving bowl. Using a spoon, gently toss to mix.

2. Add sugar to taste, toss, and sprinkle with rosewater. Toss to mix well.

3. Cover and refrigerate until ready to serve. Before serving, toss again to remix.

To serve, place bowl in the middle of the table. Have guests help themselves from the bowl using only the fingers of the right hand to pick up the fruit. According to Muslim tradition, the left hand must never touch food; it is used only for personal grooming.

Iraq

Iraq is bordered on the north by Turkey, on the east by Iran, on the southeast by the Persian Gulf and Kuwait, on the south by Saudi Arabia, and on the west by Jordan and Syria. Part of modern Iraq is situated on the ancient land of Mesopotamia, where people first began to cultivate land and where cursive writing developed. Recent history has dealt less kindly with the Iraq government, which is unfortunate for the Iraqi people.

Arabs are Iraq's largest ethnic group (approximately 75 percent), followed by a sizable Kurd population (approximately 20 percent). Both Arabs and Kurds are Muslims, but the Kurds differ from their Arab neighbors in language, dress, and customs. All life-cycle celebrations are according to their religion. (See Islam and Islamic Life-Cycle Rituals, page lxxvi.)

For Muslims, the first important life-cycle celebration is the birth of a child, especially if it's a boy. Three days after the baby's birth, visitors come to pay their respects and bring gifts for the newborn. For a boy, superstitious rituals are performed to protect the child from harm. Childless women or guests with blue eyes, the sign of a non-Iraqi, are traditionally not allowed to see the child for fear they will bring him bad luck.

As in other Muslim countries, the next big celebration for a boy is when he is circumcised. In the cities, the doctor often performs the operation in the hospital before the child is taken home. A small family dinner celebrates the event when the mother returns home with her son. In the countryside, the traditional ceremony takes place when the boy is about seven years old. The child is usually paraded through the village, and everyone is invited to a celebration feast.

The *al' Khatma* is the religious festival that celebrates the reading of the Koran (Islamic holy book) by children. Boys and girls have separate ceremonies for the *al' Khatma*. Each boy reads to men who hold a luncheon for them while women celebrate with an afternoon tea for each girl. After the reading, the young guest of honor is showered with gifts and money.

In Iraq, traditional families arrange the marriages of their children. The final decision, as to whom her sons will marry, is made by their mother. The new daughter-in-law usually moves in with her husband's parents.

Several days before the marriage ceremony, the couple is wined and dined by relatives and friends. On her wedding day, the bride, dressed in her Western-style white wedding gown, spends the day in her parent's house receiving friends and relatives—female only. According to Muslim tradition, her hands and feet will have been decorated with henna. She wears the gold jewelry given to her by her husband. Late in the day, the groom arrives with the Muslim religious leader to sign the Islamic contract; only immediate family and a few best friends are present. After the contract is signed, a convoy of buses and cars carries the noisy horn-blowing and cheering family members and friends through the streets and then onto the groom's parents' home, a wedding hall, or a hotel ballroom for the official reception. In urban areas in Iraq, Muslim men and women celebrate together, and everyone has a great time singing, dancing, and feasting until the wee hours of the morning. In the countryside, wedding celebrations are segregated, with the men and women celebrating separately.

In Iraq, as in neighboring Iran, it is the custom to arrange a bridal table, the *mez al sayed* (*sofreh-ye aghd* in Iran). On this table are set a mirror (representing fate) flanked by two candelabras, each representing the bride and groom and their bright future. When the bride enters the room where the wedding is to take place, her face is veiled. As she sits beside the groom before the *mez al sayed*, she takes off the veil. Her reflection in the mirror would be the bridegroom's first glimpse of his bride (in the past, when arranged marriages were more common, the bride and groom would not have had the chance to meet before their wedding day). On the table as well would be a Quran; flat bread specially baked for the wedding, inscribed with a calligraphed blessing; a basket of painted eggs and a basket of sugar-coated almonds and other nuts in their shells as symbols of fertility; and fruit such as pomegranates, red apples, or sometimes grapes representing the beauty of nature. There would be roses or other scented flowers or rosewater and incense for their perfume and a bowl of gold coins, sometimes mingled with rice, and a treasure box with pearls and crystals, symbols of prosperity.

Additionally, there would be two trays with seven items. The number seven is considered auspicious in Iraq, as in neighboring Iran and many other cultures.

First is a tray of seven herbs and condiments of seven different colors: poppy seeds, wild rice, angelica, salt, nigella, black tea, and frankincense.

The second tray holds seven white foods that represent purity: sugar, flour, rice, yeast, cream, cheese, and milk.

On the table as well is a cup of honey to sweeten the couple's life together: the bride and groom would each dip their little finger in the honey for the other to eat.

During the ceremony, relatives would hold a silk shawl over the heads of the bride and groom. The shawl may be embroidered with blessings.

ༀ *Quozi* (Roast lamb)

Quozi (often also *qozi* and *koozi*) is *the* Iraqi celebration dish—for weddings, for births, or for any important occasion, even a funeral. The traditional way is to stuff the lamb with the rice as it roasts. Here the lamb is not stuffed, but the rice is prepared as it would have been for stuffing. The crisped, brown layer of rice at the bottom of the cooking pot is called *h'kaka* (the equivalent of *tahdig* in other countries), and it is particularly relished and served in a separate dish.

Yield: 20 to 25 servings

10 cups **basmati rice**

½ whole lamb or 1 large leg (if it does not fit into your oven, have the butcher cut it to fit)

⅓ cup butter, melted

salt and pepper to taste

rubbing mix for lamb (recipe follows)

3 large onions, sliced

4 large carrots, **diced**

2 oranges, diced

10 garlic cloves, peeled

8 thyme sprigs

4 bay leaves

3 tablespoons olive oil

1 cinnamon stick

4 green cardamom pods

3 tablespoons pomegranate molasses

3 cups almond flakes or slivers

3 cups cashew nuts

2 cups **pine nuts**

3 cups sultanas

1 cup flat-leaf parsley, chopped

Spice rub for lamb:

1½ tablespoons cardamom seeds, ground to a fine powder

1 tablespoon whole **allspice**, ground to a fine powder

½ tablespoon cinnamon powder

½ of the *baharat* spice mix

Equipment: Medium and large mixing bowls, **mortar and pestle**, frying pan, large roasting tray, aluminum foil, large **heavy-bottomed** saucepan or Dutch oven, oven mitts, large serving platters or trays.

1. First attend to the rice because it needs to soak. Wash rice three times, until the rinse water is no longer milky white. Soak rice with enough water to cover for a minimum of 30 minutes, up to 1 hour.

Preheat oven to 425°F.

2. Prepare the *baharat* spice mix (recipe follows), and mix into the spice rub for lamb.

3. Prepare the lamb for roasting. Wash the lamb, and pat dry. Brush the lamb with melted butter, then season with salt, pepper, and the rubbing spices. In a large bowl, toss the onions, carrots, oranges, garlic, bay leaves, thyme sprigs, 1 cinnamon stick, and 4 cardamom pods with 2 tablespoons of olive oil.

4. Take a large roasting tray, and make a layer of the tossed vegetables, oranges, herbs, and spices. Place the lamb on top. Roast in preheated oven for 20 minutes.

5. Reduce oven temperature to 300°F, add 2 cups of water to the roasting tray, and cover the roasting tray tightly with aluminum foil. Let lamb roast for 4 hours. **Baste** with the pan drippings every hour. If the liquid level is getting low, add more water to the roasting tray. (The drippings will be used, together with water, for cooking the rice.) After 3 hours, remove the roasting tray from the oven, and, using a bulb baster or ladle, transfer the drippings to a bowl, leaving enough to cover the bottom of the tray. Return the lamb to the oven, and roast the lamb for another hour.

   The lamb should be very tender, almost falling off the bone. Let it rest for 30 minutes.

6. At least 1½ hours before serving, cook the rice. In a large heavy-bottomed saucepan or Dutch oven, warm the olive oil over low-medium heat, and fry 1 cinnamon stick and 3 cardamom pods. When the oil is giving off aromatic scents, stir in the rice.

7. Measure the reserved lamb drippings, and add water for a total of 15 cups of liquid (allowing for 1½ cups of water per cup of rice). Pour the lamb drippings and water over the rice. The liquid should cover the rice by ½ inch. Add more water if necessary. Stir in the remaining *baharat* spice mixture, the pomegranate molasses, and salt to taste (from 1 to 2 teaspoons for this amount of rice is the norm, but you may certainly use less).

8. Cover and cook over medium heat until the water comes to a boil, about 10 to 15 minutes.

   Reduce heat to low, and continue cooking for another 15 to 20 minutes, or until the rice has absorbed all the liquid. Turn off heat, but keep the rice covered.

9. Meanwhile, dry-fry the pine nuts over low heat in a frying pan. Once golden, transfer to a bowl, and set aside. Dry-fry the cashews next, and then the almonds, until golden. Add the cashews and almonds to the bowl with the pine nuts, and mix in the sultanas. Set aside about ½ cup of the nut and sultana mixture for garnish, and stir the rest into the rice.

10. Mound the rice nicely onto a large serving tray or platter. Do not dish up the crisped, brown layer at the bottom of the pan. Keep it to be served in a separate dish.

11. Ladle the remaining lamb juices from the roasting pan over the rice, or into a bowl or gravy boat for passing at the table. Place the lamb on top of the rice.

Garnish with the reserved nuts and sultanas and chopped parsley.

⚬ Baharat Spice Mix

Yield: 7 to 8 tablespoons

1 tablespoon paprika

1 tablespoon cumin

¼ tablespoon **coriander**

¼ tablespoon **allspice**

¼ tablespoon cinnamon

¼ tablespoon freshly ground black pepper

1½ teaspoons cardamom

2 dried limes (*loomi*), ground (remove seeds before grinding in **mortar and pestle**)

½ teaspoon cloves

½ teaspoon ginger

½ teaspoon nutmeg

½ teaspoon saffron threads, pulverized, or turmeric

Iraqis prefer to use whole spices and then grind them finely in a mortar and pestle just before use. But if whole spices are not available, powdered ones are fine. Mix the spices, and use the mixture to rub on the lamb, as directed.

Use with quozi *(recipe precedes).*

♪ *Masgouf* (Grilled Fish with Tomato Topping)

Baghdad in the past had a vibrant Jewish community. Special occasions such as weddings were celebrated at home, and it was the custom to hire specialists to prepare *masgouf* in the garden. *Masgouf* is freshwater fish grilled upright on stakes and served with a tomato sauce, and it used to be a particular specialty of boatmen on the Tigris River. *Masgouf* is considered the national dish of Iraq. The fish used for this dish used to be those caught in the river—carp and related fish, such as barbel or tench. Those who are not fond of carp or other freshwater fish can substitute sea bream or salmon (whole or fillets).

Yield: 4 servings

1 large carp, 3½ to 4 pounds, scaled, gutted, and cleaned, cut open from the belly, **butterfly** style, or 4 small sea bream, each about a pound, cleaned and cut open in the same manner

olive oil

juice of 2 lemons

salt

6 to 7 large ripe tomatoes, diced

Equipment: Aluminum foil, oil brush, oven mitts, 1 large serving platter or 4 serving plates

1. Lay the fish on aluminum foil, and brush thoroughly with olive oil on all sides. Sprinkle with salt, and let stand for 15 minutes.

2. Grill under a broiler, skin-side up, until the skin is crisp and golden, about 5 to 10 minutes.

   Turn the fish, and continue broiling for another 5 to 7 minutes, or until the flesh is almost done. The flesh should have become opaque on the surface but still raw in the center. Do not let it grill until completely done at this point. Sprinkle with lemon juice, and spread with a good layer of diced tomatoes. **Drizzle** the tomatoes with olive oil and salt.

3, Return to the broiler, and grill for another 2 minutes, or until the tomatoes are hot and the fish is completely done.

Serve on a large platter or individual platters.

Qu'meh is served as a side dish at banquets. To eat *qu'meh*, using the right hand, make a small ball of the meat or scoop it on a piece of bread, then pop it into your mouth.

According to Arab and Muslim tradition, the left hand must never touch food; it is used only for personal grooming.

₵ *Qu'meh* (Minced Meat)

Yield: serves 6

4 tablespoons butter or margarine, more if necessary

1 onion, chopped

1 pound **ground** lamb or beef

½ teaspoon turmeric

salt and pepper to taste

1½ cups tomato juice

1½ cups hot water

½ cup dried yellow split peas

¼ cup lemon juice

1 cup canned **pitted** cherries, drained

Equipment: Medium saucepan, slotted spoon, paper towels, mixing spoon, serving bowl

1. Melt butter or margarine in medium saucepan over medium-high heat. Add onion, stir, and **sauté** until well browned, 7 to 12 minutes. Using slotted spoon, transfer to paper towels to drain.

2. Add more butter or margarine to medium saucepan, if necessary. Crumble in ground meat, stir, and sauté over medium-high heat until browned, 5 to 7 minutes. Stir in turmeric, salt and pepper to taste, tomato juice, hot water, split peas, and lemon juice. Bring to boil. Reduce heat to simmer, cover, and cook 45 minutes, or until peas are tender.

3. Add sautéed onions and cherries, and stir. Cook to heat through, 3 to 5 minutes.

To serve, transfer to serving bowl, and serve with shereen polow *(recipe page 657).*

A banquet ends with fresh fruit, but during the celebration there is always a table with dozens of different cookies, cakes, and candies. Many cakes are made with dates and nuts, such as *tamriah.*

₵ *Tamriah* (Date Cakes)

Yield: 12 pieces

2 pounds **pitted** dates, **finely chopped**

½ cup walnuts, finely chopped

1 cup all-purpose **flour**

¼ cup melted butter or margarine

4 tablespoons butter or margarine, more as needed

1 cup plain yogurt, for serving

Equipment: Medium mixing bowl, mixing spoon, wax paper, work surface, large skillet, metal spatula, serving platter, small serving bowl

1. Put chopped dates, walnuts, and flour into mixing bowl. Using your hands, mix together. Stir in melted butter or margarine. Divide date mixture into 12 balls. Shape each ball into ½-inch-thick patties, and place on wax paper–covered work surface.

2. Melt 4 tablespoons butter or margarine in large skillet over medium-high heat. Fry cakes in batches, if necessary, until browned on both sides, 5 to 7 minutes. Add more butter or margarine as needed to fry each batch.

To serve, arrange cakes on serving platter around small bowl of yogurt placed in the center for dipping.

Israel

Israel occupies a narrow land area bounded on the west by the Mediterranean Sea; on the southwest by Egypt; on the east by Jordan, the West Bank territory, and Syria; and on the north by Lebanon. Israel is a young country, having celebrated 70 years as a Jewish state in 2008. About 75 percent of the population is Jewish, 18 percent Muslim, 2 percent Christian, and the remainder are Druze, Samaritans, and adherents of minor sects. The food culture of Jews and Arabs, originally quite different, has been blending into a mixed "Israeli cuisine" in which food traditions are gradually coming together. Most Israelis eat a mix of European and Middle Eastern dishes as a matter of course.

Within the Jewish population, there are major differences in ritual interpretation between ultra-Orthodox Jews (who follow detailed food preparation and consumption laws called "*kashrut*") and the more liberal and the more secular members of the Jewish Israeli public. Additionally, with regard to life-cycle rituals and celebrations, there are distinctions in the traditions of Western Jews (Ashkenazi), Sephardic Jews (those expelled from Spain in the 15th century and then went on to settle in different countries in Southern Europe), Mizrahi Jews (from North Africa), Ethiopian Jews, and Indian Jews. Even within those major communities, there are differences in practice depending on region or country of origin. (See Judaism and Jewish Life-Cycle Rituals, page lxviii.) Most ultra-Orthodox Jews (*haredim*) want Israel to be a religious state directed by rabbis (Jewish religious leaders). This is opposed by the secular or semisecular majority. The dispute affects matters of food choice, notably in public places: Pork is rarely available, milk and meat dishes cannot be served at the same public event, and events are difficult to plan on Saturdays when public transport does not operate.

Within its borders, issues relating to the life cycle—births, marriages, divorces, and burials—are regulated according to the religious rules of the religion concerned, even for secular members of the public. Rites of passage rituals must be performed according to strict orthodoxy in order to be recognized as legal by the Israeli government. Rigid and inflexible interpretation of Jewish law dictates dress codes, the segregation of boys and girls in religious schools, and stringent observances of the Sabbath (from sundown Friday evening to sundown on Saturday), and dietary laws among the 20 percent of the population who are *haredim* (ultra-Orthodox). *Haredim* maintain the ritual laws of *kashrut* (kosher, also *kasher*, which means "pure"), the ritual slaughter of all meat animals and fowl, no mixing of meat (*basari*) and milk (*chalavi*) dishes or products, and separate utensils and dishes for these foods.

Secular members of the population often resent the ultra-Orthodox bureaucracy at the Rabbinical Office, where they must register marriages, births, and deaths to make them legal: Unless done according to Orthodox traditions or abroad, these are not legal. Orthodox rituals are very complex, especially for women, who must observe periodic ritual visits to a ritual bath (*mikveh*).

To marry, non-Orthodox couples often travel out of the country, with nearby Cyprus a favorite location. The Israeli government accepts Cyprus certificates of marriage. To please their parents and friends and to enjoy the traditions of a Jewish wedding, couples, on their return, often have a token second ceremony performed by an unofficial ceremony leader in a home, hotel, or community center.

A group of young Orthodox rabbis, interested in promoting Jewish unity and serving both the secular and religious communities, have started *Tzohar* (Window), a movement to help non-Orthodox Jews get married on Israeli soil. *Tzohar* rabbis respect the variations among Jews. They reach out to give couples a positive Jewish wedding experience and one accepted as legal by the state. A *Tzohar* rabbi meets with the couples before the wedding, and, without imposing their standards of Orthodoxy, he explains the *kedushin* (sacredness) in marriage.

The half million Ethiopian Jews living in Israel have their own marriage customs. Tradition forbids marriage within an extended family that can number thousands. If a marriageable Ethiopian woman wants to marry an Ethiopian man in Israel, it is necessary to go to their council of elders for approval. If the family records show that they shared a great-great-grandparent, marriage between the young couple is unacceptable. History shows that, by adhering to such strict rules, the tribe of Israelites that wandered into Africa almost 3,000 years ago, according to their tradition, was able to maintain its religious and cultural identity without degrading its genetic pool.

Bread holds a sacred place in the traditional religious Jewish home, and at mealtime no one eats until prayer is said over the loaf or loaves. The braided bread (*Challah*, also *Hallah*) is named for the small portion of dough that is separated ritually before baking and offered traditionally to the priests of the Jewish Temple in Jerusalem. In remembrance of her origin of creation, a Jewish woman performs the "separating *challah*" ritual when making the Sabbath loaf if she uses more than three pounds of flour to make her bread. A small portion of the dough (not less than the size of an olive) is pinched off, which is called the "small *challah*." She says the blessing over it, and then she burns the piece of dough, in lieu of the Temple offering. Traditional *challah* must be made with unbleached white flour. On the Sabbath, a blessing is said over two loaves, to suffice for the day of rest, when no baking is allowed. When the Sabbath begins at sundown on Friday night, the loaves are placed under a special napkin at the head of the dinner table. The napkin covering the loaves symbolically represents the dew that collected on the manna in the morning. For a wedding, a special large challah is made. After the blessing over the wedding challah has been said, it is sliced and shared with all the guests, and this signals the start of the wedding feast.

ꙮ *Challah* (Jewish Sabbath Bread)

Yield: 1 loaf

1 package active dry **yeast**

¾ cup **lukewarm** water

2 tablespoons sugar

1 teaspoon salt

1 egg

1 tablespoon vegetable oil, more as needed

2½ to 2¾ cups unbleached or all-purpose **flour**, divided

For **glaze: egg wash**

1 tablespoon poppy or **sesame seeds**, for **garnish**

Equipment: Large mixing bowl, mixing spoon, lightly floured work surface, kitchen towel, lightly greased baking sheet, **pastry brush**, oven mitts, cloth napkin

1. In large mixing bowl, sprinkle yeast over lukewarm water, and let stand until dissolved, 5 minutes. Stir in sugar, salt, egg, 1 tablespoon oil, and 1¼ cups flour, and beat until smooth. Stir in enough remaining 1¼ to 1½ cups flour to make dough easy to handle and no longer sticky.

2. Transfer to lightly floured work surface, and **knead** until smooth and **elastic**, 5 to 7 minutes. Clean and lightly grease large mixing bowl. Place dough in lightly greased large mixing bowl, and turn to grease all sides. Cover with towel, and set in warm place to rise to double in bulk, 1½ to 2 hours. (Dough is ready if indentation remains when poked with your finger.)

3. **Punch down** dough, transfer to lightly floured work surface, and divide into 3 equal parts. Roll each part into a rope 14 inches long. Place ropes side by side on lightly greased baking sheet. Pinch ropes together at one end, and braid them gently and loosely (do not stretch). When finished braiding, pinch ends of braid together and tuck both braided ends under the loaf to keep them in place. Brush braided loaf lightly with oil, cover with towel, and let rise to double in bulk, 40 to 50 minutes.

Preheat oven to 375°F.

4. Brush loaf lightly with egg wash, and sprinkle with poppy or sesame seeds. Bake in oven for about 25 to 35 minutes, until golden. Test **bread doneness**.

To serve challah, *place the uncut loaf on the dinner table, and cover with a large white napkin. Usually the host or male guest will say the blessing as he cuts the first slice. He then cuts slices for everyone at the table, and as diners break their bread to eat it, they repeat the prayer. A second loaf is often prepared and blessed to be eaten on the day following the Sabbath.*

If there is a Jewish comfort food, it would have to be chicken soup. It is customary for the bride and groom to fast for an Ashkenazi Jewish wedding, and, to break the fast, they eat chicken soup. (Sephardi and Mizrachi Jews do not fast for their wedding.) The following recipe is a spicy chicken soup of Yemenite Jewish origin. It makes an alternative to the more commonly known Ashkenazi-style chicken soup.

⚝ *Marak Off Teimani* (Yemenite Spiced Chicken Soup)

Yield: 8 to 9 servings

3 tablespoons oil

2 large onions, finely chopped

8 garlic cloves, peeled and minced

2 tablespoons *hawaij* spice mix (recipe follows)

¼ cup tomato paste

⅓ cup *hilbe* condiment (recipe follows)

2 tablespoons *s'chug* sauce, or to taste (recipe follows)

3- to 4-pound chicken, cut into serving portions

1 large tomato, **diced**

2 stalks celery, cut into large chunks

3 carrots, peeled and cut into large chunks

16 cups water

3 potatoes, peeled and **cubed**

1 cup parsley, finely chopped

1 cup **cilantro**, finely chopped

2 tablespoons salt, or to taste

Equipment: Large stock pot with cover, **skimmer**, wooden spoon, oven mitts, bowls, food processor or **blender, mortar and pestle** (optional), small **heavy-bottomed** skillet, rubber spatula, small storage jars for condiments

Note: This recipe takes 3 days.

1. Three days before soup is needed, begin preparations for the *hilbe* condiment, *hawaij* spice mix, and *s'chug* sauce. These may occasionally (though not reliably) be found in food shops specializing in Israeli and other Middle Eastern food products.

2. Prepare the soup: In a large stock pot over medium heat, put 3 tablespoons of oil, and fry the onions and garlic until pale golden and aromatic. Stir in the *hawaij* spice mix and tomato paste. Add the chicken pieces, and mix them well to coat them with the spices and onion, garlic, and tomato mixture.

3. Let the chicken cook for about 8 to 10 minutes to brown slightly, then pour in the water, celery, carrots, and the diced tomato. Slowly bring to a boil, and assiduously skim off all scum that rises. Simmer for 45 to 60 minutes, until the chicken is tender. (You may wish to halt the cooking process here and cool the soup, so as to be able to skim off most of the fat from the surface of the stock.)

4. Add the potatoes to the boiling stock, the *s'chug*, and all but a few tablespoons of the cilantro and the parsley. Continue simmering until the potatoes are tender. Taste and adjust the seasoning, adding more salt or pepper to your taste.

Just before serving, sprinkle with the reserved cilantro and parsley. Serve with s'chug *sauce in a bowl: Each diner stirs as much as he or she wants at the table (a little goes a long way, as it is quite peppery hot).*

⚜ Hilbe (Yemenite Fenugreek Condiment)

Yield: about 1 cup

⅓ cup dried **fenugreek** seeds (available from Middle Eastern and Indian food shops)

½ cup (firmly packed) **cilantro**

2 cloves garlic, peeled

1 small semiripe tomato

juice of 1 lemon

½ teaspoon salt

freshly ground black pepper to taste

¼ cup olive oil

Equipment: Mixing bowl, food processor or **blender**, sterilized glass jar

1. In a bowl, soak dried fenugreek seeds with enough cold water to cover for 3 days. Change the water twice a day, rinsing the seeds well each time. When the seeds have completely swollen, rinse them well before placing in a food processor or blender, together with the cilantro, garlic, lemon juice, salt, pepper, and olive oil. Process or pulse to a purée.

2. Store in a sterilized glass jar with cover, and keep refrigerated. This will keep for a week or two, as long as the surface of the condiment is covered with olive oil.

⚜ Hawaij (Yemenite Spice Mix)

Yield: 5 tablespoons

Hawaij (also *hawaej*) is a traditional Yemenite Jewish spice mix. *Nigella sativa* seeds can be found in Middle Eastern or Indian food shops.

2 tablespoons black peppercorns

1 tablespoon *Nigella sativa* seeds, also called "black caraway" or "*kalonji*"

1 teaspoon cumin seeds

1 teaspoon **coriander** seeds

1 teaspoon cardamom seeds (discard the pods)

1½ teaspoons turmeric

1 teaspoon saffron threads (optional)

Equipment: **Heavy-bottomed** skillet, food processor or **mortar and pestle**

1. In a small heavy-bottomed skillet over low heat, **dry-roast** the peppercorns, cumin seeds, coriander seeds, and cardamom seeds, until they are aromatic. Keep a close eye on them, as they can quickly burn.

2. Place toasted spices in a food processor with the turmeric (and saffron threads, if using), and pulse to a fine powder. Alternatively, pound to a powder in a mortar and pestle.

Store in an airtight jar with cover.

¿ *S'chug* (Spicy Cilantro Sauce)

Yield: about 2 cups

S'chug (also *zhug;* the "ch" is pronounced like the German "ch" or an aspirated "h") is a spicy sauce made of cilantro, hot chili peppers, and other spices. Cilantro is an herb commonly used in Middle Eastern and North African Jewish cuisine (as well as in Asian and South American cuisine). Nowadays, the use of *s'chug* has spread to the general population and is commonly used as a condiment for *falafel*.

1 to 5 green serrano or **jalapeño** peppers, or to taste (1 for mildly hot and 5 for very hot)

½ cup olive oil

1 whole head of garlic, peeled

1 bunch, about 1 cup, fresh **cilantro**, rinsed and dried

1 bunch, about 1 cup, fresh flat-leaf parsley, rinsed and dried

seeds of 3 green cardamom pods

1 teaspoon cumin powder

1 teaspoon salt

Equipment: Food processor or **mortar and pestle**, sterilized glass jar

CAUTION: Use care when handling peppers. Wrap your hands in plastic wrap or slip them in plastic sandwich bags when handling peppers. Do not touch your eyes while handling peppers. If you accidentally touch your eyes, rinse them under cold running water at once.

1. Remove the stems of the peppers, as well as the seeds and pith if you want a milder result. Use the seeds and pith if you want your sauce quite hot.

2. In a food processor or blender, put the olive oil, then add the peppers, garlic, cilantro, parsley, cardamom seeds, cumin powder, and salt. Pulse until the herbs are finely chopped.

Store in a sterilized glass jar with cover. Keep the surface of the mixture covered with olive oil, and it will keep in the refrigerator for a few weeks.

Jews from India comprise three traditional communities: Cochin Jews, Baghdadi Jews, and the Bene Israel of Mumbai. The Bene Israel prepare a festive dish, *malida,* for the festival of Tu B'Shvat, also known as the New Year of Trees. The main activity during Tu B'Shvat (the ninth day of the month Shvat) is planting trees. In Israel, it is traditional to eat dried fruits and nuts, such as almonds, figs, dates, raisins, apricots, and carob, on this holiday. The colorful and sweet *malida* is also prepared by the Bene Israel Jews for special celebrations, such as a circumcision, a wedding, or a house warming. The main ingredient for *malida* is *poha,* raw rice grains that are pounded or pressed into flakes. *Poha* flakes are similar to Western breakfast cereal that can be eaten with milk and that are usually available from Indian or Asian food shops. Freshly grated coconut is essential to the taste of this dish, but thawed frozen grated coconut can be substituted. If you cannot find fresh or frozen grated coconut, soak dry grated coconut in hot milk for 15 to 20 minutes.

₡ *Malida* (Sweet Rice Flakes)

Yield: 4 to 6 servings

4 cups *poha* (dry rice flakes, available at Asian and Indian food shops)

1 cup fresh or frozen (and thawed) grated coconut (Alternatively, soak ¾cup dry grated coconut in ½ cup hot milk for 15 to 20 minutes before using.)

½ cup demerara or unrefined brown sugar

seeds from 8 cardamom pods, finely ground

½ cup any nuts, such as almond flakes, pistachios, walnuts, or cashews

⅓ cup raisins or sultanas, plumped in warm water for 10 minutes before using, and drained

⅓ cup fresh or dried dates, **pitted** and chopped

For **garnish**: any 5 to 7 temperate or tropical fruits in season—**kiwi** fruits, peeled and sliced into rings; strawberries, raspberries, or other berries; physalis fruits; grapes; banana slices; orange slices; pear slices; apple slices; pineapple slices; mango slices; lychees; passion fruit; pomegranate arils.

Equipment: Heatproof bowl (glass or ceramic), sieve, serving platter or large shallow bowl

1. In a heatproof bowl, put the *poha*, and pour boiling water to cover. Stir for a minute or two until the *poha* has softened, then drain thoroughly through a sieve.

2. Put the *poha* back into the bowl, and mix in well the coconut, sugar, cardamom, nuts, raisins, and dates. Chill before serving.

Transfer the mixture to a decorative serving platter or shallow bowl, and surround with your chosen fruit garnishes.

Ethiopian Jews celebrate special occasions and holy days with homemade beer called *t'ella* (also called *t'alla*). *T'ella* is not specific to Ethiopian Jews alone but is a widely made and drunk beer for celebrations in Ethiopia. While teff (*Eragrostis teff*), a very small grain, is most often used to brew *t'ella*, other grains, such as barley, sorghum, or wheat, can also be used. The hop-like flavor of *t'ella* comes from the leaves of the *gesho* plant (*Rhamnus prinoides*, a relative of the buckthorn). There is a special type of dark smokey *t'ella*, *zilel*, that gets its color and flavor from dark toasted bread and by being fermented in a vessel that has absorbed smoke.

₡ *Boyos de Spinaka* (Spinach and Cheese Pastries)

Boyos is the Ladino spelling of the original Spanish *bollos*, meaning "balls of pastry." Before her wedding day, a Sephardi Jewish bride goes to the ritual bath (*mikveh*), accompanied by her mother, the groom's mother, aunts, her sisters, and close friends, in a tradition called *banio* (in the Ladino language, literally "bath," from the original Spanish). After the bath and the appropriate blessing, all partake of a light festive meal of cheese *burekas*, *haminados* (hard-cooked eggs), and *boyos* (small pastries filled with cheese and spinach or chard).

Yield: about 40 pieces

2 pounds spinach or **Swiss chard**

½ tablespoon salt

2½ cups grated cheese (any)

Egg wash: 1 egg well beaten with 2 tablespoons water

½ cup grated Romano or Parmesan for sprinkling

Dough:

1 cup water, plus a bit more if needed

1 teaspoon sugar

1 teaspoon active dry **yeast**

4 cups flour, plus more for rolling out

¼ teaspoon salt

2 cups oil for greasing and soaking the dough balls

Equipment: Mixing bowl, mixing spoon, plastic wrap, baking tray, cookie sheet, oven mitts, wire rack

Note: This recipe may take 2 days.

1. A few hours or a day before pastries are needed, prepare the filling: Wash the spinach or chard, and dry well. (Only the leaves of the chard are used; the stalks can be used for another dish, such as soup.) Slice them finely, and mix well with salt and grated cheese. Set aside until needed, or refrigerate, covered with plastic wrap, for use the following day.

2. Prepare the dough: In a bowl, combine ¼ cup lukewarm water and sugar. Sprinkle the yeast into mixture, and let stand in a warm place until frothy, about 15 minutes.

3. In a large mixing bowl, put flour, and make a well (hole) in the center. Into the well, add the yeast mixture, then the remaining water and salt, and mix to a soft but not sticky dough. Adjust the consistency by adding a bit more water or flour, but try to add as little flour as possible.

   Transfer the dough to a lightly floured surface, and knead until smooth and **elastic**, 8 to 10 minutes.

4. Grease the cleaned mixing bowl with 2 tablespoons of oil, and put the dough, turning it once so that the top can also be coated with oil. Let the dough rise in the bowl, covered with plastic wrap, for about 30 minutes in a draft-free place.

5. Meanwhile, pour oil in a baking pan up to ¼ inch to soak the dough balls in. This oil "bath" is called a *"marina"* in the Ladino language. Pinch off a small piece of dough, about 1½ inches in diameter, and roll it between your oiled palms or on your work surface to a ball. Keep the rest of the dough in the bowl covered. Place the ball in the *marina*, and turn it over so that the top can also be coated with oil. Repeat making more balls with the rest of the dough, and let them rest in the *marina*.

6. Begin "opening out" the dough balls, starting with the balls that had been rolled earliest.

Take the first ball of dough, roll it out with a rolling pin to as thin and as wide a sheet as possible, taking care not to tear the dough or make any holes in it. Next, add the filling: scoop with the tips of your fingers some of the spinach or chard and cheese filling, and place in the middle of the rolled-out dough sheet. Starting at the widest side of the dough, gently lift up the dough to cover the filling. Fold in the sides to keep the filling from falling out. Continue to roll up the rest of the dough firmly like a jelly roll. Starting from one end, coil the roll into a spiral, and tuck in the other end underneath to keep it from uncoiling.

7. Lay the coiled *boyo* on a greased baking sheet. Repeat with the rest of the balls. Brush the *boyos* with egg wash, and sprinkle with grated Romano or Parmesan cheese.

Ten minutes before baking, preheat oven to 350°.

8. Bake in the middle shelf of preheated oven for 25 to 35 minutes, or until golden.

Transfer to a wire rack to cool.

Serve warm or at room temperature. The baked boyos *can also be frozen. Thaw and reheat in the oven, not a microwave, to retain the* boyos's *crisp texture.*

Prickly pears, are a popular Israeli fruit, called "*sabra*" in Hebrew, which refers to both the fruit and the plant. Native-born Israelis are called "*sabra* because, like the fruit, they are bristly (show angry defiance) outside but are sweet on the inside. In Israel, the *sabra* are chilled, cut in half, and eaten right out of the skin, seeds and all. They are also peeled, sliced, sprinkled with lemon juice, and served as dessert. To remove the barbs or prickly coating that cover the skin, wear gloves, and use a small paring knife to peel off the skin.

Today, Jews from more than 70 countries call Israel home. This diversity of people is reflected in the way food is prepared for celebration feasts. The following *basari (fleishig* in Yiddish, meaning "meat") wedding menu was served to some 500 guests at a *kibbutz* (Israeli collective farm or settlement; there are both secular and orthodox *kibbutzim*) and shows the cross-culturalism of present-day Israel.

The reception began when the Rabbi blessed the traditional *challah*, made extra large for the occasion. As he said the *mitzvah* over the loaf and cut the first slice, this signaled the guests to eat.

The menu included huge baskets and bowls of assorted yeast breads, flat breads, rolls, and an old favorite, Polish *kuchel*. The buffet tables were laden with *forspeise* (appetizers) of international flavors: Russian-style mushrooms in *smetana* (recipe page 450), and eggplant caviar (recipe page 508), and stuffed grape leaves (recipe page 640) from Eastern Europe and the Mediterranean region. Egyptian *Bedingane masri* (recipe page 652), popular throughout the Middle East, and chicken soup with *kreplach*. The main dishes included Moroccan-style sweet *couscous*, Eastern

European *fleischig tzimmes* (recipe follows), and Chinese stir-fry chicken. The dessert table was covered with cakes, cookies, such as *kikar shkedim*, and candies. Honey cakes (recipe page 678) were prepared for the occasion to celebrate symbolically the sweetness of life.

Wine is the beverage for rituals and celebrations. Festivities include a round of toasts, where everyone drinks the wine, and says "*L'Chayim*" (to life and good health). Non-wine drinkers enjoy a variety of soft drinks and juices from oranges, clementines, pomegranates, grapes, and apples all of local produce.

A typical Jewish wedding celebration includes circle dancing (the *hora*), where the bride and groom may be lifted above the circle. If either the bride or the groom is the last child of the family to be married, another special dance may be performed for the parents to celebrate their success in marrying off all their children. In Orthodox communities, where dancing with the opposite sex is prohibited, dancing may be done with dance partners holding opposite ends of a scarf.

Brisket is a relatively inexpensive cut of beef that is easy to prepare and a favorite of East European Jews. For festive occasions, meat is combined with prunes, carrots, and potatoes for the main course. There are no set rules, and every household has their own favorite combination of vegetables with the meat. A variation of this dish can be made vegetarian, without meat, and is called *tzimmes*. The Yiddish word *tzimmes* means "to make a fuss" over someone or something.

⚘ *Fleischig Tzimmes* (Roast Brisket with Vegetable Medley)

Yield: serves 6

2 tablespoons vegetable oil	salt and pepper to taste
4 onions, sliced	8 cups boiling water, more or less as needed
4 to 5 pounds **oven-ready** brisket of beef	8 carrots, peeled, cut into chunks
6 tablespoons honey	6 potatoes, peeled, quartered
juice of ½ lemon	1½ cups (¾ pound) large **pitted** prunes, soaked, if necessary, according to directions on package
1 teaspoon **ground** cinnamon	

Equipment: Large roasting pan with cover, mixing spoon, oven mitts, **bulb baster** (optional), meat knife, small sauce bowl, serving platter, cutting board

Preheat oven to 325°F.

1. Heat oil in medium skillet over medium-high heat. Add onions, stir, and **sauté** until golden, 3 to 5 minutes. Spoon onions over bottom of large roasting pan, and set meat on top. Spread honey over top of meat, sprinkle with lemon juice, cinnamon, and salt and pepper to taste. Pour 8 cups boiling water around meat, cover, and place in oven.

2. Bake in oven for 3 hours. **Baste** occasionally, and add more boiling water to keep liquid to original level in pan.

3. Using oven mitts, remove from oven, add carrots, sweet potatoes, and prunes around sides of meat. Baste, and add more boiling water, if necessary. Cover, and continue baking for 1 to 1¼ hours more, or until meat is fork tender.

To serve, transfer meat to cutting board. Let rest 20 minutes before slicing. Using meat knife, cut across the grain in thin slices, and place on serving platter. Surround meat with potatoes, carrots, and prunes. Skim and discard fat from pan juices using bulb baster or mixing spoon. Pour pan juices over meat or in sauce bowl.

Honey plays an important role in all religious celebrations, and cooking *mit lechig* (with honey) is a reminder of hope. To begin the New Year, many Jews say a blessing over an apple dipped in honey: The evening meal ends with honey cake. Honey traditionally is served at the birth of a boy, at weddings and on all happy occasions.

An old wedding custom among Eastern European Jews was to smear the doors of the homecoming newlyweds with honey. The honey symbolism has prevailed among Jews, according to Dov Noy, professor of folklore at Hebrew University of Jerusalem: "Thus the origin of the word honeymoon is derived because *isha* (woman or wife) has the value in Hebrew of *dvash* (honey).

♪ Lechig Cake (Honey Cake)

Yield: 2 loaf cakes

3 cups all-purpose **flour**	½ cup sugar
1 teaspoon baking soda	1 cup clover honey
½ teaspoon **ground** ginger	¼ cup vegetable oil
½ teaspoon ground cloves	**zest** and juice of 1 lemon and 1 orange
½ teaspoon ground cinnamon	½ cup apricot jam
1 teaspoon salt	½ cup dried apricots, soaked for 15 minutes in warm water, drained, **finely chopped**
2 large eggs	½ cup **slivered** almonds

Equipment: Flour **sifter**, medium bowl, electric mixer (optional), large mixing bowl, rubber spatula, wooden mixing spoon, 2 greased 9×5-inch loaf pans, oven mitts, wire cake rack, serving platter

Preheat oven to 350°F.

1. Sift flour, baking soda, ginger, cloves, cinnamon, and salt in medium bowl.

2. Using electric mixer or mixing spoon, beat eggs in large mixing bowl. Add sugar, honey, oil, zests and juices of lemon and orange, and apricot jam. Beating egg mixture constantly, add

flour mixture, a little at a time, alternately with water. Using rubber spatula or wooden spoon, **fold in** apricots and almonds. Transfer batter equally into 2 greased loaf pans.

3. Bake in oven for 40 to 50 minutes, or until toothpick inserted in center comes out clean. Flip cake over onto wire cake rack to cool.

To serve, slice honey cakes into ½-inch-thick slices, and place on serving platter. Eat as dessert with fresh fruit.

Jordan

Jordan lies in the heart of the Middle East. It is bordered by Syria to the north, by Iraq to the east, by Saudi Arabia to the east and southeast, and by Israel and the West Bank territory to the west. Almost all Jordanians are Muslim Arabs, and Arabic is the official language; however, English is used widely in commerce and government. Most of the population are urbanites, and their lifestyle is very Westernized. About half the population is of Bedouin descent, and they strive to maintain the traditions of their ancestors to some degree. The other half are of Palestinian origin, mainly farmers and urbanites. There are small minorities of Circassians and Rom. Women dress fashionably but conservatively. Women attend universities and have equality with men. Many women hold top-level jobs in the government and business and are well represented in the professions.

Jordanians feel strongly about their religion, and they follow Muslim life-cycle events accordingly (See Islam and Islamic Life-Cycle Rituals, page lxxvi). However, the Muslim customs and practices in Jordan are less structured than in some of the other Muslim countries.

Men and women work together and meet at social gatherings. They are able to date, and when they marry, they have a wedding reception with men and women together.

Childbirth traditions in Jordan, as in other Islamic countries, have their roots in Islam. Just prior to childbirth and especially during breastfeeding, mothers were encouraged to eat dates, in particular, *rutab* dates. The tradition stems from the Quran (Surat Maryam 19:23–26), enjoining Maryam (the Islamic name given to Mary, the mother of Jesus) to eat dates just as she is about to give birth. It appears that there is sound nutritional basis for this tradition. *Rutab* dates are named for the second stage of date fruit ripening, which is when the date fruit's sugars and organic acids are at its highest levels, thus providing more energy to the new mother and enabling her to produce a higher quality of milk.

As in Islamic tradition, the first words that an infant hears should be the call to prayer, *adhan*, whispered into the right ear by the father. On the seventh day after the birth, it is traditional to hold a celebration called *aqiqah* for the community—relatives, friends, and neighbors—though often this can take place much later. For the feast, the father is responsible for having two lamb or sheep prepared, and one-third of the meat is supposed to be given to the poor.

♀ *Mansaf* (Lamb and Rice Celebration Dish)

For celebrations, such as an *aqiqah*, or for other special occasions such as welcoming a guest, *mansaf*, a typical Bedouin dish, is usually prepared. *Samneh* is clarified butter that is made by heating butter at low heat until the milk solids precipitate and the water in the butter evaporates. Clarified butter does not need refrigeration. *Ghee* is the Indian term for the same product. If you cannot find *samneh* or *ghee*, use regular butter. *Jameed* is strained yogurt (*laban* or *labne*) that has been salted and allowed to dry to a rock-hard stage. It may be found in Middle Eastern food shops. Otherwise, a substitute (though without the flavor and aroma of the original) is to strain unflavored, full-fat yogurt overnight, refrigerated, in a fine kitchen sieve or cheesecloth to allow the whey to drain. Use the whey for another dish or during assembly of the finished *mansaf*. Diners sit on the floor on carpets or around the serving platter at a table, and help themselves only from the portion directly in front of them. Only the right hand is used for eating; make a small ball of rice and meat to pop into the mouth. The fingers must not touch the lips (this requires some practice).

Yield: 6 servings

10 tablespoons *samneh* (clarified butter or *ghee*) homemade (recipe page 142), or store bought

⅔ cup **pine nuts**

⅔ cup flaked almonds

3 large onions, thickly sliced

1½ teaspoons turmeric

⅔ teaspoon **allspice**

⅔ teaspoon cinnamon

3 pounds stewing lamb, **cubed**

water, as needed

salt and freshly ground black pepper to taste

4 cups long-grain rice

1½ pounds *jameed* (dried yogurt, or substitute full-fat unflavored, Greek-style yogurt, strained overnight)

3 tablespoons **cornstarch**, dissolved in 5 tablespoons water

6 to 7 pieces large, soft Middle Eastern flat bread (or 10 pita)

Equipment: Frying pan, large **heavy-bottomed** saucepan with cover, **heavy-bottomed** covered saucepan or automatic rice cooker, large ovenproof casserole with cover, large platter or tray or shallow bowl for serving, oven mitts

1. In a frying pan over low heat, heat 3 tablespoons of *samneh*, and quickly fry the pine nuts and almonds until golden. Remove and set aside.

2. Add 3 tablespoons of *samneh* to pan, increase heat to medium, and sauté onions until softened, about 7 minutes. Add turmeric, allspice, and cinnamon, and continue to cook, stirring constantly for 1 to 2 minutes. Set aside.

3. In a large saucepan over medium heat, place the lamb and water to cover, and simmer for 30 minutes. Season with salt and pepper, add spiced onion mixture, and continue to simmer until lamb is very tender, about 45 minutes to 1 hour.

4. Meanwhile, prepare rice. Using the same frying pan (scraped clean of onions and spices), over medium heat, warm 2 tablespoons of *samneh*, and add rice, stirring constantly for about

2 to 3 minutes, until all grains are coated with *samneh*. Turn off heat, and transfer rice to a saucepan or rice cooker.

5. Stir in 8 cups of water. Bring to a boil at high heat, cover, and reduce heat to low until rice is done, about 20 minutes. Stir in the remaining *samneh*, replace the cover, and let rice rest until assembly. If using an automatic rice cooker, use the quantity of water required, and follow manufacturer's instructions.

6. When meat is tender, transfer it to a covered dish, and mix well with *jameed* or strained yogurt. Taste and, if necessary, add salt and pepper. Keep meat warm in a low oven.

7. To the remaining broth in the saucepan where meat was cooked, add whey and cornstarch mixture, and cook over medium heat, stirring as you add the cornstarch mixture, until the broth thickens. Turn off heat.

8. To assemble: Line bottom of chosen serving dish with flat bread or pita. If using a large, shallow bowl, extend flat bread up the sides as well. Ladle broth over bread to moisten them. Place remaining broth in a gravy boat or bowl for passing at the table. Place the rice in a mound on the flat bread. Distribute meat evenly over the rice, and decorate with the reserved pine nuts and almonds. **Drizzle** remaining *samneh* over the rice.

Eat while warm, with all diners helping themselves from the central dish.

Muslim funerals are very simple, and all burials must be within 24 hours. The religion requires the deceased to be washed by authorized person(s) of the same gender. The death is announced at the mosque by a holy man. Some words are read from the Koran (the Islamic holy book), along with the deceased's name, funeral time, and place.

The body is carried to the mosque but kept outside in the courtyard. After a short service, the body is taken to the cemetery by a hearse, followed by a convoy of men. Women are forbidden from attending funerals, but, to show they are in mourning, all female family members wear white scarves over their head. The deceased is placed in the grave in only the shroud and laid facing the direction of Mecca (the holy city in Saudi Arabia). The Imam's prayers over the grave signify the end of the burial.

There are memorial services for the deceased on the seventh and 52nd days of his death, and they include Islamic readings. Sometimes big funerary meals or *halvah* (sweets) are offered to the poor to serve as a memorial for the dead. A religious or wedding feast often includes as many as 40 dishes, followed by a profusion of desserts and fresh fruits. The preparations require the work of many people and are as much a part of the celebration as the feast itself.

As in other Arabic countries, Jordanians traditionally sit on cushions on the floor and eat from dishes placed on low tables or on tablecloths spread out on the floor. Traditionally, no plates or forks are used, but flat bread is broken into pieces and used to scoop up food. Bowls of perfumed water are passed from time to time throughout the meal so that diners may cleanse their carefully licked fingers.

Muslims are forbidden, by their religion, to drink wine. On special occasions, however, such as weddings, many drink the strong alcoholic *arak* (also *araq*), locally produced in most of the Arabic countries. *Arak* is a colorless, unsweetened liquor usually distilled from grapes but may also be made from grains and is flavored with anise. It is usually mixed with two-thirds of its quantity with water, which turns its color milky. It is often served with ice and sipped from a small glass. Bite-size *mezze* (appetizers) are usually served before a celebration meal with the *arak*.

Bamieh bil zayt can be served as a *mezze* (appetizer) or as one of the dozen vegetable dishes served with roasted lamb or goat.

Bamieh Bil Zayt (Okra in Olive Oil)

Yield: serves 6

24 to 30 fresh whole okra

½ cup olive oil, divided

3 onions, chopped

4 cloves garlic, **finely chopped**

16 ounces canned stewed tomatoes

½ cup fresh **coriander**, chopped

salt and pepper to taste

water, as needed

For serving; 2 lemons, cut in wedges

Equipment: Paring knife, **colander**, large saucepan with cover or **Dutch oven**, mixing spoon, serving bowl

1. Using paring knife, trim and discard cone-shaped portion from top of okra. Put okra in colander, rinse under cold running water, and set colander in sink to drain.

2. Heat half the oil in large saucepan or Dutch oven over medium-high heat. Add onions and garlic, stir, and **sauté** until onions are soft, 3 to 5 minutes. Add tomatoes, drained okra, coriander, and salt and pepper to taste. Add enough water to cover vegetables, and bring to boil. Reduce heat to simmer, cover, and cook for 20 to 30 minutes, or until okra is tender.

To serve, transfer to serving bowl, and serve either warm or chilled, with lemon wedges as garnish.

Bread is an essential part of a meal since it is used to scoop up the food.

Khobaz Arabee (Arab Bread)

Yield: 8 thin loaves

2 cups **lukewarm** water

1 package active dry **yeast**

2 teaspoons salt

1 tablespoon vegetable oil

5 to 6 cups all-purpose **flour**, more as needed

½ cup yellow **cornmeal**

Equipment: Large mixing bowl, mixing spoon, lightly floured work surface, kitchen towel, knife, pie pan, wax paper, baking sheet, oven mitts, metal spatula, wire cake rack, napkin-lined bread basket

1. Pour lukewarm water into large mixing bowl, add yeast, and soften, 3 to 5 minutes. Stir in salt and oil. Beat in 5 cups flour, adding more if necessary to make a dough that does not stick to your hands. Transfer to lightly floured work surface, and **knead** dough until smooth. Clean and grease large mixing bowl. Put dough in lightly greased large mixing bowl, and turn to grease all sides. Cover with towel, and let rise in warm place until double in bulk, 1½ to 2 hours.

2. **Punch down** dough, and cut into 8 pieces. Knead each piece until dough is satiny. Shape each piece of dough into a ball. Put a little oil on your hands, and rub each ball lightly with oil. Place on work surface, cover with towel, and let rise for 30 minutes.

Preheat oven to 450°F.

3. In pie pan, mix cornmeal with ½ cup flour. Roll each ball in cornmeal mixture, and flatten with palms of your hands to the size of a large pancake. Place on wax paper–covered work surface, and cover with towel.

4. Place one flat bread at a time on lightly floured work surface. Using your hands, gently stretch the bread into a thin round. Repeat stretching the remaining flat breads. Place two or three side by side on baking sheet.

5. Bake in oven for 7 minutes, or until browned. Remove from oven, and turn bread over with a metal spatula. Bake second side for 5 to 7 minutes more, until browned. Continue baking breads 2 or 3 at a time. Place baked breads on wire cake rack to cool.

To serve, place 2 or 3 breads on baking sheet pan, and place under broiler to heat through, 2 to 3 minutes. Place in napkin-lined breadbasket, and set on buffet table.

Fruit is eaten at the end of a meal, and sweets are eaten as between-meal snacks. Sweets are also served at most life-cycle celebrations, especially for weddings. Trays of *deser-e toot farangi* (recipe follows) are especially liked in most Middle East countries.

Deser-e Toot Farangi (Strawberry Delight)

Yield: about 3 pounds

2½ pounds strawberries, stems left on

2 cups sugar

½ cup water

2 tablespoons **rosewater** (available at Middle Eastern food stores and pharmacies)

Equipment: Paper towels, work surface, 2 or 3 baking sheets, wax paper, small saucepan, **candy thermometer** (optional), fork or wooden skewer, dinner knife, serving platter

1. Place 3 or 4 layers of paper towels on the work surface. Rinse strawberries under cold water, and place them in single layer on the paper towels to drain. Place a paper towel over the strawberries, and gently pat dry.

2. Cover the surface of each baking pan with wax paper, and place on the work surface next to the stove. Put the sugar and water in a small saucepan, and cook over medium heat, stirring constantly until sugar dissolves, 1 to 2 minutes. Add rosewater, and, using a spoon, skim and discard any foam from the surface. When the syrup reaches the soft-ball stage, 234° to 240°F on the candy thermometer (see **sugar syrup** in the Glossary of Food Terms), reduce heat to warm. Poke a fork or wooden skewer in the stem end of a strawberry and carefully hold it over the pan of syrup. Spoon 1 teaspoon syrup over the strawberry. Let the excess drip back into the pan. Carefully place the coated strawberry on the wax paper. Repeat coating the strawberries, and place them side by side, not touching, on the wax paper.

3. When the strawberries have cooled, loosen each one from the wax paper using the tip of a dinner knife.

To serve, arrange the strawberries decoratively on serving platter.

Lebanon

Lebanon is a small country lying on the eastern end of the Mediterranean Sea. It is bordered on the north and east by Syria and to the south by Israel. Approximately 90 percent of the people living in Lebanon are Arabs, but they are almost equally divided between Christians and Muslims. Each group follows the life-cycle events according to their religion. (See Protestant and Catholic Life-Cycle Rituals, page lxxiii, and Islam and Islamic Life-Cycle Rituals, page lxxvi.)

In Lebanon, Christians and Muslims are divided into different groups, or sects. There are at least 17 officially recognized sects. The largest Christian sect is the Maronite Catholics, a part of the Roman Catholic Church. The Greek Orthodox is the next largest Christian sect. Although in business the Christians and Muslims often work together, they live in separate communities.

Both Christian and Muslim Lebanese have a high regard for family values. The mother is traditionally treated with respect, and she has a strong voice in family matters. Among the educated urbanite Christian and Muslim families, life is quite similar to the American way of life. It is acceptable, though not yet commonplace, for women to have careers, and most urban Muslim women wear Western fashions.

In the cities, some families are headed by Muslim husbands and Christian wives. Islamic law requires the children of such marriages to be brought up as Muslims. Marriage between a Christian man and a Muslim woman rarely happens, however, because it is forbidden by Islamic law.

Weddings in Lebanon tend to be grand affairs with hundreds of invited guests, and festivities often take place over three days. The festivities include prewedding parties, held in separate venues with different invited guests, for the bride and groom. The bride usually hosts a prewedding party—a *laylia*—during which her hands and feet, as well as those of the principal wedding party, are painted with intricate designs in henna to protect against the evil eye. The groom attends the bride's henna party briefly to receive some henna and soon departs. Or, alternatively, there may be a third celebration planned, combining both groom's and bride's guests at another venue, with more food and drinks, music, dancing, and the traditional celebratory ululation by women (*zhalgouta*). Although other Middle Eastern and North African cultures share the same tradition of women performing these high-pitched tongue trills, in Lebanon, the ululations are preceded by verses that praise the bride and groom. The verses compliment the couple's family, beauty, and other qualities. On the morning of the wedding, the immediate relatives of the bride gather at her house while she and the bridesmaids are getting ready for the ceremony. Her family will usually serve sweets such as *baklava*, *knafe*, and drinks. The groom fetches the bride from her house, and as they leave, loud ululations, gunfire into the air, and fireworks join with drummers to inform all and sundry that a wedding is about to take place. The neighborhood will often shower the bride and groom with rice, candied almonds, and rose petals as they depart. All the cars bearing the wedding party will have their horns blaring all the way to the church or mosque. In addition playing as the bride and groom leave their respective houses, the traditional drummers also play as the bride and groom walk together into the church or mosque for the ceremony.

As with most celebrations in Lebanon, wedding festivities will have hundreds of guests, enormous quantities of food, and professional dancers and musicians (*zaffe*) as entertainment. Interfaith marriages between Muslims and Christians are not legal in Lebanon, and therefore an interfaith marriage must be legalized outside of the country, with only the wedding feast celebrated in Lebanon.

⸙ *Ghraybeh* (Butter Cookies)

Ghraybeh (also *ghoraibi*) are butter cookies that are flavored with orange-blossom water and that are made for all festive occasions and celebratory events. You may substitute vanilla extract or almond extract for the orange-blossom water. *Ghraybeh* are baked for weddings, their white or pale color symbolizing the purity of the bride.

Yield: 60 cookies

1 cup butter, softened

1½ cups confectioners' sugar

2⅔ cups flour, **sifted**

1 tablespoon orange-blossom water, or 1 teaspoon vanilla or almond extract

60 whole **blanched** almonds

Equipment: Large bowl, electric mixer, mixing spoon, parchment paper, baking sheets or trays

Ten minutes before baking, preheat oven to 300°F.

1. In a large bowl, use a mixer to beat butter, confectioners' sugar, and orange blossom water (or vanilla or almond extract) until smooth and fluffy. Stir in the flour, and gently mix until just combined.

2. Take two teaspoonfuls of cookie mixture, roll into balls, and place on parchment-lined baking sheets. Place an almond in the center of each ball and press down gently. The cookies will spread slightly as they bake, so space them about 2 inches apart. Bake the cookies in the middle shelf of preheated oven for 12 to 15 minutes, or just until the bottoms are starting to turn a pale gold. The tops of the cookies should remain pale. Switch the baking sheets midway through baking. Leave the cookies to cool on the baking sheets.

Stored in an airtight container, ghraybeh *will keep for about a week.*

Meghli (Festive Rice Pudding)

Meghli (also *meghlie*) is a festive rice pudding made to celebrate the birth of a son. As such, it is also popularly made by Christian Lebanese during Christmas to celebrate the birth of Christ. It may also be prepared for a daughter if there has been a succession of sons before her. If fresh or frozen coconut is not available, use dry or dessicated shredded coconut soaked in ¼ cup warm milk for 15 minutes. This pudding is usually made in generous quantities, to be served to guests and well-wishers following the birth.

Yield: 6 to 8 servings

1 cup ground rice (not flour)

1 cup powdered sugar

1 teaspoon caraway seeds, powdered

1 teaspoon cinnamon powder

1 teaspoon anise seeds, powdered

8 cups water

For **garnish:**

8 tablespoons shredded fresh or frozen (thawed) coconut

Any combination of the following: ½ cup **blanched** whole almonds or almond flakes, ½ cup pecans or walnuts, ½ cup pistachios or hazelnuts, ¼ cup toasted **pine nuts**

Equipment: Medium saucepan, wire whisk, 8 glass dessert bowls or glasses, or large glass serving dish

1. In a saucepan, combine the rice flour, sugar, caraway powder, cinnamon, and aniseed powder.

   Gradually whisk in the water, taking care not to create lumps, until the mixture is smooth. Cook over low heat until the mixture begins to thicken, about 15 to 20 minutes. The pudding should not be too stiff, as it will become thicker as it cools.

2. Allow to cool for about 10 minutes, then spoon into individual bowls or large serving dish.

Sprinkle the coconut over the surface. Distribute the nuts in a decorative pattern over the coconut layer. Chill for 2 hours or overnight before serving.

The ancient combination of lentils and rice is thought to be Esau's "mess of pottage" mentioned in the Bible. In Egypt and Saudi Arabia, this same dish is called *"ruz koshari,"* where it is served with a side dish of tomato sauce. In Lebanon, it is served with vegetable dishes and salad as part of the *mezze* (appetizer) table for a wedding celebration. *Mujadarah* is also a popular dish in neighboring Syria, Israel, and other Middle Eastern countries.

⚶ *Mujadarah* (also *Moudardara*) (Rice and Lentils)

Yield: serves 4

2 tablespoons olive oil or vegetable oil

2 onions, thinly sliced

3 cups water or chicken broth

1 cup brown or green **lentils** (available at all supermarkets and health food stores)

½ cup white rice

1 teaspoon **allspice**

For **garnish**: 4 lemon wedges

For serving: 1 cup plain yogurt

Equipment: Large skillet with cover, slotted spoon, serving platter, small serving bowl

1. Heat 2 tablespoons oil in large skillet over medium-high heat. Add sliced onions, and fry until soft, 3 to 5 minutes. Add water or chicken broth, and bring to boil over high heat. Stir in lentils, rice, and allspice, and return to boil. Reduce heat to simmer, cover, and cook for 25 to 30 minutes, until rice and lentils are tender. Remove from heat, and keep covered for 10 minutes.

To serve, place rice mixture on a serving platter, and serve lemon wedges and a small serving bowl of yogurt on the side. To eat, squeeze lemon juice over the rice mixture, and spoon a little yogurt over each serving.

Syria

Syria is a large country that lies south of Turkey and is bordered on the east by Iraq, on the south by Jordan, and on the west by the Mediterranean Sea, Lebanon, and Israel. The majority of Syrians are Arabs, and almost all of the people are Muslims except for a small Christian population who belong to the Orthodox Christian Church.

In Syria, Islamic modesty laws are less stringent than in other countries. Many urban Arabs keep strict Islamic rules at home for their family and follow a modern lifestyle in business. Muslim women can wear Western clothes if they like, without fear of punishment.

Women are publicly active in Syria, and they have a prominent place in the urban workforce. Many well educated Syrian Muslim women have gone into business and the professions. In Syria, women doctors are free to set up practice and have male patients, which is unheard of in most other Muslim countries.

Since 2011, Syria has been in the grip of a civil war between the government and numerous antigovernment groups. This has led to the destruction and disruption of Syrian food traditions. The two culinary centers of the country—Damascus and Aleppo—lie in partial ruins, and many famous traditions are in abeyance or are maintained only overseas by Syrian emigrants.

In many respects, the food in Syria and neighboring Lebanon have many similarities. The difference is that Syrian dishes tend to use more meat, whereas Lebanese dishes tend to use more vegetables. The cooking traditions of Damascus and Aleppo are slightly different. Aleppo, in particular, is famous for its sweets, which used to be shipped all over the country and even abroad. Pork is the favored meat for Christian religious holidays and life-cycle celebrations. Muslims favor lamb, goat, or camel; pork is forbidden. Celebration feasts are a time for large families living apart to come together. Whole roast lamb (recipe follows) is the favorite. The patriarch of the family purchases a live lamb from the market and fattens it for a week on malt and mulberry leaves. Neighbors and friends join in for the slaughtering of the lamb and to applaud the dressing and seasoning.

✥ *Zarb* (Slow Roasted Spiced Lamb)

Aleppo is famed for its cuisine, especially for lamb, goat, or chicken slow cooked in an underground oven, a *zarb*. *Zarb* is a traditional way of cooking in the desert by nomadic Bedouins, who scooped a cavity in the sand to build a fire and lined it with stones; this style of cooking has spread to other communities, in particular Aleppo in Syria, Tripoli in Lebanon, Jordan, and elsewhere in the region. (In other parts of the Middle East as well as North Africa, a similar underground oven is called *tabun*.) The stones retain the heat for the two hours or more of cooking, and the surrounding sand serves as insulation to keep the heat in. These days, a metal frame and bricks are used when making this outdoors (or an oven, if indoors) to make the dish. The meat, whether lamb or goat or chicken, is cut into small pieces, marinated with a mixture of diverse spices, threaded on skewers, wrapped in foil (traditionally palm leaves were used), and placed vertically in the *zarb* to roast slowly and gently for two hours. Vegetables to accompany the meat, usually whole potatoes and onions, are also wrapped in foil and placed to bake surrounding the lamb in the *zarb*.

In making the marinade, use ready-ground spices or 1¾ teaspoons *baharat* spice mix to save time and effort, but cooking with whole fresh spices and grinding them just before use gives a greater depth of flavor to the dish.

Yield: 8 to 10 servings

Note: Prepare 1 day in advance

5 pounds boneless lamb, **cubed**	⅔ teaspoon salt
3 tablespoons olive oil	¼ teaspoon whole cardamom seeds
5 cloves garlic	¼ teaspoon whole cumin seeds

¼ teaspoon whole cloves

¼ teaspoon whole black pepper

¼ teaspoon freshly ground nutmeg

1 cinnamon stick, about 2 inches long

¼ teaspoon paprika

1 cup vinegar

whole potatoes, one per person

whole sweet onions, one per person

large tomatoes, one per person

Equipment: **Mortar and pestle** or food processor, parchment paper, aluminum foil, oven mitts

1. Prepare marinade: In a large mortar and pestle, pound garlic and salt to a paste, adding olive oil a teaspoon at a time. Add cardamom seeds to the mortar, and pound until finely ground. Continue with the remaining spices, adding the next when the previous spice has been finely ground. Mix finely ground spices with vinegar. If using a food processor, add all the olive oil to facilitate grinding the garlic and salt, and add vinegar with the rest of the spices.

2. In a large bowl or tray, place lamb cubes, and rub all over with marinade. Cover and refrigerate overnight.

   Ten minutes before baking, preheat oven to 400°F.

3. The following day, wrap lamb cubes in parchment paper, then enclose in foil, making individual portions. Wrap the potatoes, onions, and tomatoes individually in parchment paper and then in foil.

4. Place foil packages in preheated oven. After 15 minutes, reduce heat to 325°F, and continue baking meat and vegetables for another 45 minutes. Turn off heat, but keep packages in the oven, with door closed, for 20 to 30 minutes to rest.

To serve, place 1 meat package and 1 vegetable package on each person's plate. Diners open their packages just before eating to fully savor the spicy aromas released.

Shouraba il kuthra is fed to young Muslim boys to sooth them after their circumcision. It is also a favorite soup for breaking the fast during Ramadan. Christians serve the soup at the beginning of the wedding feast or to nourish a new mother.

Shouraba Il Kuthra (Vegetable Soup)

Yield: serves 8

1½ pounds beef, including bone

3 quarts water

2 teaspoons salt

½ head cabbage, shredded

3 carrots, **trimmed**, sliced

1 onion, **finely chopped**

3 ribs celery, including leafy tops, sliced

2 cloves garlic, finely chopped

16 ounces canned whole tomatoes

¼ cup fresh parsley, finely chopped

Equipment: Large saucepan with cover, mixing spoon, ladle, individual soup bowls

1. Put beef with bone in large saucepan, and add water and salt. Bring to boil over high heat. Remove and discard meat residue on the surface of the water. Reduce heat to simmer, cover, and cook 1 hour.

2. Add cabbage, carrots, onion, celery, garlic, and canned tomatoes. Stirring occasionally, increase heat to high, and bring to boil. Reduce heat to simmer, cover, and cook 1 hour more.

To serve, ladle into soup bowls, and serve with flat *bread (recipe page 682).*

♀ *Kibbeh bil Sanieh* (Meat and Bulgur Pie)

Kibbeh is undoubtedly the most popular celebration dish in Syria, so much so that it is regarded as the national dish. It is made for every celebratory occasion and important event.

Yield: 10 to 12 servings

Filling:

3 tablespoons olive oil

2 pounds ground lamb or beef

3 to 4 onions, finely chopped

1 teaspoon *baharat* spice (available at Middle Eastern food shops or online, or see recipe page 665)

½ teaspoon cinnamon

1 teaspoon salt

freshly ground black pepper to taste

1 tablespoon butter

¼ cup **pine nuts**

Kibbeh crust:

2 cups fine **bulgur**

2 pounds very finely minced lamb or beef (have butcher grind meat twice)

2 onions, minced

1 tsp *baharat* spice mix.

1 teaspoon salt

freshly ground black pepper to taste

2 tablespoons olive oil

Note: Prepare one day in advance

1. The day before: Soak the bulgur in 1 cup water overnight. Drain thoroughly before using.

2. Prepare filling: In a heavy-bottomed skillet over medium heat, warm oil, and add meat, stirring to break up meat into small pellets. Increase heat slightly so that the meat does not stew (release liquid). Add onions, *baharat* spice mix, cinnamon, salt, and pepper, and stir-fry until onions are very soft and aromatic. Turn off heat.

3. In a smaller skillet over low heat, melt butter, and fry pine nuts until golden. Turn off heat, and add pine nuts and butter to the meat and onion mixture. Set aside to cool.

4. Prepare kibbeh crust: With moistened hands, combine drained bulgur, meat, onion, *baharat* spice, salt, and pepper. Mix thoroughly until all ingredients are equally distributed and form a dough-like paste. Add a tablespoon or so of water to achieve this consistency, if necessary.

Ten minutes before baking, preheat oven to 350°F.

5. Grease a 12-inch tart pan or cake pan with oil. Use half of the *kibbeh* crust dough to lay a ⅛-inch-thick layer of *kibbeh* crust at the bottom of the pan. The traditional way is to take fistfuls of the *kibbeh* dough, and press each into a disk of about ⅛-inch thick between your palms. Lay the thinly pressed dough disks on the pan. Continue making more thin disks in the same manner until the bottom of the pan is fully covered. Press edges of the disks together to form a solid layer, with no gaps.

Spread meat filling evenly over the *kibbeh* crust layer. Smooth the surface of the filling, and press down gently to ensure there are no air pockets. With remaining half of the *kibbeh* crust dough, make the top *kibbeh* crust. Form thin disks as for the bottom layer, lay them over the filling, and press the disk edges together to form a solid layer. Smooth the top kibbeh layer, then make a central hole in the center with your finger to allow steam to escape during baking.

With a sharp knife, score the top layer into pie-like slices radiating from the central hole.

6. Bake in the middle shelf of preheated oven for 25 to 30 minutes, or until golden.

Serve with cucumber and yogurt salad (recipe follows).

Salatit Laban wa Khyar (Cucumber and Yogurt Salad)

This salad makes an excellent accompaniment to roasted and baked dishes, such as *kibbeh* as well as *zarb* (recipe page 688).

Yield: 4 to 5 servings

2 cups natural, thick unflavored yogurt

2 cups cucumber, peeled (if peel is thick), sliced into small cubes

¼ teaspoon salt

1 clove garlic, peeled, minced

1 teaspoon dried or 1 tablespoon fresh mint, finely chopped

For **garnish**: 2 or 3 sprigs fresh mint, finely sliced

For serving: 1 tablespoon olive oil

1. In a bowl, mix yogurt, cucumbers, salt, and dried mint together. Adjust seasoning, and add more salt if needed.

2. Chill salad, covered, at least for 30 minutes for flavors to infuse.

Garnish with fresh mint, and drizzle with olive oil.

Jaj Mishwee (Syrian Roast Chicken)

Jaj mishwee is an easy way to prepare chicken. The chicken is first cooked in water, making a flavorful broth, and then roasted. The broth should soothe the little guest of honor at a circumcision feast.

Yield: serves 6

5 pound **oven-ready** whole chicken	¼ cup honey
water, as needed	1 teaspoon **ground** cinnamon
salt and pepper, as needed	½ teaspoon ground nutmeg
½ cup butter	

Equipment: Large saucepan with cover, metal tongs, roasting pan, small saucepan, **pastry brush, bulb baster** (optional), oven mitts, serving platter

1. Remove bag with chicken gizzard from inside of chicken. Rinse chicken, inside and out, under cold running water. Put in large saucepan, and cover with water. Add 1 teaspoon salt, and bring to boil over high heat. Reduce heat to simmer, cover, and cook for 1 hour, or until tender. Using metal tongs, remove chicken from saucepan, and place in roasting pan.

Preheat oven to 350°F.

2. Melt butter or margarine in small saucepan over medium heat. Add honey, cinnamon, nutmeg, and salt and pepper to taste, and stir to mix. Remove from heat. Using pastry brush, brush surface of chicken with honey mixture.

3. Bake chicken in oven for 1 hour, until golden brown. Combine remaining honey mixture with ¼ cup chicken broth from saucepan, and use it to **baste** chicken frequently with bulb baster or mixing spoon.

To serve, set chicken on serving platter with rice or couscous (prepared according to directions on package). Serve with flat bread (recipe page 682).

♪ Ma'Mounia (Semolina Pudding)

Variations of this pudding are made throughout the Middle East, but this has become an Aleppo specialty. It is usually served to a woman who has just given birth in order to build up her strength. The original, ancient recipe was made with rice.

Yield: 4 servings

3½ cups water	4 ounces butter
2 cups sugar	1 cup **semolina**
1 teaspoon lemon juice	

For **garnish:**

1 teaspoon cinnamon, or to taste	1 cup thick clotted cream, stiffly beaten whipped cream, or unflavored thick (Greek) yogurt, for serving

Equipment: Medium saucepan, skillet or shallow saucepan, mixing spoon, oven mitts

1. In a medium saucepan, place the water, sugar, and lemon juice over medium heat, and simmer for 10 to 12 minutes, or until slightly thickened.

2. In a deep skillet or shallow saucepan over low, heat the butter, and fry the semolina for about 5 minutes. Gradually add the syrup, stirring continuously to prevent the pudding from sticking to the bottom of the pan.

3. Let it cook for another 5 minutes. Turn off heat, and let pudding stand for 15 minutes.

To serve, transfer to serving dishes, and sprinkle with cinnamon. Add a dollop of clotted cream, whipped cream, or thick yogurt over each serving.

Turkey

Turkey occupies a unique geographic position, bounded partly by European countries and partly by Asian countries. It shares borders with Georgia, Armenia, Azerbaijan, and Iran to the north and east; with Iraq, Syria, and the Mediterranean Sea to the south; and with the Aegean Sea, Greece, and Bulgaria to the west. To the north of Turkey is the Black Sea. Most of the people living in Turkey are Muslim, and unlike other predominantly Muslim countries, there is freedom of religion and a separation of church and state. Turkish Muslims are much more lenient about dietary and moral codes; the rules governing prayer, alcohol, and pork are not as formally followed. In an effort to share Islam with non-Muslims, anyone is permitted to visit a Turkish mosque. This is not permitted in strict, Islamic-ruled countries.

In 1926, the Turkish civil law was adopted, which suddenly changed the family structure. Polygamy was abolished, along with religious marriages. Only civil marriages are recognized as legal. Divorce and child custody became the right of both parents. Child marriages were outlawed, and the minimum age for marriage was fixed at 15 for girls and 17 for boys. Today, the average marrying age is about 18 for girls and at least 20 for boys. In 1926, women gained equal rights with men in the field of education. Veiling was abolished, as well as long garments that were required by the old religious beliefs. The right to vote was granted Turkish women in the early 1930s. Equal wages for both sexes was ratified by Turkey in 1966.

When a married woman announces her pregnancy for the first time, the excitement among family members grows. Upon hearing the good news, a gold bracelet comes immediately as a present from the mother-in-law. In rural areas, a pregnant woman announces her pregnancy by embroidering a design, symbolic of a baby, on her clothing or her scarf. In some regions of Turkey, there is a custom of planting a tree in the name of a newborn child. Chestnut, mulberry, and apple trees are planted for girls, poplar or pine trees for boys.

Turkish names always have meanings. Some of the children's names may derive from the time in which they were born: *Bayram* (feast), *Safak* (dawn), *Bahar* (spring); or from events during the birth: *Yagmur* (rain), *Tufan* (storm); or from the parents' feeling about the child, if they want him to be the last one: *Yeter* (enough). Sometimes names of family elders are chosen to display respect. When a name is selected, it is given by an *imam* (Islamic holy man) or a family elder by holding the child in the direction of Mecca and reading from the Koran into the left ear and repeating the name three times into the right ear.

In Turkey, Muslim boys are circumcised between the ages of 2 and 14 by licensed circumcision surgeons. The *sunnet* (circumcision) introduces a child to his religious society as a new member. When a family determines a date for their circumcision feast, they send out invitations to relatives, friends, and neighbors. Depending upon the budget, feasts might take place in a ceremonial hall or a hotel instead of at home. They prepare a highly decorated room with streamers and balloons and a nice bed for the boy. Boys always wear special costumes for this event; a suit, a red cape, a scepter and a special hat inscribed with *Masallah*, meaning "God preserve him."

On the morning of a traditional circumcision, the children of guests are all taken for a tour in a big convoy with the boy either on horseback, in a horse cart, or in an automobile. This convoy is followed by musicians playing drums and clarinets. On their return, the boy changes to a loose, long white dress. He is then circumcised by the surgeon while he is held by a person close to the family. It is a great honor to be selected as the person to hold the child. The *kirve* (honored person) will play an active role in the boy's life. Similar to the godfather in Christianity, he has nearly equal rights with the father regarding the boy's future. Although there is no blood relationship, the boy will not be allowed to marry his *kirve*'s daughter.

After circumcision, the boy is kept busy opening presents while everyone hovers around singing and dancing and telling jokes to make him forget his pain. In the meantime, words from the Koran are recited, and guests are taken to tables for the feast. There is always lamb: if not whole roasted lamb (*quozi*, see recipe page 664), then *baharatli kuzu* (recipe page 696) is the centerpiece for the occasion. There are many vegetable dishes and tables covered with sweets.

The marriage practices of the city and the countryside often differ. Many urban brides wear the long white Western-style dress with veil. In the country, brides wear traditional Muslim garments, and prearranged marriages are common. All Turkish brides prepare a complete trousseau so that, once married, they enter a house where nothing will be lacking. Traditionally, the groom's family pays for the wedding and pays a bride-price by giving money to her father. On the day of the marriage, in order to protect the couple from poverty, wedding guests hang pieces of gold and jewelry on the clothing of the bride. When couples marry, by law they must have a civil ceremony. Many couples have both civil and religious ceremonies.

♪ Çorum Düğün Çorbasi (Çorum Wedding Soup)

Each region in Turkey, as in other countries, has its distinct traditions for celebrating life-cycle events, and the foods served at such special celebrations likewise show a wide range of variation. In contrast to the previous wedding soup recipe, this wedding soup made in the

Çorum region of Turkey, near the Black Sea, has no meat, just rice or chickpeas and yogurt flavored with mint.

Yield: 8 to 10 servings

4 cups strained yogurt (also *suzme* in Turkish

3½ cups water

1 cup dry chickpeas, soaked overnight

1 teaspoon dried mint

½ teaspoon Turkish mixed sweet and spicy paprika (*cariçik biber*)

1 tablespoon **cornstarch** mixed into a slurry with 3 tablespoons water

3 teaspoons fresh mint, finely chopped

Equipment: Large **heavy-bottomed** saucepan, wooden mixing spoon, oven mitts

Note: This recipe takes 24 hours.

1. The day before, prepare strained yogurt: Place plain, unflavored Greek-type, full-fat yogurt in a fine sieve, and leave to drain into a bowl overnight, covered, in the refrigerator.

2. Into a large, heavy-bottomed saucepan, put strained yogurt, and mix with water to the consistency of light cream. Add more water if needed. Add chickpeas.

3. Heat at medium heat until mixture boils, then lower heat to simmer. Cook, stirring from time to time with a wooden spoon until chickpeas are tender. Stir in dried mint and paprika.

4. Five minutes before serving, stir in the cornstarch slurry to thicken the soup.

To serve, garnish with fresh, chopped mint leaves.

Yuvarlama (Pearl-sized Meatball Stew)

Gaziantep, a city in Turkey's Anatolia region, is noted throughout the country for its distinctive cuisine, influenced by its proximity to the Syrian city of Aleppo, whose cuisine is well renowned. One of Gaziantep's famous dishes is a stew, *yuvarlama* (or in the vernacular, *yuvalama*), that is served during the three-day celebration of *Bayram* after Ramadan. It is a must to prepare it for this festival, by rich and poor alike, and is as well served to a newly married couple after their wedding night. The pearl-sized meatballs in the stew are Gaziantep's claim to fame, as the minuscule balls require dexterity and a great deal of time to prepare. *Yuvarlama* is usually served with a rice pilaf cooked with fine noodles (vermicelli).

Yield: 5 to 6 servings

¼ cup dry chickpeas, soaked overnight

1½ pounds lamb stewing (boneless) meat, **cubed**

3 cups water

1 teaspoon salt

2 cups strained yogurt

1 egg

3 tablespoons butter

½ tablespoon dried mint

¼ teaspoon freshly ground black pepper, or to taste

Meatballs:

1 cup rice

½ pound lean lamb, finely minced

½ teaspoon salt

¼ teaspoon black pepper, freshly ground

2 tablespoons oil for hands and tray

Equipment: 3 medium-sized bowls, large **heavy-bottomed** saucepan, **skimmer**, small saucepan, food processor, tray, whisk, ladle, egg beater, large serving bowl or individual serving bowls

1. The day before, prepare the rice and chickpeas: In a bowl, soak rice in plenty of water, and in another bowl, soak chickpeas with water to cover.

2. Prepare broth: In a large saucepan, put lamb cubes with water and salt, and bring to boil over medium heat. Skim assiduously all froth that arises. Drain soaked chickpeas, and add to meat in saucepan. When water returns to a boil, lower heat, and simmer lamb and chickpeas until tender, about 1½ hours.

3. Meanwhile, prepare meatballs: Drain soaked rice, and grind finely in food processor. (Traditionally this process was done in a mortar and pestle.) Add minced meat, salt, and pepper to food processor, and mince all together until thoroughly mixed. Transfer meat and rice mixture to a bowl, and knead to a paste.

4. With oiled hands, form pea- or pearl-sized balls, laying them on an oiled tray. Add the meatballs gently in several batches to the barely simmering broth, and let them simmer for about 20 minutes.

5. Prepare yogurt: In a bowl, beat the egg with the strained yogurt, and pour into a saucepan.

6. Over low heat, warm the yogurt mixture, and add 4 spoonfuls of the broth. As soon as the yogurt starts to bubble, turn off heat under saucepan, and stir in yogurt to simmering broth. Do not allow broth to boil. Transfer stew to a serving dish or to individual serving dishes.

7. Prepare mint garnish: In a small saucepan over low heat, gently melt butter. Place mint and black pepper in a ladle, and pour melted butter over it. (Do not put mint directly into melted butter in the pan, as it will burn.)

To serve, pour mint and butter mixture over stew.

The wedding celebration is not complete unless lamb is prepared for the occasion. If whole roasted lamb is too expensive, the next best thing is *baharatli kuzu.*

⚘ *Baharatli Kuzu* (Spiced Leg of Lamb)

Note: This recipe takes 24 hours.

Yield: serves 10

3 cups plain yogurt

½ cup olive oil

1 onion, **finely chopped**

1 tablespoon sweet marjoram, finely chopped

1 tablespoon rosemary, finely chopped

salt and pepper to taste

½ cup fresh mint, finely chopped, or
1 tablespoon dried mint

½ cup fresh dill, finely chopped, or
1 tablespoon dried dill

1 teaspoon **ground** thyme

4 cloves garlic, **crushed**

juice of 1 lemon

1 leg of lamb (about 6 pounds), **trimmed**
of fat

Equipment: Medium mixing bowl, mixing spoon, paring knife, roasting pan with cover, oven mitts, **meat thermometer** (optional), **bulb baster** (optional), meat knife

1. Make **marinade**: In medium mixing bowl, combine yogurt, oil, onion, marjoram, rosemary, salt and pepper to taste, mint, dill, thyme, garlic, and lemon juice. Stir well to mix all ingredients.

2. Using the point of paring knife, make 1-inch cuts all over meat surface. Place meat in roasting pan, and completely cover with marinade. Cover and refrigerate overnight, turning meat several times to coat with marinade.

Preheat oven to 325°F.

3. Remove meat from refrigerator, and leave at room temperature for 2 hours before baking, turning meat several times in marinade.

4. Bake in oven, covered, for 1 hour. Remove cover, insert meat thermometer, if using, in thickest part of meat. Continue baking, uncovered, for 2 to 2½ hours more, or until thermometer registers 145° to 150°F for medium doneness. (Bake 30 to 35 minutes per pound.) Using bulb baster or spoon, **baste** meat several times during baking. Remove from oven and allow to rest for 30 minutes before slicing.

Serve lamb with rice and stuffed vegetables.

One of the aspirations of all Muslims is to make a pilgrimage to Mecca; the pilgrimage is called the *hajj*. It is actually an obligation for every adult Muslim who is physically and financially able to and, additionally, able to provide for his or her family during the pilgrimage. The *hajj* is an annual event, whose date changes every year according to the lunar calendar. Muslims from all over the world converge at Mecca to participate in several rituals throughout the five days designated for the Hajj. The rituals are a reenactment of the plight in the desert of Ishmael, the son of Abraham, and Hagar, his mother and Abraham's second wife, when they were banished by Abraham upon God's command. These rituals comprise: Tawaf—walking around the sacred cube (Ka'aba) seven times counterclockwise (the first three times hurriedly and the last four, leisurely); Sa'i—running seven times between the hills of Marwah and Safa, now housed inside a mosque near the Ka'aba; spending a night in the plain of Muzdalifa; symbolically stoning the devil; drinking from the nearby well at Zamzam (whose spring water saved Ishmael and Hagar from dying of thirst in the desert); and standing in vigil at the plains of Mount Arafat. Once they have accomplished these rituals, the pilgrims shave their heads, perform an animal sacrifice, and celebrate Eid al-Adha.

In Turkey, it is traditional for Muslims to bring finger food—sweet pastries, such as nightingale's nest *baklava* (*bülbül yuvasi*) (recipe page 699) and *findikli kurabiye* (hazelnut cookies) (recipe follows), as well as savory ones such as *börek*—to the mosque to share with fellow worshippers before leaving for the *hajj*. Upon returning from the pilgrimage, each *Hadji* brings similar offerings of sweet and savory finger food. (*Hadji* is a title of respect used to address a person who has completed the *hajj*. The honorific "*Hadji*" precedes the personal name.)

✣ *Findikli Kurabiye* (Hazelnut Cookies)

Yield: about 25 cookies

1 cup hazelnuts

½ cup butter, softened

1 egg

1 cup icing sugar

1½ cups flour, plus a bit more for shaping cookies and flouring the work surface

1 **egg white**, lightly beaten

¼ cup icing sugar for sifting over finished *kurabiye* (optional)

Equipment: Mixer, parchment paper, cookie sheet or baking tray, oven mitts

Preheat oven to 325°F.

1. Coarsely chop half the hazelnuts, and set aside.

2. Take remaining half of the hazelnuts, place on a baking tray or cookie sheet, and toast in preheated oven for about 7 minutes, or until lightly browned.

3. Grind toasted hazelnuts to fine powder in food processor. Pause the processor, and add soft butter, whole egg, icing sugar, and flour. Process until mixture just comes together into a soft dough. Remove dough using rubber spatula.

4. With floured hands, lightly knead dough quickly on a lightly floured surface until smooth, and shape into a ball. Cover with plastic wrap, and let dough rest for 15 minutes in the refrigerator.

5. With floured hands, pinch off walnut-sized pieces from dough, and shape into balls. Place shaped *kurabiye*, well spaced apart, on parchment-lined baking tray or cookie sheet. Press *kurabiye* slightly to flatten their tops, brush with beaten egg white, and sprinkle with reserved chopped hazelnuts.

6. Bake *kurabiye* in the middle rack of preheated oven for 10 to 12 minutes, or just until lightly golden on their bottom edges. Do not let cookies brown; they are meant to be pale. Transfer cookies still on the parchment sheet to wire rack to cool. Sift more icing sugar on them while still warm (optional).

Store in an airtight container.

♪ *Bülbül Yuvasi* (Nightingale's Nest *Baklava*)

No celebration in Turkey is complete without *baklava*, and this is shaped a bit differently from the usual.

Syrup:

2 cups sugar

1 cup water

1 tablespoon lemon juice

Pastry:

1 package **phyllo** dough, at room temperature

1½ cups chopped walnuts, pistachios, or pecans, plus ½ cup for sprinkling over baked pastries

1½ cup unsalted butter, melted

Equipment: Small saucepan, large tray or work surface, **pastry brush**, greased cookie sheet or baking tray, parchment paper, oven mitts, serving tray

1. Prepare syrup. Put sugar and water in a small saucepan over medium heat, and slowly let it come to a boil. Add lemon juice, and continue to simmer for 10 minutes more. Turn off heat, and set aside.

   Ten minutes before baking, preheat the oven to 350°F.

2. On your work surface or a large tray, lay one sheet of phyllo (usually sold in standard dimensions), and brush with melted butter. Layer two more over the first sheet, and brush each layer as well. Spread one tablespoon chopped nuts on the long side of the rectangular phyllo sheet, and roll the sheet tightly over the nuts to cover them.

3. If you want to serve the pastries as finger food, slice the roll into three. Otherwise, slice into two. Slicing them before baking makes for neater cuts; after baking, the phyllo pastry tends to splinter when sliced.

4. Coil each rolled-up pastry into a spiral. Place the spirals on to a greased cookie sheet or baking tray. If you have only one cookie sheet or tray, line it with parchment paper. The baked pastries can be lifted out while still on the parchment, leaving the cookie sheet ready for use for the next batch. Repeat until all the sheets of phyllo pastry have been used.

5. Bake on top shelf of a preheated oven, for 25 to 30 minutes, or until golden brown.

   Remove from oven, let *baklava* cool for about 10 minutes, then drizzle syrup over *baklava* tray slowly.

6. Sprinkle the spirals with your choice of nuts. These will keep in the refrigerator for about a week, if not eaten before that time.

*To serve, place pastries on serving platter. Usually Turkish coffee accompanies the sweets. Turkish coffee (*Türk kahvesi*) is similar to Middle East* kahve *(recipe page 643).*

NORTH AMERICA

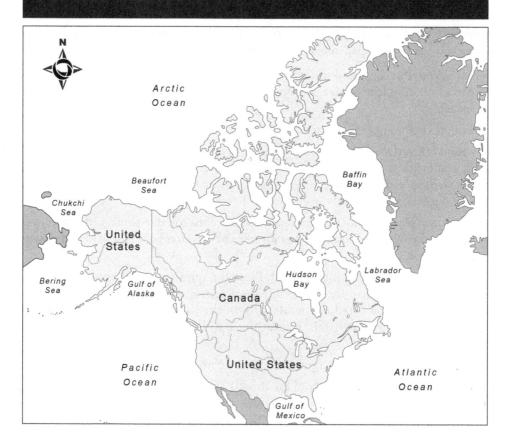

❦ 7 ❧

North America

The two countries that make up North America—Canada and the United States—were conquered and settled by people from many different parts of the world. Although Canada and the United States are similar in many ways and share some cultural traits, both countries of North America have their unique histories and cultures.

At first glance, Canada is hard to distinguish from the United States, especially along the border and the two coasts where most Canadians live. The constant interchange of peoples in those areas has led those Canadians to have a lifestyle very similar to people of the United States. But on closer examination, one finds regional communities, such as French-speaking Quebec, with completely different cultures. In addition, many indigenous peoples living in isolated areas of Canada, especially the far north, have preserved their cultures into modern times.

The United States itself is far from unified in its culture. If one travels from coast to coast and from border to border, the differences in each region's foods, culture, and even speech is readily apparent, yet all these people would refer to themselves as American.

In the pages that follow, foods and life-cycle traditions from different regions of each of these North American countries will be presented and described. The variety of cultures and foods is amazing.

Canada

Canada is the northernmost and largest of North American countries, stretching from its southern border with the United States up into the Arctic Ocean. The original inhabitants of Canada were Indians, particularly the Inuit (Eskimos) of the far north.

The first European settlers were French, and Canada was a French colony until the 1763 Treaty of Paris ceded the territory to Britain. At the time, most European inhabitants were French, and today large regions of Canada, especially the province of Quebec, retain the French culture, language, and religion.

Today, Canada is home to people from many different cultures. As people settled in Canada, they had to modify their traditional life-cycle customs, especially the celebration feasts, to fit what they could catch, hunt, raise, and store in the harsh Canadian environment. Most Canadians are Christians, so life-cycle celebrations correspond with their religious beliefs (see Protestant and Catholic Life-Cycle Rituals, page lxxiii), but some big differences can be found between the English- and French-speaking parts of Canada. The French Canadians are generally Roman Catholic and follow the traditions of their Church, while most of the English-speaking Canadians belong to various Protestant churches.

Baptism is an important ritual among French-Canadian Catholics. The child is usually dressed in a family christening gown that was worn and handed down by many other family members. The shawl blanket the child is wrapped in is usually a family heirloom. After the church service, the family celebrates with food and gifts for the infant. *Petits fours* (recipe page 707) and candies, usually Jordan almonds, *sucre a la crème* (recipe page 707), and *bâtons de noisettes* (recipe page 711) are set out for guests along with soft drinks, tea, coffee, and alcoholic beverages.

Among French Canadians, the nuptial wedding mass is generally held in the morning at the church, and the families of the bride and groom go either to the bride's home or to a hotel for the wedding luncheon. The traditional wedding cake is the same as English wedding fruitcake (recipe page 273).

At French-Canadian funerals, special prayers are often said over the casket at the funeral home. Then the casket is taken to a church for the service with a procession of male mourners, dressed in black, walking behind the hearse. Following the burial service, the funeral feast is either catered at the home of the bereaved family, or it is held in a restaurant.

The Canadian North, bordering the Arctic Ocean, is home to the circumpolar ethnic group, once called "Eskimos," now known as "Inuit" (the people). In the last half century, the Inuit have had to adjust from a Stone Age existence to a modern consumer society. Although most Inuit live by fishing and hunting, they no longer live in igloos but rather in prefabricated houses in government-built settlements. They travel by motor-powered boat instead of by kayak. Despite the availability of snowmobiles, many Inuit keep a nine-dog sled team. They consider four-pawed traction more reliable: Dogs don't stall uphill, nor do they run out of gas.

Among the Inuit, life-cycle celebrations begin with the birth of a baby, usually performed at home by a midwife. The Inuit believe dead ancestors are reborn in children, and according to tradition, the name of a dead ancestor is given to a newborn, thus keeping the spirit of the ancestor alive.

Among the Inuit, it was the practice for a pregnant woman to not sit around as soon as she woke up or to stand in a doorway; to do so was believed to make delivery difficult. It was widely believed that a prospective mother's emotions, thoughts, and diet affected the fetus directly. Likewise, the father's behavior had an impact on the coming baby. Hence, the Inuit took care not to stress a pregnant woman. Eating caribou kidneys was believed to result in a beautiful baby.

Among the Upper Nicola Okanagan nation in British Columbia, a coming of age tradition that was once commonly practiced for girls aged 11 to 12 has been revitalized. Called the "13-moon Ceremony," the coming of age training was reintroduced by a female community elder in 1994 to heal the conflicts that arose among different generations within a family due to being forced by the government to leave home to be educated in distant boarding schools. The yearlong training aims to ground modern Upper Nicola Okanagan girls and to provide them with a sense of discipline and purpose. The training teaches resilience and endurance in the face of physical hardship: for example, bathing in a frozen river with other female relatives. Other types of training teach self-reliance and the ability to be on one's own. As part of the process of entering adulthood, girls undergoing the training wear long skirts and tie their hair back in public.

Among the Blackfoot nation, there is a tradition of giving a youth a new name, or even two (considered an extraordinary honor), when an elder decides the youth is ready to exchange or abandon his childhood name (often an English name) for an adult one in the indigenous language.

Death customs and traditions vary among the different First Nations. The Sioux or Dakota nation is spread throughout the United States (North Dakota, South Dakota, Nebraska, Montana, and Minnesota) and Canada (Alberta, Manitoba, and Saskatchewan). The Dakota nation painted the deceased's face red because red is the color of life. The Ojibwe (Ojibway) or Chippewa (Chippeway) nation settled in the United States (in North Dakota, Minnesota, Montana, and Wisconsin) and in Canada (Manitoba and Ontario). For them, the deceased is a child, the hair is cut and made into a doll, for the mother to carry with her for a whole year after the child's death. The doll is called "Doll of Sorrow."

Marriage is an important part of Inuit culture, and they have a saying, "Every woman needs a hunter, and man should not be alone." When a wedding is announced, everyone in the settlement is expected not only to attend but also to help with the work. The wedding ceremony generally is a big celebration with plenty of food.

To outsiders, the Inuit seem to have unusual food and eating habits. Traditionally, groups prepared and ate only one meal a day together. Inuit used no salt, pepper, or sugar, and they preferred their food raw, even eggs. Whale oil was used for cooking, and seal oil was used for lighting. In recent years, eating habits are changing. Many have two or more meals a day, sweets are causing dental problems, especially among children, and many prefer their food cooked. Frozen TV dinners are popular and available in the local stores. Some old customs haven't changed, though. The raw liver of the seal is considered sacred, and, like candy, it is a treat for children.

Cod is caught by the Inuit, and it is usually eaten raw, especially by elderly Inuit. The younger generations seem to prefer cooked food.

Salmon features largely in First Nations' celebrations. Traditionally, it was consumed fresh during the summer, being steamed, smoked, or grilled over an open fire. It was dried and smoked for use during the winter months. The method of pit-cooking, that is, cooking in an underground heated cavity, or "oven," is common to several other traditional cultures. The ingredients are wrapped in leaves and placed on top of heated stones, covered with a thick layer of leaves and/or tarpaulin to keep the heat in, and left to slowly cook for several hours. The long waiting time allows for plenty of opportunity for guests to chat and socialize.

⚸ Traditional Pit-cooked Salmon

Yield: about 10 servings

2 whole sockeye salmon, washed, patted dry, cut into individual serving pieces

6 pounds clams, soaked in water to free them of sand, rinsed

12 pounds carrots, washed, peeled, left whole

salt and pepper to taste (optional)

good quantity of skunk cabbage leaves, cabbage leaves, seaweed

Equipment: Digging tools (spade, pick), kitchen twine or aluminum foil, heavy tarpaulin or canvas, long-handled tongs, oven mitts

1. Prepare the cooking pit: Dig a cavity in the ground, preferably on sandy clay soil, about 2 feet deep by 3 feet wide. Line the cavity with 25 to 30 round stones, each about the size of a fist. Collect another 25 to 30 stones of roughly the same size, and set aside. Build a fire inside the cavity with dry hardwood for a very hot fire (soft wood gives off less heat). Once the fire gets going, place the remaining stones around it to heat up. Keep the fire burning robustly for 2 to 3 hours.

2. While waiting for the stones to heat up sufficiently, securely wrap the salmon pieces, clams, and carrots into individual packets with the leaves, and tie securely with kitchen twine. Alternatively, use sheets of aluminum foil to further wrap the leaf-wrapped packets, and seal firmly. Take out any unburnt wood from the fire, and lay a thick layer of leaves over the hot stones.

3. Place the securely wrapped packets over the hot stones, and cover with a thick layer of leaves and/or seaweed. Lay a tarpaulin or sheet of heavy canvas over the leaf and seaweed layer, then cover with a 4-inch layer of soil to keep the heat from escaping.

Allow to slowly cook for 3 to 4 hours. Remove the soil and tarpaulin carefully, and use long-handled tongs to take out and distribute the cooked packets.

♪ *Bannock* (Bread)

"Bannock" is the English word for a staple bread eaten by the First Nations (indigenous or aboriginal Canadians). Originally, the staple was made with ground wild roots and tubers mixed with wild berries. Nowadays, it is made with wheat flour and commonly raised with baking powder or, occasionally, yeast. It can be fried, baked, wrapped around a stick and cooked over an open fire, or cooked in an underground pit oven. It is also known as "frybread" (*assaleeak*, among the Inuit) or *sapli'l* or *sepli'l* (among the Interior Salish). It is eaten like other kinds of bread—to accompany a main meal or as a snack spread with a savory or sweet spread— and eaten at daily meals and also at gatherings and celebrations. It can be served piping hot with a local jam, made with saskatoons (Canadian native berry, *Amelanchier* species), cloudberries, or cranberries, or as an accompaniment for a main meal, such as pit-cooked salmon (recipe precedes).

Yield: about 8 servings

4 cups all-purpose flour

4 tablespoons baking powder

1½ teaspoons salt

2 cups warm milk

4 tablespoons vegetable oil

Equipment: Large mixing bowl, wooden mixing spoon, pastry cutter, baking sheet or muffin pan, wire rack or paper towels for draining (if frying), oven mitts

Ten minutes before baking, preheat the oven to 450°F.

1. In a large mixing bowl, thoroughly combine the flour, baking powder, and salt.

   Make a well (hole) in the center of the flour mixture, and immediately pour in all the milk and oil. Mix only until it is smooth and all comes together into a soft dough. Do not over-mix, and do not knead.

2. Turn the dough onto a lightly floured surface, and, with a pastry cutter, divide the dough into plum-size pieces. Quickly shape the pieces into regular balls, and place well spaced on the prepared baking sheet or into muffin pans. Bake in preheated oven for 15 minutes, or until nicely browned and crusty. Alternatively, deep-fry the bannocks for a few minutes on each side until brown, and drain on a wire rack or kitchen paper towels.

Serve hot with plain or cinnamon butter or with jam.

Fish soups are popular with all Canadians, and often the wedding or funeral feast begins with soup.

♪ *Soupe à la Morue* (Cod Soup)

Yield: serves 6

8 cups water

2 potatoes, peeled, **coarsely chopped**

1 onion, **finely chopped**

1 celery rib, **trimmed**, finely chopped

salt and pepper to taste

1 pound fresh or frozen skinless fish **fillets** (cod, trout, snapper, or whiting), rinsed, patted dry with paper towels, cut into 2-inch slices

2 tablespoons butter or margarine

2 tablespoons all-purpose flour

2 cups half-and-half

For **garnish**: 3 tablespoons parsley or chives, finely chopped

Equipment: Large saucepan with cover, mixing spoon, medium skillet, whisk

1. Put water, chopped potatoes, onion, celery, and salt and pepper to taste into large saucepan. Bring to boil over high heat. Reduce heat to **simmer**, cover, and cook for 15 to 20 minutes or until potatoes are tender. Add fish, stir, cover again, and cook for 7 to 12 minutes, until fish is opaque white and done. Keep covered, and reduce heat to low.

2. Melt butter or margarine in medium skillet over medium-high heat. Remove skillet from heat, and whisk in flour until smooth and well blended. Whisk continuously, slowly add half-and-half until well mixed. Return to medium heat, and whisk constantly until smooth and thickened, 5 to 7 minutes. Slowly add cream mixture to fish mixture while stirring gently and constantly. Reduce heat to low, and cook, uncovered, for 5 to 7 minutes for flavor to develop.

To serve, sprinkle each serving with chopped parsley or chives.

ॐ *Ragout de Boulettes* (Small Meatballs)

These small meatballs are a favorite **appetizer** for all life-cycle celebrations.

Yield: serves 6 to 8

1 pound lean ground beef

½ pound lean ground pork

¾ cup dry **bread crumbs**

¼ cup milk

1 egg

1 onion, **finely chopped**

¼ teaspoon **ground** nutmeg

salt and pepper to taste

3 tablespoons all-purpose flour

1 teaspoon instant beef bouillon

¾ cup water, divided

1 cup half-and-half

2 tablespoons fresh parsley, finely chopped, or 2 teaspoons dried parsley flakes

Equipment: Large mixing bowl, mixing spoon, **baking sheet,** oven mitts, medium ovenproof bowl, large skillet

1. In large mixing bowl, combine ground beef, ground pork, bread crumbs, milk, egg, onion, nutmeg, and salt and pepper. Using mixing spoon or hands, combine ingredients.

Preheat oven to 350°F.

2. Moistening your hands with water frequently, shape meat mixture into walnut-sized balls. Place side by side on baking sheet. There should be about 48 meatballs.

3. Bake in preheated oven until lightly browned, about 20 minutes. Using oven mitts, remove pan of meatballs from oven. Transfer meatballs to ovenproof bowl, and keep warm. Save pan juices.

4. Prepare sauce: Spoon 3 tablespoons saved pan juices in large skillet. Add flour, ¼ cup water, and bouillon, and stir until smooth. Heat over low heat, stirring constantly until bubbly, or about 1 minute. Remove from heat. Stirring constantly, add remaining ½ cup water and half-and-half. Increase heat to medium-high, and continue to stir until smooth and thickened, 3 to 5 minutes.

Before serving, pour sauce over meatballs, and sprinkle with parsley. Serve while warm as an appetizer or as a side dish on the celebration table.

⚜ *Sucre à la Crème* (Sugar-Cream Confection)

This candy is served at life-cycle events from baptisms to funerals.

Yield: 64 to 100 pieces

2 pounds brown sugar or maple sugar	½ cup butter or margarine
½ cup heavy cream	1 cup walnuts, **coarsely chopped**

Equipment: Medium saucepan, wooden mixing spoon, buttered 8- to 10-inch-square cake pan, **icing spatula**, plastic food wrap

1. Put sugar and cream in medium saucepan, and, stirring constantly, bring to boil over medium-high heat. Reduce heat to **simmer**, then add butter or margarine and continue stirring until butter melts. Remove from heat, and stir in chopped walnuts.

2. Beat mixture with wooden spoon until thick and creamy, about 7 to 12 minutes. Transfer mixture to buttered baking pan, and spread evenly, using back of spoon or icing spatula. Cover with plastic wrap, and refrigerate until set, 2 to 4 hours.

To serve, cut into 1-inch squares and place in serving dish.

Petits fours are very labor intensive but well worth the effort. Adding special decorations make *petits fours* ideal for life-cycle parties. Use multicolored, chocolate, silver, or gold sprinkles (available at most supermarkets), **silver leaf**, nuts, heart-shaped candies, or edible flowers. For example, at a baby girl's baptism party, use raspberry preserves for the filling, spread pink icing over the cakes, and cover the top with pink and white sprinkles or place a pink candied heart on each cake. Before you begin, coordinate fillings (homemade and canned preserves), icing colors, and decorations for the cakes.

⚜ *Petits Fours* (Small Individual Cakes)

Yield: Five dozen 1½-inch-square cakes

½ cup all-purpose flour	6 tablespoons unsalted butter
½ cup **cornstarch**	water, as needed

6 eggs, at room temperature

1 cup granulated sugar

1 teaspoon vanilla extract

chocolate filling (recipe follows)

3 flavors of preserves (variety of colors) to be used as a filling

sweet icing (recipe follows)

dried or fresh fruits for decorating cakes (optional)

decorating icing for decorating cakes (assorted colors are available in 4.25-ounce tubes at most supermarkets) (optional)

Equipment: 17×11×1-inch jelly roll pan, paring knife or scissors, wax paper, flour **sifter**, medium bowl, small **heavy-bottomed** saucepan, spoon, small bowl, large saucepan, heatproof surface, large heatproof mixing bowl, electric mixer or whisk, rubber **spatula,** oven mitts, toothpick, ruler, 9×15-inch rectangular cardboard pattern, long **serrated knife**, plastic food wrap, wire cake rack, metal spatula

1. Prepare jelly roll pan: Grease bottom and sides of pan. Use paring knife or scissors, cut wax paper to fit bottom of pan and press smooth. Grease surface of wax paper, and sprinkle with flour to coat. Shake out and discard excess flour.

2. **Sift** flour and cornstarch together into medium bowl.

3. Melt butter in small heavy-bottomed saucepan over low heat. When butter separates, remove from heat. Skim off and discard any foam that forms on the top. Tip the pan slightly, spoon the clear butter into a small bowl, and set aside. Discard milky solids that settled in bottom of pan.

Preheat oven to 350°F.

4. Fill large saucepan halfway with water, and bring to boil over high heat. Remove from heat, and set on a heatproof surface. Put eggs and sugar in large mixing bowl, and set over pan of hot water. ***Note:*** *Bottom of large mixing bowl should not touch water; if necessary, pour some water off.* Using electric mixer or whisk, beat egg mixture until thick and foamy. When mixture is **lukewarm**, place bowl on work surface, and continue to beat until egg mixture has almost tripled in volume. The mixture should stand in peaks when the beaters or whisk is lifted from the bowl. This will take about 15 minutes with an electric mixer or, if using a whisk, about 30 minutes.

5. Using rubber spatula, **fold in** flour mixture, ¼ cup at a time. Fold in the clear melted butter, a little at a time, and add vanilla extract. Spread batter evenly over prepared paper-lined pan, and smooth top with rubber spatula.

6. Bake for 25 to 30 minutes, or until the cake begins to pull away from sides of pan and toothpick inserted in center comes out clean. Using oven mitts, remove cake from oven and flip onto sheet of wax paper placed on work surface. Carefully peel off the wax paper that is now on the top side of cake, and cool cake to room temperature.

7. Prepare chocolate filling (recipe follows). Place preserve fillings next to prepared chocolate filling.

8. Prepare sweet icing (recipe follows).

9. Center 9×15-inch cardboard pattern on cake. Using long serrated knife, cut around pattern, cutting off all edges of cake. Discard or save edges for another use. Cut 15-inch length in half, making two 7½×9-inch pieces. Cut both 7½×9-inch pieces in half, making 4 4½×7½-inch cakes.

10. Make each cake two layers by cutting through the middle horizontally, separating the top from the bottom. Place top on bottom, exactly as they were before cutting, so they don't become mixed up.

11. Add fillings: Work with one cake at a time. Carefully remove top layer, then place bottom layer, cut side up, on work surface. Spread prepared chocolate filling thinly over cut side of bottom layer and replace top layer, cut-side down. Using the preserves as a different filling for each cake, repeat filling and reassembling. Wrap each cake separately in plastic wrap, and place in freezer for at least 1 hour.

12. Remove 1 cake at a time from freezer, unwrap, and cut into 1½-inch squares. Using serrated knife, cut longest side into four strips, each 1½-inch wide. Cut each strip into three 1½-inch pieces, making 15 squares.

13. Cover cakes with sweet icing: Select a color of icing that corresponds or complements the color of the filling for each cake. Working with 1 colored icing at a time, transfer icing to heavy-bottomed saucepan. (Keep other icings covered.) Rinse and dry jelly roll pan, set wire cake rack in pan, and place on work surface. Set cake squares about 1 inch apart on wire cake rack. Warm icing over low heat to make it pourable, stirring constantly. Pour or spoon icing generously over tops of cakes, letting it run down the sides. With metal spatula, scrape up excess icing that dripped onto jelly roll pan under wire rack, and return it to saucepan. Stirring constantly, warm icing over low heat until it is pourable again. Pour or spoon it over any cakes that were not evenly coated. You can repeat, scrape, warm, and pour icing as many times as necessary until all the cakes are evenly coated. Let iced cakes dry on rack for about 10 minutes before transferring to wax paper–covered work surface. Repeat cutting and icing remaining 4½×7½- inch cakes, one at a time.

14. Each *petit four* can be decorated with pieces of dried or fresh fruit, and/or you can draw whatever designs you like using bought decorating icing tubes. Allow icing to dry at least 1 hour before lightly covering with wax paper.

To serve, arrange differently colored cakes decoratively on serving platter.

Any fruit preserves you like can be used as filling for *petits fours*. Thin each ¾ cup of preserves with 3 tablespoons apple juice. A few drops of mint extract added to *chocolate filling* also gives it a nice flavor.

ξ *Chocolate Filling*

Yield: about 2 cups

12 ounces semisweet chocolate, **coarsely chopped**

16 tablespoons unsalted butter

2 cups confectioners' sugar

Equipment: Medium **heavy-bottomed** saucepan, wooden mixing spoon

1. Melt chocolate and butter in medium heavy-bottomed saucepan over medium-low heat, stirring constantly. When mixture is fully melted, remove from heat.

2. Using wooden spoon, beat in confectioners' sugar, ½ cup at a time, beating well after each addition.

Use for petits fours *(recipe precedes)*.

Once you've decided on four flavors of preserves to be used as fillings, select a food coloring to add to the *sweet icing* that will match or complement the filling color and flavor. For instance, red or purple fruit preserves go well with pink icing. Chocolate filling (recipe precedes) or peach or orange preserves go well with yellow icing, and green icing goes well when mint extract is added to chocolate filling. White icing goes with any color filling.

♪ Sweet Icing

Yield: enough for 60 cakes

5 cups granulated sugar

2½ cups water

1½ cups light corn syrup

12 cups (4 pounds) confectioners' sugar, **sifted**

Red, green, and yellow liquid food coloring

mint extract (optional)

Equipment: Large **heavy-bottomed** saucepan with cover, wooden mixing spoon, hair-bristled (not nylon) **pastry brush**, electric mixer or whisk, rubber spatula, 4 medium bowls, plastic food wrap

1. In large heavy-bottomed saucepan, combine granulated sugar, water, and corn syrup. Stir over medium-low heat until sugar dissolves. Using a pastry brush dipped in cold water, wipe sugar crystals from around sides of pan back down into the syrup. Cover pan, and cook syrup over low heat for 5 minutes; the steam will dissolve any remaining crystals.

2. Remove cover, increase heat to medium-high, and boil syrup, without stirring, for 5 minutes. Remove from heat, and cool to room temperature.

3. Using electric mixer or whisk, beat constantly, add confectioners' sugar, about 1 cupful at a time, beating well after each addition, and continue to beat until mixture is well mixed.

4. Place sugar mixture over low heat, stirring constantly. Cook until mixture is **lukewarm** and appears smooth and shiny, 7 to 12 minutes. Do not overcook, or icing will lose its gloss.

5. Color icing: Divide icing equally among 4 medium bowls. Select a different color of food coloring for 3 of the bowls of icing, and leave the 4th bowl white. Stir in a few drops of the selected color of food coloring to that individual bowl. Cool icings to room temperature, and cover with plastic warp.

Use for petits fours.

In the afternoon after a baptism, a tray of assorted cookies is always a welcome treat for the friends and relatives who come by to see the baptized child. Cookies are also a popular addition at children's birthday parties.

♪ *Bâtons de Noisettes* (Nut Stick Cookies)

Yield: 28 to 30 pieces

1 cup unsalted butter, at room temperature

¼ cup granulated sugar

¼ teaspoon salt

2 cups all-purpose flour

2 teaspoons vanilla extract

1 cup walnuts or filberts, **finely chopped**

1 cup confectioners' sugar

Equipment: Large mixing bowl, electric mixer or mixing spoon, rubber **spatula,** wax paper, work surface, buttered cookie sheet pan, oven mitts, wide metal spatula, wire cake rack, small shallow bowl, serving platter

1. Put butter in large mixing bowl, and, using electric mixer or spoon, beat until creamy. Beating constantly, add granulated sugar a little at a time, and continue beating until light and fluffy. Sprinkle salt over flour, and add to the butter mixture about ½ cup at a time, beating well after each addition. Beat in vanilla. Using rubber spatula, **fold in** nuts.

Preheat oven to 350°F.

2. Shape cookies: Place wax paper on work surface. Divide dough into 28 to 30 equal balls, and set on wax paper. Roll each ball between the palms of your hands into a cylinder about 2½ inches long and about ½ inch thick. Place them about 1 inch apart on buttered cookie sheet.

3. Bake in oven for 10 to 12 minutes, or until light golden brown. Using oven mitts, remove pan from oven, and let cookies rest for 10 minutes. Using wide metal spatula, transfer cookies to wire cake rack to cool.

4. Put confectioners' sugar into small shallow bowl. When cookies are cool, roll each in confectioners' sugar to coat all sides.

To serve, decoratively arrange cookies on serving platter. Bâtons de noisettes *keep well for several weeks in a tightly covered container.*

United States

The United States sits between Mexico to the south and Canada to the north. Most of the original inhabitants of the country, the Native American Indians, were wiped out shortly after contact with Europeans, though some tribes survived the wars and diseases brought by Europeans. Today there are 567 federally recognized Native American Nations (also called "tribes," "communities," "bands," etc.) with their own distinctive cultures and languages. Of these, 229 are in Alaska. Although originally colonized and ruled by England, the United States has attracted immigrants from all over the world since independence was declared in 1776.

The various waves of immigration from around the world have changed the American cultural landscape, but at the same time, each wave of immigrants is assimilated into the cultural mainstream in an ever changing mix. Americans choose from the cultures their ancestors brought with them and the new culture that has developed here. At times, this process has been viewed optimistically, as seen in the popular belief in United States as a "Melting Pot," a term coined by Israel Zangwell in a 1908 play describing the assimilation of the new immigrants into the American way of life.

Another metaphor that has been used in place of the melting pot is the "breadbasket," which seems appropriate for a cookbook. Although the meaning of this metaphor implies that America is a large culture (the breadbasket) filled with many separate, distinct cultures (the breads), the literal meaning applies as well. The new American breadbasket includes breads from the many different cultures that make it up, from white bread to brioches, *challah* to dark pumpernickel, from flat breads such as pita, tortillas, and nan to hard rolls, soft rolls, sweet rolls, bagels, croissants, and breadsticks.

The reality probably falls somewhere between the two metaphors. Successive waves of immigrants have been assimilated into the mainstream culture while retaining important rituals of their home culture, including life-cycle rituals. The rest of this section will detail a few of the cultures and their life-cycle rituals that have become part of the U.S. landscape.

Acadian (Cajun)

Around 1755, a group of French settlers living in Acadia, an English colony on the North Atlantic seaboard, now known as Nova Scotia, refused to swear allegiance to the English flag; they refused to stop speaking French or to give up Catholicism, as ordered by British. The British were unhappy with the group, known as the French Acadians, and drove them out of the region.

The Acadians found a home in the French colony of Louisiana. Their Louisianan neighbors had trouble saying "Acadian," which they mispronounced "Cajun," and the name stuck. Most Cajuns are devout Roman Catholics, and all life-cycle events are celebrated according to doctrines of the Church. (See Protestant and Catholic Life-Cycle Rituals, page lxxiii.)

Weddings are big celebrations for Cajuns. Besides the bride and groom, the cakes are the most important part of a Cajun wedding. There can't be too many, and too few would be unacceptable. The cakes are made by members of the bride's family, who spend weeks before the wedding getting them baked and decorated.

If the reception is in the home of the bride's parents, they often have a room designated as the Cake Room. On the wedding day, it is filled with cakes of every description, like the *gâteau à la montagne blanche* (recipe page 717). The cakes are round, flat, square, and layered, then iced and decorated in every color imaginable. Other sweets served include trays of beautifully decorated *petits fours* (recipe page 707), crunchy brittle, fudge, and cookies, like *bâtons de noisettes* (recipe page 711).

At Cajun religious and life-cycle celebrations, the feast includes any number of spit-roasted hogs or suckling pigs (recipe page 425). Cajuns use every part of a pig except the squeal. They pickle the pig's ears and feet and make some very unusual sausages. *Boudin noir* (black sausage) is made with the blood and fat of hogs. *Boudin blanc* literally means "white pork pudding" and is a very white sausage.

Boudin Blanc (White Sausage)

Yield: makes 12 sausages

7- to 9-feet natural **sausage casing** (available at most butcher shops and some supermarkets) (When you purchase the natural casing for this recipe, it need not be in one length; allow for some waste.)

3 tablespoons vegetable oil

3 onions, **finely chopped**

2 green bell peppers, **trimmed**, **seeded**, finely chopped

2 cloves garlic, finely chopped

2 cups finely **ground** chicken or turkey meat (buy already ground, available at most supermarkets)

1½ pounds finely ground lean pork (buy already ground, available at most supermarkets)

2 cups water

3 cups cooked rice

salt and ground white pepper to taste

ground red pepper to taste

2 teaspoons ground **allspice**

1 quart water, for cooking

2 cups milk

4 tablespoons butter or margarine, more if necessary

Equipment: Large skillet with cover, mixing spoon, food processor, rubber spatula, large mixing bowl, sausage stuffer or large funnel, kitchen string, wooden spoon, large saucepan, ice pick, metal tongs, large platter, sharp knife or scissors

1. Prepare **sausage casing**. (See directions in glossary.)

2. Heat oil in large skillet over medium-high heat. Add finely chopped onions, green peppers, and garlic, stir, and **sauté** for 3 to 5 minutes, until soft. Crumble in ground chicken or turkey and ground pork. Add water, stir, and bring to boil. Reduce heat to **simmer**, cover, and cook, stirring occasionally, 12 to 18 minutes, or until done. Transfer to large mixing bowl, and cool to room temperature.

3. Add cooked rice, and sprinkle in salt and white pepper to taste, ground red pepper to taste, and allspice. Using your hands, toss to mix well.

4. Prepare to fill presoaked natural casing: Rinse casing under cold running water before filling. Insert the tube end of stuffer or large funnel into casing. Ease as much casing as possible onto the tube so it wrinkles up. Seal opposite end with a knot, or tie with string.

5. Fill casing: Work with a few cups of meat mixture at a time, push it through tube into casing, easing the filling toward the sealed end. Use wooden spoon handle or something similar to push filling into casing. Continue to fill casing until all the mixture is used and evenly distributed in casing. Do not overfill casing. Allow room for expansion, or the casing will burst during cooking. Twist and tie filled casing into 6-inch lengths.

6. In large saucepan, bring water and milk to boil over medium-high heat. Coil sausages into boiling liquid, reduce heat to simmer, and cook 25 to 35 minutes until well done and mixture has firmed up. As sausages rise to the surface, prick each section once or twice with an ice pick to keep casing from bursting. Remove sausages with metal tongs, and transfer to large platter to cool. Do not separate links. Links can be covered and refrigerated for up to 2 days.

7. At serving time, cut sausages into individual links with sharp knife or scissors. Melt 4 tablespoons butter or margarine in large skillet over medium-high heat. Sauté 3 or 4 links at a time, on both sides, to heat through and lightly brown. Sauté in batches, adding more butter or margarine, if necessary.

*To serve, cut each link crosswise in 2 or 3 pieces, and serve as an **appetizer** on the buffet table. For dinner, serve 1 or 2 links of* boudin blanc *per person with mashed potatoes.*

A large gathering for a Cajun birthday feast or other large family gathering during the crawfish season—between December and July—usually calls for a crawfish boil (*écrevisses bouillies*). Crawfish (also called crayfish, crawdads, or mudbugs) are often mistaken for lobsters because they look like miniature lobsters, typically averaging about 4 to 6 inches, about half the size of an average lobster. Unlike lobsters that live in the sea, crawfish are freshwater creatures (not to be confused with marine crayfish, also known as spiny or rock lobsters, which do not have the large claws of lobsters or the freshwater crawfish). A crawfish boil focuses on fresh crawfish poached (not really boiled) in a well flavored stock with onions, garlic, assorted herbs, and vegetables such as mushrooms, potatoes, and, depending on the cook's preference, other accompanying vegetables such as corn, beans, artichokes, cauliflower, or broccoli.

A sack of fresh crawfish typically weighs around 30 pounds. Allowing for 3 pounds live weight for an average eater, one sack may be sufficient for about 10 people. Crawfish aficionados may easily consume twice or thrice that amount. Other vegetables may be added, depending on personal preference: green beans, broccoli, carrots. Sausages are a usual addition, but they make the shells of the crawfish greasy, and some people leave them out or else cook them in the same pot after the crawfish have been taken out. Powdered and liquid crawfish seasonings often include salt, but if they do not, add salt to taste. Beer is the usual accompanying drink for adults.

It is not considered bad manners, even in polite company, to make a sound when sucking the juices from crawfish heads. Any leftover crawfish can be peeled immediately and refrigerated to make into *écrevisse étouffée* (see recipe page 717).

Écrevisses Bouillies (Crawfish Boil)

Yield: 20 to 25 servings

2 sacks live **crawfish**, 60 to 65 pounds

12 lemons, halved

6 heads garlic, left unpeeled, cut in half crosswise

8 large onions, peeled, sliced in half crosswise

2 fat bunches celery with leaves, sliced in half crosswise

15 to 20 dried bay leaves

4½-pound bag powdered crawfish boil seasoning

2 pounds liquid crawfish boil seasoning (optional)

2 ounces cayenne pepper sauce

3 pounds sweet potatoes or potatoes in a mesh bag

1 pound whole fresh mushrooms

frozen corn on the cob, halved, about 2 halves per person

1 or more link sausages per person, cut up (optional)

Equipment: High-capacity propane gas burner and gas tank, 120-quart pot with cover, 3- to 4-foot-long wooden paddle for stirring, 3-foot-long perforated cooking spoon or ladle, mesh bags (for cooking potatoes, mushrooms, corn cobs), oven mitts, long table laid with disposable plastic cover and a layer of newspapers for serving, rolls of paper towels for serving

1. Clean the crawfish thoroughly: Remove any dead ones (those whose tails are not curled; it is normal to have a few in a sack) and all traces of mud. Also wash thoroughly, and prepare all the vegetables.

2. Fill the cooking pot halfway with water, and turn on the burner to high. Squeeze the juice from the lemons straight into the water, and add the peels. Add the garlic, onions, celery, bay leaves, powdered seasoning, and cayenne sauce. Stir and bring to a boil.

3. Add the sweet potatoes or potatoes in mesh bag(s), and, when the stock returns to a boil, add the crawfish. Stir thoroughly. As soon as there are bubbles forming all over the pot but before it goes into a full rolling boil, turn off the heat.

4. Depending on the size of the crawfish, wait 2 to 3 minutes for smaller ones, up to 5 minutes for larger ones, then add the frozen corn. Cover the pot.

5. Begin timing: Let the crawfish poach (soak) in the cooking liquid between 30 to 40 minutes (depending on size). Check at 5-minute intervals to see if crawfish are done.

   Taste one: Break the head from the tail. The head should be full of juice. If the texture of the tail is rubbery, it is not yet fully cooked. If the tail is falling apart, it is overcooked. The texture of a perfectly cooked crawfish tail is firm. When the crawfish have all sunk to the bottom of the pot, they have absorbed as much of the flavoring liquid as they can.

6. Remove the crawfish and accompanying vegetables with a large strainer or long-handled perforated ladle. Drain for a few minutes at the edge of the pot to let the excess stock drip.

7. To serve: Spread the drained crawfish and vegetables in the middle of an outdoor table covered with a disposable cover and layers of newspaper or paper towels. Have rolls of paper towels (much sturdier than table napkins) handy for diners. While the stock in the pot is still hot, add the sausages (if desired) and cook for 15 to 20 minutes. Add to the piled crawfish and vegetables.

8. To eat: Separate the head from the tail. Suck the juices from the head and tail. Scoop out with a finger the red-orange coral within the head. Peel off the first segment of the tail shell, and squeeze the tail between your fingers to loosen the meat.

Serve crawfish with a favorite dipping sauce, sauce rémoulade *(recipe follows).*

♨ *Sauce Rémoulade* (Remoulade Sauce)

Rémoulade is a famous Cajun sauce served with everything from seafood to meats and vegetables. Bowls of it are always on the celebration buffet table.

Yield: 5½ to 6 cups

hot, spicy mustard, such as Creole mustard or horseradish mustard (available at most supermarkets)

4 hard-cooked eggs, peeled, **coarsely chopped**

1 tablespoon paprika

½ teaspoon **ground** red pepper to taste

2 teaspoons **kosher salt**

2 tablespoons vinegar

juice of 1 lemon

1 cup extra-virgin olive oil

1 cup green onions, **finely chopped** (including 3 inches of top greens)

¼ cup fresh Italian (flat-leaf) parsley, finely chopped

1 cup celery, **trimmed**, finely chopped

Equipment: Electric **blender**, rubber **spatula,** medium mixing bowl with cover, mixing spoon

1. In blender, combine mustard, chopped hard-cooked eggs, paprika, ground red pepper to taste, salt, vinegar, and lemon juice. **Blend** for about 30 seconds, or until well mixed and smooth.

2. With blender running on low, slowly pour oil through the feed tube in a thin line until mixture is thickened, about 1 minute. Transfer to medium bowl. Add green onions, parsley, and celery, and stir to mix well. Cover and refrigerate for at least 1 hour before serving.

Serve as dip with boiled **crawfish** *(recipe precedes), or* **crudités**.

The favorite way of serving food is called *Ambigu*, a French-Créole buffet service with all the dishes placed on the table at the same time. One of the most popular Cajun dishes served *Ambigu*-style for the wedding feast and funeral meals is *etouffée*.

♪ *Écrevisse Etouffée* (Crawfish Stew)

Yield: serves 4

½ cup butter or margarine

1 onion, **finely chopped**

1 green pepper, **trimmed, seeded,** finely chopped

1 rib celery, trimmed and finely chopped

¼ cup cream

½ teaspoon **cornstarch**

1 pound frozen **crawfish** meat, thawed according to directions on package

(available in Asian food stores and most supermarkets), or cooked leftover crawfish meat from crawfish boil (recipe page 715)

salt and pepper to taste

ground red pepper to taste

2 green onion tops, finely sliced

¼ cup fresh parsley, chopped, or ¼ teaspoon dried parsley flakes

4 cups cooked rice, kept warm, for serving

Equipment: Large **heavy-bottomed** saucepan with cover or **Dutch oven**, mixing spoon, small bowl

1. Melt butter or margarine in large heavy-bottomed saucepan or Dutch oven over medium-high heat. Add finely chopped onion, green pepper, and celery, stir, and **sauté** for 5 to 7 minutes, or until onions are soft. Reduce heat to medium.

2. Put cornstarch in small bowl, and stir in half-and-half a little at a time, until smooth. Slowly stir cornstarch mixture into onion mixture. Add thawed crawfish, salt and pepper to taste, and ground red pepper to taste, stir well. Cover and cook 10 to 12 minutes for flavor to develop, stirring frequently. Just before serving, **fold in** sliced green onion tops and parsley.

To serve, mound cooked rice in large serving bowl, and pour crawfish mixture over the top, or serve in separate bowls.

On the Cake Table, one cake is more important than the others, the wedding cake. *Gâteau de noce créole à l'ancienne* (old-fashioned Creole wedding cake) is the same as the *Caribbean black wedding cake* (recipe page 235). The following cake, *gateau à la montagne blanche*, might accompany the wedding cake on the Cake Table.

♪ *Gâteau à la Montagne Blanche* (White Mountain Cake)

Yield: serves 24

2 cups cake flour

2 teaspoons baking powder

3 **egg whites**

½ cup butter

1 cup sugar

¾ cup milk

½ teaspoon almond extract

grated rind of 1 lemon

For **garnish**: butter icing (recipe page 324) or confectioners' sugar

Equipment: Flour **sifter**, 2 medium bowls, electric mixer or whisk, large mixing bowl, mixing spoon, rubber **spatula,** buttered and floured 12×8-inch cake pan, oven mitts, wire cake rack

Preheat oven to 350°F.

1. **Sift** together flour and baking powder into medium bowl.

2. Put egg whites in medium bowl, and, using electric mixer or whisk, beat until stiff but not dry, 2 to 3 minutes.

3. Put butter into large mixing bowl, and, using electric mixer or mixing spoon, beat until creamy. Slowly add sugar, beating constantly until fluffy and light. Add flour mixture alternately with milk while continuing to beat constantly. Add almond extract, and beat until mixture is smooth. Using rubber spatula, **fold in** whipped egg whites. Transfer mixture to prepared cake pan, and spread smooth.

4. Bake for about 1 hour, or until toothpick inserted in cake comes out clean and cake has pulled away from sides of pan. Using oven mitts, remove from oven, and place on wire cake rack to cool to room temperature.

To serve, cover top with butter icing or sprinkle with confectioners' sugar, and cut into 2-inch squares.

African Americans

Unlike most immigrants to the United States who came seeking freedom or economic opportunity or fleeing trouble or persecution, the ancestors of most African Americans were brought to this country by force, as slaves. Although the slave owners discouraged the importation of African culture, many slaves kept their own traditions and created new ones in the harsh conditions of slavery.

Today, many African Americans are revisiting these traditions, and some couples have added a ritual called "jumping the broom" to their wedding ceremony.

This tradition developed during slavery when slaves were considered chattel, and they had no legal or religious rights, including marriage. To mark their passage into marriage, the slaves devised a ritual that was known as the "jumping the broom." To legitimize their union as husband and wife, the husband and wife would join hands and step over broom, signifying their passage into married life.

Today, reviving the ritual gives newlyweds a connection with their past and allows them to show pride and respect for their ancestors. The jumping the broom ritual is included in modern weddings either after vows are exchanged or later during the wedding reception.

The wedding feast often includes foods that have special meaning for African Americans. **Black-eyed peas**, for example, are said to have come to America from Africa by way of the West Indies, sometime before 1700. Today, they hold an important place in African American culinary history. For many centuries, black-eyed peas have been eaten at New Year's celebrations for good luck, and more recently they have been eaten for good luck at weddings. Hoppin' John is made with black-eyed peas. A big pot of Hoppin' John is a necessary addition to the Southern African American wedding feast. It is also commonly brought to funeral repasts.

Other African American food traditions, such as so-called soul food, developed as a result of slave cooks making do with the poorest-quality ingredients allotted to them by slave owners, such as chitlins (small intestines), hog maw (pig's stomach), and pig's feet and ears. Today, descendants of slaves are keeping traditions alive by preparing their beloved chitlins and other soul food dishes for major holiday and life-cycle celebration feasts.

ℰ *Chitlins* (also *Chitterlings*) (Skillet-fried Hog Intestines)

Note: This recipe takes 2 days.

Yield: serves 6

2 pounds chitlins (available by special order at most butcher shops)

water, as needed

2 onions, quartered

2 cloves garlic, **coarsely chopped**

½ teaspoon salt

salt and pepper to taste

juice of 1 lemon

½ cup all-purpose flour

½ cup butter or margarine, more if necessary

For **garnish**:

1 tablespoon fresh parsley, **finely chopped**, or 2 teaspoons dried parsley flakes

1 lemon, cut into 6 wedges

Equipment: Medium bowl with cover, **colander**, knife, medium saucepan with cover, fork, large skillet, metal spatula, serving platter

1. Rinse chitlins under cold running water, put in medium bowl, and cover with fresh cold water. Cover bowl, and allow chitlins to soak for 24 hours in the refrigerator. During that time, make several changes of water. Transfer to colander, and drain well.

2. Cut chitlins into 2-inch lengths. Turn inside out, and peel away and discard most of the fat, leaving a little for flavor. Rinse again under cold running water.

3. Pour 4 cups water in medium saucepan, and bring to boil over high heat. Reduce heat to **simmer**, and add chitlins, onions, garlic, ½ teaspoon salt, and lemon juice. Stir, cover, and

simmer for 2 to 2½ hours, or until tender when pierced with a fork. ***Note:*** *Do not boil chitlins, or they become tough.*

4. Transfer chitlins to colander in sink and drain thoroughly. Then, transfer chitlins to medium bowl, sprinkle with salt and pepper to taste, and toss with flour until well coated.

5. Prepare to skillet-fry: Melt ½ cup butter or margarine in large skillet over medium-high heat. Fry chitlins a few at a time, turning with metal spatula, until golden brown, about 3 to 5 minutes. Transfer to serving platter, and keep warm while frying remaining chitlins in batches. Add more butter or margarine, if necessary, to prevent sticking.

To serve, sprinkle with chopped parsley, and garnish with lemon wedges for guests to squeeze on serving if desired.

Another make-do dish came about because masters decided lemons were a luxury and therefore too good for the slaves. With no lemons to cook with, ingenious slave cooks created this pie made with vinegar, a surprisingly good substitute for lemon. Vinegar pie should be on the wedding feast table.

♘ Mock Lemon Pie (Vinegar Pie)

Yield: serves 10 to 12

9-inch baked, homemade crust or commercial, frozen (prepared according to directions on package)

1¼ cups sugar, divided

3 tablespoons all-purpose flour

¼ teaspoon salt

3 **eggs, separated**

1 cup water

2 tablespoons butter or margarine

¼ cup cider vinegar

2 or 3 drops yellow food coloring

1 tablespoon lemon extract

Equipment: Oven mitts, wire cake rack, medium **heavy-bottomed** saucepan, whisk, rubber **spatula**, electric mixer, medium mixing bowl

1. Prepare pie shell according to directions on package.

2. Set baked pie shell on wire cake rack to cool to room temperature.

3. Combine 1 cup sugar, flour, and salt in medium heavy-bottomed saucepan. Whisk in egg yolks and water. Set over low heat, add butter or margarine, and, whisking constantly, cook until smooth and thickened, 7 to 12 minutes. Remove from heat, and, whisking constantly, slowly pour in vinegar. While whisking, add 2 or 3 drops yellow food coloring. Using rubber spatula, transfer vinegar filling to cooled, baked pie shell.

Preheat oven to 350°F.

4. Prepare meringue: If using whisk to beat egg whites, wash and dry whisk thoroughly. Using electric mixer or whisk, beat egg whites in medium mixing bowl until **frothy**. Beating constantly, add remaining ¼ cup sugar, a little at a time. Add lemon extract, and beat until stiff

peaks form. Using rubber spatula, spread meringue to completely cover and seal in filling. To make a more attractive meringue, swirl it into peaks and valleys, using rubber spatula.

5. Bake in oven for 8 to 10 minutes, or until meringue peaks are golden brown.

To serve, cool to room temperature, and cut into wedges.

Today, a refreshing punch is almost always served at the wedding receptions.

₡ *Strawberry Iced Tea Punch*

Yield: serves 14 to 18

2 cups water

1 cup sugar

2 cups strong tea

6-ounces canned frozen lemon juice concentrate

8 cups apple juice

24 ice cubes

For **garnish**:

1 lemon, thinly sliced

8 strawberries, washed, **trimmed,** and sliced

Equipment: Small saucepan, mixing spoon, large punch bowl, ladle

1. Pour water into small saucepan, add sugar, astir, and cook over medium heat until liquid is clear and sugar is dissolved. Remove from heat, and cool to room temperature.

2. At serving time: Combine tea, frozen lemon juice concentrates, and apple juice, and stir well. Stir in sugar mixture, a little at a time, to sweeten punch. Add ice cubes.

To serve, place the filled on the buffet table. Float lemon slices and strawberries in the punch, for garnish. Set the ladle in the punchbowl and arrange the punch cups around the bowl. Fresh greenery and/or flowers placed around the base of the punch bowl also add a festive touch.

African American funerals are noted for being jubilant events, in contrast to the sobriety that characterizes mainstream American funerals. Particularly in the South, a funeral is a time of celebrating to the fullest the life of the deceased. In New Orleans, the birthplace of jazz, a jazz funeral is regarded as the most desirable part of a "homegoing," or Southern African American–style funeral. The jubilant mood of a Southern African American funeral originates from the days of slavery, when death was seen as a release into freedom and an end to the relentless suffering of slaves' daily life. The term "homegoing" for a funeral reflects the yearning of many slaves to go home (to their homeland, Africa), impossible in life, and made feasible, only in a metaphysical sense, by death. Hence, in the South, African Americans prefer a homegoing in style, with massive, custom-made floral arrangements, plentiful food, and, if in New Orleans or wherever there may be a jazz marching band, with a jazz parade leading from the funeral or the family home to the burial ground. In New Orleans, in addition to the "first line," that is, the musicians hired to play music, there is usually a "second line"—friends or other people in the community who may bring their own instruments and follow the first line, playing music and dancing, as the funeral parade heads toward the cemetery.

In the countryside, where there are few funeral homes or too distant, a wake would be held in the home of the deceased, and the body would lie in the receiving room until burial. The deceased are often buried with their favorite personal items.

The foods served during a wake and at Southern funerals are brought by mourning friends, neighbors, and relatives. Casseroles are easy to make and are amenable to freezing, a convenient item to bring to a mourning family, whose members may be too bereft to prepare food for themselves. Ham biscuits and tomato aspic are classic foods brought to a Southern repast (the African American term for a funeral meal). A repast (pronounced "repass") most usually is potluck style, with fried chicken, string beans, crab cakes, different types of salad (bean salad, seafood salad, hot chicken salad, **black-eyed peas** salad), traditional classics such as pig's feet cooked with sauerkraut, chitlins, and several rice dishes (from plain rice to go with greens to red rice with sausages). Some of the rice dishes have quaint names—Hoppin' John, Limpin' Susan. Those who can afford it may have a catered, sit-down meal for the repast.

♪ Chicken Purloo

This rice and chicken dish is also known as "chicken pilau." It is a classic casserole dish, originally from the Gullah community of South Carolina, which has since become popular outside its home territory. It is one of the dishes that are brought to potluck meals, such as a funeral repast.

Yield: about 6 to 8 servings

1 3-pound chicken, cut into large serving pieces

3 tablespoons oil

2 large onions, finely chopped

salt and freshly ground black pepper to taste

8 rashers bacon, **diced**

2 stalks celery, diced

3 cups long grain rice

2 large **tomatoes, peeled** and finely chopped

For **garnish**: finely chopped parsley or slices of green and yellow bell pepper

Equipment: Large **heavy-bottomed** saucepan or Dutch oven, large bowl, oven mitts

1. In a large, heavy-bottomed saucepan or Dutch oven over medium heat, briefly fry the chicken pieces in the oil, a few pieces at a time, until brown on both sides. Set aside. In the remaining oil in the pan, fry the onions, stirring frequently, until softened and aromatic.

2. Add the chicken pieces to the onions in the pan, and add enough water to cover. Add salt and pepper. Cover the pan, and bring to a boil. Skim any froth that forms. Turn down the heat, and let the chicken pieces simmer for 40 to 45 minutes, or until tender.

3. Remove the chicken pieces to a plate, and allow to cool. Transfer the chicken stock to a bowl. When the chicken is cool enough to handle, debone, and remove the skin. Slice the chicken into bite-size pieces. Taste the chicken, and, if needed, season with salt and pepper.

4. In the same saucepan over low heat, slowly cook the diced bacon until crisp and brown, stirring frequently. Add a tablespoon of oil if necessary.

5. Turn up the heat to medium, and sauté the rest of the onion and the celery, until softened. Stir in the rice, and sauté. When it has turned opaque, add the tomatoes, followed by the chicken stock. There should be enough liquid to cover the rice by an inch. Top up with water if necessary.

6. Cover the pan, and let the rice come to a rolling boil. Turn down the heat to low, and let the rice continue to cook gently for about 15 minutes, or until tender.

7. Add the reserved chicken pieces, and continue to cook, covered, for another 3 to 5 minutes until the chicken pieces are hot. Turn off the heat.

Serve garnished with parsley or slices of bell pepper.

The Amish

Early in the 1700s, southeastern Pennsylvania became a sanctuary for thousands of German Protestants of many diverse sects, such as Mennonites, Amish, Moravians, and Seventh-Day Adventists, who came to America seeking religious freedom.

The settlers, mostly from Germany, were called "Dutch," a corruption of the German word *Deutsch*, which means "German," and has nothing to do with Dutch people from the Netherlands. The Pennsylvania Dutch (Deutsch) were divided into two groups: the Plain People, such as the Amish and Mennonites, who followed a strict religious path, and the Fancy Dutch or Church People, the more worldly liberal members of the Lutheran and Reform Churches.

Both Plain and Fancy Dutch have two things in common: their local dialect, a blending of English with old south German, and their love of food. They have a word for it—*Feinschmeckers*, which roughly means "those who know how good food should taste and who eat plenty of it."

Today, Amish communities are located all over North America. The Amish have a simple lifestyle and are against the use of modern technology such as electricity and motorized vehicles. They are easily identified by their plain, nonornate style of dress. Amish women wear a white cap or bonnet over hair parted in the middle and pulled back into a bun. Amish men wear black or dark blue clothing with suspenders and black felt or straw hats with a flat crown and wide, flat brim. Most clothing is sewn by hand by the females of the community.

Eating is one of the pleasures the Amish consider legitimate, and they indulge themselves whenever an occasion arises, be it a wedding, a barn raising, or a huge dinner after Sunday church services. Throughout the year, Sunday worship takes place in a different parishioner's farmhouse each week and is always followed by a feast.

Rumspringa in Amish culture refers to a period and process of coming of age. From the ages of 14 to 16, Amish youth begin to take a greater part in the social life of the community, such as participating in Sunday night "sings." It is also a time of getting to know and courting a lifelong partner. At the age of 21 or at the end of *Rumspringa*, most Amish youth choose to be baptized to join the church. A minority prefer to leave the community, but they are welcomed back when they do choose to return in the future.

An Amish funeral is simple and somber. The deceased person is not eulogized; the Amish hold that praise is reserved for God. There are no flowers or any singing. A hymn is read (not sung) as the coffin, a plain one usually made by members of the community, is lowered into the ground. After the funeral, mourners go to the home of the deceased to comfort the bereaved family and to share a simple meal. Mourners make a point to visit every Sunday and on other days of the week for an entire year.

An Amish postfuneral meal may include sandwiches (ham, cheese), potato salad, cupcakes or cake or pie, pickled **beets**, or a very simple one of bread, coffee, and mixed peanut butter spread. In Pennsylvania, raisin pie is almost always served at funerals.

⚘ *Raisin Pie*

Raisin pie is ubiquitous at Pennsylvania Amish funerals. It is intentionally cloyingly sweet—the reason being that one needs to be distracted from sorrowful mourning by the pie's intense sweetness. If desired, the sugar can be reduced considerably, since the raisins provide sufficient sweetness.

Yield: 6 to 8 servings

pastry for a 9-inch single or double pie crust	4 eggs, separated
¼ cup butter, softened	1½ cups seedless raisins, washed, patted dry, roughly chopped
½ cup light brown sugar	
½ cup sugar	3 tablespoons cider vinegar
½ teaspoon cinnamon	pinch salt
¼ teaspoon ground **allspice** or ground cloves	For serving: whipped cream (optional)

Equipment: rolling pin, 9-inch pie pan, electric mixer, wooden spoon, rubber spatula, oven mitts, wire rack

1. Prepare the crust: On a lightly floured surface, roll out the pastry, and line a 9-inch pie pan. Trim excess pastry ½ inch from the pie pan rim. Turn the overhang under so that the fold is even with the pan rim. Flute or crimp the crust edge with a fork. Do not prick the bottom of

the pastry. (If preparing a double crust, keep the remaining pastry under a moist clean kitchen towel, and roll out the top crust only when the filling is ready.) Set aside.

Ten minutes before baking, preheat the oven to 425°F.

2. In a mixer bowl at medium speed, cream thoroughly the butter, light brown sugar, and sugar until fluffy and light colored. Blend in the cinnamon and allspice or cloves. Add the yolks, one at a time, beating well after each addition, until the mixture is smooth. Turn off the mixer, and with a wooden spoon, mix in the raisins.

3. In a separate bowl and with cleaned mixer beaters, beat the egg whites with a pinch of salt to stiff peaks. Gently fold the egg whites into the raisin mixture, until the filling is homogeneous. Transfer the filling to the pastry-lined pan.

4. Bake in preheated oven for 15 minutes, then reduce the temperature to 300°F, and bake for 20 to 25 minutes more, or until nicely browned. Remove to a wire rack to cool for at least 3 hours before cutting.

Serve with whipped cream, if desired.

When a boy and girl are of marrying age, they follow very rigid courting customs. The boy usually calls on the girl at her home where they get to know each other in the sitting room.

When a couple wants to "bond," as the Amish call marriage, it is announced at Sunday service. Traditionally, the bonding ceremony takes place after the harvest season, in the fall. The ceremony is on either Tuesday or Thursday so that everyone can attend. During the bonding service, the bride and groom sit facing each other. The bonding ritual ends with the couple standing together to accept the bonding vows.

After the late morning service, everyone enjoys the wedding feast. Usually 300 to 400 guests are fed in shifts, which can often run into more than six seatings. The newlyweds sit facing the guests and must remain seated until everyone has eaten. After the feast, the rest of the day is spent singing hymns and snacking on cold food and beverages. A huge supper is served before everyone heads for home.

Guests do not bring gifts to an Amish wedding. Instead, in the weeks following, the gifts are picked up by the newlyweds as they fulfill their obligation to visit the home of each family who attended their bonding.

Schwingfelder is considered the traditional Amish wedding cake, although it is more like bread. The saffron and turmeric give it a yellowish color.

Schwingfelder (Saffron Wedding Cake Bread)

Note: This recipe takes over 8 hours.

Yield: 2 loaves or cakes

6 saffron threads (available in spice section of most supermarkets)   ¾ cup hot water

¾ cup milk

½ cup water

1 package active dry **yeast**

13 teaspoons sugar, divided

6 cups all-purpose flour, **sifted**

1 teaspoon salt

½ teaspoon **ground** turmeric

6 tablespoons vegetable shortening

½ cup currants

½ cup seedless raisins

½ teaspoon ground nutmeg

Equipment: Plastic food wrap, mixing spoon, work surface, small saucepan, cooking **thermometer**, large mixing bowl, **pastry blender (optional)**, kitchen towel, lightly floured work surface, 2 6-inch well buttered round cake pans, oven mitts, white napkin-lined plate

1. Put saffron threads in ¾ cup hot water, cover with plastic wrap, and set on work surface for at least 8 hours.

2. In small pan, combine milk and water, and heat to **lukewarm**. Remove from heat, and let rest 5 minutes. Stir in yeast and 1 teaspoon sugar, and let stand for 5 to 10 minutes or until **frothy**.

3. Put flour, salt, ground turmeric, and remaining 12 teaspoons sugar in large mixing bowl. Using pastry blender or your fingers, cut or rub shortening into flour mixture until mixture resembles bread crumbs. Add currants, raisins, and nutmeg. Pour saffron liquid and frothy yeast mixture over flour mixture. Stir well, or use your hands to form soft dough. Cover with towel, and set in warm place to rise to double in bulk, 2 to 2½ hours.

4. **Punch down** and transfer dough to lightly floured work surface. **Knead** until smooth and firm, about 5 to 7 minutes. If dough is sticky, sprinkle lightly with flour, and knead in. Divide dough in half, and shape each piece to fit into a well greased 6-inch cake pan. Cover pans with towel, and set in warm place until dough has risen to tops of pans, 40 to 50 minutes.

Preheat oven to 400°F.

5. Bake in oven for 35 to 45 minutes, or until golden brown. Test **bread doneness**.

To serve, wrap each loaf separately in a white napkin–lined plate, and set one in front of the bride and the other in front of the groom. After the food is blessed, the newlyweds break off chunks from their loaf to share with each other. This symbolizes togetherness and that from this day forward, they will share everything in their lives.

Amish serve a great variety and quantity of farm food for the wedding feast. The menu usually includes roast chicken with stuffing, pork and sauerkraut, chicken pot pie, scrapple (recipe follows), egg noodles, fried chicken and mashed potatoes, pickled eggs (recipe page 485), pepper cabbage, *schmierkäse* (cottage cheese salad), and a great assortment of cakes, cookies, and pies, such as shoo-fly pie (recipe page 728).

✣ *Scrapple (also Ponhaws) (Fried Pork Cakes)*

Scrapple (also *ponhaws*) got its name because it was made from scraps of meat scraped from cooked hog bones (usually the head). This is a perfect way to use leftover pork.

Yield: serves 6

cold water, as needed for cooking

4 cups boiling water

1 cup **cornmeal** (available at all health food stores and most supermarkets)

1 teaspoon salt, more if necessary

1 cup cold water

1½ cups **ground**, cooked pork

1 onion, **finely chopped**

½ teaspoon ground sage

¼ teaspoon ground nutmeg

salt to taste

ground red pepper to taste

4 to 6 tablespoons butter or margarine, for frying

Equipment: **Double boiler** with cover, medium bowl, mixing spoon, heatproof surface, scissors, wax paper, large loaf pan, plastic food wrap, knife, cutting board, large skillet, wide metal **spatula**, serving platter

1. Prepare to cook in double boiler: Fill bottom pan of double boiler halfway with cold water, and bring to boil over high heat. Reduce heat to simmer.

2. Pour 1 cup cold water into a small bowl, and stir in 1 cup ground cornmeal and 1 teaspoon salt until smooth.

3. Place top pan of double boiler over the simmering water, and fill with 4 cups boiling water. Stirring constantly, slowly add the cornmeal mixture until smooth. Cover and continue cooking until mixture is thickened and cooked through, 20 to 25 minutes, stirring frequently. Remove double boiler from heat, then remove top pan with cornmeal mixture, and place on heatproof surface.

4. Crumble in cooked ground pork, finely chopped onion, ground sage, ground nutmeg, and salt and ground red pepper to taste. Using mixing spoon, stir until well mixed.

5. Cut piece of wax paper to fit the bottom of medium loaf pan. Rinse loaf pan with cold water (do not dry). Place piece of wax paper in bottom of pan, and fill with pork mixture, then press down with your hand or back of spoon and pat smooth. Cover with plastic wrap, and refrigerate until cold and firm, about 3 to 4 hours, or place in freezer for 1 to 2 hours.

6. At serving time, uncover and remove pork mixture from pan by running a knife around the sides of pan, flip onto cutting board. Remove and discard wax paper. Cut loaf crosswise into about ½-inch slices.

7. Melt 4 tablespoons butter or margarine in large skillet over medium-high heat. Reduce heat to medium, and fry slices a few at a time until golden brown on both sides, about 3 to 5 minutes. Fry in batches, adding more butter or margarine when necessary.

*To serve, transfer to serving platter. Scrapple can be eaten cold as an **appetizer** or hot as one of the many side dishes at the wedding luncheon. Scrapple keeps well, wrapped and refrigerated, up to 1 week.*

✿ *Shoo-Fly Pie* (also *Shoofly* or *Wet-bottom Pie*) (Molasses Pie)

Shoo-fly pie is sometimes called "wet-bottom pie" because the crust stays moist from the filling. It's a classic Pennsylvania Dutch pie that is included on the dessert table of the wedding feast.

Yield: serves 6 to 8

9-inch unbaked pie crust, homemade, or frozen (available at most supermarkets)

¼ cup vegetable shortening

2 cups all-purpose flour

½ cup brown sugar

1 teaspoon baking soda

1 cup hot water

½ cup light corn syrup

½ cup dark molasses

½ teaspoon **ground** nutmeg

¼ teaspoon ground ginger

¼ teaspoon ground cinnamon

¼ teaspoon ground cloves

¼ teaspoon salt

3 eggs, lightly beaten

For **garnish**: whipped cream or vanilla ice cream (optional)

Equipment: 9-inch pie pan, medium bowl, **pastry blender** (optional), large mixing bowl, mixing spoon, aluminum foil, baking sheet pan, oven mitts

Prepare pie crust: If homemade, fit crust in 9-inch pie pan. If buying frozen pie crust in pie pan, thaw according to directions on package.

1. Prepare crumb topping: Combine shortening, flour, and brown sugar in medium bowl. Using pastry blender or your fingers, cut or rub shortening into dry ingredients until mixture resembles moist bread crumbs. Set aside.

Preheat oven to 450°F.

2. Prepare filling: In large mixing bowl, stir baking soda in hot water to dissolve. Stir in corn syrup, molasses, nutmeg, ginger, cinnamon, cloves, salt, and lightly beaten eggs. Stir well, pour into unbaked prepared pie shell, and spread smooth.

3. Assemble pie: Spoon crumb mixture over top of filling in pie pan, leaving about 1-inch circle of filling exposed in the center. This opening is like a steam vent and prevents the filling from bubbling over as it bakes. To be safe, place filled pie pan on foil-lined baking sheet, and place in oven.

3. Bake 10 minutes, then reduce heat to 350°F, and continue to bake 40 to 50 minutes, or until filling thickens into custard. Wear oven mitts to test doneness. Pie should not quiver when you gently shake it from side to side. *Note: Do not overbake, or filling will become too dry.*

To serve, cut in wedges. The pie has the best flavor while still warm. Serve plain or with a whipped cream or vanilla ice cream.

Bibliography

Adams, Thatcher. 1991. *Traditional Cookery in Bermuda.* Washington, DC: Island Press.

Adeleke, Tunde. 1996. *Songhay.* Heritage Library of African People Series. New York: Rosen Publishing Group.

Africa News Service, Inc. 1985. *The Africa News Cookbook.* New York: Penguin Books.

Ayer, Eleanor H. 1996. *Germany, The Heartland of Europe.* Tarrytown, NY: Benchmark Books, Marshall Cavendish Corp.

Ayo, Yvonne. 1995. *Africa.* New York: Alfred A. Knopf.

Ayodo, Awuor. 1996. *Luo.* Heritage Library of African People Series. New York: Rosen Publishing Group.

Beckwith, Carol. October 1983. "Niger's Wodaabe: 'People of the Taboo.'" *National Geographic*, CD-ROM.

Benchley, Peter. January 1972. "New Zealand's Bountiful South Island." *National Geographic*, CD-ROM.

Bennett, Margaret. 1992. *Scottish Customs from the Cradle to the Grave.* Edinburgh, UK: Polygon.

Biddlecombe, Peter. 1994. *French Lessons in Africa.* London: Abacus, a division of Little, Brown & Co.

Broek, Jan O. M., and John W. Webb. 1978. *A Geography of Mankind.* New York: McGraw-Hill.

"Calling the Ancestors to Enter: Introducing the Garifuna Dugu." https://ambergriscaye .com/forum/ubbthreads.php/topics/445146/Introducing_the_Garifuna_Dugu .html (accessed 4 August 2017).

Chamberlain, Lesley. 1989. *The Food and Cooking of Eastern Europe*. London: Penguin Books.

"Chocolate Caliente de Cumpleaños (a la taza)." http://www.tembiuparaguay.com /recetas/chocolate-caliente-de-cumpleanos-la-taza (accessed 10 July 2017).

Clayton, Bernard, Jr. 1973. *The Complete Bread Book*. New York: Simon & Schuster.

Davidson, Alan. 1999. *The Oxford Companion to Food*. Oxford, UK: Oxford University Press.

De Mente, Boye Lafayette. 1995. *Japan Encyclopedia*. Lincolnwood, IL: Passport Books, a division of NTC Publishing Group.

Devine, Elizabeth, and Nancy L Bragant. 1995. *The Travelers' Guide to African Customs & Manners*. New York: St. Martin's Press.

Dossey, Donald E. 1992. *Holiday Folklore, Phobias and Fun*. Los Angeles: Outcomes Unlimited Press.

"Dügü o Walagallo. Principal Ceremonia Garífuna." http://pueblosoriginarios.com /meso/maya/garifuna/dugu.html (accessed 5 August 2017).

Eerdmans, W. 1982. *Eerdmans' Handbook to the World's Religions*. Grand Rapids, MI: William B. Eerdmans.

Esposito, Mary Ann. 1995. *Celebrations Italian Style*. New York: William Morrow.

Farley, Marta Pisetska. 1990. *Festive Ukrainian Cooking*. Pittsburgh: University of Pittsburgh Press.

Fisher, Angela. 1984. *Africa Adorned*. New York: Harry N. Abrams.

"Food from Portugal: Great Recipes from Portugal." http://www.foodfromportugal .com/recipe/brigadeiro-cake/# (accessed 10 January 2017).

Freeman, Bobby. 1988. *Welsh Country Cookery: Traditional Recipes from the Country Kitchens of Wales*. Talibont, Dyfed, Wales: Y Lolfa Cyf.

Gaertner, Ursula. 1995. *Elmolo*. Heritage Library of African People Series. New York: Rosen Publishing Group.

Gillison, Gillian. July 1997. "Fertility Rites and Sorcery in a New Guinea Village." *National Geographic*, CD-ROM.

Goldstein, Darra. 1983. *A La Russe*. New York: Random House.

Goodman, Jim. 1991. *Cultures of the World, Thailand*. North Bellmore, NY: Marshall Cavendish Corp.

Goossen, Benjamin W. 2016. Mennonites in Latin America: A Review of the Literature. *The Conrad Grebel Review* 34 (3): 236–265.

"Greece: Kourabiedes." https://www.196flavors.com/greece-kourabiedes/ (accessed 1 August, 2017).

Harris, Andy. 1992. *A Taste of the Aegean*. New York: Abbeville Press.

Harris, Jonathan. 1989. *France*. New York: J. L. Lippincott.

Hartley, Dorothy. 1996. *Food in England*. London: Little, Brown and Co.

Hodgson, Bryan. June 1982. "Namibia, Nearly a Nation?" *National Geographic*, CD- ROM.

Holder, Geoffrey. 1973. *Geoffrey Holder's Caribbean Cookbook*. New York: Viking Press.

Holtzman, Jon. 1995. *Samburu*. Heritage Library of African People Series. New York: Rosen Publishing Group.

Huyler, Stephen P. 1994. *Painted Prayers*. New York: Rizzoli International Publications.

Idiáquez, José. "Walagallo: Corazón del Mundo Garífuna." http://www.envio.org.ni /articulo/794 (accessed 12 July 2017).

Imbrasienè, Birutè. 1998. *Lithuanian Traditional Foods*. Lithuania: Baltos Lankos.

Jacob, Jeanne, and Michael Ashkenazi. 2007. *The World Cookbook for Students*. Westport, CT: Greenwood Press.

Jacob, Jeanne, and Michael Ashkenazi. 2014. *The World Cookbook: The Greatest Recipes from around the Globe*. Santa Barbara, CA: Greenwood/ABC-CLIO.

Jomier, Jacques. 1989. *How to Understand Islam*. New York: Crossroad.

Kamman, Madeleine. 1971. *The Making of a Cook*. New York: Atheneum.

Kornblum, William. 1988. *Sociology in a Changing World*. 3rd ed. Fort Worth, TX: Harcourt Brace College.

Kraus, Barbara. 1964. *The Cookbook of the United Nations*. London: Cookery Book Club.

Labourt, Jose. "La Mujer Dominicana despues del Parto: Creencias y Medicinas Populares Criollas." http://www.banica.net/ (accessed 4 July 2017).

Lands & People: Africa. 1995. Danbury, CT: America Grolier.

Lands & People: Central & South America. 1993. Danbury, CT: America Grolier.

Lands & People: Europe. 1995. Danbury, CT: America Grolier.

"Letter from the Editor by Arun Narayan Toké." N.d. *Skipping Stones Magazine* 9(1).

Leydet, François. August 1982. "Journey through Time, Papua New Guinea." *National Geographic*, CD-ROM.

Livingstone, Sheila. 1996. *Scottish Customs*. Edinburgh, UK: Birlinn.

Marks, Copeland. 1993. *The Korean Kitchen*. San Francisco: Chronicle Books.

Marquis, Vivienne, and Patricia Haskell. 1985. *The Cheese Book*. New York: Simon & Schuster.

Mathabane, Mark. 1994. *African Women*. New York: HarperCollins.

McDowell, Bart, Albert Moldvay, and Joseph J. Schersche. April 1971. "Hungary, Changing Homeland of a Tough, Romantic People." *National Geographic*, CD- ROM.

McGowan, Kathryn. "Jeweled Rice for a Persian Wedding." Comestibles: Kathryn McGowan on victuals and potables historical and modern. https://blog .kathrynmcgowan.com/2010/05/24/jeweled-rice-for-a-persian-wedding/ (accessed 15 July 2017).

Merchant, Ismail. 1994. *Passionate Meals*. New York: Hyperion.

Milhench, Heike. 2007. *Flavors of Slovenia: Food and Wine from Central Europe's Hidden Gem*. New York: Hippocrene Books.

Momatiuk, Yva, and John Eastcott. October 1984. "Maoris: At Home in Two Worlds." *National Geographic*, CD-ROM.

Morales, Euda. "Pepián, Platillo de Gran Arraigo y Patrimonio Cultural Intangible de la Nacion." http://entrecocinasyrecetas.blogspot.com/2011/09/pepian-platillo-de -gran-arraigo-y.html (accessed 11 June, 2017).

Moosewood Collective. 1990. *Sundays at Moosewood Restaurant*. New York: Simon & Schuster.

N.a. 1973. *Farmhouse Fare—Country Recipes Collected by Farmers Weekly*. Frome, Somerset: Countrywise Books.

The National Council of Negro Women, Inc. 1998. *Mother Africa's Table*. New York: Main Street Books/Doubleday Dell Publishing.

Newton, Alex, and David Else. 1995. *West Africa*. Oakland, CA: Lonely Planet Publications.

Njoku, Onwuka N. *Mbundu*. 1997. Heritage Library of African People Series. New York: Rosen Publishing Group.

Nwanunobi, C.O. 1996. *Malinke*. Heritage Library of African People Series. New York: Rosen Publishing Group.

Nwanunobi, C.O. 1996. *Soninke*. Heritage Library of African People Series. New York: Rosen Publishing Group.

Ojakangas, Beatrice A. 1964. *The Finnish Cookbook*. New York: Crown Publishers.

Oluikpe, Benson O. 1997. *Swazi*. Heritage Library of African People Series. New York: Rosen Publishing Group.

Ortiz, Elizabeth Lambert. 1969. *The Book of Latin American Cooking*. New York: Vintage Books by Random House.

Papashvily, Helen. 1969. *Russian Cooking*. New York: Time-Life Books.

Parris, Ronald. 1996. *Hausa*. Heritage Library of African People Series. New York: Rosen Publishing Group.

Patten, Marguerite, and Betty Dunleavy. 1965. *Cakes and Cake Decorating*. Feltham, UK: Hamlyn House; Sydney, Australia: Dee Way West.

The Picayune Creole Cookbook. 1989. New York: Weathervane Books.

"Platz (Coffee Cake with Fruit and Crumbs)." http://www.mennonitegirlscancook.ca /2008/06/platz.html (accessed 5 August 2017).

Post, Laurens van der. 1970. *African Cooking*. New York: Time-Life Books.

Prudhomme, Paul. 1984. *Chef Paul Prudhomme's Louisiana Kitchen*. New York: William Morrow and Co.

Quintana, Patricia. 1989. *Mexico's Feasts of Life*. Tulsa, OK: Council Oak Books.

Richards, Chris. 1997. *World Religions*. New York: Element Books.

Roden, Claudia. 1968. *A Book of Middle Eastern Food*. Harmondsworth, UK: Penguin Books.

Scot, Barbara J. 1993. *The Violet Shyness of Their Eyes—Notes from Nepal*. Corvallis, OR: CALYX Books.

Seah, Audrey. 1994. *Cultures of the World*. North Bellmore, NY: Marshall CavendishCorp.

Slater, Mary. 1974. *Cooking the Caribbean Way*. London: Hamlyn.

Sturgis, Ingrid. 1997. *The Nubian Wedding Book*. New York: CrownPublishers.

Taik, Aung Aung. 1993. *The Best of Burmese Cooking*. San Francisco: Chronicle Books.

Thurman, Sue Bailey (compiler & editor). 2000. *The Historical Cookbook of the American Negro*. Boston: Beacon Press.

Tope, Lily Rose R. 1991. *Cultures of the World, Philippines*. North Bellmore, NY: Marshall Cavendish Corp.

Tornquist, David. 1991. *Vietnam, Then & Now*. London: Flint River Press.

Twagilimana, A. 1998. *Hutu & Tutsi*. Heritage Library of African People Series. New York: Rosen Publishing Group.

Usta, Oktay. 2008. *Oktay Usta'Yla Lezzet Yolculuğu* [Flavor Journeys with Oktay Usta]. Istanbul: Yakamoz Publications.

Vasallo Gonzalez, Mirza. N.d. *Las Mejores Recetas de la Cocina Peruana*. Lima, Peru: Editorial Contorno.

Wanasundera, Nanda P. 1991. *Sri Lanka*. North Bellmore, NY: Marshall Cavendish Corp.

Wangu, Madhu Bazaz. N.d. *Hinduism*. World Religions. New York: Facts on File.

Warren, Janet. 1990. *A Feast of Scotland*. London: Published for Lomond Books by Reed Consumer Books.

Weeks, Gertrude S. August 1956. "In the Heart of Africa." *National Geographic*, CD-ROM.

Weiser, Francis X. 1952. *Christian Feasts and Customs*. New York: Harcourt, Brace & World.

Wells, Troth. 1990. *The Global Kitchen*. Freedom, CA: Crossing Press.

Wells, Troth. 1993. *The World in Your Kitchen*. Freedom, CA: Crossing Press.

Wentzel, Volkmar. January 1998. "Zulu King Weds a Swazi Princess." *National Geographic*, CD-ROM.

Whedon, Peggy, and John Kidner. 1987. *Great Embassies Cookbook*. Seattle: Peanut Butter Publishing.

Wolf, Burt. 1996. *Gatherings and Celebrations*. New York: Doubleday.

Wyk, Gary N. van. 1996. *Basotho*. Heritage Library of African People Series. New York: Rosen Publishing Group.

Yin, Saw Myat. 1990. *Cultures of the World, Burma*. North Bellmore, NY: Marshall Cavendish Corp.

Index

Index

Index

Index